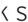 ⟨ S

WYOMING

DON PITCHER

GRAND TETON NATIONAL PARK

To West Thumb
and Yellowstone
National Park

To Togwotee
Pass and
Dubois

26 / 287

Buffalo River

BUFFALO
VALLEY RD

Moran
Junction

Two Ocean
Lake

Emma
Matilda
Lake

Oxbow
Bend

Pacific Creek

Signal Mountain
7,593ft

Snake River

Bridger-Teton
National
Forest

JACKSON LAKE
LODGE

JACKSON
LAKE DAM

POTHOLES

SIGNAL MOUNTAIN LODGE

SIGNAL MOUNTAIN

FLAGG RANCH

89
191
287

RD

Snake River

GRASSY LAKE

John D
Rockefeller Jr
Memorial
Parkway

LIZARD CREEK

Webb Canyon

Colter Canyon

Waterfalls Canyon

LEEKS MARINA

COLTER BAY

COLTER BAY
VISITOR CENTER

Jackson

Lake

Elk
Island

Ranger Peak
11,355ft

Eagles Rest Peak
11,258ft

Bivouac Peak
10,825ft

Traverse Peak
11,051ft

Mt Moran
12,605ft

Thor Peak
12,028 ft

Moose
Basin

Survey Peak
9,277ft

Moose Mtn
10,054 ft

Winegar Hole
Wilderness

Caribou-
Targhee
National
Forest

Jedediah Smith
Wilderness

Leigh

YELLOWSTONE NATIONAL PARK

DISCOVER WYOMING

The expansively rugged land called Wyoming
resonates with the spirit of the American West. For anyone who has
spent time in Wyoming, the state evokes vivid images: cattle standing in the lee of snow fences, children riding horses along dusty dirt
roads, weather-beaten ranches lit by the slanting light of late afternoon, oil-covered roustabouts struggling with the furious machinery
of a drilling rig, the sounds of drumming and singing at a powwow,
and cow towns where the area code is larger than the population.
Here is the original "Wild West," the real-life inspiration for countless
Western novels, movies, and songs.

In the vast open spaces of Wyoming, the sky takes on its own
importance, sometimes making the land seem like an afterthought.
The land changes slowly with the seasons — first a carpet of winter
white, then the mud and first luminescent green buds of spring growth,

bison within Grand Teton National Park

© DON PITCHER

followed by the verdant summer flowers, and finally the brilliance of fall cottonwood trees along a dry creekbed. But the sky follows the beat of another drummer, changing moment by moment throughout each day. Cotton-ball clouds float overhead, sending moving shadows across the landscape and coloring the sun's light. Storm clouds build on a summer afternoon, and in the distance a lightning bolt leaps to earth. Perhaps the most memorable times are the lingering sunsets, when colors seem to bounce back and forth across the sky, finally exiting as a fringe of color on the western horizon. At night, coyotes howl the same way they have for millennia, and an enormous panorama of stars arches above, undimmed by discordant city lights.

The earliest Anglo explorers described Wyoming in less than flattering terms. The image that stuck was the "Great American Desert," a place where the native peoples flourished along with buffalo, antelope, jackrabbits, and rattlesnakes, but where homesteaders and ranchers struggled to survive. Hundreds of thousands of travelers pushed across Wyoming's basins and mountain ranges in the 19th century, bound for greener pastures and gold. Very few considered staying

waterfall in Cirque of the Towers, Wind River Mountains

in such an unforgiving environment. Even today, the vast majority of those who enter Wyoming are en route to someplace else.

A frontier spirit pervades both Wyoming's landscape and its people, mixing the past and present so completely that it sometimes seems as though around the next bend you might see Chief Washakie's men circling a massive herd of bison, or Butch Cassidy and the Sundance Kid shooting it out with lawmen, or a party of fur trappers setting out for the mountains. Officially known as "The Equality State" because it was the first to allow women to vote, Wyoming actually revels in another title, "The Cowboy State." License plates carry the state emblem: a cowboy, hat in hand, atop a furiously bucking bronco. A cowboy hat and boots are acceptable dress anywhere, and the unpolished individuality embodied in the cowboy remains the state's heritage, even for those whose only connection is country-and-western music.

Covering nearly 98,000 square miles, Wyoming is America's ninth-largest state. The states of Connecticut, Delaware, Hawaii, Maryland, Massachusetts, New Hampshire, New Jersey, Rhode Island, Vermont, and West Virginia would all fit within Wyoming's borders

Sheridan's famous Mint Bar

– with room to spare. With just over 506,000 people in 2004 – the smallest population of any state – Wyoming remains a remarkably undeveloped and unsettled place. Cattle outnumber people by nearly three to one, the population density averages just over five people per square mile, and in some counties there is nearly one square mile of land for each person. With an average elevation of 6,700 feet (and a range of 3,125–13,804 feet), Wyoming is the third-highest state in the nation. Only Alaska and Colorado are higher.

Although Wyoming is bisected by three major interstate highways, the best way to see the state is from the smaller asphalt and gravel roads where the pace slows and tumbleweeds pile against fences. From the freeways, the landscape is just a blur, but along the back roads this same land becomes a thing of raw-edged, surreal beauty. Old ranches hunker in the valleys, herds of deer and antelope glance up warily at passing cars, oddly colored rock pinnacles crown the hills, and winding streams become glowing silver ribbons of light. Only the wind, singing birds, and the buzz of insects break the stillness.

Devils Tower National Monument

On back roads you'll find folks lifting a hand to wave as you pass. Small-town cafés serve down-home food, friendly motel owners greet tired travelers, and the pace of living slows measurably. You can almost feel the stress of city life dissipating. People leave their homes, cars, and bikes unlocked; they load up clothes in the launderette and come back later to move them to the dryer. They pull in at the drive-up liquor store for a six-pack. Unlike big cities, where waiting in lines becomes a way of life, the bank, grocery store, and post office queues are short or nonexistent. Try on a cowboy hat and boots, look around the local museum, or stop in for a beer at a country bar and talk politics with the locals. In a short while you'll gain an appreciation for Wyoming and the down-to-earth people who live here.

Wyoming residents

Contents

MAP CONTENTS

MONTANA

○ Mammoth

YELLOWSTONE NATIONAL PARK

○ Lovell

Powell ○

Cody ○

Greybull ○

○ Old Faithful

BIGHORN BASIN

**GRAND TETON
NATIONAL PARK**

○ Thermopolis

Jackson ○

Dubois ○

IDAHO

JACKSON HOLE

Shoshoni ○

○ Alpine

○ Moneta

Riverton ○

○ Pinedale

○ Lander

○ Afton

WIND RIVER MOUNTAINS COUNTRY

Jeffrey City ○

○ Kemmerer

Green River ○

○ Rock Springs

UTAH

○ Evanston

SOUTHWEST WYOMING

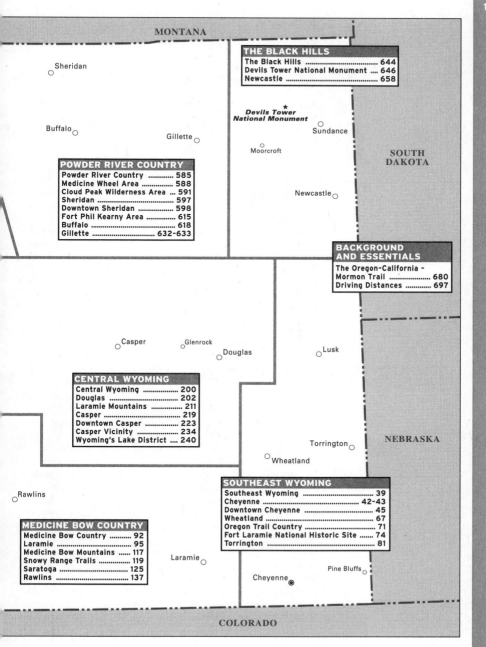

MONTANA

Sheridan

★
Devils Tower
National Monument

Buffalo

Gillette

Sundance

Moorcroft

SOUTH
DAKOTA

Newcastle

Casper

Glenrock

Douglas

Lusk

Torrington

NEBRASKA

Wheatland

Rawlins

Laramie

Pine Bluffs

Cheyenne

COLORADO

The Lay of the Land

SOUTHEAST WYOMING

The southeastern corner of Wyoming is dominated by the state's largest city—and its capital—**Cheyenne.** The city has museums, an interesting capitol building, and a strategic military base, but it is famous for its Frontier Days festivities in late July, with rodeos, parades, and other activities that draw thousands of visitors.

Much of southeast Wyoming is farm and ranch country. Explore the back roads and you'll find busy cattle ranches, abandoned mining towns, remnants of many historic trails, archaeological sites, dinosaur bones, and old sod homesteads.

Several towns—**Wheatland, Torrington,** and **Lusk**—are agricultural focal points, each with a good museum and comfortable places to stay. Historic sites abound, including **Fort Laramie,** once a vital base for the U.S. Army and a way station for Oregon Trail travelers; today it's maintained by the Park Service. Not far away are four-foot-deep ruts gouged by heavy wagons and hundreds of names carved into a cliff by the emigrants. State parks at **Glendo** and **Guernsey** are good places for hiking or water recreation.

MEDICINE BOW COUNTRY

This part of southern Wyoming is dominated by the beautiful **Medicine Bow Mountains,** also called the Snowy Range. These high peaks (some over 12,000 feet) provide a scenic destination for hiking, camping, winter skiing, or just enjoying the great outdoors. East of them lies the Laramie Basin (highest short-grass prairie in the world) and the fun college town of **Laramie,** with fascinating geology and art museums at the University of Wyoming, a restored prison that once incarcerated Butch Cassidy, and some of the state's top restaurants. West of the Snowy Range is another valley, where the pretty town of **Saratoga** has a free hot springs pool, art galleries, and historic buildings. South of here, the Grand Encampment Museum reveals the mining history of the nearby Sierra Madre Range, and to the north are classic old hotels in the tiny settlements of Elk Mountain and Medicine Bow. The busy oil and gas town of **Rawlins,** just off I-80, has several good restaurants, the old Frontier Prison, and a museum with some oddities—including shoes made from the skin of outlaw Big Nose George Parrot.

SOUTHWEST WYOMING

The southwestern corner of Wyoming exhibits a raw beauty that takes time to appreciate. Much of this land is dry and hot in the summer, particularly the **Red Desert** within the Great Divide Basin, a 90-mile-long region where the little water that falls never makes it to either ocean. Sand dunes, wild horses, and Indian petroglyphs draw photographers, and abundant oil and gas attract workers. **Green River** has a fine museum and whitewater park for kayakers. Immediately south lies **Flaming Gorge National Recreation Area,** with grand canyon scenery and recreation opportunities. Farther west is **Fort Bridger,** a small state park with many historic buildings and a popular mountain-man rendezvous on Labor Day weekend. The town of **Evanston** is just a couple of miles from the Utah border along I-80 and has a number of historic buildings, including a Chinese Joss House. Farther north is Kemmerer, home to **Fossil Butte National Monument** and a number of private fossil-fish quarries open to the public.

CENTRAL WYOMING

This is Wyoming's heartland, and the country is definitive: sage- and grass-carpeted plains, desolate badlands, impressive tree-draped mountainsides, and the big, lazy North Platte River. Ranching is important, but oil and gas provide many of the jobs, especially in places such as the town of Midwest, where hundreds of **pumpjacks** and many miles of oil pipelines cover the landscape. The second-largest city in Wyoming, **Casper** is home to several notable museums: the National Historic Trails Interpretive Center, Fort Caspar, and Nicolaysen Art Museum. It's a short but steep drive to the cool pine forests of **Casper Mountain,** and south of here are three large North Platte River reservoirs that are popular with boaters and anglers. West of Casper, the land becomes drier and more desolate, wrinkled by the badlands of **Hell's Half Acre** and the barren crests of desert mountain ranges. The **Oregon Trail** paralleled the Sweetwater River toward distant mountains, and today's visitors find fascinating Oregon Trail sights at Independence Rock and Martin's Cove, where many Mormon travelers died in an 1856 blizzard.

WIND RIVER MOUNTAINS COUNTY

The Wind River Mountains—Wyoming's highest and longest range—form a dramatic divide between two of the state's most important rivers. The east side drains into the Wind River, eventually reaching the Atlantic Ocean, and the western slopes drop into the Green River and eventually the Pacific. The north side of the mountains contains the **Wind River Reservation,** with the villages of Fort Washakie, Ethete, and Arapahoe. Nearby are the large towns of **Riverton** and **Lander.** East of the reservation is **Dubois,** an edge-of-the-mountains settlement with spectacular badlands on all sides; it's one of the gateways to Yellowstone. The state park at **South Pass** has historic buildings from an 1860s gold rush, and it was the primary crossing point for Oregon Trail travelers over the Continental Divide. The highway drops to the west to the crossroads called **Farson** (famous for its ice-cream shop) within the arid Green River Valley. North of here is **Pinedale,** both a fast-growing center for gas production and a base for adventurers heading high into the Wind River Mountains.

JACKSON HOLE

Wyoming's preeminent tourist town, **Jackson** is a destination for those who love the outdoors. The town of 9,000—plus three million tourists annually—occupies the southern end of the valley called Jackson Hole and is almost completely surrounded by Grand Teton National Park, the National Elk Refuge, and Bridger–Teton National Forest. Acclaimed as one of the top artistic centers in the nation, Jackson is crowded with more than 30 **art galleries,** and the impressive **National Museum of Wildlife Art** perches along a hillside just north of town. In the winter, sleigh rides among the elk draw visitors to the **National Elk Refuge,** while skiers and snowboarders enjoy the challenging slopes at famous **Jackson Hole Mountain Resort.** Jackson's restaurants are easily the finest (and most expensive) in Wyoming, and lodging ranges from cozy old log units to ultraluxurious hotels. In summer, the **Snake River** attracts whitewater rafters and fly-fishermen, while mountain-bikers and hikers head out on miles of paved (and unpaved) paths.

GRAND TETON NATIONAL PARK

Yellowstone may get all the acclaim, but Grand Teton National Park easily wins the battle for splendor. The main attraction here is a dramatic mountains-and-valley setting. Capped by 13,772-foot Grand Teton, the **Teton Range** rises abruptly from the valley floor, with the Snake River winding sinuously beneath ragged peaks. One of the most scenic areas is **Jenny Lake,** where boats transport hikers to Inspiration Point, a base for longer explorations into the Tetons.

There are fine vistas from the summit of Signal Mountain, and you may see moose in the sloughs at Oxbow Bend or bison on the flats near **Mormon Row.** The latter area has some of the most photographed barns in America, with a Teton Range backdrop to die for. The **Colter Bay Indian Arts Museum** on the northern end of the park houses an extraordinary collection of Native American pieces, and **Jackson Lake** is popular for fishing and boating. Park headquarters and the main visitor center are on the south end of Grand Teton National Park in the little settlement of **Moose.**

YELLOWSTONE NATIONAL PARK

America's first and most famous national park, Yellowstone is a geology lesson in the raw. The park's best-known site is **Old Faithful,** with its predictable eruptions that delight crowds every hour and a half. Old Faithful is just one of dozens of geysers and other geothermal features that fill Upper Geyser Basin, the largest concentration of geysers in the world. Near the center of the park is **Norris Geyser Basin,** where you might witness Steamboat Geyser blasting 300 feet into the air on its very rare eruptions. **Mammoth Hot Springs** is famous for an ever-changing palette of softly colored springs, and it is also home to park headquarters. Bucolic **Lamar Valley** in the northeast corner of Yellowstone is the best place to see wolves, and nearby **Tower Fall** provides a great photo op.

Grand Canyon of the Yellowstone may be the park's most spectacular feature, with the Yellowstone River plummeting 308 feet over Lower Falls. South of here is **Yellowstone Lake**—the largest high-elevation lake in North America.

BIGHORN BASIN

Bighorn Basin is an enormous intermountain desertscape reaching almost 100 miles north to south and 50 miles east to west. Mountain ranges rim the basin—the Absarokas rise as a western border, the Owl Creek Mountains line the southern horizon, and the snowcapped Big Horns gleam in the east. The basin's rolling hills are topped with oil pumpjacks, and the wind blows incessantly through the sage-covered badlands. Three lazy rivers—Big Horn, Greybull, and Shoshone—create long green corridors, and several towns line these waterways. Largest is **Cody,** founded (in part) by Buffalo Bill Cody. This small city serves as an important gateway into Yellowstone National Park (via scenic **Wapiti Valley**) but is best known for the massive **Buffalo Bill Historical Center,** the finest Old West museum in existence. **Bighorn Canyon National Recreation Area** is a good place to look for wild horses or to take in the dramatic and colorful canyons. At the southern end of the basin, **Thermopolis** is home to the world's largest hot springs, managed as a wonderful state park, and it also has an outstanding dinosaur education center.

POWDER RIVER COUNTY

The most historically interesting part of a state overflowing with history, Powder River Basin was a focal point for battles between Indians and white travelers, and later clashes between cattlemen and homesteaders. Today, this is one of the primary places for coal and coalbed methane gas development, but much of the land remains wild. The western margin of this basin abuts the **Big Horn Mountains,** with high country recreation within the **Cloud Peak Wilderness** and a mysterious Medicine Wheel created by Indians centuries ago. **Sheridan** is a pleasant small city with great restaurants and sights—including the historic mansions at Trail End and Sheridan Inn, plus a surprising collection of historic items at King's Saddlery. Now a state historic site, **Fort Phil Kearny** sits in the rolling timber-and-grass along the old Bozeman Trail and was the scene of battles between the U.S. Army and the Sioux in the 1860s. The town of **Buffalo** features an excellent museum and pleasant mountain drives, and to the south is famous **Hole-in-the-Wall country,** where Butch Cassidy and other outlaws hid their stolen horses.

THE BLACK HILLS

In Wyoming's northeast corner, the Black Hills of South Dakota roll across an arbitrary state line, their rocky knolls crowded with pine and aspen forests, while lower areas have open meadows and valleys lined with bur oak. There's a quiet beauty to the Black Hills. The Belle Fourche River cuts northeast past rich pastures before taking a sudden right angle to the southeast as it descends to the Missouri River. Only 13,000 people live in this part of Wyoming, scattered on rural ranches or in settlements nestled among forested hills. In the center of these hills, one of the most stunning of all sights—**Devils Tower National Monument**—seems almost alive in its abrupt rise from the pastoral landscape. Managed by the National Park Service, the peak draws rock climbers from all over the nation, and its distinctive profile is featured on Wyoming license plates. Several small towns surround the Black Hills, including **Sundance,** with its fine museum that houses artifacts from the Sundance Kid's time in the local jail. South of the Black Hills, the country abruptly opens into the mixed-grass prairie of the plains.

Planning Your Trip

Wyoming's topography consists of a series of mountain ranges and broad basins, and this variability creates vastly different conditions across the state, from dry deserts that are blazing hot in midsummer to chilly mountaintops where the snow never completely melts.

All sorts of travelers come to Wyoming: vans filled with families heading to Yellowstone, international vacationers in search of the legendary cowboy West, job seekers on their way to busy gas fields and coal mines, horse lovers glassing the dunes for wild horses in the Red Desert, sleepy truckers cruising along I-80, Oregon Trail enthusiasts visiting the land their ancestors rolled through, retirees looking for a place where taxes are low and mortgages reasonable, and young climbers seeking adventure in the high mountains. For each of these the state has something different to offer, whether it's a fat oil-company paycheck or the chance to see wild country on horseback.

Wyoming is big, and only those with unlimited time could ever really explore the state. So find a place that looks interesting and plan your travels accordingly. If you want to see a good variety of sights, set aside at least 10 days in Wyoming, more if possible. Those with the time (and money) should consider booking a week at one of Wyoming's old-time guest ranches.

Start planning your trip by contacting the **Wyoming Travel and Tourism Division** (800/225-5996, www.wyomingtourism.org) for maps and publications. Other phone numbers and websites are listed throughout this book, or you can visit the author's website (www.donpitcher.com) for hundreds of Wyoming web links.

WHEN TO GO

The vast majority of Wyoming visitors arrive June–August when the land is green, temperatures are warm (or hot), and local businesses and attractions are all in full swing. Summer is also when many regional festivals take place, including rodeos, county fairs, and mountain-man rendezvous. But if you visit in the summer you'll need to share the most popular areas with hordes of other wanderers, especially in the northwest corner of the state where Yellowstone National Park, Grand Teton National Park, and Jackson Hole attract three million travelers annually. On a mid-July day the benches circling Old Faithful are filled with hundreds of visitors, Snake River becomes a traffic jam of rafts, and downtown Jackson is packed with shoppers and sightseers from all over the world. But even in Jackson Hole it is surprisingly easy to find a quiet spot to escape into the surrounding wild places where few others tread. Anyone planning a peak-season summertime trip to Yellowstone and Jackson Hole should make lodging and other travel arrangements well ahead of time. The same holds true for the winter holiday ski and snowboard season in Jackson.

Other parts of Wyoming are far less crowded, though you still need to make reservations for hotels in popular edge-of-the-mountains towns such as Saratoga, Buffalo, Saratoga, Cody, Lander, and Pinedale, or for major events, particularly Cheyenne's Frontier Days in July.

Fall is a delightful time to explore Wyoming. After Labor Day weekend the crowds diminish and some tourist businesses are shuttered for the season, but the weather can be ideal. This is a great time to look for wildlife in Yellowstone, to visit Devils Tower National Monument, watch a cattle auction in Torrington, hang out with the college students in Laramie, or drive through the autumnal gold of Aspen Alley in the Sierra Madre. Peak fall colors generally arrive in early October, and the Jackson Hole Fall Arts Festival is a major September event. Temperatures drop as fall progresses and the snow gradually moves down the mountains.

Winters can be harsh—especially in the

mountains—but some parts of southern and eastern Wyoming have relatively mild winters, with little snow and temperatures often above freezing. Many mountain passes in Wyoming and most Yellowstone roads are closed by early November and don't reopen until May. Jackson Hole is a major winter destination, with three ski resorts and all sorts of other activities—from sleigh rides among the elk to dog sledding. Yellowstone is beautiful in the winter and is open to snowcoaches, skis, and guided snowmobile tours. Other parts of Wyoming—particularly the mountain ranges—are popular for snowmobiling, snowboarding, downhill skiing, and cross-country skiing.

Spring is a quiet time of year, and many mountain passes and park roads don't open till mid-May. The land gradually greens up, but trees are often not leafed out—especially at higher elevations—till the later part of May.

WHAT TO TAKE

Because of seasonal variations, when you visit dictates what you need to bring. In midsummer, short pants and Tevas might be all you need most days, while winter can push temperatures well below zero. One thing you can almost always count on is the wind, especially in the open sage and grass country across eastern and southern Wyoming. The state's average wind speed is nearly 13 miles an hour, making Wyoming the windiest state in the nation! All those wind generators along I-80 are there for a reason.

Keep it casual when it comes to clothing. Only a couple of Wyoming restaurants require a sports jacket or tie, but you may feel like Michael Moore at a Republican fund-raiser if you show up wearing shorts and a tie-dyed T-shirt while others are dressed for a night out. For summer travel, pack comfortable walking shoes, sunglasses, a hat, sunscreen, insect repellent, and prescription medications. Be sure to bring a bathing suit even if you don't plan on swimming in local lakes or pools—many hotels and B&Bs have hot tubs. You'll want long sleeve shirts and pants for cooler summer evenings and a light Gore-Tex jacket for rainy days or on-the-water trips.

For other seasons, bring several layers of noncotton clothing to adjust to varying temperatures. If you plan to spend time in Yellowstone in midwinter, come prepared for temperatures that may drop well below zero; the lowest recorded temperature there was −66°F!

Explore Wyoming

THE 16-DAY TOUR DE WYOMING

This long trip starts from Denver and follows a circuitous route across Wyoming, with a mix of hotels, motels, and camping.

DAY 1

Start from Denver and drive north to Wyoming's capital city, **Cheyenne,** spending the night at the beautifully restored Plains Hotel in the heart of town. There are many sights to see here; start with the **Capitol Building,** historic **Governors' Mansion, Wyoming State Museum, Frontier Days Old West Museum,** and **Nelson Museum of the West.** The historic railroad depot houses a visitor center and brewpub with tasty pizzas and finger food.

DAY 2

You probably didn't have time to see everything in Cheyenne yesterday, so check out a few more sights before pushing off for the hour drive to **Laramie,** stopping along the way to check out the strange rock formations at **Vedauwoo,** and then visiting the geology and art museums at the **University of Wyoming** and **Wyoming Territorial Park,** where Butch Cassidy did his time. Enjoy dinner at Jeffrey's Bistro.

DAY 3

Head west now over the gorgeous **Snowy Range** (great for an alpine hike) and then down to **Saratoga** for a dip in the hot springs before bedding down at historic Hotel Wolf.

DAY 4

Lots of driving today, so get going early. Head north to the freeway and then west on I-80, stopping in **Rawlins** for a tour of the eerie old prison and some tasty Thai food before continuing west to Rock Springs and then south into **Flaming Gorge National Recreation Area,** where campsites are available. The **Red Desert** north of Rock Springs is another fascinating place, with long sand dunes and herds of elk and wild horses.

DAY 5

Take the back way (Hwy. 414) northwest from Flaming Gorge to **Fort Bridger State Historic Site** and then north to **Kemmerer** to check out **Fossil Butte National Monument.** If you have extra time, you might want to arrange a fossil dig at one of the local quarries.

DAY 6

Next stop is **Pinedale,** with its **Museum of the Mountain Man** and spectacular mountain scenery. Lakeside campsites are available seven miles from town, or stay at Rivera Lodge in town.

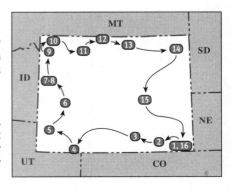

DAY 7

Head northwest to the touristy town of **Jackson** at the southern end of the valley called **Jackson Hole,** but make sure you've set up lodging well in advance. A good log cabin-style place is Wagon Wheel Village. Explore the art galleries, evening shoot-out, and elk antler arches downtown, and savor dinner at Nani's Genuine Pasta House or something lighter at Snake River Brewing Company.

DAY 8

A second day in Jackson allows time to visit the **National Museum of Wildlife Art** and drive up to **Grand Teton National Park** for a hike along **Jenny Lake** before returning for chow-down dining at always-crowded Bubba's Bar-B-Que.

DAY 9

Next stop is **Yellowstone,** where you've had the sense to book a room at beautiful Old Faithful Inn. Take the time to drive through parts of Grand Teton that you didn't see yesterday (don't miss Colter Bay Indian Arts Museum) before entering Yellowstone National Park. You'll want lots of photos of **Old Faithful** when it erupts, but also take time to explore other geysers and hot springs in the area.

DAY 10

Continue the park tour with visits to **Norris Geyser Basin** and **Mammoth Hot Springs** before ending for the night at **Grand Canyon of the Yellowstone** with its spectacular waterfalls and steep hiking paths. You can camp nearby or stay in comfortable modern lodges.

DAY 11

Exit stage east today, but first spend some time in **Hayden Valley** and around the Lake Hotel (great organic lunches), before rolling over mountains and down picturesque **Wapiti Valley** to **Buffalo Bill Dam** (jaw-dropping vistas) and the town of **Cody.** Try to get there early enough for the **Cody Nite Rodeo.** Best Value Inn West is a good midrange lodging place, and Cassie's Supper Club has prime rib and a chuck wagon buffet.

DAY 12

You could easily spend all day at the enormous **Buffalo Bill Historical Center,** probably the most famous museum in the Rockies. Don't miss this one! Also worth seeing is the less ostentatious **Trail Town.** Drive east to tiny **Lovell,** home to **Bighorn Canyon National Recreation Area,** where campsites are available in this desert setting with dramatic canyons plunging to the reservoir hundreds of feet below.

DAY 13

Take steep U.S. 14A over the **Big Horn Mountains** (be sure to see Medicine Wheel) to **Sheridan,** with its New West shops and Old West sights, including **Trail End, King's Saddlery,** and the nearby **Bradford Brinton Memorial Museum.** Enjoy great meals at Oliver's or Empire Grill. (Hot-springs lovers may prefer to add an extra day here that includes a detour to wonderful **Hot Springs State Park** in **Thermopolis** before crossing the Big Horns.)

DAY 14

Drive south to visit the site of **Fort Phil Kearny** to learn about battles between the U.S. Army and the Sioux in the 1860s, and then on to the pretty town of **Buffalo,** with a great museum and good lunch or dinner places. Time is running out, so keep driving east all the way to **Devils Tower National Monument,** a wonderful spot to camp for the night and dream of *Close Encounters.*

DAY 15

Drive southwest to **Casper,** stopping to check out the gargantuan coal mines near Wright. Be sure to visit the **National Historic Trails Interpretive Center, Fort Caspar,** and

Nicolaysen Art Museum. Casper's fine dining place is 303 Restaurant.

DAY 16

Heading southeast now, you'll have time for a short visit to **Fort Laramie National Historic Site** and other nearby Oregon Trail sites before continuing south all the way to Cheyenne, where you arrive exhausted and ready for a vacation from your 3,000-mile driving vacation!

FOLLOWING HISTORIC TRAILS

Many of America's most famous historic trails passed through Wyoming, including the Oregon/California/Mormon Trail, Pony Express, Overland Trail, Bozeman Trail, Texas Trail, and Cheyenne–Deadwood Stage Road. Reminders of these important 19th-century routes are scattered across the state in the form of old forts, trail ruts, names carved in rocks, memorial markers, and even re-created wagon train rides. Below are a few places to begin your exploration of this rich past.

NATIONAL HISTORIC TRAILS INTERPRETIVE CENTER

This modern hilltop museum houses extraordinary displays about the historic trails that traversed the West, with a special emphasis on the **Oregon Trail.** (Through Wyoming, the same route was used by gold miners en route to California and Mormons heading to Salt Lake City, so it was also known as the California Trail and Mormon Trail.) It overlooks Casper, a hub not just for the Oregon Trail heading west, but also for the Bozeman Trail used by miners heading north. Also in Casper is the reconstructed log structure called **Fort Caspar,** now a museum, but once an important crossing of the North Platte River.

FORT LARAMIE NATIONAL HISTORIC SITE

On the plains of southeastern Wyoming, this fort began as an 1834 trading post and

later served as a base for Indian treaties, Army battles with the Sioux, and as a vital way station for emigrants along the Oregon Trail and Cheyenne-Deadwood Stage Road. Today, the National Park Service manages the fort, and many of the buildings have been restored and filled with historical displays.

REGISTER CLIFF

This site just a few miles west of Fort Laramie is famous for the thousands of names that were carved in soft sandstone cliffs by Oregon Trail travelers. Nearby are some extraordinary ruts – some four feet deep – created by wagon trains as they rolled through more than 150 years ago.

INDEPENDENCE ROCK

This rounded granite rock rises from the sagebrush country 55 miles southwest of Casper and is famous as the "Great Register of the Desert," where an estimated

50,000 travelers carved, chipped, or painted their names for posterity before mounting up to continue west. Quite a few of these are still visible; the oldest dates to 1824. Its name came from the date when many travelers arrived; to make it to Oregon or California they tried to be here by the Fourth of July.

MARTIN'S COVE

Just nine miles west of Independence Rock, this rocky place along the Sweetwater River was where a party of Mormon handcart emigrants were caught by an early winter storm that dumped 18 inches of snow on the ill-prepared travelers. Before rescue parties could arrive from Salt Lake, a total of 145 men, women, and children had frozen to death. The LDS Church operates a fine **Mormon Handcart Visitor Center** at the historic Thomas Sun ranch here, and you'll see handcart replicas being pulled by families reliving the past.

SOUTH PASS STATE HISTORIC SITE

This state park is home to two dozen restored buildings, most from a gold rush to the area in the 1860s. At an easy crossing point atop the Continental Divide, South Pass was the primary crossing point for Oregon Trail travelers, and an important **Pony Express** station once stood here. West of this the trails diverged, with some wagons turning south to Fort Bridger and others west along the Lander Cutoff.

FORT BRIDGER STATE HISTORIC SITE

Named for famous mountain man and guide Jim Bridger, this fort contains a re-created log stockade and many historic buildings built by the U.S. Army in the mid-19th century. A very popular mountain-man rendezvous in early September provides a window into the past. North of here near the little town of La Barge is a small cliff known as **Names Hill,** where Bridger's name is one of many etched in the rocks.

POINT OF ROCKS

Twenty-five miles east of Rock Springs is one of the few surviving Overland Stage stations, a rustic sandstone building and corrals. It's just off I-80 and right along the route also used by the Pony Express.

FORT PHIL KEARNY

Now a state historic site, this fort had a short and violent life. Built in 1866 to protect miners heading north up the Bozeman Trail, it was under almost constant attack from the Sioux Indians, through whose land the trail passed. Several major battles were fought here, but the fort was abandoned in 1868 when most travelers stopped using the trail. Today a visitor center and archaeological digs detail the area's rich history.

YELLOWSTONE IN A DAY

Yellowstone is best seen at a leisurely pace, but many travelers passing through simply don't have the time to really explore the park. Given such constraints, you need to decide what matters most—seeing the top sights quickly or finding one place that appeals to you. Most folks probably choose the former, and the obvious choices are the three most popular attractions: Old Faithful, Grand Canyon of the Yellowstone, and Mammoth Hot Springs. One could easily spend a full day in each of these areas, but it is possible to make quick visits to all three while circling through the park. The specific routing, of course, depends upon your direction of travel, but I'll assume that you are coming in from West Yellowstone. Get an early start on the day since you'll need to cover a lot of ground and the park speed limit is 35 miles an hour.

The Yellowstone concessioner, **Xanterra Parks and Resorts,** offers full-day bus tours of the park that start from most park hotels. Some of these focus on the southern or northern half of the park, while others take you to all the sights in one long day of sensory overload. Quite a few other companies offer Yellowstone day tours from surrounding towns.

MORNING

Your first stop will be **Old Faithful,** where the world's best-known geyser erupts approximately every hour and a half. Drop by the visitor center to check on the next predicted eruption and explore the area in the interim. Paved paths lead to nearby geysers, hot springs, and other features, and something is always going on somewhere in the area, but make sure you're back well before the expected eruption of Old Faithful since the timing isn't entirely predictable. Several interesting buildings are in the area, most notably **Old Faithful Inn,** built more than a century ago and still one of the largest log structures of its kind in the world.

Drive north, stopping briefly to see the colorful bubbling mud and active small geysers at **Fountain Paint Pot.** You might also have time for fascinating **Norris Geyser Basin,** the hottest such basin in North America, but don't stop too long.

AFTERNOON

By the time you reach **Mammoth Hot Springs** it may well be lunch, so take a break with a picnic or café meal here and walk up the hillside to see which of the many colorful springs are most active. Take a quick tour of Albright Visitor Center, and turn your car east for the drive to **Tower Fall,** where a steep trail leads 0.5 mile downhill to the base of this pretty waterfall. But now it's on to something far more dramatic.

The road south from Tower Fall crosses 8,859-foot Dunraven Pass before dropping to spectacular **Grand Canyon of the Yellowstone.** The road junction at Canyon has visitor services if the kids need an ice-cream or bathroom break, and just south of here are access roads to both sides of the canyon. The most famous vista point (don't miss this one) is **Artist Point** on the south side, but others on both sides provide other options, including a steep trail that leads to the top of **Lower Falls** (twice the height of Niagara Falls).

EVENING

Now it's time to circle back to your starting point. If it's already late in the day, drive directly back to West Yellowstone via Norris and Madison, but if you still have a couple of hours of light, continue south to **Lake Yellowstone** for a big dinner or sunset drink at historic **Lake Yellowstone** Hotel before continuing past West Thum, Old Faithful, and Madison to the town of West Yellowstone.

SEVEN-DAY PARKS ADVENTURE

This tour is perfect for families and those who prefer to camp in the great outdoors. Some of the activities are a bit pricey, and it's easy to spend a small (or large) fortune visiting Jackson Hole, but it is also possible to have a wonderful time without breaking the bank if you cook your own meals and keep costly activities to a minimum.

DAY 1

Choose from five campgrounds within Grand Teton National Park; most popular is scenic **Jenny Lake Campground.** Once you're set up, drive to **Moose Visitor Center** for details on the park, maps, brochures, and guidebooks. Your entrance fee covers both Yellowstone and Grand Teton for a week. Just across the river in Moose are shops with groceries, wine, meals, and outdoor gear — including bike and canoe rentals. A nice evening drive is the winding road to the summit of **Signal Mountain,** where the panorama encompasses the majestic Teton Range.

DAY 2

This is a day to explore Grand Teton. Take a morning hike up popular **Inspiration Point,** accessible by shuttle boat across **Jenny Lake,** and return for an afternoon drive through the park, including time at **Colter Bay Indian Arts Museum,** Oxbow Bend, the old Cunningham homesteader cabin, and a couple of spectacular turnouts facing the Tetons. Turn east onto Antelope Flats Road for another photo op, this time of the picturesque barns along **Mormon Row.** Next up is pretty **Chapel of the Transfiguration** near the Moose Visitor Center, and our final stop is Jenny Lake, where you began the day.

DAY 3

Jackson is today's destination. You can't miss shady **Town Square** with its four elk-antler arches and evening shoot-outs. Art galleries abound, and just north of town is the outstanding **National Museum of Wildlife Art.** For fun, take a float or whitewater raft trip down the **Snake River,** or a horseback ride at Teton Village. Back in town, travelers will find an amazing variety of outstanding dining choices. Don't miss the **Million Dollar Cowboy Bar** with its saddle barstools and nightly country-and-western bands. Directly behind town is **Snow King Resort,** with a summertime lift (great for hikers and mountain-bikers), plus a fun alpine slide. Take the scenic route back to Jenny Lake by driving to **Teton Village** and up the narrow Moose-Wilson Road.

DAY 4

Drive north into **Yellowstone National Park,** where you've booked a rustic bath-down-the-hall room at Old Faithful Inn. Watch **Old Faithful** geyser erupt, walk the paths that circle past nearby hot springs and geysers, and enjoy a big dinner at the hotel. Afterward, sit in the gracious old building and write postcards while enjoying the ambience of the finest building in any American park.

DAY 5

Continue through the park with lots of stops along the way: taking the kids swimming in **Firehole Canyon,** watching the bubbling mud at **Fountain Paint Pot,** getting sprayed by **Echinus Geyser** in Norris Geyser Basin, and enjoying the ever-changing **Mammoth Hot Springs.** Pitch your tent at **Slough Creek Campground,** where you may hear wolves howling as the stars appear.

DAY 6

Head south over Dunraven Pass, where a side road leads to a parking area where you can hike to the top of **Mt. Washburn** for great park vistas. Next stop is spectacu-lar **Grand Canyon of the Yellowstone,** where you take the easy saunter to Artist Point, along with a 600-foot climb down to stunning Brink of the Lower Falls (but not if you're afraid of heights). Continue south through **Hayden Valley** – where bison and elk are commonly seen – to Bridge Bay Campground on the shore of **Yellowstone Lake,** but be sure to stop for an evening cocktail or gourmet dinner at historic **Lake Yellowstone Hotel.**

DAY 7

The last day lands us back at our Jackson Hole starting point. Check out the hot springs at **West Thumb** and pretty **Lewis Falls** before exiting Yellowstone and continuing south to Grand Teton, where you can unwind at peaceful **Gros Ventre Campground** after a swim in nearby **Kelly Warm Springs.**

AND NOW FOR SOMETHING COMPLETELY DIFFERENT. . .

Wyoming has its share of unusual attractions, some with a whimsical edge, others just odd. You'll find something peculiar in almost every town, from the double-ended car that sits out front of a Rawlins gas station to the Easter Island statues on a college campus in Rock Springs. Here are a few of the best.

JACKALOPES

You'll see these imaginary creatures in taxi-dermy shops across the West, but the town of Douglas takes credit for this hare-brained idea. There's an eight-foot-tall jackalope statue at Jackalope Square in the center of town, you can pick up a jackalope "hunting license" from the chamber of commerce visi-tor center, and the Exxon station in Dubois has a large jackalope with a saddle for silly kid photos.

WORLD'S OLDEST BUILDING

Wyoming is famous for its dinosaur discover-ies, and some of the first took place at Como Bluff, northwest of Laramie. A building at the site was built from broken pieces of dinosaur bones, and a small sign proclaims, "This building walked 75 million years ago!"

ACCIDENTAL OIL COMPANY

The gift shop is housed within an old oil tank at this offbeat Newcastle site. You can walk down steps to view oil seeping from the rocks. The hole was dug by hand in 1966 and is called the "world's only hand-dug oil well."

PAUL BUNYAN'S MINES

Wyoming's Powder River Basin contains vast reserves of low-sulfur coal and a number of gargantuan mines feed America's demand for energy. The equipment used is equally impressive; the haul trucks – powered by 3,500-horsepower engines – carry 400 tons of coal, and their tires are 13 feet tall. A constant stream of trains (each 110 cars long) load the coal for power plants around the nation.

PIEDMONT KILNS

One of Wyoming's more interesting ghost towns, Piedmont lies in dry sagebrush country southeast of Evanston. A few old cabins and a cemetery remain, along with three tall stone charcoal kilns. They were built in 1859 to supply a smelter in Utah and are a very odd discovery in the middle of nowhere.

MOTHER FEATHER LEGS

Out in the country a dozen or so miles southwest of Lusk is a small granite monument at the site where Mother Feather Legs – a 19th-century madam – had a dugout cabin. She was murdered by "Dangerous Dick" Davis, one of the outlaws who always seemed to be around her old place of entertainment along the Cheyenne-Black Hills Stage Line. This is probably the nation's only historical marker commemorating a prostitute.

HELL'S HALF ACRE

Forty-five miles west of Casper is one of the freaks of nature, Hell's Half Acre. Actually covering 320 acres, the area includes deeply eroded colorful badlands and was the setting for the 1997 sci-fi movie *Starship Troopers* – a space-station "city" was built on the south half of the badlands.

AYRES NATURAL BRIDGE

This odd geological formation lies 14 miles west of Douglas within a small county park. The 100-foot-long, 50-foot-high rock arches over LaPrele Creek. It was formed when a meander bend in the creek gradually eroded the base of the rock face, leaving the arch behind.

VEDAUWOO AND PYRAMID TOO

Halfway between Cheyenne and Laramie along I-80 are strange rock formations known as Vedauwoo. These oddly jumbled rocks form all sorts of shapes: mushrooms, balancing rocks, feminine curves, lizards, faces, turtles, and anything you might dream up. The area is especially popular with rock climbers.

Just two miles south of Vedauwoo is a 60-foot-tall stone pyramid in the middle of nowhere. The memorial commemorates Oakes and Oliver Ames, two influential figures in building the transcontinental railroad. A corrupt congressman who used his office for personal gain, Oakes was known as the "King of Frauds."

VIRGIN MARY

One of Wyoming's most bizarre sights is the five-story-tall Our Lady of Peace Shrine – the largest statue of the Virgin Mary in the United States. Built of cast stone by artist Robert Fida, the white monument faces I-80 and is just a few feet from the Nebraska border. While you're in the area, check out the highest "mountain" in Nebraska, a low hill called Panorama Point.

SOUTHEAST WYOMING

Southeast Wyoming is farming and ranching country, part of the vast prairie region that drapes America's heartland. In many ways, it is indistinguishable from western Nebraska or eastern Colorado—one long continuum of grass, grain, and grazing. Folks drive big American cars and Ford pickups. Instead of the saddleries and oil companies elsewhere in Wyoming, you'll find farm-equipment dealers and more feed caps than cowboy hats (they hold down better in the wind that seems to never stop blowing).

Buffalo roamed through southeast Wyoming for thousands of years, hunted by nomadic tribes of Plains Indians. Now cattle and sheep follow the same trails, and farmers grow wheat where Cheyenne Indian villages once stood. Alternating bands of wheat and fallow land give some areas a candy-striped appearance, while in others the expansive prairie extends in all directions. Old windmills, white farmhouses, hip-roofed barns, rusting retired farm machinery, and tall silos mark the old homesteads that became permanent farmsteads. The gravel roads cut straight across this gently rolling land with sudden right-angled jags around old homestead boundaries. Drive out on these roads and the pace slows to country speed and meadowlarks call from the fence posts. Folks raise a hand to wave as you pass and stop to chat on the crest of a hill. Tune in the radio and you're likely to hear country music, farm market reports, and Paul Harvey commentaries. This is Wyoming's most important agricultural region.

The capital city, Cheyenne, dominates the economy of southeast Wyoming, one of only two real cities in the state (the other is Casper).

© DON PITCHER

SOUTHEAST WYOMING

HIGHLIGHTS

State Capitol: It's grandiose, gilded, and covered with murals of the Old West, but the governor's door is usually open and one of the main attractions is the statue of a bucking bronco (page 46).

Wyoming State Museum: Free—and worth every penny—this museum has a 3-D model of the state, a kids' room, and historical exhibits (page 47).

Frontier Days Old West Museum: If you like horse-drawn carriages and wagons, don't miss this one (page 48).

Nelson Museum of the West: A downtown surprise, this private museum has amazing Western artifacts, along with some that don't seem to belong—such as the African lion (page 48).

Frontier Days: The "Daddy of 'em All" is Wyoming's most famous event, with bucking broncs, parades, the Air Force Thunderbirds, and cement-mixer pancakes (page 53).

Oregon Trail Ruts and Register Cliff: A century and a half ago 350,000 people passed through this now-quiet spot. The four-foot ruts and hundreds of names carved into the cliff are evidence of this mass migration West (page 69).

Guernsey State Park: The reservoir attracts boaters, but don't miss the hiking trails, dramatic overlooks, and grand stone structures built by the CCC, including the "million-dollar privy" (page 72).

Fort Laramie National Historic Site: A major Oregon Trail way station and military

fort, Fort Laramie was also where two important Indian treaties were signed. If only these lovingly restored old buildings could speak (page 74).

Torrington Livestock Market: Don't put up your hand unless you want to buy that cow (page 82).

Stagecoach Museum: What do Mother Feather Legs's pantaloons, an iron lung, Barbie-doll presidents' wives, and a Cheyenne and Black Hills stagecoach have in common? Head to Lusk to find out (page 86).

LOOK FOR **(** TO FIND RECOMMENDED SIGHTS, ACTIVITIES, DINING, AND LODGING.

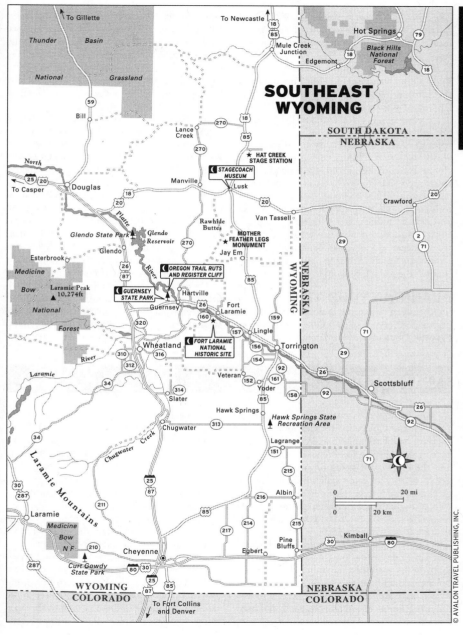

To Gillette

To Newcastle

Thunder   Basin

Hot Springs 79

National   Grassland

Mule Creek
Junction

Edgemont

Black Hills
National
Forest

SOUTHEAST WYOMING

59

Bill

Lance
Creek

270

270

85

18

SOUTH DAKOTA
NEBRASKA

HAT CREEK
STAGE STATION

North

To Casper

25 20

Douglas

Manville

18

20

STAGECOACH
MUSEUM

Lusk

20

Crawford

20

20

270

Van Tassell

Rawhide
Buttes

29

2
71

Glendo State Park

Glendo
Reservoir

MOTHER
FEATHER LEGS
MONUMENT

Esterbrook

Glendo

270

Jay Em

85

Medicine

26
87

OREGON TRAIL RUTS
AND REGISTER CLIFF

NEBRASKA
WYOMING

Bow   Laramie Peak
10,274ft

GUERNSEY
STATE PARK

Hartville

National

Guernsey

Fort
Laramie

159

Forest

320

160

26

157

Lingle

71

River

Wheatland

310

316

FORT LARAMIE
NATIONAL
HISTORIC SITE

156

154

Torrington

29

Laramie

312

Veteran

92

River

152

161

26

34

Slater

314

Yoder

158

92

Scottsbluff

85

Hawk Springs

Hawk Springs State
Recreation Area

26

92

34

Chugwater

313

Lagrange

Laramie Mountains

151

215

71

0   20 mi

0   20 km

30
287

25
87

211

Albin

216

Laramie

214

217

215

Medicine

Bow

N F

210

Cheyenne

Egbert

Pine
Bluffs

30

Kimball

80

Curt Gowdy
State Park

80 30

287

WYOMING
COLORADO

25

85

87

To Fort Collins
and Denver

NEBRASKA
COLORADO

The other significant settlements—Wheatland, Torrington, and Lusk—are small agricultural focal points and governmental centers for their respective counties.

Southeast Wyoming experiences typical high-plains weather. It is hot and windy in the summer, cold and windy in the winter. The wind—averaging more than 13 mph—is a given; this is great country for kites but not much fun when the gales of winter slice through like a knife. Partly because of this wind, however, Cheyenne has some of the cleanest air in the nation. Explore the back roads and you'll find busy cattle ranches, abandoned mining towns, remnants of many historic trails, archaeological sites, dinosaur bones, and old sod homesteads. Hiking through the gently undulating plains is a delightful experience because vast expanses of this land remain almost unchanged from the time when bison roamed the great grasslands of the West.

PLANNING YOUR TIME

Southeastern Wyoming is not a major tourist destination, except during Cheyenne's famous **Frontier Days** festivities in late July, when thousands of visitors flood the area and fill hotels for 100 miles in all directions. Travelers could see most regional sights in a few days, and many people just pick a couple of interesting places for a visit on their way to Yellowstone. Cheyenne is close enough for a weekend or one-day trip from Denver, and it's only another hour or two to other towns in the area.

In Cheyenne, be sure to visit the **State Capitol** and three excellent museums: the **Wyoming State Museum, Frontier Days Old West Museum,** and **Nelson Museum of the West.** A number of places along the Oregon Trail are well worth seeing, particularly the historic buildings of **Fort Laramie National Historic Site,** and a couple of nearby places: the deep **Oregon Trail ruts** made by wagons a century and a half ago and **Register Cliff,** where many emigrant names are inscribed. The town of Lusk has a surprisingly large **Stagecoach Museum** with one of two surviving Cheyenne and Black Hills stages, and for a down-to-earth slice of life in farming country, head to one of the weekly auctions at **Torrington Livestock Market.** State parks at **Glendo** and **Guernsey** are good places for hiking or water recreation.

Cheyenne

As you drive west toward Cheyenne (pop. 55,000), the Colorado Rockies loom on the southwestern horizon like whitecaps in a sea of barely rolling plains, snow fences, stunted grass, and the highway slashing toward the boundary of sight. You catch quick glimpses of the great mountain ranges that ramble across Wyoming. Gradually they grow larger, and finally you know that the Great Plains will soon be left behind. It's easy to imagine how this must have looked to the railroad passengers who passed this way in the 1860s, watching the mountains loom on the horizon as the train rolled into Wyoming. Suddenly you're shaken into the present by the highway sign "Cheyenne Next 4 Exits." Suburban homes crowd over the gentle hillsides, and the state capitol gleams in the setting sun.

You have arrived at Wyoming's political and transportation fulcrum.

The city of Cheyenne hunkers down in the southeastern corner of Wyoming, just 10 miles from Colorado and 40 miles from Nebraska. Its wide, tree-draped urban streets and graceful older homes form a gridwork through downtown, while suburbia spreads its tentacles into the surrounding prairie. Cheyenne is remarkably similar to (although smaller than) another state capital—Lincoln, Nebraska. For many visitors, it offers a taste of the West without leaving the Midwest. Folks in Casper or Cody view Cheyenne as the capital of eastern Wyoming and as a city whose ties are really closer to the markets of Denver or Omaha than to the sagebrush, oil, gas, and coal of Wyoming. People in Cheyenne brush aside these criticisms. They know everyone else is just jealous.

As the state capital, the largest city, home to a strategic military base, a center for various governmental agencies, and a major transportation hub, Cheyenne is a big fish in the small pond called Wyoming. The city has one of the most stable and prosperous economies in the state. Its largest employer (nearly 5,000 people) is Francis E. Warren Air Force Base, but several thousand other folks work for federal, state, and local government agencies around town. Railroad tracks of the Union Pacific and Burlington Northern Railroads head to the four points of the compass, and Cheyenne is right at the junction of two of the primary transportation routes across the Plains and the Rockies: I-25 and I-80. About 800 folks work for Union Pacific, with hundreds more employed in light industry, communications, air transport (Great Lakes Aviation is based here), and shipping firms. Both Wal-Mart and Lowe's have major distribution centers in Cheyenne, and *Inc. Magazine* recently ranked the city one of the top places to do business in America.

As the sprawl from Denver and Fort Collins heads ever outward, you'll even hear Cheyenne called a Front Range city. It's two hours away by car, but a number of business folks cut that time by flying daily to Denver. Drive out Dell Range Boulevard on the north side of town to find mile after mile of new developments, with national chains of all stripes moving in. The homogenization of America continues, even in Wyoming.

HISTORY

Like so many other Wyoming cities, Cheyenne is a creation of the railroad. It is the oldest of Wyoming's railroad towns, established as the Union Pacific raced westward in 1867. When General Grenville M. Dodge was planning the new railroad's route, he decided to establish a major rail terminal in the plains just before the long climb over the Laramie Mountains. He named the new settlement Cheyenne, for the Indians who lived in this country. The word is from the Sioux Indian term "Shey an nah," meaning "People of a Strange Tongue." (Some have suggested a less complimentary origin for the word, the French term *chienne,* meaning "bitch.") While Dodge was there, Indians attacked a Mormon grading crew, killing two men. The graveyard was started before the first building was up. By November of that year the new town of Cheyenne had swollen to 4,000 people, earning the nickname "Magic City of the Plains." It was easily the largest town in Wyoming and has remained that way for much of the state's history.

At first, Cheyenne consisted of the usual hell-on-wheels railroad settlement of tents and hastily erected buildings. Railroad workers and army men from nearby Fort D. A. Russell turned the town into a rip-roaring place—every second building was a saloon, and burlesque

CHEYENNE AREA CLIMATE

| | SNOWFALL | | MAXIMUM TEMP. |
| | RAINFALL | | MINIMUM TEMP. |

Average Maximum Temp.	57.8°F
Average Minimum Temp.	33.1°F
Annual Rainfall	15.29"
Annual Snowfall	56.1"

To Chugwater and Wheatland

RIDING CLUB RD

RD

25 85 87

219

FOUR MILE

212

RD

FRANCIS E

YELLOWSTONE

POWDERHOUSE

WARREN

STOREY   BLVD

ROUNDTOP

WYOMING GAME AND FISH

AMERICAN FAMILY LODGE

BLM OFFICE

SEE "DOWNTOWN CHEYENNE" MAP

EXIT 12

85

AVANTI RESTAURANT

AIR

DELL   RANGE

CENTRAL   AVE

Lions Park

Frontier Park

8TH   AVE

CONVERSE   AVE

WARREN ICBM & HERITAGE MUSEUM

RANDALL   AVE

FORCE

CAREY   AVE

CHEYENNE MUNICIPAL AIRPORT

CAPITOL STADIUM 12 THEATRE

HIGH SCHOOL

VA HOSPITAL

W PERSHING   BLVD

COLE SQUARE SHOPPING CENTER

STATE CAPITOL

CENTRAL   AVE

WARREN   AVE

LOGAN   AVE

CHEYENNE MOTEL

HOME RANCH MOTEL

BASE

ALT 30

FIREBIRD MOTEL

VIADUCT   AVE

To Curt Gowdy State Park and Laramie

210

HAPPY JACK   RD

ST

HAMPTON INN

DAYS INN

LA QUINTA INN

EXPRESS INN

W LINCOLNWAY

19TH   ST

85   85

LITTLE AMERICA

1ST   ST

80

EXIT 358

To Laramie

EXIT 359

EXIT 8

OTTO   RD

25 87

FOX   FARM   RD

GREELEY

COWBOY SOUTH

225

WYOMING TRAVEL INFORMATION CENTER

ROUND-UP MOTEL

TANK FARM   RD

COLLEGE

DR

212

AB CAMPGROUND

HWY

COMFORT INN

85

To Terry Bison Ranch and Denver, CO

To Greeley and Denver, CO

© AVALON TRAVEL PUBLISHING, INC.

shows were the rage. At center stage stood a 36-by-100-foot tent housing Headquarters Saloon. Reporter James Chisholm noted:

> *The wildest roughs from all parts of the country are congregated here, as one may see by glancing into the numerous dance houses and gambling halls – men who carry on the trade of robbery openly, and would not scruple to kill a man for ten dollars.*

Settling Down

Within a decade, however, Cheyenne had settled into a more urbane stage. The railroad provided access to the East, not only allowing cattle to be shipped but also keeping the town abreast of the latest fashions and furnishings and bringing news of world events. With the discovery of gold in the Black Hills, Cheyenne became the primary shipping center for supplies to the Black Hills and gold bullion from the smelters.

By the 1880s, Cheyenne had grown to a cosmopolitan small city of 14,000 people and was declared the wealthiest city per capita in the world. It was one of the first cities in the West to have electric lights; a power plant charged batteries during the day and then delivered them by wagon in time for the evening's use. In 1882, the elaborate Cheyenne Opera House opened with great fanfare. With seating for up to 1,000 people, luxurious furnishings, and a huge 52-light gas chandelier overhead, it was regarded as the equal of any in New York and attracted such performers as Lily Langtry, Sarah Bernhardt, P. T. Barnum, Buffalo Bill Cody, and the Royal Opera Company.

Despite its peripheral location, Cheyenne was the logical place for Wyoming's territorial capital. The railroad was here, as were Fort D. A. Russell and most of the wealthy cattlemen. In 1869, the first territorial governor, John A. Campbell, made Cheyenne the temporary capital, with the legislature meeting in rented quarters. Five years later it almost lost that title to Laramie in a rump session of the legislature, but after completion of the capitol building in 1888 it became obvious that the governmental seat would remain in Cheyenne.

Rule of the Cattle Barons

Destruction of the once-vast herds of bison and the eviction of Indians who had lived in Wyoming for centuries suddenly opened up nearly all of the territory to cattle grazing. At the time, Laramie County extended all the way to the border with Montana, so it was logical that Cheyenne became the focal point for hundreds of cattlemen who rushed in to make a killing on the booming cattle market. The most famous of these was Alexander Swan, founder of a spread so large that it required a special book to keep track of all its cattle brands. Other part-time residents included members of English nobility such as Moreton Frewen (uncle of Sir Winston Churchill) and Sir Oliver H. Wallop, seventh earl of Portsmouth.

Fort D. A. Russell

In 1862, President Lincoln approved creation of a military fort to guard the then-proposed transcontinental railroad against Indian attacks. When the railroad finally arrived five years later, the army established a fort near the new town of Cheyenne. Both the town and fort were officially established on the same day. Originally named for Civil War general David A. Russell, the new fort grew into America's largest cavalry outpost. Troops from the base were sent out to protect railroad survey and construction parties and later served as guards along the route. The **Cheyenne Depot,** commonly called Camp Carlin, was established adjacent to the fort, providing vital equipment for a dozen army posts scattered throughout the Indian frontier. It was abandoned in 1890.

With forced relocation of the Indians to reservations, the role of Fort D. A. Russell changed and it became a training center and strategic garrison for the Rockies. New brick barracks and officers' quarters were completed in 1885, and the dusty parade ground was planted with grass and trees. Wyoming senator Francis E. Warren had long "brought home the bacon" by gaining political plums for his constituents, and one of the biggest was continued support for the fort in Cheyenne. After his death in 1929, the fort was renamed **Francis E. Warren Air Force Base.**

The base served as a training center and POW camp in World War II and was transferred to the newly created Air Force in 1947.

The fort's current role began in 1958, when the arrival of Atlas missiles made Warren the nation's first nuclear-missile base. The event was greeted with glee by Cheyenne's then-mayor, Worth Story, who exclaimed, "Cheyenne is proud to be the nation's number one target for enemy missiles." In 1986 the base became home to 50 of the 10-warhead "Peacekeeper" MX nuclear missiles—the only place where these missiles were kept. By the 1980s, F. E. Warren controlled 40 percent of the nation's intercontinental ballistic missiles (ICBMs), making it one of the most important ICBM centers in America. The "Peacekeepers" were removed in 2005, and the base's 150 Minuteman III missiles have all been rendered unlaunchable in the post–Cold War era. Despite these changes, the base remains Cheyenne's largest employer, employing more than 4,000 military and civilian personnel.

SIGHTS

For a fine introduction to Cheyenne, take one of the **trolley tours** that depart from the historic

FRANCIS E. WARREN

One of Wyoming's best-known politicians was Francis E. Warren (1844–1929). A lifelong Republican, Warren served as both a territorial and state governor before being elected to the U.S. Senate in 1890. He was one of the millionaire cattle barons – his ranch once held more than 100,000 sheep. This land later got him in trouble when he was charged with fencing public land for his own gain, but his friendship with President Theodore Roosevelt helped keep him out of prison. While territorial governor in the 1880s, Warren ardently agitated for statehood. His 37 years in the U.S. Senate made him one of its most powerful members, and newspapers labeled him the "Boss of Wyoming." Upon his death, Fort D. A. Russell was renamed in his honor.

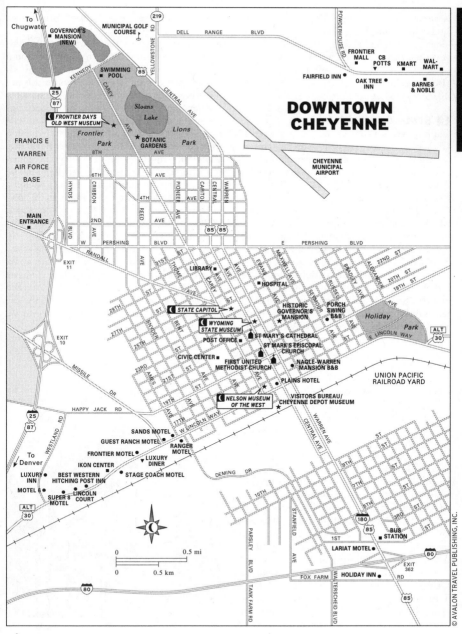

DOWNTOWN CHEYENNE

depot at 15th and Capitol 10 A.M.–4 P.M. daily mid-May to mid-September. These 90-minute loop tours cost $8 ($4 for kids) and include stops at various historic attractions. You can get on or off at any point along the way. Get tickets at the visitors bureau inside the depot (121 W. 15th St., 307/778-3133 or 800/426-5009).

State Capitol

Capitol Avenue—one of the primary streets in Cheyenne—seems to symbolize the city's history. State government buildings line the street, and at the ends are the two main reasons for Cheyenne's existence: the old Union Pacific depot to the south and the State Capitol to the north. The Capitol building is open 8:30 A.M.–4:30 P.M. Monday–Friday and informative brochures are available at the information desk. Tours are available for groups of 10 or more, but call 307/777-7220 two weeks ahead for reservations.

Wyoming's capitol falls in the tradition of ostentatious political structures and is modeled after the Capitol in Washington, D.C. The initial building was authorized with a $150,000 appropriation from the territorial legislature in 1886. The cornerstone was laid on May 18, 1887, and the central section was completed the following year, with the two wings added later. When completed in 1917, the building measured its present 300-foot length. The 146-foot-tall dome has been regilded four times, most recently in 1986. (Don't bother trying to climb up to steal any; the entire dome is covered with less than an ounce of gold.)

The capitol's central rotunda has a checkered marble floor with cherry wood staircases leading to the second story. Directly overhead is a beautiful blue stained-glass window imported from England. Interesting historical photographs line the second-floor walls. The Senate chambers are in the west wing; the House meets in the east wing. You can view the legislature from the third-floor balconies when it is in session. Inside the legislative chambers are four Western murals painted by Allen T. True—designer of Wyoming's bucking-bronco symbol—along with others by Joseph Henry Sharp and Bill Gollings. Look upward in each chamber to see the large Tiffany stained-glass ceilings with the state seal.

From the outside, the capitol dome seems strangely tall; rumor has it that architects once voted it the nation's ugliest state capitol, although Alaska's would give it a run for this dubious honor. Out front stands a bronze statue of **Esther Hobart Morris,** the person credited (incorrectly) with making Wyoming the first state to grant women voting rights. Directly behind the capitol building is the much newer **Herschler Building,** named for the only Wyoming governor to serve three terms, Ed Herschler. It has an attractive interior atrium and houses a cafeteria and various state offices. Nearby is an 18-foot-tall bronze statue by Edward Fraughton, *Spirit of Wyoming,* a bucking horse and rider that seem almost suspended in space. It is perhaps fitting that the two nicknames of Wyoming—"the Equality State" and "the Cowboy State"—are symbolized by statues on either side of the State Capitol. Wander around the flower-garnished grounds and you'll discover a monument to the Spanish-American War, a bronze bison statue, and a replica of the Liberty Bell.

© DON PITCHER

State Capitol, Cheyenne

CHEYENNE AND BLACK HILLS STAGE

With the 1874 discovery of gold in the Black Hills, a stampede of miners headed north in search of riches. A fierce competition quickly developed between Cheyenne, Wyoming, and Sidney, Nebraska, to be the jumping-off point for miners. With support for road construction from the Wyoming Territorial Legislature, a 300-mile stage route was soon laid out, and the first coach headed north on February 3, 1876. The Cheyenne and Black Hills Stage, Mail and Express Line had begun.

The line ran almost straight north from Cheyenne to the vicinity of present-day Lusk before veering into Dakota Territory and ending at Deadwood. Drivers made the trip in three days and three nights, with station stops every 15 miles that usually lasted less than three minutes – just long enough to change horses. It was a strenuous and tiring journey through Sioux Indian territory, over treacherous river crossings, and past hideouts of notorious road agents. On the long trip south from the mines, special armored coaches carried gold bullion in steel strongboxes, protected by 4-6 armed guards. Often they held up to $100,000 in gold dust and nuggets and sometimes as much as $350,000! Outlaws – including Frank and Jesse James and Big Nose George Parrot's gang – targeted these coaches, riding off with both the gold and the horses. One of the most infamous attack sites was near the Robber's Roost Stage Station, along the Cheyenne River north of Lusk. Here the stages were frequently attacked, sometimes every day.

The "Deadwood Coaches," such as the one used by Buffalo Bill in his Wild West Show, were actually the famed Concord coaches built by Abbott and Downing of Concord, New Hampshire. They could jam nine passengers inside (first and second class) for $15-20 per head and an equal number on top (third class) at $10 apiece. Riders on top sometimes had to get off and push the stage up hills. (Despite the attention given to stagecoaches, much of the traffic along the goldfields route was in freight wagons pulled by long strings of oxen.) Upon completion of the Chicago and Northwestern Railroad to Rapid City, traffic on the Cheyenne-Deadwood stage dropped, and the last coach ran on February 19, 1887. In just 11 years, the stage line had carved out a big piece of history, and its closing marked the end of one of the most romantic chapters in the history of the West.

Historic Governors' Mansion

The old governors' mansion (300 E. 21st St., 307/777-7878, http://wyoparks.state.wy.us/ HGMslide.htm, open 9 A.M.–5 P.M. Tues.–Sat. year-round, free) has been lovingly restored. The 2.5-story brick building was completed in 1905 at a cost of $33,000 and is in the Georgian style, with four Corinthian columns out front. A 10-minute video provides information about the house and its inhabitants, including the nation's first woman governor, Nellie Tayloe Ross; she lived here 1925–1927. Different rooms in the home are furnished with pieces from several periods representing the many families who called this place home through the decades; some furnishings are from 1905, but most were added in 1937.

The current governors' mansion, which was completed in 1976, sits near the intersection of Central Avenue and I-25. Tours of the new mansion are offered only for groups; call 307/777-7398 for appointments.

◖ Wyoming State Museum

Inside the Barrett Building at 2301 Central Avenue, the Wyoming State Museum (307/777-7022, http://wyomuseum.state.wy.us, free admission) features a mix of continuing and changing exhibits. Permanent displays showcase coal mining, wildlife, dinosaurs, and Indian artifacts. Visitors will also find a 3-D model of the state (showing historic sites), an impressive silver service set from the decommissioned battleship USS *Wyoming,* and a fun hands-on history room for kids. Be sure to stop by the museum gift shop for high-quality regional items and

Wyoming books. The museum is open 9 A.M.–4:30 P.M. Monday–Saturday May–October, and 9 A.M.–4:30 P.M. Monday–Friday and 10 A.M.–2 P.M. Saturday the rest of the year. (It's always closed on Sundays and holidays.)

❰ Frontier Days Old West Museum

Right next to the rodeo grounds in Frontier Park, Frontier Days Old West Museum (307/778-7290 or 800/778-7290, www.oldwestmuseum.org) is one of the most interesting museums in Wyoming. It's open 9 A.M.–5 P.M. Monday–Friday and 10 A.M.–5 P.M. Saturday–Sunday Memorial Day–Labor Day (daily 8 A.M.–8 P.M. during Frontier Days), and 8 A.M.–5 P.M. Monday–Friday and 9 A.M.–5 P.M. Saturday–Sunday the rest of the year. Admission is $5 adults, free for kids under 13. The museum's focus is on Western heritage, with changing historical and art exhibits, Indian artifacts, early clothing, old films, Frontier Days displays—including a bronc-riding saddle that you can try out—and a special "Hole in the Wall" hands-on kids' room. The museum is best known for its extraordinary collection of horse-drawn transportation of all types. More than 40 carriages, including many that appear in the annual Frontier Days parade, are displayed. The stars are a Cheyenne–Deadwood stage, a prairie schooner, sleighs, a buckboard (the name came from the lack of springs on the axles), and, of course, a surrey with the fringe on top. Be sure to check out the luxurious landau—sort of an early convertible. The gift shop sells various Frontier Days souvenirs and historical books. Out front is a sculpture of champion bull rider Lane Frost, who was killed during a 1989 ride at Frontier Days. A big **Western Spirit Art Show and Sale** takes place at the museum during Frontier Days, and other exhibits fill the galleries at other times.

❰ Nelson Museum of the West

This surprising museum (1714 Carey Ave., 307/635-7670, www.nelsonmuseum.com, $3 adults, $2 seniors, free for kids under 13) is right in the heart of downtown Cheyenne. The collection was acquired by Robert L. Nelson, a retired lawyer, big-game hunter, and owner of Manitou Gallery (across the street). It reflects his tastes, with an odd mix of Old West artifacts and memorabilia, along with big-game trophies from around the globe. You'll find a silver and gold saddle valued at $300,000 in the same room as an African lion. Despite its idiosyncrasies, the museum is well worth the price of admission, particularly if you're interested in century-old Indian and cowboy items. The museum covers three floors, so be sure to see it all, including the collection of Western movie posters, furnishings from the homes of Wyoming cattle barons, a painted buffalo robe, Mexican sombreros, cowgirl clothing, and even gruesome photos of dead outlaws. Students of the West will also want to spend time in the research library.

The museum is open 8:30 A.M.–4:30 P.M. Monday–Saturday June–August, and 8:30 A.M.–noon and 1–4:30 P.M. Monday–Friday the rest of the year.

Botanic Gardens

One of Cheyenne's lesser-known gems is the fine Botanic Gardens (307/637-6458, www.botanic.org, open 8 A.M.–4:30 P.M. Mon.–Fri., and 11 A.M.–3:30 P.M. Sat.–Sun., no charge), in Lions Park.

Troubled kids, people with disabilities, and seniors grow flowers and vegetables here. Visitors find this a pleasant place to relax, especially during the winter, when the warmth and the showy flowers are a welcome break. Inside the passively solar-heated greenhouse (look for the black metal drums filled with water) are three sections containing everything from vegetables to cacti. The central section is home to tall banana plants, tropical flowers, and a pond filled with goldfish and turtles. The angel's trumpet, with its beautiful orange flowers, is the centerpiece. Upstairs is a small library containing gardening magazines and books. Outside are pleasant picnic tables, ponds, a gazebo set among the flower beds, native plants, and shade trees. The grounds are popular for weddings, and a paved one-mile path (marked with famous Wyoming cattle brands) connects the gardens to the Old West Museum and continues around the lake.

SOUTHEAST WYOMING

Union Pacific Railroad Depot

The railroad business reached its peak in the 1940s, when Cheyenne had the finest equipment and service anywhere in America. The railroad is still an important part of the city's economy, with freight trains rumbling through day and night. Drop by the picturesque old Union Pacific Railroad depot at the south end of Capitol Avenue to see one of the finest remaining train stations in the West. Built of red and gray sandstone in 1886, the structure was at one time the largest building in the territory and the most elaborate depot between Omaha and San Francisco. It occupies an entire block, with a clock tower and Romanesque arched openings adding a touch of class. (The depot was built as a political payoff to Governor Francis E. Warren for restoring order after the 1885 massacre of Chinese workers at the Union Pacific's vital Rock Springs coal mines.)

The building reopened in 2004 after an extensive renovation, and now houses a railway museum, the Cheyenne Convention and Visitors Bureau, a coffee shop, and restaurant. The plaza out front is used for farmers markets, Friday afternoon concerts, pancake breakfasts during Frontier Days, and other events. Behind the depot is an enormous Union Pacific roundhouse built in 1931 and still used to maintain locomotives, but it's not open to the public. The plaza out front is a great place for lunch and has Saturday farmers markets and Friday night concerts. Check out the colorful eight-feet-tall **giant boots** in the plaza and scattered at other places around town through 2006.

At the **Cheyenne Depot Museum** (307/632-3905, www.cheyennedepotmuseum.org, $5 adults, free for kids under 13) the focus is—not surprisingly—on the city's fascinating railroad history through photos and exhibits. The gift shop sells rail paraphernalia, and a model railroad exhibit was to be added in 2006. The museum is open 8 A.M.–7 P.M. Monday–Friday, 9 A.M.–5 P.M. Saturday, and 11 A.M.–5 P.M. Sunday late May–early September, and 8 A.M.–5 P.M. Monday–Friday, 10 A.M.–5 P.M. Saturday, and noon–5 P.M. Sunday the rest of the year.

Holliday Park, along East 17th Street, has a **Big Boy locomotive,** one of only 25 ever

old Union Pacific Railroad Depot

© DON PITCHER

made and one of the largest steam locomotives ever built. It was used to haul freight over the mountain tracks between Cheyenne and Ogden, Utah. A couple of blocks east of here is a boxcar from the **French Merci Train,** given as a thank-you for food Americans gave the French after World War II.

Cattle Baron's Row

Cheyenne has many interesting Victorian buildings. Stop by the visitor center for a free walking-tour brochure that leads you through historic downtown. Of particular note are the Victorian homes along 17th Street, "Cattle Baron's Row."

The **Whipple House** (300 E. 17th St.) is a wonderful Victorian built in 1883 by Ithamar C. Whipple, a wealthy merchant, cattleman, mayor, and state legislator. The home was later occupied by attorney and one-time Wyoming Territorial Supreme Court Justice John W. Lacey, who defended both the notorious outlaw Tom Horn and the equally infamous oilman Harry Sinclair. Now on the National Register of Historic Places, it houses a fine-dining restaurant.

Right across the street is the **Nagle-Warren**

THE CHEYENNE CLUB

One of the most unusual organizations in frontier Wyoming was the Cheyenne Club, first established in 1880 as an exclusive English-style country club. With membership limited to 200, it included only the wealthiest of the cattlemen, men who quickly became known as cattle barons. Many came from aristocratic social backgrounds, and the club included graduates of the finest universities on the East Coast and Europe. Some were millionaires who summered in Cheyenne and then sailed back to Europe for luxurious winters. With the growing prosperity of the cattle business, the Cheyenne Club claimed the finest French Canadian chef and steward in the country and was said to be the first club in America to have electricity. Dinner dress was always formal. Despite strict rules on behavior (no card cheating, pipe smoking, or profanity), one member did manage to shoot a hole through a painting of a cow and bull—he claimed it to be an abomination against purebred cattle. Upstairs were elaborate apartments for members and guests, while the lavishly furnished downstairs included a spacious dining room, billiard room, reading room, card room, lounge, and wraparound porch. With the sudden bust that followed the harsh winter of 1886-1887, the cattle barons were brought abruptly back to reality. Many went out of business, and the club quickly followed. The historic Cheyenne Club was razed in 1936.

Mansion (307/637-3333 or 800/811-2610, www.naglewarrenmansion.com), another grand place from the same era. Built by businessman Erasmus Nagle in 1888, it later belonged to Francis E. Warren, who served as governor and U.S. senator. Warren's friend, President Theodore Roosevelt, slept here several times. Nagle built his home at the same time as the state capitol was being constructed, and he used stones that the capitol masons had rejected. Unfortunately, the masons were proven correct. The stones deteriorated when exposed to the weather and had to be covered with stucco. Today, the Nagle-Warren Mansion is an upscale bed-and-breakfast that has been lovingly restored inside and out. For a taste of gentility, attend the mansion's **English high tea,** served in Victorian style 2–4 P.M. every Friday and Saturday. The cost is $10. These gatherings usually fill up, so be sure to make reservations a day or two ahead. Guests are treated to tea, scones, cookies, tea sandwiches, tartlets, and other sweets served in the elegant parlor.

Cathedrals

Cheyenne has several of Wyoming's most ostentatious and interesting churches. **St. Mark's Episcopal Church** (1908 Central Ave., 307/634-7709) is the oldest, begun in 1886 but not completed until 1893. The exterior is of red lava stones with traditional stained-glass windows, including one by Tiffany. This was the home church for many transplanted British and Scottish cattle barons, so it is fitting that the funeral for gunman Tom Horn, who worked for some of them, was held here in 1903.

Two other impressive churches are **St. Mary's Catholic Cathedral** (2107 Capitol Ave., 307/635-9261) built in 1907 of native sandstone in the Gothic Revival style, and the **First United Methodist Church** (18th and Central Aves., 307/632-1410), completed in 1894 and also made from sandstone. The previous Methodist church, on the same site, was where marshal, gunman, and gambler Wild Bill Hickok married a circus performer, Agnes Lake Thatcher, in 1876. The officiating clergyman wrote in the registry, "Don't think they meant it." Five months later, Wild Bill was shot in the back in a Deadwood saloon. Agnes Thatcher is *not* the woman buried next to Hickok in the Deadwood cemetery; instead it's Calamity Jane.

F. E. Warren Air Force Base

The entrance to Warren Air Force Base (www.warren.af.mil) is flanked by four missiles, but the buildings are surprisingly quaint two- and three-story red-brick structures set back from the tree-lined streets—220 of these immaculate structures are on the National Register of Historic Places. Expansive green lawns give it a country-club feeling. This is essentially a self-supporting city, with child-care facilities, schools, stores, a veterinary clinic, and that old neighborhood standby, nuclear warheads. The only aircraft kept here most of the time are UH-60 Blackhawk helicopters, but during Frontier Days jets take off constantly from the airport, screaming overhead in sharp climbs that elicit gasps from the crowd.

Because of heightened security concerns, Wyoming's primary military base is generally accessible only to people with a valid military ID, although exceptions may be made; contact public affairs (307/773-3381) at least two weeks in advance. The general public *is* admitted on the first weekend of Frontier Days in July, when an air show by the U.S. Air Force Thunderbirds, base tours, a living-history camp, and mountain-man rendezvous are the featured events.

If you're able to get on base, be sure to request time at the small **Warren ICBM and Heritage Museum** (307/773-2980, www.pawnee.com/fewmuseum), with military memorabilia and missile exhibits. These include photos of the early Atlas rockets and Minuteman I missiles, a model of the MX missiles the Air Force euphemistically calls "Peacekeepers," and old launch-control equipment. Grave-gazers may want to visit the base cemetery, where soldiers and others have been interred since 1867. An interesting pamphlet available at the museum tells the stories of some who lie here, including German POWs who died on the base during World War II.

Wyoming Hereford Ranch

In 1883, cattle barons Alexander and Thomas Swan, backed by European investors, formed the Wyoming Hereford Association, placing 400 purebred Hereford bulls and cows on a ranch near Cheyenne. This was the first real attempt to bring quality cattle to the state and was at one time the world's largest herd of thoroughbred cattle. Gradually other ranches followed this lead and the rangy longhorns of Texas were replaced by the more manageable

missiles outside F. E. Warren Air Force Base

© DON PITCHER

Herefords—now the dominant breed in Wyoming. The 60,000-acre Wyoming Hereford Ranch (307/634-1905) has survived for more than 120 years and contains many historic structures in immaculate condition. It's the oldest continuously registered livestock operation in America. A small visitor center shows off awards and old photos and has a walking tour map. Out front you'll find monuments to prize bulls Prince Domino and Lerch, who sired many of the prize whiteface Herefords in America today. Prince Domino's memorial reads, "He lived and died and won a lasting name." How touching. You can wander around the showcase ranch and explore the red barns and other buildings at your leisure. Wyoming Hereford Ranch is five miles east of Cheyenne; take Campstool Road (exit 367) off I-80. Since 1980, the ranch has been owned by a local surgeon, Dr. Sloan Hales, who lives in the Tudor mansion just up the hill.

Other Attractions

Interested in learning about a real outlaw? Visit the tiny exhibit of **Tom Horn** memorabilia on the second floor of the old courthouse on the northwest corner of 19th and Carey streets.

For something a bit more genteel, hop on the free **horse-drawn carriages** that run from Depot Plaza noon–6 P.M. Wednesday–Sunday throughout the summer. Contact the Visitors Bureau (307/778-3133) for details.

The **Wyoming Department of Game and Fish** (5400 Bishop Blvd., 307/777-4600, http://gf.state.wy.us) has a small museum/visitor center with wildlife dioramas and photographs, plus an aquarium containing native trout. It's open 8 A.M.–5 P.M. Monday–Friday all year, plus 9 A.M.–5 P.M. Saturday and Sunday in the summer. No charge.

Historic **Lakeview Cemetery** has graves dating to the 1870s. Get a fascinating pamphlet on the cemetery at the visitor center and head out for a walking tour of Cheyenne's early residents, including Wyoming politicians Francis E. Warren, Joseph M. Carey, and Nellie Tayloe Ross, along with John Portugee Phillips, the man who made the famous 236-mile horseback ride from Fort Phil Kearny in 1866.

ENTERTAINMENT

During June and July, visitors gather at Lincolnway and Carey streets to watch the **Cheyenne Gunslingers** (307/635-1028, www.cheyenne–gunslingers.org) put on a Hollywood-style shoot-'em-up. Hope I don't give anything away, but the good guys invariably win. It's pretty tacky and bears absolutely no relation to Cheyenne's rather civilized history. The "gunfights" take place at 6 P.M. on weekdays and at "high noon" on Saturdays (more frequently during Frontier Days). Also here at "Gunslinger Square" is a replica of the gallows used to hang Tom Horn (no mock hangings, alas) and a nearby "Soda Saloon." A *soda saloon?* What would a real cowboy say? On Friday nights June–August, drop by Depot Plaza downtown for **free concerts.**

During July and early August, tourists fill the historic Atlas Theatre (built in 1887; 211 W. 16th St.) to watch comic Western melodramas by the **Little Theatre Players** (307/638-6543, www.cheyennelittletheatre.org). The experience includes plenty of audience participation, and popcorn, pizza, and beer are for sale. It also presents theatrical productions of musicals, comedies, and dramas throughout the year.

In existence for more than 50 years, the **Cheyenne Symphony Orchestra** (307/778-8561, www.cheyennesymphony.org) performs September–May at the Cheyenne Civic Center (510 W. 20th St.).

Nightlife

Cheyenne is a hopping town when it comes to nightlife, especially during Frontier Days, when every country-and-western band this side of the Mississippi finds a place to play. Check the Friday edition of the *Wyoming Tribune-Eagle* (www.wyomingnews.com) for this week's entertainment offerings.

Outlaw Saloon (next to the Rodeo Inn at 3839 E. Lincolnway, 307/635-7552) calls itself "Wyoming's #1 country hot spot," with live music Monday–Saturday, plus free dance lessons and nightly drink specials, and weeknight happy hours. Other attractions include dart and pool tournaments.

Rockin' Rodeo (312 S. Greeley Hwy., 307/637-3800) features classic rock bands Tues.–Sun. nights. **Goofy's Tavern** (2801 E. Lincolnway, 307/634-1501) has pool, darts, karaoke, dancing, and an array of unusual mixed drinks. **Little Bear Inn** (307/634-3684), three miles north of Cheyenne, has live music Tuesday–Saturday nights. **Cheyenne Club** (1617 Capitol Ave., 307/635-7777) is a favorite of the Air Force crowd. The big dance floor fills as the DJ spins Top 40 dance tunes nightly.

Movies

Local multiplex film-houses with stadium seating are **Frontier 9** in the Frontier Mall (1400 Dell Range Blvd., 307/634-9499, www.carmike.com) and **Capitol Stadium 12** (3410 Concord Ave., 307/638-7469, www.wyomies.com). Both **Cole Square Cinema** (517 Cole Square Shopping Center, 307/635-2923, www.carmike.com) and **Lincoln Movie Palace** (1615 Central St., 307/637-7469, www.wyomovies.com) offers second-run flicks for just $1. The latter is a classic place that opened in 1927.

◖ FRONTIER DAYS

Cheyenne Frontier Days—the "Daddy of 'em All"—is Wyoming's largest and most famous annual event, with entertainment covering the spectrum from professional rodeos to parades and free pancake breakfasts. Festivities begin the last full week of July and continue for 10 action-packed days. There's something for everyone at this memorable event, which has been in existence for more than a century, but the rodeo is the main attraction for more than 300,000 visitors from all 50 states and many other nations. The largest number commute in from Denver, while others jam the campgrounds and motels for 100 miles in all directions.

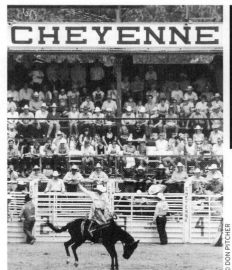

© DON PITCHER

Cheyenne's Frontier Days rodeo

History

There are several versions of the origin of Cheyenne Frontier Days, the most plausible being that it was inspired when a Union Pacific employee, F. W. Angier, watched a group of cowboys from the Swan Land and Cattle Company trying to load an ornery horse into a railroad car. The spectacle sparked his imagination, and when he suggested the idea of a Wild West buckin' and ropin' contest, others quickly jumped on the bandwagon. Just one month later (September 1897), the first Cheyenne Frontier Days celebration began. It was a rip-roaring success, with 15,000 people in attendance. In addition to various cowboy contests, Frontier Days included several events that you won't see today—a staged battle between Sioux Indians and the U.S. Cavalry, Pony Express demonstrations, and a mock stage holdup and hanging by vigilantes. Obviously, the production had been influenced by Buffalo Bill's Wild West Show, which was then touring Europe.

Most amusing of all was the dog and hare event, in which a rabbit was released to be chased by dogs. Unfortunately, the dogs in the race were quickly joined by many more from the stands, so no winner was declared, although the loser was obvious. Cheyenne Frontier Days has grown through the years to a 10-day celebration (two weekends) and is regarded as one of the top four rodeos in the world (the others being California's Salinas Rodeo, Canada's Calgary Stampede, and Oregon's Pendleton Round-Up). Local enthusiasts call it the world's largest outdoor rodeo and Western celebration.

Activities

Frontier Days centers on the daily rodeos, with the nation's top rodeo cowboys showing their stuff. The rodeo has all of the standard contests: bareback bronc riding, saddle bronc riding, Brahma bull riding, steer roping, calf roping, team roping, and steer wrestling. Other events include chaotic and amusing wild horse races and a real crowd-pleaser, the colt race (in which young colts race toward their mares). With a purse of more than $1 million, the largest regular-season payoff in rodeo, Frontier Days attracts more than 1,000 contestants, so many of the timed events must begin at 7 A.M.!

Frontier Park is the center for a range of other activities during Frontier Days, including free daily Indian dance performances, along with storytelling, handicrafts, and other popular activities at the **Indian village** on the south end of the parking lot. An Old West town springs to life at **Wild Horse Gulch** with blacksmithing, cowboy cooking, and other demonstrations.

Each evening brings **musical entertainment** by the top stars in country music (along with some rock acts). A large and well-run **carnival** provides stomach-churning rides, sugar and grease in all forms (cotton candy, candy apples, ice cream, corn dogs, burgers, ad nauseam), plus thousands of stuffed animal prizes, velvet paintings, and other necessities. Other entertainment includes comedians, balloon "sculptors," magicians, square dances, a chili cook-off, and a costume contest. After all this debauchery, try attending the **cowboy church services** held mornings at 9 A.M. on the rodeo grounds.

Also in Frontier Park is the Cheyenne Frontier Days Old West Museum (see *Sights*), where the annual **Cheyenne Frontier Days Western Art Show and Sale** offers the chance to view or buy works from more than 50 different Western artists.

Not everything happens in Frontier Park. On Monday, Wednesday, and Friday mornings during Frontier Days, a free downtown **pancake feed** stuffs more than 10,000 folks. The feeding frenzy runs 7–9 A.M. Check out the cement mixer used (in theory at least) to stir up 3,600 pounds of pancake batter and the Boy Scouts trying to catch the furiously flying flapjacks. Visitors sit on bales of hay and are treated to performances by Native American dancers and musicians of all stripes. For many children, the four **parades** (held at 9:30 A.M. on both Saturdays, Tuesday, and Thursday) are a special treat, featuring the largest collection of horse-drawn vehicles in the nation. You'll see everything from popcorn wagons to hearses.

The first weekend of Frontier Days is also the time for **Fort D. A. Russell Days** (307/773-2980) at F. E. Warren Air Force Base, the only time when the general public is admitted to the base. Featured attractions include an **air show** by the U.S. Air Force Thunderbirds, base tours, a living-history camp, and mountain-man rendezvous.

Practicalities

For information on Frontier Days, including a schedule of events, call 307/778-7222 or 800/227-6336, or visit the website www.cfdrodeo.com. Some of the night shows sell out well ahead of time, so reservations are advised. Rodeo tickets cost $12 for the bleacher seats up to $24 for prime seating over the chutes, and tickets to concerts are $30–47. Tickets are available from the ticket office south of the main grandstand or by calling the 800 number. Entrance to the midway is $2, but those holding tickets to Frontier Days events are admitted free.

Park ($6) in the huge lot along Carey and 8th avenues, or ride the shuttle from the lot near exit 10D on I-25. (Overnight camping is not allowed in the lots.) Because of the large number of participants in the calf-roping, steer-roping, and steer-wrestling contests, preliminary events are held most mornings 7–10 A.M., with no entrance fee charged. The main rodeo events start promptly at 1:30 P.M. and last three hours. Information wagons are in various locations around the park.

OTHER EVENTS

In addition to Frontier Days, Cheyenne hosts several popular events. In mid-June, the **Wyoming Brewer's Festival** (307/632-3905, www.wyomingbrewersfestival.com) attracts microbrewers and beer lovers from Wyoming and Colorado for a chance to sample the best local brews. Beer tasting is held at Frontier Park. **Super Day** on the last Saturday in June brings rides, games, a carnival, arts and crafts, and entertainment to Lions Park.

Another popular event is the **Laramie County Fair** (307/633-4534, www.laramiecountyfair.com), held the first full week in August at the fairgrounds. It has all the usual county-fair activities, including arts-and-craft contests, rodeos, exhibits, and 4-H competitions. Regional **horse shows** take place all summer at Laramie Community College (307/778-1291).

On Labor Day weekend, the **Cheyenne Cowboy Symposium and Celebration** (307/635-5788, www.cheyennecowboysymposium.com) features storytelling, cowboy poetry, music, and workshops.

The year winds down with a **Christmas**

Parade, Craft Show, and Concert (307/640-0555) in late November. The nighttime parade includes more than 100 lighted horse-drawn wagons, cars, tractors, and floats, plus a visit from St. Nick.

SHOPPING

Cheyenne is an automobile town, so most folks shop at the big malls scattered around the edges of the city. **Frontier Mall** (1400 Dell Range Blvd.) is one of the state's largest, with more than 75 stores. A Super Wal-Mart, Sam's Club, Target, and Kmart add to the town's shop-'til-you-plop allure. **Sierra Trading Post** (307/775-8050 or 800/713-4534, www.sierratradingpost.com) has a large factory outlet store at the Campstool exit off I-80, a few miles east of Cheyenne.

Western Gear

Downtown Cheyenne is home to one of the largest Western clothing stores in the state: **Wrangler** (1518 Capitol Ave., 307/634-3048, www.corralwest.com). Owned by Corral West, this is a great place to pick up a cowboy hat or boots.

Across the street from the Wrangler is **Wyoming Home** (218 W. 16th St., 307/638-2222, www.wyominghome.com) with unique Western furniture, home accessories, gifts, and artwork. It's the kind of shop you'd expect to find in Jackson (and will).

Just Dandy (212 W. 17th St., 307/635-2565) and **Snubbing Post** (1802 Dell Range Blvd., 307/638-6421) sell high-end women's Western clothing. For reasonably priced slightly used versions, visit the excellent **Donna's Wear It Again** (201 W. 17th St., 307/637-7005).

Galleries

The **Wyoming Arts Council Gallery** (2320 Capitol Ave., 307/777-7742, http://wyoarts.state.wy.us) features changing exhibits throughout the year. **Cheyenne Artist Guild** (307/632-2263) is the state's oldest art guild (since 1949) and has a nonprofit gallery at 1010 East 16th Street in Holliday Park. One of the best private collections can be found at **Manitou Gallery** (1715 Carey Ave., 307/635-0019). Also check out the Western and wildlife art at **Gallery West** (1601 Capitol Ave., 307/632-1258 or 800/786-2258, www.gallerywestframeplant.com). **DeSelm's Fine Art** (303 E. 17th St., 307/432-0606, www.deselmsfineart.com), across from the Whipple House, features original paintings, sculptures, pottery, and other works by regional artists.

Books

City News (18th and Carey Sts., 307/638-8671) has a big selection of magazines, along with some Wyoming titles. **Waldenbooks** in Frontier Mall (307/634-7099) is another good-sized shop. The largest bookstore in Cheyenne—in all of Wyoming for that matter—is **Barnes and Noble Books** (1851 Dell Range Blvd., 307/632-3000). The store has frequent book talks, signings, and poetry nights, along with a Starbucks. **The Phoenix** (1612 Capitol Ave., 307/632-3476) is a delightful little used bookstore in the heart of town.

RECREATION

Terry Bison Ranch (307/634-4171, www.terrybisonranch.com) has wagon tours, meals, horseback and pony rides, all sorts of unusual animals (including ostriches, peacocks, camels, llamas, and 2,500 bison), along with trout fishing, and even a miniature train. Horseback rides are also offered by **Dusty Bottums** (307/760-4942) and **Bit-O-Wyo Ranch** (307/638-6924); both are approximately 25 miles west of Cheyenne on Happy Jack Road.

The **Cheyenne Greenway** consists of 10 miles of paved walking and biking trails that cross the city. The trails are perfect for a romantic stroll or a morning run. One section follows Crow Creek, and the other parallels Dry Creek. Pick up a map brochure of the trails from the Visitors Bureau.

Swim or play on the water slide at Lions Park's **indoor pool** (307/637-6455) or the seasonal **Johnson outdoor pool** (307/637-6457) at 7th Street and House Avenue. The latter has two fun water slides. **Sloans Lake** in Lions Park (307/637-6361) is a summertime swimming hole and has paddleboat, kayak, and canoe rentals. Get swimming information on the web at www.cheyennecity.org/aquatics.htm. The pond is a good spot to look for birds, and a mile-long paved path circles the shoreline.

Lions Park also has a botanic garden (see *Sights*), an 18-hole **Airport Golf Course** (307/637-6418, www.cheyennecity.org/golf.htm), picnic areas, playgrounds, and ponds that turn into skating rinks in the winter. Cheyenne is home to a pair of nine-hole public golf courses: **Little America Golf Course** (307/775-8400 or 888/709-8383, www.littleamerica.com) and **Prairie View Golf Course** (307/637-6420, www.cheyennecity.org/golf.htm). The 18-hole **Warren Air Force Base Golf Course** (307/773-3556) is also accessible, but you'll need to call ahead to arrange a tee time and access through the gate.

IKON Center (1530 W. Lincolnway, 307/433-0024, www.ikoncenter.com) is an impressive facility for recreation (including lazer tag and video games), concerts, and conventions. In the winter, it houses Wyoming's best ice-skating/hockey rink. Next door is **Wyoming Adventure Miniature Golf** (307/775-0020), an enjoyable 18-hole course with a distinctive Wyoming theme.

Wyoming's only asphalt oval track, **Big Country Speedway** (4820 S. Greeley Hwy., 307/632-2107, www.bigcountryspeedway.com) just south of town, has been hosting Saturday night stock car racing since 1948.

ACCOMMODATIONS

Cheyenne has more than two dozen places to stay. The **Cheyenne Convention and Visitors Bureau**'s website (www.cheyenne.org) has web links and a summary of information for most local accommodations. Check here for a listing of available lodging during Frontier Days; it's updated daily. You can get the same information by calling the CC&VB at 307/778-3133 or 800/426-5009.

Be certain to take a look around before paying for a room at Cheyenne's cheapest motels, and also check the location. Places near the railroad—and this includes many of the less-expensive places—may suffer from noise as freight trains rumble past at all hours. Bring earplugs or look for a room away from the tracks.

The Frontier Days Shuffle

Finding a room in Cheyenne is usually easy, but when Frontier Days comes to town, motels and campgrounds book up six months in advance, and the rates often double or even triple during Frontier Days! Even towns as far away as Torrington are affected, so be sure to plan several months ahead for accommodations during the rodeo, especially for the final Saturday night. Most hotels start booking rooms in January. If you're booking a room with one of the chain hotels and folks at the national toll-free number say all of the rooms are gone for Frontier Days, don't just give up. Call the hotel directly and you may still find space.

Under $50

Don't expect the latest furnishings, but **Guest Ranch Motel** (1100 W. Lincolnway, 307/634-2137, $45–50 d) has reasonable prices, with small fridges and microwaves in all rooms. **Stage Coach Motel** (1515 W. Lincolnway, 307/634-4495, $39 s or $45–56 d) also has basic—but clean—rooms.

A good economy place is **Fleetwood Motel** (3800 E. Lincolnway, 307/638-8908 or 800/634-7763), where the clean and quiet rooms are $46 for one bed or $55 for two. A heated outdoor pool is on the premises.

For something different, stay at **Terry Bison Ranch** (307/634-4171, www.terrybisonranch.com), eight miles south of Cheyenne along I-25 and just on the Wyoming side of the state line. This 27,000-acre ranch has bunkhouse rooms ($40 d) with a shared bath, and rustic cabins ($80 for up to four) with kitchenettes and private baths.

$50-100

Express Inn (2512 W. Lincolnway, 307/632-7556 or 877/877-6807, www.expressinncheyenne.com, $50–65 d) has moderate prices, plus an indoor pool, hot tub, and wireless Internet. **Motel 6** (1735 Westland Rd., 307/635-6806 or 800/466-8356, www.motel6.com, $44–56 s or $50–62 d) includes an outdoor pool. Both Express Inn and Motel 6 are close to the busy railroad tracks.

Lincoln Court Motel (1720 W. Lincolnway, 307/638-3302 or 800/221-0125) has spacious standard rooms for $63–90 d ($159–189 during Frontier Days), including a heated outdoor pool, playground, fitness room, and light breakfast. Guests at Lincoln Court are welcome to use the hot tub and sauna at the adjacent Best Western Hitching Post Inn (same owners).

Many of the chain motels are scattered around Cheyenne, and one of your better choices is **La Quinta Motor Inn** (2410 W. Lincolnway, 307/632-7117 or 866/725-1661, www.lq.com, $79–126 d), with a little outdoor pool, wireless Internet, and a filling breakfast.

Another recommended place is the well-kept **Fairfield Inn** (1415 Stillwater Ave., 307/637-4070 or 800/228-2800, www.fairfieldinn.com, $90–100 d), across from Frontier Mall on the north side of town. Amenities include an attractive indoor pool and hot tub, Wi-Fi, and breakfast.

Cheyenne is fortunate to have one of Wyoming's few surviving historic lodging places, the five-story ◖ **Plains Hotel** (1600 Central Ave., 307/638-3311 or 866/275-2467, www.theplainshotel.com). Built in 1911 for a then-astounding $250,000, this was the political center of Cheyenne for decades, with politicians repairing to the bar to broker issues over beers and stogies. The grand lobby, marble stairway, and the tile mosaic of Chief Little Shield remain, but in 2002 The Plains underwent a multimillion-dollar reconstruction that transformed it into a boutique hotel with 131 luxury rooms and suites, two restaurants, conference rooms, and an exercise facility. Lots of little touches were added too, such as wireless Internet, large televisions, original artwork in the rooms, and custom-designed furniture and bed coverings. Standard rooms in the hotel are $89–99 d, and suites run $109–129 d ($199 for the presidential suite). The hotel also has a number of older bargain rooms (not remodeled) for $49 d. The hotel is in the heart of town and right across from the restored depot. Off-street parking is available two blocks away.

$100-150

Little America Hotel (2800 W. Lincolnway, 307/775-8400 or 888/709-8383, www.littleamerica.com) is a large, somewhat upscale hotel that feels like a resort, with 80 acres of landscaped grounds (but directly across from the rail tracks), an Olympic-size outdoor pool, an exercise facility, an airport shuttle, and a nine-hole golf course ($14). Spacious rooms start at $96 d for a standard king room, up to $159 for the presidential suite. Little America is especially popular with retirees.

A favorite of business travelers is the 244-room **Holiday Inn** (204 W. Fox Farm Rd., 307/638-4466 or 800/465-4329, www.holiday-inn.com/cheyennewy). Inside you'll find a big lobby with a fireplace, restaurant, and bar, plus an indoor pool, hot tub, sauna, exercise room, wireless Internet, and conference facilities. Guest rooms are spacious but nothing special; $100 d for standard rooms or $119 for up to four people in the suites.

One of the better local lodging places, **Best Western Hitching Post Inn** (1700 W. Lincolnway, 307/638-3301 or 800/221-0125, www.hitchingpostinn.com), has newer rooms with a cowboy motif. Attractions include indoor and outdoor pools, a hot tub, saunas, a large fitness center, wireless Internet, plus two fine restaurants, a coffeehouse, and two lounges. Rooms go for $131 d ($229 during Frontier Days) or $168 d for suites. Be sure to ask for a remodeled room; the older ones leave something to be desired.

Bed-and-Breakfasts

The friendly **Howdy Pardner B&B** (1920 Tranquility Rd., 307/634-6493, www.howdypardner.net) is out in the country just north of Cheyenne; call ahead for directions. The hilltop ranch-style home offers three guest rooms (all with private bath), a fireplace, and great views of the rolling plains. Each morning, the owners produce a robust country breakfast; bring a big appetite. Rates are $75 d, and kids and pets are welcome. For an authentically Wyoming experience, sleep inside the delightful antique sheepherder wagon for $65 d (bath in the house).

On the north side of town, **Storyteller**

Pueblo B&B (5201 Ogden Rd., 307/634-7036, www.storyteller-pueblo-bnb.com, $65–90 d) is a contemporary home with Native American art, country antiques, fireplaces, and four guest rooms with shared or private baths. It's in a quiet neighborhood and run by dynamic owners. A full breakfast is included and children are accepted.

Porch Swing B&B (712 E. 20th St., 307/778-7182, www.cruising-america.com/porch.html) is an attractive downtown bungalow built in 1917 with two rooms ($85 d) that share a bath. The back porch, surrounded by flower and herb gardens, is perfect for relaxing. Guest rooms contain antiques, and a full breakfast is served by the helpful hosts. A two-night minimum stay is required in the summer.

Adventurer's Country B&B (307/632-4087, www.bbonline.com/wy/adventurers) is a modern ranch home in the countryside 15 miles east of Cheyenne. Guests share the grounds with a variety of farm critters, including horses, geese, turkeys, ducks, cats, and dogs. The four guest rooms ($85–95 d) and a suite ($135 for up to four) are arranged around a central courtyard. A four-course breakfast and evening dessert are served, and kids, pets ($10), and horses ($15) are welcome.

Occupying a grand old home built in 1888 and listed on the National Register of Historic Places (see *Sights*), the ◖ **Nagle-Warren Mansion B&B** (222 E. 17th St., 307/637-3333 or 800/811-2610, www.naglewarrenmansion.com) provides updated Victorian accommodation near the center of Cheyenne. Owner Jim Osterfoss has transformed this grand old mansion into Cheyenne's premier B&B. Amenities include luxurious rooms with period furnishings and original artwork, a gazebo housing the hot tub, beautiful floral gardens, plus a small exercise room and conference room. The gourmet breakfast menu changes every day. The main house and adjacent carriage house contain 11 guest rooms ($142 d), plus the luxurious Teddy Roosevelt suite ($172 d) that includes a king bed, gas fireplace, and stained-glass skylight. All rooms have private baths. Children are accepted, but there's no space for roll-aways, so

they'll need to sleep with mom and dad or in a separate room. A formal English high tea ($10) is served in the parlor on Friday and Saturday afternoon, and in the off-season the B&B has monthly murder mystery dinners ($55 per person), along with four-course dinners that feature regional specialties and paired wines ($75 per person). The mansion is also a favorite spot for wedding receptions and elegant parties.

Halfway between Cheyenne and Laramie on Happy Jack Road (Hwy. 210) lie two excellent B&Bs: **A. Drummond's Ranch B&B** and **Windy Hills Guest House** (see *Curt Gowdy State Park* under *Around Cheyenne*).

Camping

Cheyenne's closest public campgrounds are 26 miles west on Hwy. 210 in **Curt Gowdy State Park** (307/632-7946; http://wyoparks.statewy.us, $12 for nonresidents, $6 for residents). Campgrounds ($10) can also be found within the scenic **Pole Mountain** area of Medicine Bow–Routt National Forest (www.fs.fed.us/r2/mbr), 30 miles west on I-80.

Showers are available at the swimming pool in Lions Park or from many of the private RV parks.

Camping and RV rates jump during Frontier Days; reserve well ahead to be sure of getting a space at that time. **AB Campground** (1503 W. College Dr., 307/634-7035, $16 tents, $28 RVs, open Apr.–mid-Oct.) is in a quiet area with plenty of trees.

Restway Travel Park (4212 Whitney Rd., 307/634-3811 or 800/443-2751, $17 tents, $24 RVs, open year-round) is one of the nicest RV parks in the area, with an outdoor heated pool, free minigolf, volleyball, and horseshoes.

Eight miles south of Cheyenne on I-25 (exit 2), **Terry Bison Ranch** (307/634-4171, www.terrybisonranch.com) is a favorite of families, with bison tours, trout fishing, horseback and pony rides, a restaurant, and miniature train. This is also the only place in Wyoming that has camels! Tent spaces are $15; RV hookups cost $25. Cabins and bunkhouse rooms are also available. Open year-round.

Other Cheyenne-area RV parks include:

Jolley Rogers RV Park (6102 E. Hwy. 30, 307/634-8457 or 800/458-7779, www.jolleyrogers.com, $18 RVs, no tents, open mid-Apr.–mid-Oct.), **Greenway Trailer Park** (3829 Greenway St., 307/634-6696, $17 RVs, no tents, open year-round), and **Hide a Way RV Park** (218 S. Greeley Hwy., 307/637-7114, open year-round).

FOOD

The city of Cheyenne offers a surprisingly diverse choice of eateries.

Coffee and Tea

Tivoli Coffee Bar (201 W. Lincolnway, 307/638-8839) offers espresso, sandwiches, wraps, and free Wi-Fi in a delightfully old-fashioned downtown setting.

In addition to caffeine jolts, **Zen's Bistro** (2606 E. Lincolnway, 307/635-1889) has vegetarian sandwiches, salads, pastries, soups, coffees, teas, and free computers to surf the web (customers only).

Visit **Nagle-Warren Mansion B&B** for a most unusual caffeinated option, English high tea, on Fridays and Saturdays.

Breakfast and Lunch

Housed within Cheyenne's oldest brick home, **Lexie's Mesa Grill** (216 E. 17th St., 307/632-9119) offers a variety of reasonably priced Southwestern food, from fajita salads and fish tacos to Santa Fe burgers. Run by a nonprofit organization, Mesa Grill serves as a training place for young people learning restaurant management. Open for lunch and dinner; most items $7–12.

Part of a small chain, **The Egg and I** (2300 Carey Ave., 307/632-5577) specializes in—surprise—eggs, with "eggceptional" omelets, frittatas, and other dishes. The atmosphere is bright and friendly, and classical tunes spill from the speakers. It also makes commendable croissant sandwiches, soups, and salads for lunch. Early birds will appreciate the 6 A.M. weekday openings.

The enormous **Little America Coffee Shop** (2800 W. Lincolnway, 307/775-8400, www.lit-tleamerica.com/cheyenne) is open 5 A.M.–midnight with better-than-average truck-stop fare, plus a Sunday buffet brunch ($22). The substantial lunchtime buffet ($10) is a favorite of the business crowd, and the adjacent Western Gold Restaurant serves prime rib, trout, and other dinner treats for $13–30.

A downtown lunch and dinner favorite of many locals is **Albany Restaurant** (1506 Capitol Ave., 307/638-3507, www.albanycheyenne.com). **Luxury Diner** (1401 W. Lincolnway, 307/638-8971) is a tiny, down-home spot for breakfast and lunch; try the breakfast burrito or a boxcar.

International

Wyoming is certainly not known for its Asian food, but Cheyenne is home to the surprisingly authentic ◖ **Twin Dragon Restaurant** (1809 Carey Ave., 307/637-6622). Its lunchtime buffet is an outstanding deal, and the dinner menu includes such specialties as sesame crispy beef and *moo-shu* pork. Keep your orders small because the portions are not. Most entrées are $7–11.

Several places in Cheyenne make very good south-of-the-border food. **La Costa** (317 E. Lincolnway, 307/638-7372) has perhaps the best Mexican meals, with all the favorites, including fajitas, *chiles rellenos,* and chalupas. Housed in Cheyenne Plaza Mall, **The Armadillo** (3617 E. Lincolnway, 307/778-0822) has been in business for more than three decades, with locally famous margaritas. Also popular is **Estevan's Cafe** (1820 Ridge Rd., 307/632-6828).

L'Osteria Mondello Italian Cucina and Pizzeria (1507 Stillwater Ave., 307/778-6068) is *the* place for authentic Southern Italian meals in Cheyenne. Excellent food.

The food isn't anything special, but stuff yourself beyond obesity at **Avanti Italian Ristorante** (4620 Grandview Ave.—between Wal-Mart and Office Max—307/634-3432), where the Italian American evening buffet is under $10 ($7 for lunch), including prime rib.

American

In business since 1977, **Poor Richard's** (2233 E. Lincolnway, 307/635-5114) serves seafood, steaks, and prime rib, and the salad bar is one of the biggest around. Enjoy a drink at the fireside lounge. Dinner entrées are $13–20.

Housed within Best Western Hitching Post, **Cheyenne Cattle Company** (1700 W. Lincolnway, 307/775-7303, www.hitchingpostinn.com) is a locals' favorite. Steaks and prime rib are the primary attractions, but the menu also offers a variety of other entrées, and a separate patio menu is available, along with a big lunchtime buffet; don't miss the bread pudding. Dinner entrées are $16–40.

The historic **Whipple House** (300 E. 17th St., 307/638-3551) has a fine-dining lunch and dinner menu of steaks, prime rib, duck, and seafood. Dinner entrées are $11–33. Built in 1883, the building is an attraction in its own right.

Looking for mass quantities of food? Head to **Country Buffet** (1400 Dell Range Blvd., 307/637-5906) for a stuff-it-in meal. Or try Avanti.

Pubs and Pizzas

The historic railway depot is home to █ **Snake River Pub and Grill** (115 W. 15th St., 307/634-7625, www.snakeriverpub.com), a fun smoke-free place for a light meal, with $6 lunchtime specials on weekdays, and a finger-friendly menu of stone-baked pizzas, sandwiches, burgers, and ribs. Be sure to order ale-battered onion rings as an appetizer or a side to your burger. Big portions, too. The high-ceilinged bar is noisy—in a fun way—but there's a quieter front section, or you can dine on the back patio next to the passing freight trains. The brewery produces 4–5 beers, all of which are worth a quaff. (This brewpub has the same owners as the popular one in Jackson Hole.) Dinner entrées are $7–12.

Sanford's Grub and Pub (115 E. 17th St., 307/634-3381) is Cheyenne's happening place, with a young crowd and live music on weekends. Part of a small chain, Sanford's exudes frat-house chic. Every square millimeter is packed with old photos, sports memorabilia, lawn-sale junk, and TV screens. The chaos ups the volume, although the 55 beers on draft

probably help. Sanford's menu is big enough to satisfy almost anyone and includes shrimp jambalaya, barbecued chicken wings, and mushroom monster burgers. On weekend evenings, get there early or be prepared for a wait.

A block up the street from Sanford's is **Grand Ave. Pizza** (112 E. 17th St., 307/635-8686) with pizzas and calzones, dartboards and pool tables. A pizza, pasta, salad, and soup lunch buffet is available on weekdays ($7) and Friday evenings ($10).

C. B. and Potts Bighorn Brewery (1650 Dell Range Blvd., 307/632-8636) is another hopping pub/sports bar with a small brewery on the premises and an eclectic menu that rambles through pasta, burgers, Tex-Mex food, salads, New York–style pizzas, nachos, and buffalo wings.

Bakeries

Get fresh bagels and sandwiches at **Mort's Bagels** (1815 Carey Ave., 307/637-5400). Best pies in town? Try **Pie Lady Bakery and Cafe** (3515 E. Lincolnway, 307/637-8838).

A longtime Cheyenne favorite—and justly so—**The Bread Basket** (1819 Maxwell Ave., 307/432-2525, www.breadbasketbakery.com) is close to downtown. Drop by for fresh-from-the-oven breads and sweets, plus filling deli sandwiches, cabbage burgers, soups, and salads.

Groceries

The **Cheyenne Farmers Market** (307/635-9291) is held 8 A.M.–1 P.M. Saturdays during August and September downtown at Depot Plaza. This is the best place to get fresh fruits and vegetables. Cheyenne has several of the regional grocery chains, including Albertsons, King's Sooper's, and Safeway.

You'll find a big selection of beer and wine at **Town and Country Supermarket Liquors** (614 S. Greeley Hwy., 307/632-8735) or downtown at **Albany Liquormart** (1506 Capitol Ave., 307/638-3507).

INFORMATION

Housed within the restored Union Pacific Depot, the **Cheyenne Convention and**

Visitors Bureau (121 W. 15th St., 307/778-3133 or 800/426-5009, www.cheyenne.org) is open 8 A.M.–7 P.M. Monday–Friday, 9 A.M.–5 P.M. Saturday, and 11–5 P.M. Sunday mid-May–early September (8 A.M.–7 P.M. daily during Frontier Days), and 8 A.M.–5 P.M. Monday–Friday the rest of the year. You'll find free wireless Internet inside the Depot building and on the plaza out front.

The state maintains a spacious **Wyoming Travel Information Center** at the College Drive off-ramp (exit 7) along I-25, 307/777-7777 or 800/225-5996. It's so windy at this exposed site that the garbage cans are all set inside concrete pipes to keep them from blowing away! The center is open 8 A.M.–5 P.M. daily all year except Thanksgiving, Christmas, and New Year's days.

Cheyenne's *Wyoming Tribune-Eagle* (www.wyomingnews.com) is one of the few daily newspapers in the state.

Online travelers should check out www.cheyennenetwork.com, with a mix of local community information, news, and events, plus a forum where you can talk politics and religion.

SERVICES

Laundromats include **Duds 'n Suds** (1802 Dell Range Blvd., 307/632-4873) and **Easy Way Laundry** (900 W. 16th St., 307/638-2177).

The expansive **Laramie County Public Library** (2800 Central Ave., 307/634-3561, www.lclsonline.org) has free Internet access. Also check out the **Wyoming State Library** (2301 Capitol Ave., 307/777-6333, www-wsl.state.wy.us).

Other services include a downtown **post office** (2120 Capitol Ave., 307/772-7080) and the **BLM's Wyoming State Office** (5353 Yellowstone Rd., 307/775-6256, www.wy.blm.gov) north of town.

Laramie County Community College (1400 E. College Dr., 307/778-5222 or 800/522-2993, www.lccc.cc.wy.us) offers classes for 2,000 students, primarily in technical fields, although there are two-year degrees in everything from accounting to wildlife conservation.

GETTING THERE AND AROUND
Bus
Cheyenne Transit Program (307/637-6253, $1) provides bus service weekdays to most parts of the city.

Powder River Transportation (307/635-1327 or 800/442-3682, http://gillette.coachusa.us) has daily service from Cheyenne's depot at 222 Deming Drive on the southeast end of town. Daily buses head to towns in northern and central Wyoming, continuing north to Billings or Rapid City and south to Denver. Greyhound no longer stops in Cheyenne, but it does serve Denver and Laramie.

Air Travel
Cheyenne Airport (www.cheyenneairport.com) is just south of Dell Range Boulevard, with the entrance at the east end of 8th Avenue. **Great Lakes Aviation** (307/433-2905 or 800/554-5111, www.greatlakesav.com) has daily flights to Denver; you'll spend more time waiting to get on the plane than in the half-hour flight. The company is headquartered in Cheyenne, and code shares with both Frontier Air and United Express.

Shamrock Airport Express (307/638-3940 or 866/482-0505, www.rideshamrock.com) provides van service six times a day to Denver International Airport for $32 one-way. It stops at the Hitching Post and Holiday Inn. **Coach USA Denver** (888/223-2877, http://denver.coachusa.us) has daily vans to Denver's Amtrak station.

Cars and Taxis
At Cheyenne airport rent cars from **Avis** (307/632-9371 or 800/831-2847, www.avis.com) or **Hertz** (307/634-2131 or 800/654-3131, www.hertz.com). In-town places include **A1 Car Rental** (307/638-3335 or 800/447-3673), **Enterprise** (307/632-1907 or 800/736-8222, www.enterprise.com), and **Thrifty** (307/637-3929 or 800/847-4389, www.thrifty.com).

Cheyenne taxi companies are **Croozer Cab** (370/221-1010) and **Impression Yellow Cab** (307/433-1661).

Around Cheyenne

CURT GOWDY STATE PARK

The 1,645-acre Curt Gowdy State Park (307/632-7946, http://wyoparks.state.wy.us) is 26 miles west of Cheyenne along Hwy. 210 (Happy Jack Road), the scenic "back way" to Laramie. The road rises slowly through the grasslands west of Cheyenne. At Curt Gowdy, the Granite Reservoir and Crystal Reservoir offer recreation for anglers, boaters, snowmobilers, and cross-country skiers. The small lakes, constructed between 1904 and 1910, are parts of Cheyenne's water supply, so no swimming is allowed. An elaborate Rube Goldberg scheme completed in 1964 now carries 12 million gallons of water from the west and across the Continental Divide, the Sierra Madre, the Snowy Range, and the Laramie Range to get it to thirsty Cheyenne.

In 1971, the two lakes at the eastern end were set aside as a state park and named for Wyoming native Curt Gowdy. Born in the town of Green River in 1919, Gowdy was a basketball player on the University of Wyoming's national championship team in 1943 and the long-time voice of the New York Yankees and Boston Red Sox. He later served as host of television's *The American Sportsman* for two decades and as a broadcaster of professional sporting events of all types, including the World Series, the Olympics, and NFL games. Day use of the park is $4 for non-Wyoming vehicles or $4 for cars with Wyoming plates. Camping costs $12 for nonresidents or $6 for Wyoming residents. Make campsite reservations ($8.50 fee) at 877/996-7275, www.wyo-park.com.

There's pleasant hiking in the surrounding pine-covered countryside, but by late summer the lakes tend to get severely drawn down. There are some interesting granitic formations to explore and climb. Also in the park is the historic **Hynds Lodge,** a stone structure completed in 1923 and available for families and groups to rent in the summer. An **ice-fishing derby** takes place in mid-February at the park.

Accommodations

The open country surrounding Curt Gowdy State Park boasts two bed-and-breakfasts well worth the drive from either Cheyenne or Laramie. An outstanding lodging option is (**A. Drummond's Ranch B&B** (399 Happy Jack Rd., 307/634-6042, www.cruising-america .com/drummond.html), just 1.5 miles away from the park and offering vistas of the Vedauwoo Rocks. Set on 120 acres, this is a fine place to splurge. The New England–style home includes four guest rooms, one of which contains a fireplace, steam sauna, and private hot tub. A second room also has its own hot tub. The Drummonds have an indoor arena for folks who bring their own horses, and guests will meet the menagerie of pets: llamas, chicken, and sheep, plus a horse, cat, and dog. Guest rooms with private baths are $88–164 or $74 d with shared baths. A delicious full breakfast is served, and kids are welcome.

One mile west of the Drummond home is **Windy Hills Guest House** (393 Happy Jack Rd., 307/632-6423 or 877/946-3944, www.windyhillswyo.com), a modern home with a deck overlooking Granite Lake and the nearby mountains. Eight guest rooms are available: one suite ($98 d) in the main house with private entrances; a log home with three guest rooms ($200 d for one room; $300 for three rooms and six people), a kitchen, and hot tub; a two-bedroom guest house ($155–175 d for one room; $200 for four people) with a kitchen, fireplace, and hot tub; and a house with an outdoor hot tub ($200 d). All rooms contain private baths. Mountain bikes are available, and a full breakfast is served. Kids are welcome.

PINE BLUFFS

Pine Bluffs (pop. 1,200) is a small agricultural center on Wyoming's eastern border. Unlike almost everywhere else in Wyoming, the local economy seems to be spiraling downward—leaving an almost abandoned downtown—even more so after a 2003 fire that destroyed a block of historic buildings—but people continue to live in graceful homes beneath spreading shade trees. The surrounding area resembles western Nebraska (which is a mile away), with ponderosa pines atop the long ridge just south of town. Wheat fields and irrigated potato fields surround Pine Bluffs, and the countryside is filled with silos, farm equipment, and rifle-racked pickup trucks, while the airwaves feature market reports and hog futures. But Pine Bluffs is a also place where you'll find racks of tortillas in the grocery store and hear Spanish spoken by migrant workers.

Archaeological Sights

Just a 10-minute walk from the I-80 rest area and information center is an ongoing archaeological excavation at a major Native American site that dates back more than 10,000 years. Indians pitched their tepees atop the pine-covered bluffs here and headed down to the fertile valley below to hunt game and collect berries. Their tepee rings are still visible. Each summer, a dozen or so University of Wyoming students under the direction of Pine Bluffs native Dr. Charles Reher arrive to slowly dig through the soil in search of a buried treasure trove of prehistory. Discoveries have included arrow and spear points, pottery, scrapers, drills, shell pendants, fire hearths, and thousands of tool-sharpening flakes.

The covered site, **Windows of the Past Interpretive Center,** is open 9 A.M.–noon and 1–5 P.M. most days mid-June–mid-August. Visitors are welcome, and the staff can answer your questions. Call 307/766-5136 for tour information or to see about joining the dig for a day (advance permission required). A couple of tepees have been erected nearby. Artifacts collected here can be seen in the **High Plains Archaeology Museum and Field Lab** (2nd and Elm, 307/245-9372) also open daily mid-June–mid-August.

The Texas Trail

Pine Bluffs lies right along the great Texas Trail; at its peak in 1871, more than 600,000 cattle were trailed north from Texas past this point. The town became not just a watering place for the stock but also a vital shipping point. For several years, more cattle were

shipped from the railroad station at Pine Bluffs than anywhere else in the world. A monument to the Texas Trail stands in the adjacent park.

The **Texas Trail Museum** (at 3rd and Market Sts., 307/245-3713, free) houses a Conestoga wagon, old photos, and a small collection of homesteading and ranching items. It's open 11 A.M.–5 P.M. Monday–Saturday Memorial Day–Labor Day, or by appointment (stop by the town hall) at other times. Next to the museum are a caboose and several historic buildings—a one-room schoolhouse, an old church, and a railroad boardinghouse.

Other Sights

Several **nature trails** with interpretive signs depart from the rest area/information center, looping up the bluff. You can also reach the hills by car by following Beech Street south under the freeway and turning right on the dirt road at the crest of the hill. This is an excellent place to watch sunrises and sunsets or to enjoy a picnic lunch amid the pines.

Pine Bluff's most bizarre sight is the five-story-tall **Our Lady of Peace Shrine**—the largest statue of the Virgin Mary in the United States. Artist Robert Fida (www.robertfida.com) built the monument in 1998 using cast stone (pulverized marble reformulated with cement). See her 180 tons of glory by heading east from town on U.S. 30 to the RV park. Turn south and she'll soon be hard to miss. She faces I-80 and is just a few feet from the Nebraska border.

A dozen miles southeast of Pine Bluffs are a pair of minor landmarks: the **Tri-State Corner Marker** where Wyoming, Nebraska, and Colorado meet, and a marker at **Panorama Point,** Nebraska's highest spot. The latter is just a small hill that crests at 5,424 feet (versus Wyoming's high point of 13,804 feet). The information center has a map with descriptions and directions for both markers. A buffalo ranch is close to Panorama Point.

Entertainment and Events

The popular **Outlaw Saloon Rodeo Series** (307/632-3626, www.outlawrodeo.com) takes place on Friday nights late May–mid-August at the rodeo grounds, with barrel racing, team roping, calf roping, and bull riding. You're also likely to see local cowboys and cowgirls practicing roping here several afternoons a week in summer. **Pine Bluffs Trail Days** comes in early August with rodeos, barbecues, a parade, melodrama, golf, mud volleyball, and dancing.

Recreation

The primary hangout in Pine Bluffs is the local bowling alley, **Pine Bowl** (3rd and Pine, 307/245-3622). The town park houses a seasonal outdoor **swimming pool** (200 E. 8th, 307/245-3783), and golfers should check out **Leaning Rock Golf Course,** with nine holes of sand and artificial turf atop the bluff.

Practicalities

Gator's Travelyn Motel (515 W. 7th, 307/245-3226, $38 s or $48–58 d) is the local lodging place. **Pine Bluff RV Campground** (307/245-3665 or 800/294-4968, $10 tents, $20 RVs) is 0.5-mile east of town and has year-round spaces; no shade but lots of wind.

Our Lady of Peace shrine in Pine Bluffs

Restaurant options are slim in Pine Bluffs. The best bet is **Uncle Fred's Place** (701 Parsons, 307/245-3443), where you'll find family meals and a salad bar. Get groceries at **Texas Trail Market** (3rd and Elm, 307/245-3302). This is a cooperatively run store, as are the auto-repair shop, local grain elevator, and electric utility. Socialism in a rock-ribbed Republican state!

Stop at the **Tourist Information Center** at the I-80 rest area (exit 401, 307/245-3695, www.pinebluffs.org) for both local and statewide information. It's open 8 A.M.–4 P.M. daily May–October, and until 5 P.M. in midsummer. The **library** is at 108 East 2nd, 307/245-3646.

NORTH FROM PINE BLUFFS

For a delightful break from busy I-80, drive north of Pine Bluffs along Hwy. 215 through the wheat and grasslands on the Wyoming–Nebraska border. The high plains landscape has a smattering of ponderosa pines capping the rocky bluffs, a handful of ranches, and to-the-horizon vistas. The road rolls past **Albin** (pop. 120) 18 miles north of Pine Bluffs, with a tiny but picturesque Catholic church. An old log homestead is worth a look west of here. Head 2.5 miles west on Hwy. 216 and then one mile north on Road 159 to the cabin. **Albin Days** takes place the second Saturday in July.

LAGRANGE

The nothing farm village of LaGrange (pop. 330) is 25 miles northwest of Albin. Established in 1889, the town was named for Kale LaGrange, a stagecoach driver on the Cheyenne to Red Cloud route. Just to the north is 66 Mountain, so called because it supposedly has the number hidden in its profile. Stop in LaGrange in June for the **Mini Fair and Rodeo.**

In the same family for six generations, **Bear Mountain Riding Ranch** (307/834-2492, www.wyobearmountain.com) has B&B accommodations, plus 8,000 acres of land on the CP Ranch. The cost is $200 d per day, including lodging, breakfast, and stables for your horse. This is a good chance for experienced riders with their own horses to ride the open range.

SWAN LAND AND CATTLE COMPANY

The most famous of all Wyoming ranching operations was the Swan Land and Cattle Company, Ltd., founded in 1883 by Alexander and Thomas Swan with enormous financial backing from Scottish investors – £600,000 the first year and an additional £1.6 million through the next three years. At its peak in the mid-1880s, the company's holdings reached from its headquarters along Chugwater Creek westward for 120 miles to the North Platte River near Rawlins. More than 110,000 cattle ranged across this vast expanse. The company bought 550,000 acres of Union Pacific Railroad land (and therefore controlled the checkerboard of public land in alternating sections) and bought government land along major creeks in the area. By doing this, it controlled access to water in this semiarid country, thus keeping others from settling on surrounding public lands. All told, the Swan Land and Cattle Company had its tentacles over nearly one million acres covering more than 30 different ranches. The company had dozens of different brands, but locals knew it as the "Two Bar." Cowboys loved the company because it always provided good working conditions and wages ($20 per month to start) and the best grub around.

In the mid-1880s, though, things began to turn sour, and by 1886 the Scottish investors accused Alexander Swan of fraud and misrepresentation; the 110,000 cattle shown on the books did not all exist on the hoof. A lawsuit eventually led to Swan's firing. Even more devastating was the severe winter of 1886-1887, which killed off thousands of the firm's cows and calves, pushing the company to the brink of bankruptcy. Amazingly, the reorganized company managed to survive for more than 50 years, although it began raising sheep instead of cattle after 1903. It was prosperous during World War I, when wool prices soared, but its fortunes gradually declined with the economy. By 1950, the vast operation had been entirely liquidated. Some folks claim that Steamboat, a wild bronc from the old Two Bar Ranch, was the inspiration for the bucking horse symbol found on Wyoming license plates. Many of the historic ranch's buildings are still intact, and the complex has been designated a National Historic Landmark.

CHUGWATER

Chugwater (pop. 240) was once headquarters for the giant Swan Land and Cattle Company, the greatest of Wyoming's cattle spreads during the 1880s. The town itself was founded in 1913 on land sold by the Swan Company. Chugwater has to have one of the strangest origins of any town name in America, coming from the Indian practice of driving buffalo over cliffs. The "chug" sound the buffalo made as they hit bottom led Mandan Indians to call it "Water at the Place Where the Buffalo Chug." The prominent flat-topped mesa over which the bison were driven rises just north of town. When the railroad was built here, thousands of buffalo bones were discovered at the base of these cliffs.

Sights

Chugwater is perhaps best known for

Chugwater Chili (307/422-3345 or 800/972-4454, www.chugwaterchili.com), a mix sold in stores throughout the Rockies or by mail order or the web. Get a free taste at 210 1st Street. The annual **Chugwater Chili Cook-Off** (307/422-3493) takes place the third Saturday in June at Diamond Guest Ranch and attracts dozens of chefs and hundreds of fire-breathing chili eaters. Other events include a rodeo and country music.

Occupying an old bank building on Main Street, the little **Chugwater Museum** (307/422-3227, open 1–4 p.m. Sat.–Sun. May–Sept.) houses a collection of brands, aging farm machinery, and various homestead-era items. An early-1900s caboose is across the road. If the museum is closed, stop across the street at the **《 Chugwater Soda Fountain** (307/422-3222) for access. In addition to great malts from one of Wyoming's oldest soda fountains, it has a limited menu of homemade soups and barbecue pork, along with T-shirts, trinkets, and liquor.

For an extraordinarily **scenic drive,** take Hwy. 211 from Chugwater to Cheyenne. It's a mix of gravel and pavement and takes longer than I-25 but is virtually free of traffic. The road passes through a Wyoming landscape of grass and sage-carpeted hills, tree-lined creeks, magnificent old ranches, and herds of deer and antelope. Stop to listen to the meadowlarks on a spring day or to watch the clouds roiling overhead in this peaceful place.

Super 8 Motel (100 Buffalo Dr., 307/422-3248 or 800/800-8000, www.super8.com, $60–80 d) has a small seasonal outdoor pool. It's considerably better than most Super 8s. The building also houses **Miss Kitty's Grill,** with three meals a day, including Chugwater chili; nothing is more than $8.

Wheatland

Wheatland (pop. 3,500) is a friendly middle-America town with a shady downtown and farming country in all directions. Despite the name, wheat is not the primary crop grown here; sugar beets, dry beans, and barley are. The largest local employer is Laramie River Station, a 1,650-megawatt coal-fired power plant five miles north of town. It supplies electricity to a grid that feeds an eight-state area. Another substantial employer is a local marble quarry that mines dolomite in the Laramie Mountains and crushes it for use in everything from aquarium gravel to cattle feed. Don't let on that I told you, but Wheatland also has Minuteman III nuclear missiles out in the country near the power plant. Perhaps for this reason, the town boasts one of the highest number of churches per capita anywhere: 23 different houses of worship crowd Wheatland.

An early settler in this part of Wyoming called it "a desolate looking place, nothing but sagebrush, cactus, rocks, mudhole, rattlesnakes, and coyotes." It took water to change all this. Wheatland is a creation of the Wyoming Development Company, founded in 1883 by several individuals, including Senators Joseph M. Carey and Francis E. Warren. In one of the few successful applications of the famous Carey Act in Wyoming, the company built a dam on Big Laramie River and canals to carry the water to 50,000 acres where homesteaders formed the Wheatland Colony. Today it remains the largest privately owned irrigation system in the nation.

In 1905 the town of Wheatland was incorporated (the name won out over Wheatdale and Wheatridge), becoming the hub of activity for the region—and later the Platte County seat. Today, Wheatland runs on a mix of agriculture, the power plant, and small businesses. Downtown may not be bustling, but it's clean and attractive. Agriculture, that old standby, continues to play a vital role in the local economy. Wyoming Premium Farms runs a gigantic hog farm a dozen miles north of Wheatland that produces 100,000 pigs annually. Hold your nose!

SIGHTS
The free **Laramie Peak Museum** (1601 16th St., 307/322-2764) is open 10 A.M.–5 P.M. Monday–Friday—till 8 P.M. Monday, Tuesday, Thursday, and Friday in midsummer—and 10 A.M.–3 P.M. Saturday late May–mid-September. It houses a variety of homestead-era flotsam and jetsam varying from early-1900s tricycles to a stuffed vulture. A saddle and cowboy hat here have burn marks from when lightning struck a local cowboy (he lived). Built in 1911, the marble-columned **Platte County Court House** at 9th and Walnut is easily the most imposing structure in Wheatland.

Country Drives
For a delightful all-day loop drive, head west from Wheatland out **Palmer Canyon Road** through the farm fields and open plains, past the old stone buildings of Muleshoe Ranch, and high into the cool Laramie Range. The first

WHEATLAND

To Glendo and Douglas

To Power Plant and Guernsey

EXIT 80

WHEATLAND TRAVEL PLAZA
ROMPOON RD
SUPER 8 MOTEL

NORTH 16TH LAUNDROMAT

ARROWHEAD RV PARK

NORTH RD

TORCHLIGHT INN
CASEY'S TIMBERHAUS
LARAMIE PEAK MUSEUM
SAFEWAY

ROWLEY ST

15TH ST · 14TH ST · 13TH ST · 12TH ST · 11TH ST · 10TH ST · 9TH ST

FARM AND MARKET RD

E OAK ST

OAK ST

CEDAR ST

SPRUCE ST — WYOMING MOTEL ST

PINE ST

WALNUT ST — LIBRARY

POST OFFICE

W WALNUT ST

Main Canal

MAPLE ST

GILCHRST ST

WATER ST — CITY HALL

AIRPORT

PLATTE COUNTY FAIRGROUNDS
ANTELOPE GAP RD

WEST WINDS MOTEL

W SOUTH ST

SOUTH ST

JOHNSTON ST

SHIEK ST

VIMBO'S MOTEL & RESTAURANT
MOTEL 8

ZORN ST — HOSPITAL

LEWIS PARK

BRICE ST

W MARIPOSA

LOOMIS ST — SWIMMING POOL

EXIT 18

MOUNTAIN VIEW RV PARK

COLE ST

E COLE ST

PLATTE COUNTY VISITORS CENTER

COLORADO-SOUTHERN RAILROAD

W COZAD RD

COZAD RD

To Sybile Canyon and Laramie

To Chugwater and Cheyenne

To Palmer Canyon

0   0.25 mi

0   0.25 km

© AVALON TRAVEL PUBLISHING, INC.

10 miles are paved. Once in the hills, the dirt road (avoid after rains or in the spring) winds through a rocky ponderosa pine–covered landscape that comes alive with springtime flowers. You can return to Wheatland the same way or do a big loop by turning north onto Cottonwood Park Road and then east again on Fletcher Park Road. Check with the visitor center for the specific route or look over Forest Service or topo maps. It also has a Laramie Peak loop tour pamphlet that describes hiking trails in the area.

A shorter country drive—on a mix of paved and gravel roads—connects Wheatland with Fort Laramie. Head north on Hwy. 320 for two miles, turning east onto Grayrocks Road, which leads past the huge **Laramie River Station** power plant (www.wmpa.org/laramie_river_station.htm). The coal-fired generating station produces 1.65 million kilowatts and is fed by an almost-constant stream of trains filled with coal from mines in the Gillette area. Call 307/322-9601 for free weekday tours. A few miles up the narrow road is **Grayrocks Reservoir,** which provides cooling water for the power plant and recreation for boaters and anglers. A small store (Cottonwood Canteen) sells gas and groceries. Beyond this you can follow the signs to historic Fort Laramie. The road follows an old stage route and is a scenic and out-of-the-way drive with little traffic. In recent years an extended drought has dropped the water level to just a fraction of its capacity, leaving campsites far from the water's edge.

ENTERTAINMENT AND EVENTS

Cinema West (609 10th St., 307/322-9032) is the local movie house. Wheatland has a big fireworks show at the fairgrounds on the **Fourth of July.** The **Platte County Fair and Rodeo** (307/322-2322, www.plattecofair.com) occurs in early August and offers a street breakfast, barbecue, parade, rodeo, entertainment, and all the usual fun of a country fair.

RECREATION

There is a fine outdoor **swimming pool** (307/322-9254) in Lewis Park, open in the sum-

mer. The nine-hole **Wheatland Golf Course** is at 1253 Cole, 307/322-3675.

ACCOMMODATIONS

Expect to pay substantially higher rates than those listed as follows during Frontier Days, even though it is an hour's drive to Cheyenne. Friendly **◖ Wyoming Motel** (1101 9th St., 307/322-5383 or 800/839-5383, www.wyomingmotel.com, $32 s or $35–42 d) has clean furnishings, in-room fridges, some microwaves, a guest computer, Wi-Fi, and a barbecue. It is well away from the highway, making it a quiet place to spend the night.

Motel West Winds (1756 South St., 307/322-2705, www.motelwestwinds.com, $39 s or $41–46 d) is another mom-and-pop place; fridges and microwaves in all rooms. **Vimbo's Motel** (203 16th St., 307/322-3842 or 800/577-3842, www.vimbos.com, $37 s or $42–45 d) has large and well-maintained rooms, plus a popular restaurant and lounge. **Best Western Torchlite Motor Inn** (1809 N. 16th St., 307/322-4070 or 800/662-3968, www.bestwestern.com, $80 d) has an outdoor pool, hot tub, and wireless Internet.

On the north end of town off I-25 exit 80, **Super 8 Motel** (2401 16th St., 307/322-2224 or 800/800-8000, www.super8.com, $79–89 d) is the newest lodging place, with an indoor pool and hot tub, wireless Internet, and light breakfast.

Camping

You can camp for free beneath the cottonwoods at 40-acre **Lewis Park** (307/322-2962) right in town along 8th Street. This quiet spot is a perfect place to relax. Showers and RV hookups are available; three-night maximum stay. Open year-round.

You'll find more free camping at **Grayrocks Reservoir,** northeast of Wheatland beyond the power plant. No RV hookups, but coin-operated showers are available. The nearby **Cottonwood Canteen** (307/322-2242) sells a few groceries, beer, gas, and bait. Open summers only. In addition, free campsites can be found along **Wheatland Reservoir** and **Rock Lake** a few miles southwest of town, as well as on Forest Service land in the Laramie Mountains west of Wheatland.

RVers may prefer to park at **Mountain View RV Park** just west of I-25 exit 78 (77 20th St., 307/322-4858, $17–20 RVs, open late Apr.–early Oct.). On the north end of town is **Arrowhead RV Park** (2005 N. 16th St., 307/322-3467, $12 tents, $20 RVs, open year-round). Showers are $3 if you aren't staying here.

FOOD

Vimbo's Family Restaurant (203 16th St., 307/322-3725) is a longtime local fixture, with dependable homemade food, a big and reasonably priced menu, and friendly waitresses. Breakfast and lunch buffets are especially popular, as is the Friday night seafood buffet ($12).

Housed in an attractive log building, **Casey's Timberhaus Family Restaurant** (1803 16th St., 307/322-4932) is another bring-out-the-gang restaurant, with a so-so salad bar and standard American burgers and steak. Breakfasts are a better bet.

Terra Grano Pizza (1557 South St., 307/322-4888) makes from-scratch bagels, sandwiches, big salads, homemade soups, espresso, pizzas, and calzones. **Pizza Hut** (1801 N. 16th St., 307/322-4001) is the only place that's open late most nights.

Groceries are available at homey **Huffer's Food Pride** (702 10th St., 307/322-3343) or the larger **Safeway** (1307 16th St., 307/322-4530).

INFORMATION AND SERVICES

The always helpful **Platte County Visitor's Center** (307/322-2322, www.plattechamber.com) is next to I-25 exit 78. Hours are 8 A.M.–5 P.M. Monday–Friday and 10 A.M.–2 P.M. Saturday–Sunday Memorial Day–Labor Day, and 8 A.M.–5 P.M. Monday–Friday the rest of the year. Pop open your laptop to use its free Wi-Fi.

Platte County Library (904 9th St., 307/322-2689) also has computers, and the **Wheatland post office** (307/332-3287) is at 852 Walnut Street. Wash clothes at **North 16th St. Laundromat,** next to Arrowhead RV Park on 16th Street. **Wheatland Travel Plaza** (81 Swanson Rd., 307/322-1884) is a truck stop with showers and laundry. **Platte County Memorial Hospital** (202 14th St., 307/322-3636, www.plattecountyhospital.com) provides emergency medical services.

GETTING THERE AND AROUND

Powder River Transportation (307/682-1888 or 800/442-3682, http://gillette.coachusa.us) has daily buses connecting Wheatland with eastern and central Wyoming, Denver, Billings, and Rapid City.

Rent cars from **Laramie Peak Motors** (307/322-2355 or 800/564-2355, www.laramiepeakmotors.com).

Guernsey and Vicinity

GUERNSEY

Guernsey (pop. 1,200) is a scenic railroad and ranching town along the once-mighty North Platte River. The river is now just a trickle in late summer, thanks to all the upstream dams. The town is named for Charles A. Guernsey, a prominent local rancher and legislator who came here in the late 19th century. The town is right in the heart of Oregon Trail country, with Fort Laramie just 11 miles east and numerous 19th-century historical markers. The

Wyoming Army National Guard maintains Camp Guernsey, a large troop-training facility just north of town that has grown in recent years. Watch your speed here; local cops strictly enforce the 30 mph limit!

Oregon Trail Ruts and Register Cliff

The Oregon Trail ran just on the other side of the North Platte River from Guernsey. One mile south of town are some of the deepest and most impressive Oregon Trail ruts anywhere along the historic route. Informative plaques describe the site in detail, and a short trail leads uphill to four-foot-deep gouges cut into the soft sandstone. The paths of bullwhackers are visible alongside. The old wagon trail is easy to follow in both directions, and the surrounding landscape has probably changed little since the last wagon train rolled past. Perhaps better than any historic photos or written descriptions, these deep ruts serve as permanent reminders of the great westward migration. Not far away is a white obelisk marking the grave of Lucindy Rollins, one of the thousands who died on the hard road west.

The 100-foot-tall Register Cliff is four miles south of Guernsey. Here the soft limestone made a perfect place for passing emigrants to carve their names, and thousands took the time to do so. The oldest—dating to the 1850s—are now behind a chain-link fence to keep folks from defacing them further. Hundreds of swallows nest on the cliff here. North of Guernsey, ruts of the historic Mormon Trail are visible along **Emigrant Hill,** where Mormon pioneers struggled to hoist their wagons up the steep slope.

Another important nearby site was **Emigrants' Washtub,** a warm springs where weary travelers stopped to bathe and wash clothes. The springs are an enjoyable place to relax even today and are reached via a two-mile walk along a dry creekbed. Access is a bit tricky because you pass through private land along the way and need to watch out for old shells left behind from National Guard training exercises. Get access information from the visitor center.

Events

Each **Fourth of July,** Guernsey comes to life with the standard small-town fun: a parade, rodeo, street dance, barbecue, and fireworks. **Labor Day** brings a demolition derby and an arts-and-crafts fair.

Accommodations

No bunkhouse accommodations at the **Bunkhouse Motel** (307/836-2356, www.bunk-

carved names at Register Cliff

© DON PITCHER

housemotel.com, $46–54 d), but there are nice motel rooms with fridges and Wi-Fi.

You'll find pleasant riverside campsites near the Oregon Trail ruts at the town-managed **Larson Park** (307/836-2255, $8 tents, $13 RVs, open Apr.–mid-Oct.). Noncampers can shower for $2.

Food

Rob's Riverview Restaurant (800 W. Laramie, 307/836-2191) is a modern place with three reasonably priced meals daily. There are specials most nights, including roast prime rib Saturday evenings. Big portions, too.

Burrito Brothers Mexican Food (307/836-2610) offers decent Mexican food. **Guernsey Lunch Box** (307/836-3188), on the east side of town, has standard American fare in a fast-food setting: burgers, chicken-fried steak, corn dogs, sandwiches, and a salad bar. Get groceries at **B&F Foods.**

Other Practicalities

Guernsey's little **visitor center/museum** (S.W. Wyoming and W. Sunrise, 307/836-2715, open

To Douglas

25 87

Oregon Trail

319

GLENDO
STATE PARK

Glendo
Reservoir

Glendo

To Esterbrook

Oregon Trail

319

To Lusk

270

MOTHER
FEATHER LEGS
MONUMENT

To Lusk

85

Rawhide
Buttes

Hartville Uplift

Jay Em

CAMP GUERNEY
TRAINING AREA

Hell Gap

OREGON
TRAIL
COUNTRY

Guernsey
Reservoir

Sunrise

Hartville

GUERNSEY
STATE PARK

Guernsey

EMIGRANTS
WASHTUB

26

North

Platte

Fort Laramie

Oregon

OREGON TRAIL RUTS

320

Grayrocks
Reservoir

River

316

REGISTER CLIFF

GRATTAN
MASSACRE
SITE

85

To
Torrington

FORT LARAMIE
NATIONAL HISTORIC SITE

Lingle   26

Trail

River

Laramie River

Wheatland

316

0   5 mi

0   5 km

To Chugwater
and Cheyenne

25

87

© AVALON TRAVEL PUBLISHING, INC.

late May–early Sept.) is right in front of the town's seasonal **swimming pool.** Tiny **Guernsey library** is open Monday–Saturday.

Get fast cash from the ATM inside the Phillips 66 station. The nine-hole **Trail Ruts Golf Course** (307/836-2255) provides a place to putt around.

Guernsey's airport is surprisingly large and well equipped, not because of any commercial service—there isn't any—but because of the nearby National Guard training facilities.

HARTVILLE AREA

Six miles north of Guernsey on Hwy. 270 is the picturesque old mining community of Hartville (pop. 80). Established in 1884, it is the oldest incorporated town in Wyoming. It was named for Colonel Verling Hart, an officer at nearby Fort Laramie and owner of a copper mine here. The Hartville Uplift—as it is known by geologists—is one of the most min-

eral-rich regions in Wyoming. Indians used its iron as pigment to make war paint. During the 1870s, prospectors found gold, silver, copper, onyx, and iron ore in these scenic pine- and juniper-dotted hills. Copper brought the first miners, but by 1887 it had been mostly mined out and they turned to iron ore. Hartville arose as a shopping, gambling, boozing, and whoring center for the miners; many of the historic stone and false-front buildings still stand.

Of note is **Miners Bar** (307/836-2008)— the state's oldest drinking establishment and the only surviving business. The cherry-wood back bar was crafted in Germany in 1864 and shipped to Fort Laramie before landing in Hartville in 1881. The bar is open only in the summer and has a horseshoe pit next door. Also in Hartville is an old stone jail.

Sunrise

The mining ghost town of Sunrise (closed to

the public) is just one mile east of Hartville. An extraordinarily rich body of iron ore was discovered here in 1887, and a dozen years later the Colorado Fuel and Iron Corp. established an open-pit iron mine, a mine that would eventually reach 650 feet in depth to become the largest glory hole in the world. It closed in 1984, and reclamation work has restored the gaping hole to a more natural contour. When the mine first opened, the company hired 750 predominantly Italian and Greek emigrants to dig the ore, which was shipped to a smelter in Pueblo, Colorado. To house the workers, the well-planned company town of Sunrise sprang up. The mine was closed in 1980 because of a lessened demand for ore, and its brick buildings now stand abandoned. It is a fascinating place to explore but isn't open to the public. You may be able to get access by asking locally for permission. Sunrise claims a minuscule footnote to history: *Ripley's Believe It or Not!* noted that the town had the longest string of car garages in the world. They are still standing, but it is doubtful that just six garages would merit such a rating today.

Spanish Diggings

The Hartville area is part of the so-called Spanish Diggings, an extensive archaeological site that covers hundreds of square miles. Early settlers believed this to be the site of a Spanish gold mine—hence the name—but it is now known to have been used instead by Native Americans gathering flint for arrowheads. They mined quartzite, jasper, moss agate, and chalcedony here for perhaps 10,000 years. Stone flakes and countless old pits up to 15 feet deep and 50 feet wide abound in this region. The material mined was carried all the way to the Missouri River. You'll find hundreds of tepee rings and rock chips here. One of the most important aboriginal places in Wyoming is in this area: an 11,000-year-old paleo-Indian site called **Hell Gap.**

Heading North

Highway 270 heads north from Hartville over pine-carpeted hills before descending through rolling grassland with a backdrop of rocky buttes and antelope grazing beside old windmills. There are dramatic views of Laramie Peak and Flattop Butte from the hilltops, plus a picturesque smattering of old stone or log houses.

At **Manville** (pop. 100) the road meets U.S. 18/20, which leads to Lusk. There's not much in Manville other than a few old buildings, including one of the smallest post offices in Wyoming, a water tower, a school, and a gas station/café/bar.

◖ GUERNSEY STATE PARK

Two state parks are found along the North Platte River in eastern Wyoming. Seven miles long and covering 6,538 acres, Guernsey is the smaller of the two but is far more interesting than its sister, Glendo State Park. Day use at Guernsey State Park (307/836-2334, http://wyoparks.state.wy.us) costs $4 for nonresident vehicles or $2 for folks with Wyoming plates.

The south entrance to Guernsey State Park is one mile northwest of Guernsey, and the road connects through to the Hartville area. The park surrounds Guernsey Reservoir, which is backed up behind a 105-foot-tall, 560-foot-long earthen dam completed in 1927. Originally, the dam stored 74,000 acre-feet of water, but half that capacity has been lost as a result of siltation. To reduce this problem, authorities now drain the reservoir each summer after the Fourth of July, killing off many of the fish and sometimes creating havoc with boaters because draining can take place with almost no warning. Don't bother bringing your fishing pole. The reservoir generally fills up again by Labor Day weekend.

Guernsey is surrounded by scenic grass-and-sage-covered hills topped with juniper and pine. The drive from Hartville through the park is a surprise after the open sage-and-grass country north of here. Pink-walled sandstone cliffs suddenly appear as the narrow, winding road (not for RVs) enters the canyon, hugs the cliffs as it passes the lake, and then climbs into the pines. There is a pleasant beach five miles west along the southern shore and 19 different campgrounds, each costing $12 for nonresidents or $6 for Wyoming residents year-round. Make

© DON PITCHER

Guernsey Reservoir, Guernsey State Park

campsite reservations ($8.50 fee) at 877/996-7275, www.wyo-park.com. The water is warm, making this a popular swimming hole.

Sights

Other than the scenery, the main attractions in Guernsey State Park are the wonderful stone structures built by the Civilian Conservation Corps (CCC) during the 1930s—some of the best examples of CCC craftsmanship in existence. Built in 1936, the **Guernsey State Park Museum** (307/836-2900, open 10 A.M.–6 P.M. daily May–Sept., free) is the finest of all, with an arched stone entrance facing impressive Laramie Peak 35 miles to the west. Inside are enormous hand-hewn timbers, wrought-iron light fixtures, and flagstone floors. This place was built to last! Inside are 14 displays created by the CCC to illustrate the geology and human use of the surrounding country. Take a look at the historical slide show.

Other park structures built of native materials include roads, overlooks, rock walls, culverts, bridges, and picnic shelters. Most impressive is a massive sandstone picnic shelter

known as **The Castle,** which faces the reservoir and Laramie Peak. Take the side road up to **Brimmer Point Overlook** for outstanding sunset vistas. Not far away is the "million-dollar privy," so named because it took so much time and money to build. Guernsey State Park also contains eight miles of hiking/mountain-biking trails and a short nature trail near the museum. Pick up a trail guide inside.

GLENDO STATE PARK

Twenty-five miles east of Douglas and 32 miles north of Wheatland, 10,000-acre Glendo State Park (307/735-4433, http://wyoparks.state.wy.us, $4 for nonresident vehicles, $2 for Wyoming vehicles) surrounds Glendo Reservoir. A 167-foot-high earthen dam backs up water for 14 miles and generates 24,000 kilowatts of electricity. This is one of the largest reservoirs on the North Platte River, and it has almost 80 miles of shoreline. Note, however, that drought years sometimes reduce the reservoir to little more than a puddle. The surrounding country is treeless and windy, but the towering 10,272-foot summit of Laramie Peak dominates the skyline to the west. The surprisingly warm water at Sandy Beach makes this a play area for families from surrounding towns. Other attractions are the Red Cliffs, where cliff divers agonize over the long drop, and Muddy Bay, where anglers look for walleye (there are some lunkers here), perch, or trout. You can explore dozens of small coves by boat or float down the river below the dam. The wind can really blow, making for good sailboarding conditions but also creating hazards for folks who go out in small boats.

There are seven state park campgrounds ($12 for nonresidents, $6 for Wyoming residents; open year-round) on the eastern end of Glendo Reservoir. Make campsite reservations ($8.50 fee) at 877/996-7275, www.wyo-park.com.

Town of Glendo

The desolate town of Glendo (pop. 230) is just two miles from Glendo State Park, near the site of the old **Horseshoe Creek Stage Station.** Built by Mormons in the 1850s, this station was later burned by them to keep it out of government hands. A tiny **Glendo Historical Museum** (open 8 A.M.–noon and 1–4 P.M. Mon.–Fri.) next to the town office displays early settlers' gear, dinosaur bones, and rocks.

Cribbage players take note: Diamond A's Lounge and Grill hosts the **Platte Valley Cribbage Tournament** in early March. It's said to be the oldest consecutive tournament in the United States. **Glendo Days** (307/735-4242) arrives in mid-June, featuring a hot air–balloon rally, parade, craft fair, games, food booths, and a street dance. The **Glendo Marina Walleye Tournament** (307/735-4216) comes around in early June, and a fireworks display takes place on the **Fourth of July.**

Cheap lodging (in mobile homes) is available just off the interstate and behind the general store at **Howard's Motel** (106 A St., 307/735-4252). The store here has an ATM. **Lakeview Motel and Trailer Court** (307/735-4461) is just north of town overlooking the lake, with RV hookups, tent sites, and basic cottages.

Hall's Glendo Marina (307/735-4216, www.hallsglendomarina.com) near the dam has rustic accommodations ($63 d) overlooking the lake, RV sites with hookups ($25), plus a restaurant and small grocery store. Hall's rents fishing boats and pontoon boats and is open late May–early September.

Rooster's Old Western Saloon (307/735-4451) serves the best dinners around, with steak, prime rib, fresh walleye, and Indian fry bread on the menu. Also worth a visit is **Mike's Steak Place** (307/735-4616), popular for country cooking, from pork tenderloin to Philly steak sandwiches. Open three meals a day.

◖ FORT LARAMIE NATIONAL HISTORIC SITE

One of the most important historic sites in all of Wyoming is old Fort Laramie, three miles southwest of the town of the same name. The fort played a variety of roles as the West was developed: Indian trading post, emigrant way station, and military center. The budding territory's first school and post office opened here, and nearly every famous citizen of the fron-

FORT LARAMIE NATIONAL HISTORIC SITE

SCALE NOT AVAILABLE

© AVALON TRAVEL PUBLISHING, INC.

tier era—from Jim Bridger to Mark Twain—stopped in. Today Fort Laramie is one of the most popular stopping points for visitors who want a taste of the rich history of this region.

In 1834, trader William Sublette halted along the banks of the Laramie River near its confluence with the North Platte. With him were 35 mountain men, their pack animals weighed down with trade items for the annual rendezvous along the Green River. Sublette had a bold plan to build a permanent trading post here, one that would make it easier to bring supplies west and beaver furs and buffalo robes back east, a place where Indians and whites could parley and profit. He left behind a dozen men to begin work on what would become Fort William—named after its founder—and hurried west to the rendezvous. The men threw up a cottonwood stockade with blockhouses on the corners and a sally port (special passageway) to the outer gate for trading with the Indians.

The post changed hands a couple of times in the next two years. Changing its name to Fort Lucien, it became an important trade center for Pierre Chouteau's American Fur Company. By 1841, competition from the Fort Platte trading post—built just one mile away—forced the company to start again. This time it spent $10,000 to build a whitewashed adobe fort near the already rotting old one. Fort John-on-the-Laramie was the official name given to the second fort, but this was quickly shortened to Fort Laramie.

During the next eight years, Fort Laramie emerged as a strategic center for trade with the Indians; more than 10,000 buffalo robes were purchased each year. (Traders generally paid the equivalent of $1 per robe in the form of gunpowder, hatchets, tobacco, coffee, sugar, blankets, and, of course, liquor. The robes were sold in St. Louis for $4 each.) But its time as a trading post gradually gave way to a new role for the fort.

Protecting the Oregon Trail

Fort Laramie stood right along the main trail to Oregon, California, and Salt Lake City. It was one-third of the way from Missouri to the Columbia River mouth and provided a much-anticipated break before the long, desolate trek over the Continental Divide. In 1843, nearly 1,000 people passed the fort. The numbers increased each year, reaching a crescendo after gold was discovered in California in 1849. Soon thereafter, more than 50,000 emigrants were trudging into Fort Laramie each summer. They stopped to repair wheels at the wheelwright and blacksmith shops, buy food, clothing, and other supplies at the store, or trade tired stock for fresh oxen and horses. The latter was the best deal for traders at the fort; all they had to do was put the "worn out" oxen and horses they had exchanged with the emigrants (generally a two-for-one deal) out to pasture

for a couple of weeks and then trade them as fresh stock to subsequent emigrants.

This great migration westward had its negative consequences. Indians complained that buffalo were being shot and forced away from their traditional migration routes and that the thousands of stock animals brought by the emigrants were destroying the grass. The inevitable conflicts began as young warriors halted wagon trains, demanding "tolls" in the form of tobacco, coffee, or sugar. Quickly, this escalated into attacks against the emigrants, and a great cry went up for protection from the "savages." Thus it was that Congress gave Fort Laramie the new role of military garrison mandated to protect the Oregon Trail.

The Army Takes Over

In 1849, the army bought Fort Laramie for $4,000, establishing the first military post in what would become Wyoming. About 180 men—both mounted rifle and infantrymen—were assigned to the post. A rapid expansion program was begun; the old adobe fort served as temporary quarters while more elaborate facilities were built. The army's Fort Laramie did not fit the Hollywood stereotype of a frontier fort—it had no log perimeter or blockhouses. The fort was instead laid out around a central parade ground, with clapboard and "lime grout" concrete buildings forming a loose perimeter. In case of attack, the army was prepared to retreat to a single, heavily fortified building. Despite this general lack of protection and the fact that Indians once brazenly drove off the fort's horses, the fort was never attacked by Indians, and most soldiers never engaged in battle with the Indians.

Fort Laramie was essentially a male bastion, although a few officers' wives were present. The only exceptions were laundresses and servant girls. The latter were said to have been hired on the basis of their physical appearance: the less attractive the better, so as to not appeal to the soldiers' prurient interests. After all, if a servant got married, her mistress had to find another one to replace her. A small group of Indians, derisively termed "Laramie Loafers,"

© DON PITCHER

Old Bedlam, Fort Laramie National Historic Site

soon attached themselves to the fort, camping nearby and providing scouts, interpreters, errand boys, and paramours. Fort Laramie—like most 19th-century military posts—was not a pleasant place. The food was adequate but lacked variety, the discipline so strict that even the smallest infraction could land a man in the guardhouse, and sanitary conditions were so bad that by 1880 it was getting hard to find a place to dig latrines that had not already been contaminated. The infrequent paydays turned into drunken brawls. No wonder so many men deserted their posts and slipped off for the promising goldfields of California or the Black Hills! The inevitable "hog ranches" also grew up near the fort and offered an escape from the day-to-day monotony of the soldiers' lives. In 1877, Lieutenant John G. Bourke described the "ranches" as:

tenanted by as hardened and depraved a set of witches as could be found on the face of the globe. Each of these establishments was equipped with a rum-mill of the worst kind and each contained from three to half a dozen Cyprians, virgins whose lamps were always burning brightly in expectance of the coming of the bridegroom, and who lured to destruction the soldiers of the garrison. In all my experience I have never seen a lower, more beastly set of people of both sexes.

For the next four decades, Fort Laramie served as the nerve center for this part of the plains, providing troops and cavalry to retaliate against Indian attacks and serving as a meeting place for treaty arrangements when the political wind shifted toward negotiation instead of confrontation. The first of these treaties came in 1851, under the inspired leadership of Indian agent Thomas Fitzpatrick, a former mountain man. More than 10,000 Indians attended, representing the Sioux, Cheyenne, Arapaho, Shoshone, Crow, Gros Ventre, and Assiniboin tribes. The treaty consisted essentially of annual bribes (annuities) to be given to the Indians to compensate them for their losses to whites. The various tribes would be assigned to distinct territories but could hunt in other areas. After signing the treaty, a mountain of presents awaited—the first of the $50,000 in annuities for each of the next 50 years. Shortly thereafter, the federal government reneged on the promise, increasing the annual amount to $70,000 per year but cutting the time to just 10 years. Peace lasted but a short while.

Grattan Fight

One of the few Indian–white conflicts to occur in the vicinity of Fort Laramie took place in 1854. It began innocently enough when a Mormon emigrant's lame cow wandered off and was butchered by a hungry Miniconjou Indian waiting for the government to dispense annuities. A hotheaded young lieutenant, John Grattan, was sent out to bring in the Indian. Unfortunately, Grattan's interpreter was drunk and began immediately shouting insults at the Sioux in whose village the man was camped. Grattan himself was anxious for a fight, hoping to gain a piece of fame, so when the Sioux refused to give up the man—offering instead to pay for the cow with two horses—Grattan would have nothing of it. His soldiers opened fire and were themselves immediately attacked by a vastly superior force of Sioux. All 29 soldiers died in the battle that followed, and Fort Laramie stood in danger of being destroyed. But the Indians instead raided local storehouses for the promised annuities and headed out. The army used the Grattan Massacre as proof that the Indians could not be trusted. In reality, the entire incident was an instance of utter stupidity on the part of the army.

More Trouble

One of the least distinguished post commanders at Fort Laramie was the hard-drinking and ill-tempered Colonel Thomas Moonlight. In 1865, he publicly hanged two Sioux subchiefs who had brought in two white women captives for reward. Their bodies were left dangling in chains for several weeks, an act that brought condemnation from the Eastern press. In retaliation, the Sioux killed several soldiers and then managed to drive off most of the horses from Colonel Moonlight's cavalry. A sullen Moonlight led his almost horseless cavalry in the 120-mile hike back to the fort. Although shortly thereafter stripped of his command, Moonlight later served as the politically appointed territorial governor of Wyoming.

With the decline in importance of the Oregon Trail, Fort Laramie became a staging area for military expeditions against the Indians. In the Treaty of 1868, signed at the fort, the Sioux were guaranteed the Powder River country "as long as the grass shall grow and the buffalo shall roam." But the discovery of gold in the Black Hills abruptly changed the picture, and whites now wanted the land itself, not just a road through it. They eventually got it, but not before Lieutenant Colonel Custer and his men were wiped out at Little Big Horn in 1876. After this, with the Indians tucked away on reservations, most of the hostilities died down and the fort lost its strategic importance. The railroad had long since supplanted the Oregon Trail as the primary route west, and during the 1880s Fort Laramie served as a way station along the Cheyenne–Deadwood stage road. During this time the fort grew more genteel with the planting of trees and completion of numerous substantial homes.

The Army Departs

By 1889, it was clear that Fort Laramie had outlived its usefulness, and it was ordered closed. The following year, the 35,000 acres of military land were opened to homesteaders and the buildings auctioned off. Because of the scarcity of wood in the area, many buildings were stripped and hauled away to become cabins or other structures. Others remained on the site and were used as homes, businesses, or barns. For the next half century the historic fort slowly deteriorated, but in 1937 the state of Wyoming bought the site and donated it to the federal government. The following year it was declared a national monument, to be managed by the National Park Service. A lengthy and difficult restoration process managed to stabilize the ruins and restore a dozen of the historic structures, but it was not until 1964 that the fort was restored to something approaching the conditions in the 1880s.

Visiting the Fort

Each year nearly 55,000 visitors come to historic Fort Laramie for a rewarding traipse back in time. The clear, tree-lined Laramie River still flows close by, and the spacious parade ground engenders a feeling of this fort's importance, while the bleak, windswept setting speaks of its hardships.

Buildings and grounds of the 830-acre Fort Laramie National Historic Site are open 8 A.M.–sunset year-round. Entrance costs $3 for adults, no charge for kids under 16 or seniors with Golden Age passes. There's no camping at the site, but there is a pleasant picnic area.

For an excellent orientation to Fort Laramie, head to the old commissary building, now the **visitor center/park headquarters** (307/837-2221, www.nps.gov/fola). Inside are excellent displays, historic photos, and an 18-minute video on the history of Fort Laramie. Ask about interpretive talks and tours and the dramatic firings of historic weapons. The center is open 8 A.M.–7 P.M. daily June–August; 8 A.M.–6 P.M. daily in May and September; and 8 A.M.–4:30 P.M. daily the rest of the year. The gift shop offers an extraordinary collection of historic books on the Old West. It also rents CD audio tours ($3) and sells such authentic items as locally made lye soap, brass cavalry spurs, military insignias, bonnets (made by Torrington seniors), wooden toys, old playing cards, and hardtack.

The **Fort Laramie Historical Association** (307/837-2662 or 800/321-5456, www.fortlaramie.com) manages the bookshop and produces a big publication describing several hundred Western history books available by mail order.

If you're in the area in early July, be sure to drop by Fort Laramie for an **Frontier Fourth of July Celebration** with old-time music, locals in period clothing, games, and dancing. In mid-August comes a **Military Encampment Weekend** with special moonlight programs.

Historical Buildings

By the time it was abandoned in 1890, Fort Laramie was approaching the size of a small town; 68 buildings of all types were scattered around the grounds. The remains of 21 of these are still visible—some simply limegrout concrete ruins maintained in a state of arrested decay. A dozen have been completely restored and refurbished with authentic period pieces behind Plexiglas doors. The Park Service has an informative *Historic Buildings Guide* available at the visitor center. Several of the buildings are particularly noteworthy: the cavalry barracks, Old Bedlam, the bakery, and the guardhouse.

Most of the men who soldiered out of Fort Laramie lived under crowded conditions with little privacy. Sometimes this meant living in tents for long periods. The **cavalry barracks** on your left as you enter the fort were an improvement, but quarters were still tight. Walk up to the restored second floor to find row upon row of cots where an entire company of 60 men slept. Then try to imagine all the snoring and the smelly feet after being out on duty for weeks at a time! Baths were taken, in theory, every Saturday night in a half barrel.

The **post trader's store** just right of the entrance provided a break from the army's monotonous food and supplies. Built in 1849, it served not only the military but also the thousands of civilians who poured west along the Oregon Trail and the Indians who traded for various items. The store owner provided everything from essential food supplies to fresh oxen for weary emigrants. He also sold alcohol and benefited from the tons of excess belongings that many overburdened travelers cast aside to lighten their loads.

The officers enjoyed far better living conditions than the cavalry and infantry, including access to a pleasant officers' club and a hired cook. The 1884 **lieutenant colonel's quarters** has been restored to the era when Lieutenant Colonel Andrew Burt and his family lived here (1887–1888). Inside you'll see some of the family's original furnishings. Next door is the **post surgeon's quarters,** completed in 1875. The surgeon had a highly respected rank in the fort and was accorded the responsibility of gathering weather data as well as scientific specimens. The surgeon dealt primarily with such problems as kicks by horses, injuries from brawls, frostbitten fingers and toes, and venereal diseases. War wounds were far less common, but when they did occur many could not be adequately treated and the men often died.

The oldest and most prominent building at Fort Laramie is **Old Bedlam,** an attractive clapboard structure that dominates the west end of the parade grounds. Built in 1849, it was the center of life at the fort. Old Bedlam served a variety of purposes when the military was here; initially it served as a bachelor officers' quarters and later as the post headquarters and commanding officers' home, before finally becoming housing for married officers and their families. The name apparently comes from the bedlam that existed with so many folks jammed together—particularly after payday, when parties raged. Old Bedlam is now refurbished to represent two different periods. The south end represents the post headquarters of the 1864 period and the living quarters of Lieutenant Colonel William O. Collins, while the north end represents a bachelor officer's quarters of the early 1850s period.

Behind the attractive **Captain's Quarters** on the south end of the parade ground is a model of adobe-walled Fort John, which stood on this spot in 1841. A footpath leads to the Laramie River. The old stone **guardhouse** on the east side of the fort could house up to 45 prisoners, varying from soldiers who had violated minor conduct rules to those charged with murder. The basement jail had no furniture, toilet, or light, and no heat even in the dead of winter. Stop by the historic **bakery**—one of four built here at different times. One loaf of bread, along with greasy salt pork or beef, beans, rice, and rotgut coffee, was the typical daily allotment · for soldiers. Fresh vegetables were often unavailable for months at a time, and scurvy was a constant threat. In the field, the rations were even worse, generally consisting of salt pork, beans, and wormy hardtack.

Oregon Trail Ruts

One of the less-visited sights in the area is **Old Bedlam ruts,** two miles northwest of

Fort Laramie. A gravel road leads to the location; get a map from park headquarters. The ruts (marked by posts) climb into the gentle hills west of the old fort, offering a marvelous panorama of a landscape that has not changed much in the last century. From here, it's easy to imagine emigrants looking back on the fort, their last touch with civilization for hundreds of miles. Laramie Peak is prominent to the west. Nearby is the grave of Mary Homsley, one of the thousands who died along the difficult trek west. The ruts can be traced all the way to Guernsey, where they grow even deeper. A similar series of ruts extends eastward from the fort. If you're heading to Wheatland from the fort, try the "back way" via **Grayrocks Reservoir**—the source of cooling water for the Laramie River Station Power Plant. The road is rough for the first eight miles or so but is paved beyond that and offers an enjoyable taste of the rugged countryside around the reservoir. Signs point the way to Wheatland.

Oregon Trail ruts, near Guernsey

© DON PITCHER

THE TOWN OF FORT LARAMIE

The town of Fort Laramie (pop. 240) lies three miles northeast of the historic fort and across the North Platte River. Wyoming's oldest post office is here, dating to the 1880s, when the army occupied the fort. One mile south of town is an **iron bridge** built in 1875. Although long superseded by a concrete span just upriver and not much to look at, the bridge bears historical importance. Funded by a $15,000 congressional appropriation, the bridge ensured the establishment of the Cheyenne–Deadwood Stage and Express through here. It remained the major route north for many years thereafter. Note how much longer the old bridge is than the new one. Upstream dams have blocked the river flow, making it barely one-third of the original width. A highway monument east of town along U.S. 26 notes the site of the Grattan Massacre.

Practicalities

A couple of places offer meals and lodging in Fort Laramie, but I'd keep on driving if I were you. Pitch tents for free at the **Fort Laramie town park** just across the railroad tracks on the south side of town; no showers.

Two miles from the fort, **Chuckwagon RV Park** (307/837-2828, www.prairieweb.com/chuckwagonrvpark, $10 tents, $16 RVs) is open May–September. Halfway between Fort Laramie and Lingle—five miles in either direction—**Pony Soldier RV Park** (307/837-3078, $16 tents, $25 RVs) is open mid-April–mid-October.

Torrington

Torrington (pop. 5,800) is a quiet farming and retirement town just eight miles from the Nebraska border. It's the seat of Wyoming's most important agricultural county—Goshen, alias "The Land of Goshen"—and lots of sugar beets, alfalfa, oats, dry beans, corn, and hay are grown here. The tree-lined North Platte River drifts lazily through town, and easy-listening "music" blares over the downtown speakers at all hours for your listening pleasure.

Torrington's economy has been relatively stable; the biggest local employer, a Western Sugar factory, is on the edge of town, and many productive farms are scattered in the surrounding countryside.

Two long waterways—Fort Laramie Canal and the Interstate Canal—provide irrigation water for much of this farmland. Trains filled with coal from Campbell and Weston counties constantly rumble through toward the south and east, a stench from the sugar refinery hangs in the air each fall, and the livestock auction is the big weekly event. A walk along Main Street is a trek through the American heartland; if the cars were older, Torrington could model for a *Saturday Evening Post* cover from the '50s. Retirees and wealthy refugees from the Colorado Front Range have moved into the area, and a 650-bed medium-security state prison—set to open in 2007—will provide many new jobs.

Although several hundred thousand emigrants passed through Goshen County on their way to Oregon, California, or Utah, none bothered to stop. The area was not settled until cattlemen came in the 1880s, followed by homesteaders around the turn of the 20th century, including many from Russia and Germany. Many of the "soddies" and wooden shacks these emigrants built still stand in the fields throughout the county. Named for Torrington, Connecticut, the town was incorporated in 1907 as a ranching and farming center. Completion of the Interstate Canal in 1915 and the Fort Laramie Canal in 1924 brought North Platte River water, making it possible to grow a wide variety of crops. The Burlington Railroad arrived from the east in 1900, but it was not until 1926 that the Union Pacific built a line connecting Torrington with Pine Bluffs to the south. That year proved pivotal because it brought a new train depot and the

TORRINGTON

HOSPITAL

EASTERN WYOMING
COLLEGE

MAVERICK MOTEL

GARRETT ST

HOUSE ST

GOSHEN COUNTY
FAIRGROUNDS

JAMES
LAUNDROMAT

To Fort
Laramie
and Guernsey

85
26

WEST VALLEY RD

E ST
D ST
C ST
B ST
A ST
MAIN ST

30TH AVE
29TH AVE
28TH AVE
27TH AVE
SHOEMAKER ST
26TH AVE
25TH AVE
24TH AVE
23RD AVE

JIRDON PARK &
SWIMMING POOL

TORRINGTON
LIVESTOCK MARKET

CHAMBER OF
COMMERCE

POST
OFFICE

GOSHEN COUNTY
COURTHOUSE

22ND AVE
21ST AVE

CITY HALL

LIBRARY

20TH AVE
19TH AVE

A ST
B ST

AIRPORT RD

Grass Roots Trail

BEST
VALUE INN

MAIN STREET
MARKET

PIONEER PARK

GOLF COURSE RD

14TH AVE

KING'S INN

ST JOSEPH
CHILDREN'S
HOME

18TH AVE
17TH AVE
16TH AVE

C ST
D ST
E ST
F ST
G ST
H ST

OREGON
TRAIL LODGE

EAST VALLEY RD

15TH AVE

Burlington Northern Railroad

River

11TH AVE

KELLY'S
SUPER MARKET

Platte

13TH AVE

PIZZA
HUT

26

North

0   0.25 mi

0   0.25 km

BOTANICAL PARK

HOLLY
SUGAR FACTORY

1ST AVE

SOUTH MAIN ST

2ND AVE

HOMESTEAD
MUSEUM

To Holiday Inn and
Scottsbluff, NE

4TH AVE

Union Pacific Railroad

To Cheyenne

85

5TH AVE

© AVALON TRAVEL PUBLISHING, INC.

Holly Sugar plant. The town has grown slowly through the years, and except for a brief flirtation with oil and gas in the 1970s has remained true to its farming and ranching roots.

HOMESTEADERS MUSEUM

Right at the crossroads of the Oregon Trail, the Cheyenne–Deadwood stage route, the Mormon Trail, and the Texas Cattle Trail, the Homesteaders Museum seems to sit atop history. It is housed in the 1926 brick-and-masonry Union Pacific depot just south of town. The last train stopped at the depot in 1964. The museum (307/532-5612) is open 9:30 A.M.–4 P.M. Monday–Friday, 9:30 A.M.–6 P.M. Saturday, and noon–6 P.M. Sunday during summer; closed Saturdays in winter. Although it contains a substantial paleo-Indian collection, the museum focuses on the thousands of early-1900s homesteaders who flocked to eastern Wyoming. The Yoder Ranch collection (artifacts from 1881 on) is particularly noteworthy, along with such oddities as a 1907 International car, a relay saddle used by Pony Express riders, a four-way Sears Roebuck mousetrap from the 1920s, and a crockpot-style fireless stove. Sit down and spend some time looking through the many historic black and white pictures; they will quickly transport you back to a simple era when pioneers scratched out a hardscrabble life on the mixed-grass prairie in wooden or sod shacks. The museum's KKK robe comes from the 1920s, when a vehemently racist and anti-Catholic spirit dominated much of rural America. Outside are an old homestead cabin, a windmill, and a caboose housing historic railroad photos and memorabilia. When I last wandered through the museum, the long-retired docent joked, "When I started working here my kids asked if I was going to be one of the displays. I said I'd rather be an artifact."

South of Torrington a sign marks the **Cold Springs Campground** used by travelers on the Oregon Trail and later the site of a stage station and a Pony Express stop. A few miles east of town is a memorial to the party of Astorians who camped nearby in the winter of 1812.

◖ TORRINGTON LIVESTOCK MARKET

More than 120,000 cattle are raised in Goshen County each year—more than in any other Wyoming county—so it is logical that Torrington should also be at the center of the state's livestock trade. Each year nearly a quarter of a million cattle are marketed at the Torrington Livestock Market (307/532-3333, www.torringtonlive.com) on U.S. 26 at West E Street. Auctions take place beginning at 10 A.M. every Friday and last into the early afternoon, with additional load lot auctions on Monday and Wednesday in the fall. All of these auctions are open to the public and are quite interesting, but don't raise your hand or you might just buy a bull. The award-winning auctioneers, brothers Lex and Shawn Madden, put on quite a show.

ENTERTAINMENT AND EVENTS

Watch movies at **Wyoming Theatre** (126 E. 20th Ave., 307/532-2226). Two local places have live country music on some weekends: **Bronco Bar** (1924 Main St., 307/532-8660) and **Tote-Away Bar** (1934½ W. A St., 307/532-5506).

Many locals also head over to the **Stateline Oasis** (307/532-4990), next to the Nebraska line, for the chance to check out the strippers Tuesday–Saturday nights. The Oasis typically has live bands on Saturday nights.

The biggest annual event in Torrington is the **Goshen County Fair** (307/532-2525), held the first full week in August and presenting everything from a parade to pig wrestling. The indoor arena here is Wyoming's largest.

SHOPPING

Head up the steps to **The Studio** (2007 Main St., 307/532-8709) for something quite unexpected in Torrington, a real art gallery. In addition to pieces by owner/artist Julie Nighswonger, you'll find a selection of locally made gifts and artwork. Head to **Pamida** on the east end of town for discount items.

RECREATION

Torrington has a summertime outdoor **swimming pool** (307/532-7798) in Jirdon Park. Kids will love the 180-foot water slide. There is also an 18-hole **municipal golf course** (307/532-3868) outside of town. Bowl at **Ten Pin Tropics** (307/532-2187) on the east side of Torrington. For a walk, saunter the paved **Grassroots Trail,** built atop an old irrigation canal that slices across the northern edge of town.

ACCOMMODATIONS

Note that noisy freight trains roll through Torrington at all hours of the night, so you may want to choose a place as far as possible from the tracks. **Oregon Trail Lodge** (710 E. Valley Rd., 307/532-2101, $32 s or $45 d) has inexpensive lodging, with fridges in all rooms.

Find affordable rooms—including some efficiencies—at **Maverick Motel** (1.5 miles west of town on U.S. 26/85, 307/532-4064, $38 s or $40–42 d).

King's Inn (1555 S. Main St., 307/532-4011, www.kings-inn.tripod.com, $52 s or $59 d) has a hot tub and boot-shaped indoor pool, wireless Internet, a hot breakfast, and fridges and microwaves in some rooms. A restaurant and lounge are on the premises.

STARVING TO DEATH ON A GOVERNMENT CLAIM

My name is Frank Taylor, a bachelor I am,
I'm keeping old batch on an elegant plan,
You'll find me out West in the county of Lane
A-starving to death on a Government claim.

Hurrah for Lane County, the land of the free,
The home of the bedbug, grasshopper and flea,
I'll sing of its praises and boast of its fame
A-starving to death on a Government claim.

My clothes they are ragged, my language is rough,
My bread is case-hardened and solid and tough,
But I have a good time and live at my ease
On common sop-sorghum and old bacon grease.

How happy am I when I crawl into bed,
With rattlesnakes rattling just under my head,
And the gay little bedbug, so cheerful and bright,
He keeps me a-going two-thirds of the night.

How happy am I on my Government claim,
I've nothing to lose and I've nothing to gain,
I've nothing to eat and I've nothing to wear,
And nothing from nothing is honest and fair.

Oh, come to Lane County, there's room for you all,
Where the wind never stops and the rains never fall,
Oh, join in the chorus and sing of her fame,
A-starving to death on a Government claim.

Oh, don't be downhearted, you poor hungry men,
We're all just as free as the pigs in the pen,
Just stick to your homestead and fight with your fleas,
And pray to your Maker to send some more breeze.

Now all you poor sinners, I hope you will stay
And chaw on your hardtack till you're toothless and grey,
But as for myself I don't aim to remain
And slave like a dog on no Government claim.

Farewell to Lane County, the pride of the West
I'm going back East to the girl I love best,
I'll stop in Missouri and get me a wife,
And live on corn doggers the rest of my life.
                    —Anonymous

Best Value Inn (1548 S. Main St., 307/532-7118 or 866/506-8181, www.bestvalue-torrington.com) provides clean and comfy rooms, along with an indoor pool, hot tub, exercise room, wireless Internet, and continental breakfast. Rates in standard rooms are $57–62 s or $74–79 d; suites with three queen beds cost $80 d.

On the east side of town, **◖ Holiday Inn Express** (307/532-7600 or 800/465-4329, www.hiexpress.com/torringtonwy) is Torrington's newest and nicest place to stay, with a breakfast bar, indoor pool, hot tub, and fitness center. Rates are $75 d in standard rooms. Suites include hot tubs, microwaves, and fridges for $120 d.

Camping

Camp for free at shady **Pioneer Park** along the North Platte River on the edge of town. It's open year-round and has electrical hookups, but during the winter you'll need to get water elsewhere. Additional sites are available year-round at the **Goshen County Fairgrounds** (307/532-2525). RV sites with hookups cost $10, and you can probably pitch a tent for free.

FOOD

Torrington has a decent choice of restaurants, but almost none are open on Sundays, and closing time is early—8 or 9 p.m. other nights. **Java Jar** (1940 N. Main St., 307/532-8541) has espresso, soup served in bread bowls, and sandwiches. It's popular for lunch but closes at 3 P.M.

Looking for southern fried chicken, burgers, shakes, and fries? Join the flock at **Chicken Hut** (650 E. Valley Rd., 307/532-4441). It's one of the only places open Sundays. Visit **Deacons Restaurant** (1558 S. Main St., 307/532-4766, open at 5 A.M. Mon.–Sat.) for dependable meals, plus a substantial salad bar and homemade pies.

Canton Dragon (2126 N. Main St., 307/532-3888) serves pseudo-Chinese food, with $5 lunch specials. **La Familia Prado** (1250 S. Main St., 307/534-1975) has Mexican meals and margaritas. Although the owners are Asian Americans, **Grandpa Chuy's** (1915 Main St., 307/532-2982) serves Mexican food: tacos, burritos, fajitas, and enchiladas. **Buck's Pizza** (300 W. Valley Rd., 307/534-4616) is the local pizza joint.

For reasonably priced steaks and seafood in an attractive setting, drive to **Little Moon Lake Supper Club** (307/532-5750) on the state line eight miles east on U.S. 26.

Get groceries from two places on South Main: **Kelly's Super Market** (307/532-3113) or **Main St. Market** (307/532-3401).

INFORMATION AND SERVICES

For local information, drop by the office of **Goshen County Chamber of Commerce** (350 W. 21st St., 307/532-3879 or 800/577-3555, www.torringtonterritory.com, open 8 A.M.–5 P.M. Mon.–Fri. year-round). Be sure to pick up its loop-tour brochure for interesting sights in surrounding areas.

Services include the **public library** (2001 E. A St., 307/532-3411) and the **post office** (2145 Main St., 307/532-2213). Wash clothes at **James Laundromat** (27th Ave. and W. C St.).

One of the oldest junior colleges in the state (but that means 1948), **Eastern Wyoming College** (3200 W. C St., 307/532-8200 or 866/327-8996, http://ewcweb.ewc.cc.wy.us) has vocational and academic programs.

SOUTH OF TORRINGTON

The town symbol for Torrington is the ring-necked pheasant—a fitting logo in this farm-ing country. **Downar Bird Farm** (17 miles south on U.S. 85, 307/532-3449) raises 11,000 pheasants each year. It is run by the Wyoming Game and Fish Department, which releases the birds each fall for area hunters. This is basically a release-and-shoot operation because the birds are let go in unfamiliar territory just in time for hunting season. The farm is an interesting place to visit and boasts 27 different pheasant breeds. Incidentally, although the ring-necked pheasant is abundant throughout the Midwest, it is a native of China.

The minuscule town of **Veteran** (pop. 30)—basically a post office and general store 15 miles southwest of Torrington—was established by Iowa veterans of World War I. A POW camp was established here in World War II. The surrounding landscape is a mixture of grass, wheat, sage, and rocky buttes, with cattle grazing the land and vultures circling above.

Hawk Springs State Recreation Area (307/836-2334, http://wyoparks.state.wy.us) lies 27 miles south of Torrington off U.S. 85. The small park contains campsites ($12 for nonresidents or $6 for Wyoming residents), picnic tables, and a boat ramp along Hawk Springs Reservoir. Fishing is good for walleye, largemouth bass, yellow perch, black crappie, and channel catfish. Boaters will discover a blue heron rookery on the south end of the reservoir. Park entrance costs $4 for nonresident vehicles or $2 for Wyoming residents.

Seven miles north is the postage stamp–size town of **Hawk Springs** (pop. 70), home to the **Longbranch Saloon and Steakhouse** (307/532-4266), open three meals a day. That's about it here; most of the town is shuttered. Five miles north of Hawk Springs and just off U.S. 85 is **Springer/Bump Sullivan Wildlife Management Area,** with more fishing, boating, and camping at Sullivan Reservoir.

LINGLE

Ten miles northwest of Torrington is the tidy farming crossroads called Lingle (pop. 500), where trains laden with coal roll through al-most continuously. An **outdoor pool** is open in the summer. The town has a couple of places to eat but no accommodations. **Lira's** (307/837-2826) offers authentic Mexican food that attracts folks from miles around. Also here are **Stagecoach Cafe** (307/837-2614), with Saturday night prime rib specials.

Five miles west of Lingle (or five miles east of Fort Laramie) is the **Western History Center** (307/837-3052, www.wyshs.org/mus-westhist-ctr.htm, $1.50 adults, free for kids under 13). This small museum has a variety of displays, including fossils, mammoth bones, and Indian artifacts. Noted anthropologist George Zeimens, who manages this private museum, also leads tours to historic and archaeological sites in eastern Wyoming ($40 per person for groups of six or more by reservation only). The museum is well worth a stop, and is open 10 A.M.–4 P.M. Monday–Saturday June–August, or 9 A.M.–3 P.M. Monday, Thursday, and Saturday the rest of the year.

Adjacent to the history center is **Pony Soldier RV Park** (307/837-3078, $16 tents, $25 RVs, open mid-Apr.–mid-Oct.).

JAY EM

North of Lingle on U.S. 85, the irrigated pastures and green fields give way to endless prairies. This is a land of sandy hillocks carpeted with short grasses, similar to the sandhill country of western Nebraska, which lies just a dozen miles eastward. Stop to take in the wind and to listen to squeaking windmills and singing meadowlarks. In summer the dark afternoon sky is accented by slashes of lightning and occasional rainbows.

Halfway between Lingle and Lusk, the road passes the almost ghost town of Jay Em (pop. 15), named for the cattle brand of rancher Jim Moore. Just to the north lies his old Jay Em Ranch. A few people still live in the old wooden houses of Jay Em, and the post office becomes a meeting place each morning, but the town is otherwise deserted. It's a peaceful spot to stop and walk along narrow Rawhide Creek among the cottonwood trees and tall grass. The town is a National Historic District, and the rustic old buildings are a photographer's treat. Get a brochure detailing the buildings from the chamber of commerce in Torrington. Tours are available by reservation; call 307/735-4364. As you continue north to Lusk, the country again opens into grassland, windmills, cattle, a few tree-topped hills, and small rocky buttes.

Lusk

Lusk (pop. 1,400) is the seat of Wyoming's least-populated county. Just 2,400 people live in rural Niobrara County—an average of almost 700 acres per person! It's remote grassland country here with long, straight highways heading out in the compass directions. Ranching provides a relatively stable—albeit limited—economic base, but the oil industry that was once so prominent has faded. The town itself has a Midwestern feel, with tree-lined streets and attractive older homes. It's quiet and safe; great for raising a family, but teenagers probably get bored quickly. Downtown businesses are clearly struggling to survive, and more than a few have given up, leaving shuttered doors in their wake. Lusk's main claim to fame is the *Legend of Rawhide,* a July extravaganza.

The first settlers in this part of Wyoming were miners in search of copper, silver, and gold. They built a small settlement around the Silver Cliff Mine but moved one mile east when the Fremont, Elkhorn, and Missouri Valley Railroad arrived in 1886. Lusk was named for Frank Lusk, a local rancher who donated land for the new townsite. In 1917, oil was discovered along Lance Creek 20 miles north of here, and almost overnight Lusk became a boomtown, reaching more than 10,000 residents during the peak years of oil production. Pipelines were built to the 200 producing wells, and a refinery was added in Lusk. By the

1940s, Lance Creek had become Wyoming's largest oil field. In 1984, the town succeeded in getting a women's correctional center built; this is now the second-largest employer in the county (after the local school district). More recently, high oil prices, a robust farm economy, and an influx of railroad workers have helped the local economy. There's even an espresso shop in Lusk now, a sure sign that newcomers are moving in.

◖ STAGECOACH MUSEUM

Lusk has one of the better historic collections in the state at the aptly named Stagecoach Museum (342 S. Main St., 307/334-3444, open 10 A.M.–5 P.M. Mon.–Sat. year-round, $2 adults, free for kids under 12). Climb up the stairs to find the reason for its name—an old coach built in 1863 by Abbott and Downing of Concord, New Hampshire. Used for many years on the famed Cheyenne and Black Hills Stage and Express Line, the stagecoach is one of only two in existence; its sister resides in the Smithsonian Institution in Washington, D.C. Next to the stage is a treasure chest broken open during the Canyon Springs Stage robbery of 1879; it contained gold bullion from the Black Hills destined for Cheyenne. Besides the standard fare—an old buggy, a sulky, a dray wagon, covered wagons, and various Indian artifacts and arrowheads—you'll also find such intriguing odds and ends as a 1950s iron lung, a 30-foot *Triceratops* (made from a mix of real bones and iron), a two-headed calf, an albino deer, an antique bedpan collection and suppository machine, 448 (count 'em) salt and pepper shakers, photos of Niobrara County's many one-room schoolhouses, and a 31-star 1876 U.S. flag. Try not to snicker at the kitschy collection of dolls dressed up as the wives of various presidents (including Barbara Bush as a busty Barbie doll). Out back is an old one-room log schoolhouse (oldest structure in the county) built in 1886.

OTHER SIGHTS

The city park at 14th and Linn contains a **homestead cabin** built in the 1880s and

originally located at Running Water Stage Station. Another site of historical interest is on the east side of town along the railroad tracks. Here you'll find a **redwood water tower** built in 1886 to supply water for steam engines of the Chicago and Northwestern Railroad. It is one of only six still standing in the nation. Today the water tower is no longer needed, but the railroad is busier than ever, with 115-car coal trains screaming their presence every few minutes.

Just west of downtown is a small hill with fine panoramic views of the area. It's posted, but ask locally for permission to climb to the top. Also of note is the big **Niobrara County building** at East 5th and South Elm streets, with its red brick walls. Etched above the entrances are words that most politicians seem to consider expendable: "A public office is a public trust."

Rawhide Buttes

Whether or not the *Legend of Rawhide* is true, the Rawhide Buttes actually do exist; they

© DON PITCHER

an old redwood water tower near Lusk

MOTHER FEATHER LEGS

Lusk has seen its share of lust through the years. The Yellow Hotel brothel occupied a place of local importance until the late 1970s; rumor has it that the madam, Del Burke, was allowed to keep it open because she owned most of Lusk's water bonds! The decrepit still-yellow building still stands across from the old train depot.

Mother Feather Legs – so named because she often rode horseback with her red pantaloons blowing in the wind – was a well-known 19th-century madam who arrived in these parts in 1876. Her dugout cabin served as a hangout for outlaws and desperados who ambushed travelers on the Cheyenne–Black Hills trail, but one of them – named, appropriately enough, "Dangerous Dick" Davis – shot her three years later and fled with her money. Dangerous Dick was later caught in the swamps of Louisiana, where he was served summary justice and hanged. Some claim that a fortune in gold Mother Feather Legs had buried still waits to be claimed. In

1990, Lusk locals swept into a Deadwood saloon and recovered Mother Feather Legs's infamous pantaloons, supposedly stolen from her grave site in 1964. Today you'll find them on display at the town museum. (Or at least that's what the tale asserts. The pantaloons certainly don't look old to me.)

A granite marker southwest of Lusk identifies her old place of entertainment along the Cheyenne–Black Hills Stage Line; it's said to be the nation's only historical marker commemorating a prostitute. Get here by heading two miles west of town on U.S. 18 and then turning south 0.5 mile west of the rest area for another 11 miles on Silver Springs Road (Road 54). The gravesite is surrounded by rocky sandstone hills topped by pines. Continue south on this untrafficked road to Whalen Canyon Road, which continues past prehistoric Indian mines near Hartville. Parts of the latter road can be a muddy mess if it has rained recently.

are 10 miles south of Lusk. Some stories give a less interesting origin of the name Rawhide Buttes, claiming they were the site where raw buffalo hides were prepared for shipment east. A highway marker notes the Cheyenne–Deadwood stage station that once stood here. Two miles west of Lusk on U.S. 18/20 is a historical marker along the Cheyenne–Deadwood Trail. The ruts are still visible for a ways here, and George Lathrop, one of the best-known stage drivers, is buried nearby.

ENTERTAINMENT AND EVENTS

The **Cowboy Mounted Shooting Sports** takes place in June with demonstrations of fast riding and gunplay by contestants dressed in late 1800s clothing. The **Niobrara County Fair** comes to town the first week of August. For rodeo action, check out the **Wyoming Junior Rodeo** in July, and the **Senior Pro Rodeo** on Labor Day. Lusk's featured event is the *Legend of Rawhide*.

Legend of Rawhide

In 1946, the people of Lusk were looking for an event to attract visitors—something, say, along the lines of Cheyenne Frontier Days, only different. A local doctor, Walter Reckling, faintly remembered a tale that had been passed down for generations—the legend of Rawhide Buttes. It was one of the enduring yarns of the Old West, one with a thousand variations, claimed by half a dozen states. In the story, an emigrant wagon train headed west to the California goldfields carryied a young man who boasted that he would shoot the first Indian he saw. He killed an innocent Indian girl—a princess, of course—and her tribe retaliated by attacking the wagon train and forcing the young man to surrender. He was skinned alive in revenge. Nobody has ever been able to substantiate the tale, but then again, nobody has proved it *didn't* happen, either.

Dr. Reckling managed to stir up considerable interest for the idea in Lusk and then found a local college student, Eva Lou Bonsell, who was studying theater in Colorado. She wrote a play to be pantomimed as a narrator described the scenes, and the *Legend of Rawhide* was off and running. The first production gained a measure of realism by being staged in the midst of a thunderstorm. The crowd of 10,000 loved it. The *Legend of Rawhide* made the covers of *Life* and *Look* magazines at various times and ran from 1946 to 1966. It was revived in 1986. Today the annual production is still a decidedly local affair, with a cast of 200 folks from the surrounding area. The spectacle has evolved through the years, with the addition of 13 "soiled doves," Father DeSmet, Jim Bridger, about 15 wagons, and several dozen Indians on ponies. The skinning alive of bad guy Clyde Pickett is the gory climax. It's also quite a trick, but I won't give away the secret.

The *Legend of Rawhide* begins at 8 P.M. on Friday and Saturday the second weekend in July every year. Other activities include a parade, art show, square dancing, country music, pancake breakfasts, and a barbecue. Get additional information at 307/334-2950 or 800/223-5875, www.luskwy.com. The *Legend of Rawhide* attracts more than 3,000 visitors, so be sure to book rooms far ahead.

RECREATION

Swim at the **Lusk Plunge** (307/334-3612) on the north side of the tracks during the summer. **Lusk Municipal Golf Course** (307/334-2438) is one of the better nine-hole golf courses in the state.

ACCOMMODATIONS

Lusk has several comfortable motels for reasonable rates, but prices may be higher during the *Legend of Rawhide*. **Town House Motel** (525 S. Main St., 307/334-2376, www.lusktownhouse.com, $40 s or $44–52 d) has fridges, microwaves, and a continental breakfast. Pets welcome ($5 extra).

A good reasonably priced option is **Rawhide Motel** (805 S. Main St., 307/334-2440 or 888/679-2558, www.rawhidemotel.net, $45–48 d).

Trail Motel is just west of town on U.S. 18/20 (305 W. 8th, 307/334-2530 or 800/333-5875, $59 s or $65 d) and has updated rooms and a heated outdoor pool. Subtract $5 for its older rooms.

◖ Sager House B&B (310 S. Main St., 307/334-2423 or 800/435-2468, www.sagerhouse.com, $79–109) is a lovely historic home in the heart of town and just up from the museum. Inside are six guest rooms, all with Victorian decor and private baths. This is a place to escape, so no TVs or phones in the rooms. Rates include a full breakfast.

Covered Wagon Motel/Best Value Inn (730 S. Main St., 307/334-2836 or 888/315-2378, www.coveredwagonmotel.com) is the nicest local motel, with an indoor pool, hot tub, sauna, guest computer, Wi-Fi, and continental breakfast. Room prices vary greatly, but average around $74–85 d in the summer.

For a unique ranch experience, spend a day at **Paleo Park** (307/334-2271, www.paleopark.com), northwest of Lusk in the heart of the Lance Creek fossil area. Fascinating two-hour tours ($40 per person) are offered in the summer, and overnight lodging is available; $100 per person per day, including three meals (see *Newcastle and Vicinity* in the *Black Hills* chapter).

Camping

Prairie View Campground (two miles west of Lusk on U.S. 18/20, 307/334-3174, $10 tents, $20 RVs, open year-round) offers a country location, friendly owner, and some shade. Showers for those not camping here are $5.

FOOD

Get good pizzas, calzones, subs, and salads at **The Pizza Place** (218 S. Main St., 307/334-3000). Next door is **Rawhide Creek Coffee Co.** (307/334-2102), with espresso drinks, plus a morning menu of breakfast burritos, biscuits and gravy, and omelets. **El Jarro Restaurant** (625 S. Main St., 307/334-5004) is the Mexican place in Lusk.

Outpost (307/334-3085) on the south end of town serves most of the standards—from pork chops to halibut, with most items under $10. Open three meals a day, and very popular with smokers (gag).

BQ Corral Drive-In (W. 7th and S. Main Sts., 307/334-0128) has carhop service and tasty, fast food. Get groceries at **Decker's Food Center** (405 S. Main. St., 307/334-3810).

INFORMATION AND SERVICES

The **Lusk Visitor Center** (119 W. 3rd St., 307/334-2950 or 800/223-5875, www.luskwyoming.com) is open 9 A.M.–5 P.M. Monday–Friday.

Find the **Niobrara County Library** in a historic multicolor brick building at 425 South Main Street, 307/334-3490, and the **post office** at 116 West 3rd Street, 307/334-3700.

HEADING NORTH

U.S. 18/85 points due north from Lusk toward Newcastle, passing through mile after mile of rolling and windy grassland with scattered rocky buttes—a few wearing top hats of ponderosa pines. For the first dozen miles the road parallels the historic Cheyenne–Deadwood stage route. Bottomland creeks curl through with cottonwoods and willows on both sides. This is gorgeous big-sky country; the land seems almost an afterthought. It's about as remote a place as you'll find, with just a few ranches, windmills, and cattle for company.

Fort Hat Creek

About 13 miles north of Lusk a sign marks the old **Fort Hat Creek Stage Station,** mistakenly built (in 1876) along Sage Creek, Wyoming, instead of Hat Creek, Nebraska! It's easy to see how the country could start to blend together here. The old stage station, on private land but right next to the road, is two miles east of here on a paved road and then one mile southwest on a gravel road. It is an impressive two-story log structure built in 1887 to replace the original buildings, which had burned. The small fort garrisoned 40 soldiers who would ride out to protect the Cheyenne–Deadwood stage from attack. Hat Creek was typical of stage stations along the route. One writer of the time, Leander P. Richardson, noted: "At any of these places a traveler can purchase almost anything, from a glass of whiskey to a four-horse team, but the former article is usually the staple of demand."

Lance Creek

Tiny Lance Creek (pop. 50) lies in the middle of Niobrara County and is surrounded by the Lance Creek oil fields. An oil boom peaked here during World War II; more recently production has declined and the community now ekes out a minimal survival. The Lance Creek area is the site of discoveries of horned dinosaurs (ceratopsians) and other fossils. Beginning in the 1880s, scientists found an incredible number of fossil plants, dinosaurs, and ancient mammals, including at least 75 different species of vertebrates, many of which were previously unknown.

Mule Creek Junction

Halfway between Lusk and Newcastle is Mule Creek Junction (no services), where you'll find a state rest area. A couple of miles north of this, U.S. 85 crosses the Cheyenne River near the site of the aptly named **Robber's Roost Stage Station.** Here outlaws sometimes attacked the Cheyenne–Deadwood stage when it slowed to cross the river. In an 1878 robbery attempt an outlaw was killed here by the shotgun messengers, but his partners managed to escape with the mail sacks.

MEDICINE BOW COUNTRY

West from Cheyenne, I-80 climbs a long, gentle ramp into the Laramie Mountains, reaches the highest point on its 3,000-mile trek across America, and then abruptly begins a steep descent onto the expansive Laramie Plains. A distinctly frontier feeling envelops this land: Mountains rim the valley, and as you continue west the grass intermixes with more and more sagebrush. You are entering the real West of mountains, sage, and sky.

Medicine Bow Country consists of Albany County—with Laramie and the Laramie Plains at its center and the Laramie and Medicine Bow Mountains on either side—and Carbon County, where Rawlins is the main town and the Sierra Madre dominate the southern horizon. The name "Medicine Bow" has a convoluted origin. The mountains in southern Wy-

oming were considered a sacred place, and each year Indians gathered nearby to celebrate powwows and build bows from the cedar wood. The Indian term for "medicine" means something spiritually powerful—symbolized by the mountains, the cedar that made fine bows, and the annual powwows. Whites combined the various tribal activities into "Medicine Bow" and applied the name to a river, a mountain range, a national forest, and a town.

The land is remarkably diverse in terms of both topography and vegetation. Laramie Basin contains the highest short-grass prairie in the world, 7,200 feet above sea level. Three mountain ranges cross through this region: the Laramie Mountains, the Medicine Bow Mountains (also called the Snowy Range), and the Sierra Madre. Mountain slopes are covered with

© DON PITCHER

HIGHLIGHTS

◖ University Art Museum: The building is downright bizarre, but the collection features works by some of the masters, including Pablo Picasso, Winslow Homer, and Paul Gauguin (page 99).

◖ Geological Museum: Meet "Big Al" the allosaurus and a multitude of other dinos that once roamed Wyoming (page 100).

◖ Wyoming Territorial Prison State Historical Site: Butch Cassidy—inmate number 187—slept here before being pardoned by the governor and promising to "never molest the state of Wyoming again." Guess he had his fingers crossed (page 100).

◖ Vedauwoo: A favorite of climbers, these oddly shaped rocks are just off I-80 and a few miles uphill from a pyramid commemorating the "King of Frauds" (page 110).

◖ Snowy Range: A National Scenic Byway climbs over these mountains; don't miss picture-perfect Sugarloaf Recreation Area (page 118).

◖ Hobo Pool: No hobos, but this free Saratoga hot springs is a delight on a chilly evening (page 124).

◖ Grand Encampment Museum: Where else could you find a stuffed dog named Teddy, Noah's Ark, and a two-story outhouse? (page 130).

◖ Frontier Prison: An hour here and you'll never run another stoplight. This was where they filmed the B movie *Prison;* ketchup "blood" still stains the floors (page 138).

◖ Carbon County Museum: Indian and Oregon Trail relics are here, but everyone wants to see the two-tone shoes made from the skin of train robber Big Nose George Parrot (page 139).

LOOK FOR ◖ TO FIND RECOMMENDED SIGHTS, ACTIVITIES, DINING, AND LODGING.

© AVALON TRAVEL PUBLISHING, INC.

lodgepole pine, Engelmann spruce, and sub-alpine fir, while alpine meadows, tundra, and rock dominate the highest elevations. To the north and west of these mountain ranges, the country is a dry landscape of sage and desert.

For many centuries this land was filled with buffalo, elk, and deer, providing a rich home for wandering tribes of Indians. By the time whites arrived in large numbers, the area was claimed and fought over by many tribes, including Oglala Sioux, Northern Arapaho, Eastern Shoshone, Northern Cheyenne, and White River Utes. Although mountain men long trapped in this part of Wyoming, it remained off the beaten path for many years, with emigrants preferring the Oregon Trail through the central part of the state. This began to change in 1862, when the Overland Trail opened across southern Wyoming. Ben Holladay's stage traversed the route, as did many thousands of emigrants who found it shorter and generally safer from Indian attack. As with the rest of southern Wyoming, the coming of the Union Pacific Railroad transformed this area from a place to get through into a place to live. The railroad provided the region's lifeblood for many years. Later, Laramie gained the University of Wyoming and Rawlins the state penitentiary.

PLANNING YOUR TIME

Medicine Bow Country has much to draw visitors, and the area could easily make a great destination, especially for weekend visits from Denver, as part of a longer trip through the Rockies, or simply as a pleasant diversion en route to Jackson Hole or Park City. Those who appreciate a comfortable lodging place and good food could easily use the towns of Laramie or Saratoga as bases for day trips into the mountains.

At Laramie, historic **Wyoming Territorial Prison** has been beautifully restored, and the University of Wyoming's **Geological Museum** and **Art Museum** are also well worth a visit. Wander around downtown Laramie's interesting shops, bookstores, and fine restaurants. The town also has a couple of great B&Bs. Ten miles east of here are the strange rock formations called **Vedauwoo** (great for rock climbers), and west of Laramie is the **Snowy Range.** The mountains—some over 12,000 feet—offer exposed rock faces, alpine lakes, and one of the prettiest drives in Wyoming. The road tops Snowy Range Pass and then down the west side to sleepy Saratoga, home to **Hobo Pool,** a delightful (and free) hot springs. South of here are a pair of little towns, Riverside and Encampment; the latter contains **Grand Encampment Museum,** with a big collection of old buildings and other reminders of the area's mining past. North of the mountains are a few scattered settlements, including hidden Elk Mountain with its beautifully restored hotel, and the town of Medicine Bow, with an interesting wind farm, country museum, and another historic hotel. The busy oil and gas town of Rawlins, just off I-80, has several good restaurants, the old **Frontier Prison,** and the **Carbon County Museum,** with some oddities—including shoes made from the skin of an outlaw.

Laramie

The countryside around Laramie (pop. 27,000) differs little from that in much of Wyoming—arid plains abruptly broken by rugged mountain ranges—but the town itself offers a real change of pace. True, Laramie does have rodeos, restaurants with names such as the Cavalryman, and great country-and-western tunes at the ever-popular Cowboy Saloon, but it also seems to violate one's expectations of a Wyoming town. It's the kind of place where you meet cops drinking mochas while munching bagels instead of hobnobbing with smokers over cheap coffee and doughnuts. Bumper stickers demand "Free Leonard Peltier" while others joke "I'm hung like Einstein and smart as a horse."

Take a stroll along downtown's Ivinson Avenue and you'll discover a shop selling fancy chocolates, an upscale children's store, art galleries, a day spa, flower shops, a yoga center, bookstores, and even an organic foods store complete with post-hippie decor. Nearby are vegetarian restaurants, bars that attract reggae and blues bands, and galleries filled with hand-crafted items from all over the planet.

Laramie is one of my favorite cities in Wyoming, a place that has a sense of intelligence without being stultified, where culture mixes with fun and games. Tourist brochures call Laramie "Gem City of the Plains." It has the laid-back college-town feel of Chico, California, or Fort Collins, Colorado, but Laramie is considerably less congested. The students add a playful, literary atmosphere—bikes on the streets, rock concerts, heady conversations over beers, and theatrical productions. Laramie has both crowded fast-food outlets and sophisticated restaurants offering more substantial fare. It's probably the only place in the state (other than Jackson) where a restaurant would dare carry wine descriptions on its menu: "A complex, medium-bodied wine with black cherry and wild berry flavors, balanced by toasty-oak nuances."

The Union Pacific Railroad splits Laramie into two distinct parts. The campus, stately older homes, and nearly the entire city lie on the east side; less pretentious quarters lie on "the other side of the tracks." Long and noisy freight trains roll through every few minutes at all hours of the day and night piled high with double-decker containerized freight boxes destined for Chicago, Denver, or Los Angeles.

Situated close to the Medicine Bow Mountains (hiking and skiing), Vedauwoo Rocks (rock climbing), Lake Hattie (sailboarding), and the Colorado Rockies (Coors), Laramie is a haven for those who love the outdoors. The only problem is the midwinter wind, which makes life in this part of the state difficult. Temperatures may be relatively mild—in the low 20s—but add in a 30-mph wind and it feels like 20 below zero. Bitter gale-force winds can howl through for days on end in this open country.

HISTORY

The city of Laramie (and several other places in eastern Wyoming) has the name of a French Canadian trapper who was killed by Indians in the mountains now also named in his honor. Nearly everything about the man is open to question. Jacques LaRamee (or was it Joseph De la Ramie?) was killed in 1820 (or 1821) by Arapahoes (or another tribe), who stuffed his body under the ice in a beaver pond (or left his corpse in his cabin). Be that as it may, he attained a far more lasting legacy through his death than through anything he did while alive.

Fort Sanders

The first permanent settlement in the Laramie area was Fort Sanders, originally known as Fort John Buford, built in 1866. Approximately two miles south of present-day Laramie, it served to protect emigrants and stagecoaches along the Overland Trail and, later, Union Pacific Railroad construction workers. At its peak, Fort Sanders housed nearly 600 soldiers. As with other posts on the frontier, desertions were rampant; 41 men went AWOL in a single month, taking with them whatever supplies

MEDICINE BOW COUNTRY

DOWNTOWN
LARAMIE DETAIL

LARAMIE

UNIVERSITY OF
WYOMING DETAIL

they could grab. As the threat of Indian attacks lessened through the years, so did the value of Fort Sanders. It was abandoned in 1882, and very little remains.

The Union Pacific Arrives

Laramie City (as it was first called) was named and established by General Grenville Dodge, the man in charge of planning the Union Pacific's route westward. The site was chosen because of a major spring that still produces millions of gallons of water, and because railroad ties could be cut in the mountains to the west and brought down the Laramie River. The proximity of Fort Sanders also influenced the location. By the time the first train rolled into

Laramie City on May 10, 1868, many "sooners" had already set up business in tents. The first passengers were met with 23 saloons, one hotel, and no churches. Within three months, Laramie had 5,000 people.

Many of the earliest to arrive were the usual end-of-the-track types: hoodlums, gamblers, prostitutes, and others out to make a fast buck. When the tracks headed on westward, the riff-raff stayed behind, kept busy by the soldiers. Within a short time, a saloon owner named Asa Moore gained the support of various gambling houses, brothels, and other bars to create a rump town government with himself as mayor. The man they appointed town marshal had recently left Cheyenne after being acquitted on a murder charge, and his assistant was caught stealing mules. Laramie quickly became one of the wildest towns on the frontier, with murders occurring almost daily. Men who were arrested often faced trial in a back room of Asa Moore's saloon, where his men robbed and then killed them, burying their bodies out on the plains. Stories tell of up to 10 men disappearing in a single night.

Seeing that the law was in the hands of criminals, the more respectable citizens decided to put an end to the mayhem. More than 500 men joined a vigilante committee that swept into the saloons, brothels, dance halls, and casinos on the night of October 18, 1868. Three men died in gun battles (including a musician and a vigilante), and dozens of others were wounded. Another three were hanged by vigilantes, including the mayor, Asa Moore. The next day, outlaw Big Steve Young met the same fate, and more than 100 crooks were piled into railroad cars and sent west. These actions calmed things down rather quickly, and thereafter Laramie City became something of a model town. It is perhaps fitting that four years later Laramie would be awarded the territorial prison.

For many years the main reason for the existence of Laramie was the presence of the railroad and the operations it established, including a roundhouse, an iron foundry, a tie-treating plant, machine shops, and a mill for

LARAMIE AREA CLIMATE

Average Maximum Temp.	54.4°F
Average Minimum Temp.	27°F
Annual Rainfall	10.87″
Annual Snowfall	48.8″

reprocessing old rails. Gold discoveries in the Snowy Range to the west helped Laramie's economy grow, but the railroad remained the largest employer in Laramie until the 1950s, when it was supplanted by the university.

Women's Suffrage

Laramie was the site of two of the most notable events in the history of women's rights. On September 6, 1870, Louisa Gardner ("Grandma") Swain became the first woman in the nation to vote in an open and public election. A few months before this, a judge in Laramie established the world's first jury with women members. (Reporters noted that the female jurors hid behind heavy veils and held crying babies on their laps.) The women brought about a change in the jury system: breaks for boozing and gambling were ended, and smoking and chewing tobacco in the jury box were also halted. The women also proved more likely to convict men of murder than their male peers, who regarded killing humans a less serious crime than rustling cattle. A stone monument near 1st and Garfield streets marks the location where the first all-woman jury met.

UNIVERSITY OF WYOMING

In 1886, Laramie received a gift from the state legislature that would eventually transform it from a cow town into a college town. Under the leadership of Colonel Stephen W. "Father of the University" Downey, the legislature voted to establish the University of Wyoming. It was part of a deal that carved up Wyoming: Laramie got the university, Cheyenne became the capital, Rawlins landed the prison, and Evanston got the state asylum. The bill was signed into law by Governor Francis E. Warren in 1886, four years before Wyoming achieved statehood. The school opened the following year with a single building—now called Old Main—built at a cost of $49,000. The new program had five professors and a coed student body of 42, who paid $7.50 each to attend. Through the years, the railroad gradually diminished in importance while the university added more and more to

the local economy, until it became the biggest local employer. It remains so today. Because of the university, Laramie has never really experienced the economic booms and busts common to much of Wyoming.

Wyoming is the only state to have just one baccalaureate-granting institution. The University of Wyoming campus in Laramie thus gains the state's undivided financial support, much to the chagrin of the two-year colleges. The university lays claim to being the highest university campus in the nation—at 7,200 feet, it makes Denver's mile-high claim to fame look puny. Although not a major research institution, UW has respected programs in atmospheric sciences (ozone-depletion studies), coal production, aquatic toxicology, oil-recovery technology, water management, agricultural research, and infrared astronomy. Approximately 11,000 students attend the university under the tutelage of 2,500 faculty and staff members.

The university offers more than 75 degree programs in seven accredited colleges: agriculture, arts and sciences, business, education, engineering, health sciences, and law. It operates on a semester system, with a summer session open to visiting students. A summertime **Elderhostel** provides classes for folks over 60, and various noncredit classes are also offered throughout the year, covering the spectrum from ballroom dancing to LSAT preparation. For a copy of the school's *General Bulletin,* call the admissions office at 307/766-5160 or 800/342-5996, or find it on the Internet at www.uwyo.edu.

Exploring the Campus

Begin your campus visit at the helpful **University of Wyoming Visitor Information Center** (1408 Ivinson Ave., 307/766-4075). It's open 7:30 A.M.–4:30 P.M. Monday–Friday in the summer and 8 A.M.–5 P.M. Monday–Friday during the school year. The center can provide maps and complete information on the university, including lectures, films, concerts, dances, and other events open to the public. Also stop here for details on one-hour **campus tours,**

MEDICINE BOW COUNTRY

BILL NYE

Laramie lays claim to one of the most popular humorists of the 19th century, Edgar "Bill" Nye (1850-1896). Born in Maine and raised in Wisconsin, Nye arrived in Laramie in 1876 and soon began writing columns for a local newspaper. His sharp wit and wry sense of humor quickly showed through the news. Local Republicans backed him in publishing his own paper, the *Laramie Boomerang* – named for a flea-bitten gray mule that kept returning no matter how hard Nye tried to get rid of him. The paper first rolled off his "lemon-squeezer" press in 1881. When the news wasn't all that interesting, Nye would embellish it: "[I] write up things that never occurred with a masterly and graphic hand. Then, if they occur, I am grateful; if not, I bow to the inevitable and smother my chagrin."

Even Nye's appointment as Laramie City postmaster (a political plum gained because of his connection with the dominant Republican party) became grist for his humor mill. He wrote the postmaster general, noting, "I look upon the appointment, myself, as a great triumph of eternal truth over error and wrong. It is one of the epoches, I may say, in the Nation's onward march toward political purity and perfection. I do not know when I have noticed any stride in the affairs of state, which so thoroughly impressed me with its wisdom..." Nye kept the position for only a year.

In 1883, an attack of spinal meningitis forced him to leave high-elevation Laramie for a lower climate. By the time he departed, Nye's newspaper was in dire financial condition, but it managed to survive under new, more responsible, management. The *Boomerang* is still published today and is one of the state's few daily papers. The old livery stable where it was originally published is on the corner of 3rd and Garfield; Nye's office was on the second floor.

Bill Nye's witty *Boomerang* columns gained a national following, and by the 1890s he had become the best-paid humorist in America. Nye would eventually write 14 books of humor; *Bill Nye's History of the United States,* published in 1894, sold an incredible 500,000 copies. Unfortunately, the intense stress of life on the road helped shorten his life. Nye died of a stroke when he was just 45 years old.

Much of Nye's humor falls flat today, and its racial stereotypes are certainly dated, but some of the short pieces still have a delightful zing, particularly when he tweaks the noses of famous people such as Oscar Wilde (whom Nye called "Thou bilious pelican from o'er the sea") or a competing newspaper editor ("We have nothing more to say of the editor of the Sweetwater *Gazette.* Aside from the fact that he is a squint-eyed, consumptive liar, with a breath like a buzzard and a record like a convict, we don't know anything against him..."). None of his works are in print, but you'll find *Bill Nye's Western Humor* in many Wyoming libraries.

The following commentary on Wyoming agriculture and "reclamation" efforts is typical of Nye's tongue-in-cheek writing:

I do not wish to discourage those who might wish to come to this place for the purpose of engaging in agriculture, but frankly I will state that it has its drawbacks. In the first place, the soil is quite course, and the agriculturist, before he can even begin with any prospect of success must run his farm through a stamp-mill in order to make it sufficiently mellow. This, as the reader will see, involves a large expense at the very outset. Hauling the farm to a custom mill would delay the farmer two or three hundred years in getting his crops in, thus giving the agriculturist who had a pulverized farm in Nebraska, Colorado, or Utah, a great advantage over his own, which had not yet been to the reduction works.

offered at 11 A.M. Monday–Friday in the summer, and at 11 A.M. and 2 P.M. Monday–Friday during the school year. At other times, just pick up the **walking-tour brochure** and head out on your own. Right next door to the visitor center you'll find the historic **Cooper Mansion,** built in 1920 in the Mission Pueblo style and now on the National Register of Historic Places.

An **information desk** (307/766-3160, www.uwyo.edu/cac) in the Wyoming Union building is open 7:30 A.M.–midnight Monday–Saturday, and noon–10 P.M. Sunday during the school year; 7 A.M.–7 P.M. Monday–Friday and 10 A.M.–7 P.M. Saturday in the summer. You can check your email or surf the web on free computers near the information desk. Also stop in the union for a listing of campus activities, stamps, cash from the ATM, or snacks. The main campus buildings center around **Prexy's Pasture,** where the school's first president grazed his personal cattle. Today Prexy's is a favorite place to relax on sunny days—and it's still legal to leave your horse here.

A **campus shuttle** (307/766-9800) provides free transport on weekdays during the school year, with stops all around the university.

◖ University Art Museum

This excellent museum (307/766-6622, www.uwyo.edu/artmuseum, free) encompasses nine large galleries, including an outdoor sculpture court. It's housed in Centennial Complex, which also contains the American Heritage Center. Art exhibits change several times a year, so you aren't likely to see the same thing twice. Some of these are from the university's collection of 6,000 paintings, pieces of sculpture, and other works of art. The permanent collection is mostly by 19th- and 20th-century artists, including paintings and drawings by Thomas Hart Benton, Charles M. Russell, Winslow Homer, Paul Gauguin, Andy Warhol, Thomas Moran, and Pablo Picasso. The museum puts on a variety of special programs, lectures, and other art events throughout the year and has a fine **gift shop** selling distinctive arts and crafts. The art museum is open 10 A.M.–5 P.M. Mon-

day–Saturday all year, plus 1–5 P.M. Sunday June–August. Closed late December–January.

Another place to view artwork on campus is **Gallery 234,** which exhibits student pieces. It's in the Wyoming Union building and is open 8 A.M.–5 P.M. Monday–Friday.

American Heritage Center

The American Heritage Center (307/766-4114, www.uwyo.edu/ahc, free) serves as both a research center and exhibition space for art and historical pieces. It is not really a tourist destination, but the building also houses the University Art Museum and a lunchtime café. The center is open 7:30 A.M.–4:30 P.M. Monday–Friday and 11 A.M.–5 P.M. Saturday June–August, and 8 A.M.–5 P.M. Monday–Friday and 11 A.M.–5 P.M. Saturday during the school year.

Designed by famed architect Antoine Predock, this multilevel conical building contains expansive art galleries and thousands of manuscripts, rare books, and artifacts from Wyoming and the West. The building was designed to represent the mountains surrounding Laramie and is oriented so that one small section is lit by the sun during the summer solstice. The building gets a decidedly mixed reaction. To be honest, I found it a big disappointment. The exterior resembles (take your pick) a Darth Vader mask or a stealth jet, and the wonderful central loggia is ruined by a claustrophobic tangle of 32 concrete columns intended—the architect claimed—to resemble a forest.

Nine oil paintings by Alfred Jacob Miller hang on the walls of the loggia, including his best-known work, *The Rendezvous Near Green River—Oregon Territory,* valued at $750,000. Miller was the only artist ever to witness a mountain-man rendezvous; he documented the West during a trip in 1837. Also in the loggia are the saddles of Hollywood cowboys William Boyd ("Hopalong Cassidy") and Duncan Renaldo ("Cisco Kid"). The George Rentschler room on this level contains nine paintings by the Western artist Henry Farney. Also nearby are a room with changing exhibits and another one containing the university's 50,000-volume rare-book repository. Wander around a bit more and you will find—surprisingly—Jack Benny's old violin.

Take the elevator to the fourth-floor reading room for access to an outstanding research collection of Western books, documents, and photographs, including the papers of Buffalo Bill Cody, F. E. Warren, Jack Benny, and Irving Wallace. Other pop-culture figures have collections here too, including Ozzie and Harriet Nelson, Don Knotts, and Andy Griffith. The fifth floor provides a dramatic view across Laramie to the Snowy Range and historic photos on the walls.

Geological Museum

Established in 1887, the Geological Museum (307/766-4218, www.uwyo.edu/geomuseum, open 8 A.M.–5 P.M. Mon.–Fri. and 10 A.M.–3 P.M. Sat.–Sun. year-round, free) is Wyoming's oldest museum and one of the most interesting campus sites. A life-size bronze *Tyrannosaurus rex* greets visitors at the entrance, while dinosaur bones surround the doorway. Inside the museum you'll find fossil and mineral displays from around the state (including fluorescent minerals). An enormous woolly mammoth skull found near Rawlins is one of the most impressive fossils, but the museum's centerpiece is "Big Al"—one of the most complete allosaurus skeletons ever discovered; it was found in 1991 near Shell, Wyoming. Also certain to appeal to dino-heads is a 75-foot-long *Apatosaurus excelsus,* better known as a brontosaurus. Excavated along Sheep Creek in Albany County, it's one of just five such skeletons on display in the world. Also here, you'll find displays on the Red Gulch dinosaur tracksite, a cast of the largest allosaurus skeleton ever found and the largest complete freshwater fossil fish in the world.

Right next door to the Geological Museum is the **Wyoming Geological Survey Building,** which sells interesting maps and guides to the state's geology.

Other University Sights

The first campus building was **Old Main,** completed in 1887 and now housing the administrative offices. The prominent tower

that once adorned the building was removed in 1915. Look for Wyoming's territorial seal over the west entrance. Head to the Anthropology Building to view the university's **Anthropology Museum,** representing a small part of the department's extensive cultural collection. The museum (307/766-5136, http://uwadmnweb.uwyo.edu/anth) is open 7:30 A.M.–4:30 P.M. Monday–Friday and focuses on the Plains Indians. A mammoth skull is here, along with a display on the Vore Site buffalo jump in northeastern Wyoming, where thousands of buffalo were trapped and killed. The Anthropology Museum was to move to a new site at 12th and Lewis in 2007.

On the fourth floor of the Agriculture Building is the **Entomology Museum** (307/766-5338), housing thousands of insect specimens. Although primarily for research, it's open to the public. At the **Rocky Mountain Herbarium** (307/766-2236)—on the third floor of the Aven Nelson Building—you'll find one of the nation's largest plant collections, but it's open to the general public only by arrangement.

The fine **Williams Botany Conservatory** (307/766-2380) fronts the Aven Nelson Building and is a warm, bright place to escape on a winter day. Inside are dozens of tropical plants, including orchids and bananas. It's open 10 A.M.–4 P.M. Monday–Thursday and 10 A.M.–3 P.M. Friday.

WYOMING TERRITORIAL PRISON STATE HISTORICAL SITE

In 1869, the territorial legislature voted to construct a penitentiary at Laramie. (Wyoming prisoners had previously been housed in the Detroit House of Correction at a cost of $1.25 per week.) The imposing three-story stone building in west Laramie off Snowy Range Road was dedicated to "evil doers of all classes and kinds"; fittingly enough, a bottle of bourbon was deposited in the cornerstone. It remained a prison until 1902, when the inmates were transferred to a new facility in Rawlins. After the prisoners were moved out, the building was turned over to the university for use as an experimental livestock farm; the cells became cattle stalls and the prison broom factory a sheep barn. The university farm moved to a more modern facility in the 1980s, and today the buildings are managed as Wyoming Territorial Prison State Historical Site (307/745-6161, www.wyoprisonpark.org, $5 adults, $2.50 ages 12–17, free for younger children, open 9 A.M.–6 P.M. daily May–Nov.; closed the rest of the year).

Prison

The cornerstone of the historic park is the beautifully restored prison. A wooden stockade surrounds the sandstone building and adjacent broom factory where prisoners were forced to work. Other prisoners made candles, furniture, or musical instruments, or braided leather. Pick up a self-guided tour brochure as you enter the prison. The interior has been reconstructed using the original cells and period fixtures. Interesting displays and short videos describe the prisoners' lives. The convicts who served time here—including inmate number 187, Butch Cassidy—glare down from giant photos on the walls. Each cell held two prisoners in a tiny 6- by 8-foot arched brick enclosure sealed with an iron door. Inmates slept on straw mattresses. Walk inside one of the cells to get a feeling for the claustrophobic conditions. No wonder Butch Cassidy promised to "never molest the state of Wyoming again" when he was pardoned after 18 months here!

Other Attractions

A number of other buildings are scattered throughout the site, including the restored horse barn with exhibits (and weekend demonstrations) on spinning and weaving. Also check out the homesteader's log cabin, one-room schoolhouse, chicken house, barn, old Rock River church, and other buildings moved to the site from surrounding areas and furnished with period pieces. The saloon building sells old-time crafts and gifts, and a 0.25-mile **Laramie River Interpretive Trail** follows the banks of the river near the prison, providing a place to relax and explore.

A cast from the university puts on a musical

the prison at the Wyoming Territorial Prison State Historical Site in Laramie

dinner theater at the horse barn theater during June and July. It's pretty foolish, but the production and singing are first rate. Performances take place Thursday–Saturday evenings; $24. The show without dinner costs $13.

IVINSON MANSION

Although its official name is the **Laramie Plains Museum,** this historic site is known to most folks as the Ivinson Mansion. The home, at 603 Ivinson, is a delightful example of the Queen Anne style of Victorian architecture. The home was built in 1892 for Edward Ivinson, a millionaire merchant turned banker and politician. It's now on the National Register of Historic Places. After his death, the mansion became an Episcopal girls' school. When the school closed, locals managed to raise more than $74,000 to buy the mansion and turn it into a museum.

The Ivinson Mansion occupies an entire city block, with a carriage house out back and attractive Victorian-style gardens. Few of the original furnishings remain, but much of the interior woodwork, including a freestanding stairway built without nails or screws, is still here. The museum is furnished with antiques, including some elaborate hand-carved furniture built at the Wyoming Penitentiary in 1901, handmade toys (including a doll from the 1840s), a piano that arrived by covered wagon, and several Indian artifacts. More unusual are a quilt that took 60 years to complete (listed in *Ripley's Believe It or Not!*), a seven-headed shower that looks like a medieval torture device, and a square Steinway grand piano. The back carriage house contains a small visitor center, carriages, old bikes, impressive fur coats, and two wonderful antique woodstoves. Also on the grounds are a one-room log schoolhouse built in 1924 and a statue/fountain honoring the events that helped bring equality to women in the West.

The museum (307/742-4448, www.laramiemuseum.org, $5 adults, $3 students and children, $15 families) is open 9 A.M.–5 P.M. Tuesday–Saturday and 1–4 P.M. Sunday mid-June to mid-August, and 1–4 P.M. Tuesday–

Saturday the rest of the year. Guided hour-long tours are given throughout the day, with the last one starting one hour before closing time. On one weekend in mid-December, the museum has a special Christmas open house in which local florists decorate the rooms and carolers stroll the halls.

MORE LARAMIE SIGHTS
Downtown

Laramie's downtown buildings—many of them dating from the 19th century—are on the National Register of Historic Places. Along Ivinson Avenue, a major renovation turned what had been a collection of sleazy flophouses and bars into a lively, attractive, and fun section of town. Pick up **walking-tour** brochures describing Laramie's historical and architectural downtown buildings from the chamber of commerce visitor center. **St. Matthew's Cathedral,** at the corner of 3rd and Ivinson, is one of Wyoming's more interesting churches. The limestone structure was built in 1868 and funded by Edward Ivinson. To get to the other side of the tracks (literally), cross the **pedestrian overpass** at Garfield and 1st; it provides a birds-eye view of the always busy (and noisy) freight yard.

The **Wyoming Children's Museum and Nature Center** (968 N. 9th St., 307/745-6332, www.wcmnc.org, open 10 A.M.–2 P.M. Tues.–Sat., $2 adults, $3 ages 4–12, $1 children under four) in La Bonte Park has fun hands-on exhibits for kids, including an Oregon Trail exhibit with a wagon, trading post, and gold panning. The nature center is home to salamanders, turtles, Hissy the great horned owl, and a crawl-through "beaver lodge."

Farther Afield

A granite monument to **Fort Sanders** stands two miles south of town along U.S. 287. Most of the fort site lies under an avalanche of residential and commercial development—the highway bisects the old parade grounds—but a few ruins from the old stone guardhouse and the powder house still stand. One of Fort Sanders's wooden buildings was moved to LaBonte

Park, at 9th and Canby streets in Laramie, where it is used as a recreation center. **Hutton Lake National Wildlife Refuge** lies six miles south of Laramie on Hwy. 230 and then three miles south on County Road 37. It is a quiet, peaceful place to look for ducks, shorebirds, swallows, and migratory birds.

A warning for motorists: If you're planning to drive U.S. 287 between Laramie and Fort Collins, try to do so in the daytime. The road has a reputation as a deathtrap, with speeding trucks and few passing lanes. It is a popular route for students heading to the bars and party scene in Fort Collins, but it can be treacherous at night or in the winter. The highway's most infamous incident came in 2001, when eight UW athletes were killed in a head-on collision with a truck driven by another student. The driver of the other vehicle, Clinton Haskins, was convicted of drunken driving and is now in prison.

ENTERTAINMENT AND EVENTS
Nightlife

In 2005 Laramie joined an increasing number of cities that have banned smoking in all public places—including bars, so take that cigarette outside and away from any entrances. I for one hope this smoke-free policy spreads to other Wyoming towns.

You'll find plenty of night action in Laramie, where bumper stickers proclaim: "I go from zero to horny in 2.5 beers." Laramie's oldest saloon—dating to 1890—is the ◖ **Buckhorn Bar** (114 Ivinson Ave., 307/742-3554). Mounted heads of all types—including a two-headed calf—adorn the walls, while students and bikers adorn the pool table and barstools. Notice the bullet hole in the mirror behind the bar—the result of a 1971 incident in which a man opened fire on the bartender (he missed). The Buckhorn is a popular place for TV sports, and when school's in session, the back room thumps to rock or blues most weekends. The bar opens early, attracting the after-school college crowd.

Coal Creek Coffeehouse (110 Grand Ave., 307/745-7737, www.coalcreekcoffee.com)

has mellower live music or poetry a couple of times a month, plus open-mike sessions every Wednesday evening.

Lovejoy's Bar and Grill (101 Grand Ave., 307/745-0141) has live bands on Friday and Saturday nights in the school year, with DJs on Thursday nights.

For hot country-and-western tunes, duded-up cowboys, and fresh-faced cowgirls, saunter on over to **The Cowboy Saloon** (108 S. 2nd St., 307/721-3165). It's a spacious place with a big dance floor, two bars, and several pool tables.

At the popular **Mingles Sports Bar** (3206 Grand Ave., 307/721-2005), you can sample the 21 beers on tap or shoot pool at any of the 14 tables (free pool 3–6 P.M. daily). It's especially crowded for happy hour.

Bud's Bar (354 W. University Ave., 307/745-5236) is a favorite with university alumni. Everyone goes there before and after university football or basketball games.

Students hang out at "Club UDub"—the **Beergarden** in the basement of the Wyoming Union building—which has live music during the school year.

Cinema

Local movie houses are the **Fox Cinema** (505 S. 20th St., 307/742-2842, www.transluxmovies.com) and the **Wyo Cinema** (309 S. 5th St., 307/742-7469). The latter features second-run and foreign films for $3.

Events

The **Laramie events hotline** (307/721-7345, www.laramie-tourism.org) provides information on upcoming activities in the area. **Summer productions** (307/766-6666) at the university include dance and music festivals and light-hearted plays. **Music in the Park Concerts** are held at the Washington Park band shell on Wednesday evenings in June and July. The **University of Wyoming Symphony Orchestra** (307/766-6666) performs concerts at the Fine Arts Center on campus October–May.

Laramie Jubilee Days (307/745-7339 or 866/876-1012, www.laramiejubileedays.com) starts on the Fourth of July and lasts a week,

MEDICINE BOW COUNTRY

bringing PRCA rodeos, parades, the biggest fireworks show in Wyoming, cowboy poetry, live music, a free pancake breakfast, street dancing, a cattle drive through the center of town, carnival, melodramas, art exhibits, a softball tournament, and other activities to celebrate Wyoming's statehood. It's easily the biggest event in Laramie, and it attracts folks from throughout the region.

The ever-popular **Albany County Fair** is held the first week of August, with 4-H contests, a carnival, and a demolition derby.

The Wyoming Territorial Prison opens for spooky nighttime **haunted prison tours** most October weekends; they're just in time for Halloween. These very popular tours focus on the real lives of men who were once incarcerated here.

SHOPPING

Mountain Woods (206 S. 2nd St., 307/745-3515) sells handcrafted aspen and lodgepole furniture. Buy hemp garments, imported items, black lights, and hippie garb from **Terrapin** (301 S. 2nd St., 307/745-3027). **The Boardwalk** (1951 Snowy Range Rd., 307/742-3977) is an old-fashioned tack and saddle shop that also carries Wyoming-made gifts.

Laramie has several small art galleries in addition to the larger ones at the university. Don't miss the **first Friday gallery walk,** when local shops have art openings and hors d'oeuvres (spring and fall only). Of particular note is **Earth, Wind and Fire Gallery** (220 S. 2nd St., 307/745-0227), which sells designer jewelry, Indian art, art prints, blown glass, and fine pottery. **Eagle Rock Pottery** (119 E. Grand Ave., 307/721-6233) exhibits distinctive works by other local potters. Other places worth a look include **Artisan's Gallery** (215 S. 2nd St., 307/745-3983), with a good selection of Wyoming-made gifts, and **Grand Bazaar Gallery** (111 Grand Ave., 307/742-9386) for gifts, collectibles, and pottery.

Laramie is home to several excellent bookstores. The spacious **University Bookstore** (in the Student Union, 307/766-3264, www.uwyobookstore.com) has many regional titles and

travel books. **Chickering Bookstore** (307 S. 2nd, 307/742-8609 or 800/742-8609) is a small and friendly bookshop in downtown Laramie. **Personally Recommended Books/ The Second Story** (105 Ivinson Ave., 307/745-4423) is a relaxing upstairs place to look over local literary favorites, and **The Grand News Stand** (214 E. Grand Ave., 307/742-5127) has a big magazine selection and quite a few Wyoming titles. **Adams and Adams Booksellers** (216 E. Grand Ave., 307/755-1955) contains an amazing selection of used Western titles and antiquarian books.

SPORTS AND RECREATION

Spectator Sports

The biggest attraction in Laramie comes each fall with the arrival of football season. Half the state seems to turn out to join in the festivities at War Memorial Stadium—tailgate parties, rooting sections, and rock-'em-sock-'em helmeted soldiers battling it out against other citadels of higher learning. Up to 30,000 fans crowd the stadium Saturday afternoons to cheer on the Wyoming Cowboys—better known as "the 'Pokes"—as in "Cowpokes." The university also competes in several other sports—men's basketball is a primary draw. The athletic facilities are among the finest in the nation and include a modern 15,000-seat arena-auditorium for basketball games, concerts, and other events. Contact the Athletic Ticket Office (307/766-4850 or 800/922-9461, www.wyomingathletics.com).

The **Laramie Colts** (307/742-2191, www .laramiecolts.com) play collegiate baseball at Cowboy Field (2623 Willet Dr.) throughout the summer.

Recreation

The brand-new **Laramie Community Recreation Center** (920 Boulder Dr., 307/721-5269, www.ci.laramie.wy.us) houses an indoor lane pool, kids' pool with lazy river and tube slide, and seasonal outdoor family pool with slides, plus a hot tub, exercise equipment, gym, and child care. Day passes are $3.50 for adults, $2 for kids and seniors. Open daily. Nearby is the **Laramie Ice Arena** (3510 E. Garfield St., 307/721-3530) with skating and skate rentals.

The paved **Laramie River Greenbelt** covers six miles along the river on the west side of Laramie. It's a fine place for a bike ride, walk, or jog. Swim or fish for kokanee and rainbow trout in the summer at shallow **Lake Hattie,** 20 miles southwest of Laramie on Hwy. 230. **West Laramie Fly Store** (1657 Snowy Range Rd., 307/745-5425 or 888/745-9565, www.flystore.net) and **Four Seasons Anglers** (334 S. Fillmore, 307/721-4047, www.fourseasonsanglers.com) sell fishing gear and offer casting and fly-tying classes and guided fishing. **Two Dogs Guide Service** (307/761-2921, www.twodogsfishing.com) offers North Platte float trips and guided fishing.

Horseback and wagon rides are available from **Two Bars Seven Ranch** (307/742-6072, www.twobarssevenranch.com).

The university's **Jacoby Park Golf Course** (on N. 30th, 307/745-3111) is an 18-hole course open to the public. **Laramie Country Club** (307/745-8490) is a nine-hole course west of town on U.S. 230 that is also open to the public. For more play, head to **Laramie Lanes** (1270 N. 3rd St., 307/745-3835), the local bowling alley, or **Oasis Mini-Golf** (15th and Skyline, 307/745-7575).

Rent skis, snowboards, snowshoes, and other winter gear from **Cross Country Connection** (221 S. 2nd St., 307/721-2851), **Westgate Ski and Sports** (1979 Snowy Range Rd., 307/742-6742 or 800/308-6742), or **Fine Edge Ski Shop** (1660 N. 4th St., 307/745-4499, www.fineedge.net).

Pedal House (207 S. 1st St., 307/742-5533, www.pedalhouse.com) has a few bikes for rent and can provide maps of local cycling routes.

ACCOMMODATIONS

Space is generally not a problem in Laramie, although you should reserve well ahead during graduation week (mid-May), Jubilee Days (Fourth of July), Cheyenne Frontier Days (mid-July), and on football weekends in the fall. The old rule of supply and de-

mand holds, so rates also rise considerably over those listed at these times. The Albany County Tourism Board (www.laramie-tourism.org) has a relatively complete listing of local lodging places.

In addition to the places below, a 125-room Hilton Garden Inn was to open in 2007 as part of a university conference center on the east side of the campus.

Under $50

For unpretentious accommodations, check out **Ranger Motel** (453 N. 3rd St., 307/742-6677, $42 s or $46–50 d) where the furnishings are old but clean. Some rooms contain fridges and microwaves.

$50-100

The plain-vanilla **Motel 6** (621 Plaza La., 307/742-2307 or 800/466-8356, www.motel6.com, $46–50 s or $52–58 d) has a small outdoor pool. Another reasonably priced chain is **Best Value Inn** (523 S. Adams St., 307/721-8860 or 888/315-2378, www.bestvalueinn.com, $55 s or $60 d).

In the heart of town, **Travel Inn** (262 N. 3rd St., 307/745-4853 or 877/310-7381, www.laramietravelinnmotels.com, $54–64 d) is an older place with a heated outdoor pool, fridges, microwaves, continental breakfast, and wireless Internet.

⟨ Gas Lite Motel (960 N. 3rd, 307/742-6616 or 800/942-6610, $55–65 d) is easily the most distinctive lodging choice in Laramie, with a playful collection of Old West flotsam and jetsam to please even the most committed packrat. Rooms are comfortable and clean, though not fancy. Extras include fridges and microwaves, a continental breakfast, and an indoor pool with a retractable roof.

First Inn Gold (421 Boswell, 307/742-3721 or 800/642-4212, www.firstinns.com, $65 s or $73 d) offers comfortable, unpretentious rooms and a surprisingly large outdoor pool, an indoor hot tub, and light breakfast.

Days Inn (1368 McCue St., 307/745-5678 or 800/329-7466, www.daysinn.com) has standard rooms for $85–95 d, and suites with whirlpool tubs for $125–135 d. Amenities include an indoor pool, fitness center, Wi-Fi, and breakfast.

$100-150

One of Laramie's newest lodging places is the three-level **Hampton Inn** (3715 E. Grand Ave., 307/742-0125 or 800/426-7866, www.hamptoninn.com) on the east end of town. Amenities include an indoor pool and hot tub, exercise room, large TVs, wireless Internet in the lobby, and a big hot breakfast. Standard rooms (one king or two queen beds) are $119 d, and suites with fridges and microwaves cost $129 d (or $139 d with a jetted tub).

Ramada Center Hotel (2313 Soldier Springs Rd., 307/742-6611 or 800/465-4329, www.ramada.com, $104 d) is on the south side of town and just off I-80. Facilities include an indoor pool, hot tub, sushi restaurant, sports bar, and workout room. The rack rates are pricy, but call to check on the daily specials; they're often considerably lower.

Bed-and-Breakfasts

Built more than a century ago, **The Brick B&B** (102 S. 5th St., 307/745-4390 or 800/788-4626, www.wyomingcompanion.com/thebrickbb, $89–109 d) is a three-block walk from downtown. The lovingly restored yellow-brick home makes a relaxing place to unwind and shake out those road jitters. Four upstairs guest rooms share two baths, and amenities include a big breakfast, an outdoor hot tub, upper deck, and evening aperitifs. Children over 12 are welcome.

◖ **Mad Carpenter Inn** (353 N. 8th St., 307/742-0870, www.madcarpenter.com) features the handiwork of co-owner Lawrence Thomas—alias the mad carpenter. This 1912 four-square home has been transformed into a real masterpiece, with attention to detail (such as rainfall showerheads, ceiling fans, plush carpeting, and Wi-Fi), and a game room that includes a pool table, antique piano, Foosball, air hockey, and table tennis. Guests stay in two Victorian-style rooms in the main house ($85–95 d), or a separate dollhouse cottage ($115 d) with jetted tub and private deck. A light breakfast with "best-west-of-the-Mississippi" granola is served, and the home is just a block from the campus, making this a good place for visiting moms and dads.

Camping

The closest public campgrounds ($10, www.fs.fed.us/r2/mbr) are in the scenic Pole Mountain section of Medicine Bow–Routt National Forest (approximately 10 miles east of Laramie). Other public campsites are 30 miles west in the Snowy Range. (See *East of Laramie* and the *Snowy Range* sections in this chapter.) **Curt Gowdy State Park** (307/632-7946, http://wyoparks.state.wy.us), 22 miles east of Laramie on Hwy. 210/Happy Jack Road, also has campsites ($12 for nonresidents, $6 for Wyoming residents; open all year; see the *Southeast Wyoming* chapter).

Laramie KOA (1171 Baker, 307/742-6553 or 800/562-4153, www.koa.com, $18 tents, $27–29 RVs, open year-round) is in a trailer park next to the noisy freeway.

FOOD

If you like reasonable prices, creative cooking, and a wide selection (who doesn't?), you're bound to appreciate all that Laramie has to offer in the way of dining out. You'll discover some of the best food in Wyoming here, from thick, juicy steaks to nouvelle cuisine.

Coffeehouses

◖ **Coal Creek Coffeehouse** (110 Grand Ave., 307/745-7737 or 800/838-7737, www.coalcreekcoffee.com) is a sweet spot to meet friends over espresso in an art-filled setting. On the menu are sandwiches, salads, soups, bagels, and freshly baked sweets. Free Wi-Fi too.

Right across the street is another student hangout, **Trinity Coffee House** (307/721-8016), with a funky mélange of old tables, light breakfasts, and lunchtime bagel melts, sandwiches, and salad, all under $6. The breakfast and lunch menu are available till 8 P.M. The Trinity name comes from the owners, not from any religious connotations.

Turtle Rock Coffee (270 N. 9th St., 307/745-

3741) has espresso, panini, salads, and desserts in a close-to-campus location. **Grounds Coffee Lounge** (171 N. 3rd St., 307/742-5208) has free computer access and Wi-Fi for customers.

American

For earthy and creative "kick-ass" breakfasts visit 〖 **The Overland Restaurant** (100 Ivinson Ave., 307/721-2800, www.overlandrestaurant.com), but be ready for a wait on weekend mornings. Try the Happy Jack sandwich—cream cheese, green chilies, and horseradish with roast beef, tomatoes, and sprouts—for lunch. Dinners feature everything from Cajun shrimp alfredo to sirloin steaks, and the extensive wine list adds to the appeal. Dinner entrées are $10–15.

Lovejoy's Bar and Grill (101 Grand Ave., 307/745-0141) serves burgers, steaks, wraps, salads, burritos, nachos, pasta, and microbrews in a pleasant setting. It's owned by the same folks who bring you Altitude Chophouse and Brewery and has a late-night menu—until 11 P.M. nightly.

You'll find inexpensive food, pizza, ice cream, and sandwiches at the **University Cafeteria,** in the Wyoming Union building on campus.

Cow-Belle Ranch Cookouts (307/745-9521, www.wyocattlewomen.org/albany) take place once a month in the summer. Just $8 gets you a ranch visit with dinner and entertainment.

International

Several places in town offer Mexican food. The best are **El Conquistador** (110 Ivinson Ave., 307/742-2377) and **Corona Village** (421 Boswell, 307/721-0167). Stop by the latter on Tuesdays for an all-you-can-eat taco bar.

Grand Avenue Pizza (301 Grand Ave., 307/721-2909) bakes pizzas and cranks out salads and daily soup specials. Get delicious Italian food, Wyoming-style, at **Vitale's Italian Cowboy** (2127 E. Grand Ave., 307/755-1500). Open for dinner only.

Three places serve Chinese food and lunch buffets (around $6.50): **The Great Wall** (1501 S. 3rd St., 307/745-7966), **The New Mandarin**

Restaurant (1254 N. 3rd St., 307/742-8822), and **Peking Chinese Restaurant** (1665 N. 3rd St., 307/742-8138).

Find fresh sushi at **Tokyo Sushi and Grill** (2313 Soldier Springs Rd., 307/745-4991), housed within Ramada Center Hotel. Most entrées are $14–20. The same menu is available in the adjacent sports bar if you want to watch football while sampling sashimi.

Eclectic

〖 **Jeffrey's Bistro** (123 Ivinson Ave., 307/742-7046, www.jeffreysbistro.com) is a personal favorite. The atmosphere is relaxed and friendly, with a mix of brick, oak, and brass. On the menu are light meals, salads, sandwiches, creative vegetarian specialties, and great homemade bread. Reasonable prices too; the most expensive full meal is $17. Try the shrimp Thai burrito for something different.

Natural Foods

Whole Earth Grainery and Truck Store (111 Ivinson Ave., 307/745-4268) is a friendly straight-from-the-'70s grocery with all sorts of organic produce, fresh fish, dried foods, teas, spices, and coffees.

A few doors down is 〖 **Medicine Bow Natural Foods and Deli** (101 Ivinson Ave., 307/742-2350, www.mbnaturalfoods.com), an upscale corner place with a natural market, hopping café, and free Wi-Fi. Try the smoothies, soups of the day, breakfast scrambles and crepes, panini sandwiches, salad bar, fresh-baked pies, breads, and scones. Dine inside or at one of the tables along Grand Avenue.

Sweet Melissa Vegetarian Cafe (213 S. 1st St., 307/742-9607) serves "comfort food for homesick vegetarians." Peruse the blackboard menu (most under $8), which includes portabella *fajitas,* linguini marinara, falafel, chili tacos, sandwiches, soups, salads, and veggie burgers. Closed Sundays and no credit cards.

Brewpubs

Altitude Chophouse and Brewery (320 S. 2nd St., 307/721-4031) combines good beer (seven or so of its own versions are usually on tap) with a menu that encompasses both standard pub grub (fish-and-chips, pizzas, bangers and mash, etc.) and more upscale fare, including rack of lamb, ahi tuna, smoked pork chops, and spinach ravioli. In the back are pool and Foosball tables. Closed Sundays.

Directly across from campus, **The Library Restaurant and Brewing Co.** (1622 E. Grand Ave., 307/742-0500) is a favorite of UW students, with fresh-brewed beers, reasonable prices, and ample servings of food.

Groceries, Bakeries, and Treats

Get groceries from **Albertsons, Safeway,** and **Wal-Mart SuperCenter** stores along the main route through town. The **Laramie Farmers Market** (307/332-0305) takes place on Grand Avenue Fridays mid-July–mid-October.

Head to **Old Town Bagels** (307 E. Grand Ave., 307/721-8965) for the best bagels in these parts, plus smoothies, ice cream, and espresso. **The Chocolate Cellar** (115A Ivinson Ave., 307/742-9278) sells imported chocolates.

INFORMATION AND SERVICES

The **Laramie Chamber of Commerce** (800 S. 3rd St., 307/745-7339 or 866/876-1012, www.laramie.org, open 8 A.M.–5 P.M. Mon.–Fri. all year) has a slew of brochures on the area. Also look for the chamber visitor center in the caboose on the south end of town; open 9 A.M.–5 P.M. daily late May–early September. If you're planning a trip to the Laramie area, contact the **Albany County Tourism Board** (307/745-4195 or 800/445-5303, www.laramie-tourism.org) for details. (See the *Sights* section for details on the University of Wyoming visitor center.)

Before heading out to the Medicine Bow Mountains, be sure to stop by the **Medicine Bow-Routt National Forest Supervisor's Office** (2468 Jackson St., 307/745-2300, www.fs.fed.us/r2/mbr) for maps and up-to-date trail and campground information.

The 100,000-watt **Wyoming Public Radio** station KUWR (91.9 FM, www.wyomingpublicradio.net) is based in Laramie, with repeaters throughout Wyoming providing in-depth news and music sans commercials.

The Wyoming Room in the **Albany County Library** (310 S. 8th, 307/745-3365, http://acpl.lib.wy.us/info.html) has a big selection of historic books and other documents. It also provides computers with free Internet. Much more impressive are the eight university libraries (www-lib.uwyo.edu) housing more than 1.1 million volumes, including the most complete collection of Wyoming books in existence, plus 150,000 maps and 13,000 periodicals. Most of these publications are in the **William Robertson Coe Library** (307/766-5312), which also has a map room, an extensive depository of government publications, and the American Heritage Center's outstanding collection of historic books about Wyoming and the West.

Other Laramie services include **Ivinson Memorial Hospital** (255 N. 30th St., 307/742-2141, www.ivinsonhospital.org), the **post office** (152 N. 5th St., 307/721-8837), and **Snowy Range Laundromat** (2275 Snowy Range Rd., 307/745-9456).

GETTING THERE AND AROUND

Great Lakes Aviation (307/433-2905 or 800/554-5111, www.greatlakesav.com) provides daily flights to Denver and Worland from Laramie Airport (www.laramieairport.com), just west of town on Hwy. 130. **France Flying Service** (307/324-2361) has charter and scenic flights.

Rent cars at the airport from **Enterprise** (307/721-9876 or 800/261-7331, www.enterprise.com) or **Hertz** (307/745-0500 or 800/654-3131, www.hertz.com).

Greyhound (307/742-9663 or 800/231-2222, www.greyhound.com) stops at the Tumbleweed Express Gas Station on East Grand at I-80. Buses head south to Denver or west to Salt Lake City.

EAST OF LARAMIE
Pole Mountain Area

Heading east from Laramie on I-80, the freeway climbs steadily into the second-growth ponderosa and lodgepole pine forests of the Pole Mountain area. It's a scenic land punctuated by unusual and colorful rock formations.

For many years much of the land here belonged to the military and was used as a target and maneuver area for the army's version of off-road vehicles—tanks. Amazingly, the land seems to show little sign of all this abuse today.

Ten miles east of Laramie is the Summit Rest Area at the highest point (8,640 feet) along I-80. A 13-foot-tall bronze bust of **Abraham Lincoln** looks over the freeway from atop a granite base. The largest bronze bust in the nation, it was created by Robert I. Russin, former art professor at the university and Wyoming's best-known sculptor. The old road through this pass was known as the Lincoln Highway and was the first transcontinental highway. The sculpture was placed in this area in 1959, on the 150th anniversary of Lincoln's birth. It was moved to the present location when the interstate highway came through in 1968. The **visitor center** here has information on nearby areas and is open 9 A.M.–7 P.M. daily mid-May–October. Also here is a small theater showing videos.

Choose from three Forest Service campgrounds ($10, open May–Sept.) in the Pole Mountain area, or camp for free on land away from the roads. **Headquarters Trail** extends 4.5 miles from the Summit Rest Area to Headquarters Road.

During the winter, the **Medicine Bow Nordic Association** (www.medbownordic.org) maintains more than 20 kilometers of groomed cross-country ski trails in the Pole Mountain area; get maps from Laramie ski shops. Many others come to play on the unofficial tubing and tobogganing hill near Happy Jack Trailhead. A $5 day-use fee is charged at trailheads and picnic areas in the Pole Mountain area.

East of the summit, I-80 follows a long open plateau and then drops gradually into the shortgrass prairie of southeastern Wyoming via "The Gangplank." The Colorado Rockies form a jagged southern horizon line. This crossing of the Laramie Range was discovered by General Grenville Dodge in 1865. While exploring the railroad's new route, an attack by a party of Indians forced his men to flee eastward. In the process they discovered this gentle ramp to the plains of Cheyenne. Unfortunately, today the route is marked for miles by a dominolike

Vedauwoo, near Laramie

line of billboards advertising everything from McDonald's to fireworks. It's too bad the billboards can't topple like dominoes to reveal the expansive grassland beyond!

◖ Vedauwoo

Just five miles east of the summit you'll find the turnoff to strange rock formations known as Vedauwoo (VEE-dah-voo), a name meaning "earthborn" in Arapaho. In this area, which is considered a sacred place where young Indian men went on vision quests, oddly jumbled rocks form all sorts of shapes: mushrooms, balancing rocks, feminine curves, rounded knolls, lizards, faces, turtles, and anything you might dream up. Imagine it as a Rorschach test. Indians believed that the rocks were created by animal and human spirits. Today, Vedauwoo is considered one of Wyoming's best and unique places for rock climbing. Climbs go from a difficulty level of 5.0 all the way to 5.14, with many easy places to practice crack climbs. For more on the area, visit www.vedauwoo.org. Nonclimbers come just to view the rocks, eat a picnic lunch, ride mountain bikes along the dirt roads, hike in the countryside, or scramble up for marvelous vistas of the surrounding land. Vedauwoo Glen Road connects with Happy Jack Road for a nice loop trip. There's a campground right at Vedauwoo. The Forest Service charges a $5 fee for day use.

PYRAMID POWER

Head two miles south from the Vedauwoo exit to one of the strangest monuments in Wyoming: a 60-foot-tall stone pyramid in the middle of nowhere. The memorial commemorates Oakes and Oliver Ames, two of the most influential figures in building the transcontinental railroad. As a U.S. congressman, Oakes Ames gained passage of a bill that allowed the railroad to sell bonds equal to the amount lent by the federal government—$60 million. The company they established to handle this financing was the infamous Credit Mobilier of America. It later came to light that Oakes had bribed fellow congressmen with discounted railroad stock and greatly exaggerated construction costs for his own gain. A congressional investigation labeled Oakes "King of Frauds" and censured him. He died before he could stand trial, and the money was never recovered.

Despite this bit of infamy, nearly $65,000 was spent in 1882 to build this monument to the Ames brothers. It was originally situated at the highest elevation of the transcontinental railroad route, near the town of Sherman, a place where trains halted to check their brakes before the long descent on either side. In 1902, the tracks were rerouted a couple of miles to the south, leaving the grandiose pile of rocks by itself. Nothing remains today from the Sherman townsite except a cemetery. The **Ames Monument** seems to bring out two conflicting emotions: dismay at the obscenity of this monstrosity and amusement at the irony that so much money was wasted on a self-aggrandizing monument soon abandoned even by the railroad the Ames brothers had helped build.

Medicine Bow Vicinity

Two roads head west from Laramie. Most people follow I-80 straight to Rawlins, but U.S. 30/287 (the old Lincoln Highway) gets you there in about the same time and provides a strong flavor of the Old West. It doesn't get much traffic and offers grand big-sky country. Highway 34 heads northeast from U.S. 30 near the dot on the map called **Bosler,** climbing over the low mountains to Wheatland 50 miles away. It's a pretty drive with little traffic. Halfway to Wheatland is the Johnson Creek Wildlife Habitat Management Area, a popular place for fishing. There are no trails, but hiking is easy in the open country.

ROCK RIVER

This almost ghost town of 180 lonely souls has the basics, including a general store and **Longhorn Lodge Motel and Restaurant** (362 N. 4th, 307/378-2555, $35–45 s or $40–45 d), with log cabin units and a good restaurant.

West of Rock River, the road sails through desolate treeless country, with sagebrush to the horizon and the impressive summit of Elk Mountain rising to the southwest. The Union Pacific Railroad parallels the highway most of the way, and antelope glance up at the passing trains and cars. Anyone coming through in the winter will appreciate the miles of snow fences along the south side of the highway. Still, the snow streams over the roadway almost constantly.

COMO BLUFF

Halfway between the towns of Rock River and Medicine Bow on U.S. 30/287 is a long, low ridge known as Como Bluff. There isn't much to distinguish this from countless other buttes in the West, but paleontologists consider it one of the most important sites ever discovered, a place one author likened to Darwin's *On the Origin of Species* in terms of its impact on scientific thought. This was the first large discovery of dinosaurs anywhere, and the first place diplodocus dinosaurs—the largest ever found—

were discovered. The mammals discovered here are prized around the world and include all but three of the 250 known Jurassic mammals found in North America. Combined, the dinosaur and mammal fossils from Como Bluff make up a major part of the collections of Yale's Peabody Museum, the Smithsonian Institution, the New York Museum of Natural History, the National Museum in Washington, D.C., and many others around the world.

History

In July 1877, Professor Othniel Charles Marsh of Yale College received a letter from two Wyoming men calling themselves Harlow and Edwards. They told of finding:

a large number of fossils, supposed to be those of the Megatherium, although there is no one here sufficient of a geologist to state for a certainty. We have excavated one (1) partly, and know where there is several others that we have not, as yet, done any work upon.... We are desirous of disposing of what fossils we have, and also, the secret of the others. We are working men and are not able to present them as a gift, and if we can sell the secret of the fossil bed, and procure work in excavating others we would like to do so. We have said nothing to anyone as yet.... We would be pleased to hear from you, as you are well known as an enthusiastic geologist, and a man of means, both of which we are desirous of finding – more especially the latter.

Marsh was in stiff competition with other paleontologists around the country, and his rival, Professor E. D. Cope from the Philadelphia Academy of Sciences, had just scooped him on a major dinosaur discovery in Colorado. The letter from "Harlow and Edwards" piqued Marsh's curiosity. An assistant sent to investigate wrote that the find was indeed substantive and suggested that Marsh immediately hire the two discoverers—actually two railroad employees, William Reed and William Carlin—to keep them from revealing the secret to others. Reed would later work for many years as a collector for the University of Wyoming and eventually as an instructor in geology and curator of the Geology Museum on the Laramie campus.

Work began almost immediately and continued right through the winter blizzards, but despite efforts to keep the find a secret, Professor Cope soon had his own men working at Como Bluff. The rivalry almost came to blows, and Marsh's men made it a point to smash any bones left behind after their digging was complete and to backfill the quarries with rocks, even if their rivals were working below. Excavations continued until 1889, by which time most of the finest specimens had been unearthed.

Today geology and paleontology classes still visit Como Bluff, but the quarries where the bones were found are now abandoned and can't be seen from the road. Como Bluff itself is visible a little more than one mile north of U.S. 30, and a sign describes the site. Travelers will want to stop to see **"the world's oldest building"** at Como Bluffs, a now-closed gift shop built from dinosaur bones. The sign on the front proclaims "This building walked 75 million years ago!"

MEDICINE BOW

The little town of Medicine Bow (pop. 270, www.medicinebow.org) is the sort of place where headlines in the weekly *Medicine Bow Post* complain of dogs getting into garbage or barking at kids. For the most part it's a nondescript town with old boxlike houses and newer boxlike trailers with a fine view to the south of the Medicine Bow Mountains. If Garrison Keillor had been born in Wyoming he'd be positively rhapsodic about this little place that time forgot. Medicine Bow is not unlike hundreds of barely surviving old settlements all over the West, but it was here that novelist Owen Wister had his legendary cowboy hero,

the Virginian, face off with Trampas. Over a game of cards, Trampas calls the Virginian a "son-of-a-bitch," leading to the famous encounter in which the Virginian pulls his pistol and says, "When you call me that, smile!" It remains one of the classic lines in American folklore. *The Virginian* became the prototype for the modern Western and was later made into three movies and a TV series.

History

The town of Medicine Bow began in the 1870s as a Union Pacific pumping station along Medicine Bow River and grew into a local supply point and minor army garrison. It has always been a center for the ranchers who run thousands of head of livestock in the surrounding countryside, so it was a logical place for Wister to base his cowboy hero. During the 1930s, Medicine Bow prospered because it lay along the Lincoln Highway (U.S. 30), but after completion of I-80, it lapsed into decay. The coal mines of Hanna (20 miles west) and uranium and oil explorations in Shirley Basin led to temporary energy booms, but the economy has now returned to its ranching base.

Sights

Medicine Bow's main attraction is the boxy, three-story **Virginian Hotel,** built in 1909—seven years after *The Virginian* came out. At the time, it was the largest hotel between Denver and Salt Lake City. It's still a marvelous building, so take a look around, even if you aren't planning on staying here. The Virginian's authentic old-time bar is one of the best in Wyoming. Just down the street is the modern **Diplodocus Bar** (307/379-2312), alias "the Dip," containing the largest jade bar in existence, cut from a 4.5-ton jade boulder discovered near Lander. Look down for the only hand-painted dance floor west of the Mississippi. While you're here for a beer, be sure to ask owner Bill Bennett to show you his unusually intricate woodcarvings. Good food too, but closed Sundays.

Across from the hotel is the **Medicine Bow Museum** (307/379-2383, www.medi-

© DON PITCHER

The Virginian Hotel is the main attraction in Medicine Bow.

MEDICINE BOW COUNTRY

cinebow.org/museum.htm, open 10 A.M.–5 P.M. Mon.–Sat. and 1–5 P.M. Sun.), housed in the circa 1913 railroad depot. Out front is a cabin built by Owen Wister—it stood in Jackson Hole until being moved here in 1976—and a petrified-wood monument to the novelist. The museum contains the typical things found in small-town museums: various homesteading items, a lamb warmer, a coyote scare made from sawdust and firecrackers, and old fire equipment. It's kind of like wandering through an old attic where you wonder how half the stuff was ever used. An old caboose is on the side.

The wind blows almost constantly in Medicine Bow, making it a great place to harness the wind for electricity. Five miles south of the town are 11 **wind turbines,** each of which produces 660 kilowatts. Together they supply enough energy for 1,200 homes in Colorado's fast-growing front-range cities. The turbines are owned by the Platte River Power Authority (www.prpa.org).

Practicalities

Upstairs rooms at the historic **Virginian Hotel** (307/379-2377, www.medicinebow.org/virgin-

ian) are remarkably inexpensive, starting at just $22 s for a tiny room with a twin bed and bath down the hall, or $45 d for a larger room with private bath. Sleep in the two-bedroom suite where Owen Wister stayed for $65 d. This is a delightfully old-fashioned place with a grandma's-house feeling, and the rooms have tubs (not showers) and lack TVs or phones. Things can get noisy when downstairs bar patrons shift into high gear. If you miss your TV, try a motel room in the annex for $45 d. The downstairs restaurant ($9–15 entrées) provides good home cooking three meals a day, or you can tip a beer in the old-time bar. Both are popular with smokers.

Pitch your tent or park RVs for free at the town park.

SHIRLEY BASIN

Highway 487 heads north from Medicine Bow across vast and remote Shirley Basin, with some of the finest cattle rangeland in Wyoming. The road is smooth with wide shoulders (perfect for bikes), and the vistas are dramatic—colorful badlands, rolling hills covered with sage and grass, and cottonwood-lined creeks. There's

MEDICINE BOW COUNTRY

lots of wildlife here, too, especially antelope and deer. The basin has large prairie-dog towns, and the endangered black-footed ferrets were released here in the early 1990s. Sylvatic plague later decimated prairie-dog and ferret populations. A few ferrets still survive in Shirley Basin, but it's highly unlikely that you would see them.

Extensive deposits of uranium have been discovered in Shirley Basin—some of the largest and richest in the world—but low prices and an oversupply have all but halted the uranium-mining business. Ask in Medicine Bow for directions to the petrified forest. Nearly every yard in town has a piece out front.

HANNA

The town of Hanna (pop. 900) lies at the center of one of the state's major coal fields. There are lots of mobile homes and company housing in Hanna, but there is nothing particularly interesting about the town, unless you care to check out the miners' memorials or the enormous Union Pacific snowplow. Mining has been a mainstay of the local economy since coal was discovered here in the late 1800s. Two disastrous explosions in 1903 and 1908 killed 228 miners, and two Hanna monuments commemorate the men who died. The mines remained open until 1954 and were reactivated in the 1970s. The last underground mine closed in 2001. Only the Arch Coal strip mine, 23 miles west, remains open, but high costs associated with the depth of the coal here may force its closure.

The mining ghost town of **Carbon**—established in 1868 as the state's first coal town—once stood a few miles east of Hanna. The coal ran out in 1902, and today only a few ruins and the graveyard remain.

Hanna Basin Museum (on Front St. below the bridge, 307/324-3915) has local memorabilia, including a collection of mine photos and details on the mine disasters. The building once served as a miner's cottage for the old company town and is open 1–5 P.M. Friday-Sunday in summer, and 1–5 P.M. Fridays the rest of the year.

abandoned motel near Hanna

© DON PITCHER

Practicalities

Hanna's fine **recreation center** houses a sauna, swimming pool, hot tub, and gym.

Golden Rule Motel (307/325-6525, $32 s or $36 d) has minimalist prefab rooms. **Hanna's Wild Wonder** (307/325-6478) and **Country Cupboard** (307/325-6022) serve three meals a day. Groceries (and an ATM) are available at **The Super Market.**

ARLINGTON

Approximately 30 miles west of Laramie, I-80 drivers are suddenly confronted with a strange apparition: towering **windmills** lining the crest of Foote Creek Rim. Completed in 1998, these 69 turbines crank out 41,000 kilowatt-hours of electricity, enough to power 20,000 homes. One of the windiest spots in America, this hilltop location is perfect for energy generation and is one of the biggest outside California.

Below the windmills is the freeway off-ramp called Arlington, a tiny place with a surprising amount of history. **Arlington Outpost Campground** (307/378-2350, $14 tents, $20 RVs, open June–Sept.) has a convenience store and gas.

Rock Creek Stage Station

You'll find several buildings from the Rock Creek Stage Station, which stood along the Overland Route, including one of the oldest structures in Wyoming, a log cabin built around 1860. Also in Arlington, on private land south of the freeway, is a combination blacksmith shop/dance hall/gambling palace.

In 1865, Indians attacked a wagon train near the Rock Creek Stage Station and captured two girls, Mary and Lizzie Fletcher. Mary was eventually sold to a white trader, but Lizzie remained with the Arapahoes for the rest of her life. It wasn't until 35 years after their parting that Mary discovered her sister alive and living on the Wind River Reservation. Having grown accustomed to the Arapaho way of life and enjoying a high status in the community, Lizzie chose to stay in her home. She is buried next to her husband, Broken Horn, in the St. Stephen's Mission Cemetery.

ELK MOUNTAIN

The tiny settlement of Elk Mountain (pop. 190) stands just off I-80 halfway between Laramie and Rawlins. Although almost within sight of the freeway, the town seems a world apart. Big cottonwoods line the quiet streets, and the Medicine Bow River, home of blue-ribbon trout fishing, flows right through town. Several buildings are noteworthy: The small New England–style community church, the Elk Mountain Trading Company (with a few groceries), and an enormous log barn are still in perfect condition after more than a century. Directly behind town is the rounded, snowcapped 11,156-foot summit of Elk Mountain, one of the most prominent natural landmarks anywhere along I-80. Unusual clouds frequently hang off its peak, making it a valuable site for the University of Wyoming's atmospheric research program. Ask in town for access information to the mountain; you'll need to get permission from local ranchers.

In late July, the **Bow River Blue Grass Festival** features regional bands in a mix of music and fun at the hotel. Unfortunately, Elk Mountain's Garden Spot Pavilion—a dance hall that in the 1930s and '40s attracted the likes of Louis Armstrong, Tommy Dorsey, Glenn Miller, and Lawrence Welk—was torn down in 2003 because it had deteriorated too much for restoration.

Founded in 1866, **Elk Mountain Ranch** (307/348-7440, www.elkmountain.com) is a working bison ranch that offers fly-fishing vacation packages and trophy big game hunts.

Accommodations and Food

Built in 1905, the **(Elk Mountain Hotel** (307/348-7774 or 888/348-7774, www.elkmountainhotel.com) is a beautifully restored lodge. Tall cottonwood trees shade the grounds, and the gazebo and big white tent host summertime weddings and concerts. Hotel rooms feature elegant furnishings and private baths; $115–135 d, including a full breakfast. The honeymoon suite has a king bed and hot tub, $155 d with breakfast. Many guests choose the hotel's packages, starting at $192 d, including lodging, dinner, a bottle of wine, and breakfast.

The hotel dining room has pressed tin ceilings, a log-burning fireplace, and delicious entrées such as steak taboo, prime rib, and chicken piccata. Dinner entrées are $20–30. Save room for the crème brûlée. Sunday brunch ($20) is especially popular.

Housed in another historic Elk Mountain building, **Wild Wonder Cafe** (307/348-7478) serves lunch and dinner most days and has an adjacent convenience store.

Into the Country

Five miles west of town, a stone monument marks the site of **Fort Halleck,** a short-lived military post built in 1862 to guard the Overland Trail. With the arrival of the transcontinental railroad, it was abandoned in 1866 and its fixtures moved east to Fort Buford (later called Fort Sanders), near present-day Laramie.

Head south from Elk Mountain on Pass Creek Road (Road 404) for a wonderful 11-mile round-the-mountain drive. The gravel road (not recommended after rains) curves south past Elk Mountain and then west along the willow-lined Pass Creek to a junction with Hwy. 130, where you can continue to Saratoga. This little-traveled road offers open hills with wide vistas of the mountains and plains. While you listen to meadowlarks singing and wind rustling through the grass, you can watch—as the song says—the deer and the antelope play. Not even a line of telephone poles breaks the view, and seldom is heard a discouraging word.

Medicine Bow Mountains

Medicine Bow–Routt National Forest is scattered over four disjunctive areas in Wyoming. (The northern section—the Laramie Mountains—is discussed in the *Central Wyoming* chapter; the Pole Mountain section is described under *Laramie* in this chapter.) The other two mountainous areas are west of Laramie: the Medicine Bow Mountains, locally called the Snowy Range, and the Sierra Madre. The Forest Service has controlled most of this land since 1902, although the name and boundaries have changed through the years. Mining was the big attraction in the late 1800s, but the major gold and copper deposits were quickly mined out, and logging became the primary use of this mountainous country. Between 1867 and 1940, millions of railroad ties were brought out of the Laramie and Medicine Bow mountains by tie hacks who logged almost every drivable creek they could find. The area provided ties for not only Wyoming but western Nebraska and Colorado as well. Logging for lumber is still important in the Medicine Bow–Routt National Forest, but recreation is increasingly becoming the dominant use of the forest as more people discover this scenic country. The supervisor's office for Medicine Bow–Routt National Forest in Wyoming is in Laramie (307/745-2300 or 800/877-9965, www.fs.fed.us/r2/mbr) with district offices in Saratoga, Encampment, and Douglas. Pick up a copy of the forest map at any of these offices before heading out.

LARAMIE PLAINS

Heading west from Laramie on Hwy. 130, you pass through some of the most desolate country in Wyoming, with flat grassland stretching in all directions, interrupted by mountains to the east, south, and west. An enormous windswept bowl here—**Big Hollow**—was created by howling winds during the last ice age. The only other place like this is in Russia. Laramie Basin is also unique in having the highest short-grass prairie in the world, 7,200 feet above sea level. Eleven miles west of Laramie, Hwy. 130 crosses the historic **Overland Trail,** which carried emigrants, mail, and freight west between 1862 and 1868, when the railroad replaced it. The wagon ruts are still visible, with markers trac-

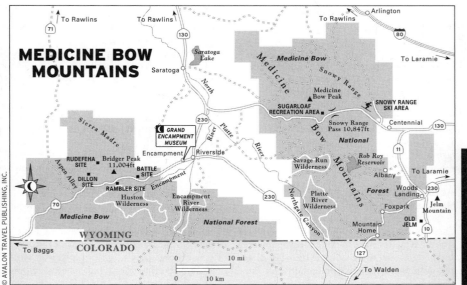

© AVALON TRAVEL PUBLISHING, INC.

MEDICINE BOW COUNTRY

ing the old route. As you approach the Medicine Bow Mountains, the highway dips to sample the tree-lined beauty of Little Laramie Creek and then begins the long ascent to Snowy Range Pass.

ALBANY

Highway 11 heads south along Little Laramie Creek to the foothills town of Albany, passing rolling grass and sagebrush country with pine-topped hills. Old ranches are sprinkled around this gorgeous little valley. **Albany Lodge** (307/745-5782, www.albanylodge.com) has a restaurant, bar, convenience store, and lodging year-round. New motel units are $70 d. Also available are a four-person cabin ($100) with private bath and kitchenette, and a guesthouse ($350) that sleeps 10 and has a full kitchen, dining room, and two baths. Rent ATVs in the summer or snowmobiles in the winter.

A dirt road continues south from Albany to Woods Landing, but blowing snows often cause its closure in the winter. Albany is a favorite base for snowmobilers, and the lodge has rentals and gas.

CENTENNIAL

Thirty-five miles west of Laramie, Hwy. 130 widens to include the funky old mining town of Centennial (pop. 190). Situated at the foot of the Snowy Range, Centennial was founded in 1875 and gained its name the following year—the centennial of the founding of America. (James Michener claimed not to have known of the town when he wrote his novel of the same name about an early Rocky Mountain town.) Prospectors came here in search of gold. That first year the Centennial Mine produced more than $90,000 worth, but when the vein ran out, only a few people stayed around. Another short boom created by infusions of cash from a Boston financier brought a fish hatchery, hotels, mining explorations, and an exclusive country club to Centennial, but the bubble burst again when the expected gold deposits failed to materialize. Eventually, Centennial became a minor ranching center. Today it's a tourist way station with a devil-may-care mix of old log homes and house trailers. It's also home to novelist Annie Proulx, the Pulitzer Prize–winning author of *The Shipping News*.

Find local information on the web at www.centennialwyoming.com.

Sights

Housed within the little 1907 railroad depot building, **Nici Self Museum** (307/742-7158, www.wyshs.org/mus-nici.htm, free) contains exhibits on the area's mining, ranching, and logging history. It's open 1–4 P.M. Friday–Monday mid-June–early September. Out front are a Union Pacific caboose and various aging farm implements. By the way, the word nici is pronounced NEE-chee.

Accommodations and Food

Mountain View Historic Hotel (307/742-5476 or 888/400-9953, www.mtnviewhotel.net) is a classic building from 1907. Most of the nicely renovated guest rooms ($75 d) have microwaves and fridges, and three suites ($100–110 d) are also available, two with full kitchens. A comfy café/espresso shop on the premises also serves a brunch menu that attracts a crowd on weekends, plus relaxed candlelight multicourse dinners on Friday nights ($16–25, BYOB). There's also a big wraparound deck for relaxing.

Old Corral Hotel and Steakhouse (307/745-5918 or 866/653-2677, www.oldcorral.com) is the biggest place in town, with 35 Western-decor rooms in the lodge for $59–69 s or $69–79 d, with access to the outdoor hot tub and game room with billiards and darts. Guests can settle into the theater for movies on the big-screen television; the hotel has 300 flicks to choose from. The restaurant—open three meals a day—serves steaks, chicken, and seafood in a comfortably Old West atmosphere and has occasional live music on Saturday nights.

Friendly Motel (307/742-6033) has eight motel rooms for $49 s or $59 d and a cabin for $90. The latter sleeps six and requires a two-night minimum. Open year-round. Tent and RV sites (with electricity only) are $10.

Across the road is **Trading Post Dinner House and Saloon** (307/721-5074 or 888/521-5074, www.centennial-tradingpost.com), where you'll find prime rib, seafood, and four-pound sirloin steaks, and dinner theater productions

throughout the year. The bar comes alive with blues, rock, or jazz some weekends. Out front is **The Phoenix Gallery** (307/742-9672) with stained glass, paintings, jewelry, and more by local artisans; open weekends only.

East of Centennial, **Vee Bar Guest Ranch** (307/745-7036 or 800/483-3227, www.veebar.com) offers luxury at the foot of the Snowy Range. Stay in comfortable old cabins or in a grand old lodge listed on the National Register of Historic Places. The emphasis is on horseback riding, but the Vee Bar also offers hayrides, trap shooting, trout fishing, and hiking. When the day is done, relax tired muscles in the outdoor hot tub. The 26,000-acre ranch attracts a clientele that includes celebrities and politicians. Accommodations mid-June–early September cost $2,900 for two people for six nights, all-inclusive. A less expensive option is to stay for Saturday night only; $150 d with breakfast. During the winter, the ranch has nightly B&B lodging for $100 d.

Rainbow Valley Resort (307/745-0368, www.rainbowvalleyresort.com) is one mile west of Centennial and another mile up Rainbow Valley Road. Accommodations include six cabins, all with full kitchens, baths, and other amenities. These vary from a simple $75 one-room cabin to an attractive new 10-person unit for $210.

◖ SNOWY RANGE

Between the Laramie Plains and the valley created by the upper North Platte River lies a section of the Medicine Bow Mountains that is locally called the Snowy Range. This name is appropriate because it can snow here at any time of the year. Ten-foot drifts are not uncommon in the winter, and snow remains on high passes until late summer. Just southwest of the Snowy Range are the **Savage Run Wilderness** (15,260 acres) and the **Platte River Wilderness** (22,749 acres), both lying close to the Wyoming–Colorado border. Get maps of these from local Forest Service offices. Most visitors simply enjoy the drive over the mountains and the chance to camp beside an alpine lake with a backdrop of 12,000-foot

SNOWY RANGE TRAILS

To Sand Lake

Deep Lake

Sheep Lake

Rock Creek Knoll 11,125ft

Black Spotted Lake

North Twin Lakes

Meadows Lakes

Cutthroat Lake

Arrowhead Lake

Qualy Lake

Qualy Lake Trail

Reservoir Lake

Crescent Lake

Vagner Lake

Glacier Lakes

North Gap Lake

Shelf Lakes Trail

Shelf Lakes

Lost Lake

BROOKLYN LAKE

Hatchet Lake

South Gap Lake

Browns Pk 11,722ft

Gap Lakes Trail

Brooklyn Lake

Heart Lake

Upper Long Lake

Telephone Lakes

BROOKLYN LAKE GUARD STATION

OPEN AIR CHAPEL

Medicine Bow Pk 12,013ft

Klondyke Lake

Lost Lake Trail

Little Brooklyn Lake

NASH FORK

Bow Peak Trail

Libby Lake

Lewis Lake

SUGARLOAF RECREATION AREA

Towner Lake

TOWNER LAKE RD

To Centennial and Laramie

Sugarloaf Mtn 11,398ft

Medicine Lakes Trail

Lookout Lake

MEDICINE BOW OBSERVATION AREA

Snowy Range Pass

Black Jack Lake

130

Mirror Lake

LIBBY FLATS OBSERVATION POINT

Lake Marie

0   5 mi

0   5 km

130

Bear Lake

To Saratoga and Encampment

Silver Run Lake

MEDICINE BOW COUNTRY

mountains. Numerous short hiking trails and outstanding trout fishing make this a favorite spot for locals.

Over the Top

The 40-mile drive on Hwy. 130 over the Snowy Range is one of the most dramatic in Wyoming and is designated a National Scenic Byway. The pass is closed by snow late October–Memorial Day but remains open year-round to just beyond the Snowy Range Ski Area on the east side and 20 miles up from the west side. Higher-elevation parts of the road are popular with snowmobilers and cross-country skiers. West of Centennial, the highway climbs sharply through lodgepole and spruce forests to beautiful Snowy Range Pass at 10,847 feet (second-highest in the state). Even taking a short hike is likely to leave you a bit out of breath unless you're acclimated to the altitude. Before heading up the road, pick up a brochure on the scenic byway from one of the local visitor centers or Forest Service offices; it details sights along the way.

Be sure to stop at **Sugarloaf Recreation Area,** just east of the pass. Sharp, glacially carved spires rise above the small lakes, and islands of stunted Engelmann spruce and subalpine fir dot the alpine country. Trails head out to nearby lakes and flower-covered alpine meadows. At the summit, a viewing platform provides panoramic vistas of **Libby Flats,** massive Medicine Bow Peak, and the valleys on both sides. Pull off at the Medicine Bow Peak Observation Point for a 0.75-mile hike to the picturesque remains of the old **Red Mask Mine.** Just west of here, **Mirror Lake** and **Lake Marie** are two of the most photographed spots in Wyoming, with a spectacular backdrop of steep mountain faces reflected in the dark blue lake waters. Campgrounds and picnic areas are all along here. A wheelchair-accessible path leads along one shore of Lake Marie, and the west parking lot acts as a trailhead for the path up **Medicine Bow Peak.** On

Mirror Lake is nestled in the Snowy Range, near Laramie.

the western side of the pass, the highway drops steadily through the forest, eventually reaching the rolling sage and grass of the Upper North Platte River Valley. A small recreation area at **French Creek** provides an accessible fishing pier and interpretive signs. Stop at the **Brush Creek Visitor Center** on the western end for directions to **Kennaday Peak Lookout,** one of the few fire lookouts still staffed in Wyoming. It's open 10 A.M.–5 P.M. Friday–Monday mid-June–October and is accessible by high-clearance cars. No RVs.

Highway 230

Another route west is Hwy. 230. While this highway is not as dramatic as the Snowy Pass trek, it's open year-round and is still quite scenic. The road curves around the southern end of the Snowy Range and passes through tiny Woods Landing en route to the Colorado border. This is the only real settlement between Laramie and Encampment—a distance of 87 miles.

Woods Landing Resort (307/745-9638, www.woodslanding.com) comprises most of the town, with a combination country store/lodge/gas station/café/bar. Park RVs for $20, or stay in the rustic cabins for $35–45 d with a shared bath. Two recently built cabins ($85–95 d) are much nicer and have decks, queen or king beds, kitchenettes, and private baths. Showers cost $5 if you aren't staying here. The floor of the bar was built atop 24 boxcar springs—courtesy of railroad workers—so the dance floor really starts rocking on Saturday nights in the summer when country-and-western bands play. Anglers will find excellent fishing for brown trout in the nearby Big Laramie River.

Several old clapboard buildings from the mining ghost town of **Old Jelm** lie on private property four miles west of Woods Landing. The university's **Jelm Mountain Infrared Observatory** (307/766-6150) is up a five-mile dirt road from here; tours by reservation only.

Beyond Woods Landing, Hwy. 230 dips south and passes **WyColo Lodge** (307/755-5160) just two miles north of the state line. Here, you'll find three rustic cabins with a shared bathhouse for $45 d, and a modern cabin that sleeps four for $85. Upstairs rooms in the lodge are $55–85 d with private baths; the largest sleeps six. A two-night minimum is required in the winter. WyColo houses a bar and restaurant and has summertime ATV rentals and wintertime snowmobile rentals. The lodge is open year-round.

South of **Mountain Home,** the road continues into Colorado for nine miles along Colorado Hwy. 127 and then back north on Colorado Hwy. 125 for another nine miles before again crossing into Wyoming on Hwy. 230. Much of this is open rangeland with hills on either side. Only a few abandoned cabins and fences mark the presence of humans on this vast landscape. The huge white hip-roofed barn of the Big Creek Ranch is one of the most beautiful in Wyoming. Turn around for outstanding views of the Colorado Rockies. See Steve Knopper's *Moon Colorado* (www.moon.com) for details on sights to the south.

Trails

The Medicine Bows are ideal for short one- to five-day hikes; get maps from Forest Service offices or visitor centers. They also have maps showing trails open to **mountain-biking,** including many on the west side of the mountains.

The 4.5-mile **Medicine Bow Peak Trail** climbs 1,600 feet to the summit of this 12,013-foot mountain, the highest in southern Wyoming, providing extraordinary vistas. The trail leaves from the west Lake Marie parking area and is in exposed alpine terrain most of the way. You can make a seven-mile loop by following this route to the top and then dropping down the east side to the **Lakes Trail,** which takes you past rock-rimmed Lookout Lake—keep a lookout for marmots—and on to Mirror Lake. Your starting point is just down the road. Medicine Bow Peak can also be climbed via a steeper and shorter trail (four miles round-trip) that leaves from the Lewis Lake Trailhead. The Forest Service charges a $5 day-use fee at the Libby Lake and Lewis Lake trailheads and picnic areas.

North Gap Lake Trail departs from the Lewis Lake parking lot in the Sugarloaf Recreation Area and follows a gentle grade past Gap Lakes, continuing to Sheep Lake. Here, you can follow the **Sheep Lake Trail** to Brooklyn Lake before returning to your starting point via **Lost Lake Trail.** Total distance for this delightful high-mountain loop is 15 miles. This entire area is crisscrossed with other alpine trails, some of which are not shown on topographic maps. Check with the Forest Service for details.

Platte River Trail, a 6.5-mile-long path, parallels the river through a deep and narrow canyon lined with ponderosa pines and Douglas firs. Access is from the south via a trailhead near Sixmile Gap Campground (22 miles south of Encampment). The trail follows the west bank of the river, but by July the river can sometimes be forded, allowing hikers to continue another two miles northward to Pickaroon Campground. Check with the Forest Service for current water levels.

Savage Run Trail crosses the wilderness area of the same name. Nine miles long, it parallels Savage Run Creek, dropping 2,400 feet along the way. Access is too convoluted to describe, but it's not that hard to find if you have a Medicine Bow–Routt National Forest map.

Snowy Range Ski and Recreation Area

In the mountains 32 miles west of Laramie on Hwy. 130, the Snowy Range Ski and Recreation Area (307/745-5750 or 800/462-7669, www.snowyrange.com) has four lifts and 27 different runs. Outside of Jackson Hole, this is the best place to ski in Wyoming, with a good variety of skiing conditions, uncrowded slopes, and soft powder snow. Snowy Range is open Thanksgiving weekend–early April and charges $35 adults, $21 kids ages 6–12 and seniors. Children under six are free with a paying adult. The area is open 9 A.M.–4 P.M. daily, with ski and snowboard rentals and lessons, along with guided snowmobile trips. The lodge has cafeteria food, beer, and a fireplace.

Cross-Country Skiing and Snowmobiling

The Forest Service maintains dozens of miles of groomed Nordic ski trails in the mountains around Snowy Range Ski Area, with a wide variety of loops and longer treks available for those willing to strike out on their own. The Forest Service's historic Little Brooklyn Lake Guard Station is a popular overnight ski-in or snowmobile-in destination.

Snowmobiling is one of the most popular winter activities in the Snowy Range, and parking lots on all sides of the range fill with vehicles on winter weekends. More than 200 miles of groomed trails follow summertime roads and are maintained by the state of Wyoming. For details on both cross-country skiing and snowmobiling, stop by Forest Service offices in Laramie or Saratoga.

Mountain Lodges

At an elevation of 10,000 feet, **Snowy Mountain Lodge** (307/742-7669 or 866/467-6699, www.snowymountainlodge.com) is just one mile beyond the Snowy Range Ski Area and seven miles west of Centennial. Built as a University of Wyoming science camp in 1927, the 9,000-square-foot lodge was totally refurbished a few years back but still retains its rustic charm. There's a grand stone fireplace, teak furniture, a pool table made in 1862, a gift shop, and a restaurant open for breakfast and lunch. Stay in nicely remodeled historic cabins ($150–175 d, plus $7 for additional guests). These sleep up to eight and have private baths and kitchenettes. Another option is the very basic "trapper cabins" ($40–50 d) with bunk beds and dry toilets, but no running water. The lodge is a popular stop for snowmobilers or cross-country skiers. More than 300 miles of snowmobile trails fan out from here, and snowmobile rentals are available. Snowy Mountain Lodge is open June–September and December–April.

Uphill 1.5 miles from Snowy Mountain Lodge is **Mountain Meadow Cabins** (307/742-6042, www.mtnmeadowcabins.com). Built in the 1950s, the eight cabins have been nicely updated with private baths and kitchenettes and are open year-round; you'll need a snowmobile or skis for winter access. The smallest ones sleep two for $50, while four-person cabins are $70, and eight-person units (two bedrooms) cost $100.

Another delightful place is **Brooklyn Lodge** (307/742-6916 in summer, 408/761-0242 at other times, www.brooklynlodge.com), eight miles west of Centennial in the Snowy Range at an elevation of 10,200 feet. Built in 1922 and refurbished in the 1990s, the log lodge is on the National Register of Historic Places. Inside, two guest rooms have king-size beds and share a bath. The living room contains a big stone fireplace, and the front porch overlooks a mountain meadow. There's a minimum two-night stay on weekends and a five-night minimum on holidays and in the winter, when access is by skis or snowmobile. The room price of $150 d includes a full country breakfast. With only two rooms, Brooklyn Lodge fills up far ahead; reserve six months in advance for summer weekends. It is also a favorite spot for summer weddings. The lodge is open late June–mid-August through 2006 and till late October in subsequent years. Children are allowed only if you rent both rooms.

Historic **Medicine Bow Lodge and Guest Ranch** (307/326-5439 or 800/409-5439, www.medbowlodge.com) is 22 miles east of Saratoga along Hwy. 130—just inside the national forest boundary. The main building opened in 1917, and refurbished historic log cabins are $300 per night for two people with a three-night minimum. This includes lodging, three home-cooked meals, horseback rides, cookouts, and fishing, plus access to a workout facility, hot tub, sauna, and cross-country skis in winter. Snowmobile rentals are available in the winter. Open all year.

Historic **Ryan Park,** 24 miles east of Saratoga, is home to **B&B Mountain Retreat** (308/235-3881, www.bbmountain.20m.com), with a four-bedroom log home. It sleeps up to six comfortably for $150, with a two-night minimum stay.

Camping

Twenty-five Forest Service campgrounds dot the Medicine Bow Mountains. Most of these are open June–October, but the season varies depending on snow conditions and budget constraints. A few of the campgrounds—those with no water or trash pickup—are free, but most cost $10 per night. Because of heavy use during the summer, you should arrive at the most popular sites early in the day. Four campgrounds along Hwy. 130 over the Snowy Range—Brooklyn Lake, North Fork, Ryan Park, and Sugarloaf—can be reserved ($9 fee) at 518/885-3639 or 877/444-6777, www.reserveusa.com. In addition to the official campgrounds, dispersed camping is permitted in most areas as long as you're off the main roads, although not along the crest of the Snowy Range. Check with local Forest Service offices for areas closed to dispersed camping. **Campfire talks** are given during the summer; visitor centers have the details.

Cabins

The Forest Service rents out several historic structures in the Medicine Bow mountains, but for all of these you'll need to bring bedding or sleeping bags, plus personal supplies. The **Bow River Ranger Station** (307/326-525, www.fs.fed.us/r2/mbr) is 15 miles south of Elk Mountain on Forest Road 101 and sleeps up to eight people for $80 per night. The cabin has two bedrooms and a kitchen, plus electricity and running water. A two-night minimum stay is required, and the cabin is available year-round. Make reservations ($9 fee) at 518/885-3639 or 877/444-6777, www.reserveusa.com.

Built in 1931, **Little Brooklyn Lake Guard Station** sits near the crest of the Snowy Range and can accommodate seven people for $40 per night. It's especially popular with cross-coun-try skiers in the winter but is available year-round. **Spruce Mountain Fire Lookout Tower** is seven miles west of Albany on a gravel road. No longer used for fire detection, the tower can sleep two people and is available mid-June–September for $40 per night. You'll need to bring water. Not far away is the **Keystone Ranger Station**, eight miles west of Albany. The cabin is available mid-November–April, with access primarily by cross-country skis or snowmobile. It can accommodate up to eight people for $120 per night and has electricity, running water, and a full bathroom, plus a large wood-burning stove and complete kitchen. Get details on these last three cabins at 307/745-2300 or 800/877-9965, www.fs.fed.us/r2/mbr. Make reservations ($9 fee) at 518/885-3639 or 877/444-6777, www.reserveusa.com.

Information

The Forest Service has detailed maps and helpful brochures at its Laramie office (2468 Jackson St., 307/745-2300 or 800/877-9965, www.fs.fed.us/r2/mbr). You'll also find Forest Service information centers on both sides of the Snowy Range along Hwy. 130. The **Centennial Visitor Center** (307/742-6023), one mile west of Centennial, is open 9 A.M.–4 P.M. daily July–August and is 9 A.M.–4 P.M. Saturday–Sunday in winter. **Brush Creek Visitor Center** (307/326-5562), 20 miles east of Saratoga, is open 8 A.M.–5 P.M. daily Memorial Day–September. Saturday evening interpretive programs, including full-moon walks, are offered at both the Centennial and Brush Creek visitor centers during the summer. Other full-moon walks are offered June–October at various sites around the forest; contact the Laramie Ranger District office (307/745-2300 or 800/877-9965, www.fs.fed.us/r2/mbr) for details.

North Platte Valley

SARATOGA

The friendly, laid-back town of Saratoga (pop. 1,700) is one of two towns in Wyoming—the other being Thermopolis—that center around hot springs. The name was borrowed from another well-known spa: Saratoga, New York. Wyoming's version of Saratoga straddles the North Platte River and putters along on a mixed economy. The Louisiana Pacific lumber mill has closed, but many cattle still graze in the beautiful river bottom country along the North Platte. Saratoga serves as a bedroom community for coal miners who work in Hanna but prefer the country around here. Others commute as far as Rawlins to work on scenic Hwy. 130, which is also a great place for cyclists and motorcyclists.

Like many places in Wyoming, Saratoga has long depended on various extractive industries for a livelihood and is only now discovering how attractive the land itself is. With mountains on both sides, "blue ribbon" trout fishing, river float trips, a free hot springs, a rich history, and lots of wildlife, it's certain that tourism will grow increasingly important. The town has become something of a retreat for executives and others in the rich-and-famous crowd who find that locals allow them a measure of privacy and anonymity. Head out to homes bordering Old Baldy Club Golf Course and you just might meet a former president, Supreme Court justice, or Hollywood star.

History

Indians called Saratoga Hot Springs "Place of the Magic Water"; it was a site of healing where various tribes could mingle without fear of attack. When whites arrived and first bathed here, the Indians noted that the waters boiled more violently than before, indicating an evil spirit. Thereafter most shunned the hot springs, but an 1874 smallpox epidemic forced some to return. Patients were soaked in the hot water in an attempt to boil out the disease and then dipped in the cold river water. When all the patients died, the Indians decided that whites had turned the waters from good medicine to bad medicine. The area was littered with the graves of smallpox victims. Thereafter, the Indians moved even farther from the hot springs.

In 1877, William H. Cadwell homesteaded near the springs, built a wooden bathhouse on the site, and offered hot baths, meals, and a place for travelers to stretch out for a night's sleep. People flocked here from all over the region—some even came from England to soak in the waters claimed to cure "rheumatism, eczema, paralysis, stomach trouble, kidney disease, nerves, and all forms of blood and skin disease." The copper-mining boom in the Sierra Madre brought prosperity as miners came to Saratoga to relax and freighters used it as a way station and supply center. A spur route from the Union Pacific line was built south to Saratoga in 1907 to haul ore from the mines, but when they closed shortly thereafter the town was forced to turn to other pursuits, becoming a ranching and logging center.

◖ Hobo Pool

The main attraction in Saratoga is Hobo Pool, on the east end of Walnut Avenue, where a sandy-bottomed outdoor pool is fed by the odorless 117–128°F water of Saratoga Hot Springs. It's open 24 hours a day and is fully accessible. No charge and no alcohol or naked bodies allowed. Heated changing rooms have showers. An adjacent swimming pool—not mineral water—is open daily June–August; $3 adults, $2 children. The mineral baths attract both old and young, with more adventurous types sprinting down to the adjacent North Platte River to cool off or to soak in smaller hot springs that feed directly into the river. All this hot water keeps stretches of the river open, and **Odd Fellows Park** at River Street and Main Avenue is a good place to find ducks and geese at all times of the year.

You can also use the luxurious spring-fed pool and hot tubs at **Saratoga Inn Resort** (601

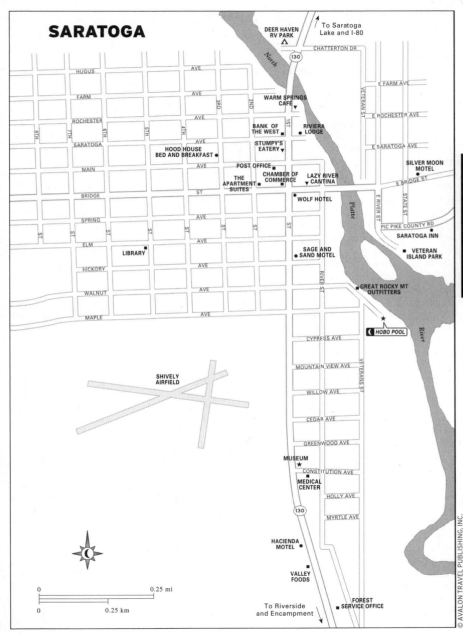

SARATOGA

To Saratoga
Lake and I-80

DEER HAVEN
RV PARK

CHATTERTON DR

North

130

HUGUS AVE

E FARM AVE

FARM AVE

VETERAN ST

3RD

2ND

WARM SPRINGS
CAFE

ROCHESTER AVE

E ROCHESTER AVE

BANK OF
THE WEST

RIVIERA
LODGE

1ST

SARATOGA AVE

E SARATOGA AVE

8TH

7TH

H19

5TH

4TH

HOOD HOUSE
BED AND BREAKFAST

STUMPY'S
EATERY

SILVER MOON
MOTEL

MAIN AVE

POST OFFICE

CHAMBER OF
COMMERCE

LAZY RIVER
CANTINA

E BRIDGE ST

THE
APARTMENT
SUITES

STATE ST

BRIDGE ST

E RIVER ST

Platte

WOLF HOTEL

PIC PIKE COUNTY RD

SPRING AVE

SARATOGA INN

ST

ST

ST

ST

ST

ST

ST

ELM AVE

SAGE AND
SAND MOTEL

VETERAN
ISLAND PARK

LIBRARY

HICKORY AVE

RIVER ST

WALNUT AVE

GREAT ROCKY MT
OUTFITTERS

MAPLE AVE

River

HOBO POOL

SHIVELY
AIRFIELD

CYPRESS AVE

MOUNTAIN VIEW AVE

VETERANS ST

WILLOW AVE

CEDAR AVE

GREENWOOD AVE

MUSEUM

CONSTITUTION AVE

MEDICAL
CENTER

HOLLY AVE

130

MYRTLE AVE

HACIENDA
MOTEL

VALLEY
FOODS

FOREST
SERVICE OFFICE

To Riverside
and Encampment

0   0.25 mi

0   0.25 km

MEDICINE BOW COUNTRY

© AVALON TRAVEL PUBLISHING, INC.

E. Pic Pike Rd., 307/326-5261 or 800/594-0178, www.saratogainn.com).

Other Sights

Saratoga's wonderful **Wolf Hotel** (101 E. Bridge St., 307/326-5525, www.wolfhotel.com) was built in 1893 by a German emigrant named Frederick Wolf. Today it's a National Historic Landmark. The old brick building with steeply gabled windows served for many years as a stage stop along the road to the mines of the Sierra Madre. Now restored with antique furnishings, the Wolf offers an enjoyable taste of the past. There are also accommodations and a restaurant and bar on the premises. **Saratoga Museum** (307/326-5511, www.saratoga-museum.org, open 1–5 P.M. Tues.–Sat. late May–early Sept. only, donation) is housed in the old railroad depot on the south end of town. Inside are items from the region's ranching, logging, and sheepherding past, along with a hands-on archaeology exhibit. Outside you'll find an old Union Pacific boxcar and caboose, along with a gazebo.

The **North Platte River** is one of the only rivers in the United States that flows predominantly north. From the Wyoming–Colorado border to the mouth of Sage Creek, 65 miles north, it is also the only "blue ribbon" trout fishery in southern Wyoming, with outstanding fishing for rainbow and brown trout. Studies have found more than 4,200 catchable wild trout averaging 13–17 inches per mile in the river. (See the *River Recreation* section.) You can find Indian petroglyphs along the bluff above the river just north of Saratoga. Fish are raised at the **Saratoga National Fish Hatchery** (307/326-5662) five miles north of town; open 8 A.M.–4 P.M. daily in the summer. Constructed in 1915, the hatchery produces fingerling cutthroat, rainbow, and brook trout for Wyoming rivers and lakes.

Entertainment and Events

Local restaurants provide most of the nightlife here (see *Food*). Otherwise, the **Rustic Bar** (124 E. Bridge St., 307/326-5965) is known for its "fighting" mountain lion mounts and has live music on summer weekends.

Start the year dressed in winter clothes for the **Saratoga Lake Ice Fishing Derby** each January. It's one of the top fishing derbies in the Lower 48. **Platte Valley Festival of Birds** attracts flocks of bird-watchers to local wetlands in early June. The three-day **Platte Valley Festival of the Arts** (www.plattevalleyarts.com) is held around the Fourth of July each year and includes a juried art show, plus a parade, box social, live music, and the obligatory fireworks.

In late August the **Wyoming Microbrewery Competition** attracts brewers from around the state. At the **Saratoga Bullfest and Taste of the West Cook-Off**—held the same weekend—you can watch the amateur rodeo, sample the chefs' treats, or two-step to live bands playing for the street dance.

Shopping

For such a small town, Saratoga has quite a few places to keep browsers happy. **Blackhawk Gallery** (100 N. 1st St., 307/326-5063, www.blackhawkgallery.com) sells quality Western paintings, bronzes, jewelry, and crafts. **Wyold Aspen Studio and Gallery** (102 W. Bridge St., 307/326-3404, www.wyoldaspenstudio.com) is a cooperative, with works by 10 local artists, including landscape paintings, jewelry, and handmade paper. **Opera House Gallery** (110 W. Bridge, 307/326-3939, www.operahousegallery.com) is a large space filled with works by more than 20 regional artisans.

Bill Naylor of **Peg Leg Mountain Furniture** (413 E. Bridge St., 307/326-5022) makes unique lodgepole items, from walking sticks to bunk beds, and **Whitney's Saddle Shop,** inside the Saratoga Inn, has quality Western gifts and clothing. Also check out **Hat Creek Trading Post** (107 W. Bridge St., 307/326-5755) with custom saddles, Western memorabilia, jewelry, and handwoven rugs.

Laura M (114 E. Bridge St., 307/326-8187 or 800/251-3505, www.lauram.com) is a Saratoga-based clothing designer with a line of stylish Western wear and furs for women. Most of the items are sewn on the premises from natural fibers and unique fabrics.

Cover to Cover Books and Things (112 E. Bridge St., 307/326-8745) has a good selection of books, along with fabrics for quilters.

River Recreation

The North Platte River forms a major focal point for visitors staying in Saratoga or Encampment. The trout fishing is excellent and the scenery grand; no wonder this is called the "Good Times Valley." Many travelers float downriver either on their own or with guides.

In Saratoga, **Stoney Creek Outfitters** (216 E. Walnut, 307/326-8750, www.fish-stoneycreek.com) sells quality Orvis fly-fishing gear and can fill you in on the latest fishing and floating conditions. All-day fishing trips run $425 for two people; overnight camping and fishing trips and boat shuttles are also available.

Hack's Tackle and Outfitters (407 N. 1st St., 307/326-9823, www.hackstackle.com) guides float trips for anglers (and bird-watchers) down the North Platte River and has a tackle shop. It also provides shuttles, raft and canoe rentals, and tours.

As the North Platte River enters Wyoming from Colorado, it drops into **North Gate Canyon,** a class III and IV stretch of whitewater with several hairy sets of rapids. Whitewater kayakers and rafters typically put in at Routt Access (just inside Colorado) and take out at Sixmile Campground, where the river broadens and becomes a gentler float. If you are a whitewater enthusiast, get here early because the water level drops after June. Check with the aforementioned companies for guided trips in May and June, or contact local Forest Service offices for river access information.

Accommodations

Built in 1893, the historic **Wolf Hotel** (101 E. Bridge St., 307/326-5525, www.wolfhotel.com) has a variety of lodging options, including a range of upstairs rooms (all nonsmoking), and all now with private baths. Basic rooms are $39–45 s or $47–52d; these are over the bar and can

© DON PITCHER

The Wolf Hotel in Saratoga is a National Historic Landmark.

MEDICINE BOW COUNTRY

get noisy when it is hopping. Two-room suites are $69 d, and a top-floor luxury suite includes a wet bar and room; $90 d or $110 for four people. Any of these choices offer a wonderful change from standard motel rooms.

The rooms are a bit old-fashioned, but you'll find clean and cozy accommodations at **Silver Moon Motel** (412 E. Bridge St., 307/326-5974), where rates are $41 s or $57 d. Full-kitchen units are $44 s or $64 d.

Riviera Lodge (303 N. 1st St., 307/326-5651) offers a riverside location with a variety of remodeled rooms. The smallest and oldest are $49 s or $55 d. Larger rooms (including some that are brand new) cost $50–65 s or $65–78 d, and suites with two beds and a deck over the river are $98 d or $113 for five guests. Wireless Internet is available in some rooms.

Hacienda Motel (1500 S. 1st St., 307/326-5751, $56 s or $66 d) is next to the grocery store on the south end of town. Some rooms contain kitchenettes.

Saratoga Inn Resort (601 E. Pic Pike Rd., 307/326-5261 or 800/594-0178, www.saratogainn.com) is the most ostentatious place in town. All rooms (some are miniscule) follow a Western theme, with rustic lodgepole furniture. The trophy room has a big central fireplace, overstuffed chairs, and Wi-Fi, and the central courtyard contains a large hot spring–fed pool and five soaking tubs, two of which are covered by tepees. The resort also features a nine-hole golf course, along with massage and spa treatments. Weekend rates for the guest rooms are $138 d; suites cost $178 d. Weekday rates are $20 lower.

B&Bs and Guesthouses

Hood House B&B (214 N. 3rd, 307/326-8901, www.hoodhousebnb.com, $85 s or $100 d) is a simple historic home with an enclosed porch and antique furnishings. The four guest rooms contain shared baths, a full breakfast is served, and kids are welcome.

❰ Apartment Suites (114 W. Bridge St., 307/329-7883, www.theapartmentsuites.com, $78 d or $87 for four) consists of two comfortable and homey downtown suites, each with two bedrooms, a kitchen, and living room, plus wireless Internet and a continental breakfast. Owner Cynthia Cannell is very accommodating.

River Cottages (216 E. Walnut St., 307/326-8750, www.fishstoneycreek.com) consists of three very nice Saratoga places: two houses with full kitchens for $100–125 d ($25 per person for additional guests) and a suite for $85 d. Hobo Pool hot springs is right next door.

The **Kingfisher House** (210 W. Saratoga Ave., 307/326-8217, www.kingfisherhouse.com, $65–90 d) is a furnished three-bedroom home in a quiet part of town. There's a full kitchen, big back porch, and barbecue grill.

Guest Ranches

Brush Creek Guest Ranch (307/327-5241 or 800/726-2499, www.brushcreekranch.com), 15 miles southeast of Saratoga, is a wonderful 6,000-acre cattle ranch that dates back almost a century. A maximum of 24 guests stay in the grand 6,500-square-foot main lodge or in comfortable modern cabins. The emphasis is on horseback riding, guided fly-fishing—it's an Orvis-endorsed lodge—hayrides, creekside barbecues, hiking, mountain-biking, and wintertime cross-country skiing. Guests can help move cattle between pastures or simply relax on the big front porch overlooking the flower-filled yard. Weekly rates are $2,550 for two people, all-inclusive; open year-round.

A-Bar-A Ranch (307/327-5454) also has a guest ranch (including a gorgeous riverside golf course) near Saratoga, but it's typically full all summer with a select clientele; call if you qualify.

Camping

Adjacent to a small lake 1.5 miles north of town, **Saratoga Lake Campground** (307/326-5629, $7 tents, $10 with electricity) has year-round campsites, but no trees or showers.

Just north of the Platte River bridge **Deer Haven RV Park** (706 N. 1st St., 307/326-8746, $20–25, open mid-May–Oct.) provides shady RV sites (no showers or tents). Some are right along the river.

Foote Recreation Area is a peaceful little spot along the North Platte River, with a couple of cottonwood-shaded free campsites, singing birds, and an outhouse. It's five miles north of Saratoga; follow the small sign to the river. Other access points are dotted along the river; get a map showing all of them from the chamber of commerce.

Food

Get savory breakfasts (including eggs Benedict or Belgian waffles) along with espresso, tasty croissant sandwiches, and 32 flavors of homemade ice cream at **Lollypops** (107 E. Bridge St., 307/326-5020).

Hang out with locals at **Donut Ranch Bakery** (307/326-8932) on West Bridge Street, with big and filling breakfasts, including the ranch burritos. Get the half size to save your waistline. Lots of food for your money, but it sometimes runs out if you get there late. Closed Sundays.

The historic ◖ **Wolf Hotel** (101 E. Bridge St., 307/326-5525, www.wolfhotel.com) is known for prime rib and steaks, but it also delivers more unusual fare such as king crab legs or veggie kabobs. Entrées run $16–23. There's a small salad bar, too. The Wolf is open Monday–Saturday for lunch and dinner (no breakfast). The bar is the local hangout, with periodic live country-and-western music.

For inexpensive pizzas, burgers, salads, and sandwiches, head to **Stumpy's Eatery** (218 N. 1st St., 307/326-8132).

Lazy River Cantina (110 E. Bridge Ave., 307/326-8472) has Mexican food—including chimichangas—pizzas, chicken-fried steaks, and a bar with darts and TV sports. Its 45-ounce Terminator margarita ($12) does a good job of finishing you off. Live music in the bar throughout the summer.

Best view in town? Try a meal at **Warm Springs Cafe** (4015 1st St., 307/326-5046), a popular family dining place with big windows and outside tables on a deck beside the North Platte River. The menu isn't extensive, but it isn't costly either; ranging from $3 hot dogs to $9 fried-chicken dinners and $10 steak sandwiches. Open breakfast, lunch, and dinner.

Best outside-town view? **Whistle Pig Saloon** (307/326-5744) is one mile south of town, with meals three times a day, big windows facing the Snowy Range, and karaoke and occasional country bands. And look out for the whistle pigs (ground squirrels) on nearby roads.

Get groceries at **Valley Foods** (307/326-5336) on the south end of town, where the deli has baked goods and the walls are lined with trophy mounts.

Information and Services

The **Saratoga Chamber of Commerce** (115 W. Bridge St., 307/326-8855 or 866/828-8855, www.saratogachamber.info) is open 9 A.M.–5 P.M. Monday–Friday.

The Forest Service's **Saratoga Ranger Station** (307/326-5258) faces the mountains on the south edge of town.

The **Saratoga Library** (503 W. Elm St., 307/326-8209) has free Internet. Find the **post office** (307/326-5611) at 105 Main Avenue, and wash clothes at **Carbon County Coin Op** (105 E. Walnut, 307/326-5384). **Corbett Medical Clinic** (1208 S. River St., 307/326-8381) has a doctor on staff.

A real surprise in Saratoga is the airport, with an 8,400-foot runway. No scheduled service, but **Saratoga Aviation** (307/326-8344) has charter flights. In the summer and fall (especially on the weekend after Labor Day), aircraft executives and other wealthy enthusiasts—alias "the conquistadors"—fly here for a rendezvous at the A-Bar-A Ranch. The tarmac is jammed with corporate jets, turning Shively Field into the third-busiest jetport in Wyoming.

ENCAMPMENT AND RIVERSIDE

The quaint ranching and tourism town of Encampment (pop. 400) lies in the gorgeous foothills of the Sierra Madre, which were once home to thousands of copper miners. Today the area abounds with ghost towns from that era. Encampment's twin settlement of Riverside (pop. 60) lies just one mile to the east. This area is popular with hunters who come for deer, antelope, and elk, for photographers who enjoy the colorful autumn leaves, and for anglers who cast about for trout. The community is decidedly conservative: Bumper stickers proclaim, "If you're out of work and hungry eat an environmentalist," and each fall finds the back roads crowded with gun-racked pickup trucks and silent, orange-capped hunters scanning the horizon for bucks. Back in town, the smoky bars fill at night with tales of the chase and chubby old men winking at the waitresses over their Budweisers.

History

Encampment takes its name from the Grand Encampment of French Canadian trappers who rendezvoused along the Encampment River in 1838. Miners had long suspected that the Sierra Madre contained a wealth of minerals, but the first significant gold strike was not made until 1896. Another mineral, however, transformed the region. Encampment itself began in 1897, when British sheepherder Ed Haggerty discovered a rich vein of copper in the Sierra Madre to the west. The mine he developed was named Rudefeha, a word concocted from the letters of the various partners' names—J. M. *Ru*msey, Robert *De*al, George *Fe*rris, and Ed *Ha*ggerty. In the first three months of digging, miners recovered $300,000 worth of copper ore. Haggerty took his 10 percent share and returned to England.

As the wealth of the discovery became known, Chicago promoter and newspaperman Willis George Emerson bought the mine and built a 16-mile-long aerial tram to haul the ore over the 10,600-foot Continental Divide and then down to the Boston–Wyoming Smelter at Encampment (elevation 7,200 feet). The tram consisted of 304 wooden towers with buckets supported on thick steel cables. Each bucket held 700 pounds of ore and moved at four miles per hour. The tram could carry almost 1,000 tons of ore per day and was powered by water flowing through a four-foot wooden pipeline. Thousands of men flocked to the mines, creating almost overnight the settlements of Battle, Copperton, Dillon, Elwood, Halfway House,

and Rambler. A railroad was completed from the smelter to the main Union Pacific line at Walcott in 1905, and by 1908 more than 23 million pounds of copper had been produced.

The main regional settlement was Encampment, situated at the foot of the mountains and numbering 1,500 rough and hardened souls at its peak. By 1900, the town featured three general stores, two lodging houses, two hotels, two restaurants, and three lumber yards, along with nine saloons and two houses of prostitution. Nearby Riverside served as a shipping center for the mines. (Originally known as Dogget, the name was changed to Riverside after folks began calling it Dog Town.) Another 1,500 people lived in the other mining towns. The mining boom came to an abrupt halt after two disastrous fires destroyed the concentrating mill, the smelter, the boiler room, and the powerhouse. Combined with falling copper prices, it forced the company into bankruptcy. Soon, all sorts of illegal actions surfaced, including overcapitalization and fraudulent stock sales.

All but a few diehards left the area, and what had once been the town of Grand Encampment was eventually reduced to simply Encampment. Logging, first for ties and mine supports and later for lumber, became an important part of the economy, but the last mill closed in the 1990s, and many locals now commute to work in the Sinclair refinery or Hanna coal mines. Tourism is becoming increasingly important in the area, and retirees are attracted to the slow pace, moderate prices, and beautiful setting.

◖ Grand Encampment Museum

On the south side of Encampment at 6th and Barnett streets, the excellent Grand Encampment Museum (307/327-5558, free) includes items from the early-1900s mining camps that filled the Sierra Madre. Displayed here are historic photographs and clothing, Indian artifacts, Forest Service memorabilia, and even a folding bathtub from the 1890s. Teddy the (stuffed) dog greets visitors. Most interesting of all are the 14 historic buildings set up as a frontier town with wooden boardwalks. These include a tie-hack cabin, a bakery, a lookout tower, and a stage

© DON PITCHER

MEDICINE BOW COUNTRY

Grand Encampment Museum, Encampment

station. The transportation barn even houses Noah's Ark, although, alas, it's probably not the original one. Oddest of all is a two-story outhouse modeled after one used in the mining ghost town of Dillon. The lower level was used in summer, with the upper floor reserved for wintertime when the snows drifted many feet deep. The Australian term for privies (long drop) is especially fitting here! Also at the museum are parts of the 16-mile-long aerial tramway that brought ore from the Rudefeha mine.

This museum is open 10 A.M.–5 P.M. Monday–Saturday and 1–5 P.M. Sunday Memorial Day–Labor Day. The rest of the year, you can see the museum by special appointment only. Retired locals provide informative tours in July and August, and you can even buy bars of homemade soap inside the main building. In mid-July the museum has living-history demonstrations and music.

At the museum, pick up a copy of the local **walking-tour** brochure, which describes some of the town's buildings. Be sure to also see the pretty white **Presbyterian Church** at 9th and Rankin.

Other Sights

For a slice of country life, head to the erroneously named **Riverside Garage,** which is not a garage but a great old country store with a few groceries, hardware, car parts, and even a box of "spotted owl helper" to amuse your redneck friends. It's hard to miss this red and yellow building in Riverside. The nearby **town park** is a great place for picnic lunches amid tall cottonwoods.

A 0.75-mile trail leads to the **Indian Bathtubs,** natural geologic formations that collect rainwater. Indian hunters used them for bathing. Get there by heading one mile west of Riverside on Hwy. 230. Turn right onto Blackhall Road and follow it one mile to the trailhead.

Events

In early February, the **Sierra Madre Winter Carnival** includes a variety of skiing contests, dances, and lots of other activities.

One of the most popular regional events is the **Woodchoppers Jamboree and Rodeo** (307/326-8855) at Encampment the third full weekend of June. Begun in 1961, this is the state's largest loggers' show, including tree-felling, chainsaw log–bucking, hand-sawing, pole-throwing, and ax-throwing contests. Other activities include a fun amateur rodeo, a parade, a barbecue, and a melodrama featuring "dance hall girls." The town erupts with lots of drunken and rowdy behavior at night, befitting such a festival. (And guess who sponsors the jamboree? Budweiser.)

Grand Encampment Cowboy Gathering is a popular cowboy music and poetry event in mid-July. In late August, the **Sierra Madre Muzzleloaders Mountain-Man Rendezvous** brings mountain men and women to Encampment.

Accommodations

Although popular with visitors all year, this area is doubly so during the fall hunting season; book ahead if you're coming through at that time, and bring your bright orange clothes to keep from getting shot. In Encampment, stay at **Vacher's Bighorn Lodge** (508 McCaffrey, 307/327-5110, $47–53 d) with fridges and microwaves and some kitchenette units.

Lazy Acres Campground and Motel in Riverside (307/327-5968, www.wyomingcarboncounty.com/lazy.htm) has motel units for $32 s or $36–39 d and a cute little cabin (shared bath) for $27 d. Open mid-May–October.

Bear Trap Cafe and Cabins (307/327-5277, $35 s or $40–45 d) in Riverside has rustic cabins (two with kitchenettes) and retro modular motel rooms.

More Riverside rusticity can be found at **Riverside Cabins** (307/327-5361), where most cabins include kitchenettes and private baths but no phones or TVs. Rates start at $40 d for a basic cabin up to $86 for a two-bedroom unit that sleeps six and has a full kitchen and two baths. Open May–October. Also in Riverside, **Cottonwood Cabins** (307/327-5151, $60–105 d) has three modern cabins with full kitchens; open May–October.

Bed-and-Breakfasts

Twelve miles south of Encampment is **Platt's Rustic Mountain Lodge B&B** (307/327-5539, www.plattoutfitting.com), an 8,000-acre ranch

where a spacious log lodge offers dramatic vistas of the Sierra Madre Range. The lodge also offers horseback trail rides, fishing, pack trips, photo safaris, cross-country skiing, snowmobiling, and incongruously, both hunting and nature retreats! Lodging rates are $50 s or $75 d, including a full breakfast. Also here is a newer cabin with a kitchen and two bedrooms for more seclusion. It sleeps four and costs $1,275 for five days. Kids are welcome.

Owned by the nationally known wildlife artist R. G. Finney, **Spirit West River Lodge B&B** (307/327-5753 or 888/289-8321, www.spiritwestriverlodge.com, $85 d) is a rambling log riverfront lodge with four guest rooms, all with private baths and access to the deck. Many of the furnishings were handcrafted, and a big country breakfast is served each morning. No kids under 12.

Camping

The BLM's **Encampment River Campground** ($7, open June–Oct.) is three miles from town, but the road may be inaccessible after recent rains. Head west from Encampment and turn south on Road 353 (Hog Park Road). Ask locally for directions to two free BLM campgrounds: Bennett Peak and Corral Creek.

The nearest Forest Service campsite ($10, open late May–Oct.) is **Bottle Creek Campground**, seven miles southwest of town on Hwy. 70. Five more campgrounds lie west of here in the Sierra Madre.

In Riverside, **Lazy Acres Campground and Motel** (307/327-5968, www.wyomingcarboncounty.com/lazy.htm, $16 tents, $21 RVs) has pleasant shady tent sites; open mid-May–October.

Food

Encampment's **Pine Lodge Saloon** (518 McCaffrey, 307/327-5203) has a pool table and three meals a day, with a patio for al fresco dining. Riverside's **Bear Trap Cafe** (307/327-5277) serves chicken-fried steak, burgers, and other Wyoming grub, but be sure to save room for the coconut cream pie. The bar has Guinness on draft and a pool table.

Information and Services

Get local details at a small **information center** (307/327-5600) at the junction of Highways 70 and 230. The hours are astoundingly long: 6 A.M.–7 P.M. daily June–October and 9 A.M.–5 P.M. Thursday–Monday the rest of the year.

Encampment's **city hall** is in the historic Opera House, a wooden building with a bell tower that looks like a lighthouse. The **Encampment Library** (202 Rankin Ave., 307/327-5775) is on the east end of town, and the **post office** (307/327-5747) sits on the corner of 6th and McCaffrey streets.

Sierra Madre and Vicinity

The historic Sierra Madre—a finger from the Medicine Bow Range that stretches south into Colorado—cover a small section of Wyoming. This is one of the lesser-known parts of the state. Worth a visit are the many mining ghost towns and historic mine sites, and hikers will find many miles of wilderness trails. The highest mountain in the range is 11,004-foot Bridger Peak, named for mountain man Jim Bridger. Before heading out, get maps and camping and hiking information from the Forest Service's **Hayden Ranger Station** (204 W. 9th in Encampment, 307/327-5481, www.fs.fed.us/r2/mbr). Also ask for the auto-tour brochure.

SIGHTS

The paved **Battle Highway** (Hwy. 70) crosses the Sierra Madre from Encampment on the east to Baggs on the west, a distance of 57 miles. The smooth, wide-shouldered road (perfect for bikes) is extraordinarily scenic, especially in the fall when the aspens turn golden. Lodgepole pines are the dominant trees at higher elevations. During the winter and spring, generally November–mid-June, Hwy. 70 is closed at the forest boundary, although snowmobilers and skiers may continue up the road. Approximately 10 miles west of Encampment the road reaches the Continental Divide at 9,916-foot Battle Pass. This is the location of **Battle,** one of many ghost towns capping the Sierra Madre. Battle is named for an 1841 fight between Indians and whites that took place near here.

A 4WD road good for mountain bikes heads north from the east side of the pass to the Bridger Peak summit and then down the western side to the Ferris-Haggerty mine site at the ghost town of **Rudefeha,** where remains of the tramway towers are still visible. One mile to the west you'll find the remains of **Dillon,** established after the company town of Rudefeha banned saloons; the saloon owners simply moved a short distance away and started anew, and in no time at all Dillon was the largest town in the Sierra Madre. Many buildings remain here, hidden in the trees.

Two miles west of the Continental Divide on Hwy. 70 is a turnout overlooking pretty Battle Lake and a monument to **Thomas A. Edison.** While vacationing here in 1878, Edison was pondering what substance to use as a filament for incandescent lights. One night he threw a broken bamboo fishing pole in the fire and was intrigued by the way the frayed pieces glowed. Carbonized bamboo would make a fine nonconducting filament for his bulbs. This tale has been passed down as fact through the years, but in reality Edison didn't come up with the idea until one year later. Maybe he remembered the old fly rod at that time.

The town of **Rambler** once stood along the lake shore, with the Doane–Rambler copper mine nearby. The mine operated from 1879 to 1902, producing one-half million tons of copper. Another six miles west are a few remains from the settlement of **Copperton.**

Aspen Alley

The western slopes of the Sierra Madre are carpeted with extensive stands of quaking aspen trees that came up after fires swept through this region during the mining era. These reach for many miles along Hwy. 70. A favorite of photographers is Aspen Alley, a 0.5-mile stretch of fabulously flamboyant fall foliage. Get here by turning north onto Deep Creek Road (Forest Road 801). The colors generally peak in late September, but call the Encampment Forest Service office (307/327-5481) for current conditions. Adventurous souls will enjoy the 50-mile drive north from Aspen Alley to Rawlins. Camping is available at the no-longer-maintained Sandstone camping area, approximately four miles up the road.

Once the gravel road emerges from the national forest, the land broadens into sage and grass before once again climbing over the Continental Divide. Stop here on a fall night and listen to the quiet. A few clouds hang on the western horizon, and a few pickups churn clouds of dust up the road—en route to either hunting grounds or a bar. The night lies over the land like a blackened canvas splattered with stars. There aren't many places like this anymore.

RECREATION
Huston Park Wilderness
The 30,726-acre Huston Park Wilderness straddles the Continental Divide just south of Battle Pass. It contains spruce, fir, aspen, and lodgepole forests, as well as open alpine country reaching to 10,500 feet. **Continental Divide National Scenic Trail** provides an enjoyable high-elevation trek along the crest of the mountains. The trail stretches 3,100 miles from Canada to Mexico, and 16 miles of it pass through this wilderness area. The route is marked with rock cairns and blazed trees. Trailheads are one mile south of the Battle townsite and 2.5 miles west of Hog Park Reservoir.

The nine-mile-long **Baby Lake Trail** is an enjoyable overnight trip through high meadows and along a mountain creek. Take in excellent vistas of the Snake River Valley from the Continental Divide. The trail is accessible from Hwy. 70 on both ends, but for the easiest hiking, start from a trailhead at the end of a two-mile gravel road just south of Battle Pass.

From here, the trail drops 2,600 feet in elevation to a second trailhead off Forest Road 811 (near Lost Creek Campground).

North Fork Encampment Trail takes you two miles up North Fork Creek to Green Mountain Falls. Get to the trailhead by driving west from Encampment to Bottle Creek Campground and then south on Forest Road 550 for 1.5 miles. This is one of the few waterfalls in the area (but it typically dries up after mid-June).

Encampment River Wilderness
At just 10,400 acres, Encampment River Wilderness is one of the smallest and least-visited wilderness areas in Wyoming. The centerpiece is the Encampment River, with its narrow canyon, rushing rapids, quiet pools, and fine fishing. Despite the Encampment's current wilderness status, much of this land was logged at the turn of the 20th century to supply railroad ties and mine timbers for the Union Pacific Railroad. Old cabins and mines offer endless opportunities to explore. The well-maintained **Encampment River Trail** is a 15-mile-long path that follows this scenic river through the heart of the wilderness. Roads provide access from either end, so the trail is easier to hike if you can shuttle a second vehicle to the other end. Start from a trailhead near the BLM's Encampment River Campground, three miles south of Encampment. The trail follows the river upstream, beginning in low-elevation sage-and-grass country and gradually climbing into dense lodgepole and spruce forests. The first five miles are considerably easier hiking than higher up, where the canyon narrows and becomes more rugged. The trail ends at Hog Park, near the Colorado state line.

Another off-the-beaten-path sight near the Encampment River Wilderness is an old abandoned fire tower at **Blackhall Mountain,** approximately 15 miles south of Riverside on Forest Road 409. The last several miles are narrow but passable. From the top are long vistas into the mountains of Wyoming and Colorado.

Winter Recreation
During winter the Forest Service maintains

many groomed miles of cross-country ski trails around the Bottle Creek Campground 5.5 miles west of Encampment and along the South Brush Creek (near the visitor center), 20 miles east of Saratoga. Call 307/326-5258 for access details. Many forest roads in the Sierra Madre are used extensively by snowmobilers, with 26 miles of groomed trails and an equal amount of ungroomed trails. Contact Forest Service offices in Encampment and Saratoga for details.

CAMPING AND CABINS

The Forest Service has six campgrounds ($7–10, open June–Oct.) in the Sierra Madre, all of which are along Hwy. 70, the main road across the mountains. These campgrounds are not nearly as crowded as those in the Snowy Range to the east.

Built in 1934, the Forest Service's **Jack Creek Guard Station** is a delightful one-room log cabin in the mountains northwest of Encampment. Facilities are rustic: two sets of bunk beds (bring sleeping bags), wood or propane heat, and propane lights. The cabin costs $40 per night and sleeps four. Nearby is the impressive **Jack Creek Crew Quarters,** a modern five-bedroom facility with space for 15 folks at $150 per night. Both buildings are along Forest Road 452 approximately 25 miles west of Saratoga. Get additional information on both of these at 307/326-525, www.fs.fed.us/r2/mbr. Make reservations ($9 fee) for both places at 518/885-3639 or 877/444-6777, www.reserveusa.com.

LITTLE SNAKE RIVER VALLEY

One of the most isolated parts of Wyoming, the Little Snake River Valley lies right on the Colorado border, with the desolate Red Desert to the west and the Sierra Madre to the east. Irrigated farmland lines Savery Creek, and solid old log cabins dot the countryside, but in the last few years this once-peaceful valley has come alive with oil and gas developments. The valley contains three small—but fast-growing—towns: Savery, Dixon, and Baggs.

Savery

Housed in an old grade school, Savery's **Little Snake River Museum** (307/383-7262, www.lsrvmuseum.homestead.com/homepage.htm, open 11 A.M.–5 P.M. daily late May–late Oct.) provides a sampling of the area's rich history, including the dugout canoe of mountain man Jim Baker and many other historical items. A distinctive two-story log blockhouse built by Baker stands out front; he and his wife are buried one mile west of town. Also on the museum grounds are a one-room schoolhouse from the Brown's Hill area and the Strobridge house, a grand two-story log structure that is more than a century old.

Not far from town is **Savery Creek Thoroughbred Ranch** (307/383-7840, www.savery-creek.com), a riding ranch for those who are serious about horses, with training in both English and Western riding. Beautiful country surrounds the ranch, which offers unpretentious lodging. The three guest rooms have shared or private baths; also available for lodging are two covered wagons. The ranch hosts only six people at a time and is open May–September. Rates are $290–355 daily for two people with a three-night minimum. This includes lodging, meals, and riding.

Ladder Ranch (307/383-2418, www.ladder-ranch.com) has accommodations and activities on a large ranch straddling the Wyoming–Colorado border. The big draws here are trout fishing and riding the range, and a variety of angler/wrangler packages are available, starting at $100/day per person including lodging, three meals, and fishing. Lodging only in a modern home is $120 d. A three-night minimum stay is required.

The **Savery Store** (307/383-2711) has groceries, supplies, and a campground ($25 RVs, $15 tents).

Dixon

Four miles west of Savery and seven miles east of Baggs, the small agricultural settlement of Dixon holds the **Little Snake River Valley Rodeo** each July. It also hosts a **Cutting Horse**

Contest, where cowboys work specially trained horses to move cattle.

Built in 1911, the classic **Dixon Club Bar** (307/383-7722) is a fun place to explore; its walls are lined with old junk and antiques. Free camping is available at **Dixon Town Park** along Main Street; no hookups or showers.

Baggs

Named for rancher George Baggs and his wife, Maggie, Baggs's isolated location and proximity to the state line made it a gathering place for outlaws. In 1900, after a $32,000 bank robbery in Winnemucca, Nevada, Butch Cassidy helped build a cabin here to serve as a refuge for his gang. The cabin, now called the **Gaddis-Matthews House,** still stands in the center of town. Another noteworthy building is the **Bank Club Bar,** listed on the National Historic Register. Built as a bank, it later became a bar. Find it off the main drag on North and Miles.

Jim Beall of **Wild Horse Tours** (307/383-6865 or 866/753-8501, www.wildhorse-tours.com) offers 4WD or horseback tours into the Sand Wash or Horse Shoe Bend area in search of the many wild horses found here.

Stay at **Drifters Inn** (307/383-2015, $60 d), where the rooms have microwaves and fridges, or pitch tents or park RVs (no hookups or showers) for free at **Baggs Park** on Hunt Street.

Northwest of Baggs is a unique area of badlands known as **Adobe Town.** The colorful terrain is fascinating, but it's easy to get lost in the maze of canyons, basins, ledges, and alcoves. Contact the Rawlins BLM office (307/328-4200, www.wy.blm.gov) for access information.

Rawlins and Vicinity

The small city of Rawlins (pop. 8,500) sits right in the center of southern Wyoming. To the east and south lie mountain ranges and rich grazing land; to the west are the Great Divide Basin and a vast expanse of desert country. During the late 1970s and early '80s, Rawlins was a hub of development as the "Oil Patch" blossomed and energy companies pumped petrodollars into the economy. But, as in so many other Wyoming towns, the inevitable bust that followed was traumatic.

As of 2006, another oil and gas boom was in full swing, creating a new Rawlins very different from those bad old days. Downtown stores that sat abandoned for two decades are now filled, and the town is clearly growing at the margins, creating the now-standard mix of fast food, discount megamarts, gas stations, and chain motels. The only question is how long these new happy days will continue before the next bust.

Rawlins is named for General John A. Rawlins, secretary of war under President Grant. In 1867, as the railroad route was being surveyed westward, the crew of General Grenville Dodge met up with soldiers under Rawlins's command. When they discovered a clear, alkali-free spring at the base of a hill, Rawlins remarked, "If anything is ever named after me, I hope it will be a spring of water." Dodge immediately decided to name this Rawlins Spring. When a division point on the Union Pacific was established here in 1868, the town was also named Rawlins Spring. Its name was later shortened to Rawlins.

In 1886, the Wyoming Legislature appropriated $100,000 for a state penitentiary in Rawlins. Two years later, construction began with enormous slabs of sandstone cut and hauled by wagon from a quarry south of town. Because of inadequate funding the new prison was not completed and occupied until December 1901, 13 years after it was begun. By that time the town had grown, and what had been a relatively remote location was now in central Rawlins. For the next eight decades this would be Wyoming's only state prison, housing its most hardened criminals. The prison

MEDICINE BOW COUNTRY

RAWLINS

TOM HORN

The story of the murderer Tom Horn will always remain something of a mystery. Through the years, Horn worked as a stage driver, an army scout, a deputy sheriff, a Pinkerton investigator, and a detective for the Wyoming Stock Growers Association. When J. M. Carey (later Wyoming governor and senator) discovered that Tom Horn was out to murder – rather than bring in for trial – accused rustlers, he had Horn fired from the association. Other cattle barons quickly moved to hire him, however, paying $500 for each man killed. Horn is generally blamed for ambushing and assassinating two ranchers (and suspected rustlers) in the Laramie Mountains in 1895, along with two others in Brown's Park, Colorado, five years later.

Wherever Horn went, a trail of dead men was left behind, but nobody was able to pin the blame on him until 1901, when a 14-year-old boy was shot in the back and killed in the Laramie Mountains. It was a case of mistaken identity because the boy had been wearing his father's hat and clothes. The older man was later shot from ambush but survived. Horn was implicated in the boy's slaying by his trademark: a small stone placed under the victim's head.

Horn would probably have escaped even this heinous crime had he not bragged about it. (The confession would never hold up in court today; Deputy U.S. Marshal Joe LeFors had plied Horn with liquor and had a court stenographer listen through a crack in the door as he boasted of the slaying.) Horn had little money himself, but his supporters spent $100,000 in his defense. They hired the finest legal counsel, John W. Lacey, who had never lost any of his 50 previous murder trials (and who, not coincidentally, also represented the Wyoming Stock Growers Association and the Union Pacific Railroad).

Despite this, Horn was adjudged guilty and sentenced to hang. Horn's supporters tried to free him with a dynamite blast, and he later did briefly escape from jail, but on November 20, 1903, Horn was hanged before a large crowd at the corner of Pioneer and 19th avenues in Cheyenne. Until the last minute, everyone expected a pardon, and many wealthy cattlemen feared what Horn might reveal. His last words were to his friend T. Joe Cahill: "Joe, they tell me you are married now. I hope you're doing well. Treat her right."

was finally abandoned in 1981, when the inmates were transferred to a new facility south of Rawlins.

◖ FRONTIER PRISON

Rawlins's main attraction is the Frontier Prison (5th and Walnut, 307/324-4422, www.wyomingfrontierprison.com), first opened in 1901 and in use until 1981; hence the prison motto: "No visitors locked inside since 1981." Actually, this was a state prison for all of its existence, but locals prefer to call it a frontier prison because construction began while Wyoming was still a territory. The prison is open 8:30 A.M.–5:30 P.M. daily late May–early September, with guided hourly tours at half past the hour. Winter tours are less frequent, but someone is generally here on weekdays. These excellent, hour-long tours cost $6 adults, $5 seniors or kids (children under

six free), and $25 families. Be sure to bring a sweater or coat with you because the stone prison is chilly even in midsummer. For a scarier visit, ask about the nighttime flashlight tours offered some summer evenings ($7) and on Halloween. Night tours are by reservation only and not recommended for young children.

The imposing turret towers and stonework of the prison's exterior give it the oppressive appearance of a medieval castle. Inside, conditions for the inmates were almost as primitive, bordering on ghastly. There was no plumbing or electricity for the first 15 years, and it wasn't until 1978 that hot water was installed in one block of cells. A special dungeon house was built for uncooperative inmates, and beatings were common in the early years. Ten prisoners were hanged—one by fellow inmates—and another five were executed in the gas chamber in Rawlins, the last in 1965. The gallows were a uniquely gruesome device in which the victim actually hanged himself through an elaborate mechanism by which his weight displaced a water counterbalance, thus releasing a trapdoor and leaving him hanging by a noose. It was built to hang notorious cattle detective and murderer Tom Horn in 1903 and moved into the prison later (Horn was never in this prison). The instrument did not always work; one man had to be strangled by the "humane" guards when he didn't die fast enough. Science marches onward: Wyoming's death-row inmates now face lethal injection instead.

The old prison was the scene of several escape attempts, including one in which four death-row inmates tunneled out as far as the west wall before being caught. The dirt was secreted away in ceiling panels, where it's still visible. Two other breakouts were successful—one involved 28 men—although nearly all of the escapees were caught or killed in the surrounding community. In later years the penitentiary housed 500 prisoners and employed 100 guards and other workers.

In 1987, the B movie *Prison* was filmed on location here with locals as extras. Parts of the movie set are still visible, and some of the prison floors are still red from the fake blood. If you missed it in the theaters, don't despair; this is one of those godawful flicks that will eventually make it to the 4 A.M. slot on some obscure cable TV station. Or, you can buy a copy in the Frontier Prison gift shop.

The Lone Bandit

The most famous inmate to spend time here was William Carlisle, the "gentleman train robber." In three Union Pacific train robberies in Wyoming, Carlisle netted barely $1,000. He never robbed female passengers, never shot or injured anyone, and was reported to have bought gifts for children with the loot. After the third robbery, he was caught and sentenced to life in prison. Carlisle was sent to Rawlins in 1916 but escaped in a shirt crate three years later. In another train robbery Carlisle was shot and wounded but still managed to remain free

for two weeks before a posse caught up with him. The last conviction landed him another life sentence, but the governor pardoned Carlisle in 1936. He walked out a changed man and eventually became a respected Laramie motel owner and author of a book about his life, *The Lone Bandit*. Carlisle died in 1964.

The Sweet Smell of Sagebrush

A section of the old prison serves double duty as the **Wyoming Peace Officers Museum,** with memorials, artifacts, and badges. Also here are photos and descriptions of various inmates, along with a souvenir shop selling postcards, books, and other items. One book well worth a look is *The Sweet Smell of Sagebrush.* This is a collection of stories by William Stanley Hudson, a man who served four separate sentences here for such crimes as horse stealing and passing stolen checks. It offers not only a glimpse of early-1900s prison life but also a fascinating account of criminal logic. The title comes from his release from prison after serving his first sentence:

i thought little of those things that august day as i walked out from the damp prison air into the glorious sunshine of this enchanted land. i felt only a desire to get away somewhere out of sight. after walking towards the buisness part of town a short way, i turned and went straight out of town untill i reached the high sagebrush. the smell of the sage was that day sweeter to me than a breath from a bed of rarest flowers. for an hour i was content to sit and breathe the pure mountain air and enjoy the warm sunshine.

Hudson's fate is unknown. After release from his fourth incarceration in 1921, he disappeared. Perhaps he was a reformed man. Or perhaps he learned enough to avoid getting caught again.

CARBON COUNTY MUSEUM

Housed in an old Mormon church at 9th and Walnut streets, the Carbon County Museum

BIG NOSE GEORGE PARROT

George Manuse, better known as Big Nose George Parrot, was a rustler from the Powder River country who joined Dutch Charley Burris and Frank James (of the James Gang) on an 1878 robbery attempt. The trio tried to derail a Union Pacific train by prying up a piece of track and waiting in ambush. Unfortunately for the outlaws, an alert Union Pacific employee discovered the missing rail before the train arrived, and a manhunt ensued. The posse tracked the gang into Rattlesnake Canyon and then stopped in a freshly deserted camp. As a deputy sheriff bent over to check the coals, he commented, "They're hot as hell." Immediately, a voice shouted from behind the bushes, "We'll show you how hot hell is." Two deputies were shot dead, and the three robbers escaped.

After the murders, the trio split up. Dutch Charlie was caught the following year and sent back via train to Carbon, Wyoming, for trial. But the trial never came; a group of masked men pulled him from the train and threw a noose around his neck. When Dutch Charlie was asked if he had any last words, the widow of one of the deputies yelled out, "No, the son-of-a-bitch has nothing to say!" and booted the barrel from under his feet. The newspaper noted, "the train was delayed only thirteen minutes by the operation."

In 1880, the law finally caught up with Big Nose George in Montana, and he too was hauled back to Rawlins in shackles. When the train pulled into town, 15 armed men forced the sheriff to release the prisoner to them and hauled him off to be hanged. Big Nose George managed to avoid his fate this time by reminding his would-be lynchers that "dead men tell no tales," but he confessed to and was convicted of the murders the following spring and was sentenced to hang. In an escape attempt shortly after the trial, George cracked the skull of a guard with his shackles before finally being subdued. When word of the escape attempt spread through Rawlins, a mob of masked men broke into the jail. Big Nose George was hauled out and lynched in the street, although it took two tries – the rope was too long the first time. The Rawlins jail register notes that Big Nose George Parrot "Went to join the angels via hempen cord on telegraph pole front of Fred Wolf's saloon."

(307/328-2740, www.carboncountymuseum.org, free) is open 10 A.M.–6 P.M. Tuesday–Friday and 1–5 P.M. Saturday May–September, and 1–5 P.M. Tuesday–Saturday the rest of the year. The museum is a mixed bag, containing Oregon Trail and Indian relics, historic photos, an Essex Motors race car from 1922, a 1920 hook-and-ladder truck, and various stage-station and Civil War artifacts. One case even contains 400-year-old Spanish artifacts discovered in a cave near Hanna. Easily the strangest object in the museum is a pair of two-tone shoes made from the skin of Big Nose George Parrot, a train robber and murderer. These were crafted by Dr. John E. Osborne, who also decided to saw open George's skull to see if the brains of desperadoes differed from those of common men. The skullcap became an ashtray now on exhibit at the Union Pacific Railroad Museum in Omaha, but the bottom of the skull is here, along with Big Nose George's death mask and a photo of the old whiskey barrel in which Osborne decided to store the body. The barrel wasn't discovered until 1950 when a construction crew found it while digging at an old Rawlins drugstore. Incidentally, this same Dr. Osborne went on to serve as Wyoming's governor from 1893 to 1895!

Looking for more criminals? Try **St. Joseph's Cemetery,** where two early train robbers are buried. Ask at the museum for the exact grave locations. Still more crooks? Try the state penitentiary, south of town; you'll meet real live ones there.

OTHER SIGHTS
Buildings
Many interesting old sandstone buildings are scattered throughout downtown, built from

© DON PITCHER

The historic Ferris Mansion was built in 1903.

ticline) rises immediately north of town, providing a textbook example of stratigraphy. Plenty of fish and invertebrate fossils are here, too. As a side note, the paint known as "Rawlins Red" originated from iron oxide mined just north of town. The color is still used for barns and buildings in the eastern United States, and this was the color originally chosen by General Rawlins to paint the Brooklyn Bridge (as Secretary of War, he approved the bridge plans).

ENTERTAINMENT AND EVENTS

For live music, try **Michael's Big City Bar and Grill** (1211 W. Spruce St., 307/324-4868); **Legends Lounge** at the Day's Inn has Top 40 DJ tunes most nights and occasional rock bands. **The Movies Triplex** (307/324-6624, www .wyomovies.com) is on the Highway 287 Bypass Road.

Crazy Days occurs in mid-July, with a motorcycle rally, outhouse races, barbecue, and street dance. The biggest local event is **Carbon County Fair and Rodeo** (307/324-6866), held the first week of August each year. Attractions include livestock and farm exhibits, rodeos, arts-and-crafts displays, parades, a carnival, street dance, and demolition derby.

RECREATION

The **Rawlins Family Recreation Center** (1616 Harshman, 307/324-7529, www.rawlins-wyoming.com/recenter.htm) has racquetball, basketball, and volleyball courts, a weight room, an indoor track, and other facilities. Swim at the **high school pool** or bowl at **Jeffrey Lanes** (1917 W. Spruce St., 307/328-0263).

Golfers will find a new 18-hole playground at **Rochelle Ranch Golf Course** (307/324-4573).

ACCOMMODATIONS

Given its relatively small size, Rawlins has a surprising number of lodging places, but if you plan to stay at one of the cheap motels—particularly those not described here—take a look at the rooms first because some may not be up to your standards.

Quite a few other budget places may be

stone quarried around Rawlins. Pick up a detailed historic downtown Rawlins walking-tour brochure of historic buildings from the chamber of commerce (517 Cedar St.). Notable ones include the **Shrine Temple** at 5th and Pine (completed in 1909), the **Elks Club** at 4th and Buffalo (completed in 1909), and the **Presbyterian** church at 3rd and Cedar (built in 1882). The beautifully restored **Union Pacific Railroad depot** (400 W. Front) was built in 1901 of granite and brick and is now used as a community meeting room. One of the most attractive buildings in Rawlins is the **Ferris Mansion** (607 W. Maple), built for the widow of an early mining pioneer, George Ferris. An old **steam locomotive** rests in Tully Park on Elm Street next to the hospital.

"Rockology"

The country around Rawlins is a geologist's and rock hound's paradise; jade, petrified wood, agate, and other minerals are here to be discovered. Of course, oil, gas, and coal are what geologists are most interested in around here. The **Rawlins Uplift** (a thrust-faulted an-

MEDICINE BOW COUNTRY

worth investigating if you want cheap rates and don't mind aging furnishings; just head west from town along Spruce Street to see what appeals to your pocketbook. A decent economy motel is **Jade Lodge** (405 W. Spruce, 307/324-2791, $40 d), where the rooms contain fridges and microwaves. **Budget Inn** (1617 W. Spruce, 307/324-2905, $70 d) has remodeled economy rooms with fridges and microwaves.

Days Inn (2222 E. Cedar, 307/324-6615 or 888/324-6615, www.daysinn.com, $70 s or $75–80) contains an enclosed heated pool and offers a hot breakfast each morning, along with Wi-Fi in the lobby.

The Lodge at Rawlins/Quality Inn (1801 E. Cedar, 307/324-2783 or 877/729-5467, www.thelodgeatrawlins.com, $75 s or $80 d) has a heated outdoor pool, wireless Internet, and updated rooms—some with king beds, microwaves, and fridges. A restaurant is on the premises. Do a little wildlife-watching while here; an active prairie dog town is right behind the hotel.

On the south edge of town (I-80 exit 214), **Best Value Inn** (1400 Higley Blvd., 307/328-1732 or 888/315-2378, www.bestvalueinn.com, $89 d) has modern rooms. Amenities include a light breakfast, sauna, game room, and wireless Internet. This is one of the better deals in town.

Rawlins's premier motel is **Best Western CottonTree Inn** (at 23rd and Spruce, 307/324-2737 or 800/662-6886, www.cottontree.net, $84–109 s or $94–114 d), with an indoor pool, hot tub, and sauna, plus passes to a local health club.

Camping

The nearest public campground (free, open June–Oct.) is at **Teton Reservoir,** 17 miles south of Rawlins. More public facilities ($4 for nonresidents, $2 for Wyoming residents, open year-round) are in **Seminoe State Park** (307/320-3013, http://wyoparks.state.wy.us), 28 miles north of Sinclair.

You'll find three parking-lot campgrounds in Rawlins, all great places to swelter in the simmering heat of summer as you listen to the freeway traffic. **Rawlins KOA** (205 E. Hwy. 71, 307/328-2021 or 800/562-7559, www.koa.com, $19 tents, $29–31 RVs) has an outdoor pool and game room. Other choices are **RV World Campground** (2401 Wagon Circle Rd., 307/328-1091, $15 tents, $22–24 RVs), and **Western Hills Campground** (2500 Wagon Circle Rd., 307/324-2592, www.trib.com/~whc, $16 tents, $25 RVs). Western Hills is open all year; the others are typically open April–October.

FOOD

In the last few years Rawlins has seen a proliferation of dining choices, including some real gems. Start the day at **Square Shooter's Eating House** (311 W. Cedar, 307/324-4380), serving standard American fare amid the ambience of mounted animal heads. Closed weekends.

Locals rave about 🌙 **Rose's Lariat** (410 E. Cedar, 307/324-5261), an old favorite with heavy and old-fashioned Mexican meals. Only one small table; everyone else sits at the counter stools, so you'll probably end up waiting to eat. Open until 7 P.M. Tuesday–Saturday with nothing over $9.

Cloverleaf Cafe (113 4th St., 307/324-9841) is a narrow downtown spot with a no-smoking setting for American breakfasts and Mexican-style lunches and dinners; around $8.

🌙 **Anong's Thai Cuisine** (210 5th St., 307/324-8967) is the most surprising place in Rawlins, with an upscale setting and delicious favorites such as spicy eggplant, roasted duck curry, *pad thai,* and asparagus shrimp. Most entrées are $8–12, and lunch specials cost $6.

Occupying a vintage 1881 building, **Blake House** (221 W. Cedar St., 307/324-6873) is an attractive fine-dining option in a romantic setting. It's open three meals a day with dinner specials that include Alaskan salmon, juniper-marinated prime rib, and wild mushroom ravioli. Dinner entrées are $15–23.

Another historic home contains 🌙 **Aspen House Restaurant** (318 5th St., 307/324-4787). The standout menu includes steaks, seafood, chicken, pasta, and Asian specialties, and the Singaporean owner brings an Eastern touch to the cookery. Open for lunch and dinner only, with $15–36 entrées.

Huckleberry Ice Cream (509 W. Cedar St., 307/324-5233 or 800/484-5808) is a very popular ice cream parlor, but it also serves espresso, sandwiches, and smoothies. Get fast service and decent truck-stop grub (including tasty pies) at **Rip Griffin's Truckstop** (I-80 at exit 215, 307/328-2103).

Groceries can be found at **City Market** (602 Higley Blvd., 307/328-1421), which also has a deli.

INFORMATION AND SERVICES

Next to City Hall is the **Rawlins-Carbon County Chamber of Commerce** (519 Cedar St., 307/324-4111, www.rawlinscarboncountychamber.com, open 9 A.M.–noon and 1– 5 P.M. Mon.–Fri. year-round).

Get regional information and publications from the **Carbon County Visitors Council** (800/228-3547, www.wyomingcarboncounty.com). Other contacts and services include the **post office** (106 5th St., 307/324-3521), **BLM district office** (1300 N. 3rd, 307/328-4200, www.wy.blm.gov), and the **Memorial Hospital of Carbon County** (2221 Elm St., 307/324-2221, www.imhcc.com).

Off the Beaten Path Bookstore (513 W. Cedar St., 307/324-3565)—a reader's bookshop—is two doors up from the chamber of commerce. Internet access is available, or head to the **Carbon County Public Library** (3rd and Buffalo, 307/328-2618).

Cedar Chest Gifts (416 W. Cedar St., 307/324-7737) is a combination gift shop and gallery. Wash clothes at **The Washboard** (504 23rd, 307/324-2434) or **Wash and Dry Laundry** (515 S. 15th Street).

GETTING THERE

Greyhound (307/324-5496 or 800/231-2222, www.greyhound.com) stops at 102 East Cedar Street, with daily service west to Salt Lake City or east to Denver. There are no commercial flights to Rawlins.

FORT FRED STEELE

Fort Fred Steele—named for Civil War hero Major General Frederick Steele—was built in 1868 as one of three Wyoming posts established to protect the transcontinental railroad from Indian attacks. Soldiers from the fort fought against the Utes in northern Colorado during their 1879 uprising against tyrannical Indian agent Nathan C. Meeker. The troops also helped reestablish peace after the 1885 anti-Chinese riots in Rock Springs.

After the fort was abandoned by the army in 1886, civilians took over the buildings and turned this into a supply base for ranchers and sheepherders. It was headquarters for the Carbon Timber Company, which controlled the enormous railroad-tie market for the Union Pacific Railroad in the Rockies and owned nearly 25,000 acres of timberland. Lodgepole pines were felled in the Medicine Bow Mountains and floated down the North Platte River during high flows each spring. At Fort Steele, they were caught by a log boom and loaded onto railway cars or used in the sawmill or box factory. The tie industry remained important well into the 20th century—300,000 ties were sent down the North Platte River in 1938 alone—but when the Union Pacific stopped using hand-hewn ties in 1940, the town of Fort Steele suffered. With the loss of its main industry and the 1939 rerouting of the Lincoln Highway, all but a few people moved away.

Fort Steele Today

Fort Steele (307/320-3013, http://wyoparks.state.wy.us, free), nine miles east of Sinclair on I-80, is now a 137-acre state park. A small visitor center in the old red bridge tender's house contains historical photos of the fort and the Carbon Timber Company. The park is open 9 A.M.–7 P.M. daily May–mid-November but closed to entry the rest of the year. Historical plaques are scattered through the grounds, but not much remains of what was a substantial settlement: just a couple of clapboard buildings, some sandstone foundations and chimneys, and the walls of a house once owned by Fenimore Chatterton, Wyoming's governor from 1903 to 1905. Stone walls from the military quartermaster's corral remain just west of the parade grounds, but a disastrous arson fire on New Year's Eve in 1976 destroyed two enlisted men's barracks that had stood here for more than a century.

Just up the hill from the fort site is a square powder magazine built in 1881 from locally quarried stone, with an adjacent cemetery containing the graves of civilians who died in the area. Only a few headstones remain. The slow-moving North Platte River right next to the fort is a great place for picnics, but there's no camping allowed. Despite the paucity of historical buildings, there's something rather nice about the authenticity of the site. Stop in at dusk on a summer evening and you'll hear the rumble of freight trains while coyotes howl from nearby hills and the North Platte River rolls away from this lonely place. It's far enough from I-80 that you can't even hear the cars and trucks.

SINCLAIR

Sinclair (pop. 420) is one of the more distinctive small settlements in Wyoming. In 1923, the Producers Oil and Refining Company (Parco) established a 50,000-barrel-a-day oil refinery here, built a town to house its employees, and named the settlement Parco. When the Sinclair Oil Company bought the refinery in 1934, the name changed, but ownership of all businesses and homes remained in corporate hands for three decades. In 1967, Sinclair finally sold the homes to renters and gave the business buildings to the town government. Today the refinery still lights up the night sky for miles around, and hundreds of giant oil tanks stand behind the facility. I-80 passes right by Sinclair, and most folks don't bother to stop here except to fill up at the Burns Brothers Truckstop one mile east of town. Actually, Sinclair is a pleasant little resting place and a nice spot for a shady picnic lunch.

Parco built the company town, including the large Parco Inn at the center, in Spanish-mission style with red-tile roofs and stucco walls. You'd think you were in Southern California. An elaborate fountain and a nice small park

stand across from the inn, now virtually abandoned but listed on the National Register of Historic Places. A pair of Civil War–vintage cannons guard the water fountain from attack by marauding oil executives. They were brought here originally to blow holes in burning oil tanks (if the need ever arose), allowing the oil to drain into the surrounding dikes before the tanks could explode from the heat.

The **Parco/Sinclair Museum** is in the old bank building and contains several local items, including clamp-on ice skates from the 1920s, old photos, and the high point, a newspaper headlined "Nixon Resigns." Open 9 A.M.–noon and 1–5 P.M. Monday–Friday. Access is through the town hall, next door. The town also has a branch library and recreation center.

Of note in Sinclair is tiny **Su Casa Cafe** (307/328-1745), which makes genuine Mexican food for lunch and dinner daily. There are no motels in town, but the road north of Sinclair leads to popular Seminoe and Pathfinder reservoirs, where camping is available. (See the *Central Wyoming* chapter.) Sinclair is also home to the nine-hole **Sinclair Golf Course** (307/324-7767) along the North Platte River. The I-80 Travel Plaza Truck Stop has an ATM and a restaurant serving trucker meals.

HEADING NORTH

U.S. 287/Hwy. 789 points north from Rawlins into Wyoming's heartland, crossing the Continental Divide twice along the way as it dips into the Great Divide Basin and then back out again. Once inside the basin, the highway throws itself straight across this sandy land from point A to point B, with not much in between to deflect it. No need to touch the steering wheel here. Fences collect both tumbleweeds and bits of miscellaneous junk. To the northeast the tilted face of 10,037-foot Ferris Mountain rises, but your sense of distance falters in the featureless desert land where only fence lines and a few gullies halt the relentless horizontal geography. Geologists love this place: long, eroded ridges and scarps in the distance, which appear so parched of water that their barren slopes could be the bleached rib cages of some prehistoric monster. Some amazing badlands formations are here as well.

Lamont and Bairoil

The diminutive settlement of Lamont lies 33 miles north of Rawlins near the Continental Divide. A paved road leads five miles west to another tiny place, Bairoil. The latter is named for Charles Bair, who discovered oil (hence the name) here in 1916. Today the surrounding area is part of Lost Soldier Oil Field, and pumpjacks sprinkle the landscape.

Bairoil lays claim to a slice of air-travel trivia. In 1989, Kevin Christopherson set a world record for foot-launched hang gliding when he took off from Whiskey Peak, caught favorable wind currents, and rode them all the way into North Dakota, 287 miles away.

Campsites and RV hookups can be found in the **Bairoil town park** (307/324-7653). In Lamont, **Grandma's Cafe and Campground** (307/324-9870) serves three meals a day (starting at 5 A.M.) and provides RV and tent sites.

Over Whiskey Gap

Forty miles north of Rawlins, the highway climbs through Whiskey Gap, with Green Mountain to the west and the Ferris Mountains to the east. The gap received its name in 1862 when Major Jack O'Farrell caught his soldiers drinking from an illegal barrel of whiskey in a trader's wagon. The whiskey was dumped on the ground, but some flowed into a spring that one soldier later called the "sweetest water he had ever tasted."

Another five miles north of Whiskey Gap is the junction of U.S. 287/Hwy. 789 and Hwy. 220 at **Muddy Gap,** where you can gas up. The road diverges, with one fork leading northeast to Casper, passing the Oregon Trail landmarks of Devil's Gate and Independence Rock (see the *Central Wyoming* chapter), and the other heading northwest to Lander, with Split Rock and Jeffrey City along the way (see *East on U.S. 287* under *Lander* in the *Wind River Mountains Country* chapter for more on Jeffrey City). In either direction you will find stereotypical Wyoming vistas—sagebrush, grass, cattle, and sky. But no whiskey barrels.

MEDICINE BOW COUNTRY

SOUTHWEST WYOMING

Southwest Wyoming is the state's forbidden quarter, a place seen primarily from the windows of cars speeding along I-80. At first glance the land appears stark, barren, and worthless. In 1866, General William T. Sherman wrote, "The Government will have to pay a bounty for people to like it up here." Others said people wouldn't come no matter how many incentives the government might offer. But despite the lack of trees, the broiling hot summers, and the wind-iced winters, people *have* settled here, primarily to extract the area's immense energy and mineral resources. Southwest Wyoming contains both the state's largest county (Sweetwater) and its smallest (Uinta), as well as Lincoln County, seemingly named for its L-shape. The Green River cuts across this part of Wyoming, eventually joining the Colorado River in Utah.

PLANNING YOUR TIME

Many visitors to this corner of Wyoming are here on business, particularly if that business has anything to do with gas, oil, coal, or trona. The town of Rock Springs promotes itself as a gateway to Yellowstone, and U.S. 191 *does* provide the quickest access if you're driving west on I-80. Evanston is just 84 miles from Salt Lake City, making it a favorite weekend place to enjoy sinful things that aren't legal in Utah.

The desert lands of Southwest Wyoming are a deterrent to many travelers, but others are drawn to their raw-edged beauty. Of particular note are the **Killpecker Dunes,** the largest active dunes in America, and dramatic **Flaming Gorge National Recreation Area,** with grand canyon scenery, monster fish, and rollicking river rafting. Farther west is **Fort Bridger**

© DON PITCHER

HIGHLIGHTS

◖ Killpecker Dunes: North America's largest active dunes are home to wild horses and elk, but don't ask where the name originated (page 151).

◖ Sweetwater County Historical Museum: Professional exhibits in this Green River museum reveal a surprising history of trona mines, massacres, outlaws, and ventriloquist dummies. And no, the one-armed statue of John Wesley Powell was not vandalized (page 161).

◖ Flaming Gorge National Recreation Area: Southwestern Wyoming's watery playground, this lake backs up behind a 502-foot-high concrete dam (page 163).

◖ Fort Bridger State Historic Site: Well worth the five-minute drive from I-80, this fort was established by famed mountain man and guide Jim Bridger. Don't miss the modern-day mountain-man rendezvous each Labor Day weekend (page 172).

◖ Fossil Butte National Monument: You wouldn't know it now, but 50 million years ago this was a giant lake. Today, millions of fossil fish and other creatures lie in these dry hills. You can't dig on the Park Service land, but nearby private quarries are open for a fee (page 186).

LOOK FOR ◖ TO FIND RECOMMENDED SIGHTS, ACTIVITIES, DINING, AND LODGING.

◖ Snake River Canyon: The highway up the canyon is a great way to enter Jackson Hole, paralleling the sinuous river beneath thick forests. The river is a favorite of whitewater rafters (page 197).

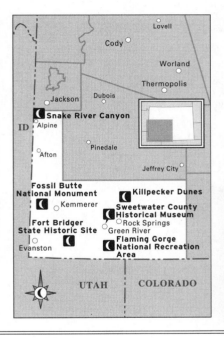

State Historic Site, with interesting buildings, a small museum, and a popular mountain-man rendezvous on Labor Day weekend.

The largest town, Rock Springs, is a booming center for energy development, and nearby Green River is home to the **Sweetwater County Historical Museum,** one of the better small museums in Wyoming. Farther north is Kemmerer, home to **Fossil Butte National Monument** and a number of private fossil-fish quarries open to the public. The town of Evanston has historic buildings, including a Chinese Joss House. Bucolic—but fast-growing—Star

Valley is sandwiched between the Idaho border and the Wyoming Range. North of here, the highway cuts through **Snake River Canyon** on its way to Jackson Hole.

HISTORY

When whites first arrived in southwest Wyoming, they found the Shoshone and Ute Indians hunting buffalo and antelope in this desert country. The first mountain-man rendezvous took place here, and many of the vital emigrant routes passed through, including the Oregon, Mormon, and Overland trails, as did

SOUTHWEST WYOMING

the Pony Express and the transcontinental telegraph. But the Union Pacific Railroad opened the land to settlement. Completion of the railroad in 1869 brought about the establishment of Rock Springs, Green River, and Evanston, and coal mines were developed in the Rock Springs, Evanston, and Kemmerer areas to fuel these trains. Men of all nationalities came to work the mines, creating a racial diversity that is still visible.

Just as the coal mines began to close in the 1950s, enormous trona deposits were developed in western Sweetwater County, and many miners simply switched employers. Other mines extract phosphates and coal, and the natural-gas fields of Sweetwater and Uinta counties are the most productive in Wyoming. Southwest Wyoming has the world's biggest coal mine, biggest coke-producing plant, biggest trona mine, and biggest helium plant. Put all this together and it's obvious that despite the desert setting and small population, southwest Wyoming is in some ways the most industrialized part of the state.

The Red Desert

The eastern half of Sweetwater County contains a vast treeless area known as the Red Desert, so named because of the brick-red soil that stretches in all directions. It's not a place to be trifled with. Less than nine inches of precipitation falls each year, and summertime temperatures frequently top 100°F in this forbidding, lonely place—the largest stretch of unfenced land in the Lower 48. Some of the largest remaining herds of wild horses roam here, along with desert elk and one of the last wild herds of bison. Antelope are found throughout this country, as are a few cattle and lots of sheep. The signs of humans are few and far between: dirt roads, oil and gas wells, and a few wind-scoured buildings.

I-80 is most folks' sole acquaintance with the Red Desert—two double-wide rivers of asphalt cracking open the desiccated land. There aren't many sights to see unless you pull off the main road and slow down. Despite its harshness, the Red Desert has a desolate beauty that grows on you. Pick what may seem the least interesting place, where the ramp ends at a cattle crossing and the road immediately turns to gravel. When you're far enough from the interstate that you can no longer hear the trucks, get out of your car and use all of your senses to grasp this place. Feel the intensity of the sun on a blistering summer day. Look at the way the thin-crusted snow lies in the lee side of the sage in winter, worn out by the incessant wind. Listen to the "scree!" cry of the red-tailed hawk. Taste a couple of the pungent sage leaves. Smell the rusty air as the first drops of a sudden shower pummel the road dust. Watch a herd of antelope bound away and then turn warily back to see who might be stopping in such a place. Or simply let the stillness of this vast land sweep over you, broken by the howl of a distant coyote. This is Wyoming without pretenses.

The Red Desert lies within **Great Divide Basin,** a 90-mile-long region where the little water that falls never makes it to either ocean. Red Lake—a salty playa—fills with water during rare rainy spells, only to have it soak into the sandy soil or evaporate in the summer sun. The Continental Divide splits south of Great Divide Basin and then rejoins on its northern margin, leaving a bowl in the middle. Highway travelers on I-80 thus cross the Continental Divide twice.

Sweetwater County Travel and Tourism Board (307/354-6457, www.tourwyoming.com) has details on the region, and the **Biodiversity Conservation Alliance** (www.voiceforthe-wild.org) has information on efforts to protect the Red Desert from development.

WAMSUTTER

As you drive the 108 miles west from Rawlins to Rock Springs, the only town worth noting—and marginally so—is Wamsutter (pop. 260). Natural-gas wells sprinkle the country to the west and south, and the town consists of a trashy collection of old trailer homes, oil field equipment, and smashed-up trucks hauled here from I-80 accidents. This is a good place to read a romance novel and pretend you're somewhere else. Butch Cassidy's Hole-in-the-Wall gang robbed a Union Pacific train near here in 1900, and freight trains still roll by every few minutes, day and night. The surrounding country is a rock hound's paradise, with petrified wood, fossils, and tortilla agate—beautiful when polished—all found on public lands in the area.

Rest your head at the pleasant **Wamsutter Motel** (307/324-7112). **Love's Travel Plaza** houses a Subway shop, or tip a beer at the **Desert Bar** (307/324-4949).

POINT OF ROCKS

At Point of Rocks (I-80 exit 130), 25 miles east of Rock Springs, the state has restored an **Overland Stage station** and adjacent stables

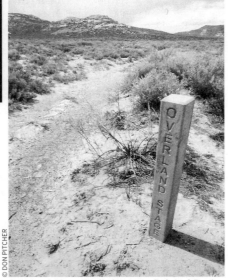

Overland Stage Trail sign near Point of Rocks

built in 1862. Constructed from sandstone, the station served as a jumping-off point for a road to South Pass City during the gold-rush years. Get here by following the sign to the historical marker for the Overland Stage Trail and then continuing another 0.5 mile over the railroad tracks (where freight trains roll through every 10 minutes or so) and south to the stage station. It sits on a hillside overlooking the railroad and freeway, and markers note the old Overland/Cherokee Trail route. The historic stone building is well worth the brief side trip from I-80.

The "town" of Point of Rocks has a gas station/restaurant/store/bar and several dozen trailer homes. Coal is dug from the ground at two enormous strip mines not far from Point of Rocks. The Jim Bridger Mine feeds directly into the equally gargantuan Jim Bridger Power Plant, built in the early 1970s to supply power for the Western United States. The smokestack here is said to be the tallest "building" in Wyoming.

SUPERIOR

For a delightful change of pace from the onward rush of commerce, take I-80 exit 122 (20 miles east of Rock Springs). Follow this winding country road through seven miles of sage and grass to the town of Superior. Movie trivia buffs might recognize the town; parts of the 1992 film *Leaving Normal* were shot here.

Superior was once home to 6,000 people, but most moved away after the coal mines closed in 1963, leaving fewer than 300 today. The only surviving businesses are Canyon Bar and Horse Thief Saloon; even the Ghost Town Bar is boarded up! Enjoy a picnic in the shady town park or just check out the many aging structures. Most interesting are the roofless remains of **Union Hall,** a trapezoidal building constructed in 1921. Interpretive signs here detail local history, and an 1867 steam engine sits out front. Additional abandoned structures can be found at Old Superior, just up the road. Find out more online at www.superiorwy.com.

One mile north of Superior are the **Natural Corrals,** an area of small corral-like enclosures in the rocks. Caves reach into the volcanic hills and often contain ice even in midsummer. Check with the Rock Springs BLM office (307/352-0256, www.wy.blm.gov) for directions.

◖ KILLPECKER DUNES

North of Rock Springs, White Mountain rises like a cresting wave over the valley through which U.S. 191 passes. Approximately 11 miles up is the turnoff to Tri-Territory Road, providing access to the Killpecker Sand Dunes, the largest active dunes in North America. The dunes—some topping 150 feet in height—extend eastward for 55 miles in a band that averages 2–3 miles wide but sometimes reaches 10. The constantly shifting dunes are formed from Eden Valley dirt that blows east on the prevailing winds. Signs point the way to most of the sights in the Killpecker Dunes area. As an aside, the Tri-Territory area received its name as the point at which three major American land acquisitions met: the Louisiana Purchase, the Northwest Territories, and the Mexican Cession.

Petroglyphs and Boars Tusk

Follow gravel Tri-Territory Road 12 miles east from U.S. 191 and head left at the turnoff to White Mountain Petroglyphs, following a very rough four-mile track. Avoid this road after rains and early in the year. The road ends at a low sandstone cliff where several hundred petroglyphs were carved into this soft rock by the Indian peoples who lived here in centuries past. Look closely to find elk, bison, horses, feather headdresses, and even a human footprint. Many petroglyphs relate to hunting. Because of the horses pictured here—horses didn't reach this region until the 16th cen-

tury—it's likely that many of the petroglyphs are of relatively recent origin. The cliff provides a safe location for several large raptor nests. Juniper and sage poke up through the remote desert landscape.

Return to the main gravel road and turn left to reach other interesting sights. Six miles to the east, the road splits. Turn right to reach the off-road vehicle (ORV) area of the dunes or left to visit Boars Tusk and dunes where vehicles are not allowed. Follow the latter road 1.5 miles to an unmarked road that leads to the base of Boars Tusk, a 400-foot-high rocky spire—a volcanic plug—that local rock climbers love. The 2.5-mile side road to Boars Tusk may be passable in a high-clearance vehicle, but I'd recommend a 4WD.

The Dunes

The dunes begin 1.5 miles beyond the turnoff to Boars Tusk, 22 miles from U.S. 191. This fascinating area is most beautiful in the early morning or at dusk, when sunlight gleams off the sand. Because it is a wilderness study area, vehicles are not allowed off the roads. Animals are surprisingly common in the Killpecker Dunes, and even a cursory examination will reveal tracks of coyotes, deer, elk, birds, and insects. Small pools of water on the lee side of some dunes are fed by melting snow that gets covered by drifting sand in the winter. This is a great place to hike, but be sure to come prepared for a desert climate: Bring food and water, a compass, and a topographic map. The dirt roads are also fine for mountain-biking. See the BLM office in Rock Springs for more details on this unusual area.

SOUTHWEST WYOMING

Rock Springs

A rapidly growing energy center, Rock Springs (pop. 23,000) is western Wyoming's largest city. It has undergone a major transformation in the last few years. The abandoned motels and boarded-up buildings that lined Dewar Drive since the last oil and gas boom ended in the mid-80s have been bulldozed. In their places stand fast-food joints, strip malls, convenience stores, espresso stands, and new-car dealers. Boom times have returned, bringing with them frenzied shopping centers—including Home Depot and a Wal-Mart Supercenter—corporate motels, and a massive Halliburton complex (said to be even larger than its Houston office) crowning a hilltop. Rock Springs has certainly become a magnet for oil and gas workers, but for travelers it still doesn't offer much beyond a place to rest up on the way to somewhere else. Like most other mining and energy towns, Rock Springs has always experienced booms and busts. Locals are enjoying the ride right now, and hoping the bad old days stay away.

Rock Springs began as a stage station along the Overland Trail but grew because of the Union Pacific's need for coal to run its trains. The Railway Act granted the Union Pacific rights to all coal along the transcontinental route. Although nearly all of Sweetwater County is underlain with coal, in Rock Springs the coal was close to the surface and easily accessible; the mines actually ran beneath the tracks in many places. Eventually the mines spread more than a mile in various directions, creating a honeycomb of tunnels under Rock Springs.

Although Rock Springs is named for flowing water, the lack of water has always been a problem. Rock Spring itself dried up once coal mining began, and Bitter Creek provided only muddy, astringent water. Killpecker Creek, a sometime stream that flows through Rock Springs, was named by soldiers who noted the alkaline water's rather painful biological effects when they visited the outhouse. Honest.

In the early years, Rock Springs was so short on drinking water that it had to be brought by train from Green River. Baths were once-a-week events despite the coal dust that blackened everyone.

Coal mining brought workers from all over the globe; locals call it the 57-variety town, and flags of many nations decorate local streets. Many arrived from Great Britain or Ireland, but others included Chinese, Italians, Scandinavians, Austrians, Hungarians, Yugoslavians, and Czechs. It was an uneasy melting

ROCK SPRINGS AREA CLIMATE

	SNOWFALL	MAXIMUM TEMP.
	RAINFALL	MINIMUM TEMP.

Average Maximum Temp.	54.7°F
Average Minimum Temp.	30.7°F
Annual Rainfall	9.09″
Annual Snowfall	45.6″

ROCK SPRINGS

BLM DISTRICT OFFICE
To Fairgrounds, Farson and Pinedale

BEST WESTERN OUTLAW INN
ECONO LODGE
DAYS INN

REGAN AVE
RECREATION CENTER
White Mountain

EXIT 103

ELK ST MOTEL
CAMP PILOT BUTTE SITE
SPRINGS MOTEL
SADDLE LITE MOTEL
SANDS CAFÉ
ECONOMY GUEST VILLAGE
SANDS INN
EXIT 107
To Airport and Railways

SLOVENSKI DOM
ROCKY MT HOTEL
BRIDGER AVE

WESTERN WYOMING COMMUNITY COLLEGE
CODY MOTEL
MUSEUM

WHITE MT LIBRARY
POST OFFICE
MOTEL 6
MEMORIAL HOSPITAL
LIBRARY/FINE ARTS CENTER

To Pilot Butte
WHITE MT MALL
THE INN
KMART
LA QUINTA INN
WAL-MART
WINGATE INN
KILLPEPPERS
BUDGET HOST INN
SUPER 8 MOTEL
MOTEL 8
HOLIDAY INN
CHAMBER OF COMMERCE
PLAZA MALL
COMFORT INN
BLM AREA OFFICE
HAMPTON INN

To Green River and Flaming Gorge
Bitter Creek
BLAIRTOWN - FLAMING GORGE RD
QUEALY RD

0   0.5 mi
0   0.5 km

© AVALON TRAVEL PUBLISHING, INC.

SOUTHWEST WYOMING

pot. They lived in company housing, riverbank dugouts, or shanties and used Bitter Creek—already notorious because of its undrinkable water—as the local cesspool and garbage dump. Rock Springs continued to expand as the Union Pacific opened more mines, and the Chinese Massacre of 1885 (see sidebar *The Chinese Massacre*) had only a minimal impact on production. By 1892, 943,513 tons of coal were being hauled out by 1,500 miners.

Although various companies mined here, the Union Pacific Coal Co. really owned Rock Springs and its miners. And Union Pacific was to blame for many of the problems: the filth, the poor housing, the lack of water, and the working conditions that spawned racial hatred. After Union Pacific engines switched from coal to diesel in the 1950s, the underground mines were closed and the economy began to fade. During another boom in the '70s, Rock Springs' population doubled, and by 1982 high-paying energy and construction jobs had made it the wealthiest city in the nation on a per capita basis. With the crash in oil prices, however, businesses fled town, and the economy went into a tailspin.

The city rebounded as coal and trona mining, a phosphate fertilizer plant, and gas and

THE CHINESE MASSACRE

Rock Springs had the dubious honor of hosting one of the most infamous incidents in Wyoming history – the Chinese Massacre. In 1875, the Union Pacific Railroad tried to step up coal production at its Rock Springs mines, but miners refused when they found their wages simultaneously being cut. To fill the gap, the company brought in Chinese contract laborers who were willing to work for less money. The Chinese immediately became targets of harassment. The railroad hired more and more Chinese while turning whites away, and within a decade more than 500 Chinese miners were in Rock Springs.

Things came to a head on September 2, 1885, when the supervisor of one of the mines began assigning Chinese workers to locations where whites had previously been working. Whites attacked the Chinese, first with picks and shovels, and then with rifles. The violence spread, and Chinatown – a ramshackle assemblage of shacks along what is now Ahsay Avenue – was burned to the ground. A mob of 60 men swept after the defenseless Chinese workers, robbing and then murdering them. Twenty-eight Chinese died in the melee and many more fled and may have died while trying to cross the desert. The sheriff came down from Green River to protect the whites but did nothing to stop the murders in Chinatown. No one ever faced trial for the attacks.

The riots spawned similar anti-Chinese violence and strikes all over the West and led Governor Francis E. Warren to call for federal troops to protect the remaining Chinese workers. As a result, Camp Pilot Butte was established to serve as a buffer between the Chinese and the whites. This was the only place in America where an international treaty post was ever established. About 250 soldiers remained here until the Spanish-American War forced the fort's abandonment in 1899.

The workers – both white and Chinese – gradually filtered back after the riots, and by December the mines had 85 whites and 457 Chinese workers. The massacre led the United States to pay the Chinese government $149,000 in compensation; it was used to fund Chinese student scholarships in America. In the 1920s and '30s, the Union Pacific Coal Co. finally rewarded the few remaining Chinese workers with passage back to their homeland and endowments to pay for their retirement. Only one of the men remained in Rock Springs all of his life. The bones of others who died were shipped home to China.

An unusual legacy of the riots is a still-burning coal mine at Potter Street in Rock Springs. During the melee, several miners stole a large amount of Chinese tea and stored it in a mine tunnel, hoping to sell it later. When the authorities came for it, the miners set it on fire, and the burning tea ignited an adjacent coal seam. Smoke still emerges from the ground at what is now called Burning Mountain.

oil production brought jobs in the 1990s. An open-pit mine east of Rock Springs provides coal for the enormous Jim Bridger Power Plant—the largest power plant in Wyoming—while the Black Butte strip mine in the same area feeds power plants elsewhere in the nation. The latter may eventually spread its tentacles across 60 square miles of desert land. There are also two underground coal mines in the vicinity.

The most recent boom—fueled by America's insatiable demand for oil and gas—has revitalized Rock Springs. But even with the good times on the edges, downtown is still pocked with empty storefronts and the mishmash of dead-end streets doesn't help; it's a legacy of the coal-mining era, when paths taken by miners walking to work gradually evolved into a road network.

SIGHTS
Rock Springs Historical Museum
The Rock Springs Historical Museum (201 B St., 307/362-3138, open 10 A.M.–5 P.M. Mon.–

The old city hall now houses the Rock Springs Historical Museum.

© DON PITCHER

The building at 432 South Main Street, now a copy shop, was once a butcher shop called Pacific Market. According to some historians, it was while working here and in other local meat shops that Robert LeRoy Parker ("Butch Cassidy") acquired his nickname. (Several other tales purport to explain the origins of his name, but nobody really knows which one is true.) The walking tour details several other Cassidy hangouts, plus the beer garden where Calamity Jane "announced her appearances in town by emptying both of her six shooters and 'shouting verbal oaths well tarnished.'" A monument to Rock Springs coal miners stands next to the old train depot downtown. The second JCPenney store ever opened (it was then called Golden Rule Mercantile) was housed in the building at 531 North Front Street.

The site of **Camp Pilot Butte** is now occupied by the Saints Cyril and Methodius Catholic Church at 633 Bridger, a major Slovenian center in the community. (Formerly part of Yugoslavia, Slovenia became an independent nation in 1991.) Only one of the original buildings from Camp Pilot Butte remains—a soldiers' barracks now used as a parish school. Chinatown was just north of here.

Slovenski Dom, the old Slovenian community center, is just down the street from Saints Cyril and Methodius Church, at 513 Bridger Street. Built in 1913, this was the home of Slovenian American fraternal lodges and was a center for dances, skits, raffles, and concerts. A few pieces of the original furniture are still here, including a long back bar in the basement. The building now houses the cooperatively run **Local Color Art Gallery** (307/382-0990), selling quality pottery, crafts, and paintings created by local artisans. Closed Sundays.

Sat., free) is housed within the old city hall. Built in 1894, this attractive sandstone building looks more like a medieval castle than a city office building. Inside, local memorabilia—some dating to the 1880s—spreads over two floors and includes exhibits on coal mining, Butch Cassidy's life in Rock Springs, moonshine stills from the 1920s, and displays on the diverse mix of people who came here for work. The old city jail cells are still in the building; check out the horsehair bedding. Be sure to pick up a copy of the excellent historical downtown walking-tour brochure while here.

Other Downtown Sights

Next to the main library is the **Community Fine Arts Center** (400 C St., 307/362-6212, free, open 10 A.M.–6 P.M. Mon.–Thurs. and noon–5 P.M. Fri.–Sat.). You'll find some surprising works here, including paintings by Conrad Schwiering, Hans Kleiber, Grandma Moses, and Norman Rockwell. Also here is a 1993 painting of the Chinese Massacre by Taylor Spence.

Western Wyoming Community College

On a hilltop overlooking town, Western Wyoming Community College (2500 College Dr., 307/382-1600, www.wwcc.cc.wy.us) is a two-year college housed in modern brick buildings. Stop here to explore the **art** gallery (open weekdays), to enjoy a light meal in the bright and spacious atrium, or to wander past imposing displays. You'll find several full-size **dinosaurs** (OK, they are actually fiberglass casts of dino bones), including triceratops and *Tyrannosaurus rex*. Also here are fish, turtle, and plant fossils and a tall pendulum. The small **Natural History Museum** (307/382-1666, open 9 A.M.–10 P.M. daily, free) houses Indian artifacts, Wyoming minerals, and more fossils. Adjacent is a collection of big-game heads from all over the world that's officially called the **Weidner Wildlife Musuem.**

The most unusual campus sight sits on the lawn out front—a nine-ton replica of an **Easter Island Statue.** The statue is an exact copy of these mysterious stone carvings and was used to test theories on how they were moved across the island. Anthropology professor Charles Love showed that 25 men could drag the piece 135 feet in two minutes by putting it upright on long log rollers. The project was featured in a *Nova* program about Easter Island.

Farther Afield

The **Reliance tipple,** five miles north of town on U.S. 191 and then two miles in on County Road 4-42, was used to load coal into railroad cars in the 1930s. Today the impressive structure is open for self-guided walking tours. A paved path leads to interpretive signs describing the facility.

Several miles northwest of Rock Springs is **Pilot Butte,** a prominent spire visible for miles in all directions and a milestone for emigrants along the Overland Trail. Get there via Gookin–White Mountain Road on the west side of town. You'll need a 4WD or a mountain bike unless you want to hoof it. A staircase leads up the rock from the east side. Another interesting rock formation stands across from Plaza Mall on Dewar Drive.

Wild Horses

More than 1,500 wild horses still run free in southwest Wyoming. Although they're often spotted east of Rock Springs along I-80, the best place to view them is along the west side of U.S. 191 approximately 28 miles north of Rock Springs and along White Mountain via County Road 4-53. The BLM has developed a 23-mile wild-horse driving tour that follows these roads between Green River and Rock Springs, with interpretive signs posted along the way. Get a brochure map of the route from local visitor centers. Note: If it has rained recently, these roads can become a quagmire. Other Wyoming places to see them are near Lander, Worland, Cody, and Lovell.

The **BLM's Rock Springs Field Office** (307/352-0256, www.wy.blm.gov) is north of town on U.S. 191 and can supply information on wild horses and the Killpecker Dunes area. Contact the office for information on adopting a wild horse (www.adoptahorse.blm.gov) from one of the BLM's Red Desert roundups.

ENTERTAINMENT AND EVENTS

In 1903, about 40 percent of the businesses in Rock Springs were bars; even during Prohibition, many "soft-drink parlors" dispensed Kemmerer moonshine. To produce this booze, 100 train cars of grapes arrived in Rock Springs within a two-month period. Many places still offer nightlife, although many tend toward the sleazy side, particularly those along the railroad tracks. The best spots for live music are **Saddle Lite Saloon** (1704 Elk St., 307/362-8704) and **Porky's Bar** (1250 Dewar Dr., 307/362-5552).

Star Stadium 8 (307/362-7827, www.wyomovies.com), next to White Mountain Mall, features state-of-the-art seating and sound systems.

Rock Springs's diverse past is celebrated in **International Day** in mid-July, with ethnic foods and entertainment, music (from polka to bagpipers), rickshaw rides, food and beer booths, and a Chinese dragon parade, all in the center of downtown.

The **Red Desert Roundup** (307/382-6323, www.rdrodeo.com), held the last weekend of July, is the second-largest professional rodeo in

Wyoming and the primary summertime event. It also features a Saturday-morning pancake breakfast followed by a big parade.

The **Sweetwater County Fair** (307/352-6789, www.sweetwaterevents.com), takes place in early August right after the Roundup. The biggest county fair in Wyoming, this eight-day festival attracts families to 4-H auctions, a carnival, food, and headline entertainers. Auto-racing enthusiasts will find stock-car racing, motocross, and demolition derbies all summer long at **Sweetwater Speedway** (3320 Yellowstone Rd., 307/352-6789, www.sweetwaterevents.com).

RECREATION

Rock Springs Family Recreation Center (3900 Sweetwater Dr., 307/352-1440) has an indoor pool and gym, ice-skating rink, racquetball and tennis courts, plus a weight room, sauna, and hot tub. **Rock Springs Civic Center** (410 N St., 307/352-1420) houses another swimming pool and a climbing wall.

The 18-hole **White Mountain Golf Course** (307/352-1415) lies three miles north of town.

ACCOMMODATIONS

The strong economy in Rock Springs is now reflected both in high lodging prices and the addition of several hotels, including two that opened in 2005.

Under $50

You'll find low rates and remodeled rooms—all with fridges and microwaves—at **Economy Guest Village** (1430 9th St., 307/362-3763, $50 d). **Springs Motel** (1525 9th St., 307/362-6683, $52 d) has reasonable prices and comfortable accommodations.

$50-100

Find decent budget accommodations at **Motel 6** (2615 Commercial Way, 307/362-1850 or 800/466-8356, www.motel6.com, $54 s or $60 d), which also has an outdoor pool.

Motel 8 (108 Gateway Blvd., 307/362-8200 or 888/362-8200) has a mix of older rooms ($76 s or $82 d) and those that were recently updated ($82 s or $88 d), all with wireless Internet, fridges, and microwaves.

Amenities at the **Comfort Inn** (1670 Sunset Dr., 307/382-9490 or 800/228-5150, www.comfortinn.com, $79 s or $90 d) include an outdoor pool, hot tub, exercise room, Wi-Fi, and continental breakfast.

Econo Lodge (1635 N. Elk St., 307/382-4217 or 800/548-6621, www.econolodge.com, $85 s or d) is a midrange place with a heated outdoor pool, hot tub, and continental breakfast.

$100-150

The Inn Hotel and Convention Center (2518 Foothill Blvd., 307/362-9600 or 800/442-9692, $95–110 d) features modern rooms, an indoor pool, wireless Internet, fridges, microwaves, and continental breakfast.

One of Rock Springs's better places to stay, **Best Western Outlaw Inn** (1630 Elk St., 307/362-6623 or 800/528-1234, www.bestwestern.com/outlawinn, $96 s or $106 d) has a fun indoor pool and atrium, plus wireless Internet.

The recently remodeled **Holiday Inn** (1675 Sunset Dr., 307/382-9200 or 800/465-4329, www.holiday-inn.com/rocksprings) features an indoor pool (with rain machine), wading pool, and hot tub. Options include standard rooms ($109 for up to four), suites ($149 d), and the more spacious executive rooms ($170 d) with jetted tubs, fridges, microwaves, and Wi-Fi.

New in 2005, **Wingate Inn Rock Springs** (517 Gateway Blvd., 307/382-5181 or 800/228-1000, www.wingateinns.com, $129 d) has such amenities as an indoor pool, hot tub, fitness center, breakfast buffet, Wi-Fi, business center, and in-room safes.

Camping

The nearest public camping is **Firehole Canyon Campground,** 27 miles southwest of Rock Springs in Flaming Gorge National Recreation Area. Camping costs $14; it's open late May–late September. Make reservations ($9 fee) at 518/885-3639 or 877/444-6777, www.reserveusa.com.

The **Rock Springs KOA Kampground** (two miles west of town on N. Service Rd.,

SOUTHWEST WYOMING

307/362-3063 or 800/562-8699, www.rock-springskoa.com, $35 RVs, $21 tents, open Apr.–mid-Oct.) provides great scenic vistas of the oil storage tanks—and you won't need to worry about trees blocking the sun. Simple cabins are $41 d, and it has a heated outdoor pool, hot tub, and wireless Internet.

FOOD

Head downtown along Broadway for a good mix of dining choices within one block, including a burger joint, soda fountain, and brewpub.

American

Rock Springs has one place you should not miss: **Grub's Drive In** (415 Paulson, 307/362-6634), where the thick shakes, grease-drenched but exceptional fried chicken, and homemade fries are favorites of both locals and visitors. This tiny old-time family operation features Shamrock burgers, loaded down with all the fixin's for $5. You can almost feel your arteries clogging.

Crueljacks Restaurant (west of Rock Springs, 307/382-9018) has good breakfasts and family dining in a truck-stop setting.

Bi-Rite Drugs (downtown at 410 S. Main St., 307/362-6601) houses a soda fountain where the burgers come with a big pile of sautéed onions.

Broadway Burger Station (628 Broadway, 307/363-5858) is where local mechanics (and lots of other folks) go for lunch. The popular '50s-style diner specializes in fountain drinks and enormous burgers ($5–9). Try the French dip or teriyaki burgers for something different.

Bitter Creek Brewing (604 Broadway St., 307/362-4782) is a noisy downtown favorite with award-winning beers. The menu features tasty pub fare, including pasta, sandwiches, and 19 different burgers for lunch, along with pizzas, steaks, pork chops, and baby-back ribs at dinner. Dinner entrées are $9–23, and six fresh brews are on tap. Brick walls, high ceilings, big front windows, and oak tables add to the charm.

International

Several places in town serve Chinese fare in quantity. Two of the better options are **Wonderful House** (1676 Sunset Dr., 307/382-5462) and **China King Buffet** (in the White Mountain Mall, 2441 Foothills Blvd., 307/382-1188). The latter has a huge lunch buffet (with Mongolian grill) for $6; dinner buffets are $8. Nice atmosphere too. **Los Cabos** (117 K St., 307/362-7744) serves good Mexican food.

Rocky Mountain Noodle (1679 Sunset Dr., 307/382-7076) has a bistro menu that includes chicken cordon bleu pasta, Italian cowboy pasta, and shrimp *portofino*. Dinner entrées are very reasonable: $7–12.

Three very good steak-and-seafood places (entrées around $13–25) operate off I-80 west of town: **Log Inn Supper Club** (307/362-7166), **Ted's Supper Club** (307/362-7323), and **White Mountain Mining Co.** (307/382-5265). You won't go wrong at White Mountain Mining. All three are closed Sundays.

INFORMATION AND SERVICES

The **Rock Springs Chamber of Commerce** (1897 Dewar Dr., 307/362-3771 or 800/463-8637, www.rockspringswyoming.net) is open 8 A.M.–5 P.M. Monday–Friday year-round. If it's closed, you can check the pamphlet rack in the entryway (open 24 hours).

The **Bureau of Land Management's Rock Springs Field Office** (307/352-0256, www.wy.blm.gov) is just north of town on U.S. 191. Stop here for information on the Red Desert and wild horses.

The **main library** (400 C St., 307/362-6212) houses a fine collection of Wyoming books and provides web access. **White Mountain Library** (2935 Sweetwater Dr., 307/362-2665) is a delightful place to enjoy the view of White Mountain or stroll through a pleasant rock garden. Find the local **post office** (307/362-9792) at 2829 Commercial Way.

Wash clothes at **Imperial Laundromat** (1669 Sunset Dr., 307/382-2774) or **9th Street Laundromat** (1215 9th St., 307/382-6092).

For medical emergencies, visit **Memorial Hospital of Sweetwater County** (1200 College Dr., 307/362-3711, www.minershospital.com).

GETTING THERE AND AROUND

The **Rock Springs airport** (www.rocksprings-airport.com) is eight miles east of town, and **Great Lakes Aviation** (307/433-2905 or 800/554-5111, www.greatlakesav.com) has daily flights to Denver.

Rent cars at the airport from **Avis** (307/362-5599 or 800/230-4898, www.avis.com), **Enterprise** (307/362-0416 or 800/261-7331, www.enterprise.com), or **Hertz** (307/382-3262 or 800/654-3131, www.hertz.com).

Greyhound (307/362-2931 or 800/231-2222, www.greyhound.com) stops behind McDonald's at 1655 Sunset Drive, heading east to Denver or west to Salt Lake City.

Green River and Vicinity

Straddling the river of the same name, Green River is a prosperous trona-mining and transportation town as well as the seat of Sweetwater County. I-80 cuts a swath just north of town, plunging through tunnels beneath memorable badlands topography. The huge Union Pacific Railroad yard divides Green River. Run-down buildings crowd the railroad tracks, but elsewhere the town appears vibrant. Wander through the older sections to find tidy wooden frame homes, while ranch-style suburbs spread to the south. During the 1970s and '80s, Green River saw an enormous growth surge as the trona mines expanded their operations, as oil and gas explorations attracted thousands of roustabouts, and as a helium facility opened nearby. The population jumped from fewer than 5,000 in 1970 to almost 13,000 in 1980 and has held relatively steady since then.

Green River was established in 1868 as workers constructed the Union Pacific Railroad across southern Wyoming. Three years later, Frederick Dellenbaugh described the town he found in less than flattering terms:

This place, when the railway was building, had been for a considerable time the terminus and a town of respectable proportions had grown up, but with the completion of the road through this region, the terminus moved on, and now all that was to be seen of those golden days was a group of adobe walls, roofless and forlorn.

The present "City" consisted of about thirteen houses, and some of these were of such complex construction that one hesitates whether to describe them as houses with canvas roofs, or tents with board sides.

In May of 1869, Major John Wesley Powell brought fame to the town when his expedition of 10 men climbed off the train at Green River City and began a long float down the Green and Colorado rivers. According to one observer, while in Green River awaiting orders, Powell and his men "tried to drink all the whiskey there was in town. The result was a failure, as Jake Field persisted in making it faster than we could drink it." They made it all the way through the Grand Canyon in stout wooden boats. Seven men survived; three who decided to hike out rather than face the treacherous rapids were never seen again. Powell returned to Green River in 1871 for a second voyage with a large contingent of scientists, who helped map this region and later directed the U.S. Geological Survey.

Green River claims title to a minor legal footnote. In 1931, Green River passed an antipeddling ordinance that achieved national notoriety and inspired similar ordinances in many other towns and cities. The "Green River Ordinance" declared uninvited peddlers or hawkers to be a nuisance punishable by a fine of $25 and higher. The Fuller Brush Company unsuccessfully fought the ordinance all the way to the U.S. Supreme Court.

SOUTHWEST WYOMING

GREEN RIVER

To Lyman and Evanston

EXIT 89

Tollgate Rock

OAK TREE INN

374

80

WESTERN MOTEL

Castle Rock

TRONA DR

HILLCREST WY

W 4TH N

W 3RD N

W 2ND N

N 1TH W

N 6TH W

SUPER 8 MOTEL

CENTENNIAL PARK PLAYGROUND

RAILROAD AVE

N CENTER ST

N 2ND E

E 3RD N

N 5TH E

LIBRARY

SWEETWATER COUNTY HISTORICAL MUSEUM

Walkway

CHAMBER OF COMMERCE

COACHMAN INN MOTEL

E 3RD S

E 2ND S

S 2ND E

S 4TH E

S 4TH S

Expedition Island

Footbridge

FLAMING GORGE WY

To Rock Springs

80

30

EXIT 91

374

Union Pacific Railroad

River

RIVER VIEW DR

Green

POST OFFICE

ASTLE AVE

E TETON BLVD

UINTA DR

Mansface Rock

RODEO ARENA

MONROE ST

CLEARVIEW LANES

SWEET DREAMS INN

HOSPITAL

FLAMING GORGE VISITOR CENTER

SHOSHONE AVE

Green

River

Greenbelt

530

UPLAND WY

To Flaming Gorge National Recreation Area

HITCHING POST DR

W TETON BLVD

BRIDGER DR

SMITH'S

PAMIDA

E TETON BLVD

STRATTON-MYERS PARK

RECREATION CENTER

COLORADO DR

0   0.25 mi

0   0.25 km

WESTERN WYOMING COMMUNITY COLLEGE

BOTTOM NATURE AREA FMC PARK

TRONA MINING

Wyoming leads the world in the mining of an obscure but important mineral: trona. With processing, trona—sodium sesquicarbonate—becomes soda ash and is used in glass, detergents, pulp and paper, metal refining, and baking soda.

Trona is found in a few widely scattered places around the globe, but one-third of the worldwide production comes from a 1,000-square-mile area 25 miles west of Green River. Most trona here occurs in a 10-foot-thick bed 1,500 feet underground. There's no chance of running out soon because there's enough here to supply the world for 2,000 years. The mineral was deposited 50 million years ago when a saline lake developed, reaching 100 by 60 miles in size and up to 2,000 feet in depth. As the climate fluctuated, the lake periodically dried out, precipitating sodium salts. The trona deposits were first discovered in 1938, when an unsuccessful natural-gas well brought up core samples containing trona. Commercial production began in 1948.

Today the four major trona mines are the region's largest employers, producing more than 10 million tons of trona and 8 million tons of soda ash annually. The world's largest trona mine is run by FMC Corporation and has 2,000 miles of tunnels, more than all the streets of San Francisco. Its tunnels are 14 feet wide and 8 feet tall, big enough to use as two-lane roads. Miners get around by driving diesel-powered jeeps or electric golf carts through the maze. Mining methods include a continuous mining machine that grinds out six tons of trona per minute; a long-wall process in which hydraulic rams hold the roof up as it is being mined and then allow the walls to collapse behind after the ore is removed; and solution mining, by which the trona is dissolved underground and pumped to the surface. Once at the surface, trona is processed and sent out on railroad tank cars or in 100-pound bags of soda ash. The production is staggering: At FMC's plant alone the mine extracts more than 900 tons per hour.

SIGHTS

◖ Sweetwater County Historical Museum

This excellent museum (3 E. Flaming Gorge Way, 307/872-6435, www.sweetwatermuseum .org, open 10 A.M.–6P.M. Mon.–Sat., free) is in the old post office. The professionally produced displays change each year but typically include exhibits on the Powell expedition, Oregon trail relics, mining and Indian exhibits, items from the Chinese massacre in Rock Springs (watch the 10-minute video), and an impressive hadrosaur footprint found in a nearby coal mine. Outlaw enthusiasts will find a rifle from Butch Cassidy's gang and the gun of Big Nose George—with two notches in it. Don't miss the fascinating write-up about the Mormon War and the Mountain Meadows Massacre—without the whitewash so often perpetrated. Lots of other unusual things are here, from the century-old ventriloquist dummies to Slovenian costumes and a complex 3-D model of a trona mine. A big statue of explorer John Wesley Powell stands out front. And no, the missing limb isn't due to vandalism; Powell lost his right arm in the Civil War.

Outdoor Attractions

Pick up the *Self-Guided Tour of Historic Green River* from the museum for a detailed walking tour of the town's oldest buildings. Be sure to also walk across the pedestrian overpass that crosses the sprawling **Union Pacific railroad yard.** It's a great place to take in the sights and very noisy engines, loud crashes, bangs, clangs, and horns of freight trains being moved around.

The most distinctive feature of the country around Green River is **Castle Rock,** the stunning rocky pinnacle that rises above the freeway north of town. Other unusual buttes are **Tollgate Rock** on the northwest end of town and **Mansface Rock** behind the post office. The visitor center has a good brochure describing the stories behind these and many other buttes in the area.

ENTERTAINMENT AND EVENTS

Given its blue-collar base, it's no surprise that Green River has plenty of bars. You'll find several along Railroad Avenue, including **((The Brewery** (50 W. Railroad Ave., 307/875-9974) housed in an amusing castle built in 1901. The building was part of Green River Brewery, Wyoming's first. **Wild Horse Saloon** has live music some weekends, and **The Other Place Restaurant** (1410 Uinta Dr., 307/875-2695) is a sing-your-heart-out karaoke spot on Friday nights.

Watch movies at **Green River Dollar Savers** (699 Uinta Dr., 307/875-4702); all seats are $3.50.

The town's **Overland Stage Stampede Rodeo** in early June attracts rodeo riders. **Flaming Gorge Days** (307/875-5711, www.flaminggorgedays.com), the last weekend of June, is the biggest local event, with a parade, bull-riding events, beauty pageant, three-on-three basketball, country and rock concerts, horseshoe contests, kayak races, and tug-of-war. On the **Fourth of July** Green River has rock concerts at the softball complex, along with the obligatory fireworks show. In late August, the **Powell Plunge** attracts kayakers and others for a river triathlon, kayak rodeo, and other events.

RECREATION

A narrow bridge on South 2nd Street leads to **Expedition Island**—a National Historic Site—close to the spot where John Wesley Powell began his expeditions down the Green River. A small plaque memorializes these voyages of discovery. Families appreciate the playground and shady picnic tables, and a footbridge crosses to the south shore. Kayakers enjoy playing in the **whitewater park** near Expedition Island, with a couple of drops that feature swirling holes.

The **Green River Greenbelt** starts at Expedition Island and continues to **Scott's Bottom Nature Area** on the southeast edge of town. Parts of this route are paved, whereas others are dirt and undeveloped. Pick up a map from the visitor center or just follow the easy path from the Expedition Island footbridge.

The big **Green River Recreation Center** (1775 Hitching Post Dr., 307/872-0511,

www.cityofgreenriver.org/parksnrec) houses an Olympic-size L-shaped pool, hot tub, sauna, steam room, gym, weight room, racquetball courts, nursery services, and even miniature golf. During the winter, rent cross-country skis here to explore the nearby Uinta Mountains. **Rolling Green Country Club** (307/875-6200) is a nine-hole public golf course three miles west of town.

Outfitters of Green River (100 E. 2nd S., 307/875-8700) sells fly-fishing gear, has up-to-date hatch information, and rents kayaks. **Highland Desert Flies** (307/875-2358) is a local river guide with float trips down the Green. **Wind River Sporting Goods** (420 Uinta Dr., 307/875-4075 or 800/568-1551) has a range of outdoor and fishing gear and guides fishing trips.

Roll black balls down the lanes at **Clearview Lanes** (1410 Uinta Dr., 307/875-2695).

ACCOMMODATIONS

In addition to the motels listed here, a few other bare-bones places are available in town, but they're primarily for long-term stays.

((Western Motel (890 W. Flaming Gorge, 307/875-2840, $45 s or $48–60 d) is a reasonably priced and well-maintained motel on the west side of town with fridges, microwaves, wireless Internet, and light breakfasts. Another good budget option is **Coachman Inn Motel** (470 E. Flaming Gorge, 307/875-3681, $55 s or $58–65 d), where all units contain fridges and microwaves.

Fill your lodging, food, and entertainment needs at **Sweet Dreams Inn** (1410 Uinta Dr., 307/875-7554), next door to the Clearview Lanes bowling alley, Liquid Emotions Lounge (with Friday night karaoke), and Other Place Restaurant. Standard motel rooms are modern and nicely furnished; $53 for one bed or $63 for two beds. Four-person suites with jetted tubs, microwaves, and fridges are $83.

Oak Tree Inn just off I-80 at exit 89 (1170 W. Flaming Gorge Way, 307/875-3500 or 888/897-9647, www.oaktreeinn.net, $63–71 s or $66–74 d) is a base for Union Pacific Railroad workers, who occupy the three front buildings. The comfortable motel has an indoor hot tub, Wi-Fi, and workout room. Out front is a gleaming 24-hour diner (fitting given all the railroad workers who stay here).

Camping

The nearest public camping is at **Buckboard Crossing Campground** ($17, open mid-May–mid-Sept.), inside Flaming Gorge National Recreation Area and 25 miles south of Green River on Hwy. 530. Make reservations ($9 fee) at 518/885-3639 or 877/444-6777, www.reserveusa.com.

Tex's Travel Camp (four miles west on Hwy. 374, 307/875-2630, $18 tents, $25–29 RVs, open year-round) is right along the river and has some shade trees. Showers are $5 if you aren't camping here.

FOOD

Some of the most popular local steak houses lie on the way east (see *Rock Springs* for details). **Sage Creek Bagels** (36 E. Flaming Gorge Way, 307/875-4877) is a local hangout. The café features an attractive exposed-brick interior, along with freshly baked breads, bagels, and sweets. The light menu includes sandwiches, schmears, salads, and espresso. Stop by for a lunchtime deli sandwich and soup.

◖ Penny's Diner (on the west side of town at 1170 W. Flaming Gorge Way, 307/875-3500) is open 24 hours a day. Built to resemble a 1950s diner, Penny's serves breakfast, burgers, sandwiches, chicken, and salads, along with soda-fountain faves. The shiny silver jukebox plays your dad's tunes. Directly behind the diner are three buildings that house workers from the Union Pacific Railroad.

For stuff-yourself lunch buffets, head to **Pizza Hut** (615 E. Flaming Gorge Way, 307/875-4562) or **China Gardens** (190 N. 5th, 307/875-3259). A longtime favorite of locals, **Don Pedro's** (520 Wilkes Dr., 307/875-7324) has reasonably authentic Mexican food.

Krazy Moose Restaurant (211 E. Flaming Gorge Way, 307/875-5124) has a big menu with all the standards three meals a day. It's a spacious family place with moose heads on the wall and a sports bar (Red Feather Bar) in the back. Dinners are $8–18.

Get groceries and baked goods from **Smith's** (905 Bridger Dr., 307/875-6900); it's open until midnight.

INFORMATION AND SERVICES

Stop by the **Green River Chamber of Commerce** (541 E. Flaming Gorge Way, 307/875-5711, www.grchamber.com, open 8 A.M.–4:30 P.M. Mon.–Fri.) for the latest information or to check out the stuffed outsize lake trout from Flaming Gorge.

The Forest Service operates a **Flaming Gorge National Recreation Area Visitor Center** (1450 Uinta Dr., 307/875-2871, www.fs.fed.us/r4/ashley). It's open 8 A.M.–4:30 P.M. Monday–Friday all year, plus 8 A.M.–4:30 P.M. Saturday late May–early September. Inside is a large relief map of Flaming Gorge, local brochures, and books for sale.

Sweetwater County Library (300 N. 1st E., 307/875-3615) is built over an old cemetery and said to be haunted. Librarians claim to have felt the ghosts, heard voices from empty rooms, and watched gates open on their own. If you don't mind the ghosts, you can surf the web or check email here.

The Green River campus of **Western Wyoming Community College** (307/875-2278, www.wwcc.cc.wy.us) sits atop a hill just south of town, providing a fine view of the surrounding badlands.

Book and Bean (79 N. 1st E., 307/875-5445) sells used (and a few new) volumes.

The local **post office** (307/875-4920) is at 350 Uinta Drive. Wash clothes at **Liberty's Laundry** (1315 Bridger Dr., 307/875-8134).

Castle Rock Medical Center (1400 Uinta, 307/875-6010 or 800/446-5684, www.crhd.org) has physicians on staff.

◖ FLAMING GORGE NATIONAL RECREATION AREA

Flaming Gorge National Recreation Area covers 94,308 acres of wild country, reaching 91 miles from the town of Green River, Wyoming, into northeastern Utah. The region was named by Major John Wesley Powell on his famous 1869 expedition down the river.

Flaming Gorge Reservoir backs up behind a 502-foot-high concrete arch dam, completed in 1964 and situated 15 miles south of the Wyoming border. The waters of the Green River back up behind this dam into a 91-mile lake that provides flood control, water storage, and irrigation for Utah farmers downstream, along with recreation for boaters, water-skiers, and anglers. Each of the dam's three enormous generators produces 50,000 kilowatts of power, electricity that powers computers, hair dryers, and factories throughout the West. Many osprey nest on the rocky pinnacles and cliffs around the edges, while below the dam is a renowned trout fishery and river-runner's funhouse. The area attracts nearly one million visitors annually.

Access

The landscape surrounding the Wyoming section of Flaming Gorge is typical high-desert country, but once you cross into Utah, the road climbs into spectacularly rugged mountains covered with forests of juniper and pinyon, lodgepole, and ponderosa pine. This area was a favorite hideout of Butch Cassidy and other outlaws who operated out of nearby Brown's Park. Flaming Gorge Reservoir is encircled by roads—total loop distance 160 miles—providing a pleasant overnight break from the grinding I-80 routine. The main roads don't come particularly close to the dramatic gorge itself except at the dam, but side roads provide access. Day use at Flaming Gorge National Recreation Area is $2 daily, $5 for 16 days, or $20 for an annual pass. Buy passes from Forest Service offices, visitor centers, or local businesses.

One of the most interesting ways to reach Flaming Gorge is via Hwy. 414 heading southeast from the town of Mountain View. The road climbs past colorful, eroded badlands topography—as though an enormous skeletal landscape were showing through—before emerging into wide-open spaces carpeted with grass and sage. Then the road dips along the Henrys Fork, where cottonwoods and willows border lush green pastures. Huge piles of hay crowd the pastures. Keep your eyes open for the many historic log structures. A sign notes the location of the **Henrys Fork Mountain-man Rendezvous** in July 1825, when 120 trappers and 680 Indians traded furs for supplies from the East. This was the first mountain-man rendezvous in America. Butch Cassidy and other outlaws later frequented Uncle Jack's Cabin Saloon, which stood nearby. Today, tiny **Lonetree** is the "smallest town in the world with a parking meter"—it was brought in from Denver—and **McKinnon** has a little store and a post office, but that's about it until you reach Manila, Utah. This is the real West!

Exploring Flaming Gorge

U.S. 191 heads south from the Rock Springs area over the dry sage-and-juniper landscape. Take the paved turnoff to **Firehole Canyon**, where there are some interesting geological treats, including the two fingerlike projections known as North and South Chimney Rocks. Look for sheepherders tending big flocks nearby. A dirt road continues south along the canyon to the Wyoming border, or you can return to U.S. 191 to eventually reach the dam. Utah Hwy. 44 meets U.S. 191 near the dam and climbs through the scenic mountain country to the west before dropping to the town of Manila, where it joins Hwy. 530 heading north.

Sheep Creek Geological Area is a side loop from the southwestern end of the National Recreation Area and provides views of dramatic geology and land formations. Spectacular rock spires run alongside the Uinta Fault, and frequent roadside signs explain the geological significance of this region. This area is also home to many bighorn sheep. A road leads west from here to **Ute Mountain Fire Tower,** an old wooden lookout with a panoramic view of the Flaming Gorge area and northeastern Uinta Mountains. Built in 1935 by the Civilian Conservation Corps, it was the first one constructed in the state of Utah and the last fire tower still in operation. It is open 10 A.M.–4 P.M. Thursday–Sunday Memorial Day–Labor Day.

Swett Ranch, just south of Flaming Gorge Lodge, is another historic site and a good place to see deer and elk. It's open 10 A.M.–5 P.M. Thursday–Monday Memorial Day–Labor Day.

Just northeast of Manila and barely in Wyoming are several unusual Indian petroglyphs; ask at the Forest Service office for directions. As you continue north along the western side of Flaming Gorge along Hwy. 530, the road passes **Haystack Buttes,** a series of beehive-shaped rocky mounds, followed by the barren, eroded badlands of **Devils Playground,** where sagebrush, sand, and cactus extend as far as you can see.

Hiking

Several trails are noteworthy in Flaming Gorge. **Little Hole National Recreation Trail** follows the north bank of Green River from just below the dam to Little Hole, seven miles away. You may want to set up a car shuttle to save having to hike back the same way. The scenic five-mile

Canyon Rim Trail connects Greendale Overlook with the Red Canyon Visitor center. The trail is also accessible from the Skull Creek, Greens Lake, and Canyon Rim campgrounds and is open to mountain bikes.

The steep **Dowd Mountain-Hideout Canyon Trail** drops five miles from Dowd Mountain Overlook to Hideout Boat Campground; it's open to mountain bikes. The overlook is four miles off the main road. A helpful brochure describing these and other trails is available from Forest Service offices and visitor centers in Manila or Green River.

A cautionary note for hikers in the Flaming Gorge area: Rattlesnakes are common in the desert and can be deadly, although bites are not common. Keep your eyes and ears open at all times.

If you want to explore further, head 30 miles west of Manila to the wonderful **High Uintas Wilderness.** This area is popular with hikers and cross-country skiers from the Evanston and Green River areas and includes Kings Peak, the highest mountain in Utah. Several access roads come in from the north, including Hwy. 150, a National Scenic Byway. See the Forest Service office in Evanston for details, or stop at the **Bear River Ranger Station** (435/642-6662), 30 miles south of Evanston and open June–October. Cabins, boat rentals, and meals are available at **Spirit Lake Lodge** (435/880-3089, open June–Oct.).

Mountain Biking

Excellent opportunities exist for mountain bikers throughout the Flaming Gorge area, particularly on trails in the more rugged southern end. Pick up a brochure describing the most popular routes at Forest Service offices or visitor centers in Manila or Green River. Rent mountain bikes from **Red Canyon Lodge** (nine miles southwest of the dam, 435/889-3759, www.redcanyonlodge.com).

Fishing and Boating

Flaming Gorge Reservoir is famous for its monster fish, including a record 51-pound Mackinaw and a world-record 33-pound brown trout.

In addition to these two species, anglers catch lake and rainbow trout, kokanee, and smallmouth and largemouth bass. **Flaming Gorge Fishing Derby** in mid-May is one of the biggest such events in Wyoming. Return on the **Fourth of July** for a popular fireworks display at Dutch John.

Three places on the reservoir rent skiffs, ski boats, and ski equipment: **Buckboard Marina** (307/875-6927 or 800/824-8155, www.fishinginthewest.com), **Cedar Springs Marina** (435/889-3795, www.cedarspringsmarina.com), and **Lucerne Valley Marina** (435/784-3483 or 888/820-9225, www.flaminggorge.com). Lucerne Valley also rents houseboats, and Buckboard rents fishing gear. Marinas are open mid-April–mid-October and carry basic supplies and fishing gear. Most fishing guides operate out of Manila and Dutch John on the Utah side; see visitor centers for a listing.

Below the dam, the Green River is considered the finest fishing in Utah, with up to 16,000 trout per mile. If you have a Wyoming fishing license and plan to fish in the Utah part of Flaming Gorge—or vice versa—you'll need to get a special Flaming Gorge Reservoir Reciprocal Stamp for $10. You can buy these at local businesses in Manila and Dutch John.

River Rafting

One of the most popular summertime activities is floating on the Green River below Flaming Gorge Dam. An entry station below the dam has safety information. The first several miles of the float are relatively gentle, although there are a half dozen small rapids, and they can be run without a guide, but life jackets are mandatory. Float tubes are not recommended.

Most folks put in just below the spillway and take out at Little Hole, seven miles downriver. Plan on three hours for the run. There's no overnight camping allowed along this stretch, but you'll find 18 campsites below Little Hole in the nine-mile stretch before you get to historic Browns Park. Check at the various visitor centers for details and precautions for these longer float trips. Get 24-hour in-

formation on lake elevation and river flow at 800/277-7571, www.usbr.gov/uc.

Rent rafts and inflatable kayaks from **Flaming Gorge Recreation Services** (in Dutch John, 435/885-3191, www.fgrecservices.com), **Flaming Gorge Lodge** (four miles south of the dam, 435/889-3773, www.fglodge.com), or **Trout Creek Flies** (in Dutch John, 435/885-3338, www.fishgreenriver.com). All of these companies offer guided float-fishing trips (around $375 per day for two people in a dory) and shuttle services (from Little Hole, $50 for up to eight people). Flaming Gorge Recreation Services and Trout Creek Flies also have hot showers. Note that varying releases from the dam may push the river up or down 3–4 feet in a matter of 15–30 minutes. Fortunately, fluctuations are rare and usually occur at night.

Winter Recreation

Snowplows keep the paved highway circling Flaming Gorge National Recreation Area clear throughout the winter, providing access to outstanding places for exploration. (Note, however, that the plows don't operate on weekends in Wyoming!) The Forest Service maintains **cross-country ski trails** at six areas along the Utah side of Flaming Gorge: Death Valley, Elk Park, Dowd Mountain, Canyon Rim, Lake Creek, and Swett Ranch. These vary greatly in length and difficulty; pick up a map from the Ashley National Forest offices in Manila (435/784-3445), Green River (307/875-2871), or the Flaming Gorge Dam Visitor center (435/885-3135). Rent snowmobiles from **Flaming Gorge Lodge** (435/889-3773, www.fglodge.com).

Accommodations and Food

Because of the popularity of this area, it's a good idea to reserve a week or two ahead during the summer to be assured of a place to stay—or in July if you need a place on Labor Day weekend.

Four miles southwest of the dam, **Flaming Gorge Lodge** (435/889-3773, www.fglodge.com) has motel rooms for $77 s or $83 d and one-bedroom condos with kitchens for $123 d (plus $6 per person for additional guests). Also here are a general store, café, and full-service restaurant. The lodge is open year-round.

One of the nicest places in the area is ◖ **Red Canyon Lodge** (435/889-3759, www.redcanyonlodge.com) near Red Canyon Overlook nine miles southwest of the dam. Lodging is available in luxurious duplex log cabins overlooking the lake. These have private baths, kitchenettes, vaulted ceilings, and covered porches; $125 d or $135 for four people. Smaller cabins with two double beds, fridges, and microwaves are $95 d or $105 for four. Also offered here are horseback rides, mountain-bike rentals, canoe and rowboat rentals (for East Greens Lake only), a fine restaurant, and a little store with groceries, souvenirs, and fishing tackle. Kids fish for free in a private lake on the grounds. The cabins are available year-round, but the restaurant and store are closed on weekdays late October–April.

The town of Manila, just three miles south of the Wyoming border on the west side of the reservoir, is home to the Forest Service's **Flaming Gorge National Recreation Area District Office** (435/784-3445). Manila offers several lodging options, including **Steinaker's Motel** (435/784-3363, $40 d) and **Vacation Inn** (435/784-3259 or 800/662-4327, $76 d for condos with kitchens, open Mar.–Oct.). Get groceries at **Flaming Gorge Market** (435/784-3582). Find additional information online at www.flaminggorgecountry.com. For more on points south, see *Moon Utah,* by W. C. McRae and Judy Jewell (www.moon.com).

Camping

The Forest Service maintains 25 roadside campgrounds ($5–17) in the Flaming Gorge National Recreation Area, although most of these are managed by concessionaires. Showers are available at the Deer Run, Firehole, and Mustang Ridge campgrounds if you aren't camping. Most campgrounds are on the Utah side of the border, particularly around the dam, and they typically open by mid-May and close in mid-September, although a few remain open year-round. Red Canyon Campground is a favorite, with spectacular canyon vistas. You can make reservations ($9 fee) for approximately

half of these campgrounds at 518/885-3639 or 877/444-6777, www.reserveusa.com. You can also camp for free in undeveloped parts of the Flaming Gorge National Recreation Area or in one of several boat-in camps.

At **Flaming Gorge KOA Kampground** (in Manila, Utah, 435/784-3184 or 800/562-3254, www.koa.com, $22 tents, $28 RVs, $40 cabins, open mid-Apr.–mid-Oct.), facilities include an outdoor pool and game room. Other places with RV sites include **Flaming Gorge Recreation Services** (in Dutch John, 435/885-3191, www.fgrecservices.com, $10 tents, $20–25 RVs), **Lucerne Valley Marina** (435/784-3483 or 888/820-9225, www.flaminggorge.com, $14 tents, $17 RVs), and **Buckboard Marina** (307/875-6927 or 800/824-8155, www.fishinginthewest.com, $22 RVs).

Visitor Centers

Flaming Gorge National Recreation Area is administered by the U.S. Forest Service. Get information, maps, and books from Ashley National Forest offices in Manila, Utah (435/784-3228) or Green River, Wyoming (307/875-2871). The offices are open weekdays. Find out more at www.fs.fed.us/r4/ashley.

The Forest Service maintains **Flaming Gorge Dam Visitor center** (435/885-3135) atop the dam; it's open 8 A.M.–6 P.M. daily Memorial Day–Labor Day, and 10 A.M.–5 P.M. daily September–mid-October and April–May, closed in winter. Free one-hour guided dam tours are offered when the center is open.

The **Red Canyon Overlook Visitor Center** (435/889-3713) is open 10 A.M.–5 P.M. daily Memorial Day–Labor Day (closed the rest of the year) and offers breathtaking canyon views. Campfire programs take place Friday and Saturday evenings in the summer.

LITTLE AMERICA

Find Little America approximately 20 miles west of Green River. From either direction along I-80, billboards announce, "Little America, only 350 (250, 150, 100…) miles ahead!" And then, out in the desolate, windblown landscape, drivers suddenly come to this oasis of consumption where you can cozy up to cable TV or enjoy fresh produce trucked in from California. The repair bays can hold half a dozen tractor-trailers at once and often do. Ten bright-red fuel tanks have "Little America" emblazoned on their sides, flanked by two emperor penguins, and a small town's worth of tidy brick buildings occupy the site, including a gift shop, restaurant, grocery mart, and café. It's as if a small suburban town had suddenly been plunked down into the middle of nowhere, with everything open 24 hours a day.

Little America had its origins in the mind of S. M. Covey, a sheepherder who spent a fearful winter near here in the 1890s. Covey resolved to build a way station for travelers, a place to escape the blizzards and wind. Many years later he saw a photo of Admiral Byrd's "Little America" in Antarctica and was inspired in 1932 to create his own Little America, adding through the years a restaurant, a motel, dozens of gas pumps—and penguins atop the hotel. He died in the 1960s and the operation was bought by Earl Holding. Other Little America stations are flung across the West—Cheyenne, Sun Valley, Flagstaff, Salt Lake City, and even San Diego—but this is the real thing, and the only one that rates a name on the map.

Practicalities

Little America Motel (307/875-2400 or 800/634-2401, www.littleamerica.com, $78–99 d) has 140 large and immaculate rooms, plus a circular outdoor pool and indoor fitness center. The coffee shop is always open and good; you'll find reasonably priced meals both here and in the restaurant. The pastries and pies are favorites, and nearly everyone gets a tall 35-cent soft ice cream cone to go. But the real reason for Little America's existence is fuel to propel you on down the road. It's fitting that a place with such a patriotic name should be built to worship the internal-combustion engine.

CHURCH BUTTES

West of Little America, I-80 lies across colorful badlands country, passing a temple of a different kind—Church Buttes. Brigham Young and

Church Buttes, near Green River

his Mormon pioneers held religious services under these churchlike spires in 1847. Take the Church Buttes exit from I-80 and head 5.5 miles north on a gravel road past several gas wells. The 75-foot-high buttes are at the intersection with Granger Road (County Road 233). The historic Mormon Pioneer Trail parallels Granger Road in this area and is marked by concrete posts.

GRANGER

The dinky town of Granger (pop. 150) is five miles north of Little America on U.S. 30 and contains the **Granger Stage Station.** The sandstone building was a stopping point on the Overland Trail and housed such visitors as Mark Twain and Horace Greeley.

The **Hams Fork Rendezvous** (307/875-5556) takes place near Granger in mid-August, with costumed mountain men and women and traditional contests of daring, including tomahawk throwing, fire-starting contests, rifle shoots, and a horse ride. Held on the site of the 1834 rendezvous, this one really strives for authenticity, with pre-1840s dress required of all the participants.

SEEDSKADEE NATIONAL WILDLIFE REFUGE

The 22,000-acre Seedskadee National Wildlife Refuge is 37 miles northwest of the town of Green River on Hwy. 372. The word comes from the Shoshone word Seeds-kee-dee, "River of the Prairie Chicken." The refuge stretches 35 miles along the Green River and contains marshes and riparian areas that provide outstanding waterfowl and wildlife habitat. It's one of the finest birding areas in the state; more than 200 species have been sighted. Canada geese are common, along with sandhill cranes, coots, shorebirds, great blue herons, and a variety of ducks. Good fishing can be found here, and canoeists and rafters will see many moose,

deer, and antelope along the banks. This is a relatively gentle float trip, although you will need to watch for boulders placed in the channel to improve the fish habitat. Make sure unoccupied boats are tied to the shore because river levels may rise suddenly as a result of releases from Fontenelle Reservoir. The reservoir backs up behind a 139-foot earthen dam a few miles upstream from the refuge.

Practicalities

Refuge headquarters (307/875-2187, http://seedskadee.fws.gov) is two miles north from the intersection of Hwy. 372 and Hwy. 28. Be sure to pick up the refuge brochure detailing Seedskadee's surprisingly rich history.

Camping is not allowed within the refuge, but you can camp just upstream at the BLM-run **Weeping Rock, Tailrace,** and **Slate Creek** campgrounds. Weeping Rock and Slate Creek campgrounds are also used as access points to float the river.

NORTHEAST TO FARSON

Highway 28 crosses the Green River at Seedskadee National Wildlife Refuge and continues for 28 little-traveled miles to the tiny settlement of Farson (see *Wind River Mountains Country* chapter). It's classic Old West country, with Pilot Butte visible to the south and the Wind River Mountains to the northeast. Amusing wildlife billboards warn of crossing critters along the way, and a roadside marker at **Simpson Hollow** gives a sanitized version of an incident that took place during the short-lived "Mormon War." In 1857, a group of Mormon guerrillas attacked a U.S. Army wagon train filled with supplies in Simpson Hollow. A second wagon train had been destroyed the previous day at the Green River as part of Brigham Young's war against the federal government. In these two incidents 74 wagons were captured and burned by the Mormons.

Bridger Valley

Bridger Valley is a large splotch of green in the midst of desert country, nourished by numerous irrigation ditches off the Blacks Fork River. This was the first place in Wyoming to be farmed, having been settled by Mormons in 1853. By the way, the various branches of the Green River—Smiths Fork, Blacks Fork, Henrys Fork, La Barge, and Hams Fork—are all named for trappers in Jedediah Smith's party of mountain men, who first spread over this country in 1824. At the time these were considered the richest beaver-trapping waters ever discovered.

LYMAN

Lyman (pop. 2,000) consists of a wide main street and not a whole lot else. Named for a Mormon leader, the town's initial settlers included many members of that religion, and a large Latter-day Saints church sits in the center of town.

Because this is a Mormon town, July 24 has a special meaning; it was on this date in 1847 that pioneers first reached what would become Salt Lake City. Lyman's **Mormon Pioneer Days** (307/787-6573) offers a week full of activities, including a rodeo, parade, and dance.

The **International Pedigree Stage Stop Sled Dog Race** (www.wyomingstagestop.org) stops here. (See the *Jackson Hole* chapter for more information.)

The town also has a public **swimming pool** (307/787-6333).

North of town—and just a mile from I-80—**KOA Kampground** (307/786-2762 or 800/562-2762, www.koa.com, $21 tents, $24 RVs, open mid-May–Sept.) has an outdoor pool. Simple cabins are $34 d. Not much shade here.

TJ's (307/787-3737) has videos on one side and fast food—including subs, thick malts, and pizzas—on the other.

Lyman's pretentious town complex houses the **Greater Bridger Valley Chamber of Commerce** (307/787-6738, www.bridgervalleychamber.com).

MOUNTAIN VIEW

The growing town of Mountain View (pop. 1,200) is appropriately named; to the south, the Uintas form a snow-capped, rough-edged horizon. Mountain View is in the heart of farming and ranching country. There's not much to see in the town itself, but it's obviously a popular place to live, with lots of new developments in the last few years.

Hoedown on the Smiths Fork (307/782-3100) comes to Mountain View on Labor Day weekend with polka and country music. The town also has a public **swimming pool** (307/782-3525).

You'll find good sub sandwiches, burgers, pasta, chicken, soups, salads, and ice cream at **Pony Express** (307/782-6782), an impressive log structure. Right out back are modern cabins for $99 d.

The closest public campground is 22 miles away along the Wyoming–Utah line. Get recreation information from the **Wasatch National Forest District Office** (307/782-6555, www.fs.fed.us/wcnf) in Mountain View.

PIEDMONT

The ghost town of Piedmont is a rarely visited part of Wyoming but worth the seven-mile drive south from I-80. Take the LeRoy Road exit (mile 24), head west on County Road 128, and follow an old railroad grade south. Continue straight at the intersection and keep your eyes open for the herd of wild buffalo that roams this country. Established as a water and wood refueling station for the Union Pacific, Piedmont was also the scene of an 1869 incident in which 300 railroad workers blocked a train carrying Union Pacific vice president Dr. Thomas Durrant en route to ceremonies at Promontory Point. The workers demanded $200,000 (some reports put the figure at $500,000) in back pay before they finally let Durrant proceed.

Around 1869, Moses Byrne built five **charcoal kilns** near Piedmont, each 30 feet

JIM BRIDGER

Legendary figures fill the history of the West, but Jim Bridger ranks as the uncrowned king of the mountain men. Like many other 19th-century frontiersmen, Bridger never learned to read or write, but his deep knowledge of the mountains and Indians gained him the name "Old Gabe" because his skills were said to rival those of the angel Gabriel. Jim Bridger has 21 different Wyoming places named for him, more than any other individual.

Bridger was born in 1804 in Virginia and later moved with his family to Missouri. When both his parents died, he was sent off to apprentice with a blacksmith, but the wild country beckoned. When William Ashley advertised for "Enterprising Young Men" to go into the Rockies to trap beaver, Bridger quickly joined up. He was on the first keelboat that headed out in 1822 and wintered that year on the Bear River of southern Idaho. When men began speculating on where the Bear River led, Bridger volunteered to find out, thus becoming the first white man to discover the Great Salt Lake. Bridger took any challenge in stride. When Ashley needed a volunteer to test the possibility of running furs down the Bighorn River, Bridger stepped forward. He nearly died taking his log raft through the wild waters of Bighorn Canyon, but the adventure added to his growing reputation.

Bridger entered the fur-trading business in 1830 when he and four others bought the Rocky Mountain Fur Company from Ashley. They in turn sold the business to William Sublette five years later. Bridger continued to lead trapping parties until the last rendezvous in 1840, after which he turned his attention to the growing tide of emigrants heading west to California and Oregon. Together with partner Louis Vásquez, Bridger built a trading post (Fort Bridger) along the Blacks Fork of the Green River. He later served as a scout for the U.S. Army in the Powder River Basin, although his sage advice was often ignored.

Like many other mountain men, Jim Bridger had several wives. His first was a white Mormon woman, but when Jim refused to join her religion they separated. He later married three different Indian women, none of whom spoke English. The first two died early, but the last one — daughter of the great Shoshone Chief Washakie — returned to Missouri with him.

Bridger's knowledge of sign language was legendary; he once kept an audience of Sioux and Cheyenne Indians in rapt attention for more than an hour as he signed a lengthy adventure. In one of his yarns, told to a naive British army captain, Bridger described how the Indians had him trapped in a canyon with his only escape up a 200-foot waterfall. When the captain insisted on discovering how he escaped this predicament, Bridger wryly went on, "Oh bless your soul, Captain, we never did get out. The Indians killed us right there!" Partly because of such yarns, few believed Bridger's true accounts of the geysers and hot springs he had found in Yellowstone or of the stream that split along the Continental Divide, with waters flowing in both directions. Bridger died on his Missouri farm in 1881 at the age of 77.

high and 30 feet across and made of stone and mortar. Wood was sealed in the ovens and slowly burned until it turned into charcoal for Utah's Pioneer smelter. Three of these massive kilns still stand, like three oversized breasts emerging from the plains. Just up the hill is the old Byrne family graveyard with the graves of many children who died young in this harsh place.

South of the kilns are a dozen buildings from old Piedmont, abandoned when the railroad tracks were moved farther north in 1901. The last store closed in 1940. A local legend claims that Butch Cassidy buried loot from one of his bank holdups near here. Treasure hunters still search for it. The father of Calamity Jane, gunned down in a saloon, lies buried in an unmarked grave in the small Piedmont cemetery.

For a surprising drive, take Piedmont Road just northeast from the Piedmont town site. This narrow gravel road (not recommended after recent rains or for RVs) climbs a high and very

© DON PITCHER

These charcoal kilns in the ghost town of Piedmont once made charcoal for a Utah smelter.

steep hill to a dramatic viewpoint before dropping into the conifers at a miniscule place called **Robertson** and then on to Mountain View and Lyman. It's easy to get on the wrong road here and end up heading toward Utah, so make sure you have a good map before heading out.

(FORT BRIDGER STATE HISTORIC SITE

The most interesting historic site in Southwest Wyoming is Fort Bridger, in the town of the same name. The Uinta Mountains form a majestic backdrop to the south, and the Blacks Fork River winds through. The old fort is just three miles off I-80 and provides an easy diversion from the interstate-highway blahs.

History

Fort Bridger was built in 1843 by the famed mountain man Jim Bridger and his Mexican partner, Louis Vásquez. The location—right on the Oregon and Mormon trails—quickly made this a vital stopping point for emigrants heading west to California, Oregon, or Salt Lake City.

The new "fort" consisted of a few crude log huts and a corral surrounded by a log stockade, while the lush riverside country provided pasturage for stock. Conflicts quickly developed between Bridger and the Mormon emigrants, who eyed his prosperous trade with envy and his good relations with the Indians as competition in their own efforts to turn them against the U.S. government. Under the pretext that Bridger was supplying weapons to Ute Indians, Brigham Young ordered Bridger arrested and sent 150 men to do the job. Bridger managed to escape, hiding in a nearby eagle nest while the men searched in vain. He finally fled with his Indian wife to Fort Laramie but lost all of his merchandise, livestock, and buildings to the raiders. The Mormons then built their own base, **Fort Supply,** 12 miles south of Bridger's trading post and established the first agricultural settlement in Wyoming. Soon Fort Supply had more than 100 log buildings surrounded by a palisade. In 1855, they bought Fort Bridger from Vásquez—without Bridger's knowledge or consent—and added a variety of structures. When the so-called Mormon War began two years later, the Saints decided to leave nothing for the U.S. Army. They burned both forts and fled to Salt Lake City.

Jim Bridger leased his land to the army in 1858 for $600 per year. The army rebuilt the fort with room for 350 resident troops. A Pony Express station was established in 1860, followed later by an Overland Stage station. The fort was the site of the first newspaper published in Wyoming (1863) and served as a base for Chief Washakie's band of Shoshone Indians until a treaty signed here in 1868 established the Wind River Reservation. Fort Bridger was abandoned by the military in 1890, and many of its buildings were sold at auction. Thirty years later, the state of Wyoming bought the site and has since restored or reconstructed many of the buildings.

Access

Fort Bridger (307/782-3842, http://wyoparks.state.wy.us) is open 9 A.M.–5:30 P.M. daily May–September and 9 A.M.–4:30 P.M. Saturday–Sunday in April and October; closed November–March. Day use costs $2 for non-residents, $1 for Wyoming residents. Several buildings are open to the public during summer, but only the museum is open the rest of the year. In June, July, and August the staff dresses in 1880s costumes and provides living-history demonstrations and historical information. Various activities take place throughout the year, including a big mountain-man rendezvous. In August, take the special moonlight tour, on which you'll meet characters from the past; call several months ahead to book these.

Sights

The attractive grounds are sprinkled with aspen and cottonwood trees and beautifully restored buildings. First stop is the **museum and visitor center,** housed in the enlisted-men's barracks. Inside you'll gain an excellent glimpse into the past with a model of the old fort, displays of army uniforms and weapons, Indian artifacts—including a bowl made from the hump of a buffalo—and a papoose board. Be sure to look for Jim Bridger's old powder

horn, vest, and other items, including a photo of a "young" Jim Bridger created by computerized reverse aging. Visitors can watch a 15-minute video on the fort's history.

The **Bridger-Vásquez Trading Co.** stands in one corner of the fort and has a working blacksmith shop in the back. It's open 9 A.M.–5 P.M. daily May–September but closed October–April. Inside this replica of Bridger's original trading post, the shop sells all sorts of interesting items: trade beads, animal furs, coyote and muskrat skulls, "church" dolls, Indian sweetgrass, old-time shirts and dresses, and even bull-scrotum bags. Ask for demonstrations of the fire steels.

Just south of the museum is a rock wall built by Mormons when they controlled the fort. Other buildings include a small commissary and two guardhouses. On the east side of the fort is the antique-filled **commanding officer's quarters,** built in 1884. Aspen trees line the alleyway connecting this building with the **log officer's quarters,** built in 1858. Look inside for the section from an aspen tree carved by Buffalo Bill Cody. On the south side of the fort is a century-old ranch home—**Goodrick House**—that was moved here and furnished with antiques.

The **post sutler's complex** contains several furnished buildings, including Wyoming's oldest schoolhouse (1860), the post trader's store, and five other structures. Not far away is the fenced-in grave of a local hero: Thornburgh the dog, who once saved a drowning boy and later warned the post of an Indian attack. A small human cemetery is near the commanding officer's quarters. A display case in the museum houses items found during archaeological excavations, including buttons, trade beads, and other items.

Fort Bridger Rendezvous

Each Labor Day weekend the largest modern-day mountain-man rendezvous in Wyoming comes to Fort Bridger. This is one of Wyoming's most enjoyable events, so don't miss it! In addition, there's a big rodeo the same weekend in Evanston, just 30 miles to the west.

SOUTHWEST WYOMING

© DON PITCHER

teepee at Fort Bridger Rendezvous

During the rendezvous, tents and tepees sprawl across the fort grounds, and hundreds of costumed revelers join in the celebration. Trader's row offers 1840s-style crafts and trade items, including beads, furs, and tomahawks. Participants take part in cannon shoots, muzzle-loading contests, Indian dancing, Dutch-oven cooking, tomahawk throwing, and acoustic music. Great cooked-over-the-fire food is offered, too. The rendezvous attracts 400 buckskinners, squaws, hunters, and pilgrims, along with thousands of spectators.

Other summer events at Fort Bridger include a parade, a rodeo, and a town dance on the **Fourth of July,** and **moonlight tours** of the fort grounds in mid-July; call 307/782-3842 for reservations.

Fort Bridger Town

The town of Fort Bridger contains **Wagon Wheel Motel** (307/782-6361) with a mix of choices: $40 d in older rooms, $50 d in newer ones (some with kitchenettes), and $75 d for a cabin with full kitchen. Park RVs for $20. A restaurant on the premises serves breakfast and lunch, or get limited groceries at **Fort Bridger Cash Store** (307/782-6744). **Fort Bridger RV Camp** (307/782-3150 or 800/578-6535, $15 tents, $19 RVs) is open all year. **Jim Bridger Trading Post** (307/782-6115) sells souvenirs, and—if you're in the market—washing machines.

Evanston

West of Fort Bridger, I-80 begins a lengthy climb into the hills, leaving the desert behind as it heads toward the Utah border. The tidy, friendly town of Evanston (pop. 12,000) lies just six miles from the Utah border and only 80 miles from Salt Lake City. Evanston's economy is a mix of gas and oil, tourism, health care, and government. On the outskirts of Evanston, fireworks stands crowd the freeway off-ramps, waiting to lure Utahans who create weekend traffic jams in pursuit of booze, bars, betting, cheap gas, and even a busy porn shop (next to Lotty's Family Restaurant, no less).

Evanston is a mix of old and new. Last time I visited the high schoolers were driving old pickups down the main drag with hip hop music shaking the windows. The town founders are probably spinning in their coffins. And that's not all that's spinning. A large wind farm consisting of 80 turbines—enough to power 43,000 homes—carpets the hills just east of Evanston and are visible from I-80 and U.S. 189. The turbines are each 330 feet tall. Many more windmills are planned for the country immediately south of town.

As the transcontinental railroad's construction crews raced across Wyoming in 1868, the settlement of Evanston was established as the last division point before the Wasatch Range. The town received its name from the railroad's surveyor, James A. Evans. In 1886, the territorial legislature offered Uinta County repre-

© AVALON TRAVEL PUBLISHING, INC.

sentatives the choice of either a university or an insane asylum. They chose the asylum. By the following year, Evanston had 1,500 people, many of whom worked at the Union Pacific car and machine shops, at an ice plant, or on the tracks. Others logged railroad ties in the mountains or raised sheep and cattle. Rich deposits of coal were discovered four miles north of Evanston, and several mines soon opened, creating the town of **Almy.** In 1869, hundreds of Chinese miners were hired as strikebreakers at the mines, creating tensions that would later erupt into race riots and force the temporary abandonment of Evanston's Chinatown.

The Almy mines became notorious for deadly methane-gas explosions. At least 60 whites and uncounted Chinese miners were killed in blasts in 1881, 1886, and 1895. The mines closed in 1906, leaving many of the fires unextinguished; you can still see evidence of the smoldering fires. Many of the old mine buildings still stand at the townsite, but the town has long since been abandoned.

THE OVERTHRUST BELT

Evanston lies at the center of the energy-rich Overthrust Belt, which extends from Canada to Mexico. This 40-mile-wide uplift was formed when two land masses smashed together, thrusting the western section atop the eastern half and creating folds that trapped oil and gas. It was long believed to contain rich energy deposits, but hundreds of dry holes were drilled before one finally hit home. In 1976, the Yellow Creek Oil Field was discovered, producing both oil and natural gas and unleashing a boomtown atmosphere. Many more oil and gas fields have been discovered since then.

SIGHTS
Depot Square

A renovation project in downtown Evanston has created an attractive central area with a fountain and open grassy lawns for relaxing. The focal point is the old **Evanston Depot.** Built in 1900, it was one of the finest along the line and had separate waiting rooms for men and women. A 1944 Union Pacific dining car and caboose stand outside the depot, and the nearby **Beeman-Cashin Implement Depot** is used for dances and community activities. Built around 1886 and restored a cen-

tury later, this unique wooden structure has no supporting posts.

The historic Carnegie library building is now home to both the **Evanston Visitor Center** and the **Uinta County Museum** (307/789-2757, free), open 9 A.M.–5 P.M. year-round Monday–Friday, plus 10 A.M.–4 P.M. Saturday–Sunday during summer. Exhibits include historic photos, arrowheads, and a variety of local items. While here, pick up a **walking-tour brochure** of Evanston that details many of the older buildings in town. Outside the museum are several old wagons.

Several large brick railroad buildings line the tracks on the northwest end of Front Street, including the old roundhouse and the adjacent **Roundhouse Machine Shop,** beautifully restored and now used for local events.

Joss House

Early in the last century, Evanston had a prominent Chinatown along the north side of the tracks. Life centered around the Joss House, a Taoist temple built in 1894 and one

© DON PITCHER

Depot Square, Evanston

of just three in the nation (the others were in San Francisco and New York). Thousands of pilgrims came from hundreds of miles away to worship. After the Chinese workers returned to their homeland, the building was destroyed in a suspicious 1922 fire that leveled much of Chinatown. A replica of the Joss House was completed in 1990 next to Depot Square and furnished with historic photos, an 1874 Chinese signboard, decorative panels from the original Joss House, opium pipes, a priceless triangular flag and century-old dragon, a Buddha figure, a gong, lanterns, and more. Check out the pottery, coins, and other artifacts found during **archaeological digs** at the Chinatown site. The digging continues each August. Be sure to ask about the video on Mormon Charlie and China Mary, the only Chinese who remained after 1922. The few Chinese Americans in Evanston today moved here more recently. Stop by the nearby museum for Joss House tours.

ENTERTAINMENT AND EVENTS

Evanston is jam-packed with liquor stores and lounges to quench the parched throats of Utahans who cross the border in droves. **Legal Tender Lounge** (at Dunmar Inn, 1601 Harrison Dr., 307/789-3770) has two bars—an upstairs disco with Top 40 tunes and a downstairs saloon where you can dance to live rock bands on weekends—and draws mainly a young crowd. **Pete's Rock-N-Rye Club,** a longtime bar east of town on U.S. 30, 307/789-2135, has occasional live music. Or just hang out in the relaxing atmosphere of **Kate's Bar** (936 Main St., 307/789-7662).

Watch movies at **Evanston Valley Cinema** (45 Aspen Grove Dr. E., 307/789-0522) or **Strand Theatre** (1028 Main St., 307/789-2974).

Events

The **International Pedigree Stage Stop Sled Dog Race** (307/734-1163, www.wyomingstagestop.org) stops here. (See the *Jackson Hole* chapter for more information.)

One of the most unusual Evanston events is **Chinese New Year,** featuring a parade, Chinese foods, fireworks, rickshaw races, and, of course, the dragon. With so few Chinese Americans in Evanston today, many of the performers are of other ancestry.

On summer weekends, **Wyoming Downs Racetrack** (12 miles north of Evanston on Hwy. 89, 307/789-0511 or 800/842-8722, www.wyomingdowns.com) has horse racing with pari-mutuel betting on Saturdays and Sundays. Wyoming's only live-meet horse track, it is particularly popular with folks from Salt Lake because horse racing is illegal in Utah. At the High Country Inn, race enthusiasts can also watch and wager off-track bets on nationwide races.

The **Evanston Rodeo Series** (307/789-5511) includes amateur rodeo events five weekends throughout the summer.

In late June, cyclists compete in the **High Uintas Classic Stage Race** (www.evanstoncycling.org), which traverses the Uinta Mountains in a spectacular 80-mile route; cyclists must climb over a 12,000-foot pass along the way. There's more cycling in mid-August, when mountain-bikers compete in the **Wolverine Ridge XC Race** on trails south of town.

Evanston's **Uinta County Fair** (www.uintacountyfair.com) the first week of August includes a greased-pig contest, 4-H animal judging, rodeos, carnival rides, concerts, and even pedal-power tractor pulls.

Cowboy Days

Evanston's main event is, predictably, the annual PRCA rodeo, here known as Cowboy Days. Labor Day weekend festivities pack all the motels in town as folks come from surrounding states to watch professional cowboys show their stuff at "the biggest little rodeo in the world." The three-day event also includes musical entertainment, dances, an arts-and-crafts fair, a parade, a pancake breakfast, a spaghetti dinner, and clowns. Labor Day is also the weekend for the popular Fort Bridger Rendezvous, just 30 miles east at historic Fort Bridger.

SHOPPING

The old Federal Building (built in 1915), on the corner of 10th and Center Streets, is home to several shops, including **Joyce Keselburg Studio,** with oil paintings, and **Common Threads** (1029 Main St., 307/789-1675), a good place to find quilts and fabrics. **Rocky Mtn. Lodgepole Furniture Co.** (1049 Main St., 307/789-9042 or 800/827-9042) creates rustic and functional chairs, benches, beds, and other furnishings.

Get books along with unique gifts from **Dee's Bookstore** (900 Main St., 307/789-0166).

Sports World (inside Jubilee Foods at 524 Front St., 307/789-6788) sells outdoor gear, and its walls are lined with big-game mounts.

RECREATION
Bear River State Park

This 300-acre park surrounds the Bear River Information Center just south of Evanston (I-80 at exit 6). The Bear River flows northward, eventually draining into Great Salt Lake. At 400 miles in length, it's the largest river in the Western Hemisphere that doesn't reach the ocean.

There's no camping, but Bear River State Park (307/789-6547, http://wyoparks.state.wy.us) has five miles of trails (one mile is paved) for hiking, walking, inline skating, and biking, and it connects with the paved Bear Parkway, which extends westward for three miles along the river. The park is also home to a small herd of bison and elk. In the winter, eight kilometers of groomed cross-country ski trails are maintained within the park, and there are a fun playground and picnic area. A **paddle-park** on the river was to open in 2006, providing a fun place for kayaking, inner-tubing, and other play; it's one of 30 or so in the nation and three in Wyoming.

More Recreation

Hamblin Park, next to the fairgrounds on Bear River Drive, is a pleasant place to enjoy a picnic lunch beneath tall cottonwood trees.

The **Evanston Recreation Center** (275 Saddle Ridge Rd., 307/789-1770, www.evanstonwy.org/parkrec) includes a swimming pool, gyms, racquetball courts, a weight room, and hot tub.

Purple Sage Golf Course (on Country Club Dr., 307/789-2383) is an 18-hole public course. **Fireside Lanes** (2631 Hwy. 150 S., 307/789-6716) is the local bowling alley.

Cross-country skiers head to groomed trails at **Lily Lake Touring Area** 30 miles south in the Uintas. A nonprofit group manages four furnished **yurts** (307/789-1770, www.evanstonoutdoors.com) at Lily Lake for overnight stays ($50 Fri.–Sat. or $25 the rest of the week). These 10-person yurts are perfect for hut-to-hut skiing but are also available in the summer.

Snowmobilers will find 40 miles of groomed winter trails starting at the Lily Lake Trailhead and continuing all the way to a snowpark on Utah Hwy. 150.

ACCOMMODATIONS

You'll find several inexpensive places to stay in Evanston. Reserve ahead on summer weekends to be sure of having a place, and on Labor Day you'll need to reserve at least one month in advance. In winter, the town provides reasonably priced lodging for skiers and snowmobilers from Park City, Utah, just 50 miles away.

Under $50

Stay at the comfortable **Vagabond Motel** (230 Bear River Dr., 307/789-2902, $42–49 d), where the well-maintained rooms have fridges and microwaves.

Motel 6 (261 Bear River Dr., 307/789-0791 or 800/466-8356, www.motel6.com, $40 s or $46 d) has standard rooms and a heated outdoor pool.

$50-100

A decent budget option is **Economy Inn** (1710 Harrison Dr., 307/789-2777, $38 s or $56 d). **Hi Country Inn** (1936 Harrison Dr., 307/789-2810 or 888/621-3220, $56–66 d) includes an outdoor pool and fitness room.

◖ Prairie Inn Motel (264 Bear River Dr., 307/789-2920, $40–50 s or $50–65 d) is a fine choice with clean rooms (half with fridges and microwaves), a continental breakfast, and attractive grounds.

Another place to hitch your wagon for the night is **Days Inn** (1983 Harrison Dr., 307/789-0783 or 800/329-7466, www.daysinn.com, $70 s or $80 d). Features include an indoor pool and hot tub, Wi-Fi, and a continental breakfast.

A recently opened **Comfort Inn** (1931 Harrison Dr., 307/789-7799 or 800/228-5150, www.comfortinn.com, $80 s or $90 d) offers attractive rooms and such features as an indoor pool, hot tub, Wi-Fi, fitness center, and light breakfast, plus in-room microwaves and fridges.

Best Western Dunmar Inn (1601 Harrison Dr., 307/789-3770 or 800/654-6509, www.bestwestern.com, $80–100 s or $90–110 d) has comfortable rooms, with an outdoor heated pool, hot tub, sauna, and Wi-Fi, plus a popular restaurant and lounge.

Bed-and-Breakfast
Evanston's homiest spot is ☾ **Pine Gables Inn B&B** (1049 Center St., 307/789-2069, www.pinegablesinn.com), built in 1883 and used as a European-style lodging place during the 1920s and '30s. The house was restored in 1981, furnished with antiques, and reopened as a delightful bed-and-breakfast. Six guest rooms are available, all with private baths. The smallest rooms are just $75 d, up to a luxurious suite with jetted tub and sitting room for $155 d. Rates include a full breakfast; no kids under 12.

Camping
The nearest public campgrounds are in the Uinta Mountains, 30 miles to the south. **Phillips RV Park** (225 Bear River Dr., 307/789-3805 or 800/349-3805, www.phillipsrvpark.com, $15 tents, $20–24 RVs) has shady sites, and is open April–mid-November.

FOOD
Breakfast and Lunch
Meet Evanston cops over coffee at **Main Street Deli** (1025 Main St., 307/789-1599). The deli also offers very good breakfasts, along with lunchtime soup, burgers, sandwiches, and cornbread.

Main St. Artisans Cafe and Gallery (927 Main St., 307/789-4991) is an earthy spot with pastries, salads, bagels, sandwiches, breakfast burritos, and espresso. The back room contains a fine-arts gallery displaying the works of regional artists. It's housed in the historic Blyth and Fargo Building.

☾ **Michael's Bar and Grill** (1011 Front St., 307/789-1088) doesn't look that inviting outside, but it's actually a fine lunch and dinner spot that fills with local business folks at the noon hour. Sandwiches, burgers, and healthy salads round out the menu.

Legal Tender Dining Room (in the Dunmar Inn, 1601 Harrison Dr., 307/789-3770) is an attractive establishment with lunch specials and reasonably priced steak-house fare.

Dinner
Lotty's Family Restaurant (1925 Harrison Dr., 307/789-9660) has a big salad bar and buffet with all-you-can-stuff-in prime rib Friday–Sunday nights. Also of note is **Bon Rico's** (925 Front St., 307/789-1753), with enormous steaks, pasta, and seafood in an upscale, romantic setting. A bit pricey ($18–26 entrées), but worth every penny.

The Old Mill Restaurant (30 Country Rd., 307/789-4040) is next to Evanston's old Chinatown, where an archaeological dig takes place in the summer. The historic building is something of a local landmark, and the restaurant serves a family menu three times a day, with karaoke twice a week in the bar.

International
It may seem a bit strange in such a small town, but Evanston has two **Don Pedro's Mexican Restaurants,** the original one at 909 Front Street, 307/789-2944, and a larger version at 205 Bear River Drive, 307/789-3322. Good and authentic Mexican fare.

Situated, appropriately enough, across the street from the Joss House is **Hunan Garden** (933 Front St., 307/789-3908), offering Chinese and American cooking. Lunch is a bargain, with

$6 specials. Get buffet-style Chinese food at **Dragon Wall** (140 Front St., 307/789-7788).

Groceries

Get groceries from the **Jubilee Super-Center** (524 Front St., 307/789-6788), **Smith's** (70 Yellow Creek Rd. N., 307/789-0532), or **Wal-Mart SuperCenter** (120 Beckers Circle, 307/789-0010).

INFORMATION AND SERVICES

Evanston has two places to go for information. If you're entering the state from the west, stop at **Bear River Information Center** (I-80 exit 6, 307/789-6540, open 8 A.M.–5 P.M. daily year-round). The center has a wealth of statewide information, a pleasant picnic area, short trails, and wind that never ceases. The information center lies within Bear River State Park.

The downtown **Evanston Chamber of Commerce** (36 10th St., 307/783-0370 or 800/328-9708, www.etownchamber.com, open 9 A.M.–5 P.M. Mon.–Fri.) provides more local information.

Check your email at **Uinta County Library** (701 Main, 307/789-2770). Wash clothes at **Sunfresh Laundro** (116 Yellow Creek Rd., 307/789-1163).

GETTING THERE AND AROUND

Sublink Stage (307/367-7433 or 800/542-2632, www.sublinkstage.com, Apr.–Nov.) provides twice-weekly van service between Salt Lake City and Pinedale, stopping in Evanston en route.

Rent cars from **Evanston Motor Co.** (2000 Hwy. 30 W., 307/789-3145).

HIGH UINTA MOUNTAINS

The **Evanston Ranger District** (1565 Hwy. 150 S., 307/789-3194, www.fs.fed.us/r4/wcnf) has maps of Wasatch National Forest, but only a tiny corner of the forest comes into Wyoming. The **High Uintas Wilderness** is 30 miles south of Evanston via Mirror Lake Hwy./Hwy. 150 (a National Scenic Byway). This wilderness area is very popular with hikers and cross-country skiers from the Evanston and Green River areas and includes Kings Peak, the tallest mountain in Utah. Get additional information from the **Bear River Ranger Station** (435/642-6662), 30 miles south of Evanston inside Utah; open late May–October. An access fee of $3 per car per day is charged in the Mirror Lake area.

Bear River Lodge (800/559-1121, www.bearriverlodge.com) has cabins, outdoor hot tubs, a general store, snowmobile rentals in winter, and ATV and watercraft rentals in summer. It's in Utah 32 miles south of Evanston. See *Moon Utah* by Bill Weir and W. C. McRae (www.moon.com) for details on the beautiful Mirror Lake Highway.

NORTH TO KEMMERER

North of Evanston, U.S. 189 follows a long valley most of the way to Kemmerer, with endless snowfences to reduce blowing snow in the winter. A hogback ridge hems you in to the east, now topped with wind turbines. Stop for a look back at the ragged snow-topped Uintas that form a southern horizon line.

Near the junction with Hwy. 412 (36 miles up) is the small **Cumberland** cemetery, enclosed within a white picket fence. Turn down Hwy. 412 to see what's left of the ghost town of Cumberland. This was a booming coal-mining town between 1920 and 1935, with four underground mines going at once. Today all that remains are the sandstone Ziller ranch buildings—the old whorehouse and saloon—and the cemetery. The buildings are not open to the public.

Kemmerer

The twin towns of Kemmerer (pop. 2,700) and Diamondville (pop. 700) are at the center of the coal industry in southwestern Wyoming. Drive west of town and you'll even pass coal seams in the road cutbank. Kemmerer is the Lincoln County seat and is on the Hams Fork River; Diamondville lies just a few yards south. The surrounding country is dotted with mining and energy plants of various types. P&M Coal Mine—the nation's largest strip mine—is several miles south, and a nearby Exxon plant is the world's largest manufacturer of helium and the state's largest consumer of electricity. Another major employer is the FMC coke plant, which provides metallurgical coke for a phosphorous plant in Pocatello, Idaho. It, too, is the largest such operation in the world. Natural gas, oil, and sulfur are also important locally, as are cattle and sheep ranching. Given this setting it should come as no surprise that this is a pickup-truck town. Either that or you better drive a Mustang with growling glaspak mufflers. But watch your speed; local cops are ever vigilant.

HISTORY
Coal Mining

Explorer John C. Frémont first chanced upon coal here in 1843, but it wasn't until 1881 that the Union Pacific opened the first underground mine. Things really began to boom when Patrick J. Quealy and his partner Mahlon S. Kemmerer established the Kemmerer Coal Company. Hundreds of men died in mine accidents; the worst was a 1923 explosion that killed 99 miners, mostly emigrants. The operation moved aboveground in 1950, and the Kemmerer mine became the Pittsburg and Midway Coal Company, now a subsidiary of ChevronTexaco. Six miles south of Kemmerer along U.S. 189, P&M is America's largest (physically, but not in terms of production) open-pit coal mine, reaching 800 feet deep and producing nearly five million tons per year. Two-thirds of the coal is used at Pacific Power's adjacent Naughton Plant, which produces 710

megawatts of power. The mine—the longest continuously operating mine in Wyoming—and the power plant are the largest employers in the region. Get details and tour information at 307/828-2200, www.kemmerer.org/pm.html. The Kemmerer family no longer lives in the area, but they are the owners of famous Jackson Hole Resort.

Moonshine and Shady Ladies

During the 1920s, Kemmerer became a national center for bootlegging and a major supplier for Chicago. Kemmerer "moon" was a favorite of speakeasies, and winemakers ordered grapes by the trainload. A 1931 bust near Kemmerer found 24,000 gallons of liquor. All this ended when Prohibition was repealed in 1933.

With all the coal miners, the ratio of men to women in Kemmerer was nearly 50 to one, prime pickings for the world's oldest profession. Into these conditions stepped Madam Isabelle Burns, fresh off the train from Salt Lake City with considerable experience in the "sporting" trade. She arrived in 1896 looking for somewhere to invest the $28,500 inheritance from her husband's suicide. With $5,000 in cash she bought a dance hall with enough convenient side rooms to house 50 prostitutes. In a short while, the Green House was a roaring success, allowing Madam Isabelle to build the most elegant house then in town, which is still standing at 301 Ruby Street. Because of the demand for "evening wear," Kemmerer's shoe store reportedly sold more high-heeled satin slippers than any shop west of the Mississippi. A nude painting of one of the Green House ladies with her brother (and lover) is now in the Golden Nugget Bar in Las Vegas. Madam Isabelle quit the business in 1926, left town, and married a New Orleans physician. Her business went on in fresh hands.

Several deaths took place at the Green House, leading to a grand conflagration when a man whose sons had been murdered there burned one of the women to death, igniting

To Lake Alice and Afton
232
To Montpelier, ID
30
233
Cokeville
PINE CREEK
Lake Viva-Naughton
NANCY HILL GRAVE
FOSSIL BUTTE NATIONAL MONUMENT
233
30
89
ULRICH'S FOSSIL GALLERY
189
To Evanston, WY and Salt Lake City, UT

KEMMERER AREA

La Barge
To Big Piney and Marbleton
189
Names Hill
Fontenelle Reservoir
Seedskadee National Wildlife Refuge
372
To Green River
189
240
Kemmerer
Diamondville
Opal
30
189
To Evanston and Lyman
Cumberland
To Green River

0   15 mi
0   15 km

© AVALON TRAVEL PUBLISHING, INC.

the building in the process and leaving it a pile of ashes. After the 1926 fire, it was replaced by the Southern Hotel. A newly elected sheriff finally shut things down in 1967, despite pleas from locals that the loss of all the Utah and Idaho clients would hurt business in town. For more on this tantalizing bit of history, see Ray Essman's *Only Count the Sunny Hours* (Winona, MN: Apollo Books).

SIGHTS
James Cash Penney House
The most unusual sights in Kemmerer relate to James Cash Penney, founder of the JCPenney chain. Penney moved to Kemmerer in 1902 from Evanston to open a dry goods store in the booming mining town, and his Golden Rule Store quickly achieved a reputation for quality

and honesty. By 1912 there were 34 Golden Rule stores; the following year their name was changed to JCPenney, and the rest is history. The company website (www.jcpenney.com) has more on JCPenney history.

The James Cash Penney House is a little six-room cottage where Penney and his family lived between 1903 and 1909. The nicely restored house is right behind the chamber of commerce office downtown and is open 9 A.M.–4:30 P.M. Monday–Saturday Memorial Day–Labor Day. No admission charge. Guides are ready to show you around and put on a video about the company's history, and one room contains family and JCPenney company memorabilia. The house is furnished as it might have been when the Penney family lived here, although the original furnishings—with

© DON PITCHER

the James Cash Penney House

the exception of a wooden cradle—are long gone. The little JCPenney "mother store" is also in Kemmerer, just a few doors up the street (JC Penney Drive, of course). If the home is closed, ask at the store for access.

Museum and Historical Buildings

Kemmerer's **Fossil Country Frontier Museum** (400 Pine Ave., 307/877-6551, www.hamsfork.net/~museum, free) is open 9 A.M.–5 P.M. Monday–Saturday in summer and 10 A.M.–4 P.M. Monday–Friday the rest of the year. It contains a variety of mining and archaeological exhibits, a walk-through underground coalmine exhibit, and dozens of kinds of barbed wire dating from the 19th century. Freak-show enthusiasts will appreciate the lamb with one head and two bodies. The small gift shop sells inexpensive fossil fish, along with Wyoming books and locally made products. Out back is a little miner's cabin from the 1920s.

The nicely restored **Lincoln County Courthouse** at Sage and Topaz streets was built in 1925 and contains a fine collection of fossils. Stop by the post office at Cedar and Sapphire streets to view the **fossil murals** painted by WPA artists in 1938. For additional historical buildings, head to "downtown" Diamondville, where several classic structures line the old main street.

Fossil Collecting

Although it's illegal to collect fossils within Fossil Butte National Monument, three local areas permit it for a fee. These are open only in summer, and children generally aren't allowed because it is considered dangerous for them. The best-known place—its fossils are exhibited in the Smithsonian—is **Ulrich's Fossil Gallery** (307/877-6466, www.ulrichsfossilgallery.com), just outside the national monument, 14 miles west of Kemmerer. Out front are enormous dinosaur tracks discovered in a coal mine. Ulrich's has a nearby quarry on state land, where you can dig your own fish fossils for $75 per couple for a half-day dig in the summer; reservations required. The staff assists diggers, and you're allowed to keep a wooden pallet full of the most common species, although the state gets any rare specimens

JAMES CASH PENNEY

One of America's best-known retail chains, JCPenney, had its start in Kemmerer, Wyoming, in 1902. The founder was James Cash Penney, a man whose life exemplified the proverbial rags-to-riches story. Born in 1875 to a devout Missouri family, Penney grew up in poverty. His father was a farmer and Baptist minister who, together with his mother – a Southern belle – instilled a Christian ethical base that emphasized the Golden Rule and self-reliance.

It didn't take long for Penney's resourcefulness to reveal itself. At age eight he needed new shoes and used his meager savings to buy young pigs that he later sold for a profit. After high school he took a job in a local dry goods store where he learned the trade, and then he moved to Colorado to open a butcher shop. The shop failed when Penney refused to continue paying bribes (in the form of a bottle of bourbon per week) to his biggest account, a local hotel.

THE GOLDEN RULE STORES

J. C. Penney's big break came in 1898 when he began work with a small chain called the Golden Rule Stores. The owners quickly recognized the skills in this ambitious young man and offered Penney a one-third interest in any new stores he would open. With $500 in savings and $1,500 in borrowed money, Penney quickly seized the chance, opening a dry goods store in Kemmerer on April 14, 1902. It wasn't much, just a one-room building away from the center of town and furnished with makeshift fixtures, but Penney was shrewd enough to recognize what people wanted: fair prices that were the same no matter who walked in the store and a cash-only operation; he was opposed to credit because it was often used by unscrupulous merchants to create a class of workers who were never able to pay off their bills. The store proved an immediate hit, and within a year he had opened another store in Rock Springs, followed by a third in Cumberland, Wyoming, in 1904.

Three years later his partners sold the entire operation to Penney, and under his guidance the company took off, quickly making him a millionaire. By the end of 1912 he was the head of a chain of 34 Golden Rule stores, and the following year the name was changed to the J. C. Penney Company. It soon became one of the fastest-growing national retail chains. By 1920, the company had 197 stores from coast to coast, and it continued to open stores throughout the next decade at the blistering pace of one new store every three days. By 1929, 1,400 Penney stores were scattered across the country. The bubble burst with the stock market crash of 1929, and Penney's financial empire collapsed around him. It took decades for Penney to recover the wealth he had lost so suddenly.

LATER YEARS

Penney was a devoted family man, but his first two wives died young – the first in 1910 from pneumonia and the second in 1924. He married a third time and remained married until his death in 1971. The loss of his wives led Penney to philanthropy and charitable projects as a way to ease his own pain by helping others. Even today, his charitable foundations continue to fund community renewal, world peace, and environmental efforts. In later years, Penney turned his attention to farming and developed an international reputation for his champion cattle, especially the Guernseys that became the basis for another company he helped found, Foremost Dairies.

Penney remained active far beyond the age when most people retire. He never forgot a name or face, and even at the age of 85 he kept up a grueling schedule of store visits, conventions, and speaking engagements. He stopped taking the city bus to work only in his nineties, and he was still coming to work within a few months of his death at the age of 95. Today the stores he founded have moved beyond the religious devotion personified in James Cash Penney, but they still bear his name and a reputation for quality merchandise. The town of Kemmerer contains both the JCPenney "mother store" and Penney's old home, now open as a small museum.

that turn up. If you don't want to dig, you can buy beautifully prepared fossils at Ulrich's gallery (open year-round). **Warfield Fossil Quarry** (307/883-2445, www.warfieldfossils.com) charges $50 for four hours. Its remote quarry (no amenities) is a 35-minute drive north of Kemmerer; get the brochure and follow the map closely.

Tynsky's Fossil Fish Shop (307/877-6885), just down from the JCPenney store in Kemmerer, has fossil fish for sale. You can also dig at Tynsky's quarry, 12 miles west of town. The cost is $75 for two hours or so, and you can keep up to 10 fossils (nothing rare). Across the street is **Creative Creations** (821 S. Main, 307/877-3901, www.earthsantiquesinc.com), downstairs inside the Pardners Memorabilia antique store (also worth a look), with inexpensive fish fossils.

Bob's Rock Shop (502 Coral, 307/877-3220) is a fun place to get petrified wood, fish fossils, and other interesting rocks.

ENTERTAINMENT AND EVENTS

The **Stock Exchange Bar** (307/877-3244) on the downtown triangle has a pool table and fills with locals most nights. Nearby, **Grumpies Bar** (815 S. Main, 307/877-5661) has pool and darts; I'm not sure if the name refers to the customers or management. For live music, try **Bon Rico's** (12 miles south of town, 307/877-4503). **Victory Theatre** (720 JC Penney Dr., 307/877-6684) shows movies downtown.

In early July, Kemmerer celebrates **Fossil Fest** with a parade, melodrama, horse-and-buggy rides, street dance, fireworks, and food and craft booths. The free **Oyster Ridge Music Festival** (307/877-9761 or 888/300-3413, www.oysterridgemusicfestival.com) in late July features an outdoor barbecue, contests, and concerts from guitar, fiddle, banjo, and mandolin musicians. The star attraction is the flatpick guitar contest, but the "band scramble" is particularly fun—musicians must play together without time to rehearse.

Anglers may want to join in the **Ice Fishing Derby** on the third weekend of February at Lake Viva-Naughton. The **International Pedigree Stage Stop Sled Dog Race** (307/734-1163, www.wyomingstagestop.org) stops here. (See the *Jackson Hole* chapter for details.)

RECREATION

Kemmerer Recreation Center (1776 Dell Rio Dr., 307/828-2365) has an indoor pool, weight room, hot tub, sauna, racquetball courts, and even an indoor climbing wall.

The outdoor pool (307/877-9641) in **Archie Neil Park** is open in summer, and you can head to Kemmerer's nine-hole **Fossil Island Golf Course** (307/877-6954) just north of town on U.S. 189. Bowl at **Sage Bowling Lanes** (918 Sage Ave., 307/877-6642).

Lions Club Park, just north of Kemmerer along scenic Hams Fork River, is a fine place for a picnic, and **Lake Viva-Naughton,** 15 miles north of Kemmerer on Hwy. 233, has good fishing.

ACCOMMODATIONS

Fossil Butte Motel (1424 Central Ave., 307/877-3996, www.fossilbuttemotel.com, $48 s or $53–58 d) has well-appointed rooms with microwaves, fridges, and wireless Internet.

Another good place where the rooms have fridges and microwaves is **Fairview Inn** (501 N. Hwy. 30 in Kemmerer, 307/877-3938 or 800/247-3938, $50–70 d).

Over in Diamondville, **Energy Inn** (307/877-6901, www.energyinn.net, $55 s or $65 d) has fridges and Wi-Fi in the rooms; some include kitchenettes.

Camping

Tent camping (no RVs) is available at **Kemmerer Community Camp** (307/828-2360, $5, open late May–early Sept.) on Hwy. 233 north of Kemmerer. Public camping is also available at **Fontenelle Creek Campground** ($5, open Memorial Day–Sept.), 25 miles northeast of Kemmerer on U.S. 189 beside Fontenelle Reservoir. In addition, three free campgrounds are along the Green River just below the Fontenelle dam, and dozens of free campsites border the lake.

Riverside RV Park (just north of town at 216 Spinel St., 307/877-3416, $20 RVs, no tents, open May–mid-Oct.) is a shadeless gravel lot. **Foothills RV Park** (310 N. U.S. 189, 307/877-6634, $25–28 RVs, open year-round) has grassy sites but no showers.

FOOD

You'll find no dining standouts in Kemmerer, but a couple of places have solid food for reasonable prices. Start your day at the smoky **Busy Bee Cafe** (919 Pine Ave., 307/877-6820); open for breakfast and lunch, with nothing over $6, including Navajo tacos. Another place with good breakfasts—plus the best local burgers—is **Polar King Drive In** (at 315 U.S. 189, 307/877-9448) on the north side of town.

Bon Rico's (307/877-4503), 12 miles south of town, is another favorite place to stuff yourself with steak or fish. Good in-town carnivorous choices are **Bootlegger's Steakhouse and Grill** (817 S. Main St., 307/828-3067) and **Ham's Fork Mesquite Grill** (307 U.S. Hwy 189, 307/877-8848).

In Diamondville, there's a **Pizza Hut** (307/877-6969) offering lunch deals. On the north side of Kemmerer, **Jubilee Foods** (307/877-3698) is the local grocery store.

INFORMATION AND SERVICES

The **Kemmerer Chamber of Commerce** is housed in a log cabin in Herschler Triangle Park at the center of town (307/877-9761 or 888/300-3413, www.kemmererchamber.com). Locals joke that Kemmerer is too small to have a town square, so it has a town triangle instead. It's open 9 A.M.–5 P.M. Monday–Saturday Memorial Day–Labor Day, and the rest of the year 9 A.M.–2 P.M. Monday–Friday, plus additional weekend hours in September and October. Inside are a few displays of fossils and historical pictures, and you can buy local books and old Wyoming license plates. The office can also provide helpful information on nearby fossil-fish quarries and details on tours of industrial plants in the area. The city's website, www.kemmerer.org, has more local information and links.

Head north on U.S. 189 to find both the Bridger–Teton National Forest's **Kemmerer Ranger District** (307/877-4415, www.fs.fed.us/r4/btnf) and the adjacent **BLM's Kemmerer Field Office** (307/828-4500, www.wy.blm.gov). Surf the bookshelves on the web at **Lincoln County Library** (519 Emerald St., 307/877-6961, www.wsl.state.wy.us/lincoln).

Sublink Stage (307/367-7433 or 800/542-2632, www.sublinkstage.com, Apr.–Nov.) provides twice-weekly van service between Salt Lake City and Pinedale, stopping in Kemmerer en route.

◖ FOSSIL BUTTE NATIONAL MONUMENT

Established in 1972 and 14 miles west of Kemmerer, Fossil Butte is an 8,198-acre natural area managed by the National Park Service. The dominant feature is an 800-foot-tall escarpment rising above the arid plains. Within this butte are millions of fossil fish, insects, snails, turtles, and plants. This is also one of the few places in the world where fossilized birds and bats have been found. The Green River Formation fossils were first collected by geologist Dr. John Evans in 1856.

Origins

Fossil Butte is not unlike countless other buttes throughout Wyoming: an exposed rocky cliff lit with the red, yellow, and buff colors representing millions of years of deposition and erosion. Despite the arid conditions today, this land once supported a subtropical climate similar to that along the Gulf Coast. During the Eocene Epoch (50 million years ago), palm trees grew along the shore of a lake, now called Fossil Lake, whose waters teemed with fish, crocodiles, turtles, stingrays, and other animals. Through a period of two million years, changing salinity levels and variations in runoff from calcium-rich streams caused calcium carbonate to precipitate out. Dead animals and plants on the lake bottom were covered with a blanket of fine sediment. Eventually they were fossilized, and when the lake dried up, the sedimentary deposits were gradually thrust upward by geological forces.

Visitor Center

The free **Fossil Butte Visitor Center** (307/877-4455, www.nps.gov/fobu) is open 8 A.M.–7 P.M. daily June–August and 8 A.M.–4:30 P.M. daily the rest of the year (closed winter holidays). The visitor center, 3.5 miles off U.S. 30 (follow the signs), houses a fossil preparation lab, along with impressive exhibits on geology, paleontology, and natural history. You'll find a 13-foot crocodile, the oldest known bat, and more than 75 other fossils on display. Watch videos on local geology, paleontology, or fossil preparation, or stop by the gift shop for natural-history books.

Visitors can assist a Park Service paleontologist in collecting fossils 10 A.M.–3 P.M. weekends June–August. You'll hike into the quarry site and actually participate in the collection of fossils and data. Be ready to work! Evening campfire programs are offered at the picnic area periodically in the summer; ask at the visitor center for specific times.

Camping is not allowed at Fossil Butte, and the nearest lodging, campground, and RV parks are in Kemmerer. You can, however, camp on nearby BLM lands; see the bureau's Kemmerer office for details.

Hiking

The 2.5-mile **Historic Quarry Trail** on the south side of the monument provides access to an old fossil quarry site (600 feet up) and has various interpretive signs along the way. It is illegal to remove fossils or other items from the monument (see *Fossil Collecting* in the *Kemmerer* section for nearby areas where it is legal).

Fossil Lake Trail begins near a pleasant picnic area three miles north of the visitor center. It provides an enjoyable 1.5-mile loop hike through open sage country and a grove of aspen trees, with descriptive placards along the way. Many varieties of flowers are blooming throughout the summer. Keep your eyes open for mule deer, coyotes, sage grouse, prairie dogs, and other animals on these paths.

Other than these two paths, you're on your own, although the open country makes hiking relatively easy. Topographic maps are sold in the visitor center. Be sure to carry water on any hike in this arid area.

OREGON TRAIL SIGHTS

Ten miles north of Kemmerer on Hwy. 233 are the still-noticeable ruts of the Oregon Trail's **Sublette Cutoff.** Named for mountain man William Sublette, who first took this route in 1826, the cutoff saved Oregon emigrants more than 50 miles of travel but bypassed the chance to rest and resupply at Fort Bridger. Wagons traversed a rough and waterless desert before finally climbing into the cool and wooded mountains. Thirteen miles west of Hwy. 233 along the Sublette Cutoff is the grave of a young emigrant, Nancy Hill. An 1852 letter written by her uncle describes how suddenly life could end on the treacherous journey west:

> *This day was called on to consign to the tomb one other of our company N. J. Hill. She was in good health on Sunday evening, taken unwell that knight worse in the morning & a corps at nine o'clock at knight. We had two doctors with her. They pronounced her complaining cholera but I believe it was nothing more than cholera with conjestion connecter.*

Names Hill

Oregon Trail travelers paused to carve their names into the rocks at three well-known places in Wyoming: Register Cliff, Independence Rock, and—westernmost of the three—Names Hill. The last of these is six miles south of the oil and gas town of La Barge, along the Sublette Cutoff at the hazardous Green River crossing. More than 2,000 old names are carved in the sandstone cliff, along with two Indian petroglyphs. The oldest name is dated 1827, when John Danks (probably a trapper) carved his still-visible appellation. Many others are from the 1840s and '50s. A fence surrounds one that reads, "James Bridger 1844 Trapper." Its authenticity is suspect because Bridger

SOUTHWEST WYOMING

could neither read nor write and always signed his name with an X. But Jim Bridger *did* run a ferry at the nearby Green River crossing, so I'll give him the benefit of the doubt; perhaps a companion carved it while he watched. Please do not add your name to this historic rock face; in all too many places modern tourists have incised their inane graffiti next to names more than 150 years old.

Fontenelle Reservoir

Fontenelle Reservoir lies just east and south of Names Hill and provides the area with irrigation water and electricity. The lake backs up behind a 139-foot earthen dam on the Green River, and it's a favorite spot for trout fishing, boating, and free camping. The river below the dam makes for a relatively gentle float trip, and the trout fishing (rainbow, brown, and cutthroat) is excellent. Van Beacham's **Solitary Angler** (307/877-9459) offers guided fly-fishing on this uncrowded stretch of the river.

COKEVILLE

Cokeville (pop. 500, www.cokevillewy.com) lies in a long, fertile valley along the Idaho border south of Star Valley. Directly behind the town is an impressive triangular mountain, **Rocky Point**. The ranching and farming country is punctuated with small white farmhouses, but many locals commute to work at the coal mine and power plant near Kemmerer. Nearly everyone is Mormon here.

The town of Cokeville was founded in 1874 with the arrival of the Oregon Shortline Railroad and is named for the coal that was used to produce coke. By the turn of the 20th century it had become the "sheep capital of the world" and claimed more millionaires per capita than anywhere on earth. Cokeville's proximity to the state line also made it a haven for outlaws—with Utah and Idaho just six miles away, lawbreakers found it easy to leave the posse behind as they fled to a different jurisdiction.

Practicalities

Pine Creek Ski Resort (307/279-3201, www .pinecreekskiresort.com, $28), six miles east of Cokeville, consists of a high-speed quad chairlift and rope tow with a 1,400-foot vertical rise. Ski rentals and instruction are available. It's open Tuesday, Saturday, and Sunday January–March. The mountains east of Cokeville also contain many miles of groomed wintertime snowmobile trails.

U.S. 30 through Cokeville is heavily traveled by trucks and cars heading north to Pocatello, Idaho, or south to I-80; because of this you'll find two gas stations and a large Flying J truck stop in town. Friendly **Hideout Motel** (307/279-3281, $40–55 d) has fridges and microwaves in standard rooms, along with several kitchenettes.

The Forest Service's **Hams Fork Campground** ($5, open Memorial Day–Oct.) is the closest public campground; it's 28 miles from Cokeville along the Smiths Fork Road. Get local specifics from the **Cokeville Visitor Center** (307/279-3200, open late May–early Sept.).

Lake Alice

Take an enjoyable side trip to Lake Alice, a pristine mountain lake at the end of a 1.5-mile trail in Bridger–Teton National Forest. Three-mile-long Lake Alice was created many centuries ago when a mountain slid across the valley and dammed the creek. Water from the lake flows underground for more than one mile before emerging in springs. Get here by heading northeast from Cokeville on Hwy. 232 and bearing right at the Y 12 miles up where the pavement ends. The gravel road continues to the trailhead 34 miles from Cokeville, where you'll find the very nice **Hobble Creek Campground** ($5, open mid-June–mid-Oct.). There's good fishing both in the creek and at Lake Alice. The road into Lake Alice is generally closed by snow October–late June. The country around here is some of the only unroaded land left in the Wyoming Range. The route to Lake Alice passes the **Kelley Guard Station** (307/877-4415, www.fs.fed.us/r4/btnf), which you can rent for $30 per night. The cabin sleeps five and is available year-round. Winter access is by snowmobile or cross-country skis, approximately nine miles in.

Heading North

The drive north from Cokeville to Star Valley follows Salt Creek from the sage-and-grass lowlands into lodgepole pine–covered mountains, eventually reaching Salt River Pass at 7,610 feet. It's a taste of the majestic mountain country that fills the north-west corner of Wyoming. On the north side of the pass, the road begins a long descent into beautiful Star Valley. Find basic rooms at **Canyon Inn Motel** (307/849-0100, $30–40 d), 24 miles north of Cokeville and just inside the Wyoming state line. Open mid-April–mid-November.

Star Valley

West of the Wyoming Range, the mountains seem exhausted as they dip into a broad, fertile farming valley that stretches across the Idaho border. This is Star Valley, a place with closer ties to Idaho—in terms of geography, farming, sheep ranching, transportation, and even religion—than to Wyoming. The valley reaches 10 miles across and 40 miles north to south. An early settler labeled it "The Star of all Valleys," and it is a very pretty place; the Salt River—named for the salt deposits and saline springs along its banks—creates an oasis of greenery, and the mountains provide a grand backdrop. Spacious old ranches, built to house large Mormon families, alternate with more modern ranch-style homes. A single main road, U.S. 89, heads north the full length of the valley, with a network of side roads and settlements.

The **Lander Cutoff** of the Oregon Trail angles through the southern half of Star Valley, follows the Salt River as far as the Auburn area, and then cuts northwest along Stump Creek. This 250-mile path—constructed in 1858 under the direction of Frederick W. Lander—was the first federal road built west of the Missouri River. Fur trappers had used the route for 45 years before Lander and his men, funded with a $300,000 appropriation from Congress, upgraded it for wagon travel. The Lander Cutoff saved Oregon-bound travelers more than 100 miles but also entailed climbing over a rugged 9,000-foot pass. You can see parts of the route along the south end of Greys River Road, where concrete posts and emigrant graves mark the way.

The first white settlers came to Star Valley from Idaho in the 1880s, fleeing laws restricting the number of wives a man could have. Polygamy, while outlawed by the federal government in 1882, was winked at by Wyoming authorities for many years. They needed all the settlers they could get, especially the conservative, hardworking Mormons. When Frank W. Mondell was running for Congress in 1894, he came to Star Valley and found that the Afton mayor was a polygamist. Polygamy has long since been outlawed, but a large brick Latter-day Saints church still stands in every small town in Star Valley.

For more than a century, Star Valley was a bucolic place with overflowing irrigation ditches, barbed wire stretched between lodgepole posts, and dairy cows dotting velvet green farm fields. Locals called it the "home of 5,000 people and 20,000 cattle." But those days are gone, and within a few years you might be able to reverse those figures. Ranches held in the same family for three generations are being subdivided into lots for baby boomers looking for a comfortable place to retire or Jackson Hole commuters searching for affordable homes. To one who first saw Star Valley 20 years ago, these changes are very disturbing, but newcomers will still find beauty in the open country that remains. One can hope that something can be done before all the farms are lost and the valley becomes one long strip of ranchettes, summer homes, and real-estate offices enticing more folks to move in.

Information

In the town of Thayne on the north end of the valley, the helpful **Star Valley Chamber**

SOUTHWEST WYOMING

of Commerce Visitor Center (229 S. Main St., 307/886-3156 or 800/426-8833, www .starvalleychamber.com) is open 9 A.M.–6 P.M. Monday–Friday and 9 A.M.–1 P.M. Saturday late May–early September, and 8 A.M.–4 P.M. Monday–Friday the rest of the year. Afton has an unstaffed visitors kiosk at 2nd and Washington. Other useful websites are www.starvalley.com and www.starvalleywy.com.

AFTON

The primary settlement in Star Valley is Afton (pop. 1,800), a typical small American town with a mix of services for both locals and for tourists en route to Jackson.

Sights

Afton's best-known attraction is the world's largest **elk antler arch,** an 18-foot-high arch that extends over the main street. Built in 1958, it contains 3,011 antlers. At today's antler prices—they're prized as aphrodisiacs in Asia—the arch would be worth more than $300,000!

Aviat (672 Washington, 307/886-3151) manufactures a variety of small aircraft in Afton, including the Pitts Special, considered the finest aerobatics plane in existence; the Eagle homebuilt kit; and the Husky A-1, similar to the famous Super Cub. The company does not officially offer tours of its aircraft manufacturing facility, but you may want to drop by on weekdays just in case.

The small **Pioneer Museum** (307/886-3730), next to the fairgrounds on the north side of town, is open 1–4 P.M. Monday–Friday late May–early September. Inside are items collected by the Daughters of the Utah Pioneers, including a loom, a spinning wheel, and other

memorabilia. The red-roofed barn next door houses old farm implements.

The enormous **Afton Tabernacle**—Latter-day Saints, of course—sits at the corner of Jefferson and 3rd and serves as a community focal point. This impressive sandstone building (architects call this a Middle English design) was begun in 1904 and received additions in the 1940s.

Periodic Spring

Afton's most unusual sight is Periodic Spring

© DON PITCHER

The elk antler arch spans Main Street in Afton.

in Swift Creek Canyon east of town (take 2nd Avenue). The six-mile drive is quite a contrast to wide-open Star Valley—it parallels a pretty tree-bordered creek and steep rocky slopes. The largest of only three intermittent springs known to exist, Periodic Spring is reached via a 0.75-mile trail. The crystalline water of this spring emerges from the base of a cliff to feed Swift Creek, the water source for Afton. When the spring is operating it seems as though there were a timer and an on-off switch buried in the mountain. Icy water gushes from a gaping opening in the cliff for approximately 18 minutes and then stops for an equal period.

The Shoshones regarded this as a sacred place of healing and said that a powerful medicine man was able to turn the waters on and off by command. Today, hydrologists believe that a large underground chamber periodically fills with and then empties of water through a natural siphon in the porous limestone rock. The spring loses its intermittence in spring and flows constantly. Best time to see it in action is in late summer or early fall.

Entertainment and Events

Watch flicks at downtown Afton's **Ford Theatre** (307/886-5684).

July kicks off with an **Independence Day** celebration that features a parade, free pancake breakfast, contests, a rodeo, and fireworks. Also in July, the community puts on a two-day **historical pageant** at the high school football field, with a homespun tale of the Mormon pioneers who settled the valley.

Held in Afton in late July or early August, the **Lincoln County Fair** has all the country fair favorites: musical entertainment, a carnival, a parade, rodeos, 4-H agricultural exhibits, and lots more. Rodeos are also held several other times each summer; see the visitor center for specifics. On Thanksgiving weekend, Afton's **Parade of Lights** is a small-town event with lighted floats.

In mid-August a cluster of activities center around **Cowboy Days,** including a bull-riding event (Erickson Capital Superbull), the Aviat's Mountain Sky Fly-in (including free plane rides for kids), a car show, and mud volleyball.

Cutter races take place at race grounds a mile northwest of Afton on winter Saturdays.

Recreation

Golfers will find the nine-hole **Valli Vu Municipal Golf Course** (307/885-3338, www.aftonwyoming.net) one mile south of Afton. Star Valley Ranch Resort (www.starvaleywy.com/svra) in Thayne has two courses open to the public, the 18-hole **Cedar Creek Golf Course** (307/883-2230) and nine-hole **Aspen Hills Golf Course** (307/883-2899).

In winter, the town operates **Snowshoe Hollow Ski Area** (307/885-9831) just east of Afton with a rope tow and snack bar.

Stop by the Forest Service office for information on the many miles of groomed **cross-country ski trails** in Star Valley. Closest are trails in Afton at Canyon View Park and one mile to the south at Valli Vu Municipal Golf Course. The Wyoming Range to the east offers unlimited opportunities for exploration by skiers and snowmobiles, with snow until the Fourth of July some years. Greys River Road is an especially popular snowmobiling area.

Accommodations

The **C Corral Motel** (161 Washington, 307/885-5424, www.thecorralmotel.com, $55–85 d, open Jan.–mid-Nov.) is an American icon, with 20 clean, well-maintained log and plaster cabins, most built in the 1940s. All are non-smoking, with fridges, microwaves, and wireless Internet; two contain kitchenettes.

At **Lazy B Motel** (219 Washington, 307/885-3187, www.thelazybmotel.com, $50–65 s or $65–77 d), all rooms contain fridges and microwaves and a heated outdoor pool awaits the kids.

South of Afton 0.75 mile, the modern **Hi-Country Inn** (307/885-3856 or 866/299-1727, www.hi-countryinn.com, $65 s or $70–75 d) has an outdoor pool, hot tub, and Wi-Fi.

Two miles south of Afton is **The Old Mill** (3497 Dry Creek Rd., 307/886-0520, www.oldmillcabins.com, $105–180), where you'll find four modern log cabins (the largest sleeps eight) set on five acres. All are nicely furnished with handcrafted log beds and gas fireplaces. Guests will also enjoy the hot tub in a lovely glass-enclosed gazebo. In the winter,

you can cross-country ski or snowmobile right from your cabin.

Seven miles south of Afton in the country close to Smoot, **Cottonwood Cottage Bed and Breakfast** (307/886-9348, $85 d) has a suite with king bed, gas fireplace, jetted tub, and continental breakfast.

Camping and Cabins

The Forest Service has three campgrounds ($7, open late May–mid-Sept.) in the Star Valley area. Closest is the attractive **Swift Creek Campground** (only 1.5 miles east of Afton (take 2nd Avenue—Periodic Spring is farther up the same road). **Allred Flat Campground** is 20 miles south of Afton, right along U.S. 89. **Cottonwood Lake Campground** is a very nice place with lakeside sites and nearby hiking trails. It's seven miles up Cottonwood Lake Road, south of Smoot.

The Forest Service rents out four guard stations (307/886-3166, www.fs.fed.us/r4/btnf) when they are not being used by field crews. These cabins are particularly popular with snowmobilers and skiers in the winter, but running water is available only in summer. The cabins are **Cozier Guard Station, Deer Creek Guard Station, McCain Guard Station,** and **Meadows Guard Station.** Each sleeps six in bunk beds and costs $40 per night.

Food

Get standard American breakfasts at **Golden Spur Cafe** (486 Washington, 307/886-9890). Try the lunchtime pizza buffets at **Pizza Hut** (228 Washington, 307/886-9794) and south-of-the-border fare at **Melina's Mexican Restaurant** (470 Washington, 307/883-2617).

Red Baron Drive-In (838 Washington, 307/886-3745) is the hangout for folks who want burgers and fries. Burger King has a big indoor playground for the youngsters.

Rocky Mt. Seafood (492 S. Washington, 307/885-2722) is a real surprise in this landlocked place, with fresh seafood, delicious fish-and-chips, and shrimp tacos for $6–7.

A few doors up is **C Star Valley Chocolates** (468 S. Washington, 307/885-1844, www.starvalleychocolates.com), selling gourmet chocolate truffles—made on the premises—plus ice cream, shakes, malts, and espresso. Great for chocoholics.

Homestead Restaurant (307/886-3878), just south of town on U.S. 89, serves the area's finest prime rib, along with rich double-fudge desserts. **Familee Thriftway** (141 N. Washington, 307/886-5550) sells groceries.

Information and Services

On the north side of town, Bridger–Teton National Forest **Greys River District Office** (307/886-3166, www.fs.fed.us/r4/btnf) dispenses local maps, natural-history books, and information on recreational opportunities.

Star Valley Library (261 Washington St., 307/886-3158) carries plenty of genealogy titles and has computers for Internet access. Find the **post office** (307/886-3625) at 31 West 4th Avenue.

If you're driving north from Afton toward Jackson, be sure to fill up with gas either here or in Thayne; it won't get any cheaper. **Lone Pine Sports** (500 Washington St., 307/885-9581) sells outdoor gear and rents cross-country skis and snowshoes in winter.

Dog-Eared Books (498 S. Washington, 307/886/885-1535) is a fine bookshop with used and new titles. Head through the back door for a delightful consignment shop called **Ditto** (307/885-4050).

Star Valley Medical Center (307/885-5800, www.svmcwy.org) is a modern hospital on the south end of town with physicians on staff and an emergency room.

GREYS RIVER LOOP ROAD

Star Valley is bordered on the east by two parallel mountain ranges: the Salt River and the Wyoming. The Greys River flows between them. Alongside it runs an exceptionally scenic 80-mile-long gravel road used by small numbers of vacationers, hikers, anglers, and hunters. This untrammeled area makes for a great escape from the Jackson Hole mob scene in the summer. The road begins a dozen miles south of Afton and continues north all the way to

Alpine. Plan to camp overnight along the way; the narrow and potholed dirt road makes for a torturous day trip. You'll fine excellent fishing for cutthroat, rainbow, brown, and brook trout in the river and good opportunities to see deer and moose along the way. All this country lies within Bridger–Teton National Forest. Considerable logging takes place in the mountains, and many thousands of sheep and cattle graze the open areas, but much of the land remains wild and beautiful. It is an almost unknown part of Wyoming. If you drive north along the Greys River Road you'll be able to watch the Greys grow from a small creek into a river. Kayakers often paddle the lower stretches of the river; see the Forest Service for specifics.

Snider Basin

Another fascinating drive (great for mountain bikes) is to continue east through Snider Basin to the town of Big Piney on Forest Road 10128. The road parallels the still-visible Lander Cutoff of the Oregon Trail for a long distance, and several emigrant graves are noted along the way. Keep your eyes open for elk and deer on the slopes and beaver dams in Piney Creek. The high country is lodgepole-pine forests, passing into open sage land as you descend toward Big Piney. Note that this route can be confusing (signs are often missing) and sometimes muddy, so be sure to get a Forest Service map and current conditions before heading out from Afton.

Recreation

More than 450 miles of trails cut across this country, including the 70-mile **Wyoming Range National Recreation Trail,** which climbs through beautiful alpine meadows and over narrow, rocky ridges. Snow covers the trail until July most years.

A side road off the Greys River Road leads to a two-mile trail that climbs 11,363-foot **Wyoming Peak,** tallest in the range. During winter cross-country skiers will find four groomed ski trails and snowmobilers can cruise on 100 miles of groomed routes in the area. See the Forest Service office in Afton for maps and recreation information, including a listing of guides and outfitters.

Accommodations

Box Y Lodge (307/654-7564, www.boxy-lodge.com) is a grand old ranch with a beautiful setting along Greys River Road 30 miles from Alpine. The ranch has a main lodge and eight comfortably rustic log cabins (each sleeps up to six) with propane heat and lights. Activities include fishing, horseback rides, float trips, and mountain-biking. All-inclusive summertime rates are $500 per day for two people. Lodging-and-three-meals rates are $230 for two people per day. The ranch is also a busy wintertime resort for snowmobilers; winter rates are $115–130 for two people per day, including lodging and three meals a day. The ranch hosts a maximum of 30 guests.

Camping

Camping is available at five places along the Greys River Road; nicest are the campgrounds at **Murphy Creek** and **Forest Park,** both of which cost $7 and are open year-round. The road is not plowed in the winter. You can camp off the road for free in most parts of the national forest.

The **La Barge Guard Station** (307/877-4415, www.fs.fed.us/r4/btnf) is approximately 22 miles from the Afton end of the road (26 miles from the La Barge side) and is available year-round. Winter access is by snowmobile or cross-country skis. The cabin sleeps six and costs $30 per night.

THAYNE

Thaye is a prosperous and fast-growing settlement best known for its cheese factory. New houses are spreading across old farms as residents flood the valley. The town's official population barely tops 350, but there are probably 2,000 or so just outside town limits.

Cutter races started here during the 1920s when dairymen used sleighs to haul milk to the local creamery. To avoid having to wait in line, the farmers often raced each other to get to the creamery first; this sparring eventually grew into a competition that now encompasses seven western states. (The "world finals" are held in Ogden, Utah.) In a cutter race, horses pull wheeled chariots over a snow-covered field at breakneck speeds; the world record stands at 21.64 seconds for the 0.25-mile run. Star Valley cutter races now take place at the race grounds north of Afton.

The Star Valley Visitor Center is in Thayne (see *Information*).

Accommodations

Snider's Rustic Inn (307/883-0222, www.snidersrusticinn.com, $55 s or $60–65 d) has renovated rooms with kitchenettes; some also feature unique log beds.

Cabin Creek Inn (307/883-3262, www.cabincreekinn.com, $79–89, open mid-Apr.–mid-Nov.) has attractive four-person log cabins with lodgepole beds, homemade quilts, kitchenettes, jetted tubs, and an outdoor pool.

Two miles north of Thayne is **Inn at Deer Run B&B** (307/883-3444, www.silverstar.com/steadman, $60–75 d), where the modern rooms are furnished with lodgepole beds. It has free Wi-Fi, and a TV is available in the central room, where a free breakfast is served each morning.

South of town, **Flat Creek RV Park** (307/883-2231, $14 tents, $25 RVs) is open year-round.

Food

Fill your belly at **☖ Star Valley Cheese** (307/883-2510), one of the most unusual eating places in Wyoming. The restaurant—an old-fashioned shop straight out of the 1950s—serves reasonably priced burgers, homemade pies, ice cream, malts, shakes, and other fare, and sells fresh cheeses and butter from the coolers. It's open for breakfast and lunch daily all year, and it's almost always filled with locals and tourists. Each day, more than 15,000 pounds of mozzarella, provolone, and ricotta cheese are made in the plant right behind the shop. Across the parking lot is **Cheese Factory Pizza** (307/883-7492), with good pizzas (with cheeses from next door), subs, and big salads.

Dad's Bar (307/883-2300) offers live music

on weekends and the finest steaks and prime rib in the area. Inside is a small collection of cutter-racing items (the sport was established by "Dad" Walton). Get groceries at **Valley Market,** which has an in-store deli.

AUBURN

The town of Auburn, eight miles north and west of Afton, contains a small area of travertine terraces and hot springs on private land. The nearby countryside is filled with old log homes, cabins, and barns. A historic **rock church,** built in 1889, sits across from the tiny Auburn post office and is used for summertime melodramas by the **Star Valley Historical Theatre** (307/883-2759). Not far away is the Davis Ranch, where Butch Cassidy and his gang holed up one winter.

West of Auburn on County Road 134 is **Auburn Fish Hatchery** (208/225-3457), where 50,000 trout are raised annually. It's open 8 A.M.–5 P.M. daily. The road to the hatchery parallels the Lander Cutoff of the Oregon Trail for several miles.

FREEDOM

Freedom (pop. 100), Star Valley's oldest settlement, straddles the Idaho–Wyoming border. The town was established by Mormons in 1879 and offered an escape from the Idaho Territory's efforts to ban polygamy. Arthur Clark named the town for his freedom to have multiple wives. Today, Freedom has a small country store just a few feet from the border where you can buy Idaho lottery tickets.

Freedom is famous in NRA circles for a small factory, **Freedom Arms** (307/883-2468, www.freedomarms.com), which makes handguns, including the massive .454 Casull, the world's most powerful revolver—and one of the most expensive at $2,000 apiece. No surprise that Clint Eastwood owns one. Don't ever get on the wrong end of this deadly instrument. Visitors can watch a short video and view a gun display here.

Free camping is available three miles west of Freedom, inside Idaho, at the Forest Service's **Tincup Campground.**

ETNA

Etna lies near the northern end of Star Valley and has a small country store and an outsized brick Latter-day Saints church that could probably house the entire population of 200. In late summer, the sweet scent of new-mown hay hangs in the air. **Etna Trading Co.** (307/883-2409) is an old-time general store. Nearby is the historic and nicely restored **Baker Cabin.**

Blue Fox Gallery (307/883-3310, www.bluefoxgallery.com) in Etna exhibits unique jewelry, raku pottery, and hand-sculpted masks by Tony Ivie and Wayne Noffsinger.

Two miles south of Etna, **Wolf Den** (307/883-2226, www.wolfdeninc.com) has modern duplex cabins ($80 d to $100 for a six-person unit) with a Western motif, and a restaurant, tepees, and a pasture with several bison. **Horse Shoe Cafe** in Etna is a classic small-town eatery, filling with locals every day and deer hunters on cool fall mornings.

ALPINE

The crossroads settlement called Alpine is an ugly place with a quickly multiplying sprawl of businesses at the intersection of U.S. 26 and U.S. 89. You'll find fireworks stands, real-estate offices, motels, restaurants, and bars strung out in all directions. During the 1990s, the population grew from 200 to 550, a 175 percent increase, and since then it just keeps going up. It's a sad sight, and all because of the tourists en route to Jackson Hole and as a home for Jackson workers. For local information, contact the Town of Alpine (307/654-7754, www.alpinewyoming.org).

The area around Alpine is called Lower Valley and borders on **Palisades Reservoir,** built at the convergence of the Snake, Greys, and Salt rivers. Water enthusiasts come here for fishing, waterskiing, camping, and picnicking.

Approximately 700 elk gather each winter at the **Elk Feedground** one mile south of Alpine on U.S. 89. You can view the elk from the parking area here: They often approach parked cars rather closely. Best time to visit is in the mornings, when they are fed.

SOUTHWEST WYOMING

Events

Alpine Mountain Days (www.starvalleywy.com/mountaindays) on the third weekend of June, is the big summer celebration, with mountain men, a black-powder shoot, country music, horseshoe tournament, arts and crafts, a Dutch-oven cook-off, and other activities.

The **International Pedigree Stage Stop Sled Dog Race** (307/734-1163, www.wyomingstagestop.org) stops here. (See the *Jackson Hole* chapter for more information.)

Recreation

Riding and Rafts (307/654-9900, www.jacksonholeoutfitters.com) has all-day horseback rides into the Greys River country for $100 with lunch. It also has unguided horse rentals and rents rafts for trips down the Snake River. Book float trips through **Nordic Inn** (307/654-7556). Most rafting operations are run out of Jackson Hole.

Accommodations

Alpine Junction has several good lodging choices at considerably lower rates than in Jackson. Reservations are advised during July and August, when everything fills up fast.

Three Rivers Motel (307/654-7551, $50 s or $55 d) has affordable rooms and kitchenettes for $5 extra.

Just west of town on U.S. 26 is **Alpine Inn** (307/654-7644, www.starvalleywy.com/alpine-inn.htm). Motel rooms in the main building are $60. Separate cabins run $45 for small units with one bed or $70 with a second bedroom and kitchenette. No phones, but most rooms sleep four (or more) people. The inn is set on 10 acres and has a hot tub and tepees.

Alpen Haus Hotel (307/654-7545 or 800/343-6755, www.alpenhaus-resort.com) is a chalet-style hotel decorated with Austrian scenes. Standard rooms cost $80 with two queen beds, or stay in the Caribbean-themed room (in an Austrian-style hotel?) with its jetted tub and pedestal bed for $149 d.

For homey and immaculate accommodations, stay at the **(Nordic Inn** (307/654-7556, www.brenthoven.com), where the nine rooms are a reasonable $78–98 d, and a stunning stone cottage has two rooms for $145 d and 225 d. The inn gets lots of repeat visitors, so be sure to reserve ahead for midsummer. Open late May–mid-October.

Bull Moose Lodge (307/654-7593 or 877/498-7993, www.bullmoosesaloon.com, $75–125 d) has a newly opened three-story hotel with hot tub, jetted tubs, decks, and continental breakfast.

You'll find very attractive and spacious rooms ($120–140 for up to four people), along with Western-themed log cottages ($180 d), at **(Best Western Flying Saddle Lodge** (307/654-7561 or 866/666-2937, www.flyingsaddle.com). Amenities include an outdoor pool, two hot tubs, Wi-Fi in the lobby, and many rooms have jetted tubs. The cottages are open only seasonally. Ask staff at the desk about famous guests through the years, including John Wayne. A fine restaurant is on the premises, and additional luxury rooms were slated for 2006.

Camping

There's plenty of public camping at nearby Forest Service campgrounds (see the *Greys River Loop Road* or *Snake River Canyon* sections of this chapter). The closest spot is **Alpine Campground** ($8, open mid-May–mid-Sept.), two miles west of town along U.S. 26. Make reservations ($9 fee) at 518/885-3639 or 877/444-6777, www.reserveusa.com). The turnoff to the Forest Service's **McCoy Campground** is three miles south of Alpine on U.S. 89 and then another five miles along Palisades Reservoir. In addition to these official campgrounds, dispersed camping spots (turnouts off the road) can be found approximately five miles up Greys River Road, which is just east of Alpine.

Food

Los Dos Amigos in the Alpen Haus (307/654-7545) has a Mexican menu, while **Gunnar's Pizza** (307/654-7778) creates sub sandwiches and pizzas, including whole-wheat and deep-dish versions. Gunnar's also offer outside dining in the summer.

Bull Moose Saloon (307/654-7593 or 877/4 98-7993, www.bullmoosesaloon.com) serves three meals a day, with sandwiches, steak, prime rib ($16), burgers, and other favorites. Check out the nightly specials and the smoke-free bar has live music on summer weekends.

The real surprise is **(Brenthoven's Restaurant** (307/654-7556, www.brenthoven.com), where specialties include exquisite dinners ($18–28 entrées), along with breakfast crepes. Save room for the signature bread pudding. The bar has a fine wine selection, and friendly owner Mike Clinger will be happy to discuss opera or tell you about his distinctive Colonial home behind the Nordic Inn. Chef Brent Johnston is also an accomplished concert pianist, and his Brenthoven quartet performs Sunday evening jazz on the lawn in July and August. The restaurant and inn are open late May–mid-October.

(SNAKE RIVER CANYON

Northeast of Alpine, the country abruptly changes as U.S. 89/26 enters Snake River Canyon, paralleling it all the way to Hoback Junction, 23 miles away. This is a delicious way to enter Jackson Hole, offering numerous pullouts where you can view the roiling, rambunctious rapids of the sinuous Snake River as it slithers through millions of years of rocky cliffs. At sunset, the river glows a silver ribbon of light. A big, powerful river, the Snake eventually feeds into the Columbia in Washington. Riverbanks are lined with ancient cottonwoods, while the higher slopes show lodgepole pines.

The whitewater of Snake River Canyon is a favorite of outdoor enthusiasts, and during the summer you're bound to meet cars with kayaks on their roofs and vans filled with happy rafters heading back to Jackson. (See the *Jackson Hole* section for details on the many river-running options.) River access is generally via the West Table Creek and Sheep Gulch boat ramps.

Hiking and Camping

Two Bridger–Teton National Forest campgrounds are along the canyon: **East Table Creek Campground** ($15) 11 miles from Hoback Junction, and **Wolf Creek Campground** ($10) 15 miles from Hoback Junction. Both are open mid-May–September. No reservations are accepted, and campsites often fill early on midsummer days.

A popular hiking trail starts six miles southwest of Hoback Junction and provides a loop trip into the backcountry. **Cabin Creek Trail** follows the creek uphill to an alpine pass filled with late-summer wildflowers and fine views of the Snake River drainage. Return the same way, or opt to head downhill along the **Dog Creek Trail,** which ends near the junction of Wilson–Fall Creek Road with U.S. 89/26. Either way, it's about six miles of hiking, but if you take Dog Creek Trail you'll need a shuttle back to your car. Get camping and hiking details from the Forest Service (307/739-5400, www.fs.fed.us/r4/btnf/teton).

CENTRAL WYOMING

The counties of Natrona and Converse enclose definitive Wyoming country: sage-and-grass-carpeted plains, desolate badlands, impressive tree-draped mountainsides, and the big, lazy North Platte River. Ranching remains important, but the dominant industry—and the one that dictates the region's economy—is energy production. It means jobs for roughnecks in dozens of oil and gas fields, but it also greases the wheels of city life, creating refinery and transportation jobs, government positions, and a wave of other effects in the local community as the wages pass on to construction workers, shop owners, and schoolteachers. Without oil and gas, Casper—Wyoming's second-largest metropolitan area—would be little more than a cattle town crossroads on the way to Yellowstone.

Geographically, central Wyoming is quite diverse. The north section is an open, expansive place. Driving across the long, straight highways that divide this land is like sailing a boat over an ocean of gentle rollers—the mountains are so far in the distance that they could well be islands. Golden eagles spin giant loops in the sky, and the coal-black clouds of distant summertime thunderheads are pierced by brilliant slashes of lightning. The wind blows on, bending the grass as it passes in waves of motion, whirling the old windmills that pump water to sheep, cattle, and deer. This is rolling mixed-grass prairie and sagebrush country, with sharp ridges appearing suddenly, topped by narrow bands of ponderosa pine and juniper.

South of this rangeland lies the North Platte River, carving a slow curve first north, then

HIGHLIGHTS

【 Pioneer Museum: This museum in Douglas is one of the state's top historical collections with a wide range of artifacts; free, too (page 203).

【 Wyoming State Fair: Held in Douglas the third week of August for more than a century, this is a fun place to check out the 4-H exhibits, country-and-western concerts, greasy food, carnival rides, and rodeos (page 206).

【 Ayres Natural Bridge Park: This tiny park in the middle of nowhere is one of nature's oddities, with a 100-foot bridge arching over LaPrele Creek (page 209).

【 Fort Caspar: Interesting exhibits and a fort replica where thousands of Oregon Trail emigrants passed. And yes, that really is the correct spelling; it's the city of Casper that has the wrong spelling (page 222).

【 National Historic Trails Interpretive Center: First-rate exhibits using the latest technology take visitors back to an era when the West was young. Set aside at least two hours for this one (page 224).

【 Nicolaysen Art Museum: Casper's surprising artistic focal point, with changing exhibits in a beautifully recycled brick power plant (page 224).

【 Casper Mountain: Stifling hot in Casper? Relief is just a 15-minute drive away. Check out Crimson Dawn Museum while you're there (page 233).

【 Salt Creek Oil Field: Ah, the pungent scent of oil and the strange apparition of mosquito-like, oil-sucking pumps sprawled across a desert landscape (page 236).

【 Independence Rock: Called the "Great Register of the Desert," this is where Oregon Trail travelers carved their names, paused for a drink from Sweetwater River, and buried their dead. Nearby is Martin's Cove, where the Mormon Handcart Visitor center tells the tragic story of some of these emigrants (page 243).

【 Hell's Half Acre: If you saw *Starship Troopers,* you've seen this colorful badlands area west of Casper. The "Half Acre" is actually 320 acres (page 246).

【 Castle Gardens: Out-of-this-world carved figures inhabit a very remote spot; don't attempt the dirt road if it's rained recently (page 247).

LOOK FOR **【** TO FIND RECOMMENDED SIGHTS, ACTIVITIES, DINING, AND LODGING.

CENTRAL WYOMING

CENTRAL WYOMING

east, and finally southeast toward Nebraska. Giant dams hold back the water for irrigation and electricity. A green stripe of riparian forests and irrigated fields borders the river. South of the Platte, the land changes again, with the Laramie Mountains rising in a rough-edged jumble of rugged canyons and pine-covered peaks. Elk stand along mountain meadows, bugling in the cool air of late fall. Pickup trucks slow as wild turkeys speed-walk across the gravel roads. Clear brooks cascade down mountain slopes. West of here, central Wyoming becomes drier and more desolate, wrinkled by the badlands of Hell's Half Acre and the barren crests of desert mountain ranges.

Casper dominates the central Wyoming economy with an oil refinery, the primary statewide newspaper, and the state's largest junior college and shopping mall. The towns of Douglas and Glenrock go their own ways, with a mixture of ranching, oil, coal, and tourism. Farther north, the tiny settlements of Midwest and Edgerton cap the vast Salt Creek Oil Field. Between these few outposts of civilization lie hundreds of square miles of sagebrush and grass, jackrabbits, and rattlers. Only the scattered roads, oil pumpjacks, windmills, and old ranch houses mark the presence of humans.

PLANNING YOUR TIME

Many travelers heading to or from Yellowstone, the Black Hills, and other regional destinations pass through central Wyoming. Casper is both the largest city and a good base for visitors, with a broad range of lodging, dining, shopping, and entertainment choices. You could easily spend a day or two here exploring historical sights. The city sits at the junction of several historic trails—including the Oregon Trail—and the recently opened **National Historic Trails Interpretive Center** provides an excellent overview. The re-created log buildings of **Fort Caspar** are right along the river, with a fine small museum. Two important Oregon Trail sights are southwest of Casper: **Independence Rock** with its thousands of carved names from 1850s emigrants, and **Martin's Cove,** where 145 Mormon handcart pioneers perished in an 1856 blizzard.

Back in Casper, the **Nicolaysen Art Museum** and several smaller collections are well worth seeing, and it's a short drive up to the cool pine forests of **Casper Mountain.** South of here are three large North Platte River reservoirs that are popular with boaters and anglers.

Little Douglas hosts the state fair in late August and has the excellent **Pioneer Museum** and historic Fort Fetterman. Two fascinating geologic areas are **Ayres Natural Bridge Park,** 14 miles west of Douglas, and the badlands of **Hell's Half Acre,** 45 miles west of Casper. Keep heading west on U.S. 20/26 to tiny Moneta, where a lonely dirt road leads to a fascinating collection of Indian petroglyphs at **Castle Gardens.**

Douglas

Douglas (pop. 5,300) epitomizes life in small-town America. It's the sort of place where the big summertime events are the state fair and weekly drag races, where a night on the town means joining a bowling league or doing the two-step at the LaBonte Inn, and where old-timers hang out in the historic College Inn Bar and drink 50-cent beers. On both ends of Douglas are more modern slices of Americana, where suburban ranch-style homes cover the hills. It's a friendly, conservative town with pickup trucks, dense American food, and an unusual history.

HISTORY

Douglas came into existence with the arrival of the Fremont, Elkhorn, and Missouri Valley Railroad. Platted in 1886, the town was named for Stephen A. Douglas, the senator from Illinois best known for his debates with

DOUGLAS

Abraham Lincoln. The town quickly boomed to 1,600 people that first year, boasting three newspapers, several restaurants and hotels, two dance halls, 12 stores, and 21 saloons (easy to see where priorities lay). Once the railroad construction had moved on down the line to Casper, the population dwindled and it became a sleepy little ranching center for the next 70 years. Only the late-summer state fair brought Douglas to life each year.

World War II

One of the strangest pieces of Douglas history is its POW camp, built in 1943 along the North Platte River. The camp contained 180 barracks-style buildings and housed up to 3,000 prisoners of war. The camp was surrounded by an electrified fence, watchtowers, German shepherds, and army guards. One prisoner was shot by a guard and a few others escaped, but they didn't get far in this remote country—2,000 miles from the sea. Although some of the prisoners at Douglas were German Nazi and SS officers, most were Italians, many of whom were happy to be away from the war.

The prisoners worked in local agricultural fields harvesting potatoes and sugar beets for

$4 per day or at a variety of art projects in the camp. Most impressive was the work of several Italian artists who painted the interior of the U.S. officers' club with 15 murals of Old West scenes. After the war, the prisoners returned home, although some returned to visit in later years. The land was sold to Converse County for $1, and the barracks were dismantled or bought by locals, who moved them to other parts of town. Today the POW camp site is an open meadow on the west bank of the North Platte south of Richards Street.

Boom and Bust

Like much of Wyoming, Douglas has watched its fortunes wax and wane through the years. In the 1950s, with the Cold War at fever pitch, prospectors combed Wyoming with Geiger counters, discovering major uranium deposits just north of Douglas. Others found oil, gas, and coal. A giant coal-fired power plant opened in nearby Glenrock, and by the late '70s the region was one of the most prosperous in the state. At the peak of the oil-and-uranium orgy of the early 1980s, the town of Douglas had doubled in size to more than 10,000 people. But then the bust hit, and within a couple of years the population plummeted back to where it had been. Long-time locals had mixed feelings when the balloon suddenly burst; they were happy to see the rabble leave town but were also suddenly burdened with paying for all the new schools, roads, and other facilities ordered up in the heady heyday. Today the economy of Douglas is back to its old mixture of energy and ranching, with some people commuting 60 miles each way to the busy coal mines near Wright while others work for the railroad, on coalbed methane operations, or at a uranium mine northwest of town.

SIGHTS
◖ Pioneer Museum

The people of Douglas point with pride to their large local museum, one of the finest in Wyoming. Just inside the fairgrounds, the spacious museum (307/358-9288, http://wy-oparks.state.wy.us, free) is open 8 A.M.–5 P.M. Monday–Friday all year, plus 1–5 P.M. Saturday June–September.

The main room is filled with old rifles and saddles, including one that belonged to outlaw Tom Horn. Check out the special "running irons" used by rustlers to alter cattle brands. Fittingly enough, the rifle of Nate Champion—a rustler murdered in the Johnson County Wars—is also here. Above one doorway is a pole from the original transcontinental telegraph line; it's one of just six known to survive. Look around the other rooms and you'll discover the bison-fur mittens worn by Portugee Phillips on his ride to get help for Fort Kearny and an army trumpet and bullets from the Custer battlefield.

The museum also contains hundreds of historic photos, a big doll collection, clothing from the 1890s, and a back room filled with impressive Indian artifacts, including baskets, pottery, Sioux and Crow war clubs, a bow from the Custer battleground, and even a tepee used in the movie *Dances with Wolves*. Downstairs are several wonderful old quilts and a collection of homestead items. The stairwell features the 64-inch-waist overalls that belonged to flamboyant C. B. Irwin, one of outlaw Tom Horn's closest friends. Irwin was a stockman, railroad detective, rodeo performer, and manager of Cheyenne Frontier Days. Outside is a schoolhouse constructed in 1886.

Douglas Railroad Interpretive Center

This center consists of seven train cars parked outside the old Chicago Elk Horn Railroad depot (built in 1886 and now home to the chamber of commerce). The collection includes a steam locomotive, dining car, sleeper, baggage car, coach, cattle car, caboose, and a little track inspection car. They represent many different eras—oldest is the 1884 caboose. The train cars are open 9 A.M.–5 P.M. Monday–Friday May–September. Be sure to pick up the amazingly detailed guide to these rail cars inside the depot visitor center.

JACKALOPES

Jackalopes are unusual mammals that move by bounding. Found originally in Converse County, Wyoming, they are now distributed throughout the western states. The critters have the horns of an antelope, the body of a jackrabbit, and the stealth of both. First observed by trapper Roy Ball in 1829, the jackalope was later noted by cowboys and others after too little sleep, too many days in the saddle, and too much cheap whiskey. Nocturnal animals, jackalopes are never seen during the day. These powerful and vicious animals are reputed to attain speeds approaching 90 mph and often sing and mate during thunderstorms. The hornless does are commonly seen by tourists, while the bucks remain elusive. Westerners, particularly members of the militias, believe that the federal government is hushing up the true story of these dangerous critters to make cowboys look like liars.

OK, I admit to liking plastic pink flamingos and tacky postcards, but jackalopes are another story. The first time you see a mounted jackalope specimen, it is mildly amusing, but with each tourist junk shop west of the Mississippi offering more jackalopes, the originality quickly fades. The town of Douglas takes credit for this hare-brained idea, although its claim is a bit suspect. In the 1920s, a Douglas resident saw a jackalope mounted in a store in Buffalo, Wyoming. He described the creature to his grandson, Douglas Herrick, who was intrigued by the animal. In 1941, he attached the antlers of a deer to the head of a large jackrabbit he had shot and sold the specimen to the LaBonte Hotel. The rest is history.

In 1960, the state of Wyoming gave the Douglas Chamber of Commerce "jackalope" as a registered trademark. Today you see jack-alopes everywhere in Douglas: The town symbol contains one; an eight-foot-tall jackalope statue greets visitors at Jackalope Square; another statue has hopped atop the LaBonte Hotel; and a roadside sign warns "Watch Out For Jackalope." You can buy cans of jackalope milk in the stores, "Rabbit Punch" at a local bar, or pick up a jackalope hunting license from the chamber of commerce visitor center. And, of course, the critters multiply like rabbits on the shelves of local shops.

jackalope statue at Jackalope Square

© DON PITCHER

More Sights

Ruts of the **Oregon Trail** are still visible nine miles south of Douglas; ask at the chamber of commerce for directions. The old **officers' club** from the Douglas POW camp is now an Odd Fellows Hall (115 S. Riverbend Dr., 307/358-2421). Ask to take a look inside at the wall-to-wall murals painted by Italian artists who were prisoners during World War II.

One of Wyoming's oldest churches is the **Christ Episcopal Church** (411 Center, 307/358-5609), built in 1896 and now on the National Register of Historic Places.

The **Plains Complex** (628 E. Richards, 307/

© DON PITCHER

Douglas Railroad Interpretive Center

358-4489) has several historic structures hauled in from all over this part of Wyoming. Included are the old officers' quarters from Fort Fetterman and a POW camp building. The ice-cream parlor served at various times as a barn, a boardinghouse, and a maternity center. Check out the doors on the ceiling of the ice-cream shop.

Douglas Park Cemetery, at 9th and Ash streets, has many interesting old graves from local characters; get a booklet describing them from the chamber of commerce office. One of those buried here is horse thief, cattle-rustler, murderer, and later saloon-keeper "Doc" Middleton. Also here is the grave of the outlaw George W. Pike, whose exploits managed to lead to at least two appearances in court annually for 15 consecutive years, although he was never convicted. His gravestone (found near the center of the cemetery) reads:

> *Underneath this stone in eternal rest*
> *Sleeps the wildest one of the wayward*
> *west*
> *He was gambler and sport and cow*
> *boy too*
> *And he led the pace in an outlaw crew.*

> *He was sure on the trigger and staid to*
> *the end*
> *But he was never known to quit on a*
> *friend*
> *In the relations of death all mankind*
> *is alike*
> *But in life there was only one George*
> *W. Pike.*

ENTERTAINMENT AND EVENTS
Nightlife

LaBonte Lounge (206 Walnut, 307/358-4343) is the place for live country bands Wednesday–Saturday nights. Pool tables and darts are available all the time. **Chutes Saloon** in the Best Western (1450 Riverbend Dr., 307/358-9790) has lounge-lizard tunes, a big-screen TV, and free appetizers on weeknights.

The historic **College Inn Bar** (103 N. 2nd, 307/358-9976) is a favorite place for major-league drinking. Drop by on Wednesday nights for 50-cent draft beers. Also try **Rex's Waterhole** (9th and Richards, 307/358-9902) for live music and comedy. For movies, head to **Mesa Theatre** (104 N. 3rd St., 307/358-6209).

CENTRAL WYOMING

◀ Wyoming State Fair

In 1905, the Wyoming Legislature appropriated $10,000 for a Wyoming State Fair (307/358-2398, www.wystatefair.com) in Douglas. With land donated by the Chicago and Northwestern Railroad, the "Show Window of Wyoming" opened that summer, offering a variety of agricultural exhibits, horseback wrestling, Roman races, and concerts. To top it off, two cavalry soldiers added their own drama by putting on an impromptu gunfight. Later, auto polo and motorcycle-riding events were added, but the big hit was Professor Carver's High Diving Girl, who leapt with her horse off a 40-foot platform into a pool of water.

The Wyoming State Fair is held the entire third week of August each year, drawing thousands of visitors from all over the nation. The 113-acre fairgrounds is right next to town and includes a 4,300-seat grandstand, an arts-and-crafts building, a cafeteria, an arena, an open-air pavilion, livestock barns and stalls, and, of course, plenty of carnival rides, cotton candy, and stuffed-animal prizes in the midway. Keep yourself entertained at the market swine evaluation, the 4-H vegetable judging, the demolition derby, or the sheep-to-shawl contest. A free "people shuttle" (tractor-pulled wagon) takes folks around the fairgrounds. Other attractions include evening country-and-western concerts, the Miss Rodeo Wyoming contest, a Saturday morning parade, and the **Douglas Invitational Art Show** (307/358-9288). Because this is Wyoming, the biggest events at the fair are the **PRCA rodeos** held the final three days.

Other Events

Both locals and visitors enjoy the **High Plains Old-Time Music Show** in April. Plenty of hot fiddle, guitar, and banjo players provide the entertainment; call 307/358-9006.

Jackalope Days (307/358-2950) in early July includes a free pancake breakfast, street dance, and beer garden, games, arts and crafts, a motorcycle and classic car show, bed races, and live music.

The **Wyoming High School Rodeo Finals**

take place in late June at the fairgrounds, and the first weekend of August brings a popular **Senior Pro Rodeo.**

Douglas Motorsports Park (307/359-8376, www.douglasmotorsportspark.com) on the southeast edge of town hosts drag races of all types May–September. On an old airport runway, it's considered one of the top 0.25-mile strips in the nation. The biggest races take place in mid-July. In early August, Douglas plays host to hundreds of motorcycle enthusiasts en route to the Sturgis Rally, with the town providing hospitality tents and other facilities.

RECREATION

A two-mile paved path follows the west bank of the North Platte River through **Riverside Park** and is a great spot for an evening stroll or bike ride. Take along your fishing pole to try for trout, walleye, or channel catfish. If you have your own raft or canoe, the river is a fun place for leisurely float trips; pick up a map of river access points from the chamber of commerce.

The free **Douglas Recreation Center** at the high school (1701 Hamilton, 307/358-4231) houses an indoor pool, gyms, racquetball courts, a sauna, and weight room. An excellent **outdoor swimming pool** in Washington Park is open in the summer, and two water slides add to the appeal. While there, check out the statue of **Sir Barton,** who in 1919 was the first horse to win the Triple Crown. He died in Douglas in 1937 at the ripe old age of 21 and is buried near the statue.

An 18-hole **golf course** (307/358-5099) is southeast of Douglas, but it has no bunkers—the fierce winter winds kept blowing the sands away. For the kid version, try **Puttin A Round Mini Golf** (119 S. 2nd St., 307/358-1123).

Rent canoes and rafts from **Curly's Leisure Sports** (219 W. Yellowstone Hwy., 307/358-9394).

ACCOMMODATIONS

For July and August you should book rooms up to two months ahead, especially for the weekend drag races and state fair week. Several locals rent out rooms in their homes to visitors while the fair is going on; get a list from the chamber of commerce (307/358-2950). Lodging rates typically rise $20 or so during fair week.

Motels

Four Winds Motel (615 E. Richards, 307/358-2322, www.4-windsmotel.com, $37–42 s or $42–49 d) is a clean and comfortable budget place with wireless Internet and fridges in all rooms.

Opened in 1914, **LaBonte Inn** (206 Walnut, 307/358-4343, www.thelabonte.com, $40–50 d) has 22 old-fashioned upstairs rooms with private baths. The bar below can be noisy when bands are playing.

Out on the east side of town (I-80 exit 135), **Alpine Inn** (2310 E. Richards, 307/358-4780, $45 s or $50 d) has affordable rooms, microwaves, fridges, free laundry, and Wi-Fi.

Best Western Douglas Inn (1450 Riverbend Dr., 307/358-9790 or 800/344-2113, www.bestwestern, $77–87 s or $87–97 d) is a fine lodging choice, with a large indoor pool, hot tub, saunas, weight room, Wi-Fi, and an atrium lobby.

Holiday Inn Express (900 W. Yellowstone Hwy., 307/358-4500 or 800/930-7829, www.hiexpress.com) has a riverside setting, the newest rooms in town, plus an indoor pool, hot tub, fridges, microwaves, Wi-Fi, and light breakfast. Standard rooms are $99 d, and suites cost $109–150.

Bed-and-Breakfast

A century-old classic, **Morton Mansion Bed and Breakfast** (425 E. Center St., 307/358-2129, www.mortonmansion.com) is a stately 1903 Queen Anne with a wraparound porch. Inside are four spacious guest rooms ($65–75 d) and a two-bedroom suite ($125 for four people), all with private baths and a Victorian decor. A full breakfast is served; kids welcome.

Guest Ranch

Two Creek Ranch (307/358-3467, www.twocreekranch.biz) is a 25,000-acre spread eight miles south of Douglas. The owners run 600 cows with their calves over this land and take on working dudes February–October. Guests ride horseback while helping out in calving, working a 75-mile cattle drive, or assisting with branding, roundups, and other ranch activities. The rates are surprisingly reasonable, around $100 per person per day all-inclusive. This is the real thing, with guests sleeping in the bunkhouse, travel trailers, or tents. Open late April–October.

Camping

Pitch tents or park RVs for free at **Riverside Park** along the North Platte River. The free showers have an amusing Western-decor bathroom covered with branded wood. Camping is limited to two nights, and the sprinklers come on at 8 A.M., so get up early! Call 307/358-9750 or 307/358-3311. During the state fair, camping is available on the fairgrounds (307/358-2398). The RV crowd heads to **Douglas KOA** (307/358-2164 or 800/562-2469, www.douglaskoa.com, $18 tents, $30 RVs, $37 d cabin) west of Douglas on Hwy. 91. It's open year-round, with a seasonal heated outdoor pool, guest computer, and Wi-Fi. (See *Laramie Mountains* in this section for details on Forest Service campsites.)

FOOD

For dependable meals and big portions three times a day, head to **LaBonte Inn** (206 Walnut St., 307/358-4343). Breakfast is available all day, or sink your teeth into dinners of steak, pasta, or seafood for $8–18.

Broken Wheel Truckstop (307/358-4446) just east of town serves breakfast 24 hours a day. Also open all the time is **Trading Post** (628 E. Richards, 307/358-4489), a so-so coffee shop and old-fashioned ice-cream parlor at the nostalgic Plains Complex.

Clementine's Restaurant (1199 Mesa Dr., 307/358-9400) serves ribs, steak, prime rib, pizza, pasta, and other all-American favorites and has a popular lunch buffet and salad bar. There are nightly specials—all-you-can-eat prime rib on Friday and Saturday nights—plus a big-screen TV for sporting events.

CENTRAL WYOMING

Chute's Eatery (at the Best Western, 1450 Riverbend Dr., 307/358-9790) has good steaks, a soup and salad buffet, and Sunday filet mignon. **Pizza Hut** (1830 Richards, 307/358-3657) offers stuff-yourself lunch specials, and **La Costa** (1213 Teton Way, 307/358-2449) is the place to go for Mexican meals.

Get supplies from **Douglas Grocery** (130 S. 4th St., 307/358-2250) or **Safeway** (1900 E. Richards St., 307/358-3446). For fresh pastries, don't miss the classic (**Home Bakery** (119 N. 3rd, 307/358-9251).

INFORMATION AND SERVICES

The **Douglas Area Chamber of Commerce** is inside the old train depot (121 Brownfield Rd., 307/358-2950, www.jackalope.org, open 9 A.M.–5 P.M. Mon.–Fri. all year). You can also pick up brochures inside on summer weekends whenever the railroad center is open.

The Forest Service's **Douglas Ranger District Office** (2250 E. Richards St., 307/358-4690, www.fs.fed.us/r2/mbr) has maps and lots of information on Medicine Bow–Routt National Forest and Thunder Basin National Grassland.

The **Converse County Library** (300 Walnut St., 307/358-3644) has Internet access, and the **post office** (307/358-3106) is at 129 North 3rd Street.

Whistle-Stop Books and Espresso (200 S. 3rd St., 307/358-3266, www.whistlestopbooks.com) has a selection of Wyoming books and gifts, with a soda fountain/coffee shop in the back. **Jen's Books** (102 N. 2nd St., 307/358-8093, www.jensbooks.com) is a fine used and rare bookstore in the heart of town.

Wash your duds at **Sudsy Duds** (1400 E. Richards St., 307/358-8022) or **Clay St. Laundry** (2nd and Clay, 307/358-8085).

For medical emergencies, head to **Converse County Memorial Hospital** (111 S. 5th St., 307/358-2122 or 800/735-8303).

GETTING THERE

Powder River Transportation (307/682-1888 or 800/442-3682, http://gillette.coachusa.us) has daily bus service to Douglas, providing connections to central and eastern Wyoming, Denver, Billings, and Rapid City.

FORT FETTERMAN

Seven miles northwest of Douglas on Hwy. 93 is Fort Fetterman State Historic Site (307/358-2864, http://wyoparks.state.wy.us). The buildings are open 9 A.M.–5 P.M. daily Memorial Day–Labor Day, and by appointment only the rest of the year. The grounds are open sunrise–sunset in summer. Entrance is $2 per person for nonresidents or $1 for Wyoming residents. A couple of simple campsites are available at no charge.

The fort was named for Lieutenant Colonel William J. Fetterman, who was killed by Indians in the Fetterman Massacre of 1866 (see the *Powder River Country* chapter). Begun in 1867, this was the last fort built in the Rockies. With the signing of the Fort Laramie Treaty of 1868, Forts Casper, Reno, Phil Kearny, and C. F. Smith were all closed, leaving Fort Fetterman the only army base in northern Wyoming. The remote hilltop location afforded commanding views along the infamous Bozeman Trail in both directions, but the location proved inhospitable. A report to headquarters the first winter noted "officers and men were found under canvas exposed on a bleak plain to violent and almost constant gales and very uncomfortable."

Even after the buildings were completed the fort remained a dreaded, windswept, lonely place, and many soldiers deserted as soon as they could get to the nearest railroad. The regimen was strict, with daily parade drills and the prospect of long rides to fight Indians in the surrounding country. Soldiers called the place "Hell Hole," while the Sioux derisively labeled it "Fort Fetterman Reservation." Not far away stood the "Hog Ranch"—sin city on the plains—where gambling, drinking, and women offered a choice of ways to spend the $13 per month the calvarymen received.

Fort Fetterman served as a supply base for the army during the mid-1870s, and both General Crook and Colonel MacKenzie led expeditions from here to attack the Sioux, but the fort itself was never the scene of any conflicts. After the battles had finally died down, the fort was abandoned in 1882. Instead of immediately disappearing, however, "Fetterman City" became the center of ranching and trade in the area. For a while, at least, it was a wide-open town with enough gunfights, hangings, whoring, gambling, and drunkenness to give Fox television stations a run for the money. In his novel *The Virginian*, Owen Wister used Fetterman as the basis for his rough-and-tumble town of "Drybone."

Alferd Packer

One of the characters attracted to Fetterman was a prospector who called himself John Swartz. When a waiter was slow in bringing water at a local restaurant, he pulled a gun, saying, "Damn you, ain't you going to bring me that water?" Service quickly improved. The man turned out to be Alferd Packer, wanted for robbing, killing, and then eating his five mining partners in Colorado during the winter of 1875. (Packer called human breast meat the sweetest he'd ever eaten.) After escaping from a Colorado jail, he remained free for the next decade before finally being recognized in Fetterman City. The sheriff captured him at a nearby ranch and spent several nervous nights on the long stage ride to Rock Creek before finally turning Packer over to Colorado authorities. Although convicted of murder, Packer managed to escape from prison again; his body was found in the Rockies in 1903.

The Fort Today

After the railroad arrived in 1886, Douglas became the new center for trade, and Fetterman quickly faded from the scene. Most of the buildings were torn down or moved to Douglas; only two of the original buildings remain: an adobe ordnance warehouse and a log officers' quarters. Inside the officers' quarters is a small state-run **museum** (free), which includes historic displays on the fort, Indian battles, and Fetterman City. The surrounding country still exudes a sense of barren loneliness, and it's easy to see how much the soldiers must have hated this windswept post. Ask the museum staff to point out the faint tracks of the "Bloody Bozeman" Trail to the south.

Fort Fetterman Days, the second weekend of July, brings military demonstrations, Indian dancing, fort tours, firing of artillery pieces, old-time music, crafts, and games. Many of the participants dress in authentic 1870s costume.

◖ AYRES NATURAL BRIDGE PARK

One of the most unusual geological formations in Wyoming lies 14 miles west of Douglas on I-25. Take exit 151 and continue five miles south to tiny 22-acre Ayres Natural Bridge Park (307/358-3532), where the main attraction is a 100-foot-long, 50-foot-high rock arch over LaPrele Creek. This natural arch was formed when a meander bend in LaPrele Creek gradually eroded the base of the rock face, leaving the upper part of the cliff unscathed. Eventually the weakened rock gave way, and the creek flowed through the hole that had been created at the bend. The ancient creekbed is 300 feet away from the present creek and 50 feet higher.

History

For the Indians who first lived in this country, the natural bridge was a deadly place. A young brave had been struck by lightning and killed while hunting in the canyon; thus began a legend that an evil spirit lived below the bridge, ready to grab anyone who ventured into his lair. When white settlers realized this, they used the natural bridge as a place to escape from Indian attacks, knowing they would not be pursued across the arch. Early-day mountain men lived in caves here, and Mormon settlers built cabins nearby in the 1850s. It took an expedition by Dr. Ferdinand V. Hayden, director of the U.S. Geological Survey in 1869, to bring the rock arch to national attention. He found it odd "that so great a natural curiosity should have failed to attract the attention it deserves." In 1881, Alva Ayres bought the land and used the lush LaPrele Creek country as headquarters for a freighting business. The natural bridge and

© DON PITCHER

Ayres Natural Bridge spans the waters of LaPrele Creek.

surrounding land were donated to Converse County in 1920 by Ayres's heirs.

Visiting the Bridge

Today, Ayres Natural Bridge offers a beautiful side trip from I-25. Box elders and cottonwoods line LaPrele Creek, fluorescent green patches against the brilliant red sandstone and the rich blue sky. Along one face of the red-walled amphitheater that circles the park are carved the names of many visitors, some dating from the 1880s. This is a popular weekend picnic and swimming spot and a great place to watch birds. Pets are not allowed, but **free camping** is available on the grounds, with a three-night stay limit. Ayres Natural Bridge Park is open 8 A.M.–8 P.M. daily April–October. Closed in the winter.

LARAMIE MOUNTAINS

The Laramie Peak section of Medicine Bow–Routt National Forest lies approximately 30 miles south of Douglas, cutting from northwest to southeast along the Laramie Mountains. The mountains are draped with stands of ponderosa, lodgepole, and limber pine and with Engelmann spruce and subalpine fir at higher elevations. Lower elevations are dominated by grass and sagebrush. It's pretty but rugged country, with deep valleys dividing the high granitic ridges and peaks—several exceeding 9,000 feet. Deer, elk, antelope, and wild turkeys are commonly seen in the Laramie Mountains, and rainbow, brook, and brown trout are found in the creeks.

Public and private lands intermingle here, with only a few large tracts of Forest Service property—the biggest being around Laramie Peak. This impressive mountain, clearly visible from Douglas, served as a landmark for travelers along the old Oregon Trail, who called this country the Black Hills. There is some logging around Esterbrook and Albany Peak, especially in insect-killed forests, but Laramie Peak is de facto wilderness.

The Medicine Bow–Routt National Forest **Douglas Ranger District Office** (2250 E. Richards St., 307/358-4690, www.fs.fed.us/r2/mbr) has maps and additional information. A $2 fee is charged for parking at Forest Service

LARAMIE MOUNTAINS

To Douglas

Labonte Creek

To Glendo

To Shirley Basin

To Wheatland

To Medicine Bow

To Rock River and Laramie

Buffalo Peak

Squaw Mountain

CAMPBELL CREEK

Warbonnet Peak

CURTIS GULCH

ESTERBROOK

BLACK MOUNTAIN FIRE LOOKOUT

FRIEND PARK

Laramie Peak

Eagle Peak

Medicine Bow National Forest

Laramie

Labonte Canyon

Big Bear Canyon

Mountains

0   5 mi
0   5 km

© AVALON TRAVEL PUBLISHING, INC.

trailheads and picnic grounds throughout the Medicine Bow–Routt National Forest, including those in the Laramie Mountains.

Esterbrook

The Esterbrook area, 32 scenic miles south of Douglas on Hwy. 94, began as a copper-mining town in 1886 but never really had much to show for its effort. Today it provides a delightful escape from the stifling summer heat at lower elevations. Don't attempt to drive on this dirt road after heavy rains or in the spring, when it becomes virtually impassable. Continuing south from Esterbrook, the road cuts through the

Laramie Mountains along beautiful Horseshoe Creek Valley, eventually depositing travelers in the town of Rock River. Along the way are numerous side roads into the mountains, including the access road to the Laramie Peak Trail.

Esterbrook is famous for its **old log church**, whose rear window frames snowcapped Laramie Peak. It's a favorite place for country weddings and is open May–October, with Sunday Episcopal services.

Esterbrook Lodge (307/351-7568) is another classic log building. Stay at small and very rustic cabins or mobile homes—no running water—for $30 d (add $7 per person for extra guests)

with a central bathhouse. Also here are tent ($10) and RV sites with hookups ($15). The restaurant has a steak-house dinner menu, and is open Friday–Sunday. The saloon and dance hall attract occasional bands, and the resort puts on events throughout the year. The lodge is open late May–October, but phone service is spotty, so you may need to write instead for reservations: Esterbrook Lodge, 32 Pine Dr., Douglas, WY 82633.

Hiking

The Forest Service office in Douglas has brochures describing local trails in detail. Some of the finest hiking in central Wyoming is found along the **Laramie Peak Trail,** a 4.2-mile (one-way) path that climbs to the top of the 10,272-foot peak. The trail begins right behind Friend Park Campground, 48 miles south of Douglas (via a gravel road for the last 20 miles). A $2 parking fee is charged. The first mile is relatively easy as the trail parallels Friend Creek, but after this it's a long, arduous climb. Be sure to bring ample water, food, clothing, and supplies because weather conditions can change rapidly. Afternoon thunderstorms occur almost daily in the summer. Two miles from the start is a small cascade; water can be hard to find above this point. Periodic forest openings offer dramatic vistas as you continue up the mountain, gaining 2,800 feet along the way. On top find expansive vistas in all directions, including into Nebraska, Colorado, and South Dakota on a clear day. Communication buildings and towers are also here. The trail is generally free of snow by late June. Plan on 4–7 hours for the round-trip hike. Note that ATVs also use the trail.

A second trailhead, 0.25 mile north of Friend Park Campground, provides access to the four-mile **Friend Park Trail,** which parallels Arapahoe Creek.

The two-mile-long **La Bonte Canyon Trail** offers both pleasant hiking and good fishing for brook trout. The trailhead is at Curtis Gulch Campground, 38 miles south of Douglas. The path drops along a gorgeous steep-walled canyon (keep your eyes open for bighorn sheep

and elk) and ends at a big-game exclosure. Along the way are meadows, forests of poplar and Douglas fir, and flowers galore. Also near the Curtis Gulch Campground is a 4WD road/hiking trail that climbs for three miles up **Big Bear Canyon** to scenic Devils Pass.

Another good climb is up the 4WD road to **Black Mountain Lookout,** one of the last operating fire towers in the nation. You'll find great views down pristine Ashenfelder Creek. Get there by following Forest Road 633 south of Esterbrook Campground for six miles to the Laramie Peak Scout Camp. Turn right onto Forest Road 667 and park inside the National Forest boundary. Hike up the 4WD road 2.5 miles to the lookout, which is staffed June–September.

The **North Laramie River Trail** starts approximately 20 miles west of Wheatland and descends for 2.5 miles into the North Laramie River Canyon, losing 1,000 feet in elevation along the way. There's good fishing for brown and rainbow trout in the river, and the remains of 15 buildings from a 1920s resort are fun to explore. Get to the trailhead by taking the El Rancho exit from I-25 (between Glendo and Wheatland) and heading west on Fish Creek Road to Fletcher Park Road. Continue past Camp Grace to the intersection of Fletcher Park and Cow Camp roads, where signs point the route to the trailhead.

Sunset Ridge Trail is a short 1.6-mile climb to a scenic view over the plains to the east. It originates from the Esterbrook Campground and gains 400 feet along the way before looping back down the hill.

Contact the Forest Service office in Douglas (307/358-4690, www.fs.fed.us/r2/mbr) for details on these and other trails, including several challenging backcountry routes near Laramie Peak.

Winter Recreation

Wintertime snow closes all roads over the Laramie Mountains, transforming the mountains into an excellent place for cross-country skiing, with many miles of scenic country and untracked snow.

Camping

Four pleasant Forest Service campgrounds ($10, open June–mid-Oct.) are in the Laramie Mountains. **Esterbrook Campground**—near the settlement of the same name—is the most accessible, and **Friend Park Campground** is a great base for hikes up Laramie Peak. **Curtis Gulch Campground** is in a scenic area with granite rock formations that are popular with rock climbers. It's 38 miles south of Douglas. **Campbell Creek Campground** is 40 miles south of Douglas in a remote area on the western end of the Laramie Mountains.

The Forest Service's historic **La Prele Guard Station** (307/358-4690, www.fs.fed.us/r2/mbr) is available for rent late June–mid-September for $70 per night. Built by the Civilian Conservation Corps 1937–1941, this two-bedroom log structure has space for six (bring sleeping bags), plus a kitchen and bath, stone fireplace, and battery-powered lamps. Make reservations ($9 fee) at 518/885-3639 or 877/444-6777, www.reserveusa.com. The cabin is 40 miles south of Douglas and close to the **Twin Peaks Trail,** which takes you 2.5 miles to a 9,000-foot mountain.

Thunder Basin National Grassland

Thunder Basin National Grassland is an expansive blend of high rolling plateaus, steep rocky escarpments, and gentle plains. It's one of the few places in Wyoming where mountain ranges are not visible, giving the countryside a North Dakota feel. The country seems to reach forever. There's virtually no traffic on some of the main routes across the grassland, especially Hwy. 450 between Wright and Newcastle. Most of the national grassland is covered with a mixture of western wheatgrass, blue grama grass, and big sagebrush, but some of the ridges have stands of ponderosa pine and juniper, while creek bottoms contain cottonwood trees or greasewood. Naturalists count 170 golden-eagle nests on Thunder Basin—one of the biggest concentrations in Wyoming—along with abundant populations of sandhill cranes, turkeys, antelope, mule deer, elk, and coyotes. Many bald eagles winter here. Look out for the jackalopes, too; lots of the antlerless variety get squashed by cars.

Thunder Basin National Grassland covers 1.8 million acres within Powder River Basin. The land is a mixture of private ranches and public land managed by the Forest Service, the BLM, and the state. The federal government owns 572,000 acres of the total. In the past, a patchwork quilt of land ownership created access and management problems for the grassland. Through a series of land trades, the grassland is now more consolidated and accessible. Get a current ownership map from the Forest Service's **Douglas Ranger District Office** (2250 E. Richards St., 307/358-4690, www.fs.fed.us/r2/mbr).

Thunder Basin came about during the glory days of the New Deal and remains today an enclave of pseudosocialism within the rock-ribbed Republican state of Wyoming. Although ranchers had grazed sheep and cattle in the area since the mid-19th century, the arrival of homesteaders caused the land to be divided into smaller parcels. In the arid mixed-grass prairies of eastern Wyoming, it was nearly impossible for a family to survive because the rains fell too infrequently for farming, and profitable cattle or sheep operations required more than 640 acres of grazing land.

Overgrazing, soil erosion, and five consecutive drought years in the 1930s combined to force many families off the land. Counties risked bankruptcy because of lost tax revenue. The Agricultural Adjustment Administration finally began buying homesteads in 1934, giving money to the counties in lieu of taxes. Programs were begun to reestablish grasses to protect the soil and to develop water sources

PRAIRIE DOGS

Prairie dogs are cat-sized rodents that live in underground communities and feed on roots and plants. Prairie dog towns sometimes cover thousands of acres with burrow holes spaced every 50 feet or so; a Texas colony was once 100 miles long and 250 miles wide! Two species are found in Wyoming: white-tailed and black-tailed. The latter occur in more than 100 towns covering 14,000 acres within Thunder Basin National Grassland, while white-tailed prairie dogs are found in parts of south-central and western Wyoming. Ranchers often complain of lost grazing range resulting from feeding and digging by the "dogs" and injuries to horses and cattle that step into the holes. Research, however, has shown that prairie dogs may actually improve grazing in some situations and that cattle seem to prefer to graze in prairie dog colonies. In addition, prairie dogs provide food for many predators and create habitat used by many other animals.

A THREATENED SPECIES

For many decades, ranchers and the Forest Service systematically poisoned prairie dog colonies in the name of "range improvement." These practices proved devastatingly effective and helped create a fragmented population that is susceptible to inbreeding and disease. A century ago, prairie dogs occupied 300 million acres of western grasslands; today they are found on just 1.8 million acres. Sightings of the endangered black-footed ferret on Thunder Basin National Grassland helped end most of the poisoning in the 1970s, and prairie dog

populations rebounded dramatically. Unfortunately, the animals are highly susceptible to sylvatic plague, an exotic Asian disease that sweeps through the colonies, killing thousands of animals in a short period. In addition, because prairie dogs are still considered varmints in many areas, "sport" hunters don't need a license to shoot them and aren't limited on how many they can kill – at least on private land.

Meanwhile, the U.S. Fish and Wildlife Service (http://mountain-prairie.fws.gov/mammals) is attempting to restore the black-footed ferret – one of the world's rarest mammals – through a captive breeding program and releases into the wild. Prairie dogs are their primary food source, and these varmint hunters may well be endangering the long-term survival of both ferrets and prairie dogs.

SEEING PRAIRIE DOGS

If you're interested in viewing prairie dogs, ask at the Douglas Forest Service office for a copy of its prairie dog town map. The largest area is along Horse Creek in the Rochelle Hills, with smaller prairie dog colonies along North Antelope Road. Perhaps the easiest place to view black-tailed prairie dogs is Devils Tower National Monument, where a colony is right along the road. Use caution if you're hiking around prairie dog colonies because the creatures may be infected with the plague bacteria, the cause of Europe's infamous "black death" in the 1300s. Fleas carry the disease, which is potentially deadly but relatively easy to halt with antibiotics.

for livestock, while private land ownership was consolidated into larger, more economically manageable units.

Today local ranchers use the grassland in a cooperative grazing scheme. Improvements such as dams, wells, and fences are cooperatively developed. In addition to livestock grazing, practically every acre of Thunder Basin has been leased for petroleum exploration. Oil and gas wells pump from 58 oil fields, and coal bed methane wells can be

seen dotting the grassland along Highway 59. Vast deposits of subbituminous coal underlie almost the entire area, and there are five gigantic strip mines, including Black Thunder Coal Mine, the largest coal mine in the nation. Bentonite—a lubricant and absorptive clay used in everything from oil-drilling muds to candy bars—is also mined on the grassland, and major uranium deposits wait for the public to forget about Three Mile Island and Chernobyl.

RECREATION

A network of more than 800 miles of gravel and dirt roads crisscrosses Thunder Basin National Grassland. No developed campgrounds are available, but you can camp for free anywhere on the public lands. A couple of areas are popular with hunters, bird-watchers, photographers, and others looking for a chance to get out and about.

As with much of Wyoming's rangelands, you should be on guard for prairie rattlesnakes, especially around rock piles and prairie-dog towns. Also, beware of thunderstorms and the lightning that can strike in this open country; this isn't called Thunder Basin for nothing. Because of the lack of drinking-water sources, carry plenty with you in your travels. The Forest Service office in Douglas has additional information on the area, including lists of birds, mammals, and wildflowers.

Rochelle Hills

The Rochelle Hills area, a forested volcanic escarpment near the intersection of Converse, Campbell, and Weston counties, is one of the prettiest parts of the national grassland. A scenic gravel road takes you on a long loop north of the tiny settlement of **Bill** (the name came from four early homesteaders, all of whom had the same first name) and then for 50 miles through the Rochelle Hills before dropping back to Hwy. 59 eight miles south of Wright. Unfortunately, landslides have destroyed a section of this road, making access difficult in one section.

Upton-Osage Area

The Upton-Osage area also contains miles of ponderosa pine–topped hills and many small ponds that attract birds. Another fascinating area is in the northern part of the grassland in the Soda Well/Weston area (30 miles north of Gillette on Hwy. 59). This is a fine place to camp or explore; see the Forest Service for access details throughout the grassland.

Glenrock

The cattle-and-coal town of Glenrock (pop. 2,200) lies halfway between Casper and Douglas at the confluence of Deer Creek and the North Platte River. The town's name comes from Rock in the Glen, a large rocky outcrop just to the west. Deer Creek was a favorite camping spot along the Oregon Trail, a place to rest up, do a little fishing, and let the stock graze on the lush creekside grass. Starting in 1847, Mormon emigrants mined the coal visible along the north bank of the river; it was the first coal mined in Wyoming. The first bridge to span the North Platte was built here in 1851 but was washed out in a flood the following year. Deer Creek Station was established in 1857, operating first as a trading post and later as a relay terminal for the Overland Stage and a home station for the short-lived Pony Express. After telegraph wires replaced the Pony Express, Deer Creek became a telegraph relay station. Indians burned the station to the ground in 1866, and it was never rebuilt.

Later years saw a series of booms and busts fueled by coal, oil, and uranium. Today, one of the largest employers is the massive coal-fired Dave Johnston Power Plant a few miles east of town.

SIGHTS
Museums

The free **Glenrock Paleontological Museum** (506 W. Birch St., 307/436-2667 or 888/461-5015, www.paleon.org, open 9 A.M.–5 P.M. Tues.–Sat.) has original bones and casts from dinosaurs found in the area, including a triceratops, hadrosaurs, nodosaurs, and even *Tyrannosaurus rex* teeth. It's a surprisingly impressive small collection that also includes the finest apatosaurus skull ever found and several dinosaur species that have been found nowhere else in the world. During summer, the museum

DISCOVERING DINOSAURS

Wyoming is prime dinosaur-hunting country, and many important specimens have been discovered, starting with diplodocus dinosaurs (the largest land animal that ever lived) at Como Bluff in 1877. Other significant dinosaur discovery sites are in the Glenrock area, the Lance Creek area southwest of Newcastle, and various places in Bighorn Basin.

The **Wyoming Geological Museum** (307/766-2646, www.uwyo.edu/geomuseum) on the University of Wyoming campus in Laramie houses a fine collection of dinosaurs, including the 75-foot-long skeleton of an apatosaurus, and "Big Al" – one of the most complete allosaurus skeletons ever discovered.

Nearby is world-famous **Como Bluff**, site of the first large discovery of dinosaurs ever found. There's even a little cabin built from dinosaur bones, the "world's oldest building."

The **Wyoming Dinosaur Center** (307/864-2997 or 800/455-3466, www.wyodino.org) in Thermopolis has a first-class museum with a camarasaurus from the area, a nearly complete *Triceratops horridus*, a cast of *Tyrannosaurus rex*, plus dinosaur eggs in a nest. Don't miss the daily tours to nearby dig sites.

Little **Glenrock Paleontological Museum** (307/436-2667 or 800/996-3466, www.paleon.org) has a surprising collection that includes triceratops, hadrosaurs, and nodosaurs. You can also join ongoing dinosaur digs nearby.

Paleo Park (307/334-2270, www.paleopark.com) lies in the heart of the Lance Creek fossil area southwest of Newcastle. Tours and accommodations are available at this site where several significant dinosaur discoveries have been made, including one of the most complete specimens of triceratops ever discovered. Also here are the intermingled tracks of both dinosaurs and birds.

Western Wyoming Community College in Rock Springs (307/382-1600, www.wwcc.cc.wy.us) exhibits some impressive dinosaur skeleton casts, including ones of triceratops and *Tyrannosaurus rex*.

Red Gulch Dinosaur Tracksite, east of Greybull, has hundreds of tracks from theropods. Guides are at the site, or you can take a tour from **Geo-Science Adventures** (307/765-2259 or 866/765-2259, www.geo-sciences.com). The nearby **Greybull Museum,** 307/765-2444, exhibits many fossils, including several dinosaur bones.

OTHER FOSSILS

Wyoming is also famous for its other fossilized animals, particularly the treasure trove of Jurassic mammals at Como Bluff and the abundant fish fossils in the Kemmerer area. At **Fossil Butte National Monument** (307/877-4455, www.nps.gov/fobu) you can learn the full story. Several quarries in the Kemmerer area let you dig your own fish fossils.

offers special dig-for-a-day programs for $50 per person. It's a great chance to get down and dirty while learning about the creatures that roamed this land more than 65 million years ago. Casts of dinosaur bones are sold, and you may see volunteers working in the prep lab. The paleo museum doubles as a visitor center.

Glenrock Deer Creek Museum (937 W. Birch St., 307/436-9443, open 10 A.M.–4 P.M. Fri.–Tues. summers only, free) occupies an old church on the west side of town. Inside is a collection of local memorabilia, along with bones from a nearby buffalo jump used by prehistoric hunters.

Other Sights

Rock in the Glen, 0.5 mile west of Glenrock, has the carved names from the 19th-century emigrants who passed by on the way to Oregon, California, or Utah. Several **graves** from this era are scattered around Glenrock, sad reminders of the thousands who never made it. One is that of A. H. Unthank, just east of the Dave Johnston Power Plant on Tank Farm Road, who died of cholera just one week after carving his name in Register Cliffs near present-day Guernsey. Four miles west of town is the grave of Ada Magill, a young girl who died of dysentery in 1864 as her parents headed west in a wagon train. Stones were piled on top of the grave to keep wolves from digging up her body.

Glenrock City Park has a granite monument to **Dr. Ferdinand V. Hayden,** a physician who devoted his life to exploration of the West. Hayden helped found the U.S. Geological Survey and led the famed Hayden Yellowstone Expedition of 1870. The Indians considered Hayden a bit wacky, calling him "Man-who-picks-up-stones-running." Hayden used the Deer Creek Station at present-day Glenrock as a base of operations for several of his expeditions around Wyoming, hence the monument—placed here in 1931 by his photographic partner on these trips, William H. Jackson.

A pleasant picnic and fishing spot is **Boxelder Canyon,** approximately 10 miles south of Glenrock on Hwy. 90. Boxelder Creek is bordered by steep rocky walls.

The country around Glenrock is laced with energy projects of all types. Immediately west of town is the Big Muddy oil field, where nearly three million barrels were pumped out in the last 40 years; production is declining now. The giant **Dave Johnston Power Plant** is six miles east of Glenrock along the North Platte River. It's one of the largest coal-fired power plants in the Rockies, generating 810,000 kilowatts of electricity for the Pacific Northwest. A private railroad feeds the plant with coal from the Glenrock Coal strip mine 16 miles to the north.

Visit the **Central Wyoming Livestock Exchange** (just east of town, 307/436-5391 or 800/967-1467, www.wyomingcattle.com), where cattle, sheep, hogs, and even a few goats are auctioned off on Thursdays year-round (every other Thursday in the summer). This is an enjoyable way to learn about ranching and to rub shoulders with local ranchers.

ENTERTAINMENT AND EVENTS

At least one of the many local bars (**Four Aces, El Diablo, Knotty Pine, Shoreliner,** or **Deer Creek Lounge**) will have a country-and-western band on most weekends. Knotty Pine has the best Bloody Marys in town, plus its "Humphrey" is not for the fainthearted.

The big annual event is **Deer Creek Days,** with a parade, car show, craft and food booths, rodeo, street dancing, and lots of drinking. It takes place the first weekend of August.

A free indoor **swimming pool** is in the middle school at 645 South 3rd Street. Golfers may want to check out the nine-hole **Glenrock Golf Course** (307/436-5560).

ACCOMMODATIONS

All American Inn (500 W. Aspen, 307/436-2772, $32 s or $43 d) has functional rooms with fridges and microwaves.

(Hotel Higgins (416 W. Birch, 307/436-9212 or 800/458-0144, www.hotelhiggins.com) is plain vanilla on the outside—red shingles on a building built in 1916—but the inside is surprisingly nice. The entire hotel has been lovingly furnished with antique brass beds, wardrobes, and lamps. Downstairs is a ticking old grandfather clock, a bearskin rug, and an upscale restaurant. Rooms cost $55 d or $75 d for two-bedroom suites, including a continental breakfast. No phones in the rooms.

Camping

Camping is free at **South Recreation Complex,** three miles south of Glenrock along the river. **Deer Creek RV Park** (on the east end of town, 307/436-8121) has RV sites with hookups for $22–24, and tent spaces for $18; open all year.

FOOD

Inside Higgins Hotel, **(The Paisley Shawl Restaurant** (307/436-9212 or 800/458-0144, www.hotelhiggins.com) is the fine-dining choice with candlelit dinners of lamb chops, grilled chicken pesto pasta, and Cuban pork tenderloin; $14–22 dinner entrées. Open for lunch and dinner, with a back deck for summer evenings. Closed Sunday and Monday.

Four Aces Bar (307/436-9010) downtown serves three meals a day and has a good steakhouse dinner menu. Most items are under $10. Get pizza at **Classic Cafe and Pizza** (201 S. 4th, 307/436-2244).

On the east side of town, **Fort Diablo Steak**

House and Saloon (307/436-2288) has Friday and Saturday night prime rib, plus buffalo steaks and seafood. Buy groceries from **Williams' Town and Country Food Center** (218 W. Cedar, 307/436-2344).

INFORMATION AND SERVICES

The **Glenrock Paleontological Museum** (506 W. Birch St., 307/436-2667 or 888/461-5015, www.paleon.org, open 9 A.M.–5 P.M. Tues.–Sat.) doubles as a visitor center, and the **Glenrock Chamber of Commerce** (307/436-5652, www.glenrockchamber.com, open 8 A.M.–3 P.M. Mon.–Fri.) is also here. The **Glenrock Library** (518 S. 4th, 307/436-2573) exhibits a few dinosaur fossils found in the area but also has something a bit newer—Internet access.

Casper

Wyoming's second-largest city, Casper (pop. 50,000) is in transition from an oil-dependent economy to a more diversified base. The city sprawls across both sides of the North Platte River and is surrounded by the outlying settlements of **Evansville** (pop. 2,300), **Mills** (pop. 2,600), and **Bar Nunn** (pop. 900), with more suburbs filling the intervening land.

For many years, Casperites trumpeted the city as "Oil Capital of the Rockies." It sits at the center of several large oil fields and is home to a refinery and a large tank farm. In the last decade, however, declining oil production has forced the city into a more diversified base, although the oil industry is still an important economic player. Open up the Casper Yellow Pages and you'll find more than 20 different types of oil-related listings—from oil and gas exploration companies to directional drilling outfits.

With its central location, substantial population, spacious convention facilities, and ties to the state's energy and ranching industries, Casper considers itself the true heart and soul of Wyoming. The only statewide newspaper, the *Casper Star-Tribune,* is based here, along with one of the state's premier medical centers. To Casperites, arch-rival Cheyenne is just a Colorado city that happened to sneak into Wyoming. The rest of Wyoming, however, views Casper with equal suspicion; in 1904 Casper aspired to become the state capital but failed miserably, coming in third behind Cheyenne and Lander in a statewide vote.

A working-class town, Casper isn't a major tourist destination, but it does have several fine museums, most notably the National Historic Trails Interpretive Center, the Nicolaysen Art Museum, Fort Caspar Museum, and two Casper College museums. The city serves as a regional hub for shopping, sporting events, and business. You'll discover outstanding recreational opportunities on nearby Casper Mountain, at local reservoirs, and on the North Platte River, plus many historic sites along the Oregon Trail. In addition, the city is filled with a variety of cultural activities, particularly in winter when symphony concerts, theatrical productions, and art receptions pepper the calendar.

HISTORY
The Astorians

Although Casper is identified today with oil, the city began as a way station along the Oregon Trail. Seven of John Jacob Astor's fur traders led by Robert Stuart first traveled through this area in 1812 on their return from Oregon, arriving in late October. Knowing they could not make it back to St. Louis in their emaciated condition, the explorers constructed a rock-walled cabin (the first Anglo building in Wyoming) and covered it with buffalo hides. Game proved amazingly plentiful. They returned from a hunting trip with 47 bison, 28 deer and bighorn sheep, and a bear! But five weeks later, a band of 23 Arapaho warriors appeared on their way to raid the Crow Indians

CASPER

To Airport and
Powder River

To Bar Nunn and Midwest

LITTLE AMERICA REFINERY

WYOMING VETERAN'S CEMETERY

To Glenrock and Douglas

COMFORT INN

SHILO INN MOTEL

WAL-MART

EASTRIDGE MALL

CASPER COUNTRY CLUB

RESHAW BRIDGE PARK

Evansville

North Platte River

CASPAR KOA EAST

FIRST INTERSTATE INN

SAFEWAY

HILLTOP SHOPPING CENTER

WALSH DR

NATIONAL HISTORIC TRAILS INTERPRETIVE CENTER

CASPER EVENTS CENTER

YELLOWSTONE MOTEL

WYOMING MEDICAL CENTER

SKYLAR INN

RECREATION CENTER AND ICE ARENA

CHAMBER OF COMMERCE

NICOLAYSEN ART MUSEUM

WERNER WILDLIFE MUSEUM

CASPER COLLEGE

MUNICIPAL GOLF COURSE

To Casper Mountain and Hogadon Ski Area

SEE "DOWNTOWN CASPER" MAP

MOTEL 6

OIL TANK FARM

OIL DERRICK

SAGE AND SAND MOTEL

ALBERTSON'S

SAFEWAY

WESTRIDGE MOTEL

SMITH'S

TATE MUSEUM

CASPER MOUNTAIN B&B

AUDUBON CENTER AT GARDEN CREEK

To Rotary Park

SALT CREEK HWY

PLATTE RIVER COMMONS

FAIRGROUNDS

SUPER 8 MOTEL

SUNRISE SHOPPING CENTER

BEACON CLUB

ROLLER RINK

MORAD PARK

BEL AIR MOTEL

WEST YELLOWSTONE

Mills

FORT CASPAR CAMPGROUND

FORT CASPAR

BLM FIELD OFFICE

ALL AMERICAN INN

To Bessemer Bend, Alcova, and Independence Rock

PARADISE VALLEY GOLF COURSE

PARADISE DR

North Platte River

ROBERTSON RD

1 mi

1 km

© AVALON TRAVEL PUBLISHING, INC.

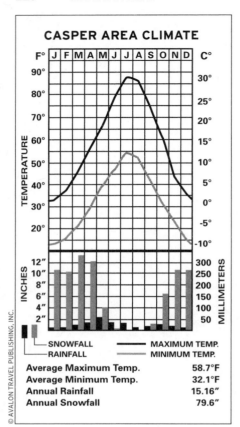

CASPER AREA CLIMATE

Average Maximum Temp.   58.7°F
Average Minimum Temp.   32.1°F
Annual Rainfall   15.16"
Annual Snowfall   79.6"

© AVALON TRAVEL PUBLISHING, INC.

summer, when the river ran dangerously high, people often died trying to cross it. Others lost their wagons or watched as their oxen and horses were swept downriver. When Brigham Young's party of Mormon emigrants arrived here in 1847, they built a 23-foot-long raft and floated their wagons across. The Mormon ferry became Casper's first business venture, with gentiles charged $1.50 per wagon. Business boomed, and by 1849, several different ferries were competing with the Mormon ferry. Despite this transporation rush, there were still delays of up to one week as California gold-rush travelers waited to cross. (This has to rate as one of Wyoming's only recorded traffic jams.)

In 1852, a French Canadian trader named John Richard (locally known as Reshaw) built a long wooden toll bridge at present-day Evansville, charging $5 in gold per wagon—less when the river was low and folks would risk fording. To stifle competition, he bought the Mormon ferry for $300 and shut it down.

In 1859, another bridge was built six miles upriver by Louis Guinard to compete for the lucrative Oregon Trail traffic. Guinard's bridge must have been one of the most impressive structures along the entire 2,000-mile route. Built at a cost of $40,000, the bridge was 17 feet wide, 1,000 feet long, and supported by 28 log and rock cribs. It soon became the preferred crossing point along the North Platte, and the old Richard bridge was cannibalized for firewood.

farther north. Intimidated, the Astorians invited them in for a meal. They stayed for a day and a half, promising to return in two weeks. The Astorians quickly decided discretion was the better part of valor and moved to a new camp just across what is now the Nebraska border. They finally reached Missouri the following spring.

Ferries and Bridges

The route pioneered by the Astorians eventually became a virtual highway to the West. The North Platte River was one of the main barriers to this migration, with many emigrants choosing to ford near what is now Casper. In early

Red Cloud's War

Platte Bridge Station served as a trading post for travelers, a Pony Express mail stop, and later a telegraph office. A volunteer force was posted to protect the telegraph and those traveling along the Oregon Trail from Indian and Mormon attacks. After a massacre of Indians at Colorado's Sand Creek in 1865, full-scale war broke out between Indians and whites. One of these battlegrounds that July was at Platte Bridge Station. Expecting a wagon train with vital supplies and ammunition, 20 men under the command of Lieutenant Caspar Collins left the fort to escort the expected convoy. Once across the bridge, the soldiers found themselves surrounded by Red Cloud and more than 1,000 Sioux, Cheyenne, and Arapaho warriors. In their flight back across the bridge, five soldiers died. Collins was killed when he stooped to rescue a fellow soldier and his horse bolted, carrying him into the onrushing warriors. Other soldiers said that when last seen, he had his reins in his teeth and was firing pistols from both hands. His body was found two days later with 24 arrows in it.

A second battle occurred that afternoon—Custard's Wagon Train Fight. When the supply wagons of Sergeant Amos Custard came within sight of the fort, the soldiers tried to warn them with cannon fire. Three men from an advance guard made it to safety within the fort, and the others quickly corralled the three wagons together. Although they put up a fierce fight, within hours Red Cloud's men had killed and mutilated the 22 defenders and burned their wagons. In honor of Caspar Collins, Platte Bridge Station was renamed Fort Caspar. (Fort Collins, Colorado, is named for his father, William Collins.) Because of a never-corrected error by an army telegraph operator—he typed a dot instead of a dot-dash—the town that eventually grew up nearby was misspelled Casper. Two years later, Fort Caspar was abandoned. Much of it was dismantled and the material used in the construction of Fort Fetterman, 40 miles to the east and a jumping-off point for the Bozeman Trail.

Lawless Days and Nights

In 1888, the Fremont, Elkhorn, and Missouri Valley Railway extended its line up the North Platte River almost to the site of old Fort Caspar. A tent city quickly sprang up, followed by more permanent buildings. For the next 17 years the town of Casper lay at the end of the tracks. It was an exceptionally violent place; employees of the first grocery store surrounded their beds with sacks of flour for protection from stray bullets, and Casper's first public building was a jail. Even the mayor got in on the act, murdering his business partner in an 1890 gun duel on Main Street. The jury let him go free. When the ruffians became too much to tolerate, a street trial was held and those who refused to leave town faced the prospect of being strung up in a "necktie party." Pinned to the shirt of one murderer lynched by a vigilance committee was the following note: "Process of law is a little slow, so this is the road you'll have to go. Murderers and sinners, Beware! People's Verdict."

Oil Changes Everything

In 1851 Jim Bridger, Cy Iba, Kit Carson, and Basil Cimineau Lajeunesse discovered an oil spring just west of Casper at Poison Spider Creek. The oil was mixed with flour and sold as axle grease for wagon trains. By 1889, when the first oil well was drilled near Casper, it was clear that much more oil lay beneath the ground. Land speculators and claim jumpers flocked to Wyoming, and battles quickly broke out over who had staked the first claim; the winner generally had more burly men, guns, and lawyers. Soon the massive Salt Creek Oil Field, 40 miles north of Casper, was producing; wagons towed by teams of up to 20 horses hauled the oil back to Casper. A small refinery was built in 1895, the first in Wyoming. It was later replaced by more modern facilities, including the now-closed Standard Oil plant, at one time the largest refinery on earth, handling 25,000 barrels of oil per day. Through time, Casper became a center for oil and refining in the northern Rockies.

Boom and Bust

Casper grew into a major industrial town with the development of Salt Creek and other oil fields. So many roustabouts flooded Casper that they had to sleep in shifts in the available tents, motels, garages, basements, or shacks. Dozens of illegal gambling houses and speakeasies helped make a trip to town memorable, and more than 2,000 prostitutes pursued their own boom times in the Sandbar district; prostitution was blatant here until the 1950s. Oil production peaked in the 1920s, but the crash of 1929 burst this economic bubble and cut the city's population in half within five years. World War II sent oil prices and Casper's economy soaring. An army air base—home to 4,000 men—opened nearby; it's now the site of Casper's airport. In the late '50s, new technology—injecting water to force the remaining oil to wellheads—helped boost recovery dramatically at Salt Creek, and there followed another boom for Casper. The discovery of massive uranium deposits in the Pumpkin Buttes, Gas Hills, and Shirley Basin areas further fueled this growth.

The roller-coaster ride continued throughout the last half of the 20th century: down in the late '60s, back up in the '70s. When oil prices soared after the OPEC oil embargo in 1973, Casper experienced such an orgy of growth that planners predicted a population rivaling that of Denver's by the year 2000. After oil prices plummeted in the 1980s, these optimistic—or apocalyptic, depending on your point of view—predictions failed to materialize. Sales-tax receipts dropped by half, many of downtown Casper's storefronts were covered with plywood, and the Amoco refinery shut down. The once-toxic site is now an 18-hole golf course, with the

hills, sand traps, and water hazards designed to help remediate the area while simultaneously challenging golfers.

The economy has improved dramatically in recent years as Casper diversified its industrial base to include everything from a copper foundry to a company building fire engines. New stores have invigorated the commercial sector, and the Nicolaysen Art Museum added an artistic focal point. Downtown is thriving, suburbs are once again creeping over the countryside, and Eastridge Mall—Wyoming's largest shopping mall—is packed with chain stores. A decade ago, you could still find a few homes for under $25,000; today the same place would probably be five times that amount and Casper home prices are above the national average.

SIGHTS
《 Fort Caspar

Although the original fort had long since disappeared, in 1936 the WPA reconstructed a half dozen of Fort Caspar's log buildings. Included are a blacksmith shop, an Overland

downtown Casper

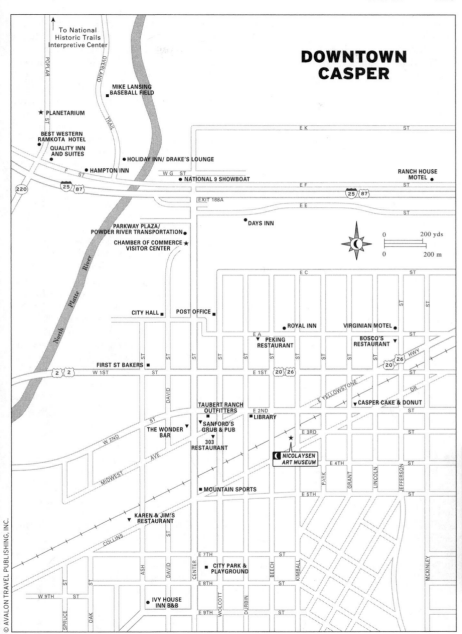

DOWNTOWN CASPER

To National Historic Trails Interpretive Center

MIKE LANSING BASEBALL FIELD

★ PLANETARIUM

BEST WESTERN RAMKOTA HOTEL
QUALITY INN AND SUITES
HOLIDAY INN/ DRAKE'S LOUNGE
HAMPTON INN
NATIONAL 9 SHOWBOAT
RANCH HOUSE MOTEL

PARKWAY PLAZA/ POWDER RIVER TRANSPORTATION
CHAMBER OF COMMERCE ★ VISITOR CENTER

DAYS INN

CITY HALL ■ POST OFFICE ■

ROYAL INN VIRGINIAN MOTEL
PEKING RESTAURANT BOSCO'S RESTAURANT

FIRST ST BAKERS ■

TAUBERT RANCH OUTFITTERS
THE WONDER BAR
SANFORD'S GRUB & PUB
303 RESTAURANT
LIBRARY
CASPER CAKE & DONUT
NICOLAYSEN ART MUSEUM

MOUNTAIN SPORTS

KAREN & JIM'S RESTAURANT

CITY PARK & PLAYGROUND

IVY HOUSE INN B&B

North Platte River

0   200 yds
0   200 m

E K ST
E F ST
EXIT 188A
E E
E C ST
E A
E 1ST
E 2ND
E 3RD
E 4TH
E 5TH
E 7TH
E 8TH
E 9TH

W G ST
W 1ST ST
W 2ND
W 9TH ST

E YELLOWSTONE

POPLAR ST
OVERLAND TRAIL
DAVID
MIDWEST AVE
COLLINS
ASH
DAVID
CENTER
BEECH
KIMBALL
WOLCOTT
DURBIN
SPRUCE
OAK
PARK
GRANT
LINCOLN
JEFFERSON
MCKINLEY

220   25 87   2 2   20 26   26 HWY

© AVALON TRAVEL PUBLISHING, INC.

Stage station, a commissary storehouse, a barracks building, and a sutler's store. Many supports from Guinard's long bridge across the North Platte are still visible as mounds of rock. Also here you'll find a replica of the Mormon ferry and a reconstruction of part of the bridge. During summer, guides dressed as 1860s cavalrymen are on hand to answer your questions.

A brick building at the fort houses an excellent small museum (307/235-8462, www.fortcasparwyoming.com, $2 adults, $1 ages 6–17) displaying a variety of items, including a reconstructed Mormon handcart, Native ceremonial pipes, and a W. H. Jackson painting of Platte Bridge Station. Be sure to check out the photos and story of the 14-inch-tall Pedro Mountain mummy, a find that seemed to bolster the "little people" stories told by many Indian tribes. The museum is open 8 A.M.–7 P.M. Monday–Saturday, noon–7 P.M. Sunday June–August; 8 A.M.–5 P.M. Monday–Saturday and noon–5 P.M. Sunday in September and May; and 8 A.M.–5 P.M. Monday–Friday, 1–4 P.M. Sunday the rest of the year. The gift shop has more than 500 Western history book titles available, along with Indian jewelry from the Wind River Reservation. The fort buildings are open May–September, but you can wander the grounds at any time of year. Kids like the fun playground that includes a stagecoach wagon.

Over in Evansville, the **Town Hall** (open 8 A.M.–5 P.M. Mon.–Fri.) also contains artifacts found along the Oregon Trail.

◖ National Historic Trails Interpretive Center

This 27,000-square-foot museum (307/261-7700, www.wy.blm.gov/nhtic) is a must-see for both Casper visitors and "rut nuts"—as Oregon Trail enthusiasts are known. More than a few travelers have dropped in for a quick break from the interstate, only to find themselves still immersed in the exhibits three hours later!

The Platte River crossing at present-day Casper was a junction for most of the major routes west, including not just the Oregon, California, Mormon, and Pony Express trails, but also the Bridger and Bozeman trails. An 18-minute multimedia presentation provides a moving introduction to the trails and to the people who traversed this land. Exhibits include one on the Indian peoples who migrated through using travois (pole-and-net handcarts), as well as the whys, wheres, and ways of 19th-century travel by the traders, explorers, trappers, missionaries, gold miners, and farmers heading west. Bigger-than-life displays and virtual-reality exhibits present the experience of these migrants. You'll get to experience the sensation of being on a moving wagon as it crosses the Platte River, step into a cold room to empathize with tragedies experienced by the Mormon handcart travelers, and sit on a stagecoach as part of the rush to California's goldfields. First-person narratives relate the pioneer and Native American experience, and present-day travelers will learn where they can find the old trails today. At the end of your trip through the past, you'll emerge to tall windows providing a great view over Casper and the surrounding country through which these trails passed.

Situated atop a hill on the north side of Casper at 1501 North Poplar Street, the center is staffed by Bureau of Land Management employees and is open 8 A.M.–7 P.M. daily April–October, and 9 A.M.–4 P.M. Tuesday–Saturday November–March. Entrance costs $6 adults, $5 seniors, $4 students, $3 ages 6–17, $1 ages 3–5, and free for tots. Entrance is free with the Park Service's Golden Eagle and Golden Age passes.

◖ Nicolaysen Art Museum

One surprising aspect of Casper is an emphasis on art and culture as exemplified by the Nicolaysen—"The Nic" (400 E. Collins, 307/235-5247, www.thenic.org, open 10 A.M.–5 P.M. Tues.–Sat. and noon–4 P.M. Sun., closed Mon.). Originally a power plant, this beautiful brick building houses six different galleries and is the finest contemporary art exhibition space in Wyoming. Exhibits change every few months, but you're unlikely to see the standard moose-in-the-meadow schlock here. The permanent collection includes more than 4,000 paintings by the late Conrad Schwiering, Wyoming's preeminent artist. His studio and samples from this collection are on display half of the year. Also of note are 1,900 drawings by German American illustrator Carl Link, along with a variety of Native American paintings, pottery, and rugs.

Children love the fun **Discovery Center,** where artistic activities and classes take place. The gift shop sells classy collectibles, and lectures, concerts, and slide shows are offered throughout the year.

Casper College

Casper College (307/268-2100 or 800/442-2963, www.caspercollege.edu) first opened its doors in 1945 and has grown into the state's largest junior college. A fine 80,000-volume **library** on campus includes a rare-book room with unusual Wyoming titles. An **Elderhostel** program operates at Casper College during the summer, and the excellent **fitness center** is open to the public. In the College Center building you'll find a cafeteria, bookstore, and other facilities.

Visitors will enjoy stops at two Casper College collections. At **Tate Geological Museum** (307/268-2447, open 9 A.M.–5 P.M. Mon.–Fri., 10 A.M.–4 P.M. Sat. all year, free), you'll find one of the largest mineralogical collections in the Rockies, including several meteorites, various types of petrified wood, Indian artifacts, dinosaur fossils, and probably the largest collection of Wyoming jade anywhere. The fossil preparation lab is a highlight, where professionals prepare bones and fossils for display. Polished stones are sold at a small gift shop here.

Werner Wildlife Museum (405 E. 15th St., 307/235-2108, open Mon., Tues., Thurs. and Fri. 1–5 P.M., free) houses the usual stuffed critters from Wyoming—dozens of antelope heads, deer mounts, bears, bison, and many birds, along with several African and Alaskan trophies.

Additional Sights

Pick up the *Art for the Streets* brochure for details on local public sculptures. Other places to see local artwork include the cooperative **West Wind Gallery** (1040 W. 15th, 307/265-2655, www.casperbusiness.com/artistsguild), **Serendipity Gallery** (105 E. 2nd St., 307/237-7205, www.mccannjewelers.com/serendipity), **Artist's Choice** (647 W. Yellowstone Hwy., 307/234-7000, www.vivicrandall.com), and the **student art gallery** at Casper College.

At the intersection of 1st and Poplar streets, a wooden **oil derrick** stands as a monument to the city's heritage. The **Casper Planetarium** (904 N. Poplar, 307/577-0310) schedules shows at 7 P.M. daily during the summer; $2.50.

Science Zone in the Sunrise Center Mall (3960 S. Poplar St., 307/473-9663, www.thesciencezone.org, open 10 A.M.–5 P.M. Tues.–Sat., $3 adults, $2 kids 2–16, free for toddlers) is a children's science center where you can create six-foot-long bubbles, visit the reptiles, or explore changing exhibits.

One of Casper's minor claims to fame is **Casper Events Center** (307/577-3030 or 800/442-2256, www.caspereventscenter.com), where you might run across a mining trade show, rock concert, wrestling tournament, cat show, or even a wedding. On a hill overlooking the city, the center is a spacious, modern building with room for more than 10,000 people.

The visitors guide produced by the Casper CVB includes a map identifying wildlife-viewing areas. Springtime visitors will enjoy a detour from Casper out Hat Six Road (Hwy. 253) east of town, where **sage grouse** perform spectacular mating displays mid-March–mid-May. Farther out this road is a large **prairie dog town.** The visitor center also has a detailed booklet with self-guided tours of Casper's historic buildings.

For a guided taste into Casper's history—from painted ladies to ghosts—join one of the candlelight tours offered throughout the summer by **Painted Past** (307/267-7243, www.paintedpast.org).

The **Wyoming Veteran's Memorial Museum** (307/472-1857, open 1–5 P.M. Thurs.–Sun.) is at the airport (eight miles northwest of Casper on U.S. 20/26) and displays military memorabilia. During World War II, the building was used by men who trained B-17 and B-24 bombing crews, and it includes a mural painted by the soldiers.

ENTERTAINMENT AND EVENTS

Nightlife

See the *Casper Star-Tribune* for the latest on local nightlife. The biggest and best-known place for live music Tuesday–Saturday is the **Beacon Club** (4100 W. Yellowstone Hwy., 307/577-1503) with country or rock tunes and a rowdy crowd.

The **Wonder Bar** (256 S. Center St., 307/234-4110, www.thewonderbar.com) has live rock bands at an upstairs dance club called The Attic. **Sidelines Sports Bar** (1121 Wilkins Circle, 307/473-7427) has a DJ Wednesday–Saturday nights. **Metro Coffee** (241 S. David St., 307/472-5042, www.metrocoffeeco.com) is a popular no-alcohol place for live music.

The Arts

The state's only professional orchestra, the **Wyoming Symphony Orchestra** (307/266-1478, www.wyomingsymphony.com) presents eight performances October–May at the high school auditorium, 930 South Elm Street. During the summer, the **Casper Municipal Band** plays free concerts at 7 P.M. on Thursdays in Washington Park.

Stage III Community Theatre (904 N. Center St., 307/234-0946, www.stageiii-theatre.com) puts on plays on weekends throughout the year. More actors can be found on stage at Casper College's 465-seat **Gertrude Krampert Theatre** (307/268-2365, www.caspercollege.edu). In the summer, the theater is home to musicals, dance performances, and comedies. Also on campus are free recitals scheduled by the Casper College Music Department (307/268-2606). Contact **Artcore** (307/265-1564) for tickets to upcoming concerts, literary events, and theatrical productions in Casper.

The **Casper Troopers Drum and Bugle Corps** (307/472-2141, www.troopersdrum-corps.org)—one of the finest in the nation—often performs around Wyoming during June before heading out on tour. In existence since 1957, the corps struts its stuff at sporting events and parades around the nation, including the past Tournament of Roses and presidential inaugural parades.

Movies

Eastridge 4 (601 S.E. Wyoming Blvd., 307/472-7469, www.wyomovies.com) has second-run flicks for just $3. For first-run movies, head to **Fox Movie Palace** (150 W. 2nd St., 307/235-0900), **Rialto Theatre** (100 E. 2nd St., 307/472-7469), or **Iris Stadium 8 Movie Theater** (230 W. Yellowstone Hwy., 307/472-4747). The Iris has stadium seating, as does the downtown **America Stadium** (119 S. Center, 307/235-5440); the America is the largest screen in Wyoming. All of these can be found on the web at www.wyomovies.com.

Events

Casper features a multitude of enjoyable events throughout summer, so there's bound to be something going on when you visit. Find a complete listing of upcoming events at www.casperwyoming.info.

The year's most unusual event is **Midsummer's Eve** atop Casper Mountain during the June summer solstice (see *Crimson Dawn Museum* in the *Casper Mountain* section).

Casper is home to the **College National Finals Rodeo** (800/442-2256, www.cnfr.com) in mid-June. This event attracts 400 of the best young cowboys and cowgirls from all over the United States and Canada with a full range of events.

Up on Casper Mountain the **Beartrap Summer Festival** (307/235-9325, www.bear-trapsummerfestival.com) brings folk, jazz, country, and blues, and even classical music in late July.

Casperites kick up their heels at the city's biggest annual event, the **Central Wyoming Fair and Rodeo** (307/235-5775 or 888/225-2600, www.centralwyomingfair.com) the second week of July. The various arts-and-crafts displays, farm animals, rodeos, a demolition derby, and midway attract thousands of locals and visitors. Rodeo festivities include a downtown parade and all the standard PRCA rodeo events. In mid-September, **Brewfest** takes place along the Platte River Parkway. The Nicolaysen Art Museum's **Arts and Crafts Festival** on the first weekend of November is a good place to shop for Christmas.

SHOPPING

Casper is Wyoming's version of shop-'til-your-car-dies. Sprawling suburbia, fast food, and a half dozen park-anywhere malls combine to make Casper indistinguishable from Modesto, California, or Columbus, Ohio. This is the sort of place where even the Highland Park Community Church is housed in what looks like an old Kmart store. **Eastridge Mall** (at Wyoming Blvd. and E. 2nd St., www.shopeastridge.com) is Wyoming's largest, with 90 stores, including Macy's, Sears, JCPenney, and Target. If Norman Rockwell were alive today, he would be painting the high-school girls eyeing the hunks on parade and the over-60, post–heart-attack crowd doing their fast walks around the mall. A Wal-Mart and Sam's Club are right across the street from Eastridge.

OK, so not all of Casper's stores are in shopping malls. Downtown is the impressive **Lou Taubert Ranch Outfitters** (125 E. 2nd St., 307/234-2500 or 800/447-9378), a four-floor department store with everything from cowboy boots (10,000 pairs in stock!) to classy gifts. It's a great place to try on a new cowboy hat or shop for fashionable clothing in one of the biggest Western shops anywhere.

Casper has a number of good antique shops, including **CY Avenue Antique Mall** (1905 CY Ave., 307/237-2293), with booths from 40 different dealers.

Mountain Sports (543 S. Center, 307/266-1136 or 800/426-1136, www.wyomap.com) sells quality outdoor gear and rents downhill and cross-country skis. While you're there, take a look at the various rock-climbing maps and books.

A fine downtown reader's spot is **Blue Heron Books and Espresso** (201 E. 2nd St., 307/265-3774 or 800/585-3774). **The Book Exchange** (323 S. Center St., 307/237-6034) offers Wyoming's largest selection of used books and is a great place to browse.

SPORTS AND RECREATION
Spectator Sports

An affiliate of the Colorado Rockies, the **Casper Rockies** (307/232-1111, www.casper-rockies.com) play minor-league professional ball at the Mike Lansing Baseball Field on the north side of town.

Watch the state's only arena football team, the **Wyoming Cavalry** (307/472-5030, www.wyomingcavalry.com), play at the Casper Events Center March–June. In the fall, the center hosts the **Wyoming Golden Eagles** (307/234-2082) of the All American Professional Basketball League.

Edness Kimball Wilkins State Park

Six miles east of Casper on Hwy. 256, the 1,420-acre Edness Kimball Wilkins State Park (307/577-5150, http://wyoparks.state.wy.us, $4 for nonresident vehicles, $2 for cars with Wyoming plates) is perfect for quiet picnics among the cottonwoods, bird-watching (more than 200 species have been observed), and fishing and canoeing in the North Platte River. The park began as a rock quarry but has been transformed into a delightful place to explore. No camping is allowed, but several trails—including a three-mile paved path—provide pleasant day hikes or bike rides, and on hot summer weekends families crowd the sandy beach along the swimming pond. Oregon Trail wagon ruts are visible near the entrance to the park.

Biking and Climbing

Mountain-bikers will find many miles of roads and trails on the Casper and Muddy mountains south of town. For maps and information, contact **Backcountry Mountain Works** (4120 S. Poplar, 307/234-5330). Unfortunately, these maps do not show the land ownership status, so you need to make sure you're riding on public land. The BLM's maps show land ownership but don't have trails marked. Rent bikes on Casper Mountain at **Broken Spur Café** (307/473-8707).

The Peak (408 N. Beverly St., 307/472-4084) has a big indoor climbing gym, rock-climbing equipment, and lessons.

Horse and Wagon Trips

Looking for a taste of the Old West? **Historic Trails West** (307/266-4868 or 800/327-4052, www.historictrailswest.com) leads various Conestoga wagon and horseback rides—3 hours–5 days—along the Oregon Trail. All of these trips include guided tours of Fort Caspar and plenty of historical stories. The four-hour trips (with lunch) are $45 adults, $35 kids. Overnight rides are $85 adults, $65 kids, and a three-day wagon ride costs $600 adults ($700 on horseback) and includes all meals and tepees; bring your own sleeping bag. These trips are about as authentic as you can get.

SpiritRider Wagon Train Adventure (307/472-5361 or 866/873-9397, www.spiritriderwagontrain.com) offers a wide range of adventures, from a two-hour Bessemer Bend wagon ride, music, and meal ($35 adults, $23 kids) to complete five-day trips along the Oregon Trail ($1,200 adults, $600 kids all-inclusive). Its six-day Hole-in-the-Wall trips ($1,500 adults, $900 kids) include time in the beautiful country where Butch Cassidy and his outlaw gang hid out. The dynamic owner, Mikel Carmon, also runs a variety of motivational workshops and corporate seminars using "equine assisted learning" as part of the therapeutic process.

Water Recreation

If you're looking for a little water activity, check out one of Casper's half dozen **swimming pools** (307/235-8383, www.casperwy.gov). Five summer-only outdoor pools ($2.50) are scattered throughout the city. The Paradise Valley pool (5200 W. Iris, $4.50) also has a popular corkscrew water slide. Indoor pools can be found at Kelly Walsh High School and the YMCA (315 E. 15th, 307/234-9187). Trivia note: Casper's high school was the first in the nation to have an indoor swimming pool, built in 1929. (This was also the high school from which Vice President Dick Cheney graduated in 1959.)

New in 2005, the **Casper Family Aquatic Center** (1801 E. 4th St., $5) is a beautiful year-round indoor facility with a lap pool, spash pool, water slide, lazy river, and hot tub.

The **North Platte River** flows right through the city of Casper, providing both the city's drinking water and recreational opportunities. The Platte's slow current and shallow depth—just 2–4 feet in most places—make for a gentle and scenic float trip with plenty of wildlife along the way: beaver, muskrats, ducks, geese, hawks, eagles, mule deer, and antelope. For a helpful map describing public landings, camping, and parking areas along the 60-mile stretch of the Platte between Alcova Reservoir and Glenrock, contact the Bureau of Land Management (2987 Prospector Dr., 307/261-7600, www.wy.blm.gov). The **Platte River Trust Whitewater Park** covers a 0.5-mile stretch of the river in Casper, with boulders and other obstacles for kayakers.

Platte River Raft N Reel (307/267-0170, www.raftnreel.com) offers guided fishing and float trips, plus canoe and raft rentals. Fishing is excellent for both German brown and rainbow trout; locals call the North Platte one of the West's largest and finest trout fisheries. Drop by the visitor center for a listing of other local fishing guides. Two good fishing shops are **Ugly Bug Fly Shop** (240 S. Center St., 307/234-6905, www.crazyrainbow.net) and **Platte River Fly Shop** (7400 Alcova Hwy., 307/237-5997, www.wyomingflyfishing.com).

Casper is one of the nation's windiest cities; winds averaging 13 mph make this a great place for kite flying, hang-gliding, and sailboarding. Pathfinder and Alcova Reservoirs are both popular sailboarding spots.

Golf

Golfers will have fun at the 27-hole **Casper Municipal Golf Course** (2120 Allendale Blvd., 307/234-2405, www.casperwy.gov). Designed by Robert Trent Jones Jr., the beautiful 18-hole **Three Crowns Golf Course** (307/472-5591, www.threecrownsgolfclub.com) opened in 2005 on the site of what was once an Amaco refinery. For the kid-size version, check out **Old Town Mini Golf** with a fun Old West theme at Parkway Plaza Hotel (123 W. E St., 307/266-4653, www.parkwayplaza.net). Also here is a go-cart course, climbing wall, and video arcade.

More Recreation

The paved 11-mile **Platte River Parkway** (307/577-1206, www.platteriverparkway.org) extends from Paradise Valley Park on the west end to the North Casper Athletic Complex and is a fine place to walk, inline skate, or bike. Get a map from the visitor center or just look for it along the river.

The fine **Casper Recreation Center** (1801 E. 4th St., 307/235-8383, www.casperwy.gov, $2.50) provides racquetball and walleyball courts, a weight room, gym, and game room. Next door is **Casper Ice Arena** (307/235-8484) with year-round skating. Wyoming's largest roller-skating palace, **Wagon Wheel Roller Skating** (305 Vanhorn Ave., 307/265-4214) is in Mills.

ACCOMMODATIONS

Casper accommodations cover the complete quality spectrum, from dumpy little holes-in-the-wall to elaborate new hotels. In general you'll find prices in Casper to be quite reasonable, though they have risen because of a strong economy in recent years. The Casper Area Convention and Visitors Bureau's website (www.casperwyoming.info) has brief descriptions and web links to most local accommodations.

Under $50

Red Arrow Motel (308 S.W. Wyoming Blvd., 307/234-5293, $32 s or $42 d) is a little 10-room place with functional rooms containing microwaves and fridges. **Sand and Sage Motel** (901 W. Yellowstone, 307/237-2088, $35 s or $42 d) is one of the older motels in town, with simple but refurbished rooms.

A good downtown choice for budget travelers is **Royal Inn** (440 E. A St., 307/234-3501 or 877/234-3501). Standard rooms go for $35 s or $40–45 d, and amenities include an outdoor pool (not heated), fridges, microwaves, and Wi-Fi. Kitchenettes are $55 d, with the larger ones sleeping six. Not fancy, but a fair value.

For a few bucks more, stay at the predictable **Motel 6** (1150 Wilkins Circle, 307/234-3903 or 800/466-8356, www.motel6.com, $40–50 s or $46–56 d), which also has an outdoor pool.

$50-100

With its distinctive riverboat front, it's hard to miss **National 9 Inn Showboat** (100 W. F St., 307/235-2711 or 866/999-1309, www.national9casper.com, $53–58 s or $67 d) just off the interstate. Rooms are clean and fairly large, with free Wi-Fi and a continental breakfast.

Next to the Wyoming Medical Center, **Skyler Inn** (111 S. Wilson St., 307/232-5100 or 866/500-1110, www.skylerinn.com) is primarily for patients' relatives needing extended stays, but the oversized no-smoking rooms, full kitchens (with dishes), fitness center, central location, and guest computer make the modern hotel attractive to travelers as well. Standard rooms cost $66 d, suites $77 d, and two-bedroom suites $97.

Days Inn (301 E. E St., 307/234-1159 or 888/307-0959, www.daysinn.com, $79 d) is a well-kept, moderately priced facility with a heated outdoor pool, small exercise room, Wi-Fi, and light breakfast. There's even a popcorn machine.

$100-150

At the large ((**Holiday Inn on the River** (300 W. F St., 307/235-2531 or 877/576-8636, www.casperhi.com $99–114 d), many rooms face the central atrium. The hotel also contains an indoor pool, hot tub, sauna, wireless Internet, fitness center, and continental breakfast. Head out back for a pleasant riverside stroll.

The **Best Western Ramkota Hotel** (800 N. Poplar, 307/266-6000 or 800/937-8376, www.casper.ramkota.com) is popular with business travelers who appreciate the large rooms (the lower floors open onto the central atrium), meeting rooms, lounge (free appetizers on weekday evenings), restaurants, indoor pool, hot tub, exercise facility, Wi-Fi, and airport shuttle. Standard rooms are $94 s or $99 d; suites cost $129–229 d.

Bed-and-Breakfasts

The ((**Ivy House Inn** (815 S. Ash St., 307/265-0974, www.ivyhouseinn.com) is a 1941 Cape Cod–style home furnished in art deco pieces. Three guest rooms share two baths and

CENTRAL WYOMING

rent for $60–70 s or $65–75 d, and two suites with private baths, living rooms, and entrances are $105 d. A full breakfast is included, well-behaved kids are welcome, and a hot tub awaits in the backyard.

At **Casper Mountain B&B** (4471 S. Center St., 307/237-6712, www.caspermountainbnb.com, $60–65 d), two guest rooms share a bath in a south Casper neighborhood. A full breakfast is served, and kids are welcome.

Camping

The nearest public camping ($7) is in the pines atop Casper Mountain, 10 miles south of Casper and 3,000 feet higher in elevation—well worth the drive. (See *Casper Mountain* section for details.) RVers also park overnight at local shopping mall lots, but be sure to ask first.

The **Fort Caspar Campground** (307/234-3260 or 888/243-7709, www.ftcasparcamp.org, $18 tents, $31 RVs) operates year-round at a peaceful spot along the river just beyond the old fort site. Deer and other critters are common sights here.

Casper East RV Park and Campground at exit 186 (2800 E. Yellowstone, 307/237-5155 or 888/294-8551, www.caspereastrvpark.com, $18 tents, $26–28 RVs, $32 cabins) has a heated outdoor pool, indoor hot tub, and minigolf, along with buffalo barbecue dinners in the summer. It's open year-round.

Casper North KOA in Bar Nunn (1101 W. Prairie La., 307/577-1664 or 888/562-4704, www.koa.com, $20 tents, $26 RVs, open Apr.–Oct.) has an indoor pool and hot tub, along with basic cabins ($34 d).

FOOD

Casper has a wide range of dining options that will suit almost any taste, and it shows greater diversity every time you visit.

Breakfast and Lunch

For a home-style, reasonably priced breakfast, visit **West Side Cafe** (5755 CY Ave., 307/266-2027). On the other end of town is the **Red and White Cafe** (1620 E. Yellowstone,

307/234-6962), a little greasy spoon. Not recommended if you don't smoke.

Eggington's (229 E. 2nd St., 307/265-8700) is a busy breakfast and lunch place in the heart of town. Breakfast includes all the usuals, plus great pecan rolls and fresh-squeezed orange juice. Lunchtime sandwiches, burgers, soups, and salads complete the offerings. It's open till 2 P.M. daily, and is especially popular on weekends.

Another local fave for three meals a day is **Johnny J's Diner** (1705 E. 2nd St., 307/234-4204). It's a modernized nonsmoking version of the classic '50s diner, with gleaming silver sides and a menu that includes 20 kinds of burgers and salads, sandwiches, chicken, and creamy malts.

During the school year, visitors will find Casper's cheapest lunch eats at the **Casper College cafeteria.** Notable soup, sandwich, and salad places in town are at **Cottage Cafe** (116 S. Lincoln St., 307/234-1157) and **Cheese Barrel** (544 S. Center, 307/235-5202), which also serves good breakfasts.

For the best sub sandwiches, head to **Mountain View Sub Shop** (239 E. 1st St., 307/237-7999).

Coffeehouses

A couple of caffeine joints are notable downtown. **Mojo Coffee** (2nd at Center Sts., 307/235-5396) serves mochas, teas, chai, and smoothies in a classy but cozy setting with a window bar to watch the passers by.

Metro Coffee (241 S. David St., 307/472-5042, www.metrocoffeeco.com) is an eclectic spot with computer rentals, free Wi-Fi, art on the walls, and casual conversation areas in an old downtown building. The late hours—till midnight most nights)—are a big draw for teens and 20-somethings. In the summer, the adjacent parking lot is transformed into an open-air theater with classic films every other Thursday night.

Steak Houses

The best local top-carnivore eateries are **Poor Boys Steak House** (739 N. Center St.,

307/237-8325) and **Dorn's Fireside** (1745 CY Ave., 307/235-6831).

In the same vein is **Goose Egg Inn** (307/473-8838, www.gooseegginn.com), nine miles southwest of Casper on Hwy. 220, where prime rib, lamb, sefood, and pan-fried chicken are house specialties. Well worth the drive.

Sedar's Restaurant (4370 S. Poplar, 307/234-6839) in Sunrise Mall serves prime rib, cabbage rolls, lobster, and steak. Behind the Mountain View Shopping Center, **Fred's Bar-B-Que** (4925 W. Natrona Ave., 307/577-1600) has tasty barbecue pork.

Greek

Families flock to ◖ **Karen and Jim's Restaurant** (520 S. Collins Dr., 307/266-4976), with a movie decor, tasty favorites three meals a day, and an adjacent lounge with Saturday night karaoke. The big menu cruises over more than a dozen burgers, along with steaks, chops, tamales, chicken, seafood, and the always popular gyros. Most menu items are $6–8, which helps explain the crowds.

Fine Dining

◖ **303 Restaurant** (303 S. Wolcott, 307/233-4303, www.303grill.com) has quickly established itself as *the* the dining experience in Casper. The atmosphere is classy, with a seasonal menu that usually includes fresh seafood, game meats, and prime steaks. Dinner entrées are $17–27. The tapas menu is great for something lighter, or try the 303's dine-around-the-world five-course meals that focus on a different culinary region each month; $50–75 per person with wine pairings. Be sure to check out the "hidden" cloak room and the distinctive bathroom sinks; where does that water go?

Italian and Pizza

Casper has several decent Italian restaurants. In business for more than three decades, downhome **Bosco's** (847 E. A St., 307/265-9658) fills with a business crowd on weekday lunches and offers such specialties as veal scallopini, eggplant parmigiana, and chicken piccata; $10–19 entrées. Check out the photos of political types who've eaten here, including President George Bush; OK, he ordered out and ate onboard Air Force One.

Botticelli Ristorante Italiano (129 W. 2nd, 307/266-2700) is one of a small chain of Northern Italian restaurants, with paninis, pastas, and pizza in a pleasantly romantic setting.

If you're looking for good pizza in Casper, try **Barry's Italian Pizzaria** (123 W. E St., 307/237-8523) at the Parkway Plaza Hotel, or **Daddy O's Italian Grill** (128 E. 2nd St., 307/473-5588).

Mexican

El Jarro's (500 W. F St., 307/577-0538) offers low prices, big margaritas, crispy chips, tangy salsa, and mass quantities of food, but this is Americanized Mexican food.

Get more authentic Mexican fare at **La Cocina** (1040 N. Center St., 307/266-1414). Everything is freshly made, including the hand-rolled tortillas. Also of note is **La Costa** (1600 E. 2nd St., 307/235-6599), a classy little place with Tex-Mex fare. If you're just looking for a quick and tasty burrito, drop by **Tacos Mexico** (112 E. 2nd St., 307/235-0042) for home-cooked Mexican food and the hottest chilies in town. It's housed within the Moonlight Bar.

Chinese

J. S. Chinese Restaurant (116 W. 2nd St., 307/577-0618) has a central downtown location next to the Fox Theater, and a dine-in or take-out menu of authentic and dependably good Chinese food, including sizzling pork and chicken with pine nuts. Most items are $8–9.

Dragon Wall Chinese Buffet (2025 E. 2nd St., 307/235-8899) serves a big Asian buffet for lunch and dinner.

Pubs

In the heart of town, the historic **The Wonder Bar** (256 S. Center St., 307/234-4110, www .thewonderbar.com) is a big and busy place with a menu featuring burgers, nachos, sandwiches, and salads. Entrées are $9–13. Directly across the street is another bustling beer house, **Sanford's Grub and Pub** (307/234-4555), part of a small chain of cluttered joints. On the menu you'll find dozens of sandwiches, all the standard bar appetizers (along with some that aren't so standard such as gizzards and fried pickle spears), burgers, salads, pasta, and more. Both Wonder Bar and Sanford's are smoke-free.

Banjo Bob's BBQ in the Sidelines Sports Bar (1121 Wilkins Circle, 307/473-7427) is a hot spot for families in the dining room, singles in the bar, or pool sharks on the upstairs tables.

Groceries and Baked Goods

Casper has several giant grocery stores scattered across the city, including Albertsons, Safeway, Smith's, and Wal-Mart SuperCenter; all have in-store bakeries and delis. If you're looking for fresh produce, be sure to check out the **farmers market** at the fairgrounds every Saturday morning during the summer. **Alpenglow Natural Foods** (109 E. 2nd St., 307/234-4156) has natural fare downtown.

First Street Bakers (260 W. 1st St., 307/472-0255) crafts bagels, breads, and sweets—including enormous cinnamon buns—along with lunchtime sandwiches.

INFORMATION AND SERVICES

The friendly **Casper Area Chamber of Commerce Visitor Center** (500 N. Center, 307/234-5311, www.casperwyoming.org) is the place to go for tourist paraphernalia. It's open 8 A.M.–6 P.M. Monday–Friday and 10 A.M.–6 P.M. Saturday–Sunday late May–early September, and 8 A.M.–5 P.M. Monday–Friday the rest of the year. Contact the **Casper Area Convention and Visitors Bureau** (307/234-5362 or 800/852-1889, www.casperwyoming.info) for information on Casper before your trip.

Wyoming's only statewide paper, the *Casper Star-Tribune* (www.casperstartribune.net) is an excellent source for regional news.

Check your email or surf the web on computers at the **Natrona County Library** (307 E. 2nd, 307/237-4935, www.library.natrona.net); open daily. The **BLM's Casper Field Office** (307/261-7600, www.wy.blm.gov) is at 2987 Prospector Drive. The **post office** (307/266-4000) is at 411 North Forest Drive.

Local launderettes include **Clay Street Laundry** (N. 2nd at Clay Sts., 307/358-8085), **Hilltop Laundromat** (2513 E. 3rd St., 307/234-7331), and **Millview Laundromat** (Millview Shopping Center, 307/472-0117).

The **Wyoming Medical Center** (1233 E. 2nd St., 307/577-7201 or 800/822-7201, www.wmcnet.org) is one of the largest hospitals in the state. For walk-in medical needs, try **Instacare** (900 CY Ave., 307/237-2273) or **Urgent Care Now** (2546 E. 2nd St., 307/265-1110).

GETTING THERE AND AROUND

Airlines

Natrona County Airport (307/472-6688, www.casperairport.com) is eight miles northwest of Casper on U.S. 20/26. Three airlines fly into Casper: **Delta/Skywest** (800/221-1212, www.deltaair.com) from Salt Lake City, **Northwest** (800/225-2525, www.nwa.com) from Minneapolis, and **United/United Express** (800/241-6522, www.unitedairlines.com) from Denver. **Bighorn Airways** (307/235-1212, www.bighornairways.com) has charter service.

Bus Service

Powder River Transportation (307/266-1904 or 800/442-3682, http://gillette.coachusa.us) has daily bus service between Casper and towns in eastern and northern Wyoming, continuing to Billings, Cody, Rapid City, Cheyenne, and Denver. Buses stop at Parkway Plaza Hotel, 123 West E Street.

The Bus (307/265-1313, www.casperarea-transportation.com, $1) has weekday transportation around Casper.

Rental Cars and Taxis

Avis (307/237-2634 or 800/331-1212, www.avis.com), **Budget** (307/266-2251 or 800/527-0700, www.budget.com), and **Hertz** (307/265-1355 or 800/654-3131, www.hertz.com) all have airport counters. Car rentals are also available from **Around Town Rent-a-Car** (307/265-5667) and **Enterprise** (307/234-8122 or 800/325-8007, www.enterprise.com).

Call **RC Cab** (307/235-5203) for local taxi service.

◖ CASPER MOUNTAIN

Scenic mountain country is just a hop, skip, and a drive away from Casper. When the thermometer tops 100°F, Casperites escape to the cool mountains just a 15-minute drive from town. Snow often lingers here until July. Rotary Park, seven miles south of Casper on South Poplar Street (Hwy. 252), has several official and unofficial trails that climb the steep canyon cut by Garden Creek. The creek drops 50 feet over **Garden Creek Falls,** one of the few waterfalls in this part of Wyoming. A viewpoint is just a short distance up the trail, or you can cross the bridge and follow a second path (actually a maze of routes) to the top of the falls, one mile up. Other trails head out to a ridge offering views of the surrounding country.

The steep, winding drive up Casper Mountain has turnouts offering panoramas that stretch all the way to the Big Horn Mountains 125 miles north. Casper Mountain's flattened 8,100-foot-summit is carpeted by ponderosa pine trees and pleasant grassy meadows. **Broken Spur Café** (307/473-8707) serves meals (including Wednesday night rib eye for $12) and has mountain-bike rentals near the entrance to Hogadon Ski Area.

Crimson Dawn Museum

This evocative place lies atop Casper Mountain, 12 miles south of Casper along Hwy. 251; follow the signs to Crimson Dawn. As the name suggests, this place is best experienced early in the morning or at sunset, when the crimson light brushes across the ochre-colored earth and streams into the dark green forests. Come here alone to really feel the magic that captivated Neal Forsling more than 75 years ago. After growing up in Independence, Missouri—and nearly marrying Harry Truman—she headed west to Casper. There Neal married a lawyer, but a bitter divorce sent her fleeing to then-remote Casper Mountain with her two children, looking to start anew as a homesteader. She quickly fell in love with the country and

© DON PITCHER

The road up Casper Mountain leads to cool pine forests.

CENTRAL WYOMING

later fell in love with local rancher Jim Forsling. They were married and settled into a fiercely independent life without electricity or running water and with but a few neighbors. The idyll was broken one bitterly cold winter day when Jim was skiing back from town with a backpack filled with supplies. Caught in a blizzard, he froze to death just a few miles from the cabin. He was 38 years old.

Neal adjusted to the loss by turning inward to grasp the spirit of the land, by painting out her emotions, and by opening outwardly to her own and neighboring children with stories. Through the years these grew into a complex series of fairy tales that detailed the good and evil witches, leprechauns, and trolls who inhabit these woods and fields. Midsummers' Eve was a special time when children and adults could enter this magical spirit world through her storytelling. In 1973, Neal Forsling gave her land and cabin to Natrona County for use as a park. She died a few years later and is buried nearby, but her extraordinary love for the earth is revealed in the small cabin, mystical paintings, fairy tales, and the trails that lead through the woods to shrines celebrating the good witches, magical creatures, and witty forest spirits who haunt this land. Neal's philosophy is summed up by a sign in her cabin:

What I had, I lost
What I saved, I spent
What I gave, I have.

Today, her old log home is a small museum (307/235-1303, open 10 A.M.–7 P.M. Sat.–Thurs. mid-June–mid-October).

Inside the cabin are several of Forsling's somewhat crude paintings, seemingly inspired by both Vincent van Gogh and Grandma Moses, which reveal her mystical sensibilities. A framed letter from Missouri childhood friend Bess Truman hangs on one wall. You may want to buy a copy of *Crimson Dawn,* a collection of Forsling's tales. And be sure to wander along the nearby woodland trails to enjoy the 20 shrines she created (my favorite is Sean the leprechaun). The graves of Jim and Neal Forsling overlook the green mountains. His epitaph reads:

In this red earth I loved so well
Where I worked and made my home
I am glad my body can rest at last
In this place I loved so well.
But my soul is free to climb
up through the sky's blue arch
free to explore those far away peaks
that once my eyes looked on.
For any land that a man has looked on,
and worked and claimed for his own
Part of that man will always remain
as long as the wind will blow.

On **Midsummer's Eve** (around June 21), be sure to visit Crimson Dawn for a mystical celebration of Casper Mountain's witches and spirits. The celebration has gone on every year since 1929. Visitors get to meet the local denizens in person and are invited to throw handfuls of the dark red earth into the bonfire; if it burns, your wish will come true. Hundreds of Casperites will also be there to celebrate, along with a handful of pompous preachy protesters from Sonlight Ministries.

Birding

Audubon Center at Garden Creek (101 Garden Creek Rd., 307/235-3485, www.audubonwyoming.com) is a 450-acre ranch in the foothills below Casper Mountain. This is a great place to watch birds and walk a path along Garden Creek. Check in at the office. For the latest bird sightings, call the local Audubon Society's bird hot line (307/265-2473 or 888/265-2473, www.murieaudubon.org).

Hogadon Ski Area

First opened in 1959, the city-run Hogadon Ski Area (307/235-8499, www.casperwy.gov) is nine miles south of Casper near the top of the mountain. A family area, it includes hills varying from the easiest bunny slope to black diamonds. Eleven different runs (and a boarders' terrain park) are fed by two chairlifts and a Poma lift, with a vertical rise of 600 feet. Ski and snowboard rentals and lessons are available, and there's a cafeteria. Lift tickets cost $30 adults, $26 ages 12–18, $17 ages 5–11; free for younger kids. Half-day rates are $23 for all age groups, and a Poma-only ticket costs $12. Hogadon is open 9 A.M.–4 P.M. Wednesday–Sunday Thanksgiving–early April.

Cross-Country Skiing and Snowmobiling

Casper Mountain often has surprisingly good powder conditions. **Natrona County Parks** (307/235-9325, www.caspernordic.com) maintains 15 miles of groomed cross-country ski trails ($5 per day) and a warming lodge. A short loop trail is lit at night. In addition, you'll find extensive undeveloped areas where more adventurous backcountry skiers can practice telemarking. Rent cross-country skis from **Mountain Sports** (543 S. Center, 307/266-1136) or **Backcountry Mountain Works** (4120 S. Poplar, 307/234-5330). Mountain Sports also has cross-country rentals at Hogadon Ski Area. Snowmobilers will find more than 60 miles of groomed trails atop Casper Mountain.

Camping

Several county parks—Casper Mountain, Crimson Dawn, Beartrap Meadow, and Ponderosa—are very popular getaways where deer and elk are found. The four **campgrounds** (307/235-9325) on Casper Mountain cost $7 per night; all are generally open Memorial Day–mid-October. Water is available only at Beartrap Campground (the nicest) and Casper Mountain Campground. Red Valley separates Casper Mountain from its neighbor five miles to the south, **Muddy Mountain.** The gravel road climbs Muddy Mountain, where the BLM (307/261-7500, www.wy.blm.gov) maintains **Rim Campground** and **Lodgepole Campground,** both of which cost $5 and are open June–October. Also atop Muddy Mountain is a self-guided nature trail and other scenic paths. For more information on the various Casper Mountain parks, call 307/234-6821. The short **Lee McCune Braille Trail** has 39 plaques describing the natural world in Braille and English. Nearby is a summer camp for the blind.

BESSEMER BEND

The bucolic Bessemer Bend area—10 miles southwest of Casper along Hwy. 220—abounds in history, both real and imagined. A lazy curve in the North Platte River, Bessemer Bend was an important 19th-century crossing point for wagon trains. Rock walls from a shelter built in 1812 by the Astorians are still visible on a knoll overlooking the river. Between 1860 and 1861, the Red Butte Pony Express station stood at the river bend, site of the longest of all Pony Express rides, a 320-mile gallop by Buffalo Bill Cody that lasted a grueling 21 hours and 40 minutes. The nearby Red Buttes were also where Custard's Wagon Train Fight took place (see *History* in this section). Bessemer City sprang up along the bend in 1888, calling itself "Queen City of the Plains." It lasted only a couple of years, and when Casper was voted the Natrona County seat, Bessemer

City quietly faded away. Many of its buildings were moved to Casper, and today Bessemer City is just a field of alfalfa.

Along the east side of the North Platte River at Bessemer Bend is the site of the famed **Goose Egg Ranch,** once one of Wyoming's largest cattle spreads. In *The Virginian,* Owen Wister used Goose Egg Ranch for a memorable scene in which two drunken cowboys switch blankets on a dozen babies while their parents are dancing, creating havoc when the ranch families drive home with the wrong children. Owned for many years by the Carey family—both father Joseph M. Carey and son Robert Carey served as governor and U.S. senator—it was later renamed the CY Ranch. The southern half of Casper is built on what was once CY land—hence CY Avenue, one of the city's main thoroughfares. Ironically, the old Goose Egg ranch house died partly because of the fame brought to it in *The Virginian.* The abandoned stone buildings gradually deteriorated as tourists chipped away for mementos. Fearing that the buildings might collapse, the owners finally tore down the ranch in 1951. John Wayne's oilfield firefighter movie, *Hellfighters,* was filmed not far away in 1968.

Today folks come to Bessemer Bend to enjoy a steak at **Goose Egg Inn** (307/473-8838) or to watch wintering golden and bald eagles in nearby Jackson Canyon—named for famed Yellowstone photographer William H. Jackson. Another five miles down Hwy. 220 is **Dan Speas Fish Hatchery** (307/473-8890), Wyoming's largest trout-rearing facility. The hatchery produces millions of rainbow, brown, and cutthroat trout and is open 8 A.M.–5 P.M. daily year-round.

Also nearby scenic **Red Butte Ranch** (307/472-3784, www.casperwyoming.org/redbutte-ranch, $130 d) rents a private cottage with kitchen and bath. It's right on the North Platte River, and breakfast is included.

◖ SALT CREEK OIL FIELD

Forty miles north of Casper is the Salt Creek Oil Field, considered the largest light-oil field in the world. The 10-mile-long field covers a land of sage, sand, and rock that has produced more than 600 million barrels of oil and 700 million cubic feet of gas. Much more oil has been found nearby. A drive up Hwy. 259 is a trip through a bizarre alien world of desert land carpeted with giant grasshopper-like electric pumpjacks spaced every couple of 100 feet to the horizon. Actually, they look more like the little plastic ostriches sold in tourist shops—the ones that keep tipping down to a bowl of water to "drink." The pumpjacks don't run all the time, allowing the oil to accumulate in the well before pumping resumes. West of the company town of Midwest, things get even stranger, with an incredible grid of pumpjacks, dirt roads, power lines, and storage tanks crisscrossing the harsh land.

History

This famed oil field occupies a classic anticlinal structure that traps oil—100-foot cliffs surround the field. Wyoming's territorial geologist, Samuel Aughey, discovered these unusual structures and brought the first speculators here to file placer claims in 1884. The first well in the area was drilled in 1889 by a Pennsylvania oilman, M. P. Shannon. The oil was hauled by horse-drawn wagon to Casper, 50 miles away. In 1904, Shannon sold his small Casper refinery and 105,000 acres of Salt Creek leases to European speculators for $350,000.

Four years later the real boom came when a Dutch-financed company struck black gold at 1,050 feet in the Salt Creek Field, spouting oil in a massive gusher. When the news hit, battles over land claims quickly escalated to the shouting and shooting stage. The Midwest Oil Company was formed and built the first pipeline to Casper in 1911 to feed the new Midwest refinery there. The Fransco Company added another refinery the following year, and Standard Oil of Indiana built a cracking plant to retrieve more gasoline from the crude.

As World War I steamed over the horizon, the field suddenly gained vital national importance; oil shipped to the Allies from Salt Creek was considered an important factor in the defeat of Kaiser Wilhelm. After the war, Standard Oil (now Amoco) bought out all of Midwest's Salt Creek properties, but the 14 remaining companies competed with each other for the crude, with oil derricks within spitting distance of each other.

Production declined as the companies attempted to pump the oil too fast, trying to get it before it flowed into neighboring wells. Finally, in 1939, Salt Creek became the first oil field in America to run as a unified operation with joint management of the various wells for greater efficiency and conservation. Production in Salt Creek reached a peak in 1923 (when it produced 5 percent of the nation's oil), but the introduction of gas injection in the 1920s and water flooding in the 1950s helped push more oil to the wellheads. Today, more than 100 years after its discovery, workers have recovered just one-third of the oil at Salt Creek. Culling the remaining oil will require more sophisticated techniques, such as flooding with carbon dioxide. Even still, Salt Creek is Wyoming's third-largest producing field.

Midwest and Edgerton

The twin oil towns of Midwest (pop. 400) and Edgerton (pop. 170) lie near the center of the Salt Creek Oil Field. A paved road north of Midwest leads to the Shannon Pool Oil Field, where oil was first discovered. Thousands of drill holes surround the towns, laced together by a grid of dirt roads, power lines, and pipes. It's an alien landscape where the pungent odor of oil hangs in the air.

The company town of Midwest is named for Midwest Oil Company. Its four straight streets contain rows of identical wooden houses built in the 1920s and now showing their age. The stench of sulfur from a gas-recovery plant south of town permeates the air. Midwest's golf course is dotted with oil pumps, and folks attending Mass at the Catholic church can hear the quiet, rhythmic "ker-thunk" of a pumpjack just 100 feet away. Midwest was especially hard hit by the slide in oil prices in the '80s; assessed valuation plummeted from $9.2 million in 1987 to $1.5 million in 1989! Anadarko now owns the fields and is using carbon dioxide injection to boost production. Rising oil prices in

CENTRAL WYOMING

recent years are bringing the area back to life as new wells are drilled, though nobody would ever confuse Midwest with Jackson Hole. Midwest claims one trivial historical footnote: In 1925 the nation's first nighttime interscholastic football game was played under artificial lights here.

Worth a look is the small **Salt Creek Museum** (531 Peake St., 307/437-6633, open 9 A.M.–5 P.M. Mon.–Fri.). Inside, you'll find a fun collection of memorabilia and junk, including bedpans, historic photos, farm tools, trophies, old high-school lockers, and even dinosaur eggs. Behind the museum is a fun playground for the kids.

The big local event—including parades, dancing, food, and various sporting events—comes in August, when both towns celebrate **Salt Creek Days** (307/437-6513). (Points northwest of Midwest and Edgerton are covered in the *Powder River Country* chapter.)

The **Midwest General Store** sells groceries, booze, and gas and has an ATM. Next door is a café called **Whiners,** serving burgers, malts, and shakes.

Just six miles east of Midwest, dumpy little Edgerton has a bit more to offer, with a grocery, a bank, two bars, a library, a gas station, and a bowling alley. Find motel rooms at **Tea Pot Motor Lodge** (307/437-6541, $36 s or $46 d), or park RVs at **Bob's Trailer Court** (307/437-6449). For meals, try **Edgerton Cafe.**

Tempest in a Teapot

Twenty-five miles north of Casper along U.S. 87 is a distinctive butte, **Teapot Rock.** Until a 1962 windstorm knocked down the "spout" that bent away from one side, the rock resembled a teapot. In the first decades of the 20th century, rapid growth in the oil industry sent prospectors and speculators all over the West in search of black gold. To ensure adequate fuel supplies for the navy's ships after World War I, the government set aside three large oil reserves—Elk Hills and Buena Vista in California and Wyoming's Teapot Dome Oil Field (named for Teapot Rock).

In 1921 and 1922, Secretary of the Interior Albert B. Fall secretly leased Teapot Dome to Edward Doheny and Harry Sinclair, owners of Mammoth Oil Company. Could anyone have ever come up with a more fitting name for a corrupt corporation? Although the action was technically legal, the $100,000 bribe paid by Doheny to President Harding's interior secretary was decidedly not legal, and Fall was forced to resign. The action brought a plethora of charges against the giant oil companies, and political cartoonists had a heyday with Teapot Dome. Interior Secretary Fall was convicted of accepting bribes and spent a year in prison. Harry Sinclair—for whom both the oil company and the Wyoming town are named—hired detectives to spy on a jury investigating Teapot Dome and was sent to jail in 1929 for contempt of court. He also spent three months in jail for refusing to testify before a Senate committee investigating the scandal. Today, the U.S. Navy still owns thousands of acres at Teapot Dome, and there are hundreds of oil wells a few miles east of the highway. A sign points out Naval Petroleum Reserve Number 3, but you won't find any historical signs mentioning this rather sordid piece of Wyoming history. The mailboxes and nearby white buildings of Teapot Dome Ranch mark the site of Teapot Rock.

Wyoming's Lake District

The 655-mile-long North Platte River rises in Colorado, heads north into Wyoming, and then curves in a long lazy loop to the east, cutting across western Nebraska and finally joining the South Platte River near the city of North Platte. The entire basin covers 32,000 square miles and in Wyoming is fed by the Sweetwater, Medicine Bow, and Laramie rivers. The name "Platte" is French for "Broad"; Indians called the river "Nebraska," meaning "flat." Both are appropriate titles along much of the river's path. Cottonwood trees line the banks, and the river offers an essential watering hole for wildlife. (Early settlers in Wyoming called the Platte "a mile wide and an inch deep" and "too thick to drink and too thin to plow.")

Once one of the most impressive rivers in the Plains states—at flood stage it ran 150 yards wide and 10–15 feet deep—the North Platte has been reduced to little more than a creek through much of Wyoming. Near Fort Laramie, where wagon trains in the 1850s found a treacherous crossing, the river today sometimes ceases to flow at all, lying in shallow puddles in the late summer sun. A look at the map makes it obvious what has happened to the water: Agriculture has siphoned it all away.

Get details on current water levels behind the dams and river flow rates from the **Bureau of Reclamation** (800/253-8737, www.usbr.gov/gp).

RECLAMATION

Without irrigation, farming was difficult or impossible in much of the arid West, and the thousands of homesteaders who tried to survive on 640 acres soon saw their hopes and dreams fizzle in the withering summer heat. Irrigation seemed natural for these desert lands. John Wesley Powell's idea of reclamation of arid lands through dams and irrigation canals gradually gained favor, and by the 1890s Wyoming's politicians were claiming that irrigation could turn 12–15 million acres of the state into productive farmland. The Carey Act—named for

Wyoming's senator Joseph M. Carey—tested these claims by having the federal government donate land to the states to be reclaimed by settlers. Wyoming became the first state to try out the new law, but only 10 percent of the two million acres in the program were finally patented. The costs were simply too high and the return too low; funding for the massive dams and irrigation canals could only come from the federal government. The Reclamation Act of 1902 was designed to do just that.

When Reclamation Act money started flowing, the North Platte was one of the first to be dammed (or damned, depending on one's perspective). It seemed a potential godsend for farmers who had long used waterwheels to lift water from the river into adjacent irrigation ditches. Today, eight giant dams hold back the river and its tributaries in Wyoming: the Seminoe, Kortes, Pathfinder, Alcova, and Gray Reef above the city of Casper, and the Glendo, Guernsey, and Grayrocks farther downstream. Two long irrigation canals—the Interstate Canal and the Fort Laramie Canal—supply water to farms east of Wheatland. Ironically, nearly 80 percent of the water behind Wyoming dams on the North Platte goes to fields in neighboring Nebraska. This is also true at most of the other large reclamation projects in Wyoming: Bighorn Canyon water goes to Montana, Keyhole Reservoir water to South Dakota, Jackson Lake water to Idaho, and Flaming Gorge water to Utah. Meanwhile, more than 100,000 acres of once-valuable farming and grazing land in Wyoming lie under these massive reservoirs. Wyoming, one of the driest states in the nation, has become an exporter of huge quantities of water to surrounding states.

SEMINOE RESERVOIR

The 295-foot-high concrete arch Seminoe Dam was completed in 1939 and is the farthest upstream of the North Platte River dams. It holds back more than one million acre-feet

CENTRAL WYOMING

of water, which drives a power plant that produces 45 megawatts of electricity. The reservoir is bounded by 3,821-acre **Seminoe State Park** (307/320-3013, http://wyoparks.state.wy.us), named for the nearby Seminoe Mountains, which in turn were named after the French trapper Basil Cimineau Lajeunesse—folks apparently had a hard time spelling his middle name. Day use of the park costs $4 for nonresident vehicles, $2 if you're driving a Wyoming vehicle.

The reservoir stretches almost 20 miles south of the dam through desolate, rocky mountains and gigantic dunes of white sand. Sandy beaches along the shoreline attract swimmers in late summer. Juniper and ponderosa pine trees dot the hills, while sagebrush, greasewood, yucca, and salt sage grow on the lower slopes. The steep 500-foot knife edge of Horseshoe Ridge is visible on the eastern shore. Golden eagles nest along the southern arm of Seminoe Reservoir, and bighorn sheep and elk have been reintroduced. The area also abounds with sage grouse.

Practicalities

Seminoe has two state park **campgrounds** ($12 nonresidents, $6 Wyoming residents, open year-round) along its northwest shore. Water, toilets, and boat ramps are available at each. You can also camp for free on Bureau of Reclamation sand dunes along the lake's southern arm. The reservoir is popular for fishing (rainbow, brown, and cutthroat trout, and walleye) and water-skiing. Gas, RV hookups ($25), a café, and limited provisions are available at **Seminoe Boat Club** (307/320-3043, open May–early Sept.). Access from Rawlins and Sinclair to the western shore of Seminoe is relatively easy via a 34-mile-long paved road, but the 70 miles of mixed pavement and gravel from Casper are a bit harder to take. The eastern shore is even less accessible.

An overlook at the dam site provides views into the steep rocky canyon and the dam that spans the chasm. North of this point, the road drops steeply into the canyon and then climbs

through Morgan Creek Canyon, where big ponderosa pines, willows, and cottonwoods line the creek. A few miles beyond this site, the road descends over a pass and then down through Hamilton Creek Canyon, finally emerging into open sagebrush country near the **Miracle Mile** of the North Platte River. You'll find free camping among the cottonwoods that line the riverbank and excellent trout fishing. More free camping is at Sage Creek Road, 0.5 mile north of the river crossing. The name Miracle Mile—actually three miles of free-flowing river—refers to this popular "blue ribbon" fishery, maintained by regulated flows from the 244-foot-high **Kortes Dam** power plant just upstream. In reality, the miracle is that any stretch of the North Platte still has anything resembling natural flows.

PATHFINDER RESERVOIR

Pathfinder Reservoir is 30 miles southwest of Casper on Hwy. 220 and then another 10 miles in along County Road 409. In 1905, the federal government provided funds for this dam, the first in eastern Wyoming, to be built near the junction of the Sweetwater and North Platte rivers. Proponents claimed that the reservoir would irrigate more than 700,000 acres, primarily in Wyoming, but instead, only 130,000 acres were irrigated, nearly all in Nebraska.

Completed in 1909, Pathfinder Dam is considered an engineering marvel for its time and is listed on the National Register of Historic Places. The 214-foot-high arched structure is made up of large granite blocks quarried from adjacent hills and held together with cement and steel hauled by wagon teams from Casper, 45 miles away. (The trip sometimes took three weeks.)

Pathfinder is named for explorer John C. Frémont, "Pathfinder of the West." In 1842 he ventured down the river and—against the advice of his guides—decided to run the canyon below the present dam site (now Fremont Canyon). He and his men narrowly escaped alive, as Frémont described:

> To go back was impossible; the torrent before us was a sheet of foam; and, shut up in the chasm by the rocks, which in some places seemed to almost meet overhead, the roar of the waters was deafening... the boat struck a concealed rock immediately at the foot of the fall, which whirled her over in an instant....For a hundred yards below, the current was covered with floating books and boxes, bales of blankets, and scattered articles of clothing.... For a moment, I felt somewhat disheartened. All our books – almost every record of the journey – our journals and registers of astronomical and barometrical observations – had been lost in a moment.

Practicalities

Pathfinder Reservoir splits into two arms, following the upstream path of the Sweetwater

The West Platte River runs near Pathfinder Reservoir.

© DON PITCHER

CENTRAL WYOMING

and North Platte rivers. **Pathfinder National Wildlife Refuge** covers 16,807 acres of land around scattered parts of the reservoir and is home to many mammals and birds. Canada geese nest along the shore, and white pelicans nest on an island here. **Camping** is available at four campgrounds on the east shore of Pathfinder Reservoir (307/235-9325, $7, open all year), or you can camp for free along much of the lake's 100-mile shore (except within the refuge). The deep-blue lake is a popular place for anglers in search of cutthroat, brown, and rainbow trout or walleye. Sailboarders find some of Wyoming's finest sailing conditions. **Pathfinder Marina** has rental boats, fishing gear, gas, and a snack bar.

Not far from the dam is an old stone building that once housed the dam tender but is today used as the **Pathfinder Interpretive Center** (307/261-5628). Summer hours are 11 A.M.–5 P.M. Saturday and 10 A.M.–4 P.M. Sunday; ask at the adjacent frame house for a peek inside at other times. A pleasant 1.5-mile loop trail crosses the dam, follows Fremont Canyon (lined with hundreds of cliff-swallow nests), and then recrosses the river over an impressive swinging footbridge before returning to the interpretive center. The interpretive center has a brochure describing sights along the path.

ALCOVA RESERVOIR

Although much smaller than Pathfinder or Seminoe reservoirs, Alcova is a favorite recreation spot for the people of Casper. Sailboarding, sailing, water-skiing, and ice fishing are all popular sports on this windy lake 30 miles southwest of Casper. The upper section of the reservoir reaches into famed **Fremont Canyon,** a mini–Grand Canyon whose red vertical cliffs rise 500 feet above the river. Access is via dirt roads from both sides. The water makes for exciting river-running if you have a kayak and the necessary skills. Golden eagles nest here. It's also very popular with rock climbers. You'll find dozens of climbs here, up to a rating of 5.13. For details, stop by Mountain Sports in Casper for a copy of Steve Petro's *Climber's Guide to Fremont Canyon and Dome Rock.* A

good place to watch climbers is the Fremont Canyon bridge. Anglers try their luck with the rainbow and cutthroat trout and walleye.

The name Alcova comes from **Alcova Hot Springs** (129°F water), so named because of its location within a series of coves. At the turn of the 20th century, developers tried to turn the hot springs into a spa, but the propensity of Wyomingites to take baths but once a week made the venture a failure. The springs were covered by the reservoir, but an artesian well below the dam pours forth the naturally heated water. Bring your swimsuit!

Practicalities

The 265-foot-high Alcova Dam, part of the Depression-era Kendrick Project, was completed in 1938; a 36-megawatt power plant was added in the 1980s. Facilities here include picnic areas, swimming beaches, five summertime campgrounds ($7), and an RV site ($15 with hookups; reservations required) near the marina; call 307/235-9325 for details or to make a reservation. At **Alcova Lakeside Marina** (307/472-6666, www.alcovalakeside-marina.com), you can rent boats or personal watercraft and buy gas or supplies; open mid-April–mid-September.

Water leaves Alcova Dam and flows into small **Gray Reef Reservoir,** used to control the fluctuating discharges from Alcova and to generate additional power. From here some of the water is diverted into the 62-mile Casper Canal to irrigate 24,000 acres of alfalfa, barley, oats, and corn west of Casper. A campground (307/235-9325, $7, open all year) below Gray Reef Dam is a favorite place to launch canoes for a leisurely float down the river.

Inn at Alcova (29 miles west of Casper on Hwy. 220, 307/234-2066, www.sloanesatal-cova.com, $65 s or $80 d) has a general store and two-room cabins with full kitchens. It's within walking distance of the North Platte River.

Riverview Inn (307/472-3200, $54–64 d) is across from the Gray Reef fishing area, with a restaurant and bar, plus showers for campers ($2).

North Platte Lodge (307/237-1182, www

.northplattelodge.com), a mile below the dam along the river, has a variety of fishing-package options.

Bucking S Ranch (307/325-6280, www.buckingsranch.com) is an authentic working cattle ranch on 40,000 acres of land. Guests take part in cattle drives or just head out for a day of riding in the wide-open country south of Alcova. All-inclusive stays are $2,600 for two people per week.

Oregon Trail Landmarks

Three of the most famous landmarks along the entire Oregon Trail lie within Natrona County: Independence Rock, Devil's Gate, and Split Rock. Travelers anticipated these landmarks because they marked the start of a long, gentle approach to the Continental Divide 80 miles west. The route past these landmarks paralleled the Sweetwater River— a ribbon of lush grass in a rugged, desolate landscape. The names applied to adjacent mountains and creeks offer clues to the land's harshness: Rattlesnake Mountains, Poison Spider Creek, Greasewood Creek, Sulfur Creek, and Stinking Creek. Steamboat Lake, just a few miles north of Independence Rock, was a source of bicarbonate of soda used to bake bread. Cattle that drank the lake's putrid water died, while bread made with this baking soda took on a greenish cast. But along the Sweetwater, horses and oxen could find forage, firewood was available, and the clean mountain water offered a relief from the alkaline springs to the east. (The name Sweetwater arose when a mule team carrying sugar lost its load in the river.) Today, Hwy. 220 crosses the old Oregon Trail several miles east of its junction with U.S. 287 at Muddy Gap. The highway parallels the trail for the next 45 miles west.

◖ INDEPENDENCE ROCK

Head southwest from Casper along Hwy. 220 for 55 miles until the granitic dome of Independence Rock rises above the flat surrounding plain. Although not as spectacular or colorful, the setting seems reminiscent of Australia's Ayers Rock. Independence Rock is 1,950 feet long by 850 feet wide; its smoothly rounded top reaches to 136 feet over the surrounding plain. Travelers could not resist the chance to note their passing on this gigantic billboard; an estimated 50,000 names were carved, chipped, or painted on Independence Rock during the mid-19th century. Father Jean Pierre DeSmet, a famed Jesuit missionary, labeled it "the Great Register of the Desert." His initials, along with the names of Captain Bonneville, John C. Frémont, and many other explorers, were etched into the rock face.

Independence Rock apparently received its name from explorer and mountain man William Sublette, who arrived here on July 4, 1830, leading the first wagon train across the overland route. Oregon Trail emigrants tried to reach the rock around July 4 to be on schedule for Oregon. When the rock came into view, it was a source of rejoicing because it offered a welcome place to rest alongside the Sweetwater River. During the heyday of migration along the Oregon Trail, dozens of wagon trains would find themselves at the rock on Independence Day, and the celebrations included patriotic flag-waving, the firing of guns, big dinners, and other festivities. Many people did not make it beyond Independence Rock; many unmarked graves surround the rock.

Exploring the Rock

Today the state has a modern rest area next to Independence Rock with signs detailing the area's rich history. Hundreds of the original names carved into Independence Rock are still visible, although weathering and lichen have obliterated thousands more. Unfortunately, more recent travelers have added their names, sometimes covering up names more than 100 years old. Independence Rock can be climbed from several points along the perimeter, providing fine views of the surrounding countryside. Some of the oldest and best-preserved names are on top; the oldest known is dated 1824. A path circles the rock, making for an interesting mile-long hike. You can spot names on all sides, and you're bound to see deer and other wildlife along the Sweetwater River. A small footbridge crosses the still-visible Oregon Trail route here. Beware of rattlesnakes around Independence Rock.

Enchanted Homestead Adventures (307/ 267-3335) leads horseback rides near Independence Rock.

DEVIL'S GATE

Visible from Independence Rock and just seven miles to the southwest is another famed Oregon Trail landmark, Devil's Gate. Through the centuries, the Sweetwater River has gradually sliced a giant cleft through the Rattlesnake Mountains, leaving 330-foot cliffs on both sides of a 1,500-foot-long canyon. (An Indian legend offers an alternative origin for Devil's Gate: A gigantic tusked beast had roamed Sweetwater Valley, and when the Indians finally managed to mortally wound the animal, it gouged out the nearby mountains in its death agony.) Devil's Gate was another favorite emigrant campsite. The cut is hard to miss, especially from the east—the direction of most Oregon Trail travelers. Today, the BLM maintains a historic site along Hwy. 220 with a short loop trail and signboards. At least 20 emigrant graves are nearby.

MARTIN'S COVE
Disaster on the Plains

Just two miles northwest of Devil's Gate, Martin's Cove is the site of the most disastrous experience along the Oregon and Mormon trails. In 1856, a group of 1,620 British converts to the Mormon religion sailed from Liverpool for America, intent on reaching Salt Lake City before winter. The total cost of the trip to Utah, including ship passage from England and Scandinavia, was just $45 per person.

Devil's Gate and Sweetwater River

CENTRAL WYOMING

© DON PITCHER

Instead of the usual wagons, many of these destitute emigrants pushed or pulled small handcarts that held their meager possessions. The converts left Iowa in five groups that summer, but the last two were delayed because their handcarts had not been completed in time. Finally, a company led by James G. Willie left Iowa City on July 15, and a group of 576 people under the direction of Edward Martin departed on July 26. The emigrants knew they were taking a big risk by leaving so late, but they were eager to reach "Zion" in Salt Lake City.

Trouble started early. The hurriedly built handcarts had been constructed of unseasoned wood that shrank and cracked as the carts rolled across the hot plains of Nebraska. When some broke down, the load was transferred to others, weakening them as well. Then, near present-day Glenrock, the emigrants decided to lighten their carts by discarding extra food, clothing, and blankets—items they would shortly need. Unable to afford the bridge toll at present-day Casper, they waded across the freezing North Platte River on October 19. Soon a blizzard dumped 18 inches of snow on them and the weather turned bitterly cold, with temperatures dropping to −14°F. The elderly and children died first; eventually even the strongest began to perish. Some bodies were covered with stones to protect them from wolves, but others were simply left on the frozen ground, strewn over 60 miles of trail. When a rescue wagon from Salt Lake City finally arrived on November 1, they found the survivors huddling in Martin's Cove, a protected area near Devil's Gate. Rescuer Daniel W. Jones wrote:

There were old men pulling and tugging their carts, sometimes loaded with a sick wife or children, women pulling along sick husbands; little children six to eight years old struggling through the mud and snow.... The provisions we took amounted to almost nothing among so many people, many of them now on very short rations, some almost starving.

The company of foolhardy emigrants finally reached Salt Lake City in late November, but 145 members had died along the way, and many others lost limbs from frostbite. The handcart company led by James G. Willie suffered a similar fate, losing 67 people to the elements at South Pass. Despite the attention that the handcarts continue to receive, they were really used by only 3,000 of the 80,000 Mormons who headed to Utah in the great migration.

Mormon Handcart Visitor Center

In 1872 the French Canadian trapper Thomas De Beau Soleil (Thomas Sun) established a ranch in the Martin's Cove area. Many of the Tom Sun Ranch buildings survive, including Soleil's original cabin (now on the National Register of Historic Places). The buildings were purchased by a private corporation connected with the Mormon church in 1996, and the old ranch house was transformed into the Mormon Handcart Visitor Center (307/328-2953, www.handcart.com). Stop here to learn more about the handcart companies in this excellent free facility, open 8 A.M.–7 P.M. daily June–early September, and 9 A.M.–4 P.M. daily the rest of the year. A genealogy center provides a way to research your family history, and an old schoolhouse contains artifacts from the Sun family. Visitors can borrow a handcart to walk a 4.5-mile section of the Oregon/Mormon Trail. Also here is a log replica of **Seminoe's Fort,** a trading post that operated 1852–1855, with artifacts found during a 2001 excavation of the site. All of these, and the exhibits, are free—and you don't even need to become a Mormon.

SPLIT ROCK

The final of the three geologic landmarks that lined the Oregon Trail through present-day Natrona County is Split Rock, a bite taken out of a solid granite mountain. The cleft was visible for two days as emigrants trudged along; it seemed to be a gunsight aimed toward the west. In the early 1860s, a Pony Express station, an Overland Stage station, a telegraph station, and a garrison of troops were nearby. Today, Split Rock is noted at a turnout 10 miles

CENTRAL WYOMING

west of Muddy Gap Junction along U.S. 287. Tourists sail past in minutes what took the emigrants many long and treacherous days to accomplish. (See *East on U.S. 287* under *Lander* in the *Wind River Mountains Country* chapter

for points west of here on U.S. 287, including Jeffrey City and Ice Slough. If you're heading south to Rawlins on U.S. 287, see *Heading North* under *Rawlins and Vicinity* in the *Medicine Bow Country* chapter.)

West from Casper

West of Casper, U.S. 20/26 passes through the heart of Wyoming, a dry landscape of sage and grass. For a fascinating diversion, follow the BLM's **Big Horn/Red Wall Byway** in a 100-mile loop over country roads with grand vistas and an outlaw past (Butch Cassidy hid out here). The road starts from the intersection of U.S. 20/26 and County Road 125, 13 miles northwest of Casper; get a route map from the BLM office in Casper (307/261-7600, www.wy.blm.gov). The road is rough in places, and high-clearance vehicles are recommended. No services are available along the way, so be sure to carry food, water, and extra clothes. Don't attempt this route in rainy weather when the roads become slick. It's remote and amazingly scenic.

POWDER RIVER

The tiny settlement of Powder River (pop. 50) lies along U.S. 20/26 where it crosses this famous river 35 lonely miles west of Casper. Not much is here today; writer James Conaway called the town "little more than a Texaco station and a bunch of pronghorn antelope looking at it." On the third weekend in July, however, several hundred people flock (pun intended) to town for the annual **Sheepherder Fair.** It features sheepdog trials, sheep roping and hooking, a free barbecue, and sheepherding demonstrations of all sorts. Calcutta wagering goes on for most events, and a band plays country-and-western favorites late into the evening for a happy throng of dancers.

The town has a convenience store, post office, a motel for oil-field workers, and a strip joint to keep them entertained.

◀ HELL'S HALF ACRE

Forty-five miles west of Casper is one of the freaks of nature, Hell's Half Acre. Actually covering 320 acres, the area includes a strange collection of deeply eroded and colorful badlands surrounded by featureless sage-covered plains. Ancient coal deposits within the badlands caught on fire and burned for many years, and when explorer Captain Bonneville passed by in 1833, he labeled it Devils Kitchen because of these sulfurous fumes. The name Hell's Half Acre was a later title. Indians used these badlands as a buffalo trap, driving herds to their deaths over the canyon walls. In the late 19th century, after whites had slaughtered the bison to the brink of extinction, bone pickers gleaned thousands of these bones from Hell's Half Acre for eastern fertilizer plants. Archaeologists later discovered additional bison bones, along with arrowheads and other artifacts. Hell's Half Acre was the setting for the 1997 sci-fi movie *Starship Troopers*—a space-station "city" was built on the south half of the badlands. Visitors today enjoy wandering through these colorful badlands. Hell's Half Acre is well worth a stop, but be forewarned that a kitschy souvenir shop, café, motel (307/473-7773), and RV park detract from the view. It's a great place to meet busloads of tottering tourists from hell.

LYSITE AND MONETA

Slow-paced Lysite is decidedly off the beaten track, eight miles north of another nowheresville place, Moneta (pop. 10). At one time the main route into the Bighorn Basin and Yellowstone lay along the Lysite road, but with completion of a highway through Wind River

Canyon in 1927, traffic bypassed this area. Lysite has an old-time country store and is the sort of town where horses are still a means of transportation. The Lysite library is housed in a building slightly larger than a shoebox.

LOST CABIN

Three miles east of Lysite is the flyspeck of a town called Lost Cabin, named for a gold mine in the Big Horn Mountains. Miner Allen Hulburt and two partners discovered a stream filled with gold, but Indians killed his partners and partially burned their cabin. The dazed miner scooped up as much gold as he could carry and fled to Casper, where his tale pricked more than a few ears. Despite repeated efforts by Hulburt and others, the Lost Cabin mine was never again found. (This is only one of many such tales about the fabled mine.)

Lost Cabin is centered around the elaborate mansion of John B. Okie. He came to Wyoming as a cowboy with only the clothes on his back, decided sheep were a better bet, and gradually became a millionaire. Okie once ran 30,000 sheep through the surrounding country, gaining the title of "Sheep King." His mansion—called "The Big Tepee" by local Indians—was built in 1900 for $30,000 and contained carved fireplaces, Asian chandeliers, imported furniture, stained-glass windows, and Persian prayer rugs. Surrounding it were a greenhouse with flowers tended by Japanese gardeners, a roller rink, a dance hall, and even an aviary housing 140 exotic birds. A power plant was built to supply electricity for Okie's town. In 1930, Okie drowned in a nearby reservoir while hunting ducks. The beautiful old home isn't open to the public but can be viewed from the gate.

◖ CASTLE GARDENS

A remote and little-known archaeological site is Castle Gardens, in desolate country south of Moneta. Head south from Moneta (bear right at the first Y in the road, 0.5 mile south of town) for 16 miles on a gravel road, and then turn east on a dirt road that takes you another six miles to the site. The latter road is quite

© DON PITCHER

mansion of John B. Okie in Lost Cabin

CENTRAL WYOMING

rutted and not recommended for RVs or after rains, when the road turns into a quagmire. Signs at Moneta and at the turnoff keep you from getting lost. At Castle Gardens are all sorts of odd sandstone formations: Toadstools, spires, and various creatures seem to appear. It's easy to see how this would be a sacred spot for the Indians who came here centuries ago. Small juniper and limber pines grow amid the gray rocks and sand, creating a garden in the castles of Castle Gardens. There's no camping here, but you will find picnic tables and an outhouse.

Dozens of Indian pictographs (presumably Shoshonean in origin) have been sharply incised into the soft rock walls. They include many in the shield motif, believed to represent the round shields of Indian warriors. Although they may be up to 900 years old, these figures are probably more recent than the pecked style of pictographs present in the Dinwoody Creek and Legend Rock areas. Castle Gardens figures that show horses or tepees are clearly from the period after A.D. 1700. The most elaborate shield found here—the figure of a turtle painted green, yellow, and red—is now in the State Museum in Cheyenne. The remaining pictographs are protected by chain-link fences, but vandals have marred many of these priceless artifacts with graffiti. The site leaves you with mixed emotions: a multitude of questions about what the images represent, a feeling of closeness to the natural world in this remote and fascinating place, and an utter disgust for those who would destroy this cultural heritage.

WEST TO SHOSHONI

The 85 miles of highway (U.S. 20/26) that connect Casper with Shoshoni cross an almost featureless plain, a place that seems to define the word "bleak." With no trees in sight, the clouds throw moving shadows across a landscape of sage and grass. This is antelope country. Even the ranches are few and far between out here, and cattle take slow, desultory steps in the summer heat or brace against the bitter winds of winter. For many travelers this is pedal-to-the-metal country, a place to crank up the country tunes and roll on west.

WIND RIVER MOUNTAINS COUNTRY

The Wind River Mountains—Wyoming's highest and longest range—form a dramatic divide between two of the state's most important rivers. The east side drains into the Wind River, eventually reaching the Atlantic Ocean, and the western slopes drop into the Green River and eventually the Pacific. The name Wind River Mountains originated as a Crow Indian reference to the warm Chinook winds that blow down the Wind River Valley.

This chapter covers Fremont and Sublette counties, named for two of the state's most famous explorers. Fremont County is a land of sharp contrasts. The eastern end consists of a spacious, arid landscape of sage, grass, and antelope, while to the west you'll find the fluorescent green of irrigated fields along the Wind River and the pastel badlands near Du-

bois. Along the southern and western borders rise the snow-crested Wind River and Absaroka mountains.

The centerpiece of Fremont County is the Wind River Reservation, home to both the Eastern Shoshone and the Northern Arapaho peoples. Within the reservation itself lie the tiny towns of Fort Washakie, Ethete, and Arapahoe, as well as the larger non-Indian settlement of Riverton. Lander borders it on the southeast; farther south stand the historic mining towns of South Pass and Atlantic City.

The Wind River Valley is farming and ranching country. Thousands of acres of alfalfa hay (considered some of the best in America), malt barley, sugar beets, and oats are under irrigation each year. This is Wyoming's

© DON PITCHER

HIGHLIGHTS

◖◗ **Yellowstone Drug Store:** Since when does a drug store in a little desert town merit must-see status? When it sells more than 60,000 malts and shakes annually! Get in line for your own; you won't regret it (page 258).

◖◗ **Sinks Canyon:** The Popo Agie River disappears into a cave, only to reemerge in a spring 0.5 mile down. Ask a local how to pronounce the name (page 269).

◖◗ **Indian Powwows:** Wind River Reservation hosts these fascinating cultural events throughout the summer; don't miss Eastern Shoshone Indian Days Powwow and Rodeo in June (page 275).

◖◗ **Fort Washakie:** Featured attractions include the Shoshone Tribal Cultural Center, the graves of Sacagawea and Chief Washakie, a hot springs pool, and historic buildings surrounded by the beautiful Wind River Reservation (page 279).

◖◗ **National Bighorn Sheep Interpretive Center:** After a visit here, head out to Whiskey Basin to see the live version (but they're in the high country by June) (page 284).

◖◗ **Togwotee Pass:** One of the prettiest mountain passes in Wyoming, Togwotee provides a grand entryway into Grand Teton and Yellowstone national parks (page 291).

◖◗ **Green River Lakes:** A long, partly gravel-road drive from Pinedale, but worth it for the lakeside campground with views of Square Top Mountain (page 295).

◖◗ **South Pass City:** The weathered buildings of this ghost town/state historic site have been here since the gold-mining heyday of the 1860s (page 304).

◖◗ **Museum of the Mountain Man:** This museum in Pinedale is a great way to learn about the rugged explorers whose beaver traps supplied London's hat shops and led to the opening of the West (page 313).

◖◗ **Granite Hot Springs:** Definitely out of the way, but definitely worth going out of your way. Best appreciated at the end of a midwinter dogsled run (page 325).

LOOK FOR ◖◗ TO FIND RECOMMENDED SIGHTS, ACTIVITIES, DINING, AND LODGING.

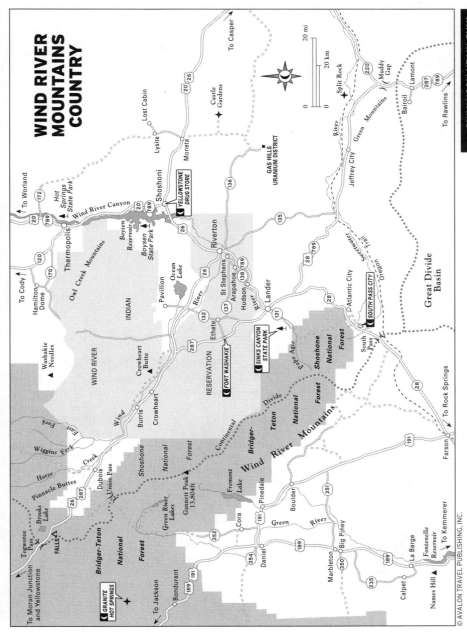

© AVALON TRAVEL PUBLISHING, INC.

WIND RIVER MOUNTAINS

second-biggest agricultural county and home to the largest number of horses in the state. A substantial amount of oil and natural-gas production also takes place here.

Until recently, Sublette County on the west side of the Wind River Mountains was a quiet and strikingly beautiful place where cattle exceeded people by a large margin. Today, the towns of Pinedale, Big Piney, Marbleton, and Boulder are almost unrecognizable. Hotel rooms are packed with gas-field workers, new homes crowd the countryside in all directions, and drilling rigs sprout above the sagebrush. Boom times have come to the Green River Valley, fueled by high prices and loosened environmental regulations under President Bush. Tourism still plays a role in the economy, and there are some gorgeous vistas of the Winds with old ranches in the foreground, but you'd better get here soon since they may be gone by the end of this decade.

PLANNING YOUR TIME

Main highways traverse both the Wind River Valley and Green River Valley, providing access to Jackson Hole, Grand Teton, and Yellowstone. Many travelers en route to these destinations overnight in Pinedale, Lander, Dubois, and Riverton, while others are drawn to this region for its own beauty. Wilderness areas in the Wind River Mountains attract hikers, campers, horseback riders, rock climbers, and other adventurers from both sides of the range.

Before your trip, contact **Wind River Visitors Council** (307/856-7566 or 800/645-6233, www.wind-river.org) and **Sublette County Visitors Council** (307/367-6763, www.sublette.com) for details on accommodations, tours, events, driving tours, and more. Another useful online source is www.windrivercountry.com.

On the north side, the mountains dip into Wind River Valley. Riverton—largest town in the region—has an interesting museum, and tiny Shoshoni contains **Yellowstone Drug Store,** an extremely popular stop for malts and ice-cream floats. Lander is a base for Wind River Mountain treks, with a central location, outdoor gear shops, headquarters for the National Outdoor Leadership School, and hip restaurants. A favorite climbing area with a disappearing stream, **Sinks Canyon,** is a few miles away, and the scenic Loop Road leads to **South Pass City,** a state historic site with a rich mining and Oregon Trail history.

In the heart of the Wind River Reservation, the village of **Fort Washakie** contains the graves of Sacagawea and Chief Washakie, along with the Shoshone Tribal Cultural Center. Summertime **powwows** provide a fascinating window into traditional Shoshone and Arapahoe cultures. Surrounded by colorful badlands, Dubois has both the **National Bighorn Sheep Center** and a small museum. The highway continues northwest from here over gorgeous **Togwotee Pass** before dropping into Jackson Hole.

Southwest of the Wind River Mountains, the Green River Valley's largest town is Pinedale, home to the **Museum of the Mountain Man.** A gravel road heads north of Pinedale to spectacular **Green River Lakes,** and U.S. 189/191 takes travelers to Jackson Hole and Yellowstone. Along the way is the turnoff to another gravel road, this time to **Granite Hot Springs,** a delightful spot for a wilderness soak.

Riverton and Vicinity

Near the confluence of the Big Wind River and Little Wind River, aptly named Riverton (pop. 9,000) is the largest settlement in the region. The Wind River Reservation surrounds Riverton on all sides. It's mid-American suburbia where chain stores and fast-food outlets dominate the outskirts. Even Riverton city hall is housed in a strip mall! Modern Central Wyoming College attracts students from throughout the area.

The Riverton area was the site of two trapping and trading rendezvous, in 1830 and 1838. The land became part of the Wind River Reservation in 1868, but a section was ceded by the Shoshone and Arapaho tribes in 1904. Almost overnight, the town of Riverton sprang up as would-be farmers drew lots for prime farmland. Canals were dug and fields planted with crops; more than 100,000 acres of irrigated farmland surround Riverton today.

During the 1960s and '70s, enormous uranium deposits were developed in the nearby Gas Hills area. Hundreds of millions of dollars poured into the local economy created rapid growth, but when nuclear power suddenly lost its luster, so did Riverton. After the bust that followed, the town diversified and now includes the Brunton Company (binoculars, spotting scopes, etc.), a college, big-box retailers, and various government agencies. The area is becoming increasingly popular with retirees.

SIGHTS

Local historical exhibits in the rambling, surprisingly large **Riverton Museum** (700 E. Park Ave., 307/856-2665, open 10 A.M.–4 P.M. Tues.–Sat. year-round, free) include a tepee containing a buffalo robe and powwow drum, an Indian cradle board with saddle, a model of the Carissa Mine at South Pass, various old farm and mining equipment, and an interesting exhibit on oil drilling. Take a gander at Desert Demon, a stuffed wild mustang that proved untamable—hence his current, more sedate, bullet-tamed condition. While you're here, also check out the photos of Leslie King, the father of former president Gerald R. Ford and a prominent Riverton-area rancher. (President Ford's parents were divorced, and his mother later married Mr. Ford.) Gerald Ford worked as a Yellowstone National Park ranger after graduating from college in Michigan but is not known to have fallen into any geysers.

WIND RIVER MOUNTAINS

RIVERTON

© AVALON TRAVEL PUBLISHING, INC.

RIVERTON AREA CLIMATE

SNOWFALL
RAINFALL
MAXIMUM TEMP.
MINIMUM TEMP.

Average Maximum Temp.	59°F
Average Minimum Temp.	26.9°F
Annual Rainfall	8.85"
Annual Snowfall	33.1"

Riverton Livestock Auction (609 Fairground Rd., 307/856-2209, www.riverton-livestock.com) is Wyoming's second-largest livestock auction barn, after Torrington. Its monthly horse sales are the most enjoyable. Tuesday is sale day.

The 109-acre campus of **Central Wyoming College** (307/855-2000 or 800/442-1228, www.cwc.cc.wy.us) is on the west edge of town along U.S. 26. Founded in 1966, it offers two-year programs, and the campus **Arts Center** houses a small gallery.

ENTERTAINMENT AND EVENTS

A half-mile south of Riverton, **Wind River Casino** (307/856-3964 or 866/657-1604) has bingo, blackjack, craps, poker, several hundred video gaming machines, plus a restaurant. This is the only casino in Wyoming.

The bar at Riverton's bowling alley, **Star Lite Lanes** (837 N. Federal, 307/856-5944) has live music Saturdays and karaoke most other nights.

Watch movies at **Acme Theatre** (312 E. Main, 307/856-3415, www.gabeltheatres.com) or the four-screen **Gem Theatre** (119 S. 3rd St. E., 307/856-9589). Central Wyoming College's **Peck Summer Theatre** (307/855-2002 or 800/735-8418, www.cwc.cc.wy.us) puts on plays.

Each February, the **Wild West Winter Carnival** includes an ice-sculpture contest, chariot races, winter golf, hockey, tethered balloon rides in Riverton, plus many other events at Boysen Reservoir.

Summer kicks off with the **Mountain Man Rendezvous** (307/856-7306, www.1838rendezvous.com) the first weekend in July on the site of the 1838 rendezvous. Events include shooting matches, basket-making, beading, Indian dancing, a mini-powwow, and other old-time activities.

The **Riverton Rendezvous** covers the second and third weekends of July. The rendezvous features food and craft booths, fireworks, a rodeo, live music, a demolition derby, stock car races, and a big **Hot Air Balloon Rally** (third weekend), where you're likely to see more than two dozen colorful balloons lifting off at sunrise.

The **Fremont County Fair and Rodeo** (www.fremontcountyfair.org) comes to the Riverton Fairground the first full week of August, with a carnival, parade, demolition derby, PRCA rodeo, musical entertainment, pig wrestling, and fun for all ages. You can have more Western fun at the **Cowboy Poetry Roundup** in mid-September, where the cowpokes spin tales at the largest cowboy poetry event in Wyoming.

SHOPPING

Wind River Gallery (312 E. Main St., 307/856-1402) displays pieces by local artists. **Books and Briar** (313 E. Main, 307/856-1797) is a surprisingly nice shop in downtown Riverton, with Wyoming books, along with hundreds of magazine titles.

RECREATION

The 23-mile **Wyoming Heritage Trail** follows an old railroad grade from Riverton to Shoshoni, providing the chance to hike or mountain-bike. The trail cuts diagonally across Riverton along the route of the old Chicago–Northwestern Railroad. It's paved through town and gravel the rest of the way.

Riverton has a fine indoor **Aquatic Center** at the high school on West Sunset Drive, 307/856-4230, with a sauna and a whirlpool. **Out Sportin'** (412 E. Main, 307/856-1373 or 800/371-1373) sells bikes and supplies, and **Wyoming Outdoor Adventures** (307/856-4867, www.wyoarentals.com) rents boats, campers, and four-wheelers.

Golfers should check out the 18-hole **Riverton Country Club** (4275 Country Club Dr., 307/856-4779, www.rivertoncountryclub.net). The nine-hole **Renegade Golf Course** (307/857-0117) is west of town.

ACCOMMODATIONS

Riverton has more than a dozen places to bed down for the night, all priced quite reasonably.

Under $50

Paintbrush Motel (1550 N. Federal, 307/856-9238 or 800/204-9238, www.paintbrushmotel.com, $42 s, $49–52 d, $69 suites) has remodeled units with fridges and microwaves, plus Wi-Fi.

Roomers Motel (319 N. Federal, 307/857-1735 or 888/857-4097, $35 s or $45–60 d) features comfortable and clean rooms with fridges and microwaves. Another good choice is **South Federal Inn** (221 S. Federal, 307/856-7455 or 866/383-6931, www.southfederalinn.com, $38–45 or $42–52 d) with fridges and microwaves in all rooms.

Thunderbird Motel (203 E. Fremont, 307/856-9201 or 888/498-9200, www.tbirdmotel.com, $40–44 d) has a quiet location, a guest computer, and wireless Internet. Rooms contain fridges and microwaves.

$50-100

Tomahawk Motor Lodge (208 E. Main, 307/856-9201 or 800/637-7378, www.tomahawkmotorlodge.com, $55–65 d) is a good mid-range place, with comfortable rooms, most with fridges and microwaves.

Popular with both business travelers and vacationers, **Sundowner Station Motel** (1616 N. Federal, 307/856-6503 or 800/874-1116, $67 s or $70 d) has attractive rooms, an exercise facility, sauna, fridges, microwaves, and Wi-Fi.

Holiday Inn (900 E. Sunset, 307/856-8100 or 877/857-4834, www.blairhotels.com) has rooms for $99 d. A honeymoon suite—complete with in-room hot tub—is $150 d. Amenities include an indoor pool and fitness center, Wi-Fi, guest computer, an outdoor courtyard, plus a restaurant and lounge.

Riverton's newest lodging choice is **Comfort Inn and Suites** (2020 N. Federal Blvd., 307/856-8900 or 800/424-6423, www.comfortinn.com), with an indoor pool and hot tub, hot breakfast, fridges, microwaves, and Wi-Fi. Standard rooms are $70–90 d, and suites (some with hot tubs) sleep four for $109–119.

Camping

The nearest public camping ($12 for nonresidents, or $6 for Wyoming residents, open year-round) is 20 miles north in **Boysen State Park** (307/876-2796, http://wyoparks.state.wy.us).

Five miles northeast of Riverton on U.S. 26, **Owl Creek Kampground** (307/856-2869, www.campowlcreek.com, $20 for tents or RVs) has shady in-the-trees sites; showers for noncampers are $4. Open mid-May–mid-September.

Wind River RV Park (1618 E. Park Ave., 307/857-3000 or 800/528-3913, www.windriverrvpark.com) has pleasant riverside tent sites (or tepees) for $16, and RV sites for $21–31. Showers cost $5 for noncampers; open year-round.

FOOD

Breakfast and Lunch

One of the better local eateries is, surprisingly, **Airport Cafe** (307/856-2838) at the airport, where cinnamon rolls and pies are specialties. Fly out here for an inexpensive homestyle breakfast. **The Cove Restaurant** (301 E. Main, 307/856-9813) makes dependably good home-style breakfasts and lunches.

The Ledge (307/856-1294) is a hangout for the young crowd that features smoothies, espresso, delicious earthy sandwiches, and memorable pies. There's a big screen TV and occasional music.

American

The smoke-free **Claimsteak,** inside Sundowner Station Motel (1616 N. Federal, 307/856-6503), serves standard American meals and is popular for Sunday breakfast buffets ($6) and Wednesday night Mexican buffets ($8).

On the west side of town, **Perrett's** (519 W. Main St., 307/857-7306) is a pleasant family spot for pizza, calzones, pasta bowls, subs, and salads. Dine in or on picnic tables outside. Reasonable prices too, mostly under $10.

The Bull Steakhouse (1100 W. Main, 307/856-4728) has fine filet mignon, seafood, soup, a salad bar, and daily lunch specials in a casual atmosphere. Save room for dessert. Head to **Golden Corral** (400 N. Federal Blvd., 307/856-1152) for stuff-it-in meals from a sprawling salad bar/buffet.

International

Housed in the old railroad station, **(The Depot** (1101 S. 1st St., 307/856-2221) is a pleasant lunch and dinner spot for tasty Mexican meals. Don't order too much; the enchiladas and chimichangas (most items $9–13) are substantial enough for two people. The cozy bar makes good margaritas.

China Panda (300 N. Federal Blvd., 307/856-7666) has a popular lunchtime Chinese buffet Monday–Saturday.

Groceries

Get groceries from **Safeway** (708 N. Federal Way, 307/856-6524), **Smith's** (1200 W. Main, 307/856-4931), or **Wal-Mart SuperCenter** (1733 N. Federal Blvd., 307/856-3261).

INFORMATION AND SERVICES

Get local information from the friendly folks at **Riverton Chamber of Commerce** (213 W. Main, 307/856-4801 or 800/325-2732, www.rivertonchamber.org, open 8 A.M.–5 P.M. Mon.–Fri. year-round).

Riverton Public Library (1330 W. Park Ave., 307/856-3556, www.fremontcountylibraries.org) has computers to check email. Wash clothes at **American Dry Cleaning and Laundry** (515 S. Federal Blvd.) or **Riverton Laundromat** (470 E. Pershing Ave.).

Riverton Memorial Hospital (2100 W. Sunset Dr., 307/856-4161 or 800/967-1646, www.riverton-hospital.com) has a 24-hour emergency room.

GETTING THERE AND AROUND

Riverton Airport (www.flyriverton.com) is two miles northwest of town. **Great Lakes Aviation** (307/433-2905 or 800/554-5111, www.greatlakesav.com) has daily service to Denver. The company code shares with United and Frontier. Rent cars at the airport from **Hertz** (307/856-2344 or 800/654-3131, www.hertz.com) or **Jim's Aircraft Service** (856-3599).

The **Wind River Transportation Authority** (WRTA, 307/856-7118 or 800/439-7118, www.wrtabuslines.com) has a mix of services, including summertime shuttles ($15) between the Riverton Airport and Lander.

SHOSHONI

During the late 1970s Shoshoni (pop. 630) was a booming oil and uranium town, but the bust of the '80s left abandoned streets with tall grass and peeling paint and plywood windows on much of downtown. Tumbleweeds rolled down Main Street, and locals joked that no one wanted to be the last to turn out the lights because they were afraid of getting stuck with the electric bill! People are now moving back to Shoshoni, and things have turned around in the last few years.

WIND RIVER MOUNTAINS

[Yellowstone Drug Store

Shoshoni's main attraction is the Yellowstone Drug Store (307/876-2523). During summer, legions of tourists stop here for ice-cream floats and ultrathick malts at the old-time soda fountain. In a typical year the store makes and scoops 13,000 gallons of ice cream (with a high 12 percent butterfat content) for more than 62,000 malts and shakes! In addition to ice cream, the store sells everything from cowboy hats to teddy bears. Trivia tidbit: Former President Gerald Ford's grandfather once owned this store.

More Sights

Certainly the most surprising local place is **Wind River Mushrooms** (307/876-2700), where white button, crimini, and portabella mushrooms are grown commercially and harvested by inmate workers from the Riverton Honor Farm. Buy fresh mushrooms from the retail shop on the west side of town; tours are sometimes available.

Also in Shoshoni is the interesting little **2nd Chance Rock-N-Shop.** You can still find ancient tepee rings northwest of town, and rock hounds enjoy looking for petrified wood, agate, tourmaline, and other stones in the area. Shoshoni is bordered on the north by Badwater Creek and on the south by Poison Creek. East of Shoshoni is an arid landscape of badlands topography. (See *West from Casper* in the *Central Wyoming* chapter for points east of Shoshoni, including the minuscule towns of Lysite, Lost Cabin, and Moneta.)

Events

The **Wyoming State Championship Old-Time Fiddle Contest** comes to town on Memorial Day weekend. You'll find rodeo action during summer at Shoshoni's rodeo arena, along with the **Flywheelers Antique Engine and Tractor Show** in June.

Practicalities

Desert Inn Motel (605 W. 2nd St., 307/876-2273, $42–65 d) has clean and comfortable rooms with small fridges and wireless Internet. Some units contain full kitchens. Just a

© DON PITCHER

Yellowstone Drug Store, Shoshoni

few miles north is **Boysen State Park,** with year-round camping.

Powder River Transportation (307/682-1888 or 800/442-3682, http://gillette.coachusa.us) has daily bus service to Shoshoni, providing connections to central and eastern Wyoming, Denver, Billings, and Rapid City.

BOYSEN STATE PARK

Established in 1956, Boysen State Park (307/876-2796, http://wyoparks.state.wy.us) surrounds a reservoir named for Asmus Boysen, a Danish emigrant who built the first dam here in 1907–1908. When the water from his dam covered tracks of the Burlington Railroad, the railroad sued and had his dam blown up. The dam that now backs up the Wind River is a 230-foot-high earthen structure completed in 1961 at the entrance to Wind River Canyon. Boysen Reservoir is a motorboat playground popular with water-skiers and anglers (it's home to the biggest walleye in Wyoming; a 17-pound monster was caught in 1991). Its relatively warm waters attract swimmers to the beach near park headquarters.

Boysen Reservoir lies primarily within the Wind River Indian Reservation and is surrounded by open desert country. A nearly straight highway (U.S. 20) rolls north from Shoshoni over the arid hills and rocky buttes, providing a few good vistas across the lake. Southwest of Shoshoni, U.S. 26 crosses an arm of the reservoir. **Boysen Lake Marina** (307/876-2772, open mid-Apr.–Sept.), on the north end near the entrance to Wind River Canyon, has a restaurant, grocery store, and boat rentals.

The reservoir is surrounded by a dozen state park campgrounds ($12 for nonresidents or $6 for Wyoming residents, open year-round). Make campsite reservations ($8.50 fee) at 877/996-7275, www.wyo-park.com. Day use costs $4 for nonresidents or $2 for cars with Wyoming plates.

The **Wild West Winter Carnival** comes to Boysen in early February, with souped-up snowmobile races, ice golf, ATV and motorcycle races, and a carnival, plus additional events in Riverton. In August, the **Governor's Cup Walleye Tournament** at Boysen hands out a $5,000 grand prize.

HUDSON

You could easily drive through Hudson (pop. 400) without paying any attention to this rather run-down little place, but the town really deserves a stop. Although many shops are shuttered, **Blue Heron Gallery** (307/332-6153) is worth a visit, and the aging Sinclair sign painted on the side of a brick building makes a good photo op. Hudson has a distinct sense of decay, but off the main drag lie quiet, cottonwood-lined streets, simple frame homes, and gardens filled with tall yellow sunflowers. This place overflows with character and characters.

Food

Hudson was established in 1905 and became a major coal-mining center in the early part of the 20th century. Most of those who settled here were European emigrants, and the town still maintains a strong ethnic flavor; the old fire truck says "Dago Red" on the front. Nowhere is this ethnic heritage as evident as in the Slavic steak house that attracts folks from all over the region: **Svilar's** (307/332-4516). Mama Bessie Svilar founded the restaurant in the 1920s to serve the hungry local miners, but it soon began drawing travelers out of their way to tiny Hudson. Restaurant critic Red Fenwick noted that Svilar's "put Hudson on the map in big red letters that dripped with gravy and honey and meat juices." Mama Svilar died in 1981, but the food is still great (especially the famous prime rib), and the bar remains a popular place for drinks. Entrées are $15–40. Closed Sundays. A few doors down is **Union Bar,** another popular Hudson hangout, and home to a 32-point deer.

After stuffing yourself with a steak dinner, ask about the badlands country east of Hudson. You'll find some fascinating eroded formations just a few miles out.

Lander

Friendly Lander (pop. 6,900) lies along the banks of the Popo Agie River, with the majestic Wind River Mountains rising just to the west. The town has a state training school for the developmentally disabled that employs more than 500 people, and there are many jobs in government, ranching, and construction. Smaller and much more homey than nearby Riverton—where Kmart and Wal-Mart reign supreme—Lander seems to epitomize the changing face of Wyoming. It has undergone a rebirth as younger folks move in to raise families, opening shops, restaurants, and small businesses.

Lander is home to several organizations geared to the outdoors, including the National Outdoor Leadership School, a significant local employer. The relatively mild winters and lack of wind here make it an attractive place to retire, and Lander's proximity to the Popo Agie Wilderness makes it a jumping-off place for

LANDER

mountain treks into the high country. I still can't figure out how it does it, but Lander somehow has managed to rope in some of the most affable locals anywhere. It's a delightful town.

Lander began in 1869 when the army established a small military post, Camp Augur (later Camp Brown), to protect Shoshones from attacks by the Sioux and Arapaho. Two years later the post was moved to Fort Washakie. The rich valley along the Popo Agie River proved easy to irrigate and grew ample crops to feed hungry miners in nearby South Pass. Settlers moved here from the dying gold mines

of South Pass in the late 1870s, creating the crossroads settlement of Pushroot (named because the vegetables grew so well here). It was later renamed Lander, after Colonel Frederick W. Lander, who had surveyed the Oregon Trail's Lander Cutoff. One of the town's early denizens was the outlaw Butch Cassidy, who bought a ranch near Dubois and was often seen at Lander poker tables and dance halls. The town grew more rapidly once the railroad arrived in 1906, but it took local farmers a while to adjust. When the first train rolled into town, people crowded around, and the engineer jok-

© DON PITCHER

downtown Lander

ingly yelled from his cab, "Stand back, I'm gonna turn around." The crowd scattered in fear. During the 1960s and '70s, Lander became a mining boom town as hundreds of workers commuted to the Columbia–Geneva iron mine and mill near Atlantic City. The mine closed in 1983.

National Outdoor Leadership School

Established in 1965 by the late legendary mountaineer Paul Petzoldt, the National Outdoor Leadership School (NOLS, 307/332-5300 or 800/710-6657, www.nols.edu) is headquartered in an old brick building at 284 Lincoln Street. In the intervening years this nonprofit school has grown to become the nation's leading source for training in wilderness skills and outdoor leadership. Staff members at NOLS have achieved a reputation as the purists in the field, emphasizing low-impact camping, respect for the land, and safety. This training has practical applications in developing leadership skills; fully half of all NASA astronauts have attended NOLS courses! The school publishes

several excellent books on wilderness mountaineering, backcountry first aid, and minimizing your impact. The Wilderness Medicine Institute is also owned by NOLS and based in Lander. Trivia facts: NOLS is the fourth-largest buyer of U.S. Geological Survey maps in the country and the largest outfitting permittee on federal lands anywhere.

Today NOLS offers classes all over the world, lasting 2 weeks–3 months and covering everything from Alaska sea kayaking to a semester in Australia. These are *not,* however, glorified adventure trips; you'll need to carry your own gear, help with cooking and cleanup, and be willing to work hard. You can rent equipment from NOLS for the classes. The school also owns a grand old hotel in downtown Lander that is used to house students and instructors when they aren't in the backcountry. College credit is available for some courses.

In addition to the main headquarters at Lincoln and 3rd streets, Lander is also home to the **NOLS Rocky Mountain Branch** (502 Lincoln St., 307/332-1421, open 8 A.M.–5 P.M. Mon.–Fri.) just up the street. More than 1,100 students come here each year to take part in backpacking, horsepacking, and mountaineering trips to the Wind River Mountains and Absaroka Range. The branch office sells new and used gear of all types and bulk food for backcountry cooking. It also rents tents, backpacks, sleeping bags, clothes, hiking boots, stoves, fishing poles, and other outdoor supplies. Other NOLS regional offices are in Alaska, Arizona, Idaho, and Washington, and the organization has international bases in Australia, Brazil, Canada, Chile, India, Mexico, and New Zealand.

Environmental Groups

Partly because of its proximity to the Wind River Mountains, Lander has become a center for the environmental movement in Wyoming. The town is home to the **Wyoming Outdoor Council** (262 Lincoln St., 307/332-7031, www.wyomingoutdoorcouncil.org), an organization founded in 1967 that emphasizes conservation education and environmental lobbying, especially on such issues as wilderness, wildlife, mining, oil and gas development, growth impacts, and waste management. Tax-deductible memberships start at $25 per year.

The **Nature Conservancy** (258 Main St., 307/332-2971, www.nature.org/wyoming) works with landowners to protect important habitats through conservation easements, land donations, and acquisitions. More than 400,000 acres in Wyoming have been protected. Several of these areas are open to the public, including the Tensleep Preserve and Heart Mountain Ranch (see the *Bighorn Basin* chapter), Sweetwater River Project (see *East on U.S. 287* in this section), and Red Canyon Ranch Preserve (see *South Pass* in this chapter).

SIGHTS

Lander's primary sights aren't in town but just a short drive away in Sinks Canyon.

The **Pioneer Museum** (1445 W. Main St., 307/335-8778) on the north end of town has a dozen historic buildings. They aren't open, but you can walk the grounds.

In a strip of shops next to a Foursquare Gospel Church, the small **Lander Children's Museum** (445 Lincoln St., 307/332-1341 or 800/332-1341, www.landerchildrensmuseum.org, $2) is open 10 A.M.–4 P.M. Tuesday and Friday in summer, and 10 A.M.–noon Saturday in winter.

The **One-Shot Evans-Dahl Memorial Museum** (545 W. Main St., 307/332-6862 or 800/768-7743) has memorabilia from this bizarre organization for antelope hunters. You may want to also visit the Department of Game and Fish's **Wildlife Education Center** (260 Buena Vista Dr., 307/332-2688) for wildlife dioramas and interactive displays.

Bronze Foundry

In recent years Lander has gained notoriety for the larger-than-life bronze statutes that line Main Street, the creations of **Eagle Bronze Foundry** (130 Poppy St., 307/332-5436). The foundry's pieces can be found in such places as NFL stadiums and outside the headquarters of Cabela's. One piece it completed (now in Dallas) is the largest bronze monument on the planet. The foundry—one of the biggest in the United States—has a small showroom, and tours ($2) are offered Monday, Wednesday, and Friday at 9:30 A.M.

Getting Jaded

The Jeffrey City area (60 miles east of Lander) is world-famous for its nephrite jade, a mineral found only in Asia, British Columbia, and Wyoming. The jade comes from Crooks Mountain, and much of it was discovered in the 1930s and '40s by Bert Rhoads, who established **Rhoads' Jewelry** (423 Main, 307/332-4439). His wife, Verla, discovered the largest piece of jade ever found—a 3,366-pound boulder that required heavy mining equipment to haul out. Wyoming jade varies greatly in value depending on color and rarity. Some of it sells cheaply, but Wyoming emerald jade can sell for several thousand dollars per carat. Warning: Much of the jewelry sold as "Wyoming jade" actually comes from British Columbia. Buy only from reputable dealers.

ENTERTAINMENT AND EVENTS

Lander Art Center (221 S. 2nd St., 307/332-5772, www.landerartcenter.org) provides space for art classes and workshops, with a small gallery space exhibiting changing works by regional artists.

Gannett Grill/Lander Bar (126 W. Main St., 307/332-8228, www.landerbar.com) brings in live bands—from bluegrass and country to hard-core rock—on weekends. No smoking.

The family-friendly **Global Cafe** (360 Main St., 307/332-7900 or 866/312-7900, www.landerglobalcafe.com) also has frequent live music—from tribal drumming to jazz—plus an upstairs game room with a pool table, Foosball, and table tennis.

Watch flicks at **Grand Theatre** (250 W. Main St., 307/332-3300, www.gabeltheatres.com).

The **International Pedigree Stage Stop Sled Dog Race** (307/734-1163, www.wyomingstagestop.org) stops here. (See the *Jackson Hole* chapter for more information.)

Lander hosts the **Wyoming State Winter Fair** the first weekend in March, with livestock exhibits, dog weight–pulling contests, horse shows, entertainment, and dancing. **Lander Brew Fest** in mid-June is a great chance to sample beers from regional brewers and to hear live music.

Native American Cultural Programs are offered Wednesday evenings July–mid-August at the Pioneer Museum.

Pioneer Days, a three-day party around the Fourth of July, is Lander's big event. It features a big parade with dozens of floats, marching bands, vintage autos, and performers, along with a buffalo barbecue, Indian dancing, street dances, and evening fireworks. The primary event is the nightly rodeo, the oldest paid rodeo on earth, first established in 1893.

An **International Climbers' Festival** (307/332-4541 or 888/284-5968, www.climbersfestival.org) attracts rock climbers to Lander the second weekend of July with clinics, slide shows and films, a trade fair, and more. The **Chokecherry Festival** in mid-August brings live music and booths to City Park.

The **One-Shot Antelope Hunt** attracts hunters in mid-September; teams of three head out to see how quickly they can bring down an antelope with just one shot. The governors of Wyoming and Colorado are "team captains," and celebrities sometimes participate. All sorts of convoluted rules and ridiculous ceremonies make this akin to a fraternity initiation rite. Old men find strange ways to amuse themselves, including cross-dressing!

SHOPPING

Lander is a town with enough book readers to support three good bookshops. **Main Street Books** (300 W. Main St., 307/332-7661, www.mainstreetbooks.com) is the largest, with an outstanding choice of books, plus espresso (best in town), educational toys, and Internet access. **The Book Basket** (325 W. Main, 307/335-7997) is a fun used bookstore, and **Cabin Fever Books** (163 S. 5th, 307/332-9580 or 800/836-9580) offers both new and used titles.

Stop by **Wild Iris Mountain Sports** (333 W. Main St., 307/332-4541 or 888/284-5968, www.wildirisclimbing.com) for outdoor gear and climbing books, including guidebooks to climbing areas in Fremont Canyon, Dome Rock, Sinks Canyon, Baldwin Creek, and Wild Iris. Owner Todd Skinner is a world-renowned rock climber; in 1999 he and six others were the first to free-climb a 3,800-foot cliff in Greenland, the tallest cliffs in the world. Check the shop's bulletin board for climbing partners or used gear.

RECREATION
Rock Climbing

When most folks think of recreation in Lander, they think of the wonderful mountain country just a few miles away. **Wild Iris Mountain Sports** (333 Main St., 307/332-4541 or 888/284-5968, www.wildirisclimbing.com) sells books detailing local climbing areas, including the **Wild Iris Climbing Area,** 29 miles south of Lander on Limestone Mountain. This area has about 150 different climbs, with pitches from 5.7 to 5.14.

Fifteen miles west of Lander is the BLM's **Baldwin Creek Rock Climbing Area,** another challenging area with climbs ranging in difficulty from 5.11 to 5.14. Get a map and access details (high-clearance vehicles are recommended) from the BLM office (1335 Main St., 307/332-8400, www.wy.blm.gov). Climbers will want to talk with folks at Wild Iris about other rock faces in Sinks Canyon and at Fossil Hill.

Other Recreation

Rent cross-country and downhill skis, snowboards, or snowshoes from **Freewheel Ski and Cycle** (378 W. Main St., 307/332-6616).

Lander's Olympic-size **swimming pool** (450 S. 9th, 307/332-2272) is open year-round. You'll also find a weight room and hydrotherapy pool here. The 18-hole **Lander Golf and Country Club** (307/332-4653) is on Capitol Hill. During the winter, skate for free at City Park, where you'll also find a warming hut and skate rentals.

ACCOMMODATIONS

Silver Spur Motel (1240 W. Main St., 307/332-5189 or 800/922-7831, $45 d) is one of the better budget places in town, with comfortable (but older) furnishings and a seasonal outdoor pool. Kitchenettes and family rooms are also available.

A friendly, easygoing place to stay is **Holiday Lodge/National 9 Inn** (210 McFarlane Dr., 307/332-2511 or 800/624-1974, www.holidaylodgelander.com). Rates are $45 s or $50–55 d, and all rooms are nicely appointed with fridges and microwaves. Kitchenettes cost $5 extra, and an indoor hot tub is available, along with a continental breakfast.

At the **Downtown Motel** (569 W. Main St., 307/332-3171), rooms cost $49 for one queen bed or $69 for two. Family rooms with two bedrooms and four beds are $89. A guest computer is available and some rooms contain microwaves and fridges.

Pronghorn Lodge/Budget Host (150 E. Main St., 307/332-3940 or 800/283-4678, www.pronghornlodge.com) has quality rooms

for $78 d, kitchenettes (no dishes) for $90 d, and four-person suites for $125. Amenities include a hot tub, continental breakfast, Wi-Fi, and an exercise room. A monumental bronze elk greets visitors to the motel.

The Inn at Lander Best Western (260 Grand View Dr., 307/332-2847 or 800/452-6337, www.bestwestern.com, $79 s or $89 d) is a modern place with comfortable rooms, plus an outdoor pool, hot tub, a small exercise room, Wi-Fi, and a light breakfast.

Bed-and-Breakfasts

In a quiet neighborhood a few blocks from downtown, **Blue Spruce Inn B&B** (677 S. 3rd St., 307/332-8253 or 888/503-3311, www.bluespruceinn.com, $70 s or $85 d) is a large brick home built in 1920 and nicely furnished with period pieces. It has four guest rooms with private baths, as well as a rec room housing a dartboard and pool table. Outside are flower gardens, tall spruce trees, and a front porch swing. Friendly and helpful owners, too. Rates include a full breakfast, wireless Internet, and even a massage chair. Kids older than age 12 are welcome.

Just two miles from downtown, **◖ Bunk House B&B** (307/332-5624 or 800/582-5262, www.landerllama.com) seems a world away. An old barn has been transformed into a comfortably rustic place to spend the night. Although it isn't spacious and has no phone, this is a perfect spot for families. A branch of the Popo Agie River flows through the property, and llamas are right outside the door. Breakfast is a make-it-yourself affair, but the ingredients—along with a stove and fridge—are provided. The bunkhouse costs $95 per night for up to five people. Owners Scott and Therese Woodruff run Lander Llama Company, and the nearby pastures contain 60 or so llamas used for backcountry trips. Guests, and especially kids, will love the chance to feed and pet the baby llamas.

Baldwin Creek B&B (307/332-7608, www.wyomingbandb.com) is set in the scenic foothills of the Wind River Mountains five miles west of Lander. Here you'll find a historic log home with two guest rooms ($80 d) and four modern cabins ($80 d; $10 each for extra guests), all with private baths. The cabins contain microwaves, fridges, and small porches facing the Wind River Mountains. A continental breakfast is included, and kids are welcome.

Guesthouses and Cabins

For privacy with a view of the Wind River Mountains, stay at **Outlaw Cabins** (five miles west of Lander, 307/332-9655, www.outlawcabins.com). Two cabins—one of which dates back more than a century—are available on this working cattle ranch. Both are nicely furnished, with lofts that are perfect for kids, and have decks to relax in the shade. Each also includes a kitchenette and private bath. Rates are $85 d or $95 for four guests. A two-night minimum is required.

Ten miles northwest of Lander along the North Fork of the Popo Agie River, **Black Mountain Guestranch** (307/332-6442, www.blkmountainranch.com) is an attractive home set on 150 acres, with four beautifully furnished bedrooms, three baths, a full kitchen, and screened porch. It's available for $750 d per week ($950 for up to nine people) or $120 d per night ($160 for up to nine people). There's a two-night minimum. Black Mountain is a favorite of fly fishers, with the river just steps away. Open May–October.

Mountain Rose Cabin (2986 Sinks Canyon Rd., 307/332-2830, $100) is seven miles from town and near the Popo Agie River. The modern cabin has all of the amenities of home, including a bedroom and sleeping loft (space for six), kitchenette, screened porch, phone, and TV. The cabin is just 0.5 mile from Sinks Canyon State Park.

Cottage House of Squaw Creek (307/332-5003, www.cottagehouseoftails.com) is on Squaw Creek Llama Ranch, five miles west of Lander. The modern log cottage has a view of the mountains. Inside, an upstairs bedroom fills the upper level, and downstairs you will find a kitchen, living room, bath, and laundry. The cottage sleeps six and can be rented as a guesthouse for $65 s or $78 d. Extra people are $15 each. The owners raise llamas, and guests enjoy the chance to feed them.

Chalet on Main (834 Main, 307/332-5372, www.thechaletonmain.com) is a charming downtown guesthouse with two bedrooms, two baths, and a full kitchen. It sleeps up to six; $100 d, plus $10 per person for additional guests.

Guest Ranches

At an elevation of 9,200 feet on the edge of the Popo Agie Wilderness, ■ **Allen's Diamond Four Ranch** (307/332-2995, www.diamond4ranch.com) provides a delightful outdoors adventure. The owners are NOLS instructors, and the ranch emphasizes horseback riding, natural-history hikes, wildlife-watching, and fishing. Overnight or extended pack trips are also available. The ranch has basic accommodations with woodstoves and propane lights, but no electricity. No swimming pools or golf courses at this ranch! The ranch is open mid-June–early September and can accommodate up to 12 guests. All-inclusive weekly rates (lodging, food, and horseback rides) are $1,800 for two people.

Twin Creek Ranch and Lodge (307/335-7485, www.twincreekranch.com) is 25 miles southeast of Lander on the edge of the Red Desert. This 17,000-acre ranch covers a mixture of rugged country that includes arid rangeland, lush valleys, and crimson-red sandstone bluffs. It's a working cattle ranch where the emphasis is on turning grass into beef while preserving the environment. Activity centers on horseback riding, and guests take part in checking or rounding up cattle on the open range, saddling horses, and branding calves. This is a great place to experience a no-frills taste of the West with a maximum of just six people at a time in the gorgeous log lodge. All-inclusive rates are $280 d per day, or $2,300 for two people per week. The ranch also offers gourmet dining ($40–50 per person) for the general public, but it's available only when the ranch does not have other guests (primarily in the winter). Call two days ahead for dining reservations. Twin Creek is open year-round.

Camping

Camping costs nothing at **Lander City Park** (405 Fremont St.), right along the banks of the Popo Agie River. Pitch tents on the shady grass here or park RVs in the lot. Local high-schoolers often pull in for a bit of extracurricular activity, so don't expect a quiet night. Camping is available May–September. Take showers at the Lander swimming pool, next to the junior high school, or at local RV parks.

Sinks Canyon State Park (307/332-6333, http://wyoparks.state.wy.us), six miles southwest of Lander on Hwy. 131, has two campgrounds ($12 for nonresidents or $6 for Wyoming residents) open May–October.

Several private campgrounds operate in the Lander area. Riverside tent sites ($8 per person, no RVs) are available behind (and down a steep hill) from **Holiday Lodge** (210 McFarlane Dr., 307/332-2511 or 800/624-1974, www.holidaylodgelander.com). Tenters can use the motel's hot tub for free. Noncampers can take a shower for $5. Open June–September.

Pioneer RV Park (176 Sunflower St., 307/332-0155 or 888/875-5238, www.pioneerrv.com, open mid-Apr.–Oct.) is a newly opened place on the south side of town with RV hookups for $24; no tent sites. No shade or showers, but perfect for big rigs.

On a hill along the east end of town, **Sleeping Bear RV Park and Campground** (715 E. Main, 307/332-5159 or 888/757-2327, www.sleepingbearrvpark.com) is open all year. The same folks also run **Sleeping Bear Ranch RV Resort,** nine miles southeast on U.S. 287, open May–October. A number of reconstructed buildings from the ghost town of Dallas, Wyoming, have been moved to the grounds, which also has a café. Same prices for both places: $17 for tents, and $29 for RVs. If you aren't staying here, showers are $4.50.

Nine miles northwest of town on U.S. 287, **Ray Lake Campground** (307/332-9333, $8 d tents, $15 RVs, open May–Sept.) has a country location (but no trees) and a small café. Showers for noncampers cost $3.

FOOD

Lander is blessed with several excellent restaurants to please almost any taste.

Breakfast and Lunch

For a light start on the day, drop by **The Magpie** (159 N. 2nd, 307/332-5565). You'll find healthy breakfasts (except Sundays) and creative lunchtime salads and espresso. It's a great place to hang out, with a couple of computers in the back for web surfing. Another recommended caffeine-and-computer hot spot (best lattes and mochas) is **Main Street Books** (300 W. Main St., 307/332-7661 www.mainstreetbooks.com).

On the south end of town, **Highwayman Cafe** (730 E. Main St., 307/332-2566) opens at 5:30 A.M. and is known for its sourdough pancakes and home cooking.

Chocolates for Breakfast (329 W. Main St., 307/332-9273) has smoothies, espresso, teas, gourmet chocolates, candles, and gifts. For ice cream, stop by **Mom's Malt Shop** (351 W. Main, 307/332-5535).

◖ WildFlour Bagels and Bread (545 W. Main, 307/332-9728 or 877/532-9728) is a great bakery, specializing in bagels, delicious fresh breads, and sweets. It's open for breakfast and lunch with bagel sandwiches, wraps, panini sandwiches, soups, a salad bar, and iced mochas.

American

The Hitching Rack (0.5 mile south on U.S. 287, 307/332-4322) has a big salad bar and homemade soups. This is the place locals go for steak and seafood dinners (it's not open for other meals). Actually, one of the most popular night-out places is 10 miles northeast in Hudson: Svilar's.

Tony's Pizza Shack (637 W. Main, 307/332-3900) makes good pizzas, pasta, and strombolis. Its breadsticks are a local favorite, and the rooftop deck is popular in the summer.

Eclectic

Meet the NOLS outdoorsy gang at ❰ **Gannett Grill** (126 W. Main St., 307/332-8228, www .landerbar.com). The café offers pizzas of all sizes, sandwiches (with names such as cluck boob and hungry hippie), half-pound burgers, salads, and bar munchies (including crinkle-cut battered fries). The historic **Lander Bar** (same building) pours regional microbrews and has a pool table. Gannett Grill overflows on summer evenings with an informal and noisy crowd, and live music fills the air on weekends. Entirely smoke-free.

Next door, in an 1888 brick building that once housed a Chinese laundry, is **Cowfish** (148 W. Main St., 307/332-8227, www.lander-bar). It has the same owners as Gannett Grill and shares a pleasant patio where folks from both places can mingle. Cowfish offers a hip setting and the sort of perfectly prepared meals you'd expect in Jackson. The bistro menu varies from cow (or fish) burgers and grass-fed beef steaks to salads, grilled Alaska salmon, Baja fish tacos, and Indian chicken curry. Most dinner entrées are $9–20. In addition to Cow-fish, the building houses the award-winning **Lander Snake River Brewery**.

❰ **Global Cafe** (360 Main St., 307/332-7900 or 866/312-7900, www.landerglobal-cafe.com, open 2–10 P.M. Tues.–Sat.) provides a no-alcohol setting that blends healthy home-cooked dinners with live music and a coffee-house atmosphere. The menu changes daily, so check the blackboard for today's offerings, typically under $9. Vegetarian specials dominate, along with organic beef, chicken and dumplings, and a wonderful rice pudding. The en-closed courtyard provides a quiet escape, and Wi-Fi is available.

International

China Garden (162 N. 6th St., 307/332-7666) has a Chinese lunch buffet ($7), reasonable dinners ($10–12), and vegetarian dishes. Quite authentic, too. Closed Sunday. **El Sol de Mexico** (453 Main St., 307/332-9298) is a good Mexican place.

Big Noi Restaurant (8125 N. Hwy. 789, 307/332-3102) serves Thai food and more standard American fare (including surprisingly good breakfasts). This is one of just five Thai restaurants in Wyoming; the others are in Jackson and Rawlins.

Groceries

Mr. D's Food Center (725 W. Main St., 307/332-2964) has groceries, an in-store deli, and bakery.

INFORMATION AND SERVICES

In the old railroad depot, the **Lander Chamber of Commerce** (160 N. 1st St., 307/332-3892 or 800/433-0662, www.landerchamber.org) is open 9 A.M.–5 P.M. Monday–Friday all year, plus 10 A.M.–2 P.M. Saturday June–August.

Visit the Shoshone National Forest's **Washakie Ranger District Office** (333 E. Main St., 307/332-5460, www.fs.fed.us/r2/ shoshone). It offers forest maps and hiking information, and there are natural-history ex-hibits in the lobby. The staff can also provide a list of permitted horsepackers, llama outfit-ters, and even a local company that provides pack goats (www.goatpacking.com) for use in the backcountry. For additional public lands information, head to the BLM's **Lander Field Office** (1335 W. Main St., 307/332-8400, www.wy.blm.gov).

Lander's **post office** (307/332-2126) stands at the junction of U.S. 287 and Hwy. 789. The **Lander Library** (2nd and Amoretti, 307/332-5194, www.fremontcountylibrar-ies.org) has computers where you can surf the web or check email. Wash clothes at **American Dry Cleaning and Laundry** (175 N. 5th St., 307/332-5454).

The **Lander Valley Medical Center** (1320 Bishop Randall Dr., 307/332-4420, www.landerhospital.com) has 24-hour emer-gency services.

GETTING THERE AND AROUND

The nearest airport with scheduled flights is in Riverton, 25 miles from Lander.

Rent cars from **Fremont Motors** (555 E.

Main St., 307/332-4355 or 877/450-9490, www.fremontmotors.com) or **Rent-a-Wreck** (323 N. 2nd St., 307/332-9965 or 888/332-9965, www.sleepingbearrvpark.com).

The nonprofit **Wind River Transportation Authority** (WRTA, 307/856-7118 or 800/439-7118, www.wrtabuslines.com) has summertime shuttles to Riverton Airport ($15), trips to Salt Lake City ($115), Jackson ($100), or Rock Springs ($50), and a school-year schedule connecting Riverton, Lander, and Wind River Reservation towns. Salt Lake trips are primarily for NOLS students but are open to the general public; reservations required.

EAST ON U.S. 287

A few miles east of Lander on U.S. 287, the highway passes an impressive vermilion sandstone butte. Near here is a beautiful, century-old red-rock barn that once stabled horses used on the stage route through here. In 1884, Wyoming's first oil well was drilled not far away. The site—now called the Dallas Dome Oil Field—was known to Indians and described in Washington Irving's *Adventures of Captain Bonneville* as the "Great Tar Springs." Nineteenth-century emigrants used the oil to grease wagon axles, in lamps, and as a balm for their aches.

As you continue eastward, the Wind River Mountains gradually diminish in magnitude. Stop to look up at them for a while. It is easy to see how the pioneers from the east—where a mountain is anything over 1,000 feet—would watch these mountains grow closer with each day's travel and wonder at their rugged crowns. It's also easy to see why they would choose to go around the southern end of this range—at South Pass—instead of crossing over the top.

Sweetwater Preserve

One mile west of the junction of U.S. 287 and Hwy. 135 is the Nature Conservancy's **Sweetwater River Project** (www.nature.org/wyoming), a 3,000-acre natural area that preserves six miles of riparian habitat along the Oregon Trail. For access information, call the Conservancy in Lander at 307/332-2971.

Ice Slough

Forty miles east of Lander, the highway passes a marker describing Ice Slough, one of many landmarks along this section of the Oregon Trail. Dense grasses in a small marsh kept ice all through the summer, a real treat for emigrants on a hot summer day. The trail is visible just to the right of the historical sign that describes Ice Slough; it's just north of the wire gate. In *Roughing It,* Mark Twain described Ice Slough as follows:

> In the night we sailed by a most notable curiosity, and one we had been hearing a good deal about for a day or two, and were suffering to see. This was what might be called a natural ice-house. It was August, now, and sweltering weather in the daytime, yet at one of the stations the men could scrape the soil on the hillside under the lee of a range of boulders, and at a depth of six inches cut out pure blocks of ice – hard, compactly frozen, and clear as crystal.

Jeffrey City

The bleak, almost ghost town of Jeffrey City is a casualty of the bust that followed the uranium-mining boom of the 1970s. First called Home on the Range, the town was renamed for a Rawlins philanthropist, Dr. Charles W. Jeffrey. The town was built on the nuclear industry, and as a company town its survival was tied to the fortunes of Western Nuclear Company. By 1980, the population had swollen to 4,000. Today you'd be lucky to find 50 folks around here, and weeds grow through the concrete sidewalks around empty bunkhouses with plywood-covered windows. The gas station and modern grade school survived for a while, but they too closed a few years back. Ranching, oil, and gas keep Jeffrey City from drying up and blowing away. Rock hounds should ask for directions to the famed jade deposits around the city, but make sure you're on public land or have permission from landowners.

East of Jeffrey City lies definitive Wyoming country with rolling sage and grassland, a few weathered old homesteads, and distant mountains on all sides. A sign notes the turnoff to **Cottonwood Campground** ($6, open June–Oct.), a BLM camp six miles east of Jeffrey City and then 11 miles south on Green Mountain Loop Road. Campsites are set in a surprisingly pleasant aspen forest. You aren't likely to meet many folks here, but you may come across some wild horses (look for their long manes and tails), particularly near a picnic area at the aptly named Wild Horse Point, eight miles from the campground. Free campsites are at county-run **Green Mountain Park** on the road to Cottonwood Campground.

For a glimpse of the **Oregon Trail** head eight miles east of Jeffrey City on U.S. 287 and turn north up Agate Flat Road. In less than one mile you'll see a concrete post marking the trail ruts. (See the *Central Wyoming* chapter for more on the country east and north of Jeffrey City, including the Oregon Trail sites of *Independence Rock, Devil's Gate,* and *Split Rock,* and the Indian pictographs at *Castle Gardens*.)

☪ SINKS CANYON

Highway 131 climbs south from Lander through fascinating Sinks Canyon and then over the mountains to Atlantic City. A popular loop trip is to follow this road to Atlantic City, returning to Lander via Hwy. 28, a total distance of 56 miles. Plan to spend at least one full day if you want to savor the many sights along the way. Locally known as the Loop Road, it is very popular with both visitors and residents. Bighorn sheep were transplanted into Sinks Canyon in 1987 and a dozen or so survive; look for them along the road. Rock climbers practice their skills on the steep cliffs of the canyon. Of interest to climbers and geologists are the three different types of rock in a five-mile stretch: sandstone, limestone, and granite. You'll find several campgrounds here, lots of lakes, trails, and big mountain country. Get to Hwy. 131 by heading south on Lander's 5th Street. Sinks Canyon begins seven miles away.

The Sinks

The Popo Agie River (usually pronounced

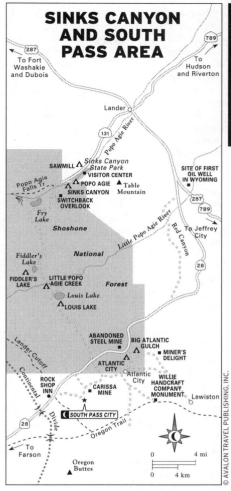

po-PO-zha, but you'll hear lots of other versions) begins in the snowfields of the Wind River Mountains and drops northeast to its junction with the Wind River near Riverton. **Sinks Canyon State Park** contains one of Wyoming's geological wonders. Here the Middle Fork of the Popo Agie plunges into a cave (the "Sinks"), only to emerge again 0.5 mile down in a gigantic spring (the "Rise"). The river's name—Popo Agie—is a Crow

Indian word meaning "Beginning of the Waters." Apparently, the stream originally flowed aboveground—it still does during high spring runoff—but through time a cave formed in the water-soluble Madison Limestone that underlies this region, allowing the water to disappear into enormous underground caverns or convoluted passages from which it slowly drains. In 1983, researchers put dye in the Sinks. The dye did reappear at the rise, but not until two hours later! The water was also a few degrees warmer, and more water appeared than entered the cavern. Lots of fat rainbow and brown trout congregate in the pool at the Rise, waiting for visitors to toss them bits of food. A vending machine sells fish food (fish do not live by bread alone). No fishing is allowed. Also keep your eyes open for the muskrat that lives in the spring here.

Sinks Visitor Center (307/332-3077, http://wyoparks.state.wy.us, open 9 A.M.–7 P.M. daily late May–early Sept.) houses displays of fish and animals, along with geological exhibits. The windows face down this steep-walled canyon, offering dramatic vistas. The cave into which the stream disappears is directly behind the visitor center. This area is a fine place to watch birds. Look for dippers—the odd birds that walk underwater—on the rocks above the Sinks.

Three nearby campgrounds operate April–October: state-run **Sawmill Campground** and **Popo Agie Campground** ($12 for non-residents or $6 for Wyoming residents, http://wyoparks.state.wy.us), and just up the road, the Forest Service's **Sinks Canyon Campground** ($8). Get brochures at the visitor center for the mile-long **nature trail** near Popo Agie Campground. More interesting is the **Popo Agie Falls Trail,** which takes off from Bruce's parking area one mile above Popo Agie Campground. This fairly easy 1.5-mile trail climbs 600 feet to a series of attractive waterfalls, the largest being 60 feet. Horses and mountain bikes are allowed on the trail, and during winter, skiers enjoy groomed cross-country trails in the canyon at Sinks Canyon Campground.

Into the Mountains

Several miles above the state park, the road turns to gravel and switchbacks steeply up the canyon's south face. The Owl Creek Mountains—50 miles to the north—are visible from the overlook. The road is usually open mid-June–mid-October and gets washboarded in sections, so be ready for a buckin'-bronc ride and lots of traffic on summer weekends. The rough ride is made worthwhile by excellent vistas and several attractive lakes (enlarged by dams). This is primarily lodgepole and limber pine country, but around Louis Lake you'll discover some huge old Engelmann spruce and subalpine fir trees.

The Forest Service maintains five delightful campgrounds ($8) along the Loop Road: **Fiddler's Lake** (open July–mid-Sept.), **Louis Lake** (open mid-June–mid-Sept.), **Popo Agie** (open July–mid-Sept., no water), **Sinks Canyon** (open May–Oct.), and **Worthen Meadows** (open mid-June–mid-Sept.). Fiddler's Lake has fully accessible facilities and, at 9,400 feet, is the highest. Louis Lake is easily the most popular, made more scenic by a sharp granite cliff that rises directly behind the lake. There's good fishing for brown and Mackinaw trout, and moose are commonly seen around Louis Lake's margins. Other folks car-camp for free around Frye Lake or off the road. Hiking trails head west from Loop Road to the lake-dotted Popo Agie Wilderness.

The Resort at Louis Lake (307/330-7571 or 888/422-2246, www.louislake.com) rents rustic four-person cabins (built in 1937) with oil lanterns, handmade furnishings, and a shared bathhouse for $70. Newer cabins—these sleep up to eight—contain kitchens and private baths and cost $175, and several rooms ($80 d) are available in the modern lodge. The resort offers horse- and llama-pack trips, drop-pack trips, tent sites ($20), and rentals of fishing boats, kayaks, and canoes in the summer, or snowshoes, cross-country skis, and snowmobiles when the snow flies. This is a classic Wyoming lodge with a peaceful mountain setting and friendly owners. Book well ahead, though, because it's full all summer long! The cabins are available all year and make a favorite winter base for cross-country skiing and snowmobiling. Winter access is by snowmobile only.

South from Louis Lake the road opens into a high plateau with limber pine trees and wide vistas south to the Oregon Buttes. An-telope are common in the sagebrush country, and moose are seen in the aspen stands along the road and in the marshes around Fiddler's Lake. The Loop Road meets Hwy. 28 beside the now-abandoned U.S. Steel iron-ore mine. From here you can continue back to Lander on the highway or visit historic South Pass.

Wind River Indian Reservation

At more than 2.2 million acres, the Wind River is one of America's largest Indian reservations. Home to both the Northern Arapaho (www.northernarapaho.com) and the Eastern Shoshone (www.easternshoshone.net) tribes, it reaches 70 miles from north to south and 55 miles east to west. You'll find some of the most unforgettable vistas in Wyoming here: fabulous badlands on the western edge; the beautiful Wind River, where the cottonwoods glow a brilliant yellow in the cool fall air; deep green irrigated pastures where horses, sheep, and cattle graze; and desolate, wide-open spaces where only cactus, sagebrush, jackrabbits, and rattlesnakes grow. Bright yellow sunflowers add color to the roadsides in late summer, and horses seem to be everywhere. All this is backdropped by the enormous, snowcapped Wind River Mountains. The eminent guide Jim Bridger reportedly attempted to convince Brigham Young that this basin would be a far better home for the Mormons than the deserts around Salt Lake. Young refused to listen. It is just as well because this was—and still is—Indian country.

The Wind River Reservation was the scene for the classic Zane Grey western *War Paint,* a film that featured Tim McCoy and hundreds of Arapaho and Shoshone Indians. Today, hundreds of people, both Indian and non-native, come to watch a different form of entertainment—the many powwows that occur throughout the summer on the reservation. The annual sun-dance ceremonies are more intense, spiritual events at which outsiders are only tolerated. The Shoshone and Arapaho peoples maintain separate sun dances and powwows; absolutely no cameras or tape recorders are allowed during the sun dances.

Despite the proximity of the reservation to Lander and Riverton, there isn't really a lot of mixing between Indians and nonnatives, except in business situations. After more than 125 years, the various cultures—Arapaho, Shoshone, and Anglo—are still like oil and water. Some whites continue to view the Indians as disorganized, drunken, and lazy, while some Indians regard whites as pushy, materialistic, selfish, and disrespectful. Even between the Shoshones and Arapaho, relations are still somewhat strained.

Public Access

Although you can drive through with no problems, access to many parts of the reservation is controlled by Indian authorities, and trespassers may be fined. If you want to explore the reservation, pick up a copy of the fishing regulations from sporting-goods stores in Lander, Riverton, and Dubois, or from the **Tribal Fish and Game Office** (307/332-7207) in Fort Washakie. These regulations detail not only fishing, but also hiking, boating, camping, and other recreation options on the reservation. For most of these activities you'll need a $5 recreation stamp, and anyone planning to fish will also need to buy a fishing permit (nonresidents $20 for one day or $60 for a week). Restrictions apply, and several areas, including the entire northern end of the reservation near the Owl Creek Mountains, are closed to the non-Indian public. Hunting by

CHIEF WASHAKIE

The history of Wyoming in the 19th century is one that resonates with battles between Indians and the invading white settlers. Only one tribe – the Shoshone – provided an exception to this rule. The reason for this stems from Chief Washakie (WASH-a-key), a man whose life spanned the entire tumultuous century. Washakie was born in 1798 of Shoshone and Flathead parents. His birth name was Pina Quanah, but later in life he gained the name Washakie – literally, "The Rattler" – a reference to a rattle made from the dried scrotum of a buffalo that he used to scare Sioux ponies during his daring raids. Because the Blackfeet tribe killed his father, Washakie lived something of an orphan's existence, growing up among both the Lemhi and Bannock peoples. He eventually joined the Eastern Shoshones and quickly proved himself a fearless and extraordinary warrior.

In the 1830s, Washakie, who was fluent in sign language, met and became a close friend of famed mountain man Jim Bridger, and one of his daughters became Bridger's third wife. From Bridger and other trappers, Washakie learned English, along with a realization that a union with whites against his enemies was wiser than trying to fight the countless hordes coming across the plains from the east. Around 1843, after the death of the previous chief, Washakie gained control over a band of Shoshones based in the Upper Green River. As their lifelong chief, he was recognized as an extraordinarily charismatic and forceful leader and a skilled orator. Because of his skills, white settlers sought Washakie out whenever trouble appeared with other tribes.

Washakie's people had been devastated through the years by smallpox, cholera, and other diseases, and they were no match for the Sioux, Cheyenne, and Arapaho. Because of this, Washakie viewed an allegiance with whites as a way to push back other tribes. When some of his young warriors began to complain that the old man was losing his warrior abilities and becoming a lackey, Washakie disappeared for a few weeks and returned with seven enemy scalps. The grumbling ended. Those Shoshones who attacked whites became instant outcasts.

In 1876, Washakie's Shoshones joined with General Crook against the Sioux and Cheyenne in the Battle of the Rosebud. The battle was a standoff, but Washakie's sage advice almost certainly prevented Crook's troops from facing what befell General Custer one week later. When President Chester Arthur visited Wyoming in 1883, he asked Chief Washakie to meet him at a reception in Fort Washakie. The proud chief demurred, instead insisting that the president come to him. They met in Washakie's tepee.

Chief Washakie died on the Wind River Reservation on February 22, 1900, and was buried with a full military funeral, the only Indian chief ever to be so honored. The procession, which was escorted by the U.S. cavalry, stretched nearly two miles. He was 102 years old and had led his people for more than 60 years. With Washakie died the tradition of having one man as chief of the Shoshones. Although his name is not nearly as well known today as that of Red Cloud or Crazy Horse, Washakie deserves a place as one of the great warriors and peacemakers of American history. A dozen different Wyoming places are named in his honor, including the Washakie Wilderness and Mt. Washakie.

outsiders on the reservation is strictly verboten. The map that comes with the permit lists public camping areas on the reservation.

SHOSHONE HISTORY

Originally peoples of the Great Basin, the Shoshones first entered southwestern Wyoming in the 16th century, and then gradually pushed northward until they controlled most of the land now known as Wyoming, as well as territory all the way into Canada. As they moved onto the plains, and with the acquisition of the horse, Shoshone life changed drastically from a simple Stone Age culture of grubbing for roots and eating whatever they could catch by hand to a sophisticated buffalo-centered livelihood.

Because Shoshone culture extended far to the south, they came into contact with Spanish traders and were some of the first Indians to have horses. The Shoshone introduced horses to the northern plains region around 1700, forever transforming Plains Indian culture. To the trappers and traders who first encountered them, the Shoshone were known as "the Snakes" because of the serpentine hand signals they used to signify their tribal name. The word *Shoshone* refers to the simple willow-and-sagebrush lodges in which they lived before the great flowering of their culture in the 18th and 19th centuries. The Eastern Shoshone occupied western Wyoming, while their cousins the Western Shoshone lived in Idaho.

In the late 18th century, the expanding Shoshone culture was halted when their enemies—the Sioux, Crow, and Arapaho—forced the Shoshone west of the Laramie Mountains. The Wind River and Fort Bridger vicinities became wintering areas. After a spring sun dance and buffalo hunt, the various tribal members would move into the mountains of northern Utah to hunt, fish, and gather berries and roots. Each fall the entire tribe would gather in the Great Divide Basin and head across the Continental Divide for the fall buffalo hunt in the Wind River and Bighorn basins. Led by Chief Washakie, the Eastern Shoshone—unlike most other Plains Indians—maintained an unbroken friendship with the invading whites.

Onto the Reservation

The Shoshones were not recognized in the great Fort Laramie Treaty of 1851, and the Wind River Basin and Bighorn Basin where they had long lived were assigned to the Crows. The Fort Bridger Treaty of 1863 gave the Shoshones and Bannocks a reservation covering parts of Colorado, Utah, Wyoming, and Idaho. In 1868, this enormous, 45-million-acre spread was whittled down to just the 2.2-million acre Wind River region, and the Bannocks were given a separate Idaho reservation.

Several years later, the government lopped off 600,000 acres around the rich gold region of South Pass City, paying Chief Washakie

$500 a year and $5,000 worth of cattle for five years—around $0.04 per acre. More land—Thermopolis Hot Springs—was ceded to the government in 1897 for $60,000, and in 1905 1.4 million acres were opened to homesteaders north of the Wind River. In exchange for the latter, the Shoshones and Arapaho received per capita payments, schools, payment for water rights, and an irrigation system on what remained of their reservation. The reservation and adjacent lands are now some of the state's most important agricultural regions.

In 1878, Wyoming's territorial governor asked Chief Washakie if the destitute Arapaho—archenemies of the Shoshone—could be allowed to stay temporarily on the Wind River Reservation. Washakie's sympathetic heart finally gave in:

> It is plain they can go no further now. Take them down to where Popo Agie walks into Wind River and let them stay until the grass comes again. But when the grass comes again take them off my reservation. I want my words written down on paper with the white man's ink. I want all you to sign as witnesses to what I have said. And I want a copy of that paper. I have spoken.

Despite this agreement, the "temporary" arrangement became permanent, and urgent pleas by Washakie went unheeded. Once again the government had abused its most loyal friend.

Many years after Chief Washakie's death, the Shoshones sued over this gross injustice. In 1937, the tribe was awarded $6.4 million for the land given to the Arapaho, minus the expenses for every building ever built by the government on the reservation and any services rendered. The cheapskate federal government even deducted $125 for a silver saddle given by President Grant to Chief Washakie as a token of appreciation! What was left amounted to a grand total of $2,350 per capita, distributed almost entirely in various Bureau of Indian Affairs (BIA)-run programs.

ARAPAHO HISTORY

The Arapaho (a Blackfeet Indian term meaning "Tattooed People") always called themselves simply "Our People." They originally lived a farming life in what is now northern Minnesota, but the arrival of whites on the East Coast created a domino effect among eastern Indians, pushing tribes westward on top of each other. Because of this pressure, the Arapaho, along with the Sioux and Crow, migrated onto the Great Plains in the late 18th century. They quickly adopted the nomadic life associated with Plains Indian culture, a life centered on the buffalo and made possible by the horse. Pressure from the Sioux, who numbered perhaps 25,000 individuals versus 3,000 Arapaho, forced the Arapaho to join with the Cheyenne and move south to the Arkansas and Platte River regions.

Around 1830, the Arapaho split into northern and southern divisions, partly because of the establishment of Fort Laramie on the Laramie River in Wyoming and Bent's Fort on the Arkansas River in Colorado. For many years, the Northern Arapaho wintered in northern Colorado, scattering along the North Platte River with the coming of spring and then gathering again in late summer to hunt buffalo and prepare for winter. In the 1851 Fort Laramie Treaty, the Arapaho and Cheyenne tribes were assigned the area east of the Rockies between the Arkansas and North Platte rivers, but as gold was discovered in the Rockies, whites began to push the Arapaho off this land.

After Cheyenne and Arapaho warriors began raiding white ranches in Colorado during the early 1860s, the governor demanded action. In the Sand Creek Massacre of 1864, a peaceful Cheyenne and Arapaho village was viciously attacked by U.S. cavalry soldiers under Colonel John M. Chivington. The action sparked a massive retaliation—Arapaho, Sioux, and Cheyenne warriors sacked Julesburg, Colorado, tore down miles of telegraph wire, stampeded cattle herds, and burned ranches and stage stations throughout the Rockies.

After this event, the Arapaho shifted their living patterns and began spending winters along Wyoming's Powder River and summers in the Medicine Bow country to the south. They continued to attack Shoshones on the Wind River Reservation, emigrant trains along the Overland Trail, and miners around South Pass until the early 1870s, but they gradually lessened their raids as the futility of their condition became more apparent.

The end came in the Bates Battle of 1874, when the Shoshones and the U.S. Army attacked the Arapaho, leaving them demoralized and without horses or supplies. In the late 1870s, many Arapaho served as army scouts, and some even joined an Arapaho unit of the army during the 1880s. Best-known of the Arapaho scouts was Friday, an orphan Arapaho boy adopted by mountain man and Indian agent Thomas Fitzpatrick and taught in eastern schools. He returned to his tribe and became their most important translator and a force for peace. Friday's friendship with Chief Washakie probably led Washakie to finally tolerate Arapaho on his reservation.

Onto the Reservation

With the buffalo gone and their way of life under constant pressure from white settlers and the deadly diseases they brought, the Arapaho were in desperate straits, shuttling from one temporary home to another. The government refused to set aside a separate reservation, insisting that they live with the Cheyenne in Oklahoma or the Sioux in South Dakota, far from their Wyoming home.

In 1878, the Northern Arapaho were shoehorned onto the Wind River Reservation with their hated enemies in what was to be a "temporary" stay. Only 913 Arapaho, mostly women and children, remained from the tribe that had once been so powerful. (Interestingly, the Arapaho now outnumber the Shoshones on the reservation.) The two bands of Arapaho that settled on the Wind River Reservation were led by Chief Black Coal, whose people settled in present-day Arapahoe, and Chief Sharp Nose, whose people settled around present-day Ethete. Chief Sharp Nose served with the U.S. Army and later lobbied in Washington for the General Allotment Act of 1887, which issued parcels of land (160 acres to the head of a house, 80 acres to single people over 18, and 40 acres to those under 18) to everyone on the reservation. Sharp Nose even named one of his sons after General Crook, whom he fought alongside during the Sioux wars of the 1870s.

The two tribes continue to jointly occupy the Wind River Reservation, with the Arapaho holding the eastern half (the towns of Ethete and Arapahoe) and the Shoshones the west (the towns of Fort Washakie, Burris, and Crowheart). In 1891, the Arapaho were given equal rights on the reservation, despite Shoshone Chief Washakie's continued attempts to have them removed. Although Chief Washakie's son married an Arapaho woman, there is still very little intermarriage between the tribes and little blending of the two cultures, even after more than a century.

RESERVATION LIFE

In the early reservation years every effort was made to break the spirit of the "savages" and make them into red-skinned Europeans (today's derogatory term is "Apples"—red on the outside, white on the inside). Even that most basic attribute—one's name—was taken away in the 1890s by the Commissioner of Indian Affairs. Thus Yellow Calf became George Caldwell and Night Horse became Henry Lee Tyler. Even William Shakespeare and Cornelius Vanderbilt suddenly became tribal members! The effort was not entirely successful: William Shakespeare was credited with bringing Peyotism—an important Native American religion today—to the Wind River Reservation. Other measures helped weaken the culture, including the repression of sun dances and other native religious practices, indoctrination by Christian missionaries, prohibition of face painting, and the forced cutting of young boys' long black hair. Today the nation is paying the price for these all-too-successful attempts to destroy Native American culture.

Most of the 5,000 Arapaho and 2,500 Shoshones live in housing built by the tribal council or in the hundreds of mobile homes that dot the reservation. From a non-Indian point of view, they are decidedly untidy, with junk of all sorts piled outside, but the folks who live here really don't care what outsiders think. You'll find older log cabins all over the back roads, their sod roofs collapsing and their log walls slowly returning to the earth. Several missions are scattered throughout this area, marked by attractive log or stucco churches.

Oil and gas revenues from major fields on the reservation provide millions of dollars each year in the form of monthly dividend payments. These royalties—along with various BIA assistance programs, ranching, farming, and tribal-owned businesses and leases—are the main source of income, though a new casino near Riverton will probably change that. An elected Business Council serves as the manager of tribal income.

The reservation is a center for fine beaded clothing and moccasins much prized by collectors. Arapaho patterns are geometric in nature, with rectangles and triangles appearing frequently. Arapaho women generally use red, black, blue, yellow, orange, and white as the main colors, with mountains, tepees, and butterflies as common motifs. Eastern Shoshone patterns tend to be more circular, with the rose a popular theme.

◀ INDIAN POWWOWS

Powwows fill the calendar on the Wind River Reservation, with events nearly every summer weekend; for details, contact the **Wind River Visitors Council** (307/856-7566 or 800/645-6233, www.wind-river.org). Shoshone Indian Days and the Ethete Powwow are the biggest of these.

The **Arapahoe Community Powwow** takes place the second weekend of June in the town of Arapahoe. On the fourth weekend of June, Fort Washakie is home to the **Treaty Day Celebration,** which includes Indian games, dancing, and a feast. It is immediately followed by the **Eastern Shoshone Indian Days Powwow and Rodeo,** with participants from across the West. In existence for more than 40 years, this all-Indian rodeo features bull riding,

POWWOWS

The Indian "powwow" (an Algonquian term meaning "medicine man") is a colorful celebration of Native American culture that cuts across tribal boundaries. Nobody knows the exact origin of powwows, but they may have developed from the Grass Dance of the Omaha and Pawnee tribes, who passed the dance on to various Plains tribes. The dance was used as a way of communicating with the Great Spirit, and the rhythmic beat of the drum helped send prayers skyward. Buffalo Bill Cody first introduced Indian dancers to audiences all over America and Europe, and in 1887 the Ponca Tribe began the first Indian fair and powwow. Other tribes joined in, and powwows became increasingly popular with the coming of the 20th century. The creation of "fancy dancing" allowed more personalized costumes and dances. Women were allowed to dance, and by the 1940s, Indians began traveling long distances to join other tribal powwows.

Dancers perform to a beat set up by different groups of drummers, who sing a repetitious song as they pound out the rhythm. The chant evokes images of somber ceremonies far out on the plains and of a lost culture. The dances originated from different tribes but have been adapted using the more colorful synthetic fabrics and beads of today. Professional dancers travel a circuit throughout the western states, and even non-Indians take part in powwows. Contestants wear numbers similar to those at track meets or rodeos and compete for cash awards (up to $5,000 at the biggest national powwows).

TRADITIONAL AND FANCY DANCING

Two main styles of powwow dance exist. In **traditional dancing,** the movements are slow and graceful, and dancers adhere to more authentic costumes and traditional dance steps. Male dancers wear bustles of eagle feathers, representing the birds of prey that once gathered over battlefields to feed on dead warriors. They also wear head roaches made from porcupine guard hairs. **Fancy dancing** is more casual — sort of an anything-goes dance in which the steps are chosen by the individual dancers. It generally involves lots of spins, bows, and head movements. Men's costumes are equally free-form, with all sorts of gaudy additions, particularly colorful bustles added to the shoulders and arms. Women's costumes for both traditional and fancy dancing are not as showy as men's, although they do include bells, elk teeth (or plastic copies), and shell decorations on the dresses, along with shawls and necklaces of hairpipe (originally small hollow bones, now often plastic).

POWWOW ACTIVITIES

The Wind River Reservation has a half dozen powwows throughout the year, most of which are held outdoors in arbor arenas. Tepees are set up, and the event becomes a joyful celebration of life and culture. Most of these are three-day-weekend events involving not just singing and dancing, but also traditional games, parades, and a "giveaway ceremony." Activities last all day and late into the evening. Things generally begin with a festive parade that includes a military honor guard and a powwow queen seated atop a car hood. Visitors are welcome at powwows, and photos are not usually a problem, although this is less true at Arapaho powwows. Be sure to stand when the eagle staff is brought in during the grand entry, and those wearing hats should remove them. If an eagle feather drops to the ground, all action must stop until it has been properly returned.

For information on powwows and other events on the reservation, contact the **Shoshone Tribal Cultural Center** (307/332-9106) or the **Wind River Visitors Council** (307/856-7566 or 800/645-6233, www.wind-river.org).

saddle bronc and bareback riding, calf roping, team roping, and the favorite—Indian relay horse racing, in which bareback riders rocket around the track in a chaos of flying dirt and colliding horses.

Ethete is home to the **Wyoming Indian High School Powwow** in May and the **Ethete Powwow** in July. The latter is one of the biggest in the area. The **Northern Arapaho Powwow** (oldest on the reservation) is held in Arapaho the first weekend of August. Summer ends with a **Labor Day Powwow** in Fort Washakie.

In addition to the powwows, **sun dances** take place in July and August at Ethete and Shoshone, but these are not really open to the public.

ARAPAHOE AND ST. STEPHENS

The town of Arapahoe is a small village on the southeastern edge of the reservation. It arose from animosity between the tribes as a subagency through which annuities could be distributed to the Arapaho without their having to face the taunts of "beggar" or "dog eater" from the Shoshones at Fort Washakie. The town's prominent white water tower is visible for miles.

St. Stephens Mission

In 1884, the St. Stephens Mission was established by Father John Jutz, a Jesuit missionary. Chief Black Coal consented to allow a mission to be built and later proved an ardent supporter of the school for Arapaho children. Until 1939, the Catholic Church operated a boarding school here. It was replaced by a day school that ran until the 1970s, when it became increasingly difficult to find priests and nuns to run the mission.

Visitors entering St. Stephens Mission pass a modern grade school built in 1983 and run by a secular corporation with an entirely Indian leadership. The most interesting sight at the mission is **St. Stephens Church,** built in 1928. Its white stucco exterior is covered with brilliant Arapaho geometric symbols. If the doors are unlocked, take a look at the colorful interior painted by local high-school students. Mass is held at 8 A.M., 10 A.M., and 5 P.M. on Sunday.

The **St. Stephens Mission Heritage Center** (307/856-4330) contains a small museum and gift shop. Some of the most interesting items for sale are locally made beadwork and collector dolls dressed in Arapaho costumes. The center is open 9 A.M.–noon and 1–4 P.M. Monday–Wednesday and Friday year-round. While here, pick up a copy of the quarterly magazine *Wind River Rendezvous* (307/856-6797) published by the mission; subscriptions are just $10 per year. Although this is a religious organization, the magazine deals with a range of historical and social issues.

A cemetery near the mission contains the graves of Chief Lone Bear, Francis Setting Eagle, and John Broken Horn, along with that of his wife, Sarah Broken Horn—a white woman (born Lizzie Fletcher) who had been captured as a child and raised as an Indian. (See *Arlington* in the *Medicine Bow Country* chapter for more on this story.) The outlaw Butch Cassidy was a frequent visitor to Chief Lone Bear's camp.

St. Stephens Church

© DON PITCHER

SACAGAWEA

Fictional books about Sacagawea (sak-uh-juh-WEE-uh) describe her as a beautiful Indian maiden, a guide, a peacemaker, a heroine, and a mother – sort of the original Superwoman. Historian James Truslow Adams declared her one of the six most important women in American history. The reality is a bit less romantic but still fascinating. Sacagawea – her name meant "Bird Woman" in Shoshone – was born around 1784 in what is now eastern Idaho. As a child, she was captured by the Minnetaree tribe and later sold to a French Canadian trapper and interpreter named Toussaint Charbonneau. He eventually made her one of his many wives.

THE LEWIS AND CLARK EXPEDITION

In 1803, President Thomas Jefferson negotiated the Louisiana Purchase from the French. For the fire-sale price of $16 million he suddenly doubled the size of the young United States of America. Captains Meriwether Lewis and William Clark were selected to lead a secret exploration of this vast land. They left St. Louis in late 1804 and camped that first winter in North Dakota, where they met Sacagawea and her husband Charbonneau. Lewis and Clark didn't think much of the ill-tempered and untrustworthy Charbonneau, but they realized the value of having with the expedition a Shoshone woman who was fluent in English and French. Charbonneau was hired, with the stipulation that his wife come along.

During the winter, Sacagawea gave birth to a baby boy (Baptiste), and when the troupe headed out two months later, the child was on her back in a cradle board. Contrary to the romanticized novels, her role was not so much that of guide as interpreter, as one who knew the edible plants along the way, and as a symbol of the expedition's friendly intentions. When the expedition reached the Continental Divide, they happened upon Sacagawea's sister and brother, whom she had not seen since being kidnapped six years before. The Shoshones agreed to provide guides and horses to cross the Rockies.

After an arduous journey, the exploration party reached the Pacific Ocean that fall and established winter quarters near the mouth of the Columbia River. They returned across the mountains the following summer, and Sacagawea, Charbonneau, and their son returned to their old existence in Mandan country. The rest of the expedition party reached St. Louis on September 23, 1806, long after everyone but President Jefferson had given them up for dead. The trip proved a vital step in bringing the Northwest under the U.S. flag.

LATER YEARS

From here, Sacagawea's story becomes murkier. Some researchers claim that she died in 1812 of "putrid fever" at Fort Mandan in North Dakota. Dakota folks generally tell this version. Wyoming partisans prefer another story: that the woman who died so young was one of Charbonneau's other wives, and that Sacagawea continued to live for many more years. After

ETHETE

Ethete (EE-thuh-tee) is the primary Arapaho settlement on the reservation. People live in trailer homes scattered on small plots around town or in ticky-tacky box houses built by the BIA. (The prefabricated houses are known as the "Easter Egg Village" because of the bright colors.) Tepee poles lean against the barns, and the bright tribal colors and geometric patterns dominate the launderette/video store. "Downtown" Ethete consists of a stoplight—the only one on the reservation—surrounded by a grocery store, a gas station, a community hall, a

high school, and the launderette. All of this is entirely forgettable, but not nearby St. Michael's Mission.

St. Michael's Mission

Established in 1887 by Reverend John Roberts of the Episcopal Church, this mission is the town's reason for existence. When Chief Sharp Nose was asked for his approval to build here, the response was *Ethete,* meaning "Good." Constructed between 1910 and 1917, the buildings are arranged in a circle around a grassy lawn. Most are fabricated leaving her abusive husband, she wandered all over the West – gaining the name Wad-ze-Wipe (Lost Woman) – before finally ending up on the Wind River Reservation with her fellow Shoshones. She served a crucial role as translator for Chief Washakie in negotiations to establish the reservation and was often seen wearing one of the peace medals given out by Lewis and Clark. Sacagawea (or at least the Wyoming version) died on April 9, 1884, and was buried near Fort Washakie in a cemetery overlooking the Wind River. Although the Shoshones had heard her tell of the expedition many times, it wasn't until 25 years later that Anglo historians began to realize who the "Lost Woman" really was. The 13,569-foot Mt. Sacagawea in the Wind River Mountains is named for the remarkable woman who remained unrecognized much of her life. An image representing Sacagawea also appears on America's rarely seen one-dollar coins.

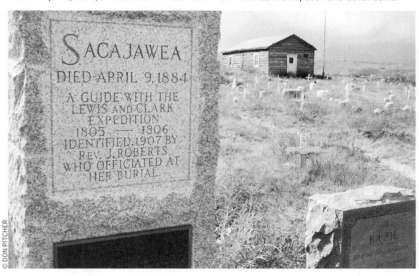

© DON PITCHER

from cobblestones, with Arapaho designs on the doors, but the **Church of Our Father's House** is made of log. Inside this fascinating building built in the shape of a cross are rustic handmade wooden benches and a central Arapaho drum. Altar seats are made of elk antlers, and the back window faces the great Wind River Mountains.

Across the circle is the **Arapaho Cultural Museum,** housing a small but remarkable collection of artifacts that encompasses beaded garments, medicine pouches, peace pipes, photographs, and warbonnets, including that of Yellow Calf, last chief of the Arapahos. The museum is open only by appointment; call 307/332-2660 2–3 days ahead to visit.

◖ FORT WASHAKIE

Fort Washakie is the center of activity on the Wind River Reservation. The BIA compound is here (locals insist the initials stand for Boss Indians Around) and so is the tribal council headquarters. Fort Washakie was the home of Chief Washakie, the longtime leader of the Shoshones. Behind Chief Washakie's town are a series of dramatic escarpments and canyons, and through a gap in the hills you can peer into the mighty Wind River Mountains.

In 1869, the U.S. Army established a fort, Camp Augur (later Camp Brown), along the Popo Agie River to protect the Shoshones from attacks by Arapaho and Sioux warriors. The fort was later moved a dozen miles west and renamed Fort Washakie, making this the only fort ever named for an Indian chief. It remained open until 1909, when the threat of conflict between the Shoshones and Arapaho had diminished. A number of interesting structures still stand, including a **stone guardhouse.** They are now used by the BIA.

Sights

Despite its minuscule size, Fort Washakie has an array of interesting sights. The **Shoshone Tribal Center** (307/332-9106, open 9 A.M.–4 P.M. Mon.–Fri. year-round, donation), next to the elementary school, contains historical photos, Chief Washakie's eagle-feather headdress, leather shirt, pipe, and pipe bag, along with other historical items. A dramatic statue of the chief stands in front of the tribal building; it's identical to one at the U.S. Capitol Building.

Built in 1913, Fort Washakie's historic **White House** is another interesting building. South Fork Road west from Fort Washakie passes the **Washakie Graveyard,** where a substantial granite memorial notes that Washakie was "Always loyal to the government and his white brothers. A wise ruler." Washakie was buried here with full military honors, the only chief of his time to be so recognized by the U.S. government. Directly across the road from the cemetery is the **R. V. Greeves Art Gallery** (307/332-3557, open by appointment only). Greeves is one of the state's most famous sculptors; his *The Unknown* is in the Buffalo Bill Historical Center in Cody.

Continue another mile along this road (stay left at the Y and turn left again at the Full Gospel Revival Center's log church) to the **Sacagawea Cemetery,** perhaps the most beautiful cemetery in Wyoming. The remote setting offers views of the Wind River Mountains. When I last visited, the sun was play-

ing behind darkly rumbling thunderheads atop the Wind Rivers while horses whinnied in the fields below. Sacagawea's gravesite (the Wyoming version) is marked by an impressive granite headstone, and one of her sons, John Baptiste, is buried alongside. A granddaughter and other descendants are up the hill. The graveyard also contains an old log church, a statue of Sacagawea, and far too many recent graves of young people from the reservation.

The historic **Shoshone Episcopal Mission** is on Trout Creek Road, 1.5 miles southwest of Fort Washakie (turn east just beyond the Hines General Store), and was founded in 1883 by Reverend John Roberts, a Welsh missionary known as "White Robe." A boarding school for Indian girls was built in 1891. The two-story brick-and-stone building still stands, although the school closed in 1945. A simple log mission chapel is nearby.

Hot Springs

Three miles east of Fort Washakie on the way to Ethete is **Chief Washakie Plunge** (307/332-4530, $5 adults, $2.50 seniors and kids, free for anyone under seven), where 110°F sulfur-rich water flows from a hot springs into an outdoor swimming pool complete with a water slide, diving board, and hot tub. The springs were a favorite place of Chief Washakie. Maybe these mineral waters are what helped him live for 102 years! Private indoor tub baths are also available, and the facilities are wheelchair-accessible. Open 9 A.M.–9 P.M. Tuesday–Sunday in the summer and 9 A.M.–5 P.M. Wednesday–Sunday the rest of the year.

Practicalities

Wind River Trading Co. (307/332-3267), next to Hines General Store, has tacky mass-produced beadwork, moccasins, blankets, and baskets. Fortunately, the store also houses **Gallery of the Wind** (307/332-4321), containing peace pipes, beaded jewelry (both Shoshone and Arapaho designs), flutes, and honey from the Wind River Reservation. An impressive historical collection of feathered warbonnets and other cultural items (not for sale) are along the walls. The

Shoshone Tribal Service Station has a deli and sells locally made crafts and beadwork.

Camping is available at Ray Lake, Red Rocks, and along the Little Wind River just north of Wind River Agency. You'll need a $5 recreation stamp from the Tribal Fish and Game Office (307/332-7207).

Ray Lake Campground, at the intersection of U.S. 287 and Hwy. 132 (307/332-9333, $8 d tents, $15 RVs, open May–Sept.) has a country location (but no trees) and a small café. Showers for noncampers cost $3. It's run by friendly folks, and the remote country setting provides classic Wyoming scenery.

WEST TO DUBOIS

As you head northwest along U.S. 26/287, the Wind River Mountains and Absarokas grow ever closer, and the Wind River Valley begins to narrow. Crowheart Butte dominates the skyline to the north for many miles, and then you drop over a rise to discover a stunning landscape of red-rock badlands accented by the green of cottonwoods along the Wind River. For the next 20 miles, travelers are treated to a constantly changing panorama of gloriously colorful badlands topography, with 11,635-foot Ramshorn Peak rising in the distance. It's a geologist's dreamscape. Several reservoirs provide irrigation and recreation on the Wind River Reservation. Largest is **Bull Lake,** along the western margin. The Shoshones say that it is haunted by a supernatural water buffalo. The aquamarine waters of **Ocean Lake** are well known for bass and crappie fishing. Other people come to swim, water-ski, sailboard, hunt, or watch birds. Seven free camping areas are scattered around the lakeshore.

Crowheart Butte

The tiny settlement of **Crowheart** consists of an old-fashioned country store and gas station surrounded by irrigated fields and grazing cattle. A couple of miles northeast of the store—and visible for many miles in any direction—is a regal summit, Crowheart Butte, looking like a pyramid whose top got caught in a giant lawnmower.

The name comes from an 1866 battle in the Wind River Valley. The Shoshones and Bannocks fought the Crows over hunting rights. The Crows had been "given" the valley in the Fort Laramie Treaty of 1851, while the Shoshones and Bannocks were "given" the same land in the 1863 Fort Bridger Treaty. Four days of intense fighting led to a standoff, and to prevent further bloodshed the chiefs declared a winner-takes-all fight near this butte. Charging each other on horseback with lances drawn, both were thrown in the collision, and the fight turned into a hand-to-hand struggle. In the battle, Shoshone Chief Washakie killed Crow Chief Big Robber and then carried his heart around on a lance, a gesture of admiration for a brave fighter. Hence the name Crowheart Butte. When Chief Washakie was later asked about the story, he replied, "When a man is in battle and his blood runs hot, he sometimes does things that he is sorry for afterwards. I cannot remember everything that happened so long ago." Washakie later took one of the captured Crow girls as one of his wives.

Crowheart Butte is regarded as something of a sacred place by local Indians and is used as a place of spiritual renewal for young men on vision quests. A small rock shelter stands on the top for this purpose. Non-Indians are legally forbidden to climb Crowheart Butte, and legends claim that those who do so may disappear.

Whiskey Basin

The highway continues its slow and scenic climb to Dubois, crossing the cottonwood-lined Wind River three times en route. Approximately 25 miles west of Crowheart (five miles east of Dubois), a sign points the way to Whiskey Basin. Follow the gravel road two miles to the **Dubois State Fish Hatchery** (307/455-2431, open 8 A.M.–5 P.M. daily), where rainbow, cutthroat, golden, brook, and brown trout as well as grayling are raised. The bucolic setting is hard to beat: a tree-lined creek surrounded by sage, mountains, and badlands.

A short distance up the road is a wildlife-viewing kiosk for the **Whiskey Basin Wildlife Habitat Area.** During winter the valley is home to the largest population of Rocky Mountain bighorn sheep anywhere on earth. About 650 sheep congregate here because of the mild winters and the shallow snow. Although you're likely to find sheep all winter, the best time to photograph them is in the breeding season, late November–December. During this period you'll see rams charging headfirst into each other over the chance to mate. It's enough to give you a headache. The lambs are born in late May and early June high on rocky slopes. Bighorn sheep are also sometimes seen in the meadows along the highway or in the hills just above Dubois. The National Bighorn Sheep Interpretive Center in Dubois leads wildlife tours of Whiskey Basin.

Beyond the wildlife-viewing kiosk, the road follows Torrey Creek up past a string of three small bodies of water: Torrey, Ring, and Trail lakes. These were created by retreating glaciers centuries ago, but small dams have enlarged them. State Game and Fish **campsites** (free) lie along Ring and Trail lakes. **Ring Lake Ranch** (307/455-2663, www.ringlake.org) houses an ecumenical religious facility used for a variety of retreats, seminars, and other activities.

A very popular trailhead at the end of the road up Whiskey Basin (12 miles from the turnoff) provides access to the primary route up to Dinwoody Glacier and 13,804-foot Gannett Peak (Wyoming's highest). At mile 8, be sure to visit the historic buildings of **Lucius Burch Center at Trail Lake Ranch** (307/455-2353 or 877/891-2357, www.traillakeranch.org), a nonprofit environmental camp with multiday workshops on natural history throughout the summer. Six-night programs cost $800 per person, including lodging, meals, and activities.

You'll discover quite a few **Indian pictographs** on large boulders in the Trail Lake vicinity; look for them along the hillside between Trail Lake and the south end of Ring Lake. (Unmarked wooden posts are near some of them). These figures—some four feet tall—are elaborate otherworldly creations with horns and headdresses, and they are believed to represent shamans performing ceremonies under altered states of consciousness. While their age is unknown, they are probably at least 2,000 years old and of Athapaskan (a Canadian tribe) rather than Shoshonean origin. This is some of the oldest rock art in Wyoming. Do not touch, make rubbings, or put anything in contact with the pictographs since it could cause damage to these irreplaceable signs from the past.

Dubois

Approaching Dubois (pop. 1,000, elev. 6,917 feet) from either direction, you drive through the extraordinary red, yellow, and gray badlands that set this country apart. The luxuriant Wind River winds its way down a narrow valley where horses graze in the irrigated pastures and old barns and newer log homes stand against the hills, while the tree-covered Absaroka and Wind River mountains ring distant views. The town of Dubois consists of a long main street that makes an abrupt elbow turn and then points due west toward the mountains. The log buildings and snatches of wooden sidewalks give the place an authen-

tic frontier feel. Locals live in cabins, trailer homes, and simple frame houses. Dubois weather is famously mild; warm Chinook winds often melt any snow that falls. Grand scenery reigns in all directions. Snowmobilers, hunters, and anglers have discovered that Dubois provides a good place to relax in Wyoming's "banana belt" while remaining close to the more temperamental mountains. The area basks in an average of 300 days of sunshine each year. By the way, Dubois is pronounced "DU-boys"; other pronunciations will reveal your tenderfoot status. Locals sometimes jokingly call it "Dubious."

To Yellowstone and Jackson Hole

TOGWOTEE PASS

To Double Cabin Campground

Brooks Lake

BROOKS LAKE

DUBOIS VICINITY

BROOKS LAKE LODGE

Pinnacle Buttes

Du Noir Creek Rd.

FALLS

Ramshorn Peak 11,635ft

HORSE CREEK

TIE HACK MEMORIAL

HORSE CREEK RD.

WARM SPRINGS RD.

Continental Divide

Wind River

SCENIC OVERLOOK

NATIONAL BIGHORN SHEEP INTERPRETIVE CENTER

Bridger-Teton National Forest

Shoshone National Forest

Badlands

Dubois

To Lander and Riverton

HATCHERY

Union Pass 9,210ft

WHISKEY BASIN HABITAT AREA

Torrey Lake

Ring Lake

0   5 mi

0   5 km

To Green River Lakes and Pinedale

Trail Lake

© AVALON TRAVEL PUBLISHING, INC.

HISTORY

Dubois began in the 1880s when pioneer ranchers and more than a few rustlers, including Butch Cassidy, settled in the area, followed by Scandinavian hand-loggers who cut lodgepole for railroad ties. The town that grew up along the juncture of Horse Creek and the Wind River was first known as Never Sweat, but when citizens applied for a post office the Postal Service refused to allow the name and suggested Dubois instead—the name of an Idaho senator who just happened to be on the Senate committee that provided funding for the post office.

Like many edge-of-the-mountain towns, Dubois is in transition. For most of its existence, it served as a logging and ranching center. After the sawmill closed in 1987, loggers blamed environmentalists and the Forest Service for sharply reducing the timber available; environmentalists countered that the company was simply using the reductions as an excuse to close an aging mill. After they all ran out of mud to sling, they decided to look at what Dubois had to offer and discovered that, lo and behold, they just happened to be sitting in an almost-undiscovered recreational and retirement gold mine. The transformation of Dubois to a visitor-oriented economy certainly has its downside—elaborate "trophy" log summer homes are beginning to overrun the lush pastures on both ends of town—but so far this pretty little place has been spared the onslaught of "industrial tourism." Still, old attitudes die hard, and you'll see pickup trucks with bumper stickers saying "Save Wyoming's wildlife. Shoot a tree hugger" or "Wolves—Government sponsored terrorists."

WIND RIVER MOUNTAINS

SIGHTS

Just west of Dubois is a signed turnoff to a **scenic overlook**. The gravel road climbs sharply (no RVs) for approximately one mile to the viewpoint, where displays note the surrounding peaks. Enjoy marvelous views of 11,635-foot Ramshorn Peak from here. **Rocky Mountain bighorn sheep** crowd the Dubois area in the winter. Many are visible on the hills just south of town, with hundreds more gathered in the Whiskey Basin Habitat Area, five miles east.

The magnificent badlands on both sides of Dubois, but especially to the east, are well worth exploring. The fascinating **Badlands Interpretive Trail** heads up Mason Draw, 2.4 miles northeast of town. Pick up a booklet describing the trail (not well maintained) at the chamber of commerce office.

Rock hounds will find all sorts of petrified wood, agates, and other colorful rocks up the Wiggins Fork and Horse Creek drainages; ask at the chamber of commerce for directions.

One thing you certainly would not expect to find in Dubois is a training center for lawyers, but famed Wyoming attorney Gerry Spence has one on his Thunderbird Ranch east of town. His nonprofit (!) **Trial Lawyers College** (760/322-3783 or 800/688-1611, www.trial-lawyerscollege.com) puts about 50 lawyers through an intense four-week session each summer, with mock trials and professional actors. Watch your step with all these lawyers around Dubois.

〔 National Bighorn Sheep Interpretive Center

The National Bighorn Sheep Interpretive Center (907 W. Ramshorn, 307/455-3429 or 888/209-2795, www.bighorn.org, $2 adults, $0.75 kids under 12, or $10 families) houses displays on desert bighorn, Rocky Mountain bighorn, stone sheep, and Dall sheep. The museum details how the population was brought back from the brink of extinction, and it includes hands-on exhibits and interactive displays on how bighorns live. Also here is a diorama of a Sheepeater Indian trap and mounted specimens around a 16-foot-high cen-

THE HARD DAY'S WORK OF TIE HACKS

Many of the trees cut in Wyoming's forests between 1870 and 1940 went to supply railroad ties for an ever-expanding network of rails throughout the Rockies. The men who cut these ties – tie hacks – spent long, hard months in the mountains, working through the winter. Most the woodsmen were emigrants from Sweden, Norway, Finland, Austria, and Italy. Tie hacks first felled a suitable lodgepole pine using a bucksaw, then limbed the tree and used a broadax to hew the tie into shape, finally peeling the remaining bark from the sides and cutting it to length. Hundreds of thousands of ties – each eight feet long and at least five inches on each side – were produced annually by tie hacks. Horses dragged the ties down to a creek bank or flume to await high spring flows, when thousands of ties could be sent downriver at once. The enormous log jams that resulted sometimes required dyna-

mite to loosen. Downstream booms caught the logs, where they could be hauled up and loaded onto railway cars.

Tie hacks found work in many parts of Wyoming, but especially in the Medicine Bow Mountains, Laramie Mountains, Sierra Madre, Big Horn Mountains, and Wind River Mountains, where major streams provided a way for the ties to reach the railheads. In the upper Wind River country, the industry spanned three decades, from 1914 to 1946. During this time, more than 10 million ties were cut and floated downstream to Riverton, where the Chicago and Northwestern Railroad used them. A stone monument to the tie hacks stands along U.S. 26/287 approximately 18 miles west of Dubois. The visitor center in Dubois has a handout that provides a self-guided tour of historical sights associated with the tie hacks.

tral "mountain." A theater shows videos on bighorn sheep and other topics, and a gift shop sells books and other items. The center is open 9 A.M.–8 P.M. daily Memorial Day–Labor Day and 9 A.M.–5 P.M. daily the rest of the year. Free Wednesday evening campfire talks are put on by the center in the summer.

The center offers wildlife tours of the **Whiskey Basin Habitat Area** just west of town November–March. These four-hour van-and-hiking trips cost $25 per person and include binoculars and spotting scopes to view the animals. Reservations are required. The center also has brochures describing self-guided tours of Whiskey Basin.

Dubois Museum

Just up the street from the Bighorn Sheep Interpretive Center, the Dubois Museum (909 W. Ramshorn, 307/455-2284, www.dubois-museum.org, $1 adults or $0.50 kids under 12) is open 9 A.M.–6 P.M. daily June–September and 10 A.M.–4 P.M. Tuesday–Saturday the rest of the year. The small museum houses a handful of exhibits on the Sheepeater Indians and their pictographs, with other displays on ranch life, geology, and wildlife. Be sure to check out the hilarious photo of 1930s movie star Tim McCoy teaching golf to a rather skeptical group of Shoshone Indians! Out front are seven historic log cabins and an old gas station, all containing interesting displays. Next to the museum is the **Headwaters Arts and Conference Center,** where an upstairs gallery (307/455-3404, www.wrvag.org) exhibits works by regional artists. It's open daily in the summer.

ENTERTAINMENT AND EVENTS

Dubois is a hopping place during the summer, especially on weekends. Find country-and-western bands at **Rustic Pine Tavern** (119 E. Ramshorn, 307/455-2430), a classic Western bar with elk and moose heads, plenty of old wood, and a pool table. Check out the ashtrays, which note, "God spends his vacation here." **Outlaw Saloon** (204 W. Ramshorn, 307/455-

2387) has music some nights, plus famous Tuesday-night **square dances** that bring in dudes from local ranches in July and August. You may want to avoid this night if you don't want to be overwhelmed with fellow visitors.

The first weekend of February brings **Winterfest** with sled dog and skijoring races (cross-country skiing while being pulled by a dog), a bread and soup cook-off, cowboy storytelling, and a hootenanny. In mid-May **Dubois Antler Rendezvous** brings five days of elk antler–selling in Dubois's town park. The **Swedish Smorgasbord** in mid-June celebrates the Scandinavian tie hacks with a big dinner of Scandinavian favorites.

Spur Spangled Celebration on Fourth of July weekend brings the biggest local event, with a parade, ice-cream social, rodeo, chariot races, Western barbecue, fireworks, and rubber-ducky races down the river. In mid-July, **Dubois Museum Day** is a folk art festival with Indian dancing, frontier crafts demonstrations, and lectures.

A **National Art Show** comes to town on the last week of July, attracting both professionals and amateurs. It's been going on for more than 50 years. Also don't miss the always popular Dubois firefighters' **Buffalo Barbecue,** held the second Saturday of August. Get specifics on these and other events from the Dubois Chamber of Commerce, 307/455-2556.

On Friday evenings mid-June–mid-August, you'll find **rodeos** at the town arena. **Archaeology Days** in August brings guest lectures and workshops at the Dubois Museum.

SHOPPING

Trapline Gallery (120 E. Ramshorn, 307/455-2800) sells Indian-crafted beadwork, jewelry, and artwork, as well as furs. **Tukadeka Traders/Horse Creek Gallery** (104 E. Ramshorn, 307/455-3345) has an impressive collection of antique trade beads for sale, along with tacky antler carvings and Indian trinkets.

A few doors down is a nice bookshop, **Two Ocean Books** (128 E. Ramshorn, 307/455-3554). **Water Wheel Gift Shop** (113 E. Ramshorn, 307/455-2112) also carries a selection of

Wyoming titles. Drop by **Wind River Gear** (19 N. 1st St., 307/455-3468) for outdoor clothing and backpacking gear.

Buy stylish Western wear inside the historic **Welty's General Store** (113 W. Ramshorn, 307/455-2377). The hours are haphazard. Be sure to ask about Butch Cassidy's priceless old pistol, although you won't be able to see it because it's locked away.

For fishing supplies, head to **Whiskey Mountain Tackle** (1428 Warm Springs Dr., 307/455-2587).

RECREATION

Dubois sits at the confluence of the Wind River and Horse Creek, and both streams provide good trout fishing right in town. Hot springs keep the Wind River flowing all year, and a shady riverside park is next to the National Bighorn Sheep Center. The visitor center has descriptions of local fishing holes and brochures from local outfitters who offer pack trips and horseback rides.

The nine-hole **Antelope Hills Golf Course** (307/455-2888) is on the western end of Dubois.

Winter Play

The Absarokas and Wind River Mountains around Dubois are crowded with **snowmobilers** during winter, and several places rent "sleds" in town and nearby. Don't expect peace and quiet with all of these machines roaring through the backcountry! More than 300 miles of trails head out in all directions, with the Union Pass area a particular focus.

For something quieter, **cross-country skiers** will find trails near Falls Campground and Brooks Lake (both 23 miles west of town) and Togwotee Mountain Lodge (40 miles west) and in backcountry wilderness areas off-limits to snowmobiles.

ACCOMMODATIONS

Dubois makes an excellent stopping point on the way to Yellowstone and Grand Teton national parks, with lodging prices well below those in Jackson Hole. All places are open year-round unless noted otherwise.

If you're looking for quietude, head three miles east of town to **Riverside Inn and Campground** (307/455-2337 or 877/489-2337, www.riversideinnandcampground.com), where the motel rooms start at $35 s or $45 d; units with full kitchens are $54 d. Guests have fishing access to a private stretch of the river and the inn sits on 50 acres. Riverside is open May–November.

Wind River Motel (519 W. Ramshorn, 307/455-2611 or 877/455-2621, www.dte-world.com/windriver, $35–75 s or $45–75 d) has a mix of rustic cabins, comfy motel rooms (some with kitchenettes), and suites. There's a relaxing riverside deck in the back. Most units contain fridges and microwaves; open May–October.

A fine riverside place is **Black Bear Country Inn** (505 W. Ramshorn, 307/455-2344 or 800/873-2327, www.blackbearcountryinn.com), where rooms (all with fridges and microwaves) cost $45–60 d. A kitchenette apartment sleeps up to eight people for $100.

Branding Iron Inn (401 Ramshorn, 307/455-2893 or 888/651-9378, www.brandingironinn.com, $60–85 d) has cozy and well-maintained duplex log cabins that were built in the 1940s, but that aresubstantially updated. Some units contain kitchenettes, and out back are corrals for folks traveling with horses.

Trail's End Motel (511 Ramshorn, 307/455-2540 or 888/455-6660, www.trailsendmotel.com) has remodeled rooms starting for $54 s or $59 d. The nicest rooms ($84–109 d) have decks facing the Wind River and include in-room fridges and microwaves. Also available are two-room family units that sleep eight for $144.

For historic rooms, stay at **C Twin Pines Lodge and Cabins** (218 Ramshorn, 307/455-2600 or 800/550-6332, www.twinpineslodge.com, $65 s or $70–80 d). Built in 1934 and listed on the National Register of Historic Places, the lodge has both modern and rustic cabins. Amenities include a filling breakfast, fridges, VCRs, and Wi-Fi throughout. Everything is immaculate in this place that gracefully blends the old and new.

Find attractive accommodations at the largest motel in town, **Stagecoach Motor Inn** (103 Ramshorn, 307/455-2303 or 800/455-5090, www.stagecoachmotel-dubois.com). Rates are $70 d, six-person kitchenettes cost $98, and king suites run $85 d. Wireless Internet is available throughout the motel, and families appreciate the outdoor pool, hot tub, and shady backyard play area.

One-half mile east of Dubois, **Chinook Winds Mountain Lodge** (307/455-2987 or 800/863-0354) has motel units for $75 d and cabins with full kitchens and jetted tubs for $80 d. The Wind River is right out the back door.

Bed-and-Breakfast

Just two blocks from downtown Dubois is **The Stone House B&B** (207 S. 1st St., 307/455-2555, www.duboisbnb.com). Inside this stately home are two guest rooms ($50–65 s or $55–65 d) with shared baths, along with a basement suite ($70 s or $75 d) that has a private bath. Adjacent is a three-room cottage; $85 d or $105 for four people. A full breakfast is served each morning, and the sitting room faces Whiskey Mountain, a good place to watch for bighorn sheep. Open May–October.

Dude Ranches and Mountain Lodges

Quite a few dude ranches/mountain lodges are found in the Dubois area, including the country west of here on the way to Togwotee Pass.

Ten miles out East Fork Road, **Lazy L&B Ranch** (307/455-2839 or 800/453-9488, www.lazylb.com) is a century-old ranch offering creekside log cabins, horseback riding, a swimming pool, hot tub, stocked fishing ponds, kids' programs, volleyball and pool, fly-fishing, and a rifle range. The ranch's horseback-riding program is excellent, and guests can choose trips through the badlands or high into the mountains. Lazy L&B is open late May–mid-September, with all-inclusive weekly rates of $2,500 for two people; adults only after Labor Day. The ranch also operates **Bear Basin Wilderness Camp** (www.bearbasincamp.com), a wonderful base from which

to explore the Washakie Wilderness on horseback. A maximum of eight guests stay in wall tents during these backcountry trips.

Sixteen miles north of Dubois in gorgeous Dunoir Valley, **Absaroka Ranch** (307/455-2275, www.absarokaranch.com) has all of the typical guest-ranch offerings: horseback riding, guided fly-fishing, hiking, and cookouts. The ranch accommodates just 18 guests and emphasizes the personal touch. It is surrounded by national forest land and has a comfortable main lodge (built in 1910), attractively restored log cabins, and a redwood sauna. The ranch is open mid-June–mid-September. All-inclusive weekly rates are $2,800 for two people.

Bitterroot Ranch (307/455-2778 or 800/545-0019, www.bitterrootranch.com) emphasizes horseback riding for riders at all levels of ability; each guest gets to ride several different horses. The owners breed Arabian horses and offer cross-country jumping courses, pack trips, cattle drives, fly-fishing, and kids' programs. Both French and German are spoken here, attracting an international clientele. The ranch is open June–September and has space for 32 guests in a dozen cabins. All-inclusive weekly rates are $3,000–3,500 for two people. The owners also run Equitors (www.equitours.com), a travel agency specializing in horseback rides all over the globe.

South of Dubois in beautiful Jakeys Fork Canyon, **CM Ranch** (307/455-2331 or 800/455-0721, www.cmranch.com) is one of Wyoming's oldest dude ranches; it's been here since 1927. The ranch offers dramatic badlands topography and a variety of fossils, making it a favorite of geologists (and amateur rock hounds). Trails lead into the adjacent Fitzpatrick Wilderness, a destination for horseback trips. Fishing is another popular activity, and a fishing guide is available. The immaculate lodge buildings have space for 55 guests, and kids love the big outdoor pool and a hot tub. All-inclusive weekly rates at this delightful old-time ranch are $2,600–2,800 for two people. The ranch is owned by the Kemmerer family, whose ancestors founded the town of Kemmerer, Wyoming. The Kemmerers also own Jackson Hole Mountain Resort.

Operating as a dude ranch since 1920, **T-Cross Ranch** (307/455-2206 or 877/827-6770, www.tcross.com) is 15 miles north of Dubois near Horse Creek and is open mid-June–September. Surrounded by the Shoshone National Forest, this remote ranch has weekly accommodations at $2,750 for two people, including horseback riding, all meals, activities for kids, trout fishing, and a hot tub. Backcountry pack trips and other activities are also available. Lodging is in eight comfortable log cabins, and the main lodge has a massive stone fireplace and spacious front porch.

Sixteen miles west of Dubois is **Mackenzie Highland Ranch** (307/455-3415, www.mackenziehighlandranch.com), where accommodations are offered in a variety of cabins and other rustic buildings. The simplest cabins share a bathhouse and cost $45 for up to four people. Considerably nicer are the two-bedroom cabins with space for seven, full kitchens, baths, and living rooms that sleep up to seven for $215. The finest is a modern four-bedroom home (it sleeps eight) with two baths and a full kitchen for $245. There's a three-night minimum stay. This isn't an all-inclusive dude ranch, but trail rides, meals, ATV rentals, and guided fishing trips are offered in the summer, and the ranch is a base for snowmobilers, cross-country skiers, and hunters at other times of the year. A section of Mackenzie Highland Ranch is used for lepidopterology research each summer, with graduate-level classes offered through Sam Houston State University. This unique program is run by professor Karölis Bagdonas, a specialist in moths and butterflies; he discovered the surprisingly vital importance of moths in the diet of Yellowstone grizzlies.

In the mountains 18 miles west of Dubois, **Triangle C Dude Ranch** (307/455-2225 or 800/661-4928, www.trianglec.com) was established as the first tie-hack camp in the region and now operates as a summertime guest ranch and wintertime snowmobiling and cross-country skiing center. In summer, the main emphasis is horseback riding, but guests will also enjoy fishing, hiking, children's activities, wagon rides, and evening entertainment. Weekly rates are $3,400 for two people. The ranch is open Memorial Day–Labor Day for summer fun, plus mid-December–March for snowmobiling.

Twenty miles west of Dubois is **Lava Mountain Lodge** (307/455-2506 or 800/919-9570, www.lavamountainlodg.com), where motel rooms are $65 d, and cabins with kitchenettes (but no TVs) go for $75 d, or $130 in five-person cabins. You'll also find a restaurant with home-cooked meals three times a day, along with camping spaces ($8 tents, $27 RVs). Open year-round, with snowmobile rentals in the winter, and corrals in the back for folks traveling with horses.

(See *Mountain Resorts* in the *Jackson Hole* chapter for information on Brooks Lake Lodge—on the lake of the same name—and Togwotee Mountain Lodge—a few miles west of Togwotee Pass.)

Camping

The closest public camping spot is **Horse Creek Campground** ($8; open late May–Sept.), 12 miles north of Dubois on Horse Creek Road.

Dubois Wind River KOA (225 W. Welty, 307/455-2238 or 800/562-0806, www.koa.com, $20 tents, $30–34 RVs, $40–45 cabins, open May–Sept.) is one of Wyoming's better private campgrounds, with an indoor pool and a riverside location, plus occasional Western music concerts. Showers for noncampers are $5.

Riverside Inn and Campground (307/455-2337 or 877/489-2337, www.riversideinnandcampground.com, $16 tents, $24 RVs, open May–Nov.) has a quiet location three miles east of town.

FOOD
Breakfast and Lunch

Popular with both locals and tourists, **Cowboy Café** (115 E. Ramshorn, 307/455-2595) has good home-style breakfasts with big helpings of biscuits and gravy, and delicious lunches that include homemade soups and pies made by the French chef.

Village Cafe/Daylight Donuts (515 W. Ramshorn, 307/455-2122) offers doughnuts and coffee in the morning and pizza and fried-chicken dinners when evening rolls around.

Kathy's Koffee (306 W. Ramshorn, 307/455-3862) operates from a little log cabin with a deck and picnic tables in the back, and a light menu of salads, sandwiches, wraps, smoothies, shakes, espresso, and bagels. This is where the fishing outfitters hold court.

American

Next to the Super 8 on the west end of town, **Chandler's Ranch House Cuisine** (1408 Warm Springs Dr., 307/455-2115) opens at 6 A.M. every day, and it doesn't close until 10 P.M. You'll find down-home cooking, fast service, and all-American meals for reasonable prices.

Rustic Pine Steakhouse (119 E. Ramshorn, 307/455-2772) is a carnivore's delight, with prime rib on Friday and Saturday nights; open for dinner only. Get malts and sundaes from the old-time soda fountain inside the **Dubois Drugstore** (126 E. Ramshorn, 307/455-2300).

The Really Wild Bunch Grill and Bar (206 W. Ramshorn, 307/433-3670) has a family atmosphere, burgers, steaks, fish, fried chicken, and a big salad bar.

Fine Dining

C Café Wyoming (106 E. Ramshorn, 307/455-3828, www.cafewyoming.com, closed Sun.–Mon.) sits back from the street along Horse Creek. The "cowboy-country-French" food is distinctive and creative, with a lunch and dinner menu that changes every week. Chef Ken Wolfe always has pastas, chicken, seafood, sandwiches, and vegetarian specials, along with a couple of house favorites: broiled rib eye with blue cheese sauce, and Cajun catfish. There's a diverse wine list, and dinner entrées run $17–23. Reservations are highly recommended. House-made sauces are sold here too.

Two places are fine-dining destinations near the top of Union Pass, 13 scenic miles west of Dubois: **Line Shack Lodge** (307/455-3232 or 888/266-4695, www.lineshack.com) and **The Sawmill Lodge** (307/455-2171 or 866/472-9645, www.thesawmill.org). Both

are open three meals a day; Sawmill is probably a better bet.

Groceries and Sweets

Get groceries at **Dubois Super Foods** (610 W. Ramshorn, 307/455-2402.

It's hard to miss the **Country Store Exxon** station (404 W. Ramshorn, 307/455-2677) on the west side of town with the Jackalope out front. Head inside for ice cream or slice of pie and the chance to plunk your kid on the giant Jackalope inside for a goofy photo. Only in Wyoming.

INFORMATION AND SERVICES

The **Dubois Chamber of Commerce** (616 W. Ramshorn, 307/455-2556, www.duboiswyoming.org) is open 9 A.M.–5 P.M. Tuesday–Saturday late May–early September and noon–5 P.M. Tuesday–Saturday the rest of the year. Ask for a self-guided tour map of old logging flumes, tie-hack cabins, and other historic structures.

Stop by the Shoshone National Forest **Wind River Ranger District** office (1403 W. Ramshorn, 307/455-2466, www.fs.fed.us/r2/shoshone) one mile west of town for maps of Shoshone and Bridger–Teton national forests and information on local trails. It also has a listing of local horsepacking outfitters. (For more on the Washakie Wilderness, see the *Bighorn Basin* chapter; see *Fitzpatrick Wilderness* under *Wind River Mountains* in this chapter.)

Open weekdays, the **Dubois Medical Center** (307/455-2516), just east of town on Hwy. 26, has a part-time doctor and nurse practitioners. Wash clothes at the **Laundromat** at 410 W. Ramshorn (across from Branding Iron Motel).

Check your email or surf the web for free at **Dubois Library** (201 1st St., 307/455-2032, www.fremontcountylibraries.org), or for a fee at **Cyber Cafe** (116 E. Ramshorn, 307/455-4011).

DUBOIS VICINITY

Anyone who loves the outdoors will discover an abundance of pleasures around Dubois. There's good fishing for rainbow, cutthroat, brown, and brook trout in Wind River and for rainbow, brook, and Mackinaw trout in the many alpine lakes. You'll also see lots of deer, elk, and bighorn sheep. Hikers and horsepackers will find hundreds of miles of Forest Service trails in the area. Photographers love the brilliantly colored badlands that frame Dubois on both the east and west sides. Each winter, hundreds of snowmobilers climb on their "sleds" and cross-country skiers strap on their boards to enter the world of deep powder in the Absarokas.

Horse Creek Area

Horse Creek Road heads north from Dubois, with scenic views of the Absarokas and nearby badland country. Several dude ranches are in the area. **Horse Creek Campground** ($8; open late May–Sept.) is 12 miles north. Forest Road 504 continues another five miles, providing access to the Washakie Wilderness via Horse Creek Trail. Forest Road 508 splits off near Horse Creek Campground and leads another 17 miles to **Double Cabin Campground** ($8; open late May–Sept.). Several trails head into the wilderness from here; the most popular are Frontier Creek Trail and the Wiggins Fork Trail. You'll find remnants of a petrified forest six miles up the Frontier Creek Trail, but they have been rather picked over by illegal collectors. (It's unlawful to remove petrified wood from a wilderness area. Please leave pieces where you find them.) For other Washakie Wilderness trails information, ask at the Dubois Ranger Station.

Union Pass

The first road across the Absarokas headed through Union Pass southwest of Dubois. The pass forms a divide between the waters of the Columbia, Colorado, and Mississippi rivers and marks the boundary of the Absaroka, Wind River, and Gros Ventre mountain ranges. Near the pass are an interpretive sign and a nature trail through a flower-filled meadow. Union Pass Road (gravel) leaves U.S. 26/287 eight miles northwest of Dubois and climbs across to connect with Hwy. 352 north of Pinedale. A major reconstruction project has dramatically improved the road in recent years, providing a beautiful over-the-mountains con-

nection between Pinedale and Dubois in the summer. The road isn't plowed in winter, but it is popular with snowmobilers.

A scenic 20-mile side road begins a few miles up Union Pass Road, heads along Warm Springs Creek, and eventually reconnects with U.S. 26/287. Find fantastic views of the Absaroka and Wind River ranges along this route. The remains of an old tie-hack logging flume are visible, and a warm spring (85°F) flows into the creek.

The Union Pass area is popular with mountain-bikers, cross-country skiers, and hordes of wintertime snowmobilers. Five miles up the road near the 8,600-foot summit, **Line Shack Lodge** (307/455-3232 or 888/266-4695, www.lineshack.com) has a wonderful setting, an inviting interior with tall windows facing the mountains, and a deck that's especially popular for summertime weddings. A variety of rooms and suites are available for $75 d in summer or $120–150 d in winter. Peak season is January and February, when you'll need to book a room up to a year in advance! The Line Shack has a full-service restaurant that gets packed with folks from Dubois for their Friday night prime rib and salad bar. The saloon has live music December–February, and there's a snowmobile shop on the grounds.

One-quarter mile downhill from Line Shack is **The Sawmill Lodge** (307/455-2171 or 866/472-9645, www.thesawmill.org) with attractive condo-style rooms ($75 d) and two-level suites ($115 d). A fine restaurant and bar are on the premises, and horseback rides are offered in the summer.

Crooked Creek Ranch (307/455-3035 or 888/238-2647, www.crookedcreek-gr.com) is 0.5 mile beyond Line Shack on Union Pass Road. In summer, the ranch has horseback rides, ATV rentals, hiking, and fishing. In winter it's the haunt of snowmobilers; the Continental Divide Snowmobile Trail is very close. The ranch rents snowmobiles, sells gas, and has a restaurant, lounge, and convenience store. Guests stay in modern log cabins ($100–150 d) or motel rooms ($75 d).

The nonprofit **Teton Valley Ranch Camp**

(307/733-2958, www.tvrcamp.org) provides a summertime Western experience for boys and girls. Formerly in Jackson Hole, the ranch moved to a 2,300-acre spread west of Dubois in 2005.

◖ TOGWOTEE PASS

The enjoyable drive west from Dubois first cuts through the colorful badlands, playing tag with the Wind River as it begins a long ascent to 9,658-foot Togwotee Pass (TOE-go-tee). The pass is named for a subchief under Chief Washakie. Togwotee was one of the last independent Sheepeater Indians—a branch of the Shoshones—and the man who led a U.S. government exploratory expedition over this pass in 1873. He even guided President Chester Arthur on his monthlong visit to Yellowstone in 1883.

Togwotee Pass (www.gotogwoteetrail.com) is one of the most scenic drives imaginable, with Ramshorn Peak peeking down from the north for several miles until the road plunges into dense lodgepole forests (Shoshone National Forest) with lingering glimpses of the Pinnacle Buttes. At the crest it emerges into grass-, willow-, and flower-bedecked meadows with Blackrock Creek winding through. Whitebark pine and Engelmann spruce trees cover the nearby slopes. As the highway drops down the western side into the Bridger–Teton National Forest, another marvelous mountain range—the Tetons—dominates the horizon in dramatic fashion. Snow lies along the roadsides until early July; notice the high posts along the road used by snowplows. Togwotee Pass is a complete shock after all the miles of sagebrush and grassland that control the heartland of Wyoming. It's like entering another world—one of cool, forested mountains and lofty peaks instead of the arid land with horizonwide vistas.

The highway over Togwotee Pass was undergoing reconstruction in a process that wasn't to be completed until 2012. The new road will have better shoulders and more passing lanes, but expect 15-minute delays.

Pinnacle Buttes and Brooks Lake

Dominating the view along U.S. 26/287 for perhaps 15 miles are the castlelike Pinnacle Buttes. Twenty-three miles west of Dubois, you'll come to the turnoff to Brooks Lake, elevation 9,100 feet. Take it, even if you don't plan on camping here. A five-mile gravel road leads to the cliff-rimmed lake, and a clear creek flows east and south from here. The Forest Service's excellent **Pinnacles** and **Brooks Lake** campgrounds are along the lakeshore and cost $8 per night; open mid-June–mid-September. Facing the lake is historic Brooks Lake Lodge (see *Mountain Resorts* in the *Jackson Hole* chapter).

Back on the main highway, you'll want to stop at **Falls Campground** (also $8, open June–mid-Sept.). Here, Brooks Creek tumbles into a deep canyon. Catch impressive views of **Brooks Creek Falls** along the short trail beginning from the parking lot. In winter, cross-country skiers will find an easy but ungroomed ski trail that heads out two miles from here. **Wind River Lake** is another five miles up the hill, just below the pass. It's a gorgeous place for picnics and fishing, with deep blue water and the sharp cliffs of Pinnacle Buttes behind. There's even a wheelchair-accessible float for anglers.

Wind River Mountains

The Wind River Mountains begin near South Pass and continue 100 miles northwest to Union Pass, forming part of America's Continental Divide backbone. The range is visible for more than 100 miles across the sagebrush country of central and southwestern Wyoming, its rugged snowcapped peaks gleaming in the light. The Shoshones traversed this range each spring and fall, and Sheepeater Indians hunted in the high country, but to most of the white pioneers whose wagon trains rolled across South Pass the peaks represented a forbidding, mysterious place. In 1868, writer James Chisholm offered a description of the range that rings true today:

I think the best inspired painter that ever drew would fail in attempting to describe these mighty mountains. He may convey correctly enough an impression of their shape, their vast extent and sublime beauty. But there is something always left out which escapes all his colors and all his skill. Their aspects shift and vary continually. Their very shapes seem to undergo a perpetual transformation like the clouds above them. There is a mystery like the mystery of the sea – a silence not of death but of eternity.

Today, the Wind River Mountains are considered Wyoming's premier backpacking area, offering perhaps 700 miles of trails. Much of the country is well above timberline, featuring glacially carved mountains and countless small lakes. Mountain climbers enjoy practicing moves on thousands of granitic precipices representing all degrees of difficulty. The Wind River Mountains contain Gannett Peak—at 13,804 feet the tallest in Wyoming—and all but one of the state's 15 other highest peaks. The 150 extant glaciers in the mountains all formed during the Little Ice Age, between A.D. 1400 and 1850. The glaciers that actually carved these mountains were far larger—so

massive, in fact, that they covered the mountaintops to great depths and spilled over to create the hanging valleys, cirques, alpine lakes, U-shaped valleys, and steep cliffs of today.

Three different Forest Service wilderness areas cap these mountains: The largest is Bridger Wilderness, on the western side of the Continental Divide (in Bridger–Teton National Forest); the other two are Popo Agie and Fitzpatrick wilderness areas east of the crest (in Shoshone National Forest). Add in the BLM's Scab Creek Wilderness Study Area for a total of more than 735,000 roadless acres. The lower elevations of the Wind Rivers are also U.S. Forest Service lands but are managed for other purposes—primarily timber harvesting and grazing. On the northeast border is the Wind River Reservation, which includes some of the high mountain country, but access is restricted. Contact the **Tribal Fish and Game Office** (307/332-7207) in Fort Washakie to buy a limited hiking, fishing, and camping permit and recreation stamp ($25 per day or $65 per week for nonresidents).

WILDLIFE

Most of the streams and larger lakes in the Wind Rivers have been planted with rainbow, cutthroat, California golden, brook, German brown, or Mackinaw trout and grayling and mountain whitefish. Although grizzlies are only infrequently sighted, black bears are still in these mountains—mainly below tree line—and have caused irresponsible campers problems in recent years. Always hang food out of their reach; check with local Forest Service offices for current conditions and precautions. Other creatures, such as mosquitoes and biting flies, are more common annoyances in the mountains. Be sure to bring insect repellent during July and August, when they are at their worst. Other critters you might see include bighorn sheep, moose, elk, mule deer, and coyotes. Pikas and yellow-bellied marmots are common in the high-country boulder fields.

© DON PITCHER

Wind River Mountains near Pinedale

ACCESS

Three highways circle the Wind River Range: U.S. 26/287 on the northeast, U.S. 191 on the southwest, and Hwy. 28 on the southeast. The mountains are traversed by only one road, gravel Union Pass Road. Most people cross the relatively gentle southern slopes at South Pass or over Togwotee Pass to the northeast. You can gain access to the three wilderness areas from either side, but the high passes and long distances keep many hikers on one side or the other. (See the sections on the three wilderness areas in this chapter for specific access points.)

Most trails in the Wind Rivers are relatively free of snow by early July and remain so until mid-September, but the high passes may not open until late July. Because of the open country in the alpine, off-trail travel is relatively easy here but is advised only for experienced hikers who know how to read topographic maps and can take care of themselves in an emergency. Be prepared for the thunderstorms that often roll in during the afternoon; lightning is a real problem above timberline, and lightning fatalities have occurred. It can snow at any time in this mountain country, and night temperatures can drop below freezing even in midsummer. You won't find a lot of wood in many parts of the range, so be sure to bring a gas stove to cook on. In addition, wood fires are prohibited at many of the most heavily used sites.

Unlike in the mountain country farther north, most of the people who head into the Winds do so on foot rather than atop a horse. Horses are used by a minority of the people, and for drop camps, in which horses carry supplies for base camps but everyone hikes in on foot, are a popular way to get into the backcountry without carrying everything on your back. Many outfitters offer these services; stop by local Forest Service offices for a listing. Most backcountry users do not need permits, but visitor permits (free) are required for groups using stock animals and organized groups such as the Boy Scouts and schools.

INFORMATION

Three Forest Service offices have details on backcountry areas in the Winds. The Southern Shoshone National Forest, www.fs.fed.us/

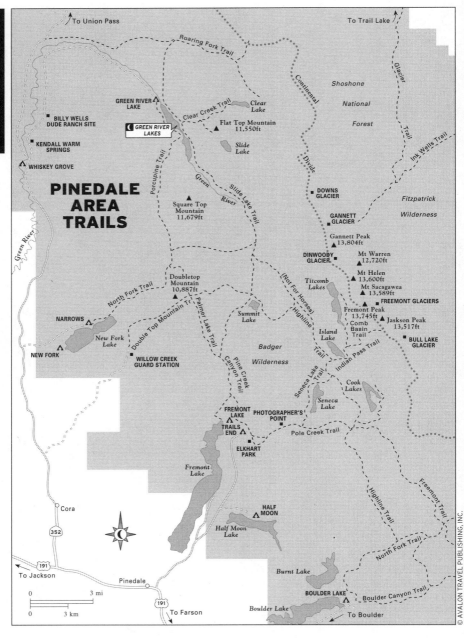

PINEDALE
AREA
TRAILS

To Union Pass

To Trail Lake

Roaring Fork Trail

Glacier

Continental

Shoshone

GREEN RIVER
LAKE

Clear Creek Trail

Clear
Lake

National

BILLY WELLS
DUDE RANCH SITE

GREEN RIVER
LAKES

Flat Top Mountain
11,550ft

Forest

KENDALL WARM
SPRINGS

Slide
Lake

Divide

Ink Wells Trail

Porcupine Trail

WHISKEY GROVE

Green

Slide Lake Trail

River

DOWNS
GLACIER

Fitzpatrick

Square Top
Mountain
11,679ft

GANNETT
GLACIER

Wilderness

Gannett Peak
13,804ft

DINWOODY
GLACIER

Mt Warren
12,720ft

North Fork Trail

Doubletop
Mountain
10,887ft

(Not For Horses)

Titcomb
Lakes

Highline

Mt Helen
13,600ft
Mt Sacagawea
13,589ft

FREEMONT GLACIERS

Fremont Peak
13,745ft
Comb
Basin
Trail

Jaskson Peak
13,517ft

NARROWS

Double Top Mountain Tr

Palmer Lake Trail

Summit
Lake

Island
Lake

BULL LAKE
GLACIER

New Fork
Lake

NEW FORK

WILLOW CREEK
GUARD STATION

Pine Creek Canyon Trail

Badger

Wilderness

Indian Pass Trail

Trail

Cook
Lakes

Seneca Lake Trail

Seneca
Lake

FREMONT
LAKE

PHOTOGRAPHER'S
POINT

TRAILS
END

Pole Creek Trail

ELKHART
PARK

Fremont
Lake

Cora

352

HALF
MOON

Half Moon
Lake

Highline Trail

Freemont Trail

191

To Jackson

Pinedale

North Fork Trail

Burnt Lake

0   3 mi

0   3 km

191

To Farson

BOULDER LAKE

Boulder Canyon Trail

Boulder Lake

To Boulder

Green River

© AVALON TRAVEL PUBLISHING, INC.

r2/shoshone, has a district office in Lander (307/332-5460) that covers the Popo Agie and Southern Fitzpatrick wilderness areas, and another one in Dubois (307/455-2466) for the Northern Fitzpatrick Wilderness. The Bridger–Teton National Forest's Pinedale district office, 307/367-4326, www.fs.fed.us/r4/btnf, covers the Bridger Wilderness. All these offices sell maps of the wilderness areas and can provide copies of backcountry use regulations, Leave No Trace literature, and lists of approved outfitters for pack trips.

You'll find brief descriptions of the most popular hikes in this chapter, but with literally hundreds of treks available in the Winds, don't think these are your only options. In fact, to avoid the crowds you should probably pick up a few topo maps and discover your own trails. The late Finis Mitchell's *Wind River Trails* (www.upress.utah.edu) is a folksy, inexpensive guide by a man who hiked this country from 1909 nearly until his death in the 1990s. Mitchell personally planted trout in dozens of high-country lakes during the 1930s and even had a mountain named for him. Pick up this guide if you plan to do any fishing. *Climbing and Hiking in the Wind River Mountains* by Joe Kelsey (www.globepequot.com) has accurate information on most of the hiking trails and describes hundreds of technical climbs. For a guide directed to hiking and fishing—not climbing—see *Walking the Winds: A Hiking and Fishing Guide to Wyoming's Wind River Range,* by Rebecca Woods (www.alpenbooks.com). Topographic maps are available from sporting-goods stores in the surrounding towns.

C GREEN RIVER LAKES

The long drive to Green River Lakes is one of the most popular getaways in the Wind River Mountains. The road parallels the Green River as it first drifts northward and then makes a U-turn to meander across southwestern Wyoming, eventually joining the Colorado River in Utah. Willows line the riverbanks in this open valley, while sagebrush and aspen cover the hills. Cattle and horses graze on the lush grasses.

Get to Green River Lakes by driving seven

miles west of Pinedale on U.S. 191, and then north up Hwy. 352. The first 26 miles of the road to Green River Lakes are paved and kept plowed all winter. Approximately 15 miles up, a sign points the way to **New Fork Lake,** four miles away on a gravel road. Camp here at either **New Fork Lake Campground** ($7, open June–mid-Sept.) or the popular **Narrows Campground** ($12, open June–mid-Sept.). Make reservations ($9 fee) for Narrows Campground at 518/885-3639 or 877/444-6777, www.reserveusa.com. **New Fork Trail** takes off from the Narrows Campground, providing one of many routes into the Winds.

At mile 20, **Green River Guest Ranch** (307/367-2314, www.grguestranch.com) has guest cabins ($80 d), plus a restaurant, bar, liquor, and limited groceries. It also offers horseback rides and guided fishing. Open year-round.

At the Forest Service border, state maintenance ends and the road becomes gravel and gets rougher and more washboarded as you go the remaining 18 miles (a total of 51 miles from Pinedale). Watch the weather because this upper section can become a quagmire after heavy rains. It's especially a problem if you're towing a trailer. Fantastic scenery makes the trip worthwhile despite the road conditions. Look for some enormous "erratic" boulders a couple of miles up the road from here, evidence of the glaciers that once scoured this valley and carried the boulders along with them.

Just inside the Forest Service border, a signboard describes the tie drives that sent several hundred thousand railroad ties down the Green River between 1869 and 1871. They made it all the way to Green River City (130 miles away), where a boom caught them and they were loaded on railcars. The crew boss, Charles Deloney, later became first superintendent of the Yellowstone Preserve and opened the first store in Jackson. The Green River Lumber and Tie Company came here in the 1890s, employing at least 50 men who lived in the town of Kendall. The company lasted only until 1904, but you can still find the tall stumps in the second-growth forests nearby.

Approximately three miles beyond the Bridger–Teton National Forest border, a rough gravel road splits off and heads over **Union Pass** to Dubois. Although this route was used by Indians and mountain men, today it probably sees more use by snowmobiles in the winter than cars in summertime. Although very rough in spots and muddy each spring, the road is passable in midsummer, even for two-wheel-drive cars. Union Pass Road is especially popular with elk hunters in the fall. The Forest Service's **Whiskey Grove Campground** ($7, open mid-June–mid-Sept.) is just west across the bridge at the site of the old logging town of Kendall.

Kendall Warm Springs

Back on Green River Lakes Road, you pass Kendall Warm Springs 1.5 miles above the turnoff to the campground, its 85°F waters issuing from a few hundred feet up the hill. This is the only place in the world where you can find **Kendall dace.** Fully grown, these tiny fish are just two inches long, or, as the Forest Service notes, shorter than their scientific name, *Rhinichthys osculus thermalis.* The water drops over a 12-foot-high travertine terrace into Green River. The terrace was built up through thousands of years; at the same time the river was cutting into its banks, thus separating these fish and allowing them to survive away from larger predators. To protect them, wading is not allowed in the waters of Kendall Warm Springs.

More Sights

Another two miles up the road are the log and red-sandstone remains of **Gros Ventre Lodge,** one of Wyoming's first dude ranches. Billy Wells built a hunting lodge here in 1897 and operated it until 1906, when stricter enforcement of game laws made it more difficult to attract clients. The lodge drew wealthy big-game hunters from England and the East Coast who enjoyed the chance to slaughter wildlife. (Bannock Indians who hunted out of season in nearby Jackson Hole were shot at, while rich white "sportsmen" could take whatever they wanted for trophies.)

The road ends at the popular **Green River Lakes Campground** ($12, open mid-June–mid-Sept.). Weekends and the Fourth of July holiday may fill the campground to overflowing. Several unofficial campsites are just off the road below the lake. **Square Top Mountain** stares back across the lake and is especially beautiful at sunrise, when the water is calm and the first light catches its cliff faces. When winter comes, ice drapes the front of Square Top, creating the longest single-pitch ice route in the nation. It has never been climbed. (See *Bridger Wilderness* for information on trails in the Green River Lakes area.)

BRIDGER WILDERNESS

The 428,169-acre Bridger Wilderness reaches 90 miles along the western side of the Wind River Mountains, encompassing 27 active glaciers, 2,300 alpine lakes, and 600 miles of trails. It's named for famed mountain man and guide Jim Bridger and was first designated a primitive area in 1931, gaining wilderness status with the original Wilderness Act of 1964. Despite this status, a considerable amount of sheep grazing still takes place in the Bridger Wilderness; it was "grandfathered" in with the wilderness legislation. Sheep are allowed to graze on the southern end of the wilderness (south of Raid Lake), while cattle graze north of there. The Forest Service office in Pinedale is now trying to control sheep grazing more and reduce the conflicts between backcountry hikers and the herds.

Regulations and Access

Before heading out, be sure to pick up a copy of Bridger Wilderness regulations from the Pinedale Forest Service office, 307/367-4326, www.fs.fed.us/r4/btnf. Call ahead for the latest on trail conditions and snow depths in the high country and for recommendations on avoiding crowded areas. The office also lends out bear-resistant food-storage containers. These are available on a first-come, first-served basis, or you can buy your own at the Great Outdoor Shop in Pinedale. Habituated black bears are becoming a problem in many backcountry camps, and some have even learned how to obtain properly hung food.

To keep from polluting the water, pitch your tent at least 200 feet from lakes or trails in the wilderness and 100 feet from streams. Campfires are allowed only below timberline and only then with dead and down wood; gas stoves are recommended. Organized groups, such as Scouts or school groups, and groups traveling with horses, mules, llamas, and pack goats must all get a free visitor permit from the Pinedale District office. If you're using an outfitter to pack in your supplies, make sure the Forest Service permits it to operate within the wilderness.

Access to the Bridger Wilderness comes from nine entrances along the western side of the range. The three most popular points of entry are described as follows, as are several favorite trails. If you're looking for solitude, you may want to avoid these popular paths. Note that the open alpine country means that anyone with topographic maps and a good sense of orientation can strike off in interesting directions and quickly escape the crowds. If you plan to do any fishing, be sure to pick up the Forest Service's guide to fishing lakes in the Bridger Wilderness, with details on which species are where.

Green River Lakes Trails

Easily the most scenic entry into the Winds is from Green River Lakes, on the end of a paved-then-dirt road that leads north from Cora. The road ends at a campground ($12, open mid-June–mid-Sept.) facing onto Lower Green River Lake, where the unforgettable 11,679-foot summit of Square Top Mountain dominates the view.

For an easy five-mile day hike, follow the trails that circle Lower Green River Lake (**Highline Trail** on the east and **Lakeside Trail** on the west). You'll have excellent views of Flat Top Mountain (not to be confused with Square Top Mountain) from the Lakeside Trail and of the Clear Creek Falls along the Highline Trail. Keep your eyes open for moose and osprey. An interesting side trip is the short hike to Upper Green River Lake, where Square Top proves

even more startling. Another side trip heads up **Clear Creek Trail;** it takes off from the southeastern end of Lower Green River Lake, climbs two miles to a natural bridge, and then continues an equal distance to Clear Lake. Some of this country was burned in a 1988 fire. Flat Top is relatively easy to climb; see one of the trail guides for specifics.

Those interested in longer hikes will find several trails in the Green River Lakes area. **Roaring Fork Trail** climbs to Faler Lake, 14 miles away and 2,200 feet higher. The **Highline Trail** follows the northeast shore of Lower Green River Lake and then continues south to the uppermost headwaters of the Green River. From there, the trail stays in the alpine much of the way to its destination at the **Big Sandy Trailhead** on the southern end of the Bridger Wilderness. The total distance is 72 miles, but few people actually follow it that far, preferring to branch off to other sights. Another popular trek is up **Porcupine Trail** to Porcupine Pass and then down **New Fork Trail** to New Fork Lake (a total of approximately 17 miles). Porcupine Trail begins at the upper end of Lower Green River Lake, splitting off from Lakeside Trail.

Elkhart Park Trails

Skyline Drive is a paved road that heads northeast from Pinedale along the eastern side of Fremont Lake, ending 17 miles later at **Elkhart Park Trailhead** (elevation 9,100 feet). The Forest Service generally has someone around to answer questions at the big parking area that fills with cars in July and August. An overlook along the way provides vistas across Fremont Lake and Bridger Wilderness. The **Trails End Campground** at Elkhart Park ($12) is open late June–mid-September. For a pleasant day hike that ends with a bang-up vista of Fremont Peak and the Wind River Range, hike four miles out the **Pole Creek Trail** to **Photographer's Point.**

Backcountry trails head out from Elkhart in two directions. **Pine Creek Canyon Trail** leads north, providing a relatively direct connection with Summit Lake (13 miles) and then down into Green River Lakes (30 miles total). Because of its steepness, it is not recommended for stock use. The main drawback to this trail is that it loses 2,000 feet by dropping into Pine Creek Canyon—elevation that you must regain to reach Summit Lake. You can make a nice loop by heading east from Summit Lake along the **Highline Trail** to Elbow Lake and Seneca Lake, where you follow the **Seneca Lake Trail** and **Pole Creek Trail** back to Elkhart Park. This loop takes you through some of the more scenic areas in the wilderness and covers approximately 31 miles.

The most popular destination from Elkhart is **Titcomb Basin.** Access from Elkhart Park is via a series of connected trails: the Pole Creek Trail, Seneca Lake Trail, **Indian Pass Trail,** and **Titcomb Basin Trail.** Many hikers and climbers overnight at Island Lake, making for crowded conditions much of the summer. It is 15 miles from Elkhart Park to Upper Titcomb Lake, a mountain cirque with abundant wildflowers. A side hike goes up through gorgeous Indian Basin to Indian Pass (three miles). Mountaineers can then descend to the Knife Point and Bull Lake glaciers within the Fitzpatrick Wilderness.

The valley above Titcomb Basin is open, giving climbers access to the west side of a whole row of peaks, including Mt. Helen (13,600 feet), Mt. Sacagawea (13,569 feet), Jackson Peak (13,517 feet), and Fremont Peak (13,745 feet). Climbers can tackle the last two without technical expertise, although Fremont does require some rough scrambling in places. It is most easily climbed from the southwest side; see a topographic map to find the route. Those with greater expertise will find many outstanding opportunities to test their skills on the cliff faces here. Warning: Some folks have died climbing Fremont Peak; use extreme caution when rock scrambling, and never push beyond your skills or ability.

Fremont Peak is named for John C. Frémont, the son-in-law of Senator Thomas Hart Benton, promoter of the Manifest Destiny that would lead Americans all the way to the Pacific. Because of this familial association, Frémont was given the task of exploring and mapping the western territories, work that brought him the nickname the "Great Pathfinder." Some of his ventures—such as floating through the wild waters of Fremont Canyon on the North Platte River or crossing the Rockies in the dead of winter—were downright stupid, and his guides tried to stop him. Frémont's best asset was his wife, who painted his adventures in such a heroic light that his presidential ambitions were nearly realized.

In 1842, Frémont and his men climbed what appeared to be the highest mountain in the Wind River range, a summit they called Snow Peak (now Fremont Peak). From the west, it is obvious why Frémont and his men would mistake this for the highest: Gannett Peak (59 feet taller) is barely visible from a distance, hidden behind other summits. It was not until years later that the mistake was discovered. Frémont was led on his wilderness treks by men with far more experience, including Kit Carson and Tom Fitzpatrick, and his real role was to transfer their innate knowledge of the land onto maps. (Although most people believe Frémont did climb the peak bearing his name, others say he climbed another peak instead, or none at all. One of his scouts, Basil Lajeunesse, stated bluntly, "Frémont never ascended the peak." Perhaps that would account for the discrepancies between what Frémont described and what is actually there.)

Big Sandy Trails

One of the most popular entry points into the Bridger Wilderness is from **Big Sandy Trailhead.** Access is from several different directions, but all require traversing long stretches of gravel road. Easiest access is from the north. From the town of Boulder, take Hwy. 353 where it turns west off U.S. 191 and follow it until it turns to gravel (16 miles). Bear left at the intersection 0.5 mile up and go another nine miles to another junction (signed), where you again turn left and go seven more miles to the turnoff (left) to the Forest Service's Dutch Joe Guard Station and then on to Big Sandy Opening. The road ends at **Big Sandy**

Campground ($7, open mid-June–mid-Sept.), where the trails begin. The Forest Service generally has someone stationed here in the summer. Note that the rough road into Big Sandy becomes slick and hazardous when it rains, so watch the weather reports closely. This is especially a problem if you're towing a trailer.

Near the end of end of Big Sandy Road—44 miles from Boulder at an elevation of 9,100 feet—is historic 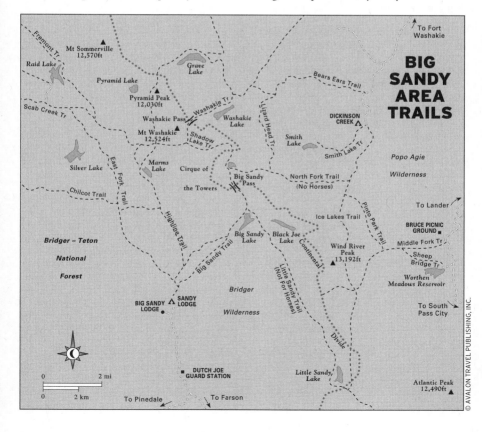 **Big Sandy Lodge.** The centerpiece is a trophy head–filled log building, built in 1929, with two stone fireplaces. It's just a mile from the Bridger Wilderness. Ten rustic log cabins ($60–85 d) lack electricity or running water but have woodstoves and kerosene lamps. Three meals per day are available for guests; others can eat here by reservation. Horseback rides, spot-pack trips, and guided pack trips are available, or a better option may be a three-night package: $490 for two people, including lodging, meals, and half-day horseback rides. Because of its proximity to backcountry trails, Big Sandy Lodge is also a popular place to ship supply packages for hikers heading up the Continental Divide Trail. There are no phones here, but you can leave messages at 307/382-6513, or email them through the website www.big-sandy-ldoge.com; it may take a couple of days for a reply either way. This place is the real McCoy, a classic old-time Wyoming lodge that seems never to change. It's open late May–early October.

BIG SANDY AREA TRAILS

To Fort Washakie

Mt Sommerville 12,570ft

Raid Lake

Fremont Tr.

Grave Lake

Pyramid Lake

Pyramid Peak 12,030ft

Scab Creek Tr

Washakie Tr.

Washakie Pass

Washakie Lake

Bears Ears Trail

Lizard Head Tr.

DICKINSON CREEK

Mt Washakie 12,524ft

Shadow Lake Tr.

Smith Lake

Smith Lake Tr.

Popo Agie

Silver Lake

East Fork Trail

Marms Lake

Cirque of the Towers

Big Sandy Pass

North Fork Trail (No Horses)

Wilderness

Chilcot Trail

To Lander

Ice Lakes Trail

Pinto Park Trail

BRUCE PICNIC GROUND

Bridger – Teton

Highline Trail

Big Sandy Lake

Black Joe Lake

Continental

Wind River Peak 13,192ft

Middle Fork Tr.

Sheep Bridge Tr.

National

Big Sandy Trail

Forest

Bridger

Little Sandy Trail (Not For Horses)

Worthen Meadows Reservoir

SANDY LODGE

BIG SANDY LODGE

Wilderness

To South Pass City

Divide

DUTCH JOE GUARD STATION

Little Sandy Lake

Atlantic Peak 12,490ft

0   2 mi

0   2 km

To Pinedale

To Farson

© AVALON TRAVEL PUBLISHING, INC.

A maze of trails departs from **Big Sandy Opening Trailhead.** The **Highline Trail** heads north, extending across the Bridger Wilderness to Green River Lakes, and continues from there to Union Pass, 100 miles away. The trail connects with numerous others, including **Shadow Lake Trail,** a 2.5-mile route to this alpine lake. More adventurous types can continue over Texas Pass and down to Lonesome Lake in the Cirque of the Towers, a distance of 15 miles. (See *Popo Agie Wilderness* for information on the very popular *Cirque of the Towers* area.)

Another side route off the Highline Trail is the **Washakie Trail,** a path used by this famous Shoshone chief during his people's biannual migration between the Wind River Valley and the Green River country. This trail goes into the South Fork area of the Popo Agie Wilderness, where you can connect with the Bears Ears Trail.

The most popular trail out of Big Sandy Opening is **Big Sandy Trail,** a 5.5-mile trek to crowded Big Sandy Lake, where it meets a spiderweb of trails and cairn-marked paths to other high-country lakes. Beyond the lake, **Jackass Pass Trail** climbs steeply up North Creek and over the pass before dropping into Lonesome Lake and Cirque of the Towers (total distance 8.5 miles). Jackass Pass Trail is a steep—but beautiful—slog. A strenuous loop trip consists of the Big Sandy Trail–Jackass Pass Trail route combined with the Texas Pass–Shadow Lake Trail–Highline Trail route. Total distance is 24 miles.

FITZPATRICK WILDERNESS

The 191,103-acre Fitzpatrick Wilderness occupies the northeast side of the Wind River Mountains, sandwiched between the Bridger Wilderness just over the Continental Divide and the Wind River Indian Reservation to the east. The wilderness is a rugged landscape of rock and ice, with dozens of mountain lakes and cascading mountain brooks. Wyoming's highest mountain, Gannett Peak, forms part of the western border, and 44 active glaciers crowd against the summits; the largest cov-

ers 1,220 acres. The Fitzpatrick is a favorite of folks with considerable backpacking or mountaineering experience.

Although long maintained as a primitive area, the Fitzpatrick Wilderness was officially established by Congress in 1976 and is named for Tom Fitzpatrick, a respected mountain man, guide, head of the Rocky Mountain Fur Company, army scout, and Indian agent. To the Indians, he was "Broken Hand," a name received after he lost three fingers in a rifle accident while being pursued by Blackfeet Indians; despite this loss, he still managed to kill two of his attackers. As an Indian agent, Tom Fitzpatrick pushed for several important treaties, including the 1851 Fort Laramie Treaty. His untimely death from pneumonia in 1854 was a blow to the peace process, and few of the agents who followed could match Fitzpatrick's diplomatic skills or knowledge of the West. Fitzpatrick's adopted Arapaho son, Friday (named for the day of the week on which Fitzpatrick found him), later became a respected chief and translator for his people.

Access

The primary entrance point into the Fitzpatrick Wilderness is from **Trail Lake.** Head five miles southeast from Dubois on U.S. 26/287 and turn right (south) onto a gravel road. The road leads into Whiskey Basin, with a rutted dirt road continuing to the left past a string of small lakes, the last being Trail Lake. The trails begin here, 12 miles off the highway. Note that access to the Cold Springs/Burris Trailhead requires that you cross Wind River Reservation land. You'll need to hire an Indian outfitter to drive you to the trailhead, and you'll have to obtain a reservation fishing/hiking permit and recreation stamp (nonresidents of Wyoming pay $25 per day or $65 per person for a week). Contact the Tribal Fish and Game Office (307/332-7207) in Fort Washakie for details.

Forest Service regulations in the Fitzpatrick Wilderness prohibit camping within 100 feet of trails or lakes. In addition, no campfires or overnight horse use is allowed above the confluence of Dinwoody and Knoll Lake creeks. For details, contact the Forest Service's Wind River Ranger District office in Dubois (307/455-2466).

Trails

Three major trails lead from Trail Lake into the high country. The **Whiskey Mountain Trail** climbs over the peak of the same name and then on to heavily used Simpson Lake, a dozen miles away. From here it's possible for experienced hikers to continue over a pass above Sandra Lake (another 3.5 miles) and then down into the Roaring Fork drainage of the Bridger Wilderness. The **New Glacier Trail** leads from **Trail Lake Trailhead** to the Dinwoody Glacier. A side trip off this trail is the Bomber Lake route. This bushwhack goes from Bomber Basin and terminates at Bomber Lake, six miles and numerous downfalls later. The route requires sound route finding and off-trail hiking skills. The basin is named for a B-17 bomber that crashed here during World War II when its crew was practicing a strafing run on either a bear or a bighorn sheep. The plane wreckage is still visible.

A popular horse trail to the Fitzpatrick high country is the **Old Glacier Trail** to Dinwoody Glacier. Once obliterated by a landslide, this trail was resurrected by local mule-packers as an alternative to the less stock-friendly New Glacier Trail. Both the new and old trails converge near Arrow Pass and continue to the glaciers. No matter which you choose, old or new trail, it is a sweaty and difficult 24 miles to Gannett country, but it passes lots of lakes and ruggedly beautiful alpine country. Bighorn sheep are sometimes seen along the way. The first five uphill miles of the old trail are without water, so be sure to bring plenty with you. The trail ends at the glacier, providing access for mountaineers who want to scale 13,804-foot Gannett Peak, the highest in Wyoming. (The peak is named for Henry Gannett, chief topographer for the Hayden Survey of the 1870s, and it was first climbed in 1922 by Arthur Tate and Floyd Stahlnaker.) Because Gannett is a glaciated mountain, proficiency in the use of ice axes and crampons is mandatory. Experience in technical climbing—including ropes and protection—is required for most routes.

Many mountaineers come up this trail to climb Gannett and the cluster of peaks over 13,000 feet just to the south, including Mt. Woodrow Wilson, the Sphinx, Mt. Warren, Doublet Peak, and Turret Peak. See Joe Kelsey's *Climbing and Hiking in the Wind River Mountains* for details. If you want to go with the pros, two first-rate mountaineering operations based in Jackson Hole lead climbs up Gannett Peak: **Exum Mountain Guides** (307/733-2297, www.exumguides.com) and **Jackson Hole Mountain Guides** (307/733-4979 or 800/239-7642, www.jhmg.com). These guides aren't cheap; expect to pay $1,400 per person for a six-day trip with three clients.

POPO AGIE WILDERNESS

The Popo Agie Wilderness is a 101,991-acre parcel of magnificent mountain real estate with jagged peaks, deep valleys, and more than 240 lakes. At least 20 peaks rise above 13,000 feet; Wind River Peak is the tallest at 13,225 feet. Popo Agie was first established as a primitive area in 1932 and enlarged and reclassified as wilderness in 1984. The Popo Agie is bounded to the west by the Bridger Wilderness and to the north by the Wind River Indian Reservation. Access to the Popo Agie Wilderness is generally from the east side, in the Lander vicinity, although it is possible to cross the Continental Divide from the Bridger Wilderness via several passes. Special regulations are intended to protect the wilderness. Camping is not allowed within 200 feet of trails, lakes, or streams. Anyone bringing in horses, mules, llamas, or pack goats will need to get a free livestock-use permit from the Forest Service. Get this and other Popo Agie Wilderness information from the Washakie Ranger District Office (307/332-5460, www.fs.fed.us/r2/shoshone) in Lander.

Dickinson Park Access

The primary jumping-off point into the Popo Agie Wilderness is the Dickinson Park area, northwest of Lander at an elevation of 9,300 feet. Get here by turning west on Moccasin Lake Road (paved) just south of Fort Washakie at the Hines Store. Stay right where the road turns to dirt and continue to Moccasin Lake/Dickinson Park junction, a total of 19 very rough and rutted miles. Turn left here and head another four miles to **Dickinson Creek Campground** (free, open July–mid-Sept., no water), passing the Dickinson Park Work Center along the way. Note that you'll pass a "No Trespassing Without Proper Tribal Travel Permit" sign on Moccasin Lake Road; it's OK to ignore this if you're en route to Dickinson Park. This road may be closed periodically by the tribe.

Close to the Dickenson Park Campground, **Allen's Diamond Four Ranch** (307/332-2995, www.diamond4ranch.com) offers rustic dude-ranch accommodations and drop-pack trips for those who want to hike while still enjoying the pleasures of a horse-packed base camp. All-inclusive weekly rates are $1,800 for two people.

The **Bears Ears Trail** takes off from the end of a 0.5-mile dirt road that turns west at the Dickinson Park Work Center and climbs quickly into the alpine before going over Adams Pass. It passes Bears Ears Mountain (look for the "ears") and follows through the alpine before dropping into the lake-filled headwaters of the South Fork of the Little Wind River, 14 miles away. Along the way are all sorts of connections to other trails, including a variety of loops.

From the **North Fork/Smith Lake Trailhead** near Dickinson Creek Campground, the popular **Smith Lake Trail** heads south and then west to Smith and then Cathedral Lakes (eight miles). The **Smith Fork Trail** splits off the **North Fork Trail** approximately 0.25 mile up. The North Fork Trail will eventually (15 miles) take you straight to Lonesome Lake at the base of the soaring Cirque of the Towers. Unfortunately, the hike requires four different fordings of the North Fork of the Popo Agie River, a treacherous proposition when the water is high. It's best to wait until late summer to attempt this one.

Loop Road Access

The Loop Road (Hwy. 131) cuts south from

Cirque of the Towers in the Popo Agie Wilderness Area

© DON PITCHER

Lander through Sinks Canyon and then over the mountains to South Pass, providing several entry points into the Popo Agie Wilderness. **Middle Fork Trail** begins at **Bruce Picnic Ground,** 13 miles south of Lander on the Loop Road, and follows the Middle Fork of the Popo Agie River upstream to Sweetwater Gap (16 miles), where you enter the Bridger Wilderness. Many people use this trail to reach the Cirque of the Towers area via the **Pinto Park Trail** and **North Fork Trail** (total one-way distance approximately 23 miles). The **Middle Fork Trail** crosses the river at Three Forks Park and continues up Tayo Creek 3.5 miles or so to Tayo Park. From there it is possible to take day hikes to the surrounding lakes. The **Sheep Bridge Trail** begins at Worthen Reservoir, 20 miles south of Lander on the Loop Road, and heads north for three miles to its junction with the Middle Fork Trail. Many people use this trail to cut distance and elevation off their trek into the Tayo Lake or Cirque of the Towers areas. (It starts 1,200 feet higher than the Middle Fork Trail.)

Cirque of the Towers

This is one of the best-known and most-visited places in the Wind River Mountains, an incredible semicircle of pinnacles at the headwaters of the North Fork of the Popo Agie River. **Lonesome Lake** is in the center, backdropped by peaks with such names as Warbonnet, Pingora, Sharks Nose, Camels Hump, Lizard Head, and Watch Tower. All of these peaks are well-known in the climbing community and attract folks from around the globe. Lonesome Lake is not so lonesome these days; on a typical day in early August you're likely to find a small town of tents in the vicinity. To help protect the area, the Forest Service prohibits camping within 0.25 mile of the lake, and no campfires are allowed.

The most popular way to reach Cirque of the Towers is from the Big Sandy Opening Trailhead (see *Bridger Wilderness* section), but the longer North Fork Trail is also commonly used and does not require traversing any passes. The other popularly used route is the Sheep Bridge Trail. Campers often choose to base themselves at Big Sandy Lake and then day hike into Cirque of the Towers. It makes for a long day, but at least you won't need to carry a heavy pack over challenging Jackass Pass.

South Pass

At the southern end of the Wind River Mountains, a broad, relatively gentle pass provides a corridor across the Continental Divide. This part of Wyoming is packed with history, particularly around South Pass, which is now traversed by Hwy. 28.

Red Canyon

Approximately 15 miles southwest of Lander, Hwy. 28 climbs to an overlook above Red Canyon, where maroon sandstone rocks rise like a backbone out of the sage and grass rangeland. A separate route, Red Canyon Road, follows Red Canyon Creek for a close-up view of this colorful valley. The 5,000-acre **Red Canyon Ranch Preserve** (307/332-3388, www.nature.org/wyoming) is a working cattle ranch maintained by the Nature Conservancy. It's a center for research on the ecological effects of different grazing techniques.

Over the Pass

West of Red Canyon, the highway passes just north of the almost ghost towns of Atlantic City and South Pass before starting the long descent into the Green River Basin and the junction town of Farson. Winters on the pass are long, cold, and windy; the snow fences stretch for miles along the highway.

Gold was first mined here during the 1860s, and a long series of booms and busts followed. For a brief time in 1867–1868, the **Sweetwater Mines** attracted national attention, and thousands of men (and a few women) flocked to the area. The land was officially part of the Wind River Reservation at the time, but legalities didn't matter much when gold could be found. South Pass was ceded by the Shoshones in 1878. Prospectors still head out each spring in search of the elusive mother lode, and various schemes to reopen the old mines surface periodically. Today the area is enjoyed by thousands of tourists and others attracted by the rich historical and recreational opportunities.

History

South Pass was first discovered by the game animals who traversed this country and the Indian hunters who followed them. The first whites to traipse through were the Astorians, fur traders led by Robert Stuart in 1812. The first wagon wheels rolled over South Pass in 1824, and between 1841 and 1866 more than 350,000 emigrants followed what had become the primary route west. Of all the sights along the Oregon Trail, South Pass was one of the most anticipated. West of here the waters flow to the Pacific Ocean, and the entire country

SOUTH PASS IN 1861

In 1861, Mark Twain rumbled west through Wyoming on a stagecoach, a trip later made famous in his book *Roughing It*. At South Pass, Twain found that the settlement in the days before mining was not exactly a hubbub of activity:

Toward dawn we got under way again, and presently as we sat with raised curtains enjoying our early-morning smoke and contemplating the first splendor of the rising sun as it swept down the long array of mountain peaks, flushing and gilding crag after crag and summit after summit, as if the invisible Creator reviewed his gray veterans and they saluted with a smile, we hove in sight of South Pass City. The hotelkeeper, the postmaster, the blacksmith, the mayor, the constable, the city marshal and the principal citizen and property holder, all came out and greeted us cheerily, and we gave him good day.... South Pass City consisted of four log cabins, one of which was unfinished, and the gentleman with all those offices and titles was the chiefest of the ten citizens of the place. Think of hotelkeeper, postmaster, blacksmith, mayor, constable, city marshal and principal citizen all condensed into one person and crammed into one skin. Bemis said he was "a perfect Allen's revolver of dignities." And he said that if he were to die as postmaster, or as blacksmith, or as postmaster and blacksmith both, the people might stand it; but if he were to die all over, it would be a frightful loss to the community.

---

became known as the Oregon Territory (hence the **Oregon Buttes** south of South Pass). Travelers took great pleasure in stopping at Pacific Springs, happy in the knowledge that its waters eventually reached the Pacific. An important stage and Pony Express station stood here; some of the buildings from a later ranch are still standing.

Today, Hwy. 28 traces a similar route across South Pass. Signboards denote various historic sites along the way. At the signboard that describes the Oregon Trail, a rough dirt road leads one mile back to the clear waters of Pacific Creek, where posts mark the historic route. Don't believe everything you read on the signs, however: The **Parting of the Ways** monument actually marks the South Pass City–Green River stage road where it intersects the Oregon Trail rather than the famous point where the Sublette Cutoff took Oregon- and California-bound travelers west while Mormon voyagers (and others in need of supplies) diverged southwest to Fort Bridger. The true Parting of the Ways lies 10 miles southwest of

this marker. The highway west to Farson rolls up and down the sage-carpeted hills, cutting straight as a carpenter's plumb line. The Wind River Mountains dominate the northern horizon, while to the south the distant Killpecker Sand Dunes slide into view.

◖ SOUTH PASS CITY

At 7,800 feet above sea level, South Pass City is one of Wyoming's highest settlements. Tall snow fences line the roads here in an attempt to halt the snow that blows all winter long. Although commonly called a ghost town, South Pass City never really died out. The town is now a State Historic Site, providing one of the most interesting and authentic historical settings in Wyoming.

Gold in the Hills

During the days of 1849, many thousands of would-be miners streamed through South Pass on their way to California, little knowing that gold lay beneath their feet. Gold was first found in 1842, but its discoverer was killed by Indians;

other miners faced similar fates. First to file a claim was Henry Reedal, who discovered what became known as the Carissa Lode in 1867. Shortly thereafter, the Miner's Delight Lode was discovered. The finds attracted an onslaught of miners, and by that fall the town of South Pass City had mushroomed into Wyoming's largest settlement, with nearly 3,000 residents.

The discovery of gold at South Pass helped propel the effort to make Wyoming a territory separate from Dakota, a move that took place the following year. At its rip-roaring peak, there was even an effort to make South Pass the Wyoming territorial capital. The town included six general stores, three butcher shops, several restaurants, two breweries, seven blacksmith shops, five hotels, and dozens of saloons and "sporting houses." In 1868, writer James Chisholm described his return to the town after an absence:

Late at night we arrived at Miner's Delight where everything was just as we had left it. The card table in the corner was in full blast. The parties whom we had left on a drunk were now sobering off and those we had left sober were getting on a drunk.

The Carissa Mine's shafts would eventually reach 400 feet down, and the mill would produce gold worth more than $6 million. But this was primarily hard-rock mining, requiring large capital investments and long hours. The lack of water in this arid country meant that placer mining was possible only in the spring, while summers were spent toiling in the hard-rock mines for $5 per day. The Sweetwater mines were a short-lived bubble that burst almost as quickly as it grew. Instead of the hoped-for mother lode, miners found only small pockets of gold. Within five years most of the miners gave up and moved away. By 1875, fewer than 100 people remained, but South Pass City refused to die. There were more booms (followed by busts) in the 1880s, 1890s, 1930s, and 1960s. Miners still come to these hills in search of gold.

Women's Suffrage

Given the rough mining crowd that jammed the streets of South Pass City, it seems odd to find the town at the center of the effort to gain equal rights for women. In late 1869, the first territorial representative from South Pass City, William Bright, introduced a women's-suffrage bill before the first territorial legislature. It was a measure supported by his wife and other South Pass women but probably opposed by many of the local men. The measure surprised almost everyone by being passed and signed into law by Governor John Campbell. In anger, the local judge resigned his post as justice of the peace for South Pass City, only to be replaced by a woman, Esther Hobart Morris. She was the first woman judge in America. In her 8.5 months of service, Morris tried 26 cases and gained recognition for her fairness, along with considerable national exposure.

The more exalted claim that Morris was the "Mother of Women's Suffrage" is suspect. In 1869, she is supposed to have held a tea party in which the South Pass City women extracted a promise from then-candidate William Bright to introduce legislation to grant women the right to vote. The tea party tale somehow made it into the history books, even though her son—a newspaper editor—concocted it after her death. A statue of Morris in front of the state capitol credits her with the bill. Morris never claimed any such thing, and in fact was not an active suffragist. According to Bright, the reason he introduced the legislation was not because of lobbying by local women but because, "If Negroes had the right to vote, women like [his] wife and mother should also."

South Pass State Historic Site

In 1965, South Pass City's buildings risked being carted off to Southern California's Knott's Berry Farm theme park. With the help of Alice "Flaming Mame" Messick, a committee of Wyoming folks outbid the Californians for the buildings and managed to keep them. The following year, the state bought the site and began the process of restoration.

CALAMITY JANE

Calamity Jane – born Martha Jane Canary in 1852 – is surely one of the most unusual characters to come out of the 19th-century West. In an era when the few women who found their way west almost invariably fell into one of three categories – housewife, washerwoman, or prostitute – Calamity Jane was all three, plus a lot more. At age 12, Martha Canary's family trekked west from Missouri to Montana. The trip took five months, and by the time they reached Virginia City, she noted: "I was considered a remarkable good shot and a fearless rider for a girl of my age." Her mother died shortly after they arrived, and the family had a hard time surviving the harsh winter; Martha and her sisters were forced to beg on the streets. Her father died the following spring, and from that time on, Martha Canary was on her own. She landed in Miners Delight (near South Pass City) in 1870-1871; here, some claim, she "entertained" men at Hyde's Hall Saloon. She certainly occasionally worked in "the sporting profession."

It was around this time that Calamity Jane gained her nickname. She claimed in a brief autobiography to have signed on as a scout for General Custer in Fort Russell, Wyoming, and to have soon thereafter "donned the uniform of a soldier. It was a bit awkward at first but I soon got to be perfectly at home in men's clothes." At other times she even masqueraded as a man and could by all accounts work, shoot, drink, and cuss as hard as the rough-edged men around her. While employed as a scout for General Crook's campaign near Sheridan she supposedly rescued the post commander, Captain Egan, from an Indian raid, helping him to safety. Egan then named her "Calamity Jane, the heroine of the plains." The name stuck for life.

Whether the story is true or not, Calamity Jane did live up to the sobriquet many times in later years. She was often found nursing men down with smallpox – she was immune to the disease – buying meals for the destitute, or assisting ill "soiled doves," even if it meant rolling a man for his money to pay the bills. She saved many lives at a time when life was short and cheap. This is not to suggest that Calamity Jane was the Mother Teresa of the Plains; the same woman who could care so much for others could also be loud and obnoxious when drunk. Her binges were legendary and landed her behind bars on numerous occasions, including a monthlong stint in the Rawlins jail for a drunken brawl with one of her many husbands and an eight-day trip to the Laramie jail for drunkenness. Beer would never do: "Give me a shot of booze and slop her over the brim" was always the bartender's order. As a friend (Deadwood madam Dora DuFran) noted:

Her many friends – she had no enemies – would buy her drinks until she reached the howling stage. Then someone would steer her to the next saloon. Her time was limited in each one when that howling began. She would finally wind up by howling up and down Main Street. Even the law was paralyzed. Nothing could quell the howling completely, so some friend would escort her home with a quart of whiskey hugged to her breast to act as a night cap and put her to sleep. In the morning she would awaken with a hangover and start all over again. The only way to sober her up was to tell her someone was sick and needed her services. Not another drink would she take. Next day she would be ready for business.

In her autobiography, Calamity Jane said she married Clinton Burk in El Paso and went on to give birth to a girl "the very image of its father... but who has the temper of its mother." Nobody knows what became of the girl in later life, but Calamity went on to marry several other men. DuFran noted that "Jane had a very affectionate nature. There were very few preachers around to bother her, so whenever she got tired of one man she soon selected a new one." Calamity also alludes in her autobiography to an affair with famed gambler and gunfighter Wild Bill Hickok, and after her death a woman professed to be their illegitimate child raised by a wealthy East Coast family. Most folks put little stock in Calamity's relationship with Wild Bill, although the two did end up in Deadwood in 1876. A desperado shot Wild Bill in the back while he was seated at a gambling table; Calamity claimed to have helped capture the murderer.

In later years, Calamity Jane seemed to spin her way across the West, stopping long enough to make money as a prospector, stagecoach driver, laundress, or some less seemly trade before getting the urge (or urging) to move on. Given the regimented code of behavior under which women lived in her era, it's easy to see how her appearance caused such a stir. Newspapers trumpeted her arrival in town, and saloons attracted crowds as her exploits grew with each telling. Someone was always willing to buy a round of drinks for the chance to hear Calamity's tales. As a young woman she was certainly attractive, but the years of hard drinking and rough living were not especially kind. As author Ellen Mueller put it, however, "perhaps the men standing in a saloon dead broke and hankering for a drink would have found the

woman beautiful who would get drinks 'on the house' for everybody."

Although she spent a brief period with Buffalo Bill's Wild West Show, Calamity Jane's biggest moment of glory came in an 1895 return to Deadwood after a 17-year absence. A masquerade ball was held in her honor, and the local newspaper noted:

She was in great demand by the Dancers, many who were anxious to spend 25¢ to dance with her, just to have it to say they had danced with "Calamity Jane." She had a fair sized jag on board, and this, together with a vile cigar which she smoked, made her look anything but the beautiful woman which novelists and story writers have said so much about.

Calamity died in 1904, just 52 years old. Her deathbed plea was to be buried next to Wild Bill Hickok, whom she said was the only man she had ever loved. Her funeral was one of the largest ever for Deadwood. Today, they lie next to each other at the Mt. Moriah Cemetery overlooking town. The testimony of fellow tough-living Dora DuFran again sums up Calamity's life best:

It is easy for a woman to be good who has been brought up with every protection from the evils of the world and with good associates. Calamity was a product of the wild and woolly west. She was not immoral; but unmoral. She took more on her shoulders than most women could. She performed many hundreds of deeds of kindness and received very little pay for her work. With her upbringing, how could she be anything but unmoral.

© DON PITCHER

South Pass State Historic Site

South Pass State Historic Site (307/332-3684, www.southpasscity.com) contains about 25 old buildings and 30,000 authentic artifacts, 90 percent of which actually came from the area. The buildings are open 9 A.M.–6 P.M. daily May 15–September; $4 for nonresident adults, $2 for Wyoming residents, and free for kids under age 18. The rest of the year, visitors can wander the streets, but many items are in storage and the windows are covered with plywood.

On summertime days the old town comes alive with gold-panning demonstrations by modern-day prospectors. The **Gold Rush Days** celebration at South Pass is great fun, with country dancing, a barbecue, bake sale, horseshoe pitching, old-time music, exhibits, and lots of folks in old-time costumes. The **Vintage Base Ball Tournament** the last weekend of July features local players in old-time uniforms competing with 1900-era equipment and rules.

Entrance fees are collected at the **visitor center** in what was once an 1890 dance hall. Inside are interpretive displays and a book and gift shop. Pick up a brochure here describing the buildings. A short way up the street is the **Smith Sherlock Co. Store,** where you can check out the exhibits or buy boulder-size jaw breakers, English marbles, homemade soap, gold pans, bonnets, distinctive candies and jellies, plus historical books. The nonprofit Friends of South Pass runs the store (which is also an official post office).

Just up from the Smith Sherlock Co. Store is a small mining museum that details the process of prospecting, locating and filing claims, and working placer and hard-rock mines in the Sweetwater Mining District. Other interesting buildings that have been restored and furnished with original items include a blacksmith shop, a restaurant, a butcher shop, a hotel, a miner's cabin, a saloon, a newspaper office, a school, and a dugout cave used to keep perishables cool. A gold-mining exhibit on the hill behind town has a huge stamp mill, a short mine tunnel, carts, and railroad track, along with other mining equipment. Gold-panning demonstrations are given by request throughout the summer. The **Sweetwater County Jail,** built in 1870, is the oldest nonmilitary government building in Wyoming, and the "**pest house**" was a place where patients with contagious diseases were left in isolation.

The reconstructed **Esther Morris cabin** stands at the eastern end of the row of buildings. Out front is a granite marker from 1939 that credits her with originating women's suffrage. Next to it is a more recent disclaimer. Adding more insult to injury is the fact that the reconstructed cabin is now believed to be in the wrong place; the actual Morris cabin site is not far away, and this was the location of a print shop instead.

Just east of the Morris cabin is a six-mile **nature trail** along Willow Creek offering the chance to explore the Carie Shields Mine (it produced $35,000 worth of gold) and other mines, cabins, and mill sites. Be careful where you walk around these old structures. Along the creek you're likely to see all sorts of animals, from beavers and ducks to mule deer and moose. Pick up a trail map at the entrance. Also here is a 10-km **Volksmarch trail.**

Practicalities

Outside the State Historic Site is a cluster of old log cabins owned by a handful of locals. Stop by the seasonally open **South Pass Mercantile** (307/332-9935, www.south-pass.com) for a selection of locally made soaps, candles, and pottery, plus gifts, books, snacks, and T-shirts.

Great Divide Tours (307/332-3123 or 800/458-1915, www.dtoutfitting.com) has fascinating six-night wagon train adventures over South Pass each July for around $1,000 per person, including meals, equipment, and tents.

ATLANTIC CITY

Funky and friendly Atlantic City has dirt streets, log-and-stone buildings, and a delightfully infectious country atmosphere. It's the sort of town where old-timers plunk themselves atop the Merc's barstools to talk cattle, football, and the old days, where many homes (and the church, too) still have outhouses, and where the big event is the volunteer fire department picnic in late August. Residents pile up huge stacks of firewood to make it through the long, cold winters. The snow can get deep here near the top of the Continental Divide (elevation 7,660 feet). One winter, the drifts topped 27 feet and the snowplows didn't get in for several weeks! Most residents like the quiet beauty that winter brings to Atlantic City and depend on snowmobiles and skis to get around. This is one of the few places left in Wyoming where the past seems so immediately present.

History

Atlantic City was formed in 1868 when gold mines had attracted thousands of miners to the Sweetwater Mining District. As miners arrived in South Pass, they spread out over the surrounding country in search of other gold deposits, founding the settlements of Atlantic City, Miner's Delight, and Lewiston at promising locations. As with most frontier towns, saloons vastly outnumbered churches in early Atlantic City. The first county sheriff owned a local brothel! **Fort Stambaugh** was established a few miles to the east in 1870 to protect miners from Sioux and Arapaho raids. It lasted only until 1878, and the buildings were auctioned off four years later.

In the 1880s, another miniboom hit as French capitalist Emile Granier built a 25-mile-long ditch from the Wind River Mountains to Atlantic City for hydraulic mining. The effort failed when the money ran out before gold could be found. Another boom hit in the late 1920s and '30s when a dredge worked its way down Rock Creek (leaving behind enormous piles of gravel). By the early 1960s, Atlantic City's population had been reduced to a handful of folks. Development of a U.S. Steel iron-ore (taconite) strip mine nearby brought prosperity after 1962, but the mine closed in 1983 and left behind a gaping pit now filled with water. Today Atlantic City depends on tourism and summer homes. But as a local brochure notes, "The wind of this old gold town always whispers of another boom on its way."

Sights

Atlantic City's main attractions are its mining-era buildings, many dating from the turn of the

WIND RIVER MOUNTAINS

© DON PITCHER

St. Andrews Episcopal Church in Atlantic City

20th century. The centerpiece is **Atlantic City Mercantile,** built in 1893 from adobe brick. Its false front is covered with old metal siding, and the interior is stuffed with stuffed heads, historic photos, mining artifacts, a big woodstove (usually in use), and a rich sense of the past. Pick up a brochure at the kiosk describing the town's many other historic buildings.

The stone structure one block to the east of the Merc housed the **McAuley Store,** later Hyde's Hall. Calamity Jane once provided the entertainment in the saloon here. Up the hill is **St. Andrews Episcopal Church,** a rustic old log church built in 1913 and still used today. Sunday services start at 10 a.m. The **Gratrix Cabin,** one block east of the church, was built in the late 1860s and was home to Judge Buck Gratrix, a man who noted that he lived in three different counties, two territories, and one state while living in one place!

Nearby Sights

Rock Creek flows through Atlantic City, and on the west end of town the banks are lined with huge piles of boulders left behind by the gold-dredging operations of the '30s. Fort Stambaugh Road heads east from Atlantic City and follows a 12-mile loop past the site of Fort Stambaugh (not marked) and the ghost town of Miner's Delight. A side road leads to **Lewiston,** another abandoned gold-mining town. The loop road is a scenic drive through open grassland and scattered patches of young aspen and lodgepole. (Miners wiped out previous stands.) Antelope are sure to be seen along the way. The settlement called **Miner's Delight** consists of a dozen log buildings in various states of decay. A small beaver pond and graveyard are also in Miner's Delight, with other old mining buildings visible just west of here.

The road west from Atlantic City to South Pass City passes more old gold mines, notably the **Duncan Mine** (two miles out) and the famous **Carissa Mine,** just before dropping to South Pass City. Most of the mines and buildings are on private land, and many contain hazardous structures and shafts without covers. Watch your step!

A little more than seven miles south of Atlantic City is a monument to the **Willie Handcart**

Company. In 1856, a large group of Mormon emigrants led by James G. Willie was caught in a series of early winter storms and camped here awaiting help and provisions from Salt Lake City. Sixty-seven of them died before they could reach the promised land. This and the Mormon handcart monuments at Rocky Ridge and Rock Creek are described in a pamphlet available at South Pass State Historic Site. (See *Martin's Cove* under *Oregon Trail Landmarks* in the *Central Wyoming* chapter for details on another Mormon handcart disaster.)

Accommodations and Food

The **"Merc"** (307/332-5143) rents A-frame cabins for $65 d, plus $5 per person for additional guests; open April–November. The bar has occasional live music in the summer, along with a piano where you can display your own tuneful talents at other times. Maybe someone decided to shoot the piano player and missed because the mirror behind the bar has a bullet hole. The Merc's dinners are well-known throughout this part of Wyoming. In the front, you can munch on inexpensive but very good burgers and sandwiches for lunch. (The lunch menu is sometimes available at dinnertime.) Back-room guests, on the other hand, are treated to an old-timey setting of oil lanterns and pine walls and a menu (entrées $12–36) that includes aspen-grilled steaks and fresh seafood daily in the summer, or Thursday–Sunday in winter. Reservations are required.

One of the most attractive buildings in Atlantic City is the mint-condition **Miner's Delight B&B** (307/332-0248 or 888/292-0248). Originally known as the Carpenter Hotel, it was constructed in 1895 and run as a boardinghouse for miners and others until 1961. Today it's a cozy B&B with two Victorian-style rooms with private baths in the main building ($75 d), a small room with twin beds and a shared bath ($75 d), plus four rustic hand-chinked log cabins ($60 d) with shared baths. A full country breakfast is included, and Miner's Delight is open all year.

The BLM maintains two attractive campgrounds ($6, open June–Oct.) in young aspen stands—brilliantly yellow in the fall—along the Fort Stambaugh Loop Road: **Atlantic City Campground** and **Big Atlantic Gulch Campground.**

Adjacent to the Merc is **Dredge Saloon and Cafe** (307/332-7404) with a breakfast and lunch menu, homemade bread for the sub sandwiches, and delicious thick steaks, plus a few groceries and local crafts for sale. Bar patrons hang out at the pool table or in front of the big-screen TV.

Groceries are not available in either Atlantic City or South Pass, so stock up elsewhere.

FARSON AND VICINITY

Farson (pop. 240) stands at the busy highway junction where Hwy. 28 and U.S. 191 greet each other. All around are long straight roads, flat sagebrush desert, a few irrigated pastures, and antelope. It's a long way to anywhere else, so almost everyone stops for a road break at this oasis of sorts. In the simmering summer sun, **Farson Mercantile** (307/273-9511) is crowded with people buying ice-cream cones to eat in the shade of the olive trees out front. In addition to the ice-cream shop, the old brick building houses a classic country market. Also worth a look is the historic and picturesque log church in Farson.

Sitzman's Motel (307/273-9246) charges $48 d but is often full with workers. Park RVs for $16 at **Oregon Trail Campground** (307/273-5586). **Mitch's Cafe** (307/273-9606) serves standard road grub and features burlwood seats at the counter.

Heading South

Four miles south of Farson is tiny **Eden,** where irrigated green fields bring the arid landscape alive. Of note here is the old **Oregon Trail Baptist Church,** with its brown log walls, quaint bell tower, and back window facing the Wind River Mountains. The view probably makes it hard to concentrate on the service. Catercorner across the road is the **Eden Saloon,** where the view may not be as great, but after a few beers it really doesn't matter. Bicentennial Park makes a shady place to enjoy

© DON PITCHER

Farson Mercantile, Farson

a picnic. South of Eden, U.S. 191 cruises into the bleak Bad Lands Hills country on its way to Rock Springs. Killpecker Dunes rise on the eastern horizon.

Heading North

Immediately north of Farson, the highway crosses Big Sandy River, which is little more than a creek much of the year, with Big Sandy Reservoir (free camping) holding back much of its water for irrigation. Flat irrigated fields of hay surround Farson. As you continue north to Pinedale (58 miles), the jagged snow-topped crowns of the Wind River Mountains loom ever larger and the sagebrush grows more abundant on the arid landscape rolling away to the mountains. The highway crosses both the **Sublette Cutoff,** one of the original routes to Oregon Country, and the 1858 **Lander Cutoff,** the first federal road west of the Mississippi. Tune in to KQSW (96.5 FM) for country tunes to speed you on your way.

A gravel road that begins two miles east of Farson and heads north along Little Sandy Creek and then northwest to Boulder is even

more dramatic, passing along the foothills of the Winds. It's used for access to the Big Sandy Trailhead into the Bridger Wilderness. This is one of my favorite drives in Wyoming. Clouds often drape the distant mountains, but when they part—like curtains at a Broadway premier—they reveal the 13,000-foot crest of the Wind River Mountains in all its majesty. This is truly one of the classic Western vistas, and the interplay of land, light, and sky creates an unforgettable scene.

The land knocks you out: Mountains climb above the distant plain, crowning the eastern horizon with slanting patches of enormous rock faces and snow-mantled slopes, reflecting back the light from a westering sun. Antelope glance up as you drive past; a rough-legged hawk hunches on a fence post; several horses paw the ground. Periodically a narrow set of pickup-truck tracks angles over the horizon to some remote ranch. In places like this, it is hard not to love the wildly beautiful state of Wyoming.

I wrote the above paragraphs several years ago, and they remain basically true. Unfortunately, this part of Wyoming is changing, and changing fast. The wide-open sagebrush country north of Farson and south of Pinedale holds vast quantities of natural gas within the Pinedale Anticline Field and the Jonah Field; these are some of the largest recently discovered gas fields in the nation. By 2005, Sublette County had become Wyoming's biggest producer of natural gas (with 2 percent of the U.S. total), and dozens of drilling rigs were scattered across the land in a frenzied search for additional gas. Thousands of gas wells are already in place, with many thousands more planned, bringing a maze of roads and pipelines. So get here soon if you want to see what's left of the Old West before it's entirely chewed up in the mill of progress.

Pinedale and Vicinity

In the upper Green River Valley, with the Wind River Mountains providing a backdrop, Pinedale (pop. 1,400) has long served as a center for local ranchers, a stop for tourists heading to Jackson Hole, and a minor governmental center. In the 1990s, wealthy people bought up old ranches around the valley, built large summer homes, and landed their Lear jets at the little airport south of town. Residents feared Pinedale might become "another Jackson." That should have been the least of their worries. Today, Pinedale is being transformed by the latest rush—a boom spurred by high energy prices, the Bush administration's loosening of environmental regulations, and the discovery of massive natural gas resources beneath the sagebrush.

In the last few years Pinedale has seen a wave of development and prosperity. The town is swarming with pickup trucks and beer drinking, red meat–lovin' men who like their Coors cold and their steaks slightly rare. Jobs are plentiful and wages are substantial working for ExxonMobile, BP America, Shell, or EnCana. The old days of quiet country roads, endless vistas, and crusty cowboys are going fast. Say hello to the New West. Like it or not, it's coming.

The first inhabitants of the Upper Green River Valley were the Shoshone, Gros Ventre, Sheepeater, and Crow Indians, who hunted buffalo, elk, and antelope in this rich country. Whites first came as explorers and fur trappers in the early 1800s, and by the 1830s this was the "capital" of the fur trade in the Rockies. Six different rendezvous were held along the Upper Green River. The first white settler arrived with his cattle in 1878, and within a few years a small trading center sprang up alongside Pine Creek. The town prospered with development of the tie-hack industry in the late 19th century. Pinedale was platted in 1904, and within a year the town consisted of a general store, newspaper, blacksmith shop, saloon, photography studio, and other businesses. It later became the Sublette County seat.

SIGHTS
Catching the Drift
The Upper Green River is still important cattle country; in fact, it's the largest range allotment in the entire national forest system, home to 7,500 cattle. Get here in June to watch cowboys (locals more commonly use the term "riders") pushing the cattle into the mountains. Some are driven as far as 90 miles from the winter range in the desert. Cattle graze in the mountains all summer, watched over by a handful of riders who stay in cabins or trailers. Each fall, the cattle drift back down from their summer home in the mountains when cool mid-October weather hits the high country. Six miles west of Pinedale at the junction of U.S. 191 and Hwy. 352 (the Cora Y), cowboys from 20 local ranches sort out the 300–700 cattle that pile up against fences in the "Green River Drift."

◖ Museum of the Mountain Man
Pinedale's Museum of the Mountain Man

PINEDALE

To Jackson

To Farson and Rock Springs

To Fremont Lake, Half Moon Lake, and Elkhart Lake

FREMONT LAKE RD

MEDICAL CLINIC
MUSEUM OF THE MOUNTAIN MAN
SKYLINE ST
WASHINGTON ST
RODEO GROUNDS
PINE ST
WAGON WHEEL MOTEL
CANAL ST
FOREST SERVICE OFFICE
FALER'S THRIFTWAY
BLM OFFICE

FALER AVE
BRIDGER AVE
HIGH SCHOOL
NORTH ST
TETON COURT MOTEL
HALF MOON LODGE
SUNDANCE MOTEL
GAME AND FISH OFFICE
SUBLETTE AVE
FREMONT AVE
FREMONT AVE
B ST

SWIMMING POOL
TYLER AVE
LOG CABIN MOTEL
MAGNOLIA ST
INFORMATION HUT
WASHINGTON ST
TYLER AVE

BUFFALO ST
BEAVER ST
HENRICK ST
MAYBELL AVE
CHAMBERS HOUSE BED AND BREAKFAST
MCGREGOR'S PUB
WILL ST
LIBRARY
CHARLES ST
Creek

FRANKLIN AVE
LAKE AVE
GREAT OUTDOOR SHOP
Town Park
MARILYN ST
RIVERA LODGE

POST OFFICE

Pine

AMERICAN LEGION PARK
STUART ST
MADISON AVE
PINE ST
PINE CREEK INN
WILSON ST
ADAMS ST
WASHINGTON ST
SHANLEY AVE
LINCOLN AVE
MADISON AVE
JADE ST
AGATE ST

JACKSON AVE
JACKSON AVE
ASHLEY AVE

ASHLEY AVE
CLARK ST
COLTER AVE
BONNEVILLE ST
HOBACK ST
LEWIS AVE
BEST WESTERN PINEDALE INN
THE LODGE AT PINEDALE
PINEDALE CAMPGROUND
PINEDALE ENTERTAINMENT CENTER

COUNTRY CLUB LN
COUNTRY CLUB RD

AMERIHOST INN

RENDEZVOUS MEADOWS GOLF COURSE

0.2 mi
0.2 km
0

(700 E. Hennick St., 307/367-4101 or 877/686-6266, www.museumofthemountainman.com, open 9 A.M.–5 P.M. daily May–Sept., $5 adults, $4 seniors, $3 ages 6–12, free children under age six) sits on a hill overlooking town. This modern, spacious museum contains displays, artifacts, and memorabilia from the fur-trapping era. One of Jim Bridger's rifles (he probably owned several) is here, along with a covered wagon and a fascinating educational video about the fur trade. You'll learn about the daily lives of trappers, how they trapped beaver and processed furs, and how the market for hats helped open the American West. Be sure to check out the inscribed section from an Aspen tree cut along the old Lander Cutoff of the Oregon Trail. Downstairs are changing displays on the history of Sublette County, and a small gift shop sells historical books. The museum puts on special programs, living-history demonstrations, and lectures on the history of the West during the Green River Rendezvous.

Day Trips

Pinedale is a perfect base for explorations of the Wind River Mountains, with a multitude of day trips and overnight—or longer—adventures in all directions. Of particular note is **Skyline Drive,** a paved road that follows the eastern side of Fremont Lake (a destination in its own right), ending 17 miles later at a campground on the edge of the Bridger Wilderness. Hiking trails fan out from here, including a four-mile path to the aptly named **Photographer's Point.** Also high on my list of scenic attractions is **Green River Lakes,** 51 miles up a paved and then gravel road—and worth every rut along the way. (See the *Wind River Mountains* section for descriptions of both of these roads.)

ENTERTAINMENT AND EVENTS

Cowboy Bar (104 W. Pine, 307/367-4520) is a classic Old West drinking joint, with a pool table and live music most Friday and Saturday nights. **Corral Bar and Grill** (30 W. Pine

St., 307/367-2469) has pool, Foosball, darts, and live country-and-western tunes some summer weekends. **Fort William Guest Ranch** (307/367-4670, www.fort-william.com), eight miles east of Pinedale, is a popular place to unwind in a cozy atmosphere; it's open late May–September.

Pinedale Entertainment Center (153 S. Entertainment La., 307/367-6688) has two stadium-seating movie theaters, a bowling alley, an arcade room, and billiards.

The **International Pedigree Stage Stop Sled Dog Race** (307/734-1163, www.wyomingstagestop.org) stops here. (See the *Jackson Hole* chapter for more information.)

Another popular winter event is **Green River Winter Carnival** in late February or early March, with a kids' Olympics, various adult contests of strength, a dance, and even a drag-queen contest. The **Pinedale Blues Festival** (www.pinedaleblues.com) in June attracts top national acts.

Pinedale's acclaimed **Green River Rendezvous** (307/367-4101 or 877/686-6266, www.meetmeonthegreen.com) takes place on the second weekend in July each year. Established in 1936, this is one of the oldest celebrations of the era of mountain-man rendezvous and commemorates the raucous activities of the 1830s on nearby Horse Creek. The highlight is the rendezvous pageant (don't miss this one), along with parades, mountain-man encampment, living-history demonstrations, guest speakers, a rodeo, and craft booths.

SHOPPING

In business since 1947, the **Cowboy Shop** (137 W. Pine, 307/367-4300, www.cowboyshop.com) has an outstanding selection of Western clothes, boots, and other necessities of life.

Rock Rabbit Art Gallery (36 W. Pine St., 307/367-2485 or 888/303-5082, www.rockrabbit.com) is a good place to find contemporary Western oil paintings, fine art photography, metal sculptures, watercolors, and carvings from regional and national artists.

WIND RIVER MOUNTAINS

© DON PITCHER

Green River Rendezvous

RECREATION
Summer Recreation

In the summer you can ride the **White Pine Ski Area** (307/367-6606, www.whitepineski.com) chairlift to the top Friday–Sunday for $5. Mountain-bike rentals are available for a fast downhill ride on the trails. The resort is 10 miles northeast of town, and also has a restaurant and horseback rides.

Other outfits with trail rides include **Fort William Guest Ranch** (307/367-4670, www.fortwilliam.com), **Half Moon Lake Resort** (307/367-6373, www.halfmoonlake.com), and **Boulder Lake Lodge** (307/537-5400 or 800/788-5401, www.boulderlake.com).

Golfers will enjoy Pinedale's nine-hole **Rendezvous Meadows Golf Course** (307/367-4252).

Stop by the Bridger–Teton National Forest **Pinedale Ranger District** office (29 E. Fremont Lake Rd., 307/367-4326, www.fs.fed.us/r4/btnf) for maps and hiking information on trails in the nearby Bridger Wilderness.

The Adventure Cycling Association's **Great Divide Mountain Bike Route** (www.adv-cy-cling.org) passes through Pinedale, and the town serves as a restocking point before heading south into very remote county between South Pass and Rawlins.

The **Great Outdoor Shop** (332 W. Pine, 307/367-2440, www.greatoutdoorshop.com) sells quality outdoor gear of all types, along with topo maps. Ask about equipment rentals in the summer, including tents, sleeping bags, climbing equipment, and fishing gear. It also operates a shuttle service with rides to Wind River Mountain trailheads and can arrange llamas and guided pack trips. **Faler's Thriftway** (341 E. Pine, 307/367-2131) has additional outdoor supplies.

Pack a picnic lunch and head to the **town park** at Franklin and Tyler, with a kid's fishing pond and playground and a paved path along Pine Creek. **American Legion Park** on the north side of Pine Creek also has picnic tables, plus a gazebo and a pretty streamside view.

On the Water

The eastern slope of the Wind River Mountains contains several large lakes created when glaciers retreated after the last major ice age 10,000 years ago. The terminal moraines they left behind acted as dams, although some have been enlarged with human-created dams in recent years. The lakes are very popular with anglers. **Fremont Lake** is Wyoming's second-largest natural lake, reaching 11 miles in length, 0.5 mile across, and up to 600 feet deep. There's even a nice sandy beach. It's just three miles northeast of Pinedale and is famous for Mackinaw that approach 40 pounds. Fremont has three Forest Service campgrounds along its shore (free–$12; one accessible only by boat). Rent a fishing boat, canoe, kayak, or pontoon boat from **Lakeside Lodge Resort and Marina** (307/367-2221, www.lakesidelodge.com, open mid-Apr.–mid-Dec.). Comfortable cabins and a restaurant are also here.

Other lakes of note are **Half Moon Lake, Willow Lake,** and **Boulder Lake.** (See *Wind River Mountains* section in this chapter for information on the Green River and New Fork lakes.) All of these lakes have Forest Service campgrounds (free–$12) and trails that lead into the Bridger Wilderness. In addition, the BLM maintains free camping areas on the west end of Boulder Lake and at Scab Creek (southeast of Boulder Lake). **Half Moon Lake Resort** (307/367-6373, www.halfmoonlake.com) rents canoes, pontoon boats, and canoes.

The lakes and streams near Pinedale offer outstanding fishing for cutthroat, rainbow, brook, Mackinaw, golden, and brown trout, plus grayling and whitefish. Several local outfitters offer float-fishing trips down the Green River; see the chamber of commerce for a listing. **Two Rivers Emporium** (307/367-4131 or 800/329-4353, www.2rivers.net) is a good place to find fly-fishing supplies and conditions or to book a drift trip. Canoeists or kayakers will also enjoy floating stretches of the Green River. The Forest Service office has details.

Swim at Pinedale's Olympic-sized **indoor pool** (307/367-2832) at the high school on the corner of Hennick Street and Tyler Avenue.

Winter Recreation
Ten miles northeast of Pinedale near Fremont Lake, **White Pine Ski Area** (307/367-6606, www.whitepineski.com) has two triple chairlifts and 25 ski trails. All-day lift tickets cost $26. The modern-day lodge houses ski and snowboard rentals, a restaurant, and lounge. In addition, 35 kilometers of groomed cross-country ski trails are accessible from the base lodge parking lot.

Cross-country skiers should pick up a copy of the *Skyline Drive Nordic Touring Trails* map from the Forest Service office in Pinedale. Maps are available on the web at www.pinedaleonline.com/x-countryskiing.htm. The 60 kilometers of trails are marked but not always groomed. More adventurous skiers will find all sorts of places to explore in the Bridger Wilderness just a few miles east of Pinedale. Rent cross-country skis from the **Great Outdoor Shop** (332 W. Pine, 307/367-2440, www.greatoutdoorshop.com).

The lower elevations of the Wind River Mountains are also extremely popular with snowmobilers; trails head out right from town. See the chamber of commerce for a list of local companies offering snowmobile rentals and tours. The 365-mile **Continental Divide Snowmobile Trail** passes through Pinedale, continuing north to Yellowstone and around the Wind River Mountains to Lander. **Green River Outfitters** (307/367-2416, www.greenriveroutfitters.com) leads snowmobile tours into the mountains around Pinedale, including overnight trips to a mountain cabin.

ACCOMMODATIONS
Pinedale has several attractive places offering friendly and clean rooms in pleasant settings. It's a good idea to book a month ahead for July and August to be sure of space, particularly during the Green River Rendezvous in July or the Pinedale Blues Festival in June. Go to www.pinedaleonline.com for web links to most local motels and other accommodations.

Motels
Rivera Lodge (442 W. Marilyn, 307/367-2424 or 888/819-1053) is right in town but off the main street and quiet. The cozy and

well-maintained cabins ($70–120 d) sit along Pine Creek and are open May–September. Most have kitchenettes. The friendly owners put on a free creekside breakfast every Sunday morning.

Teton Court Motel (123 E. Magnolia, 307/367-4317 or 877/841-0499, www.teton-court-motel.com) has 18 rooms—all with fridges, microwaves, and Wi-Fi—for $85 d. Kitchenettes cost $100 for up to four guests.

The appropriately named **◖ Log Cabin Motel** (49 E. Magnolia, 307/367-4579 in summer or 928/768-5262 in winter, www.thelogcabinmotel.com, $90–125 d, open May–Sept.) features 10 attractive and beautifully maintained cabins. Built in 1929, they are now on the National Register of Historic Places. Larger two-bedroom units sleep five and have kitchenettes.

Pinedale's newest lodging place is **AmeriHost Inn** (1624 W. Pine St., 307/367-8300 or 800/434-5800, www.amerihostpinedale.com), with an indoor pool, hot tub, fitness room, a hot breakfast, and Wi-Fi. Large standard rooms are $130 d, and suites with either kitchenettes or jetted tubs are $150–200 d.

Bed-and-Breakfasts

Right in town you'll find **◖ Chambers House B&B** (111 W. Magnolia St., 307/367-2168 or 800/567-2168, www.chambershouse.com, $85–125 d), an elegant two-story 1933 log home that is a local landmark. Inside are five guest rooms (private or shared baths) and two sitting rooms. One room is wheelchair-accessible. Rates include a full breakfast and kids are welcome.

Three miles southeast of Pinedale, **Pole Creek Ranch B&B** (307/367-4433, www.polecreekranch.com) is a modern log home in the country with an outdoor hot tub, a barn, and corrals. Two guest rooms share a bath and a third has its own; horseback riding and buggy rides are available by arrangement. The view of the Wind River Mountains is impressive, and the friendly owners will be happy to share their Christianity. Rates are very reasonable: $50 s or $65 d ("married couples"), including a full breakfast. Kids and pets welcome.

Guest Ranches and Resorts

Half Moon Lake Resort (307/367-6373, www.halfmoonlake.com) is a full-service resort overlooking the lake for which it is named. It's 10 miles northeast of Pinedale. Stay in modern log cabins with fridges and microwaves ($85–135; the largest sleeps six or more comfortably), and enjoy meals in a pleasant restaurant with a redwood deck along the shore. Fishing boats, pontoon boats, and canoes are available for rent, or you can head out on a horseback ride for two hours or all day. There's even a paddle-wheel boat with nightly dinner cruises in the summer. The lodge is closed in November and April.

Five miles northeast of Pinedale on the south end of Fremont Lake is **Lakeside Lodge Resort and Marina** (307/367-2221 or 877/755-5253, www.lakesidelodge.com). Accommodations include rustic log cabins ($65 d) with a shared bathhouse, along with a dozen deluxe shorefront log cabins with fireplaces and private baths for $139 d. RV hookups are $22, and you can rent kayaks, canoes, pontoon boats, and fishing boats. The lodge is open mid-April–mid-December and has a restaurant and lounge with a great deck along the lake.

Overlooking the Green River 30 miles north of Pinedale, **Elk Ridge Lodge** (307/367-2553, www.elkridgelodge.com) has guest ranch accommodations in modern log buildings on the edge of the national forest. Six-night all-inclusive stays (lodging, meals, horseback rides, four-wheeling, fishing, and float trips) cost $1,800 for two people. The lodge is also a winter destination for snowmobilers and cross-country skiers.

Fort William Guest Ranch (eight miles east of town, 307/367-4670, www.fort-william.com) is a very rustic lodge with accommodations ($85 d with breakfast), a restaurant and lounge, plus horseback riding and fly-fishing. Open late May–September. Call ahead for dinner reservations.

Twenty-nine miles north of Pinedale, the secluded and historic **DC Bar Guest Ranch** (307/367-2268 or 888/803-7316, www.bwo.com) nestles within the Upper Green River Valley at an elevation of 8,200 feet. The ranch is surrounded by national forest land and has room for up to 40 guests in seven cabins and a new luxury lodge. Horseback riding, fishing, kids' activities, archery, and other fun fill the agenda. All-inclusive rates are $2,250 for two people for a six-night stay. The ranch is open year-round and is popular for wintertime snowmobiling and fall hunting trips. It also offers a series of natural-history workshops though the Bridger Institute, including wildlife-sculpting, wilderness skills, and wild animal tracks.

Flying A Ranch (307/367-2385 in summer, 307/336-3339 in the off-season, or 888/833-3348, www.flyinga.com) has space for just 14 adults (no kids unless you book the entire ranch) in a casual Western atmosphere. Horseback rides are the featured attraction, but guests also enjoy wildlife-watching, hiking, fishing, mountain-biking, or simply relaxing with a book or luxuriating in the hot tub. The ranch was built in 1929, and both the main lodge and cabins have been lovingly restored. Each cabin features handmade furniture, a private bath, kitchenette, and fireplace or woodstove. Some provide extraordinary views of the Wind River Mountains. Six-night rates at Flying A are $2,600–3,000 for two people, all-inclusive. Open late June–late September.

Lozier's Box R Ranch (near Cora, 307/367-2291 or 800/822-8466, www.boxr.com) is a working cattle ranch with accommodations for 20 guests. The emphasis is on horseback riding, with the opportunity to help move cattle and otherwise pretend to be a cowboy. Optional excursions take you to gorgeous mountain country on horseback, and Box R also has spring cattle drives and fall cattle roundups. It's open late May–mid-September, with all-inclusive weekly rates of $2,200–2,800 for two people.

Camping

The closest public camping is **Fremont Lake Campground** ($12, open late May–mid-Sept.), seven miles northeast of Pinedale along the lake. Even if you aren't staying here or planning any wilderness hikes from the trailheads, *do* take the 15-mile (paved) drive from Pinedale to road's end, where you'll find the free Upper Fremont Lake Campground. The road is narrow but delivers gorgeous views of several lakes

and the rugged crest of the Wind River Mountains, and it has a good turnaround space for RVs and horse trailers at the upper end. Make campground reservations ($9 fee) at 518/885-3639 or 877/444-6777, www.reserveusa.com.

Half Moon Lake Campground ($7, open June–mid-Sept.) is on the northwest shore of Half Moon Lake, 10 miles northeast of Pinedale. A dozen other Forest Service and BLM campgrounds are dotted all along the western side of the Wind River Mountains.

Lakeside Lodge Resort and Marina at Fremont Lake, five miles northeast of town (307/367-2221 or 877/755-5253, www.lakesidelodge.com, $22 RVs) is open May–October.

FOOD

Pinedale is a bustling steak and pork chop sort of town where the beer flows freely.

Breakfast and Lunch

In existence for more than three decades, **Patio Grill** (35 W. Pine, 307/367-4611) serves dependably good family breakfasts, along with lunch. For a filling lunchtime pizza buffet, head to **Wind River Rendezvous Pizzeria** (4 Country Club La., 307/367-6760).

A favorite of travelers, **McGregor's Pub** (25 N. Franklin Ave., 307/367-4443) serves buffalo burgers, veal enchiladas, chicken, pasta, and even seafood. It's quiet and relaxing, with an outside deck in the summer. Most dinner entrées cost $16–25.

Los Cabos (120 Westpine, 307/367-6781) is a busy family Mexican restaurant with all the standards for $8–12. No alcohol and no smoking. Things are just the opposite at **Bottoms Up Brewery and Grill** (402 W. Pine St., 307/367-2337), where the smoke is thick and the fresh-brewed beers flow freely. There's a light menu—most items under $8—that includes bratwurst, fajitas, fish and chips, and pizzas. It's a fine place to relax with the locals.

Stockman's Restaurant (117 W. Pine, 307/367-4563) has the finest local steaks, plus a salad bar, prime rib, pork chops, veal, seafood, and chicken. Most dinner entrées are $13–25. Smokers rule here.

For a meal and drink with a view, drive five miles northeast of Pinedale along Fremont Lake to **Lakeside Restaurant** (307/367-3555) at Lakeside Lodge Resort. Enjoy steaks, chicken, pasta, and nightly specials (most around $12–18) while taking in the view from the big deck that fronts Fremont Lake and the Wind River Mountains. The upstairs lounge houses a big-screen TV. Open May–October.

Also of note is **Half Moon Lake Resort** (307/367-6373, www.halfmoonlake.com), 10 miles northeast of Pinedale, with fine dining and drinks on the lakeside deck.

Groceries
Get groceries at **Faler's Thriftway** (341 E. Pine, 307/367-2131), which has a deli and one of the largest collections of critter heads anywhere.

INFORMATION AND SERVICES
The **Sublette County Visitor Center** (25 N. Tyler Ave., 307/367-2242 or 888/285-7282, www.visitsublettecounty.com) is open 9 A.M.–7 P.M. Monday–Friday and 11 A.M.–5 P.M. Saturday late May–early September, and 9 A.M.–5 P.M. Monday–Friday the rest of the year. For additional Pinedale information on the web, visit www.pinedaleonline.com and www.sublette.com.

A fine online source for information on the various communities around Pinedale is www.sublette.com.

Government offices include the Forest Service's **Pinedale Ranger District Office** (29 E. Fremont Lake Rd., 307/367-4326, www.fs.fed.us/r4/btnf) and the **BLM's Pinedale Field Office** (432 E. Mill St., 307/367-5300, www.wy.blm.gov).

Check your email on computers at the beautiful new **Sublette County Library** (155 S. Tyler St., 307/367-4114). Wash clothes at **Highlander Center Laundromat** on Pine Street.

GETTING THERE AND AROUND
Drivers en route to Jackson should fill up in Pinedale; gas prices only get higher from here north. There is no commercial bus service to Pinedale, and the nearest commercial airports are in Jackson and Rock Springs. Shuttle services are available through **Pinedale Cab** (307/367-7668). The **Great Outdoor Shop** (307/367-2440, www.greatoutdoorshop.com) provides shuttles to Wind River Mountain trailheads and can also move your vehicle.

Sublink Stage (46 N. Franklin St., 307/367-7433 or 800/542-2632, www.sublinkstage.com) has van service on Saturdays and Wednesdays between Salt Lake City and Pinedale April–November. Its Pinedale office has computers to check your email.

BOULDER
A dozen miles south of Pinedale is Boulder. On the drive down (about halfway between the two towns) you'll pass two roadside telephone poles topped by active osprey nests. Boulder (pop. 30) holds a handful of businesses, including the century-old **Boulder Store** (307/537-5480), home to a restaurant with three meals a day (closed weekends). Much of the once-wild country between Pinedale and Boulder is being rapidly developed into tract homes to house the area's fast-growing economy. Fortunately, most of this ugliness ends (at least for now) south of Boulder, providing dramatic mountain-and-plains vistas.

The BLM's free **Stokes Crossing Campground** is two miles east on Hwy. 353, and then eight miles north on a gravel road. Along Boulder Creek, this is a relaxing place for anglers. A mile north of Boulder is **Wind River View Campground** (307/537-5453, $25 RVs, open June–mid-Sept.). There's no shade on this exposed and windy site, but the views are noteworthy.

Twelve miles up Hwy. 353, **Boulder Lake Lodge** (307/537-5400 or 800/788-5401, www.boulderlake.com, open June–Oct.) is a modern ranch with guest rooms for $70 d. In addition to accommodations, it serves family-style meals (call ahead for reservations) and offers horseback rides, along with pack trips. Also available are all-inclusive one-week stays at $3,050 for two people.

DANIEL

Head 11 miles west of Pinedale and then another mile south on U.S. 189 to tiny Daniel, where the **Green River Bar** makes some of the best Bloody Marys in Wyoming. The community is within spittin' distance from the original Green River rendezvous grounds and is home to a historic **little red schoolhouse,** in use 1920–1939.

A roadside marker north of Daniel notes the site of **Fort Bonneville,** constructed in 1832 to serve as a fur-trade center run by Captain Benjamin Bonneville. It lasted only a year but gained the nickname "Fort Nonsense" because of the severely cold and snowy winters that made life difficult for Bonneville's men. The fort consisted of two blockhouses guarding a perimeter of tall log posts and was used as a storage site for men and their supplies. Although nothing remains of the fort today, it was significant as one of the earliest "forts" in Wyoming.

Practicalities

The BLM's **Warren Bridge Campground** ($6, open all year, 307/367-5300) sits beside the Green River nine miles north of Daniel on U.S. 191/189. Another dozen rustic campsites (free) are spread out along 10 miles of the gravel road that parallels the river upstream. These grassy sites are popular with anglers; ask the attendant at Warren Bridge Campground which ones are available.

1840 RENDEZVOUS SITE

Two miles south and then 2.5 miles east of Daniel is the site of the 1840 rendezvous, the last grand gathering of mountain men and Indians. The dirt access road cuts through barren sage and grass country, but the vista changes abruptly as you reach the site. Below you, the Green River twists its way through a lush landscape of grass, cattle, and cottonwoods. It's pretty easy to see why the rendezvous was held in this area! Get here for a summer sunrise, when you can imagine a multitude of Indians and mountain men spread out below for the annual festivities. The meadow contains a memorial to missionaries Narcissa Whitman and Eliza Spalding, who in 1836 became the first white women to venture by land across the American continent.

A tiny shrine overlooks the meadow, marking Wyoming's first Mass, performed by Belgian Jesuit missionary Father Pierre Jean DeSmet during the 1840 rendezvous. An idealist of the first order, DeSmet spent more than three decades working with Indians in an attempt to protect them from being subsumed by America's territorial ambitions. His goal was to create communities where Indians could preserve their culture while adopting some of the technological advantages of Western civilization. Although the mission failed miserably, DeSmet was one of the few 19th-century men who maintained lifelong friendships with the Indians. "Blackrobe," as he was known, always traveled unarmed throughout the West and served as a peacemaker during treaty negotiations. The shrine on the site of DeSmet's 1840 service is used during a commemorative Mass on the second Sunday of each July.

Pinckney Sublette, one of four brothers from the famous family of fur trappers, is buried not far from the DeSmet monument. Just up the dirt road are the red log barn and white log home of the historic Quarter Circle 5 Ranch, a definitive Wyoming spread.

BIG PINEY

When the first edition of this book came out in 1989, Big Piney (pop. 500, www.bigpiney.com) was down for the count. The oil boom of the 1970s was long gone, half the stores were boarded up, and you could get a room for $18. As of 2006, the situation was completely reversed as another boom roared through the region—this time one fueled (so to speak) by high gas prices and the Bush Administration's green light to drill, drill, drill. House trailers crowd the edges of Big Piney and nearby Marbleton, big pickup trucks idle on the streets, and all the motel rooms are chock-a-block with hard-working men and women. But after every boom comes a bust....

MOUNTAIN MEN

The era of the fur trapper is one of the most colorful slices of American history, a time when a rough and hardy breed of men took to the Rockies in search of furs and adventure. Romanticized in such films as *Jeremiah Johnson*, the trappers actually played but a brief role in history and numbered fewer than 1,000 individuals. Their real importance lay in acting as the opening wedge for the West, a vanguard for the settlers and gold miners who would follow their paths – often led by these same mountain men.

THE FUR BUSINESS

Fashion sent men into the Rockies in the first place, since the waterproof underfur of a beaver could be used to create the beaver hat, which was all the rage in the early part of the 19th century. Beavers in the eastern United States were soon trapped out, forcing trappers to head farther and farther west. Several companies competed for the lucrative fur market, but John Jacob Astor's American Fur Company proved the most successful. In 1811, Astor sent a party of men across the Rockies to the mouth of the Columbia to build a trading post and then set up a chain of posts across the West. The men – known as the Astorians – were probably the first whites to follow the route that would later become the Oregon Trail.

John Jacob Astor's trappers went head to head against the Rocky Mountain Fur Company, which was owned at various times by some of the most famous mountain men – Jedediah Smith, David Jackson, William and Milton Sublette, Jim Bridger, Thomas Fitzpatrick, and others. Competition for furs became so intense that Astor's men began following Jim Bridger and Tom Fitzpatrick to discover their trapping grounds. After trying unsuccessfully to shake the men tailing them, Bridger and Fitzpatrick deliberately headed into the heart of Blackfeet country, where Indians killed the leader of Astor's party and managed to leave Bridger with an arrowhead in his shoulder that was not removed until three years later.

A large number of Indians (particularly from the Flathead and Nez Perce tribes) were also involved in the fur trade, and a standard Indian trade value was 240 beaver pelts for a riding horse. In the mountains, anything from the world back east had considerable value: Guns sold for $100 each, blankets for $40 apiece, tobacco for $3 per pound, and alcohol (often diluted) for up to $64 per gallon. After just two years of such trading, William Ashley retired with an $80,000 profit. Control of the fur market continued to change hands as the Rocky Mountain Fur Company and the American Fur Company competed with each other and with a mysterious company headed by Captain Benjamin Bonneville, which some believe was a front for the U.S. Army to explore the West.

Most of the men who trapped in the Rockies were hired and outfitted by the fur companies, but others worked under contract and traded furs for overpriced supplies. Many men found themselves in debt to the company at the end of a season. At the top of the heap were the free trappers, men who worked either alone or with others but who sold their furs to whomever offered the highest prices. Some men, primarily those who brought trade goods to the rendezvous, became rich in the process. Others, such as John Colter, Jim Bridger, James Beckwourth, Jedediah Smith, Thomas Fitzpatrick, and Kit Carson, would achieve fame for their rich knowledge of the land and their ability to survive against insurmountable odds. Many trappers married Indian women, learned sign language and various Indian tongues, and lived in tepees.

A good trapper could take in more than 150 beaver in a year, worth $4–6 apiece. It was an arduous job, and the constant threat of attacks by the Blackfeet Indians made it even more difficult. The great letting-go came with the summer rendezvous, an event anticipated for months ahead of time.

THE RENDEZVOUS
William H. Ashley, founder of the Rocky Mountain Fur Company, was one of the most important figures in the fur trade. Ashley's company of men – along with $10,000 in supplies – made it up into the Yellowstone River country that summer, and the success of the trappers led to the first rendezvous in 1825 on the Henrys Fork near its confluence with the Green River, along the present-day Wyoming-Utah border. Thus began the first rendezvous. They would take place every summer until 1840. Ashley failed to bring booze that first summer, and the rendezvous lasted only two days. In future years, however, the whiskey flowed freely, and the festivities lasted for weeks.

The rendezvous – a French word meaning "appointed place of meeting" – was a time when both white and Indian trappers could sell their furs, trade for needed supplies and Indian squaws (the women had little say in the matter), meet with old friends, get rip-roaring drunk, and engage in storytelling, gambling, gun duels, and contests of all sorts. Horse racing, wrestling bouts, and shooting contests were favorites – Kit Carson killed Shunar, a big French bully, in a duel during one of the Green River rendezvous. Debauchery reigned supreme in these three-week-long affairs, and by the time they were over, many of the trappers had lost their entire year's earnings.

During the heyday of the fur trade, a common saying was "all trails lead to the Seeds-keedee [Green River]." Six rendezvous were held here in the 1830s, others were held in the Wind River/Popo Agie River area, on Ham's Fork of the Green River, and in Idaho and Utah. Sites were chosen where there was space for up to 500 mountain men and 3,000 Indians, plenty of game, ample grazing for the thousands of horses, and good water. Not coincidentally, all were held in Shoshone country rather than farther east or north, where the hostile Sioux, Blackfeet, and Crow held sway. Despite such precautions, more than half of Ashley's men were scalped by Indians.

CHANGING TIMES
The end of the rendezvous system – and most of the Rocky Mountain fur trapping – came about for a variety of reasons: overtrapping, the financial panic of 1837, and the growing use of other materials, particularly the South American nutria and Chinese silk, for hats. In addition, permanent trading posts such as Fort Laramie drew Indians away from the mountains to trade for buffalo robes instead of beaver furs. By 1840, when the last rendezvous was held on the banks of the Green River near present-day Pinedale, it was obvious there would be no more. One of the longtime trappers, Robert Newell, said to his partner, Joseph Meek:

We are done with this life in the mountains – done with wading in beaver dams, and freezing or starving alternately – done with Indian trading and Indian fighting. The fur trade is dead in the Rocky Mountains, and it is no place for us now, if ever it was. We are young yet, and have life before us. We cannot waste it here; we cannot or will not return to the States. Let us go down to the Wallamet and take farms.

Green River Valley Museum (307/276-5343, www.grvm.com, open noon–4 P.M. Tues.–Sat. mid-June–mid-Oct.) has a sampling of the area's ranching, homesteading, and oil and gas history. The main annual event is the **Big Piney Chuckwagon Days** on the Fourth of July. Festivities include a kid's rodeo, parade, fireworks, and free barbecue. A public **swimming pool** is at the high school on the west side.

Wyoming Range

Bridger–Teton National Forest's **Big Piney Ranger District Office** (307/276-3375, www.fs.fed.us/r4/btnf) has details about the route west into the Wyoming Range. Three of its classic old cabins ($30 for up to four) are available for rent year-round.

Triple Peak Lodge (307/276-3408 or 866/302-7753, www.triplepeak.com) is 20 miles west of Big Piney on South Cottonwood Creek near the Wyoming Range. This lodge is open year-round and resembles an Old West hotel. It offers guest rooms, along with outfitting and guide services, fishing, a cow camp each fall, and wintertime snowmobiling. Lodging is $65 s or $70 d; add $25 per person for three meals daily.

High Wide and Lonesome (307/260-7990 or 877/276-3485, www.hwl.net) emphasizes horseback adventures in some of the most remote parts of the state, including the Red Desert and Pony Express Trail. These are for experienced riders who don't mind roughing it and camping under the stars at night. All-inclusive five-night trips cost $1,500 per person. Groups are kept to eight guests or fewer.

Practicalities

Big Piney Motel (307/276-3352, $46–56 d) has standard rooms with fridges and microwaves. The BLM maintains a handful of free riverside sites at **New Fork River Campground,** 12 miles east of Marbleton on Hwy. 351.

Happy Trails Cafe (307/276-5776) is open for lunch and dinner, with pizza, chicken baskets, sandwiches, and ice cream. **Burney and Co.** (307/276-3321) is the local grocery store, and the town has a library.

MARBLETON

Marbleton (pop. 700) is just a couple of hundred yards up U.S. 189 from Big Piney. There's not much to do here, but you can watch flicks at **The Flick Theatre** (307/276-5404). The **Waterhole** (307/276-9977) is the center of nightlife in the area and puts on a popular cowboy open golf tournament each summer.

Marbleton is home to the **Sublette County Fair** (www.sublette.com/countyfair), held the first weekend of August each year. One of the attractions here is the **Little Buckaroo Rodeo** for children. Other rodeos take place throughout the summer at the fairgrounds.

Country Chalet Inn (307/276-3391, $45 s or $52 d) is a comfortable place to stay. For a few bucks more, **Marbleton Inn** (307/276-5231, $65 s or $73 d) offers the best accommodations in the area. Camp at **Rob's Roost RV Park** (307/276-3611, $15 tents, $20 RVs, open year-round).

The restaurant at the Marbleton Inn serves good all-American meals in a smoke-free setting. Just up the street is **Rio Verde Grill** (307/276-5353) with Southwestern-style food.

Hot showers are available at **Laundry Basket Laundromat.**

Sublink Stage (307/367-7433 or 800/542-2632, www.sublinkstage.com, Apr.–Nov.) provides twice-weekly van service between Salt Lake City and Pinedale, stopping in Marbleton en route.

LANDER CUTOFF

North of Marbleton, the enormous Wind River Mountains become more conspicuous and the highway crosses the Lander Cutoff, its ruts still discernible across the sagebrush. Built in 1858 by Colonel Frederick W. Lander and his soldiers, it served as both a shorter route to California and Oregon and a way to bypass the Mormon communities in Utah. The route offered good grazing and water as well as abundant game, and quickly became the preferred route to California and Oregon. It was also the only section of the Oregon Trail funded with government money.

Many miles of the old Lander Cutoff can still be driven and are denoted with Oregon Trail markers. These roads are readily visible and used today by locals for hunting access, ranching, and recreation. You'll need a high-clearance, four-wheel-drive rig to do it, and expect to poke along at five miles per hour, but it's a very interesting trip. Sections that go into private land are gated off, and roads bypass those places and take you to the more improved roads. The Lander Cutoff is also good for explorations by mountain-bikers, but be sure to bring plenty of water. Contact the BLM in Pinedale for details.

Wagons A+Cross Wyoming (307/859-8629 or 888/818-3581, www.wagonsacrosswyoming.com) guides historical five-day wagon-train trips along the Lander Cutoff in July and August for $950 per person.

TO JACKSON HOLE

U.S. 189/191 provides a scenic route to Hoback Junction and Jackson Hole, crossing the Green River and then slowly climbing into the hills. Aspens begin to appear on the hilltops, and willows line the creeks. The 11,000-foot-tall Gros Ventre Mountains are visible to the northwest. Gradually, lodgepole pine and aspen begin to replace the sagebrush. At **the Rim,** the road enters Bridger–Teton National Forest. West of here, the land drains into the Hoback River, which joins the Snake River at Hoback Junction 40 miles away. The road curves gradually down through this mountainous country, crossing the Hoback River repeatedly.

Bondurant

The spread-out town of Bondurant (pop. 160) straggles along the road through a gorgeous mountain valley, its pastures dotted with piles of hay, creekside willows, and grazing horses. The Gros Ventre Mountains form a dramatic northern backdrop, but the developments consist of just a few scattered log homes. Bondurant is named for Sarah Ellen and Benjamin Franklin Bondurant, the first settlers here. Between 1907 and 1927, they ran a popular dude ranch and had as pets all sorts of wild animals: antelope, elk, and even young bears.

The **Bondurant Barbecue** at the end of June includes a big barbecue feast at the

Church of St. Hubert the Hunter, a classic log structure built in 1943.

Green River Outfitters (307/367-2416, www.greenriveroutfitters.com) leads horseback trail rides and overnight pack trips from Bondurant.

On the west end of "town," **Elkhorn Bar and Trading Post** (307/733-8358, www.elkhornbondurant.com) consists of a friendly general store, gas station, café, country watering hole, and launderette. Six small cabins ($65 d) contain fridges and microwaves and are open year-round. The bar has a pool table and darts, or you can sit down for a meal at Dell Creek Diner, serving steak, seafood, sandwiches, chicken, and salads for $10–16.

Near Bondurant, the Forest Service's **Hoback Guard Station** (307/276-3375, www.fs.fed.us/r4/btnf) is available for rent year-round and sleeps four for $30. It includes two rooms with a seasonal bathroom and running water. Access is by skis or snowmobile in the winter.

Cow Cabins (307/267-2428, www.cowcabins.com) consists of a log lodge ($200) and a smaller cabin ($120) on a beautiful 2,000-acre ranch a few miles east of Bondurant near Hoback Rim.

Hoback Canyon

A few miles west of Bondurant, the road clings to the walls of Hoback Canyon as it passes the high face of Battle Mountain, site of one of the few conflicts between Indians and whites in this part of Wyoming. It was here in 1895 that whites from Jackson Hole attacked Bannock Indians who had been hunting "out of season" along the Hoback River. Just before you reach Hoback Junction, a signpost describes John Hoback, the trapper and guide who led the Astorian trappers of Wilson Price Hunt through here in 1811.

The canyon is occasionally blocked by avalanches in the winter but is a great place to see deer, moose, and bighorn sheep.

【 Granite Hot Springs

Just west of Battle Mountain on U.S. 189/191 is the turnoff to Granite Hot Springs

(307/734-7400). *Do* take this very scenic side trip! A well-maintained gravel road follows Granite Creek for 10 miles, affording impressive views of the Gros Ventre Range and the 50-foot drop of **Granite Falls.** The road ends at a parking lot just a short walk from the hot springs. The deep pool was built in 1933 by the CCC and recently improved with a deck and changing rooms. The pool stays around 93°F in the summer but rises to 112°F in winter when the water flow slows. The springs are open 10 A.M.–8 P.M. June–October, and 11 A.M.–5 P.M. December–March; closed in the fall and spring. No showers or running water are available at the pool, but vault toilets are nearby. The cost is $6 adults, $4 ages 3–12, and free for infants. Suits and tow-

els can be rented, and a few snacks are sold here. Granite Canyon Road is not plowed in winter but is groomed for use by both snowmobilers and cross-country skiers. A nearby campground ($15) is open late June–September. The campground almost never fills up and is managed by folks from the hot springs. Dispersed camping is allowed on the road to Granite Hot Springs, except along the final 1.3 miles before the springs.

During the winter, you can ride a dog sled to the hot springs. Iditarod musher Frank Teasley's **Jackson Hole Iditarod Sled Dog Tours** (307/733-7388 or 800/554-7388, www.jhsled-dog.com) offers all-day trips for $225 per person, including a big dinner cooked while you relax in the springs.

JACKSON HOLE

Jackson Hole is one of the most-visited slices of wild country in North America, attracting well more than three million travelers each year. They come here for a multitude of reasons: to camp under the stars in Grand Teton National Park, to play and shop in the New West town of Jackson, to hike flower-bedecked trails up forested valleys, to ride sleighs among thousands of elk, to raft down the Snake River, to ski or snowboard at one of the local resorts, or to simply stand in wonderment as the sun colors the sky behind the mountains. Many continue north to Yellowstone National Park, another place on everyone's must-see list. Drive north from Jackson toward Yellowstone and you'll quickly discover the biggest reason so many people are attracted to this place—its beauty. The Tetons act as a magnet, drawing

your eyes away from the road and forcing you to stop and absorb some of their majesty. Welcome to one of the world's great wonderlands.

In the lingo of the mountain men, a "hole" was a large valley ringed by mountain ranges, and each was named for the trapper who based himself there. Jackson Hole, on Wyoming's far western border, is justifiably the most famous of all these intermountain valleys. Although Jackson Hole reaches an impressive 48 miles north to south and up to 16 miles across, the magnificent range of mountains to the west is what defines this valley. Shoshone Indians who wandered through this country called the peaks Teewinot (Many Pinnacles); later explorers would use such labels as Shark's Teeth or Pilot Knobs. But lonely French Canadian trappers arriving in the early 1800s

© DON PITCHER

JACKSON HOLE

HIGHLIGHTS

◖ Art Galleries: Jackson reveals its "Art Center of the Rockies" status with more than 30 local galleries and a massive new Jackson Hole Center for the Arts. There's something for every taste (page 339).

◖ Town Square: Where else could you mix three million tourists, hundreds of elk antlers arranged in arches, and a faux shoot-out on summer evenings (page 340)?

◖ National Museum of Wildlife Art: One of Wyoming's top museums, with works by all the American masters, from Alfred Jacob Miller to Robert Bateman (page 340).

◖ National Elk Refuge: Winter is the peak season, with and horse-drawn sleighs among the elk in a scene straight out of Currier and Ives (page 342).

◖ Jackson Hole Rodeo: Hard-riding cowboys and cowgirls strut their stuff at twice-weekly night rodeos all summer. Lots of spills and thrills, and kids love the calf scramble (page 345).

◖ Snake River Rafting: A major summertime attraction, with many companies providing the raft and guide for a whitewater rock-and-roll or a gentle float trip past the Tetons (page 350).

◖ Jackson Hole Mountain Resort: Famous for it's steep slopes and long downhills,

this wintertime ski and snowboard resort is also fun at other times; don't miss the summer-long classical music festival (page 358).

◖ Alaska Basin: This one's for backpackers, with access from Driggs, Idaho, to the heart of the Teton Range. It's a gorgeous alpine valley, where high trails lead into Grand Teton National Park (page 393).

LOOK FOR ◖ TO FIND RECOMMENDED SIGHTS, ACTIVITIES, DINING, AND LODGING.

provided the name that stuck: les Trois Tetons (literally, the Three Tits).

The valley—originally called Jackson's Hole—was named for likable trapper David E. Jackson, one of the men who helped establish the Rocky Mountain Fur Company. When Jackson and his partners sold out in 1830, they realized a profit of more than $50,000. Jackson's presence remains in the names of both Jackson Hole and Jackson Lake. Eventually,

more polite folks began calling the valley Jackson Hole in an attempt to end the ribald stories associated with the name Jackson's Hole. (It's easy to imagine the jokes with both Jackson's Hole and the Tetons in the same place.) By the way, in 1991, a group calling itself the Committee to Restore Decency to Our National Parks created quite a stir by suggesting that Grand Teton National Park be renamed. A letter sent to the Park Service and various members of Congress noted: "Though a great many Americans may be oblivious to this vulgarity, hundreds of millions of French people around the world are not! How embarrassing that these spectacular, majestic mountains are reduced to a dirty joke overseas." After a flurry of letters in response, the hoax was revealed; it was a prank by staff members of *Spy* magazine.

PLANNING YOUR TIME

Wyoming's preeminent tourist town, Jackson is both an important access point for Yellow-stone and Grand Teton national parks, and a destination in its own right. Visitors should probably plan on at least two days, but you could easily spend a couple of weeks just having fun in Jackson Hole (if your credit card doesn't get maxed out). Jackson has two peak seasons, in summer when families and international travelers stay here as part of a Yellowstone trip, and winter, when skiing and snowboarding are the big draws.

Before your trip, contact the **Jackson Hole and Greater Yellowstone Visitor Center**

JACKSON AREA CLIMATE

	Average Maximum Temp.	53.8°F
	Average Minimum Temp.	22.9°F
	Annual Rainfall	15.98"
	Annual Snowfall	74.8"

Acclaimed as one of the top artistic centers in the nation, Jackson is crowded with more than 30 **art galleries,** and the impressive **National Museum of Wildlife Art** perches along a hillside just north of town.

Wintertime sleigh rides among the elk draw visitors to the **National Elk Refuge,** while skiers and snowboarders enjoy the slopes at famous **Jackson Hole Mountain Resort** or smaller Snow King Resort, right in town. The deep powder of Grand Targhee Resort is a morning bus ride away on the west side of the Tetons. Jackson's restaurants are easily the finest (and most expensive) in Wyoming, and lodging varies from cozy old log units to ultraluxurious hotels. In summer, the **Snake River** is a major center for **whitewater rafting** and fly-fishing, while mountain-bikers and hikers head out on miles of paved (and unpaved) paths. Horseback rides and chuck wagon cookouts are other summertime favorites, along with twice-weekly **Jackson Hole Rodeos.** At Teton Village, visitors enjoy classical music performances during the Grand Teton Music Festival in July and August. More adventurous visitors enjoy extended backcountry trips into Grand Teton National Park and national forest lands, including beautiful **Alaska Basin** on the west side of the Tetons.

HISTORY

The first people to cross the mountain passes into Jackson Hole probably arrived while the last massive glaciers were still retreating. Clovis stone arrowheads—a style used 12,000 years ago—have been found along the edges of the valley. These early peoples were replaced in the 16th and 17th centuries by the Shoshone, Bannock, Blackfeet, Crow, and Gros Ventre tribes, who hunted bison from horses. When the first fur trappers tramped into Jackson Hole, they found Indian paths throughout the valley.

Because of the abundance of beavers along tributaries of the Snake River, Jackson Hole became an important crossroads for the Rocky Mountain fur trade. Although no rendezvous was ever held in the valley, many of the most famous mountain men spent time here. They

(307/733-3316, www.jacksonholechamber.com) for publications, maps, and detailed web information. For more comprehensive coverage of Jackson, Grand Teton, and Yellowstone, see Don Pitcher's *Moon Yellowstone and Grand Teton* (www.moon.com).

Shady **Town Square** in the heart of Jackson has picturesque elk antler arches on the corners, and a nearby street corner closes for entertaining shoot-outs each summer evening.

VISITING JACKSON HOLE WITH CHILDREN

Those traveling with children will find an abundance of kid-friendly options in Jackson Hole. A few noteworthy examples include:

- the hands-on Children's Discovery Gallery at the National Museum of Wildlife Art
- playgrounds at Mike Yokel Jr. Park (Kelly and Hall streets), Miller Park (Powderhorn Lane and Maple Way), and Baux Park (base of Snow King Mountain)
- the excellent swimming pool and corkscrew water slide at the Teton County Recreation Center
- the fine children's section of the library
- chuck wagon dinners at Bar-T-Five or Bar J
- pizzas at the Calico (where the lawn is great for kids)
- comedies and melodramas at Jackson Hole Playhouse or Off-Square Theatre Company
- the Alpine Slide at Snow King Resort
- the chairlifts at Jackson Hole Resort
- the evening shoot-outs at Town Square
- horseback or wagon rides
- a trip to the fish hatchery
- a night at the rodeo (including the kids-only calf chase)
- a boat ride and hike at Jenny Lake inside Grand Teton National Park
- day camp at the rec center (grades 1–6)

For those traveling with tots, **Baby's Away** (307/739-4711 or 888/616-8495) rents all sorts of baby supplies, including car seats, cribs, gates, backpacks, swings, and high chairs. You'll find more stroller and backpack rentals – along with kids' clothing – at **Teton Kids** (130 E. Broadway, 307/739-2176). Just down the street is a large toy shop, **Broadway Toys and Togs** (48 E. Broadway, 307/733-3918. **Second Helpings** (141 E. Pearl Ave., 307/733-9466) has an excellent selection of quality used baby and children's clothes. For child care, contact **Babysitting by the Tetons** (307/733-0754 or 866/733-0754, www.babysittingbythetetons.com), or **Jackson Hole Babysitting** (307/733-7720, www .jacksonholebabysitting.com).

Jackson Hole Mountain Resort (307/733-2292 or 888/333-7766, www.jacksonhole .com) operates a Kids Ranch day camp mid-June–early September, with activities and child care for ages 6 months–10 years old. Programs are geared to different ages, and cost around $75 per day.

first trapped beavers in Jackson Hole in 1811, but it was not until the 1820s that fur trapping really came into its own as mountain men fanned throughout the wilderness in search of the "soft gold." This quest continued for the next two decades, finally dying out when overtrapping made beavers harder to find and silk hats replaced fur hats. After the last rendezvous in 1840, most of the old trappers headed on to new adventures, the best becoming guides for those en route to Oregon and California. Because Jackson Hole was not near the Oregon Trail or other routes west, the area remained virtually deserted until the late 19th century.

Settlers

The first Jackson Hole homesteaders arrived in 1884, followed quickly by a handful of others fleeing the law. The settlers survived by grazing cattle, harvesting hay, and acting as guides for rich hunters from Europe and eastern states. Gradually they filled the richest parts of the valley with homesteads. Conflicts soon arose between the Bannock Indians, who had been hunting in Jackson Hole for more than 100 years, and the new settlers who made money guiding wealthy sportsmen.

By 1895, Wyoming had enacted game laws prohibiting hunting during 10 months of the year. Claiming that the Indians were taking

JACKSON HOLE

JOHN COLTER

Transport yourself back to the early 19th century, a time when people from the new nation called America saw the world west of the Mississippi River as just a blank spot on the map. In 1803, Thomas Jefferson bought the Louisiana Territory from France, and to learn more about this gigantic piece of real estate he sent Meriwether Lewis and William Clark on a military expedition to the Pacific coast, a trip that took nearly 2.5 years. Although the expedition skirted around Wyoming – heading across Montana instead – it proved the opening wedge for the settlement of the West and, indirectly, the discovery of Jackson Hole. On the return trip, the party met two fur trappers en route to the upper Missouri River. One of Lewis and Clark's respected scouts, John Colter, was allowed to join the trappers, "provided no one of the party would ask or expect a Similar permission."

After a winter of trapping with his partners, Colter headed alone down the Platte River, but before he could get back to civilization he met a company of trappers led by Manuel Lisa. They were on their way to the Rockies, determined to cash in on the huge demand for beaver furs by trapping the rich beaver streams that Lewis and Clark had described. Wealth beckoned, and John Colter gladly turned around again, guiding Lisa's men up to the mouth of the Big Horn River, where they built a small fort. From there Colter was sent on a mission: Contact Indians throughout the region, trading beads and other items for beaver furs.

His wanderings in the winter of 1807-1808 were the first white exploration of this region. A map produced by William Clark in 1814 and based on Colter's recollections shows an incredible midwinter journey around Yellowstone and Jackson lakes, across the Tetons twice, and up through Jackson Hole. He did not get back to the fort until the following spring, telling tales of huge mountain ranges and a spectacular geothermal area that others quickly laughed off as "Colter's Hell."

Colter went on to become one of the most famous of all mountain men, and his later harrowing escape from the Blackfeet in Montana has become the stuff of legend. After being captured and stripped naked, he was forced to literally run for his life. Somehow he managed to outdistance his pursuers for six miles before hiding in a pile of logs until dark. He walked barefoot the 300 miles back to Manuel Lisa's fort, surviving on roots and tree bark. Shortly thereafter, Colter was reported to have thrown his hat on the ground, declaring, "I'll be damned if I ever come into [this country] again." He returned to St. Louis, married, and established a farm near that of fellow explorer Daniel Boone. Colter lived long enough to give William Clark a description of the country he had visited, but he died from jaundice just three years later, in 1813.

---

elk out of season, Constable William Manning and 26 settlers arrested a group of 28 Indians (mostly women and children) who had been hunting in Hoback Canyon. When the Bannocks attempted to flee, an elderly Indian was shot four times in the back and died. Most of the others escaped. Settlers in Jackson Hole feared revenge and called in the cavalry, but the Indians who had been hunting in the area all returned peaceably to their Idaho reservation. Astoundingly, *The New York Times* headlined its report of the incident, "Settlers Massacred—Indians Kill Every One at Jackson's Hole—Courier Brings the News—Red

Men Apply the Torch to All the Houses in the Valley." Absolutely none of this was true, but the attack by whites succeeded in forcing the Indians off their traditional hunting grounds, an action eventually upheld in a landmark U.S. Supreme Court case.

Jackson Hole Comes of Age

By the turn of the 20th century, the Jackson Hole settlements of Jackson, Wilson, Kelly, and Moran had all been established. The towns grew slowly; people survived by ranching, guiding, and engaging in the strange new business of tending to wealthy "dudes" from back east.

Eventually, tourism would vastly eclipse raising cattle in importance, but even today Teton County has nearly as many cattle as people.

Jackson, Jackson Hole's primary settlement, was named by Maggie Simpson, who opened a post office here in 1894. Three years later Grace Miller—wife of a local banker known derisively as "Old Twelve Percent"—bought a large plot of land and planned a townsite, but the town wasn't officially incorporated until 1914. In an event that should come as no surprise in "The Equality State," Jackson later became the first town in America to be entirely governed by women. The year was 1920, and not only was the mayor a woman (Grace Miller), but so were all four council members, the city clerk, the treasurer, and even the town marshal. They remained in office until 1923.

Through the years Jackson has grown, spurred on by the creation of Grand Teton National Park and the development of Jackson Hole Mountain Resort. In the last 25 years, Jackson Hole has seen almost continuous growth; tourists have flooded the region to play, investors have built golf courses and ostentatious hotels, and wealthy families have snatched up their own parcels of paradise. Today, Teton County has the highest per capita income of any county in America (around $70,000), and locals quip that the billionaires are buying land so fast that they're driving the millionaires out of Jackson Hole.

Although much of the area is public land and will remain undeveloped, rapid growth on private land is transforming Jackson Hole into the Wyoming version of Vail or Santa Fe. Even the formerly quiet town of Wilson failed to fight off the development onslaught, with a massive new grade school and a collection of modest new homes that locals call Whoville (after those in the Dr. Seuss book). As a former resident of Wilson, I can appreciate the joke going the rounds: How many Wilsonites does it take to change a light bulb? Seven. One to screw it in, and the other six to talk about how good the old one used to be.

Growth in Jackson Hole has forced land values sky-high, and affordable housing has become an oxymoron, unless you consider $680,000—the median single-family home price—affordable. Despite all of the problems brought on by growth, the area is still remarkably beautiful, and the surrounding public lands will remain wild. Locals like to point out that this is more than a place to visit; for them it is a place to live surrounded by the best of the old (and new) West.

Saving Jackson Hole

The Jackson Hole economy has been stuck in permanent high gear for the last few decades as Jackson has grown from a sleepy burg to a national focal point for outdoor fun. From 1990 to 2000, the population nearly doubled, and today the area is home to almost 9,000 people. Expensive homes now spread across old ranch lands, retailers such as Kmart have moved in, and development reaches for miles south from Jackson itself. Surrounding towns such as Alpine and Driggs have become bedroom communities for those willing to endure the long commute to Jackson, and their growth spreads the problems outward from Jackson.

Although 97 percent of the land in Teton County is in the public domain, the 70,000 acres of private land that remain are rapidly being developed, and Jackson Hole is in grave danger of losing the wild beauty that has attracted visitors for more than a century. This dilemma is immediately obvious to anyone arriving in Jackson. Instead of the wide-open spaces that remain protected by public land ownership, the edges of Jackson are falling under a proliferation of trophy homes, real-estate offices, chain motels, fast-food outlets, megamarts, gas stations, and elaborate banks, all competing beneath a thicket of signs. Summertime traffic jams are becoming all too common in this once-quiet place, where more than 35,000 visitors can be found on a summer afternoon.

In 1994, Jackson voters got fed up with the pace of development and voted to scrap the town's 2 percent lodging tax, which had provided more than $1 million per year in funding to promote Jackson Hole around the world.

JACKSON HOLE

THE WHITE SHOSHONE

The little Jackson Hole town of Wilson is named for one of Wyoming's most fascinating characters, "Uncle Nick" Wilson. Born in 1842, Wilson grew up in Utah, where he made friends with a fellow sheepherder, an Indian boy, and learned to speak his language. Then, suddenly, Nick's life took a strange twist. The mother of Chief Washakie (from Wyoming's Wind River Reservation) had recently lost a son, and in a dream she was told that a white boy would come to take his place. Unable to convince her otherwise, Washakie sent his men out to find the new son. They came across Nick and offered him a pinto pony and the chance to fish, hunt, and ride horses all he wanted. It didn't take much persuading, and for the next two years he lived as a Shoshone, learning to hunt buffalo, to use a bow and arrow, and to answer to his new name, Yagaiki. He became a favorite of Chief Washakie, but when word came (falsely) that

Nick's father was threatening to attack the Shoshones with an army of men to retrieve his son, the chief reluctantly helped Nick return home.

At age 18, Nick Wilson became one of the first Pony Express riders, a job that nearly killed him when he was struck in the head during a Paiute Indian attack. A doctor managed to remove the arrow point, but Wilson remained in a coma for nearly two weeks. Thereafter, Wilson always wore a hat to cover the scar, even inside buildings. He went on to become an army scout and a driver for the Overland Stage before returning to a more sedate life as a farmer. Many years later, in 1889, Nick Wilson led a party of five Mormon families over steep Teton Pass and down to the rich grazing lands in Jackson Hole. The town that grew up around him became Wilson. In later years, "Uncle Nick" recounted his adventures in *The White Indian Boy*.

Despite this lack of promotional effort, growth shows no signs of slowing down. A large new Albertsons store went up in 1999, followed by an even more impressive Smiths in 2003, next to the sprawling new high school. Housing costs continue to spiral upward, pushed by a wealthy clientele willing to drop $2 million or more for a Jackson Hole home.

The **Jackson Hole Conservation Alliance** (307/733-9417, www.jhalliance.com) is an 1,800-member environmental group that works to preserve the remaining natural areas of Jackson Hole. Membership starts at $25 per

year and includes triannual newsletters and a chance to help control the many developments that threaten this still-beautiful valley.

Another influential local group is the **Jackson Hole Land Trust** (307/733-4707, www.jhlandtrust.org). Established in 1980, this nonprofit organization obtains conservation easements to maintain ranches and other land threatened by development. The group has protected more than 15,000 acres in the valley in this way, including the 1,740-acre Walton Ranch, visible along the highway between Jackson and Wilson.

Sights

The town of Jackson (pop. 9,000) lies near the southern end of Jackson Hole, hemmed in on three sides by Snow King Mountain, the Gros Ventre Range, and East Gros Ventre Butte. At 6,200 feet in elevation, Jackson experiences cold snowy winters, wet springs, delightfully warm and sunny summers, and crisp but color-filled falls. Jackson is unlike any other place in Wyoming; on a typical summer day more than 35,000 tourists flood the town. Sit on a bench in Town Square on a summer day and you're likely to see cars from every state in the Union. Tourists dart in and out of the many gift shops, art galleries, fine restaurants, Western-style saloons, and trendy boutiques. The cowboy hats all look as if the price tags just came off.

In other parts of Wyoming, Jackson is viewed with a mixture of awe and disdain—awe over its gorgeous scenery, but disdain that Jackson is not a "real" town, just a false front put up to sell things to outsiders. Yes, Jackson is almost wholly dependent on the almighty tourist dollar, but as a result it enjoys a cultural richness lacking in other parts of the state. Besides, if you don't like all the commercial foolishness, it's easy to escape to a campsite or remote trail in the wonderful countryside of nearby Grand Teton National Park or Bridger–Teton National Forest.

Keep your eyes open around Jackson and you're likely to see well-known residents such as Hollywood stars Harrison Ford, Danny De-Vito and his wife, Rhea Perlman, Connie Stevens, and Sandra Bullock, along with former Secretary of the Interior James Watt (who resigned in disgrace in 1983), attorney Gerald Spence (of Karen Silkwood and Imelda Marcos notoriety), Yvon Chouinard (mountaineer and founder of Patagonia), industrial heir Charles DuPont, and members of the extended Rockefeller family. Vice President Dick Cheney has a luxury home in Teton Pines and is a frequent visitor, which explains all of the Blackhawk helicopters, Secret Service agents, and Suburbans with dark-tinted windows.

ART

Artists have long been attracted by the beauty of Jackson Hole and the Tetons. Mount Moran, the 12,605-foot summit behind Jackson Lake, is named for Thomas Moran, whose watercolors helped persuade Congress to set aside Yellowstone as the first national park. The late Conrad Schwiering's paintings of the Tetons have attained international fame; one was even used on the Postal Service's Wyoming Centennial stamp in 1990. Ansel Adams's photograph of the Tetons remains etched in the American consciousness as one of the archetypal wilderness images. A copy of the image was included in the payload of the *Voyager II* spacecraft en route out of our solar system. Today many artists live or work in Jackson Hole, and locals proclaim it "Art Center of the Rockies," ranking it with New York, San Francisco, Santa Fe, and Scottsdale.

Jackson Hole Center for the Arts

If you have any doubts that Jackson Hole is an arts mecca, look no further than the sparkling new Jackson Hole Center for the Arts (240 S. Glenwood, 307/734-8956, www.jhcenterforthearts.org). This 41,000-square-foot masterpiece opened in 2005, with space for 20 different nonprofit arts organizations under one roof. It's the first phase of a $27 million privately funded project that also includes a performing arts facility, public park, and housing for visiting artists.

One of the primary tenants is the **Art Association** (307/733-6379, www.artassociation.org), which offers dozens of classes and workshops year-round in everything from photography and ceramics to stained glass and woodworking. **ArtSpace Gallery** displays changing exhibitions by local and national artists, and is open 8:30 A.M.–5:30 P.M. Monday–Friday all year.

Dancer's Workshop (307/733-6398, www.dwjh.org) occupies much of the second floor, with classes in modern, ballet, Pointe, hip hop, ballroom, jazz, country-and-western, and other forms. The facilities also house Contemporary

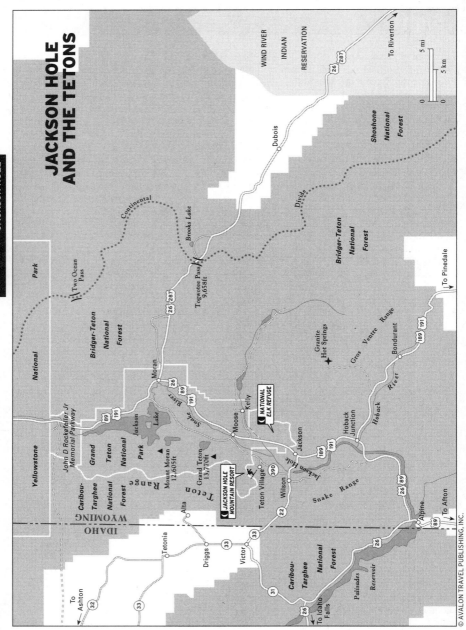

JACKSON HOLE AND THE TETONS

© AVALON TRAVEL PUBLISHING, INC.

JACKSON HOLE

© AVALON TRAVEL PUBLISHING, INC.

JACKSON HOLE

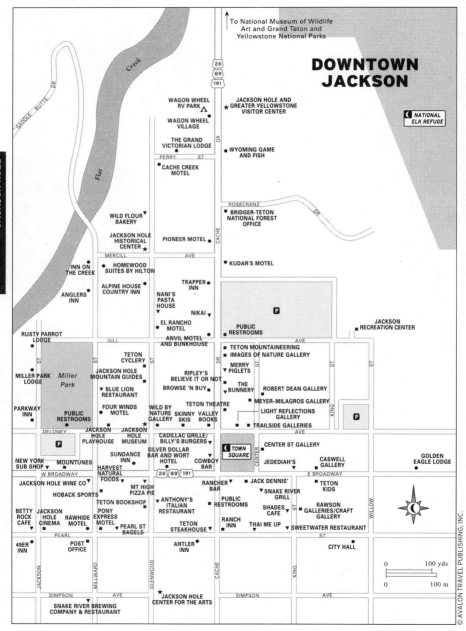

To National Museum of Wildlife
Art and Grand Teton and
Yellowstone National Parks

DOWNTOWN JACKSON

NATIONAL ELK REFUGE

WAGON WHEEL RV PARK

WAGON WHEEL VILLAGE

JACKSON HOLE AND GREATER YELLOWSTONE VISITOR CENTER

THE GRAND VICTORIAN LODGE

PERRY ST

WYOMING GAME AND FISH

CACHE CREEK MOTEL

ROSECRANZ

WILD FLOUR BAKERY

BRIDGER-TETON NATIONAL FOREST OFFICE

JACKSON HOLE HISTORICAL CENTER

PIONEER MOTEL

MERCILL   AVE   CACHE

KUDAR'S MOTEL

INN ON THE CREEK

HOMEWOOD SUITES BY HILTON

ALPINE HOUSE COUNTRY INN

TRAPPER INN

ANGLERS INN

NANI'S PASTA HOUSE

NIKAI

JACKSON RECREATION CENTER

EL RANCHO MOTEL

RUSTY PARROT LODGE

ANVIL MOTEL AND BUNKHOUSE

PUBLIC RESTROOMS

GILL   AVE

TETON MOUNTAINEERING

IMAGES OF NATURE GALLERY

TETON CYCLERY

MERRY PIGLETS

MILLER PARK LODGE

Miller Park

JACKSON HOLE MOUNTAIN GUIDES

RIPLEY'S BELIEVE IT OR NOT

THE BUNNERY

ROBERT DEAN GALLERY

BLUE LION RESTAURANT

BROWSE 'N BUY

MEYER–MILAGROS GALLERY

PARKWAY INN

PUBLIC RESTROOMS

FOUR WINDS MOTEL

WILD BY NATURE GALLERY

SKINNY SKIS

VALLEY BOOKS

TETON THEATRE

LIGHT REFLECTIONS GALLERY

TRAILSIDE GALLERIES

DELONEY   AVE

JACKSON HOLE PLAYHOUSE

JACKSON HOLE MUSEUM

CADILLAC GRILLE/ BILLY'S BURGERS

CENTER ST GALLERY

NEW YORK SUB SHOP

MOUNTUNES

SUNDANCE INN

SILVER DOLLAR BAR AND WORT HOTEL

COWBOY BAR

TOWN SQUARE

JEDEDIAH'S

CASWELL GALLERY

GOLDEN EAGLE LODGE

W BROADWAY

HARVEST NATURAL FOODS

26 89 191

E BROADWAY

JACKSON HOLE WINE CO

MT HIGH PIZZA PIE

RANCHER BAR

JACK DENNIS'

TETON KIDS

HOBACK SPORTS

ANTHONY'S ITALIAN RESTAURANT

SNAKE RIVER GRILL

TETON BOOKSHOP

PUBLIC RESTROOMS

SHADES CAFE

RAWSON GALLERIES/CRAFT GALLERY

BETTY ROCK CAFE

JACKSON HOLE CINEMA

RAWHIDE MOTEL

PONY EXPRESS MOTEL

PEARL ST BAGELS

TETON STEAKHOUSE

RANCH INN

THAI ME UP

SWEETWATER RESTAURANT

PEARL

POST OFFICE

ANTLER INN

CITY HALL

49ER INN

JACKSON

MILLWARD

GLENWOOD

CACHE

KING

WILLOW

SIMPSON   AVE

JACKSON HOLE CENTER FOR THE ARTS

SIMPSON   AVE

0   100 yds

0   100 m

SNAKE RIVER BREWING COMPANY & RESTAURANT

SIGHTS **339**

Dance Wyoming, the state's only professional dance company.

Off Square Theatre Company (307/733-3670, www.offsquare.org) is a professional repertory company with comedies in the summer, and a variety of productions and workshops throughout the winter. It will be one of many organizations using the 500-seat **Performing Arts Pavilion** that was to open in 2006 at Jackson Hole Center for the Arts.

Art Galleries

More than 30 galleries crowd the center of Jackson, their collections covering the spectrum from Indian art of questionable authenticity to impressive photographic exhibits and shows by nationally acclaimed painters. Unfortunately, many of these galleries offer recycled ideas now manufactured in mass quantity with every possible cliché thrown in. Particularly egregious examples are the Southwestern-style pastel pottery, the campy cowboy sculptures, and the prints of sexy Indian maidens with windblown hair and strategically torn garments. Pick up a free *Jackson Hole Daily* for a complete rundown of current exhibitions and displays, along with maps showing gallery locations, but don't believe everything the galleries say about themselves in their ads.

Several Jackson galleries are worth a visit, most notably the outstanding National Museum of Wildlife Art. The **Jackson Hole Gallery Association** (www.jacksonholegalleries.com) produces a helpful gallery guide; get one from local galleries or the visitor center.

Just off Town Square, **Trailside Galleries** (307/733-3186, www.trailsidegalleries.com) focuses on grandiose Western works, but you'll also find everything from impressionism to wildlife art in this big gallery at the corner of Center and Deloney. Other traditionalist galleries worth a look are **Mountain Trails Gallery** (150 N. Center St., 307/734-8150, www.mtntrails.net), **Di Tommaso Galleries** (172 Center St., 307/734-9677, www.ditommasogalleries.com), and **Legacy Gallery** (75 N. Cache, 307/733-2353, www.legacygallery.com).

More unusual is **Center Street Gallery** (30 Center St., 307/733-1115 or 888/733-1115, www.centerstreetgallery.com), where the emphasis is on vivid contemporary art and jewelry.

Meyer-Milagros Gallery (155 Center St., 307/733-0905 or 877/681-8900, www.meyermilagrosgallery.com) presents contemporary paintings and bronze sculptures by respected Western artists. These artworks are well worth seeing but are priced for serious art patrons only.

Jack Dennis' Wyoming Gallery (50 E. Broadway, 307/733-7548, www.jackdennis.com) specializes in wildlife and traditional landscape paintings and photography.

Also downtown, the **Caswell Gallery and Sculpture Garden** (145 E. Broadway, 307/734-2660, www.caswellgallery.com) is home to Jackson's only outdoor sculpture garden, with wildlife bronzes by Rip Caswell. These are not my cup of tea (or espresso for that matter), but you may appreciate the innovative sculptures from 60 other artisans displayed in this gallery.

For art from the natural world, head across the street to **Fossil Portal** (150 E. Broadway, 307/733-1019 or 307/733-3613, www.fossilportal.com). Inside are beautifully prepared fish fossils from the Kemmerer area (where the Ulrich family has a fossil quarry), including tabletops, flooring tiles, wall pieces, and other prepared specimens.

Rawson Galleries (50 King St., 307/733-7306) features traditional watercolors, displayed in a crowded space; open July–October. The same building also houses **Craft Gallery** (307/734-2747, www.jacksoncraft.com), with a gorgeous selection of hand-blown glass, woven textiles, wooden baskets, raku pottery, and other items.

Robert Dean Gallery (172 Center St., 307/733-9290) is known for its quality Indian artwork, with pottery, silver and gold jewelry, leather belts, and more.

Nearby Galleries

The **Hennes Studio and Gallery** (5850 N. Larkspur Dr., 307/733-2593) off Spring Gulch

JACKSON HOLE

Road near the Jackson Hole Golf and Tennis Club, features oil and watercolor paintings of the Tetons by Joanne Hennes, whose commissioned works hang in the Moose Visitor Center and Jenny Lake Lodge.

One of Jackson's largest private exhibition spaces is **Wilcox Gallery** (one mile north of town on U.S. 26/89, 307/733-6450, www.wilcoxgallery.com). Inside are traditional oil paintings by Jim Wilcox, along with works by other prominent Western painters and sculptors.

Photo Galleries

Many nationally known photographers live or work in Jackson Hole. Tom Mangelsen displays his outstanding wildlife and landscape photos at **Images of Nature Gallery** (170 N. Cache Dr., 307/733-9752 or 888/238-0177, www.mangelsen.com) and has galleries at 15 other locations around the country.

Inside **Light Reflections** (35 E. Deloney, 307/733-4016 or 800/346-5223, www.lightreflections.com) are many of Fred Joy's large-format visions of the American West. Also well worth a visit is **Wild by Nature Gallery** (95 W. Deloney, 307/733-8877 or 888/494-5329, www.wildbynature.com), where photographer Henry H. Holdsworth shows strikingly beautiful wildlife and nature imagery.

In Gaslight Alley at 125 North Cache, **Brookover-Muench Gallery** (307/733-3988, www.brookover-muench.com) exhibits grandiose landscapes by photographers David Brookover and David Muench. **Wild Exposures Gallery** (60 E. Broadway Ave., 307/739-1777, www.wildexposuresgallery.com) shows large-format and panoramic works from three local photographers. It's upstairs near Snake River Grill.

◖ TOWN SQUARE

In 1932, the local Rotary Club planted trees in the center of Jackson, adding four picturesque arches made from hundreds of elk antlers in the 1950s and '60s. Today the trees offer summertime shade, and at any time of day or night you'll find visitors admiring or posing for photos in front of the arches that mark the corners of Town Square. During winter, the snow-covered arches and trees are draped with lights, giving the square a festive atmosphere. Surrounded by dozens of boardwalk-fronted galleries, bars, restaurants, factory outlets, and gift shops, the square is the focal point of tourist activity in Jackson.

During summer, **stagecoaches** wait to transport you on a leisurely ride around town, and each evening "cowboys" put on a free **shoot-out** for throngs of camera-happy tourists. The shoot-out starts at 6:15 P.M. Monday–Saturday nights all summer. They've been killing each other like this since 1957. With stereotypical players and questionable acting, the "mountain law" system seems in dire need of reform. Most folks love the sham; Canon and Olympus love it even more. Warning: The sound of blanks is surprisingly loud and can be frightening for small children.

◖ NATIONAL MUSEUM OF WILDLIFE ART

Jackson is home to the magnificent National Museum of Wildlife Art (307/733-5771 or 800/313-9553, www.wildlifeart.org), two miles north of town along U.S. 26/89 and directly across from the National Elk Refuge. Built from brown Arizona sandstone, the exterior blends in with nearby rock outcroppings. Step inside the doors of this 51,000-square-foot museum to discover a marvelous interior. As visitors enter the main gallery, a larger-than-life bronze mountain lion crouches above, ready to pounce. Kids will have fun in the hands-on Children's Discovery Gallery. Adults will appreciate the artwork spread throughout a dozen galleries, along with the video theater, Rising Sage Cafe (tasty lunches), 200-seat auditorium, and gift shop.

The museum collection features pieces by Carl Rungius, George Catlin, Albert Bierstadt, Karl Bodmer, Alfred Jacob Miller, N. C. Wyeth, Conrad Schwiering, John Clymer, Charles Russell, Robert Bateman, and many others. Of particular interest are the reconstructed studio of John Clymer and the spacious Carl Rungius Gallery, where you'll find

© DON PITCHER

the National Museum of Wildlife Art

the most complete collection of his paintings in the nation. Also of note is the exhibit on American bison, which documents these once vastly abundant animals and their slaughter; the museum's bison collection is the largest in the world. Six galleries showcase photography, painting, and other art that changes throughout the year. Spotting scopes in the lobby and the cozy members' lounge (open to the public) are useful for watching residents of the adjacent National Elk Refuge.

Admission to the museum costs $8 adults, $7 seniors and students, $16 families; admission is free for kids under six. Pick up a free one-hour audio tour for details of the pieces. The museum is open 9 A.M.–5 P.M. daily year-round, with the exception of April, May, and November, when the hours are 1–5 P.M. Sunday and 9 A.M.–5 P.M. Monday–Saturday. Free audio tours detail works in the permanent collection, and you can watch films on wildlife and artists on Thursdays in the summer.

Wildlife films, slide lectures, talks, concerts, kids' programs, and other activities take place throughout the year in the auditorium and gal-leries; pick up a schedule of upcoming events at the entrance desk or from the website. One of the most popular events is the **Miniature Show and Sale** in mid-September; it attracts more than 100 of the country's leading artists.

HISTORICAL MUSEUMS

The small **Jackson Hole Museum** (105 N. Glenwood, 307/733-2414, www.jacksonhole-history.org) has a surprising homespun charm. Inside are displays and collections illustrating the days when Indians, trappers, cattlemen, and dude ranchers called this magnificent valley home. Check out the Paul Bunyan–size bear trap, the old postcards, and a replica of the "Colter stone." Admission costs $3 adults, $2 seniors, $1 ages 3–18, and $6 families. Hours are 9:30 A.M.–6 P.M. Monday–Saturday and 10 A.M.–5 P.M. Sunday late May–September; closed the rest of the year. The museum sponsors hour-long **historical walking tours** ($3 adults, $2 seniors and $1 kids, or $6 families) of Jackson's downtown several days a week in the summer.

Also managed by the local historical society, the **Jackson Hole Historical Center** (105

Mercill Ave., 307/733-9605, open 8 A.M.–5 P.M. Mon.–Fri. year-round; free) is a small research facility housing photo archives, a library of old books from the area, and rotating exhibits throughout the year.

INFORMATION CENTER

Anyone new to Jackson Hole should be sure to visit the spacious **Jackson Hole and Greater Yellowstone Visitor Center** (532 N. Cache Dr., 307/733-3316, www.jacksonholechamber.com) on the north side of town. Hours are 8 A.M.–7 P.M. daily Memorial Day–Labor Day, and 8 A.M.–5 P.M. daily the rest of the year. (The phone is answered only on weekdays, but on weekends you can leave a message and you'll be mailed an information packet.)

The information center is a two-level, sodroofed wooden building—jokingly called the "little prairie on the house"—with natural-history displays, a blizzard of free leaflets extolling the merits of local businesses (including one offering *feng shui* consulting), a gift shop selling books and maps, and an upstairs rear deck overlooking the National Elk Refuge. Ducks and trumpeter swans are visible on the marsh in the summer, and elk can be seen in the winter. The information center is staffed by the Jackson Hole Chamber of Commerce, along with Fish and Wildlife Service and Forest Service personnel in the summer. Free nature and history talks are generally given several times a week during the summer.

In addition to the main information center, you'll find brochure racks at the airport, at the stagecoach stop on Town Square, and the Mangy Moose in Teton Village.

◖ NATIONAL ELK REFUGE

Immediately north of Jackson is the National Elk Refuge (307/733-9212, http://nationalelkrefuge.fws.gov), winter home for thousands of these majestic animals. During summer, the elk range up to 65 miles away to feed on grasses, shrubs, and forbs in alpine meadows. But as the snows descend each fall, the elk move downslope, wintering in Jackson Hole and the surrounding country. The chance to view elk up close from a horse-drawn sleigh makes a trip to the National Elk Refuge one of the most popular wintertime activities for Jackson Hole visitors.

History

When the first ranchers arrived in Jackson Hole in the late 19th century, they moved onto land that had long been an elk migration route and wintering ground. The ranchers soon found elk raiding their haystacks and competing with cattle for forage, particularly during severe winters. The conflicts peaked early in the 20th century when three consecutive severe winters killed thousands of elk, leading one settler to claim that he had "walked for a mile on dead elk lying from one to four deep."

Fortunately, local rancher and hunting guide Stephen N. Leek had been given a camera by one of the sportsmen he had guided, George Eastman (founder of Kodak). Leek's disturbing photos of starving and dead elk found a national audience and helped pressure the state of Wyoming to appropriate $5,000 to buy hay in 1909. Two years later the federal government began buying land for a permanent winter elk refuge that would eventually cover nearly 25,000 acres. Today it's administered by the U.S. Fish and Wildlife Service. Famed biologist, illustrator, and conservationist Olaus Murie came to Jackson Hole in 1927 to begin his studies of the elk, remaining here until his death in 1963. Murie and his wife, Margaret "Mardy" Murie, chronicled their adventures in *Wapiti Wilderness*. Conservationist Mardy Murie died in 2003 at the age of 101, and her ranch is now a center for environmental workshops.

Today more than 7,000 elk (two-thirds of the local population) typically spend November–May on the refuge. Because development has reduced elk habitat in the valley to one-quarter of its original size, refuge managers try to improve the remaining land through seeding, irrigation, and prescribed burning. In addition, during the most difficult foraging period, the elk are fed alfalfa pellets paid for in part by sales of elk antlers col-

See elk up close from a horse-drawn sleigh at the National Elk Refuge.

lected on the refuge. During this time, each elk eats more than seven pounds of supplemental alfalfa per day, or 30 tons per day for the entire herd. Elk head back into the mountains with the melting of snow each April and May; during summer you'll see few (if any) on the refuge.

Visiting the Refuge

The National Elk Refuge is primarily a winter attraction, although it's also an excellent place to watch birds and other wildlife in summer. Trumpeter swans nest and winter here. The refuge has staff members on duty year-round in the visitor center.

The main winter attraction here is the chance to see thousands of elk up close from one of the **horse-drawn sleighs** that take visitors through the refuge. The elk are accustomed to these sleighs and pay little heed, but people on foot would scare them. A tour of the National Elk Refuge is always a highlight for wintertime visitors to Jackson Hole. In December and January the bulls have impressive antlers that they start to shed by the end of

February. The months of January and February are good times to see sparring matches. You might also catch a glimpse of a wolf or two because a pack now lives in the area year-round and hunts elk in winter. Morning is the best time to look for wolves.

Begin your wintertime visit to the refuge at the **Jackson Hole and Greater Yellowstone Visitor Center** (532 N. Cache Dr.), where you can buy sleigh-ride tickets; $15 adults, $11 ages 6–12, free for kids under age six. Rides are on a first-come basis, but group reservations are available through **Bar-T-Five** (307/733-5386 or 800/772-5386, www.bart5.com), the folks who run the sleighs. The visitor center shows an interpretive slide show about the refuge while you're waiting for a shuttle bus to take you to boarding area. Sleighs run 10 A.M.–4 P.M. daily mid-December–March (closed Christmas), heading out as soon as enough folks show up for a ride—generally just long enough for the early-comers to finish watching the slide show. The rides last 45–60 minutes. Be sure to wear warm clothes or bring extra layers because the wind can get bitterly cold.

Four miles north of town and next to the elk refuge is the **Jackson National Fish Hatchery** (307/733-2510, http://jackson.fws .gov), which rears a half million cutthroat and lake trout annually. It's open 8 A.M.–4 P.M. daily year-round.

Entertainment and Events

NIGHTLIFE

Barflies will keep buzzing in Jackson, especially during midsummer and midwinter, when visitors pack local saloons every night of the week. At least one nightclub always seems to have live tunes; check Jackson's free newspapers to see what's where. Cover charges are generally $3–5 on the weekends, and most other times you'll get in free.

The famous **Million Dollar Cowboy Bar** (on the west side of Town Square, 307/733-2207, www.milliondollarcowboybar.com) is a favorite of real cowboys and their wannabe cousins. Inside the Cowboy you'll discover burled lodgepole pine beams, four pool tables (nearly always in use), display cases with stuffed dead bears and other cuddly critters, bars inlaid with old silver dollars, and barstools made from old saddles. Until the 1950s, the Cowboy was Jackson's center for illegal gambling. Bartenders kept a close eye on Teton Pass, where messengers used mirrors to deliver warnings of coming federal revenuers, giving folks at the bar time to hide the gaming tables in a back room. Today the dance floor fills with honky-tonking couples as the bands croon lonesome cowboy tunes six nights a week. Looking to learn swing and two-step dancing? You can join an excellent free beginners' class at 7:30 P.M. every Thursday, and then dance up a storm when the band comes on at 9.

Just across the square and up the stairs is **Rancher Spirits and Billiards** (307/733-3886), where the room is filled with tables for chain-smoking billiards aficionados, and a small deck overlooks Town Square. Tuesday night $1.50 drafts and $5 pitchers are a big draw.

Silver Dollar Bar and Grill (50 N. Glenwood St., 307/733-2190, www.worthotel.com) inside the Wort Hotel offers a setting that might seem more fitting in Las Vegas: Gaudy pink neon lights curve around a bar inlaid with 2,032 (count 'em!) silver dollars. It tends to attract an older crowd with nightly drink specials (best martinis in Jackson), and the music is generally of the piano, bluegrass, or acoustic variety.

In Teton Village is **Mangy Moose Saloon** (307/733-4913, www.mangymoose.net), Jackson Hole's jumpingest pickup spot and *the* place to rock out. The Moose attracts a hip skier/outdoorsy crowd with rock, blues, or world beat bands Wednesday–Saturday both summer and winter. This is also where you'll hear nationally known acts.

Jammed against the hill on the west end of town, **Sidewinders Tavern and Sports Grill** (802 W. Broadway, 307/734-5766, www.sidewinderstavern.com) is a bar/restaurant with pub grub (including buffalo wings, burgers, pizzas, and chicken-fried steak), many beers on draft, and big-screen TVs for sports enthusiasts. Smokers head to the cigar bar.

The **Shady Lady Saloon** at Snow King Resort (400 E. Snow King Ave., 307/733-5200) typically serves up live music most Wednesday nights, along with a Tuesday DJ and open mike Fridays. More popular is the Monday night **Jackson Hole Hootenanny,** held in the lodge room of the Snow King Center (307/733-5200) throughout the summer, or at the nearby ice rink in spring and fall. Local and visiting musicians get together to jam in an all-acoustic set, and anyone can join the onstage fun if he or she has musical talent—or can pretend. The music starts at 7 P.M.; $3 cover.

Not far away is **43 North** (645 S. Cache, 307/733-0043), with live music most nights, including Monday jam sessions, Wednesday bluegrass, and Thursday jazz; no cover.

Over in Wilson, **The Stagecoach Bar** (307/733-4407) is *the* place to be on Sunday nights, when locals call it "the church." In the 1970s, when hippies risked getting their heads shaved by rednecks at Jackson's Cowboy Bar, they found the 'Coach a more tolerant place. Today tobacco-chewing cowpokes show their partners slick moves on the tiny dance floor as the Stagecoach Band (jokingly known as the "worst country-western band in the U.S.") runs through the country tunes one more time; the band has performed here every Sunday since February 16, 1969! Outside you'll find picnic tables and a volleyball court for pickup games in the summer, or pick up a cue stick and show off your billiard skills indoors. The bar food is notable, especially the buffalo burgers. Also popular are the Thursday-night disco parties (a great time to dress up in *Saturday Night Fever* garb) and Monday bluegrass bashes.

CLASSICAL MUSIC

In existence since 1962, the **Grand Teton Music Festival** (307/733-3050, www.gtmf.org) takes place at Walk Festival Hall in Teton Village, with performances of classical and modern works by a cast of 200 world-renowned symphony musicians. Concerts take place at 8 P.M. during July and August each year, with chamber music on Tuesday and Wednesday, small ensembles on Thursday, and festival orchestra concerts on Friday and Saturday. They also perform a free outdoor "Music in the Hole" patriotic concert on the Fourth of July, plus special young people's concerts in July and August. The three-hour-long Friday morning rehearsals are just $10.

MUSICALS AND MOVIES

In addition to the bar scene, summers bring several lighthearted acting ventures to Jackson. For family musicals such as *Paint Your Wagon, Nunsense,* or *Cat Ballou,* head to **Jackson Hole Playhouse** (145 W. Deloney, 307/733-6994, www.jhplayhouse.com). Shows take place Monday–Saturday evenings in a campy 1890s-style setting. A family saloon (no alcohol) and "spaghetti Western" restaurant are next door.

A professional repertory group, the **Off Square Theatre Company** (307/733-3670, www.offsquare.org) puts on Broadway comedies in the summer at the Jackson Hole Center for the Arts, with dramatic productions the rest of the year. Both Off Square and Jackson Hole Playhouse are very popular with families, and reservations are strongly recommended.

Watch flicks downtown at **Teton Theatre** (120 N. Cache Dr.) and **Jackson Hole Twin Cinema** (295 W. Pearl St.), or south of town at **MovieWorks** (860 S. U.S. 89). All three of these have the same movie line: 307/733-4939.

◖ JACKSON HOLE RODEO

On Wednesday and Saturday nights in summer you can watch bucking broncs, bull riders, barrel racers, rodeo clowns, and hard-riding cowboys at the Jackson Hole Rodeo (307/733-2805, www.jhrodeo.com) on the Teton County Fair Grounds. Kids get to join in the amusing calf scramble. The rodeo starts at 8 P.M. and costs $11 adults, $8 ages 4–12, free for kids under four, or $35 for the whole family. Rodeos take place late May–early September, with Saturday night rodeos all summer and Wednesday night rodeos starting in mid-June.

CHUCK WAGON COOKOUTS

Jackson Hole is home to several chuck wagon affairs offering all-you-can-eat barbecue cookouts and Western musical performances in the summer. Each has its own advantages, but reservations are highly recommended at all of these.

Run by the Thomas family since 1973, **Bar-T-Five** (790 Cache Creek Rd., 307/733-5386 or 800/772-5386, www.bart5.com) is one of the best chuck wagon feeds. Horse-drawn Conestoga-style wagons depart just east of Snow King, carrying visitors along Cache Creek past costumed mountain men, cowboys, and Indians. At the in-the-trees cookout site, cowboys serenade your meal, tell stories, and crack corny jokes that aren't entirely politically correct. It's great fun for families and busloads of Japanese tourists. Rates are $35 adults, $28 ages 5–12, and free for kids under five. Open mid-May–September, with

Bar-T-Five chuck wagons

departures at 5:30 and 6:30 P.M. Monday–Saturday. Recommended.

Ten miles south of Jackson near Hoback Junction, **A/OK Corral** (307/733-6556, www.horsecreekranch.com) has 45-minute horseback or wagon rides that end at an outdoor cookout. Big ranch breakfasts and steak suppers are on the menu. Breakfast rides cost $49 adults, $44 kids; dinner rides are $57 adults, $44 kids. Covered-wagon dinner rides are also available for a lower rate. Western musical entertainment is provided with the evening meals.

Along the Teton Village Road near Teton Pines, the **Bar J** (307/733-3370 or 800/905-2275, www.barjchuckwagon.com) does a land-office business throughout the summer, with seating for up to 750 people in a cavernous building, including busloads of gray-haired Gray Liners. In existence for almost three decades, Bar J is famous for its first-rate musicians who fiddle (one is a two-time national fiddle champion), sing, yodel, and regale the audience with cornball jokes and dollops of cowboy poetry. Before the show everyone queues up for heaping servings of barbecued beef, roast

chicken, or rib-eye steak served with baked potatoes, beans, biscuits, applesauce, spice cake, and lemonade (but no alcohol). Amazingly, it manages to feed the entire crowd in a half hour. The picnic-table seating is cramped, but after dinner you're treated to 90 minutes of rollicking entertainment. The cost is $17–25 for adults (depending on your meal), $7 for kids under eight, or free for tots. Bar J is open late May–September, with dinner at 7:30 P.M.; many folks arrive earlier to get front-row seats for the show. It's a good idea to make reservations at least one week ahead. The Bar J does not offer wagon or horseback rides.

In beautiful Buffalo Valley, 45 miles northeast of Jackson, **Castagno Outfitters Covered Wagon Cookouts** (307/543-2407, www.castagnooutfitters.com) start with a 30-minute ride in covered wagons. The wagons stop at an isolated aspen grove, where guests enjoy a dinner of steak, beans, baked potato, salad, and dessert. Dinners cost $25 adults, $20 kids, and run mid-June–late August; closed Sunday. It also has breakfast rides for $15 adults, $12 kids.

© DON PITCHER

EVENTS

Jackson Hole is packed with entertaining events almost every day of the year. Some of these are homegrown affairs such as the county fair, whereas others attract people from near and far. Of particular note are the International Pedigree Stage Stop Sled Dog Race (IPSSSDR), the Pole-Peddle-Paddle Race, the Elk Antler Auction, the Grand Teton Music Festival, and the Jackson Hole Fall Arts Festival. (In addition to the events listed, see *Grand Targhee Ski Resort* in this chapter for a year-round calendar of events on the other side of the Tetons.)

Winter

December is a particularly beautiful time in downtown Jackson. Lights decorate the elk antler arches, and a variety of events take place. Buy arts and crafts during the **Christmas Bazaar** early in the month, or take the kids to visit Saint Nick and his elves on Town Square starting in mid-December; they're there 5– 7 P.M. daily.

Kick the year off by watching (or participating in) the annual **torchlight ski parades** at all three local ski areas. They take place on Christmas evening and New Year's Eve at both Jackson Hole Mountain Resort and Grand Targhee Ski Resort, and on New Year's Eve at Snow King.

The **International Pedigree Stage Stop Sled Dog Race** (307/734-1163, www.wyomingstagestop.org) is the largest sled dog race in the lower 48 states and a qualifying event for the Iditarod. Unlike the Iditarod and many other mushing events, this one is run in short 30- to 60-mile legs, with teams operating from a different town each day. As with the Tour de France, it's the total time that counts in this stage race. The eight-day race starts in Jackson in late January and then goes on to Lander, Pinedale, Alpine, Kemmerer, Evanston, and Lyman before ending in Park City, Utah.

Each February, local Shriners hold horse-drawn **cutter races** (307/733-1938)—essentially a wild chariot race on 0.25 mile of ice—at Melody Ranch, six miles south of Jackson.

The ski season ends the first weekend of April with the **Pole-Pedal-Paddle Race** (307/733-6433, www.polepedalpaddle.com), combining alpine skiing, cross-country skiing, cycling, and canoeing in a wild, tough competition. It's the largest such event in the West and great fun for spectators and contestants, many of whom dress up in goofy costumes.

Spring

Spring in Jackson Hole is the least favorite time of the year for many locals. The snow is going, leaving behind brown grass and trees; biking and hiking trails aren't yet passable; and the river is too cold to enjoy. For many folks, this is the time to load up the car and head to Utah for a desert hike in Canyonlands. Despite these conditions, April and May can be a good time to visit, especially if you want to avoid the crowds, need to save money on lodging, or are planning to stay for the summer and need a job and a place to live. (Housing gets progressively more difficult to find after April.)

Summer

Summer begins with a series of events during **Elkfest** (307/733-3316, www.elkfest.org) on the third weekend of May, including a **mountain-man rendezvous** and chili cook-off. The main event, however, is the world's only public **elk antler auction,** which attracts hundreds of buyers from all over the globe to Jackson's Town Square. Local Boy Scouts collect five tons of antlers from the nearby National Elk Refuge each spring, with 80 percent of the proceeds helping to fund feeding of the elk. This may sound like an odd event, but the take is more than $60,000! Prices average $10 per pound, and the bidding gets highly competitive; perfectly matched pairs can go for more than $2,000. The antlers are used in taxidermy, belt buckles, furniture, and most important, to satisfy the high demand for antlers in the insatiable (pun intended) South Korean and Chinese aphrodisiac markets. There's more than a touch of irony in the Boy Scouts making money from the sale of sexual stimulants!

Memorial Day weekend brings **Old West**

Days (307/733-3316), complete with a horse-drawn parade, brew fest, chuck wagon dinner, and draft horse pull. The **Jackson Hole Film Festival** (307/733-8144, www.jhff.org) showcases independent films, shorts, and world premiers for five days in mid-June.

Fourth of July is another big event in Jackson, with a parade, rodeo, and an impressive fireworks show from Snow King Mountain. Another very popular Independence Day event is the free **Music in the Hole** (307/733-1128, www.gtmf.org) outdoor classical concert by the Grand Teton Music Festival orchestra.

The **Jackson Hole Rodeo** (307/733-2805, www.jhrodeo.com) brings spills and thrills to town, with Saturday night rodeos all summer and Wednesday night rodeos starting in mid-June. Another ongoing event is the **Grand Teton Music Festival** (www.gtmf.org), providing summertime classical music at Teton Village. (These latter two activities are detailed in their respective categories in this section.)

The **Mountain Artists' Rendezvous Art Fair** (307/733-8792, www.artassociation.org) is a great late-July event, with more than 100 artisans displaying their works at Miller Park. This is a highly competitive, juried event.

The last week of July brings an always fun **Teton County Fair** (307/733-5289, www.tetoncountyfair.com) with 4-H exhibits (from lambs to photography), pig wrestling in the mud, a horse show, pony rides and a petting zoo, watermelon- and pie-eating contests, live music and comedy acts, a carnival, rodeos, monster trucks, and everyone's favorite: a bang-up demolition derby ($17) on the final Sunday night.

Fall

Jackson Hole is at its most glorious in the fall, as aspens and cottonwoods turn into a fire of yellow and orange against the Teton backdrop. Most tourists have fled back home, leaving locals and hardier visitors to savor the cool autumn nights. The peak time for **fall colors** is generally the first week of October—considerably later than most people expect.

The primary autumn event is the **Jackson Hole Fall Arts Festival** (307/733-3316, www.jacksonholechamber.com), which takes place over a 10-day period in mid-September. Featured activities include exhibits at the National Museum of Wildlife Art and local galleries, a juried art fair, a miniature art show, art and cooking demonstrations, silent auctions, cowboy poetry and old-time cowboy music, "Taste of the Tetons" with delectable food from local restaurants, and tours of a half-dozen exquisite multimillion dollar homes. Also fun is a "quickdraw" in which artists paint, draw, and sculpt while you watch; the pieces are then auctioned off. The festival's **Arts for the Parks National Art Competition** (307/733-2787 or 800/553-2787, www.artsfortheparks.com) attracts thousands of paintings representing scenes from America's national parks. This isn't for amateurs; the top prize is $25,000. The banquet and silent auction seats fill by mid-August; reservations required.

Shopping

If you have the money (or a credit card), Jackson is a great place to buy everything from artwork to mountain bikes. Even if you just hitchhiked in and have no cash to spare, it's always fun to wander through the shops and galleries surrounding Town Square.

OUTDOOR GEAR

Outdoor enthusiasts will discover several excellent shops in Jackson. Climbers, backpackers, and cross-country skiers head to America's oldest climbing shop, **Teton Mountaineering** (170 N. Cache Dr., 307/733-3595 or 800/850-3595, www.tetonmtn.com), for quality equipment, maps, and travel guides. It also rents tents, sleeping bags, backpacks, cookstoves, climbing shoes, ice axes, cross-country skis, and even climbing and skiing videos. Check the bulletin board for used items.

Jack Dennis' Outdoor Shop (50 E. Broadway, 307/733-3270 or 800/570-3270, www.jackdennis.com) is a large upscale store with fly-fishing and camping gear in summer and skis and warm clothes during winter. It also rents almost anything: tents, stoves, lanterns, cookware, sleeping bags, fishing poles, fly rods, waders, float tubes, backpacks, skis, snowboards, snowshoes, and more.

Skinny Skis (65 W. Deloney Ave., 307/733-6094 or 888/733-7205, www.skinnyskis.com) has more in the way of high-quality clothing and supplies, especially cross-country ski gear. Rent sleeping bags, tents, climbing shoes, ice axes, inline skates, baby carriers, and backpacks here. The same folks run the summer-only **Moosely Seconds Mountaineering** (307/739-1801) in Moose, with climbing and outdoor gear, along with rentals of trekking poles, ice axes, crampons, rock shoes, approach shoes, plastic boots, day packs, and snowshoes.

Another place to rent outdoor gear of all types—including volleyball sets, fishing gear, float tubes, tents, sleeping bags, backpacks, campstoves, and lanterns—is **Leisure Sports** (1075 S. U.S. 89, 307/733-3040, www.leisuresportsadventure.com).

Gart Sports (485 W. Broadway, 307/733-4449, www.gartsports.com) is a large store with a variety of outdoor and sports gear. The least expensive place to buy rugged outdoor wear, cowboy boots, and cowboy hats is **Corral West** (840 W. Broadway, 307/733-0247).

BARGAINS

Buy used clothing and other items at **Browse'N Buy Thrift Shop** (139 N. Cache Dr., 307/733-7524) or the more chaotic **Orville's** (285 W. Pearl, 307/733-3165). Orville's sometimes sells old Wyoming license plates—a big hit with European tourists.

BOOKS

Unlike many Wyoming towns where the book selection consists of a few bodice-buster romance novels in the local pharmacy, Jackson is blessed with several fine bookstores. **Valley Bookstore** (125 N. Cache Dr., 307/733-4533, www.valleybook.com) is the largest local bookshop, with a big choice of regional titles, plus occasional author signings and readings.

Main Event (980 W. Broadway, 307/733-7112) in the Powderhorn Mall sells new books and CDs and rents videos. A few doors away in the mall is **Jackson Hole Book Trader** (307/734-6001 or 800/722-2710), with a surprising selection of used and rare books.

KITSCH

If you're a fan of the *National Enquirer,* check out the weird and wacky collection at **Ripley's Believe It or Not** (140 N. Cache, 307/734-0000, www.ripleys.com). Here you'll discover a shrunken head, six-legged buffalo calf, six-foot-long cigar, antique bedpan collection, and even art created from dryer lint. Who says art is only for the elite? Entrance costs a steep $8 adults, $5 ages 5–12, free for kids under five. The family rate is $28, a bargain price for families of 10 from Salt Lake City. Ripley's is open

JACKSON HOLE

9 A.M.–10 P.M. daily in summer and 10 A.M.–6 P.M. daily the rest of the year.

For more foolishness, have the kids drag you to the **Teton Maze** (307/734-0455 or 877/629-3786) across from the Snow King chairlift. As the ads proclaim, it's a-Maze-ing.

Summer Recreation

◖ SNAKE RIVER RAFTING

Jackson Hole's most popular summertime recreational activity is running Wyoming's largest river, the Snake. Each year more than 150,000 people climb aboard rafts, canoes, and kayaks to float down placid reaches of the Snake or to blast through the boiling rapids of Snake River Canyon. (As an aside, the name "Snake" comes from the Shoshone Indians, who used serpentine hand movements as sign language for their tribal name—a motion trappers misinterpreted as a snake and applied to the river flowing through Shoshone land.)

Almost 20 different rafting companies offer dozens of raft trips each day of the summer. Although you may be able to walk up and get a raft trip the same day, it's a good idea to reserve ahead for any river trip in July and August. In general, try to book a trip three or four days in advance if possible and at least one week ahead if you need a specific time, prefer an overnight float trip, or are traveling with a larger group. One or two people are more likely to get onboard at the last minute.

You may want to ask around to determine the advantages of each company. Some are cheaper but require you to drive a good distance from town; others offer more experienced crews; still others provide various perks such as fancy meals, U-paddle trips, overnight camps along the river, interpretive trips, or boats with fewer (or more) people. Several operators also lead seven-hour combination trips that include a lazy float followed by a meal break and a wild whitewater run.

The rafting companies generally operate mid-May–late September, and river conditions change throughout the season. Highest flows—and the wildest rides—are generally in May and June. Get a complete listing of float-

ing and boating outfits, along with descriptive brochures, from the visitor center in Jackson.

Float Trips

The gentlest way to see the Snake is by taking one of the many commercial float trips. Along the way, you'll be treated to stunning views of the Tetons and glimpses of eagles, ospreys, beavers, and perhaps moose or other wildlife along the riverbanks. Several companies—Will Dornan's Snake River Float Trips, Barker-Ewing, Grand Teton Lodge Co., Heart Six, Signal Mountain, Solitude, and Triangle X—offer 10-mile scenic float trips along the quiet stretch within Grand Teton National Park, generally putting in at Deadman's Bar and taking out at Moose; $45–50 adults, $30–35 kids. (Flagg Ranch Resort has rafting on the Snake River above Jackson Lake, and Grand Teton Lodge Company puts in at Pacific Creek.)

Several other rafting operations offer 13-mile South Park float trips outside the park (these typically include a lunch), putting in at the bridge near Wilson and taking out above Hoback Junction; $42 adults, $32 kids. Companies offering this trip include Barker-Ewing, Dave Hansen, Flagg Ranch, Lewis and Clark, Sands, Snake River Kayak and Canoe School, and Teton Expeditions. The in-the-park trips are considerably more scenic, so know what you are getting before you sign up because the differences are not usually emphasized by the rafting companies (at least not by those who don't operate inside the park). Some companies add options such as breakfast cookouts or overnight trips with camping along the way.

Age limits vary, but kids must generally be at least eight to float the river. Raft companies usually have folks meet up in either Jackson or Moose, but Heart Six departs from its ranch in

© DON PITCHER

whitewater rafting on the Snake River

Buffalo Valley, 45 miles northeast of Jackson. A wide variety of special voyages are also available from the various companies, including overnight camping and fish-and-float trips.

Call one of the following rafting outfits for details or pick up their slick brochures at the visitor center or from their offices scattered around town: **Barker-Ewing Float Trips** (307/733-1000 or 800/448-4202, www.barker-ewing.com), **Dave Hansen Whitewater** (307/733-6295 or 800/732-6295, www.davehansenwhitewater.com), **Will Dornan's Snake River Float Trips** (307/733-2583 or 888/998-7688, www.jacksonholefloattrips.com), **Grand Teton Lodge Float Trips** (307/543-2811 or 800/628-9988, www.gtlc.com), **Lewis and Clark Expeditions** (307/733-4022 or 800/824-5375, www.lewisandclarkexpeds.com), **Sands Wild Water** (307/733-4410 or 800/358-8184, www.sandswhitewater.com), **Signal Mountain Lodge and Marina** (307/733-5470 or 307/543-2831, www.signalmountainlodge.com), **Mad River Boat Trips** (307/733-6203 or 800/458-7238, www.mad-river.com), **Snake River Kayak and Canoe School** (307/733-9999 or 800/529-2501, www.snakeriverkayak.com),

Solitude Scenic Float Trips (307/733-2871 or 888/704-2800, www.solitudefloat-trips.com), **Teton Expeditions** (307/733-1007 or 888/700-7238, www.tetonexpeditions.com), and **Triangle X Float Trips** (a.k.a. National Park Float Trips, 307/733-5500 or 888/860-0005, www.trianglex.com).

Flagg Ranch Resort (307/543-2861 or 800/443-2311, www.flaggranch.com) offers 10-mile floats down the upper Snake River ($50 adults; $30 kids), starting at Flagg Ranch and heading downriver to Jackson Lake.

You can also float the river with any of the local fishing outfitters and combine angling with drifting downriver. One good company—it gives a really personalized tour—is **Wooden Boat River Tours** (307/732-2628, www.woodboat-tours.com), which has classic wooden dories.

Note that a few of the raft operators are regarded as "training grounds" for other companies; recommended outfits with good records include Barker-Ewing, Solitude, Grand Teton Lodge Co., and Triangle X.

Whitewater Trips

Below Jackson, the Snake enters the wild Snake

anyon, a stretch early explorers labeled "cursed mad river." The usual put-in point itewater "rapid-transit" trips is West Table Creek Campground, 26 miles south of Jackson. The take-out point is Sheep Gulch, eight miles downstream. In between, the river rocks and rolls through the narrow canyon, pumping past waterfalls and eagle nests and then over the two biggest rapids, Big Kahuna and Lunch Counter, followed by the smaller Rope and Champagne rapids. For a look at the action from the highway, stop at the paved turnout at milepost 124, where a trail leads down to Lunch Counter. The river changes greatly throughout the season, with the highest water and wildest rides in June. By August the water has warmed enough for a quick dip. Be sure to ask your river guide about the Jeep that sits in 60 feet of water below Lunch Counter!

Whitewater trips last around 3.5 hours (including transportation from Jackson) and cost around $45 adults, $35 children (age limits vary). Seven-hour combination trips covering 16 miles include a float trip, meal, and whitewater run for around $70 adults, $60 kids. You'll find discounted rates early or late in the summer and with operators who use *Titanic*-size 16-person rafts. The U-paddle versions are more fun than letting the guide do all the work in an oar raft, and the smaller eight-person rafts provide the most challenging (and wettest) runs. Most companies include round-trip transportation from Jackson.

Expect to get wet, so wear lightweight clothes and bring a jacket for the return ride. Most rafting companies provide wetsuits and booties. Note that this is not exactly a wilderness experience, especially in mid-July, when stretches of the river look like a Los Angeles freeway with traffic jams of rafts, kayaks, inner tubes, and other flotsam and jetsam. The river isn't as crowded on weekdays and early in the morning; take an 8 A.M. run for the fewest people.

Don't save your own camera along unless it's waterproof; bankside float-tographers are positioned along the biggest rapids to shoot both commercial and private rafters. Stop by **Float-O-Graphs** (130 W. Broadway, 307/733-6453 or 888/478-7427, www.floatographs.com) for

a photo from your run. Another company with a similar service is **Whitewater Photos and Video** (140 N. Cache Dr., 307/733-7015 or 800/948-3426, www.snakeriverphotos.com). Both companies also post photos online.

For details on whitewater raft trips, contact one of the following companies: **Barker-Ewing Whitewater** (307/733-1000 or 800/448-4202, www.barker-ewing.com), **Dave Hansen Whitewater** (307/733-6295 or 800/732-6295, www.davehansenwhitewater.com), **Jackson Hole Whitewater** (307/733-1007 or 800/700-7238, www.jhww.com), **Lewis and Clark Expeditions** (307/733-4022 or 800/824-5375, www.lewisandclarkexpeds.com), **Mad River Boat Trips** (307/733-6203 or 800/458-7238, www.mad-river.com), **Sands Wild Water** (307/733-4410 or 800/358-8184, www.sands-whitewater.com), **Snake River Kayak and Canoe School** (307/733-9999 or 800/529-2501, www.snakeriverkayak.com), or **Snake River Park Whitewater** (307/733-7078 or 800/562-1878, www.srpkoa.com). In addition to these, **Flagg Ranch Resort** (307/543-2861 or 800/443-2311, www.flaggranch.com) guides three-hour scenic floats down the upper Snake River above Jackson Lake.

Recommended companies with good safety records and well-trained staff include Barker-Ewing, Dave Hansen, and Sands. The largest local rafting company, Mad River, has a reputation as a proving ground for novice guides (but its prices are typically lower than those of other operators). It's your choice, but I personally would not raft with Snake River Park Whitewater.

FISHING

Jackson Hole has some of the finest angling in Wyoming, with native Snake River cutthroat (a distinct subspecies) and brook trout in the river, along with Mackinaw (lake trout), cutthroat, and brown trout in the lakes. The Snake is a particular favorite of beginning fly-fishing enthusiasts; popular shoreside fishing spots are just below Jackson Lake Dam and near the Wilson Bridge. Jackson Lake may provide higher odds for catching a fish, but you'll need to rent a boat from one of the marinas. This is the place parents take kids. Another very popular fishing hole is just below the dam on Jackson Lake. Flat Creek on the National Elk Refuge is an acclaimed spot for fly-fishing. Note that Wyoming fishing licenses are valid within Grand Teton National Park but not in Yellowstone, where you'll need a separate permit.

Fishing Guides

Many local companies offer guided fly-fishing float trips down the Snake River and other area waterways. Two people (same price for one person) should expect to pay $375 per day for a guide, rods and reels, lunch, and boat. Your fishing license and flies are extra. The visitor center has a listing of local fishing guides and outfitters, and its racks are filled with their brochures.

On Your Own

If you'd rather do it yourself, pick up a copy of the fat and free *Western Fishing Newsletter,* which offers descriptions of regional fishing areas and advice on which lures to try. Find it at **Jack Dennis' Outdoor Shop** (50 E. Broadway, 307/733-3270 or 800/570-3270, www.jackdennis.com). While there, you may want to buy a regional guide to fishing such as *Flyfisher's Guide to Wyoming* by Ken Retallic (Wilderness Adventures Press; www.wildav.com) or *Fishing Wyoming* by Kenneth Lee Graham (Globe Pequot Press; www.globepequot.com).

Jackson has several excellent fly-fishing shops, including the aforementioned Jack Dennis' Outdoor Shop. **Westbank Anglers** (3670 Teton Village Rd., 307/733-6483 or 800/922-3474, www.westbank.com) is a nationally known fly-fishing dealer with a slick mail-order catalog, excellent fishing clinics, and float trips. Both **High Country Flies** (185 N. Center St., 307/733-7210 or 866/733-7210, www.highcountryflies.com), and **Orvis Jackson Hole** (485 W. Broadway, 307/733-5407, www.orvis.com) offer fly-fishing classes and sell quality gear. Rent fishing rods, fly rods, float tubes, and waders from Jack Dennis, High Country Flies, or **Leisure Sports** (1075 S. U.S. 89, 307/733-3040, www.leisuresportsadventure.com).

BOATING
Kayaking and Canoeing

In business for more than 25 years, **Snake River Kayak and Canoe School** (365 N. Cache, 307/733-9999 or 800/529-2501, www.snakeriverkayak.com) offers a wide variety of river kayaking and canoeing classes for all levels of ability, plus fishing trips and raft trips. Full-day private lessons—including transportation, boats, paddles, wet suit, rubber booties, and life jackets—cost $340 for two students (lower rates if you have more people). Beginners may want to start out with one of the three-hour "rubber duckie" inflatable kayak river trips for $60. In addition, the school has sea kayak tours of all lengths in Yellowstone National Park. It rents practically anything that floats: canoes, sea kayaks, whitewater kayaks, inflatable kayaks, drift boats, and rafts, all with paddles and roof racks included. Also available are dry bags and life jackets.

The folks at **Rendezvous River Sports/ Jackson Hole Kayak School** (945 W. Broadway, 307/733-2471, www.jacksonholekayak.com) teach a wide range of kayaking courses from the absolute beginner level to advanced "hairboating" for experts. Classes include kayak roll clinics ($80), river rescue ($275), and special women's clinics and kids' classes. Two-day introductory classes cost $275; four days of instruction is $525. Private lessons are available, and the company rents sea kayaks and whitewater kayaks, plus inflatable kayaks.

Leisure Sports (1075 S. U.S. 89, 307/733-3040, www.leisuresportsadventure.com) rents rafts, canoes, inflatable kayaks, water skis, wet suits, dry bags, life jackets, and all sorts of other outdoor equipment (including personal watercraft). **Adventure Sports** (in Moose, 307/733-3307) also rents canoes and kayaks.

HORSEBACK RIDING
Trail Rides

Think of the Wild West and one animal always comes to mind—the horse. A ride on Old Paint gives city slickers a chance to saunter back in time to a simpler era and to simultaneously learn how ornery and opinionated horses can be. If

'll also learn why cowboys are so
th cowboy hats. In Jackson Hole
e from brief half-day trail rides in
...u Teton National Park all the way up to
weeklong pack trips into the rugged Teton Wilderness. The visitor center has a brochure listing
more than a dozen local outfitters and stables
that provide trail rides and pack trips.

For rides by the hour or day (approximately
$30 for a one-hour ride or $75 for a half-day), try **Scott's Jackson Hole Trail Rides**
(307/733-6992) in Teton Village, **Snow
King Stables** (behind Snow King Resort,
307/733-5781, www.snowking.com), **Spring
Creek Ranch** (307/733-8833 or 800/443-6139, www.springcreekranch.com) atop Gros
Ventre Butte off Spring Gulch Road, **A/OK
Corral** (in Hoback Junction, 307/733-6556,
www.horsecreekranch.com), **Mill Iron Ranch**
(10 miles south of Jackson, 307/733-6390 or
888/808-6390, www.millironranch.net),
Jackson Country Outfitters (307/413-5267 or 800/434-0368, www.jacksoncountryoutfitters.com) 14 miles south of town
near Hoback Junction, or **Goosewing Ranch**

© DON PITCHER

trail rides at Teton Village

(25 miles east of Kelly near the Gros Ventre
Wilderness, 307/733-5251 or 888/733-5251,
www.goosewingranch.com).

Of these, Scott's Jackson Hole Trail Rides,
Spring Creek Ranch, and Mill Iron Ranch are
the most popular, but you probably won't go
wrong with any of these companies. Mill Iron
Ranch, Spring Creek Ranch, and A/OK Corral
also offer rides that include breakfast or dinner
cookouts. Farther afield are several companies
offering trail rides, including three that operate out of Buffalo Valley (45 miles northeast
of Jackson): **Buffalo Valley Ranch** (307/543-2062 or 888/543-2477), **Castagno Outfitters**
(307/543-2407, www.castagnooutfitters.com),
and **Yellowstone Outfitters/Wagons West**
(307/543-2418 or 800/447-4711, www.yellowstoneoutfitters.com). More trail rides are offered
at **Togwotee Mountain Lodge** (307/543-2847
or 800/543-2847, www.togwoteelodge.com), 48
miles northeast of Jackson on the way to Togwotee Pass. The minimum age for horseback riding
is typically 5–6; these young children typically
ride while the horse is being led around by a parent. Prices may be substantially lower for rides
away from Jackson such as Yellowstone Outfitters ($55 for a half-day ride!).

Chuck wagon cookouts are a very popular family option in Jackson Hole during the
summer. Guests travel in horse-drawn wagons (or by horseback) and are treated to a
delicious all-you-can-eat meal and entertainment. (See *Chuck Wagon Cookouts* in *Entertainment and Events* for details.)

Wagon Trains

Two local companies lead overnight wagon-train rides (in wagons with rubber tires) into
the country around Jackson Hole. Guests split
their time between riding in the wagons and riding on horseback. **Wagons West** (307/543-2418
or 800/447-4711, www.wagonswestwyo.com)
heads up into the Mt. Leidy Highlands for 2–6
days. The shortest trips (two days and one night)
are $365 adults, $325 kids under 14. Four-day,
three-night trips are $690 adults, $610 kids;
and six-day, five-night trips run $905 adults,
$805 kids. **Teton Wagon Train/Double H Bar**

(307/734-6101 or 888/734-6101, www.teton-wagontrain.com) charges $795 adults ($695 ages 9–14, and $645 for younger kids) for a three-night package that includes horseback and wagon riding, meals, and camping gear.

HIKING

The country around Jackson abounds with hundreds of miles of hiking trails, providing recreation opportunities for all levels of ability. Many of the most popular local trails are within nearby **Grand Teton National Park.** Notable in-the-park hikes are found in the Taggart Lake and Jenny Lake areas, at Colter Bay, and off the Moose–Wilson Road. The visitor center in Jackson has a brochure detailing these hikes.

A local outdoors shop, **Skinny Skis** (65 W. Deloney Ave., 307/733-6094 or 888/733-7205, www.skinnyskis.com) produces an excellent free summertime guide to hiking in the area called *Trailhead.*

Closest to town are the trails at **Snow King,** where you can either hike up the mountain or ride the chairlift ($9) to the summit and hike back down. Once on top, you'll find a 0.5-mile nature trail and wonderful across-the-valley views of the Tetons. Nearby is the **Cache Creek Trail,** which follows this pretty creek uphill for six miles along an old road that's closed to motor vehicles. It's a great family hike or mountain-bike ride. For an alternate loop back (four miles round-trip), turn onto the **Putt-Putt Trail** two miles up. Cyclists often use Cache Creek Trail to connect with **Game Creek Trail** for a loop around Snow King Mountain. All of the trails in the Snow King area are open to mountain bikes, and you can transport bikes on the chairlift.

Guided Hikes

The **Teton County Parks and Recreation Department,** inside the Recreation Center (155 E. Gill St., 307/739-9025, www.teton-wyo.org/parks), sponsors a wide range of outdoor activities throughout the summer. Adult hikes ($15) take place every Tuesday May–October, plus on Thursdays June–August. Longer hikes (including an overnighter) take place several times a summer, and free senior walks are offered on Monday mornings during May and June. For a break from the young 'uns (grades 1–6), take them to the summer day camp at the rec center, available weekdays for $35 per day. You don't need to be a local resident to take part in any of these activities, but make reservations because some fill up. The Parks and Rec office also rents out volleyballs, horseshoes, boccie ball, and croquet sets.

Educational nature walks into the mountains around Jackson are offered by **The Hole Hiking Experience** (307/690-4453 or 866/733-4453, www.holehike.com). Rates start at $70 ($55 for kids) for a four-hour hike. For a free version, Grand Teton National Park offers guided walks and nature talks throughout the year.

MOUNTAIN-BIKING

Jackson Hole offers all sorts of adventures for cyclists, particularly those with mountain bikes. Most local bike shops provide maps of local mountain-bike routes, or you can buy a waterproof Jackson Hole mountain-biking map. Note that mountain bikes are not allowed on hiking trails in Grand Teton National Park or in Forest Service wilderness areas. The main road in Grand Teton National Park is plowed but closed to cars and other motorized traffic during April. It's great for an easy and scenic ride.

Bike Paths

Jackson is fast becoming a destination for cycling enthusiasts, thanks in part to the **Jackson Hole Community Pathways** (307/732-8573, www.tetonwyo.org/pathways), an expanding network of paved paths that cover 26 miles now, with plans to double in length by 2010. Its website provides detailed maps of the routes, and local bike stores sell a plasticized map ($12) showing paths and trails open to bikes on both sides of the Tetons. Get additional details from Friends of Pathways (www.jhpathways.com), a local nonprofit.

A seven-mile paved trail heads south of town, paralleling the highway to the Snake River bridge; it should be completed to Hoback Junction by 2009. A fun loop ride is to use this

JACKSON HOLE

path for a connection to the very popular Game Creek Trail, which meets the Cache Creek Trail, circling back to Jackson behind Snow King. (Some of this route is not paved.) The longest continuous paved bike path goes from Wilson westward to the summit of Teton Pass (a gain of 2,000 feet in 3.5 miles), with a second arm continuing from Wilson to Teton Village and the southern end of Grand Teton National Park parallel to the Moose–Wilson Road.

A four-mile path starts behind the main post office on Maple Way, crosses U.S. 89, and continues past the high school before turning north to meet the road to Wilson (Hwy. 22). This road has wide shoulders but gets lots of traffic.

The trails at Snow King Resort are open to mountain-bikers, and you can either peddle uphill or ride the chairlift with your bike ($9). Jackson Hole Mountain Resort has seven miles of bike trails on the lower sections of the mountain for all levels of ability. Access is via the Teewinot chairlift, which operates in the summer.

Bike Rentals and Tours

Rent mountain bikes from **Hoback Sports** (520 W. Broadway Ave., 307/733-5335, www.hobacksports.com), **The Edge Sports** (490 W. Broadway, 307/734-3916), **Wilson Backcountry Sports** (307/733-5228), **Adventure Sports** (307/733-3307) in Moose, **Jackson Hole Sports** (307/739-2687, www.jacksonholesports.com) in Teton Village, and **Boardroom of Jackson Hole** (225 W. Broadway Ave., 307/733-8327, www.boardroomofjacksonhole.com). All of these places rent bikes and helmets for around $25 per day, $40 per half day, and some also rent bike trailers, car racks, and kid bikes. Most also sell and repair bikes. Boardroom also rents skateboards, wakeboards, and inline skates.

Half-day mountain-bike tours are available for $45–66 per day from **Fat Tire Tours/ Hoback Sports** (307/733-5335, www.hobacksports.com); one of the tours includes a chairlift ride to the top of Snow King. **Teton Mountain Bike Tours** (307/733-0712 or 800/733-0788, www.tetonmtbike.com) offers scenic half- or all-day bike trips through Grand Teton and

Yellowstone national parks as well as Bridger– Teton National Forest and the National Elk Refuge. These trips are for all levels of ability, with prices starting at $45 for a four-hour ride in the Antelope Flats area.

ALPINE RIDES

Jackson Hole Resort

The tram will have ceased operation after the summer of 2006, but the **Bridger gondola** remains open for summertime rides. It doesn't reach the top of the mountain, but it does afford panoramic vistas over Jackson Hole and access to hiking trails. The **Teewiniot chairlift** ($15 all day) is also open summers, providing uphill transport for bikers and hikers.

Snow King

At Snow King Mountain right on the edge of Jackson, the resort's main **chairlift** operates late May–early September, taking folks for a 20-minute ride to the summit of the 7,751-foot mountain for $9 ($7 kids) round-trip. The chairlift runs 9 A.M.–8 P.M. daily in midsummer. On top you'll find a short nature trail and panoramic views of the Tetons.

Also at Snow King is the 2,500-foot-long **Alpine Slide** (307/733-7680 or 800/522-5464, www.snowking.com), a favorite of kids. For anyone older than six, the cost is $10 for one ride or $27 for three rides. For children under six (riding with an adult) it's just $1 per ride.

Grand Targhee Ski Resort

On the other side of the Tetons at Grand Targhee Ski Resort (307/353-2300 or 800/827-4433, www.grandtarghee.com), you can ride the **chairlift** ($8 adults, $5 kids) to the 10,200-foot summit of Fred's Mountain, where Grand Teton stands just seven miles away. The lift operates daily late June–mid-September, plus Wednesdays, Saturdays, and Sundays in June.

SWIMMING AND GYMS

Jackson is home to **Teton County/Jackson Recreation Center** (155 E. Gill St., 307/739-9025, www.tetonwyo.org/parks, open 6 A.M.–9 P.M. Mon.–Fri., noon–9 P.M. Sat., and noon–7 P.M. Sun.), which includes an indoor aquatics complex with a lap pool, 185-foot corkscrew water slide, and hot tub, plus a wading pool featuring a waterfall, slide, and water geyser. Basketball and volleyball courts are also inside the Rec Center, and after your workout, relax in the sauna and steam room. Nonresident prices are $6.25 adults, $5 ages 13–17, $4 seniors and ages 3–12, and $20 families; free for tots under three. The rec center also offers a variety of courses and activities, including yoga, toddler swimming, basketball, volleyball, and aerobics.

Out of the way is the wonderful hot mineral pool at **Granite Hot Springs** (307/734-7400, $6), 35 miles southeast of Jackson. The springs are open daily summers and winters (see *To Jackson Hole* under *Pinedale and Vicinity* in the *Wind River Mountains Country* chapter).

Rock Climbing

Jackson Hole is home for two highly regarded climbing schools: **Jackson Hole Mountain Guides** (165 N. Glenwood, 307/733-4979 or 800/239-7642, www.jhmg.com) and **Exum Mountain Guides** (307/733-2297, www.exumguides.com), with a summertime office at the south end of Jenny Lake. Both offer a wide range of classes—including ones for children—plus guided climbs up Grand Teton and wintertime courses in avalanche safety and ice climbing.

Teton Rock Gym (1116 Maple Way, 307/733-0707) has large indoor climbing walls, a weight room, and gear rentals. An **outdoor climbing wall** (307/739-2753, $5 per climb) is in the heart of Teton Village next to the pond. (See the *Grand Teton National Park* chapter for additional rock-climbing options, including Blacktail Butte, a popular place to practice your moves.)

UP IN THE AIR

Wyoming Balloon Co. (307/739-0900, w.. .wyomingballoon.com) takes off from the Jackson Hole side of the mountains. An hour-long flight is $225 adults, $175 kids (six and older). Operating out of the Jackson Hole Airport, **Soaring Eagle Glider Flights** (307/732-2359 or 877/454-3371, www.soaringeaglegliderflights.com) uses a powered glider; the engine gets you airborne and then shuts down for silent flight.

GOLF AND TENNIS

Jackson Hole Golf and Tennis Club (307/733-3111, www.gtlc.com), one mile north of town, has a public 18-hole golf course designed by Robert Trent Jones Jr. and rated one of the 10 best in America. Also here are a private swimming pool, tennis courts, and The Strutting Grouse Restaurant and Lounge, a perfect place for summertime patio dining.

Teton Pines Country Club (on Teton Village Rd., 307/733-1773 or 800/238-2223, www.tetonpines.com) is Jackson Hole's other golf spot open to the public. Its Arnold Palmer–designed 18-hole championship course is very challenging; 14 of the holes require over-water shots. The club also features a grand clubhouse, tennis courts, a large (and private) outdoor pool, and fine dining at The Pines restaurant. Both Teton Pines and Jackson Hole Golf and Tennis Club have rentals and lessons for golfers and tennis aficionados. **Public tennis courts** are on the east end of the rodeo grounds along Snow King Drive, and within Miller Park at Deloney and Gill streets.

For the serious professional golfer, **Alpine Miniature Golf** (307/733-5200 or 800/522-5464, www.snowking.com) has a Lilliputian 18-hole hillside course next to the Alpine Slide at Snow King Resort.

Winter Recreation

Jackson Hole has an international reputation as a winter destination. As access has become easier and the facilities more developed, many people have discovered the wonders of a Jackson Hole winter, especially one centered on a week of skiing or snowboarding. Three very different ski resorts attract the crowds: Grand Targhee for down-home, powder-to-the-butt conditions; Jackson Hole Mountain Resort for flashy, world-class skiing; and Snow King for steep, inexpensive, edge-of-town slopes. All three places have rental equipment, ski schools, and special programs for kids. Snowboarders and telemarkers are welcome on the slopes. These resorts, combined with an incredible abundance of developed and wild places to ski cross-country, make Jackson Hole one of the premier ski and snowboard destinations in America.

See your travel agent for package trips to any of the Jackson-area resorts. For daily ski reports, including information on both downhill and Nordic areas and the backcountry, listen to KMTN (FM 96.9) in the morning.

DOWNHILL SKIING AND SNOWBOARDING

If you plan to spend more than a couple of days in the area, it is probably worth your while to join the **Jackson Hole Ski Club** (307/733-6433, www.jhskiclub.com). In return for a $30 annual membership, you receive an impressive number of premiums, including reduced rates for lift tickets and season passes at all three local ski areas, plus discounted lodging, meals, drinks, snowmobile trips, and shopping at dozens of local stores. Join up at any local ski shop or its office at Snow King Resort.

Grand Targhee Ski Resort (307/353-2300 or 800/827-4433, www.grandtarghee.com)—just five miles above Alta, Wyoming—is the main attraction for the Teton Valley area. The resort offers excellent skiing and snowboarding in winter, along with a wide range of summer activities. (Get the complete scoop, including

details for on-mountain lodging and meals, in the *Teton Valley* section in this chapter.)

Ski and Snowboard Rentals

Rent or buy downhill skis and snowboards from **Hoback Sports** (520 W. Broadway Ave., 307/733-5335, www.hobacksports.com), **Gart Sports** (485 W. Broadway, 307/733-4449, www.gartsports.com), **Jack Dennis' Outdoor Shop** (50 E. Broadway, 307/733-3270 or 800/570-3270, www.jackdennis.com) and in Teton Village (307/733-6838), **Jackson Hole Sports** (in Teton Village, 307/739-2687, www.jacksonholesports.com), **Pepi Stiegler Sports** (in Teton Village, 307/733-4505), **Wildernest Sports** (in Teton Village, 307/733-4297, www.wildernestsports.com), or **Teton Village Sports** (307/733-2181 or 800/874-4224, www.tetonvillagesports.com). Rentals are also available at all three ski areas.

Snowboarders will find the latest gear and rentals at **Boardroom of Jackson Hole** (225 W. Broadway Ave., 307/733-8327, www.boardroomofjacksonhole.com), **Hole in the Wall Snowboard Shop** (307/739-2689), **Lowrider Board Shop** (at Pepi Stiegler Sports in Teton Village, 307/733-4505), and **Teton Village Sports** (307/733-2181 or 800/874-4224, www.tetonvillagesports.com). At Grand Targhee Ski Resort, rent boards from **Phat Fred's** (307/353-2300 or 800/827-4433, www.grandtarghee.com).

◖ Jackson Hole Mountain Resort

Just 12 miles northwest of Jackson is Jackson Hole Mountain Resort (307/733-2292 or 888/333-7766, www.jacksonhole.com), the largest and best-known Wyoming ski area. A true skiers' and snowboarders' mountain, Jackson Hole is considered the most varied and challenging of any American ski area. The powder is usually deep (average snowfall is 38 feet), lift lines are short, the slopes are relatively uncrowded, and the vistas are unbelievable. First opened in 1965, Jackson Hole Mountain Resort

© DON PITCHER

The Jackson Hole tram ceases operations after summer 2006.

JACKSON HOLE

that exceed four miles in length, and 24 miles of groomed trails, Jackson Hole Mountain Resort is truly a place of superlatives. Half of the resort's 60 runs are in the advanced category—including several of the notorious double-diamonds—but it is so large that even rank beginners will find plenty of bunny slopes on which to practice.

Rendezvous Mountain (10,450 feet) is where experts strut their stuff on these steep and fast slopes. Yes, those death-defying cliff-jumping shots are real; check out infamous **Corbet's Couloir,** a rocky gully that requires a leap of faith and suicidal urges. Fortunately, intermediate skiers and boarders are not given short shrift at Jackson Hole Mountain Resort, particularly on the friendlier slopes of 8,481-foot **Apres Vous Mountain.** Intermediate (and advanced) downhillers could spend all day playing on these slopes, and a high-speed quad here means that riders can blast to the summit of Apres Vous in just five minutes. Because of the speed of this and other lifts, the wait at the base is usually just a few minutes.

In addition to these lifts, you can ride a gondola, three other quad chairs, two triple chairs (one of which is new as of 2006), double chair, and Poma lift. Snowboarders will appreciate the half-pipe and boarders' terrain trail. The resort's **Kids Ranch** provides supervised day care, including a spacious play area; it's the only drop-off day-care center in Jackson Hole, and it's open seven days a week. Not far away is a special "magic carpet" (a conveyer belt of sorts) for children learning to ski or snowboard.

For four decades, the main attraction at Jackson Hole Resort was the 52-passenger **aerial tram** that climbed the summit of Rendezvous Mountain, providing jaw-dropping views across Jackson Hole. But all things must pass. In 2005, Jackson Hole Resort stunned local residents—and skiers around the country—by announcing that the aerial tram would be retired at the end of summer 2006. In operation since 1966, the tram had simply become too worn out to repair without a massive infusion of cash. As of this writing, any tram replacement was an open question, a $20 million question that will be replaced by a bi-cable gondola or an all-new tram. Neither

has become one of the nation's favorite ski areas. The resort has invested many millions of dollars in the last decade or so, upgrading facilities, adding lifts, expanding snowmaking, completing a spacious children's center, and building an ice rink and snowboarding half-pipe. These improvements have enhanced the resort's reputation as an expert's paradise to also include facilities that are more friendly to families and intermediate skiers. (Jackson Hole Mountain Resort is owned by the Kemmerer family, whose ancestors founded the town of Kemmerer, Wyoming, and is one of the few major American ski resorts that is still independently owned.)

The mountain has one unusual feature that occurs in midwinter: A temperature inversion frequently develops over the valley, meaning that when it's bitterly cold at the base of the mountain, the top is 15–20°F warmer. Skiers often remain on the upper slopes all day to enjoy these warmer temperatures.

With an unsurpassed 4,139-foot vertical drop (longest in the United States), 2,500 acres of terrain spread over two adjacent mountains, runs of these options will happen until the winter of 2008–09 at the earliest. In the meantime, the resort will keep the upper mountain accessible through a temporary double chairlift connecting from the top of existing chairlifts in the winter. Jackson Hole Resort will still be a great place to ski and snowboard, but the crown jewel is gone. The loss of the tram will also affect summer visitors who will no longer be able to ride to the summit for hikes and mountain vistas, though they can still ride the Bridger gondola to excellent hiking at the 9,095-foot level of the mountain, and a new restaurant at that location provides outstanding vistas from the deck.

Rates and Services: Get to Teton Village from the town of Jackson by hopping on the START bus ($3 each way; 307/733-4521, www.startbus.com). This is the only inexpensive part of a visit to Jackson Hole Resort, where prices for lift tickets approach the stratosphere. Single-day tickets are $70 adults ($52 per half day), $56 ages 15–21 ($41 per half day), and $35 kids under 14 and seniors older than 65 ($26 per half day). Multiday all-lift tickets—the most common kind bought—are $330 per week (five days of skiing) for adults, $265 for ages 15–21, and $165 for kids under 15 and seniors. Lifts are open 9 A.M.–4 P.M. daily Thanksgiving–early April.

Skis and snowboards can be rented at shops in Jackson or Teton Village. The ski school offers a special Kinderschule program for children, and beginning snowboarders can learn from the pros. Jackson Hole Resort even has special steep snowboarding and skiing camps, where you learn from extreme downhill fanatics. Tommy Moe—gold and silver medalist at the 1994 Winter Olympics—teaches a "Steep and Deep" ski camp and is a ski ambassador for the resort.

Ski hosts are scattered around the mountain, ready to provide information and free hourly tours of the slopes from the top of Rendezvous Mountain. Racers and spectators will enjoy NASTAR events, along with various other competitions throughout the winter.

For more information on Jackson Hole Mountain Resort, call 307/733-2292 or 888/333-7766. Get recorded snow conditions by calling 307/733-2291; the messages are changed each morning before 5 A.M. The resort's website, www.jacksonhole.com, is packed with additional details, including the current weather and snow conditions.

Teton Village

At the base of the mountain is the Swiss-style Teton Village—alias "the Vill." Everything skiers and boarders need is crowded together here: lodges, condominiums, espresso stands, restaurants, après-ski bars, gift shops, groceries, ski, snowboard, and snowshoe rentals and lessons, storage lockers, car rentals, a skating pond, child care, personal trainers, dogsled tours, and even a travel agency for escapes to Hawaii. Tune your radio to FM 100.1 "Teton Village Radio" for parking and transportation information.

On-the-mountain facilities include a fine dining establishment at the top of Bridger gondola, Casper Restaurant at the bottom of Casper Bowl, and snack bars at the base of Thunder chairlift and the top of Apres Vous chairlift. Casper Restaurant serves a barbecue picnic most days and is a popular place to join friends for lunch.

Snow King Resort

Snow King Resort has three things that other local ski areas lack: location, location, and location. The resort sits directly behind town and just seven blocks from Town Square. This is the locals' place, Jackson's "town hill," but it also offers surprisingly challenging runs. It may not be the largest or fanciest place around, but the King's ski runs make up in difficulty what they lack in size. From below, the mountain (7,808 feet at the summit) looks impossibly steep and narrow. High atop the big chairlift, the vista provides a panoramic tour of Jackson Hole and the Tetons.

Snow King was the first ski area in Wyoming—it opened in 1939—and one of the first in North America. The original chapter of the National Ski Patrol was established here in 1941. The mountain has a 1,571-foot vertical drop. You'll find more than 400 acres of skiable terrain at Snow King, with the longest run stretching nearly a mile. A triple chair, two double chairs, and a Poma lift climb the mountainside. Other features include snowmaking, a tubing park, and a very popular 300-foot half-pipe and terrain park for snowboarders. It's the only local resort with lighted runs.

Rates and Services: Prices for lift tickets at Snow King are well below those at other Jackson Hole resorts: $35 per day ($23 per half day) for adults and $25 per day ($15 per half day) for kids under 15 and seniors. Hours of operation are 9:30 A.M.–4:30 P.M., with night skiing (4:30–8:30 P.M. Mon.–Sat.) available on the lower sections of Snow King for an additional $15 adults or $10 kids and seniors. In addition, the King has special two-hour rates for lift tickets ($17 adults, $12 kids and seniors); these are perfect for skiers and boarders who arrive late in the afternoon and want to hit the slopes for a bit. With some of the best snowmaking in Wyoming, the resort usually opens by Thanksgiving and remains in operation through March.

At the base of Snow King you'll discover a lodge with reasonable ski-and-stay packages, starting at $498 d for three nights of lodging, plus breakfasts and two days of skiing; add $200 to this for the holiday season. Also at Snow King are two restaurants, the Shady Lady Saloon, ski and snowboard rentals and lessons, plus a variety of other facilities, including an indoor ice rink and mountaintop snack shack. Jackson's START buses (307/733-4521, www.startbus.com) offer frequent service to town (free) or Teton Village ($3). For more information on Snow King Resort, call 307/733-5200 or 800/522-5464, or find it on the web at www.snowking.com.

CROSS-COUNTRY SKIING

For many Jackson Hole residents the word "skiing" means heading across frozen Jenny Lake or telemarking down the bowls of Teton Pass rather than sliding down the slopes of the local resorts. Jackson Hole has become a center for cross-country enthusiasts and offers an impressive range of conditions—from flat-tracking along summertime golf courses where a gour-

met restaurant awaits to remote wilderness settings where a complete knowledge of snowpack structure, avalanche hazards, and winter survival techniques is essential. Beginners will probably want to start out at a Nordic center, progressing to local paths and the more gentle lift-serviced ski runs with experience. More advanced skiers will quickly discover incredible snow in the surrounding mountains.

Cross-Country Ski Rentals

Rent or buy cross-country skis from **Skinny Skis** (65 W. Deloney Ave., 307/733-6094 or 888/733-7205, www.skinnyskis.com), **Teton Mountaineering** (170 N. Cache Dr., 307/733-3595 or 800/850-3595, www.tetonmtn.com), or **Wilson Backcountry Sports** (Wilson, 307/733-5228). Local Nordic centers also rent equipment. Most places rent both classical cross-country skis and skate skis (much faster and a better workout), along with telemarking and randonnée (alpine touring) skis.

Nordic Centers

Nordic skiing enthusiasts will find three different developed facilities near Jackson and others at Grand Targhee and near Togwotee Pass. The largest is **Jackson Hole Nordic Center** (307/739-2629, www.jacksonhole.com), with 17 kilometers of groomed trails—both set track and skating lanes—that cover a wide range of conditions. Call 307/733-2291 for the snow report. In Teton Village, this is the best place to learn cross-country skiing. Daily trail passes are $10 per day. Traditional cross-country skis, skate skis, and telemarking equipment are available for rent, and the center offers a wide spectrum of lessons and tours. Hours are 8:30 A.M.–4:30 P.M. daily. You can exchange your alpine lift ticket at Jackson Hole Mountain Resort for one at the Nordic center (but, hey, it better be for no extra charge since you've already dropped $70!).

Along Teton Village Road, **Teton Pines Cross-Country Ski Center** (307/733-1005 or 800/238-2223, www.tetonpines.com) features 13 kilometers of groomed track (both classical and skating) on a summertime golf course.

AVALANCHE SAFETY

Backcountry skiing is becoming increasingly popular in the mountains surrounding Jackson Hole. Unfortunately, many skiers fail to take the necessary precautions and more than a few have paid with their lives. Between 1995 and 2004, avalanches killed 26 people in Wyoming. Given the enormous snowfalls that occur, the steep slopes the snow piles up on, and the high winds that accompany many storms, it should come as no surprise that avalanches are a real danger.

Nearly all avalanches are triggered by the victims. If you really want to avoid avalanches, ski only on groomed ski trails or "bombproof" slopes that, because of aspect, shape, and slope angle, never seem to slide. Unfortunately, this isn't always possible, so an understanding of the conditions that lead to avalanches is imperative for backcountry skiers. The Forest Service produces a useful booklet called *Basic Guidelines for Winter Recreation,* available in many of its offices around Wyoming.

The best way to learn about backcountry safety is through an avalanche class. These are offered in the Jackson Hole area by **American Avalanche Institute,** 307/733-3315, www.ava-lanchecourse.com), **Exum Mountain Guides** (307/733-2297, www.exumguides.com), and **Jackson Hole Mountain Guides** (307/733-4979 or 800/239-7642, www.jhmg.com). Failing that, you can help protect yourself by following these precautions when you head into the backcountry:

• Before leaving, get up-to-date avalanche information. Visit www.avalanche.org for links to avalanche forecasting sites throughout the western states. For the Jackson Hole area, check the Forest Service's 24-hour **Backcountry Avalanche Hazard and Weather Forecast** (307/733-2664, www.jhavalanche.org). For areas around Yellowstone – including West Yellowstone and Cooke City on the margins and the Washburn Range inside the park – contact the **Gallatin National Forest Avalanche Advisory Center** (406/587-6981, www.mtavalanche.com) in Bozeman. If the message says avalanche danger is high, ski on the flats instead. **Jackson Hole Snow Observations** (www.jhsnowobs.org) provides an online forum where backcountry users share observations on snowpack conditions and avalanche activity.

Daily trail passes cost $10 adults or $5 children and seniors, and ski rentals and lessons are available. Hours are 9 A.M.–5 P.M. daily. The clubhouse here has a restaurant for gourmet après-ski lunches and dinners.

On the west side of the Tetons 42 miles out of Jackson, **Grand Targhee Nordic Center** (307/353-2300 or 800/827-4433, www.grandtarghee.com, has 20 kilometers of groomed cross-country ski trails (classical and skating) covering rolling terrain. Trail passes are $10 adults and $5 seniors and kids. Lessons and ski rentals are also available. Hours are 9:30 A.M.–4 P.M. daily. Guests with Targhee lodging packages can ski free on the cross-country tracks.

On Your Own

Nordic skiers who would rather explore Jackson Hole and the mountains that surround it on their own will discover an extraordinary range of options, from beginner-level treks along old roads to places where only the most advanced skiers dare venture. Because Jackson has so many cross-country fanatics (and visiting enthusiasts), tracks are quickly broken along the more popular routes, making it easier for those who follow. For complete coverage of all these options, pick up a copy of the helpful free winter outdoors guide *Trailhead* at **Skinny Skis** (65 W. Deloney Ave., 307/733-6094 or 888/733-7205, www.skinnyskis.com). If you're heading out on your own, be prepared for deep snow (four feet in the valley) and temperatures that often plummet below zero at night.

The **Teton County Parks and Recreation Department** (155 E. Gill, 307/739-9025, www.tetonwyo.org/parks) leads all-day cross-

- Be sure to carry extra warm clothes, water, high-energy snacks, a dual-frequency avalanche transceiver (make sure it's turned on and that you know how to use it!), a lightweight snow shovel (for digging snow pits or excavating avalanche victims), an emergency snow shelter, cell phone, first-aid supplies, a Swiss Army or Leatherman knife, a topographic map, an extra plastic ski tip, a flashlight, matches, and a compass or GPS unit. Many skiers also carry that cure-all, duct tape, wrapped around a ski pole. Let a responsible person know exactly where you are going and when you expect to return. It's also a good idea to carry special ski poles that extend into probes in case of an avalanche. Check with local ski shops or talk to Forest Service or Park Service folks for details on specific areas.

- Check the angle of an area before you ski through it. Slopes of 30-45 degrees are the most dangerous; lesser slopes do not slide as frequently.

- Watch the weather; winds over 15 mph can pile snow much more deeply on lee slopes, causing dangerous loading on the snowpack. Especially avoid skiing on or below cornices.

- Avoid the leeward side of ridges, where snow loading can be greatest.

- Be aware of gullies and bowls; they're more likely to slip than flat open slopes or ridgetops. Stay out of gullies at the bottom of wide bowls; these are natural avalanche chutes.

- Look out for cracks in the snow, and listen for hollow snow underfoot. These are strong signs of dangerous conditions.

- Look at the trees. Smaller trees may indicate that avalanches rip through an area frequently, knocking over the larger ones. Avalanches can, however, also run through forested areas.

- Know how much new snow has fallen recently. Heavy new snow over older weak snow layers is a sure sign of extreme danger on potential avalanche slopes. Most avalanches slip during or immediately after a storm.

- Learn how to dig a snow pit and how to read the various snow layers. Particularly important are the very weak layers of depth hoar or surface hoar that have been buried under heavy new snow.

JACKSON HOLE

country ski outings most Tuesdays mid-December–mid-March; $15. Bring your own skis and a lunch; it provides the guide and transportation. The department also offers a full-moon ski tour once each winter.

ICE-SKATING

Each winter, the town of Wilson floods a hockey rink–size part of the town park for skating, hockey, and broomball. A warming hut stands next to the rink. Jackson maintains ice rinks at Snow King for figure skaters and general playing around, plus a little one at Powderhorn Park (Powderhorn Lane at Alpine Lane) for broomball. All three of these are free and lighted most winter evenings. Call 307/733-5056 for details.

All three local ski resorts have ice-skating and skate rentals. You'll find skating ponds in Teton

Village at the base of **Jackson Hole Mountain Resort** and over in Alta at **Grand Targhee Ski Resort.** For the out-of-the-elements version, skate over to **Snow King Resort,** where the indoor ice-skating rink is open in the winter and offers skate rentals and lessons.

SNOWSHOEING

Snowshoeing began as a way to get around in the winter, but the old-fashioned wood-and-rawhide snowshoes were bulky and heavy. In recent years snowshoeing has become a popular form of recreation, as new technology created lightweight and easily maneuverable snowshoes. Snowshoeing requires no real training: Just strap them on, grab a pair of poles, and start walking. But be careful where you walk (see the sidebar, *Avalanche Safety,* for tips).

Rent snowshoes from **Skinny Skis** (65 W.

Deloney Ave., 307/733-6094 or 888/733-7205, www.skinnyskis.com), **Teton Mountaineering** (170 N. Cache Dr., 307/733-3595 or 800/850-3595, www.tetonmtn.com), **Wilson Backcountry Sports** (Wilson, 307/733-5228), **Boardroom of Jackson Hole** (225 W. Broadway Ave., 307/733-8327, www.boardroomofjacksonhole.com), and **Grand Targhee Ski Resort** in Alta, 307/353-2300 or 800/827-4433.

Guided Trips

Grand Teton National Park has excellent naturalist-led **snowshoe hikes** several times each week during winter. Snowshoes are provided at no charge, and no experience is necessary. These trips generally depart at 2 P.M. from the visitor center in Moose, but for specifics call 307/739-3399. Reservations are required; no kids under eight are permitted. Free naturalist-led snowshoe tours are offered at **Grand Targhee Ski Resort** (307/353-2300 or 800/827-4433, www.grandtarghee.com).

Teton County Parks and Recreation Department (155 E. Gill, 307/739-9025, www.tetonwyo.org/parks) leads all-day snowshoe tours most Thursdays mid-December–mid-March for $15. Bring your own skis and a lunch; it provides the guide and transportation.

Snowshoe walks into the mountains around Jackson are also offered by **The Hole Hiking Experience** (307/690-4453 or 866/733-4453, www.holehike.com), the only company permitted to guide snowshoeing trips in nearby national forests. Its most popular trips go to Shadow Mountain north of Kelly. Rates start at $70 ($55 for kids) for a four-hour snowshoe trek.

The Saddlehorn Activity Center at **Jackson Hole Mountain Resort** (307/733-2292 or 888/333-7766, www.jacksonhole.com) has snowshoe rentals and guided snowshoe tours. In addition, a snowshoe trail ($10) parallels Nordic Center ski tracks, and Forest Service naturalists lead snowshoe hikes in the area on Wednesdays, Fridays, and Saturdays.

SLEIGH RIDES

Several companies offer romantic dinner and horse-drawn sleigh rides in the Jackson Hole area mid-December through March. Make reservations well in advance for these popular trips. If you don't have the cash for one of these, take a daytime sleigh ride at the National Elk Refuge.

Jackson Hole Mountain Resort (307/739-2603, www.jacksonhole.com) picks up Teton Village guests for a romantic 30-minute ride to a rustic log cabin, where they are served a four-course roast prime rib or broiled salmon dinner (vegetarian options available) with nightly entertainment. Prices are $61 adults, $17 children under 11, and $15 infants. There are two seatings nightly, and reservations are required.

Spring Creek Ranch (307/733-8833 or 800/443-6139, www.springcreekranch.com) has 45-minute afternoon sleigh rides at the top of Gros Ventre Butte for $20 per person. It also has packages ($60) that combine a sleigh ride with a meal at the Granary Restaurant. This is one of Jackson's finer restaurants, so bring your dress clothes.

Mill Iron Ranch (307/733-6390 or 888/808-6390, www.millironranch.net) is a friendly family-run operation with evening sleigh rides in a down-home setting 10 miles south of Jackson. Guests get a 45-minute ride that takes you past an elk herd to the lodge for a big T-bone steak dinner; $63 adults, $50 kids. In scenic Horse Creek Canyon, this is the most authentic of the local sleigh rides. Call for reservations.

Dinner sleigh rides are also offered at **Grand Targhee Ski Resort** (307/353-2300 or 800/827-4433, www.grandtarghee.com), where a horse-drawn sleigh transports you to a remote yurt for a Western-style meal; $35 adults, $15 kids.

Spotted Horse Ranch (307/733-2097 or 800/528-2084, www.spottedhorseranch.com) offers sleigh rides in conjunction with nearby Camp Creek Inn; a ride and candlelit dinner is $45 per person. The ranch is 16 miles south of Jackson along the beautiful Hoback River.

TUBING

Two local ski areas have sliding parks with customized inner tubes and rope tows. At Snow

King Resort it's called **King Tubes** (307/734-8823 or 800/522-5464, www.snowking.com) and is available on weekday evenings and weekends after noon. Rates are $10 per hour for adults, $7 per hour for kids. The **Grand Targhee tube park** (307/353-2300 or 800/827-4433, www.grandtarghee.com) is open for après-ski fun only (after 5 P.M.) and costs $8 per hour.

DOGSLEDDING

Founded by eight-time Iditarod musher Frank Teasley, **Jackson Hole Iditarod Sled Dog Tours** (307/733-7388 or 800/554-7388, www.jhsleddog.com) offers excellent half-day trips ($150 per person including lunch) and all-day trips ($225 per person including a big steak dinner). The main destination is wonderful Granite Hot Springs, but when snow conditions are right, the teams also run in the Grays River, Shadow Mountain, and Gros Ventre areas. All trips include round-trip transportation from Jackson. Overnight trips are also available.

Another Iditarod veteran, Billy Snodgrass, operates **Continental Divide Dogsled Adventures** (307/739-0165 or 800/531-6874, www.dogsledadventures.com), with dog teams in Teton Village, Grand Targhee Ski Resort, Togwotee Mountain Lodge (48 miles north of Jackson), and Brooks Lake Lodge (65 miles northeast of Jackson). Prices start at $120 per person for a 90-minute dogsled ride at Teton Village or Grand Targhee. Full-day tours in the gorgeous country around Brooks Lake cost $250 (including transportation from Jackson). Longer trips are also available, including an adventure on which you stay overnight in a surprisingly comfortable yurt; $540 per person, all-inclusive.

SNOWMOBILING

Snowmobiling is one of Jackson Hole's most popular wintertime activities. Hundreds of miles of packed and groomed snowmobile trails head into Bridger–Teton National Forest. Some of the most popular places include the Togwotee Pass area 48 miles north of Jackson, Cache Creek Road east of town, and Granite Hot Springs Road 25 miles southeast. Only guided snowmobile groups are allowed into Yellowstone, with all-day tours around $250 for one rider or $350 for two riders. Tours to other areas are usually less expensive, and some motels offer package deals. The Visitor center has brochures and a complete listing of local snowmobile-rental companies, plus maps of snowmobile trails.

JACKSON HOLE

Accommodations

As one of the premier centers for tourism in Wyoming, Jackson Hole is jam-packed with more than 70 motels, hotels, and B&Bs, plus many more condominiums and guest ranches. Other lodging can be found just to the north within or near Grand Teton National Park. The Jackson Hole Chamber of Commerce's website (www.jacksonholechamber.com) has brief descriptions and web links for most local places. Don Pitcher's *Moon Yellowstone and Grand Teton* (www.moon.com) has a more comprehensive listing of Jackson lodging places.

Because of the town's popularity, Jackson accommodations command premium prices. With a few exceptions, you'll pay at least $90 d during the peak visitor seasons of July–August and late December–early January. Rates can drop more than 50 percent in the off-season, so if you can visit March–May or late September–mid-December, you'll save a lot of cash. (The same Super 8 Motel rooms that go for $150 in July cost just $55 in early November!) In the town of Jackson, the highest rates are usually in July and August, while at Teton Village, skiers and snowboarders send room rates to their peak between mid-December and early January. You will need to add a 6 percent sales tax to all the lodging rates below.

Reservations are highly recommended. For midsummer, book rooms at least two months ahead, or longer if you really want to be certain of a place. During the Christmas–New Year's period you should probably reserve six months in advance to ensure a spot. Summer weekends tend to be the most crowded, with many families driving up from Salt Lake City for a cooling break in the mountains.

If you're overwhelmed by all the lodging choices, try one of the reservation services, such as **Jackson Hole Central Reservations** (307/733-4005 or 800/443-6931, www.jacksonholewy.com). Looking for other opinions? Head online to Tripadvisor (www.tripadvisor.com) for reviews of many Jackson Hole lodging places.

UNDER $50

Jackson's least-expensive option, the **Bunkhouse** (307/733-3668 or 800/234-4507, www.anvilmotel.com) is in the basement of the Anvil Motel at 215 North Cache Drive. Right in town, the year-round hostel almost always has space. It costs $25 per person and includes a TV room and a kitchen with a refrigerator and microwave (but no stove or dishes). The big sleeping room contains 27 bunk beds with linen, a towel, and adjacent storage lockers; bring your own lock. No kids under 16. Although men's and women's showers and restrooms are separate, the sleeping space is coed. It can get pretty noisy with all those snoring bodies in one room at night, so earplugs are a smart buy. Check in after 3 P.M. and be out by 11 A.M. Alcohol is not allowed, but there is no curfew. No reservations (except for groups of 10 or more), but you can call the day of your arrival to reserve a bed. Hostel guests also have access to the Anvil Motel hot tub, upstairs. Backpackers and others who aren't staying here can take showers for $6.

Despite the name, **Hostel X** (307/733-3415, www.hostelx.com) really isn't a hostel, but it does provide budget rates in a scenic location. Private rooms cost $55 s or d, or $68 for up to four people. The very small plain-vanilla rooms lack TV or phones, but there's a central lounge for camaraderie. The lounge includes a TV, pay phones, a pool table, table tennis, a children's play area, a fireplace, a microwave, games, Internet access, and a ski-waxing room. Because of its Teton Village location at the foot of Jackson Hole Mountain Resort, Hostel X is very popular with skiers on a budget; reserve three months ahead for midwinter rooms, but space is typically available in the summer.

$50-100

Despite its name, **The Cottages at Snow King** (470 King St., 307/733-3480) doesn't have cottages, but it does rent modest but comfortable motel rooms in a residential part of town. These vary from rooms with one queen bed for $68 s or d, up to full-kitchen units that sleep four for $98. All rooms have microwaves and fridges, and pets are welcome ($15 extra). Winter rates provide skiers with some of the best deals in Jackson: starting at $140 d for a week! The motel is entirely nonsmoking.

A recommended budget place is **Anvil Motel** (215 N. Cache Dr., 307/733-3668 or 800/234-4507, www.anvilmotel.com), where the modern rooms start at $103 d for a room with one queen, or $129 for up to four people in a room with two queen beds. Two suites ($165 and $235) are also available, and all rooms here have microwaves and small fridges, plus access to the outdoor hot tub. Wi-Fi is available in some rooms.

Ranch Inn (45 E. Pearl St., 307/733-6363 or 800/348-5599, www.ranchinn.com) offers a wide variety of accommodations just one block from Town Square, all with fridges and microwaves. These include remodeled standard rooms ($98 d), tower rooms with balconies facing Snow King, fridges, and microwaves ($155 d), and suites with king beds, wood-burning fireplaces, balconies, and jetted tubs ($165–170 d). Extra guests are $5 per person. Amenities include indoor and outdoor hot tubs, Wi-Fi Internet access in the lobby and some rooms, plus a continental breakfast. Some of the tower rooms are wheelchair-accessible.

One of Jackson's better deals for standard motel rooms is—not surprisingly—**Motel 6** (1370 W. Broadway, 307/733-1620 or 800/466-8356, www.motel6-jackson.com), but even here the summertime rates are $90-93 s or $96–99 d. You'll find humdrum rooms and an outdoor pool, but you should reserve six months in advance for July and August. Off-season rates ($30 s or $35 d) are a much better bargain.

Twelve miles south of Jackson in Hoback Junction, **Hoback River Resort** (307/733-5129, www.hobackriverresort.com) has large no-smoking motel rooms and cabins on attractive grounds facing the Hoback River. The rooms are very clean and well maintained, but the location—away from busy downtown Jackson—is the real draw here. Rates are $80–90 d in motel rooms with decks, or $120–160 d in rustic cabins with full kitchens (but no maid service). Modern cottages—also with full kitchen—are $140–180 for up to six guests. A three-night minimum stay is required in the cabins and cottages. No phones in the rooms.

On the south end of Jackson at the Y intersection of highways 89 and 22, **Pony Express West Motel** (1075 W. Broadway, 307/733-3835 or 800/526-2658, www.ponyexpresswest.com) has a seasonal heated outdoor pool, along with standard motel rooms ($95 for units with a queen bed and bunks for kids) and units with full kitchens ($85 d). Open May–September.

$100-150

Many Jackson accommodations fall in the $100–150 range, with pricing factors being location, type of room, quality of furnishings, and presence of amenities such as pools and hot tubs. Several comfortable midrange options are described as follows. These are not the corporate lodging giants, but they offer good value and down-home friendliness.

Downtown

Elk Country Inn (480 W. Pearl, 307/733-2364 or 800/483-8667, www.elkcountryin.com) is popular with families and small groups. Spacious motel rooms (a bit old-fashioned but nicely maintained) contain two queen beds and cost $120 d. Basic rooms with one bed are just $75 d. Also available are loft units that sleep six for $150. Add $6 to these prices for a kitchenette unit. Modern log cabins with full kitchenettes (including dishes) and lodgepole

furnishings go for $179 d or $188 for four. Other facilities include an indoor hot tub, a shady picnic area with playground, and a free wintertime shuttle to Teton Village.

Golden Eagle Inn (325 E. Broadway, 307/733-2042 or 888/748-6937, www.goldeneagleinn.com) is a quiet out-of-the-way family motel with standard rooms for $99–125 d, and larger rooms for $140–180 d. All include microwaves and small refrigerators, plus access to the heated seasonal pool. Adjacent is a two-bedroom house with a full kitchen for $275 d.

Anglers Inn (265 N. Millward St., 307/733-3682 or 800/867-4667, www.anglersinn.net) has pleasant rooms with Western-style fixtures, lodgepole beds and chairs, and small baths. This cozy motel is right on Flat Creek but just a couple of blocks from Town Square. Rates are $105–130 d, and all rooms contain fridges and microwaves. A computer is available in the office.

Jackson Hole Lodge (420 W. Broadway, 307/733-2992 or 800/604-9404, www.jacksonholelodge.com) has a diverse mixture of rooms, but the featured attractions are a large indoor swimming pool, wading pool, two hot tubs, sauna, and game room on attractive grounds. Standard motel rooms are a bit dated but clean and in good condition for $109–139 d. Condo-type units are much nicer, with an upscale decor that includes log furniture; $169 for a studio unit, $249 for a one-bedroom unit (sleeps four) with a living room, fireplace, and full kitchen. Two-bedroom units cost $309 for up to eight people. A computer is available in the lobby, which also has free Wi-Fi.

Miller Park Lodge (155 N. Jackson, 307/733-4858 or 800/429-8873, www.millerparklodge.net) is an attractive and modern 12-unit motel right across the street from a kid-friendly park. Guests appreciate the outdoor hot tub and continental breakfast. Standard rooms have two queen or a king bed, microwaves, and small fridges, and go for $139 d; add $30 for a deluxe king room that also includes a fireplace and large jetted tub. Spacious family rooms ($219) sleep six, with a separate dining nook.

On the quiet north side of town, **Cache**

Creek Motel (390 N. Glenwood, 307/733-7781 or 800/843-4788, www.cachecreekmotel.com) is a well-maintained and moderately priced lodging choice. All rooms include full kitchens (with dishes and pans). Standard rooms run $110 d or $150 for four people. One-bedroom suites cost $175, and two-bedroom suites are $190; the suites sleep up to six for the same price.

Nearby

Two midpriced motels are adjacent to each other and one mile north of Jackson on U.S. 89. Both face the Elk Refuge (and the busy highway). **Elk Refuge Inn** (307/733-3582 or 800/544-3582, www.elkrefugeinn.com) is the smaller and more homey of the two, with a mixture of rooms and friendly management, plus corrals where horses can be boarded at no additional charge. Rates are $128 d, and all rooms contain fridges, microwaves, and a small deck. A family room ($150 for six) and units with kitchenettes and private balconies ($168 d) are also available. All rooms have drive-up access, and a free wintertime shuttle is offered to Teton Village.

Flat Creek Inn (307/733-5276 or 800/438-9338, www.flatcreekinn.com) is a large two-level motel just a few hundred feet north of Elk Refuge Inn. The rooms are functionally furnished, and all include microwaves and small fridges. Standard rooms cost an affordable $104 d or $123 for up to four guests, and spacious kitchenettes are $150 for up to five. Amenities include a continental breakfast, sauna, indoor hot tub, and ski-waxing room.

In the heart of Teton Village action, **Village Center Inn** (307/733-3990 or 800/443-8613, www.jhresortlodging.com) charges $130 d for studio or loft units and $185 for two-bedroom units that sleep six. All units include full kitchens. Peak-season winter rates rise to $210 d for a one-bedroom unit, up to $280 for two bedrooms. The decor is fairly utilitarian, but other than Hostel X, this is the cheapest Teton Village accommodation.

Log Cabin Motels

Several local motels offer log cabin accommo-dations for a step back to the Old West while keeping such newer amenities as televisions and private baths. Set amid tall cottonwood trees, **Wagon Wheel Village** (435 N. Cache Dr., 307/733-2357 or 800/323-9279, www.wagonwheelvillage.com) has well-maintained and cozy log cabins and log motel units. These go for $100–160 d, depending on the amenities. The most luxurious are modern log cabin–style suites ($175 for up to six people), each with a fireplace, fridge, microwave, and small deck facing Flat Creek. All guests have access to two outside hot tubs at this friendly, family-run place. Free winter shuttle to Teton Village.

Near a busy Jackson intersection, **Cowboy Village Resort** (120 Flat Creek Dr., 307/733-3121 or 800/962-4988, www.cowboyvillage.com) has 82 modern but jammed-together cabins with kitchenettes and sleeper sofas. The cabins cost $152 for up to four people in a studio unit with two queen bunk beds, or $182 for a cabin with a separate bedroom. Guests have access to two enclosed hot tubs, an office computer, and wireless Internet. During the winter a continental breakfast is available, along with a free shuttle to Teton Village.

(Elk Country Inn and Hoback River Resort also have log units.)

$150 AND UP

It should come as no surprise that tony Jackson Hole has several elaborate, pricey, and sumptuous places to stay, with rooms starting around $150 and hitting the stratosphere at $4,000 per night!

Downtown

Close to Town Square, the **Wort Hotel** (50 N. Glenwood St., 307/733-2190 or 800/322-2727, www.worthotel.com) has been a Jackson favorite since 1941 and is the only downtown hotel earning a four-diamond rating from AAA. A disastrous 1980 fire—started by a bird that built a nest too close to a neon sign—destroyed the roof and upper floor. The hotel was completely restored within a year, and today it's better than ever, with such modern amenities as a modern fitness center and two small hot tubs.

© DON PITCHER

JACKSON HOLE

Downtown's Wort Hotel, rebuilt after a disastrous fire, is better than ever.

The lobby, with its grand central staircase and stone fireplace with crackling fire, makes a fine place to meet friends. The Silver Dollar Bar and Grill serves meals, or you can sidle up to the famous curving bar—inlaid with 2,032 uncirculated silver dollars from 1921. The Wort's spacious rooms are attractively decorated with a New West motif that includes lodgepole-pine beds, creative fixtures, and barbed wire–patterned wallpaper. Rates are $275 d for standard rooms (with two queens or one king bed), or $325 d for larger and more luxurious rooms. Spacious junior suites with king beds and wet bars cost $375, while the three-bedroom luxury suite will set you back $550 d. Wireless access costs $10, or guests can use the lobby computer to surf the web.

An outstanding in-town choice is **Parkway Inn** (125 N. Jackson St., 307/733-3143 or 800/247-8390, www.parkwayinn.com). This midsize lodge has a delightful Victorian ambience with antique furniture and quilts in every room. The rooms are immaculate, and guests will also enjoy a small indoor lap pool, two hot tubs, two saunas, and a gym in the

basement. A light breakfast is served in the lobby each morning. Rates are $195 d for standard rooms with two queen beds or a king bed, $235 for larger suites, or $275 d for two-room suites; $25 each for additional guests (maximum of four in a room).

An excellent nine-room lodge just a few blocks from Town Square, **Inn on the Creek** (295 N. Millward, 307/739-1565 or 800/669-9534, www.innonthecreek.com) has a peaceful location beside Flat Creek. Standard rooms ($179–199 d) feature designer furnishings, down comforters, and VCRs. The deluxe rooms ($219–269 d) also include balconies, fireplaces, and in-room hot tubs, while a gorgeous suite ($449) sleeps four and has a full kitchen, jetted tub, and private patio. A light breakfast is delivered to your door each morning, and all guests have access to the outdoor hot tub facing the creek. Check your email on the inn's computer; Wi-Fi is an additional $25.

The acclaimed **◖ Rusty Parrot Lodge and Spa** (175 N. Jackson, 307/733-2000 or 800/458-2004, www.rustyparrot.com) offers sumptuous accommodation just two blocks from Town Square. The 31 rooms are highlighted with handcrafted furniture, original artwork, oversize tubs, and goose-down comforters; some also contain wood-burning fireplaces or jetted tubs. An unforgettable breakfast—it's never the same—is served each morning in the cozy dining room, and guests can relax in the hot tub on a deck overlooking Jackson, borrow a book from the library, or pamper themselves with a massage, aromatherapy session, or facial from Body Sage Day Spa (extra charges). Rates are $325–370 d for standard rooms, or $625 d for the luxurious master suite. No children under age 12. The lodge also serves epicurean dinners at Wild Sage Restaurant each evening. It doesn't get much better than this.

Jackson's newest—and one of its fanciest lodging places—is **Homewood Suites by Hilton** (207 N. Millward St., 307/739-0808 or 800/225-5466, www.homewoodsuites.com, $300–409). All units are two-room suites with separate living and sleeping areas, top-of-the-line beds, a fireplace, two TVs and phones, free airport shuttle, an indoor pool, fitness center, and hot tub, plus fully equipped kitchens, Wi-Fi, and a big breakfast buffet. On Monday–Thursday nights guests are served light entrées and salads.

RESORTS

At the base of Jackson's in-town ski hill, and just a few blocks from downtown, **Snow King Resort** (400 E. Snow King Ave., 307/733-5200 or 800/522-5464, www.snowking.com) includes more than 200 hotel rooms and 130 condos, plus such amenities as a year-round heated outdoor pool and two hot tubs, a sauna, an exercise facility, restaurants facing the slopes, a bar, a concierge, a business center (with Internet access), game room, spa, and Wi-Fi. Additional condos, a spa, and an upscale restaurant were to open in 2007. A free shuttle provides connections to the airport and Teton Village (winters), and guests receive discounted passes for Snow King Ski Area. The main resort building has a '70s feel, but guest rooms are comfortable and updated.

Hotel rooms at Snow King cost $230–240 d, and two-room suites are $250–430 d. Condos start at $260 d, up to an ultraluxurious three-bedroom Love Ridge condo that will set you back $720 per night.

Some of the most dramatic vistas of the Tetons are from the luxurious **Spring Creek Ranch** (307/733-8833 or 800/443-6139, www.springcreekranch.com). On a 1,000-acre estate, the resort sits high atop Gros Ventre Butte four miles west of Jackson and includes a wide range of lodging options. Hotel rooms are $310 d, and suites cost $340 for four people. Studio units and one-bedroom condos run $305–375 d; two- and three-bedroom condos are $550–1,200 and sleep 4–8. Also available are executive four-bedroom homes that sleep eight and cost a mere $2,000–2,200 per night. All rooms at Spring Creek Ranch contain fireplaces and lodgepole furnishings, and the condos and studios have full kitchens. Other amenities include a private pond, tennis courts, an outdoor pool, hot tub, fitness center, and day spa with massage and other offerings (for a fee). Breakfast at the Granary Restaurant is included for guests in the hotel and studio units.

Four miles south of Teton Village, **Teton Pines Resort and Country Club** (307/733-1005 or 800/238-2223, www.tetonpines.com) features the amenities you'd expect in a year-round resort, including an 18-hole golf course, tennis center, and classy restaurant. The accommodations are varied, but all include a continental breakfast, access to the outdoor pool and hot tub, athletic-club privileges, concierge service, and an airport shuttle. Most of the resort's condos are now privately owned, but two large (2,100-square-foot) three-bedroom town houses are offered on a nightly basis. Each includes a kitchen, dining room, two decks, fireplace, hot tub, washer and dryer, and garage. These sleep up to eight for $950 per night. Golf packages are also available.

Atop Gros Ventre Butte near Spring Creek Ranch is stunning **Amangani** (307/734-7333 or 877/734-7333, www.amangani.com), the only representative of Amanresorts in America.

(Most of the company's other lavish resorts are in Southeast Asia.) Aman groupies and business travelers know to expect the utmost in luxury, and they will certainly not be disappointed here, starting with dressed-in-black employees and spare-no-expenses construction. Guests who come here expect pampering, and the somewhat snooty staff obliges. The three-story sandstone-faced hotel contains 40 suites, each with a patined-metal fireplace, mountain-facing balcony, king-size bed, deep soaking tub (with a window view), minibar, and terrazzo dining table. Amangani's central lobby is particularly impressive, blending sandstone columns, redwood accents, custom furnishings, and soaring two-story windows. Outside, those soaking in a whirlpool and heated 35-meter pool enjoy a remarkable view of the Tetons. Among other amenities are a complete health center (exercise facility, gym, steam rooms, yoga and meditation classes, and massage), a gourmet restaurant (The Grill) specializing in steaks, chops, and seafood, and a lounge. Amangani's accommodations include suites ($700 d), six deluxe suites ($875 d), four large luxury suites with two baths and spacious balconies ($1,050 d), and the premier Sena suite ($1,300 d) for the utmost in sumptuousness. The health center and restaurant are open to the general public.

TETON VILLAGE LODGES

If you're looking for beautifully appointed accommodations in Teton Village instead of downtown Jackson, you can't go wrong at **《 Snake River Lodge and Spa** (307/733-3657 or 800/445-4655, www.snakeriverlodge.com). The lodge features a New West–style lobby with stone fireplaces and whimsically carved bears, plus rooms that continue the theme with rustic lamps, pine furniture, and colorful prints. A gorgeous free-form indoor/outdoor heated pool has a cascading waterfall, and other attractions include indoor and outdoor hot tubs, a sauna, ski lockers, a ski-in concierge service, and a five-story spa and health club with exercise equipment, facials, manicures, hydrotherapy, massages, soaking

tubs, and steam baths. Peak-season summertime rates are $289–550 d in the guest rooms or $800–1,300 d in the condominiums. Peak winter rates run $359–550 for the standard rooms, or $1,200–3,000 for the condos. Snake River Lodge is owned by Rock Resorts.

Also in Teton Village, **Alpenhof Lodge** (307/733-3242 or 800/732-3244, www.alpenhoflodge.com) exudes a European ambience, and its owners come from Switzerland and Germany. Summertime rates start at $159 d for the simplest rooms on the top floor with sloping ceilings, or $214–259 for rooms with Bavarian furnishings and space for four guests. A two-room suite is $439. Peak winter ski-season rates are $229–569 d. Guests have access to the heated year-round outdoor pool, hot tub, sauna, and computer, and Wi-Fi is available. The resident golden retriever is a favorite of dog lovers.

Another of Jackson Hole's upmarket lodging options, **Teton Mountain Lodge** (307/734-7111 or 800/801-6615, www.tetonlodge.com) sits at the base of the mountain in Teton Village. The lodge offers an array of amenities and services, including indoor and outdoor heated pools, hot tubs, a fitness center/spa, concierge service, valet parking, free Wi-Fi in the lobby, and underground parking. Guests can choose lodge rooms or studios for $300–329 d, or one-, two-, or three-bedroom suites for $500–1,200.

Another Teton Village option is **The Inn at Jackson Hole/Best Western** (307/733-2311 or 800/842-7666, www.innatjh.com), where standard rooms with log furnishings cost $199 d, while rates are $229 for units with kitchenettes and fireplaces (plus $10 per person for additional guests). Family-friendly loft suites with fireplaces and kitchenettes are $269 for up to six guests. The hotel also has an outdoor heated pool and hot tub, a sauna, ski lockers, and two upscale restaurants. Free Wi-Fi is available in the lobby.

Four Seasons Resort (307/732-5000 or 800/732-5000, www.fourseasons.com/jacksonhole) includes a 124-room luxury hotel with ski-in access, an elegant restaurant

JACKSON HOLE

(Westbank Grill), après ski bar for slope-side drinks, gorgeous outdoor heated pool, three whirlpools, full health club, spa, and concierge. They're all under one roof in Wyoming's third-largest building. Rates start at $400 d for not-so-standard, standard rooms—which come with a king bed, marble bath and soaking tub, in-room safe, minibar, private terrace or gas fireplace—all the way up to $4,000 for the presidential suite (it's bigger than many houses). Wi-Fi Internet access ($10) is available.

BED-AND-BREAKFASTS

Jackson hosts many fine B&Bs, where those who can afford it can relax in comfort at the homes of locals. Be sure to reserve space far ahead during the peak summer season, although you might get lucky at the last minute if someone cancels. The **Jackson Hole Bed and Breakfast Association's** website (www.jacksonholebnb.com) has links to a number of local B&Bs.

You'll find outdoorsy owners at **Alpine House Country Inn** (285 N. Glenwood, 307/739-1570 or 800/753-1421, www.alpinehouse.com); both Hans and Nancy Johnstone were skiers for U.S. Olympic teams and are highly knowledgeable about adventure options in the Tetons. The modern timber-frame lodge is just two blocks from Jackson's Town Square and has 22 guest rooms in two connected buildings. Both are bright and modern, accented by Swedish-style stenciling on the walls. All rooms have private baths and balconies, plus access to the outdoor hot tub and a central computer. A healthy full breakfast is served. Rates are $165 d in the original rooms, and $185–225 d in the new building, which also features TVs and air-conditioning, along with gas fireplaces and hot tubs in most rooms. Suites cost $270 for up to four guests. Children are $25 extra. Closed in November.

On the road to Teton Village, **The Painted Porch** (3755 N. Moose–Wilson Rd., 307/733-1981, www.jacksonholebedandbreakfast.com) was built in 1901 in Idaho and moved here many years later. Situated on three acres and surrounded by a white picket fence and tall aspen trees, this rambling red farmhouse has two guest rooms ($175–200 d) and a two-room suite ($300 d). Each has a microwave, fridge, TV/VCR, and private bath with jetted tub. For more privacy, stay in the adjacent cottage ($240 d), which has a living room, kitchen, bedroom, and bath. Children are welcome in the suite and cabin, and a big breakfast is served in the main house. Other amenities include an outdoor hot tub and game room with pool table. A two-night minimum stay is required; closed November– late December and April–mid-June.

Near the Aspens along the road to Teton Village, **The Sassy Moose Inn** (307/733-1277 or 800/356-1277, www.sassymoose.com) is a modest log house with five guest rooms, each with private bath, TV, and VCR. A full breakfast is served each morning, along with wine and fruit in the evening. An indoor hot tub and wireless Internet are also available. Rates are $159–189 d; the larger have two beds and are fine for families. Pets are welcome (a rarity for B&Bs).

A personal favorite—it gets high marks from all who visit—is **Teton Treehouse B&B** (307/733-3233, www.cruising-america.com/tetontreehouse), a gorgeous four-story hillside home in Wilson. This spacious open-beam B&B sits up 95 steps—needless to say, it's not accessible for people with disabilities—and contains six guest rooms with private baths. It really does offer the feeling of living in a treehouse, and it's a great place for bird-watchers. Decks provide impressive views across the valley below, and you can soak in the outdoor hot tub each evening and enjoy a healthy full breakfast each morning. Rooms cost $175–210 d. No young children, but ages 10 and older are welcome. There's a three-night minimum stay in July and August.

On the way to Teton Village, **Teton View B&B** (2136 Coyote Loop, 307/733-7954 or 866/504-7954, www.tetonview.com) features a guest room ($159 d) and suite ($195 d), both with private baths. Guests enjoy a big breakfast and a dramatic view of the Tetons from both the indoor whirlpool tub and outdoor hot tub. The owners also offer a perfect-for-familes cabin with a kitchen, wood-burning stove, and private; $245 d plus $20 per person for additional guests. The cabin is available only in the summer.

At the base of the mountains in Wilson, **Trail Creek Ranch** (307/733-2610, www .jacksonholetrailcreekranch.com) operated as a dude ranch for 50 years and recently reopened as a B&B. Guests stay in five rooms and three cabins (all with private baths) scattered around the 280-acre ranch. Summertime rates are $175–275 in the rooms, or $325–375 in the cabins, two of which are large enough for families. A filling ranch breakfast is served in the main lodge, and guests enjoy the heated outdoor pool and use of a computer for Internet access. Horseback rides are available by the hour. Trail Creek is open June–September with a three-night minimum, making this a good alternative to traditional dude ranches where one-week stays are required. It reopens February–mid-March for winter guests; $175 per person/night, including three meals a day.

The rambling **Wildflower Inn** (307/733-4710, www.jacksonholewildflower.com) sits on three acres of country land along Teton Village Road, with five bright guest rooms. Four rooms have private decks, and all contain private baths and handcrafted lodgepole beds. One of the rooms is actually a suite with a separate sitting room, hot tub, and gas fireplace. Wildflower's hot tub occupies a plant-filled solarium. The owner/builders are an Exum climbing guide and a former ski instructor. Rates are $250–300 s or $280–310 d ($360 d in the suite) and include an earthy breakfast served family-style. Children are welcome and Wi-Fi Internet is available.

One of the most impressive local lodging options is **⬛ Bentwood B&B** (307/739-1411, www.bentwoodinn.com), just north of the junction on the road to Teton Village. This massive 6,000-square-foot log home sits amid tall cottonwood trees and is a favorite place for weddings and receptions. The grand living room is centered on a three-story stone fireplace, and each of the five el-egant guest rooms has a fireplace, TV, deck or balcony, and jetted tub. The loft room is perfect for families. The interior is filled with Western styling and English antiques, not to mention gracious hosts. Drinks and hors d'oeuvres are served each evening, and morning brings a creative breakfast. Rates are $255–295 d, or $325 for up to four in the family room. Both children and pets (even horses) are welcome in this very special place. A three-night minimum stay is generally required in the summer.

CONDOMINIUM RENTALS

Condominiums provide a popular option for families and groups visiting Jackson Hole. These privately owned places are maintained by several local property-management companies and vary from small studio apartments to spacious five-bedroom houses. All are completely furnished (including dishes) and have fireplaces, cable TV, phones, and midstay maid service. The nicest also include access to pools and hot tubs and have balconies overlooking the spectacular Tetons. Many of the condominiums are in Teton Village (adjacent to the ski area) or just to the south in Teton Pines or the Aspens; others are scattered around Jackson Hole.

Condo prices vary widely depending upon location and amenities, but during the winter holiday season (Christmas–early January), expect to pay $170–310 per night for studio or one-bedroom condos (1–2 people). Two-bedroom Teton Village units (up to four people) cost $325–465 per night, and full four-bedroom/four-bath condos (these sleep eight) are $835–870. The most sumptuous places will set you back $1,400 per night in the peak winter season! Summer and off-peak winter rates are typically 35–50 percent lower, with spring and fall rates 50–75 percent less than peak-season prices. In fall or spring, condos offer a real bargain for traveling families looking to stay several nights in the area. Minimum stays of 2–7 nights are required throughout the year, with the longest minimum stays required in the peak winter season. Midstay maid service is generally offered if you remain more than five nights.

If you have the luxury of time, do a little comparison shopping before renting a condo. Things to ask include whether you have access to a pool and hot tub, how close you are to the ski slopes, how frequent the maid service is, and whether the units include such amenities as VCRs and washing machines. Also be sure to find out what beds are in the rooms because couples might not enjoy sleeping in twin bunk beds.

Condo Companies

For condo rental information, including prices and available dates, you can go to www.jacksonholenet.com and click on lodging for connections to most of the larger condo companies. The largest of these companies—and a good place to begin your search—is **Jackson Hole Resort Lodging** (307/733-3990 or 800/443-8613, www.jhrl.com). Owned by Jackson Hole Mountain Resort, it manages about 250 places. Other large management companies include Black Diamond Vacation Rentals, Jackson Hole Lodge, Rendezvous Mountain Rentals, and Snow King Resort Condominiums.

GUEST RANCHES

Several of Wyoming's best-known and most luxurious dude ranches are in Jackson Hole, providing wonderful places for families who are looking to rough it in style. In addition to the local places listed alphabetically, many more guest ranches are just over Togwotee Pass in the Dubois area and to the south in the Pinedale area (see the *Wind River Mountains Country* chapter for details on these ranches).

At the base of Sheep Mountain, **Flat Creek Ranch** (307/733-0603 or 866/522-3344, www.flatcreekranch.com) is packed with history. The land was originally homesteaded by cowboy, hunting guide, and rustler Cal Carrington, but he sold it to his close friend, "Countess" Cissy Patterson, in 1923. Previously married to a Polish count, Cissy came from a wealthy Chicago newspaper family, but her love of the West and horses matched Cal's. For two decades Cissy and Cal were grist for the gossip mill, mostly during her trips to Wyoming, but also when she took him along on a grand tour of Europe. Cissy died in 1948, and her relatives now own the ranch. After a long hiatus and extensive improvements in 2001, this historic ranch in a gorgeous setting is once again open for guests, with five renovated cabins and three gourmet meals daily. The emphasis is on fly-fishing in legendary Flat Creek; the ranch owns 1.5 miles along the stream. Other activities include horseback rides and hikes into the Gros Ventre Wilderness, boating, and a wood-fired sauna for chilly evenings. There's a three-night minimum stay in the summer; $550 for two people per night, all-inclusive. The ranch is 15 miles up a bumpy dirt road, but the ranch provides transportation (Mondays and Fridays only) if you don't have a four-wheel-drive with high clearance. Open late May–late September.

Looking for a peaceful place to really relax? Twenty miles up a dirt road in undeveloped Gros Ventre Valley (30 miles northeast of Jackson), **Goosewing Ranch** (307/733-5251 or 888/733-5251, www.goosewingranch.com) is one of the most remote guest ranches in Jackson Hole. The well-appointed modern log cabins have fireplaces, private baths, and decks. Guests can use the outdoor hot tub all year and the outdoor heated pool in the summer. Popular summertime activities include horseback excursions, fly-fishing, mountain-biking, and hiking. All-inclusive weekly summertime rates are $2,000 for two people. There's a three-night minimum stay, and the ranch accommodates a maximum of 30 guests. When winter arrives, the ranch becomes a favorite destination for snowmobiling, with a variety of packages available.

Gros Ventre River Ranch (307/733-4138, www.grosventreriverranch.com) is a small ranch with accommodations for up to 34 guests in modern log cabins and a homestead house and is known for its delicious meals. The ranch sits up undiscovered Gros Ventre River Valley, 18 miles northeast of Jackson near Slide Lake. The main activities are horseback riding, world-class fly-fishing, cookouts, canoeing, and mountain-biking. The lodge has a pool table, table tennis, and large-screen television.

Weekly all-inclusive rates are $3,000–5,700 for two people. The ranch is open May–October.

A classic family summer destination, **Heart Six Ranch** (307/543-2477 or 888/543-2477, www.heartsix.com) is in the heart of Buffalo Valley, 12 miles east of Moran Junction and 43 miles northeast of Jackson. Horseback rides are a star attraction, along with kids' programs, day trips to Yellowstone National Park and the Jackson Hole rodeo, and a range of evening activities including cookouts, nature programs, and country music. All-inclusive weekly rates are $3,100–3,300 for two people. The ranch takes in up to 50 guests at a time and is open year-round. Only weekly stays are available June–August, but at other times of the year the ranch offers nightly lodging ($75–200 d). This is a favorite base for snowmobilers mid-December–March.

Wyoming's most elaborate—and expensive—guest ranch, **Lost Creek Ranch** (307/733-3435, www.lostcreek.com), is 21 miles north of Jackson. This showplace resort emphasizes fitness, with a spa facility that includes exercise classes, a weight room, steam room, sauna, and hot tub, along with massage and facials (extra charge). Guests stay in modern duplex log cabins and enjoy gourmet meals in the main lodge's patio overlooking the Tetons. Amenities include such nontraditional items as a heated swimming pool, tennis courts, and a skeet range, in addition to more standard horseback riding, kids' programs, float trips, hiking, Yellowstone tours, and fly-fishing. It's all a bit too Disneyesque for my tastes, and the prices are too Madison Avenue. Weekly all-inclusive rates run $5,850 for two people in a duplex cabin or an astounding $13,700 for up to four people in a luxurious two-bedroom, two-bath cabin with a living room and fireplace. Some consider this a small price to pay for such pampering. The ranch hosts a maximum of 60 guests at a time and is open late May–September, with a one-week minimum stay.

Another historic dude ranch is **R Lazy S Ranch** (13 miles northeast of Jackson, 307/733-2655, www.rlazys.com), with space for 45 guests, who enjoy horseback rides, fishing, and other Western adventures. A one-week minimum stay is required. All-inclusive rates are $2,575–3,480 for two people per week, and the ranch is open mid-June–September. Tykes under age seven are not allowed.

Located along the rolling Gros Ventre River, **Red Rock Ranch** (307/733-6288, www.theredrockranch.com) faces spectacular orange-red badlands. The ranch is 32 miles northeast of Jackson, and the quiet location and drop-dead-gorgeous scenery are reason enough to stay here. Guests settle into comfortable log cabins with woodstoves, and they can take part in horseback riding, cookouts, and other activities. The ranch also features kids' programs, stocked fishing ponds, a large swimming pool, and hot tub. There's space for a maximum of 30 guests, and a six-night minimum stay is required. Open June to mid-September. All-inclusive weekly rates are $3,450 for two adults.

On the banks of the Hoback River, 16 miles south of Jackson, **Spotted Horse Ranch** (307/733-2097 or 800/528-2084, www.spottedhorseranch.com) exudes a comfortable rusticity. The main lodge and cabins contain lodgepole furniture, and a maximum of 35 guests stay in log cabins with modern conveniences. Activities include horseback riding (some Appaloosas), fly-fishing, cookouts, and river trips, and you can unwind in the hot tub or sauna. A one-week minimum stay is required; $4,400 d per week, all-inclusive. Open mid-May–October.

Within Grand Teton National Park, 25 miles north of Jackson, **◖ Triangle X Ranch** (307/733-2183 or 888/860-0005, www.trianglex.com) is a classic family-oriented ranch with unmatched Teton views. The ranch has been in the Turner family for more than 75 years, and the acclaimed author Barry Lopez once worked as a wrangler here. Horseback riding is the main focus, but it also offers kids' programs and nightly events such as Dutch-oven cookouts, naturalist presentations, square dancing, and campfire sing-alongs. All-inclusive weekly rates are $3,000 for two

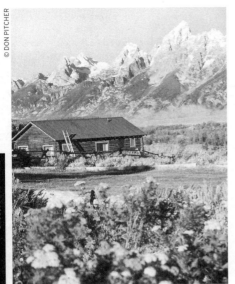

© DON PITCHER

Triangle X Ranch

adults. The ranch is open May–October and January–March. In winter Triangle X goes upscale, with fewer guests (maximum of 35 versus 80 in the summer), a hot tub, and three gourmet meals a day. The nightly winter rate is $210 d, including lodging, meals, and use of cross-country skis and snowshoes. There's a two-night minimum stay in winter and a one-week minimum stay in summer (four nights in spring and fall).

A longtime favorite—it began taking guests in the 1920s—is **Turpin Meadow Ranch** (307/543-2496 or 800/743-2496, www.turpinmeadowranch.com). The ranch's Buffalo Valley location provides impressive Teton vistas, along with all of the traditional ranch activities: horseback riding, cookouts, fly-fishing, day trips to Yellowstone, and pack trips, plus weekly nature programs by Forest Service naturalists. Guests stay in modern cabins and have access to an indoor hot tub. Summertime all-inclusive rates are approximately $550 per day for two adults, with a three-night minimum stay. The ranch is open year-round and is a favorite snowmobile spot in winter.

MOUNTAIN RESORTS

East of Moran Junction at Togwotee Pass (9,658 feet), U.S. 26/287 tops the Continental Divide and then slides eastward toward Dubois and the Wind River Valley. The Togwotee Pass area is famous for luxuriously deep snow all winter and is a destination for snowmobilers, cross-country skiers, and dogsledding enthusiasts. Just north of the pass is Teton Wilderness, a place to discover what solitude means. As you face west from the pass, the Teton Range offers a jagged horizon line. This entire area provides a delicious escape from hectic Jackson and is home to two noteworthy, attractive high-elevation resorts: Togwotee Mountain Lodge and Brooks Lake Lodge.

Forty-eight miles northeast of Jackson and just a few miles west of Togwotee Pass is **Togwotee Mountain Lodge** (307/543-2847 or 800/543-2847, www.togwoteelodge.com), a pleasantly rustic place to spend a night or a week. The resort offers horseback rides, and the staff can set up mountain-bike trips, whitewater rafting, fly-fishing, backcountry pack trips, and other summertime adventures, along with wintertime snowmobiling (the primary winter activity), dogsledding, and cross-country skiing when the snow flies. Togwotee has a variety of accommodations, and guests will enjoy the sauna and two large hot tubs. Summer rates are $129–139 d for rooms in the lodge, $149–159 d for minisuites, and $189–199 d for one-bedroom cabins. The minisuites and cabins sleep up to six people ($10 per person for more than two). In winter, the resort specializes in package deals that include lodging, breakfast and dinner, snowmobile guide, and free airport shuttle. The resort also houses a steak house, bar, gas station, gift shop, and convenience store. Togwotee is closed early April–mid-May, and mid-October–November.

Brooks Lake Lodge (307/455-2121, www.brookslake.com) may have the finest location of any Wyoming resort, with a placid lake in front and the cliffs of Pinnacle Buttes nearby. Built in 1922, it has long served travelers en route to Yellowstone, and its enormous great hall contains big-game trophies from all over the world. The lodge was completely restored in the late 1980s and is now on the National Register of Historic Places. Seven guest rooms are available in the main lodge, and eight attractive cabins are hidden in the trees; all are tastefully furnished with handmade lodgepole furniture.

The turnoff for Brooks Lake Lodge is 65 miles northeast of Jackson (34 miles east of Moran Junction) and another five miles off the highway via Brooks Lake Road. The lodge is open mid-June–mid-September and late December–mid-March. There's a three-night minimum stay (though shorter visits may be possible), and rates are $660 d per day in the lodge, $726 d per day in the cabins (large enough for families). These rates include gourmet meals, horseback riding, hiking, guided hiking, canoeing, and fly-fishing in summer. A casting pond is available for working on your technique. The spa features a small workout room, sauna, and outdoor hot tub; massages are extra. Winter rates are $560–626 per day for two people, including meals, cross-country skis, ice-fishing, and snowshoes in winter. Snowmobile rentals and dogsled tours are available. Brooks Lake Lodge is open to the public for winter lunches, making this a popular stop for snowmobilers.

PUBLIC CAMPGROUNDS

Both the National Park Service and the U.S. Forest Service maintain campgrounds around Jackson Hole. The Jackson Hole Public Campgrounds chart shows two dozen public campgrounds within 50 miles of Jackson. For more specifics on public sites, contact Bridger–Teton National Forest in Jackson (340 N. Cache Dr., 307/739-5500, www.fs.fed.us/r4/btnf) or Grand Teton National Park (307/739-3603, www.nps.gov/grte) in Moose. In addition to these sites, many people camp for free on dispersed sites on Forest Service lands; contact the Forest Service for locations and restrictions.

RV PARKS

Jackson has several RV parks scattered around town and in surrounding areas, but the rates are shockingly high in midsummer. Additional privately run campgrounds are at Colter Bay and Flagg Ranch Resort inside Grand Teton National Park.

None of the private RV parks in the town of Jackson is really noteworthy; "parking lots" would be a better term. They can also be surprisingly expensive: Some places charge more for a tent space than it would cost to stay in a motel room in many Wyoming towns! Even more expensive is a ticket for parking RVs overnight on Jackson city streets. It's illegal to do so, and local police strictly enforce the ordinance.

Virginian RV Park (750 W. Broadway, 307/733-7189 or 800/321-6982 in summer or 800/262-4999 in winter, www.virginian-lodge.com) is the biggest RV parking lot in the area, with more than 100 sites (including many pull-through sites) on the south end of town. Full hookups cost $45–50; no tents. Guests at the RV park can use the Virginian Lodge's outdoor pool and hot tub. The park is open May–mid-October.

Wagon Wheel RV Park and Campground (525 N. Cache, 307/733-4588 or 800/323-9279, www.wagonwheelvillage.com) is along Flat Creek on the north end of town. Behind the motel of the same name, it has both RV hookups ($50 d) and grassy tent spaces ($25 d) and is open May–mid-October.

Teton Village KOA (307/733-5354 or 800/562-9043, www.jacksonholecamping.com) is five miles south of Teton Village and six miles from Jackson. It is out of the way and quiet, with trees providing shade (lacking in other local RV parks). Full RV hookups cost $47 d, tent sites are $35 d, and basic "kamping kabins" run $58–65 d. It's open May–September. Also here are a game room and playground, and the KOA is right across the road from the golf course at Teton Pines.

Grand Teton Park RV Resort (307/733-1980 or 800/563-6469, www.yellowstonerv.com) is 37 miles northeast of Jackson (six miles east of Moran Junction) along Hwy. 26/287. There are fine views of the Tetons, and facilities include a heated seasonal pool and hot tub, recreation room, and grocery

JACKSON HOLE PUBLIC CAMPGROUNDS

The following public campgrounds are available on a first-come, first-served basis with no reservations. Most are open through September. They are listed by distance and direction from Jackson. Get details for each from Bridger-Teton National Forest (BTNF; 307/739-5400, www.fs.fed.us/r4/btnf/teton), Grand Teton National Park (GTNP; 307/739-3603, www.nps.gov/grte), or Caribou-Targhee National Forest (CTNF; 208/354-2312, www.fs.fed.us/r4/caribou). See the text for private RV campgrounds in the area.

CAMPGROUNDS NORTH OF JACKSON

Curtis Canyon Campground: seven miles northeast of Jackson; open mid-May–mid-September; $12; BTNF; six miles of gravel road with a fine view of the Tetons.

Gros Ventre Campground: 10 miles northeast of Jackson; open May–mid-October; $15; GTNP; along Gros Ventre River; dump station; campground often fills by evening in midsummer.

Atherton Creek Campground: 18 miles northeast of Jackson; open mid-May–September; $12; BTNF; seven miles northeast of Kelly up Gros Ventre Road along Slide Lake.

Jenny Lake Campground: 20 miles north of Jackson; open mid-May–late September; $15;

GTNP; tents only (no RVs); campground fills by 8 A.M. in midsummer.

Red Hills Campground: 22 miles northeast of Jackson; open mid-May–mid-September; $10; BTNF; 12 miles up Gros Ventre Road (partly dirt) along Gros Ventre River.

Crystal Creek Campground: 23 miles northeast of Jackson; open mid-May–September; $10; BTNF; five miles up Gros Ventre Road (gravel) along Gros Ventre River.

Signal Mountain Campground: 32 miles north of Jackson; open early May–mid-October; $15; GTNP; on Jackson Lake; dump station; no vehicles over 30 feet; campground fills by 10 A.M. in midsummer.

Colter Bay Campground: 40 miles north of Jackson; open late May–late September; $15; GTNP; on Jackson Lake; coin-operated showers and laundry nearby, dump station; campground fills by noon in midsummer.

Hatchet Campground: 40 miles northeast of Jackson; open mid-May–September; $10; BTNF; in Buffalo Valley eight miles east of Moran Junction.

Box Creek Campground: 46 miles northeast of Jackson; open mid-May–September; $10; BTNF; on Buffalo Valley Road, no potable water.

Pacific Creek Campground: 46 miles north of Jackson; open mid-May–September; $5;

---

store. The cost is $48 d for RVs with hookups, $35 d for tents. Simple camping cabins go for $60 d. Open year-round.

Two private campgrounds are in the Hoback Junction area, 12 miles south of Jackson. **Lazy J Corral** (307/733-1554) is right on the highway at Hoback Junction, but the rates are low: RV sites with full hookups are just $23.

It does not have tent spaces and is open May–October. **Hoback Junction KOA** (307/733-7078 or 800/562-1878, www.koa.com), 12 miles south of Jackson at Hoback Junction, has RV spaces for $49 d, tent sites for $33 d, and simple "kamping kabins" for $60–70 d. Open mid-April–September. The KOA has a riverside location and a game room.

BTNF; nine miles up Pacific Creek Road (enter through Grand Teton National Park).

Lizard Creek Campground: 48 miles north of Jackson; open early June–early September; $15; GTNP; on Jackson Lake; no vehicles over 30 feet; campground fills by 2 P.M. in midsummer.

Turpin Campground: 48 miles northeast of Jackson; mid-May–September; $10; BTNF; in Buffalo Valley 10 miles east of Moran Junction.

Angles Campground: 49 miles north of Jackson; open mid-May–September; $10; BTNF; small site 0.5 mile northeast of Cowboy Village Resort on U.S. 287.

Sheffield Creek Campground: 55 miles north of Jackson; open mid-May–September; $5; BTNF; small campground off U.S. 89/191/287 near Flagg Ranch Resort; poor road access until late summer.

CAMPGROUNDS SOUTH OF JACKSON

Hoback Campground: 22 miles southeast of Jackson; open mid-May–September; $15; BTNF; along Hoback River eight miles east of Hoback Junction.

East Table Creek Campground: 24 miles south of Jackson; open mid-May–September; $15; BTNF; along Snake River 11 miles southwest of Hoback Junction.

Station Creek Campground: 24 miles southeast of Jackson; open mid-May–September; $15; BTNF; along Snake River 11 miles southwest of Hoback Junction. Reservations ($9 fee) at 518/885-3639 or 877/444-6777, www.reserveusa.com.

Wolf Creek Campground: 26 miles southwest of Jackson; open mid-May–September; $10; BTNF; along Snake River Canyon six miles from Hoback Junction.

Kozy Campground: 19 miles southeast of Jackson; open mid-May–September; $12; BTNF; along Hoback River seven miles southeast of Hoback Junction.

Granite Campground: 35 miles southeast of Jackson; open mid-May–September; $15; BTNF; near Granite Hot Springs, nine miles up Granite Creek Road (gravel).

CAMPGROUNDS WEST OF JACKSON

Trail Creek Campground: 20 miles west of Jackson; open mid-May–mid-September; $10; CTNF; on the west side of Teton Pass. Reservations ($9 fee) at 518/885-3639 or 877/444-6777, www.reserveusa.com.

Mike Harris Campground: 21 miles west of Jackson; open mid-May–mid-September; $10; CTNF; on the west side of Teton Pass.

JACKSON HOLE

Food

Jackson stands out from the rest of Wyoming on the culinary scene: Chicken-fried steak may be available, but it certainly isn't the house specialty! You won't need to look far to find good food; in fact, the town seems to overflow with memorable (and even more memorably priced) eateries. If you stood in Town Square and walked in any direction for a block you would find at least one restaurant that would be a standout in any other Wyoming town. More than 70 local restaurants do business here—in a town that contains just 9,000 people.

To get an idea of what to expect at local res-taurants, pick up a copy of the free *Jackson Hole Dining Guide* (www.jacksonholenet.com) at the visitor center or local restaurants. The guide includes sample menus and brief descriptions of many local establishments. If you don't find a place to your liking among those listed below or in the dining guide, be assured that all of the major fast-food outlets line Jackson's streets, ready to grease your digestive tract.

BREAKFAST

The best breakfast place in Jackson isn't in Jackson, but in Wilson, where **◖ Nora's**

Fish Creek Inn (307/733-8288, www.jacksonholenet.com/noras) attracts a full house each morning. The food (including *huevos rancheros,* biscuits and gravy, and omelets) is great, the setting is authentically rustic, and the waitresses are friendly and fast. Nora's also serves tried-and-true lunches and dinners at very good prices, from $4.50 patty melts to nut-crusted trout for $16. Unfortunately, you'll have to contend with a smoky atmosphere at the counter in the morning (smoke-free for dinner).

Very popular for breakfast and lunch is **Jedediah's House of Sourdough** (135 E. Broadway, 307/733-5671), where, as the name implies, sourdough pancakes are the morning specialty. Housed in a 1910 log cabin, the restaurant gets noisy and crowded in the morning, making it perfect for families with young kids. The lunch menu stars burgers, sandwiches, and salads, while the summer-only dinners include steaks, chicken, trout, and burgers. A half dozen tables are on the deck, shaded by tall cottonwoods.

Another longtime breakfast and lunch standout is **The Bunnery** (130 N. Cache Dr., 307/733-5474 or 800/349-0492, www.bunnery.com), with good omelets and delicious sandwiches on freshly baked breads, along with fresh salads and homemade soups.

LUNCH

One of the most popular noontime spots in Jackson—it's been here more than 30 years—is **Sweetwater Restaurant** (85 King St., 307/733-3553). The cozy log cabin has several tables on the front deck and a lunch menu ($9–12) of dependably good salads, homemade soups, and a variety of earthy sandwiches. For dinner, try buffalo pot roast, pistachio salmon, or mustard-marinated pork tenderloin. Dinner entrées are $16–25.

Get delicious sub sandwiches on tangy homemade bread at **New York City Sub Shop** (20 N. Jackson St., 307/733-4414). It's a little pricey ($6 for a half hoagie or more than $10 for a whole), but the service is fast, and the hot sandwiches are always vastly better than Sub-

way. You'll recognize the owner by his famous handlebar mustache.

Pearl Street Bagels (145 Pearl St., 307/739-1218) serves home-baked bagels (they're on the small side, however) along with good espresso and juices. Open daily until 6 P.M. in summer. It has a second shop in Wilson (307/739-1261)—it's *the* groovy place to be seen in Wilson (OK, so are Nora's and the 'Coach).

If you're in search of a substantial vegetarian breakfast or lunch, try the café at **Harvest Natural Foods** (130 W. Broadway, 307/733-5418). The salad-and-soup bar in the back is a favorite lunch break for Jacksonians. Great sandwiches, fruit smoothies, and baked goods are offered, too. You won't go wrong here.

ESPRESSO AND LIGHT MEALS

The hip crowd heads for breakfast and lunch to two excellent local cafés: Betty Rock and Shades. **Betty Rock Cafe and Coffeehouse** (325 W. Pearl, 307/733-0747) is a great and noisy place for breakfast or lunch, with blueberry pancakes, omelets, delectable homemade breads, chicken pot pies, turkey havarti paninis, veg-head wraps, salads, soups, and espresso.

You'll find similar food and service at **Shades Cafe** (82 S. King St., 307/733-2015). This tiny log cabin has a shady summer-only patio on the side. Breakfasts feature waffles, egg dishes, fruit, and yogurt, plus lattes, mochas, and other coffee drinks. At lunch, the standouts are salads, quiches, burritos, and paninis. Shades is a relaxing place to hang out with the latte habitués, although it does close early in the fall, winter, and spring.

Out in Teton Village, **Village Cafe** (307/733-2233) serves very good breakfasts, baked goods, sandwiches, wraps, pizza by the slice, espresso, and microbrewed beer. Open summers and winters only.

Better known as DOG, **Down on Glen** (307/733-4422) is a miniscule eatery next to Mountain High Pizza at Glenwood and Broadway serving to-go breakfast burritos, buffalo burgers, Philly cheesesteaks, and other homemade fare. Most of the ingredients are organic, and the bread comes from Wild Flour Bakery. Everything is freshly made, so be ready to wait.

AMERICAN

Jackson's most popular family eatery is ◖ **Bubba's Bar-B-Que Restaurant** (515 W. Broadway, 307/733-2288). Each evening the parking lot out front is jammed with folks waiting patiently for a chance to gnaw on barbecued spare ribs, savor the spicy chicken wings, or get the turkey plate; $10–15 entrées. The big salad bar is just $6.50, but get here before 6:30 for shorter lines. Lunch is a real bargain, with specials for less than $7. Drinks come in recycled Mason jars, but it doesn't serve alcohol, so BYOB (no corkage fee). Cheap breakfasts, too.

Get great all-American burgers at the '50s-style **Billy's Burgers** (55 N. Cache Dr., 307/733-3279, www.cadillac-grille.com), adjacent to the more upscale Cadillac Grille. The Billy burger ($5) is a half-pound monster. Not on the menu, but recommended if you aren't absolutely famished, is the one-third-pound Betty burger. Ask for it.

Next door to Billy's and in the basement of the bar of the same name, the **Million Dollar Cowboy Steakhouse** (307/733-4790, www.cowboysteakhouse.net) specializes in "casual Western elegance" and great steaks, from porterhouse to filet mignon. In addition, the menu includes salads, rack of lamb, seafood, pasta, ribs, and even vegetarian specials. The bar offers a dozen different single-malt scotches, plus seasonal drink specials. Not for kids or smokers, and not cheap: entrées are $23–43. Reservations advised.

Also recommended is **Gun Barrel Steakhouse** (862 W. Broadway, 307/733-3287, www.gunbarrel.com), where the meaty mesquite-grilled steaks, elk, and buffalo are served in a great hunting-lodge atmosphere with trophy game mounts; they came from a wildlife museum that previously occupied the site. You'll find lots of historic guns and other Old West paraphernalia around the Gun Barrel too, making this an interesting place to explore

even if you aren't hungry. It's a bit on the pricey side, with dinner entrées for $22–34. The bar has a wide choice of beers on tap.

A very popular place with both locals and ski bums is the **Mangy Moose** (in Teton Village, 307/733-4913, www.mangymoose.net), where you'll find a big salad bar and fair prices on steak, prime rib, pasta, chicken, and fresh fish (dinner entrées $16–33). It's a fun and lively place. Downstairs is The Rocky Mountain Oyster (don't ask), offering killer breakfasts and inexpensive burgers, pizza, and sandwiches for lunch.

The menu and setting at **Teton Steakhouse** (40 W. Pearl St., 307/733-2639, www.teton-steakhouse.com) reflect this restaurant's previous incarnation as a Sizzler, but that doesn't faze anyone. The central location (one block off Town Square), stuff-yourself meals, and noisy, kid-friendly setting bring a crowd every day. Line up to put in your order for steaks, ribs, or chicken, or just sidle up to the big salad, soup, and dessert bar to fill your plate. Steaks are $13–27, and there also is a cheap breakfast buffet. No booze is sold here, but bring your own beer or wine and you'll be provided the glasses (no corkage fee). This is where the motorcoach tours unload, so you won't have it to yourself. Free Wi-Fi too.

Housed in an old Denny's building at 380 South U.S. 89, **Rendezvous Bistro** (307/739-1100) has a strong local following for all-better-than-mom's meat loaf, citrus glazed halibut, eggplant cannelloni, duck confit, and a rather pricy oyster bar. Entrées are $13–20.

(See *Chuck Wagon Cookouts* under *Entertainment and Events* for outfits that combine cowboy cookery with Old West entertainment.)

PASTA AND PIZZA

One of the tried-and-true local eateries is **Anthony's Italian Restaurant** (62 S. Glenwood St., 307/733-3717). In business since 1977, Anthony's has built a reputation for simple food (a bit heavy for some tastes) and attentive, efficient service. Vegetarians will find several good menu items. Meals come with homemade soup, salad, and fresh-baked garlic bread—guaranteed to fill you up and then some. Open for dinner only, with $13–20 entrées.

Hidden away on the north end of town next to the Anvil Motel, **((Nani's Genuine Pasta House** (242 N. Glenwood, 307/733-3888, www.nanis.com) is Jackson's gourmet Italian restaurant—but without the pretense. Meals are served in a charming little home with an old-country ambience, big portions, and friendly service. Prices are surprisingly reasonable, with most entrées for $13–33. The menu features specialties from a different region of Italy each month, so it is constantly changing. Vegetarian and vegan dishes are available, along with a choice of Italian wines and beers. Nani's is open for dinner year-round; reservations recommended.

Several pizza places stand out in Jackson. You'll find **Calico Italian Restaurant and Bar** (307/733-2460, www.calicorestaurant.com) in a garish red-and-white building 0.75 mile north on Teton Village Road. The menu has gone a bit upscale, but prices are still manageable: $11–19 entrées. The bar at Calico is a very popular locals' watering hole, and kids love the 2.5-acre lawn/playground.

Mountain High Pizza Pie (120 W. Broadway, 307/733-3646) is a favorite downtown place offering all the usual toppings (and some not so, including the Thai pie), plus calzones, subs, salads, and free delivery in Jackson and Teton Village. Large pizzas start around $13.

For other notable pizza places, see Old Yellowstone Garage and Grand Teton Brewing Company.

CONTINENTAL/ NOUVELLE CUISINE

If you want fine continental dining and aren't deterred by entrées costing $20 or more, Jackson has much to offer.

Just off Town Square, **Snake River Grill** (upstairs at 84 E. Broadway, 307/733-0557, www.snakerivergrill.com) is one of Jackson's finest gourmet restaurants—with prices to match ($18–43 entrées). The meals are exquisite, and the seasonal menu typically contains a variety of seafood, free-range beef, and organic vegetables that are artfully presented. The wine list is equally impressive, and a few outside tables face the square. Reservations are a must; reserve one week in advance for prime-time seatings in the summer. Try the warm chocolate tart for dessert. Snake River Grill is a good place to watch for Jackson's best-known resident, Harrison Ford. Closed November and April.

For views so spectacular they make it difficult to concentrate on your meal, don't miss **The Granary Restaurant** (307/733-8833 or 800/443-6139, www.springcreekranch.com), atop East Gros Ventre Butte west of Jackson with tall windows opening to the Tetons. This is also a very popular place for evening cocktails romantic dining. Dinner entrées run $26–35 and include rack of lamb, fresh seafood, and a very popular elk tenderloin. The separate lounge menu serves lighter fare, including a $5 burger during the Sunday happy hour.

Jackson's most popular nouvelle cuisine restaurant is **((Cadillac Grille** (55 N. Cache on the square, 307/733-3279, www.cadillacgrille.com). The food is artfully prepared and includes a changing menu of seafood, grilled meats, and wild game. The art deco decor of the Cadillac helps make it one of the most crowded tourist hangouts in town, but it also attracts a devoted following of locals, especially during the nightly happy hour when two-for-one drinks are the draw. The restaurant includes a bar and rear patio for summertime dining under the stars. Dinner entrées run $18–36.

Old Yellowstone Garage (115 Center St., 307/734-6161, www.oyg.com) serves exceptional Italian meals—particularly the grilled lamb shank—that can be matched with its select Italian wines. The restaurant was formerly in an old garage in Dubois, hence the name. It has outside dining in the summer and a changing cast of entrées for $18–42. Yellowstone Garage is famous for its all-you-can-eat Sunday pizza fest ($16). Servers come around as each pie emerges from the oven, offering slices to diners. Don't come here expecting to eat and run because the pizzas are served at a leisurely pace. The owners say this is in keeping with the Italian ambience, but it also means you'll probably be ordering drinks and salads while you wait. The restaurant is open for dinners only and closed Mondays. It's also closed November, April, and May, when the owners are in Italy in search of new wines.

At the base of Snow King Mountain, **43 North** (645 S. Cache, 307/733-0043) has quickly established itself with locals who appreciate the away-from-the-Square setting, great food, a lively pub atmosphere, live music most nights, and a big rooftop deck and front patio for summertime dining. The restaurant is for open lunch and dinner daily, with burgers, fish tacos, open-faced sandwiches, salads, and notable daily specials; $7–20. Good drinks, too, especially its Irish coffees and martinis.

Housed within Rusty Parrot Lodge, the acclaimed **《 Wild Sage Restaurant** (175 N. Jackson, 307/733-2000 or 800/458-2004, www.rustyparrot.com) serves gourmet dinners in an intimate setting (just 21 seats). This is AAA's only four-star restaurant in Wyoming, and chef Jeffrey Blackwell offers a delectable array of regional cuisine and fresh seafood. The menu changes, but typically includes pan-seared beef tenderloin, juniper spiced wapiti, and wild huckleberry crème brûlée, plus a fine choice of wines. Dinner entrées are $26–36, and reservations are required; call a month ahead in mid-summer. Lunches are a bargain, with lighter fare such as Reubens, chicken wraps, burgers, soups, and salads. Breakfast is primarily for lodge guests.

MEXICAN

For the fastest Mexican food in town (with the possible exception of Taco Bell), drop by **Pica's Mexican Taqueria** (1160 Alpine La., 307/734-4457, $6–8). You'll find tasty tacos, bodacious burritos, enchanting enchiladas, and tempting *tortas* in a hip setting full of locals. The shop is in Buffalo Junction strip mall near Albertsons.

In business since 1969, **The Merry Piglets** (160 N. Cache Dr., 307/733-2966, www.merrypiglets.com) serves very good Tex-Mex meals,

fajitas, and cheese crisps—the house specialty. Excellent margaritas, pitchers of beer, and an open front section add to the appeal. Most items run $9–12, but you can get a simple burrito for $4.

ASIAN
Chinese

In Grand Teton Plaza on the south end of town, **Chinatown Restaurant** (850 W. Broadway, 307/733-8856) serves good Chinese dishes—particularly the *mu shu* vegetables, lemon chicken, and pot stickers—and offers $6 weekday lunch specials.

Ocean City China Bistro (340 W. Broadway, 307/734-9768) provides a pleasant downtown setting and more than 120 choices—from honey walnut prawns with pork to Szechuan three delight—for $8–12. Lunch combo plates ($6) are a bargain.

Japanese

Get delicious freshly rolled sushi—including vegetarian rolls and a unique hot spicy tuna roll—at **Masa Sushi** (307/733-2311), inside The Inn at Jackson Hole in Teton Village. The setting is intimate and inviting.

Nikai (225 N. Cache, 307/734-6490, www.nikaisushi.com) is open for dinner only, and reservations are advised. Creatively prepared sushi is the main attraction, but the restaurant also has a menu of Asian fusion items from the open kitchen, including miso black cod, pork *gyoza,* and *wakame* seaweed salad. The atmosphere is contemporary and stylish.

Housed within the Jackson Hole Wine Company, **Koshu Wine Bar** (200 W. Broadway, 307/733-5283) serves pan-Asian cuisine nightly in a classy setting. The menu changes often; most items are $9–27. You can choose from more than a dozen wines by the glass, or buy a bottle from the shop's extensive selection ($10 corkage fee).

Thai

Jackson is one of only three towns in Wyoming with Thai restaurants; the others are, rather surprisingly, in Lander and Rawlins.

Thai Me Up (75 E. Pearl St., 307/733-0005) has a gimmicky name and U.S.-born chefs, but the food is spicy, creative, and delicious. It's open for dinners only seven days a week and has a few sidewalk tables, plus a tiny bar with great drinks, including the Bigglesworth Typhoon, a blow-me-down 45-ounce blend of seven different alcohols that's set afire. The location is a bit quieter than places on the Square, but entrées aren't cheap: $10–18. Lunches are more reasonable, with $7 specials. Try the drunken noodles (*pad kee mow*) for a spicy favorite. Thai Me Up is closed April–mid-May.

For the downscale version, check out **Teton Thai Restaurant** (135 N. Cache Dr., 307/733-0022) across the street from Teton Theater. The tiny retro eatery has a handful of stools along the counter where you can watch the busy chefs and a few picnic tables out front. The food is simple and authentic, with specials such as chicken saté or *tom yum koong* for $8–10. No credit cards.

BREWERIES

Grand Teton Brewing Company (208/787-4000, www.grandtetonbrewing.com) now brews just over Teton Pass in Victor, Idaho, where you can sample Teton Ale, Old Faithful Ale, Moose Juice Stout, Teton Golden Ale, Teton Huckleberry Wheat, and Sweetgrass IPA. You'll find them on tap at many Jackson-area bars and restaurants and for sale in six-pack bottles.

An old warehouse two blocks from Town Square has been beautifully transformed into **◖ Snake River Brewing Co. and Restaurant** (265 S. Millward St., 307/739-2337, www.snakeriverbrewing.com). The bright and cavernous setting fills with a convivial crowd of young outdoors enthusiasts most evenings, and the bar generally has seven or eight of its award-winning beers on tap. Particularly notable—they've all won gold medals at various brew festivals—are Zonker Stout, Snake River Lager, and Snake River Pale Ale. The lunch and dinner café menu includes delicious thin-crust pizzas baked in the apple-wood–fired oven, flavorful appetizers, daily pasta specials, panini sandwiches, and salads. It's great food in a lively atmosphere, and one of *the* places to be seen in Jackson. Most dinner entrées run $9–12, but it has a variety of $6 lunch specials.

WINE SHOPS

The most complete local wine and beer shops are **Westside Wine and Spirits** (307/733-5038) in the Aspens along Teton Village Road, **The Liquor Store** (next to Albertsons on W. Broadway, 307/733-4466, www.wineliquorbeer.com), and **Dornan's Wine Shoppe** (307/733-2415, ext. 202, www.dornans.com) in Moose. The Liquor Store features an impressive upstairs wine department and a bar with free wine tastings Friday evenings. You can even use the computer to check your email.

Jackson Hole Wine Company (200 W. Broadway, 307/739-9463) also has a fine selection and offers free Friday evening wine tastings, with a different choice of wines each week (except in April, May, and November). It's a great way to learn about various vintages from wine experts. Koshu Wine Bar is in the back.

BAKERIES

The Bunnery (130 N. Cache Dr., 307/733-5474 or 800/349-0492, www.bunnery.com) bakes a big variety of treats and sweets, but it's best known for its hearty-flavored OSM (oat, sunflower, and millet) bread—on the pricey side at almost $5 a loaf. Bunnery's restaurant is a hectic breakfast and lunch destination.

Another place for fresh-baked—and organic—breads and pastries is **Harvest Natural Foods** (130 W. Broadway, 307/733-5418, www.harvestorganicfoods.com).

The location is a bit out of the way, but a visit to **Wild Flour Bakery** (345 N. Glenwood, 307/734-2455) is a must if you're in search of French baguettes and other breads (different choice every day). Great pies, focaccia, pastries, cookies, and muffins, too. You'll find the company's goods in local grocers, and it bakes the house bread for several of Jackson's gourmet restaurants.

GROCERIES AND NATURAL FOODS

Get groceries from the large **Albertsons** (307/733-5950) on the south end of town at the corner of Buffalo Way and Broadway. Inside you'll find a bakery, pharmacy, deli, one-hour photo lab, bank branch, and coffee bar. This is the most lucrative Albertsons in the entire chain of 2,300 stores; sales are said to be three times higher than at the second-most-successful store! A few blocks farther south (right in front of the high school) is an even larger **Smith's** (1425 S. U.S. 89, 307/733-8908, www.smithsfoodanddrug.com) with the same features as Albertsons and a deli with fresh sushi.

Meet the locals at the less ostentatious (and generally cheaper) **Food Town** (970 W. Broadway, 307/733-0450) in the Powderhorn Mall. The best spot for fresh vegetables and fruit is the little **Fruit Market** next to the Maverik gas station on the south end of town. It's open only in the summer but has better prices and higher quality than local grocers.

In business since 1947, **Jackson Hole Buffalo Company** (1325 S. Hwy. 89, 307/733-8343 or 800/543-6328, www.buybuffalomeat.com) sells smoked buffalo salami, jerky, sausage, steaks, and burgers, along with buffalo meat gift packs and New Zealand elk steaks. It's in the Smith's mall.

For organic produce and health foods, head downtown to **Harvest Natural Foods** (130 W. Broadway, 307/733-5418, www.harvestorganicfoods.com).

Jackson's popular **Farmers Market** (307/690-2657) comes to Town Square 8–11 A.M. Saturdays July–September. Shop for fresh veggies, fruits, flowers, and baked goods. Live music and cooking demonstrations add to the attraction.

Information and Services

INFORMATION

On the north side of town is the **Jackson Hole and Greater Yellowstone Visitor Center** (532 N. Cache Dr., 307/733-3316, www.jacksonholechamber.com, open daily; see details in *Sights*). Immediately south of the visitor center is an impressive building housing the **Wyoming Game and Fish** (307/733-2321) offices.

The **Bridger-Teton National Forest** supervisor's office (340 N. Cache Dr., 307/739-5500, www.fs.fed.us/r4/btnf) is open 8 A.M.–4:30 P.M. Monday–Friday. Get information and Forest Service maps from the visitor center.

Newspapers

Jackson's outstanding local newspaper—the *Jackson Hole News and Guide* (307/733-2047, www.jhnewsandguide.com)—is produced in tabloid format. Free Monday–Saturday editions can be found all over the valley, and a fat weekly edition ($0.50) comes out on Wednesdays with more detailed local and regional coverage.

Planet Jackson Hole (307/732-0299, www.planetjh.com) is a free weekly with a focus on local music and entertainment.

Jackson Hole on the Web

A great place to begin your web tour is the chamber of commerce site: www.jacksonholechamber.com. Also very useful are www.jacksonholetraveler.com and www.jacksonholenet.com. All three of these contain links to dozens of local businesses of all types. You may also want to check out www.jacksonnetwork.com, and the Teton County website, www.tetonwyo.org.

Library

Spacious **Teton County Library** (125 Virginian La., 307/733-2164, www.tclib.org) is the kind of library every town should have. Inside this modern building is a large collection of books about Wyoming and the West, plus a great kids' section (complete with a fenced-in children's garden with a tepee). Computers

JACKSON HOLE

provide free Internet access and are available by reservation or on a walk-up-and-wait basis. In the summer the queue can get long if you don't have a reservation. The library takes reservations up to one week in advance. Library hours are 10 A.M.–9 P.M. Monday–Thursday, 10 A.M.–5:30 P.M. Friday, 10 A.M.–1 P.M. Saturday, and 1–5 P.M. Sunday. If you plan to be in the Jackson area for a week or more, it may be worth your while to get a visitor's library card. For a one-time fee of $5 you can check out up to four books at a time.

SERVICES
Trip Planning
Several local travel agencies offer reservation services for those who prefer to leave the planning to someone else. They can set up airline tickets, rental cars, lodging, horseback riding, fishing trips, whitewater rafting, ski vacations, and all sorts of other packages. The biggest is the long-established **Jackson Hole Central Reservations** (307/733-4005 or 800/443-6931, www.jacksonholewy.com), which produces a slick glossy publication of featured properties. Also helpful for trip planning are **Llama Lou's Reservations** (307/733-1617 or 800/709-1617, www.jhsummerfun.com) and **Jackson Hole Reservations** (307/733-6331 or 800/329-9205, www.jacksonhole.net).

Banking and Currency Exchange
Get fast cash from **ATMs** at many locations around town, including banks, Albertsons, downtown in front of Sirk Shirts, at the airport, and in Teton Village and the Aspens.

International travelers will appreciate the currency exchange where you can swap those Euros or colorful Canadian bills at all three Jackson State Bank (307/733-3737, www.jacksonstatebank.com) locations: 112 Center Street, 50 Buffalo Way, and in the Aspens on Teton Village Road.

Post Office
Jackson's main post office (1070 Maple Way, 307/733-3650) near Powderhorn Lane is open 8:30 A.M.–5 P.M. Monday–Friday, 10 A.M.–1 P.M. Saturday. Other post offices are downtown (220 W. Pearl Ave., 307/739-1740), in Teton Village (307/733-3575), in Wilson, 307/733-3335), and in Kelly (307/733-8884).

Internet Access
To keep in touch with folks via email, use the free terminals in the library. Another option is **Mountunes** (265 W. Broadway, 307/733-4514 or 800/982-2241, www.mountunes.com). In addition to a diverse collection of new and used CDs for sale, it has an Internet café where computer time costs $5 per half hour. Wi-Fi is free if you buy an espresso drink.

Medical
Because of the abundance of ski and snowboard accidents, orthopedic specialists are in high demand in Jackson and are some of the best around. The specialists at Orthopaedics of Jackson Hole are official physicians for the U.S. and French national ski teams! Head to **St. John's Hospital** (625 E. Broadway, 307/733-3636, www.tetonhospital.org) for emergency medical attention. Medical service on a walk-in basis is available at **Emerg-A-Care** (975 W. Broadway, 307/733-8002) in Powderhorn Mall.

Laundry and Showers
Wash clothes at **Soap Opera Laundry** (850 W. Broadway, 307/733-5584) in Grand Teton Plaza or **Ryan Cleaners** (545 N. Cache Dr., 307/733-2938). You'll find public lockers at Jackson Hole Mountain Resort during winter. **Showers** ($6 with towel) are available in the Bunkhouse section of **Anvil Motel** (215 N. Cache Dr., 307/733-3668 or 800/234-4507, www.anvilmotel.com).

Getting There and Around

Access to Jackson Hole has become easier in recent years, with several airlines and daily buses now serving the valley. Most summer visitors arrive by car, although a few more adventurous souls pedal in on bikes. If you're looking for or offering a ride, KMTN (96.9 FM, 307/733-4500, www.jacksonholeradio.com/kmtn.htm) has daily ride-finder announcements during its Trash and Treasure radio program. Tune in weekdays 9:30–9:50 A.M.

BY AIR

Jackson Hole Airport (307/733-7682, www.jacksonholeairport.com) is eight miles north of Jackson inside Grand Teton National Park. It's the only commercial airport within any national park, and the Grand Teton Natural History Association maintains a gift shop here. The airport is small and cozy but offers daily jet service to several U.S. cities. In addition, the tarmac is often crowded with Lear and Gulfstream jets and other noisy transportation symbols of the elite.

Delta/Skywest (800/221-1212, www.delta.com) has year-round flights from Salt Lake City, with additional winter flights out of Atlanta. Some of the Salt Lake flights are in smaller turboprops, others in jets; all Atlanta flights are jets. **American** (800/433-7300, www.aa.com) has nonstop summer and winter service from Dallas and Chicago. **Northwest** (800/225-2525, www.nwa.com) flies from Minneapolis/St. Paul year-round; off-season flights make a stop in Billings. **United/United Express** (800/241-6522, www.ual.com) offers year-round turboprop service from Denver, with jets in the summer and winter seasons. **Big Sky Airlines** (800/237-7788, www.bigskyair.com) has daily nonstop commuter service between Boise and Jackson.

Jackson Hole Aviation (307/733-4767 or 800/437-5387, www.jhaviation.com) offers charter air service.

If you're flying in from the West Coast, you will need to go through either Salt Lake City (275 miles away) or Idaho Falls (90 miles away). The latter airport is served by Horizon Air (Alaska Airlines). Many travelers opt to fly to either Salt Lake or Idaho Falls and pick up a rental car for the drive to Jackson.

Airport Shuttles and Taxis
Alltrans/Gray Line of Jackson Hole (307/733-4325 or 800/443-6133, www.jacksonhole-alltrans.com) provides airport shuttle service to and from motels in Jackson ($15 one-way or $26 round-trip per person) and Teton Village ($22 one-way or $38 round-trip per person). The shuttles meet nearly all commercial airline flights in winter and most summertime flights, but you should make reservations to be sure of an airport pickup. Make outgoing reservations for a motel pickup 24 hours in advance.

Local taxis provide direct service from the airport to your hotel. The one-way rates for 1–2 people are $27 to Jackson, or $47 to Teton Village. Local taxi companies include **Airport Taxi/Alltrans** (307/733-1700 or 800/443-6133, www.jacksonholealltrans.com), **Airport Shuttle Service and Taxi** (307/413-1200), **All Star Taxi and Transportation Services** (307/733-2888), **Buckboard Transportation** (307/733-1112 or 877/791-0211, www.buckboardtrans.com), **Bullseye Taxi** (307/730-5000), **Cowboy Cab** (307/413-1000), **Elk Country Cab** (307/733-8181), **Late Night Early Morning Taxi** (307/690-1004), and **Teton Taxi and Backcountry Shuttle** (307/733-1506, www.tetontaxi.com).

CAR RENTALS
Most of the national chains offer rental cars in town or at the airport. These include **Alamo** (307/733-0671 or 888/426-3299, www.alamo.com), **Avis** (307/733-3422 or 800/831-2847, www.avis.com), **Budget** (270 W. Pearl St., 307/733-2206 or 800/237-7251, www.budget.com), **Dollar Rent A Car** (345 W. Broadway, 307/733-9224 or 877/222-7736, www.dollar.com), **Hertz** (307/733-2272 or 800/654-3131, www.hertz.com),

JACKSON HOLE

© DON PITCHER

Wyoming stop sign

National (220 N. Millward St., 307/733-7961 or 888/868-6204, www.nationalcar.com), and **Thrifty** (307/734-9306 or 800/847-4389, www.jackson.thrifty.com). Alamo, Avis, Hertz, and Thrifty all have counters at the airport, while the others provide a free shuttle to their offices in town.

Local companies include **Eagle Rent-a-Car** (890 W. Broadway, 307/739-9999 or 800/582-2128, www.eaglerentals.net, mostly SUVs), **Grand Teton Rentals** (1180 S. Gregory La., 307/734-7979), and **Leisure Sports** (1075 S. Hwy. 89, 307/733-3040, www.leisuresportsadventure.com). **Jackson Hole Recreational Rentals** (375 N. Cache St., 307/734-5110 or 866/734-5110, www.jhrr.com) rents an odd mix of vehicles—from Harleys to Hummers.

BY BUS
START Buses
Local buses are operated by Southern Teton Area Rapid Transit (START, 307/733-4521 www.startbus.com) and serve Jackson and Teton Village all year. START fares are free within town and $3 to Teton Village (cheaper for seniors and children). Discount coupons are available for multiple rides. Hours of operation are generally 6 A.M.–10:30 P.M. During summer, buses run seven days a week, with in-town service every 30 minutes. Service to Teton Village is eight times a day in summer and more often in winter. Reduced bus service is available in fall and spring. Get bus schedules and route maps in the visitor center. Buses stop near most Jackson hotels and motels and are equipped to carry skis (in winter) and bikes (in summer) on outside racks. Wintertime service is also offered to the National Museum of Wildlife Art and National Elk Refuge. Unfortunately, START buses do not run to the airport, Kelly, or Moose, but winter service is available to Wilson.

Long-Distance Buses
Greyhound buses don't come even close to Jackson; the nearest stopping place is the regional hub at Salt Lake City. **Alltrans/Jackson Hole Express** (307/733-1719 or 800/652-9510, www.jacksonholealltrans.com) connects Jackson with Salt Lake City ($66

one-way), Idaho Falls ($38 one-way), and Pocatello ($46 one-way) daily.

TOURS AND SHUTTLES

Grand Teton Lodge Company (307/543-2811 or 800/628-9988, www.gtlc.com) has five-times-daily summer shuttles between Jackson and Jackson Lake Lodge for $20 one-way (plus a $10 park entrance fee) and on to Colter Bay Village for an additional $4 one-way. Transportation between the airport and Jackson Lake Lodge is $20 one-way (plus a $10 park entrance fee heading north). Reservations are required for all of these. The company also offers three-hour bus tours of Grand Teton National Park and eight-hour tours of Yellowstone National Park. (See *Park Access* in the *Grand Teton National Park* chapter for details on other companies offering park tours from Jackson.)

Bridger-Teton National Forest

One of the largest national forests in the Lower 48, Bridger–Teton ("the B–T") National Forest stretches southward for 135 miles from the Yellowstone border and covers 3.4 million acres. Parts of the forest are described elsewhere (see *Bridger Wilderness* in the *Wind River Mountains Country* chapter and *Greys River Loop Road* in the *Southwest Wyoming* chapter). In Jackson Hole, the two areas of most interest for recreation are the Teton Wilderness and the Gros Ventre Wilderness, but nonwilderness areas offer additional opportunities for recreation.

The Bridger–Teton National Forest **supervisor's office** (307/739-5500, www.fs.fed.us/r4/btnf) is at 340 North Cache Drive in Jackson. The visitor center, a couple of blocks north on Cache, usually has a Forest Service worker on duty who can provide recreation information. The center also sells Bridger–Teton maps and has a good choice of outdoor books. Local ranger stations are the **Jackson Ranger District** (directly behind the supervisor's office, 307/739-5400) and the **Blackrock Ranger Station** (nine miles east of Moran Junction, 307/543-2386).

Forest Service lands around Jackson provide an amazing array of hiking and mountain-biking options. Pick up a copy of *Top 10 Trails* from the Forest Service office in town for descriptions of the most popular trails, or find an updated version at www.fs.fed.us/r4/btnf.

TETON WILDERNESS

The Teton Wilderness covers 585,468 acres of mountain country, bordered to the north by Yellowstone National Park, to the west by Grand Teton National Park, and to the east by the Washakie Wilderness. Established as a primitive area in 1934, it was declared one of the nation's first wilderness areas upon passage of the 1964 Wilderness Act. The Teton Wilderness offers a diverse mixture of rolling lands carpeted with lodgepole pine, spacious grassy meadows, roaring rivers, and dramatic mountains. Elevations range from 7,500 feet to the 12,165-foot summit of Younts Peak. The Continental Divide slices across the wilderness, with headwaters of the Yellowstone River draining the eastern half and headwaters of the Buffalo and Snake rivers flowing down the western side. Teton Wilderness has a considerable amount of bear activity, so make sure you know how to avoid bear encounters and bring pepper spray.

Natural events have had a major effect on the Teton Wilderness. On July 21, 1987, a world-record high-elevation tornado created a 10,000-acre blowdown of trees around the Enos Lake area, and it took years to rebuild the trails. A series of fires followed—including the Huck and Mink Creek fires that burned 200,000 acres. Don't let these incidents dissuade you from visiting; this is still a marvelous and little-used area, and more than 60 percent of the land was not burned. Herds of

LONE HIGHWAYMAN OF YELLOWSTONE

Because of its remote location, Teton Valley became a rendezvous place for rustlers and outlaws in the 1880s. Horses stolen from the soldiers at Fort Hall, along with cattle "liberated" from Wyoming and Montana ranches, made their way through Pierre's Hole to the railroads. Hiram C. Lapham was the first to try his hand at ranching in the valley, but his cattle quickly disappeared. With the help of a posse from Rexburg, Lapham tracked down the culprits, one of whom was killed in the ensuing gunfight. The others surrendered but escaped from jail when the wife of bandit Ed Harrington smuggled a gun to her husband in clothing worn by his baby. Harrington and partner Lum Nickerson were eventually tracked down and sent to jail.

Although Harrington was sentenced to 25 years, the governor pardoned him after just three. Harrington went on to become Teton Valley's first postman, but his criminal activity continued. Using the alias Ed Trafton, Harrington went on to rob stores throughout Teton Valley and eventually spent another two years behind bars. After getting out, he turned his attention to the tourism business in Yellowstone, but not in the standard way. Although it was never proven, he was suspected of being behind a string of stagecoach robberies in 1908 in which cash and jewelry were taken from tourists at gunpoint. Harrington's most brazen feat came on July 29, 1914, when he single-handedly robbed 15 stages, earning the nickname "the lone highwayman of Yellowstone." The tourists were particularly impressed with his gentlemanly manner as he asked them to "please" hand over all their cash and jewelry. Harrington made off with $915.35 in cash and $130 in jewelry, but he made the mistake of posing for photos in the process. He was caught the following year and spent five years in Leavenworth Prison.

When Harrington died, a letter in his pocket claimed that he had been Owen Wister's model for the Virginian in the famous novel of the same name. Others suspected that he was more likely to have been Wister's model for the villain, Trampas.

elk graze in alpine areas, and many consider the Thorofare country abutting Yellowstone National Park the most remote place in the Lower 48. This is prime grizzly habitat and you may well encounter them, so be very cautious at all times. Poles for hanging food have been placed at most campsites, as have bear-resistant boxes or barrels. Use them, and always keep a clean camp. You can rent bear-resistant backpacker food tubes or horse panniers from the Blackrock Ranger District (307/543-2386), but it's a good idea to make reservations for these items before your trip.

Access

Three primary trailheads provide access to the Teton Wilderness: Pacific Creek on the southwestern end, Turpin Meadow on the Buffalo Fork River, and Brooks Lake just east of the Continental Divide. Campgrounds are at each of these trailheads. Teton Wilderness is a favorite of Wyomingites, particularly those with horses, and in the fall elk hunters from across the nation come here. Distances are so great and some of the stream crossings so intimidating that few backpackers head into this wilderness area. No permits are needed, but it's a good idea to stop in at the **Blackrock Ranger District** (307/543-2386) nine miles east of Moran Junction on U.S. 26/287, for topographic maps and information on current trail conditions, bear problems, regulations, and a list of permitted outfitters offering horse or llama trips.

For a shorter trip, you could take a guided horseback ride with one of two companies based at the Turpin Meadow Trailhead: **Yellowstone Outfitters** (307/543-2418 or 800/447-4711, www.yellowstoneoutfitters.com), or **Teton Wilderness Outfitters** (307/543-0120). Additional rides are available from nearby **Turpin Meadow Ranch** (307/543-2000 or 800/743-

2496, www.turpinmeadowranch.com), **Buffalo Valley Ranch** (307/543-2062 or 888/543-2477). All four of these have horses available for hourly or all-day rides into the Teton Wilderness. **Teton Horseback Adventures** (307/856-3628 or 307/739-7176, www.horsebackadv.com) has horseback rides and wilderness trips out of the Pacific Creek Trailhead.

Unfortunately, USGS maps don't show the many Teton Wilderness trails built and maintained (or not maintained) by private outfitters and hunters. These can make hiking confusing since not every junction is signed. Forest Service maps for the wilderness have been updated with most trail locations. A few of the many possible hikes are described as follows.

Whetstone Creek
Whetstone Creek Trail begins at the Pacific Creek Trailhead, on the southwest side of Teton Wilderness. An enjoyable 20-mile round-trip hike leaves the trailhead and follows Pacific Creek for 1.5 miles before splitting left to follow Whetstone Creek. Bear left when the trail splits again another three miles upstream and continue through a series of small meadows to the junction with Pilgrim Creek Trail. Turn right here and follow this trail two more miles to Coulter Creek Trail, climbing up Coulter Creek to scenic Coulter Basin and then dropping along the East Fork of Whetstone Creek. This rejoins the Whetstone Creek Trail and returns you to the trailhead, passing many attractive small meadows along the way. The upper half of this loop hike was burned in 1988; some areas were heavily scorched, while others are patchy. Flowers are abundant in the burned areas, and this is important elk habitat.

South Fork to Soda Fork
A fine loop hike leaves Turpin Meadow and follows South Buffalo Fork River to South Fork Falls. Just above this point, a trail splits off and climbs to Nowlin Meadow (excellent views of Smokehouse Mountain) and then down to Soda Fork River, where it joins the Soda Fork Trail. Follow this trail back downstream to huge Soda Fork Meadow (a good

place to see moose and occasionally grizzlies) and then back to Turpin Meadow, a distance of approximately 23 miles round-trip. For a fascinating side trip from this route, head up the Soda Fork into the alpine at Crater Lake, a six-mile hike above the Nowlin Meadow-Soda Fork Trail junction. The outlet stream at Crater Lake disappears into a gaping hole, emerging as a large creek two miles below at Big Springs. It's an incredible sight.

Cub Creek Area
The Brooks Lake area just east of Togwotee Pass is a popular summertime camping and fishing place with magnificent views. Brooks Lake Trail follows the western shore of Brooks Lake and continues past Upper Brooks Lakes to Bear Cub Pass. From here, the trail drops to Cub Creek, where you'll find several good campsites. You can make a long and scenic loop by following the trail up Cub Creek into the alpine country and then back down along the South Buffalo Fork River to Lower Pendergraft Meadow. From here, take the Cub Creek Trail back up along Cub Creek to Bear Cub Pass and back out to Brooks Lake. Get a topographic map before heading into this remote country. Total distance is approximately 33 miles round-trip.

GROS VENTRE WILDERNESS
The 287,000-acre Gros Ventre Wilderness was established in 1984 and covers the mountain country just east of Jackson Hole. This range trends mainly in a northwest-southeast direction and is probably best known for Sleeping Indian Mountain (maps now call it Sheep Mountain, but locals never use that appellation), the distinctive rocky summit visible from Jackson Hole. Although there are densely forested areas at lower elevations, the central section of the wilderness lies above timberline, and many peaks top 10,000 feet. The tallest is Doubletop Peak at 11,682 feet. The Tetons are visible from almost any high point in the Gros Ventre, and meadows line the lower-elevation streams. Elk, mule deer, bighorn sheep, moose, and black bears are found here, and a

© DON PITCHER

Granite Hot Springs is nestled in the Bridger-Teton National Forest south of Jackson.

few grizzlies have been reported. The Forest Service office in Jackson has more information on the wilderness, including brief trail descriptions and maps.

Access and Trails

Several roads provide good access to the Gros Ventre Wilderness: Gros Ventre River Road on the northern border; Curtis Canyon Road on the western margin; and Granite Creek Road to the south. Flat Creek is rough and accessible only in a 4WD vehicle. Hikes beginning or ending in the Granite Creek area have the added advantage of nearby Granite Hot Springs, a great place to soak tired muscles.

For a beautiful hike, follow **Highline Trail** from the Granite Creek area across to Cache Creek, a distance of 16 miles. This route passes just below a row of high and rugged mountains, but because it isn't a loop route, you'll need to hitchhike or set up a shuttle back. Plan on three days for this hike. The area is crisscrossed with game and cattle trails, making it easy to get lost, especially on the headwaters of Little Granite Creek. Talk with Forest Service folks before heading out, and make sure that you know how to read a map and compass.

A third hike begins at the **Goosewing Ranger Station,** 12 miles east of Slide Lake on Gros Ventre River Road. Take the trail from here to Two Echo Park (a fine camping spot) and then continue up to Six Lakes. You can return via the same trail or take the Crystal Creek Trail back to Red Rock Ranch and hitch back to Goosewing. The trail distance is approximately 23 miles round-trip.

Caribou-Targhee National Forest

Covering nearly three million acres, Caribou–Targhee National Forest extends from Montana to Utah. Most of the forest lies within Idaho, but it also includes the western edge of Wyoming along the Tetons. Much of the forest is heavily logged, but two wilderness areas protect most of the Wyoming section. Contact the Forest Service office in Driggs, Idaho (208/354-2312, www.fs.fed.us/r4/caribou) for more recreation information.

JEDEDIAH SMITH WILDERNESS

The 123,451-acre Jedediah Smith Wilderness lies on the west side of the Teton Range, facing Idaho but lying entirely within Wyoming. Access is primarily from the Idaho side, although trails breach the mountain passes at various points, making it possible to enter from Grand Teton National Park. This area was not declared a wilderness until 1984. A second wilderness area, the 10,820-acre **Winegar Hole Wilderness** (WINE-a-gur), lies along the southern border of Yellowstone National Park. Grizzlies love this country, but hikers will find it uninteresting and without trails. In contrast, the Jedediah Smith Wilderness contains nearly 200 miles of paths and some incredible high-mountain scenery.

Several mostly gravel roads lead up from the Driggs and Victor areas into the Tetons. Get a map ($7) showing wilderness trails and access points from the Caribou–Targhee National Forest ranger station in Driggs, Idaho (208/354-2312) or from the Forest Service offices in Jackson. Be sure to camp at least 200 feet from lakes and 100 feet from streams. Group size limits are also in place; check with the Forest Service for specifics on these and other backcountry regulations. In addition, anyone planning to cross into Grand Teton National Park from the west side will need to get a park camping permit in advance. Wilderness permits are not required for the Jedediah Smith Wilderness. Both grizzly and black bears are present throughout the Tetons, so all food must be either hung out of reach or stored in bear-resistant containers.

(Alaska Basin

The most popular hiking trail in the Jedediah Smith begins near the **Teton Canyon Campground** ($10, 518/885-3639 or 877/444-6777 for reservations, www.reserve-usa.com, open late May–mid-Sept.) and leads through flower-bedecked meadows to mountain-rimmed Alaska Basin. It's great country, but don't expect a true wilderness experience because many others will also be hiking and camping here. Get to the campground by following the Grand Targhee Ski Resort signs east from Driggs, Idaho. A gravel road splits off to the right approximately three miles beyond the little settlement of Alta. Follow it to the campground. (If you miss

© DON PITCHER

breathtaking Alaska Basin in the Jedediah Smith Wilderness

the turn, you'll end up at the ski area.) For an enjoyable loop, follow Alaska Basin Trail up the canyon to Basin Lakes and then head southwest along the Teton Crest Trail to the Teton Shelf Trail. Follow this trail back to its junction with the Alaska Basin Trail, dropping down the Devils Stairs—a series of very steep switchbacks. You can then take

the Alaska Basin Trail back to Teton Camp-ground, a round-trip distance of approxi-mately 19 miles. You could also use these trails to reach the high peaks of the Tetons or to cross the mountains into Death Canyon within Grand Teton National Park (camp-ing permit required). Campfires and horse camping are not allowed in Alaska Basin.

Teton Valley

The west side of the Tetons differs dramati-cally from nearby Jackson Hole. As the road descends from Teton Pass into Teton Valley, Idaho, the lush farming country spreads out before you, 30 miles long and 15 miles across. This, the "quiet side" of the Tetons, offers a slower pace than bustling Jackson, but the Teton Range vistas are equally dramatic.

In recent years the growth in Jackson Hole has spilled across the mountains. The potato farms, horse pastures, and country towns are now undergoing the same transformation that first hit Jackson in the 1970s. As land prices soar and affordable housing becomes more difficult to find in Jackson, more people have opted to move over the pass and com-mute from Idaho. The primary town here—it's the county seat—is Driggs, Idaho, with Victor nine miles south and tiny Tetonia eight miles north.

A couple of good lodging choices in Driggs are **Movin' Sol Hostel** (208/354-5454, www.tetonhostel.com) for budget travelers, and **The Pines Motel Guest Haus** (208/354-2774 or 800/354-2778) for something nicer. The For-est Service's **Teton Canyon Campground** is 11 miles east of Driggs in the Tetons. For meals, try **Miso Hungry Cafe** (208/354-8015) in town or **Warbirds Cafe** (208/354-2550, www.tetona-viation.com) at the airport. The **Teton Valley Chamber of Commerce** (91 E. Little Ave., 208/354-2500, www.tetonvalleychamber.com) has additional info on the area.

See Don Root's *Moon Idaho* (www.moon.com) for coverage of eastern Idaho, including the

Swan Valley to the south and the Island Park area to the north.

ALTA

The little place called Alta sits right along the Wyoming border and just six miles northeast of Driggs, Idaho. There are no stores in Alta, but the settlement does have a stellar restau-rant and several places to stay. East from Alta, the road climbs through heavily timbered country, with periodic views of the Big Hole Mountains to the west and up-close looks at the Teton Range.

Also in Alta is the nine-hole **Targhee Village Golf Course** (208/354-8577 or 307/353-8577).

Accommodations

Right on the state line, **Alta Lodge B&B** (307/353-2582, www.pdt.net/altalodge) is a large modern home with tall picture windows framing the Tetons. It has four guest rooms (two with private baths), and a hot tub is avail-able. Rates are $75 d with a shared bath, or $85–95 in the larger rooms. Kids over age 10 are welcome, and a full breakfast is served.

Teton Teepee Lodge (470 W. Alta Rd., 307/353-8176 or 800/353-8176, www.teton-teepee.com) is a winter-only place with a spacious common area at the center of a tepee-shaped building. Twenty-one guest rooms (no TV or phones in rooms) surround it, and two large dorm rooms—primarily used by kids—occupy a lower level. The lodge is a favorite of skiers and snowboarders, with a large central stone fireplace, dining area, pool table, game room, TV room, and outdoor hot tub. The lodge is open only during ski season, mid-November–April; call for rates.

Also in Alta is **Wilson Creekside Inn B&B** (130 Alta North Rd., 307/353-2409, www.wilsoncreeksideinn.net), where you'll find a century-old home on a 200-acre sheep farm. Four guest rooms are available and all contain family heirlooms. One costs $85 d and includes a king-size bed and private bath; the others share a bath and run $75d or $85 for four people. Guests are served an ample country breakfast. Kids are welcome.

Food

Lost Horizon Dinner Club (307/353-8226) is one of the standout places in the Teton Valley area. The restaurant/home has space for just a dozen guests, who sit down to a memorable 10-course Japanese and Chinese meal ($40 plus wine) prepared by co-owner and chef Shigako Irwin. This isn't for vegetarians or for those in a hurry; expect to be here for three leisurely hours. Dinners are served Friday and Saturday nights at 7, and reservations are required. No credit cards are accepted. Formal dress isn't necessary, but don't come in shorts, sandals, or T-shirts.

GRAND TARGHEE SKI RESORT

On the west side of the Tetons 42 miles from Jackson, Grand Targhee Ski Resort (307/353-2300 or 800/827-4433, www.grandtarghee.com) offers the friendliness of a small resort with the amenities and snow you'd expect at a major one. To get here you'll need to drive into Idaho and turn east at Driggs. The resort sits at the end of a beautiful road (recently rebuilt) 12 miles east of Driggs and just six miles inside Wyoming. Its motto says it all: "Snow from heaven, not from hoses." With an annual snowfall topping 500 inches (42 feet!)—most of which is champagne powder—Targhee became the spot where powderhounds got all they could ever want. Ski magazines consistently rank it as having North America's best (or second-best) snow. In fact, the resort guarantees its snow: If you find conditions not to

your liking, you can turn in your ticket within an hour of purchase and get a "snow check" good for another day of skiing. By the way, the official name is Grand Targhee Ski and Summer Resort, but most folks call it Grand Targhee, or simply Targhee.

The biggest drawback to Grand Targhee Ski Resort is the same thing that makes it so great—the weather. Lots of snow means lots of clouds and storms, and because it snows so much there are many days when the name cynics apply—"Grand Foghee"—seems more appropriate. Many folks who have returned to Targhee year after year have still not seen the magnificent Grand Teton backdrop behind the ski area! Be sure to bring your goggles. The quad lift up Peaked Mountain provides intermediate skiing on slopes that are more protected and suffer less wind and fog.

Skiing and Snowboarding

The resort has two quads, one double chairlift, and a surface lift on Fred's Mountain, plus a quad on adjacent Peaked Mountain. The top elevation is 10,230 feet, with the longest run dropping 2,822 feet over almost three miles. About 750 acres are groomed, but you'll always find track-free skiing on the remaining 2,250 acres of ungroomed powder, so bring your snorkel. In addition, snowcat skiing ($300 per day including lunch and guide) is offered on a 1,000-acre section of Peaked Mountain reserved for powderhounds.

Lift tickets at Grand Targhee cost $55 per day ($39 half day) for adults and $35 per day for children ages 6–14 and seniors (free under age six). Substantial discounts are offered for multi-day lift tickets or lodging-and-ski packages.

Fully 70 percent of Targhee's groomed runs are intermediate to advanced-intermediate, but advanced skiers will find an extraordinary number of deep-powder faces to explore. Snowboarders can play at the half-pipe. The ski school offers lessons for all abilities, and children's programs make it possible for parents to leave their kids behind. Cross-country skiers enjoy the Nordic center, and ski and snowboard rentals are available at the base of the mountain. The ski area usually opens in mid-November and closes in late April, although some years you may be able to ski even into July. Lifts operate 9:30 A.M.–4 P.M. daily.

Other Winter Activities

Dogsled tours leave from the lodge in winter, with a 90-minute trip for $115 per person. Guided **snowshoe wildlife tours** (free) will appeal to amateur naturalists, and on the **sleigh-ride dinner** ($35 adults, $15 kids), you'll ride in a horse-drawn sleigh to a yurt where a Western-style meal is served. Targhee's **tubing park** ($8 per hour; opens at 5 P.M.) is a fun place for kids to slide down a snowy hill, and the resort also has an outdoor **skating pond** and skate rentals. A **Kid's Club** at Targhee provides supervised childcare for children under six ($51 per day), and teens can join special programs that include skiing and other fun on the mountain.

Summer Activities

Not far from Grand Targhee are several popular summertime hiking trails within the Jedediah Smith Wilderness.

The resort is a popular place to relax in the summer and offers many activities. A quad chairlift ($8 adults, $5 kids) takes you up the 10,200-foot summit of Fred's Mountain for strikingly close views of the Tetons. The lift operates daily late June–mid-September, plus Wednesdays, Saturdays, and Sundays in June. A Forest Service naturalist leads guided walks on weekends, or by request Wednesday–Friday.

Horseback rides and lessons are a favorite Targhee summertime activity; one-hour rides are $28. The area is also a fun mountain-biking destination, with bike rentals; you can also take them up the ski lift. The climbing wall ($6 for an introductory climb) is open to all abilities and is a good place to learn some basic—or advanced—moves. Even more challenging is the adventure ropes course, for those who have always wanted to walk the high wire. Other summer activities and facilities at Targhee include a zip line, basketball courts, an outdoor swimming pool and hot tubs, a fitness center, horse-

shoes, tennis, and volleyball. The nine-hole **Targhee Village Golf Course** is just down the road. After all this excitement, you'll probably want to relax with a massage, aromatherapy, facial, or steam bath from the on-site spa.

Based at the resort, the nonprofit **Targhee Institute** (307/353-2233) directs the Science Explorers Day Camp for ages 3–12, with tons of fun activities. The institute also offers weeklong Elderhostel programs throughout the year, covering everything from snowshoeing to photography.

Events

End the year—and start a new one—with **Torch Light Parades** at Grand Targhee on the evenings of December 25 and 31. Also on New Year's Eve is a fireworks display over the mountain. Each March, the resort celebrates telemark skiing with the **Nordic Festival.** Ski races of all sorts take place, and Targhee rocks to great music, an outdoor barbecue, and fun events. The **Spring Snow Games** is a three-day mid-March event with races and other play for all ages. It's followed in early April by the **Cardboard Box Derby,** with participants swooshing down the ski hill on cardboard creations of all types.

The resort pulls out the stops for the popular **Targhee Bluegrass Festival** in mid-August, with nationally known acts. Bring your dancin' shoes! The music attracts hundreds of people, so call the resort well ahead of time for camping or lodging reservations. Other big summertime events at Targhee include the **Grand Teton Summer Festival** around Fourth of July and the **WYDAHO Mountain Bike Race,** at the same time.

Accommodations

Contact Targhee (307/353-2300 or 800/827-4433, www.grandtarghee.com) for details on lodging options at or near the resort. The three lodges at the base of the mountain—Targhee Lodge, Teewinot Lodge, and Sioux Lodge—offer ski-in, ski-out access, a large heated outdoor pool, a hot tub, and a workout room. Rates quoted are for the winter holiday season; they're approximately 40 percent lower in summertime.

Most lodging places are closed October–mid-November, and mid-April–mid-June.

Get standard motel accommodations at **Targhee Lodge** with holiday winter rates of $172 d. Deluxe hotel rooms with lodgepole furnishings and access to an indoor hot tub are $220 d at **Teewinot Lodge.** The lobby here is a fine place to relax in front of the fire on winter evenings. **Sioux Lodge** continues the Western theme with lodgepole furnishings, but it also has kitchenettes, adobe-style fireplaces, and small balconies. Studio units are $294 for up to four people, loft units $394 for four people, and two-bedroom units run $514 for up to eight.

Summer packages are good bargains, including two nights of lodging with breakfast, a scenic chairlift ride, and a one-hour horseback ride; $356 for two adults and two kids. A wide variety of wintertime package deals are also available for stays longer than three nights. One that provides seven nights of lodging and six days of skiing costs $1,870 for two adults (and their kids under 14) during the holiday season at Targhee Lodge; rates are considerably higher at Teewinot or Sioux Lodge. You can cut these rates substantially if you ski in the "value" season before mid-December and after late March, with a complete seven-night package for just $1,168 d.

The resort also has off-site condo lodging available approximately 10 miles down the hill at **Teton Creek Resort** and **Powder Valley Condominiums.** Choose from one-, two-, and three-bedroom condominiums, each with a fireplace, kitchen, private patio, and VCR. Outdoor hot tubs are also available. Nightly holiday-season rates start at $219 d for the one-bedroom units, up to $529 for eight people in a three-bedroom unit. Rates are, of course, lower if you can come at other times.

In addition to the places at the base of the resort, lodging is available just down the hill in Alta, Wyoming, and in the nearby Idaho towns of Driggs, Victor, and Tetonia.

Food

At the base of Grand Targhee is a compact cluster of shops and places to stay. You won't have to walk far to find a cafeteria, pizza place, and burger joint. The nicest place is **Targhee Steakhouse,** serving hearty breakfasts and lunches, along with cozy dinners. Grand Targhee's social center is the **Trap Bar,** featuring live music Wednesday –Sunday all winter, along with pub grub on the menu all the time. Guests at Targhee can also take a **horse-drawn sleigh** on a 15-minute ride to a Mongolian-style yurt for a home-cooked steak or chicken dinner. The price is $35 ($15 for kids ages 7–12), and reservations are required. Other shops here sell groceries, ski and snowboard gear, clothing, and gifts. **Lost Horizon Dinner Club** (307/353-8226) five miles below the resort in the town of Alta, is highly recommended for a relaxing formal dinner with an Asian flair.

Getting There

Grand Targhee is 42 miles northwest of Jackson on the western side of the Tetons in Alta, Wyoming. Get there by driving over Teton Pass (occasionally closed by winter storms), north through Victor and Driggs, Idaho, and then east back into Wyoming.

The **Targhee Express/Alltrans** bus makes daily wintertime trips (90 minutes each way) to Grand Targhee from Jackson Hole. Buses pick up skiers from Jackson and Teton Village hotels shortly after 7 A.M., returning from Targhee at 4:30 P.M. for a round-trip fare of $69, including a full-day lift ticket. Round-trip bus fare without a lift ticket costs $25. Reservations are required; make them before 9 P.M. on the night before by calling 307/733-4325 or 800/443-6133, or book online at www.jacksonholealltrans.com. Van service is also available year-round to airports in Jackson or Idaho Falls, Idaho.

JACKSON HOLE

GRAND TETON NATIONAL PARK

Please see front color map Grand Teton National Park

Grand Teton National Park remains one of the preeminent symbols of American wilderness. The Tetons rise abruptly from the valley floor, their bare triangular ridges looking like broken shards of glass from some cosmic accident of creation. With six different summits topping 12,000 feet, plus some of the finest climbing and hiking in Wyoming, the Tetons are a paradise for lovers of the outdoors. They have long been a favorite of photographers and sightseers and once even appeared in an ad promoting Colorado tourism! The Tetons change character with the seasons. In summer the sagebrush flats are a garden of flowers set against the mountain backdrop. When autumn arrives, the cottonwoods and aspens become swaths of yellow and orange. Winter turns everything a glorious, sparkling white, set against the fluorescent blue sky.

PLANNING YOUR TIME

Travelers to Grand Teton National Park typically see it at the same time they're visiting Yellowstone National Park and the town of Jackson. Backcountry hikers are attracted to the scenic canyons and alpine areas within the park, and the 13,772-foot Grand Teton is a goal of mountain climbers. Photographers can't resist the mountain-and-river **Teton Viewpoints** that captivated millions of earlier visitors, including Ansel Adams. A couple of days are sufficient to see park sights.

One of the most scenic areas within the park is **Jenny Lake,** where a boat transports hikers to **Inspiration Point and Hidden Falls,**

© DON PITCHER

HIGHLIGHTS

◖ Chapel of the Transfiguration: Built in 1925, this quaint log church has a back window that frames the Tetons. You won't find a better wedding chapel than this (page 406)!

◖ Jenny Lake: You won't be the first—or last—person to discover this idyllic lake in the heart of Grand Teton National Park (page 406).

◖ Signal Mountain: It's too narrow for RVs, but the road up Signal Mountain provides panoramic vistas of the Tetons; it's best at sunrise or sunset (page 407).

◖ Colter Bay Indian Arts Museum: Tucked away in a nondescript visitor center, this amazing collection includes quality Indian artistry; open summers only (page 408).

◖ Teton Viewpoints: Ansel Adams wannabees, take note: This is where that famous photo of the Tetons was taken (page 411).

◖ Blacktail Butte and Mormon Row: The historic farm buildings provide a picture-perfect setting and a good spot to see bison (page 411).

◖ Moose-Wilson Road: Rough in places, narrow, and winding (no RVs), it's a fine place for wildlife-watching and hiking (page 413).

◖ Inspiration Point and Hidden Falls: Getting there is half the fun with a shuttle-boat trip across Jenny Lake followed by a 0.5-mile hike to this scenic point. Expect a queue in midsummer, or just hike around the lake to avoid the crowds (page 414).

LOOK FOR ◖ TO FIND RECOMMENDED SIGHTS, ACTIVITIES, DINING, AND LODGING.

GRAND TETON

a base for longer explorations into the Tetons. Historic Jenny Lake Lodge has upscale accommodations and gourmet meals; it's one of several good choices in the park.

There are fine vistas from the summit of **Signal Mountain,** and you may see moose in the sloughs at Oxbow Bend or bison on the flats near **Mormon Row.** The latter area has some of the most photographed barns in America, with a Teton Range backdrop to die for. The **Colter Bay Indian Arts Museum** on the northern end of the park houses an extraor-

dinary collection of Native American pieces. Jackson Lake is popular for fishing and boating. Park headquarters and the main visitor center are on the south end of Grand Teton National Park in the little settlement of Moose. Nearby is **Chapel of the Transfiguration,** a rustic log church with a dramatic backdrop. The narrow and winding **Moose-Wilson Road** heads south to Teton Village and Wilson.

Before your visit, contact Grand Teton National Park (307/739-3600, www.nps.gov/grte) for publications and maps, or use its website to learn more about the area. For more comprehensive coverage of Grand Teton, Yellowstone, and Jackson Hole, see Don Pitcher's *Moon Yellowstone and Grand Teton* (www.moon.com).

GEOLOGY
Building a Mountain Range

The precipitous Teton Range contains perhaps the most complex geologic history in North America. Although the Tetons are ancient by any human scale, they are the youngest mountains in the Rockies, less than 10 million years old (versus 60 million years for the nearby Wind River Mountains). The Tetons are a fault-block range, formed when the earth's crust cracked along an angled fault. Forces within the earth have pushed the western side (the Tetons) up, while the eastern part (Jackson Hole) dropped down like a trapdoor. Geologists believe the fault could slip up to 10 feet at a time, producing a violent earthquake. All this shifting has created one of the most dramatic and asymmetric mountain faces on earth.

Unlike in typical mountain ranges, the highest parts are not at the center of the range but along the eastern edge, where uplifting continues. The western slope, which drops gently into Idaho, is much less dramatic, although the views are still impressive. This tilting-and-subsidence process is still going on today, pushed by the movement of a plume of magma beneath Yellowstone as the continental plate slides over the top. Because of this subsidence, the town of Wilson in Jackson Hole now lies 10 feet below the level of the nearby Snake River; only riverside dikes protect the town from flooding.

As the mountains rose along this fault, millennia of overlying deposits were stripped away by erosion, leaving three-million-year-old Precambrian rock jutting into the air above the more recent sedimentary deposits in the valley. Because of this shifting and erosion, sandstone deposits atop Mt. Moran match those 24,000 feet below Jackson Hole. Although the most recent major earthquake on the Teton Fault was at least 2,000 years ago, geologists are convinced that Jackson Hole could experience a major temblor at any time.

Rivers of Ice

In counterpoint to the uplifting actions that created the general outline of the Tetons, erosional forces have been wearing them down again. Glaciers, which are created when more snow falls than melts off, have proven to be one of the most important of these erosional processes. After a period of several years and under the weight of additional snow, the accumulated snow crystals change into ice. Gravity pulls this ice slowly downhill, creating essentially a frozen river that grinds against whatever lies in the way, plucking loose rocks and soil and polishing hard bedrock. This debris moves slowly down the glacier as if on a conveyer belt, eventually reaching the glacier's terminus.

When a glacier remains the same size for a long period, large piles of glacial debris accumulate at its end, creating what glaciologists call a terminal moraine. One of these created Jackson Lake, when a huge glacier dumped tons of rock at its snout. After the glacier melted back, this terminal moraine became a natural dam for the

Mount Moran and aspens in fall

waters of the Snake River. Similar mounds of glacial debris dammed the creeks that formed Jenny, Leigh, Bradley, Taggart, and Phelps lakes within Grand Teton National Park.

The earth has experienced cyclical periods of glaciation for hundreds of thousands of years, probably because of changes in the earth's orbit around the sun. During the colder parts of these cycles, glaciers appear and advance. The entire Yellowstone region has undergone a series of massive glaciations, the last of which is called the Pinedale Glaciation. It began around 70,000 years ago and had essentially disappeared by 15,000 years ago. At its peak, the Pinedale Glaciation covered all of Yellowstone and reached well into Jackson Hole.

Streams flowed from the ends of these glaciers, carrying along gravel, sand, silt, and clay. The cobbles and sands from these streams were dropped on the flat valley below, while the finer silts and clays continued downstream, leaving behind soils too rocky and nutrient-poor to support trees. Only sagebrush grows on this plain today, while the surrounding hills and mountain slopes (which were spared this rocky deposition) are covered with lodgepole and subalpine fir forests. Trees can also be found covering the silty terminal moraines that ring the lakes.

Other reminders of the glacial past are the "potholes" (more accurately termed "kettles") that dot the plain south of Signal Mountain. These depressions were created when large blocks of ice were buried under glacial outwash. When the ice melted, it left a kettle-shaped pond surrounded by glacial debris. Only a dozen or so small glaciers remain in the Tetons; the largest is the 3,500-foot-long Teton Glacier, visible on the northeastern face of Grand Teton. For a far more detailed picture of Teton geology, read *Interpreting the Landscape: Recent and Ongoing Geology of Grand Teton and Yellowstone National Parks,* by John Good and Kenneth Pierce (Moose, WY: Grand Teton Natural History Association, 1996).

WILDLIFE

Grand Teton National Park is an excellent place to look for wildlife, especially in the early morning or at dusk. Moose are often seen at Willow Flats along Jackson Lake just north of the dam, at Oxbow Bend, south of the settlement of Moose, and along the Snake River. Look for bison along Antelope Flats Road, Teton Park Road, and near Moran Junction. Herds of pronghorn antelope are common on the sagebrush flats near Kelly. Elk are frequent sights in fall as they migrate down from the high country to the elk refuge near Jackson, but smaller numbers are in the park during summer. (Grand Teton is the only national park outside of Alaska that allows hunting. The rules are pretty strange, however, requiring elk hunters to become temporarily deputized park rangers before they head out!) Grizzlies are found only on the park's northern margins, but black bears are present in wooded canyons and riverbeds, so be careful when hiking or camping in the park. Other animals to look for are bald eagles and ospreys along the Snake River and trumpeter swans and Canada geese in ponds and lakes. Look for mule deer in meadows and at forest edges, such as those near Colter Bay.

Bison

Herds of bison (buffalo) are commonly seen in the Moran Junction area and in the Mormon Row area. They were present historically (hence the name Buffalo River) but had been extinct for perhaps a century when eight bison were released into Grand Teton National Park in 1969. The population grew slowly for the first decade until they discovered the free alfalfa handout at the elk refuge north of Jackson. Partly because of this winter feeding, the population has grown to almost 600 animals—much to the chagrin of the elk-refuge managers. A few bison are hunted outside the park to control their numbers.

Wolves

Wolves were reintroduced to Yellowstone National Park starting in 1995 and have continued to expand into surrounding areas, including Grand Teton National Park. They're most easily seen in winter, particularly on the adjacent National Elk Refuge where they prey on elk,

GRAND TETON

© DON PITCHER

About 600 bison live in Grand Teton National Park.

but they may sometimes be seen during summer inside the park.

HISTORY

Once the wonders of Yellowstone came to widespread public attention, it took only a few months for Congress to declare that area a national park. But the magnificent mountain range to the south proved an entirely different story. Early on, there were suggestions that Yellowstone be expanded to include the Tetons, but it would take decades of wrangling before Jackson Hole would finally be preserved.

"Damning" Jackson Lake

Jackson Lake represents one of the sadder chapters in the history of northwestern Wyoming. Jackson Lake Dam was built in the winter of 1910–1911 to supply water for Idaho potato and beet farmers. The town of Moran was built to house construction workers for Jackson Lake Dam and at one time included more than 100 ramshackle structures. Virtually nothing remains of the town. The 70-foot-tall dam increased the size of the natural lake, flooding

out more than 7,200 acres of trees and creating a tangle of floating and submerged trunks and stumps. To some, the dam seemed like the serpent in the Garden of Eden, a symbol of the development that would destroy the valley if not stopped. The trees remained in Jackson Lake for many years, creating an eyesore until the Park Service and the CCC finally launched a massive cleanup project in the 1930s. The dam was completely rebuilt in 1988–1989, and while the lake now looks attractive, it remains yet another example of how Wyoming provides water for farmers in surrounding states. Late in the fall, especially in dry years, the lake can drop to a large puddle with long stretches of exposed bottom at the upper end. Fortunately, Idaho irrigators did not succeed in their planned dams on Jenny, Leigh, and Taggart lakes in what is now Grand Teton National Park.

Dudes and Development

Because of the rocky soils and long winters, Jackson Hole has always been a marginal place for cattle ranching, and only in the southern end of the valley are the soils rich enough to support a decent crop of hay. This poor soil and harsh climate saved Jackson Hole from early development and forced the ranchers to bring in dudes to supplement their income. (One old-timer noted, "Dudes winter better than cattle.")

Louis Joy established the first Jackson Hole dude ranch, the JY, in 1908 along Phelps Lake. It was followed a few years later by the Bar BC Ranch of Struthers Burt, an acclaimed East Coast author who had come west as a dude but learned enough to go into the business for himself. The dude ranchers were some of the first to realize the value of Jackson Hole and to support its preservation. Burt proposed that the valley and mountains be saved not as a traditional park but as a "museum on the hoof," where ranching and tourism would join hands to stave off commercial developments. The roads would remain unpaved, all homes would be log, and Jackson would stay a frontier town. Needless to say, that didn't happen.

The movement to save Jackson Hole coalesced in a 1923 meeting at the cabin of Maude Noble. Horace Albright, superintendent of Yellowstone National Park, was there, along with local dude ranchers, businessmen, and cattlemen who were eager to save the remote valley from exploitation. To accomplish this goal, they proposed finding a wealthy philanthropist who might be willing to invest the $2 million that would be needed to buy the land. Fortunately, one of Struthers Burt's friends happened to be Kenneth Chorley, an assistant to John D. Rockefeller Jr. Burt used this contact to get Rockefeller interested in the project.

Rocky to the Rescue

In 1926, Rockefeller traveled west for a 12-day trip to Yellowstone. Horace Albright used the chance to take him on a side trip into Jackson Hole and to proselytize for protection of the valley. What they saw portended badly for the future: the Jenny Lake dance hall, roadside tourist camps and hot dog stands, rusting abandoned cars, and a place that billboards proclaimed "Home of the Hollywood Cowboy." Rockefeller was angered by the prospect of crass commercial developments blanketing Jackson Hole and

quickly signed on to the idea of buying the land and giving it to the Park Service.

To cover his tracks as he bought the land, Rockefeller formed the Snake River Land Company; if ranchers had known that the Rockefeller clan was behind the scheme, they would have either refused to sell or jacked up the price. Only a few residents—mostly supporters—knew of the plan. The local banker, Robert Miller, served as land-purchasing agent, although even he opposed letting the Park Service gain control of the valley. Miller used his position to buy out ranches with delinquent mortgages at his Jackson State Bank and then resigned, claiming the whole thing was part of a sinister plot to run the ranchers out and halt "progress." In 1929, Congress voted to establish a small Grand Teton National Park that would encompass the mountains themselves, which stood little chance of development, but not much else. Conservationists knew that without preservation of the valley below, the wonderful vistas would be lost.

A National Battleground

Rockefeller and Albright finally went public with their land-buying scheme in 1930, releasing a tidal wave of outrage. Antipark forces led by Senator Milward Simpson (father of recently retired Senator Alan Simpson) spent the next decade fighting the park tooth and nail, charging that it would destroy the economy of Jackson Hole and that ranchers would lose their livelihoods. Rockefeller's agents were falsely accused of trying to intimidate holdouts with strong-arm tactics. Congress refused to accept Rockefeller's gift, and local opposition blocked the bill for more than a decade.

Finally, in 1943, President Roosevelt made an end run around the antipark forces; he accepted the 32,000 acres purchased by Rockefeller, added 130,000 acres of Forest Service land, and declared it the Jackson Hole National Monument. The move outraged those in the valley, prompting more hearings and bills to abolish the new national monument. Wyoming's politicians attacked Roosevelt's actions. A bill overturning the decision was pocketvetoed by the president, but for the next several years, the Wyoming delegation kept reintroducing the measure.

Things came to a head when Wallace Beery—a Reaganesque Hollywood actor—threatened to "shoot to kill" park officials. Beery, who had to use a stepladder to climb on his horse, organized a cattle drive across the monument. Unable to find anyone to fire on in the new monument, his cadres sat on a creek bank and drank a case of beer, cussing out the damn bureaucrats. So much for the Wild West.

By 1947, the tide had turned as increasing postwar tourism revitalized the local economy. Finally, in 1950, a compromise was reached, granting ranchers lifetime grazing rights and the right to trail their cattle across the park en route to summer grazing lands. The new-and-improved Grand Teton National Park had finally come to fruition.

Postmortem

Some of the early fears that Rockefeller would use the new park for his own gain seemed partly justified. For many years his descendants owned the old JY Ranch and used Phelps Lake as something of a semiprivate playground, though it has now been donated to the Park Service. Rockefeller also built the enormous Grand Teton Lodge along Jackson Lake and facilities at Colter Bay Village and Jenny Lake, leading some to accuse the family of attempting to monopolize services within the park. The company, Grand Teton Lodge Company, is now owned by Vail Resorts, which manages Jackson Lake Lodge, Jenny Lake Lodge, and Colter Bay Village, along with Jackson Hole Golf and Tennis Club (near Jackson).

Looking back on the controversial creation of Grand Teton National Park, it's easy to see how wrong park opponents were. Teton County has Wyoming's most vibrant economy, and millions of people arrive each year to enjoy the beauty of the undeveloped Tetons. As writer Nathaniel Burt noted, "The old enemies of the park are riding the profitable bandwagon of unlimited tourism with high hearts and open palms." Park opponents' claims that the Park Service would "lock up" the land ring as hollow as similar anti-wilderness claims today by descendants of the same politicians who opposed Grand Teton National Park half a century ago. Without inclusion of the land purchased by Rockefeller, it is easy to imagine the valley covered with all sorts of summer-home developments, RV campgrounds, souvenir shops, motels, billboards, and neon signs. Take a look at the town of Jackson to see what might have been without Rockefeller's philanthropy.

EXPLORING THE PARK

Grand Teton National Park has fewer "attractions" than Yellowstone—its big sister to the north—and an easy day's drive takes you past the road-accessible parts of the park. The real attractions are the mountains and the incomparable views one gets of them from Jackson Hole. This is one backdrop you will never tire of seeing.

Entrance Stations

Grand Teton National Park (307/739-3600, www.nps.gov/grte) has two entrance stations. One is just north of the Moose Visitor Center on Teton Park Road, and the second is on U.S. 89/191/287 at Moran Junction. Entrance to the park is $20 per vehicle or $10 for individuals entering by bicycle, foot, or as a bus passenger. Motorcycles and snowmobiles are $15. The pass covers entrance to both Yellowstone and Grand Teton national parks and is good for seven days. If you're planning to be here longer or to make additional visits, get an annual pass covering both parks for $40, or the National Parks Pass—good for all national parks—for $65 per year. A Golden Age Passport for all national parks is available to anyone over 62 for a one-time fee of $10, and people with disabilities can get a free Golden Access Passport. Both of these also give the holders 50 percent reductions in most camping fees.

At the entrance stations, park visitors receive a copy of *Teewinot,* the park newspaper. It lists park facilities and services, along with interpretive programs, nature walks, and other activities. Family favorites for generations are the evening campfire programs held at campground amphitheaters throughout the summer.

The park also produces a helpful *Easy Access* brochure with details on wheelchair-accessible visitor centers, trails, sights, picnic areas, activities, campsites, and accommodations.

Visitor Centers

Grand Teton National Park headquarters is in the settlement of Moose near the southern end of the park. **Moose Visitor Center** (307/739-3399) is open 8 A.M.–7 P.M. daily early June–early September, and 8 A.M.–5 P.M. daily (except Christmas) the rest of the year. **Jenny Lake Visitor Center** is open 8 A.M.–7 P.M. daily early June–early September; closed the remainder of the year.

On the east side of Jackson Lake, **Colter Bay Visitor Center** (307/739-3594) is open 8 A.M.–7 P.M. daily late May–early September, and 8 A.M.–5 P.M. daily for most of May and for most of early September–mid-October; closed the rest of the year.

Jenny Lake Visitor Center is open 8 A.M.–7 P.M. early June–early September, and 8 A.M.–5 P.M. daily the rest of September). Coin-operated storage lockers are next to the store.

Just north of Grand Teton inside John D. Rockefeller Jr. Memorial Parkway is **Flagg Ranch Information Station** (307/543-2372) open 8:30 A.M.–5 P.M. daily early June–early September, and with varying hours mid-December–mid-March.

Tours

As of 2006 the Park Service was developing a transportation plan for Grand Teton National Park that may include the addition of a public bus service from Jackson to the park and the addition of paved pathways and bike lanes. Don't expect any major changes till at least 2008.

Grand Teton Lodge Company (307/543-3100 or 800/628-9988, www.gtlc.com) has five-times-daily summer shuttle buses connecting Jackson with Jackson Lake Lodge for $20 one-way, and on to Colter Bay Village for an additional $4 one-way. Transportation between the airport and Jackson Lake Lodge is $30 one-way (plus a $10 park entrance heading north). Reservations are required for all of these shuttles. In Jackson, the buses depart from the Home Ranch parking lot on the corner of Gill Street and North Cache Drive. The company also offers three-hour bus tours of Grand Teton National Park on Mondays, Wednesdays, and Fridays for $33 ($16 kids under 12) and eight-hour tours of Yellowstone National Park on Tuesdays, Thursdays, and Saturdays for $52 ($30 kids). Tours depart from Jackson Lake Lodge at 8:30 A.M.

Summertime bus tours of Grand Teton and Yellowstone national parks are available several times a week from **Alltrans/Gray Line of Jackson Hole** (307/733-4325 or 800/443-6133, www.jacksonholealltrans.com). Yellowstone tours last 11 hours and cost $90 plus park entrance fees. Eight-hour Grand Teton tours are $75 plus the park entrance. **Powder River Tours** (307/527-3677 or 800/442-3682, http://gillettecoachusa.us) has all-day tours of Grand Teton out of Cody for $74.

Operated by Teton Science School, **Wildlife Expeditions** (307/733-2623 or 888/945-3567, www.wildlifeexpeditions.org) leads an array of wildlife-viewing safaris throughout the region, from four-hour sunset trips for $95 to four-day tours through Yellowstone and Grand Teton for $1,700. Its trips change seasonally—depending upon which animals are visible—and are offered in customized vehicles with multiple roof hatches for better wildlife-viewing.

Roads

Grand Teton National Park is bisected by the main north-south highway (U.S. 26/89/191) and by the road heading east over Togwotee Pass (U.S. 26/287). Both of these routes are kept open year-round, although wintertime plowing ends at Flagg Ranch Resort, just south of the Yellowstone boundary. In addition, a paved park road cuts south from Jackson Lake Dam to Jenny Lake and Moose. Only the southern end of this road is plowed in winter; the remainder becomes a snowmobile and cross-country ski route. South of Moose, a narrow, winding road (the Moose–Wilson Road) connects the park to Teton Village, nine miles away. It is rough dirt in places—no trailers or RVs—and is closed in winter.

Sights

Moose

The following tour takes you past points of interest along the main roads. The route follows a general clockwise direction beginning at the **Moose Visitor Center** (307/739-3399, www.nps.gov/grte). Before heading out, step inside the center (open daily year-round) for a fine introduction to the park and a look at the natural-history videos, books, and oil paintings. A large three-dimensional map here reveals the lay of the land. A brand new 23,000-square-foot Grand Teton Discovery and Visitor Center was to open in 2007, with state-of-the-art exhibits showcasing the natural world, and 30-foot-high windows providing a spectacular Teton Range vista.

The commercial center at Moose is across the Snake River bridge and just east of the visitor center. Here you'll find a plethora of operations run by **Dornan's** (307/733-2415, www.dornans.com): a general store, gift shop, lodging, restaurant and bar, wine shop, bike shop (with rentals), canoe and kayak rentals, and a chuck wagon eatery. Also here is a sporting-goods store (Moosely Seconds, 307/739-1801) and fishing shop (Snake River Angler, 307/733-3699, www.snakeriverangler.com). Moose has pretty much everything you might need for a day in the park.

(Chapel of the Transfiguration

Just inside the South Entrance to Grand Teton National Park, a side road leads to Chapel of the Transfiguration and Menor's Ferry. The rustic log church (built in 1925) is most notable for its dramatic setting. Episcopal services are held on summer Sundays, with Eucharist at 8 and 10 A.M.

The back window faces directly toward the Tetons, providing ample distractions for worshippers (or wedding guests). The bell out front was cast in 1842. Nearby **Menor's Ferry** is named for William D. Menor, who first homesteaded here in 1894 and later built a cable ferry to make it easier to cross the river.

His old whitewashed store still stands. You can cross the river in a reconstructed version of the old ferry when the water level is low enough; check out the ingenious propulsion mechanism that uses the current to pull it across. For many years, Menor's ferry served as the primary means of crossing the river in the central part of Jackson Hole. Wagons were charged $0.50, while those on horseback paid $0.25. (William Menor's brother, Holiday, lived on the opposite side of the river, but the two often feuded, yelling insults across the water at each other and refusing to acknowledge one another for years at a time.)

Also here is the 0.5-mile **Menor's Ferry Trail;** a brochure describes historic points of interest along the path. Bill Menor's cabin houses a small country store that sells the old-fashioned supplies he stocked at the turn of the 20th century. It is open 9 A.M.–4:30 P.M. daily late May–late September; closed the rest of the year.

Menor sold out to Maude Noble in 1918, and she ran the ferry until 1927, when a bridge was built near the present one in Moose. Her cabin now houses an excellent collection of historical photos from Jackson Hole. Maude Noble gained a measure of fame in 1923 when she hosted the gathering of residents to save Jackson Hole from development (see *Park History*).

Heading northwest beyond the Menor's Ferry area, the main road climbs up an old river bench, created by flooding from the rapid melting of the glaciers, and passes the trailhead to the turquoise waters of **Taggart Lake.** The land around here was burned in the 1,028-acre Beaver Creek lightning fire of 1985, and summers find a riot of wildflowers.

(Jenny Lake

The most loved of all Grand Teton lakes is Jenny Lake, nestled at the foot of Cascade Canyon and surrounded by a luxuriant forest of Engelmann spruce, subalpine fir, and lodgepole pine. Jenny Lake is named for Jenny

© DON PITCHER

A moose and calf wander along the Snake River.

Leigh, the Shoshone wife of Beaver Dick Leigh. A one-way loop road leads south past Jenny and String lakes, providing excellent views of the **Cathedral Group:** Teewinot, Grand Teton, and Mt. Owen. This is the most popular part of the park, and day-hikers will find a plethora of trails to sample, along with crowds of fellow hikers. Paths lead around both Jenny and String lakes, while another nearly level trail follows the east shore of **Leigh Lake** to several pleasant sandy beaches. **String Lake** is narrow but very pretty and makes a fine place for canoeing or swimming. Get supplies from the small store at Jenny Lake and information or guidebooks from the **Jenny Lake Visitor Center,** open 8 A.M.–7 P.M. early June–early September, and 8 A.M.–5 P.M. daily the rest of September. Coin-operated storage lockers are next to the store. Frequent shuttle boats provide access to hiking trails to the Inspiration Point and Cascade Canyon areas (see *Hiking* for details). Scenic boat cruises and fishing-boat rentals are also available at Jenny Lake.

Beautiful **Jenny Lake Lodge** sits on the northeast end of the lake and provides the finest lodging in the park, and the gourmet meals are legendary.

◖ Signal Mountain

As the road approaches Jackson Lake, a paved but narrow side road (no RVs or trailers) turns east and leads to the summit of Signal Mountain, 800 feet above Jackson Hole. On top are panoramic views of the Tetons, Jackson Lake, the Snake River, and the long valley below. To the south lies **The Potholes,** a hummocky area created when retreating glaciers left behind huge blocks of ice. The melting ice created depressions, some of which are still filled with water. Signal Mountain was burned by a massive 1879 fire and offers a good opportunity to see how Yellowstone may look in a century.

Hugging the southeast shore of Jackson Lake, **Signal Mountain Lodge** (307/733-5470 or 307/543-2831, www.signalmountainlodge.com) includes cabins and campsites, plus a gift shop, convenience store, gas station, marina with boat rentals, restaurant, and bar. Just east of the lodge is **Chapel of the Sacred Heart,** a small Roman Catholic church that

BEAVER DICK LEIGH

Around 1863, Richard "Beaver Dick" Leigh became the first white man to attempt a permanent life in Jackson Hole. An Englishman by birth, Beaver Dick lived in a log cabin with his Shoshone wife, Jenny, and their four children, scraping out the barest existence by hunting, trapping, and guiding. As guide for the 1872 Hayden Survey of the Jackson Hole area, Beaver Dick gained the respect of the surveyors, who named Leigh Lake for him and Jenny Lake for his wife. Today a local bar denigrates this remarkable man by calling itself Beaver Dick's and using a cartoonish image of him in its ads. The real man was nothing like this, and reading his diaries and letters is a lesson in how difficult life was for early Wyoming settlers. On one terrible Christmas in 1876, Beaver Dick watched his entire family – Jenny, their newborn baby, and the four other children – all slowly die from smallpox. Their deaths left him badly shaken.

But the human spirit is remarkably resilient. Beaver Dick later married a Bannock girl, raised another family, and guided for others, even meeting Theodore Roosevelt on one of his hunting trips. Beaver Dick Leigh died in 1899 and was buried on a ridge overlooking Idaho's Teton Basin.

has summer services at 5:30 P.M. on Saturdays and at 10 A.M. Sundays. The road then crosses **Jackson Lake Dam,** which raises the water level by 39 feet, alters the river's natural flow, and inundates a large area upstream. Many conservationists fought to have Jackson Lake excluded from the park, concerned that it would establish a bad precedent for allowing reservoirs in other parks. Nevertheless, once you get away from the dam, the lake appears relatively natural today (except in drought years when it gets the "bathtub ring" effect).

Along Jackson Lake

A turnout near Jackson Lake Junction provides views over **Willow Flats,** where moose are frequently seen, especially in the morning. Topping a bluff overlooking the flats is **Jackson Lake Lodge,** built in the 1950s with the $5 million financial backing of John D. Rockefeller Jr. Architects are not thrilled about the design (one author termed it "the ugliest building in Western Wyoming"), but the 60-foot-tall back windows frame an unbelievable view of the Tetons and Jackson Lake. Immediately across from the lodge is a trail leading to **Emma Matilda** and **Two Ocean** lakes. It is 14 miles round-trip around both lakes, with lots of wildlife along the way, including moose, trumpeter swans, pelicans, and ducks. You may have to contend with large groups on horseback.

〖 Colter Bay Indian Arts Museum

Colter Bay Village is one of the most developed parts of Grand Teton National Park, with a full marina, stores, a gas station, cabins, a campground, restaurants, and acres of parking. The main attraction here is the Colter Bay Indian Arts Museum (307/739-3594, free) housed in the visitor center. It's open 8 A.M.–5 P.M. daily mid-May–Memorial Day and Labor Day–September; 8 A.M.–8 P.M. daily early June–Labor Day. The museum is closed the rest of the year. Inside you will find the extraordinary David T. Vernon collection of Indian arts, the finest of its kind in any national park and one of the best in Wyoming. The collection spreads through several rooms on two floors and includes exquisitely beaded buckskin dresses, moccasins, masks, ceremonial pipes, war clubs, shields, bows, baskets, headdresses, and other decorated items. Stop to chat with Native artisans as they work on paintings, beaded items, wood carvings, pottery, and weaving. They're at the museum daily Memorial Day–Labor Day. This museum should not be missed! Step out back to join the shoreside fun or to rent a canoe or boat from the nearby marina.

Rockefeller Memorial Parkway

North of Colter Bay, the highway cruises along the shore of Jackson Lake for the next nine miles, providing some fine vantage points of the Tetons. The burned area on the opposite

GRAND TETON

photographers near Willow Flats in Grand Teton National Park

shore was ignited by lightning in the 1974 Waterfalls Canyon Fire, which consumed 3,700 acres. By late fall each year, Idaho spud farmers have drawn down water in the lake, leaving a long, barren shoreline at the upper end.

Shortly after the road leaves the upper end of Jackson Lake, a signboard announces your entrance into John D. Rockefeller Jr. Memorial Parkway. This 24,000-acre parcel of land was transferred to the National Park Service in 1972 in commemoration of Rockefeller's unstinting work in establishing Grand Teton National Park. The land forms a connection between Grand Teton and Yellowstone and is managed by Grand Teton National Park. Much of this area was severely burned by the 1988 Huck Fire, which began when strong winds blew a tree into power lines. Despite immediate efforts to control the blaze, it consumed 4,000 acres in the first two hours and later grew to cover nearly 200,000 acres, primarily within the Forest Service's Teton Wilderness. Dense young lodgepole pines now carpet much of the land.

On the northern end of Rockefeller Parkway is **Flagg Ranch Resort** (307/543-2861 or 800/443-2311, www.flaggranch.com), where the modern facilities include a gas station, convenience store, gift shop, cabins, restaurant, and campground with RV hookups. The park service operates the **Flagg Ranch Information Station** here early June–Labor Day. During the winter, Flagg Ranch is the jumping-off point for snowcoach and snowmobile trips into Yellowstone, and snowmobiles are available for rent.

Grassy Lake Road

Grassy Lake Road takes off just north of Flagg Ranch Resort and continues 52 miles to Ashton, Idaho. It's a scenic drive, but don't attempt this narrow and rough dirt road with a trailer or an RV. This route provides a shortcut to the Bechler River area of Yellowstone and is a popular wintertime snowmobile route. Huckleberry Hot Springs, a short hike north from the Grassy Lake Road bridge over the Snake River, was the site of a public swimming pool until 1983, when it was razed by the Park Service. The hot springs are accessible via an unmaintained trail, but you'll need to wade Polecat Creek to reach them. Although they remain popular with hikers and cross-country skiers, it's worth noting that the springs may pose a risk from dangerously high radiation levels.

Jackson Lake to Moran Junction

Heading east and south from Jackson Lake, the road immediately passes **Oxbow Bend,** where the turnout is almost always filled with folks looking for geese, ducks, moose, and other animals. The oxbow was formed when the meandering river cut off an old loop. The calm water here is a delightful place for canoes, although the mosquitoes can be a major annoyance in midsummer. Come fall, photographers line the shoulder of the road for classic shots of flaming aspen trees with Grand Teton and **Mt. Moran** in the background. Mt. Moran is the massive peak with a flattened summit, a skillet-shaped glacier across its front, and a distinctive black vertical diabase dike that looks like a scar from some ancient battle. It rises 12,605 feet above sea level and is named for Thomas Moran, whose beautiful paintings of Yellowstone helped persuade Congress to set aside that area as the world's first national park.

At **Moran Junction** you pass the park's Buffalo Entrance Station and meet the road to Togwotee Pass and Dubois. A post office and school are the only developments remaining here. The epic Western *The Big Trail* was filmed nearby in 1930, starring an actor named John Wayne in his first speaking role. (Wayne had never ridden a horse before this.) An interesting side trip is to head east from Moran on U.S. 26/287 for three miles to **Buffalo Valley Road.** This narrow and scenic road leads to Turpin Meadow, a major entryway into the Teton Wilderness (see *Bridger–Teton National Forest* in the *Jackson Hole* chapter). It is very pretty, especially in early summer when flowers carpet the fields. Buck-and-rail fences line the road, and the pastures are filled with horses and cattle. Beyond Turpin Meadow, the road turns to gravel and climbs sharply uphill, rejoining the main highway a couple of miles below Togwotee Mountain Lodge. The Blackrock Ranger Station of Bridger–Teton National Forest is eight miles east of Moran Junction on U.S. 26/287. Nearby

is historic **Rosie's Cabin,** built early in the 20th century by Rudolph Rosencrans, an Austrian emigrant who was the first forest ranger in this part of the Tetons.

Moran Junction to Moose

Heading south from Moran, U.S. 26/89/191 immediately crosses the Buffalo River (a.k.a. Buffalo Fork of the Snake River), where bison were once abundant. With a little help from humans, bison have been reestablished and are now often seen just south of here along the road.

The turnoff to the **Cunningham Cabin** is six miles south of Moran Junction. The structure actually consists of two sod-roofed log cabins connected by a covered walkway called a "dogtrot." Built around 1890, it served first as living quarters and later as a barn and smithy. A park brochure describes the locations of other structures on the property.

Pierce Cunningham came here as a homesteader and, with his wife, Margaret, settled to raise cattle. Although this was some of the better land in this part of the valley, the soil was still so rocky that they had a hard time digging fencepost holes. Instead, they opted to build the buck-and-rail fences that have become a hallmark of Jackson Hole ranches. Cunningham Ranch gained notoriety in 1893 when a posse surrounded two suspected horse thieves who were wintering at Cunningham's place while he was away. Vigilantes shot and killed George Spencer and Mike Burnett in an example of "mountain justice." Later, however, suspicions arose that hired killers working for wealthy cattle barons had led the posse and that the murdered men may have been innocent. **Spread Creek** is just north of the Cunningham cabin; it gained its name by having two mouths, separated by a distance of three miles.

The highway next rolls past **Triangle X Ranch,** one of the most famous dude ranches in Jackson Hole. Although it's on park land, the Turner family has managed Triangle X for more than 60 years. (One of the owners, John Turner, was director of the U.S. Fish and Wildlife Service under the first President Bush.) Stop by just after sunup to watch wranglers

© DON PITCHER

horseback riders at Triangle X Ranch

driving 120 head of horses to the corrals. It's a scene straight out of an old Marlboro ad.

Southwest from Triangle X, the road climbs along an ancient river terrace and passes **Hedrick Pond,** where the 1963 Henry Fonda movie *Spencer's Mountain* was filmed. Although the book on which the movie was based was set in Virginia, the producers found the Tetons a considerably more impressive location. Trumpeter swans are often seen on the pond. Hedrick Pond isn't really visible from the road and there are no signs pointing it out, but you can get there by parking near the S-curve road sign 1.4 miles south of Triangle X. The pond is a good example of a kettle pond, created when retreating glaciers left behind a block of ice covered with gravel and other deposits. The ice melted, leaving behind a depression that filled to become Hedrick Pond.

◖ Teton Viewpoints

Several turnouts provide popular photo-opportunity spots, the most famous being **Snake River Overlook.** Ansel Adams's famous shot of the Tetons was taken here and has been repeated with less success by generations of photographers. Throughout the summer, a progression of different flowers blooms in the open sagebrush flats along the road, adding brilliant slashes of color. They're prettiest in late June; in the high country, the peak comes a month or more later than elsewhere.

Just north of Snake River Overlook is the turnoff to **Deadman's Bar.** A steep partially dirt road (not for RVs) drops to one of the primary river-access points used by river rafters. The river bar received its name from an incident in 1886. Four German prospectors entered the area, but only one—John Tonnar—emerged. Bodies of the other three were found along the Snake River, and Tonnar was charged with murder. The jury in Evanston believed his claim of self-defense and he was set free, an act that so angered locals that they vowed to take care of future Jackson Hole criminals with a shotgun. A skull from one of the victims is on display in the Jackson Hole Museum.

Schwabacher Landing sits at the end of a one-mile gravel road that splits off just north of the Glacier View Turnout. It's a pleasant place for riverside picnics and some of the most famous Teton Range photos—the ones you see in local galleries—were taken just a few hundred yards upstream from the parking area. Schwabacher Landing was formerly a common starting point for rafting trips, but the river channel has shifted westward, making access difficult. Most floaters now put in at Pacific Creek or Deadman's Bar.

◖ Blacktail Butte and Mormon Row

One mile north of the turnoff to Moose, Antelope Flats Road heads east along Ditch Creek. Just south of here lies Blacktail Butte, a timbered knoll rising over the surrounding sagebrush plains. It's a favorite of rock climbers and has a hiking trail up the back (east) side. You will want to stop at the much-photographed old farm buildings known as Mormon Row. The farmland here was homesteaded by predominantly Mormon settlers in the early 1900s but was later purchased by Rockefeller's Snake

River Land Company and transferred to the Park Service. Only one set of buildings—an acre of the Moulton Ranch—is still in private hands. The other buildings were allowed to decay until the 1990s, when the Park Service recognized their value and stepped in to preserve the structures. Herds of bison often wander past the old farmsteads in summer, providing one of the best places to view them. Also keep your eyes open for small groups of pronghorn antelope in the vicinity.

Teton Science Schools

Hidden away in a valley along upper Ditch Creek is Teton Science Schools (TSS; 307/733-4765, www.tetonscience.org), a fine hands-on school for both young and old. Founded in 1967 as a summer field-biology program for high-school kids, it has grown into a year-round program with classes that run the gamut from elementary-school level all the way up to intensive college courses and a residency program. Summertime visitors will enjoy their one- to five-day adult seminars on such diverse subjects as entomology for fly-fishing, bird-watching, the biology of bugs, wildflower identification, river channels, and grizzly bear biology. These classes are limited to 12 students and fill up fast, so make reservations in the spring to be sure of a spot. The school's excellent monthlong wilderness emergency medical technician (EMT) course in early winter ($610 per person) is one of the few programs of its kind in the nation.

Based at the old Elbo dude ranch (started in 1932), TSS includes two dormitories, a central kitchen, a dining area, and other log structures. Visitors to the school should visit the **Murie Natural History Museum,** which displays thousands of specimens of birds, mammals, and plants. Included are casts of animal tracks used by famed wildlife biologist Olaus Murie in producing his *Peterson's Guide to Animal Tracks.* It's open to the public, but call ahead to arrange an appointment.

A new **Jackson Campus** of TSS opened in 2006 on an 860-acre parcel west of town along Hwy. 22. Built at a cost of $23 million, this ecofriendly facility provides much-needed room for additional programs and staff housing. Teton Science Schools offers a fine **winter speaker series** at the National Museum of Wildlife Art and at the Jackson campus, covering a spectrum of scientific, environmental, and social issues. In addition, the school operates **Wildlife Expeditions** (307/733-2623 or 888/945-3567, www.wildlifeexpeditions.org), with wildlife safaris throughout the Grand Teton and Yellowstone area.

Shadow Mountain Area

North from the TSS turnoff, the paved road splits. Turn left (west) on Antelope Flats Road to head back to Mormon Row and the main highway, or continue straight to climb Shadow Mountain (8,252 feet). The name comes from the shadows of the Tetons that fall across the mountain's face each evening. The road is paved for the first mile or so, but it turns to gravel as it snakes rather steeply up the mountain. The road is definitely not recommended for RVs or trailers, or for any vehicles after rains, when some sections turn to slippery mud. The views from the top of Shadow Mountain are truly amazing, with the Tetons in all their glory. Several dispersed campsites can be found along this route on Forest Service land.

Kelly and Vicinity

The small settlement of Kelly borders on the southeastern end of Grand Teton National Park and has log homes and a cluster of Mongolian-style yurts—certainly the most unusual dwellings in Wyoming. Folks living in the yurts share a common bathhouse and rent the land. The town has a shoebox-size post office and a couple of rental cabins. The Park Service's **Gros Ventre Campground** is three miles west of here.

Gros Ventre Road leads east from the Kelly area, passing **Kelly Warm Spring** on the right. Its shallow and warm waters are a favorite place for local kayakers to practice their rolls or for families to swim on a summer afternoon. A short distance up the road and off to the north (left) are the collapsing remains of the *Shane cabin,* where a scene from the classic 1951

Western was filmed. Beyond this point, the road enters Bridger–Teton National Forest and the Slide Lake area, where there is a Forest Service campground.

Gros Ventre Slide

One of the most extraordinary geologic events in recent Wyoming history took place in the Gros Ventre (GROW-vont—"Big Belly" in French trapper lingo) Canyon, named for the Gros Ventre Indians of this area. Sheep Mountain, on the south side of the canyon, consists of sandstone underlain by a layer of shale that becomes slippery when wet. Melting snow and heavy rains in the spring of 1925 lubricated this layer of shale, and on June 23 the entire north end of the mountain—a section 2,000 feet wide and one mile long—suddenly slid 1.5 miles downslope, instantly damming the river below and creating Slide Lake. A rancher in the valley, Guil Huff, watched in amazement as the mountain began to move, but he managed to gallop his horse out of the way as the slide roared within 30 feet. Huff's ranch floated away on the new lake several days later.

For two years folks kept a wary eye on the makeshift dam of rock and mud. Then, on May 18, 1927, the dam suddenly gave way, pushing an enormous wall of water through the downstream town of Kelly. Six people perished in the flood, and when the water reached Snake River Canyon nine hours later it filled the canyon to the rim with boiling water, trees, houses, and debris. Today a smaller Slide Lake still exists, and the massive landslide that created it more than 75 years ago remains an exposed gouge visible for miles around. Geologists say that, under the right conditions, more of Sheep Mountain could slide. Dead trees still stand in the upper end of Slide Lake. The Forest Service has a **Gros Ventre Geological Trail** 10 miles up Gros Ventre Road. This 0.25-mile path leads to an incredible viewpoint overlooking the slide and is marked with interpretive signs.

Gros Ventre River Valley

Above Slide Lake (six miles up), the road turns to gravel, becoming quite rutted in places. Surprising scenery makes the sometimes bone-jarring route easier to take. The landscape here is far different from that of the Tetons, with brilliant red-orange badland hills rising sharply above the Gros Ventre River. Two more Forest Service campgrounds (Red Hills and Crystal Creek) are four miles above Slide Lake, or you can camp in dispersed sites off the road. **Grizzly Lake Trail** starts at the Red Hills Campground and continues for 3.5 miles to this small mountain lake. There are wonderful vistas of the Red Hills and Gros Ventre River valley below.

The road continues another 15 beautiful miles along the river above the lake, getting rougher at the upper end. Several remote guest ranches are up here. Beyond Cow Creek Trailhead (29 miles from Kelly) the route is virtually impassable unless you have a high-clearance 4WD and are ready to get stuck. Hard-core mountain-bikers sometimes continue up this road/trail and then drop into the Green River watershed north of Pinedale. Cow Creek Trail and other paths lead into the Gros Ventre Wilderness, which borders the south side of the road. On the drive back down the Gros Ventre River valley you will discover some fine views across to the Tetons.

◖ Moose-Wilson Road

This narrow and winding road heads south from park headquarters in Moose, continuing nine miles to Teton Village. It is paved most of the way, but a 1.5-mile section is dirt. Keep your speed down to reduce the amount of dust in the air and to keep the backseat passengers from getting ill from all the curves. No trailers or RVs are allowed, and the road is not plowed in the winter. It is especially pretty in the fall when the aspens are turning. This is also a good place to watch for moose and other animals in summer or for easy cross-country ski adventures on a sunny winter day.

Two backcountry trailheads—Death Canyon Trailhead and Granite Canyon Trailhead—are accessible from the Moose–Wilson Road (see *Recreation* for details).

The Rockefeller family's JY Ranch (built in 1908) stood along Phelps Lake until 2005, when the land was donated to the Park Service and the buildings removed. One of these cabins has been moved along the road and now serves as a seasonal visitor center focusing on the importance of philanthropy, noting especially the Rockefeller family's donations that led to the establishment of Grand Teton National Park.

Recreation

HIKING

The precipitous Tetons that look so dramatic from the roads are even more impressive up close and personal. Grand Teton National Park is laced with 200 miles of trails, and hikers can choose anything from simple day treks to weeklong trips along the crest of the range. Unlike nearby Yellowstone, where most of the country is forested, the Tetons contain extensive alpine scenery. This means, however, that many of the high passes won't be free of snow until late July and may require ice axes before then. Check at the visitor centers or Jenny Lake Ranger Station for current trail conditions. In addition, this high country can be dangerous when frequent thunderstorms roll through in summer. Several people have been killed by lightning strikes in the Tetons. Most storms hit in the afternoon, so it's good to get an early start to avoid them if possible. Besides, trailhead parking spots fill early, especially on warm summer weekends.

Get the helpful *Grand Teton Day Hikes* pamphlet from park visitor centers or online at www.nps.gov/grte. For the guided version, get a schedule of free ranger walks and hikes (including special ones for kids) from visitor centers or in the park newspaper. These are offered daily throughout the summer.

JENNY LAKE AREA HIKES
◖ Inspiration Point and Hidden Falls

The fun trek to Inspiration Point is one of the most popular day hikes in Grand Teton National Park. The trail starts on the west side of Jenny Lake. It's 2.4 miles by foot from the Jenny Lake Ranger Station on the east side, or you can ride one of the summertime shuttle boats (307/734-9227, $7.50 adults round-trip, $5 ages 5–12, free for younger kids) that cross the lake every 20 minutes or so 8 A.M.–6 P.M. daily mid-May–September. In midsummer, the shuttle boat lines lengthen around 11 A.M., so get here early in the morning to avoid the crush and to better your odds at finding a parking spot. Boat tickets are not available in advance. Afternoon thunderstorms frequently build up over the Tetons, which is another good reason to start your hike early.

From the boat dock on the west side, the trail climbs 0.5 mile to picturesque Hidden Falls, and then continues steeply another 0.5 mile to Inspiration Point, which overlooks Jackson Hole from 400 feet above Jenny Lake. Avoid the crowds on the way down from Inspiration Point by following a second trail back to Jenny Lake. If you miss the last boat at 6 P.M., it's a 2.4-mile hike around the lake to the parking area.

Cascade Canyon

Many day-hikers continue at least part of the way up Cascade Canyon beyond Inspiration Point on this strenuous hike. The trail climbs gradually, gaining 640 feet in the next 3.6 miles, and provides a good chance to fish for trout or watch for moose and other animals along Cascade Creek. Those with strong legs can make a *very* long day hike all the way up to Lake Solitude (14 miles round-trip with shuttle boat) or even Hurricane Pass (19 miles round-trip with shuttle boat, and gaining almost 3,600 feet on the way up). If you're into hiking that far, it probably makes more sense to reserve a backcountry campsite and take things a bit more leisurely. (See *Backcountry Hiking* for details.)

Taggart and Bradley Lakes

A very popular day hike follows Taggart Lake Trail to the lake and then back via the Beaver Creek Trail, a distance of 4.4 miles round-trip. A side loop to Bradley Lake adds about two miles to this journey. These trails provide a fine way to explore the damlike glacial moraines that created the lakes. You can also continue beyond Bradley Lake on a trail that climbs to beautiful Amphitheater Lake, the primary access point for climbs up Grand Teton. (Climbers generally begin from Jenny Lake, however.)

Amphitheater Lake

Looking for a fast climb into the mountains? Amphitheater Lake is only five miles up the trail but is 3,000 feet higher, making this the quickest climb to the Teton treeline. Many folks day-hike the Amphitheater Lake Trail to savor the wonderful vistas across Jackson Hole along the way. Camping is available at Surprise Lake, 0.5-half mile below Amphithe-ater Lake, but you'll need a backcountry permit. The mountain behind this alpine cirque is 11,618-foot Disappointment Peak, directly in front of Grand Teton. It was named in 1925 by a group of climbers who mistakenly thought they were on the east face of the Grand. The trailhead is accessible off Teton Park Road just south of Jenny Lake.

COLTER BAY AREA HIKES
Colter Bay Trails

A spiderweb of mostly level trails heads south from the Hermitage Point Trailhead at the south end of Colter Bay Visitor Center parking lot, passing beaver ponds and willow patches where trumpeter swans, moose, and ducks are commonly seen. The longest destination is Hermitage Point (nine miles round-trip), on the tip of a peninsula jutting into Jackson Lake. Get a map of Colter Bay trails from park visitor centers to see the various options. Shorter loop paths include the two-mile Lakeshore Trail and the three-mile Swan Lake-Heron Pond Trail.

GRAND TETON

the Colter Bay Marina on Jackson Lake

MOOSE-WILSON ROAD AREA HIKES
Phelps Lake

Death Canyon Trailhead (three miles south of Moose off the Moose–Wilson Road) is a popular access point for backpackers heading into the wilderness, but shorter hikes are possible. It's 1.8 miles round-trip to Phelps Lake Overlook, where you get a view across this beautiful mountain lake 600 feet below. From Phelps Lake Overlook you can hike steeply down for a lakeside picnic on the sandy beach, and then back the same way.

Death Canyon Patrol Cabin

This challenging eight-mile round-trip hike covers some of the same country as the Phelps Lake hike, but it continues beyond Phelps Lake Overlook to Death Canyon Patrol Cabin at the junction of Death Canyon Trail and Static Peak Trail. Getting to the cabin requires climbing 420 feet to the overlook, losing 400 feet in elevation, and then climbing 1,000 feet higher. And you've got to go back the same way. The small log cabin was built by the Civilian Conservation Corps in the 1930s and is still used by trail maintenance crews. Continue 0.5-half mile beyond the cabin up Death Canyon Trail for a dramatic vista into Death Canyon.

BACKCOUNTRY HIKING

The most popular backcountry hiking area centers on the crest of the Tetons and the lakes that lie at its feet, most notably Jenny Lake. Teton Crest Trail stretches from Teton Pass north all the way to Cascade Canyon, with numerous connecting paths from both sides of the range. Three relatively short (two- to three-day) loop hikes are described below. For more complete descriptions of park trails, see *Jackson Hole Hikes* by Rebecca Woods (Jackson: White Willow Publishing) or *Teton Trails* by Katy Duffy and Darwin Wile (Grand Teton Natural History Association, www.grandteton-park.org). Get topographic maps at the Moose Visitor Center or Teton Mountaineering in Jackson. Best is the waterproof version produced by Trails Illustrated.

The backcountry trails of Grand Teton National Park are some of the most heavily used paths in Wyoming, and strict regulations are enforced. Backcountry-use permits are required of all overnight hikers, and you'll need to specify a particular camping zone or site for each night of your trip. Get permits and detailed backcountry brochures from the visitor centers in Moose or Colter Bay or the Jenny Lake Ranger Station. Get there early in the morning during summer for permits to popular trails. A limited number of backcountry permits can be reserved in advance January 1–May 15 by writing the Permits Office, Grand Teton National Park, P.O. Drawer 170, Moose, WY 83012. For faster service, send a fax to 307/739-3438. You'll need to pick the permit up in person and pay a $15 service fee for reservations. There's no charge for permits if you get them the day of your trip. Get more information on permits and reservations by calling 307/739-3309. Be sure to also request its *Backcountry Camping* publication (also available online at www.nps.gov/grte) with details on regulations, snow conditions, minimizing impacts, and bear safety issues. On the back is a trail map that shows camping zones and access.

Safety in the Backcountry

Grizzlies are primarily found in the northern end of Grand Teton National Park, but you still need to hang all food because black bears roam throughout the park, particularly in the forested areas along the lakes. Special boxes are provided for food storage at some backcountry campsites. Campfires are not allowed at higher elevations, so be sure to bring a cooking stove. Bikes are not permitted on trails anywhere in the park.

Backcountry hikers (and day-hikers for that matter) need to be aware of the dangers from summertime thunderstorms in the Tetons. A common weather pattern is for clear mornings to build to blustery thunderstorms in late afternoon, followed by gradual clearing as evening arrives. Lightning is a major threat in the park's exposed alpine country, and rain showers can be surprisingly heavy at times. Make sure all of your gear is wrapped in plastic (garbage

BACKCOUNTRY HIKING

Jackson Lake

Cirque Lake

Mt Moran ▲

Caribou-Targhee National Forest

Leigh Canyon

Leigh Lake

Trail

GRAND TARGHEE RESORT

Freds Mtn ▲

Lake Solitude

Paintbrush Divide

Paintbrush Canyon

Rockchuck Peak

To Jackson Lake Dam

Mt St John ▲

JENNY LAKE LODGE ●

☾ INSPIRATION POINT

☾ JENNY LAKE

TETON CANYON ⌂

To Alta and Driggs

Teton Range

Cascade Canyon Trail

☾ HIDDEN FALLS

JENNY LAKE

Table Mtn ▲

Mt Owen ▲

Grand Teton ▲

Teewinot Mtn ▲

LUPINE MEADOWS ■

Grand Teton National Park

Hurricane Pass

Middle Teton ▲

Ampitheater Lake

Jedediah Smith

Alaska Basin

Wilderness

DEVIL'S STAIRS

South Teton ▲

Bradley Lake

Alaska Basin Trail

Snowdrift Lake

Taggart Lake

CLIMBERS RANCH ■

To Moran

Darby Canyon

Teton Crest Trail

Static Peak Trail

Valley Trail

☾ CHAPEL OF THE TRANSFIGURATION

Jackson Hole

Death Canyon Trail

WHITE GRASS RANGER STATION

MENOR'S FERRY

Fox Creek

DEATH CANYON PATROL CABIN

MOOSE VISITOR CENTER

DORNAN'S

Teton Crest Trail

Fox Creek Pass

Phelps Lake

☾ MORMON ROW

Mt Hunt ▲

Canyon Trail

J Y RANCH ■

Open

Granite Canyon Trail

☾ BLACKTAIL BUTTE

GROS VENTRE ⌂

JACKSON HOLE MOUNTAIN RESORT

Snake River

Teton Village

Lake Creek

✈

National Elk Refuge

Rendezvous Mtn ▲

☾ MOOSE-WILSON RD

Teton National Forest

Gros Ventre River

26 89 191

COAL CREEK ⌂

Fish Creek

390

Teton Pass

To Jackson

0   2 mi
0   2 km

GRAND TETON

bags work well), and carry a rain poncho or other rainwear. Many hikers carry cell phones for emergencies, but coverage is spotty in the mountains. Unfortunately, the phones can also create a false sense of security for those who are not familiar with backcountry travel. Don't head unprepared into the mountains thinking you can always call for a rescue if you sprain your ankle.

Cascade Canyon to Paintbrush Canyon

One of the most popular hikes in Grand Teton National Park is this 19-mile loop trip up Cascade Canyon, over Paintbrush Divide, and down Paintbrush Canyon (or vice versa). The trip offers a little of everything: dense forests, alpine lakes, flower-covered meadows, and magnificent views of the Tetons. This trip is best done in late summer because a cornice of snow typically blocks Paintbrush Divide until the latter part of July. Most folks do it as an overnight trip, but it's possible to do the entire loop in a single very long day if you're in good shape and have a masochistic streak. Be sure to bring plenty of water along.

Begin at the String Lake Trailhead and head south around Jenny Lake, stopping to enjoy the views (and crowds) at Inspiration Point before heading up along Cascade Creek. The trail splits at the upper end of this canyon; turning left takes you to Hurricane Pass and the Teton Crest Trail, where you'll discover wonderful views of the back side of Grand Teton. Instead, turn right (north) and head up to beautiful Lake Solitude. Behind you, Teewinot, Mt. Owen, and Grand Teton are framed by the glacially carved valley walls. Above Lake Solitude, the trail climbs sharply to Paintbrush Divide and then switchbacks even more quickly down into Paintbrush Canyon. The trail eventually leads back to String Lake. Be sure to stop at beautiful Holly Lake on the way down.

Death Canyon Loop

Another fine loop trip departs from the Death Canyon Trailhead, approximately three miles south of park headquarters on the Moose–Wilson Road. Many hiking options are available here, with trails leading to Phelps Lake, up Open Canyon, or into Death Canyon. (The name came about when a survey party was in the area in 1899 and one of the men disappeared. He was never seen again.) Despite the name, Death Canyon provides a wonderful 26-mile loop hike that takes you over three high passes and into spectacular alpine country. From the trailhead, hike to Phelps Lake Overlook before dropping to a junction, where you turn right to hike up Death Canyon. Bear left at a patrol cabin built in the 1930s, and continue climbing all the way to Fox Creek Pass (9,520 feet). After this the going is fairly easy for the next three miles along Death Canyon Shelf to Mt. Meek Pass, where you drop into famous Alaska Basin (see *Caribou–Targhee National Forest* in the *Jackson Hole* chapter). Return to your starting point by climbing east from Alaska Basin over Static Peak Divide (10,800 feet) and then switchbacking downhill to the CCC cabin and the trailhead. This is a late-season trek because snow often blocks the passes until July; get snow conditions at the Jenny Lake Ranger Station.

MOUNTAIN CLIMBING

The Tetons are considered some of the premier mountaineering country in the nation, with solid rock, good access, and a wide range of climbing conditions. Hundreds of climbing routes have been described for the main peaks, but the goal of many climbers is Grand Teton, better known as "the Grand." At 13,772 feet, this is Wyoming's second-highest summit, exceeded only by 13,804-foot Gannett Peak in the Wind River Mountains.

Several thousand people climb the mountain each summer, many with no previous climbing experience (but with excellent guides and a couple of days of training). The record time is an unbelievable three hours, six minutes, and 25 seconds for Bryce Thatcher in 1983. This time includes starting—and returning—to the parking lot at the foot of the mountain! And just to prove that it could be done, in 1971 one fanatic actually skied the Grand (he's the ski-school director at Snow King Resort), followed in 1989 by a snowboarder. Both lived to tell the tale.

Most climbing takes place after the snow has melted back (mid-July) and before conditions again deteriorate (late September). Overnight mountain climbing or off-trail hiking requires a special permit available from the **Jenny Lake Ranger Station,** staffed daily June–mid-September. There's no need to register if you're climbing or doing off-trail hiking for the day only, just for overnight trips. (Still, it's a good idea to leave a detailed trip itinerary with a responsible person in case of an emergency.) Winter climbers should register at the Moose Visitor Center. The climbing rangers—one of the most prestigious and hazardous jobs in the park—are all highly experienced mountaineers and can provide specific route information for the various summits. Call 307/739-3604 for recorded climbing information, or talk to folks at the Jenny Lake Ranger Station, 307/739-3343, for weather conditions, route information, and permits.

Many climbers who scale Grand Teton follow the Amphitheater Lake Trail from Lupine Meadows to its junction with the Garnet Canyon Trail. This leads to the **Lower Saddle,** which separates Grand Teton and Middle Teton. Exum and the Park Service have base-camp huts and steel storage boxes here. No outhouses at Lower Saddle, and climbers are required to use high-tech carry-out bags for human waste—complete with a system that breaks down feces (www.whennaturecalls.com).

Other folks pitch tents behind boulders in the extraordinarily windy mountain gap at Lower Saddle. See Park Service handouts for camping restrictions and recommendations in this fragile alpine area, where heavy use by 4,000 climbers each year has caused considerable damage. The final assault on the summit of Grand Teton requires technical equipment and expertise. No motorized drills are allowed for placing climbing bolts.

Mountaineers who have registered to climb the Grand can stay at **Climbers' Ranch,** near Taggart Lake, for $10 per night. Lodging is in small log cabins with 4–8 bunks; hot showers and a cooking shelter are close by, but you'll need to bring your own sleeping bag and food. The ranch is open June–mid-September. Call 307/733-7271 after June 1 for reservation information, or visit the American Alpine Club's website (www.americanalpineclub.org) for details.

Climbing Schools

Jackson Hole is blessed with two of the finest climbing schools in North America: **Jackson Hole Mountain Guides** (165 N. Glenwood, 307/733-4979 or 800/239-7642, www.jhmg.com) and **Exum Mountain Guides** (307/733-2297, www.exumguides.com) with a summertime office at the south end of Jenny Lake near the boat dock. Both are authorized concessions of the National Park Service and the U.S. Forest Service and offer a wide range of classes, snow training, and climbs in the Tetons and elsewhere—even as far away as Alaska and the Himalayas. Exum has been around since 1931, when Glenn Exum pioneered the first solo climb of what has become the most popular route to the top of the Grand, the Exum Route. It's the only company permitted to guide all Teton peaks and routes throughout the year. Exum's base camp is in the busy Lower Saddle area, while Jackson Hole Mountain Guides' base camp is 450 feet lower in elevation in a more secluded location (it takes an extra hour of climbing on the day of your ascent). Exum has some of the most experienced guides in the world, but they take up to four clients in a group, while Jackson Hole limits its Grand Teton ascent parties to three clients.

During midsummer, you'll pay around $720–1,000 (depending on the number of people in the group) for an ascent of Grand Teton; this includes two days of basic and intermediate training followed by a two-day climb up the Grand and back. Food, gear, and shelter are also included. If you're planning to climb the Grand during the peak summer season, be sure to make reservations several months in advance to be assured of a spot. For July and August, make Grand Teton climbing reservations before the end of March.

Reservations generally are not needed for the companies' one-day basic ($120) and intermediate ($140) climbing schools. Also available are climbs of other faces, such as Baxter's Pinnacle, Symmetry Spire, and Cube Point, along with more advanced classes and climbs in the Wind River Mountains and up Devils Tower and other precipices throughout the western states. In addition, both companies offer many winter classes, such as avalanche safety and ski or snowboard mountaineering.

On Your Own

If you already have the experience and want to do your own climbing, the most accessible local spot is **Blacktail Butte,** just north of Moose near Ditch Creek. The parking lot here fills on warm summer afternoons as hang-dogging enthusiasts try their moves on the rock face. Get climbing supplies at **Moosely Seconds Mountaineering** (307/739-1801) in Moose, or in Jackson at **Teton Mountaineering** (170 N. Cache Dr., 307/733-3595 or 800/850-3595, www.tetonmtn.com). Both stores rent climbing shoes and other gear. **Teton Rock Gym** (1116 Maple Way, 307/733-0707) has challenging indoor climbing walls where you can practice your moves. It also rents climbing gear and has special kids' climbing classes in the summer.

For complete details on local climbing, see Reynold Jackson's *A Complete Guide to the Teton Range* (The Mountaineers Books, www.mountaineerbooks.org), *Rock Climbing Jackson Hole and Pinedale, Wyoming* by Wesley Gooch (www.climbingwyoming.com), or the smaller *Teton Classics,* by Richard Rossiter (Chockstone Press). Online, check out **Way Wired Mountaineer** (www.way-wired.com) for details on climbing and skiing in the Tetons.

ON THE WATER
Floating the River

Several rafting companies lead scenic half-day 10-mile float trips (around $45–50 adults, $30–35 kids) down the Snake River inside the park, generally putting in at Deadman's Bar and taking out in Moose. (See the *Jackson Hole* chapter for details on these very popular river floats.)

Boating

Canoeists will discover several excellent places to paddle within Grand Teton, particularly the Snake River Oxbow Bend, String Lake, and Leigh Lake. Canoes are available for rent both in the park at Colter Bay Marina and Signal Mountain Lodge, and in Jackson.

Boaters within Grand Teton will need to buy a permit; seven-day permits cost $10 for motorboats, $5 for nonmotorized craft. Motorboats are allowed only on Jackson Lake, Jenny Lake (10-horsepower max), and Phelps Lake. Sailboarding, water-skiing, jet skis, and sailing are permitted on Jackson Lake, but no personal watercraft are allowed anywhere in the park. See the park boating brochure for details.

Marinas

Jackson Lake has three marinas, all of which are generally open sometime in May–late September. **Signal Mountain Lodge Marina** (307/733-5470 or 307/543-2831, www.signalmountainlodge.com) rents a range of floating objects, including sea kayaks, canoes, motorboats, runabouts, pontoon boats, and deck cruisers. **Colter Bay Marina** (307/543-3100 or 800/628-9988, www.gtlc.com) is near a Park Service campground, cabins, and the Colter Bay Indian Arts Museum. It's an exceptionally busy place in the summer, with motorboat, rowboat, and canoe rentals, along with guides to take you to the hot fly-fishing spots. Scenic **Jackson Lake cruises** ($18 adults, $8.50 kids under 12) are also available from Colter Bay Marina, as are breakfast or evening cruise-and-dine trips ($30 for breakfast; $50 for dinner).

A short distance north of Colter Bay is **Leek's Marina** (307/543-2494, www.signalmountainlodge.com), a simple place with a couple of docks, a pizza restaurant, and gas pumps.

Fishing

Grand Teton National Park rivers and lakes contain cutthroat, lake, and brown trout, along with whitefish. Park anglers must have a valid Wyoming state fishing license, available for $11 for one day if you aren't a resident. Pick up a handout describing fishing regulations and seasons from park visitor centers. Fishing licenses and supplies are available at park marinas and stores. (For more on fishing in the park, see the *Jackson Hole* chapter.)

Kayaking

O.A.R.S. (209/736-4677 or 800/346-6277, www.oars.com) offers multiday sea kayaking trips around Jackson Lake—perfect for beginning kayakers and families. You don't need any paddling experience for these trips, which are supported by a motorized skiff. Overnight trips cost $226 adults or $182 youths; two-night kayak trips are $359 adults or $290 kids. O.A.R.S. also has combination trips that include kayaking on the lake and rafting down the Snake River. Its two-day combo trips cost $382 adults or $317 youths; four-day trips run $664 adults or $570 kids. It supplies kayaks, a guide, and dry bags, with tents and sleeping bags available for rent. Reserve well ahead for these popular trips.

Swimming

Swimming is allowed in all park lakes, but they can be quite cold. Jenny, String, and Leigh lakes all have delightful spots for swimming on the east side, including some sandy or gravelly beaches. The Snake River is dangerous and swimming isn't recommended. Jackson Lake Lodge has a large outdoor pool, but it's open only for guests at the lodge or nearby Colter Bay Village. In addition, the town of Jackson has a wonderful recreation center with pools, and the pond at Kelly Warm Spring is a fun spot to splash around.

BIRDING

The diversity of habitat types within Grand Teton National Park means that birdwatchers can find everything from trumpeter swans to calliope hummingbirds. The park produces a free *Bird-Finding Guide* with descriptions of birding hot spots. A couple of the best places are Willow Flats and Blacktail Ponds. A checklist of park birds is also available from visitor centers.

BICYCLING

The main roads through Grand Teton get heavy traffic, and the shoulder width varies (although it is wide from Moose to Jenny Lake). Pick up the park's bicycling pamphlet for details on cycling options. Bikes are not allowed on any trails within Grand Teton

GRAND TETON

© DON PITCHER

Bison are encountered frequently throughout Grand Teton.

National Park, but you *can* ride mountain bikes on several wonderful dirt roads, including Two Ocean Lake Road (three miles), Grassy Lake Road (52 miles from Flagg Ranch to Ashton, Idaho), and the River Road (15 delightfully remote miles in the heart of the park). In addition, the paved secondary roads in the Antelope Flats-Mormon Row-Kelly area see less traffic and provide the opportunity to see bison and spectacular mountain vistas. Shadow Mountain Road is an off-the-beaten-path dirt road that takes off from the Antelope Flats area and climbs through Forest Service land to splendid vistas.

The main park road is closed to cars and other motorized traffic until May, and during April it is plowed and open to cyclists, walkers, and in-line skaters. When the weather warms up, this is a wonderful traffic-free way to see the park.

TRAIL RIDES

Horseback and wagon rides, including popular breakfast and dinner rides, take place at **Jackson Lake Lodge Corral** and **Colter Bay Village Corral.** Trail rides start at $30 for 1.5 hours,

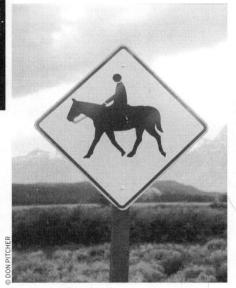

© DON PITCHER

horse crossing sign

with dinner wagon rides for $36. Get details on both of these activities from Grand Teton Lodge Company (307/543-3100 or 800/628-9988, www.gtlc.com). In the Rockefeller Parkway between Grand Teton and Yellowstone, **Flagg Ranch Resort** (307/543-2861 or 800/443-2311, www.flaggranch.com) offers hour-long horseback trail rides in the summer for $30.

WINTER RECREATION

The snow-covered landscape of Grand Teton National Park draws cross-country skiers, snowshoers, and snowmobilers throughout the winter.

Skiing

Cross-country skiing is popular on park roads and trails in the winter. The main thoroughfare—Teton Park Road—provides stellar views of the Teton Range and is regularly groomed for both parallel and skate skiing (with sections for hikers and snowshoers) from Taggart Lake to Signal Mountain, a distance of 14 miles. Park three miles northwest of Moose at the Taggart Lake Trailhead, where plowing ends. More adventurous skiers will enjoy side trails to Jenny Lake (eight miles round-trip) or the more challenging Taggart Lake-Beaver Creek loop (three miles with an elevation change of almost 400 feet). Another fun area is the Moose–Wilson Road, an easy four-mile round-trip ski from the Granite Canyon Trailhead (where plowing stops). A good optional side route is the trail to Phelps Lake overlook (five miles round-trip with an elevation change of 520 feet). Other enjoyable places to ski include Antelope Flats Road and trails at Taggart Lake, Flagg Ranch, and Colter Bay.

Most park ski routes (other than Teton Road) are not machine-groomed but are often well packed by other skiers. After a new snowfall you'll need to break trail as you follow the orange markers. Pick up a brochure describing ski trails from the Moose Visitor Center or find the information on the park website (www.nps.gov/grte). If you're planning to camp overnight in the park, you'll need to get a free permit from the visitor center.

Snowshoeing

Park naturalists lead two-hour snowshoe hikes late December–March and provide snowshoes at no charge. No experience is necessary. The hikes generally depart from the Moose Visitor Center at 2 P.M. several times a week. Reservations are required; no kids under age eight. Call 307/739-3399 for reservations and details on other winter activities in the park.

Snowmobiling

Snowmobiles are allowed on the **Continental Divide Snowmobile Trail,** which cuts through Grand Teton National Park and provides a link between the Wind River Mountains and Yellowstone National Park. Within Grand Teton the trail is generally open early January–mid-March and parallels U.S. 26/287 from the east park boundary to Moran Junction and then along U.S. 89 north to Yellowstone. Restrictions on snowmobile access within Yellowstone have greatly reduced the number of snowmobilers heading through Grand Teton National Park in the last few years. For the latest, pick up the snowmobiling handout at the Moose Visitor Center.

Winter Access

During winter, **Alltrans/Gray Line of Jackson Hole** (307/733-4325 or 800/443-6133, www.jacksonholealltrans.com) has daily bus runs between Jackson and Flagg Ranch Resort for $40 one-way or $60 round-trip, arriving in time to meet the snowcoach departures for Yellowstone. Reservations are required. Taxi companies in Jackson can also provide shuttles to Flagg Ranch in the winter, including **Buckboard Transportation** (307/733-1112 or 877/791-0211, www.buckboardtrans.com) and **All Star Taxi** (307/733-2888).

OUTDOOR GEAR

The little settlement of Moose has several businesses in addition to the Dornan's shops and eateries. **Adventure Sports** (307/733-3307, www.dornans.com) rents mountain bikes, canoes, and kayaks. Next door is **Moosely Seconds** (307/739-1801), with good deals on outdoor clothing and climbing gear; open May–September. It also rents ice axes, crampons, rock shoes, trekking poles, approach shoes, plastic boots, day packs, and snowshoes. **Snake River Angler** (307/733-3699, www.snakeriverangler.com) sells and rents fishing supplies and camping equipment.

GRAND TETON

Accommodations

Several places provide concessioner lodging inside Grand Teton National Park. As in all national parks, none of the lodge rooms contains TVs or radios. Reserve at least nine months ahead to be sure of getting a room in the peak summer season. Dozens of additional accommodations are south of the park in Jackson, and the pleasant **Hatchet Resort** (307/543-2413 or 877/543-2413, www.hatchetresort.com) has cozy and moderately priced rooms in the heart of Buffalo Valley.

JACKSON LAKE LODGE

Built on a grand scale, the 385-room Jackson Lake Lodge (307/543-3100 or 800/628-9988, www.gtlc.com) occupies a bluff above Willow Flats on the southeast side of Jackson Lake. Sixty-foot-high windows look across to the Tetons, and fireplaces flank the spacious central hall. Outside is a large swimming pool and kiddie pool (major attractions for families), and inside you'll find restaurants, a lounge, a gift shop, a newsstand, a clothing shop, and an ATM. All rooms contain two double beds and phones; some also have small fridges. Rooms in the lodge without a view (unless you count the parking lot) are $141 d, while those with big windows fronting the Tetons are $249 d. Cottages cost $173–181, or $239 d for ones with mountain vistas.

Luxury suites in the lodge are $425–575 d. Extra guests (beyond two) in any of these rooms are $10 per person. The lodge is open late May–early October.

JENNY LAKE LODGE

For four-star accommodations a stone's throw from the Tetons, stay at Jenny Lake Lodge (307/733-4647 or 800/628-9988, www.gtlc.com), where 37 comfortably appointed cabins surround a cozy Old West main lodge. This is a marvelous honeymoon or big-splurge place, and the $385 s or $475 d price includes horseback rides, bikes, breakfast, and a marvelous six-course dinner. (Note, however, that the meals are served only at specific times, so you'll need to adjust your schedule accordingly.) For the ultimate in extravagance, choose the lodge's luxurious suites; $635–680 d. Jenny Lake Lodge is open June–early October.

COLTER BAY VILLAGE

Family-oriented Colter Bay Village (307/543-3100, ext. 1080, or 800/628-9988, www.gtlc.com) has 166 rustic cabins of varying sizes and types, some of which sleep six people. There are no phones or cooking facilities in any of these cabins. The most basic are canvas-and-log structures with outdoor grills and picnic tables, indoor woodstoves, and bring-your-own-linen bunk beds. Restrooms are nearby, and the showers are coin-operated. These tent cabins cost just $37 d ($5 for each additional person up to six). Sleeping bags and other camping supplies are available for rent. The tent cabins are open early June–early September.

Slightly nicer are little one-room cabins that share a bath for $38 d. Cabins with a private bath start at $75 d for those with a double bed, up to $112 d for those with two double beds and a twin bed. Two-room cabins with a bath are $118 d or $140 for up to four. Additional guests are $9 each in all of these, and the cabins are open late May–late September. Guests at Colter Bay Village can use the big swimming pool at nearby Jackson Lake Lodge.

DORNAN'S

Near park headquarters in Moose, Dornan's Spur Ranch Cabins (307/733-2522, www.dornans.com) has a dozen modern log cabins filled with handcrafted lodgepole pine furniture. One-bedroom cabins are $155 d or $185 for up to four people, and two-bedroom cabins cost $230 for up to six people. There's a three-night minimum stay in the summer. All cabins include full kitchens and are open year-round.

SIGNAL MOUNTAIN LODGE

On the south shore of Jackson Lake, Signal Mountain Lodge (307/733-5470 or 800/672-6012, www.signalmountainlodge.com) offers a variety of lodging options. Simple and rustic log cabins start at $99 d, up to $148 for a two-room unit that sleeps six. Motel-style rooms with fridges and microwaves are $132 for up to four people or $179 for a nicer room with a fireplace and king bed. The lodge's finest options include lakefront suites for $199–210, cozy bungalows with kitchens and private decks for $140 d, and a three-room cabin with fireplace in the living room, full kitchen, and laundry for $255. Signal Mountain Lodge is open early May–mid-October.

FLAGG RANCH RESORT

On Rockefeller Parkway just three miles south of Yellowstone, Flagg Ranch Resort (307/543-2861 or 800/443-2311, www.flaggranch.com) has modern four-plex log cabins with patios and two queen beds or a king bed. Rates are $150–160 d, plus $10 for additional adults. The main lodge houses a convenience store, restaurant, deli, gift shop, and central area with couches and a large fireplace. Flagg Ranch is open mid-May–mid-October and mid-December–mid-March, but lodging is available only in summer.

CAMPING

Grand Teton National Park has five campgrounds, with sites in all of these costing $15 ($7.50 for Golden Age/Golden Access cardholders). These are available on a first-come, first-served basis with no reservations, and by midafternoon in the peak summer season all park campgrounds may well be full. The maximum stay is seven days at Jenny Lake or 14 days at other campgrounds. Camping (or overnight parking) is not allowed along roadsides, overlooks, or parking areas within the park. Off-the-road camping is restricted to specific sites and requires a special permit (see *Backcountry Hiking* for specifics).

The largest park campground—and last to fill—is Gros Ventre Campground near the town of Kelly. The most scenic location—and quickest to fill—is Jenny Lake Campground. Showers and a launderette are available at Colter Bay Village. Several special hiker/biker sites are at Jenny Lake and Colter Bay for $5. Group sites can be found at Colter Bay and Gros Ventre campgrounds, but reservations are required. All Grand Teton National Park campgrounds are closed in winter, but limited tent camping and RV parking ($5, restrooms and water but no hookups) are available near the Colter Bay Visitor Center. (For details on Park Service and nearby Forest Service campgrounds, see the sidebar, *Jackson Hole Public Campgrounds,* in the *Jackson Hole* chapter.)

Grand Teton rangers lead popular evening campfire programs at all five campgrounds throughout the summer. All campgrounds have running water but no utility hookups. Get park campground information at 307/739-3603, or on the web at www.nps.gov/grte.

Camping Options

In addition to the five NPS campgrounds, park concessioners maintain two seasonal RV parks with full hookups, showers, washers, and driers. **Flagg Ranch Resort** (307/543-2861 or 800/443-2311, www.flaggranch.com) in Rockefeller Parkway has 100 pull-through RV sites with full hookups for $45, and 75 tent sites for $20. The resort is open late May–September, and reservations are highly recommended.

On the south shore of Jackson Lake, **Colter Bay RV Park** (307/543-3100 or 800/628-9988, www.gtlc.com, $42 RVs) is open late May–mid-September. No tent spaces are available here, but evening nature programs are offered in the summer.

Not far from the park is **Grand Teton Park RV Resort** (307/733-1980 or 800/563-6469, www.yellowstonerv.com), six miles east of Moran Junction along Hwy. 26/287. Facilities include a heated seasonal pool and hot tub, recreation room, and grocery store; $48 for RV hookups, $35 for tents. Simple camping cabins go for $60 d. Open year-round. Showers for those not camping here are $5.

The Forest Service has quite a few campgrounds in the surrounding country, and several private RV parks are available in Jackson.

Food

RESTAURANTS AND BARS

Several dining options exist at **Jackson Lake Lodge** (including the Mural Room with its 60-foot windows fronting the Tetons. The restaurant serves three meals a day, while the nearby Blue Heron Lounge offers equally impressive views and musicians provide accompaniment for your cocktails most evenings. Dinner reservations are required in summer; call 307/543-2811, ext. 1911. Casual meals are available at Pioneer Grill, also inside Jackson Lake Lodge, or the very popular Pool Snack Bar, next to the big outdoor swimming pool. The latter has an all-you-can-eat dinner buffet ($25 adults, $12 kids) with steaks, barbecue chicken and ribs, and other Western grub daily during July and August.

Marvelous old **◖ Jenny Lake Lodge** (307/543-3300, www.gtlc.com) has impeccable service, windows that face the mountains, and a cozy setting. Five-course dinners are the featured attractions, and the wine list is extensive. Lunch is à la carte, but breakfast and dinner are fixed price (and pricey: $60 for dinner,

$19 for breakfast). Jenny Lake Lodge is open early June–early October, and reservations are required. This is a dress-up place, so a jacket is recommended for dinner.

Colter Bay Village has two dining choices: the Chuckwagon for steaks and pasta and the John Colter Cafe Court for chicken, pizza, deli sandwiches, salads, and snacks.

An old favorite with an egalitarian setting—look for the tepees—is **Dornan's Chuck Wagon Restaurant** (307/733-2415, www.dornans.com), offering reasonable meals every summer since 1948. The all-you-can-eat breakfasts ($6–9) include pancakes, ham, bacon, biscuits, and eggs. Sandwiches are the main lunch attraction, and dinners ($14–22) include grilled-to-order barbecue ribs, chicken, steaks, salmon, or trout, plus a big outdoor salad bar. The Chuck Wagon is open mid-June–mid-September.

Across the street—and open all year—is Dornan's ◖ **Spur Bar/Moose Pizza and Pasta Co.** (307/733-2415), offering a wide range of superb homemade pizzas ($10–13), sandwiches, calzones, and pastas. Dining is available on two outside decks with can't-beat-the-view Teton vistas, and folk musicians perform once or twice a month. During the off-season (Oct.–May) the bar puts on monthly wine tastings ($5) on the first Sunday of the month, along with occasional wine-paired dinners. Check out the club on the wall. In 1944, local resident Farney Cole used it to defend himself from a bear attack. He survived, as did the bear.

Signal Mountain Lodge (307/733-5470 or 307/543-2831, www.signalmountainlodge.com) houses Trapper Grill, with casual fare and a popular deck for al fresco dining, and Peaks Restaurant, with an upscale menu and spectacular vistas of the Tetons. Deadman's Bar at Signal Mountain is famous for blackberry margaritas and also serves a pub menu.

Leek's Marina (307/543-2494, www.signalmountainlodge.com) is home to a very popular pizzeria that also serves calzones, sandwiches, salads, and beer on tap. Musicians drop by every other Wednesday evening for an open mike session. Open summers only.

The main lodge at **Flagg Ranch Resort** (307/543-2861 or 800/443-2311, www.flaggranch.com) houses Bear's Den Restaurant, serving three meals a day. Also here are a deli, saloon, and grocery store.

GROCERIES AND SUPPLIES

The best in-the-park store is **Dornan's Trading Post** (307/733-2415, www.dornans.com), near park headquarters in Moose. The store is open all year and stocked with groceries, tasty deli sandwiches, fresh baked goods, and camping supplies. The cart out front has espresso, and next door is **Dornan's Wine Shoppe,** with the biggest selection of fine wine and beer in Jackson Hole, including more than 1,700 different wines. Other nearby Dornan's operations include Moose Pizza and Pasta Co. and the Chuck Wagon, and a gift shop. In winter, the gift shop rents cross-country skis, snowshoes, and pull-behind sleds. It also has computers for Internet access.

Colter Bay General Store (307/543-3100) has a good choice of groceries and supplies, and convenience stores operate at Signal Mountain, Flagg Ranch Resort, and Jenny Lake. The store at Flagg Ranch Resort is open in both summer and winter seasons (mid-May–mid-Oct. and mid-Dec.–mid-Mar.). All of the others are open only for summer.

Information and Services

Support Organizations

The **Grand Teton Natural History Association** (307/739-3403, www.grandtetonpark.org) operates bookstores in park visitor centers and the store at Menor's Ferry. It also has a mail-order service for Grand Teton books.

The nonprofit **Grand Teton National Park Foundation** (307/739-0629, www.gtnpf.org) provides support for park projects that would not otherwise be funded, and all contributions are tax-deductible. Its big project is helping fund the new visitor center at Moose.

Medical

Get emergency medical assistance at the **Grand Teton Medical Clinic** (307/543-2514) near the Chevron station at Jackson Lake Lodge. It's open 10 A.M.–6 P.M. daily late May–early October. The nearest hospital is St. John's Medical Center in Jackson.

Other Practicalities

Gas is available year-round at Dornan's in Moose, summer and winter at Flagg Ranch Resort, and summers only at Colter Bay Village, Signal Mountain Lodge, and Jackson Lake Lodge. You'll find gift shops at Signal Mountain, Flagg Ranch Resort, Jackson Lake Lodge, Moose, and Colter Bay. Year-round post offices are in Moran, Moose, and Kelly. Get cash from ATMs at Dornan's in Moose, Jackson Lake Lodge, Colter Bay Village, Flagg Ranch Resort, and Signal Mountain Lodge.

GRAND TETON

YELLOWSTONE NATIONAL PARK

Please see front color map Yellowstone National Park

The words "national park" seem to stimulate an almost Pavlovian response: Yellowstone. The geysers, canyons, and bears of Yellowstone National Park are so intertwined in our collective consciousness that even 1960s American cartoons used the park as a model: Jellystone Park, where Yogi Bear and Boo Boo were constantly out to thwart the rangers. One source estimated that nearly one-third of the U.S. population has visited the park, and each year three million people roll through its gates.

Yellowstone has always been a place of wonder. There is considerable evidence that the Indians who first lived in this area viewed it as a place of great spiritual power and treated it with reverence. Yellowstone was later to become the birthplace for the national-park movement, and Americans today still love the park, although they don't always treat it with reverence.

There is something about Yellowstone National Park that calls people back again and again, something more than simply the chance to see the curiosities of the natural world. Generations of parents have brought their children to see the place that they recall from their own childhood visits. Other cultures have the Ganges River, Rome, or Mecca as places with deep spiritual meaning. In America, our national parks have become places for similar renewal, and as the nation's first national park, Yellowstone remains one of our most valued treasures.

HIGHLIGHTS

◖ Norris Geyser Basin: Yellowstone's hottest and oldest geyser basin is home to the world's tallest geyser (but don't wait for an eruption, or you may be here for years). Echinus Geyer is the real crowd-pleaser (page 447).

◖ Mammoth Hot Springs: Ever-changing, with water trickling over multihued terraces, Mammoth is a moving watercolor painting. Albright Visitor Center houses an interesting museum (page 450).

◖ The Northeast Corner: Peaceful and away from the big Yellowstone sights, this is not only a good place to see bison and elk, but wolves as well (page 454).

◖ Tower Fall: Hike down the steep 0.5-mile path to get soaked by this tall, narrow, and very accessible waterfall (page 455).

◖ Grand Canyon of the Yellowstone: No adjectives can really describe the power and beauty of this painted canyon where the Yellowstone River drops over two high waterfalls. Lots of viewpoints from all angles, but acrophobics should avoid the Brink of the Lower Falls (page 456).

◖ Mud Volcano Area: Think of this as a bad case of geological heartburn. The names tell all: Dragon's Mouth Spring, Churning Caldron, and Sulphur Caldron (page 459).

◖ Yellowstone Lake: America's largest high-elevation lake, it occupies an ancient volcanic caldera. Boat tours and fishing are popular, or just relax with a drink inside historic Lake Yellowstone Hotel's Sunset Room (page 459).

◖ Old Faithful Geyser: This is the big enchilada. The eruptions are more-or-less predictable, always crowded, and always fun. But don't miss the many other sights in the area, particularly Riverside Geyser and Morning Glory Pool (page 465).

◖ Old Faithful Inn: This massive log structure is Yellowstone's most majestic lodge and a delightful place to soak up the ambience. Don't miss it (page 467).

◖ Midway Geyser Basin: The featured attractions are spectacular Great Fountain Geyser and brilliantly colored Grand Prismatic Spring (page 468).

LOOK FOR ◖ TO FIND RECOMMENDED SIGHTS, ACTIVITIES, DINING, AND LODGING.

YELLOWSTONE

So, into the park we come in our cars with our crying babies in the back—babies who suddenly quiet down at the sight of a bison or elk. I recall bringing relatives to Yellowstone after I had worked in the vicinity all summer and had become a bit jaded. Their emotional reaction surprised me, and more than a decade later they still tell stories of the bison calves, the astounding geysers, the rush of the waterfalls, and the night they spent at Old Faithful Inn. Yellowstone is a collective religious experience that sends us back to our roots in the natural world. The smell of wood smoke from a campfire, the picnic lunch on the shore of Yellowstone Lake, the backcountry horseback ride, the hike down to the lip of Lower Falls, the quick strike of a trout on the line, the gasp of the crowd as the first spurt of Old Faithful jets upward, the herds of bison wading Firehole River, the evening piano tunes drifting through the air at Lake Yellowstone Hotel, the howl of a distant wolf, and even the cheesy Yellowstone trinkets—all of these things combine to leave an indelible mark on visitors to Yellowstone National Park.

PLANNING YOUR TIME

America's first and most famous national park, Yellowstone is the primary regional destination. Travelers often take a cursory tour of the park in a single day, but try to set aside a minimum of three days to discover this diverse and geologically fascinating place. If you have only a day or two, pick a couple of spots and see them right. Don't just check out the views everyone else sees; find a nearby trail and do a little exploring on your own. It would be easy to spend a full week in Yellowstone, plus another week in nearby Grand Teton National Park and Jackson Hole. Before visiting, contact Yellowstone (307/344-7381, www.nps.gov/yell) for a copy of the park newspaper and other information. For more comprehensive coverage of Yellowstone and other sights in the region, see Don Pitcher's *Moon Yellowstone and Grand Teton* (www.moon.com).

Near the center of the park, **Norris Geyser Basin** is home to Steamboat Geyser, which blasts 300 feet into the air on its extremely rare eruptions, along with playful Echinus Geyser and others that are more predictable. **Mammoth Hot Springs** is famous for its ever-changing palette of softly colored springs, and it also contains park headquarters and an interesting small museum. Bucolic Lamar Valley in the **northeast corner** of Yellowstone is a good place to see bison, elk, and wolves, and nearby **Tower Fall** provides a great photo-op.

Grand Canyon of the Yellowstone may be the park's most spectacular feature, with the river plummeting 308 feet over Lower Falls. South of here is Hayden Valley (look for bison, elk, and occasional bears), along with the belching geysers and hot springs of **Mud Volcano** and **Yellowstone Lake**—largest high-elevation lake in North America. On its north shore is picturesque and graceful Lake Yellowstone Hotel.

Yellowstone's best-known site is **Old Faithful Geyser,** with its predictable eruptions that delight crowds every hour and a half or so. Step inside the equally acclaimed **Old Faithful Inn**—a delightful century-old log structure—for meals and lodging, or just to soak up the ambience. Old Faithful is the most famous of dozens of geysers, hot springs, and other geothermal features that fill Upper Geyser Basin, the largest concentration of geysers in the world. Five miles north of Old Faithful, take time to visit **Midway Geyser Basin** with its massive **Grand Prismatic Spring,** the park's largest hot spring.

THE SETTING

On a map, Yellowstone appears as a gigantic box wedged so tightly against the northwest corner of Wyoming that it squeezes over into Montana and Idaho. The park measures 63 by 54 miles and covers 2.2 million acres, making it one of the largest national parks in the Lower 48 (although it is dwarfed by Alaska's Wrangell–St. Elias National Park and Preserve, which covers almost six times as much land). The United Nations has declared Yellowstone both a World Biosphere Reserve and a World Heritage Site.

The park is accessible from all four sides, and a loop road provides easy access to all of the best-known sights. Because of its popularity as a destination, tourist towns surround Yellowstone: Jackson to the south, Cody to the east, Gardiner and Cooke City on the northern margin, and West Yellowstone on its western border. Also because so many people visit the park, there is a well-developed network of facilities inside the park, including visitor centers, campgrounds, hotels, restaurants, a hospital, gift shops, ATMs, one-hour photo shops, espresso stands, and other supposed necessities of modern life. Although less than 2 percent of the park is developed, Yellowstone contains more than 2,000 buildings of various types. In some spots (most egregiously around Old Faithful), these developments have grown to the point that the natural world seems simply a backdrop for the human world that pulls visitors in to buy T-shirts or to watch park slide shows on wildlife or geysers while missing the real thing just outside the door.

More than any other national park, Yellowstone seems to provide the oddities of nature, creating, as historian Aubrey L. Haines noted,

YELLOWSTONE

"a false impression that the park is only a colossal, steam-operated freak show." Yellowstone is a mix of the real and the unreal, a place where our fantasies of what nature should be blend with the reality of crowds of fellow travelers and the impact we have on the place we love so much. In midsummer, a trip into Yellowstone can be something less than a natural experience. Long lines of cars back up behind RVs creeping up the narrow roads, and throngs of visitors crowd the benches around Old Faithful Geyser waiting for an eruption, while dozens of others cluster around bewildered elk to get photos to email their friends. Despite this crowding—or perhaps because most folks prefer to stay on paved paths—many parts of the park remain virtually uninhabited. In the Yellowstone backcountry, one can still walk for days without seeing more than a handful of other hardy hikers.

A PLACE OF CONTROVERSY

Yellowstone National Park evokes a torrent of emotions in anyone with a knowledge of and concern for the natural world. Perhaps more than any other wild place in America, the park seems to be in a perpetual state of controversy, be it over fire policies, bison and wolf management, snowmobile use, or some other issue; there's always something getting folks stirred up. Perhaps it is because so many Americans have visited the park that we feel a vested interest in what it means to us. Writer Paul Schullery in his wonderful book *Searching for Yellowstone* put it best when he noted, "Caring for Yellowstone National Park brings to mind all the metaphors of growth and change; it is a process more organic than political; a crucible of ideas, ambitions, dreams, and belief systems; a cultural, intellectual, and spiritual crossroads at which we are forever debating which way to turn." As visitation has risen in recent decades, more and more folks have begun to suggest some sort of limits on numbers to preserve the experience and protect the park. Don't-tread-on-me Westerners consider the idea of limits an example of environmental extremism for the elite, but as visitation increases, conflicts and controversies are a natural outcome.

GEOLOGY

Yellowstone is, without a doubt, the most geologically fascinating place on this planet. Here the forces that elsewhere lie deep within the earth seem close enough to touch. They're palpable not only in the geysers and hot springs but also in the lake that fills part of an enormous caldera, the earthquakes that shake this land, the evidence of massive glaciations, and the deeply eroded Grand Canyon of the Yellowstone.

The Yellowstone Hot Spot

When geologists began to study the Yellowstone area in depth, they found a surprising pattern. Extending far to the southwest was a chain of volcanic fields, the most ancient of which—16 million years old—lay in northern Nevada. In addition, geologic fault lines created a 100-mile-wide semicircle around the Yellowstone area, as if some deep-seated force were pushing the land outward and upward the way a ripple moves across a pond.

Both the volcanic activity and the wavelike pattern of faults are caused by the same source: a plume of superheated material moving up from the core of the planet through a narrow tube, creating a hot spot beneath the earth's crust. As the North American continent slid to the southwest through the eons, this plume traced a line of volcanoes across the West, and as the land continues to move, the plume causes massive deformations in the crust that show up as mountain ranges, fault lines, and earthquakes. It's a little like somebody tugging a piece of cloth across a candle. Approximately 40 such hot spots are known to exist around the globe, but most are beneath the seas. Other than Yellowstone, the best-known example is the chain of Hawaiian Islands. The earth has been moving over the Yellowstone hot spot at the rate of 15 miles per million years for the last 10 million years, and on the present track, the spot might eventually end up in Hudson Bay in 100 million years or so. Don't hold your breath.

Tambora on Steroids

The volcanic activity revealed by Yellowstone's geysers, hot springs, and fumaroles is not always benign. Within the last two million years there have been three stupendous volcanic eruptions in the area, the most recent taking place 640,000 years ago. The largest of these eruptions took place two million years ago and created an event beyond the realm of imagination: 600 cubic miles of ash were blasted into the atmosphere! This eruption—probably one of the largest to ever occur on Earth—ejected 17 times more material than the massive Tambora eruption of 1815, an explosion that was heard 1,600 miles away. Compared to an explosion that is better known to Americans, the 1980 eruption of Mt. St. Helens, the first Yellowstone event was 2,400 times as large. Ash from this first Yellowstone eruption carried east to Iowa, north to Saskatchewan, south to the Gulf of Mexico, and west to California. This titanic infusion of ash into the atmosphere undoubtedly affected the global climate for years to follow.

The process that creates these explosions starts when molten rock pushes up from the center of the earth, bulging the land upward into an enormous dome. Eventually the pressure becomes too great and fractures develop around the dome's margins, sending hot gases, ash, and rock blasting into the atmosphere. After the most recent eruption (640,000 years ago), the magma chamber collapsed into a gigantic, smoldering pit reaching 28 by 47 miles in surface area and perhaps several thousand feet deep. Through time, additional molten rock pushed up from underneath and flowed as thick lava over the land. The most recent of these lava flows was 70,000 years ago.

Two resurgent domes—one near Old Faithful and the other just north of Yellowstone Lake near LeHardys Rapids—have been discovered by geologists. Measurements at LeHardys Rapids showed that the land rose almost three feet from 1923 to 1985, although it has since been subsiding. This upsurge raised the outlet of Yellowstone Lake, creating new beaches on the north shore while flooding forests along the lake's southern margins. Obviously, Yellowstone's volcanism is far from dead, and scientists believe another eruption

is possible or even likely, although nobody knows when it might occur.

The **Yellowstone Volcano Observatory** (http://volcanoes.usgs.gov/yvo)—a partnership of the USGS, Park Service, and University of Utah—monitors Yellowstone's ever-changing volcanic system and produces an excellent small publication about the park's geologic origins; find it in visitor centers.

Glaciation

Not everything in Yellowstone is the result of volcanic activity. The entire Yellowstone region has undergone a series of at least eight major glaciations during the last million years, the last of which—the Pinedale Glaciation—began about 70,000 years ago. At its peak, the Pinedale Glaciation covered almost all of Yellowstone and reached southward into Jackson Hole and north much of the way to Livingston, Montana. Over Yellowstone Lake the icefield was 4,000 feet thick and covered 10,000-foot mountains. This period of glaciation ended about 15,000 years ago, but trees did not appear in the Yellowstone area until 11,500 years ago, and it wasn't until about 5,000 years ago that the landscape began to appear as it does today.

Geysers

Yellowstone is famous for geysers, and geyser-gazers will not be disappointed. At least 60 percent of the world's geysers are in the park, making this easily the largest and most diverse collection in existence. Yellowstone's more than 300 geysers are spread through nine different basins, with half of these in Upper Geyser Basin, the home of Old Faithful.

Geysers need three essentials to exist: water, heat, and fractured rock. The water comes from snow and rain falling on this high plateau, while the heat comes from molten rock close to the earth's surface. Massive pressures from below have created a ring of fractures around the edge of Yellowstone's caldera. This is one of the hottest places on the planet, with heat flows more than 60 times the global average.

Geysers operate because cold water is dense and sinks, while hot water is less dense and

CONSTRICTION

BOILING

CONSTRICTION

BOILING

CONSTRICTION

BOILING

SUPERHEATED WATER AND STEAM

BOB RACE

YELLOWSTONE

rises. The periodic eruption of geysers is caused by constrictions in the underground channels that prevent an adequate heat exchange with the surface. Precipitation slowly moves into the earth, eventually contacting the molten rock. Because of high pressures at these depths, water can reach extreme temperatures without vaporizing (as in a pressure cooker). As this superheated water rises back toward the surface, it emerges in hot springs, fumaroles, mud pots, and geysers. The most spectacular of these phenomena are geysers. Two general types of geysers exist in Yellowstone. Fountain geysers (such as Great Fountain Geyser) explode from pools of water and tend to spray water more widely, whereas cone-type geysers (such as Old Faithful) jet out of nozzlelike formations.

In a geyser, steam bubbles upward from the superheated source of water and expands as it rises. These bubbles block the plumbing system, keeping hot water from reaching the surface. Eventually, however, pressure from the bubbles begins to force the cooler water above out of the vent. This initial release triggers a more vio-

lent reaction as the sudden lessening of pressure allows the entire column to begin boiling, explosively expelling steam and water to produce a geyser. Once the eruption has emptied the plumbing system, water gradually seeps back into the chambers to begin the process anew. Some of Yellowstone's geysers have enormous underground caverns that fill with water; in its rare eruptions, massive Steamboat Geyser can blast a million gallons of water into the air!

As an aside, the term "geyser" is one of the few Icelandic terms in the English language; it means to "gush forth." There are probably 30 active geysers in Iceland, many more on Russia's Kamchatka Peninsula, and a few in New Zealand, where geothermal development has greatly lessened geyser activity. A fine online source with details about Yellowstone's geysers—and others around the globe—is maintained by the nonprofit **Geyser Observation and Study Association** (www.geyserstudy.org).

Unfortunately, some of Yellowstone's geysers have been lost because of human stupidity or vandalism. At one time, it was considered great sport to stuff logs, rocks, and even chairs into the geysers for a little added show. Others poured chemicals into them to make them play. As a result of such actions, some geysers have been severely damaged or destroyed, and some hot springs have become collection points for coins, rocks, sticks, and trash. It shouldn't be necessary to point out that such actions ruin these thermal areas for everyone and destroy something that may have been going on for hundreds of years.

Other Geothermal Activity

Although geysers are Yellowstone's best-known features, they make up only a tiny fraction of perhaps 10,000 thermal features in the park. **Hot springs** appear where water can reach the ground surface relatively easily, allowing the heat that builds up in the chambers of geysers to dissipate. When less groundwater is present, you may find **fumaroles,** vents that shoot steam, carbon dioxide, and even hydrogen sulfide gas. **Mud pots** (also called paint pots) are essentially wet fumaroles. Hydrogen sulfide gas combines with water to produce hydrosulfuric acid. This acid breaks down surrounding rocks to form clay, and the clay combines with water to create mud. As gas passes through the mud, it creates the bubbling mud pots. Probably the best examples of these different forms are at Fountain Paint Pot in Lower Geyser Basin, where geysers and hot springs are found in the wetter areas below, while mud pots and fumaroles sit atop a small hill. Hydrogen sulfide is, of course, poisonous, and toxic fumes sometimes kill bison and elk who cluster around the geothermal areas in the winter. Scientists joke that Norris Geyser Basin would be considered an EPA Superfund site if it weren't within a national park!

The colors in Yellowstone's hot springs come from a variety of sources, including algae and bacteria as well as various minerals, particularly sulfur, iron oxides, and arsenic sulfide. The algae and bacteria are highly temperature-specific and help create the distinct bands of colors around many hot springs. Interestingly, many of these algal species are found only in hot springs, although they exist around the world. The bacteria have proven of considerable interest to science because of their ability to survive such high temperatures. One such organism, *Thermus aquaticus,* was discovered in a Yellowstone hot springs in 1967, and scientists extracted an enzyme that was later used to develop the increasingly important technique of DNA fingerprinting. Above 190°F, even these hot-water bacteria and algae cannot survive, so the hottest springs may appear a deep blue because of the water's ability to absorb all wavelengths of light except blue, which is reflected back into our eyes.

More Terminology

A couple of other terms are worth learning before heading out to see the sights of Yellowstone. **Sinter** (also called "geyserite") is a deposit composed primarily of silica. The silica is dissolved by hot water deep underground and brought to the surface in geysers or hot springs. At the surface the water evaporates, leaving behind the light gray sinter, which

can create large mounds (up to 30 feet high) around the older geysers. The rate of accumulation is very slow, and some of the park's geysers have obviously been active for many thousands of years. The other precipitate that is sometimes deposited around Yellowstone's hot springs and geysers is **travertine,** consisting of calcium carbonate that has been dissolved underground. (See *Mammoth Hot Springs* for more on this process.)

A Note of Warning

The surface around many of the hot springs and geysers is surprisingly thin, and people have been killed or seriously injured by falling through into the boiling water. Stay on the boardwalks in developed areas, and use extreme caution around backcountry thermal features. If in doubt, stay away!

FLORA AND FAUNA

One of the largest intact temperate-zone ecosystems on the planet, Yellowstone was for decades viewed as an island of nature surrounded by a world of human development. Unfortunately, this attitude has led to a host of problems. Despite its size, Yellowstone alone is not large enough to support a viable population of all the animals that once existed within its borders, and developments outside the park pose threats within. In recent years, there have been increasing calls to treat the park as part of the larger Greater Yellowstone Ecosystem—18 million acres of land at the juncture of Wyoming, Montana, and Idaho covering both public and private lands. With each year that passes it has become more obvious that Yellowstone can never be simply an island. Most of the issues that have made headlines in the last decade or so—from fisheries problems to snowmobile use—have been ones that spread beyond the artificial park boundaries.

Within surrounding lands, conflicts between development and preservation are even more obvious than within the park itself. Logging is one of the most apparent of these, and along the park's western border aerial photos reveal a perfectly straight line, with lodgepole pines on the park side and old clear-cuts on the Forest Service side. One of these was the largest timber sale ever made outside of Alaska! Near the park boundaries, housing developments, the massive growth of the tourism industry, oil and gas drilling, mining, a grizzly bear and wolf theme park, and other activities all create potential problems within the park and for the Yellowstone ecosystem as a whole.

Plants

Yellowstone National Park is primarily a series of high plateaus ranging 7,500–8,500 feet in elevation. Surrounding this gently rolling expanse are the Absaroka Mountains along the east and north sides and the Gallatin Range in the northwestern corner. Elevations are lowest along the northern end of the park, where the Yellowstone River and other rivers cut through, and highest on the eastern and northwestern margins. The plants that carpet Yellowstone are predominantly determined by the amount of precipitation and the type of soils in which they grow: Areas underlain by Absaroka volcanic bedrock have more nutrient-rich soils than areas with Yellowstone rhyolites. Vegetation types within the park include sagebrush-steppe, lodgepole pine forests, spruce-fir forests, and subalpine areas.

Wildlife

Yellowstone provides a marvelous natural setting in which to view bison, elk, moose, wolves, coyotes, pronghorn antelope, bighorn sheep, and other wild animals. One of the easiest ways to find wildlife is simply by watching for the brake lights, the cars pulled half off the road, and the cameras all pointed in one direction. Inevitably, you'll find an elk or a bison placidly munching away, trying to remain oblivious to the chaos that surrounds it. Be sure to bring binoculars for your trip to Yellowstone. A spotting scope is also helpful in searching for distant bears and wolves.

The park contains about 60 species of resident mammals, varying from shrews and bats to bison and grizzlies. In addition, 309 species of birds have been recorded, along with 18 species

© DON PITCHER

Visitors should stay 25 yards from bison and elk.

of fish (five of which are nonnative), four amphibians, and six reptiles. The only poisonous animal is the prairie rattlesnake, found at low elevations in the northern end of Yellowstone. Oh yes, countless insect species live here, too. Some Yellowstone critters are friendlier than others, most notably the mosquitoes that show up in large numbers early in the summer. By mid-August they're much less of a hassle, and winter visitors will have no problems at all.

The Park Service has a free pamphlet showing where you're most likely to see wildlife in Yellowstone. Pick one up at any visitor center. During summer, the best wildlife-viewing hours are early in the morning and in the late afternoon to early evening.

Safety

Because of the constant parade of visitors and the lack of hunting, many of Yellowstone's animals appear to almost ignore the presence of people, and it isn't uncommon to see visitors approach an animal without respecting its need for space. Although they may appear tame,

Yellowstone's animals really are wild, and attacks are not uncommon. Those quiet bison can suddenly erupt with an enormous ferocity if provoked by photographers who come too close. Between 1983 and 1994, four people were killed by bison in Yellowstone and Grand Teton national parks. **Stay at least 25 yards away from bison and elk and at least 100 yards away from bears.** Do not under any circumstances feed the park's animals. This creates an unnatural dependency, is unhealthy for the animal, and may even lead to its death. You'll find some entertaining (and simultaneously scary) wildlife safety videos of wildlife encounters with foolish tourists on the Yellowstone website (www.nps.gov/yell).

Bears

Both black and grizzly bears are found throughout Yellowstone, but the days of bear jams along the park roads are long past because rangers actively work to prevent bears from becoming habituated to people. Most bears have returned to their more natural ways of living, although problems still crop up with individuals wandering through campgrounds in search of food. You're more likely to encounter a bear in the backcountry areas, and some places are closed to hiking for extended periods each year for this reason. The best places to watch for grizzlies along the road system are in the Hayden and Lamar valleys, near Mt. Washburn, and in the Antelope Creek drainage (just south of Tower Fall). (For details on staying safe around bears, see *Health and Safety* in the *Essentials* chapter.)

Bighorn Sheep

About 250 bighorns live within Yellowstone National Park, with much larger populations in the surrounding national forests. Look for bighorn sheep on cliffs in the Gardner River Canyon between Mammoth Hot Springs and the town of Gardiner. Ewes and lambs also frequently appear just off the road on Dunraven Pass north of Canyon, and day-hikers commonly encounter rams up close on the slopes of Mt. Washburn. Another place to see bighorns is along Specimen Ridge.

Birds

Trumpeter swans—beautiful white birds with seven-foot wingspans—are a fairly common sight in Yellowstone, particularly on the Madison and Yellowstone rivers and on Yellowstone Lake. Many trumpeter swans winter in hot-spring areas. These are some of the largest birds in America, weighing 20–30 pounds. Another large white bird here is the ungainly-looking and bulbous-billed **white pelican,** a common sight on Yellowstone Lake and near Fishing Bridge. More than 350 pairs of pelicans nest on the Molly Islands in Yellowstone Lake; this is one of the largest white-pelican breeding colonies in the Rockies. **Bald eagles**—America's national bird—and **ospreys** have managed comebacks in recent years and are frequently seen along the Yellowstone River and above Yellowstone Lake. Look for **golden eagles** flying over the open grasslands of Lamar Valley or Hayden Valley.

Bison

When Yellowstone was established in 1872, hundreds of mountain bison (also called wood bison) still ranged across this high plateau. Sport and meat hunting—legal until 1894—and later poaching reduced the population so that by 1902 perhaps fewer than 25 remained. That year, 21 plains bison were brought in from private ranches in Montana and Texas to help restore the Yellowstone herd, and today there are more than 4,000 in the park, making this the largest free-ranging herd of bison anywhere on earth. Unfortunately, interbreeding between the mountain and plains bison means that the animals in Yellowstone today are genetically different from the original inhabitants.

Bison are found in open country throughout Yellowstone, including Hayden, Lamar, and Pelican valleys, along with the Firehole River Basin (including Old Faithful). A favorite time to see bison in Yellowstone is late May, just after the new calves have been born. The calves' antics are always good for laughs. Be sure to use caution around bison; many people have been gored when they've come too close. Always stay at least 25 yards away, preferably farther.

YELLOWSTONE

Coyotes

Although wolves get the media attention, visitors to Yellowstone are probably more likely to see another native of the dog family: the coyote. Keep your eyes open for coyotes anywhere in Yellowstone but especially in open grassy areas, where they are more easily spotted. During summer, you'll often see them in small packs or alone as they hunt small mammals such as mice, voles, and pocket gophers. At other times of the year they prey on larger animals, including the calves of elk and pronghorn antelope, and scavenge carrion. Good places to look for coyotes are in the Blacktail Plateau area and Lamar Valley, along with the Upper and Lower Geyser basins near Old Faithful.

Deer

Mule deer (also known as black-tailed deer) are common in many parts of Yellowstone during summer, but most migrate to lower elevations when winter comes. They are typically found in open areas containing sagebrush or grass.

Mule deer are named for their long mulelike ears. They also have black-tipped tails and a peculiar way of pogoing away when frightened.

The smaller **white-tailed deer** are far less common in Yellowstone. You are most likely to find them along rivers or in brushy areas at low elevations, such as around Mammoth Hot Springs or in Lamar Valley. Other places to watch for them are along Yellowstone Lake and in the Upper Geyser Basin.

Elk

One animal virtually every visitor to Yellowstone sees is elk. About 30,000 of these regal animals summer in the park, and approximately 15,000 remain through the winter, primarily on the north end of Yellowstone. In summer, look for elk in Mammoth Hot Springs, Elk Park, and Gibbon Meadows, but you're certain to also see them elsewhere in Yellowstone. The bugling of bull elk is a common autumn sound in Yellowstone, as anyone who visits Mammoth at that time of year can attest. Winter snows push the elk to lower elevations

Elk relax on the terraces at Mammoth Hot Springs.

© DON PITCHER

YELLOWSTONE

on the north side of Yellowstone or out of the park into surrounding areas.

Moose

The largest members of the deer family, moose are typically seen eating willow bushes in riparian areas inside Yellowstone National Park. The best places to look for moose are Hayden Valley, around Yellowstone Lake, the Willow Park area north of Norris, the southwestern corner along the Bechler and Falls rivers, and along the Gallatin, Lamar, and Lewis river drainages.

Pronghorn Antelope

These speedy and colorful ungulates (hoofed mammals) are common sights on the plains of Wyoming, but most of Yellowstone doesn't provide adequate habitat. Pronghorn antelope are found only in sagebrush and grassy areas on the northern end of the park from Lamar Valley to the Gardiner area.

Wolves

The best place to look for wolves is the open

© DON PITCHER

pronghorn antelope near Mammoth Hot Springs

terrain of Lamar Valley, where the **Druid Peak Pack** and others have taken up residence and are visible at many times of the year. Visit early in the morning or near dusk to increase your odds of seeing them. You may well hear their plaintive cry from your campground late at night, particularly at Slough Creek or Pebble Creek campgrounds. Binoculars or spotting scopes are helpful for roadside wolf-watching. Rent quality scopes ($20 for the first day, plus $10 for subsequent days) from **Silver Gate General Store** (406/838-2371, www.silver-gate-cabins.com) in the town of Silver Gate, Montana, just outside the northeast corner of the park.

Wolf-watchers should follow the advice listed in the park newspaper. Noise can be a problem, especially in popular wolf-viewing areas, so avoid slamming car doors and keep other sounds to a minimum. And yes, it is illegal to imitate a wolf howl in the park. Do not follow the wolves around because this may disturb them and affect their survival. Denning activity typically takes place early April–early May, with active denning areas closed to humans; check with the Park Service for closed areas.

YELLOWSTONE NATIONAL PARK HISTORY

Yellowstone National Park has a rich and fascinating history that reaches back through thousands of years of settlement.

Sheepeater Indians

The last major glaciation ended around 15,000 years ago, and the first peoples may have reached Yellowstone while the ice was still retreating. There is good evidence that the country was occupied for at least 10,000 years, although the tribes apparently changed through time. By the mid-19th century, the country was surrounded by Blackfeet to the north, Crow to the east, and Shoshone and Bannock to the south and west. These tribes all traveled through and hunted in Yellowstone, building temporary shelters, called wickiups, made of aspen poles covered with pine boughs; a few of these still exist in the park. The

YELLOWSTONE

THE NEZ PERCE WAR

One of the saddest episodes in the history of Yellowstone took place in 1877 and involved the Nez Perce Indians of Oregon's Wallowa Valley. When the government tried to force the people of Chief White Bird and Chief Joseph onto an Idaho reservation so that white ranchers could have their lands, the Indians stubbornly refused. A few drunken young Indians killed four whites, and subsequent raids led to the deaths of at least 14 more. The army retaliated but was turned back by the Nez Perce. Rather than face government reinforcements, more than 1,000 Nez Perce began an 1,800-mile flight in a desperate bid to reach Canada. A series of running battles followed as the Indians managed to confound the inept army using their geographic knowledge and battle skills. The Nez Perce entered Yellowstone from the west, and a few hotheads immediately attacked vacationing tourists and prospectors. Two whites were killed in the park, others were kidnapped, and another man nearly died from his wounds.

The Nez Perce exited Yellowstone two weeks after they arrived, narrowly missing an encounter with their implacable foe, General William T. Sherman, who just happened to be vacationing in Yellowstone at the time. East of the park, the Indians plotted a masterful escape from two columns of army forces, feinting a move down the Shoshone River and then heading north along a route that left their pursuers gasping in amazement – straight up the narrow Clarks Fork Canyon, "where rocks on each side came so near together that two horses abreast could hardly pass." Finally, less than 40 miles from the international border with Canada, the army caught up with the Nez Perce, and after a fierce battle the tribe was forced to surrender (although 300 did make good their escape).

Chief Joseph's haunting words still echo through the years: "Hear me, my chiefs, I am tired; my heart is sick and sad. From where the sun now stands, I will fight no more forever." Despite promises that they would be allowed to return home, the Nez Perce were hustled onto reservations in Oklahoma and Washington while whites remained on their ancestral lands. Chief Joseph spent the rest of his life on Washington's Colville Reservation and died in 1904, reportedly of a broken heart. Yellowstone's Nez Perce Creek, which feeds the Firehole River, is named for this desperate bid for freedom.

primary inhabitants of this high plateau were the Sheepeater Indians, who may have been here for more than 2,000 years. Of Shoshone stock, the Sheepeaters hunted bighorn sheep (hence the name) and made bows from the sheep horns, but their diet also included other animals, fish, roots, and berries. Because they did not have horses, the Sheepeaters used dog-pulled travois to carry their few possessions from camp to camp. Summers were spent in high alpine meadows and along passes, where they hunted migrating game animals or gathered roots and berries. They wintered in protected canyons.

The Sheepeaters were smaller than other Indians and have achieved an aura of mystery because so little is known of their way of living. Yellowstone was at the heart of their territory, but with the arrival of whites came devastating diseases, particularly smallpox. The survivors joined their Shoshone brothers on the Wind River Reservation or the Bannock Reservation in Idaho. The last of the tribe left Yellowstone in the 1870s.

Fur Trappers

The word "Yellowstone" appears to have come from the Minnetaree Indians, who called the river "Mi tsi a-da-zi," a word French Canadian trappers translated into "Rive des Roche Jaunes"—literally, "River of Yellow Rock." The Indians apparently called it this because of the yellowish bluffs along the river near Billings, Montana (not because of the colorful Grand Canyon of the Yellowstone). The term "Yellow Stone" was first used on a map made in 1797.

When the Lewis and Clark Expedition traveled through the country north of Yellowstone in 1805–1806, the Indians told them tales of this mysterious place: "There is frequently heard a loud noise like thunder, which makes the earth tremble, they state that they seldom go there because children Cannot sleep—and Conceive it possessed of spirits, who were adverse that men Should be near them." (This certainly was not the attitude of all the native peoples, for the park had long been inhabited.) The first white man to come through Yellowstone is believed to be John Colter, a former member of the Lewis and Clark Expedition who wandered through the region in the winter of 1807–1808. A map based on Colter's recollections shows Yellowstone Lake ("Eustis Lake"), along with an area of "Hot Spring Brimstone."

As fur trappers spread through the Rockies in the 1820s and '30s, many discovered the geysers and hot springs of Yellowstone, and stories quickly spread around the rendezvous fires. The word of the trappers was passed on to later settlers and explorers but not entirely believed. After all, mountain man Jim Bridger described not just petrified trees, but petrified birds singing petrified songs! His tales of a river that "ran so fast that it became hot on the bottom" could well have referred to the Firehole River. When Bridger tried to lead a party of military explorers into Yellowstone, they were stymied by deep snows. Still, word gradually got out that something very strange could be found in this part of the mountains. Little remains today from the mountain-man era, although in 1880 the letters "J.O.R. Aug. 19, 1819" were found carved in a tree near the Upper Falls of the Yellowstone, and later a cache of iron beaver traps similar to those used by the Hudson's Bay Company was discovered near Obsidian Cliff.

Expeditions

National attention finally came to Yellowstone with a series of three expeditions to check out the wild claims of local prospectors. In 1869, David E. Folsom, Charles W. Cook, and William Peterson headed south from Bozeman, finding the Grand Canyon, Yellowstone Lake, and the geyser basins. When a friend pressured them to submit a description of their travels for publication, the *New York Tribune* refused to publish it, noting that the paper "had a reputation that they could not risk with such unreliable material."

The adventures of this first expedition led another group of explorers into Yellowstone the following year, but this time money was the motive. Jay Cooke's Northern Pacific Railroad needed investors for a planned route across Montana. A good public-relations campaign was the first step, and it happened to coincide with the visit of a former Montana tax collector named Nathaniel P. Langford, who had heard of the discoveries of Folsom, Cook, and Peterson. The party of 19 soldiers and civilians, including Langford, headed out in August of 1870 under General Henry D. Washburn. They were thrilled by what they discovered and proceeded to give the geysers names—Old Faithful, Castle, Giant, Grotto, Giantess—which became permanently attached to the features. The joy of the trip was marred when one man—Truman Everts—became separated from the others and then lost his horse. He was not found until 37 days later, by which time he weighed just 50 pounds. His rescuer did not even recognize him as human. Amazingly, Everts survived and recovered.

With the return of the Washburn Expedition, national newspapers and magazines finally began to pay attention to Yellowstone, and Langford began lecturing in the East on what they had found. One of those listening was Dr. Ferdinand V. Hayden, director of the U.S. Geological Survey. Hayden asked Congress to fund an official investigation. With the help of Representatives James G. Blaine (coincidentally a supporter of the Northern Pacific Railroad) and conservationist Henry M. Dawes, Congress appropriated $40,000 for an exploration of "the sources of the Missouri and Yellowstone Rivers." Thus began the most famous and influential trip into Yellowstone—the 1871 Hayden Expedition. The troop included 34 men, an escort of cavalry, painter Thomas Moran, and photographer William H. Jackson.

Establishing the Park

When Hayden returned to Washington to prepare his report, he found a letter from railroad promoter Jay Cooke. In the letter, Cooke proposed that "Congress pass a bill reserving the Great Geyser Basin as a public park forever—just as it has reserved that far inferior wonder the Yosemite valley and big trees." (Abraham Lincoln had established Yosemite earlier as a state park.) In an amazingly short time, a bill was introduced to set aside the land, and Hayden rushed to arrange a display in the Capitol rotunda of geological specimens, sketches by Moran, and photos by Jackson. The bill easily passed both houses of Congress and was signed into law on March 1, 1872, by President Ulysses S. Grant. The first national park had come into existence, a culmination not just of the discoveries in Yellowstone but also of a growing appreciation for preserving the wonders of the natural world.

Because of the difficult access, fewer than 500 people visited in each of Yellowstone's first few years as a park, most to soak in tubs at Mammoth Hot Springs. Not a few decided to take home souvenirs, bringing pickaxes and shovels for that purpose. Meanwhile, hunters—including some working for the Mammoth Hotel—began shooting the park's abundant game. Two brothers who had a ranch just north of the park killed 2,000 elk in a single year. Superintendent Langford did little to stop the slaughter and bothered to visit the park only twice. Finally, in 1877, the Secretary of the Interior fired him, putting Philetus W. Norris in charge instead. Norris proved a good choice, despite a knack for applying his name to everything in sight. (Most of his attempts at immortality have been replaced by other titles, but Norris Geyser Basin, Norris Road, and even the town of Norris, Michigan, remain.)

Norris oversaw construction of the first major road in Yellowstone, a rough 60-mile route built in just 30 days to connect Upper Geyser Basin with Mammoth and the western entrance. The next decade was tumultuous, as railroad tycoons attempted to control access to the park for their own financial gain, and as poachers decimated park wildlife and fish. Finally, Congress grew fed up and the Secretary of the Interior was forced to request the aid of the military in 1886. It proved a fortuitous step.

The Army Years

The U.S. Army finally brought a semblance of order to Yellowstone, eliminating the political appointees who viewed the park as a place to get rich. That first year, a temporary fort—Camp Sheridan—was thrown up and a troop of soldiers arrived, but it wasn't until 1891 that work began on a permanent Fort Yellowstone at Mammoth. By 1904, the fort consisted of some 26 buildings housing 120 men. The soldiers had clear objectives—protecting wildlife (or at least bison and elk) from poachers, fighting fires, stopping vandalism, and generally achieving order out of chaos. These goals were accomplished with a fervor that gained widespread respect, and in a way that would later influence the organization of the National Park Service. One of the major accomplishments of the soldiers was completion of the Grand Loop Road, which passes most of Yellowstone's attractions. The basic pattern was completed by 1905.

Fort Yellowstone was a favorite station for soldiers, and it was considered something of an honor to be sent to such a setting. The life of the soldiers was not always easy, however, and some died in the bitter winters or in accidents. A series of 16 soldier stations—actually little more than large cabins—was established around the park, and each was manned year-round, usually by four soldiers.

Before the arrival of cars, many visitors to Yellowstone were wealthy people from the East Coast or Europe intent on doing the grand tour of the West. The railroads (Northern Pacific to the north, Union Pacific to the west, and the Burlington to the east) deposited them near park borders, where they were met by carriages, Tallyhos (26-passenger stagecoaches), and surreys. In 1915, 3,000 horses were in use within the park! Most "dudes" paid approximately $50 for a six-day tour that included transportation, meals, and lodging at the hotels. They paid another $2.50 for the privilege of sailing across

Yellowstone Lake on the steamship *Zillah*. By contrast, another group, the "sagebrushers," came to Yellowstone in smaller numbers, arriving in their own wagons or hiring a coach to transport them between the "Wylie Way" campgrounds. These seasonal tent camps were scattered around the park, providing an inexpensive way to see the sights—just $35 for a seven-day tour. Even as early as 1908, Yellowstone was being seen by 18,000 visitors per year.

The first car entered Yellowstone in 1915, and it became clear that horses and cars could not mix, so motor buses replaced the old coaches. From then on, the park would be increasingly a place for "autoists." Within a year, the park would come under the jurisdiction of the newly created National Park Service.

The Park Service Takes Over

After years of army control, supporters of a separate National Park Service finally had their way in 1916. The congressional act created a dual role for the new park system: to "conserve the scenery" and to "provide for the enjoyment of the same," a contradictory mandate that would later lead to all sorts of conflicts. The first couple of years were tenuous, as management flip-flopped between the army and civilians; the final changeover came in 1918 and ended three decades of military supervision. The management of Yellowstone fell on the shoulders of two men, Horace M. Albright and his mentor, Stephen Mather, both of whom had been heavily involved in lobbying to create the new agency. Mather became the Park Service's first director, while Albright served as superintendent at Yellowstone and later stepped into Mather's shoes to head the agency.

Albright quickly upgraded facilities to meet the influx of motorists who demanded more camping facilities but also cabins, lodges, cafeterias, and bathhouses. Forty-six camps of one sort or another were constructed (only 12 survive today), fulfilling Albright's dream of "a motorist's paradise." The focus of the new Park Service was clearly visitation rather than preservation. Albright assembled a first-rate force of park rangers and instituted the environmental-education programs that have been the agency's hallmark ever since.

As the automobile took over Yellowstone, the railroads gradually lost their sway, and the final passenger train to the park's gateway towns stopped in 1960. In the 1950s, the Park Service initiated "Mission 66," a decade-long project to upgrade facilities and add lodging. By the late '60s, a growing appreciation for the natural world was shifting public opinion away from such developments, and the 1973 master plan scaled back proposed developments. From day one, Yellowstone National Park had been set up for what Edward Abbey called "industrial tourism." The park had come into existence in part because of a railroad promoter who hoped to gain from its development, and it grew to maturity on a diet of roads, hotels, and curio shops. In recent years, Americans have taken a second look at this heritage and have begun to wonder which matters more: providing a public playground or preserving an area that is unique on this planet. The inherent conflict between the need for public facilities and services in Yellowstone and the survival of a functioning ecosystem will continue to create a tug-of-war between various factions.

Certainly the most famous recent event was the series of massive fires that swept across nearly half of Yellowstone in 1988. The land has recovered surprisingly well since then, and in recent years other issues came to the fore: wolf reintroduction, the killing of bison on the park boundaries, snowmobile and other winter use, and problems caused by exotic species and fish disease. There's always something stewing in the mud pots of Yellowstone! Some things have been improving in recent years, including efforts to repair aging roads and to replace outdated buildings in the park. Despite any problems and controversies, the park is just as fascinating as ever. The geysers never cease to amaze visitors, the scenery remains majestic, the Grand Canyon of the Yellowstone is still just as stunning, and the superb wildlife-viewing continues to make this the Serengeti of America.

Exploring Yellowstone

Yellowstone is perhaps the most accessible large national park in America. Nearly all of the famous sights are within a couple of hundred feet of the Grand Loop Road, a 142-mile figure-eight through the middle of the park. Whatever you do, *don't* see Yellowstone at 45 miles per hour; that's like seeing the Louvre from a passing train.

For all too many visitors, Yellowstone becomes a checklist of places to visit, geysers to watch, and animals to see. This tends to inspire an attitude that treats this great national treasure as a drive-through theme park, where the animals come out to perform and the geyser eruptions are predicted so everyone can be there on time. If you're one of this crowd, give yourself a giant kick in the rear and take a walk, even if it is just around Upper Geyser Basin where you see something beyond Old Faithful.

The sights listed in this section begin on the west side of the park (the most popular entrance is via West Yellowstone) and traces a clockwise path around the Grand Loop, with several side trips.

PARK ACCESS

Entrance to Yellowstone (307/344-7381, www.nps.gov/yell) costs $20 per vehicle, or $10 for individuals entering by bicycle, foot, or as a bus passenger. Motorcycles are $15. The pass covers both Yellowstone and Grand Teton national parks and is good for seven days. If you're planning to be here longer or to make additional visits, get an annual pass covering both parks for $40, or the National Park Pass—good for all national parks—for $65 per year. A Golden Age Passport for all national parks is available to anyone older than 62 for a one-time fee of $10, and people with disabilities can get a free Golden Access Passport. Both of these passes also give you 50 percent reductions in most camping fees.

Upon entering the park, you'll receive a Yellowstone map and a copy of *Yellowstone Today,* a quarterly newspaper that describes facilities and services and provides camping, fishing, and backcountry information. This is the best source for up-to-date park information. It's also packed with enough warnings to scare off a platoon of Marines. Examples include cautions against falling trees, bathing in thermal pools (infections and/or amoebic meningitis), unpredictable wildlife, improper food storage, health problems from the altitude, narrow roads, theft, spotlighting elk, imitating wolf howls, and scalding water. And, oh yes, "swim at your own risk." Pets are prohibited on trails or boardwalks anywhere in Yellowstone. Kennel facilities are not available in the park but can be found in Jackson and Cody.

If you are planning a trip to Yellowstone, request a copy of the annual *Yellowstone National Park Trip Planner* booklet for an overview of sights, visitor centers, what to do, services, camping, and more. It's also available on the park website, www.nps.gov/yell. Call 307/344-2113 for a recorded park weather forecast.

Visitor Centers

The Park Service maintains visitor centers at Mammoth Hot Springs, Norris Geyser Basin, Old Faithful, Canyon Village, Fishing Bridge, and Grant Village. All of these sell maps and natural-history books covering the park and surrounding areas. In addition, you'll find smaller information stations at Madison and West Thumb and a Park Service ranger at the West Yellowstone Visitor Center. (Hours, seasons, and phone numbers for all of these are listed with the descriptions of the centers.)

GETTING AROUND BY CAR

The **speed limit** on all park roads is a vigilantly enforced 45 mph (or less); exceed this and you're likely to get a ticket! Be especially cautious on the south side of the park, where rangers seem to wait most evenings and the relatively straight road makes it easy to speed. During summer you're not likely to approach the speed limit because long lines of traffic form behind monstrous RVs or when wildlife is visible.

Gas stations are at Old Faithful, Canyon Village, Mammoth Hot Springs, Fishing Bridge, Grant Village, and Tower Junction, while repair services are available at all of these except Mammoth Hot Springs and Tower Junction. Additional service stations are in towns surrounding the park.

Seasonal Road Closures

Most roads in Yellowstone close on the Monday after the first Sunday in November and usually open again by mid-May. Only the road between Mammoth and Cooke City is kept plowed all winter; other roads are groomed for snowmobiles and snowcoaches (snow conditions permitting) by mid-December. Plowing begins in early March, and the roads reopen in sections. The roads connecting Mammoth to West Yellowstone open first, while Dunraven Pass is plowed last. Spring storms may cause closures or restrictions on some park roads, so get current road conditions at entrance stations and visitor centers, or by calling 307/344-7381.

The Construction Maze

Yellowstone's roads have long been a source of irritation. Much of the roadbed was built at the turn of the 20th century, when horses and carriages were the primary means of travel. Increasing traffic and larger vehicles contributed to deterioration of park roads, as did stretched-thin park maintenance budgets. Yellowstone is now well along on a massive 20-year road reconstruction program, and each summer you'll find a different section undergoing rebuilding, so be ready for delays up to 30 minutes somewhere during your journey. As the Park Service notes, "park roads have either been recently repaired or reconstructed, or are scheduled for repair or reconstruction." Fortunately, all this work means that the roads are vastly better than they were a decade ago. Contact the park (307/344-7381, www.nps.gov/yell) for the latest on the road situation and this year's construction delays, or check the park newspaper.

TOURS

During summer, most people come into Yellowstone in private cars or RVs, but there *are* other ways of getting around. An interpretive bus tour provides a quick overview of the park while leaving the driving to an expert. This is especially true for RVers who can park at Fishing Bridge RV Park or Bridge Bay Campground and then don't need to worry about driving on narrow park roads.

In-Park Tours

From mid-May to late September, **Xanterra Parks and Resorts** (307/344-7311, www .travelyellowstone.com) offers full-day bus tours from Canyon Lodge, Lake Yellowstone Hotel, Old Faithful Inn, Fishing Bridge RV Park, Bridge Bay Campground, and Grant Village. Tours of either the lower loop road are $44 adults or $24 ages 12–16 (free for younger kids). A longer Grand Loop tour (not recommended unless you're into sensory overload and more than nine hours of riding around) costs $50 adults or $25 teens. The Grand Loop tour is available only from Mammoth or Gardiner. Also available is an all-day "Teton Vista Rendezvous" tour ($48 adults, $24 teens) that heads south through Grand Teton National Park, and professionally taught **Photo Safari** ($52 adults for four hours, or $27 teens) provided several times a week out of Old Faithful Inn, Mammoth, and Lake Yellowstone Hotel.

Also available are three-hour **Firehole Basin** tours ($23 adults, $11 teens) and two-hour **Hayden Valley twilight tours** (a top time to find bears) for $19 adults or $10 teens. All-day trips to **Mt. Washburn** and **Lamar Valley wildlife excursions** were to be available once the road construction over Dunraven Pass is complete (after 2006). The latter cover three or four hours and provide an opportunity to catch a glimpse of wolves.

One of the most distinctive tour offerings is to ride a classic **1937 Yellowstone touring bus** on sunset tours around Lake Yellowstone. The vehicles get almost as much attention as the scenery during these fun voyages back in time. These trips cost $25 adults or $12 kids.

Other Bus Tours

Upper or lower loop tours are available out of West Yellowstone from **Buffalo Bus Touring Co.** (406/646-9564 or 800/426-7669, www.yellowstonevacations.com, $45 adults or $32 kids under 16). Park entrance fees are additional.

Additional Yellowstone tours leave out of Cody ($74) aboard **Powder River Tours** (307/527-3677 or 800/442-3682, http://gillette.coachusa.us) and from Jackson ($75) aboard **Alltrans/Gray Line** (307/733-4325 or 800/443-6133, www.jacksonholealltrans.com). Those without vehicles can use Gray Line or Powder River tours for access to the parks from Jackson or Cody; the bus can pick you up at many places along the road system, but you'll need to schedule this in advance.

Karst Stage (406/388-2293 or 800/287-4759, www.karststage.com) has daily wintertime shuttles between the Bozeman airport and Mammoth Hot Springs; rates depend upon the number of passengers.

Natural-History Tours

In addition to traditional classes, the Yellowstone Association Institute (307/344-2294, www.yellowstoneassociation.org) offers a popular series of **Lodging and Learning** packages. These two- to five-day programs blend education, recreation, and comfortable lodging. Naturalist-guides from the association lead excursions, and participants are provided accommodations in park hotels, plus breakfasts and lunches. The programs include special ones for families, winter ski treks, winter wildlife, and hiking. For the private touch, the institute has **Educational Adventures,** tours in which a wildlife biologist travels along in your own vehicle. It's sort of like having a personal trainer for Yellowstone wildlife.

For a listing of licensed tour operators offering wildlife, natural-history, and photography tours in the park, contact the Park Service (307/344-738, www.nps.gov/yell). Operated by the highly respected Teton Science School, **Wildlife Expeditions** (307/733-2623 or 888/945-3567, www.wildlifeexpeditions.org) leads a variety of wildlife-viewing safaris

throughout the region, including multiday wildlife tours into Yellowstone. Also highly recommended are naturalist Carl Swoboda's **Safari Yellowstone** (800/723-2747, www.safariyellowstone.com), geologist Dr. Keith Watts of **Earth Tours** (307/733-4261, www.earthtours.com), and **Tory and Meredith Taylor** (307/455-2161), who provide personalized wildlife package tours.

MADISON

The tourist town of **West Yellowstone, Montana,** is right outside the park's western boundary. **West Entrance** is the busiest of all the park entry stations, handling more than one-third of the nearly three million people who enter Yellowstone each year. A 14-mile road heads east to Madison Junction, closely paralleling the scenic Madison River (a major tributary of the Missouri River) in which geese, ducks, and trumpeter swans are common. Bison and elk are other critters to watch for in the open meadows. The Madison River is open only to fly-fishing and is considered one of the finest places in the nation to catch trout (although they can be a real challenge to fool). On warm summer evenings you're likely to see dozens of anglers casting for wily rainbow and brown trout and mountain whitefish.

At Madison Junction, the road splits, heading south to Old Faithful and north to Mammoth. This is where the Gibbon and Firehole rivers join to form the Madison River. The 406,359-acre North Fork Fire of 1988 ripped through most of the Madison River country, but the land is recovering well in most places, and wildflowers are abundant in midsummer.

Madison Canyon is flanked by mountains named for two photographers who had a marked influence on Yellowstone. To the north is 8,257-foot **Mt. Jackson**—as in William H. Jackson, whose photos helped bring the area to national attention—and to the south is distinctive, 8,235-foot **Mt. Haynes,** named for the man who held the park photo concession for nearly four decades. These mountains and the surrounding slopes were created by rhyolite lava flows.

The Northwest Corner

From West Yellowstone, Montana, U.S. 191 heads north to Bozeman, passing through a small corner of Yellowstone National Park en route. There are no entrance stations or developed facilities here, but the area provides backcountry access for hikers and horsepackers from several trailheads. The drive itself is scenic, and the road is wide and smooth. The road enters the park approximately 10 miles north of West Yellowstone and gradually climbs through stretches that were burned in the fires of 1988 before emerging into unburned alpine meadows near tiny Divide Lake. North of here, U.S. 191 follows the growing Gallatin River downhill through a pretty mix of meadows, sagebrush, rocky outcrops, and forested hillsides with grassy carpets beneath. Approximately 31 miles north of West Yellowstone, the road exits Yellowstone and enters Gallatin National Forest. It's another 17 miles from here to the turnoff for Big Sky Resort or 60 miles from the park boundary to Bozeman.

Madison Junction to Norris

The **Madison Information Station** (307/344-2821) near Madison Junction is open 9 A.M.–5 P.M. daily early June–September and closed the rest of the year. A small bookstore is also here. Directly behind Madison Campground is 7,500-foot **National Park Mountain,** named in honor of a fabled incident in 1870. Three explorers were gathered around the campfire, discussing the wonders that they had found in this area, when one suggested that rather than letting all of these wonders pass into private hands, they should be set aside as a national park. Thus was born the concept that led to the world's first national park. The tale was passed on as the gospel truth for so long that the mountain was named in honor of this evening. Unfortunately, the story was a complete fabrication. Cynics may read something into the fact that National Park Mountain was torched by the fires of 1988.

North of Madison Junction, the road follows the Gibbon River nearly all of the 14 miles to Norris. It crosses the river five times and hangs right on the edge through Gibbon Canyon. The pretty, 84-foot-high **Gibbon Falls** is approximately five miles up the road and situated right at the edge of the enormous caldera that fills the center of Yellowstone. The 1988 fires consumed most of the trees around the falls, but the new lodgepoles are now topping 20 feet. Another five miles beyond this point, the road emerges from the canyon into grassy **Gibbon Meadows,** where elk and bison are commonly seen. The prominent peak visible to the north is 10,336-foot Mt. Holmes. On the west end of Gibbon Meadows is a barren area that contains **Sylvan Springs Geyser Basin.** No maintained trail leads to this small collection of pools and springs, but hikers sometimes head across the north end of the meadows at the Gibbon River Picnic Area. The path is wet most of the summer.

An easy 0.5-mile trail leads to **Artist Paint Pots,** filled with colorful plopping and steaming mud pots and hot springs. Although it's a short hike, the paint pots see far fewer visitors than roadside sites, making it a nice place to escape the crowds. The forest was burned in the North Fork Fire, so it's also a good place to see how the lodgepole pines are regenerating. Just south of the parking area for Artist Paint Pots is a trail to **Monument Geyser Basin,** where there isn't much activity, but the tall sinter cones form all sorts of bizarre shapes, including Thermos Bottle Geyser. The mile-long hike climbs 500 feet and provides views of the surrounding country. Another attraction is **Chocolate Pots,** found along the highway just north of Gibbon Meadows. The reddish-brown color comes from iron, aluminum, and manganese oxides. Just before you reach Norris, the road crosses through the appropriately named **Elk Park.**

◖ NORRIS GEYSER BASIN

Although Old Faithful and the Upper Geyser Basin are more famous, many visitors to Yellowstone find Norris Geyser Basin equally interesting. Norris sits atop the junction of several major fault lines, providing conduits for heat from the molten lava below. Because of this, it is apparently the hottest geyser basin in North America, if not the world; a scientific team found temperatures of 459°F at 1,087 feet underground and was forced to quit drilling when the pressure threatened to destroy the drilling rig! Because of considerable sulfur (and hence sulfuric acid) in the springs and geysers, the water at Norris is acidic; most of the world's acid geysers are here. The acidic water kills lodgepole trees in the basin, creating an open, nearly barren place. Norris Basin has been around at least 115,000 years, making it the oldest of any of Yellowstone's active geyser basins. It is a constantly changing place, with small geysers seeming to come and go on an almost daily basis.

The paved trail from the often crowded parking area leads to **Norris Geyser Basin Museum and Information Station** (307/344-2812), built of stone in 1929–1930. The small museum houses exhibit panels on hot springs and geothermal activity and is open 10 A.M.–5 P.M. daily late May–September and closed the rest of the year. Be sure to pick up the detailed brochure ($0.50) describing the various features at Norris. Ranger-led walks are given several times a day in the summer, and there's usually one in the area ready to answer your questions. A little bookstore is housed in a nearby building. From the museum, the Norris Basin spreads both north and south, with two rather different trails to hike. Take the time to walk along both. The Norris Campground is only 0.25 mile from the geyser basin.

Porcelain Basin

Just behind the museum is an overlook that provides an impressive view across the always-changing Porcelain Basin. The path descends into the basin, passing hissing steam vents, bubbling hot pools, and small geysers, including **Constant Geyser,** with frequent and sudden bursts to 20 feet or more. **Whirligig Geyser** is another one that is often active, spraying a noisy fan of water. (Watch your glasses and camera lenses in the steam; silica deposits can be difficult to remove.) For an enjoyable short walk, follow the boardwalk around the mile-

long loop through Porcelain Basin. Stop to admire the bright colors in the steaming water, indicators of iron, arsenic, and other elements, along with algae and cyanobacteria.

Back Basin

A mile-long loop trail takes you to the sights within the Back Basin south of the museum. Before heading out, check at the museum for the latest on geyser activity. Most people follow the path in a clockwise direction, coming first to **Emerald Spring,** a gorgeous green pool with acidic water just below boiling. A little way farther down the path is **Steamboat Geyser.** Wait a few minutes and you're likely to see one of its minor eruptions, which may reach 40 feet. On rare occasions, Steamboat erupts with a fury that is hard to believe, blasting more than 300 feet into the air—more than twice the height of Old Faithful—making this the world's tallest geyser. Eruptions can last up to 20 minutes or more, enough time to pour out a million gallons of water, and the explosions have been heard up to 14 miles away. Steamboat's unforgettable eruptions cannot be predicted; a 50-year span once passed between eruptions, while several eruptions may occur in one year. If you ever see this one erupt, consider yourself incredibly lucky!

The path splits just below Steamboat; on the right is **Cistern Spring,** whose deep blue waters are constantly building deposits of sinter and have flooded the nearby lodgepole-pine forests, killing the trees. If you turn left where the trail splits, you come to **Echinus Geyser,** a personal favorite. (It's pronounced e-KI-nus.) The name—Greek for "spiny"—comes from the pebbles that lie around the geyser; resembling sea urchins, they are a result of sinter accumulation. The eruptions of Echinus have varied in recent years. Sometimes it settles into a regular pattern, with eruptions every hour or two, but at other times you may wait four hours for an eruption. Whatever the case, it's certainly worth the wait. When Echinus does erupt, the geyser sends explosions of acidic steam and water (pH 3.5) 40–60 feet. These generally last 3–

5 minutes but sometimes continue for much longer. Unlike Old Faithful, this is one geyser where you can get up close and personal. Bench-sitters may get splashed, although the water is not hot enough to burn.

Continue along this trail beyond Echinus to see many more hot springs and steam vents. **Porkchop Geyser** was in continuous eruption for several years, but in 1989 it self-destructed in an explosion that threw rocks more than 200 feet, leaving behind a bubbling hot spring.

Norris Junction to Canyon

From Norris Geyser Basin to Canyon, the road cuts across the center of the park on the high Solfatara Plateau, an area scorched in the 1988 North Fork Fire. The lodgepole pines had been uprooted in a wild 1984 windstorm, and four years later the wind-whipped fires arrived, creating a holocaust. Now, almost 20 years later, lodgepoles are well established in many areas and the land is recovering.

Virginia Cascades Road is a 2.5-mile-long, one-way road that circles around this blowdown area and provides a view of the 60-foot-tall Virginia Cascade of the Gibbon River. Back on the main highway heading east, keep your eyes open for elk and bison as the road approaches Canyon. Also note the thick young forest of lodgepole pines that was established after a fire burned through in 1955.

Norris Junction to Mammoth

The park road between Norris and Mammoth Hot Springs provides some interesting sights, although much of this country burned in the 1988 North Fork Fire. Just beyond the highway junction is the **Norris Soldier Station.** Built by the army in 1897 and modified in 1908, it is one of just three stations still standing in the park. The attractive log building now houses the small **Museum of the National Park Ranger** (307/344-7353) with displays and a video on the history of park rangers. It is open 9 A.M.–5 P.M. daily late May–late September and closed the rest of the year.

Just up the road is **Frying Pan Spring** (named for its shape), where the water is actu-

ally not that hot. The bubbles are from pungent-smelling hydrogen-sulfide gas. **Roaring Mountain** is a bleak, steaming mountainside four miles north of Norris. In 1902, the mountain erupted into activity with fumaroles that made a roar audible at great distances. It is far less active today and is best seen in winter, when the temperature difference results in much more steam.

Obsidian Cliff

Stop at Obsidian Cliff to see the black glassy rocks formed when lava cooled rapidly. One mountain man (not, as many sources claim, Jim Bridger) told tall tales of "Glass Mountain," where his shots at an elk kept missing. When he got closer, he found he had actually been firing at a clear mountain of glass. The elk was 25 miles away, but the mountain was acting as a telescope to make the animal appear close. Obsidian Cliff was an important source of rock for Indians in making fine arrowheads and other tools. The obsidian from here was of such value that Indians traded it extensively; obsidian points made from this rock have even been found in Ohio and Ontario. (It is illegal to remove obsidian; leave it for future generations to enjoy.) North of here the countryside opens up along Obsidian Creek at **Willow Park,** one of the best places to see moose, especially in the fall.

Sheepeater Cliff and Golden Gate

Approximately 13 miles north of Norris, the road passes Indian Creek Campground (one of the quietest in the park) and the basalt columns of Sheepeater Cliff, named for the Indian inhabitants of these mountains. North of this point, the country opens into Swan Lake Flats, where you get a fine gander at 10,992-foot Electric Peak nine miles to the northwest.

At Golden Gate the road suddenly enters a narrow defile, through which flows Glen Creek. Stop to look over the edge of **Rustic Falls** and to note how the road is cantilevered over the cliff edge. Acrophobics should *not* stop here. Instead, have someone else drive, close your eyes, and say three Hail Marys.

Bunsen Peak and the Hoodoos

Just south of Mammoth is Bunsen Peak, an 8,564-foot inactive volcanic cone. Any chemistry student will recognize the name because Robert Wilhelm Eberhard von Bunsen not only first explained the action of geysers but also invented the Bunsen burner. Parts of Bunsen Peak look like a chemistry experiment run amok. The North Fork Fire of 1988 swept through this area in a patchy mosaic, leaving long strips of unburned trees next to those that are now just blackened telephone poles.

North of Golden Gate, the main road soon passes the Hoodoos, a fascinating jumble of travertine boulders leaning in all directions. The rocks were created by hot springs thousands of years ago and toppled from the east face of Terrace Mountain. Just before Mammoth, turn left onto Upper Terrace Drive, a 0.5-mile loop road providing access to the upper end of Mammoth Hot Springs. (No trailers or large RVs.)

◖ MAMMOTH HOT SPRINGS

Mammoth Hot Springs lies at an elevation of 6,239 feet near the northern border of Yellowstone, just five miles from the town of Gardiner, Montana. Here you'll find park headquarters, a variety of other facilities, and delightfully colorful hot springs. The Mammoth area is an important wintering spot for elk, pronghorn antelope, deer, and bison. During the fall, at least one bull elk and his harem can be seen wandering across the green lawns, while lesser males bugle challenges from behind the buildings or over the hill. The bugling may even keep you awake at night if you're staying in the Mammoth Hotel.

Origins

Mammoth Hot Springs consists of a series of multihued terraces down which hot, mineral-laden water trickles. This water originates as snow and rain that falls on the surrounding country, although some is believed to come from the Norris area, 20 miles to the south. As it passes through the earth, the water comes into contact with volcanic magma containing massive amounts of carbon dioxide, creating carbonic acid. The now-acidic water passes through and dissolves the region's sedimentary limestone, and the calcium carbonate remains in solution until it reaches the surface at Mammoth. Once at the surface, the carbon dioxide begins to escape into the atmosphere, reducing the acidity and causing the lime to precipitate out, forming the travertine terraces that are so prominent here. As the water flows over small obstructions, more carbon dioxide is released, causing accumulations that eventually grow into the lips that surround the terrace pools. The rate of accumulation of travertine (calcium carbonate) is astounding: more than two tons a day at Mammoth Hot Springs. Some terraces grow by eight inches per year. The first explorers were fascinated by these terraces; mountain man Jim Bridger noted that they made for delightful baths. A later operation—long since ended—coated knickknacks by dipping them in the hot springs!

The springs are constantly changing as underground passages are blocked by limestone deposits, forcing the water in new directions. As a result, old dried-out terraces stand on all sides, while new ones grow each day. Areas that were active just a few years ago may now be simply gray masses of crumbling travertine rock, and new areas may appear and spread in a matter of days. Mammoth is guaranteed to be different every time you visit. One of the most interesting aspects of the hot springs here is the variety of colors, results of the many different species of algae and bacteria that live in the water. Various factors, including temperature and acidity, affect the survival of different species; bright yellow algae live in the hottest areas, whereas cooler waters are colored orange and brown by other algae.

Visiting the Springs

Mammoth Hot Springs covers a steep hillside and consists of a series of colorful springs in various stages of accretion or decay. The area is accessible by road from below or above (Upper Terrace Drive), and a boardwalk staircase

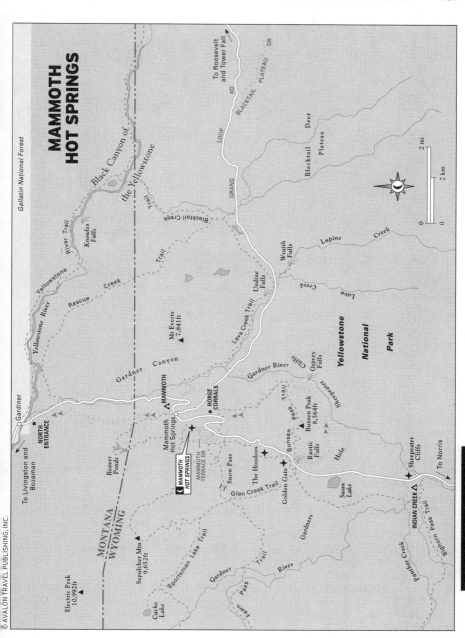

MAMMOTH HOT SPRINGS

Gallatin National Forest

Black Canyon of the Yellowstone

To Roosevelt and Tower Fall

BLACKTAIL PLATEAU DR

LOOP RD

GRAND

Blacktail Creek

Knowles Falls

River Trail

Yellowstone River

Trail

Rescue Creek

Deer

Blacktail Plateau

Lupine Creek

Wraith Falls

Undine Falls

Lava Creek

Lava Creek Trail

Mt Everts 7,841ft

Gardner Canyon

Gardner River

Osprey Falls

Cliffs

Yellowstone National Park

MAMMOTH

HORSE CORRALS

Mammoth Hot Springs

MAMMOTH HOT SPRINGS

MAMMOTH TERRACE DR

Bunson Peak Trail

Silvergate

Bunson Peak 8,564ft

Sheepeater

To Gardiner

NORTH ENTRANCE

To Livingston and Bozeman

Beaver Ponds

Snow Pass

The Hoodoos

Golden Gate

Rustic Falls

Hole

Glen Creek Trail

Swan Lake

Sheepeater Cliffs

To Norris

MONTANA
WYOMING

Sepulcher Mtn 9,652ft

Sportsman Lake Trail

Gardner River

Gardners

Panther Creek

INDIAN CREEK

Bighorn Pass Trail

Electric Peak 10,992ft

Cache Lake

Gardner Pass Trail

Fawn Pass Trail

0   2 mi
0   2 km

N

© DON PITCHER

Mammoth Hot Springs

connects the two. At the bottom of Mammoth Hot Springs and off to the right is a 37-foot-tall mass of travertine known as **Liberty Cap** for its faint similarity to the caps worn in the French Revolution. The spring that created this formation no longer flows.

The springs at Mammoth change continuously, and every visit brings something new. For details on currently active areas, pick up the Park Service's informative brochure ($0.50) from the box at the parking area. The most interesting areas are **New Blue Spring** and **Canary Spring** in the vicinity of the overlook, **Angel Terrace** along Upper Terrace Drive, and **Palate Spring** near the base.

All of the water flowing out of Mammoth terraces quickly disappears into underground caverns. In front of the Mammoth Hotel are two sinkholes from which steam often rises. Caverns above the terraces were once open to the public but later were closed when it became apparent that they contained poisonous gases. Dead birds are sometimes found around one of the small pools in this area appropriately named Poison Spring.

Albright Visitor Center

The Albright Visitor Center (307/344-2263) is named for Horace Albright, the first National Park Service superintendent at Yellowstone. The center is housed in the army's old bachelor officers' quarters and is open 8 A.M.–7 P.M. daily late May–early September, 8 A.M.–5 P.M. daily the rest of September, and 9 A.M.–5 P.M. daily the remainder of the year. Spread over the two floors are exhibits on park wildlife and history, but the real treats are the works of two artists who helped bring Yellowstone's magnificent scenery to public attention. Twenty-three of painter Thomas Moran's famous Yellowstone watercolors line the walls, and his studio has been re-created in one corner. Equally impressive are 26 classic photographs—including one of Thomas Moran at Mammoth Hot Springs—taken by William H. Jackson during the 1871 Hayden Survey. The paintings and photos are must-sees for anyone with an artistic bent. The center also has an information desk, racks of books, and films about the park and Moran. Check at the information desk for schedules of wildlife talks and frequent ranger-led walks to surrounding sights in the summer.

Historic Buildings

Mammoth contains several other historic structures built during the army's tenure at **Fort Yellowstone.** The most distinctive are the six buildings (all in a row) constructed between 1891 and 1909 as quarters for the officers and captains. Most of the grunt soldiers lived just behind here in barracks, one of which is now the park administration building. The U.S. Engineers Department was housed in an odd stone building with obvious Asian influences; it's right across from the visitor center. The visitor center has an informative pamphlet ($0.50) that describes the Fort Yellowstone Historic District in detail. Displays around the grounds provide additional details.

Although one wing survives from a hotel built in 1911, most of the **Mammoth Hot Springs Hotel** was constructed in 1937. Step inside to view the large map of the United States built from 15 different types of wood. Mammoth also features a Yellowstone General Store, post office, gas station, restaurant, fast-food eatery, and medical clinic. Mammoth Campground is just down the road. Just up the hill—less than one mile from the hotel—is the Mammoth corral, where horseback rides are offered. Also here is a small **cemetery** populated mostly by infants and a few civilians who died here in the early 1900s.

North Entrance Road

The main road north from Mammoth Hot Springs follows the Gardner River, dropping nearly 1,000 feet in elevation before reaching the town of Gardiner, Montana. (Both the river and the misspelled town are named for Johnson Gardner, a ruthless trapper from the 1820s.) The river is a favorite of fly-fishing enthusiasts. A turnout near the Wyoming-Montana border notes the "boiling river" section of the Gardner River; it's always worth a stop, and the 0.5-mile hike has a big reward at the end. Sometimes during the winter you can spot bighorn sheep on the mountain slopes just north of the river as you head down to Gardiner.

The "back way" to Gardiner is the **Old Gardiner Road,** a five-mile gravel road (great for mountain bikes, but not for RVs or trailers) that starts behind Mammoth Hot Springs Hotel. Traffic is downhill only, so you'll need to take the main road for your return into the park; mountain bikes can go in both directions. This is one of the best places to spot pronghorn antelope in the park, and it also provides a fine escape from the crowds at Mammoth.

To Tower Junction

The 18-mile drive from Mammoth to Tower Junction takes visitors through some of the driest and most open country in Yellowstone. Two waterfalls provide stopping places along the way. Beautiful **Undine Falls** is a 60-foot-high double falls immediately north of the road. Just up the road is a gentle 0.5-mile path to the base of **Wraith Falls,** where Lupine Creek cascades 90 feet. Look for ducks and trumpeter swans in **Blacktail Pond,** a couple of miles farther east.

Blacktail Plateau Drive, approximately nine miles east of Mammoth, turns off from the main road. The rough seven-mile dirt road is a one-way route that loosely follows the Bannock Trail, a path used by the Bannock tribe on their way to buffalo-hunting grounds east of here. Their travois trails are still visible. The Bannocks used this route from 1838 to 1878, but it was probably used for hundreds or thousands of years by various tribes crossing the high plateau. Much of Blacktail Plateau Drive is through open sagebrush, grass, and aspen country, where you're likely to see deer and pronghorn antelope. The trees are very pretty in the fall. On the east end, the road drops back into a forest burned by a severe crown fire in 1988 but now containing young aspen and lodgepole trees and abundant summertime flowers.

The Park Service has developed a two-thirds–mile boardwalk **Forces of the Northern Range Self-Guiding Trail,** approximately six miles east of Mammoth Hot Springs. Trailside exhibits describe the natural world. Half a mile beyond where Blacktail Plateau Drive rejoins the main road is the turnoff to the **petrified tree.** The 20-foot-tall stump of an ancient redwood tree (50 million years old) stands behind iron bars; a second petrified tree that used to stand nearby was stolen piece by piece through the years by thoughtless tourists. The **Tower Ranger Station,** originally occupied by the U.S. Army, is just before Tower Junction where the road splits, leading to either Northeast Entrance Road or Canyon.

◖ THE NORTHEAST CORNER

Of the five primary entryways into Yellowstone, the Northeast Entrance is the least traveled, making this a great place to escape the hordes in midsummer. It is also one of the few places to see tall mountains in Yellowstone. The road heads east from Tower Junction and immediately enters **Lamar Valley,** an area of grass and sage along the sinuous Lamar River.

This is one of the best places in Yellowstone to view bison, with a gorgeous backdrop of open country and wooded mountains. Elk and mule deer are also commonly seen, and the reintroduction of wolves has added another dimension to wildlife-viewing. The valley contains several small ponds created when the retreating glaciers left large blocks of ice that formed "kettles." Erratic glacial boulders are scattered along the way. There are campgrounds at Slough Creek and Pebble Creek and very good fishing in Slough Creek, too. But look out for one other critter: the ubiquitous ground squirrels that dart into the road, playing chicken with your tires.

Yellowstone River Picnic Area

Picnic areas don't generally merit a mention, but this one—1.5 miles east of Tower Junction on the Northeast Entrance Road—is an exception because of its proximity to a grand view. A two-mile trail takes off from here for Grand Canyon of the Yellowstone River. The hike is easy and provides a good chance to see bighorn sheep, but be careful to stay away from the canyon rim. For a loop hike (four miles round-trip), continue to the Specimen Ridge Trail, where you turn left and follow it back to your starting point.

Yellowstone Association Institute

The nonprofit Yellowstone Association Institute (307/344-2294, www.yellowstoneassociation.org) offers many classes out of Lamar Valley's historic Buffalo Ranch, approximately 10 miles east of Tower Junction. To augment the park's small wild herd, bison were brought here in 1902 from private ranches. The bison stayed in pens at night and were herded during the day. After 1915, they were allowed to roam freely in summer, although all of the park's bison were rounded up and driven here for winter. After 1938, the roundups ended, but the bison were fed hay every winter in Lamar Valley. Finally in 1952, even this practice was halted and the bison were allowed to roam throughout the park. The historic buildings are worth a look, or better still, take one of the institute's excellent classes.

Specimen Ridge

Just east of the historic Buffalo Ranch is a turnout across from Specimen Ridge, where explorers discovered the standing trunks of petrified trees that had been buried in volcanic ash and mudflows 50 million years ago. Through the centuries, the trunks literally turned to stone as silica entered the wood. The process was repeated through the centuries as new forests gradually developed atop the volcanic deposits, only to be buried by later flows. Scientists have found 27 different forests on top of each other, containing walnut, magnolia, oak, redwood, and maple—evidence that the climate was once more like that of today's Midwestern states. Erosion eventually revealed the trees, many of which are still standing. This is one of the largest areas of petrified trees known to exist.

There is no trail to the petrified forest, but during summer rangers lead hikes into the area. Check with the Albright Visitor Center for upcoming treks. Mark Marschall's *Yellowstone Trails* provides a description of the 1.5-mile route if you want to try it on your own. A lesser-known petrified forest in the northwest corner of Yellowstone is accessible via U.S. 191.

Wolf-Watching

Between the Slough Creek and Pebble Creek campgrounds, wolf aficionados fill roadside turnouts each morning and evening, waiting patiently for members of the Druid Peak Pack (and other packs) to appear. Bring your binoculars and spotting scope! During the wolf denning season, the Park Service prohibits parking or walking along certain stretches of the road, but two turnouts are available.

Northeast Entrance

At the east end of Lamar Valley, the road continues northeast up Soda Butte Creek and between the steep rocky cliffs of **Barronette Peak** (10,404 feet) and **Abiathar Peak** (10,928 feet). Stop at **Soda Butte,** where you'll find a substantial travertine mound similar to those at Mammoth. Although the springs are no longer very active, the air still reeks of hydrogen sulfide, the "rotten egg" gas. South of Soda Butte and several miles up a backcountry trail is **Wahb Springs,** found within Death Gulch. Here poisonous gases are emitted from the ground, killing animals in the vicinity. Early explorers reported finding dead bears that had been overcome by the fumes. Less than one mile north of Soda Butte is a pullout where a 0.5-mile trail leads to pretty **Trout Lake.** It's a nice afternoon break from the crowds elsewhere in Yellowstone.

North of Pebble Creek Campground, the road squeezes through beautiful **Icebox Canyon,** past Barronette Peak, and into the (unburned) lodgepole pine forests. It follows the creek all the way to the edge of the park, crossing into Montana two miles before the park border. The **Northeast Entrance Station** is a classic log building built in 1935 and now designated a National Historic Landmark. The twin gateway towns of Silver Gate and Cooke City are just up the road.

TOWER FALL/ROOSEVELT
Roosevelt Lodge

Lying at the junction of the roads to Canyon, Mammoth, and Lamar Valley, Roosevelt Lodge was built in 1920 and named for President Theodore Roosevelt, who camped a few miles to the south during his 1903 visit. A lifelong supporter of Yellowstone, Roosevelt helped push through legislation that clamped down on the rampant destruction of park wildlife early in the 20th century.

The Roosevelt area is a favorite of families, wolf-watchers, and anglers, many of whom return year after year. The main building has the rough-edged flavor of a hunting lodge and a peacefulness that you won't find at Old Faithful, Canyon, or Mammoth. Inside are two large stone fireplaces, and the porch out front has comfortable rocking chairs that fill each evening. Folks plop their feet on the rail, nurse a beer, and watch the evening roll in. Heavenly. Rustic cabins—most built in the 1920s—provide simple accommodations, and Roosevelt has a restaurant and little gift shop/ general store, along with horseback rides. It's also the only place in Yellowstone to offer wagon rides and Old West cookouts; call well ahead for reservations.

Stop at the overlook to **Calcite Springs,** two miles southeast of the junction, where a walkway provides dramatic views into the canyon of the Yellowstone River, with steaming geothermal activity far below. The cliff faces contain a wide strip of columnar basalt, some of which overhangs the highway just to the south.

◖ Tower Fall

On summer afternoons the parking lot at Tower Fall fills with cars as folks stop to see Tower Creek plummeting 132 feet before joining the Yellowstone River. The towerlike black rocks of the area are volcanic basalt. Nearby are a campground and a Yellowstone General Store. Tower Fall overlook is just a couple of hundred paved feet from the parking area, or you can follow the path 0.5 mile down the switchbacks to the canyon bottom, where the vista is far more impressive and a rainbow is sometimes visible. Be prepared to get wet in the spray! A ford of the Yellowstone River—used by Bannock Indians in the 19th century—is just 0.25 mile away. For more than 100 years, a

© DON PITCHER

Tower Fall

huge boulder stood atop Tower Fall; the water and gravity finally won in 1986.

Dunraven Pass and Mt. Washburn

Continuing southward, the road climbs along Antelope Creek and eventually switchbacks up the aptly named Mae West Curve. The North Fork Fire swept through this country in 1988, but the area is now verdant with new trees, grasses, and flowers. Ten miles south of Tower Junction, the old Chittenden Road turns off and leads a mile uphill to a large parking area and trailhead for popular day hikes up Mt. Washburn, the 10,243-foot peak that dominates this part of Yellowstone.

South of this is Dunraven Pass (8,859 feet), named for the Earl of Dunraven, who visited the park in 1874 and whose widely read book *The Great Divide* brought Yellowstone to the attention of wealthy European travelers. This is the highest point along any park road, even higher than the three other places where the road crosses the Continental Divide! Look for whitebark pines near the road, and be sure to stop just south of here

for a view across to the distant Grand Canyon of the Yellowstone.

◖ GRAND CANYON OF THE YELLOWSTONE

Yellowstone is best known for its geysers and animals, but for many visitors the Grand Canyon is the park's most memorable feature. This 20-mile-long canyon ranges 1,500–4,000 feet across and has colorful yellow, pink, orange, and buff cliffs that drop as much as 1,200 feet on either side. The river itself tumbles abruptly over two massive waterfalls, sending up a roar that's audible for miles along the rims. Grand Canyon is accessible by road from both the north and south sides, with equally amazing views. The lodgepole pine forests around here escaped the 1988 fires.

Carving a Canyon

After a massive volcanic eruption 650,000 years ago, rhyolite lava flows came through what is now the Grand Canyon. The flows eventually cooled, but geothermal activity within the rhyolite weakened the rock with hot steam and gasses, making it susceptible to erosion. Through the centuries, a series of glaciers blocked water upstream, each time creating a lake. As each glacier retreated it undammed the stream, allowing the water in the lake to empty suddenly. The weakened rhyolite was easily eroded by these periodic floods of water and glacial debris, thus revealing pastel yellow and red canyon walls colored by the thermal activities. The **Lower Falls** are at the edge of the thermal basin, above rock that was not weakened by geothermal activity. The **Upper Falls** are at a contact point between hard rhyolite that does not erode easily and a band of rhyolite that contains more easily eroded volcanic glass. Today the canyon is eroding more slowly, having increased in depth just 50 feet during the last 10,000 years.

Canyon Village

Canyon Village on the north rim is a forgettable shopping mall in the wilderness, complete with a visitor center, various stores and eat-

YELLOWSTONE

GRAND CANYON OF THE YELLOWSTONE

ing places, a post office, a gas station, cabins, lodges, and a campground. It's a good place to come on a rainy summer afternoon when the kids are starting to scream for ice cream. Horseback rides are available less than one mile south of here. Step into the newly built **Canyon Visitor Center** (307/242-2550) for park information or to see the natural-history exhibits. Hours are 8 A.M.–7 P.M. daily late May–early September and 9 A.M.–6 P.M. daily for the rest of September. It's closed in winter.

North Rim Vistas

A one-way road takes visitors to a series of extremely popular overlooks along the north rim of Grand Canyon of the Yellowstone. Farthest east is **Inspiration Point,** where the views of the canyon and Lower Falls are, well, inspirational. A wheelchair-accessible canyon view

is available from the edge of the parking lot. **North Rim Trail** leads along the rim from Inspiration Point up to Chittenden Bridge, three miles away, and some sections of this scenic and nearly level path are paved. Just a couple of hundred feet up from Inspiration Point, be sure to look for a 500-ton boulder deposited by a glacier during the glaciation that ended 15,000 years ago. The glacial erratic (as such rocks are called) originated in the Beartooth Mountains at least 30 miles north of here and was carried south atop a moving river of ice.

The one-way road continues westward to overlooks at **Grandview Point** and **Lookout Point.** From Lookout Point, a 0.5-mile trail drops 500 hundred feet to **Red Rock Point** for a closer view of Lower Falls—you can feel the spray. Farthest west along the one-way North Rim Road is the trail to the **Brink of**

the Lower Falls. The trail is 0.5-mile long and paved, descending 600 feet to a viewing area where you can peer over the edge as the water plummets in a thunderous roar over the 308-foot precipice (twice the height of Niagara Falls). This is probably the most breathtaking sight in Yellowstone, but if you suffer from vertigo don't even think about peering over the brink! Just south of where the one-way road rejoins the main highway is a turnoff to the **Brink of the Upper Falls,** where a short walk leads to a less dramatic but still beautiful view of the 109-foot-high Upper Falls.

A party of prospectors wandered north into this country in 1867, following the Yellowstone River downstream without suspecting the canyon below. A. Bart Henderson wrote in his diary of strolling down the river and being

> *very much surprised to see the water disappear from my sight. I walked out on a rock & made two steps at the same time, one forward, the other backward, for I had unawares as it were, looked down into the depth or bowels of the earth, into which the Yellow plunged as if to cool the infernal region that lay under all this wonderful country of lava and boiling springs.*

South Rim Vistas

The south rim is lined with additional dramatic views into Grand Canyon. Cross the Chittenden Bridge over the Yellowstone River (otters are sometimes seen playing in the river below) and continue 0.5 mile to Uncle Tom's parking area, where a short trail leads to views of the Upper Falls and Crystal Falls. More unusual is **Uncle Tom's Trail,** which descends 500 feet to Lower Falls. The trail is partly paved, but it's steep and includes 328 metal steps before you get to the bottom—good exercise if you're in shape. It was named for "Uncle" Tom Richardson who, with the help of wooden ladders and ropes, led paying tourists to the base of the falls around the turn of the 20th century. Because there was no bridge, Uncle Tom also rowed his guests across the river near the pres-

ent Chittenden Bridge. After his permit was revoked in 1903, visitors had to make do on their own.

One mile beyond Uncle Tom's parking area, the road ends at the parking area for **Artist Point,** the most famous—and crowded—of all Grand Canyon viewpoints. A short paved path leads to an astoundingly beautiful spot where one can look upriver to the Lower Falls or down the opposite direction into the canyon. Look for thermal activity far below. The point is apparently where artist Thomas Moran painted some of his famous watercolors. Avoid the crowds and afternoon thunderstorms by getting here early in the morning; it's almost always deserted at sunrise.

HAYDEN VALLEY

Just a few miles south of Canyon, the country abruptly opens into beautiful Hayden Valley, named for Ferdinand V. Hayden, leader of the 1871 expedition into Yellowstone. Reaching eight miles across, this relatively level part of the park was once occupied by an arm of Yellowstone Lake. The sediments left behind by the lake, along with glacial till, do not hold sufficient water to support trees. As a result, the area is occupied primarily by grasses, forbs, and sage. This is one of the best areas in the park to see wildlife, especially bison and elk. The Yellowstone River wanders across Hayden Valley, and streams enter from various sides. The waterways are excellent places to look for Canada geese, trumpeter swans, pelicans, and many kinds of ducks. Although they are less common, grizzly bears sometimes can be found feeding in the eastern end of the valley. Because of the bears, hikers need to be especially cautious when tramping through the grasses and shrubs, where it is easy to surprise a bear or to be likewise surprised. On the north end of Hayden Valley, the road crosses **Alum Creek,** named for its highly alkaline water, which could make anything shrink. In the horse-and-buggy days, Yellowstone wags claimed that a man had forded the creek with a team of horses and a wagon but came out the other side with four Shetland ponies pulling a basket!

◖ Mud Volcano Area

Shortly after the road climbs south out of Hayden Valley, it passes one of the most interesting of Yellowstone's many thermal basins. On the east side of the road, a turnout overlooks **Sulphur Caldron,** where a highly acidic pool is filled with sulfur-tinted waters and the air is filled with the odor of hydrogen-sulfide gas. Directly across the road is the Mud Volcano area, where a two-thirds–mile loop trail provides what could be a tour through a bad case of heartburn. Pick up a Park Service brochure ($0.50) from the box for descriptions of all the bizarre features here. The area is in a constant state of flux as springs dry up or begin overflowing, killing trees in their path. **Churning Caldron** is a frothing pool where periodic jets send superheated water into the air. Just up the trail is one of the most interesting features, **Black Dragons Caldron,** where an explosive spring blasts constantly through a mass of boiling black mud. The wildest place at Mud Volcano is **Dragon's Mouth Spring,** which the Park Service notes is named for "the rhythmic belching of steam and water shooting from the cavernous opening." It's easy to imagine the fires of hell not far below this spring. The waters are 180°F. During winter (and often in summer), the Mud Volcano area is a good place to see elk or bison.

Along the Yellowstone

South of Mud Volcano, the road parallels the Yellowstone River. At **LeHardys Rapids** a boardwalk provides an overlook where early-summer visitors see blush-red spawning cut-throats. In late summer, this part of the Yellowstone River is a very popular fly-fishing spot—some call it the finest stream for cutthroat fishing in the world—and a good place to view ducks and swans. Earlier in the year, it's open only to the bears that gorge on the cutthroats. By the way, the Yellowstone River, which begins at Yellowstone Lake, is the longest free-flowing (undammed) river in the Lower 48.

◖ YELLOWSTONE LAKE

When first-time visitors see Yellowstone Lake, they are stunned by its magnitude. The statistics are impressive: 110 miles of shoreline,

Yellowstone Lake near Bridge Bay

© DON PITCHER

YELLOWSTONE

20 miles north to south and 14 miles east to west, with an average depth of 139 feet and a maximum depth of 390 feet. This is the largest high-elevation (over 7,000 feet) lake in North America; Lake Tahoe is bigger, but lower. Yellowstone Lake can seem like a sheet of glass laid to the horizon at one moment and just a half hour later be a roiling ocean of whitecaps and wind-whipped waves. These changeable waters can be dangerous to those in canoes or small boats; several people have drowned, including experienced park rangers. The water is covered by ice at least half of the year, and breakup does not come until late May or early June. Even in summer, water temperatures are often only in the 40s.

Fishing Bridge

The area around famous Fishing Bridge (built in 1937) was for many years a favorite place to catch cutthroat trout. These same fish are a major food source for grizzlies, and this area is considered some of the most important bear habitat in Yellowstone. Conflicts between bears and humans led to the death of 16 grizzlies here. To help restore trout populations and to provide food for the grizzlies, the Park Service banned fishing from Fishing Bridge in 1973 and tried to move the developments to the Grant Village area. Lobbying by folks from Cody (worried lest they lose some of the tourist traffic) kept some of the facilities at Fishing Bridge from closing. Remaining facilities include an RV park, Yellowstone General Store, and gas station. **Fishing Bridge Visitor Center** (307/242-2450) houses exhibits of birds, animals, and geology. It's open 8 A.M.–7 P.M. daily late May–early September and 9 A.M.–6 P.M. daily for the rest of September. It's closed the remainder of the year. The bridge itself is still a popular stopping point and a good place to see large cutthroat trout in the shallows.

Lake Yellowstone Hotel

Lake Yellowstone Hotel, the oldest extant park hostelry, was built in 1889–1891 by the Northern Pacific Railroad and originally consisted of a simple boxlike structure facing Yellowstone Lake. The hotel was sold to Harry Child in 1901, and two years later Robert Reamer—the architect who designed Old Faithful Inn—was given free rein to transform this into a more attractive place. Hard to believe that the same architect could create a grand log masterpiece and a sprawling Southern colonial mansion with distinctive ionic columns in the same park! Lake Yellowstone Hotel is the second-largest wood-framed building in North America and requires 500 gallons of paint each year to keep it in shape.

Today, Lake Yellowstone Hotel is one of the nicest places to stay in the park, with fine vistas out over the lake and comfortable quarters. Relax with a drink in the sunlit **Sun Room** while a pianist or a string quartet provides the atmosphere. Free 45-minute historic **tours of Lake Yellowstone Hotel** are given at 5:30 P.M. Monday–Friday early June–late September. The hotel also houses a restaurant, gift shop, and snack bar.

Be sure to take a walk along the lakeshore out in front of the hotel, where the Absaroka Range forms a backdrop far to the east. The highest mountain is Avalanche Peak (10,566 feet). Almost due south is the 10,308-foot summit of Mt. Sheridan, named for General Philip Sheridan, a longtime supporter of expanding the park to include the Tetons. Watch for the big white pelicans catching fish on the lake.

Just east of Lake Yellowstone Hotel is the **Lake Ranger Station,** built in 1922–1923 and now on the National Register of Historic Places. Inside the octagonal main room you will find a massive central fireplace, exposed log rafters, and rustic light fixtures. A short walk away is **Lake Lodge,** another rustic log structure that houses a reasonably priced cafeteria with grand windows fronting the lake. A Yellowstone General Store stands nearby, and dozens of plain cabins are behind it.

To West Thumb

The highway south from Lake Junction to West Thumb follows the lakeshore nearly the entire distance. A campground and boat har-

The Lake Yellowstone Hotel is the second largest wood-framed building in North America.

bor are at **Bridge Bay,** along with a ranger station, marina, and store. Stop here for hour-long boat tours of Yellowstone Lake, offered several times a day throughout the summer, or for guided fishing trips and boat rentals.

Back on the main road, keep your eyes open for Canada geese and trumpeter swans as you drive south. **Gull Point Drive,** a two-mile-long side road, offers views of **Stevenson Island** just offshore; farther south, **Frank Island** and tiny **Dot Island** become visible. The small **Potts Hot Springs Basin,** just north of West Thumb, is named for fur trapper Daniel T. Potts, one of the first white men to explore the Yellowstone country. His travels here in 1826 were described the following year in a Philadelphia newspaper article. It was perhaps the first published mention of Yellowstone Lake and the hot springs.

East Entrance Road

Heading east from Fishing Bridge, the road follows the shore of Yellowstone Lake past country that escaped the 1988 fires. Three miles east of the bridge are Indian Pond—popular with birders—and the trailhead for Storm Point Trail. North of here, Pelican Valley is considered important grizzly habitat and is closed to all overnight camping year-round. Even daytime use is not allowed until July 4, and then only between 9 A.M. and 7 P.M. Before venturing out on the Storm Point Trail or into Pelican Valley, check at the Lake Ranger Station for current bear information. The 0.5-mile **Pelican Creek Nature Trail** starts one mile east of Fishing Bridge and provides an easy hike to a beach along Yellowstone Lake. Much of the way is on boardwalk over a marshy area.

At **Steamboat Point** the road swings out along the shore, providing excellent views across the lake and of a noisy fumarole. For an even better view (don't miss this one!), take the **Lake Butte Overlook** road, which continues one mile to a small parking area 1,000 feet above the lake. This is a fine place to watch sunsets and to get a feeling for the enormous size of Yellowstone Lake. Back on the main highway and heading east, you soon leave Yellowstone Lake behind and it is visible in only a few spots as the road climbs gradually, passing scenic **Sylvan Lake,** a nice place for picnics. Just up the road is tiny Eleanor Lake (little more than a puddle) and a steep trail to 10,566-foot **Avalanche Peak.**

Immediately east of Eleanor Lake, the main road climbs to 8,530-foot **Sylvan Pass,** flanked by Hoyt Peak on the north and Top Notch Peak to the south. Steep scree slopes drop down both sides. East of Sylvan Pass, the road descends quickly along Middle Creek (a tributary of the Shoshone River), providing good views to the south of Mt. Langford and Mt. Doane. **East Entrance Ranger Station** was built by the army in 1904. For many years, the road leading up to Sylvan Pass from the east took drivers across Corkscrew Bridge, a bridge that literally looped over itself as the road climbed steeply up the narrow valley. (The road continues eastward to Cody through beautiful Wapiti Valley; see the *Bighorn Basin* chapter for details.)

WEST THUMB AND GRANT VILLAGE

The South Entrance Station consists of several log structures right along the Snake River. Just 1.5 miles beyond the entrance is an easily missed turnout where you can walk down to 30-foot-high **Moose Falls.** Beyond this point, the road climbs a long, gentle ramp to Pitchstone Plateau, passing green forests of lodgepole pine. Stop at a turnout to look back at the majestic Tetons. Abruptly, this gentle country is broken by the edge of **Lewis River Canyon,** with rhyolite walls that rise to 600 feet. The fires of 1988 burned hot throughout much of this area, and dead trees line both sides of the canyon in all directions, although young trees are now carpeting many areas.

The road parallels the river for the next seven miles. Nearly everyone stops for a look at 29-foot-high **Lewis Falls.** Camping is available at the south end of **Lewis Lake,** which—like the lake, falls, river, and canyon—was named for the Lewis and Clark expedition's Meriwether Lewis. Lewis Lake is the park's third-largest body of water (after Yellowstone Lake and Shoshone Lake) and is popular with canoeists,

kayakers, and anglers. The clear waters contain brown trout and Mackinaw (lake trout). Approximately four miles north of Lewis Lake, the highway tops the Continental Divide, 7,988 feet above sea level. This is one of three such crossings that roads make within Yellowstone.

Grant Village

This odd scattering of buildings is named for President Ulysses S. Grant, who signed the act establishing Yellowstone and whose terms in office were marked by massive corruption scandals. Grant Village was built in the 1980s to replace facilities at Fishing Bridge, an area of important grizzly habitat. Unfortunately, instead of one bad development, Yellowstone now has two because some of the buildings at Fishing Bridge still stand. Unlike some of the more historic places in Yellowstone where a natural rusticity prevailed, Grant Village has less charm than most Wal-Marts. An ugly steakhouse restaurant and waterside cafeteria face Yellowstone Lake, but the marina that was once here is closed. Also sprawled around Grant Village are a campground, rows of chintzy condos, a Yellowstone General Store, a gas station, and post offices. Much of the area around here was consumed in the 1988 Snake River Fire; unfortunately, the fire missed this scar on the Yellowstone landscape.

Grant Village Visitor Center (307/242-2650) houses an informative exhibit and film on the role of fires in the park, particularly the massive 1988 fires. These provide a good background to help understand the changes taking place as the burned areas recover. The visitor center is open 8 A.M.–7 P.M. daily late May–early September and 9 A.M.–6 P.M. daily for the rest of September. It's closed the rest of the year.

West Thumb

If you look at a map of Yellowstone Lake, it's possible to imagine the lake as a giant hand with three mangled fingers heading south and a gnarled thumb hitching west. Hence the name West Thumb. This section of Yellowstone Lake is the deepest (to 390 feet) and is actually a caldera that filled with water after erupting 150,000 years ago. Considerable heat is still just below the surface, as revealed by **West Thumb Geyser Basin.** Get a Park Service booklet ($0.50) from the box for details on the area's geothermal origins and attractions.

A short loop trail leads past steaming hot springs and pools at West Thumb. Right on the shore is **Fishing Cone,** where tourists once caught fish and then plopped them in the cone to be cooked; after several clowning tourists were injured, the Park Service put a stop to this stunt. The **West Thumb Information Station** is open 8 A.M.–7 P.M. daily late May–early September and 9 A.M.–5 P.M. daily the rest of September, when it closes for the season. A small bookstore is housed here, and in winter the station is used as a warming hut.

West Thumb to Upper Geyser Basin

Heading west from West Thumb, the highway climbs over the Continental Divide twice. Most of these forests escaped the 1988 fires. A few miles beyond the eastern crossing of the divide is a turnout at **Shoshone Point,** where you catch glimpses of Shoshone Lake and the Tetons.

Approximately 14 miles beyond West Thumb, pull off to see the Firehole River as it drops over **Kepler Cascades.** The western crossing of the Continental Divide is at **Craig Pass,** where a tiny pond (Isa Lake) empties into both the Atlantic and Pacific oceans through its two outlet streams.

OLD FAITHFUL AND UPPER GEYSER BASIN

As you approach Old Faithful from either direction, the two-lane road suddenly widens into four, and a cloverleaf exit takes you to Yellowstone's most fabulous sight. Welcome to Upper Geyser Basin, home of Old Faithful, about 400 buildings of all sizes, and a small town's worth of people. For many folks, this is the heart of Yellowstone, and a visit to the park without seeing Old Faithful is like a baseball game without the national anthem. If you came to Yellowstone to see the wonders of nature, you're going to see more than your share

OLD FAITHFUL AREA CLIMATE

SNOWFALL	MAXIMUM TEMP.	
RAINFALL	MINIMUM TEMP.	
Average Maximum Temp.	49.4°F	
Average Minimum Temp.	18.1°F	
Annual Rainfall	25.38"	
Annual Snowfall	228.3"	

here, but you'll probably have to share your share with hundreds of other folks. On busy summer days more than 25,000 visitors come through the Old Faithful area! Fortunately, the Upper Geyser Basin contains the largest concentration of geysers in the world, and the adventurous will even discover places almost nobody ever visits. But be very careful: The crust can be dangerously thin around some of the hot springs and geysers, and people have

YELLOWSTONE

OLD FAITHFUL AND UPPER GEYSER BASIN

	PAVED TRAIL
	UNPAVED TRAIL
	BOARDWALK

To Madison Junction

To Mystic Falls

Biscuit Basin

Mustard Spring
Avoca Spring
Sapphire Pool
Shell Geyser
Jewel Geyser

Little Firehole River

Firehole River

Mirror Pool

Gem Pool

Atomizer Geyser
Artemisia Geyser

River

Morning Glory Pool

Far, Mortar, and Spiteful Geysers

Riverside Geyser

Grotto Geyser

Comet Geyser
Daisy Geyser
Splendid Geyser

Giant Geyser

Punch Bowl Spring

Round Spring

Chromatic Spring
Beauty Pool

Solitary Geyser

Black Sand Pool

Firehole River

Grand Geyser

OBSERVATION POINT

Sunset Lake
Opalescent Pool
Rainbow Pool
Cliff Geyser

Crested Pool

Castle Geyser

Lion Geyser

Geyser Hill

Giantess Geyser

Black Sand Basin
Emerald Pool

Beehive Geyser

Chinese Spring

STORE

OLD FAITHFUL GEYSER

OLD FAITHFUL INN

OLD FAITHFUL LODGE

VISITOR CENTER

Iron Spring Creek

RANGER STATION/ CLINIC

SNOW LODGE

STORE

POST OFFICE

To Fern Cascades

To Lone Star Geyser

To West Thumb

0   0.5 mi
0   0.5 km

YELLOWSTONE

© AVALON TRAVEL PUBLISHING, INC.

been badly scalded and even killed by missteps. Stay on the boardwalks and trails.

Old Faithful Geyser

The one sight seen by virtually everyone who comes to Yellowstone is Old Faithful Geyser, easily the most visited geyser in the world. Old Faithful is neither the tallest nor the most frequently erupting geyser in Yellowstone, but it always provides a great show and is both highly accessible and fairly predictable. Contrary to the rumors, Old Faithful never erupted "every hour on the hour," but for many years its period was a little more than an hour. It has slowed in recent years and is now averaging around 92 minutes per cycle, but varies from 45 to 120 minutes. In general, the longer the length of the eruption, the longer the interval until the next eruption. Check at the visitor center for the latest prognostications on this and other geysers in the basin.

An almost level paved path circles Old Faithful, providing many different angles from which to view the eruptions, although none of these is particularly close to the geyser because of the danger from hot water. Along the north side is **Chinese Spring,** named in 1885 for a short-lived laundry operation. Apparently, the washman had filled the spring with clothes and soap, not knowing that soap can cause geysers to erupt. One newspaper correspondent claimed—although the tale obviously suffered from embellishment and racism—that,

> *The soap awakened the imprisoned giant; with a roar that made the earth tremble, and a shriek of a steam whistle, a cloud of steam and a column of boiling water shot up into the air a hundred feet, carrying soap, raiment, tent and China-man along with the rush, and dropping them at various intervals along the way.*

Old Faithful provides a textbook example of geyser activity. The first signs of life are when water begins to splash out of the vent in what is called preplay. This splashing can last up to 20 minutes, but it's generally only a few minutes

© DON PITCHER

Yellowstone's most famous geyser, Old Faithful, erupts about once every 90 minutes.

before the real thing. The water quickly spears into the sky, reaching 100–180 feet for 1.5–5 minutes before rapidly dropping down. During a typical eruption, between 3,700 and 8,400 gallons of water are sent skyward.

On any given summer day, the scene at Old Faithful is almost comical. Just before the predicted eruption time, the benches encircling the south and east sides are jammed with hundreds of people waiting expectantly for the geyser to erupt, and with each tentative spray the camera shutters begin to click. Listen closely and you'll hear half the languages of Europe and Asia. Once the action is over, there's a mad rush back into the visitor center, the stores, and Old Faithful Inn, and within a few minutes the benches are virtually empty. A tale is told of two concessioner employees who once decided to have fun at Old Faithful by placing a large crank atop a box and putting the contraption near the geyser. When they knew it was ready to erupt, they ran out and turned the crank just as Old Faithful shot into the air. Their

YELLOWSTONE

employer failed to find humor in the prank, and both were fired, or so the story claims.

Geyser Hill Area

Upper Geyser Basin is laced with paved trails that lead to dozens of nearby geysers and hot springs. The easiest path loops around Geyser Hill, just across the Firehole River from Old Faithful. Here are more than 40 different geysers. Check at the visitor center to get an idea of current activity and predicted eruptions, and while you're there pick up the excellent Upper Geyser Basin map ($0.50), which describes some of them. Several geysers are particularly noteworthy. When it plays, **Beehive Geyser** (it has a tall, beehive-shaped cone) vents water as high as 180 feet into the air. These spectacular eruptions vary in frequency; one time you visit they may be 10 days apart, while the next time you come they may be happening twice daily. **Lion Geyser Group** consists of four different interconnected geysers with varying periods of activity and eruptions up to 80 feet. Listen for the roar when Lion is ready to erupt. **Giantess Geyser** may not be active for years at a time—or may erupt several times a year—but the eruptions are sensationally powerful, sending water 100–200 feet skyward. **Doublet Pool** is a beautiful deep-blue pool that is a favorite of photographers. Not far away is **Sponge Geyser,** which rockets water an astounding 2.29 billion angstroms into the air (that's nine inches for the nonscientific crowd). It's considered the smallest named geyser in Yellowstone and gets its title by sending up a spurt of water big enough to be mopped up with a sponge.

Observation Point Loop Trail splits off shortly after you cross the bridge on the way to Geyser Hill and climbs to an excellent overlook where you can watch eruptions of Old Faithful. This is also a good place to view the effects of, and recovery from, the 1988 North Fork Fire. It's two miles round-trip to Observation Point from the visitor center. Another easy trail splits off from this path to **Solitary Geyser,** which is actually just a pool that periodically burps four-foot splashes of hot water. This is not a natural geyser. In 1915, the hot

spring here was tapped to provide water for Old Faithful Geyser Bath, a concession that lasted until 1948. The lowering of the water level in the pool completely changed the plumbing system of the hot springs and turned it into a geyser that at one time shot 25 feet in the air. The system still hasn't recovered, although water levels have been restored for many decades.

More Geyser-Gazing

Another easy, paved path follows the Firehole River downstream from Old Faithful, looping back along the other side for a total distance of three miles. Other trails head off from this loop to the Fairy Falls Trailhead, Biscuit Basin, and Black Sand Basin. The loop is a very popular wintertime ski path, and sections are open to bikes in the summer. Twelve-foot-high **Castle Geyser** does indeed resemble a ruined old castle. Because of its size and the slow accretion of sinter (silica) to form this cone, it is believed to be somewhere between 5,000 and 50,000 years old. Castle sends up a column of water and steam 75 feet into the air and usually erupts every 11–13 hours. Check at the visitor center for a guess at the next eruption.

Daisy Geyser is farther down the path and off to the left. It is usually one of the most predictable of the geysers, erupting to 75 feet approximately every 120–150 minutes. The water shoots out at a sharp angle and is visible all over the basin, making this a real crowd-pleaser.

Just east of Daisy is **Radiator Geyser,** which isn't much to look at—eruptions to two feet—but was named when this area was a parking lot and the sudden eruption under a car led people to think its radiator was overheating. A personal favorite, **Grotto Geyser** is certainly the weirdest of all the geysers, having formed around a tangle of long-petrified tree stumps. It is in eruption one-third of the time, but most eruptions reach only 10 feet.

Look for **Riverside Geyser** across the Firehole from the path and not far downstream from Grotto. This picturesque geyser arches spray 75 feet over the river and is one of the most predictable, with 20-minute-long eruptions approximately every six hours. The paved trail crosses the river and ends at famous **Morning Glory Pool.** For many years, the main road passed this colorful pool, which became something of a wishing well for not just coins but also trash, rocks, logs, and other debris. Because of this junk, the pool began to cool, and the beautiful blue color is now tinged by brown and green algae, despite efforts to remove the debris.

Turning back at Morning Glory, recross the bridge and head left where the path splits at Grotto Geyser. **Giant Geyser** is on the left along the river. Years may pass between eruptions of Giant (or it might erupt every week or so), but when it does go, the name rings true because the water can reach 250 feet. Cross the river again and pass **Beauty Pool** and **Chromatic Pool,** which are connected below the ground so that one declines as the other rises. Very pretty.

Grand Geyser is a wonderful sight. The water column erupts in 1–4 towering bursts lasting 9–12 minutes and sometimes reaching 200 feet. It's the tallest predictable geyser on the planet; see the visitor center for the next eruption or wait with the crowds if the pool looks full. When Grand isn't playing, watch for smaller eruptions from nearby **Turban Geyser.** Two little fun geysers are a short distance to the south: **Sawmill Geyser** and **Tardy Geyser.** The latter is just 10 feet or so from the trail, providing an up-close look at a small but active geyser. Cross the river again just beyond these two geysers and pass **Crested Pool** on your way back to Castle Geyser. The pool contains deep-blue water that is constantly boiling, preventing the survival of algae.

Black Sand Basin

Just one mile west of Old Faithful is Black Sand Basin, a small cluster of geysers and hot springs. Most enjoyable is unpredictable **Cliff Geyser,** which often sends a spray of hot water 25–30 feet over Iron Spring Creek. Three colorful pools are quite interesting in the basin: **Emerald Pool, Rainbow Pool,** and **Sunset Lake. Handkerchief Pool** is now just a small spouter but was famous for many years as a

place where visitors could drop a handkerchief in one end and then recover it later at another vent. In 1929, vandals jammed logs into the pool, destroying this little game. The pool was covered with gravel in subsequent eruptions of Rainbow Pool.

Biscuit Basin

Three miles north of Old Faithful, this basin is named for biscuitlike formations that were found in one of the pools; they were destroyed in an eruption following the 1959 Hebgen Lake earthquake. From the parking lot, the trail leads across the Firehole River to pretty **Sapphire Pool** and then past **Jewel Geyser,** which typically erupts every 7–10 minutes to a height of 15–20 feet. The boardwalk follows a short loop through the other sights of Biscuit Basin. From the west end of the boardwalk, a one-mile trail leads to **Mystic Falls.**

◖ Old Faithful Inn

Matching one of the great sights of the natural world is one of America's most majestic hotels, Old Faithful Inn. One of the largest log structures of its kind in existence, the inn has delighted generations of visitors and continues to enthrall all who enter. Now more than a century old, the building was designed by Robert Reamer and built in the winter of 1903–1904. Its steeply angled roofline reaches seven stories high, with gables jutting from the sides and flags flying from the roof. Surprisingly, the hotel does not face the geyser. Instead, it was built facing sideways to allow newly arriving visitors the opportunity to view the geyser as they stepped from carriages. As you open the rustic split-log front doors with their hand-wrought hardware, you enter a world of the past. The central lobby towers more than 75 feet overhead and is dominated by a massive four-sided stone fireplace that required 500 tons of stone from a nearby quarry. Four overhanging balconies extend above, each bordered by posts made from gnarled lodgepole burls found within the park. Above the fireplace is an enormous clock designed by Reamer and built on the site by a blacksmith.

Reamer also designed the two wings that were added in 1913 and 1928.

On warm summer evenings, visitors stand out on the porch where they can watch Old Faithful erupting, or sit inside at the hand-crafted tables to write letters as music spills from the grand piano. It's enough to warm the heart of even the most cynical curmudgeon. A good restaurant is on the premises, along with a rustic but comfortable bar, a gift shop, fast-food eatery, ice-cream shop, and ATM. Free 45-minute **tours** of Old Faithful Inn are given several times daily during the summer; check the activity desk for times. Old Faithful Inn closes during the winter; it would be hard to imagine trying to heat such a cavern when it's 30° below zero outside! The building was undergoing a major renovation through 2007, with structural upgrades to protect the building from earthquakes and a variety of other improvements. The inn was to have a shorter operating season during the construction period: open only July–mid-September.

Another nearby building of interest is **Old Faithful Lodge.** Built in 1928, this is the large stone-and-log building just south of the geyser of the same name. The giant fireplace inside is a joy on frosty evenings, and cafeteria windows face the geyser—unlike those at the inn.

Much newer, but an instant classic, is the award-winning **Old Faithful Snow Lodge,** which opened in 1999. This large building offers a sense of rustic elegance, with heavy timbers, a window-lined main entrance, a large stone fireplace, overstuffed couches, and hand-made wrought-iron light fixtures and accents. It is one of just two places (the other being Mammoth Hot Springs Hotel) open in winter.

Old Faithful Services

The Park Service's **Old Faithful Visitor Center** (307/545-2750) is generally open mid-April–early November and mid-December–mid-March. It's open 8 A.M.–7 P.M. daily (information window till 8 P.M.) late May–early September and 8 A.M.–6 P.M. daily the rest of September. During the fall, winter, and spring when park gates are open, the visitor center op-erates 9 A.M.–5 P.M. daily. Various films about Yellowstone are shown throughout the day, and the center has a fine selection of books, maps, and other park publications. In summer, be sure to check the board for the predicted eruptions of six major geysers in the area: Old Faithful, Grand, Daisy, Riverside, Great Fountain, and Castle. The rangers can provide you all sorts of other information, from where to see bighorn sheep to where to find the restrooms. A much-needed new visitor center was being built at Old Faithful, with construction on the $15 million facility in 2006 and 2007. During the construction, temporary buildings near Old Faithful Lodge were to house visitor facilities. Don't expect completion until 2008.

Backcountry permits are available from the ranger station, while food, supplies, and postcards can be purchased at either of the two Yellowstone General Stores. Old Faithful Inn has a gift shop, restaurant, snack bar, ice cream parlor, lounge, and ATM. Cafeteria meals, espresso, and baked goods are available at Old Faithful Lodge, and Old Faithful Snow Lodge houses a restaurant and snack bar. Both of these also have gift shops. In addition, the Old Faithful area has two gas stations, a post office, photo shop, and medical clinic. (See the *Accommodations* section for lodging details.) Note that camping is *not* available in the Old Faithful area, and it's illegal to stay overnight in the parking lots. The closest campgrounds are in Madison (16 miles north) and Grant Village (19 miles southeast).

MIDWAY AND LOWER GEYSER BASINS

Heading north from Upper Geyser Basin, the road follows the Firehole River past Midway and Lower Geyser Basins, both of which are quite interesting. This stretch of the river is popular with fly-fishing enthusiasts, and several side roads provide access to a variety of hot springs and other sights.

◖ Midway Geyser Basin

Midway is a large and readily accessible geyser basin with a loop path leading to most of the

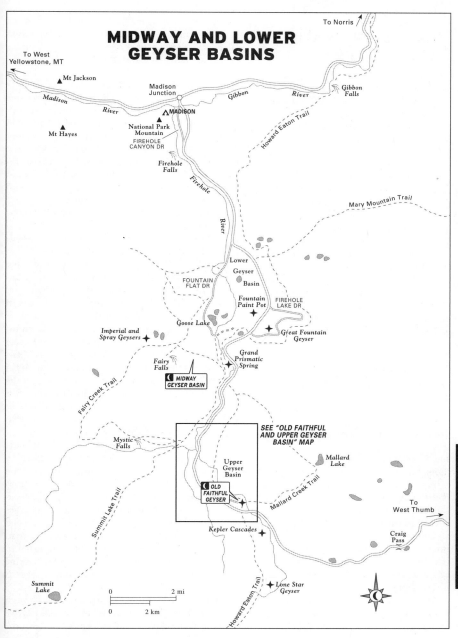

MIDWAY AND LOWER GEYSER BASINS

To Norris

To West
Yellowstone, MT

Mt Jackson

Madison
Junction

Madison River   *Gibbon River*   Gibbon
Falls

MADISON

Mt Hayes

National Park
Mountain
FIREHOLE
CANYON DR

Howard Eaton Trail

*Firehole
Falls*

Firehole

Mary Mountain Trail

River

Lower
Geyser
Basin

FOUNTAIN
FLAT DR

*Fountain
Paint Pot*

FIREHOLE
LAKE DR

Goose Lake

Imperial and
Spray Geysers

*Great Fountain
Geyser*

*Fairy
Falls*

☾ **MIDWAY
GEYSER BASIN**

*Grand
Prismatic
Spring*

Fairy Creek Trail

*Mystic
Falls*

SEE "OLD FAITHFUL
AND UPPER GEYSER
BASIN" MAP

Upper
Geyser
Basin

*Mallard
Lake*

☾ **OLD
FAITHFUL
GEYSER**

Summit Lake Trail

Mallard Creek Trail

To
West Thumb

Kepler Cascades

*Craig
Pass*

*Summit
Lake*

0   2 mi

0   2 km

Howard Eaton Trail

*Lone Star
Geyser*

YELLOWSTONE

GRAND PRISMATIC SPRING, 1839

At length we came to a boiling Lake about 300 ft in diameter forming nearly a complete circle as we approached on the south side The steam which arose from it was of three distinct Colors from the west side for one third of the diameter it was white, in the middle it was pale red, and the remaining third on the east light sky blue Whether it was something peculiar in the state of the atmosphere the day being cloudy or whether it was some Chemical properties contained in the water which produced this phenomenon I am unable to say and shall leave the explanation to some scientific tourist who may have the Curiosity to visit this place at some future period – The water was of deep indigo blue boiling like an imense caldron running over the white rock which had formed the edges to the height of 4 or 5 feet from the surface of the earth sloping gradually for 60 or 70 feet. What a field of speculation this presents for chemist and geologist.

—Mountain man Osborne Russell

sights. **Excelsior Geyser** is actually an enormous hot spring that pours 4,000 gallons per minute of steaming water into the Firehole River. The water is a deep turquoise. During the 1880s, this geyser was truly stupendous, with explosions that reached 380 feet in the air and almost as wide. These violent eruptions apparently damaged the plumbing system that fed them, and the geyser was dormant for nearly a century until smaller eruptions took place in 1985.

At 370 feet across, **Grand Prismatic Spring** is Yellowstone's largest hot spring. The brilliant reds and yellows around the edges of the blue pool are from algae and bacteria that can tolerate temperatures of 170°F. It's difficult to get a good perspective on this spring from the ground; see aerial photos to really appreciate its beauty.

Firehole Lake Drive

This road (one-way heading north) goes three miles through Lower Geyser Basin, the park's most extensive geyser basin. **Great Fountain Geyser** is truly one of the most spectacular geysers in Yellowstone. Charles Cook, of the 1869 Cook-Folsom-Peterson Expedition, recalled his impression of the geyser: "We could not contain our enthusiasm; with one accord we all took off our hats and yelled with all our might." Modern-day visitors would not be faulted for reacting similarly.

Great Fountain erupts every 9–12 hours (although it can be irregular) and usually reaches 100 feet, but it has been known to blast more than 200 feet. Eruptions begin 70–100 minutes after water starts to overflow from the crater and last for 45–60 minutes in a series of decreasingly active eruptive cycles; but don't leave too early or you may miss the real show! Eruption predictions are posted at the geyser and in the Old Faithful Visitor Center. While you're waiting, watch the periodic eruptions of **White Dome Geyser** just 100 yards down the road. Because of its massive 30-foot cone, this is believed to be one of the oldest geysers in the park. Eruptions occur every 10 minutes to three hours and spray 30 feet into the air.

Another mile ahead, the road literally cuts into the mound of **Pink Cone Geyser,** which now erupts every 6–20 hours and reaches a height of 30 feet. The pink color comes from manganese oxide. Just up from here at the bend in the road is **Firehole Lake,** which discharges 3,500 gallons of water per minute into Tangled Creek, which in turn drains across the road into **Hot Lake. Steady Geyser** is unusual in that it forms both sinter (silica) and travertine (calcium carbonate) deposits. The geyser is along the edge of Hot Lake and, true to its name, erupts almost continuously, although the height is only five feet. Firehole Lake Drive continues another mile to its junction with the main road right across from the parking area for Fountain Paint Pot. In the winter, Firehole Lake Drive is popular with skiers but is closed to snowmobiles.

Fountain Paint Pot

Always a favorite of visitors, Fountain Paint Pot seems to have a playfulness about it that belies the immense power just below the surface. Pick up a trail guide ($0.50) as you head up the walkway for the full story. **Silex Spring,** off to the right as you walk up the small hill, is colored by different kinds of algae and bacteria. The spring has been known to erupt as a geyser (to 20 feet) but is currently dormant.

The famous Fountain Paint Pot is a few steps up the boardwalk and consists of colorful mud that changes in consistency throughout the season depending on soil moisture. The pressure from steam and gases under the Paint Pot can throw gobs of mud up to 20 feet into the air. Just north of here are fumaroles that spray steam, carbon dioxide, and hydrogen sulfide into the air.

Continuing down the boardwalk, you come upon an impressive overlook above a multitude of geysers that change constantly in activity, including **Morning Geyser,** which has been known to erupt more than 200 feet. The most active is **Clepsydra Geyser,** which is in eruption much of the time. **Fountain Geyser** explodes in a stunning display that can last 30 minutes and reach up to 50 feet. Eruptions are unpredictable but impressive, particularly at sunset. The rest of the loop trail passes dead lodgepole pines that are being petrified as the silica is absorbed, creating a bobby-socks appearance.

Fountain Flat

Fountain Flat Drive provides access to meadows along the Firehole River and is a good place to see bison and elk. The paved road ends after one mile at a parking area, but hikers and cyclists (or skiers in winter) can continue another four miles on Old Fountain Freight Road to its junction with the main road again near Midway Geyser Basin. The road ends in a parking area near **Ojo Caliente**—a small hot springs with a big odor—right along the river. Several more hot springs are upstream from here, and the **Fairy Falls Trail** starts three miles south of the parking area (see *Old Faithful Area Hikes* under *Recreation*).

Firehole Canyon Drive

This one-way road (south only) curves for two miles through Firehole Canyon, where dark rhyolite cliffs rise hundreds of feet above the river. The road begins just south of Madison Junction and was intensely burned in the 1988 North Fork Fire, giving the canyon's name a dual meaning. **Firehole Falls,** a 40-foot drop, is worth stopping to see, as is **Firehole Cascades** a bit farther up. Kids of all ages enjoy the popular hot springs–warmed swimming hole a short distance up the road. It's one of the few places along the Yellowstone road system where swimming is openly allowed (albeit not encouraged). No lifeguard is provided, of course.

Recreation

DAY HIKING

Short nature trails (0.5 mile or less) are briefly described in the *Exploring Yellowstone* section, but Yellowstone also has a wonderful diversity of day hikes that are perfect for all levels of ability. Park visitor centers distribute free handouts for trails covering Mammoth, Old Faithful, Grant Village, Canyon, and Lake Yellowstone areas. You can also buy a day-hike sampler pamphlet ($0.25) or various hiking books. Good ones are *Yellowstone Trails* by Mark C. Marschall and *A Ranger's Guide to Yellowstone Day Hikes* by Roger Anderson and Carol Shively Anderson.

The Park Service offers free naturalist-led programs and interpretive walks, along with half-day Ranger Adventure Hikes ($5) most days; see your copy of *Yellowstone Today* for the current schedule.

MAMMOTH AREA HIKES
Bunsen Peak

This trail begins a short way up the Bunsen Peak Road (closed to motor vehicles) from the Golden Gate entrance and climbs through forest and meadow to the top of Bunsen Peak, where you'll find panoramic vistas of the entire region. Return via the same path for 4.2 miles round-trip. The trailhead is five miles south of Mammoth on the Mammoth–Norris Road, across from the Glen Creek Trailhead.

Osprey Falls

This dirt track is open to hikers and mountain-bikers but closed to cars. Follow it 2.5 miles to the Osprey Falls Trail, where a steep path (no bikes allowed) drops 700 feet in less than a mile to the base of this 150-foot waterfall. You'll need to climb back out the same way, so don't get too late of a start. The trailhead is five miles south of Mammoth on the Mammoth–Norris Road, across from the Glen Creek Trailhead.

Beaver Ponds Loop

This five-mile round-trip trail begins with a 350-foot climb up and above Clematis Gulch.

Turn right at the junction with Sepulcher Mountain Trail, and the trail soon levels out and rambles through meadows and aspen to a series of beaver ponds. Past here, the route loops back to Mammoth through forests and grassland. This trail provides a good opportunity to see mule deer, elk, pronghorn antelope, and moose, but it is best hiked in the spring or fall when temperatures are lower. Black and grizzly bears are sometimes seen along the way, so be sure to make noise while you walk. The trailhead is between Liberty Cap and the stone house next to Mammoth Terraces.

Sepulcher Mountain Trail

Follow the Beaver Ponds Trail to the Sepulcher Mountain Trail junction and then climb sharply (you'll be sweating) through forest and meadows to the top of this 9,652-foot peak just northwest of Mammoth. Return the same way or via a loop trail that continues along the opposite side of the mountain through an open slope to the junction of Snow Pass Trail, which descends to the Howard Eaton Trail, and then back to Mammoth. You'll find abundant late-summer flowers in the expansive meadows on the south side of Sepulcher Mountain (named for several strange rocks at its summit). Before heading out, check at the visitor center to see if there are any major bear problems in the area and to get a topographic map and hiking tips. This is a strenuous, 11-mile round-trip hike. The trailhead is between Liberty Cap and the stone house next to Mammoth Terraces.

NORTHEAST CORNER HIKES
Slough Creek Trail

This trail—actually a wagon road—makes for a delightful day hike through Douglas fir forests and open meadows. The first mile gains 400 feet in elevation, but it's mostly downhill on the way back. The road continues all the way to the park boundary, 11 miles north of the campground, and is used for access to Silver Tip Ranch. This is the only way into the ranch, and because no motor vehicles are allowed you may meet folks on a horse-drawn wagon during your hike. Day-hikers often go up the road as far as the first meadow, but more adventurous hikers continue to the second meadow (10 miles round-trip). The trailhead is on the dirt road toward Slough Creek Campground, where the road turns left.

Pebble Creek Trail

This remote area is far from the crowds around Old Faithful or Canyon. The strenuous trail climbs 1,000 feet in 1.5 miles before dropping into flower-filled mountain meadows along Pebble Creek. A second trailhead at Pebble Creek Campground anchors the other end of this trail, but at 12 miles it's too long for most day-hikers. Backpackers use this route for longer trips into the area (see *Backcountry Hiking* for details). The trailhead is at Warm Creek Picnic Area, 1.5 miles west of the Northeast Entrance station.

TOWER/ROOSEVELT HIKES
Lost Lake Trail

This moderate trail climbs through forested hills to Lost Lake, where you can either return via the Roosevelt Horse Trail (four miles round-trip) or contour along the hillside to the Petrified Tree parking area, where another path loops back to the lodge. Black bears are often seen in the area, so stay alert. The trailhead is behind Roosevelt Lodge.

Mt. Washburn

This outstanding and extremely popular day hike is accessible from two different trailheads along the Tower–Canyon Road, both of which are equal in length (six miles round-trip) and in elevation gained. Either route ascends 10,243-foot Mt. Washburn on a wide path, and the north end is open to mountain bikes. The summit provides commanding vistas in all directions, with a shelter at the base of the fire lookout (which has telescopes, water, and toilets). Many wildflowers bloom in midsummer, and bighorn sheep are frequently seen right along the trail. Bring warm clothes and rain

gear because conditions on top may be much cooler and windier than below. Mornings are better times to climb Mt. Washburn since afternoon thunderstorms often roll in during the summer. Trailheads are at Dunraven Pass parking area (14 miles south of Tower Junction on the Tower–Canyon Road) or Chittenden Road parking area (nine miles south of Tower Junction). The Dunraven Pass parking area is often full, but space is generally available at the north trailhead.

GRAND CANYON OF THE YELLOWSTONE HIKES
Seven Mile Hole Trail

This strenuous, 11-mile round-trip trail provides fantastic views for the first mile or so, minus the crowds at nearby Inspiration Point. Look for Silver Cord Cascade, a thin ribbon of water dropping over the opposite wall of the canyon, but be careful not to go too close to the very loose edge. It's a very long way down! The trail switchbacks steeply to the Yellowstone River, passing odoriferous thermal areas en route. Many anglers come to Seven Mile Hole (it's seven miles downriver from Lower Falls) while other folks come to relax along the river. Save your energy for the strenuous 1,400-foot climb back up, and bring lots of drinking water. Three campsites are available near the base of the trail for those who want to make this an overnight hike (backcountry permit required). The trailhead is at the Glacial Boulder pullout on the road to Inspiration Point.

South Rim Trail

This six-mile round-trip hike follows the almost-level and partly paved South Rim Trail two miles to Artist Point, providing many viewpoints en route, including an optional hike down Uncle Tom's Trail, a steep 500-foot drop to Lower Falls. The least-traveled part of the trail (it's called Ribbon Lake Trail) continues eastward along the top, providing an abrupt escape from the mob scene at Artist Point, as well as a chance to see the kaleidoscopically colored canyon, hear the roar of the river from far below, and watch for squirrels and birds. But be careful to stay away from the edge where the rocks are loose. It's doubtful that anyone could survive such a fall, and I once came perilously close to testing that postulate. The trail continues to Lily Pad Lake, where a spur path leads uphill for a wonderful view of the canyon and Silver Cord Cascade. With a drop of 1,200 feet, Silver Cord is the highest falls in Yellowstone. You can return the same way or via a number of loop hikes in the area; get the park's *Canyon Area Trail Guide* for details. (As an aside, the old trail to Point Sublime has been closed because of unsafe conditions along the canyon rim.) The trailhead is at the east end of Chittenden Bridge across from Wapiti Lake Picnic Area.

YELLOWSTONE LAKE AREA HIKES
Natural Bridge

An easy three-mile round-trip hike brings you to a 51-foot-high span of rock that was carved by the waters of Bridge Creek. The trail meanders through the forest 0.25 mile and then follows a paved road the rest of the way. A short, but steep, switchback trail to the top of the bridge starts in front of the interpretive exhibit. Above the bridge, the trail crosses the creek and continues along the cliff before rejoining the road. Cyclists can ride bikes to Natural Bridge on a separate trail that begins south of the marina. The Natural Bridge area is closed in spring and early summer when bears are feeding on spawning trout in the creek. The trailhead is at the Bridge Bay Marina parking lot near the campground entrance road.

Storm Point Trail

This pleasant 2.3-mile loop trail is essentially level and goes past a large colony of yellow-bellied marmots before reaching windswept Storm Point, where waves often pound against the rocks. Following the shoreline to the west, the trail eventually loops back through the lodgepole forest to Indian Pond. The trail may be closed in spring and early summer because of grizzlies, and mosquitoes may make a June or July trip less enjoyable. The trailhead is at the Indian Pond pullout, three miles east of Fishing Bridge Visitor Center.

Elephant Back Mountain Trail

This nice 3.6-mile round-trip hike climbs 800 feet in elevation through dense lodgepole forests to panoramic views across Yellowstone Lake and into Pelican Valley. After a mile the trail splits into a loop, both sides of which join at the overlook. The trailhead is at the pullout one mile south of Fishing Bridge Junction.

Avalanche Peak Trail

This strenuous four-mile round-trip hike begins on the east side of Middle Creek and climbs very steeply. It emerges from the forest halfway up at the base of a large bowl, and then it continues to the left and switchbacks over talus slopes to an open area below the summit. Follow the trail up the narrow ridgeline and cross it with extreme caution. At the summit, you can see most of the peaks in the Absarokas and Tetons, but snow is present on top until mid-July. Hiking isn't recommended here in September and October because of the presence of grizzly bears feeding on whitebark pinenuts. The trailhead is across the road from the pullout at the west end of Eleanor Lake (eight miles west of East Entrance).

WEST THUMB AND GRANT VILLAGE HIKES
Lewis River Channel/ Dogshead Loop

Choose between two trails—or combine them into a loop hike—to Shoshone Lake. The 4-mile-long Dogshead Trail is more direct, while the 7-mile Lewis Channel Trail takes a much more scenic trek via the channel connecting Shoshone and Lewis lakes. This slow-flowing creek is popular with anglers who come to fish for brown and cutthroat trout during the fall spawning season, and it's also used by canoeists and kayakers heading into Shoshone Lake. Much of the Lewis Lake area was burned in the 1988 fires. Dogshead Trailhead is just north of Lewis Lake on the west side of road (five miles south of Grant Village).

Yellowstone Lake Overlook

This fine two-mile round-trip hike gains 400 feet in elevation in a mile, enough for a commanding vista across the lake, with the Absaroka Mountains behind.

DeLacy Creek Trail

This six-mile round-trip hike provides access to Shoshone Lake—Yellowstone's largest backcountry lake—which is circled by more trails. Keep your eyes open for moose, sandhill cranes, and other animals in the meadows along the way. DeLacy Creek Trailhead is nine miles west of West Thumb Junction.

OLD FAITHFUL AREA HIKES
Lone Star Geyser Trail

A wide paved trail (actually an old road) leads to this popular geyser. It's a favorite of bicyclists in the summer and skiers in the winter. Lone Star Geyser erupts every three hours from a distinctive nine-foot-high cone, with eruptions generally reaching 45 feet and lasting for 30 minutes. Bikes are not allowed beyond the geyser. Hikers can also get to Lone Star via the Howard Eaton Trail out of Old Faithful (6 miles round-trip). For a longer hike, you can continue south from Lone Star on Shoshone Lake Trail to Shoshone Lake, eight fairly easy miles from the main road. Lone Star Geyser Trailhead is 3.5 miles south of Old Faithful Junction (just east of Kepler Cascades).

Mystic Falls Trail

This path follows a pretty creek to where the Little Firehole River cascades 70 feet over Mystic Falls. You can switchback farther up the trail to the top of the falls and then connect with another trail for the loop back to Biscuit Basin (three miles round-trip). This is a very nice short hike and can be lengthened into a trip to Little Firehole Meadows (10 miles round-trip), where bison are often seen in the summer. The trailhead is at the back of the Biscuit Basin boardwalk (two miles north of Old Faithful Junction).

Fountain Freight Road/Fairy Falls

The four-mile-long Fountain Freight Road is closed to cars, but it's a great place for mountain-bikers and those out for a relatively level walk. A steel bridge crosses the Firehole River at the southern trailhead, and the road soon passes the west side of Grand Prismatic Spring; rough trails lead up the hillside for a better view. One mile up from the trailhead you'll come to Fairy Falls Trail on your left. It's an easy walk to the falls, a 200-foot ribbon of water cascading into a large pool. The hike to Fairy Falls can be combined with longer treks to Little Firehole Meadow and Mystic Falls or to a pair of small peaks called Twin Buttes. Half a mile beyond Fairy Falls are Imperial Geyser, with periodic small eruptions. Nearby Spray Geyser erupts frequently, sending water six feet in the air. For a longer version of the hike to Fairy Falls (10 miles round-trip), start from the north end, where Fountain Flat Drive ends. The trailhead is one mile south of Midway Geyser Basin (4.5 miles north of the Old Faithful Interchange).

BACKCOUNTRY HIKING

Most Yellowstone visitors act as though they were chained to their cars with a 100-yard tether—as if by getting away from their vehicles they might miss some other sight down the road. For the 2 percent or so who *do* abandon their cars, Yellowstone has much to offer beyond the spectacular geysers and canyons for which it is famous. Although many parts of the Yellowstone backcountry are heavily visited, regulations keep the sense of wildness intact by separating campsites and limiting the number of hikers. If you head out early or late in the season, you'll discover solitude just a few miles from the traffic jams.

Much of Yellowstone consists of lodgepole (or burned lodgepole) forests on rolling terrain. With a few exceptions, anyone looking for dramatic alpine scenery would probably be better off heading to Grand Teton National Park, the Beartooth Mountains, or the Wind River Mountains. The Yellowstone backcountry is still enjoyable to walk through, however, and many trails lead past waterfalls, geysers, and hot springs. Besides, this is one of the finest places in America to view wildlife—including bison, elk, grizzlies, and wolves—in a setting other than a zoo.

Before August, when they start to die down, you should be ready for the ubiquitous mosquitoes. Ticks are a nuisance mid-March– mid-July in lower-elevation parts of Yellowstone. The fires of 1988 created some problems for backcountry hikers but also offer a good opportunity to see how the land is recovering.

Rules and Regulations

The Park Service maintains more than 300 campsites in the Yellowstone backcountry, most of which have pit toilets and fire rings, along with storage poles to keep food from bears. Hikers may stay only at designated campsites. Wood fires are not allowed in many areas and are discouraged elsewhere, so be sure to have a gas stove for cooking. Bear-management areas have special regulations; they may be for day-use only, include seasonal restrictions, or specify minimum group sizes. Pets are not allowed on the trails within Yellowstone, and special rules apply for those coming in with horses, mules, burros, and llamas. Because of wet conditions and the lack of forage, no stock animals are permitted before July.

A free **backcountry-use permit** is required of each overnight party and is available in person from various Yellowstone ranger stations and visitor centers within 48 hours of your hike. Because of the popularity of backcountry trips, you should make reservations before your arrival in the park. Unfortunately, the Park Service has taken a lesson from the IRS and makes the process as complex as bureaucratically possible. Try to follow me here. Reservations cost $20 per trip, and the reservation forms are available from the Backcountry Office, P.O. Box 168, Yellowstone National Park, WY 82190, 307/344-2160. Campsite reservation requests must be mailed in, using these forms; reservations are not accepted by phone, fax, or over the Internet (but there is a printable version on the park website, www.nps.gov/yell). You'll receive a confirmation notice by return mail and will exchange the notice for a permit when you get

there; the permit must be obtained in person at a ranger station within 48 hours of your first camping date. Before receiving your permit, you will be given a lengthy rundown on what to expect and what precautions to take, and you'll be shown a bear-safety video. The ranger stations are generally open 8 A.M.–4:30 P.M. seven days a week June–August.

For backcountry rules, bear-safety tips, and suggestions for hiking and horsepacking, pick up (or find it on the web) Yellowstone's *Backcountry Trip Planner,* which shows locations of campsites throughout the park and provides detailed information on wilderness access and precautions. You may want to also pick up or request the free park pamphlet *Beyond Road's End.*

Those interested in horsepacking or llama trips should contact the park (307/344-7381, www.nps.gov/yell) for a list of outfitters authorized to operate in Yellowstone. The outfitters offer everything from day trips to weeklong adventures deep into the backcountry.

Before you head out you will probably want to look over your hiking options. Two excellent source books are *Yellowstone Trails,* by Mark Marschall, and *Hiking Yellowstone National Park,* by Bill Schneider. Get them from park gift shops or visitor centers, which also sell topographic park maps. The best maps are those produced by Trails Illustrated; these feature all of the major trails and show the severity of burn from the 1988 fires—a considerable help when planning hiking trips.

FISHING

In the early years of the park, fish from Yellowstone Lake were a specialty at the various hotels, and because there was no limit on the take, up to 7,500 pounds of fish were caught each year. After commercial fishing was halted, park policy shifted to planting nonnative species. But by the 1970s, Yellowstone Lake had been devastated by overfishing, and new regulations were needed. Beginning in 1973, bait fishing was banned, Fishing Bridge was closed to anglers, and catch-and-release rules were put into place. Increased fish populations have been a boon for wildlife, especially grizzlies, bald eagles, and osprey. Because of these regulations, Yellowstone National Park has achieved an almost mythical status when it comes to fishing. Each year 75,000 visitors spend time fishing in the park. The most commonly caught fish in Yellowstone are cutthroat, rainbow, brown, lake, and brook trout, along with mountain whitefish. Montana grayling are found at only a few small lakes within the park, most notably Grebe Lake. All native species in the park—including Montana grayling, cutthroat trout, and mountain whitefish—are now catch-and-release only. Fishing regulations are complex and are described in a booklet available at park visitor centers or on the web at www.nps.gov/yell.

The Yellowstone River is still considered one of the best places in the world to catch cutthroat trout, and the Madison River is a justifiably famous fly-fishing river with a wide range of conditions. Yellowstone Lake is where the lure anglers go to catch cutthroats and lake trout. Beginners may have luck in the Gallatin River, but they're less likely to do well in the Firehole River, where the fish are smart and wary. Peaceful Slough Creek in the northeast corner of Yellowstone is filled with fat rainbows and cutthroats, attracting fly-fishers from around the globe.

Fishing Regulations

In most parts of Yellowstone, the fishing season extends from Memorial Day weekend in late May to the first Sunday of November, but Lake Yellowstone opens June 15, and the Yellowstone River opens July 15. Hayden Valley and some other areas are entirely closed to fishing, and only artificial lures and flies are allowed in the park. Lead cannot be used. All native species in the park—Montana grayling, cutthroat trout, and mountain whitefish—are catch-and-release only. Barbless hooks are preferable for catch-and-release fishing because they cause less damage and are easier to remove. Some rivers, including the Madison River, the Firehole River, and the Gibbon River (downstream from Gibbon Falls) are open only to fly-fishing. For complete details, request the park's fishing regulations brochure, or find it online at www.nps.gov/yell.

Anglers don't need a state fishing license but must obtain a special Yellowstone National Park permit, available from visitor centers, ranger stations, and Yellowstone General Stores, plus fishing shops in surrounding towns. The adult **fishing fee** is $15 for a three-day permit, $20 for a seven-day permit, or $35 for a season permit. Kids ages 12–15 get permits for free, and younger children do not need a permit. Park visitor centers and ranger stations have copies of current fishing regulations.

BOATING

Bridge Bay Marina runs hour-long scenic **boat tours** of Yellowstone Lake ($10.50 adults, $6.75 ages 2–11) several times a day in the summer, providing a fine introduction to the area. Also available at the marina are **guided fishing charters** ($66–85 per hour for up to six people) and **boat rentals** ($8 per hour for a 16-foot rowboat; $37 per hour for a 18-foot motorboat with a 40-horsepower outboard).

The best Yellowstone Lake fishing is from boats rather than from the shoreline. If you're bringing your own boat or canoe to Yellowstone, pick up a park boat permit—and check out the regulations—at the Lake Ranger Station or Grant Village Visitor Center. Boat slips are available at Bridge Bay Marina. All streams are closed to watercraft, with the exception of the Lewis River Channel between Shoshone and Lewis lakes. Motorboats are allowed only on Lewis Lake and parts of Yellowstone Lake.

Kayaking

Several companies offer guided kayak trips in the park. **Snake River Kayak and Canoe School** (307/733-9999 or 800/529-2501, www.snakeriverkayak.com) leads a variety of trips on Yellowstone Lake, starting with three-hour sunset paddles ($95) and half-day paddles in the West Thumb area ($175), all the way up to eight-day paddling trips that leave the crowds behind as you explore the lake; these cost $1,200 per person, all-inclusive. It also guides kayaking tours of Lewis and Shoshone lakes and has a full range of kayaking classes taught in Jackson and Grand Teton National Park.

Jackson Hole Kayak School (307/733-2471, www.jacksonholekayak.com) has day tours of Yellowstone Lake or Lewis Lake for $350 per person. It also offers three-day tours of Yellowstone Lake for $800 per person, and three-day tours of Lewis and Shoshone lakes for $700 per person. The overnight trip prices include transportation from Jackson, kayaking and camping gear, supplies, and all meals.

O.A.R.S. (209/736-4677 or 800/346-6277, www.oars.com) offers half-day kayak trips from Grant Village for $75 adults or $50 kids. In addition, it guides multiday trips in the Yellowstone-Grand Teton region, including five-day paddle-and-hike adventures for $894 adults or $775 kids. Tents and sleeping bags are available for rent, or bring your own.

BIKING

Cycling provides a unique way to see Yellowstone up close. Unfortunately, park roads tend to have narrow shoulders and traffic is heavy, making for dangerous conditions. These problems are exacerbated early in the year by high snowbanks, so bikes are not allowed on certain roads. Call 307/344-7381 for current road conditions. The Park Service produces a helpful "Bicycling in Yellowstone National Park" handout with details on bicycle routes and safety, plus a map showing road conditions; get it from visitor centers or online at www.nps.gov/yell.

If you're planning a cycling trip through Yellowstone, be sure to wear a helmet and high-visibility clothing. A bike mirror also helps. If you want to avoid some of the hassles and don't mind spring conditions, visit the park between late March and the third Friday in April, when motorized vehicles are usually prohibited from entering the park (except for park administrative vehicles). During this period, cyclists are allowed to ride only on the stretch between the West Entrance and Mammoth Hot Springs; other roads are closed to cycling because they're being plowed. Fall is also a good time to ride because traffic is much lighter than in summer.

The best times to ride in summer are in the morning before traffic thickens or late in the afternoon before the light begins to fade and you become less visible to motorists.

Where to Ride

The best main park roads to ride (less traffic or better visibility and shoulders) are the following sections: Mammoth to Tower, Tower to Cooke City, Canyon to Lake, and Lake to Grant Village. Bikes are not allowed on backcountry trails or boardwalks inside Yellowstone. Several relatively short but fun mountain-bike rides are available around the park, including the paved trail from Old Faithful to Morning Glory Pool (two miles), the partly paved trail to Lone Star Geyser in the Old Faithful area (two miles), Fountain Flat Drive to the vicinity of Midway Geyser Basin (six miles), the old Chittenden Road up Mt. Washburn (three miles each way, but gaining 1,400 feet on the way up), Bunsen Peak Road near Mammoth (six miles and steep in places), the Old Gardiner Road from Mammoth to Gardiner (five miles), and Blacktail Plateau Drive (seven miles) east of Mammoth. Of these routes, cars are allowed only on the Old Gardiner Road and Blacktail Plateau Drive, but traffic is light on these two.

Bike Rentals and Tours

Unfortunately, there are no bike rentals inside Yellowstone, although they are available in the surrounding towns of West Yellowstone, Jackson, Gardiner, and Cody. **Backroads** (800/462-2848, www.backroads.com) has six-day multisport trips into Yellowstone and Grand Teton that include biking, hiking, rafting, and kayaking. These are offered as either camping trips ($3,400 for two people including meals) or trips on which you stay at local inns ($4,400–5,200 for two people including meals). Contact the Park Service for a list of other permitted bicycle-tour operators.

HORSEBACK RIDING

Summertime trail rides are available from the corrals at Mammoth Hot Springs, Canyon Village, and Roosevelt Lodge. These cost $31 for

trail ride near Mammoth Hot Springs

one hour or $50 for a two-hour ride. Kids must be at least eight years old and 48 inches tall, and there is a 250-pound weight limit, much to the relief of the horses. Roosevelt also has **stagecoach rides** ($8.75 adults, $7.25 ages 2–11) several times a day in the summer. In addition, **Old West dinner cookouts** at Roosevelt combine a horseback or wagon ride with a filling steak dinner.

For details on trail rides, contact Xanterra Parks and Resorts (307/344-7311, www.travel-yellowstone.com). Several outfitters provide backcountry pack trips inside Yellowstone; get a list from Park Service visitor centers (307/344-7381, www.nps.gov/yell).

HOT SPRINGS

Many people are disappointed to discover that there are no places in Yellowstone where you can soak in the hot springs. Not only is "hot-potting" illegal, but it can also be dangerous because temperatures often approach boiling and bathers can cause severe damage to these surprisingly fragile natural wonders. Legal bathing pools are found in cold-water streams that have hot springs feeding into them. You're not allowed to enter the source pool or stream itself. Families often stop for a swim in the Firehole River along Firehole Canyon Drive near Madison. The Park Service doesn't encourage this, and there are no lifeguards, so parents need to watch children closely.

WINTER RECREATION

Winter transforms Yellowstone into an extraordinarily beautiful place where the fires and brimstone of hell meet the bitter cold and snow of winter. The snow often averages four feet in depth but can exceed 10 feet on mountain passes. The snow is usually quite dry, although late in the season conditions deteriorate as temperatures rise. Early in the winter or after major storms, backcountry skiing can be difficult because of the deep powder. Temperatures are generally in the 10–25°F range during the day, while nights frequently dip below zero. (The record is -66°F, recorded on February 9, 1933.) Winds can make these temperatures feel even lower, so visitors should come prepared for extreme conditions.

YELLOWSTONE

The thermal basins are a real wintertime treat. Hot springs that are simply colorful pools in summer send up billows of steam in the winter, coating nearby trees with thick layers of ice and turning them into "ghost trees." The geysers put on astounding displays as boiling water meets frigid air; steam from Old Faithful can tower 1,000 feet into the air! Bison and elk gather around the hot springs, soaking up the heat and searching for dried grasses, and bald eagles are often seen flying over the heated waters of Firehole River. The bison are perhaps the most interesting to watch as they swing their enormous heads from side to side to shovel snow off the grass. Grand Canyon of the Yellowstone is another place transformed by the snow and cold. Although the water still flows, the falls are surrounded by tall cones of ice, and the canyon walls lie under deep snow. A good resource on winter access to Yellowstone is *Yellowstone Winter Guide* by Jeff Henry (www.roberts-rinehart.com).

Roads

Most of Yellowstone's roads officially close to cars on the Monday after the first Sunday in November and remain shut down all over except for the 56 miles between Mammoth and Cooke City. Roads don't open for cars again until sometime between mid-May and early June. The roads are groomed for snowmobiles and snowcoaches mid-December–mid-March. The rest of the winter you'll find only skiers and park personnel on the roads. During winter, the most popular (and crowded) times to visit Yellowstone are around Christmas and New Year's and the Presidents' Day weekend in February. If you plan to arrive at these times, make lodging reservations six months in advance. The rest of the winter, you should probably reserve at least three months ahead.

Services

Only the Mammoth and Old Faithful visitor centers are open during winter. Free ranger-led activities include evening programs at Mammoth and Old Faithful. Check the winter edition of *Yellowstone Today* for details, or find it on the web at www.nps.gov/yell.

Xanterra Parks and Resorts (307/344-7311, www.travelyellowstone.com) offers a variety of guided ski and snowmobile tours and provides wildlife bus or van tours. In addition, the Yellowstone Association Institute (307/344-2294, www.yellowstoneassociation.org) has outstanding winter classes.

The Mammoth Clinic (307/344-7965) is open weekdays—except Friday afternoons—in the winter for medical emergencies.

Supplies and Warming Huts

The Yellowstone General Store at Mammoth is open for groceries and supplies year-round, but only meals and gas are available at Old Faithful. Warming huts are at Old Faithful, Madison Junction, Canyon, West Thumb, Fishing Bridge, and Indian Creek (south of Mammoth Hot Springs). All contain restrooms and snack machines (except Indian Creek and West Thumb), and all are open 24 hours (except for Old Faithful, where other facilities are available). The huts at Madison and Canyon also have snack bars selling hot chili or soup. Park rangers are often at the warming huts during the middle of the day.

SNOWCOACHES

The easiest and most enjoyable way to get into Yellowstone in the winter is on the ungainly snowcoaches—machines that look like something the Norwegian Army might have used during World War II. Most were actually built by a Canadian company, Bombidier. They can be noisy, and the windows fog up (hence the spray bottles of antifreeze). But despite their ancient condition and spartan interiors, these beasts still work well and can carry 10 passengers, gear (two suitcases per person), and skis. You will also see (or ride in) several other oversnow vehicles, including vans on tracks.

A variety of snowcoach tours are provided by Xanterra Parks and Resorts (307/344-7311, www.travelyellowstone.com). All snowcoach tours and transportation are half price for kids ages 2–11 and free for toddlers. Adult per-person rates to Old Faithful are $60 round-trip from Flagg Ranch (where the plowing ends just south of Yellowstone), $51 round-trip from West Yellowstone, and $60 round-trip from Mammoth. It also provides all-day tours most days of the week from Mammoth to Canyon for $110 round-trip, Mammoth to Old Faithful for $120 round-trip, and Old Faithful to Canyon for $115 round-trip.

Shorter snowcoach tours depart two or three times a week from Old Faithful for the Firehole River/Fountain Flats area (three hours; $27.50 round-trip). Three-hour winter wildlife bus tours to the Lamar Valley ($24) depart from Mammoth on Wednesdays, providing a good opportunity to see wolves. Also available from Mammoth is a daybreak bus tour (3.5 hours; $27 with a continental breakfast). See below for combination snowcoach and cross-country skiing trips. For any of these trips, be sure to make reservations well in advance.

During the winter, **Alltrans/Gray Line** (307/733-4325 or 800/443-6133, www.jacksonholealltrans.com) has daily bus runs from Jackson to Flagg Ranch for $60 round-trip, arriving in time to meet the snowcoach departures for Yellowstone. Reservations required.

Yellowstone Alpen Guides (406/646-9591 or 800/858-3502, www.yellowstoneguides.com) leads snowcoach tours from West Yellowstone. All-day trips are $99 adults, $89 seniors, $79 kids to either Grand Canyon of the Yellowstone or Old Faithful. Guests on the latter run have an option of getting dropped at Biscuit Basin, where they can ski to Old Faithful and meet the rest of the group for the return trip. Special snowcoach-and-guided-snowshoe tours are $110 per person (four-person minimum). Ski or snowshoe rentals are available. The classic snowcoaches (one built in 1953) have been modernized, but they are still a charming anachronism.

Buffalo Bus Touring Co. (406/646-9564 or 800/426-7669, www.yellowstonevacations.com) operates modern snowcoach vans, with all-day tours from West Yellowstone to Old Faithful ($89 adults, $69 kids) or Canyon ($99 adults, $79 kids).

For a truly unique experience, book a trip with another West Yellowstone–based company, **Yellowstone Expeditions** (406/646-9333 or 800/728-9333, www.yellowstoneexpeditions.com). It runs converted vans and has a remote base camp near Canyon that is perfect for those who want to really explore Yellowstone in winter. Guests stay in eight heated tent cabins, with two yurts providing a central kitchen and dining/social area. These trips start at $1,600 for two people for three nights and four days, up to $2,600 for two people for seven nights and eight days. The price includes lodging, food, bedding, round-trip transportation from West Yellowstone to the base camp near Canyon, and backcountry ski guides. Ski and snowshoe rentals are extra. Days are spent skiing or snowshoeing in the Canyon area or along trails around Hayden Valley, Norris, or Mt. Washburn. The cedar sauna is perfect after a long day in the backcountry. This is the only overnight accommodation at the Canyon area during the winter.

SKIING AND SNOWSHOEING

Cross-country skis and snowshoes provide the finest ways to see Yellowstone in the winter. Rent them from Old Faithful Snow Lodge or Mammoth Hot Springs Hotel. Both places also provide lessons and guided tours for groups or individuals. The towns surrounding Yellowstone also have shops that rent skis and snowshoes. The Old Faithful area is the center for skiing within Yellowstone, with trails circling the Upper Geyser Basin and leading to nearby sights. You'll find similar ski trails (marked but not groomed) in the Tower Fall, Canyon, Northeast, and Mammoth areas. Get free ski-trail maps at park visitor centers. Old Faithful Snow Lodge is open in winter, providing an excellent base for day trips into nearby areas or for a snowcoach tour of the park.

Skiers and snowshoers sometimes assume that they can't possibly cause problems for Yellowstone's wildlife, but studies show that elk and bison often move away from skiers, which forces the animals to expend energy they need to survive through the bitterly cold winters. It's best to stay on the trails and to keep from skiing into areas where elk or bison may be disturbed by your presence. For more on skiing and winter visitation in the park, see Jeff Henry's *Yellowstone Winter Guide* (www.roberts-rinehart.com), or *Winter Tales and Trails: Skiing, Snowshoeing and Snowboarding in Idaho, the Grand Tetons and Yellowstone National Park* by Ron Watters (Great Rift Press).

Shuttles and Tours

Xanterra Parks and Resorts (307/344-7311, www.travelyellowstone.com) operates **skier shuttles** ($14 round-trip) from Mammoth eastward by van to Blacktail Plateau and Tower Junction, or southward by snowcoach to Golden Gate and Indian Creek. From these last two folks choose to ski back to Mammoth because it's mostly downhill. A similar snowcoach shuttle is available from Old Faithful to Fairy Falls Trailhead or the Continental Divide area for $13. In these last two trips you ski back to the Snow Lodge on your own; the Continental Divide run is eight miles long and primarily downhill.

In addition, Xanterra has all-day Grand Canyon snowcoach-and-guided-ski tours ($115 round-trip) twice a week from Old Faithful and once weekly from Mammoth. **Afternoon ski-daddles** are guided five-hour ski tours from Old Faithful to Fairy Falls or DeLacey Creek. They're offered twice a week and cost $40.

Guided snowshoe tours ($27 with snowshoes) are offered twice weekly from Old Faithful and Mammoth. They last three hours and are a great way to explore the country. Besides these concessioner-run tours, park naturalists sometimes lead ski trips from Old Faithful to nearby sights. Stop by the visitor center for details.

Safety on Skis

Before your trip, call Yellowstone (307/344-7381) to request the informative *Winter Back-country Trip Planner,* with details on trails, equipment, weather, and avalanche safety. Yellowstone's roads are traveled by snowmobiles and snowcoaches, making for potential conflicts with skiers. Be sure to keep to the right while skiing. Most trails are identified by orange metal markers on the trees. If you're planning a backcountry trip, pick up a use permit from one of the ranger stations. A thorough understanding of winter camping and survival is imperative before you head out on any overnight trip, and avalanche safety classes are a wise investment of your time.

Get avalanche-safety information from the **Gallatin National Forest Avalanche Center** (406/587-6981, www.mtavalanche.com) in Bozeman. The recording does not cover the entire park, but it does include the Washburn Range and areas near Cooke City and West Yellowstone. It's updated daily in the winter. Call 307/344-2113 for a recording of the latest park weather forecast.

SNOWMOBILING

Yellowstone's temporary winter-use plan allows a maximum of 720 guided groups (no private individuals) on snowmobiles with clean-burning four-stroke engines. This plan was to stay in effect through the 2006–07 winter, when a final winter management plan was to come into force.

Snowmobiles are available for rent from all four sides of the park and inside Yellowstone at Mammoth and Old Faithful, with the majority of snowmobilers—all guided—coming in from West Yellowstone, where prices are usually a bit lower and access is quicker. Contact chamber of commerce offices in West Yellowstone, Jackson, or Cody for a listing of companies offering snowmobile tours.

Accommodations

Yellowstone accommodations vary from extremely basic cabins with four thin walls starting at $47 up to luxury suites that will set you back $465. Following a fine old Park Service tradition, the rooms do not have TVs, and most lack phones. Web access is limited to slow phone connections (where available). What they do offer is the chance to relax in comfortable accommodations and explore the magical world outside. Most are open early June–mid-September, with additional winter lodging at Mammoth Hot Springs Hotel and the Old Faithful Snow Lodge. Several hundred more motels and other places to stay operate outside park boundaries in the towns of Jackson, Cody, West Yellowstone, Gardiner, and Cooke City.

Xanterra Parks and Resorts (307/344-7311, www.travelyellowstone.com) is Yellowstone's lodging concessioner. **Make Yellowstone lodging reservations six months ahead** for the park's prime hotels, or you may find that the only rooms available are in Grant Village, the laughingstock of park lodges. Those traveling with small children should also request cribs when making reservations. Wheelchair-accessible (ADA-compliant) rooms are available at most of the park's cabins and hotels. (As an aside, several web-based companies purport to make reservations for hotels and lodges inside Yellowstone, but all of these charge a service fee. Save yourself money and hassles by just going direct to Xanterra.)

At the turn of the 20th century, most visitors to Yellowstone stayed in park hotels rather than roughing it on the ground. Three of these wonderful old lodging places remain: Old Faithful Inn, Lake Yellowstone Hotel, and Mammoth Hot Springs Hotel. Standard motel rooms can be found at Grant Village. In addition, three nicer places opened in the 1990s: the Old Faithful Snow Lodge and two small lodges at Canyon Village. All told, more than 2,200 rooms and cabins provide overnight accommodations in Yellowstone.

Not all lodging options inside the park are nearly as pleasant, however. Hundreds of simple boxes are clustered in the Lake, Mammoth, Old Faithful, and Roosevelt areas. Most of these cabins offer a roof over your head, simple furnishings, and communal showers, but the more expensive cabins are considerably nicer, and two of them even include private hot tubs. Fortunately, prices are fairly reasonable for all of the cabins, and the park concessioner is gradually renovating the oldest units.

Lodging rates are listed for two people; children under age 12 stay free. Add $10 per person for additional older kids or adults in the hotel rooms or cabins. Prices at some park lodging places are lower in May when snow still covers much of the park, but you need to book before April 1. Also available are a variety of winter and summer package deals that include lodging, tours, hikes, and more. Especially noteworthy are the four-day **Lodging and Learning** packages that combine tours, educational activities, and hikes led by naturalist-guides from the Yellowstone Association Institute (307/344-2294, www.yellowstoneassociation.org) with accommodations in park hotels, plus breakfasts and lunches.

Rates listed are without tax, which is 6 percent on the south half of the park (inside Teton County—including Old Faithful, Grant Village, and Lake Village) and 8 percent on the north half (inside Park County—including Roosevelt, Mammoth Hot Springs, and Canyon Village).

CANYON VILLAGE

The centrally situated **Canyon Lodge** is just 0.5 mile from Grand Canyon of the Yellowstone, one of the park's premier attractions. The main lodge is part of a late-1950s complex of ugly structures built around a large parking lot. The area has all the charm of an aging shopping mall from an era when bigger meant better. The lodge itself covers the space of a football field and houses a dining room, cafeteria, lounge, and snack shop, but no guest rooms.

Cabins

Behind the lodge in the trees (at least the setting is peaceful), the road circles past three sprawling clusters of cabins, all with private baths. You'll find 540 cabins here. The most basic "pioneer" units cost $47–64 d and aren't much to look at outside but are actually fairly roomy and comfortable inside. Two newer types of cabins are available at Canyon: the "frontier" units for $87 d and the "western" cabins for $127 d. The western cabins are being renovated over several summers; ask for an updated one if available.

Lodges

Providing far better accommodations are two 1990s additions: **Dunraven Lodge** and **Cascade Lodge.** Rooms at both of these attractive log- and rock-trimmed structures are furnished with rustic lodgepole pieces and have two double beds and private baths. Rooms in the lodges cost $149 d. The cabins and lodges at Canyon are open early June–mid-September.

GRANT VILLAGE

The southernmost lodging in Yellowstone, Grant Village offers accommodations in condo-type units from the 1980s, with exceptional parking-lot views from the rooms. These buildings would be completely out of place in *any* national park, especially Yellowstone. Six hideously ugly lodge buildings contain updated motel-type units for $122 d. All of these have two double beds and private baths, and several wheelchair-accessible rooms are available. A park visitor center and campground are in the area, along with a variety of concessioner facilities, including a restaurant, waterside café, general store, lounge, snack shop, and gift shop. Grant Village is open late May–September and has 300 units.

LAKE VILLAGE

The Lake Village area has a full range of lodging options for travelers. The fascinating Southern colonial–style **◖ Lake Yellowstone Hotel** delivers a magnificent view across Yellowstone Lake. Begun in 1889, the building

expanded and changed through the decades to yield its current configuration of 158 guest rooms. The hotel has been lovingly restored and exudes a grandeur and charm rarely found today. It's the sort of place where Fred Astaire and Ginger Rogers would feel comfortable dancing—if they were still alive.

The Lake Yellowstone's inviting hotel rooms all contain updated furnishings, private baths, and in-room phones. Standard units cost $188 d on the backside or $202 d facing the lake, and a delightfully spacious two-bedroom suite is the most elaborate (and most expensive) accommodation in the park at $465 for four people. For the best vistas, ask for a third-floor room on the lake side when making your reservations.

Downstairs is a good restaurant (reservations required for dinner), along with a fast-food eatery; the cafeteria at Lake Lodge is only a short walk away. The real treat at Lake Yellowstone Hotel is the **Sun Room,** where rows of windows front the lake. The room's ambience is further enhanced by period wicker furnishings and evening chamber music or classical piano. It's a great place to sip a martini or write a postcard. The hotel is open mid-May–mid-October.

Out back is the **Lake Yellowstone Hotel Annex,** where the recently refurbished rooms cost $130 d. No view, but each room has two double beds, phones, a bath, and pleasant furnishings. Some of these are wheelchair-accessible.

Also behind Lake Yellowstone Hotel are more than 100 rather dingy old boxes from the 1950s, each with two double beds and private baths. These have been jammed together in row after identical row to create the **Lake Yellowstone Hotel Frontier Cabins.** Fortunately, they're fairly reasonable ($106 d), and cabin guests can pretend they're traveling on a more ample budget by spending time in the hotel dining room and the Sun Room. Lake Yellowstone Hotel Cabins are open mid-May–mid-October.

Lake Lodge Cabins

A short distance east of Lake Yellowstone Hotel is Lake Lodge. Built in the 1920s, this archetypal log building has a gracious lobby containing two stone fireplaces, comfortably rustic furnishings, an open ceiling where the supporting log trusses and beams are visible, and a delightful front porch. One end of the building houses a large and reasonably priced cafeteria with picture windows framing Lake Yellowstone, and the other end contains a recreation hall for employees. Lodging options at Lake Lodge are not nearly as gracious, consisting of plain-vanilla "pioneer" cabins from the 1920s and '30s, each with a double bed and private bath for $64 d, and a bit more comfortable "western" cabins built in the 1950s and '60s that include two double beds and private baths with showers for $127 d. The 186 cabins at Lake Lodge are open mid-June–late September. Guests here often walk over to the nearby Lake Yellowstone Hotel for fine dining and the chance to relax in the Sun Room.

MAMMOTH HOT SPRINGS

The rambling **Mammoth Hot Springs Hotel** sits in the northwest corner of Yellowstone near park headquarters in the settlement of Mammoth. Built in 1937 (one wing was constructed in 1911 and the original hotel was built even earlier), the hotel has 222 rooms in a variety of configurations. Elk are a common sight on the grounds, and in the fall the bulls' bugling may wake you in the morning. There's live piano music downstairs in the map room most summer evenings as a counterpoint to the elk songs. (The room is named for a distinctive map of the United States crafted from 16 types of wood; it's on the northern wall.) Also just off the lobby is a gift shop. Just steps away are Park Service headquarters, the fine Albright Visitor Center and other historical buildings, along with places to eat and buy groceries, gas, and trinkets.

Mammoth Hotel rooms are comfortable but modest. Walls are not entirely soundproof, furnishings show some wear, and the hallway floors squeak, but baths are large and the hotel exudes a graceful aura that fits the setting well. Several rooms on each floor provide low-cost accommodations ($79 d) with communal baths down the hall, but most have two beds and private baths ($104 d); ask for a corner room if available. The hotel also houses two

the "frontier" cabins at Mammoth Hot Springs

© DON PITCHER

luxury suites ($316 d). It is open mid-May–mid-October and late December–mid-March.

Rates are the same in summer and winter, but early-season discounts are available. In the winter, "Frosty Fun" packages are a better bet, including one that provides two nights' lodging, two breakfasts, hot tub access, and ice skates, at $198 for two people. Hot tubs are available on an hourly basis during winter, offering a great way to relax after a day of cross-country skiing. Mammoth Hotel and Old Faithful Snow Lodge offer the only wintertime hotels inside the park.

Behind the hotel is 🄲 **Mammoth Cabins,** with 116 cabins including budget units ($68 d) with a shared bathhouse and delightful "frontier" cottages (from $99 d) with small porches and private baths. Most of these accommodations were built in 1938, and all contain two double beds. Some are duplex units that can be joined for families or friends traveling together. Dozens of ground squirrels populate the grounds, providing endless entertainment for the kids. Two units also have private outdoor hot tubs and are the nicest cabins in Yellowstone ($172 d). The Mammoth cabins are open mid-May–mid-October.

At the junction of the roads to Canyon, Mammoth, and Lamar Valley, 🄲 **Roosevelt Lodge** is *the* place to escape the crowds and return to a quieter and simpler era. Roosevelt Lodge is decidedly off the beaten path to the major Yellowstone sights, and that suits folks who stay here just fine. Named for President Theodore Roosevelt—perhaps the most conservation-minded president ever—the lodge has the well-worn feeling of an old dude ranch, and many families treat it as such. More than a few folks book cabins for several weeks at a stretch, enjoying the wolf-watching, fly-fishing, horseback and wagon rides, and barbecue cookout dinners. (Cookouts book up six months ahead, so reserve your space when you make a Roosevelt Lodge reservation.)

The main lodge features two large stone fireplaces, a family-style restaurant with notable meals, a lounge, a gift shop, a little general store, and a big front porch with old-fashioned rocking chairs. Surrounding it are 82 utilitarian cabins, most of which were built in the 1920s. Most basic—and just a step up from camping—are the "Roughrider" cabins, with one, two, or three beds, a writing table, and a woodstove (the only ones in any Yellowstone lodging). These cabins share a communal bathhouse, cost $60 for up to six guests, and fill up quickly. Call far ahead to reserve one of these classics! The same price will also get you larger cabins without the woodstove (but still no private bath). Nicer "Frontier" cabins with hardwood floors, 1–2 double beds, and private baths go for $99 d. All of these cabins can get stuffy in midsummer, and the windows lack screens. Two of the Roosevelt cabins are wheelchair-accessible. The Roosevelt Lodge and cabins are open mid-June–early September.

OLD FAITHFUL

The Old Faithful area contains a plethora of lodging options, including two large hotels—Old Faithful Inn and Old Faithful Snow Lodge—and several dozen cabins.

Built in 1903–1904, the timeless 🄲 **Old Faithful Inn** (see the *Exploring Yellowstone* section of this chapter) is easily the most delightful place to stay inside Yellowstone—if not in all of America. I wouldn't trade it for a thousand Hiltons. If you're able to get a room here during your visit to the park, do so; you certainly won't regret it! The hotel contains 327 guest rooms to suit all budgets. Even those staying in the simplest rooms here will enjoy the five-star lobby with its towering stone fireplace, the old-fashioned writing tables, cushy overstuffed chairs, a classy bar and restaurant, and evening piano music.

Most rooms in the original section of the hotel are cramped spaces with a brass double bed, dresser, in-room sink, bare-bulb lighting, older carpets, log walls, and communal baths down the hall; these go for $85 d. Of the cheap rooms, the best ones (these are often reserved a year ahead) are the dormer rooms on the second floor—particularly room 229—but those who stay there must walk past folks in the lobby to take a shower! Many other types of rooms are

© DON PITCHER

Old Faithful Inn

available throughout this sprawling hotel. The attractively appointed midrange rooms ($111 d) are comfortable and contain two double beds, phones, and tub baths with colorful tiles. Premium rooms vary in price from $148–202 d depending in part on whether they face the geyser, but personally I don't think they are much better than the midrange units. If you have the money, rent a suite for $305–404 d. When booking, ask for a room or suite in the East Wing facing the geyser if possible. Good choices include numbers 2002, 2010, 2012, 2014, and 2016; all have notable views of Old Faithful Geyser. Old Faithful Inn is generally open early May–mid-October, though the season was to be shortened in 2006 because of construction.

Although it is an attractively rustic building that would be a major focal point almost anywhere else, **Old Faithful Lodge** is overshadowed by its grand neighbor, Old Faithful Inn. The lodge does not contain guest rooms but houses a large cafeteria (open for lunch and dinner only), recreation hall, gift shop, bake shop, ice-cream stand, espresso cart, and showers. Unlike the inn, the lodge has enormous windows that face the geyser, providing those eating in the cafeteria with dramatic views of the eruptions. The lodge's massive fir logs and stone pillars add to a feeling of permanence. Behind and beside Old Faithful Lodge are approximately 130 moderately priced but cramped cabins. These contain older (but functional) furnishings, and most have two beds. The simplest budget units share communal bathhouses and cost just $60 d; they're some of the cheapest rooms in Yellowstone and just a few steps from Old Faithful. Slightly nicer (but still small) cabins have one or two beds and private baths and cost $89 d. There is even a pair of handicapped-accessible cabins here. The cabins at Old Faithful Lodge are open early May–early October.

Completed in 1999, the 100-room ☾ **Old Faithful Snow Lodge** provides accommodations in both summer and winter (Mammoth Hot Springs Hotel is Yellowstone's only other wintertime hotel). Both inside and out, Snow Lodge evokes the spirit of "parkitecture" from the early 1900s. The building blends the past and present, with timbers (recycled from

YELLOWSTONE

old buildings), hardwood floors, a central stone fireplace, custom-designed overstuffed couches, and wrought-iron accents, along with all the modern conveniences you expect from a fine hotel—unless you're expecting TVs, which no park hotels contain. Rooms are beautifully appointed and comfortable, and all have private baths. The hotel also houses a restaurant, snack shop, lounge, and gift shop, along with a ski shop and snowmobile rentals in winter. Rates are $169 d.

In addition to the hotel, 34 four-plex Snow Lodge Cabins are available behind the building, costing $127 d. Built in 1989, these **Western Cabins** have standard motel furnishings, with two double beds and a full bath. In addition, duplex **Frontier Cabins** provide simple accommodations with bath for $87 d. The Snow Lodge and Cabins are open early May–late October and late December–mid-March. Rates are the same in summer and winter, but early-season discounts are available in May. During winter, "Frosty Fun" packages are a better bet, including one that provides two nights' lodging, two breakfasts, and a round-trip snowcoach transport to Old Faithful at $458 for two people.

WINTER ACCOMMODATIONS

Only two places offer wintertime lodging inside Yellowstone. **Mammoth Hot Springs Hotel,** on the north end of the park, is the only accommodation accessible by road and has ski and snowshoe trails nearby, while the modern **Old Faithful Snow Lodge and Cabins** puts you close to the geysers and many miles of ski trails. Each has a restaurant, lounge, gift shop, and rentals of skis and snowshoes. Mammoth has a couple of advantages over Old Faithful: far fewer snowmobiles so it's much quieter, and road access to the Lamar Valley, where wolves, bison, and elk are major attractions. You might even see a pack of wolves take down an elk.

A wide variety of two-night **Winter Getaway** package trips are available out of Mammoth or Old Faithful. In addition, the Yellowstone Association Institute has excellent **Lodging and Learning** packages throughout the winter, no-

tably a three-night winter wolf-discovery trip ($850 d) that includes lodging at Mammoth, breakfasts and lunches, snowshoes, and naturalist-led treks in Lamar Valley. Get details on various winter lodging, learning, and play options from **Xanterra Parks and Resorts** (307/344-7311, www.travelyellowstone.com).

Many winter lodging options are available in the nearby towns of Jackson, West Yellowstone, Gardiner, Cooke City, Silver Gate, and Cody; they're described elsewhere in this book.

The only wintertime camping place is Mammoth Campground, where temperatures are milder and the snow lighter.

CAMPING

Tent camping in Yellowstone's early days left a bit to be desired. One 1884 tourist noted that during the height of summer, "the principle upon which the beds are populated is said to be the addition of visitors so long as they may arrive, or until the occupants'go for their guns.' The plan is simple, and relieves the authorities of responsibility." It's still crowded in the park, but at least guns are prohibited today!

Camping is available at a dozen sites scattered along the Yellowstone road network (see the sidebar, *Yellowstone National Park Campgrounds,* for specifics.) Most of these campsites are open from at least Memorial Day to mid-September, but only Mammoth Campground remains open throughout the year. Generators are allowed in more than half of the campgrounds but can be used only between 8 A.M. and 8 P.M. Roadside or parking-lot camping is prohibited, and rangers vigorously enforce this rule.

Reservations are available—and advised— for five concessioner-managed campgrounds: Bridge Bay Campground, Canyon Campground, Grant Village Campground, Madison Campground, and Fishing Bridge RV Park. Contact Xanterra Parks and Resorts for reservations (no extra charge) at 307/344-7311, www.travelyellowstone.com. The other seven (Park Service–managed) campgrounds inside Yellowstone are available on a first-come, first-camped basis with no reservations. You can pay with cash, checks, or credit cards.

YELLOWSTONE NATIONAL PARK CAMPGROUNDS

Bridge Bay Campground: $17; fills early, flush toilets, dump station, generators permitted, open late May-mid-September; reservations at 307/344-7311, www.travelyellowstone.com

Canyon Campground: $17; fills early, laundry facilities, showers $3, flush toilets, dump station, generators permitted, open June-mid-September; reservations at 307/344-7311, www.travelyellowstone.com

Fishing Bridge RV Park: $33; fills early, hard-sided RVs only, full hookups, laundry facilities, showers $3, flush toilets, sewer system, generators permitted, open mid-May-September; reservations at 307/344-7311, www.travelyellowstone.com

Grant Village Campground: $17; fills early, showers nearby for $2, flush toilets, dump station, generators permitted, open late June-September, reservations at 307/344-7311, www.travelyellowstone.com

Indian Creek Campground: $12; vault toilets, open early June-mid-September

Lewis Lake Campground: $12; vault toilets, fills early, open mid-June-early Nov.

Madison Campground: $17; fills early; flush toilets, dump station, generators permitted, open May-October; reservations at 307/344-7311, www.travelyellowstone.com

Mammoth Campground: $14; near a residential area and along the park road, flush toilets, generators permitted, open year-round

Norris Campground: $14; fills early, flush toilets, generators permitted, open mid-May-late September

Pebble Creek Campground: $12; vault toilets, open June-late September

Slough Creek Campground: $12; vault toilets, open late May-October

Tower Fall Campground: $12; fills early, vault toilets, open mid-May-late September

During July and August, virtually all campsites in Yellowstone fill *before noon,* so get there early or reserve a space! The busiest weekends are—not surprisingly—around Fourth of July and Labor Day, but Yellowstone's most popular campgrounds fill up even in late fall and early summer. Call the Park Service at 307/344-2114 for a recording noting which campgrounds are full.

When everything else is packed, folks head to campgrounds on surrounding Forest Service and Grand Teton National Park lands or to private campgrounds and motels in the gateway towns. (All are described elsewhere in this book.) The farther you get from Yellowstone, the more likely you are to find space. If you reach Nebraska, you should have no trouble at all. Campers can take showers ($3) at Old Faithful Lodge, Mammoth Hotel, Grant Village, Fishing Bridge RV Park, and Canyon Village Campground.

Food

RESTAURANTS

You'll find restaurants at Mammoth Hot Springs, Lake Yellowstone Hotel, Old Faithful Inn, Old Faithful Snow Lodge, Grant Village, Roosevelt Lodge, and Canyon Lodge. All of these are open for three meals a day throughout the summer, and some are open to mid-October. Dining is available at the Snow Lodge mid-April–October and for the winter season mid-December–early March. All restaurants and lounges in Yellowstone are entirely nonsmoking.

The enormous **(Old Faithful Inn Dining Room** is a wonderful option, with impressive all-you-can-eat breakfast ($9) and lunch ($11) buffets, plus a dinner menu that stars prime rib, halibut, chicken, steaks, and pork chops ($17–30 entrées). The cozy lounge serves single-malt scotches, tequilas, and cognacs.

Yellowstone's fine-dining choice is the **(Lake Yellowstone Hotel Dining Room,** with breakfast buffets, plus upscale lunches and dinners that emphasize seasonal and organic foods such as wild Alaskan salmon, hormone-free Montana beef, and a variety of organic ingredients, from vegetables to goat cheeses.

Meals in other restaurants throughout the park are also reasonably priced, but the quality can vary from so-so to quite good. Typical menus include steaks, burgers, seafood, pasta, chicken, and vegetarian dishes. The filling breakfasts and chocolate pecan pie at **Mammoth Hot Springs Dining Room** are noteworthy, and **Roosevelt Lodge Dining Room** emphasizes down-home carnivore fare such as barbecue ribs, country-fried steaks, sandwiches, chili, and fried chicken. The dinner menu at **Grant Village Dining Room** includes huckleberry chicken, rib eye steak, polenta lasagna, prime rib, and trout. It also has a substantial breakfast buffet. The building is one of the newer ones in the park, with a bland exterior but big windows facing the lake (although trees obscure the view). **Obsidian Dining Room** at the Snow Lodge has a fun Western flair. In addition to an extensive breakfast menu, the restaurant serves specialty burgers, steaks, and seafood. Unfortunately, the quality isn't stellar.

Dinner reservations are *required* in the summer at Old Faithful Inn Dining Room (307/545-4999), Lake Yellowstone Hotel Dining Room (307/242-3899), and Grant Village Dining Room (307/242-3499), and they should be made before your arrival. For a dinner table at Old Faithful Inn, reserve a week ahead if you want a choice of seating times. You can also call 307/344-7311 for dining reservations at any of park restaurants.

CAFETERIAS AND FAST FOOD

Yellowstone has always catered to families, and several park cafeterias provide dependably good food for decent prices. Your kids' noise will almost certainly be drowned out by racket from the rest of the hoi polloi (I'm speaking from experience here). Of particular note are **Lake Lodge Cafeteria** and **Old Faithful Lodge Cafeteria,** both of which are housed in grand stone-and-timber buildings with tall windows. Lake Lodge overlooks Lake Yellowstone, and Old Faithful Lodge faces the geyser. Less distinguished are **Canyon Lodge Cafeteria**—with a 1960s design that hasn't aged well—and the **Grant Village Lake House.** At the latter, big windows open onto Yellowstone Lake (great for sunsets), and you can graze a pasta and salad bar in the evenings or order a pizza. In addition to these options, you'll find snack shops or delis selling burgers, veggie burgers, sandwiches, espresso, and ice cream in Mammoth, Old Faithful, Lake, and Canyon. All these places can also put together picnic lunches.

Many of the park's **Yellowstone General Stores** have food services of the burger, fries, and milkshake variety, and can put together box lunches for a to-go meal.

OLD WEST COOKOUTS

The **(Old West Wagon Cookouts** at Roosevelt Lodge are a longtime family favorite and so popular that you'll need to make reservations at least six months in advance of your visit. These events take place every evening mid-June–early September, and you either hop on board the horse-drawn wagons or astride a horse for a saunter into history. Cookouts take place in Pleasant Valley, three miles from the lodge, and include cowboy music, a campfire, and a big buffet dinner of steak, baked beans, coleslaw, potato salad, corn, corn muffins, watermelon, apple cobbler, and beverages. Top it off with a cup of cowboy coffee. No discounts are given for vegetarians, but the staff can make substitutions if you notify them in advance. Covered seating is available in case of rain.

Wagon rides with dinner last 1.5 hours round-trip and cost $50 adults, $40 ages 5–11, or free for younger kids. Horseback riders can choose either a one-hour trail ride and meal at $60 adults, $50 ages 8–11, or a two-hour trail ride at $70 adults or $60 kids. Make reservations at 307/344-7311, www.travelyellowstone.com. If you're in the area and don't have a reservation, ask to get on the waiting list. You might get lucky and have a last-minute cancellation.

LOUNGES

Just because you're in a national park doesn't mean you can't tip back a gin and tonic. **Old Faithful Tavern** inside Old Faithful Inn is a fine place for a drink in the evening. Beverage service is also available on the upstairs mezzanine and the outside deck facing Old Faithful. Another good place for a drink is **Firehole Lounge** at the nearby Old Faithful Snow Lodge.

Lake Yellowstone Hotel's aptly named **Sun Room** fills a large wing of the lobby and is surrounded on three sides by picture windows. It exudes a casual elegance, making this a wonderful spot to while away the hours reading a book, writing postcards, or just listening to the piano tunes with a drink in your hand.

Smaller bars are off the dining rooms at Mammoth Hot Springs, Roosevelt Lodge, Lake Lodge, Grant Village, and Canyon Lodge. The little corner bar at Mammoth has the only public TV inside Yellowstone; none of the in-park hotel rooms have televisions. Smoking is prohibited in Yellowstone lounges.

GROCERIES AND SUPPLIES

The park's 12 Yellowstone General Stores are at Mammoth, Canyon Village, Old Faithful, Fishing Bridge, Grant Village, Lake, Tower Fall, Bridge Bay, and Roosevelt. Each outlet has its own personality, and several of these—most notably the Lower Basin store at Old Faithful and the ones at Lake and Fishing Bridge—are grand old log structures. The Mammoth general store is another historic structure, here for nearly a century.

In addition to groceries, beer, and liquor, these stores sell a variety of merchandise, clothing, souvenirs, film and photo supplies, T-shirts, and accessories. Featured items include locally made arts and crafts, and they even offer interpretive programs. The larger ones also have popular soda fountains with burgers, shakes, and other fast food. General stores at Canyon and Old Faithful deliver the best selection, and the Mammoth store is open year-round. The others are generally open mid-May–September. The stores are managed by Delaware North Park Service (www.yellowstonegeneralstores.com).

YELLOWSTONE

Information and Services

RANGER-NATURALIST PROGRAMS

Park naturalists lead slide shows, films, guided walks, kids' programs, campfire talks, and other activities at the campgrounds and visitor centers. These are always favorites of visitors, and on summer days you can choose from more than a multitude of Yellowstone activities, all of which are free. In keeping with the government's increasing make-'em-pay-for-services policy, there is a $5 fee to join half-day Ranger Adventure Hikes offered most summer days. Get a complete listing of ranger programs in the *Yellowstone Today* paper you receive upon entering the park or online at www.nps.gov/yell. Evening slide programs are also offered in winter at Mammoth and Old Faithful. For a more in-depth look at the park, take a class through the Yellowstone Association Institute (www.yellowstoneassociation.org) or join one of its popular **Lodging and Learning** packages.

SUPPORTING THE PARK

The **Yellowstone Association** (307/344-2289, www.yellowstoneassociation.org) is a nonprofit organization that assists with education, research, publishing, and book sales inside the park. The organization also teaches classes through the Yellowstone Association Institute.

The **Yellowstone Park Foundation** (406/586-6303, www.ypf.org) is another nonprofit group that works with the National Park Service by providing funds for projects and programs that would not be otherwise supported. Its biggest project is helping to raise the $15 million needed for a new visitor center at Old Faithful. All funding comes from individuals and corporations, not from the government.

The primary environmental group involved with protecting Yellowstone and the surrounding public lands is the **Greater Yellowstone Coalition** (406/586-1593, www.greateryellowstone.org), based in Bozeman, Montana. This private nonprofit organization is involved in all sorts of environmental issues within the 10-million-acre Greater Yellowstone Ecosystem, including such hot-button issues as logging, mining, winter use, and bison management. It represents more than 13,000 members and publishes a quarterly newsletter detailing various issues. Annual membership costs $25.

SERVICES
Shopping

Nearly every road junction in Yellowstone has some sort of general store, gas station, or gift shop. **Yellowstone General Stores** are especially interesting because they tend to be in rustic old log structures and staffed by friendly retired folks and fresh college kids. The stores are being modernized but still retain the historic charm from past eras. Here you'll find all of the standard tourist supplies and gifts, plus groceries, snack bars, booze, camping equipment, books, fishing supplies, and locally made arts and crafts. The largest general stores are at Old Faithful and Canyon.

The **Old Faithful Inn Gift Shop** is well worth a visit, with a good selection of items from apparel to artwork. It often has book signings and guest presentations during summer. **The Shop at Old Faithful Lodge** features artists in residence creating paintings or pottery (for sale, of course). Additional gift shops can be found in the other hotel complexes at Lake Lodge, Mammoth Hot Springs, Roosevelt Lodge, Canyon Lodge, and Grant Village.

Money

You'll discover ATMs at most of the settled areas, including Old Faithful Inn, Old Faithful Snow Lodge, Fishing Bridge, Lake Yellowstone Hotel, Mammoth Hot Springs Hotel, Mammoth General Store, Canyon General Store, Canyon Lodge, and Grant Village. Park lodges and hotels are able to provide a limited currency exchange for international travelers 8 A.M.–5 P.M. Monday–Friday.

YELLOWSTONE ASSOCIATION

Founded in 1933, the nonprofit Yellowstone Association (307/344-2293, www.yellowstoneassociation.org) assists in educational, historical, and scientific programs. The organization publishes several natural-history publications and provides funds to produce trail leaflets and park newspapers, along with the excellent *Yellowstone Science* magazine. In addition, the association manages book sales at visitors centers, funds park exhibits and research, and otherwise assists the park in educating the public. The organization is best known for the **Yellowstone Association Institute,** operating out of the historic Buffalo Ranch in Lamar Valley.

Instructors at the institute lead more than 100 different natural-history and humanities classes in the summer, along with several others in winter. Most of these last 2-5 days and typically cost around $75 per day – a real bargain. Courses cover the spectrum from wolf ecology to fly-fishing and provide a great way to learn about this wonderful wild place. Class size is small; most classes contain 10-15 students. Participants typically stay at the Buffalo Ranch in comfortable log cabins ($25 per person per night) and cook meals in the shared kitchen.

In addition to these classes, the Yellowstone Association Institute also offers **Lodging and Learning** programs, 2-5-day packages that blend education, recreation, and lodging. Naturalist-guides from the association lead small-group excursions (13 people maximum), and participants are provided with accommodations in park hotels, plus breakfasts and box lunches. Its *Yellowstone for Families* program ($1,144 for two adults plus $348 per child) is especially popular, with a mix of activities for both kids and parents over five days: animal tracking, wildlife-watching, photography, painting, hiking, and more.

For folks who really want the personalized touch (and can afford it), the institute offers **Personal Ed-Ventures,** private tours in which a wildlife biologist travels with you in your vehicle for 6-8 hours, providing an introduction to park wildlife and ecology. The charge is $350 for up to seven people.

Membership in the Yellowstone Association starts at $30 per year and is tax-deductible. Members get discounts on classes taught by the Yellowstone Association Institute and can sign up early. They also receive quarterly newsletters and discounts for purchases of items sold by the association.

Publications

If you're planning a trip to Yellowstone, call the park at 307/344-7381 to request a copy of the *Yellowstone National Park Trip Planner.* It provides detailed up-to-date information on hiking and camping, fishing, services, road construction, safety issues, park highlights, and lots more. The same information (and much more) is available online at www.nps.gov/yell. Also be sure to request the latest version of the park paper, *Yellowstone Today;* it's issued quarterly.

Several print and online sources provide unofficial information on Yellowstone. One of the better private sources is the Lander-based *Yellowstone Journal* (307/332-2323 or 800/656-8762, www.yellowstonepark.com). The publication comes out five times a year and is sold in stores inside and around the park. A good freebie publication called simply *Yellowstone Park,* is published annually by the *Billings Gazette* and is available online at www.billingsgazette.com. Find it in regional visitor centers outside the park. Also check out the web-only *Yellowstone Traveler* (www.yellowstoneparktraveler.com), maintained by Circumerro Publishing.

Medical Services

For medical emergencies 24 hours a day, the park manages **Lake Hospital** (307/242-7241), a 10-bed acute-care facility. It's open mid-May–September; also here are a clinic and pharmacy. Outpatient services are available both here and at the **Old Faithful Clinic** (307/545-7325), open early May–mid-October.

Open weekdays year-round and daily in the summer, the **Mammoth Hot Springs Clinic** (307/344-7965) has a physician available. Call 911 for emergencies anywhere in the park.

Laundry and Showers

In summer, find coin-operated washers and dryers at Fishing Bridge RV Park, Canyon Village Campground, and Grant Village Campground. Public showers ($3) are at Fishing Bridge RV Park, Lake Lodge, Old Faithful Lodge, Mammoth Hotel, Grant Village, and Canyon Village Campground.

Other Services

For a complete directory of the many other Yellowstone visitor services, see *Yellowstone Today*, which you receive upon entering the park. You can also download a copy off the web from the Yellowstone site, www.nps.gov/yell.

A year-round post office is in a 1930s-era stone building at Mammoth Hot Springs, and seasonal post offices can be found at Old Faithful, Lake Village, Canyon Village, and Grant Village.

Check the visitor centers for a schedule of church services. Cell phone users will find spotty service in many parts of Yellowstone—and nonexistent in much of the backcountry—but your phone will probably work in the country around Old Faithful, Lake, and Mammoth (and possibly elsewhere). Internet access is even more limited, though you can use phones for dial-up service from a laptop.

West Yellowstone, Montana

West Yellowstone (elev. 6,650) is the definitive Western tourist town. With a year-round population of only 1,000 (three times that in the summer) but more than 50 places to stay, it's pretty easy to see what makes the West Yellowstone cash registers ring. The West Entrance gate—most popular of all Yellowstone entrances—lies just a couple of hundred feet away. "West," as the town is known locally, isn't particularly attractive, and in the 1990s a major development brouhgt several corporate hotels and other ugly additions to an already crowded mix of restaurants, motels, T-shirt stores, and gift shops.

West Yellowstone may be decidedly middlebrow, but the surrounding land is anything but, with Gallatin (GAL-a-tin) National Forest lying north and west, Caribou–Targhee National Forest just a few miles to the south, and Yellowstone National Park just a few feet to the east. It's just a couple of miles east from West Yellowstone to the Wyoming border, and the Idaho border lies only nine miles west.

SIGHTS

Yellowstone Historic Center

The Yellowstone Historic Center (104 Yellow-stone Ave., 406/646-1100, www.yellowstonehistoriccenter.org) is a stone-and-log structure from the railroad days that served for decades as the town's train depot. The museum is open 9 A.M.–9 P.M. daily mid-May–early September, and 9 A.M.–7 P.M. daily the rest of September–early October, and closed the rest of the year. Entrance is $6 adults, $5 seniors, $4 students and kids, and $15 families; free for kids under three. Inside are exhibits on the history of park transportation (including railroads and stagecoaches), the 1959 Hebgen Lake earthquake, the fires of 1988, and wildlife displays, including "Old Snaggletooth" the grizzly and an enormous cave bear skull. Videos and movies about Yellowstone are shown in the theater, and the museum offers a variety of free tours when enough people are interested. These include 45-minute historic walking tours, along with afternoon nature or history talks, and tours in the classic 1938 White touring bus; it was used in the park until 1959. Also here is a good collection of regional books for sale.

Right next door is another wonderful stone structure (built in 1925) that served until the late 1950s as an elegant Union Pacific Dining Lodge. The building has a spacious dining hall containing an enormous fireplace, a 45-foot-tall vaulted ceiling, and handmade light fixtures. Also worth a look-see is an **Oregon Short Line Railroad car** housed at the Holiday Inn Sunspree Resort (315 Yellowstone Ave., 406/646-7365, www.doyellowstone.com). Built in 1903, the railroad car has been beautifully restored and forms a centerpiece for the restaurant and lounge here.

Grizzly and Wolf Discovery Center

The Grizzly and Wolf Discovery Center (201 S. Canyon St., 406/646-7001 or 800/257-2570, www.grizzlydiscoveryctr.com, open 8 A.M.–dusk daily all year, $10 adults, $9 seniors, $5 ages 5–12, free for kids under five) is home to eight Alaskan and Canadian grizzlies and six captive-born gray wolves. Not all of the bears are visible at any given time, but visitors are bound to see at least one in the pseudo-natural habitat. This center attracts throngs of visitors and photographers who might otherwise never see a grizzly or wolf, and there's always a staff member out to answer any questions. In addition to the bears and wolves, the center has wildlife exhibits, a 40-minute video on bears, plus the obligatory gift shop.

Yellowstone IMAX Theatre

Directly in front of the Grizzly and Wolf Discovery Center is the Yellowstone IMAX Theatre (406/646-4100 or 888/854-5862, www.yellowstoneimax.com, $8 adults, $6 ages 3–11, free for younger children, open 8:30 A.M.–9 P.M. daily late May–early October, reduced hours the rest of the year), where you can watch the big-budget production of *Yellowstone* on the 60- by 80-foot screen; other movies typically are on wolves, bears, Lewis and Clark, or some other nature or Old West topic. The featured attraction is a 35-minute movie that presents Yellowstone history and geology, complete with stirring music and a cast of dozens. If you haven't seen IMAX flicks before, hold onto your seat—lots of jaw-dropping scenes here.

Eagle's Store

Family-run Eagle's Store (406/646-9300, www

.eagles-store.com) on the corner of Canyon and Yellowstone, is definitely worth a stop. Built in the 1920s, this historic log building contains all of the standard tourist knickknacks, along with quality Western clothing, jewelry, fishing tackle, and a delightful old-fashioned soda fountain open in summer.

ENTERTAINMENT AND EVENTS

During summer, you can attend lighthearted comedies and musicals for the whole family at **Playmill Theatre** (124 Madison Ave., 406/646-7757, www.playmill.com). It's been in operation for more than four decades.

Watch flicks at **Bears Den Cinema** (15 Electric St., 406/646-7777). **Yellowstone IMAX Theatre** (406/646-4100 or 888/854-5862) shows movies especially formatted for the three-story screen.

The bar at **Stage Coach Inn** (209 Madison Ave., 406/646-7381) has a pool table and the occasional live band, or try **Iron Horse Saloon** inside the West Yellowstone Conference Hotel (315 Yellowstone Ave., 406/646-7365). **Lionshead Super 8** (seven miles west of town, 406/646-9584, www.wyellowstone.com/lionshead) has square dancing in May and September.

Events

On the second weekend of March, the **Rendezvous Marathon Ski Race** (406/646-7245, www.rendezvousrace.com), a nationally known Nordic ski race, attracts hundreds of participants. The following weekend brings a very different event, the **World Snowmobile Expo** (406/646-7001, www.snowmobileexpo.com), with races, demos, and other activities.

A fun parade, live music, and fireworks highlight the town's **Fourth of July** festivities, and the **Yellowstone Rod Run** takes place on the first full weekend of August, bringing vintage cars of all types to the oldest such event in the Pacific Northwest.

The **Wild West Yellowstone Rodeo** features bareback riding, team roping, saddle bronc riding, bull riding, and more in the rodeo arena on several weekends June–August.

The ever-popular **Knothead Jamboree** attracts more than 1,000 square dancing enthusiasts for calling, clapping, and fun on Labor Day weekend; it's been happening annually since 1955.

Thanksgiving weekend in November means **Yellowstone Ski Festival** (www.yellowstoneskifestival.com), attracting hundreds of spandex-clad cross-country ski enthusiasts. The event also attracts major Nordic ski manufacturers, giving the public a chance to demo their latest toys.

SHOPPING

Many West Yellowstone shops sell the obligatory Yellowstone souvenirs, corny T-shirts, and other items with mass appeal. You'll probably get bored after one or two of these gift shops, but many more await your exploration. Fortunately, the town does have several more distinctive places, including **Seldom Seen Knives** (115 Yellowstone Ave., 406/646-4116, www.seldomseenknives.com) and **Homeroom** (121 Madison St., 406/646-4338, www.yellowstoneshop.com).

The Book Peddler (106 Canyon St., 406/646-9358), is a large and attractive bookstore with an abundance of regional titles. A pleasant café sells espresso, bagels, and pastries in the back. This is a great place to hang with the locals. **Bookworm Books** (14 Canyon St., 406/646-9736) is another good shop with both new and used titles, including many first editions; it's open nightly until midnight all summer. Check out its collection of vintage Yellowstone tourist antiques, particularly the collectable spoons, plates, and stereo views. The small **West Yellowstone Library** (200 Yellowstone Ave., 406/646-9017), inside the railroad's old stone dining lodge, has Internet access.

RECREATION
Horseback Riding and Biking

Horseback trail rides are available from **Parade Rest Guest Ranch** (seven miles north of town, 406/646-7217 or 800/753-5934, www.paraderestranch.com), **Diamond P Ranch** (seven miles to the west, 406/646-7246), and **Yellowstone**

Mountain Guides (406/646-7230, www.yellowstone-guides.com). Several other ranches farther afield also offer horseback rides; contact the chamber of commerce for details.

The 30-km Rendezvous Trail System becomes mountain-bike central when summer rolls around. It starts from the southern edge of town; get a map at the visitor center. Rent mountain bikes from **Yellowstone Bicycles** (132 Madison Ave., 406/646-7815) or **Free Heel and Wheel** (40 Yellowstone Ave., 406/646-7744, www.freeheelandwheel.com). Free Heel also rents bike trailers, bike racks, and baby joggers.

Fishing

You'll find five different **fly-fishing shops** in town, a reflection of the sport's importance in the Yellowstone area. In business for more than 50 years, **Bud Lilly's Trout Shop** (39 Madison Ave., 406/646-7801 or 800/854-9559, www.budlillys.com) is the best-known local place, with fishing tackle, clothing, guides, and even a gallery. Also well worth a look are **Arrick's Fly Shop** (37 Canyon St., 406/646-7290, www.arricks.com), **Eagle's Tackle Shop** (3 Canyon St., 406/646-7521, www.eagles-store.com), **Jacklin's Fly Shop** (105 Yellowstone Ave., 406/646-7336, www.jacklinsflyshop.com), and **Madison River Outfitters** (117 Canyon St., 406/646-9644, www.flyfishingyellowstone.com). All of these offer guided fishing (around $350 for two people per day) and equipment.

Cross-Country Skiing

West Yellowstone is infamous for its bitterly cold winters, when the thermometer can drop to −50°F. Fortunately, it doesn't always stay there, and by March the days have often warmed to a balmy 20°F. In November, West Yellowstone becomes a national center for cross-country skiers, with the U.S. Nordic and biathlon ski teams training here.

Two trail systems provide a wide variety of Nordic skiing conditions. The 30-km **Rendezvous Ski Trail** system (www.rendezvousskitrails.com) takes off from the southern edge of town and is groomed with both classical and skating tracks early November–April.

The nine-kilometer **Riverside Trail** begins on the east side of town and leads to the Madison River within Yellowstone National Park. This trail is partially groomed and provides a good opportunity to see bison, elk, and possibly moose; it's closed to skate skiing. You can also ski the snowpacked streets in winter. Find many more places for flat tracking or telemarking in adjacent Yellowstone National Park and the Gallatin and Caribou–Targhee national forests. Before heading out, get recorded avalanche-safety information from the **Avalanche Advisory Hotline** (406/587-6981). It's updated daily in the winter.

Rent skinny skis from **Bud Lilly's Trout Shop** (39 Madison Ave., 406/646-7801 or 800/854-9559, www.budlillys.com), or **Free Heel and Wheel** (40 Yellowstone Ave., 406/646-7744, www.freeheelandwheel.com). Free Heel also rents snowshoes.

Dogsledding

For a delightfully different way to explore the Gallatin National Forest backcountry, take a sled dog tour from **Spirit of the North Sled Dog Adventure** (406/682-7994, www.huskypower.com). Half-day tours are $110 adults or $76 kids.

Snowcoach Trips

Yellowstone Alpen Guides (406/646-9591 or 800/858-3502, www.yellowstoneguides.com, leads snowcoach tours from West Yellowstone. All-day trips are $99 adults, $89 seniors, $79 kids to either Grand Canyon of the Yellowstone or Old Faithful. Guests on the latter run have an option of getting dropped at Biscuit Basin, where they can ski to Old Faithful and meet up with others. Special snowcoach-and-guided-snowshoe tours are $110 per person (four-person minimum). Ski or snowshoe rentals are available. The classic snowcoaches (one built in 1953) have been modernized but are still a charming anachronism.

For a truly unique experience, book a winter trip with another West Yellowstone–based company, **Yellowstone Expeditions** (406/646-9333 or 800/728-9333, www.yellowstoneexpedi-

tions.com). The company has homey tent-cabins at the Canyon area during the winter, with a variety of multi-night adventures for skiers.

Snowmobiling

Enthusiasts refer to West as "snowmobile capital of the world," and each winter day hundreds of 'bilers show up to roar across nearby Forest Service lands or to join park tours. Because of new Park Service restrictions, all trips inside Yellowstone must be with guided groups, including a number of local companies. The West Yellowstone Chamber of Commerce (406/646-7701, www.westyellowstonechamber.com) can provide current snow and trail conditions, a detailed map of local trails, and a listing of companies that offer guided snowmobile trips into the park.

Snowmobile rentals for use on Forest Service lands outside the park are available from more than a dozen local companies. Hundreds more folks bring in their own "crotch rockets" to ride on national forest lands, and local motels offer snowmobile/lodging packages.

ACCOMMODATIONS

The proximity to Yellowstone makes the town of West Yellowstone an extremely popular stopping place for vacationers in both summer and winter. More than 1,700 rooms are available, starting around $80 in midsummer. The streets are lined with more than three dozen motels, so I won't try to describe all of them, although you'll find general information and links from the **West Yellowstone Chamber of Commerce** (406/646-7701, www.westyellowstonechamber.com).

Although rooms are generally available most summer nights, reservations are advisable; motels can even be full on late September weekends. To ensure your best choice of accommodations, reserve a room in April or May for the peak summer season. **West Yellowstone Central Reservations** (406/646-7077 or 888/646-7077, www.yellowstonereservation.com) books rooms at many local places and can also set up a range of activities, from snowcoach tours to whitewater rafting.

Hostel

Budget travelers will be happy to discover the West Yellowstone International Hostel (not affiliated with AYH) in the historic **Madison Hotel** (139 Yellowstone Ave., 406/646-7745 or 800/838-7745, www.wyellowstone.com/madisonhotel). On the National Register of Historic Places, the hotel has friendly owners and a delightfully rustic lobby crowded with deer and moose heads. Presidents Harding and Hoover stayed here (though it wasn't a hostel at the time, of course). Travelers stay in clean and comfortable bedrooms (3–4 beds in each, with bedding provided) that have been furnished with handmade lodgepole furniture. The classic hotel rooms are a delightful mix of old and new, providing the ambience of a place that has been here since 1912. No televisions or phones are provided in the rooms, but there is a small fridge and microwave for hostelers in the back, plus a TV in the lobby and a barbecue grill out back. A computer is available to check your email ($5 per hour). Lodging costs $25 per person in three-bed dorm rooms. Make hostel reservations a few days ahead in midsummer or get here before evening to be sure of a space in the dorms.

In addition to hostel rooms, the hotel has a range of other economical options, starting with a basic room with a bath down the hall and no TV for $40 d, or $60 for a room with space for four and a private bath. Behind the hotel is a separate building with standard motel accommodations (private baths and TVs) for $59 d or $79 for a room with three double beds. The Madison Hotel is open late May–early October only.

$50-100

A good economy choice, **◖ Lazy G Motel** (123 Hayden, 406/646-7586, www.wyellowstone.com/clients/lazyg, $56–76 d) offers clean and quiet rooms with fridges and phones (but no air-conditioning); kitchenettes are $15 extra. Friendly owners too. Closed in April.

Also recommended is another affordable place, **Al's Westward Ho Motel** (16 Boundary St., 406/646-7331 or 888/646-7331, www.wyellowstone.com/alswestwardho), which charges $56–60 d, and some rooms contain kitchenettes. Open May–October; no in-room phones.

A little nicer but still reasonably priced is **◖ City Center Motel** (408/646-7337 or 800/742-0665, www.yellowstonevacations.com), where the big rooms (no phones) are $69 for one queen bed or $89 for two. A community kitchen and indoor hot tub are available for guests.

Wagon Wheel Cabins and Campground (408 Gibbon, 406/646-7872, www.wagonwheelrv.com) has a collection of 10 attractive cabins, most containing full kitchens. The cabins are on large lots surrounded by trees, and each has a barbecue grill and picnic table. Basic bring-your-sleeping-bag cabins cost $55 d, and a one-bedroom unit starts at $84 d. The largest unit has three bedrooms, a full kitchen, and fireplace; it sleeps six for $196. There's a four-night summertime minimum on the larger cabins. The cabins at Wagon Wheel fill early, so book several months ahead if possible. It may be closed in the winter.

Three Bear Lodge (217 Yellowstone Ave., 406/646-7353 or 800/646-7353, www.threebearlodge.com) is probably best known for its popular restaurant of the same name. The 73-room motel features contemporary rooms, plus four indoor hot tubs and an outdoor pool. A wide variety of rooms are available, starting at $85–99 for standard rooms, up to $110 for units that include a king bed and jetted tub. Two-room family units with fridges and microwaves are $115–158); the largest sleeps six. Open year-round.

$100-150

You'll find very good accommodations at **Brandin' Iron Inn** (201 Canyon St., 406/646-9411 or 800/217-4613, www.brandiniron.com, $104–114 d). The spacious, clean rooms include fridges, a big hot breakfast, and access to two indoor hot tubs.

Yellowstone Lodge (251 Electric St., 406/646-0020 or 877/239-9298, www.yellowstonelodge.com, $139–169 d) is one of the newest places in town, with oversize rooms, fridges, microwaves, an indoor pool, spa, and light breakfast.

At **Hibernation Station** (212 Gray Wolf Ave., 406/646-4200 or 800/580-3557, www.hibernationstation.com) the 40 modern cabins—each a bit different inside—feature handmade log furniture and down comforters. Some also contain kitchenettes. Prices are high, starting at $109 d for a cabin with a queen bed, or $169 for one that sleeps four and contains a queen-size bunk bed, fireplace, and kitchenette. Families (not on a budget) will appreciate the large condo unit with room for eight, a full kitchen and dining area, fireplace, and jetted tubs for $279. A big outdoor hot tub is available for all guests.

The motel chains have moved into West Yellowstone in a big way. One of the nicest is **Comfort Inn** (638 Madison Ave., 406/646-4212 or 888/264-2466, www.westyellowstonecomfortinn.com). The featured attraction here is the biggest indoor pool in town, but the motel also has large rooms, a hot tub, exercise room, and breakfast. Rates are $139–149 d in standard rooms, or $189–199 for six-person suites.

The most elaborate local place is the ludicrously named **West Yellowstone Conference Hotel Holiday Inn Sunspree Resort** (315 Yellowstone Ave., 406/646-7365 or 888/633-1724, www.doyellowstone.com), with spacious rooms with fridges and microwaves, wireless Internet, an indoor pool, exercise room, sauna, and hot tub. Standard rooms cost $139–149 d, two-room family suites are $191–200 and sleep six, and luxurious executive suites (king bed, jetted tub, and wet bar) run $175–200.

Over $150

Another relatively new place with a fine reputation is **(Kelly Inn West Yellowstone** (104 S. Canyon St., 406/646-4544 or 800/259-4672, www.yellowstonekellyinn.com, $149–189), which features huge rooms, fridges, microwaves, an indoor pool, sauna, Wi-Fi, a guest computer, and continental breakfast. Some rooms also include a whirlpool and wet bar.

Camping

The nearest Park Service camping place is inside Yellowstone at **Madison Campground,** 14 miles east of West Yellowstone. The cost

is $17, and it's open early May–October. Make reservations (advised) at 307/344-7311, www.travelyellowstone.com.

Gallatin National Forest (406/823-6961, www.fs.fed.us/r1/gallatin) has several campgrounds in the West Yellowstone area. The closest camping spot is **Baker's Hole Campground** ($13, open mid-May–mid-Sept.), just three miles north of West Yellowstone. It's open for RVs and other hard-sided vehicles only because of bear problems. Tent campers will need to go north of town to **Hebgen Lake,** where five different tenting areas are strung westward along the lake; closest is the **Lonesomehurst Campground** ($13, open mid-May–mid-Sept.), 12 miles from West Yellowstone. No reservations are taken at these Forest Service sites.

West Yellowstone has a half dozen private campgrounds right in town, and several more are west or north of town. Most of the in-town places are just RV parking lots. Far nicer are two places with shady trees and quiet sites: **Rustic Wagon Campground** (634 U.S. 20, 406/646-7387, www.rusticwagonrv.com, $27 for tents or $36–38 for RVs); and **Wagon Wheel Cabins and Campground** (408 Gibbon Ave., 406/646-7872, www.wagonwheelrv.com, $26 tents, $34–36 RVs). Noncampers can shower at either of these for a few dollars. Rustic Wagon is open mid-April–October, and Wagon Wheel is open late May–October.

FOOD

West Yellowstone has many restaurants, but prices are generally higher than in Wyoming towns and the menu is plebeian, with burgers and fries as the dominant food group.

Breakfast and Lunch

For omelets, buckwheat pancakes, biscuits and sausage gravy, or other good breakfasts, run on over to **Running Bear Pancake House** (538 Madison Ave., 406/646-7703) but be ready for a long wait in midsummer. Tasty lunches too; open 7 A.M.–2 P.M. only.

Ernie's Deli and Bakery (406 U.S. 20 W., 406/646-9467) is the local doughnut shop in the morning, and it makes unbeatable sandwiches for lunch. Ernie's will put together a big box lunch if you're heading into the park and want to leave the sandwiches to the experts.

Stop by **Mocha Mammas** (40 Yellowstone Ave., 406/646-7744)—inside Free Heel and Wheel—for espresso and bagels. Another good latte destination is **The Book Peddler** (106 Canyon St., 406/646-9358) with several tables in the back for bagels, sweets, and coffee. It's open until 10 in the summer.

American

If you're searching for a down-home greasy spoon serving good food three meals a day, your hunt will end at **Old Town Cafe** (18 Madison, 406/646-9633). Chicken-fried steaks, biscuits and gravy, buffalo burgers (recommended), and hot open-faced sandwiches grace the menu, and pine paneling decorates the walls. Fans of '50s diners will appreciate the simple and filling meals here.

Beartooth BBQ (111 Canyon St., 406/646-0227) is a popular no-smoking eatery with a top-carnivore menu of beef brisket sandwiches, spare ribs, and smoked sausage for $8–16.

Pig out cheaply at tiny **Mountain Mike's Cafe** (38 Canyon, 406/646-9462) with all-American faves: burgers, sandwiches, steak, and chicken, plus freshly baked pies for dessert. A few picnic tables sit out back.

(**Three Bear Restaurant** (205 Yellowstone Ave., 406/646-7811, www.threebearlodge.com) is a friendly place with an up-market dinner menu of shrimp, fresh seafood, trout, chicken, and steaks. It has a good salad-and-soup bar ($9), a children's menu, and apple brown Betty à la mode for dessert. Open for breakfast and lunch and entirely nonsmoking. Dinner entrées are $13–25.

The most unusual local eatery is rustic **Eino's Bar** (406/646-9344), nine miles north of town on U.S. 191. It's a cook-your-own steak, burger, and chicken place with a big indoor grill and a motley, hard-drinking crowd. The bar is famous for its bloody Marys and is popular with snowmobilers. Open for lunch and dinner year-round. The patio features a view across Hebgen Lake, and the bar has a big-screen TV and pool tables.

Pizza and International

Pete's Rocky Mountain Pizza (104 Canyon St., 406/646-7820) serves pizzas, chicken Parmesan, vegetarian lasagna, and other Italian-style meals for $11–14.

Wild West Pizza (20 Madison Ave., 406/646-4400, www.wildwestpizza.com) is another good spot for pizzas and calzones. I'm not sure how they came up with the pizza names, but somehow the "Sacajawea" has fresh spinach, feta, kalamata olives, and artichoke hearts! Medium pizzas run $10–16. Both Wild West and Pete's offer free delivery if you just want to eat a pizza in your motel room. See also Wolf Pack Brewing Co. for pizzas.

Chinatown (110 Madison Ave., 406/646-7088) serves surprisingly authentic Chinese meals and has $6 lunch specials. **La Hacienda** (215 N. Canyon St., 406/640-1437) is the best place for Mexican meals in West.

At the airport 1.5 miles north of town, **TJ's Bettoa** (406/646-4700) serves Italian cuisine, steaks, and seafood for lunch and dinner.

Brewpub

(**Wolf Pack Brewing Co.** (139 N. Canyon St., 406/646-7225) has 10 of its German-style beers on draft, including award-winning Storm Council Irish Stout, Old Snaggletooth Scwartzbier, and Kölsch. The menu features pub fare such as bratwursts, fish-and-chips, burgers, and Polish sausages, but the real stars are New York–style pizzas, crafted with house-made sauces. Try the Thai chicken pizza (with peanut sauce instead of tomato sauce) for something different. For munchies, choose from 10 different kinds of buffalo wings. Most items run $10–20. The brewery is open year-round, but get here early since it closes at 8 nightly because of idiotic Montana state laws that prohibit breweries from serving alcohol after this time. This is the only state in the union with such policies.

Groceries

Market Place (22 Madison Ave., 406/646-9600, and **Food Roundup Supermarket** (107 Dunraven, 406/646-7501) are the local grocery stores. Market Place also contains a deli and bakery. For sweet treats, head to **Arrowleaf Ice Cream Parlor** (29 Canyon St., 406/646-9776). In addition to homemade ice cream, shakes, banana splits, and waffle cones, Arrowleaf serves burgers, chili dogs, and surprisingly good soups. Open summers only.

INFORMATION AND SERVICES

The **West Yellowstone Chamber of Commerce Visitor Center** (30 Yellowstone Ave., 406/646-7701, www.westyellowstonechamber.com) is open 8 A.M.–8 P.M. daily Memorial Day–Labor Day, 8 A.M.–5 P.M. daily in May and Labor Day–October, and 8 A.M.–5 P.M. Monday–Friday the rest of the year. The office is also staffed by Park Service employees (406/646-4403) whenever Yellowstone is open. Daily ranger talks are a feature late May–mid-September, and during the winter rangers lead twice-weekly snowshoe walks.

In addition to the chamber's website, you'll find useful information at www.westyellowstonetraveler.com, maintained by Circumerro Publishing, and Yellowstone Park Net's www.westyellowstonenet.com. The chamber office has a computer to surf the web, along with free Wi-Fi if you brought a laptop. The **library,** a block west at 200 Yellowstone Ave., also has free computers.

The **Hebgen Lake Ranger District Office** (406/646-7369, www.fs.fed.us/r1/gallatin) is just north of town on U.S. 191/287.

West Yellowstone's **post office** (406/646-7704) is at 209 Grizzly Avenue.

Wash clothes at **Canyon Street Laundromat** (312 Canyon St., 406/646-9733), where you'll also find showers.

West Yellowstone Family Medical Center (236 Yellowstone Ave., 406/646-7668) takes walk-in patients. It generally has a nurse practitioner or a doctor on duty, and it is open weekdays.

GETTING THERE AND AROUND
By Air
Delta/Skywest (406/646-7351 or 800/453-9417, www.delta.com) has two flights a day to West Yellowstone airport (just north of town) from Salt Lake City June–September. The rest of the year, the closest air service is in Bozeman, Idaho Falls, or Jackson Hole.

By Bus and Car
Karst Stage (406/556-3500 or 800/287-4759, www.karststage.com) provides daily winter shuttles between the Bozeman airport and West Yellowstone for $75 per person round-trip.

West Yellowstone has some of the highest gas prices in the region; fill up before you get here! Rental cars are available at the airport from **Avis** (406/646-7635 or 800/831-2847, www.avis.com) and **Budget** (406/646-7882 or 800/527-0700, www.budget.com), or in town from **Big Sky Car Rentals** (415 Yellowstone Ave., 406/646-9564 or 800/426-7669, www.yellowstonevacations.com).

PARK TOURS
Buffalo Bus Touring Co. (429 Yellowstone, 406/646-9564 or 800/426-7669, www.yellowstonevacations.com) has summertime loop tours of Yellowstone for $45 adults or $32 kids under 16. It does the lower park loop daily and the upper loop on Mondays, Wednesdays, and Fridays. In the winter, it operates modern snowcoach vans, with all-day tours to Old Faithful ($89 adults, $69 kids) or Canyon ($99 adults, $79 kids). Park entrance fees are additional.

Yellowstone Country Van Tours (406/646-9310 or 800/221-1151, www.yellowstone-tours.com) takes smaller groups (maximum 12) on van tours of the park for a bit more: $50 for the lower loop, $55 for an evening wildlife tour of the upper loop (including Lamar Valley), and $70 for a tour to Grand Teton and Jackson Hole. Park entrance fees are additional.

Yellowstone Alpen Guides (555 Yellowstone Ave., 406/646-9591 or 800/858-3502, www.yellowstoneguides.com) leads personalized tours, from day trips to multiday excursions. The company provides the naturalist-guide, and you travel around the park in the company van or your car.

Gardiner, Montana

The little tourist town of Gardiner, Montana (pop. 800), lies barely outside the northwest entrance to Yellowstone, just three miles from the Wyoming line. The Yellowstone River slices right through town. Park headquarters at Mammoth Hot Springs is just five miles away, and the large warehouses of park concessioner Xanterra Parks and Resorts dominate the vicinity. Gardiner is the only year-round entrance to Yellowstone, and the Absaroka-Beartooth Wilderness lies just north of here. The town sits at an elevation of 5,300 feet—about 900 feet lower than Mammoth—and has warm, dry summers and relatively mild winters.

SIGHTS
Roosevelt Arch

Gardiner was founded in 1880, and three years later the Northern Pacific Railroad extended a line to the edge of Yellowstone, making the town the first major entryway into the park. A reporter of that era described Gardiner as having "200 hardy souls, with 6 restaurants, 1 billiard hall, 2 dance halls, 4 houses of ill-fame, 1 milk man and 21 saloons." Today, the most distinctive structure in town is the monumental stone park entryway—similar to France's Arc de Triomphe—which was the primary entry point into Yellowstone for many years. Built in 1903, Roosevelt Arch was dedicated by President Theodore Roosevelt, a man regarded by many as Yellowstone's patron saint. A tablet above the keystone is inscribed, "For the Benefit and Enjoyment of the People." (The arch was actually built to offset the park visitors' initial disappointment at finding the rather ordinary country in this part of Yellowstone!) Just downhill from the arch is a small park with picnic tables.

Yellowstone Heritage and Research Center

On the edge of town is the Park Service's massive 32,000-square-foot Yellowstone Heritage and Research Center (307/344-2563, www.nps.gov/yell), home to archives, museum collections, and the park library. The five million (!) artifacts include Thomas Moran watercolors, historic photos, early park souvenirs and postcards, and many old vehicles—from horse-drawn carriages to a fire engine. It's hard to miss the building, just below the Roosevelt Arch; it's easily the largest building in town. A few of the historic objects are displayed in the lobby, and the library is open 9 A.M.–4 P.M. Tuesday–Friday, but the collection is primarily for research purposes by appointment only.

ENTERTAINMENT AND EVENTS

Look for live bands on occasional weekends at the **Two-Bit Saloon** (406/848-7743).

The big annual event in town is the **Gardiner Father's Day Rodeo,** which comes around the third weekend of June. Throughout the summer, Arch Park gazebo is home to **evening programs** a couple of times a week; contact the chamber of commerce (www.gardinerchamber.com) for upcoming events. End summer with a Labor Day blast at the **Yellowstone Music Festival** (www.yellowstonemusicfest.com), offering plenty of live folk, bluegrass, rock, and roots music in Arch Park. In late September, return for **Brew Fest** (406/848-7541), an event that combines food, microbrews from regional breweries, and live bands.

SHOPPING

Tumbleweed Bookstore and Cafe (501 Scott St., 406/848-2225) sells new and used titles and serves bagels, deli sandwiches, espresso, and smoothies. It also has rental computers for web surfing. You'll also find Western books and gifts—along with espresso—downtown on Park Street at **High Country Trading** (406/848-7707).

Yellowstone Gallery and Frameworks (406/848-7306, www.yellowstonegallery.com)

© DON PITCHER

Roosevelt Arch, Gardiner

is an excellent place for quality pottery, jewelry, paintings, and photography.

Flying Pig Camp Store (406/848-7510 or 866/807-0744, www.flyingpigrafting.com) sells quality outdoor gear, offers river-rafting trips, and has rental computers and Wi-Fi to check your email.

RECREATION

Kids will appreciate the playground at the K–12 school in Gardiner. There are two fly-fishing shops in Gardiner: **Park's Fly Shop** (406/848-7314, www.parksflyshop.com) and **Big Sky's Flies and Guides** (107 S. 2nd St., 406/848-9998 or 888/315-3789, www.bigsky-flies.com); check Park's website for current fly-fishing conditions in Yellowstone. During the winter, Park's also rents cross-country skis.

For horseback rides and backcountry pack trips, contact **North Yellowstone Outfitters** (406/848-7651, www.northyellowstoneout-fitters.com), **Rendezvous Outfitters** (406/848-7697 or 800/565-7110), or **Flying Pig Adventure Company** (406/848-7510 or 866/807-0744, www.flyingpigrafting.com).

River Rafting

During summer, three rafting companies offer whitewater trips from Gardiner down the Yellowstone River. **Yellowstone Raft Company** (406/848-7777 or 800/858-7781, www.yellowstoneraft.com) has been running trips since 1978. Other good companies are **Flying Pig Adventure Company** (406/848-7510 or 866/807-0744, www.flyingpigrafting.com), **Montana Whitewater** (406/763-4465 or 800/799-4465, www.montanawhitewater.com), and **Wild West Rafting** (406/848-2252 or 800/862-0557, www.wildwestrafting.com).

The rapids in this stretch of the Yellowstone River are relatively gentle, in the Class II–III range, and the featured attractions are half-day eight-mile trips or all-day 17-mile trips. Expect to pay around $35 adults, $25 kids for three-hour trips, or $75 adults, $55 kids for a full-day voyage.

Mountain-Biking

Rent mountain bikes at **Sawtooth Deli** (406/848-7600) to explore a pair of fine cycling options. The Old Gardiner Road to Mammoth gains 900 feet in a distance of five miles and makes for a fun ride back down. Also worth a ride is the old road to Livingston, a gravel road that follows the west side of the Yellowstone River out of Gardiner. It starts near the arch and passes an interesting old cemetery with century-old graves a few miles up.

ACCOMMODATIONS

Gardiner has many places to stay, but be sure to make reservations in the summer; rooms may be hard to find even in mid-September. Rates plummet after (and before) the gold rush of seasonal tourists; $90 summertime rooms suddenly go for $45!

$50-100

Yellowstone River Motel (406/848-7303 or 888/797-4837, www.yellowstonerivermo-tel.com, open May–Oct.) has a garden patio overlooking the river. Economy rooms in the older building are $63 s, $68 d, or $94 for a three-bedroom family unit with full kitchen.

YELLOWSTONE

Rooms in the new addition have air-conditioning and cost $85 d.

Jim Bridger Motor Court (406/848-7371 or 888/858-7508) is a classic Western place with clean and well-kept log cabins built in 1937. Smaller cabins are $69 d, or $79 for two-room units that sleep four. No phones or air-conditioning in the cabins, but they do have fans and small fridges. Open late May–mid-October.

Originally built in the 1950s but updated with newer furnishings, **Hillcrest Cottages** (200 Scott St., 406/848-7353 or 800/970-7353, www.hillcrestcottages.com) has 15 cozy little units, all with kitchenettes and picnic tables. Most have showers, but a few contain tubs. No phones. Rates are $70–80 d, or $120 for a two-room cottage with space for six. Open May–October.

Riverside Cottages (406/848-7719 or 877/774-2836, www.riversidecottages.com) has a mix of motel units ($69–89 d), cottages ($109–139 d) with full kitchens, and suites with whirlpool bath($149 for up to six). Rooms are in good condition, and guests will appreciate the gazebo out back that contains a hot tub overlooking the Yellowstone River. Open June–September.

$100-150

◖ Absaroka Lodge (406/848-7414 or 800/755-7414, www.yellowstonemotel.com), is a modern motel with immaculate rooms for $95 d, and suites with kitchenettes that cost $105 d, or $115 for four people. All rooms have balconies or decks with a great view of the Yellowstone River. The hotel is especially popular with families.

Out in the country four miles northwest of Gardiner, **◖ Yellowstone Basin Inn** (406/848-7080 or 800/624-3364, www.yellowstonebasininn.com) is a charming, recently built lodge with a variety of accommodations. Standard rooms are $113–135 d, and two-room suites with a jetted tub and king bed are $185 d. Also offered are townhouses with full kitchen, living room, and loft: $235 for four in a two-bedroom unit, or $280 for up to seven guests in a three-bedroom town house.

All units have private decks where you can sit on a rocking chair with a view of Electric Peak inside Yellowstone. An outdoor hot tub is available, and a light breakfast is served in the lobby. The inn is open mid-May–mid-October.

Bed-and-Breakfasts

Yellowstone Suites B&B (506 4th St., 406/848-7937 or 800/948-7937, www.yellowstonesuites.com, $85–129 d) is a stone house that's a century old. Features include Victorian antique furnishings, hardwood floors, a veranda, a hot tub, and full breakfasts. The four guest rooms have shared or private baths; one contains a kitchenette. Kids are welcome.

North Yellowstone B&B (406/848-7651, www.northyellowstone.com) is a delightful country place, with two modern log cabins two miles up Jardine Road. The cabins are $90 for up to six, including a full breakfast that is served at the main house. No phones and only a TV are provided, but the cabins have private baths, small fridges, and barbecue grills. Outside, weeping willow trees provide shade, and gorgeous sagebrush country heads out in all directions.

Headwaters of the Yellowstone B&B (406/848-7073 or 888/848-7220, www.headwatersbandb.com) is a large house on three acres of land along the Yellowstone River. It's a mile north of the Gardiner airport and has four guest rooms ($100–110 d) and a suite ($140 for up to four) along with two modern cabins with full kitchens ($135–160 for up to six). All of these rooms have private baths, and the rate includes a full breakfast for guests in the rooms and suites.

Guesthouses

◖ Above the Rest Lodge (406/848-7747 or 800/406-7748, www.abovetherestlodge.com) has five modern and well-appointed cabins less than two miles north of Gardiner up Jardine Road. Smallest is a one-bedroom unit with a spiral staircase and full kitchen; $125 for four people. Largest is a spacious three-bedroom home that sleeps 14 people for $260 per night. All of these have full kitchens and decks facing

Yellowstone. Open year-round. This is a great, secluded place to get away from it all.

Camping

Yellowstone National Park's **Mammoth Campground** is five miles up the hill at Mammoth Hot Springs and costs $14. The campground is open year-round but sits close to a busy road. No reservations are taken.

Closer—and more peaceful—is the small **Eagle Creek Campground** ($7, open year-round), less than two miles northeast of Gardiner up the gravel road on the way to Jardine. This Gallatin National Forest campground (406/848-7375, www.fs.fed.us/r1/gallatin) is approximately 500 feet higher than Gardiner, and you will need to bring water from town or treat water from the creek here. Two other Forest Service campgrounds (free, open mid-June–Oct.) are a few miles up Jardine Road.

Park RVs at **Rocky Mountain Campground** (406/848-7251 or 877/534-6931, www.rocky-mountaincampground.com, $25 tents, $42 RVs, open Apr.–Oct.), with free wireless internet. Showers for noncampers cost $5, and a public launderette is on the site.

FOOD

K Bar Club (406/848-9995) doesn't look like much either outside or inside, but the from-scratch pizzas are very good in this locals' hangout; kids and families are welcome. Also popular with families is **Outlaw's Pizza** (in the Outpost Mall on the northwest end of town, 406/848-7733) for pizzas, pasta, and calzones, with a small salad bar.

Two Bit Saloon (406/848-7743) serves the best greasy-spoon breakfasts, but it can be smoky and a bit pricy.

The downtown **Sawtooth Deli** (406/848-7600) serves tasty breakfasts, along with subs, grilled sandwiches, soups, salads, and espresso for lunch. Daily specials are generally your best bet. The covered deck is a favorite hang-out. Closed Sunday and Monday and mid-October–May.

At the aging yellow **Corral Drive Inn** (406/848-7627), Helen and her sons serve the biggest, juiciest, and messiest (grab a handful of napkins) hamburgers anywhere around.

🄲 **Park Street Grill and Café** (406/848-7989) seems out of place in down-home Gardiner. Most of the menu isn't your standard Old West fare, although it does serve steaks and prime rib. Instead, it's Italian food with flair, including such delights as shrimp fra diavolo (large shrimp sautéed with garlic, peppers, and tomatoes served over linguine) or Crazy Mt. Alfredo with chicken breast, *soppressata,* Italian sausage, and hot peppers. Also check out the daily fresh seafood specials. Meals come with a big house salad, and the atmosphere is rustic elegance. Park Street Grill is open for dinners only ($14–18 entrées) and is closed October–April.

Shop for groceries, fresh baked goods, and deli items at **Food Farm** (406/848-7524) across the river on the northwest end of town.

INFORMATION AND SERVICES

The **Gardiner Chamber of Commerce** (222 Park St., 406/848-7971, www.gardinerchamber.com) has local information and is open 10 A.M.–8 P.M. Monday–Friday and 10 A.M.–5 P.M. Saturday–Sunday late May–early September, and 10 A.M.–3 P.M. Monday–Friday the rest of the year. If the office is closed, check the information kiosk next to Outlaw Pizza on the north end of town for maps, brochures, and events. You can use its computer to surf the web ($1 per half hour). The town library (open Tuesday and Thursday only) has computers with free Internet access.

The **Gardiner District Office** of Gallatin National Forest (406/848-7375, www.fs.fed.us/r1/gallatin) has maps and information on the 930,584-acre **Absaroka-Beartooth Wilderness.** The part around Gardiner is lower in elevation and covered with forests, while farther east are the alpine peaks of the Beartooth Mountains.

The **post office** is on the north end of town (along U.S. 89, 406/848-7579). Get fast cash at the ATM inside the Exxon station just north of the river or from the First Interstate Bank on the northwest end of town. Wash clothes at **Arch Laundrette** (next to High Country Trading on Park St.). Both Yellowstone Village Inn and Rocky Mountain Campground also have washers and driers available to the public. The closest medical facility is in Mammoth Hot Springs.

GETTING THERE AND AROUND

Karst Stage (406/388-2293 or 800/287-4759, www.karststage.com) has daily winter-time shuttles between the Bozeman airport and Gardiner; rates depend upon the number of passengers.

Mid-May–September, **Xanterra Parks and Resorts** (307/344-7311, www.travelyellowstone.com) operates full-day bus tours of Yellowstone out of Gardiner. Rates are $50 adults, $25 ages 12–16, and free for kids under 12; park entrance fees are extra. These tours are a bit grueling because you leave at 8:30 A.M. and don't get back until 6:15 P.M.

Cooke City and Silver Gate, Montana

Shortly after you exit Yellowstone's northeast corner along U.S. 212, the road widens slightly as it passes through two settlements: Silver Gate and the larger Cooke City, Montana. The towns are just three miles apart and almost within spitting distance of the Wyoming line. The area code—406—is larger than the combined population of both settlements! Although they depend on tourism, these quiet, homespun places lack the hustle and bustle of West Yellowstone and have a more authentic feel. No leash laws exist here, so you're likely to see dogs sleeping on the sidewalks or wandering lazily down the middle of the road. Most establishments are built of log, befitting the mining heritage of this area. Silver Gate even has a building code that requires all structures to be of log or rustic architecture—it's the only municipality in the country with such a code. Pilot Peak and Index Peak are the prominent rocky spires visible along the highway east of Cooke City. Dramatic Amphitheater Peak juts out just south of Silver Gate.

During winter, the road is plowed all the way from Gardiner, through the northern part of Yellowstone, and into Cooke City, making this a popular staging area for snowmobilers and skiers heading into the Beartooth Mountains. East of Cooke City, the Beartooth Highway across 10,947-foot Beartooth Pass is closed by the first of November (often earlier) and doesn't open again until late May.

SIGHTS

It's hard to miss the red ◖ **Cooke City General Store** (406/838-2234, www.cookecitystore.com), one of the oldest buildings in the area. Built in 1886, this classic country market sells groceries, quality T-shirts, and gifts that include Indian jewelry and imported items from all over the globe. It also has Yellowstone and Wyoming fishing licenses. Open May–September only. Up the street is another summertime place that is well worth a look. **Blain Gallery** (406/838-2474) features original watercolors by Mary Blain, along with pottery, baskets, and photographs.

RECREATION

Yellowstone is less than four miles away, and it's the obvious site for recreation in the Cooke City-Silver Gate area during the summer. The **Absaroka-Beartooth Wilderness** is accessible from Cooke City and various points to the east along the gorgeous Beartooth Highway.

Summertime horseback rides, pack trips into the Absaroka–Beartooth Wilderness, and guided fly-fishing expeditions are provided by several local outfitters; get a listing from the visitor center in Cooke City.

Biking and Skiing

Cooke City Bike Shack (406/838-2412, www.cookecitybikeshack.com) is a hub for the outdoor adventure crowd. Friendly owner Bill

downtown Cooke City

Blackford is a jack of all trades, running the espresso machine one minute and fixing a bike or selling outdoor gear the next. In the winter he rents snowshoes, high-end backcountry skis, avalanche transceivers, and other supplies, and guides telemarking and cross-country ski trips; $85 per person for an all-day trek. Backcountry skiers and snowboarders who want to head out on their own can catch a five-mile snowmobile ride ($15 per person) into the high country at Daisy Pass, gaining 2,100 feet of elevation along the way. This makes for a great day of skiing and a fun downhill run back to town.

Snowmobiling

Cooke City has become a hub for winter sports. Pick up a map of groomed cross-country ski trails and snowmobile routes from local businesses. The area consistently ranks among the top snowmobiling destinations in America. Snowmobile rentals (and summertime ATV rentals) are available from **Cooke City Exxon** (406/838-2244) and **Cooke City Motorsports** (406/838-2231). The local snowmobile club grooms approximately 60 miles of trails in the

surrounding mountains. Be sure to also check the **Avalanche Advisory Hotline** (406/587-6981, www.mtavalanche.com) for the latest on backcountry conditions before heading out.

ACCOMMODATIONS

Cooke City and Silver Gate have quite a few old-fashioned motels and cabins that provide a delightful Old West feeling. As with other towns surrounding Yellowstone, reservations are always a good idea in midsummer or midwinter.

Cooke City

Three miles east of Cooke City, **Big Moose Resort** (406/838-2393, www.bigmooseresort .com, $65–80 d) has a mix of old and new year-round cabins; two include kitchenettes. Right across the road, **Big Bear Lodge** (406/838-2267 or 888/341-2267, www.montanabigbearlodge.com) is primarily a fishing and hunting lodge but offers nightly accommodations throughout the year. Guests stay in six older but well-kept log cabins ($50 d), each of which has two double beds.

Antler's Lodge (406/838-2432 or 866/738-2432, www.cookecityantlerslodge.com, $55–120 d) has 18 cabins in various sizes and configurations, some with kitchens and lofts. Wireless Internet is available; open year-round.

Absaroka Cabins (406/838-2018) rents out three modern cabins with kitchenettes. These cost $85 d, or $95 for four people, and are open year-round.

You'll find spacious, clean, and comfortable rooms and cabins at ◖ **High Country Motel** (406/838-2272, www.cookecityhighcountry.com, $55–85 d). Some units contain kitchenettes. Open all year.

Hoosier's Motel (406/838-2241, $64 s or $69 d) has good rooms and is open mid-May–mid-October.

Alpine Motel (406/838-2262 or 888/838-1190, www.ccalpinemotel.com) is also open all year and has rooms for $62–77 d, plus apartment-style units with two bedrooms and full kitchens for $92 d, plus $10 per person (maximum of six). The motel also has a guest computer and wireless Internet.

With 32 guest rooms on two floors, **Soda Butte Lodge** (406/838-2251 or 800/527-6462, www.cookecity.com, $65–75 d) is one of the largest lodging places in the area. The hotel contains one of the better restaurants in these parts (Prospector), and guests are welcome to use the seasonal hot tub. Open year-round.

The friendly 🄒 **Elk Horn Lodge** (406/838-2332, www.beartooths.com/elkhorn) has attractive and spotless motel rooms ($60 s or $65 d) with microwaves and fridges, plus two cabins ($75 d or $85 for four guests) with kitchenettes. Open year-round.

Silver Gate

For a quiet step into the past, book one of the 15 🄒 **Silver Gate Cabins** (406/838-2371, www.silver-gate-cabins.com, $72–120 d). Built in 1933, these attractive log cabins (most with kitchenettes) vary widely, from basic two-person units ($55) where Daniel Boone would feel at home, to an attractive six-person cabin ($120). The secluded honeymoon cabin ($85) has a creekside location. Also here are five motel units for $72 d. Outside, you'll find barbecue grills, volleyball and horseshoes, and a playground for kids. Some of the cabins are available year-round. This is a quiet place where snowmobiles and four-wheelers are not allowed. Also here is **Silver Gate General Store,** with supplies, a good selection of books and Montana-made products. The store rents high-quality spotting scopes ($20) for folks heading into Yellowstone to watch wolves.

Right on the river and close to the Yellowstone border in Silver Gate, **Grizzly Lodge** (406/838-2219, www.yellowstonelodges.com, $60–80) is a century-old log building. Guests stay in a variety of motel-style rooms (including kitchenettes, two-bedroom units, and rooms with lofts) inside the lodge; the largest sleeps six. The sauna and hot tub here may—or may not—be operational. Open late May–early October.

Camping

Heading east from Cooke City, you'll find four Forest Service campgrounds ($9, open July–Sept.) within 10 miles of town. Closest is **Soda Butte Campground,** just 0.5 mile from town; another mile to the east is **Colter Campground** (406/848-7375, www.fs.fed.us/r1/gallatin).

No RV parks are in the area, but two lodging places have summertime RV sites with water and electric hookups: **Big Moose Resort** (406/838-2393, www.bigmooseresort.com), and **Antler's Lodge** (406/838-2432 or 866/738-2432, www.cookecityantlerslodge.com). Showers are available from Soda Butte Lodge in Cooke City.

FOOD

Inside Cooke City's Soda Butte Lodge (406/838-2251 or 800/527-6462, www.cookecity.com), **Prospector Restaurant** is well known for prime rib cooked to perfection, but it's also open for breakfast and lunch. Dinner entrées are $11–30. Also here is the **Ore House Saloon,** with sports on the TV and video poker and keno machines to take your money. Everything at Soda Butte Lodge is open year-round.

Cooke City Bike Shack (406/838-2412) cranks out espresso coffees and is a great place to meet locals. Nearby 🄒 **Bistro Cafe** (406/838-2160) serves standard American fare for breakfast and lunch, but dinner is when this authentically French bistro shines, with quality steaks, veal, lamb, and seafood; $13–24. Closed in fall and spring.

Beartooth Cafe in Cooke City (406/838-2475) has good sandwiches for lunch, dinners that star free-range Angus beef steaks, a popular deck, and more than 130 kinds of beer. It serves breakfast on weekends and is open summers only. Next door is **Buns'N Beds** (406/838-2030), with year-round deli sandwiches, soups, and salads. Also in Cooke City, **The Grizzly Pad Grill** (406/838-2161) has reasonable prices, three meals a day, and locally famous milk shakes, burgers, and fries.

In peaceful Silver Gate, **Log Cabin Cafe** (406/838-2367) is a consistent favorite, with well-prepared trout, pasta, barbecued beef, steaks, and homemade soups. Open mid-May–mid-September.

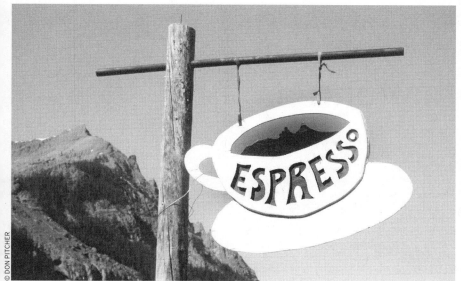

© DON PITCHER

an enticing sign in Cooke City

Cooke City's 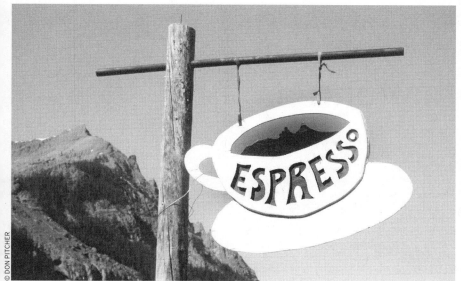 **Miner's Saloon** (406/838-2214) is a classic Old West bar where the stools are filled with locals and tourists. Pull the handles on the keno and poker machines, or Texas hold 'em poker, or try a game of pool, Foosball, or air hockey. The menu includes surprisingly good pizzas and burgers.

For groceries and supplies, head to Cooke City General Store (see *Sights*).

INFORMATION AND SERVICES

The **Cooke City, Colter Pass, and Silver Gate Chamber of Commerce** (406/838-2495, www.cookecitychamber.org) has a small sum-mertime visitor center in Cooke City that's open 11 A.M.–6 P.M. daily late May–mid-September. When it's closed, drop by High Country Motel or Elk Horn Lodge for local information. Put away your cell phone in Cooke City and Silver Gate; there's no service here. If you're heading here from other areas, fill your tank because gas prices here are some of the highest in the region.

Despite its remoteness, you'll discover several ATMs in Cooke City. Laundry facilities are inside Soda Butte Lodge and **Cooke City Sinclair** (406/838-2000, www.ccsinclair.com) has Internet access.

YELLOWSTONE

BIGHORN BASIN

Bighorn Basin is an enormous intermountain desertscape reaching almost 100 miles north to south and 50 miles east to west. Mountain ranges rim the basin—the Absarokas (ab-SOR-kas) rise as a western border, the Owl Creek Mountains line the southern horizon, and the snowcapped Big Horns gleam in the east. The basin's rolling desert hills are topped with oil pumpjacks, and the wind blows incessantly. Cactus and sagebrush struggle up through a hardened surface of small rocks, and rugged badlands buttes rise above dry creekbeds. The countryside looks like southern Nevada.

Much of the basin gets less than 10 inches of precipitation per year; in some places just half that, and even in midwinter there isn't much snow on the ground. Three lazy rivers—Big Horn, Greybull, and Shoshone—create long green corridors through this desolation, offering an oasis in the dry desert country. Because of the lack of water, this was one of the last parts of Wyoming to be settled, and most of the towns did not spring up until the 1890s, when passage of the Carey Act brought a flood of irrigation speculators, investors, and farmers. The Carey Act, named for Wyoming Senator Joseph M. Carey, allowed the federal government to donate land to the states for reclamation by settlers. Canals have created wide swatches of irrigated green around the towns and along the rivers. Much of this water comes from the Buffalo Bill Reservoir just west of Cody and a series of canals supplying water to sugar beet and barley farms along the Big Horn and Greybull rivers.

In the early part of the 20th century, boom

© DON PITCHER

HIGHLIGHTS

◖ Beartooth Mountains: Some call the Beartooth Highway the most scenic highway in America. High (10,947 feet) and dramatic, and closed September–May (page 518).

◖ Buffalo Bill Historical Center: It started with items from Buffalo Bill's life, but now it covers 300,000 square feet in five distinct museums focusing on Western art, the Plains Indians, natural history, firearms, and of course, Buffalo Bill. It's one of the finest museums in North America (page 528).

◖ Trail Town: The perfect counterpoint to BBHC, with old wagons, rustic cabins—including one used by Butch Cassidy and the Sundance Kid—plus a treasure trove of other items. Check out the dugout canoe that just might have been used by Lewis and Clark (page 533).

◖ Cody Nite Rodeo: Still going strong after seven decades, the rodeos take place nightly all summer. Get there early for a seat in "buzzards roost" (page 536).

◖ Bighorn Canyon National Recreation Area: Featured attractions include wild horses and bighorn sheep, but your jaw will drop when you peer over the 1,000-foot-cliffs at Devil Canyon Overlook (page 555).

◖ Medicine Lodge State Archaeological Site: Occupied for 10,000 years, the site has a cliff covered with petroglyphs and pictographs. Pleasant creekside camping, too (page 567).

◖ Hot Springs State Park: Join the geriatric set in the hot pools here, or the schoolkids at two adjacent commercial areas with long water slides and swimming pools. This is the world's largest hot springs (page 574).

LOOK FOR ◖ TO FIND RECOMMENDED SIGHTS, ACTIVITIES, DINING, AND LODGING.

◖ Wyoming Dinosaur Center: The museum houses specimens—including a nearly complete Triceratops—and informative displays, but most interesting is the chance to tour a nearby dig site (page 577).

◖ Legend Rock Petroglyph Site: Bison, elk, humans, and even a flying rabbit appear at this remote sacred place northwest of Thermopolis (page 578).

◖ Wind River Canyon: Narrow and dramatic, with high cliffs on both sides and the Wind River rolling through. A fun place for river rafting (page 581).

© AVALON TRAVEL PUBLISHING, INC.

times came to the basin with discoveries of oil and natural gas at Grass Creek and Byron. Along with cattle and sheep ranching (important since the 1880s), these industries still dominate the economy of Bighorn Basin. To most tourists, the basin (with the exception of Cody) is a place to get through on the way to Yellowstone or the Black Hills. Locals, however, call it a retirement haven and offer as proof the dry, sunny climate (more than 300 days of sun per year), relatively mild winters, moderately priced housing, low crime rate, and proximity to the recreational

wonderlands of Yellowstone and the Absaroka and Big Horn mountains. (In case you're confused, the word "Bighorn" is used for the national forest, canyon, river, lake, and basin, while "Big Horn" is the correct spelling for the mountain range, town, and county. Even Wyoming state maps get these spellings wrong!)

PLANNING YOUR TIME

Bighorn Basin is one of the primary transit routes for Yellowstone visitors, and the basin's towns—particularly Cody, Greybull, Powell,

Worland, and Thermopolis—all have a good mix of lodging, RV parks, and restaurants. Plan at least two nights in Cody, and one or two in Thermopolis.

Cody is the main regional draw and the home to massive **Buffalo Bill Historical Center,** the finest Old West museum anywhere. Up the road is low-key **Trail Town** with historic cabins and wagons. The **Cody Nite Rodeo** takes place throughout the summer, and whitewater rafting on the Shoshone River lets visitors do their own bucking. Cody serves as a good center for day trips or dude-ranch visits up scenic **Wapiti Valley** or to Sunlight Basin and the dramatic alpine pass over the **Beartooth Mountains.** Some travelers also use Cody as a base for long day-trips into Yellowstone National Park.

The towns of Powell, Greybull, Meeteetse, and Worland all have smaller museums, and Greybull is also home to a fleet of historic aircraft. **Bighorn Canyon National Recreation Area** is a good place to look for wild horses or to take in the dramatic plunge of Devil Canyon. At the southern end of the basin, quiet Thermopolis has the world's largest hot springs, managed as **Hot Springs State Park,** as well as two local museums and the extraordinary **Wyoming Dinosaur Center.** Approximately 20 miles northwest of town is **Legend Rock Petroglyph Site** and south of Thermopolis the highway cuts through dramatic **Wind River Canyon. Medicine Lodge State Archaeological Site** is in the foothills of the Big Horn Mountains near the town of Hyattville.

Shoshone National Forest

Shoshone National Forest encompasses more than 2.4 million acres and extends along a 180-mile strip from the Montana border to the Wind River Mountains. Sagebrush dominates at the lowest elevations, but as you climb, lodgepole, Douglas fir, Engelmann spruce, and subalpine fir cover the slopes. Above 10,000 feet, the land opens into alpine vegetation and barren rocky peaks. The **Shoshone National Forest Supervisor's Office** (307/578-1200, www.fs.fed.us/r2/shoshone) is in Cody. Get information and forest maps there or from ranger stations in Cody, Dubois, and Lander.

Shoshone is America's oldest national forest. On March 30, 1891, President Benjamin Harrison signed a proclamation creating Yellowstone Park Timberland Reserve adjacent to Yellowstone National Park. At first this title meant very little, but in 1902 President Theodore Roosevelt appointed rancher and artist A. A. Anderson to control grazing and logging and catch poachers. His strong management almost got him lynched. Three years later under Gifford Pinchot, the forest reserves were transferred to the Department of Agriculture

and renamed national forests. The land was renamed Shoshone National Forest in 1908.

More than half of Shoshone National Forest lies inside wilderness boundaries; the Absaroka-Beartooth, North Absaroka, and Washakie wilderness areas cover much of the country east of Yellowstone National Park, while the Wind River Mountains contain the Fitzpatrick and Popo Agie wildernesses (see the *Wind River Mountains Country* chapter for more on these areas). Part of the credit for the surprising expanse of wilderness areas in the national forest goes to Buffalo Bill. By bringing people into the area to hunt, fish, and explore, he helped create what one author called a "dude's forest." In addition, the Buffalo Bill Dam (which he vociferously supported) prevented logs from being sent down the North Fork of the Shoshone River and thus made logging less important.

More than 1,500 miles of trails offer hiking and horseback access to much of this country. Shoshone has more than 50 campgrounds, most costing $5–10 per night. Once the water has been shut off for winter (generally Oct.–Apr.), you can camp for free but will have to

To Red Lodge

Cooke City
Silver Gate
Absaroka-Beartooth Wilderness
Beartooth Pass
MONTANA
WYOMING
212
120

To Tower Fall
CLAY BUTTE LOOKOUT
Shoshone National Forest

212
Beartooth Mtns
296

North Absaroka Wilderness
Windy Mtn Trail
Windy Mtn
Sunlight Basin
Dead Indian Pass

Yellowstone National Park
SUNLIGHT RANGER STATION
Heart Mountain
To Powell

CAMP MONACO
Dead Indian Trail
Trout Peak
14A

Pahaska-Sunlight Trail
Cody

To Yellowstone Lake
Pahaska
WAPITI RANGER STATION
Cedar Mountain
14 16 20

14 16 2
SLEEPING GIANT
Wapiti
Buffalo Bill Reservoir

Eagle Peak
Eagle Creek Trail
Kitty Creek Trail
Washakie Wilderness
Elk Fork Trail
291
120

Thorofare Trail
Open Creek Trail
SOUTH FORK RD
Shoshone National Forest

Deer Creek Trail
DEER CREEK
10 mi
10 km

Thorofare Plateau
JACK CREEK TRAILHEAD
To Meeteetse
WOOD RIVER RD

Continental
Absaroka Range
BROWN MOUNTAIN
WOOD RIVER

Divide
South Fork Trail
Washakie Wilderness

Bridger-Teton National Forest
Wiggins Fork Trail

To Grand Teton National Park
Togwotee Pass
Brooks Lake
PINNACLE BUTTES
DOUBLE CABIN

BROOKS LAKE
SHOSHONE NATIONAL FOREST

26 287

WIND RIVER INDIAN
RESERVATION

Dubois

haul out your own trash. Space is generally available even at the busiest times of year. In addition, free dispersed camping is possible at undeveloped sites throughout the forest, with the exception of heavily traveled U.S. 14/16/20, where you must be 0.5 mile off the road.

Although uncommon, black bears roam throughout the forest, and grizzlies are found within the northern sections, including the North Absaroka and Washakie wilderness areas. Be sure to take the necessary bear precautions anywhere in the backcountry. Bears also sometimes wander into campgrounds along U.S. 14/16/20 near Yellowstone National Park. You are much more likely to encounter mosquitoes, deer flies, and horse flies in mid-summer, so be sure to bring insect repellent.

NORTH ABSAROKA WILDERNESS

The 350,488-acre North Absaroka Wilderness is one of the lesser-known wild places in Wyoming. It abuts Yellowstone National Park to the west and is bordered by the Sunlight Basin Highway and Beartooth Highway to the north and U.S. 14/16/20 to the south. North Absaroka Wilderness is primarily used by hunters who arrive on horseback. The few hikers here tend to be quite experienced with backcountry travel and willing to tolerate the lack of trail signs and the steep and frequently washed-out paths. Much of the wilderness is relatively inaccessible, and snow may be present on passes until mid-July. Ask at the ranger stations for current trail conditions, and be sure to get topographic maps before heading out. Large populations of grizzly and black bears, bighorn sheep, moose, and elk are found in the Absaroka Mountains, and golden eagles are a common sight. The tough landscape is of volcanic origin, and the topsoil erodes easily, turning mountain creeks into churning rivers of mud after heavy summer rainstorms.

Hiking

The 1988 Clover-Mist Fire that began in Yellowstone burned through a large section of the North Absaroka Wilderness, but the land is recovering. Many hikers begin from trailheads near the Crandall Ranger Station along the Chief Joseph Scenic Highway. The **North Crandall Trail** is the most popular, a 16-mile hike up the North Fork of Crandall Creek. It is primarily used by horsepackers and offers great views of Hurricane Mesa along the way. Another popular wilderness path is **Pahaska-Sunlight Trail,** an 18-mile trek that begins at Pahaska Campground on U.S. 14/16/20 and heads north through historic Camp Monaco to Sunlight Basin.

WASHAKIE WILDERNESS

Covering 704,529 acres, Washakie Wilderness is one of the largest chunks of wild land in Wyoming. Named for Shoshone Chief Washakie, it lies between U.S. 14/16/20 (the road connecting Yellowstone and Cody) and U.S. 26/287 (Dubois area). To the west are Yellowstone National Park and Teton Wilderness. The Washakie is a land of deep narrow valleys, mountains of highly erodible volcanic material, and steplike buttes. The mountains—a few top 13,000 feet—are part of the Absaroka Range. About half of the land is forested. One of the unique features of Washakie Wilderness is a petrified forest, a reminder of the region's volcanic past.

Hiking

Numerous trails run through the Washakie Wilderness, but most require that you either return the same way or end at a location far from your starting point. Several trails stretch into Yellowstone National Park and are popular with extended horsepacking trips. The most popular Washakie Wilderness hikes are from U.S. 14/16/20 in Wapiti Valley. Most folks use them for short day hikes or horseback rides rather than attempting longer backcountry treks.

Kitty Creek Trail leaves from the Kitty Creek summer home area, nine miles east of Yellowstone. Low-clearance vehicles will need to park along the highway. The trail follows the creek past two large scenic meadows to Flora Lake, 6.5 miles and 2,500 feet higher. This is the shortest hike in the area and one of the most popular.

The 21-mile-long **Elk Fork Trail** starts at Elk

Fork Campground and crosses Elk Creek several times en route to remote Rampart Pass at nearly 11,000 feet. It is steep and rocky in the higher elevations. West of the Continental Divide you enter the Teton Wilderness. For the really ambitious, the Open Creek Trail and Thorofare Trail continue into Yellowstone National Park.

Deer Creek Trail departs from the free Deer Creek Campground, 42 miles southwest of Cody on Hwy. 291 (South Fork Rd.). The trail switchbacks very steeply uphill at first and after two miles reaches an attractive waterfall. Continue another eight miles from here to the Continental Divide and the Thorofare section of the Teton Wilderness. This is probably the quickest route into this remote country and is popular with both horsepackers and hikers.

South Fork Trail takes off from the South Fork Guard Station across the creek from Deer Creek Campground. (Take a signed spur road to get there.) It climbs up along South Fork Creek to Shoshone Pass on the Continental Divide (9,858 feet). From here you can continue on several trails to the south, rambling over three more passes to eventually reach Double Cabin Campground, 27 miles north of Dubois. Another long hike into Washakie Wilderness leaves from this campground and follows the **Wiggins Fork Trail** up into a connecting series of paths: Absaroka, Nine Mile, East Fork, and Bug Creek trails. It ends back at Double Cabin Campground. Total length is 60 miles. Along the way you're likely to see hundreds of elk in the high country as well as bighorn sheep.

SUNLIGHT BASIN

The **Chief Joseph Scenic Highway** (Hwy. 296) is a 46-mile route through a magnificent Wyoming landscape. Popularly known as Sunlight Basin Road, it is paved and most of it remains open year-round, providing access for backcountry skiers and snowmobilers to the beautiful Beartooth Pass area. (An eight-mile section between Cooke City, Montana, and Pilot Creek, Wyoming, is not plowed in the winter. It typically opens by early May.) Chief Joseph Highway begins 17 miles north of Cody off Hwy. 120, with Heart Mountain prominent to

---

WYOMING DESIGN

Wyoming seems to be the doing of a mad architect – tumbled and twisted, ribboned with faded, deathbed colors, thrust up and pulled down as if the place had been startled out of a deep sleep and thrown into a pure light.

–Gretel Ehrlich in
The Solace of Open Spaces

---

the southeast, and climbs sharply from the dry east side, passing a brilliant red butte en route to **Dead Indian Pass,** named for an incident during an 1878 fight between Bannocks and the U.S. Army. After the battle, Crow scouts found a wounded old Bannock warrior here. They killed and scalped him, burying the body under a pile of rocks. Other tales claim that the name came from the body of an Indian propped up as a ruse to trick the army during Chief Joseph's attempted escape to Canada in 1877. Chief Joseph *did* lead the Nez Perce through this country, avoiding the cavalry by heading up Clarks Fork Canyon, a route the army had considered impassable. An overlook on top of Dead Indian Pass provides a panoramic vista of the rugged mountains and valleys below. The river forms a boundary between the volcanic Absarokas to the south and the granitic Beartooth Mountains to the north.

Indians weren't the only ones killed in this era. In 1870, two miners, Marvin Crandall and T. Dougherty, headed into the Upper Clarks Fork after reports of gold in the area. When they failed to meet up with other miners, a search party was sent out. The searchers were themselves attacked by Indians, but they later found the bodies of Crandall and Dougherty—scalped and decapitated, with their heads atop mining picks. In a macabre bit of humor, tin cups sat in front of each skull and the right hand of each man held a spoon. The men had apparently been killed while eating and the bodies were left as a warning against further white exploration of the area.

West of the overlook, the road switchbacks down hairpin turns into remote and beautiful Sunlight Basin. The name came about in the 1840s. Fur trappers worked this area for beaver and discovered a place flooded with light, but it was so remote that "the only thing that can get into this valley most of the year is sunlight." Today it is considerably more accessible but still just as beautiful. A gravel side road leads seven miles up the valley to **Sunlight Ranger Station,** built in 1936 by the CCC. It's open summers only. This is some of the finest elk winter range anywhere and the home of several scenic old guest ranches.

Back on the main road, a bridge—highest in Wyoming at 300 feet above Sunlight Creek— spans deep, cliff-walled **Sunlight Gorge.** Sorry, no bungee jumping allowed. The highway then continues northwest past Cathedral Cliffs and through a scenic ranching and timbering valley, offering views into the deep gorge that belongs to the Clarks Fork of the Yellowstone River. In some sections, sheer cliffs tower 1,200 feet above the water. Part of the area burned by the 1988 Clover-Mist Fire is visible near **Crandall Ranger Station.** This area also contains the only large herd of mountain goats in Wyoming. Eventually you reach the junction with U.S. 212, the Beartooth Highway (see the *Beartooth Mountains* section for a description of this beautiful route).

Hiking

The Forest Service's Lake Creek, Hunter Peak, and Dead Indian campgrounds ($5–10, open mid-May–Sept.) are found along Chief Joseph Scenic Highway. **Dead Indian Trail** (just uphill from Dead Indian Campground) goes two miles to a fine overlook into Clarks Fork Canyon. Also of interest is **Windy Mountain Trail** which climbs 10,262-foot Windy Mountain. It starts from a trailhead four miles east of the Crandall Ranger Station (interesting old log buildings here), is approximately seven miles one-way, and gains 3,700 feet in elevation. Windy Mountain can also be climbed from the other side near the Sunlight Ranger Station. Trailheads into the North Absaroka Wilderness are at the Crandall Ranger Station and beyond the Little Sunlight Campground (free; open year-round) on Forest Road 101.

River-Running

Clarks Fork of the Yellowstone River (named for William Clark, of the Lewis and Clark expedition) is Wyoming's only designated Wild and Scenic River. Experienced kayakers will find a couple of great stretches of class IV–V whitewater in the upper Clarks Fork; however, use considerable caution because there are several big drops. Be sure to pull out before dangerous Box Canyon, which is considered unrunnable. Find more class IV waters farther down the river. Check with the Forest Service for specifics. Below the rapids are quieter stretches. Based in Cody, **Red Canyon River Trips** (1374 Sheridan Ave., 307/587-6988 or 800/293-0148, www.imt.net/~rodeo/raft.html) leads gentle float trips down a scenic 12-mile section of the Clarks Fork. The half-day trip ($55) is offered late May–early August.

Accommodations

In the heart of beautiful Sunlight Basin, **Seven D Ranch** (307/587-9885, www.7dranch.com) is a family-oriented guest ranch offering horseback rides, cookouts, fly-fishing, hiking, and pack trips, and something parents will really appreciate: free child care for tots during riding periods, along with a special program for older kids. The setting is spectacular—it's where some of the Marlboro ads were shot— and the cabins are comfortable and cozy. Weekly all-inclusive rates are $3,120 for two people. The ranch has space for a maximum of 32 guests. Open early June–late September; adults only in September.

K Bar Z Guest Ranch (307/587-4410, www.agonline.com/kbarz) is off the Chief Joseph Scenic Highway in the Crandall Creek area. Nightly log-cabin accommodations are available for $90 d (lodging only), or two people can stay for six nights for $2,000, including meals, lodging, horseback rides, and Yellowstone sightseeing; extra charge for backcountry pack trips and guided fishing trips. The ranch is open June–mid-December and has room for a maximum of 30 guests.

Hunter Peak Ranch (4027 Crandall Rd., 307/587-3711, www.nezperce.com/ranchhp .html) is on the banks of the upper Clarks Fork River and offers lodging in rustic log cabins or motel-style rooms. Unlike most dude ranches, this one operates on an à la carte basis. Lodging is $120 d per night or $713 d per week, with extra charges for meals, horseback rides, and pack trips. The main lodge was built from hand-hewn logs in 1917. Open year-round.

Also in Sunlight Basin, **Elk Creek Ranch** (307/587-3902 in summers or 207/384-5361 in winter, www.elkcreekranch.com) provides a unique coed opportunity for teenagers to gain a wide range of ranching and wilderness skills. Ranch stays ($3,300 per person all-inclusive for a four-week session) include lots of time on horseback; they also build cabins, cut hay, and learn other ranch work. The backpacking adventures ($3,200 per person all-inclusive for a four-week session) give kids plenty of time in the backcountry, where they learn a range of outdoor and mountain-climbing skills—including a chance to summit Grand Teton. Two monthlong sessions are offered each summer with a maximum of 30 kids at a time.

(See *Hiking* for campground information.)

Services

The little settlement called **Painter** is 21 miles southeast of Cooke City on Chief Joseph Highway and right along the Clarks Fork River. Here you'll find a general store and gas pumps, along with year-round campsites ($25 for RVs, $14 for tents) at **Painter Outpost** (307/527-5510, www.painteroutpost.com). Its restaurant, named—appropriately enough—**Clark's Fork and Spoon,** serves three homestyle meals a day. Showers are $5 if you aren't camping here.

SOUTH FORK AREA

South Fork Road heads southwest from Cody and follows the South Fork of the Shoshone River for 42 miles to the edge of the Washakie Wilderness. It's a beautiful drive through definitive Western country with tree-covered mountains and the rich valley below. During winter, the South Fork area has one of the largest collections of frozen waterfalls in the Lower 48, with more than 200 world-class multipitch climbs. Ice climbers are here all winter, and the **Water Fall Ice Roundup** (www.southfork-ice.com) takes place each February.

Accommodations

Bison Willy's Bunkhouse (307/587-0629 or 877/587-0629, www.bisonwillys.com) is open mid-October–mid-April and is primarily used by ice climbers. The hostel has two coed bunk rooms at $24 each, plus kitchenettes and showers. You'll need to bring your own sleeping bag. The cabin is part of the American Alpine Club's national hut system (www.americanalpineclub.org). Also available are two more-upscale cabins: $75 d or $90 for four guests. Call ahead for reservations.

Rustler's Roost Guest House (307/587-8171 or 800/667-6352, www.rustlersroost .homestead.com/guesthouse.html) is a small furnished house with a deck overlooking the South Fork, plus a full kitchen, and a bath with jetted tub. It sleeps four for $110, with a two-night minimum stay.

◖ BEARTOOTH MOUNTAINS

Spectacular Beartooth Highway (U.S. 212) connects Cooke City and Yellowstone National Park with the historic mining town of Red Lodge, Montana (www.redlodge.com). Along the way, it passes through the Beartooth Mountains on a road built by the CCC in the 1930s. Some have called this the most scenic route in America. If you like alpine country, towering rocky spires, and a landscaped dotted with small lakes and scraggly trees, you're going to love this drive. A small corner (23,750 acres out of a total of 945,334 acres) of the **Absaroka-Beartooth Wilderness** lies in Wyoming just north of the highway—the rest is right across the Montana border.

Over the Top

A national scenic byway, Beartooth Highway sails across a high plateau and then over the

© DON PITCHER

Beartooth Pass area in Shoshone National Forest

twin summits of **Beartooth Pass**—the east summit is 10,936 feet, and a short distance farther is the west summit at 10,947 feet. A scenic overlook at west summit provides views of the Absarokas to the south and west, the Beartooths to the north, and Bighorn Basin to the east. Majestic rock faces rise in all directions, the most obvious being Beartooth Mountain (its sharp point resembles the tooth of a bear), Pilot Peak, and Index Peak. This is the highest highway pass in Wyoming and one of the highest in North America. A major rebuilding of the highway will bring construction delays for the next several years; call 888/285-4636 for current conditions, or go to www.mdt.mt.gov.

As the road enters Montana, it passes Beartooth Mountain and begins a rapid elevator ride down folded ribbon curves into the resort town of Red Lodge. On top, keep your eyes open for moose, mule deer, mountain goats, bighorn sheep, marmots, and pikas. Be ready for strange weather at this elevation, including snow at any time of year. The highway is closed with the first heavy snow-

fall (generally in September) and doesn't open until June. The flowers don't really get going until mid-July.

Twin Lakes Race Camp sits near the Wyoming–Montana border and provides Olympic ski training for teens in June and July. South of the summit is the appropriately named Top of the World Store, and another mile or so farther south is the turnoff to an old fire lookout tower at **Clay Butte,** where you'll discover horizon-to-horizon views of the surrounding countryside. A narrow gravel road climbs three miles to the tower, perched at an elevation of 9,811 feet. The small visitor center here is staffed July–mid-September.

Hiking

The open country at this elevation is dotted with whitebark pines and Engelmann spruce, and it delivers marvelous cross-country hiking opportunities. Anglers should bring a fishing pole to take a few casts for the brook, cutthroat, and rainbow trout in the alpine lakes. Two major trail systems are found in the High Lakes area.

The **Beartooth High Lakes Trail**—actually a series of trails—connects Island Lake, Beartooth Lake, Beauty Lake, and many smaller alpine ponds and puddles. A good place to start is from the boat ramp at Island Lake; see topographic maps for specific routes. This is a very popular late-summer area for day hiking or for access to the Absaroka-Beartooth Wilderness. Be sure to bring a compass, topo map, and warm clothes before heading out on a day hike; the weather can close in very quickly at this elevation, and afternoon thunderstorms are frequent. Always be aware of lightning activity when hiking in this exposed country.

Beartooth Loop National Recreation Trail is just two miles east of Beartooth Pass. This 15-mile loop traverses alpine tundra and passes several lakes and a century-old log stockade of unknown origins.

Practicalities

Top of the World Store (307/899-2482, www.topoftheworldresort.com) sits along the highway between the two Forest Service campgrounds. It's a popular stopping point for cyclists and other travelers crossing the pass. The general store has a limited selection of food, gifts, camping supplies, and gifts, plus gas pumps. Three motel rooms ($35 d) and a handful of RV spaces ($14 with hookups) are also available. The store and motel are open late May–mid-October.

There are four developed campgrounds ($10, open July–Labor Day) along this stretch of U.S. 212, and more once you drop into Montana. **Beartooth Lake** and **Island Lake** campgrounds border alpine lakes. In addition, dispersed camping is allowed for free once you get off the main roads. Grizzlies inhabit this country, so be sure to store your food safely.

Wapiti Valley

Wapiti Valley provides one of the most popular and scenic routes into or out of Yellowstone National Park, connecting Cody with the park's East Entrance. President Theodore Roosevelt came here often and called it "the most scenic 50 miles in the U.S." The valley is bisected by the North Fork of the Shoshone River, which U.S. 14/16/20 parallels for the entire 50 miles from Yellowstone to Cody. Heading east out of Yellowstone, the highway drops through high forests and past an array of volcanic pinnacles and cliffs as the country becomes drier and more open. Cottonwoods line the gradually widening river, and Douglas firs intermix with sage, grass, and rock at lower elevations. Trailheads provide access to two backcountry areas that border the highway: North Absaroka Wilderness and Washakie Wilderness. The road is in excellent condition the entire distance from Cody to Yellowstone.

Wapiti Valley—the tourism promoters have recently started promoting it as **"East Yellowstone Valley"**—is dotted with lodges, dude ranches, and resorts, many of which offer family-style meals, barbecue cookouts, horseback rides, pack trips, fishing, hiking, river rafting, and other outdoor recreation. If you aren't staying on an all-inclusive plan, most of these perks will cost extra, and some—such as meals or horseback rides—are often available to both guests and the general public. The lodges generally do not have TVs or phones in the rooms, but most will provide transportation from Cody on request. Those Wapiti lodges and guest ranches that are open in winter are favorite bases for snowmobiling and cross-country skiing. Get additional Wapiti Valley information from the **East Yellowstone Valley Chamber of Commerce** (307/587-9595, www.yellowstone-lodging.com).

On the western end of the valley are Shoshone National Forest campgrounds and hiking trails. The fishing is great in the river and at Buffalo Bill Reservoir on the eastern end of Wapiti Valley.

SIGHTS

Below Sleeping Giant Ski Area the road passes a whole series of delightfully weird volcanic rock formations. Signs point out several of the most obvious. Stop at the **Firefighters' Memorial,** which honors 15 firefighters who were killed nearby in the Blackwater Fire of 1937. The picnic area here has a special pond for anglers with disabilities.

Eight miles farther east is the historic **Wapiti Ranger Station.** Built in 1903, it was the nation's first Forest Service ranger station. Just a few hundred feet away and right along the highway is **Wapiti Wayside Visitor Center** (307/587-3925, open late May–early Sept.). Pull in for details on local camping and recreation opportunities, and watch the informative video on safety in bear country. Check the board for recent bear sightings. A few miles to the west (not marked and on an old section of the highway) is Mummy Cave, where a 10,000-year-old mummified body was discovered in 1957.

Next up is a parking area at **Holy City,** an impressive group of dark red volcanic rocks with the North Fork of the Shoshone River cutting away at their base. Try to pick out Anvil Rock, Goose Rock, and Slipper Rock here. The highway leaves Shoshone National Forest and then passes the scattered settlement called **Wapiti**—an Indian word meaning "elk"—20 miles east of Cody. As you might guess, a large elk herd winters in this valley. An unusual volcanic rock ridge near here is locally called Chinese Wall. The eastern half of the road between Cody and Yellowstone passes through this broad and fertile valley; it's quite a change from the rock-lined route to the west. On the east end, the road borders Buffalo Bill Reservoir before plunging through three tunnels on the descent into Cody.

RECREATION

Just four miles from Yellowstone's East Gate, **Sleeping Giant Ski Area** (307/587-4044 information or 307/527-7669 ski report) is a small skiing and snowboarding hill with a chairlift and T-bar providing a 500-foot vertical rise. Lifts operate mid-December–early April, and tickets cost $20 adults, $10 kids under 12. Snowboards, alpine skis, and Nordic skis are available for rent.

Also based here is **North Fork Nordic Trails** (307/527-4044, www.nordicskiclub.com), with more than 50 kilometers of groomed cross-country ski trails for both classical and skate skiing. No charge, and the grooming is generally completed in time for the weekend rush of skiers. Trails cover a widely varied terrain along the river and right to the edge of Yellowstone National Park.

ACCOMMODATIONS

Less than three miles from Yellowstone's East Entrance (48 miles west of Cody), **◖ Pahaska Tepee** (307/527-7701 or 800/628-7791, www .pahaska.com) was built in 1904 to house Buffalo Bill's guests and others on their way to the park. Pahaska (pa-HAZ-ka) was Buffalo Bill's nickname, a Crow Indian word meaning "Long Hair."

The original Pahaska Tepee is a two-story log building that contains a few of Buffalo Bill's original items, including an old buffalo skull over the stone fireplace and several flags that were given to him. Although it is no longer used and in need of major repairs, the main lodge is open for fascinating free tours on weekdays during the summer. The bar inside Pahaska Tepee is small but contains a stunning Thomas Molesworth chandelier crafted in 1938; it's said to be worth $2 million. Look around for other furnishings from Molesworth and a beautiful stained-glass window.

On one of Buffalo Bill's many hunting treks with European royalty, he led the Prince of Monaco into the North Fork country. **Camp Monaco,** 15 miles up the Pahaska-Sunlight Trail from Pahaska Tepee, was named in his honor. Unfortunately, the old spruce tree inscribed with the words "Camp Monaco" was killed when the Clover-Mist Fire burned through here in 1988.

Pahaska Tepee Resort has a mix of old and new cabins, along with tiny A-frame motel rooms. Summer rates start at $93 d in a little housekeeping cabin up to $495 for a two-bedroom condo (two-night minimum for this one). Also here are a restaurant, gift shop, gas pumps, and limited supplies. Pahaska is open

© DON PITCHER

Buffalo Bill's Pahaska Tepee was built in 1904 and is open for tours in the summer.

year-round. In winter the road is not plowed beyond Pahaska, and the lodge becomes a popular place to rent cross-country skis for trips into Yellowstone or on nearby trails.

Upper North Fork Ranches

More than 20 lodges, motels, and guest ranches line the road between Yellowstone and Cody. Lodging places west of the midpoint between Cody and Yellowstone are in the more secluded and wooded canyon country of the upper North Fork of the Shoshone River. These places are listed as follows, arranged by their distance from downtown Cody on U.S. 14/16/20, starting with those nearest the East Entrance to Yellowstone. Places east of the midpoint between Cody and Yellowstone are situated in the broad and beautiful Wapiti Valley and are typically visible from the highway. Pahaska Tepee is the closest lodge to Yellowstone (see *Sights*).

Shoshone Lodge (46 miles west of Cody, four miles east of Yellowstone, 307/587-4044, www.shoshonelodge.com) is a classic mountain lodge with rustic log cabins and home-cooked meals served in the main lodge. The cabins have been updated with Western furnishings, and they range in size from 1–3 rooms; some contain kitchens. Nightly lodging rates start at $100 d or $119 for four guests, although the nicest cabins are considerably more expensive (up to $274 for a three-bedroom cabin that sleeps six). Horseback rides are available, and Shoshone Lodge is open May–early November. The owners also run Sleeping Giant Ski Area, directly across the road.

Established in 1898, **Crossed Sabres Ranch** (307/587-3750, www.crossedsabres.com), 42 miles west of Cody (eight miles east of Yellowstone), has a beautiful main lodge (rebuilt after a fire in 2004), plus space for 40 guests in modernized two-bedroom cabins with log furniture and Western decor. After a day of horseback riding, hiking, river rafting, square dancing, or exploring Yellowstone, guests can relax with an evening cookout or soak in the hot tub. All-inclusive weekly packages are $3,000 for two adults; open late May–early September.

Stay in deluxe log cabins at **Goff Creek Lodge** (307/587-3753 or 800/859-3985, www.goffcreek.com) 40 miles west of Cody or 10 miles east of Yellowstone. Cabins are offered on either a nightly basis ($119 d) with activities and meals extra, or by the week ($2,300 for two people) on an all-inclusive basis. Goff Creek is open mid-May–mid-September. A variety of outdoor adventures fill the bill here, including horseback rides, fly-fishing, trips to Yellowstone, and chuck wagon cookouts. All of these options, including meals at the restaurant, are also open to the general public.

Forty miles west of Cody or 10 miles east of Yellowstone, **Elephant Head Lodge** (307/587-3980, www.elephantheadlodge.com) is a no-frills dude ranch with a gracious main lodge built in 1910. Guests stay in 15 modernized cabins, all with private baths and most with decks. Because of its proximity to the park, Elephant Head makes a good base for exploring Yellowstone. Peak-season lodging-only rates start at $115 d per day. The largest cabin—it's actually more like a luxury apartment—sleeps eight people comfortably and has a full kitchen; $250. All-inclusive packages with lodging, meals, and horseback rides are $360 for two people per day. Elephant Head's restaurant is open for breakfast and dinner and is locally famous for steaks, pork chops, and other carnivorous fare. It's a frequent destination for Cody folks looking for an evening out. Horseback rides are also available for both guests and the general public. The ranch is open mid-May–September.

Find old-time hospitality and adventure at **Absaroka Mountain Lodge** (307/587-3963, www.absarokamtlodge.com) 38 miles west of Cody (12 miles east of Yellowstone). Guests stay in comfortable log cabins with private baths and dine in the historic main lodge, built in 1910. Nightly rates start at $101 for one bed, up to $175 for a two-bedroom cabin that sleeps eight. The package plan includes lodging, three meals a day, and four hours per day of horseback rides for $147 per person per day. Open mid-May–September. Folks who aren't staying here can join the trail rides of all types or eat in the full-service restaurant, or join the Wednesday and Saturday night all-you-can-eat outdoor barbecue for $15.

A classic Western dude ranch, **UXU Ranch** (307/587-2143 or 800/373-9027, www.uxu-ranch.com) is 33 miles west of Cody or 17 miles east of Yellowstone. It offers horseback riding, hiking, fly-fishing, mountain-biking, and day trips to Yellowstone and Cody. Guests stay in comfortable cabins containing private baths and porches; some also have fireplaces or gas stoves. After a day of trail riding, you can relax in the big hot tub or visit with new friends in the main lodge. Special children's activities and nature talks are available, and the gourmet meals are memorable. All-inclusive six-night stays cost $3,050 for two people, or four people can stay in the luxurious Hollister cabin (featured in *Architectural Digest*) for $6,400. The ranch is open June–September.

Halfway between Cody and Yellowstone—25 miles in either direction—**Bill Cody Ranch** (307/587-6271 or 800/615-2934, www.bill-codyranch.com) has graceful log cabins, a comfortable lodge, horseback rides, creekside cookouts, and trout fishing. All-inclusive stays are $290 for two people per night; lodging-only rates are $125 d. Looking for more room and privacy? The ranch also rents out two comfortable fully furnished homes with space for up to 13 guests at $425 per day, with a three-night minimum stay. Meals, chuck wagon cookouts, and horseback rides are also offered to those not staying at Bill Cody Ranch. The guest ranch is open mid-May–September.

Twenty-five miles west of Cody or 25 miles east of Yellowstone, **Rimrock Dude Ranch** (307/587-3970, www.rimrockranch.com) is a classic place with creekside log cabins, horseback riding, a large swimming pool and hot tub, river rafting, hearty family-style meals, and grand mountain country. In the winter, this is a popular destination for snowmobilers; the ranch rents snowmobiles and leads tours into Yellowstone. Rimrock is open May–mid-September and December–March.

Lower Wapiti Valley Accommodations

The places listed here are east of the midpoint between Yellowstone and Cody, in the broad and open part of Wapiti Valley; those listed under *Upper North Fork Ranches* are west of the midpoint, in the more secluded and wooded canyon country.

Built in 1922, **Trail Shop Inn and Cafe** (307/587-3741) 23 miles west of Cody or 27 miles east of Yellowstone, sits off the road and along the North Fork Shoshone River. Rustic cabins with private baths are $35–75 d. Open May–September.

Green Creek Inn and RV Park (307/587-5004 or 877/587-5004, www.greencreekinn.com), 22 miles west of Cody or 28 miles east of Yellowstone, has roadside motel rooms with rustic log furniture for $60–70 d. Also available is a six-person log cabin with bunk beds for $88. The setting is pretty, and children will appreciate the fun playground and horseshoe pit. RV sites (no tents) are $21, but they lack showers or a restroom. Open May–mid-November.

Stay in modern log cabins at **DNR Ranch at Rand Creek** (307/527-7176 or 888/412-7335, www.dnrranch.com) 19 miles west of Cody (31 miles east of Yellowstone). Nightly rates in small cabins are $110 for up to four guests; the largest can sleep eight for $260. All-inclusive stays are also available; a full week is $1,160–2,210 for two people, including horseback rides, lodging, and breakfast (dinners are additional). Built in 1905, DNR Ranch's main lodge is the oldest building in the area. The ranch is open mid-May–mid-September. Trail rides are also offered to folks who are not staying here. **Wapiti Lodge and Steak House** (18 miles west of Cody or 32 miles east of Yellowstone, 307/587-6659) is "downtown" Wapiti, with a bar, full-service restaurant, and post office in the same building.

At **Yellowstone Valley Inn** (307/587-3961 or 877/587-3961, www.yellowstonevalleyinn.com), 18 miles west of Cody or 32 miles east of Yellowstone, small cabins are $99–149 d, tent spaces are $20, and RV sites with full hookups run $30–37. The attractive inn sits right on the North Fork Shoshone River and has an outdoor pool, indoor hot tub, restaurant, launderette, and lounge (with live music on summer weekends). Open year-round.

Streamside Inn (307/587-8242 or 800/285-1282, www.streamsideinn.com) is 15 miles west of Cody (35 miles east of Yellowstone) near the east end of Buffalo Bill Reservoir. Modern motel rooms go for $74 s or $78 d, including a continental breakfast. Kitchenettes are $10 extra. A few RV sites are also available for $35, and guests can use the large outdoor pool; no air-condiitioning. Horseback rides start at $25 for a one-hour ride. The inn is open May–November.

Red Pole Ranch (307/587-5929 or 800/587-5929, www.redpoleranch.com), 11 miles west of Cody or 39 miles east of Yellowstone, has eight updated log cabins starting for $75 d, up to $110 for units that sleep five and include a full kitchen.

Camping

Nine Shoshone National Forest campgrounds provide rustic accommodations along the North Fork of the Shoshone River. Most of these are open mid-May–September (some remain open through October) and cost $5–10 per site; no reservations are taken. All sites have picnic tables, fire rings, potable water, and outhouses. In areas where bears are a problem, the campgrounds also contain bear-proof food-storage boxes. All of these Forest Service campgrounds are on the west half of the 50-mile stretch of highway between Cody and Yellowstone. Of these, **Big Game Campground** is closest to Cody at 25 miles to the west, and **Three Mile Campground** is closest to the park, just three miles from Yellowstone's East Gate. Get details on public campgrounds from the Forest Service's Wapiti Wayside Visitor Center. Dispersed camping outside designated campsites is not allowed anywhere between Cody and Yellowstone along U.S. 14/16/20.

Two campgrounds are within Buffalo Bill State Park. Two Wapiti Valley lodges also have RV campgrounds: Green River Inn and Yellowstone Valley Inn.

BUFFALO BILL STATE PARK

Six miles west of Cody on U.S. 14/16/20, **Buffalo Bill Reservoir** is a popular place for local boaters and fishermen. Buffalo Bill State Park (307/587-9227, http://wyoparks.state.wy.us) encompasses the reservoir and includes two campgrounds ($12 for nonresidents or $6 for Wyoming residents, open May–Sept.) on the north shore. Make campsite reservations ($8.50 fee) at 877/996-7275, www.wyo-park.com. Day use of the park is $4 for nonresident vehicles or $2 for those with Wyoming plates.

Atop the dam, the impressive **Buffalo Bill Dam Visitor Center** (307/527-6076, www.bbdvc.org) has historical displays and jaw-dropping views into the canyon, which plummets 350 feet below you. Borrow the headphones for a 30-minute audio tour ($4) of the area. The center is open 8 A.M.–8 P.M. Monday–Friday and 8 A.M.–6 P.M. Saturday–Sunday June–August, 8 A.M.–6 P.M. daily in May and September, and closed the rest of the year. Even if it's closed, stop for the view over the dam.

Fishing is good for rainbow, cutthroat, brown, and Mackinaw trout in Buffalo Bill Reservoir. The lake also offers some of the finest **sailboarding** conditions anywhere, with nearly constant 30 mph winds; *Outside* magazine once rated it among the country's 10 best spots. The water's cold: You'll need a wetsuit until mid-June.

History

In 1899, Buffalo Bill Cody acquired the rights to build canals and irrigate 60,000 acres of land near the new town of Cody. With passage of the Reclamation Act of 1902, the project was taken over by the Reclamation Service and an enormous concrete-arch dam was added to provide water. The 328-foot-high dam was begun in 1904 and required five years to finish. It cost nearly $1 million and when finally completed was the tallest dam in the world. Seven men died along the way, including a chief engineer, and the first two contractors were forced into bankruptcy as a result of bad weather, floods, engineering difficulties, and labor strife. A lack of sand and crushed gravel forced them to manufacture it from granite, and 200-pound boulders were hand-placed into the concrete to save having to crush more gravel.

Originally named Shoshone Dam, the impoundment was renamed in honor of Buffalo Bill in 1946. A hydroelectric plant and a 25-foot addition to the top were completed in 1993, bringing the total dam height to 353 feet and increasing water storage by 50 percent. The dam irrigates more than 93,000 downstream acres through the Shoshone Reclamation Project, making it one of the only Wyoming irrigation schemes that actually benefits the state's farmers to a large extent.

Cody

The city of Cody (pop. 8,800, elev. 5,095 ft) marks the transition point between the forested mountains of northwest Wyoming and the sage-covered plains of Bighorn Basin. It's a favorite stopping place for Yellowstone tourists. The park is just 54 miles due west of town, and other magnificent country spreads in all directions—the Beartooth Mountains and Sunlight Basin to the north, the Absaroka Range and Wapiti Valley to the west and south. Established as an agricultural and tourism center, Cody retains both roles today, although tourism gains in importance with each passing year.

Cody has several attractions, including the justly famous Buffalo Bill Historical Center, along with Trail Town and other local sights. The Shoshone River flows right through town, providing the opportunity for scenic float trips. Lots of events crowd the summer calendar, from nightly rodeos and shoot-outs to parades and powwows; biggest of all is the annual Cody Stampede in July. The town also takes pride in a long list of artists that includes Charles Cary Rumsey and Harry Jackson. Famed abstract expressionist Jackson Pollock was born here but achieved his reputation in New York and never returned to his birthplace.

HISTORY

Just west of Cody—past the Wal-Mart, RV parks, fireworks stands, and gas stations—are the Absaroka Mountains, named for the Native Americans who first lived here. They called themselves the Absaroka, or "Children of the Large Beaked Bird." Whites interpreted this as crow, and the natives have been called Crow Indians ever since. Explorer John Colter passed through this region in 1808 while recruiting Indians to supply beaver furs. When Colter returned to the semblance of civilization called Fort Manual Lisa, everyone laughed at

his tales of a spectacular geothermal area along the "Stinkingwater River." Soon everyone was calling it "Colter's Hell." But the geysers were real, and they still steam along the Shoshone (formerly the Stinkingwater) just west of present-day Cody. Other mountain men came later, followed by miners who found copper and sulfur in Sunlight Basin. The first real settler in the area was a Prussian, Otto Franc, who developed a large cattle spread at the famous Pitchfork Ranch. (Franc is said to have helped finance the Wyoming Stock Growers during the Johnson County War. He was later murdered, and some blamed men affiliated with the homesteaders.)

Because of desertlike conditions, Bighorn

CODY AREA CLIMATE

	Average Maximum Temp.	58.8°F
	Average Minimum Temp.	32.6°F
	Annual Rainfall	10.03″
	Annual Snowfall	39″

SNOWFALL — MAXIMUM TEMP.
RAINFALL — MINIMUM TEMP.

© AVALON TRAVEL PUBLISHING, INC.

Basin was one of the last parts of Wyoming to be settled, and most of the towns did not spring up until the 1890s, when passage of the Carey Act brought a flood of irrigation speculators, investors, and farmers. In 1895, William F. "Buffalo Bill" Cody and two partners began plans for the Shoshone Land and Irrigation Company, with headquarters along the Shoshone River just west of the present city of Cody. Cody had spent much time in the Bighorn Basin, guiding parties of wealthy sportsmen, and was convinced that a combination of tourism and irrigated farming could transform this desert land. The name Cody was a natural choice for this new settlement, officially founded in 1896. At the urging of Buffalo Bill,

the Chicago, Burlington, and Quincy Railroad arrived in 1901, bringing in thousands of tourists who continued west up Shoshone Canyon to Yellowstone by stagecoach. Between 1904 and 1909, construction of massive Buffalo Bill Dam employed hundreds of workers, and the reservoir later provided water to irrigate farmland in Bighorn Basin. Oil was first discovered near Cody in 1904, and Park County remains an important oil producer. Other local businesses include a wallboard manufacturing plant, a lumber mill, and a pharmaceutical manufacturer. One of the biggest employers (after the hospital, the school district, and Wal-Mart) makes—I kid you not—ear tags for livestock. Tourism remains a cornerstone of Cody's

YOUNG BUFFALO BILL CODY

For many people today, the name "Buffalo Bill" brings to mind a man who helped slaughter the vast herds of wild bison that once filled the West. But William F. Cody cannot be so easily pigeon-holed, for here was one of the most remarkable men of his or any other era – a man who almost single-handedly established the aura of the "Wild West." More than 800 books – many of them the dime-store novels that thrilled genera-tions of youngsters – have been written about Cody. In many of these, the truth was stretched far beyond any semblance of reality, but the real life of William Cody contains so many adventures and plot twists that it seems hard to believe one person could have done so much.

Born to an Iowa farm family in 1846, William Cody started life as had many others of his era. His parents moved to Kansas when he was six, but his abolitionist father, Isaac Cody, soon be-came embroiled in arguments with the many slaveholders. While defending his views at a public meeting, Isaac Cody was stabbed in the back and fled for his life. When a mob learned of his father's whereabouts, the eight-year-old Will Cody rode on his first venture through enemy lines, galloping 35 miles to warn of the impending attack. Three years later, when Isaac Cody died of complications from the stabbing, 11-year-old Will Cody became the family's bread-winner. There were four other children to feed. Will quickly joined the company of Alexander Majors, running dispatches between army supply wagons and giving his $40 monthly wages to his mother. In Cody's autobiography he claimed to have killed his first Indian on this trip, an action that gave him the then-enviable title "youngest Indian slayer of the plains."

On his first long wagon trek west, the army

economy, fueled both by its status as an entry point into the park, and also because of the world-famous Buffalo Bill Historical Center. Interestingly, the town is also attracting quite a few retirees who appreciate the mild weather and abundant recreational opportunities.

◖ BUFFALO BILL HISTORICAL CENTER

Each year, more than 220,000 people visit Cody's main attraction, the Buffalo Bill His-torical Center (BBHC). The center actually houses five separate museums covering Buffalo Bill, the Plains Indians, Western art, firearms, and natural history, plus a research library, the boyhood home of Buffalo Bill, and two sculp-ture gardens. This is the largest and most im-pressive museum in Wyoming and the finest Western museum in the world. Nowhere else in America is such a major museum situated in a town with so few people. The late author James Michener once labeled the BBHC "the Smith-sonian of the West," and his term is even truer today with the addition of a natural-history wing a few years back. The museum's collec-tion focuses—not surprisingly—on the West-ern frontier and includes thousands of artifacts and works of art, culture, and natural history spread throughout more than 300,000 square feet of space.

The original Buffalo Bill Museum opened in 1927 in what is now the chamber of commerce log cabin. Opening in 1959, the Whitney Gal-lery of Western Art formed a nucleus for the current museum location; later additions in-cluded the Buffalo Bill Museum, the Plains In-dian Museum, the Cody Firearms Museum, and the Draper Museum of Natural History.

Buffalo Bill Historical Center (307/587-4771 or 800/227-8483, www.bbhc.org) is open year-round. In the busy summer season, June–mid-September, it's open 7 A.M.–8 P.M. daily. At other times, hours are reduced: 8 A.M.–5 P.M. daily mid-September–October; 10 A.M.–5 P.M. daily in April; and 8 A.M.–8 P.M. daily in May. The museum is open 10 A.M.–3 P.M. Tuesday–Sunday November–March. Closed Thanksgiv-ing, Christmas, and New Year's Day.

Admission costs $15 adults, $13 seniors, $10 students age 13–17, and $6 ages 5–12. The $40 family rate is a great value, and children under six get in free. The admission is good for two supply wagons were attacked by Mormon zealots who took all the weapons and horses, forcing Cody to walk much of the 1,000 miles back to his Kansas home. It was apparently on this walk that Cody met Wild Bill Hickok. At Wyoming's Fort Laramie, young Will sat in awe as famed scouts Jim Bridger and Kit Carson reminisced about their adventures. The experience was a turning point in Cody's life; he resolved to one day become a scout. Cody's next job offered excellent training: He became a rider for the Pony Express. At just 15 years of age he already was one of the finest riders in the West and a crack shot with a rifle. On one of his Pony Express rides, Cody covered a total of 320 miles in just 21 hours and 40 minutes – the longest Pony Express ride ever. The Civil War had begun, and at age 18 Cody joined the Seventh Kansas Regiment, serving as a scout and spy for the Union Army.

After the Civil War, Will Cody tried his hand at the hotel business and then briefly joined General George Custer as a scout before returning to Kansas to do a little land speculating along the route of the newly built railroad. Cody and a partner bought land and laid out a town that they named Rome. For a short while it boomed. One day a man appeared in Rome, offering to take over the town while leaving Cody with only a small part of the place he had founded. Thinking it was only intimidation from a shady operator, Cody laughed at the man, not knowing that he was president of the railroad's town-site company. The railroad quickly chose another town site, and three days later all the inhabitants of Rome moved east to the new site, taking their buildings with them. Cody was left with a worthless patch of land.

days, and it may well take you that long to explore this massive collection! Tours are generally offered only for school groups and VIPs, but the historical center often has summertime demonstrations, and the helpful docents can provide additional information.

On the Museum Grounds

Flanking the museum on the right side is *The Scout,* a dramatic, larger-than-life statue of larger-than-life Buffalo Bill. This tall bronze piece was created by New York sculptor Gertrude Vanderbilt Whitney and was unveiled in 1924. Her family later donated 40 acres of surrounding land to the Buffalo Bill Museum. Directly in front of the historical center are three colorfully painted tepees, a treat for kids.

Buffalo Bill Museum

The Buffalo Bill Museum is a real joy. In it, the life of Buffalo Bill Cody is briefly sketched with all sorts of memorabilia from his Wild West Show, including the famous Deadwood stage, silver-laden saddles, enormous posters, furniture, guns, wagons, and buffalo hide coats. Be sure to look for "Lucre-

tia Borgia," the Springfield rifle that helped William Cody gain his nickname. Also here are some of the gifts given to Buffalo Bill by European heads of state—including a fur carriage robe from Czar Alexander II—and by Wild Bill Hickok and Sitting Bull. Original film footage from the Wild West Show runs continuously, offering a fascinating and sometimes unintentionally comical glimpse into the past. Amazingly choreographed marching soldiers, fake Indian battles, sign-language conversations, and bucking broncos make it easy to see how the Wild West Show helped inspire Western movies.

Whitney Gallery of Western Art

The Whitney Gallery contains a stunning collection of masterworks by such Western artists and sculptors as Charles Russell, Frederic Remington, Carl Bodmer, George Catlin, Thomas Moran, Albert Bierstadt, Alfred Jacob Miller, Edgar Paxson, N. C. Wyeth, and others. The studios of Frederic Remington and W. H. D. Koerner have been re-created, and Gertrude Vanderbilt Whitney's *The Scout* is visible from a large window on the north end. The collections of both "cowboy artist" Charles Russell and Frederic Remington—best known for his paintings of battles during the Indian wars—are the most complete here; the museum has more than 100 of each man's paintings. Next to the Whitney Gallery is the **Joseph Henry Sharp Garden,** where you'll find his "Absarokee Hut" filled with the painter's paraphernalia.

The **Kriendler Gallery of Contemporary Western Art** is upstairs from the entrance to the Whitney Gallery and contains a diverse collection of pieces, including several with a delightfully whimsical twist. Well worth the detour.

Plains Indian Museum

The largest exhibition space in the historical center encloses the Plains Indian Museum, with items from the Sioux, Cheyenne, Blackfeet, Crow, Arapaho, Shoshone, and Gros Ventre tribes. At first it may seem incongruous that a museum featuring the man once called the "youngest Indian slayer of the plains" should include so much about the culture of Indians, but Cody's later maturity forced him to the realization that Indians had been severely mistreated and that their culture was of great value. His Wild West Shows re-created some semblance of that lost society, if only for show. Some of the more important items here were given to Buffalo Bill by various Indian performers through the years, and the collection of artifacts is now one of the finest in America.

On exhibit are an extraordinary painted buffalo robe from 1890 that depicts the Battle of Little Big Horn, elaborately decorated baby carriers, ghost-dance dresses, beaded arrow quivers, dance shields, leather garments, war bonnets, ceremonial pipes, and even a Pawnee grizzly claw necklace. One of the more unusual items is Lone Dog's Winter Count, with figures representing a 71-year sequence of events affecting the Sioux; it was created in 1877. The Hitatsa earth lodge is another highlight. One easy-to-miss area is the special exhibitions gallery downstairs and to the left of the Crow tepee village display. The exhibits change but are always well

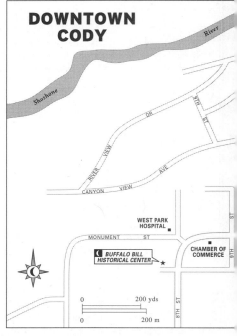

worth viewing. On the other side of the tepees is a room containing computers and additional displays.

Walking through this remarkable collection always leaves me with mixed emotions. I'm impressed at the beauty of the items and their historical and cultural significance, but I'm saddened by the way all museums—of necessity—remove things from their environments and create a visually enticing setting, but one that is devoid of the living, breathing people who created these objects. If only we could step back into the past to see how life really was, dirt and all.

Draper Museum of Natural History

This newest addition to the BBHC opened in 2002 to rave reviews. The $17-million museum covers 55,000 square feet, with state-of-the-art exhibits on the Greater Yellowstone Ecosystem and the integral role of humans. Guests

© AVALON TRAVEL PUBLISHING, INC.

begin at a pair of cabins, one of which serves as a naturalist's field station. The other serves as a classroom (of sorts), with a seismograph and computer stations to learn about glaciers, volcanoes, and other natural forces. The main section of the Draper descends along a spiraling path through a giant rotunda, with exhibits describing alpine areas, forests, meadows, and lowland plains ecosystems in the Yellowstone landscape. It's like taking a virtual safari through the area. Multidisciplinary exhibits invite interaction, with lots of kid-friendly audio and video stations, a walk-in beaver lodge, a wolf den, a prairie dog colony, and much more. The winding path ends at a colorful tile map of the Yellowstone ecosystem and an exhibition of children's art.

Cody Firearms Museum

The Cody Firearms Museum houses one of the most comprehensive collections of American firearms in the world, including everything from 16th-century matchlocks to self-loading semiautomatic pistols. This is one museum where the men outnumber the women. Start your visit by viewing *Lock, Stock, and Barrel,* a 10-minute video that describes the history of guns and how they work; it's interesting even for those of us who consider the proliferation of guns a national menace. In fact, the entire firearms collection is remarkably informative and well worth taking time to view.

The museum now contains more than 5,000 weapons, but these aren't just rows of guns in glass cases. Some of the more unusual items include a 10-shot repeating flintlock rifle made for the New York Militia around 1825 and a 17th-century windlass crossbow. There are all sorts of displays to explore, including a colonial gun shop, a Western stage station, an early-1900s firearms factory, and a truly extraordinary collection of embellished arms. One of the most lavish is an intricately carved flintlock sporting carbine presented by

BUFFALO BILL CODY: HUNTER AND SCOUT

In 1867, Buffalo Bill Cody found work hunting buffalo to supply fresh meat for the railroad construction crews, a job that soon made him famous as "Buffalo Bill" and paid a hefty $500 per month. With 75 million bison spread from northern Canada to Mexico, and herds so vast that they took many days to pass one point, it seemed impossible that they could ever be killed off. Cody was one of the best hunters in the West; in just eight months, he slaughtered 4,280 buffalo, often saving transportation by driving the herd toward the camp and dropping the animals within sight of the workers. Cody's name lives on in the jingle: "Buffalo Bill, Buffalo Bill; never missed and never will; always aims and shoots to kill; and the company pays his buffalo bill..."

After this stint, Cody finally got the job he wanted – chief scout for the U.S. Army in the West, a job packed with excitement and danger. Conflicts with Indians had reached a fever pitch as more and more whites moved into the last Indian strongholds. Cody worked as scout for General Philip Sheridan, providing information on the Indians' movements, leading troops in pursuit of the warriors, and joining in the battles, including one in which he supposedly killed Chief Tall Bull. His men considered Buffalo Bill good luck because he managed to keep them out of ambushes.

During the Indian campaigns, the writer/preacher/scoundrel Ned Buntline began writing of Cody's exploits for various New York papers, giving Buffalo Bill his first taste of national acclaim. Soon Buntline had cranked out several romantic novels loosely based on Cody's adventures. America had a new national hero. European and Eastern gentry began asking Cody to guide them on buffalo hunts. On the trips, Cody referred to them as "dudes" and to his camps as "dude ranches" – perhaps the first time anyone had used the terms for such hunters. One of Wyoming's most unusual businesses had begun. Cody's incredible knowledge of the land and hunting impressed the men, but they were stunned to also discover in him a natural showman. In

1872, the Grand Duke Alexis of Russia came to the United States and was guided by Cody on a hunt that made national headlines and brought even more fame to the 26-year-old. On a trip to New York in 1872, Cody met Buntline again and watched a wildly distorted theater production called *Buffalo Bill*. Amazingly, Cody adjusted quickly to the new surroundings. Dressed in the finest silk clothes but with his long scout's hair under a Western hat, Cody suddenly entered the world of high society.

In a short while, Cody was on the stage himself, performing with Ned Buntline and fellow scout Texas Jack in a play called *Scouts of the Plains*. Although meant to be serious, the acting of all three proved so atrocious that the play had audiences rolling in the aisles with laughter. A New York reviewer called the play "so wonderfully bad it was almost good. The whole performance was so far aside of human experience, so wonderful in its daring feebleness, that no ordinary intellect is capable of comprehending it." Audiences packed the theaters for weeks on end. But Cody was suddenly called back west, for the Sioux were again on the warpath.

Shortly after Cody had returned to guide General Eugene Carr's forces, they learned of the massacre of Custer's men at the Battle of the Little Big Horn. In revenge, Carr's men set out to pursue Indians along the border between Nebraska and Wyoming. Under Cody's guidance, they surprised a group of warriors at War Bonnet Creek. Cody shot the chief, Yellow Hand, and immediately scalped him, raising the scalp above his head with the cry "first scalp for Custer!" (Cody later claimed that he scalped the chief because he was wearing an American flag as a loincloth and had a lock of yellow hair from a white woman's scalp pinned to his clothing.) The Sioux immediately fled. If Cody had been famous before, this event propelled him to even more acclaim. It became the grist for countless dime-store novels and was embellished in so many ways through the years that the true story will never be known.

Empress Elizabeth I of Russia to King Louis XV of France. The Boone and Crockett Club's collection of trophy animal heads is here, including an elephant-sized moose housed in a re-created hunting lodge. Take the elevator to the basement for even more gun displays. All told, this museum houses more implements of destruction and mayhem than you're likely to see at an NRA convention.

Additional Exhibits

Downstairs from the Buffalo Bill Museum is a spacious gallery used for special exhibitions (always worth a look), along with the **Harold McCracken Research Library,** open 8 A.M.–noon and 1–5 P.M. Monday–Friday May–October, or by appointment. The library houses 250,000 historical photos and 15,000 books, including more than 300 volumes about Buffalo Bill—mostly dime novels and comic books. Buffalo Bill's **boyhood home**—a tiny yellow building built in 1841 by Isaac Cody—is in the garden area. The house stood in LeClarie, Iowa, for almost a century. In 1933 it was sawed in half, loaded on two railcars, and hauled to Cody to be reassembled and refurbished. The **Photography Gallery** near the entrance to the Draper features changing exhibits.

Other facilities at the Buffalo Bill Historical Center include an excellent **gift shop and bookstore,** plus a café. Head to the sculpture garden for a lunchtime buffalo burger or Polish dog at the **Western cookout** beneath the aspen trees.

Activities and Events

During summer you'll find a wide range of demonstrations every day, including wool-spinning demonstrations, historical talks, cowboy singing, storytelling, and various lectures. Get a brochure at the front desk for today's activities. The **Larom Summer Institute in Western American Studies** is an in-depth two-week history course with two sessions offered each June. The BBHC also hosts many events (see *Entertainment and Events* for details).

OTHER SIGHTS
◖ Trail Town

Point your horses toward the mountains and head 'em two miles west of Cody to a unique collection of historic buildings at Trail Town (307/587-5302, www.museumoftheoldwest.org, open 8 A.M.–8 P.M. daily mid-May–Sept. only; $7 adults, $6 seniors, $3 for kids under 13). Trail Town is the creation of Bob Edgar, the man who discovered Mummy Cave—one of the most important archaeological finds in the West—in 1957. Edgar bought the old Arland and Corbett trading post, and then began dragging in other historic Wyoming cabins. Some were transported whole, others were disassembled and then put back together at Trail Town. The site now holds 26 buildings dating from 1879 to 1901, plus 100 wagons.

For those who love history, Trail Town is an incredible treasure trove without the fancy gift shops and commercial junk that tag along with most such endeavors. This is the real thing, low-key and genuine. Probably the most famous building here is an 1883 cabin from the Hole-in-the-Wall country that Butch Cassidy and the Sundance Kid used as a rendezvous spot. Also at Trail Town is the oldest saloon (another hangout of the gang) from this part of Wyoming, complete with bullet holes in the door, and a cabin where Jim White—one of the most famous buffalo hunters—was murdered in 1879. The log home of Crow Indian scout Curley stands along the main street, too. (Curley was the only one of General Custer's command who escaped alive from the Battle of the Little Big Horn.) Be sure to step inside **Museum of the Old West,** a more recent log cabin filled with artifacts that include a black hearse, rifles found at Indian battlefield sites, arrowheads, beaded necklaces, a cradleboard, and items from the fur traders. Look above the display cases for what may be the most significant discovery, a dugout canoe that was found buried along the Yellowstone River in Montana. It might have belonged to a trapper but is remarkably similar to the ones used by Lewis and Clark. They buried canoes while heading west, planning to dig them up on their return

© DON PITCHER

historic buildings at Trail Town in Cody

trip. The wood dates to that era; could this be one they left behind?

The bodies of buffalo hunter Jim White and several other historic figures have been reinterred in a small graveyard at Trail Town. One of the most interesting of these is Belle Drewry, a prostitute known as "The Woman in Blue." After bouncing around several 19th-century mining towns, she ended up in the lawless and now-abandoned town of Arland, northwest of Meeteetse. One night in 1897 she shot a cowboy to death during a dance. The following night his outlaw friends took retribution by murdering her. Belle was buried in the blue dress that she always wore. Also buried in the cemetery is **John "Liver Eating" Johnston,** the mountain man portrayed by Robert Redford in the movie *Jeremiah Johnston.* Those who have seen the film will be surprised to learn that Johnston died in 1900 at the Old Soldiers' Home in Los Angeles! Friends sent him there by train from Montana when his health deteriorated, but he spent only a month in California before his death at the age of 76. After the movie came out, schoolchildren in Los Angeles

helped promote moving Johnston's body closer to his mountain home. Nearly 2,000 people showed up for the reburial in 1974, including Robert Redford. A memorial to explorers John Colter and Jim Bridger also stands near the graveyard. The historic buildings, artifacts, and graves at Trail Town provide a fine counterpoint to the glitzier Buffalo Bill Historical Center. Directly in front of Old Trail Town is **Colter's Hell Trail,** a pleasant 0.5-mile loop through the prairie within Stampede Park.

Irma Hotel

Named for Buffalo Bill Cody's daughter, the Irma Hotel was built in 1902 to house tourists arriving by train and was one of three way stations to Yellowstone that Cody built. The luxurious saloon has a French-made cherrywood back bar given to Buffalo Bill by Queen Victoria. The queen spent $100,000 to have it built—no doubt helping to fuel rumors of a romance between her and Buffalo Bill. Many famous people have gathered at the bar through the years.

The **Cody Gunfighters** (307/587-4221,

www.irmahotel.com) perform in front of the Irma Monday–Saturday June–September. Cody was established long after the era of gunfights in the streets, so this isn't particularly authentic, but it does attract a crowd each evening. The gunfight officially starts at 6 P.M., but the first 15 minutes or so are typically wasted on ads for local businesses. You know you're in America when the advertising even delays a gunfight!

Harry Jackson Art Museum

Cody's most famous living artist, Harry Jackson (602 Blackburn St., 307/587-5508, www.harry-jackson.com, open 8 A.M.–5 P.M. Mon.–Fri., $8) has a large and interesting gallery. It doesn't look like much outside, but inside you'll discover an amazing diversity of works, covering the palette from abstract expressionist paintings, dark World War II pieces, collages, and cubist studies to his more recent paintings and sculptures (many of which contain distinctively painted surfaces). His other sculptures include the monumental *Sacajawea* at the Buffalo Bill Historical Center and *Horseman* in Beverly Hills. Jackson's pieces have been exhibited throughout the United States and in Italy, where his works are cast. Now something of a living legend, Jackson divides his time between Cody and Italy. All bronzes (but not his paintings) displayed here are for sale, but they're only for serious art patrons willing to spend thousands of dollars—a 10-foot painted Sacagawea goes for $400,000.

Art Galleries

The **Buffalo Bill Historical Center** houses a fine gift shop with art prints, Indian jewelry, and reproductions of bronze sculptures. Next to the chamber of commerce office, the **Cody Country Art League** (836 Sheridan Ave. 307/587-3597, www.codyart.vcn.com) has paintings, sculptures, photos, and crafts for sale. It also offers workshops and juried art shows.

Bison Legacy (1191 Sheridan Ave., 307/587-4199, www.bisonlegacy.com) is a fine downtown gallery with beautiful bison leatherwork and pieces by regional artists.

Simpson Gallagher Gallery (1161 Sheridan Ave., 307/587-4022, www.simpsongallaghergallery.com) is another of the best in Cody, with works that go well beyond the standard Western clichés. Just down the street is **Wyoming Artisans** (307/527-7000), a cooperative where everything is made in Wyoming, including paintings, pottery, lamps, jewelry, and carvings.

Two distinctive photographic galleries are across from each other downtown: **Open Range Images** (1201 Sheridan Ave., 307/587-8870, www.openrangeimages.com), and **Traces of Light Gallery** (1280 Sheridan Ave., 307/527-6912, www.tracesoflight.com).

Old West Miniature Village

Cody has an abundance of offbeat attractions, from talking sheep to sanctified ceilings. The most unusual—and actually worth a visit—is Old West Miniature Village and Museum, a.k.a. Tecumseh's Trading Post (142 W. Yellowstone Ave., 307/587-5362, www.tecumsehs.com, open 8 A.M.–8 P.M. daily mid-May–mid-Sept and 9 A.M.–6 P.M. daily the rest of the year, donation requested). Owner Jerry Fick spent decades creating an enormous diorama that offers a truncated version of Wyoming and Montana history. The term "kitsch" quickly enters your head when you step inside, but you've got to appreciate the effort that went into creating thousands of hand-carved figures and an array of miniature villages. Of considerably more interest is his collection of artifacts that includes a knife from the Battle of Little Bighorn, old-time cowboy garb, the bow and arrows that belonged to Geronimo, and many Plains Indian artifacts.

ENTERTAINMENT AND EVENTS

The downtown City Park band shell is the place to be for Friday evening **Concerts in the Park** during July and August. These free musical performances—in a variety of genres—start at 6 P.M.

Find flicks at **Cody Theatre** (1171 Sheridan Ave., 307/587-2712) or **Big Horn Cinemas** (2525 Big Horn Ave., 307/587-8001 or 888/878-3549).

Nightlife

On the West Strip, **Cassie's** (214 Yellowstone Ave., 307/527-5500, www.cassies.com) has Wednesday night country-swing dance lessons on the big dance floor, along with country-and-western and mellow rock tunes nightly throughout the summer. Hang around the bar long enough and you can join in that old Cassie's favorite, barroom brawling.

Silver Dollar Bar (1313 Sheridan Ave., Cody, 307/527-7666) offers great burgers and accompanies them with rock bands Friday and Saturday nights all year. **Cooter Brown's** (1134 13th St., 307/587-6261) is the party-down spot in Cody, with a DJ Friday and Saturday nights, and karaoke on Thursdays.

Events

Summer is a busy time in Cody, with special events nearly every weekend. The **Cody Gunslingers** perform downtown at the Irma Hotel at 6 P.M. Monday–Saturday in the summer. The mock gunfights are Western-style entertainment. They're worth a look if you haven't seen one before, but still corny and quite out of character for settled-down Cody.

Cowboy Songs and Range Ballads (307/587-4771, www.bbhc.org/events) is a unique Western musical festival held the second weekend of April at the Buffalo Bill Historical Center. You'll hear true cowboy music (not country-and-western), along with poetry and stories from cowboys, ranchers, musicians, and folklorists.

Held in the Robbie Powwow Garden in front of the Buffalo Bill Historical Center in mid-June, the **Plains Indian Powwow** (307/587-4771, www.bbhc.org/events) attracts several hundred participants from all over the Rockies and Canada vying for $15,000 in prize money. It includes daylong singing and dancing in tribal regalia and various dance competitions. Visitors can buy Indian arts and crafts and taste Indian tacos and fry bread.

The **Old West Show and Auction** (307/587-9014, www.codyoldwest.com) in late June offers a chance for collectors to buy quality old cowboy gear. It's considered the finest such

event in the nation and attracts a wealthy crowd. The **Yellowstone Jazz Festival** (www.yellowstonejazz.com) in mid-July brings both regional and national jazz groups.

The **Buffalo Bill Art Show and Sale** (307/587-5002 or 888/598-8119, www.buffalobillartshow.com) in late September is the largest art event of the year, with exhibitions, a symposium, receptions, and an auction.

Cody Nite Rodeo

Cody calls itself "Rodeo Capital of the World," and it packs the calendar with nightly summertime rodeos, plus the famous Cody Stampede. The rodeo grounds are one mile west of town on U.S. 14/16/20. After nearly 70 years of operation, the Cody Nite Rodeo (307/587-5155 or 800/207-0744, www.codyniterodeo.com) is still one of the best in a state filled with rodeos. Shows begin at 8:30 P.M. nightly June–August and always attract a crowd. A crowd favorite is the calf scramble, starring kids from the stands. Tickets cost $15 adults and $8 children; free for kids under seven. For top-of-the-action seats, be sure to get there early and follow the signs to the "buzzards roost" section.

Cody Stampede

Independence Day sets the stage for Cody's main event, the Cody Stampede (307/587-5155 or 800/207-0744, www.codystampederodeo.org), held July 1–4. Established in 1922, it attracts thousands of visitors from all over the nation. Parade fans are treated to one each morning (including a kiddie parade), with dozens of marching bands, mountain men, vintage autos, floats, cowboys, and tons of free candy. Special PRCA rodeo performances, a street dance, art shows, running events, fireworks, and a carnival complete the schedule.

SHOPPING

As you might expect from a tourist town, Cody has more than its share of shops dealing in clunky jewelry, crass T-shirts, and fake Indian trinkets. Fortunately, it's also home to several places with a bit more class. Get fancy Western duds at **Custom Cowboy Shop** (1286

Sheridan Ave., 307/527-7300), or saunter over to **Corral West Ranchwear** (1625 Stampede Ave., 307/587-4493, www.corralwest.com) for inexpensive hats and clothes.

Traditions West Antique Mall (1137 12th St., 307/587-7434) and **Old West Antique Mall** (1215 Sheridan Ave., 307/587-9014) are good places to look for Western antiques.

New books are available from **Cody Newsstand** (1121 13th St., 307/587-2843) and **The Thistle** (1243 Rumsey, 307/587-6635). Cody Newsstand also has one of the best magazine selections in Bighorn Basin. **Wyoming Well Book Exchange and Oilfield Supply** (1902 E. Sheridan Ave., 307/587-4249) has the oddest combination in town: bodice-buster novels and oil-drilling equipment!

Outdoor Gear

For quality backcountry equipment, especially if you travel by horse, be sure to drop by **Wyoming Outdoor Industries** (1231 13th St., 307/527-6449 or 800/725-6853, www.wyomingoutdoors.com). You won't find Gore-Tex jogging bras here, just tough equipment for backcountry use (especially horsepacking), including folding woodstoves, pack saddles, bear-resistant panniers, and wall tents.

Sunlight Sports (1131 Sheridan Ave., 307/587-9517, www.sunlightsports.com) is the largest outdoors shop in town, with tents, climbing equipment, clothes, topographic maps, and more. It also rents cross-country and downhill skis, snowboards, and snowshoes during the winter.

North Fork Anglers (1438 Sheridan Ave., 307/527-7274, www.northforkanglers.com) has anything you might need for fly-fishing, including a full-service retail shop, professional fishing guides, and fly-tying clinics.

RECREATION

Cody Quad (1402 Heart Mountain St., 307/587-0400, www.cityofcody-wy.gov) is an impressive recreation center on the south side of town. It houses a large indoor pool with a long spiral slide, hot tub, wading pool, basketball and racquetball courts, an indoor track, exercise machines, and

child care. Nonresident rec center passes are $10 adults, $5 youths. Next door is the **Victor J. Riley Arena and Community Events Center** (307/587-1400), which serves as a summertime convention center and winter ice rink.

Absaroka Bicycles (2201 17th St., 307/527-5566, www.absarokabike.com) has mountain-bike rentals, bike trail maps, and guided bike tours. Boarders will appreciate the impressive **Cody Skateboard Park** on Blackburn Street in east Cody.

The 18-hole **Olive Glenn Golf and Country Club** (802 Meadow La., 307/587-5308, www.oliveglenngolf.com) is a PGA championship course with a complete golf shop and upscale restaurant. Families enjoy playing **miniature golf** (307/587-3685) at the downtown city park; open seasonally.

River-Rafting

One of the most popular summertime activities in Cody is floating the class I and II Shoshone River. Beware, however, that even with these mild conditions, you should plan on getting soaked in the rapids. Expect to pay around $25 adults ($23 kids) for a seven-mile run that lasts 90 minutes, or $61 for a 13-mile (three-hour) float. For details, contact **Wyoming River Trips** (233 Yellowstone Hwy., 307/587-6661 or 800/586-6661, www.wyomingrivertrips.com), **River Runners** (1491 Sheridan Ave., 307/527-7238 or 800/535-7238, www.riverrunnersofwyoming.com), or **Red Canyon River Trips** (1374 Sheridan Ave., 307/587-6988 or 800/293-0148, www.imt.net/~rodeo/raft.html).

If you want to try rafting or kayaking on your own, you'll find several miles of technical class IV water with some class V drops below the dam and above DeMaris Springs. Above the dam are stretches of class I and II water with good access from the main highway. Ask locally for flow conditions before heading out because snowmelt and dam releases can dramatically affect water levels. The rafting companies offer half-day whitewater trips down the North Fork above the reservoir for $60 including lunch. These trips run only late May–July, when the water level is high.

Most rafters put in three miles west of Cody off Demaris Street. Just upstream from the put-in point is DeMaris Springs, a part of "Colter's Hell" that is on private property and not open to the public. The area was once far more active, with hot springs bubbling out of the river and sulfurous smoke rising all around. People actually died from the poisonous gas. Today the geothermal activity has lessened, but the air still smells of sulfur and small hot springs color the cliff faces. Miners worked over nearby hillsides in search of sulfur; the diggings are still apparent. It's also pretty obvious why they first called this the Stinkingwater River.

Open seasonally, **Gradient Mountain Sports** (1723 Sheridan Ave., 307/587-4659, www.gradientmountainsports.com) has kayak rentals and sales, gear, lessons, and guided trips to Buffalo Bill Reservoir and the Shoshone River.

Horse and Wagon Rides

Horseback rides are available from **Cedar Mountain Trail Rides** (307/527-4966) at Cody KOA two miles east of town, or at the rodeo grounds on the west side, or **Big Bear Motel** (139 W. Yellowstone Ave., 307/587-3117 or 800/325-7163, www.bigbearmotel.com). Hour-long trail rides are $20. Many of the lodges in Wapiti Valley also offer horseback rides. Get a complete listing of Cody-area outfitters and guides from the chamber of commerce, and a list of permitted outfitters from local Forest Service offices.

If you just want to see wild horses, contact photographer Ken Martin of **Red Canyon Wild Mustang Tours** (307/587-6988 or 800/293-0148, www.wildmustangtours.com). His two-hour trips cost $24 adults or $21 kids.

Climbing

Core Mountain Sports (1019 15th St., 307/527-7354, www.coremountainsports.com) sells ice tools, rock equipment, and climbing gear and has a climbing wall ($7/day plus shoe rental). This is the place to get details on winter ice climbing (www.codyice.com) in the South Fork area.

Jackson Hole Mountain Guides (1019 15th St., 307/877/587-0629, www.jhmg.com) has a summertime operation out of Cody, leading climbing classes in the Beartooth Mountains or in the Shoshone River Canyon, along with Heart Mountain day hikes.

ACCOMMODATIONS

The tourist town of Cody is jam-packed with places to stay, but be ready to pay more than anyplace in Wyoming except Jackson Hole. Budget accommodations are hard to find during the summer, although rates plummet with the first cold nights of fall. Most of the year, finding lodging in Cody is not a problem as long as you check in before 4 P.M., but during July and August you should reserve a week ahead—and longer for the Cody Stampede in early July. The **Park County Travel Council**'s website (www.yellowstonecountry.org) has details and links for most local lodging places.

Cody Area Central Reservations (307/587-0200 or 888/468-6996) makes reservations for many local motels, mountain lodges, and B&Bs. It's a good one-stop place to plan your trip to the Cody and Jackson Hole area.

In addition to the places below, you will find many dude ranches and lodges in the mountain country around Cody (see *Sunlight Basin* and *South Fork Area* under *Shoshone National Forest* and the *Wapiti Valley* section).

Under $50

Cody's newest lodging place is a homey hostel: **Bison Willy's Base Camp** (1625 Alger Ave., 307/250-0763 or 877/587-0629, www.bisonwillys.com). The backstreet location is just a few blocks from the center of town, but it is quiet, with a delightful yard and deck, plus an attractive interior, a full kitchen, and commons area. No TV, and the hostel is closed daily 10 A.M.–2 P.M. A small back building serves as a coed six-person dorm ($20/person) with bunk beds and its own kitchen and bath. The main house has a four-person dorm ($30/person) with bath, and a larger room with queen bed and private bath for $75 d. Bedding is provided, and the hostel is open all year. Reservations are recommended in the summer. Owner and climbing guide Kenny

Gasch also runs a wintertime ice climbers' hostel in the South Fork area.

Built in 1900, **Pawnee Hotel** (1032 12th St., 307/587-2239, www.cjswalkerswyoming.com) contains 22 old-fashioned but clean rooms, including four with clawfoot bathtubs. Least expensive are two rooms that share a bath down the hall: $32 s or $34. Rooms with private baths start at $35 s or $40 d, and a four-person suite is $52. The owner is very accommodating.

$50-100

Skyline Motel (1919 17th St., 307/587-4201 or 800/843-8809, $52 s or $62 d) has older furnishings, but large rooms and a fenced play area for children.

Stay in attractive log cabins from the 1920s at **(C Carriage House Motel** (1816 8th St., 307/587-2572 or 800/531-2572, www.carriagehousevillas.com). The cabins are small and don't have phones, but they have been lovingly remodeled. Rates are $65 for one queen bed, $75 for two beds, or $90 for a two-room suite that sleeps five. Open May–October.

Big Bear Motel (139 W. Yellowstone Ave., 307/587-3117 or 800/325-7163, www.bigbearmotel.com, $70 s or $75 d) is an older place with dated—but clean—rooms and friendly owners. No phones in the rooms, but Wi-Fi Internet is available and most rooms include fridges and microwaves. Families love the large outdoor pool.

On the National Register of Historic Places, Buffalo Bill Cody's **Irma Hotel** (1192 Sheridan Ave., 307/587-4221 or 800/745-4762, www.irmahotel.com) has a great downtown location and all the ambience you could want. It's the real thing—a classic Old West hotel. Given the historic importance of the Irma, the guest rooms are a major disappointment. The 15 suites in the original building ($113 s or $120 d) are tolerable, or you can stay in the basic motel rooms in the annex for $73 s or $80 d. At least they're cheap. Be sure to ask about the ghost (of Buffalo Bill?) that supposedly haunts the hotel.

Carter Mountain Motel (1701 Central Ave., 307/587-4295, www.cartermountainmotel.net),

atop the hill near Albertsons, features very nicely maintained rooms. Standard units (some with fridges) are $74–87 d. Suites with full kitchens are $98–183; the largest can sleep nine.

(C Best Value Inn West (720 W. Yellowstone Ave., 307/587-4208 or 888/315-2378, www.bestvalueinn.com) is indeed one of the best values in town, with attractive rooms, a small heated outdoor pool (seasonal), and a continental breakfast in the lobby. Standard rooms (some with king beds) are $80–96 s or $84–96 d. A two-bedroom family suite sleeps six for $118. Open March–November. Same owner for **Best Value Inn East** (1807 Sheridan Ave., 307/587-4258 or 888/315-2378), where the prices are $10 lower for similar rooms. This one lacks a pool, but it is in a quiet part of town and is open year-round.

$100-150

New in 2006, **Cody Legacy Inn and Suites** (1801 Mountain View Dr., 307/527-7119, www.codylegacyinn.com) features 50 spacious rooms, most with two queen beds for $99–119 d. A king suite with jetted tub is $129 d. Amenities include an outdoor heated pool (seasonal), indoor hot tub, and continental breakfast.

Sunrise Motor Inn (1407 8th St., 307/587-5566 or 877/587-5566, www.sunriseinn-cody.com) is another comfortable place, with a heated outdoor pool (seasonal), continental breakfast, and wireless Internet. Rates are $89–99 d, or $120 for rooms that sleep up to six. Open May–mid-October.

Buffalo Bill Village Resort consists of three separate operations that total nearly 350 rooms: Holiday Inn, Comfort Inn, and Buffalo Bill Village Resort. All three are in the heart of Cody at 1701 Sheridan Avenue and share the same toll-free number and website: 800/527-5544, www.blairhotels.com. Guests at all three facilities can use the outdoor heated pool at the Holiday Inn and are welcome to join the free wine and champagne reception each evening. The beautifully remodeled 189-room **Holiday Inn at Buffalo Bill Village Resort** (307/587-5555) charges $159 d for rooms with

THE WILD WEST SHOW

Buffalo Bill's days in the real Wild West were over, and he returned to staging shows, eventually starting his famed Wild West extravaganza. This was unlike anything ever done before – an outdoor circus that seemed to transport all who watched to the frontier. One newspaper remarked that Cody had "out-Barnumed Barnum." There were buffalo stampedes, cowboy bronc riding, Indian camps, a Deadwood stage and outlaws, crack shooting by Annie Oakley, and, of course, Buffalo Bill. At its peak in the late 1890s, the show made Cody more than a million dollars in profit each year.

Amazingly, Sitting Bull and Buffalo Bill became good friends. Cody, who had earlier bragged of his many Indian killings, changed his attitude, eventually saying, "In nine cases out of 10 when there is trouble between white men and Indians, it will be found that the white man is responsible." Cody's other attitudes also continued to evolve. He criticized the buffalo hunters of the 1870s and 1880s for their reckless slaughter, and he later became an ardent supporter of game preserves and limitations on hunting seasons.

The Wild West Show became one of the most popular events anywhere in America and Europe, attracting crowds of up to 40,000 people. Queen Victoria was a special fan (although rumors of an affair are probably false). At the peak of his fame around the turn of the 20th century, Buffalo Bill was arguably the world's best-known man. Cody, however, continued to drink heavily. One day, an obviously drunken Buffalo Bill insisted that his cowboys ride Monarch, a massive and dangerous bison in the entourage. When they refused in front of thousands of spectators, Cody himself climbed on top and was immediately thrown to the ground. He spent the next two weeks in a hospital. For the next decade the show continued to tour but gradually lost its novelty as other forms of entertainment, especially movies, came along. Cody used his money to buy the 40,000-acre TE Ranch in northwestern Wyoming near Yellowstone National Park. For him the Bighorn Basin was paradise. The town that he helped establish here was named Cody in his honor, and he backed the massive Shoshone irrigation project.

Unfortunately, Buffalo Bill seemed to have no comprehension of how to save his wealth. He was a notoriously soft touch and would

---

two double or one king bed. Amenities include wireless Internet, a guest computer, and fitness center. **Comfort Inn at Buffalo Bill Village Resort** (307/587-5556) charges $159 d, including a filling breakfast and free Wi-Fi (but thin walls). The most distinctive of this Cody lodging triumvirate is ◖ **Buffalo Bill Village Cabins** (307/587-5544), which consists of 83 cozy log cabins. These cabins were built in the 1920s to house workers and their families for nearby Buffalo Bill Dam. They were later moved here and have since been updated to include phones, TVs, private baths, and air-conditioning. Small cabins have a queen or king bed for $129 d. Family cabins ($149) have two bedrooms with three or four double beds. The cabins are open May–September, and Wi-Fi is available in some units.

One of Cody's nicer motels, **Beartooth Inn** (2513 Greybull Hwy., 307/527-5505 or 800/807-8522, www.beartoothinn.com) is a mile east of town. Spacious standard rooms (biggest in town) are $99 s or $115 d, six-person family rooms go for $149, and minisuites with hot tubs cost $145 d. Hotel amenities include a sauna and hot tub, exercise equipment, free wireless Internet, guest computer, and a big breakfast (fresh waffles), plus microwaves and fridges in most rooms. Ground-floor rooms have both outside and interior entrances.

You'll find excellent accommodations at **Best Western Sunset Motor Inn** (1601 8th St., 307/587-4265 or 800/624-2727, www.bestwestern.com/sunsetmotorinn), where standard rooms start at $119 d, up to $189 for family suites that sleep six. Amenities include give money to almost anyone who asked. As his fortune slipped away and his show became more dated, Cody was finally forced to join up with H. H. Tammen, the crooked owner of the *Denver Post*. Tammen used the aging Cody's fame to attract people to his own circus. He forced Cody's Wild West Show into bankruptcy in 1913, sold off all of the incredible collection of historical artifacts that had been amassed through the years, and left workers to find their own ways home. Buffalo Bill was heartbroken but, still trusting Tammen (or in desperation), agreed to join his circus almost as a sideshow act.

Three years later, Cody died while visiting his sister in Denver and was buried on Lookout Mountain near Denver. Cody had wanted to be buried on Cedar Mountain above the town of Cody, but even this wish was denied by Tammen, who apparently paid Cody's widow Louisa $10,000 for the privilege of choosing the burial site (and to use the funeral parade to the burial site as an advertisement for his circus troupe). When rumors came that folks from Wyoming intended to dig up Cody's body and take it back to its rightful burial place, Tammen had tons of concrete dumped on top of the grave. Louisa

Cody went on to outlive not only her husband but also all four of her children. She ended up caring for her four grandchildren.

Despite the unhappy ending to Buffalo Bill's life, there are few individuals who lived such a diverse and adventure-filled life and who could count so many people as their friends, from the lowliest beggar to the richest king. Cody's life spanned one of the most remarkable eras in American history, and his impact on American culture is still felt today, not just in the image of the West that he created, which lives on in hundreds of Western movies, but also in the Boy Scouts (an organization inspired partly by his exploits), in the city of Cody, and even in the dude ranches that dot Wyoming.

Late in life, Cody was asked how he wanted to be remembered. He replied:

> I don't want to die and have people say, "Oh, there goes another old showman." When I die I want the people of Wyoming who are living on the land that has been made fertile by my work and expenditure to remember me. I would like people to say, "This is the man who opened up Wyoming to the best of civilization."

indoor and outdoor pools, a hot tub, wireless Internet, guest computers, a playground, and fitness facility.

AmericInn Lodge and Suites (508 Yellowstone Ave., 307/587-7716 or 800/634-3444, www.americinn.com) is one of the newest places to stay in Cody and offers some of the finest (and quietest) rooms. All 64 are large, with standard rooms (king or two queen beds) for $150 d, and luxurious suites—some with jetted tubs and fireplaces—for $189–210. Other amenities include an indoor pool, hot tub, sauna, and fitness center, plus a light breakfast.

Guesthouses, Cabins, and Apartments

Families may want to stay in one of 40 nicely furnished homes, cottages, apartments, and lodges

managed by **Cody Lodging Company** (307/587-6000 or 800/587-6560, www.codyguesthouses.com). Prices start at $100 d for a small cottage, up to $450 for a luxurious three-bedroom home near Buffalo Bill State Park.

Bed-and-Breakfasts

The website for **Cody Country Bed and Breakfast Association** (www.codybedandbreakfast.com) has links to most local B&Bs. Several historic buildings are now part of the Cody B&B scene, offering a taste of the genteel past. **Parson's Pillow B&B** (1202 14th St., 307/587-2382 or 800/377-2348, www.cruisingamerica.com/parsonspillow) is one of the most interesting and enjoys a fine central location. Completed in 1902, the building served for many years as a Methodist-Episcopal Church.

Today it's a cozy and well-maintained B&B with antique furnishings, five guest rooms, private baths, and full breakfasts; $95 d. One room has space for four ($120) and bunk beds that are popular with families. Kids older than age five are accepted.

Built in 1924 by Cody Mayor P. E. Markham, **Lambright Place B&B** (1501 Beck Ave., 307/527-5310 or 800/241-5310, www.lambrightplace.com) exudes an old-fashioned charm. Three rooms in the large main house are available for $95–120 d, and a Western-themed cottage/bunkhouse sleeps five for $160. All rooms have private baths, and the breakfasts are memorable. Kids are welcome, and the bunkhouse works well for families.

Also recommended is **Robin's Nest B&B** (1508 Alger Ave., 307/527-7208 or 866/723-7797, www.robinsnestcody.com, $115–135 d). On a quiet street just a few blocks from the heart of town, this 1928 brick and frame home features a relaxing and shady backyard, a large living room, and three guest rooms with private baths, plus a guest computer and wireless Internet. Unique is the treehouse suite, situated on an upstairs porch. A full breakfast is served each morning, and well-behaved kids are accepted.

For lodging in a classic Cody home, stay at **C The Mayor's Inn** (1413 Rumsey Ave., 307/587-0887 or 888/217-3001, www.mayorsinn.com), built in 1909 by Frank Houx, the town's first mayor. In 1997 it was moved to the present site and restored to its original opulence. The four guest rooms ($115–205 d) include private baths with jetted tubs, down comforters, terrycloth robes, and heated floors. The nicest room has a king bed and jetted tub. A full breakfast is served each morning; no young children allowed. Also available is a separate cottage with full kitchen for $100 for families (no breakfast). Mayor's Inn also serves gourmet dinners.

Angel's Keep B&B (1241 Wyoming Ave., 307/587-6205 or 877/320-2800, www.angelskeep.com) is housed within a restored 1930s Assembly of God church and has three rooms with queen beds and TV/VCRs for $99–135 d. Guests are served a filling country breakfast,

with snacks and beverages each evening. A gift shop here offers locally made items.

K3 Guest Ranch (307/587-2080 or 888/587-2080, www.k3guestranch.com) sits on 33 acres of land along the outskirts of Cody. The modern home has three Western-themed guest rooms ($150–175 d), all with private baths and windows facing the hayfield. One even features a chuck wagon bed. Owners Jerry and Bette Kinkade cook a big ranch breakfast over an open fire each morning and also offer a day ranch for wanna-be cowboys: $175/person for a mix of horsemanship, target practice, roping, fishing, and more. Open May–mid-November.

Southfork Bed and Breakfast (797 Southfork Rd., 307/587-8311, www.southforkbb.com) is a large home eight miles southwest of town near Buffalo Bill Reservoir. The two guest rooms ($100–125 d) contain private baths and entrances, and guests are served a full breakfast by the owner—who is also a professional chef. A third room ($50 extra) can be combined with the others for families. Other amenities include a home theater, full bar, outdoor pool, indoor lap pool and hot tub, and spacious great room with a stone fireplace. Horse lodging is available, or you can just visit with the owner's (formerly) wild mustangs.

Camping

The closest public campground ($12 for nonresidents, or $6 for Wyoming residents) is 11 miles west in Buffalo Bill State Park. Make campsite reservations ($8.50 fee) at 877/996-7275, www.wyo-park.com. Find many more campgrounds ($5–10) in Shoshone National Forest; the nearest is 28 miles west of Cody in the upper North Fork.

You'll find a number of private RV park/campgrounds in Cody, but the finest is **Ponderosa Campground** (1815 8th St., 307/587-9203, www.codyponderosa.com, open May–mid-Oct.), with attractive, shady sites ($18 tents or $30–34 RVs) along with tepees ($21) and simple cabins ($34 for four people).

Cody KOA (two miles east on U.S. 14/16/20, 307/587-2369 or 800/562-8507, www.codykoa.com) opened in 1964 as the first franchised KOA. Rates are $30 for tents and $44–49 for RVs, and $54–62 for simple cabins. Open May–September, with an outdoor pool, hot tub, Wi-Fi, $1 pancake breakfasts, and a rodeo shuttle.

Noncampers can take showers at Gateway Campground or Ponderosa Campground.

FOOD

Because Cody is a tourist town, it's no surprise to find many fine places to eat, covering the spectrum from buffalo burgers to Chinese won-tons.

Breakfast and Lunch

Hang out with the farmers over a good breakfast or lunch at the smoke-free **Our Place** (148 W. Yellowstone, 307/527-4420).

Although **Peter's Cafe** (1219 Sheridan Ave., 307/527-5040) is open for dinner, the main attractions come earlier, with inexpensive breakfasts and lunchtime subs on freshly baked breads, plus homemade soups, buffalo burgers, and 32-plus flavors of ice cream. Banana splits, smoothies, and malts are big draws on hot summer afternoons.

The Beta Coffeehouse (1132 12th St., 307/587-7707) is the best local espresso joint, with a hip setting, good smoothies, homemade pastries (cinnamon rolls, scones, and muffins), and free Wi-Fi for customers.

Dinner

Proud Cut Saloon (1227 Sheridan Ave., 307/587-7343) is a fine Wyoming bar and restaurant offering unusual lunchtime sandwiches and burgers (try the jalapeño burger) and outstanding steak and prime rib for dinner, or as the saloon calls it, "kick ass cowboy cuisine." It's the real thing, with a rustic and woodsy Old West decor. And—amazingly enough—smoking isn't allowed. Most dinners are $16–24.

Irma Hotel (1192 Sheridan Ave., 307/587-4221, www.irmahotel.com) is an old favorite for lunch and dinner, but the food is nothing special—except for the prime rib. Drop by in the morning for the big breakfast buffet.

Bubba's Bar-B-Que (512 Yellowstone Ave.,

307/587-7427) has the best salad bar in town, big breakfasts (including smoked pork chop and eggs), along with reasonably priced barbecued ribs, steak, or chicken for dinner ($10–18). This is a great stuff-yourself spot.

In existence since 1922, **Cassie's Supper Club** (214 Yellowstone Ave., 307/527-5500, www.cassies.com) is famous locally for steaks, prime rib, shrimp, and its summer-only chuck wagon buffet ($11). Tuesday Mexican and Thursday barbecued rib lunch specials attract a crowd. Most dinner entrées are $25–30.

Eclectic

The ever-popular **Maxwell's Fine Food and Spirits** (937 Sheridan Ave., 307/527-7749) dishes up homemade lunches that include sandwiches, pasta, and salads. It's a bright and homey place, with a patio for sunny days, and a small bakery/coffee shop. The dinner menu features pasta, seafood, chicken, beef, offbeat pizzas, and vegetarian dishes; $12–18. Closed Sunday.

Of particular note is **The Mayor's Inn** (1413 Rumsey Ave., 307/587-0887 or 888/217-3001, www.mayorsinndinnerhouse.com), where fabulous gourmet dinners are served Thursday–Saturday evenings in a quaint Victorian setting. The limited menu changes every couple of weeks but always includes steaks and other regional fare. Prices are surprisingly reasonable, with most entrées at $14–20. Open May–October only. Reservations recommended.

Open for lunch and dinner, **Wyoming Rib and Chop House** (1367 Sheridan Ave., 307/587-7731) specializes in baby-back ribs, Angus steaks, and fresh seafood. The atmosphere is upscale and romantic; dinner entrées cost $10–22, but you can also get buffalo burgers and other munchies for $7.

International

Two blocks north of the Irma Hotel—and a world away from the crush of tourists—is **The Noon Break** (927 12th St., 307/587-9720). This may be Cody's best-kept secret, with simple, flavorful, and inexpensive (under $6) Mexican fare for breakfast and lunch. Specialties include *huevos rancheros,* steak quesadillas, taco salads, and "code 10 chili." Service is slow, so don't come here in a hurry. Open 7 A.M.– 2 P.M. Tuesday–Saturday. Be sure to check out the license plate collection that fills one wall.

For decent Chinese food—including a lunch buffet and family-style dinners—visit **Hong Kong Restaurant** (1201 17th St., 307/587-6420).

Adriano's Italian Restaurant (1244 Sheridan Ave., 307/527-7320) may not have the friendliest or fastest service, but this is the real thing, with a big menu that features veal marsala, scampi, chicken Florentine, and very good New York–style pizzas.

Groceries and Specialty Foods

Cody's grocers include an **Albertsons** (on the south side of Cody at 1825 17th St., 307/527-7007) and a big **Wal-Mart SuperCenter** on the west end at 321 Yellowstone Ave., 307/527-4673). For natural foods and Wyoming-made gifts, head to **Whole Foods Trading Co.** (1239 Rumsey, 307/587-3213). **Wyoming Buffalo Company** (1270 Sheridan Ave., 307/587-8708 or 800/453-0636, www.wyomingbuffalocompany.com) specializes in buffalo jerky, salami, sausage, and fresh meat, with a variety of gift packages. Stop in for a free sample.

INFORMATION AND SERVICES

Get local information from the **Cody Country Chamber of Commerce** (836 Sheridan Ave., 307/587-2777 or 800/393-2639, www.codychamber.org). Hours are 8 A.M.– 6 P.M. Monday–Saturday and 10 A.M.–3 P.M. Sunday Memorial Day–Labor Day, and 8 A.M.– 5 P.M. Monday–Friday the rest of the year. This log building—on the National Register of Historic Places—housed the original Buffalo Bill Museum from 1927 to 1969 and was built as a replica of Cody's TE Ranch. In addition to tons of brochures and a helpful staff, the building houses computers where you can check your email. A regional tourism organization, **Park County Travel Council** (307/587-2297 or 800/393-2639, www.yellowstonecountry.org) is also based here. Another useful web source is www.codywyomingnet.com.

Government offices include the **BLM's Cody Field Office** (1002 Blackburn Ave., 307/578-5900, www.wy.blm.gov), **Shoshone National Forest Supervisor's Office** (808 Meadow La., 307/527-6241, www.fs.fed.us/r2/shoshone), and the **North Zone Ranger District Office** (203 W. Yellowstone, 307/527-6921).

The **Park County Library** (1501 Stampede Ave., 307/527-8820, http://will.state.wy.us/park) has regional titles and computers for Internet access.

Cody's **West Park Hospital** (707 Sheridan Ave., 307/527-7501 or 800/654-9447, www.westparkhospital.org) is the largest in Bighorn Basin and one of the finest in the state. The hospital's **Urgent Care Clinic** (702 Yellowstone Ave., 307/587-7207) is open daily and evenings. No appointment needed.

Wash clothes at **Eastgate Laundry** (1813 17th St., 307/587-5355) next to Albertsons, **Quick Coin-Op Laundromat** (930 12th St., 307/587-6519), or **Cody Laundromat** (1728 Beck Ave., 307/587-8500).

GETTING THERE AND AROUND

Yellowstone Regional Airport (www.flyyra.com) is just east of town on U.S. 14/16/20. **SkyWest/Delta** (307/587-9740 or 800/221-1212, www.delta.com) has daily flights to Salt Lake City, while **United Express** (307/587-9740 or 800/241-6522, www.united.com) has daily service to Denver. **Spirit Mountain Aviation** (307/587-6732) offers scenic flights and charter service.

Shuttle Services (307/899-3960) provides transportation to the Billings airport ($85 s or $110 d), along with in-town taxi service.

Rent cars at the airport from **Budget** (307/587-6066 or 800/527-0700, www.budget.com), **Hertz** (307/587-2914 or 800/654-3131, www.hertz.com), or **Thrifty** (307/587-8855 or 800/847-4389, www.cody.thrifty.com). In town, find lower rates at **Rent-a-Wreck** (2515 Greybull Hwy., 307/527-5549 or 800/452-0396).

Cody Over Land Transit (COLT, 307/527-7043) provides public bus service across town for just $1 per ride or $2 for all day. Buses operate daily June–mid-September, coming by every 45 minutes or so.

Buses from **Powder River Transportation** (307/682-1888 or 800/442-3682, http://gillette.coachusa.us) stop at Palmers Outpost (1521 Rumsey Ave.), providing service to most Bighorn Basin towns, along with central and eastern Wyoming, Billings, Denver, and Rapid City.

Tours

The **Cody Trolley** (307/527-7043, www.codytrolleytours.com) takes you on a very informative hour-long tour of town (and up to Buffalo Bill Dam) for $15, or a combo $25 ticket that includes entrance into the Buffalo Bill Historical Center. These tours are offered several times a day in summer.

During summer, **Powder River Tours** (307/527-3677 or 800/442-3682, www.powderriverbuslines.com) has daily tours of Yellowstone National Park for $74 adults, $68 seniors, and $40 kids. Three tour options are offered: the southern park loop, the northern part, or a tour into Grand Teton National Park. With notice, you can overnight in Yellowstone and return on a later bus for no extra charge (space-available basis) or transfer to **Alltrans/Gray Line** (307/733-4325 or 800/443-6133, www.jacksonholealltrans.com) buses for Jackson, or **Buffalo Bus Touring Co.** (406/646-9564 or 800/426-7669, www.yellowstonevacations .com) for West Yellowstone.

For a more personalized trip, call **Grub Steak Expeditions** (307/527-6316 or 800/527-6316, www.grubsteaktours.com). The company leads 12-hour auto tours of the park, along with visits to Sunlight Basin, Wapiti Valley, and the South Fork. One-day tours cost $390 for two people, plus $100 for each additional guest. These tours are popular with families looking for a unique perspective on the park, and some are led by co-owner Bob Richard, a retired Yellowstone park ranger.

Wildlife biologist Sean Sheehan leads **Wyoming Nature Tours** (307/250-0251, www.wyomingnaturetours.com) with natural-history trips throughout the Big Horn Basin, including Bighorn Canyon. **Wyoming Touring Adventures** (307/587-5136) and **High Country Advetures** (307/587-7669, www.yellowstoneadventuretours.com) offer similar services.

HEART MOUNTAIN

Halfway between Cody and Powell is Heart Mountain, so named because its twin summits faintly resemble the traditional valentine. The mountain is visible for many miles in all directions and was one of the few identifiable topographical features on maps drawn by Lewis and Clark in 1811. Geologists scratch their heads over this seemingly upside-down mountain. The Heart Mountain detachment fault stretches for more than 100 miles, cutting southwest from near Cooke City, Montana. To the east are enormous blocks of land that have slid onto the top of more recent deposits, reversing the normal situation in which older rocks lie beneath more recent ones. Scientists know that these limestone and dolomite blocks moved around 45–50 million years ago, but none have been able to adequately explain how entire mountains, including Heart, could have slid for dozens of miles.

The Nature Conservancy's 15,000-acre **Heart Mountain Ranch** (307/754-8446, www.nature.org/wyoming) encompasses the north and east slopes of the mountain, along with part of the surrounding plains. The region supports a surprising diversity of plants, including several rare species. An enjoyable seven-mile trail climbs to the summit of Heart Mountain.

Heart Mountain Relocation Center

For Americans of Japanese ancestry, Heart Mountain might as well have been called Broken Heart Mountain. After the Japanese attack on Pearl Harbor in 1941, Japanese Americans found their patriotism under increasing suspicion, and the following spring President Roosevelt signed an executive order establishing the War Relocation Authority to move them away from the coasts. The authority built 10 remote "relocation centers" to imprison anyone of Japanese ancestry; one such center went up just east

© DON PITCHER

Heart Mountain

of Heart Mountain and housed 10,767 Japanese Americans (two-thirds of them born in America). The camp became Wyoming's third-largest settlement. It took just 62 days to complete the 468 barracks, 40 laundry-toilet buildings, Buddhist and Christian churches, a high school, fire station, recreation hall, power station, mess hall, hospital, sewage plant, administrative offices, and numerous other structures. (No environmental impact reports on this baby!) Barbed wire surrounded the perimeter, and military police staffed nine guard towers with high-beam searchlights and machine guns.

Camp Life

Most of the Japanese Americans took the forced relocation with remarkable aplomb, realizing the futility of any escape attempt. It almost seemed the patriotic thing to do; *shi-kata-ga-nai* ("I guess it cannot be helped") became the accepted phrase. Although life in the camp maintained a sense of normalcy—some kids came to enjoy their peaceful high-school years and the picnics in Yellowstone—the camp was far from idyllic. Three or four peo-

ple were jammed into each room, furniture was minimal, people had to share communal bathhouses, and the winter winds blew through the uninsulated tar-paper buildings. Local folks resented the Japanese Americans but appreciated the cheap farm labor that they provided while Wyoming's sons were off fighting the Germans and Japanese.

After the War

With the war's end in 1945, the camp was closed and the internees were given $25 and a one-way bus ticket home (or rather, to what remained; many found their homes ransacked or sold to others). During the next four years the 740 acres of land was opened to homesteading, and the barracks were sold at two for $1. Most of the buildings ended up as temporary homes for the new settlers. None of the Japanese American internees remained in the area, and most of the survivors have little desire to even visit what seemed such a desolate, godforsaken place. They would rather try to forget. See Gretel Ehrlich's *Heart Mountain* for a fictional treatment of life inside the camp.

The Camp Today

Today the only reminders of the Heart Mountain Relocation Center are three buildings, the largest of which is the old hospital heating plant with its tall brick chimney. Several plaques also mark the camp's site, one noting the more than 600 men who left Heart Mountain camp to join the U.S. Army in Europe. Twenty-one internees and a camp teacher died while fighting in Europe.

The site is 11 miles east of Cody on U.S. 14A. Barley fields now surround the former camp, while Heart Mountain stands guard over the western flank. Based in Powell, the nonprofit **Heart Mountain, Wyoming Foundation** (307/754-2689, www.heartmountain.net) works to preserve the memory of this painful era lest it be repeated. An interpretive center was in the discussion stages, but don't look for it anytime soon.

HEADING EAST FROM HEART MOUNTAIN

The historic **Eagles Nest Stage Station** stands east of the relocation camp as you continue toward Powell. The log cabins and barns were built a century ago by the Lanchbury family, which homesteaded here. Their ranch served as a stage station midway between Meeteetse (then the largest town in Bighorn Basin) and Red Lodge, Montana. Today a fifth generation of Lanchburys lives in the restored buildings of historic Eagles Nest.

If you're looking for trivia, stop in the tiny settlement of **Ralston** to see the railroad bridge over a highway bridge, atop a creek. This odd collection made it into *Ripley's Believe It or Not!* The town is home to **Mule Days** (www.saddlemule.com) in mid-June, a chance to learn about the ornery critters and to enjoy the unique all-mule rodeo and auction.

Meeteetse

Along the western edge of Bighorn Basin is a charming little ranching center called Meeteetse (pop. 350). The name is a Shoshone Indian word meaning "Meeting Place of the Chiefs." The Absaroka Mountains rise gently to the south and west, and the Greybull River flows right through town, cottonwood trees on either side. To the north, the highway crosses a rolling land of sage and greasewood, while to the south are rugged badlands. Meeteetse has wooden sidewalks and hitching rails, occasional cattle drives right down Main Street, and an interesting museum.

The last wild black-footed ferrets were discovered just a dozen miles to the west at the famed Pitchfork Ranch. They were captured in 1987 after an outbreak of canine distemper threatened to kill all of the remaining wild ferrets. A bronze ferret statue guards tiny but picturesque Riverside Park in town, but it may be many decades (if ever) before living ferrets return.

SIGHTS

One of the oldest towns in Bighorn Basin, Meeteetse was first settled in the late 1870s by homesteaders and wealthy European cattle barons. By 1890 it was the largest community in the basin. Several original buildings are still standing, including the impressively large **Meeteetse Mercantile,** built in 1899 but now closed. A few doors away is the **Cowboy Bar,** with more than a century of rough-and-tumble history. The saloon opened in 1893, and it still has the original rosewood and cherrywood back bar. Historical artifacts and local brands fill the walls. More than a few guns have gone off here through the years; at last count the bar contained 56 bullet holes and a shotgun blast! Many well-known people have spent time in this bar, including Buffalo Bill Cody, Tom Horn, Butch Cassidy, and Amelia Earhart.

The **Beldon and Meeteetse Museum** (307/868-2423, www.meeteetsemuseum.org) is open 10 A.M.–4 P.M. Monday–Saturday late May–early September, and Monday, Tuesday,

Thursday, and Friday 10 A.M.–4 P.M. the rest of the year. Inside are artifacts from the famous Pitchfork Ranch, including the collection of Charles Beldon's classic cowboy photographs from the 1930s. Also here is one of the largest grizzlies ever taken in the Lower 48 (it's eight feet tall), items from early settlers of the area, plus early photos from the mining town of Kirwin. It also has the (stuffed) ferret that was dragged in by a dog in 1981.

Down the street is the historic **Bank Museum,** now restored to the way it looked in 1901, with banking artifacts, the original safe, and Meeetetse photos. Open Saturdays in summer.

PRACTICALITIES
Events
Visit Meeteetse on **Labor Day weekend** in September for a small-town parade, street games, a barbecue, arts and crafts, live music, dancing, and a grand finale rodeo. Great fun, and its been going on for more than 90 years.

Recreation
An indoor **swimming pool** (307/868-2603, www.meetrec.org) is at the high school. **Pine Rock Golf Course** (307/868-2177, www.pine-rockgolf.com) is a new nine-hole course just south of town.

Accommodations
Oasis Motel and RV Park (1702 State St., 307/868-2551 or 888/868-5270, www.oasis-motelwyoming.com) has clean and well-maintained motel rooms for $40 s or $45 d; cabins with kitchenettes for $51 s or $56 d; campsites for $8; and RV spots for $17. Ask about its chuck wagon dinners. The riverside location is a plus, and there's even a corral for those traveling with horses.

Vision Quest Motel (2207 State St., 307/868-2512 or 866/478-2987, www.vqmotel.com) is another friendly place, with attractive rooms—most with kitchenettes—for $49 d, and six-person suites for $79 d. RV parking is $15.

Food
Elkhorn Bar and Grill has the best local burgers and is a meeting spot for local folks, especially on weekend evenings, when country bands sometimes play. Other times you can try your hand at pool or darts.

Outlaw Parlor Cafe at the Cowboy Bar also has good pizzas and steaks, along with old photos from early-day Meeteetse. Be sure to ask the bartender at the Cowboy for the "true" origins of the word Meeteetse.

Information
Just up the hill from the Bank Museum is the **Meeteetse Visitor Information Center** (2044 State St., 307/868-2454, www.meeteet-sewy.com) with brochures on the area. It's open 9 A.M.–5:30 P.M. daily in summer, and 9 A.M.–5:30 P.M. Monday–Friday the rest of the year.

WOOD RIVER VALLEY
Southwest of Meeteetse, beautiful Wood River Valley is an enjoyable drive or bike ride. It's a great place to watch for moose and elk in the bottomlands, along with a variety of smaller animals. Two free Forest Service **campgrounds** (open June–Nov.) are available near the end of the road. From here you can hike into the **Washakie Wilderness** along any of several different trails (see *Shoshone National Forest* in this chapter for details).

Wood River Valley Ski Touring Park (307/868-2603, www.meetrec.org, free) is 22 miles southwest of town on Wood River Road. The Meeteetse Recreation District runs the park and provides ski rentals in town. The cross-country ski area includes 25 kilometers of groomed trails, wonderful mountain scenery, a warming hut, and a small cabin (donation) for overnight stays.

Wood River Lodge (307/868-9211, www.tc-twest.net/~woodriver) is 20 miles out and just three miles from the National Forest boundary. It's a great base for hiking, biking, or wintertime skiing. Accommodations include four modern cabins ($70 d) with private baths, or small rooms ($35 d) in a bunkhouse with a shared bath. Meals are available upon request. Closed December–January.

KIRWIN

The abandoned mining town of Kirwin is accessible from the Brown Creek Campground at the end of Wood River Road. You'll need a 4WD (or at least a high-clearance vehicle) to continue the 11 miles past the campground to Kirwin, at an elevation of 9,200 feet. Mountain-bikers in good shape will also enjoy this challenging road. The road is typically accessible late June–early October.

Gold was discovered in the Kirwin area in 1885, and within a few years more than 200 miners were living in this remote high-elevation site. A 1907 avalanche killed three people and proved the last straw for miners who had been struggling for years with little or no profit. Most of them abandoned their cabins and claims with what they could carry on their backs, never to return. Now within Shoshone National Forest, the old mining town is a fascinating place to explore, with the decaying remains of a hotel and cabins, along with rusting farm and mining machinery.

On the drive into Kirwin you pass what remains of Double D Dude Ranch, established in 1931. Famed aviatrix Amelia Earhart was having a summer cabin built near here shortly before her 1934 disappearance during an around-the-world flight. The cabin was never finished, and only a few rotting logs remain. A monument to Amelia Earhart stands in Meeteetse, and the flight jacket she wore when she became the first woman to cross the Atlantic alone is in the Buffalo Bill Historical Center.

MORE NEARBY SIGHTS

Another historic place—**Palatte Ranch**—is at the end of Pitchfork Road, a gravel road paralleling the Greybull River. The road ends 30 miles west of Meeteetse at Jack Creek Campground (free). A six-mile hike from the campground takes you to **Anderson Lodge,** an archetypal log home that was restored by the Forest Service. Palatte Ranch was once owned by A. A. Anderson, first superintendent of the Yellowstone Park Timberland Reserve (now Shoshone National Forest). Check with the Forest Service office in Cody for more information on this area.

Northwest of Meeteetse is an important archaeological site, the **Great Arrow,** a 58-foot-long arrow made from rocks and placed atop a long hogback ridge. Of unknown age, the arrow points toward the Medicine Wheel in the Big Horn Mountains 70 miles to the northeast. The Great Arrow is on private land and not accessible to the public. The turnoff to impressive **Legend Rock Petroglyph Site** is 32 miles southeast of Meeteetse along Hwy. 120 (see *Thermopolis*).

Powell

One of the most pleasant settlements in Bighorn Basin, Powell (pop. 5,300) is a clean and prosperous farming, oil, and college town halfway between Cody and Lovell. Declared an All-America City in 1994, it sits at the center of a rich farming region where sugar beets, dry beans, and malting barley (grown for Coors and Anheuser-Busch) are raised. Because these crops are harvested at different times of the year, many farmers grow all three. Tall bean elevators border the railroad tracks on the south edge of town, and a dozen miles to the north is the giant Elk Basin Oil Field. First discovered in 1915, it had 150 wells pumping more than 4,200 barrels a day within five years. The field has proven a major factor in the growth of the northern Bighorn Basin, although production is declining as the supply is exhausted.

Powell was named for Major John Wesley Powell (1834–1902), the famed one-armed explorer of the Colorado River and an early director of the U.S. Geological Survey. His 1889 report on the agricultural potential of Western desert lands had asserted the value of irrigation in "reclaiming" these areas and

© AVALON TRAVEL PUBLISHING, INC.

proposed a system of dams and canals funded by the government. One of the earliest of these was the mammoth Shoshone Project, involving Buffalo Bill Dam and a series of canals to feed water to the fields along the Shoshone River. Powell is right at the center of all this irrigation, and homesteaders flocked here in the first two decades of the 20th century. The town sprang up at a campsite used by workers on the Shoshone Project. With the arrival of the Chicago, Burlington and Quincy Railroad (now Burlington Northern), Powell became an agricultural shipping point.

SIGHTS

The **Homesteader Museum** (on the corner of 1st and Clark Sts., 307/754-9481, free) is open 10 A.M.–5 P.M. Tuesday–Friday and 10 A.M.–3 P.M. Saturday May–September, and 10 A.M.–4 P.M. Tuesday–Saturday the rest of the year except for January and February, when it is closed. The museum captures the hardscrabble life of early-1900s homesteaders in the northern Bighorn Basin. You'll find interesting old photographs, a beautiful collection of dryhead agate, some Indian artifacts, a century-old porcelain doll, and a German grandfather clock, chairs, and bench covered with carved bears. There's more junk to check out, but take the time to watch the videotape detailing the history of the nearby Heart Mountain Relocation Center. An adjacent building is filled with horse-drawn machines and old tractors, while outside are a caboose and various pieces of old farm equipment.

The chamber of commerce (307/754-3494 or 800/325-4278) offers individualized **agricultural tours** of the farms and ranches around Powell, providing a good way to learn about irrigation systems, dairy farms, feed lots, sheep and cattle breeding, irrigation, and crop production. These reasonably priced trips in-

EARL DURAND

Folks still talk about "Tarzan of the Tetons," a local kid gone bad. Earl Durand was a crack shot and a mountain man of sorts. He had once traveled by horse and foot to Mexico and bragged that he could survive on practically anything, even raw bobcat meat. Durand hated being cooped up inside buildings, so when he was arrested for poaching in 1939, he escaped the Cody jail. Five people died in the shooting rampage that followed, and the murders attracted intense national attention. The climax came when Durand robbed a Powell bank and suddenly found himself surrounded. A 17-year-old kid shot – but didn't kill – Durand as he came out of the bank with a screen of hostages. Sensing the futility of the situation, Durand went back inside and committed suicide. Powell's Homesteader Museum has lots of old newspaper clippings on this sad story, and the incident inspired *The Legend of Earl Durand*, a minor 1974 movie starring Slim Pickens, Peter Haskell, and Martin Sheen.

clude transportation, a guide, and lunch; the cost depends on the trip length and group size.

Founded in 1946, **Northwest College** is one of the state's top junior colleges. The 124-acre campus has modern brick buildings and fluorescent green lawns (at least in the summer). Northwest is a cultural and social center for Powell and the surrounding area, bringing a variety of theater productions and entertainment, plus art exhibits at the **Northwest Gallery** (307/754-6111 or 800/442-2946, www.northwestcollege.org).

ENTERTAINMENT AND EVENTS

For movies, drop by **Vali Cinema** (204 N. Bent St., 307/754-4211) or, for the outdoor version (a rare treat these days), **American Dream Drive-In Theatre** (1070 Rd. 9, 307/754-5133).

May Fest in early May is a community event with booths, a car show, and Cinco de Mayo fes-

tivities. The popular **Foxtrotter Horse Show and Sale** takes place at the fairgrounds on Father's Day weekend in June. The last full week of July brings the **Park County Fair** (307/754-3494), with parades, pig mud wrestling, 4-H shows, a demolition derby, tractor pulls, a horse pull, dancing, headline acts, and a carnival. **Wings and Wheels** comes to town the third week of August, with a fun fly-in and car show at the airport. If you happen to be in the area on the first weekend of December, stop by for **Country Christmas,** a three-day festivity with activities and craft exhibits as well as a torchlight parade and a parade with lighted floats.

SHOPPING

Basin and Range Book Co. (109 N. Bent, 307/754-4504) is a pleasant little bookshop in the center of town with used (and a few new) titles, plus amazingly thin pottery crafted by the owner's daughter.

Also check out **The Merc** (227 N. Bent, 307/754-5888), a unique clothing store that is co-owned by many locals; they sold 800 shares to start the store in 2002. Down the street and up the stairs is **Rising Sun Art** (129 N. Bent, 307/754-2225), a fun little shop in a sliver of a building.

Get camping and hiking supplies at **War Surplus** (130 N. Bent, 307/754-2694); there always seems to be a surplus of wars, so you might as well buy a couple while you're in town.

RECREATION

Homesteader Park has a kids'll-love-it green frog slide at the wading pool. In winter, there is a free ice arena here with skate rentals and a warming hut. The public **swimming pool** is in the high school. The 18-hole **Powell Golf Club** (307/754-3039 or 800/325-4278) is five miles east of town.

ACCOMMODATIONS

Although it is just 24 miles from Cody, travelers will find distinctly less expensive accommodations in Powell. **Best Choice Motel** (337 E. 2nd St., 307/754-2243 or 800/308-8447, $45–55 d) has microwaves and fridges in all rooms. **Lamplighter Inn** (234 1st St., 307/754-2226, $59–79 d) is another affordable choice. Similarly priced is **Park Motel** (737 E. 2nd St., 307/754-2233, $60–68 s or $70–95 d), with comfortable rooms, half of which contain fridges and microwaves.

Nicest in town is **King's Inn** (777 E. 2nd St., 307/754-5117 or 800/441-7778, $69–77 d), with a seasonal heated outdoor pool and fridges in all rooms.

Camping

Park County Fairgrounds (307/754-5421, open mid-Apr.–mid-Sept.) has RV sites ($15) and shower facilities. RVers park for free (no hookups) at the highway rest area in the 57-acre **Homesteader Park** on the east end of town. You can also pitch a tent on the grass here, but the sprinklers come on at night. Open all year.

FOOD

Start your day with an espresso from **Parlor News Coffeehouse** (135 E. 2nd St., 307/754-0717). It's a cozy spot to relax; stop by for ice cream on a warm summer afternoon. Meet the locals for breakfast at **Skyline Family Dining** (141 E. Coulter, 307/754-2772), where you'll also find a mean chicken-fried steak for dinner, a decent salad bar, and breakfast buffets on Saturday and Sunday mornings.

Powell Drug (140 N. Bent, 307/754-2031) has an old-fashioned soda fountain where the root-beer floats, malts, and cheeseburgers still attract kids.

In business since 1973, **Hansel and Gretel's** (113 S. Bent, 307/754-2191) serves spaghetti, soups, sandwiches, and delicious homemade pies. Head to **El Tapatio** (112 N. Bent, 307/754-8085) for good south-of-the-border eats.

The **Lamplighter Inn** (at the corner of 1st and Clark, 307/754-2226) is the fanciest place in town, with sandwiches, burgers, and daily specials for lunch, along with prime rib, steaks, chicken, and seafood for dinner.

Chinatown Restaurant (151 E. Coulter, 307/754-7924) has surprisingly good Asian food to eat in or take out, and big buffets for lunch ($6) or dinner ($9) weekdays.

Pick up groceries at **Blair's Market** (311 W. Coulter Ave., 307/754-3122) or **Food Basket IGA** (421 E. 1st, 307/754-3602). Blair's contains a good deli and bakery.

INFORMATION AND SERVICES

The **Powell Valley Chamber of Commerce** (111 S. Day, 307/754-3494 or 800/325-4278, www.powellchamber.org) is open 8 A.M.–5 P.M. Monday–Friday year-round. Pick up its walking-tour map for historical tidbits on downtown Powell. If you're driving west, fill your tank in Powell since gas prices in Cody are usually substantially higher.

Relax with a book or surf the web at **Powell Public Library** (217 E. 3rd, 307/754-2261) or the **John Hinkley Memorial Library** on the Northwest College campus (307/754-6207). (No, it isn't named for the man who shot President Reagan.)

GETTING THERE

Powder River Transportation (307/682-1888 or 800/442-3682, http://gillette.coachusa.us) has daily bus service to Powell, providing connections to central and eastern Wyoming, Denver, Billings, and Rapid City.

EAST TO LOVELL

A tangle of roads wanders through the country between Lovell and Powell, tying together a cluster of agricultural and oil settlements established by Mormon emigrants in the early 1900s.

Cowley

This settlement of fewer than 600 people has several impressive old sandstone buildings. One of the nicest—built in 1909—began as the Mormon stake office and tithing building, but it now houses the town office and **Pioneer Museum** (307/548-7700, open 9 A.M.–1 P.M. Mon., Wed., and Fri.). Not far away is another stone building built by the LDS that same year—**Big Horn Academy**—and a beautiful **Log Community Building** constructed in 1933 by the Works Progress Administration. The local event is **Pioneer Day** in late July.

Cowtown Cafe (307/548-2990) serves daily

specials, homemade pies, and gargantuan cinnamon rolls. Ask for directions to ancient Indian petroglyphs north of town in Blue Wash.

Other Towns

Byron (pop. 560) has quite a few old log buildings and is surrounded by dairy farms and oil wells.

Just two miles south of the Montana border on U.S. 310, **Frannie** (pop. 200) straddles the line between Park and Big Horn counties. Residents say it's "The Biggest Little Town in Wyoming because it takes two counties to hold the people." Stop by **Frannie Tack Shop** (307/548-2344 or 800/552-8836) to see the saddles.

Deaver has a population of 180 folks, and the main attractions are the bright red general store (built in 1919) and the new playground.

The dot of a place called **Garland** (pop. 100) is home to a boxy old schoolhouse (now occupied by a church) that was built in the early 1900s.

Just east of Lovell, the pungent odors of sulfur and oil hang in the air, and the dry badlands are punctuated by oil pumpjacks in the large Byron Oil Field, discovered in 1918. The other business here is farming. Much of this desert land is now under irrigation, and the lush green farmlands are filled with sugar beets, beans, malting barley, alfalfa, and corn. A sign along U.S. 14A notes the **Sidon Canal,** built in 1900 by Mormon settlers of the Bighorn Basin. The 37-mile-long canal was entirely self-financed with land donated by the government and transports water from the Shoshone River to 20,000 acres of farmland. Mormons claim that Prayer Rock, a large impediment to the canal's construction, was miraculously split as a result of their supplications.

Lovell and Vicinity

The sleepy little burg of Lovell (pop. 2,300; LOVE-ul) calls itself the "City of Roses," a title that comes from Dr. William Horsley, who lived here from 1924 until his death in 1971. Horsley loved roses and in the course of a lifetime of cultivating them became one of the nation's foremost authorities. The "Rose Doctor's" enthusiasm rubbed off on others, and today gardens around town are packed with roses. Oil fields surround Lovell, and a Georgia Pacific wallboard plant and two bentonite plants are substantial local employers, but farming is king. The Western Sugar factory stands on the edge of town, providing jobs for workers and a market for local farmers who contract with the plant to grow sugar beets. In late fall, huge mounds of straw-covered beets pile up beside the factory, and the rancid/sweet odor of cooking beets fills the air. Stray beets, spilled from overloaded farm trucks, lie along the highway for miles.

Downtown Lovell seems to specialize in empty storefronts, and the settlement doesn't offer much for tourists. It's one of the few towns in Wyoming without a museum and is known for an insular attitude toward outsiders, but the surrounding country includes fascinating Bighorn Canyon National Recreation Area and the majestic Big Horn Mountains. A state-run fish-rearing station at Tillett Springs, 17 miles north of Lovell, raises cutthroat and rainbow trout.

Like most towns in the northern Bighorn Basin, Lovell is dominated by Mormons. An enormous brick Latter-day Saints church fills an entire block along the main drag and is often mistaken for an imposing office building. Lovell has wide, clean streets crowded with summertime flower boxes.

History

The town of Lovell has its roots in the enormous ML Ranch, founded in 1880 by Anthony L. Mason and Henry Clay Lovell (see *Bighorn Canyon National Recreation Area*). In 1900, Mormon settlers moved to the remote Bighorn Basin (partly to escape prosecution for polygamy), working on the Burlington

Railroad and developing irrigation projects. The area boomed with the discovery of natural gas and the opening of various factories. A few years later, German emigrants provided labor for the farm fields and then settled down to acquire their own land. Yellowtail Dam on the Bighorn River was built in 1965, and the surrounding land became a national recreation area the following year.

Lovell is said to have the lowest crime rate in Wyoming, but nowhere in the tourist brochures does the city mention the history of two of its most prominent doctors. A few years before his 1971 death, Dr. William Horsley, the famed "Rose Doctor," was forced to resign from the local hospital after a series of homosexual incidents with boys. (You *definitely* won't read this in the glowing stories about Horsley's life in the local press.) But another respected physician, Dr. John Story, gained considerably more notoriety for his actions. Story arrived in 1958 to practice general medicine, joined the local Baptist church, and became a strong conservative community·leader. Unfortunately, during the next 25 years he also raped or molested dozens (some say hundreds) of women and girls in his office. A combination of strict Mormon upbringing, sexual ignorance, shame, and fear prevented the victims from talking, and the few who did speak up were called liars. Finally, in 1983, the charges began to surface. The trial turned Lovell inside out. Despite intense pressure from local and state politicians (then-Governor Ed Herschler called the victims' testimony "hogwash"), Story was convicted in April 1985 on several rape charges and served 20-year sentence in the Wyoming State Penitentiary. Jack Olson's harrowing book, *Doc,* describes this sorry chapter in Wyoming history.

ENTERTAINMENT AND EVENTS

Hy Art (307/548-7021) is Lovell's movie palace.

The big annual event in Lovell is **Mustang Days,** held the last full week in June. Activities include a parade, fireworks, barbecue, a follies show, rodeo, and demolition derby.

RECREATION

You'll find an Olympic-size indoor **swimming pool** (307/548-6466) and other recreation facilities on the southwest end of town. **Foster Gulch Golf Course** (307/548-2445) is a nine-hole course in the same area.

ACCOMMODATIONS
Motels

Cattleman Motel (470 Montana Ave., 307/548-2296, $36 s or $42–48 d) has budget lodging off the main drag, plus an outdoor hot tub. **Horseshoe Bend Motel** (375 E. Main St., 307/548-2221 or 800/548-2850) has comfortable rooms (most with microwaves and fridges) along with a heated outdoor pool, gazebo, grill, and picnic tables. Standard rooms sleep four for $65, and kitchenettes run $58 d. **Super 8 Motel** (595 E. Main St., 307/548-2725 or 800/800-8000, www.super8.com, $53–60 s or $64–68 d) has predictable rooms and a continental breakfast.

Guest Ranches

A 45,000-acre cattle ranch, the **TX Ranch** (406/484-2583, www.txranch.com) offers a unique chance to take part in the cowboy life. It isn't a dude ranch, and visitors end up joining in during spring or fall cattle drives, branding calves and doing roundups. You'll be riding 6–10 hours per day here, and you'll stay in wall tents at the cow camps. There are no electricity, phones, TVs, fax machines, or other modern conveniences to interfere with a real Old West adventure. The ranch is primarily in Montana, but some of the operation is in Wyoming. All-inclusive weekly rates are $2,100 for two people. There's a seven-day minimum stay, for a maximum of 18 guests. Open mid-April–mid-October.

The **Dryhead Ranch** (307/548-6688, www .dryheadranch.com) is a 30,000-acre ranch on the eastern side of the Pryor Mountains and just across the Montana border. Guests can take part in a 50-mile cattle drive each spring or fall, or help in a variety of ranch chores at other times. It's a great way to learn about the real West. One-week rates are $2,200 for two people all-inclusive, $2,600 for two people during the cattle drives. Unique are the horse drives in spring and fall, when you can help move a herd of horses into or out of the mountains; $3,000 for two people. There's room for a maximum of 14 guests in rustic cabins with a central bathhouse. The guest ranch is open mid-April–October.

Camping

The best campsites in the Lovell area lie within nearby Bighorn Canyon National Recreation Area ($5); closest is Horseshoe Bend Campground, 14 miles from Lovell. In town, camp for free (including showers) at **Lovell Camper Park** on Quebec Avenue north of Main Street. It's a quiet place surrounded by cottonwoods. RVers can pay to stay behind the Super 8 Motel at **Camp Big Horn RV Park** (595 E. Main St., 307/548-2725, $15 tents, $22 RVs, open all year).

FOOD

Lange's Kitchen (483 Shoshone Ave., 307/548-9370) is popular for breakfast and lunch. For pizzas, run across the street to **Pizza on the Run** (307/548-2206).

Queen Bee Honey Candy (262 Main St., 307/548-2543 or 800/225-7553, www.queen-beegardens.com) harvests its own honey to create a variety of unique and supersweet candies, available at the shop or mail order. Drop by to see the folks here at work or for a sample.

Get groceries and deli food at **Red Apple Supermarket** (9 E. Main St., 307/548-9907), which also houses a War Memorial.

INFORMATION AND SERVICES

For local attractions, visit the **Lovell Information Center** (287 E. Main, 307/548-7552, www.lovellchamber.com). Hours are 8:30 A.M.–4:30 P.M. Monday–Friday late May–early September, and 8:30 A.M.–12:30 P.M. Monday–Friday the rest of the year.

Bighorn National Forest's **Medicine Wheel/Paintrock Ranger District Office** (604 E. Main, 307/548-6541, www.fs.fed.us/r2/bighorn) has information on the Medicine Wheel and Bighorn National Forest.

The town **library** is at 3rd Street and Oregon Avenue, 307/548-7228, and the **post office** is at 167 West 3rd, 307/548-7605. Wash clothes at **Mustang Laundry** (340 E. Montana Ave.). **North Big Horn Hospital** (115 La. 12, 307/548-2271, www.nbhh.com) has physicians on staff.

GETTING THERE

Powder River Transportation (307/682-1888 or 800/442-3682, http://gillette.coachusa.us) stops in Lovell, providing daily bus connections to central and eastern Wyoming, Denver, Billings, and Rapid City.

◖ BIGHORN CANYON NATIONAL RECREATION AREA

Just east of Lovell is one of America's lesser-known but most stunning sights, Bighorn Canyon. Through the eons, the Bighorn River has slowly carved out a 2,200-foot-deep chasm through the desert country. Since 1967, when water backed up behind the 525-foot-tall Yellowtail Dam, the canyon has lain under a deep blanket of water—water that provides 250,000 kilowatts of electricity for the western United States and irrigates thousands of acres of Montana farmland. The dam itself is—as the raven flies—more than 20 miles north of the Wyoming–Montana border, but its impact reaches 70 river miles upstream, creating Bighorn Lake.

The 120,000-acre Bighorn Canyon National Recreation Area (307/548-2251, www.nps.gov/bica) is managed by the National Park Service. A $5 per-vehicle entrance fee is charged, and it's good for 24 hours from the time of purchase. An annual Bighorn Canyon pass is $30, or pay $65 for a National Park Pass that provides access to all Park Service areas. The fee (or pass) covers camping, boat launching, hiking, and other activities in the recreation area.

Separate facilities on both ends of the recreation area are linked by a circuitous 180-mile route that takes you through Billings, Montana. (A shorter route includes 18 miles of gravel road.) Because of the distances, most road-bound visitors come to either the Montana side or the

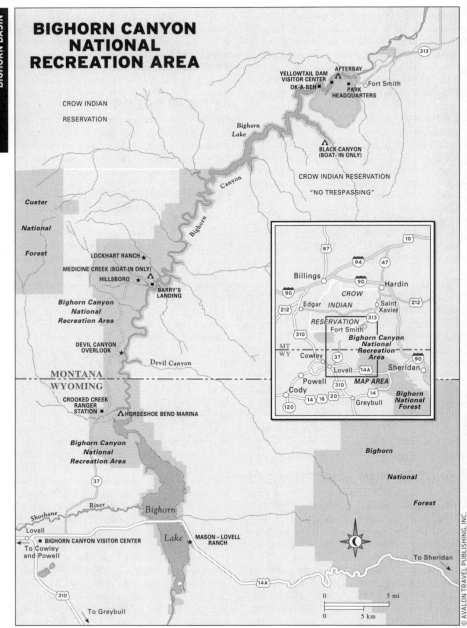

BIGHORN CANYON NATIONAL RECREATION AREA

CROW INDIAN
RESERVATION

YELLOWTAIL DAM
VISITOR CENTER
OK-A-BEH
AFTERBAY
PARK
HEADQUARTERS
Fort Smith

Bighorn
Lake

BLACK CANYON
(BOAT-IN ONLY)

Canyon

CROW INDIAN RESERVATION

"NO TRESPASSING"

Custer

National

Forest

Bighorn

LOCKHART RANCH
MEDICINE CREEK (BOAT-IN ONLY)
HILLSBORO
BARRY'S
LANDING

Bighorn Canyon
National
Recreation Area

DEVIL CANYON
OVERLOOK

Devil Canyon

MONTANA
WYOMING

CROOKED CREEK
RANGER
STATION
HORSESHOE BEND MARINA

Bighorn Canyon
National
Recreation Area

37

Shoshone

River

Bighorn

Lovell

Lake
MASON – LOVELL
RANCH

BIGHORN CANYON VISITOR CENTER
To Cowley
and Powell

310

To Greybull

0   5 mi

0   5 km

Inset map

10

87

94

47

Billings
90
Hardin

90
CROW

212
Edgar
INDIAN
Saint
Xavier
212

313

RESERVATION
Fort Smith

310
Bighorn Canyon
National
Recreation
Area

MT
WY
Cowley
37
90

Powell
Lovell
14A
Sheridan

MAP AREA

Cody
310

120
14 16   20
14

Greybull
Bighorn
National
Forest

Bighorn

National

Forest

To Sheridan

© AVALON TRAVEL PUBLISHING, INC.

Wyoming side but not both. Boaters can traverse the entire reach of the canyon.

Attractions accessible only from Montana include a visitor center at the dam (406/666-2412), a short nature trail, and the site of two Bozeman Trail features: Fort C. F. Smith and the Hayfield Fight (both on private land).

From the Wyoming side, things are considerably more interesting, even though some of the sights actually lie across the Montana border. A paved road extends 27 miles along the western side of the recreation area, with a rough dirt road continuing 15 more miles to the Crow Indian Reservation. Along the way are a couple of campgrounds, the historic Bad Pass Trail, two old ranches, magnificent Bighorn Canyon, and a good chance to see bighorn sheep and wild horses. The road cuts through impressive red and gray badlands carpeted by juniper, sagebrush, and mountain mahogany.

Devil Canyon Area

The pièce de résistance of Bighorn Canyon National Recreation Area is **Devil Canyon Overlook,** where Devil Canyon joins Bighorn Canyon. From the overlook, the earth drops suddenly away. More than 1,000 feet below, motorboats look like miniature toys in a bathtub. A real treat in the canyon is the chance to see **bighorn sheep** up close; more than 100 of these majestic animals live in the national recreation area. Although the more impressive rams tend to hang out in remote parts of the Pryor Mountains in the summer, you can spot ewes and lambs along the road between the state line and Layout Creek. The rams are more likely to be seen during the November–December rutting season, but some will probably be visible until late May.

Precipitous Bighorn Canyon was known as **Bad Pass** by the Indians. The trail they used to reach the buffalo herds followed the canyon rim for many miles and was marked by rock cairns. Some of these cairns are still visible between Devil Canyon Overlook and Barry's Landing, as are some of the caves where they wintered near the canyon bottoms.

Before it was dammed, the river offered a

© DON PITCHER

More than 100 bighorn sheep live in the national recreation area.

torrent of rushing rapids and falls, with jagged rocks waiting to punch holes in any boat and a canyon so deep that the sun reached the bottom for only a few hours each day. In 1825, the famed mountain man and guide Jim Bridger decided to take a wooden raft down the canyon to see if it could provide a way to ship furs back east. It was a feat that was not matched for many decades, when a motorboat finally ran the wild currents.

Hillsboro

The ghost settlement of Hillsboro is about one mile above Barry's Landing and is accessible only by foot. Established around the turn of the 20th century by a self-proclaimed physician, Grosverner William Barry, the site was originally promoted as a gold-mining center. When that didn't pan out (they didn't get enough gold to pay for the operation of a dredge), he turned to dude ranching and promoted his ranch as a place where guests could cruise through Bighorn Canyon in motorboats or ride his English Hackney horses. The dude ranch flourished until the 1930s, but the collection of antique furniture and paintings was destroyed by a fire in the winter of 1947–1948. Still standing are the old post office and various cabins.

ML Ranch

The great ML Ranch was founded in 1883 by Anthony L. Mason and Henry Clay Lovell. Lovell trailed herds of cattle up from Kansas to this newly opened country, building his main headquarters along the Bighorn River just east of the community that was later named for him. The vast unfenced ranch became known as the "Big Outfit" and employed hundreds of cowhands. Grazed by 25,000 cattle, it stretched from Thermopolis all the way to the Crow Reservation in Montana, 90 miles away.

Most of the buildings from the old ML Ranch are now gone, but you can still visit the restored bunkhouse, the blacksmith shop, and two cabins. Most interesting is the bunkhouse—actually three cabins connected by dogtrots (covered breezeways). The end cabins acted as sleeping quarters, the middle one as a

cook shack and mess hall. Get here by heading east from Lovell across the bridge over Bighorn Lake. A sign points out the ranch.

Lockhart Ranch

The Lockhart Ranch was where writer Caroline Lockhart lived off and on from 1926 until 1955. North of the Barry's Landing area, it's accessible via a two-mile dirt road. The road is fine for cars but not advised for large RVs. A 0.25-mile path leads down to the ranch, where you'll find more than a dozen log buildings set among the cottonwoods and box elder trees along Davis Creek (a.k.a. Medicine Creek). It's a fascinating and bucolic place to explore. (See the sidebar *Caroline Lockhart* to learn more about her life.)

Other Sights

Adjacent to the Bighorn Canyon National Recreation Area is the 19,424-acre **Yellowtail Wildlife Habitat Management Unit** (307/548-6650), a popular place for hunters and birdwatchers. Many dirt roads and trails crisscross the area, and wildlife of all types abounds. During fall migration, the wetlands here are jammed with up to 10,000 ducks. The Park Service and Wyoming Game and Fish departments cooperatively manage the land, and maps of Yellowtail roads and trails are available at the Bighorn Canyon Visitor Center.

Caves create a latticework under sections of the recreation area. On the east side of Bighorn Lake is **Bighorn Caverns.** Access is limited to experienced spelunkers and requires 4WD vehicles; get the gate key and directions at the Bighorn Canyon Visitor Center. Not far away is **Horsethief Cave.** Although closed to the public, **Natural Trap Cave** is of paleontological value. Thirty-five miles northeast of Lovell, a 12- by 15-foot opening drops into the 80-foot-deep cavern. Through the centuries many animals—from prehistoric horses to rabbits—have fallen in here.

Hiking

Although there are only a few trails in Bighorn Canyon, the open badlands country makes hiking relatively easy. Some trails lead to spec-

CAROLINE LOCKHART

The West overflows with famous men, but women sometimes get unjustly shunted aside in the accolades. One of the most interesting was Caroline Lockhart (1871-1962), a woman who began her career as an actress but turned quickly to journalism as a writer for a Boston newspaper. Using the pen name "Suzette," she became one of the country's first female newspaper reporters. The job led her into all sorts of adventures, from entering a circus cage with a lion that had killed his trainer the previous day to testing the Boston Fire Department's new fire nets by jumping out of a fourth-story hotel window. When she heard of a "Home for Intemperate Women" where the women were being severely mistreated, Caroline decided to investigate by posing as a derelict. She got her story all right, but it took considerable convincing from her editor to get her out. "Release!" shouted the matron running the house. "We can't! She's not cured yet." One of Lockhart's most lasting impacts was the creation of Mother's Day. Although Anna Jarvis came up with the concept, Caroline Lockhart made it a reality by tirelessly promoting the idea in the newspapers.

In 1904, Lockhart took a bold step. After an interview with Buffalo Bill Cody in the town named for him, she decided to move to Wyoming. She bought the local newspaper, the *Cody Enterprise*, and quickly made a name for herself as a crusader against Prohibition and "game hogs" (hunters who killed everything in sight). She also founded the Cody Stampede, the big annual event in Bighorn Basin. Lockhart wrote seven novels, including *The Lady Doc*, a book that managed to ruffle local feathers with its too-close-to-the-truth descriptions of real-life Cody people. Despite this controversy, her witty, humorous, and insightful writing gained a national reputation.

In 1925, she sold the *Cody Enterprise* and acquired a ranch that eventually included 7,000 acres of land along the Bighorn River north of Lovell, dividing her time between her Cody home (now the Lockhart Bed and Breakfast) and her ranch. She died at the age of 92. Today her old ranch lies within Bighorn Canyon National Recreation Area.

---

tacular canyon rim overviews. Best times are in the fall or in February and March, when temperatures are milder and you're less likely to meet a rattler. Prairie rattlesnakes and black widow spiders are both common in this desert country, so be aware, especially when exploring old buildings. Ask at the visitor center for its free booklet detailing 10 local places to hike in Bighorn Canyon. In addition to the trails listed, you can also hike the mile-long dirt path to the ghost town of Hillsboro.

Crooked Creek Nature Trail, a 0.5-mile path with self-guiding brochures, takes off from the Horseshoe Bend campground. The appropriately named **State Line Trail** is an easy one-mile hike that starts just north of the Montana state line. Rock cairns mark the path through juniper forests to the canyon rim for dramatic vistas. **Sullivan's Knob Trail** is another delightful one-mile hike that leads to the canyon rim. The rock cairn–marked route starts one mile north of the Devil Canyon Overlook and cuts along the base of a geological feature called Sullivan's Knob. **Upper Layout Creek Trail** is another interesting two-mile (each way) path. It starts five miles north of the turnoff for Devil Canyon Overlook and follows an old road along the creek before entering Layout Creek Canyon. The route isn't well marked once you get off the road, but you just follow the creek uphill.

On the Water

Most visitors come to Bighorn Canyon to play on the water. You'll see lots of people tooling around in powerful boats, towing water-skiers, trolling for fish, or sailboarding. Fishing is the biggest attraction; walleye, rainbow, and brown trout, yellow perch, ling, crappie, and catfish are commonly caught. Because the lake straddles the state line, you'll need a fishing license for whichever state you are in. If you fish both sides of the border, you'll need to buy licenses for both Wyoming and Montana. Launch ramps are at Barry's Landing and Horseshoe Bend, plus Ok-A-Beh Marina at the north end of the lake. Swimmers hang out at the Horseshoe Bend beach, the only place with a lifeguard; check with the visitor center to see when one is on duty.

Droughts are common in Wyoming, and when they occur lake levels may be too low for boating or other water activities. But as locals like to say, it is always a fluid situation (ha, ha), so call the National Recreation Area for the latest.

Ok-A-Beh Marina (406/665-2349), on the Montana side, has limited fishing supplies, plus food, boat gas, and boat rentals. Hours are 10 A.M.–7 P.M. Monday–Friday and 8 A.M.–8 P.M. Saturday–Sunday Memorial Day–Labor Day.

Camping

There are three campgrounds in the southern half of Bighorn Canyon and two in the northern half. No extra charge to camp; it's included in your $5 entrance fee. Folks in RVs park at **Horseshoe Bend,** which has water, toilets, picnic tables, a playground, and shelters to ward off the wind and sun. The rocky surface and windy conditions make this a challenging place for anyone in a tent. The drive in to Horseshoe Bend passes lovely red sandstone badlands. Campfire programs are generally offered at Horseshoe Bend amphitheater on Saturday evenings in the summer.

Barry's Landing Campground has fewer sites but is a much nicer place to stay. Bring your own water. RVers can park overnight above the boat ramp. Firewood is usually available at both Horseshoe Bend and Barry's Landing. In addition, you can pitch a tent at **Medicine Creek Campground,** although you'll need to hike in along a two-mile dirt road or float in by boat.

Backcountry camping is available throughout the southern end of the recreation area; check at the visitor center for current restrictions and access information. Also be sure to avoid trespassing on the nearby Crow Indian Reservation.

Information

For a good orientation to the area, stop by **Bighorn Canyon Visitor Center** (307/548-2251, www.nps.gov/bica, open 8 A.M.–6 P.M. daily Memorial Day–Labor Day, and 8:30 A.M.–5 P.M. daily the rest of the year; closed Thanksgiving, Christmas, and New Year's Day), just east of Lovell along U.S. 14A. The solar-heated center is an attraction in itself; 70 percent of its heat comes directly from the sun. Inside are a three-dimensional relief map of the canyon, displays on local animals, books and topo maps for sale, and movies on Bighorn Canyon, Pryor Mountain Wild Horse Range, and Medicine Wheel. Check the notice board for other talks or hikes in the recreation area, including the weekend **campfire programs** at Horseshoe Bend Campground (summer only). Be sure to pick up a copy of *Canyon Echoes,* the free visitor guide with current information. A ranger station is at Crooked Creek, just south of the Horseshoe Bend junction. The **Ewing-Snell Historical Site** at Layout Creek contains a restored one-room schoolhouse.

PRYOR MOUNTAIN WILD HORSE RANGE

Pryor Mountain Wild Horse Range covers almost 40,000 acres on the western side of Bighorn Canyon. Established in 1968 as the nation's first public wild horse range, it is managed by the Bureau of Land Management (406/896-5013, www.wildhorseandburro.blm.gov). Pryor Mountain's desert country supports three subherds, and periodic roundups keep the population near the carrying capacity of around 100 horses. Most horses remain out of sight in remote box canyons, but you're likely to see some relatively tame ones along the road between Horseshoe Bend and Layout Creek Ranger Station. Two other wild horse ranges also exist, in Nevada and Colorado, and there are another 3,000 wild horses in the Red Desert of southwestern Wyoming.

All together, the BLM manages more than 38,000 wild horses across the West.

Most "wild horses" of the West are of mixed origin. Some are primarily domestic horses that were released into the wild by local ranchers, but many others can trace at least some of their bloodlines to Spanish mustangs brought to the New World in the 16th century. Studies of wild horses have found that the mustangs at Pryor Mountain are the most uniformly Spanish of any wild horse herd in America, although there is some intermixing from more recent breeds. This Spanish influence is exhibited in the distinctive colors that include dun, blue roan, *grulla,* and *sabino.* Many have dark manes and tails. Other common characteristics are dark leg stripes and a dorsal stripe running down the back.

Before protection of the wild horses, many were rounded up for use on ranches or for the pet-food industry. After 1971, when it became illegal to harass or kill wild horses, their numbers began to grow rapidly. Each year's colt crop increases the herd by 20 percent, placing increasing demands on a limited forage supply. Today, the BLM controls numbers through its adopt-a-horse program, removing 40–50 horses every few years from Pryor Mountain and offering them to the public. Contact the BLM for details on adopting a wild horse.

The **Pryor Mountain Wild Mustang Center** (307/548-9453, www.pryormustangs.org) was planning to open a small visitor center on land adjacent to the Park Service's Bighorn Canyon Visitor Center.

Greybull

For travelers en route to Yellowstone, the crossroads town of Greybull (pop. 1,800) is a splotch of irrigated green surrounded by desert country. Greybull lies near the junction of Shell Creek and the Bighorn River and at the intersection of U.S. 14 and 16/20. As such, it is both an agricultural center and a commercial center. Most of the town lies along the western shore of the river behind a long levee; barren rocky bluffs line the opposite bank. There are bentonite processing plants just north of town, oil pumpjacks farther afield, and irrigated farms along the river. Tip: If you're heading west to Cody and Yellowstone, fill up here because gas prices get more expensive as you approach the mountains.

The land around Greybull was first settled in the 1880s by stockmen, with several hundred Mormon homesteaders moving in a decade later to dig irrigation ditches and establish the minuscule farming settlements of **Burlington** (pop. 250) and **Otto** along the Greybull River. Nearby **Emblem** was established by 600 German farmers in the late 1890s. A diversion of the Greybull River was begun in 1895, the first reclamation project

under the Carey Act. Originally called Germania, the name was changed to Emblem (a reference to the American flag) during the anti-German hysteria of World War I.

The origins of the name Greybull are unclear, although the town was named for the nearby Greybull River. Some say that it was named for a huge albino buffalo that once roamed this country. A more likely explanation is that the river was named after a Crow Indian medicine man, named Chief Grey Bull, who spent considerable time in the area.

The town is primarily a creation of the Burlington Railroad in 1909–1910, but much of its growth has been fueled by oil and gas developments in the surrounding country. Completion of U.S. 14 across the Big Horn Mountains in the 1930s brought tourists and led to Greybull's development as a way station for folks heading east to the Black Hills or west to Yellowstone. Beginning in 1934, scientists excavated a dozen complete skeletons of dinosaurs near Greybull, and in 1991 Swiss paleontologists excavated one of the largest allosauruses ever found; it's now at the university's geology museum in Laramie. The railroad is still a major employer in

Greybull, as are two bentonite plants, along with Hawkins and Powers Aviation. The town isn't exactly prosperous, but it makes a quiet resting point en route to Cody or Yellowstone.

SIGHTS
Greybull Museum
The local museum is in the same building as the library (325 Greybull Ave., 307/765-2444). It's open 10 A.M.–8 P.M. Monday–Friday and 10 A.M.–6 P.M. Saturday June–September, 1–5 P.M. Monday–Friday in the spring and fall, and 1–5 P.M. Monday, Wednesday, and Friday in the winter. No charge. Inside are agate collections and polished petrified-wood pieces, a fine fossil collection that includes one of the largest fossil ammonites ever found, fossil turtles, and dinosaur bones. Also here are various Indian arrowheads and other historical artifacts, including a New England church made from royal icing!

Museum of Flight and Aerial Firefighting
South Big Horn County Airport, atop a hill just north of town, is the home of Hawkins and Powers Aviation, for many years a major source of planes used to drop fire retardant on forest fires throughout the West, including three of the four PB4Y-2s still able to fly. During World War II, PB4Ys played an important role in routing the Japanese from the South Pacific. Hawkins and Powers planes appeared in several movies, including the Steven Spielberg firefighting film *Always,* in which a C-119 was used. The company experienced disastrous losses in 2002 when two of its air tankers—a PB4Y-2 and a C-130—crashed while fighting fires. Five crew members perished and the company was forced to reorganize. Today it is busy repairing C-130s and other aircraft for the Air Force.

Fourteen retired aircraft are included in a display behind the rest area and just west of the airport. It's called the Museum of Flight and Aerial Firefighting (307/765-4322, www.tctwest.net/~flight, open 9 A.M.–5 P.M. daily May–Sept., donation). Tours are available of the old aircraft—including planes used

© DON PITCHER

fire-fighting aircraft at the Museum of Flight and Aerial Firefighting in Greybull in fighting fires and three C-97 Deliverances that were part of the Berlin airlift. If it's closed, you can always look through the fence.

Other Attractions

Five miles northeast of Greybull is **Devil's Kitchen,** a fascinating arroyo filled with brilliantly colored badlands and many fossils. Get a map and directions from the chamber of commerce and follow it closely; the last turn-off is easy to miss.

Sheep Mountain, a 15-mile-long hogback of eroded land just north of Greybull, is a favorite of geologists, who marvel at this fossil-packed anticline. Photographers love the vivid reds, browns, and yellows of this desert landscape. A bit farther afield is the Red Gulch Dinosaur Tracksite (see the *Shell Valley* section for details on this important discovery).

A couple of **Indian petroglyphs** are 0.5 mile north of town and just east on a dirt road. Look for the bluff across from the bentonite plant, where you'll see a bison with an arrow in it and a couple of human figures, along with more recent graffiti and gunshots courtesy of jerks.

You'll find an attractive flower garden in the shape of the Wyoming state flag at the west end of Greybull Avenue. Folks traveling with children should make a detour to the **city park,** with its extensive play area, skateboard park, picnic tables and grills, jogging path, restrooms, and a lonely chimney from the first house built in Greybull.

ENTERTAINMENT AND EVENTS

For live music, try **Smokehouse Saloon** (562 Greybull Ave., 307/765-2232) or **Silver Spur** (445 Greybull Ave., 307/765-2300). A favorite of bikers, the Smokehouse has a 19th-century cherry-wood back bar, plus pool tables, darts, and pub grub.

Greybull's big annual event is **Days of '49**—1949 that is—held the second weekend in June. There's a top-notch rodeo, a parade, barbecue in the park, locally famous lawn-mower races, dancing, tug-of-war contests, and demolition derby.

SHOPPING

Probst Western Store (547 Greybull Ave., 307/765-2171 or 888/765-2171) has a great selection of cowboy hats, boots, and Western clothes, plus gifts and jewelry. It's been in business since 1945. A few doors up, **Big Horn Quilts** (532 Greybull Ave., 307/765-2304 or 877/586-9150, www.bighornquilts.com) is a surprisingly complete and bustling quilt shop. The walls are lined with intricate quilts from local artisans, and quilting bees take place every Thursday.

RECREATION

A marvelous **1920s log building** houses the **Greybull Roller Rink** (527 S. 1st Ave., 307/765-2761). Swim and take showers at the **pool** across from the high school (N. 6th St., 307/765-9575). There's also a great kids' **playground and skateboard area** at the city park (3rd Ave. S. and S. 2nd St.). Five miles south of Greybull, **Midway Golf Club** (307/568-9575) is a nine-hole course open to the public.

ACCOMMODATIONS

A Maverik Motel (625 N. 6th St., 307/765-4626, $40–50 s or $45–65 d) is hard to miss, with its odd collection of antique flotsam and jetsam decorating the exterior. The owner found some of these items in the storerooms and when he put them out, neighbors started bringing in more junk till he had more than 500 items. The seven rooms are simple and reasonable, some with efficiencies.

Antler Motel (1116 N. 6th St., 307/765-4404, www.antlermotel.com, $50–65 d) is a quiet place with Western-themed rooms, microwaves, fridges, Wi-Fi, and a fun minigolf course on the front lawn. Comfortable **Greybull Motel** (300 N. 6th St., 307/765-2628, $58–68 d) has microwaves and fridges in most rooms, nicely maintained grounds, with flowers and shade trees. Rooms are all no-smoking.

Yellowstone Motel (247 Greybull Ave., 307/765-4456, www.yellowstonemotel.net, $60–95 d) offers a heated outdoor pool and Wi-Fi, plus fridges and microwaves in the larger rooms.

On the north end of town next to a 24-hour restaurant, **Budget Host Wheels Motel** (1324 N. 6th St., 307/765-2105, www.wheelsmotel.com, $62–72 s or 69–79 d) is one of the better local motels, with attractive rooms (some brand new), many with fridges and recliners.

West of Greybull near the town of Burlington, **Wayfaring Traveler Ranch** (307/762-3536, www.tctwest.net/~wtr) is a working llama ranch (organic produce and an ostrich, too) that offers a secluded guesthouse, guided llama treks to nearby Sheep Mountain, and llama rentals. It's a quiet getaway with more than 40 llamas. The guesthouse has a kitchenette and bath. Up to four guests can stay for $80, and kids are welcome.

Camping
Green Oasis RV Park (540 N. 12th Ave., 307/765-2856 or 888/765-2856, www.greenoasiscampground.com) has tent sites for $17, RV sites for $27. Showers for noncampers cost $5. Open year-round.

Greybull KOA (333 N. 2nd Ave., 307/765-2555 or 800/562-7508, www.koa.com) charges $20 for tent sites, $32–40 for RVs, and has basic cabins for $40 d. Open mid-April–October, with trees, an outdoor heated pool, wireless Internet, and a playground in a quiet setting. Showers are available for noncampers.

FOOD
For family lunches and dinners, it's hard to fault **Buffalo Rose Restaurant** (601 N. 6th St., 307/765-4781). Prices are reasonable ($9–20 dinners), the setting is kid-friendly and smoke-free, and the food is quite good. There are daily specials and homemade pies, plus prime rib Friday and Saturday nights.

Right downtown next to the stoplight, **Uptown Cafe** (536 Greybull Ave., 307/765-2152) is the local greasy spoon, with the best biscuits and gravy in town, plus daily specials and homemade soups and pies. It's smoky—even in the no-smoking section—but dirt cheap: breakfast under $5 and most dinners under $9.

Open 24 hours a day, **Ernesto's Fine Dining** (1336 N. 6th St., 307/765-2456) serves standard American fare, with breakfast at any hour, plus an authentic Mexican menu three meals a day. **Beijing Garden** (510 Greybull Ave., 307/765-9826) serves tasty—and spicy hot—Chinese meals, with more than 100 items on the menu.

Step back in time to the **Sugar Shack** (509 Greybull Ave., 307/765-9650), a 1950s soda fountain and gift shop with banana splits, sundaes, ice cream sodas, lattes, *chai* tea, and locally made items.

Ron's Food Farm (909 N. 6th St., 307/765-2890) has groceries and a deli with hot lunch specials.

INFORMATION AND SERVICES
In the heart of town, **Greybull Chamber of Commerce** (521 Greybull Ave., 307/765-2100 or 877/765-2100, www.greybull.com) is open mornings in summer, with local artwork and handcrafted Western items on display. Check your email at the chamber for free, or use a computer at **Greybull Public Library** (325 Greybull Ave., 307/765-2551).

Find the local **post office** at 401 Greybull Avenue, 307/765-4771. Wash clothes at **Northside Laundromat,** across the street from the A&W on North 6th Street. Four miles south of Greybull, **South Big Horn County Hospital** (307/568-3311) has a 24-hour emergency room.

GETTING THERE
Powder River Transportation (307/682-1888 or 800/442-3682, http://gillette.coachusa.us) has daily bus service to Greybull, providing connections to central and eastern Wyoming, Denver, Billings, and Rapid City.

BASIN
South of Greybull, the highway parallels the Bighorn River. Sharp bluffs rise along the eastern side of the river, and cottonwoods and willows crowd the banks. As you head away from the broad river valley, the endless hills are covered with dry grass, sage, and greasewood. It's a plain-Jane, arid landscape. Eight miles away lies the struggling town of Basin (pop. 1,200), puttering along on its status as

Big Horn County seat and the presence of a large state retirement center. The shady town park has a nice kids' playground.

Established in 1896, the town has always been an agricultural center, with both farming and ranching in the surrounding land. In 1897, a bitter custody battle for the county seat split voters between Basin City, as it was then known, and the older town of Otto. Basin City won by 38 votes.

The first weekend of June brings **Pioneer Expo and Festival** (www.pioneerexpo.com), with a mountain-man rendezvous, demonstrations, chuck wagon breakfast, and races at the fairgrounds.

In early August, Basin hosts the **Big Horn County Fair** (307/568-2968, www.tctwest.net/~bhfair), with livestock judging, pig wrestling, demolition derby, zucchini carving contest, and more small-town fun.

There's an outdoor **swimming pool** at the high school.

Practicalities

The **Lilac Motel** (710 W. C St., 307/568-3355, $39 s or $45 d) has a quiet location off the main drag, along with microwaves and fridges in all rooms.

Park RVs for free next to the Big Horn River boat ramp off the east end of B Street, or pay at **Rose Garden RV Park** (307/568-2589) on the south end of town.

Start your day with a fine breakfast (served anytime) at **Tom's Cafe** (602 S. 4th St., 307/568-2246). Lunch and dinner include such Wyoming favorites as chicken-fried steak, burgers, sandwiches, and a chicken basket with fries and cole slaw. **Wheeler's IGA Market** (114 S. 4th St., 307/568-2325) has groceries and an ATM.

For books, stop by **Big Horn County Library** (103 W. C St., 307/568-2388). Wash clothes at the **launderette** on D and 4th streets.

Powder River Transportation (307/682-1888 or 800/442-3682, http://gillette.coach-usa.us) stops in Basin, providing connections to central and eastern Wyoming, Denver, Billings, and Rapid City.

Manderson

Hwy. 789 heads south from Basin to dinky Manderson (pop. 100), where **Hiway Bar and Cafe** (307/568-2384) has a Sunday buffet and salad bar. South of here the road splits and continues on both sides of Bighorn River to Worland. The main road (on the east side of the river) plays tag with the irrigation ditch much of the way, passing eroded desert bluffs to the east and flat farm country closer to the river. A thin strip of trees runs right down the middle; in fall they look like skeletons against the skyline. Lots of barley, sugar beet, and hayfields can be seen here.

SHELL VALLEY

Shell Valley is farming and ranching country, its lush irrigated hayfields contrasting sharply with the arid landscape to the west. The tiny town called Shell has a country store/bar and several places to stay. Several old log-and-stone buildings are in Shell, including the Community Church, built in 1903. Also from that same era is a distinctive old stone school several miles west of Shell; it served as a one-room school until the 1950s.

Big Horn Wilderness Rides (307/765-9319 or 888/770-8769, www.bighornwildernessrides.com) guides horseback trips from one-day rides to weeklong horseback adventures in the mountains. This a great chance to really experience the Old West.

Head a mile east of Shell for **Dirty Annie's** (307/765-2304) with three meals a day, and **Wagonwheel Restaurant and Lounge** (307/765-2561), with a dinner menu of prime rib, seafood, and steaks. Summer visitors will enjoy the outdoor patio.

Red Gulch and Dinosaur Tracks

The Bureau of Land Management's **Red Gulch/Alkali Scenic Byway** is a 32-mile dirt road through remote and striking country. The northern access point starts on the south side of U.S. 14 four miles west of Shell (10 miles east of Greybull) and is well-marked. The first 10 miles of the byway are the most interesting, with spectacular red badlands of the Chugwater

Formation on both sides of the road. The road gets slick and muddy when wet, so don't venture out after a day of rain. If it hasn't rained in awhile the road is usually passable in a two-wheel-drive vehicle. This is some of the most remote country in Wyoming; even ranches are few and far between. No phones, gas, or other services are available until Hyattville, 32 miles from your starting point. The area is rich in Indian history; tepee rings and pictographs are scattered over the countryside.

Five miles south of the turnoff from U.S. 14 is a parking area (with picnic tables, restrooms, and a wooden walkway) for **Red Gulch Dinosaur Tracksite.** In 1997, geologist Erik Kvale was looking over this area when a relative asked him if dinosaur tracks might be found in this formation. "No," he responded. But when he looked at the rocks at his feet, he corrected himself, "But here is one right in front of me." Dr. Kvale's discovery attracted national attention, and the site has become a major attraction for both paleontologists and anyone interested in dinosaurs. Hundreds of three-toed tracks crisscross more than 40 acres. The tracks were apparently made when theropods (meat-eating dinosaurs) walked in mud along a lakeshore. Most are 2–10 inches in length, fairly shallow, and easiest to see in the low-angled light of morning or dusk. Volunteer guides are at the site 6–8 P.M. Wednesday–Saturday in the summer.

The discovery of these tracks has changed the way paleontologists view the geologic history of Bighorn Basin. Previously it was believed that this entire area had been underwater during the middle Jurassic period (165 million years ago), but these tracks are from land-dwelling dinosaurs. For more information on the tracks and Red Gulch, contact the BLM's Worland Field Office (307/347-5100, www.wy.blm.gov). **Geo-Science Adventures** (307/765-2259 or 866/765-2259, www.geo-sciences.com) conducts multiday educational workshops on regional geology and paleontology, plus informative tours of dinosaur tracksites.

Accommodations
Trapper's Rest Guest Cabin (307/765-9239 or 877/765-5233, $55, open June–Oct.) has two-bedroom cabins with bath; one has a kitchenette. The five-person cabins are three miles southeast of Shell in a peaceful and quiet setting with a tree-lined trout stream nearby. A cook-tent is nearby, complete with a well-supplied kitchen.

At the foot of the Big Horns, **The Hideout at Flitner Ranch** (307/765-2080 or 800/354-8637, www.thehideout.com) is a fifth-generation working cattle ranch in operation since 1906. Exceptionally popular with European travelers in search of a Wild West experience, the ranch has an incredible 250,000 acres of leased or deeded land, so you'll find an abundance of country to explore, from 4,200-foot valleys to 11,000-foot mountain peaks. Guests stay in modern log cabins with all the amenities, including private baths, phones, televisions, wireless Internet, and a hot tub. Activities center on horseback riding, fly-fishing, and trap shooting, and there's an indoor riding arena, along with an airboat for river trips (extra charge). All-inclusive six-night rates are $4,400 for two people in the peak season, and the ranch has space for a maximum of 24 guests. Open late April–October. Also at the ranch is historic **Trapper Creek Lodge,** a luxurious retreat center that is perfect for weddings or business gatherings at $1,200/day. All-inclusive one-week stays in the suites here are $6,400 for two people. Great for folks with their own Lear Jets who can appreciate the ultimate in amenities, including the $3,000 bedspreads.

Wagonwheel Restaurant and Lounge (307/765-2561) has a pair of simple roadside cabins—baths but no TV or phones—two miles east of Shell; $30 d. The restaurant is open for lunch and dinner.

Shell Campground (307/765-9924, www.shellcampground.com, $18 tents, $23 RVs) has year-round shady campsites, along with new duplex cabins with private baths for $55 d. Showers cost $4 for those not camping here. The campground is a base for workers at nearby dinosaur digs, and folks here can set up tours of the dig sites.

HYATTVILLE AREA

Twenty-one miles east of Manderson on Hwy. 31 is the tiny ranching center of Hyattville. Check out the **Hyattville Old-Timers Picnic** on the last weekend of July at nearby Medicine Lodge State Archaeological Site. Bring a salad or dessert and join in the fun; it's been going on for nearly a century.

Built in 1905, **Paintrock Creek Inn** (307/469-2335) has dinners and alcohol, with simple lodging in rooms and a cabin. **Hyattville Cafe** (307/469-2242) is popular for breakfast and lunch.

Medicine Lodge State Archaeological Site

One of Wyoming's most famous archaeological sites, Medicine Lodge (307/469-2234, http://wyoparks.state.wy.us, free) is well worth the detour. Get here by heading north from Hyattville and turning right onto Cold Springs Road. After four miles, turn left again at the "Medicine Lodge" sign and follow the dirt road 1.5 miles to the park (the road gets slippery when it rains).

The main attraction at Medicine Lodge is a 750-foot-long low cliff that served as a backdrop to 10,000 years of Indian settlements. The cliff is covered with dozens of petroglyphs and pictographs. A small log **visitor center**—built a century ago as a cowboy bunkhouse—is open 8 A.M.–5 P.M. Monday–Friday and 9 A.M.–8 P.M. Saturday–Sunday May–Labor Day. Inside are displays on the area's incredibly rich archaeological history. Beginning in 1969, researchers uncovered 60 cultural levels and thousands of artifacts and bones here. It's considered one of the most significant archaeological sites in the West.

A delightful creekside **campground** ($12 for nonresidents or $6 for Wyoming residents) is just a short distance from the petroglyphs and has restrooms, water, and good fishing for brown trout in the creek. Make campsite reservations ($8.50 fee) at 877/996-7275, www.wyopark.com. Wheelchair fishing access is also provided. Ask at the visitor center to pick fruit from the old apple trees next to the cabin.

A 0.75-mile **nature trail** begins near the visitor center, or you can hike up the trail/4WD road along Dry Medicine Lodge Creek. This route passes a natural arch approximately three miles up and goes through a BLM wilderness study area. It's a great place for mountain-biking or a peaceful evening walk.

Staying on Cold Springs Road—instead of turning off to Medicine Lodge State Archaeological Site—takes you 15 miles to Paint Rocks Lakes, a jumping-off point for Cloud Peak Wilderness (see *Big Horn Mountains* in the *Powder River Country* chapter).

Trapper Canyon

North of Hyattville, another interesting place awaits folks willing to do a lot of adventuring. Trapper Canyon, on public land, has colorful walls rising 1,200 feet above Trapper Creek. No trails, and tough access requires serious 4WD vehicles; check with the BLM office in Worland for details.

Worland

The prosperous community of Worland (pop. 5,300) depends on a mixture of agriculture (primarily malt barley and sugar beets), sheep and cattle ranching, oil production, and manufacturing. Sheep glean plowed fields near town, there's a big Coors barley elevator just north of town, and the Wyoming Sugar Company's plant on the southwest edge of Worland provides economic stability, keeping more than 20,000 acres in beets. Ever wonder where cat litter comes from? The Scoop Away bentonite plant is in Worland. Also important is a major aluminum-can factory that produces three million cans per day, and a Pepsi bottling plant that fills many of these. The town has a pleasant Midwestern feel, with nightly baseball games throughout the summer, tree-bordered streets and simple homes in the center, and suburban ranch-style homes spreading across the surrounding countryside. The slow Bighorn River twists its way along the edge of Worland, but just a few miles away is painted-desert country with dry rocky buttes, sagebrush, and sheep.

Worland is named for Charlie "Dad" Worland, one of the first homesteaders in this part of the Bighorn Basin and the manager of a stage station and saloon built along the old Bridger Trail in 1900. It wasn't much to look at—a cave dug into the riverbank, with log walls out front. His bar quickly acquired the nickname "The Hole-in-the-Wall." A cigar box just behind the bar served as the local bank, and anyone needing money could borrow it and leave behind an IOU. Other folks settled around Dad Worland, and A. G. Rupp added a general store nearby, also built into the side of the riverbank to save precious timber. Ray Pendergraft, in *Washakie: A Wyoming County History*, relates the following story about early Worland:

> Once a compactly-built man rode into the settlement, refreshed himself at Worland's saloon, then went on to Rupps for some supplies. On one wall of the store
> was a poster, complete with a picture. It read, "$5,000 Reward, Dead or Alive Robert Leroy Parker, alias Butch Cassidy." The visitor examined it. "It's not a very good likeness," he told Rupp. Rupp examined the poster, looked at the man, and readily agreed. "You don't want it up there do you, Mr. Rupp?" the man politely asked. "No, I don't," replied Mr. Rupp. "I'll take it down for you," the man said, did so and went on about his selection of supplies.

Originally on the western side of the Bighorn River, Worland moved to the other side after the Chicago, Burlington, and Quincy Railroad announced plans to build along the east bank. The nucleus of Worland, 10 buildings, was slid across the river on the ice during the winter of 1905–1906. The following year, construction was finished on the 54-mile-long Big Horn irrigation canal, opening 30,000 acres to agriculture. It had been begun almost 20 years earlier. A new sugar beet processing plant in 1917 attracted more farmers and workers from the Midwest and many Germans and Ukrainians. The discovery of oil in the Hidden Dome Field in that same year brought boom times as speculators flooded the area. Oil and agriculture, especially sugar beets, have remained important ever since, although oil production has declined while natural gas production increases.

SIGHTS

Housed in an old Mormon church, the **Washakie Museum** (1115 Obie Sue Ave., 307/347-4102, www.washakiemuseum.com, donation) is open 9 A.M.–7 P.M. Tuesday–Friday and 11 A.M.–7 P.M. Saturday–Monday in summer, and 10 A.M.–4 P.M. Tuesday–Saturday the rest of the year. Inside are Indian artifacts from cave sites near Ten Sleep, a re-creation of the A. G. Rupp Store, old photos, cowboy and ranch equipment, and a fine geology and fossil collection. The museum's highlight is a Sheepeater Indian lodge constructed in the 1860s from 130 poles. It was moved here from its original location near Soapy Peak. Also here are mammoth bones from the 11,000-year-old Colby Site, three miles east of Worland. This was one of the largest and oldest known mammoth kills in North America. Kids will enjoy the Family Discovery Center, with art activities and other hands-on fun. Across the street is a pleasant **city park** with picnic tables, shade trees, and a playground.

Next to the County Court House, at the corner of Big Horn Avenue and 10th Street, is a fountain fed by a 4,330-foot-deep **artesian well** 23 miles north of Worland. The well flows at an impressive 14,000 gallons per minute and with sufficient pressure to push water all the way to Worland. Also on the courthouse

grounds is a grotesque 15-foot-tall **Indian statue** carved out of wood by Peter Toth and placed here in 1980. **Pioneer Square,** just across the road, has unusual metal sculptures depicting pioneer settlers.

Head two miles north on Hwy. 433 to **Duck Swamp,** with picnic tables, a paved interpretive trail, and an overlook. A sign describes the Bridger Trail that passed through here.

Both east and west of Worland in the Painted Desert, you'll find some of the most interesting badlands country in Wyoming. Of particular note are the **Gooseberry Badlands** (a.k.a. 15-Mile Badlands) on Bureau of Land Management property west of town near Squaw Teats and right along Hwy. 431. The BLM has developed a 1.5-mile nature trail through the colorful hoodoo formations here;

pick up a descriptive handout from its office in Worland or local visitor centers. There's plenty of eroded country to explore, including arches and a variety of bizarrely carved shapes, and the bones of a prehistoric horse, *Eohippus,* have been found in the area. Get details from the BLM in Worland (307/347-5100, www.wy.blm.gov/wfo/index.htm).

ENTERTAINMENT AND EVENTS

Mikell's Office Lounge (1515 Big Horn Ave., 307/347-8171) has live music most weekends, or head to **Cottonwood Twin Cinemas** (401 Robertson, 307/347-8414), the local movie palace.

Worland's big annual event is the **Washakie County Fair** on the first week of August, with a parade, country music, and other country-fair fun.

RECREATION

During summer, many people float and fish the **Bighorn River** north from Worland. The river is gentle in many stretches, but get detailed information and a map of access sites from the BLM office before putting in. Upstream from Worland to Thermopolis, the river has many hazards, and this stretch is not recommended for novices.

There's a community **swimming pool** at the high school (1706 Washakie Ave., 307/347-4113) and an 18-hole **Municipal Golf Course** (307/347-2695) next to the airport. Roll black balls toward white pins at **Hurricane Lanes** (612 S. 12th, 307/347-4044).

ACCOMMODATIONS

If cheap and basic are what you need, try **Town House Motor Inn** (119 N. 10th St., 307/347-2426, $45 s or $48 d) with fridges, microwaves, and a seasonal outdoor pool.

One of the better places in town is **Days Inn** (500 N. 10th St., 307/347-4251 or 800/329-7466, www.daysinn.com, $90 d) with a light breakfast, fridges, microwaves, and wireless Internet.

Worland's newest and nicest motel is **Comfort Inn** (100 N. Rd. 11, 307/347-9898 or 800/228-5150, www.comfortinn.com, $90 s or $95 d, suites $145 d), a mile east of downtown. Amenities include an indoor pool, outdoor hot tub, light breakfast, and limited Wi-Fi.

Camping

No public campgrounds are near Worland (although you can pitch a tent on nearby BLM lands), but the private **Worland Campground** (2311 Big Horn Ave., 307/347-2329, www.worlandcowboycampground.com, $15 tents, $20–26 RVs, open May–Oct.) has shady sites on the east side of town. Showers for noncampers cost $5.

FOOD

Downtown Worland has several good restaurants within a block of each other along Big Horn Avenue: Rams Horn, Maggies, Ranchito, and Golden Dragon. **Maggie's Cafe** (541 Big Horn Ave., 307/347-3354) has reasonable breakfasts and lunches, including homemade soups and breads. It opens at 5 A.M. for early birds. Smoke-free, too. **Golden Dragon** (616 Big Horn Ave., 307/347-6168) has big buffet lunches ($6) and dinners ($9).

Ram's Horn Cafe (629 Big Horn Ave., 307/347-6351) serves a big menu three meals a day for reasonable prices; most dinners are $6–13, and it always has nightly specials and homemade pies. Sunday brunch is popular, along with the Friday night all-you-can-eat buffets for just $8.

Ranchito Mexican Food (544 Big Horn Ave., 307/347-8501) serves authentic south-of-the-border fare, or try **Los Cabos** (1110 Big Horn Ave., 307/347-2685) for Baja-style lunches and dinners. Get lunchtime sandwiches (homemade bread) at **Mikell's Office Lounge** (1515 Big Horn Ave., 307/347-8171) or drop by on Friday night for the prime rib special.

Season's Supper Club (1620 Big Horn Ave., 307/347-9261) serves some of the best grilled steaks in these parts.

Get groceries at **Jon's IGA** (221 N. 10th St., 307/347-3628) or **Blair's Market** (1801 Big Horn Ave., 307/347-8500. Both have in-store delis.

INFORMATION AND SERVICES

The **Worland-Ten Sleep Chamber of Commerce** office (120 N. 10th St., 307/347-3226, www.worlandchamber.com, open 8 A.M.–noon and 1–5 P.M. Mon.–Fri.) is downtown in front of the county courthouse.

The **Washakie County Library** (1019 Coburn Ave., 307/347-2231) has Internet access. Drop by the **BLM's Worland Field Office** (101 S. 23rd St., 307/347-5100, www.wy.blm.gov/wfo/index.htm) for information on scenic back roads and nearby places to hike or mountainbike. The building also houses Bighorn National Forest's **Worland Information Office** (307/347-5105, www.fs.fed.us/r2/bighorn).

Wash clothes at **Coin-Op Laundry** (1401 Big Horn Ave.). For medical emergencies, head to **Washakie Medical Clinic** (400 S. 15th St., 307/347-3221).

GETTING THERE AND AROUND

The Worland Airport is two miles south of town and is served by **Great Lakes Aviation** (307/433-2905 or 800/554-5111, www.greatlakesav.com), with daily flights to Denver and Laramie. Rent cars from **Big West Autoplex** (545 N. 10th Ave., 307/347-4229).

Powder River Transportation (307/682-1888 or 800/442-3682, http://gillette.coach-usa.us) has daily bus service to Worland, providing connections to central and eastern Wyoming, Denver, Billings, and Rapid City.

TEN SLEEP

Ten Sleep (pop. 300) has one of the most picturesque settings in all of Wyoming. The drive in from Worland offers a traipse across dry desert badlands crowded with oil pumpjacks and then up into rolling grass and sagebrush country with the tree-covered Big Horn Mountains marking the distant horizon. Great views can be seen from atop the long hills before the road descends sharply into a lush green valley cut through by Nowood and Tensleep creeks. Because of its mountain valley location, the town of Ten Sleep offers an escape from the oppressive summer heat of Bighorn Basin. This

© DON PITCHER

the sleepy town of Ten Sleep

verdant valley is one of the few places in Wyoming where apple, peach, and pear trees grow. Rustic log buildings fill this tiny ranching and tourism center. Take away the cars and the asphalt and it's easy to imagine Ten Sleep as the location for some Hollywood film about the Green Valley.

The name Ten Sleep comes from the Sioux Indians, who frequently stopped in this valley during their travels between a permanent camp along the Clarks Fork River in Montana and another one along the Platte River. Halfway between the two was Ten Sleeps, so named because they measured distances in the number of nights it took to get to a place. The town of Ten Sleep was established as a trading center for the Scottish and Irish sheepmen who came here in the 1890s.

Sights

The main sights in Ten Sleep are the comfortable, slow-paced town itself and its pretty setting. **Pioneer Museum** behind the Flagstaff Cafe has local artifacts and is open 9 A.M.–5 P.M. daily in the summer. An old sheriff wagon sits on the main street ready to haul off the bad guys. Ask at the museum for directions to the Indian pictographs on the Walt Patch Ranch. Lions Club Park has an artesian well that is a favorite place to fill jugs with cold water.

Drop into the **Ten Sleep Saloon** (307/366-9208) or the **Big Horn Bar** (307/366-9222) for a cold one with local ranchers and cowboys. Ten Sleep Saloon has a bar inlaid with 5,052 pennies (oldest is from 1906) and 233 nickels; the bartender claims that they started out with inlaid silver dollars, but this is all they had left after the taxes!

Just west of Ten Sleep is the turnoff to **Castle Gardens,** a scenic area of wind-carved sandstone badlands in all sizes and shapes. It's an eight-mile drive via a dirt road that may become impassable when wet. Castle Gardens has two free campsites, picnic tables, and an outhouse. A few miles south of Castle Gardens are the **Honeycombs,** where the landscape is pockmarked with holes. Not far away, **Big Cedar Ridge** contains an abundance of fossil-

ized leaves and flowers on BLM land. You can dig in existing pits, but don't start new holes.

Another great drive connects Ten Sleep with tiny Lysite, 60 miles to the south. The first 21 miles are paved to a spot on the map called Big Trails. South of here, the road turns to gravel and takes you along lazy Nowood River through dramatic canyons and past grand old ranches. As you approach Lysite the landscape turns desertlike, with cactus mixing with sage and sand. It's a classic Wyoming drive and passable in two-wheel-drive vehicles.

Salt Lick Trail is an enjoyable short hike (1.25 miles) into an open forest of ponderosa pine and juniper, with fine views across Bighorn Basin. The trailhead is 5.5 miles east of Ten Sleep.

Tensleep Canyon

Six miles east of town, U.S. 16 passes the entrance to the 8,500-acre **Tensleep Preserve** (307/366-2671, www.nature.org/wyoming), managed by The Nature Conservancy. The preserve follows a 12-mile stretch of Canyon Creek and is a great place for day hikes. Workshops and conservation projects take place here throughout the summer, with lodging in cozy wall tents and delicious meals in the beautiful lodge. The preserve is open to visitors May–mid-October.

Shortly beyond the turnoff to the Tensleep Preserve, the highway climbs up spectacular Tensleep Canyon toward 9,666-foot Powder River Pass in the Big Horn Mountains. **Wigwam Fish Rearing Station,** run by the Wyoming Game and Fish Department, is five miles east of town. Another six miles up is the turnoff to the old log buildings that house **Ten Sleep Fish Hatchery.** Both of these operations are open daily for tours. (See the *Powder River Country* chapter for sights east of here as U.S. 16 climbs over the majestic Big Horns.)

Events

Come to Ten Sleep on the **Fourth of July** for a popular rodeo, parade, outdoor dances, and a kids' sheep ride. The **Nowood Stock Music Fest** (get it?) takes place the second weekend

THE TEN SLEEP RAID

Cattlemen have always viewed sheep with disdain, regarding them as despoilers of the range, "locusts with hooves" or "range maggots." Cattle reached Wyoming's grazing lands first, and when sheep began to arrive in large numbers around the turn of the 20th century, the cattle owners fought back with intimidation and violence. In many places, the cattlemen declared a "dead line," and any sheep or sheepherder that came into that area risked being killed. (One such line existed in Jackson Hole; even today the county has just 300 sheep as opposed to 12,000 cattle.) Despite these threats, sheep ranching was simply too lucrative to pass up; by 1889, Bighorn Basin was overrun with more than 387,000 sheep – and boasted fewer than 22,000 cattle.

Perhaps 10,000 sheep throughout the state were killed by cattlemen; some flocks were driven over cliffs, others were dynamited or attacked by dogs, and thousands more died from gunshots. Many of Wyoming's sheepherders were viciously attacked, and at least 16 were murdered. The most notorious of all these incidents took place along Spring Creek near Ten Sleep in 1909. Joe Emge, a hotheaded cattleman turned sheepman, announced plans to trail his sheep across the dead line set up

in the Nowater Creek area. One April night just after the sheep had reached the grazing grounds, at least half a dozen masked men burst into the camp and murdered Emge, his partner, and a herder. The killers set the wagons afire and shot many sheep before disappearing into the night, leaving a grisly scene to be discovered the next morning.

The investigation pointed directly at a local cattleman, and after testifying before a grand jury one of the suspected raiders was found dead. Officials judged it a suicide, but many suspected that the cattleman had been waylaid by others seeking to silence anyone who might tell the truth. Eventually, two men broke the silence and fingered five others, including several prominent ranchers. All five were convicted and spent from three years to life in prison for the murders. Like the Johnson County War two decades earlier, this incident helped turn many people against the cattlemen. Sheep continued to grow in importance for a while – Wyoming became the largest wool producer in the country – but overgrazing, the severe winter of 1911–1912, and the removal of a wool tariff the next year led to a long decline. Even today, though, Wyoming is America's second-largest producer of wool.

---

of August, with a variety of jazz, blues, country, and rock bands.

Practicalities

Contact the **Ten Sleep/Worland Visitors Council** (307/347-3226, www.tensleepworlandwyoming.com) for local information. **Log Cabin Motel** (307/366-2320, www.tensleepwyoming.com/logcabin, $45–75 d) has comfortable rooms, some with microwaves and fridges.

Pitch your tent in town at **Ten Broek RV Park** (307/366-2250, $14 tents, $21 RVs, open Apr.–Oct.), which also has simple cabins ($35 d) and a horse corral.

The closest public camping is eight miles east of Ten Sleep inside Bighorn National Forest at **Tensleep Creek Campground.** Only five sites are available ($10, open mid-May–Oct.) at this peaceful riverside spot surrounded by tall cottonwoods. You can also stay at a dozen other Forest Service campgrounds farther east.

Ten Sleep Saloon serves meals, as does **L and L's Hitchin' Post** (307/366-2696). A classic country store, **Ten Sleep Mercantile** (307/366-2224) sells groceries and supplies.

Thermopolis

The town of Thermopolis (pop. 3,200) lies on the southern edge of the Bighorn Basin surrounded by the Owl Creek Mountains. It's one of two Wyoming towns established because of a hot springs; the other is Saratoga. Thermopolis comes from the words *thermae* (Latin for "hot springs") and *polis* (Greek for "city"). It is a fitting title because the world's largest hot springs are the centerpiece of Thermopolis. Hot Springs State Park is right in town, encompassing both a wonderful public bathhouse and several commercial endeavors. The economy of Thermopolis was for a long while dependent on oil and ranching, but tourism has become increasingly important.

Thermopolis came into existence with the 1896 purchase of Big Springs from the Shoshone and Arapahoes. Streets were laid out wide enough for a 16-mule team to turn around in the middle of the block—something still obvious today, although you don't often see mule teams on the streets. Because of their medicinal value, the hot springs attracted many people, and the town became a health center, particularly for those suffering from arthritis and polio. There wasn't much timber around here, so the first lodging place, the Sage Brush Hotel, was made from a wooden frame laced with sagebrush and covered with a thatched roof of more sage.

◖ HOT SPRINGS STATE PARK

Shoshone legend tells of a young warrior and his lover who were standing in the Wind River Canyon when an eagle feather—earned in battles with the enemy—blew out of his hair and wafted down the canyon. They raced after it and found it floating in an enormous hot spring with steam gushing from its mouth. The springs were a gift from the Great Spirit.

Originally a part of the Wind River Reservation, Big Springs and 10 square miles of surrounding land were sold to the U.S. government in 1896 for the bargain-basement price of $60,000. The treaty was signed by Shoshone Chief Washakie and Arapaho Chief Sharp Nose. In it, Washakie stipulated that some of the water must remain free to all people and that a campground be set aside for Indians: "I, Washakie, chief of Shoshones, freely give to the great white father these waters, belov'd by my people; that all may receive that great blessing of bodily health in the bathing." Thus was established Wyoming's first state park.

Today the park is the third-most popular attraction in Wyoming; only Yellowstone and Grand Teton national parks bring in more visitors. The park includes a variety of facilities: a state-run bathhouse, two commercial establishments, a senior center, a rehabilitation center, and even a small herd of buffalo. Adjacent is the Holiday Inn spa facility. Park headquarters is the A-frame structure at the corner of Park Street and U.S. 789. Just behind here is an impressive travertine cone created when workers put in a vent pipe.

Big Springs

Big Springs flows at a rate of approximately 2,575 gallons per minute at 135°F and is considered the largest hot springs in the world. The springs are at the base of a small butte; just in case there might be some confusion, someone has placed white rocks along the hillside spelling out "World's Largest Mineral Hot Spring." Several cooling ponds spread out in front of the springs, dropping water over terraces of lime and gypsum to the Bighorn River. (Because of the hot water, this stretch of the Bighorn River remains open throughout the winter, attracting ducks and other birds.) The cooling ponds are colorful, with algae and minerals (particularly calcium carbonate, bicarbonate, sulfate, and sodium) adding splashes of reds, greens, browns, and yellows. A concrete path winds around the terraces and along the river, leading to a scenic swinging bridge. Many people who drink the mineral-rich water claim an array of medicinal benefits.

THERMOPOLIS

© DON PITCHER

Hot Springs State Park

State Bath House

For an incredibly relaxing soak, be sure to visit the very nice State Bath House (307/864-3765, www.wyoparks.state.wy.us, open 8 A.M.–5:30 P.M. Mon.–Sat. and noon–5:30 P.M. Sun. and holidays, free). The facilities are always exceptionally clean, and there are lockers to store your clothes. Rent towels and swimsuits here if you didn't bring your own. Soak in private tubs inside the locker rooms (where you can temper the 104°F mineral water with cooler water), or head to the central indoor pool or a seasonal outdoor soaking pool. The pools are fully accessible. Attendants make sure folks don't stay in the hot water for more than 20 minutes because the heat can be weakening. This is not a place to clean up, and no soap is allowed—even in the showers.

More Park Attractions

Hellie's Teepee Spa (307/864-9250) in the white domed building next to the state bathhouse has indoor and outdoor pools, two spiraling water slides, four hot tubs, a steam room, a sauna, mineral spa, weight room, and snack bar. Adults and children over age five pay $9, seniors $7, and kids ages 4–5 $5; it's free for children under four. Hellie's is open 9 A.M.–9 P.M. daily all year.

Even bigger is **Star Plunge** (307/864-3771), also inside the state park, with indoor and outdoor pools, three slippery water slides, a high dive, steam room, vapor cave, three hot tubs, and tanning booths ($5 extra). The 500-foot-long outdoor slide is one of the longest in the nation. Admission to Star Plunge costs $9 for ages five to adult, $7 seniors, and $4 kids under five. Towels, swimsuits, and inner tubes can also be rented. It's open 9 A.M.–9 P.M. daily year-round. (The state's largest outdoor mineral swimming pool is at Fountain of Youth RV Park.)

Also on the grounds of the state park are **Gottsche Rehabilitation Center** (307/864-2147 or 800/743-0736, www.gottsche-rehab.com), an outpatient treatment facility established in 1959 to make use of the medicinal properties of the hot springs; **Big Horn Basin Children's Center** for children with severe disabilities; and a **Wyoming Pioneer Home** for the elderly. A small **museum** in the basement of the

Pioneer Home features arrowheads, baskets, and other Indian artifacts, as well as antiques from nearby ranches. A statue commemorating Chief Washakie's "gift of the smoking waters" stands in front of the home. Washakie would be proud of all the good his gift has done.

In addition to facilities associated with the hot springs, the park includes shady picnic tables and playgrounds. A rough trail cuts to the top of **Monument Hill** right behind Big Springs. The northeast section of Hot Springs State Park includes a pasture where a herd of 20 or so buffalo roam. A loop road through the pasture gives you a chance to drive by them. They are fed at 8:30 A.M. daily.

OTHER SIGHTS
Hot Springs Historical Museum
The Hot Springs Historical Museum (700 Broadway, 307/864-5183, www.trib.com/~history) calls itself "one of the best small museums in the country" and lives up to this billing with an impressive collection of ranching and cowboy gear, historical photos, wagons, Indian artifacts, and much more. The museum is open 9 A.M.–5 P.M. Monday–Saturday and 1–5 P.M. Sunday June–August, and 9 A.M.–5 P.M. Monday–Saturday the rest of the year. Entrance costs $4 adults, $2 seniors and youths. Kids under six get in free.

The museum sprawls throughout two floors of the main building and across the street to include an agriculture building, an old schoolhouse, a petroleum building, and a caboose. The main museum houses various displays of frontier life: a newspaper shop, dentist's office (complete with frightening tools), blacksmith shop, and general store. The cherry-wood bar from the Hole-in-the-Wall Saloon is particularly popular; here members of the famous outlaw gang tipped their glasses with sympathetic locals.

The Indian artifact collection downstairs is impressive, not just because of the thousands of arrowheads but also because it includes an elk hide painted by Shoshone Chief Washakie. Outside, the 1920 Middleton Schoolhouse comes complete with old desks; check out the amusing letters from present-day schoolchildren. Kids of all ages love traipsing through the old Burlington Northern caboose and trying to figure out how the agriculture building's amazing 1926 Case threshing machine worked. The petroleum building houses exhibits on drilling for and refining oil, including old gusher photos and a gigantic power unit once used to pump oil before the arrival of electric pumps.

◀ Wyoming Dinosaur Center
In 1992, three Germans formed a prospecting company to search for fossils in the Bighorn Basin. With the help of an American fossil expert they found a promising site just out of Thermopolis and the following year discovered a sauropod (a plant-eating dinosaur from the Jurassic Period). Realizing that many more dinosaurs lay below the surface, the leader, Dr. Burkhard Pohl (a Frankfurt veterinarian), bought the 7,000-acre Warm Springs Ranch and began digging, later unearthing the most complete skeleton of a brachiosaur ever found, along with many more species. The discoveries led to the creation of the Wyoming Dinosaur Center (307/864-2997 or 800/455-3466, www.wyodino.org), housed in a warehouse-type metal building on the eastern edge of town. The facility displays more than a dozen full-size skeletons and casts from dinosaurs found not only nearby but also in Russia, Germany, and China. These include a 19-foot skeleton of a camarasaurus from the site, a nearly complete *Triceratops horridus*—the only known specimen of this species—and a cast of *Tyrannosaurus rex,* plus 13 dinosaur eggs in a nest, and marine reptiles.

Although this is a for-profit venture with a gift shop selling educational dinosaur toys, it's not just a gee-whiz exhibit to wow the kids; the emphasis is heavily on science. Excellent displays reveal the evolution of life on the planet. Visitors can watch workers prepare specimens in the lab or take a tour of the Warm Springs Ranch dig sites two miles away, where excavations continue every summer. There's no chance of running out of specimens; the deposit contains an estimated 100,000 bones. The informative, hour-long tours (mid-May–Sept.) include a bus ride from the Dinosaur

Center and details about the local geology and digging techniques. One of the sites contains a feeding ground with tracks. Tours are offered hourly throughout the day and cost $10 adults, $7 kids and seniors, and free for children under four. Entrance to the Dinosaur Center is $6 adults, $3.50 kids and seniors, and free for children under four. A better option is a combination tour and museum entrance; $12 adults, $8 seniors and kids, free for children under four. Special Kids' Digs take place several times each summer and include classes, geology lessons, and fossil digging. The museum is open 8 A.M.–6 P.M. daily mid-May–mid-September, and 10 A.M.–5 P.M. daily the rest of the year.

Budding paleontologists can join the Dig for a Day program; you pay $125 per person to help on a dino dig. And no, you don't get to keep what you find.

Wax History and Teddy Bears

Thermopolis seems to attract an unusual mix of attractions, the strangest conglomeration being the **Old West Wax Museum and Dancing Bear Folk Center** (119 S. 6th, 307/864-9396, www.westwaxmuseum.com). The 250 teddy bears hang out downstairs, and some are arranged in "historical" settings—including teddy bears on the *Titanic*. Other oddities include the third-largest barbed wire collection in the United States, the biggest collection of marbles west of the Mississippi, and a room with model trains. Also here is a textile studio with quilts and looms, plus classes and demonstrations. Upstairs is a wax museum that was in Jackson for 30 years, with various Old West figures such as Butch Cassidy, Chief Washakie, Jim Bridger, Big Nose George, and General Custer. A bit bizarre, but the displays are actually quite informative.

This odd juxtoposition of wax figures and stuffed bears is open 9 A.M.–5 P.M. daily mid-May–mid-September and 10 A.M.–4 P.M. daily the rest of the year. Entrance to both costs $4.50 adults, or $3 senior, $12 for families, and free for children under five. The museum also houses the chamber of commerce office.

A couple of other downtown sights are worth a look, including the big statue of a **cowboy and horse** on Broadway, and the **swastikas** embedded in the bricks at 509 Broadway. The latter are actually Indian symbols from a pre-Nazi era; represented the four directions and the sun.

◖ Legend Rock Petroglyph Site

One of the finest sites for Indian rock art in Wyoming lies in the foothills of the Owl Creek Mountains. Get there by driving 21 miles northwest from Thermopolis on Hwy. 120. Turn left at the *second* Hamilton Dome turnoff (marked with a High Island Ranch billboard) and after 5.5 miles, turn right onto the gravel Cottonwood Creek Road. Continue two miles, and just past the second cattle guard take the road on your left. Follow it a short distance to a parking area in front of a green gate marked "Legend Rock." The petroglyphs are a 0.5-mile walk down from here. (If you want to drive down the hill, borrow the key for the gate from the Hot Springs State Park office in Thermopolis, 307/864-217.) The total distance from Hwy. 120 to the petroglyph site is eight miles.

Hundreds of petroglyphs covering several time periods and styles have been found on the nearby sandstone cliffs. There are deer, bison, elk, and various human figures, but most unusual is a rabbit, the only one known in Wyoming rock art. The rabbit is similar to ones on Mimbres ceramic items from A.D. 1000; the Mimbres are from New Mexico. The rock art at Legend Rock may have been associated with shamanism and ritual healing, and some sections have been dated to 2,000 years old. Please do your part to protect this sacred site by not touching the petroglyphs. Owl Creek flows not far away, and oil pumpjacks dot the nearby hills (Hamilton Dome is one of the most important oil fields in Bighorn Basin).

West of Legend Rock is **Anchor Dam,** a major engineering blunder. Shortly after the dam was completed in 1960, a 300-foot-wide sinkhole developed in the porous limestone underlying the reservoir. The hole was filled with dirt and rock, but it collapsed again. The second time the repair held, but new sinkholes appear each year. After decades of this—and millions of dollars down the proverbial sink-hole—the reservoir still fills only halfway in the best years.

Ghost Towns

Ghost town aficionados shouldn't miss the old coal-mining settlement of **Gebo**, where you'll find eight stone buildings, a fascinating grave-yard, and various other structures. The town was established in 1906 and abandoned in the 1950s. Get to Gebo by driving 10 miles north of Thermopolis on U.S. 20 and turning west onto Sand Draw Road. The remains are approximately four miles in. A mile or so south of Gebo is another ghost town, **Crosby,** with additional mine ruins. The Hot Springs Historical Museum has historical photos from the mines.

ENTERTAINMENT AND EVENTS

Catch the latest flicks at **The Ritz Theater** (309 Arapahoe, 307/864-3118).

Held the first weekend in August at Hot Springs State Park, the **Gift of the Waters Pageant** commemorates the transfer of Big Springs to the federal government in 1896. The pageant has been presented every summer since 1950, with a cast that includes both local residents and Shoshone from the Wind River Indian Reservation in full regalia. A tepee camp is set up near the hot springs for the festivities. Other events during Gift of the Waters include Indian dancing, a parade, PRCA rodeo, and an arts-and-crafts fair. **Hot Springs County Fair** starts on the pageant weekend and goes through the following weekend, with all the standard agricultural and ranching exhibits.

SHOPPING

Sunshine Gallery (517 Broadway, 307/864-3727) exhibits beautiful jewelry and hammered metal pieces by owner Pamela Sundstrom, along with works by other Wyoming artists.

RECREATION

Most of the recreation in Thermopolis takes place around the hot springs pools, but there are other things to do as well. **Roundtop Mountain,** the distinctive butte that dominates the area, is an enjoyable but fairly steep hike. Take 7th Street to Airport Hill and turn at the first left. After the cemetery, turn right on a gravel road that takes you to the trailhead.

The nine-hole **Legion Town and Country Club** (307/864-5294) is on Airport Hill north of town. Miniature golfers may prefer **Sweet Spot Mini Golf** (510 Park St.). The local bowling alley is also the A&W stand; look for **A&W Bowling Center** (942 Shoshoni, 307/864-3887). Got kids? Make sure to take them to the fantastic wooden playground at the **Community Playpark** on Araphoe Street immediately south of the football field.

HorseWorks Wyoming (307/867-2367 or 877/807-2367, www.horseworkswyoming.com) leads five-day trail rides and cattle drives into the mountains around Grass Creek, 40 miles northwest of Thermopolis.

A unique way to discover the Old West is the **Outlaw Trail Ride** (307/864-2287 or 888/362-7433, www.rideoutlawtrail.com), a weeklong not-for-profit adventure in early August. This 100-mile trip follows the "Outlaw Trail" from the Hole-in-the-Wall country of Butch Cassidy and the Sundance Kid to Thermopolis. It isn't for dudes—you'll need to bring your own horse (although they can also be rented from HorseWorks), bedroll, and gear—but excellent meals are provided. A trail ride fee of $875 covers catered meals, horse feed, nightly entertainment, and more.

ACCOMMODATIONS

Because of the popularity of Thermopolis during the summer, it's a good idea to make reservations to be assured of a place.

Under $50

Cactus Inn (605 S. 6th St., 307/864-3155 or 877/621-7811, www.cactusinn.com) charges $40 s or $45 d for nicely maintained standard rooms, or $75 for a two-room suite that sleeps four. All rooms contain fridges and microwaves, and the suite has a full kitchen.

Find newly updated rooms, microwaves, fridges, and Wi-Fi at **El Rancho Motel** (924

Shoshoni Rd., 307/864-2341 or 800/283-2777), where standard units are $40–60 d, and six-person suites run $105. The owners opened a 40-unit **Motel 6** adjacent to the El Rancho in 2006.

Moonlighter Motel 600 Broadway, 307/864-2321, $42–52 d) is another decent place with affordable rooms.

$50-100

Elk Antler Inn (501 S. 6th, 307/864-2325 or 800/320-4028) has nicely remodeled rooms ($50–60) with log furnishings, fridges and microwaves, along with two-room suites ($70–80).

Roundtop Mountain Motel (412 N. 6th, 307/864-3126 or 800/584-9126, www.roundtopmotel.com) charges $55–69 d for motel rooms, or $69 for funky four-person log cabins with kitchenettes. They definitely aren't for everyone, but do offer an Old West experience.

The attractive **Super 8 Motel,** on the southern edge of town (La. 5, Hwy. 20 S., 307/864-5515 or 800/800-8000, www.thermopolissuper8.com), is a fine midrange choice, with an indoor pool, hot tub, wireless Internet, and a hot breakfast. Most rooms go for $90 d, but it also has a couple of family rooms with bunk beds, microwaves, and fridges for $100 d. Suites and wheelchair-accessible rooms are also available.

In the heart of town, **Nuss Broadway Inn** (342 Broadway St., 307/864-2786, www.nussbroadwayinn.com, $75 d) has four guest rooms with private baths. A light breakfast is included.

$100-150

C **Best Western Plaza Hotel** (307/864-2939 or 888/919-9009, www.wyomingvacations.com, $89–129 d) is a beautifully restored historic brick building within Hot Springs State Park. Bright and spacious rooms ($99–119 d) feature custommade lodgepole furniture and ultracomfortable beds. Two-room luxury suites—all with fridges and microwaves and many with fireplaces—cost $129–139 for up to four guests. Rates include wireless Internet and a filling breakfast. The

courtyard contains a small swimming pool and hot mineral spa.

Right across the street is a favorite of the senior set, **Holiday Inn of the Waters** (307/864-3131 or 800/465-4329, www.thermopolis-hi.com). Summertime room rates are $98–129 d, but the rest of the year the hotel offers reasonable two-night packages ($160–180 d) that include a prime rib dinner and bottle of champagne. Facilities include an outdoor seasonal pool, an exercise room, mineral spa, soaking tubs, a steam room, and Wi-Fi.

Ranch

The 130,000-acre **High Island Ranch and Cattle Co.** (307/867-2374 in summer or 307/864-5389 in winter, www.highislandranch.com) is a working ranch with a gorgeously remote setting at Hamilton Dome north of Thermopolis. Guests can take part in cattle drives four times a year. Especially popular are the authentic 1800s cattle drives—no vehicles used. No hot tubs here: This is the real thing, with guests staying in canvas tents along the trail (bring your sleeping bag) and rustic cabins or bunkhouses at the ranch. Ranch visits are by the week only and cost $2,800–3,400 per person, all-inclusive. There's room for a maximum of 25 guests, and guest ranch activities take place late May–mid-September.

Camping

The closest public camping is 17 miles south in Wind River Canyon. **Fountain of Youth RV Park** (two miles north of Thermopolis on U.S. 20, 307/864-3265, www.trib.com/~foyrvpk, $26 RVs or tents) boasts Wyoming's largest mineral swimming pool, fed by what was intended to be an oil well. In 1918, C. F. Cross began drilling, but instead of hitting oil he struck hot mineral water, blowing the pipe casing out of the ground. Eventually a small travertine cone formed around the old casing. The "Sacajawea" well still flows at a rate of 1.3 million gallons per day. Not surprisingly, this is a popular place with the "snowbird" RV crowd. The Labor Day breakfast in the pool is a favorite event. Open mid-March–September.

Because of its proximity to both the highway and rail tracks, the campground can be noisy, especially for tent campers.

Eagle RV Park on the south edge of town (307/864-5262 or 888/865-5707, www.eaglervpark.com, $17 tents, $23 RVs, $35 cabins, open year-round) has wireless Internet.

Country Campin' (307/864-2416 or 800/609-2244, www.trib.com/~camp, $18 tents, $23 RVs, open May–Sept.) lives up to its name with a quiet country location five miles northeast of Thermopolis along the Bighorn River. Kids will love to pet the miniature horses.

FOOD

Open three meals a day, **((Pumpernick's** (512 Broadway, 307/864-5151) has some of the best meals in Thermopolis. The diverse menu encompasses teriyaki chicken, steaks, seafood, prime rib on weekends, and homemade pies. Dinner entrées run $11–20. Its outside patio is a pleasant place for summer dining.

For quick eats, stop by the little seasonal trailer at 600 South 6th Street, **Henry Lee's Smoked Ribs and BBQ.** Also popular is **Dairyland** (510 Park St., 307/864-2757), an old-fashioned burger and shake stand. The minigolf place is right next door, making this a good kid stop.

Find a good selection of books, free Wi-Fi, and espresso at **The Storyteller** (528 Broadway, 307/864-3272).

Las Fuentes Mexican Restaurant (530 Arapahoe, 307/864-2695) has so-so fajitas, chimichangas, burritos, and margaritas, plus outdoor dining in the summer. Most items are $6–13.

The Safari Club (307/864-3131), at the Holiday Inn within Hot Springs State Park, has reasonably priced buffet breakfasts, a salad bar, and a diverse dinner menu that includes blackened prime rib, Alaskan king crab, and buffalo burgers. The walls are lined with dozens of big-game trophy mounts and pictures of great white hunters standing over their deceased quarry. Owner Jim Mills killed most of the animals hanging around here, creating what might be called a low-maintenance zoo.

It's either appealing or appalling, depending on your perspective. Bands sometimes play in the adjacent bar, where you can join the locals watching a game on the big-screen TV or at the pool table.

One of the best and most popular local eateries isn't actually in Thermopolis. **Butch's Place** (307/864-2669) has family dining—and a bar—12 miles north in the "town" of Kirby. The menu includes buffalo burgers, shrimp, chicken, steaks, big burgers, and more Tuesday–Saturday evenings.

The Prospector Pizzeria (500 Broadway, 307/864-3343) serves pizza by the slice or pie, plus pasta, sandwiches, and salads. Open for lunch and dinner; $9–11.

Get groceries from **Consumers' Supermarket** (600 S. 6th, 307/864-3112) or **Don's IGA** (225 S. 4th, 307/864-5576). Don's also houses a small deli and bakery.

INFORMATION AND SERVICES

The **Thermopolis Chamber of Commerce** (119 S. 6th St., 307/864-3192 or 800/786-6772, www.thermopolis.com) has its office in the Old West Wax Museum building. While you're here, pick up its historic Thermopolis walking-tour brochure to learn more about the town's interesting buildings. Hours are 8 A.M.–5 P.M. Monday–Friday, but the brochure racks are available whenever the Wax Museum is open.

Hot Springs County Library (344 Arapahoe St., 307/864-3104) has web access. Wash your clothes at **Wishy Washy Laundromat** (630 Shoshoni; open 24 hours a day in the summer).

For medical emergencies, head to **Hot Springs County Memorial Hospital** (150 E. Arapahoe, 307/864-3121, www.hscmh.org).

((WIND RIVER CANYON

South of Thermopolis, the highway cuts across lush irrigated farm fields. Turn around and you'll see the steep slopes of Roundtop Mountain dominating the vistas. The highway bridges the Bighorn River and then, four miles south of town, abruptly enters magnificent Wind River Canyon. At this point the river's name changes just as abruptly. Lewis and

Wind River Canyon

2815) in Thermopolis sells permits, along with fishing, boating, and camping gear.

Wind River Canyon Whitewater (307/864-9343 or 800/246-9343, www.windrivercanyonraft.com) leads exciting raft trips through the canyon during summer, with the biggest water generally in June and July. Trips vary from a quick 1.5-hour drenching ($35) to five-hour trips that take you through the entire canyon and include lunch ($75). In addition, this Indian-owned company offers guided fishing. See the chamber of commerce in Thermopolis for a listing of other fishing outfitters.

Geologic History Lesson

The drive through Wind River Canyon is one of the most dramatic in Wyoming; U.S. 20 clings to the eastern bank of the river, and canyon walls rise up to 2,500 feet overhead. Tracks of the Burlington Northern Railroad (built in 1913) parallel the river on the other side, threading in and out through several tunnels. This place is a geologist's dream, slicing through rocks that grow progressively older as you continue south, with the oldest dating to the Precambrian era, 2.7 billion years ago. A succession of roadside signs notes the various rock formations, and the Thermopolis Chamber of Commerce can provide you a descriptive log of the canyon's complex geology.

At the upper end of the canyon, the road quickly climbs past Boysen Dam and into the open country of Boysen State Park (see the *Wind River Mountains Country* chapter). Within the canyon you'll find two attractive **campgrounds,** Upper and Lower Wind River State Park ($12 for nonresidents or $6 for Wyoming residents). The river flows right alongside, and there are many big old cottonwoods, but highway noise may keep you awake at night.

Clark had named it the Bighorn River, Crow Indians the Wind River. Early explorers somehow concluded that they were two separate waterways and in the confusion Wind River Canyon became the "Wedding of the Waters." Above this point the river is called the Wind, below it the Big Horn. A bit confusing.

Floating and Fishing

Many people float the Bighorn River, putting in at the Wedding of the Waters and taking out in Thermopolis. It's an enjoyable and leisurely drift with nice scenery and excellent fishing for rainbow trout (average size 15 inches). A special permit is required to fish in the canyon above Wedding of the Waters because it is part of the Wind River Indian Reservation. **Canyon Sporting Goods** (903 Shoshoni, 307/864-

POWDER RIVER COUNTRY

Powder River country is the most historically interesting part of a state overflowing with history. For the Indians who made this area their home, the basin was paradise, a place of massive bison herds and abundant forage for horses. Because of this richness, the area became a confrontation point between various Indian tribes and later between Indians and invading whites along the Bozeman Trail. Still later, the clashes were among the whites: cattlemen versus homesteaders, outlaws against lawmen. Today the clashes have faded into memory, but the rich country remains. Coal, coalbed methane gas, cattle, and sheep rule.

The Powder River Basin stretches from the crest of the Big Horn Mountains to the Black Hills and then south to Casper. The three largest settlements—Gillette, Sheridan, and Buffalo—dominate the region's economy. Sheridan and Buffalo provide gateways to the magnificent Big Horn Mountains, a recreation paradise capped by barren alpine peaks. Rolling grassland predominates across the Powder River Basin, accented by steep-sided buttes and lush riversides. The land is grazed extensively by cattle and sheep, although alfalfa and wheat are grown in many places. Coal, oil, and methane gas resources are vital to the economy of the area, especially around Gillette, making this the most important energy region in Wyoming. Despite the many large coal mines, the land remains relatively undeveloped. Nearly everyone chooses to live in the cities and smaller settlements, leaving enormous open expanses of land.

© DON PITCHER

HIGHLIGHTS

◖ Medicine Wheel: Do the 28 stone spokes create a stone calendar to predict the solstice or was this a place for religious ceremonies? High in the Big Horn Mountains, this mysterious site still draws Native people seeking renewal (page 588).

◖ Trail End State Historic Site: Built by a wealthy politician in 1908, this graceful brick mansion has a third-floor ballroom with a separate loft for musicians (page 598).

◖ King's Saddlery: Walk through the front store, across the alley, and past the lariats and ropes to an amazingly crowded collection of saddles and cowboy memorabilia (page 600).

◖ Bradford Brinton Memorial Museum: Hidden in lush country south of Sheridan, this bucolic old ranch houses a remarkable collection of Western art (page 612).

◖ Jim Gatchell Memorial Museum: This surprising collection focuses on battles between the U.S. Army and the Sioux at Fort Phil Kearny, but it also houses displays on the Johnson County War and outlaws. It's perhaps the finest small museum in Wyoming (page 619).

◖ Occidental Hotel: Tour (or stay in) the wonderfully restored rooms where Teddy Roosevelt, Calvin Coolidge, Buffalo Bill, and Calamity Jane once slept, or enjoy a gourmet dinner in the downstairs restaurant (page 619).

◖ Coal Mine Tours: Marvel at the gargantuan trucks, 110-car coal trains, and 80-foot-thick coal seams that supply the nation's power plants. Be sure to ask your guide how burning coal affects global warming; the guides love that topic (page 634).

LOOK FOR ◖ TO FIND RECOMMENDED SIGHTS, ACTIVITIES, DINING, AND LODGING.

© AVALON TRAVEL PUBLISHING, INC.

PLANNING YOUR TIME

I-90 cuts across Powder River Basin, providing a popular corridor for travelers on the Mt. Rushmore–Devils Tower–Yellowstone circuit. The main towns—Gillette, Sheridan, and Buffalo—all have lodging, RV parks, and good restaurants. Long an overnight stop for travelers en route to Yellowstone, Buffalo and Sheridan are fast becoming places where folks stop for a couple of days to explore the fascinating country and historical sights.

The western margin of the Powder River Basin abuts against the Big Horn Mountains, home to mysterious **Medicine Wheel,** the Cloud Peak Wilderness, and three National Scenic Highways that cross the mountains. At the foot of the Big Horns, the small city of Sheridan has fine restaurants and interesting sights—including historic mansions at **Trail End State** Historic Site and Buffalo Bill's Sheridan Inn. **King's Saddlery** houses an amazing collection of historic items, or you can head south to tiny Big Horn for another remarkable private collection, **Bradford Brinton Memorial Museum.**

Another edge-of-the-mountains town, Buffalo is smaller, but equally interesting. The main attractions are outstanding **Jim Gatchell Memorial Museum** and the gorgeously restored **Occidental Hotel.** Now a state historic site, **Fort Phil Kearny** sits in the rolling timber-and-grass between Buffalo and Sheridan. Tiny Kaycee has a museum, and west of here is the famous Hole-in-the-Wall country where Butch Cassidy and other outlaws hid their stolen horses. Prosperous Gillette is Wyoming's center for coal mining and coalbed methane gas production. You can book an eye-opening **coal mine tour** through the visitor center.

Big Horn Mountains

Sandwiched between two broad basins—Bighorn to the west and Powder River to the east—are the majestic Big Horn Mountains. To the early explorers, this 70-mile-long range was the Shining Mountains, a name inspired by its snowcapped peaks, some topping 13,000 feet. The Indians called it "Ahsahta," meaning "The Big Horns," after the Rocky Mountain bighorn sheep found here. Eventually, whites applied the name to all sorts of places in the region. The mountain country here is carpeted primarily with lodgepole pine, with Engelmann spruce and subalpine fir at higher elevations. Although much of the country here is not as rugged as the mountains on the western border of Wyoming, the Big Horns do contain many rocky peaks above 9,000 feet, with 13,175-foot Cloud Peak crowning the skyline. Hundreds of small lakes reflect this dramatic scenery within the Cloud Peak Wilderness.

Nearly the entire range lies within **Bighorn National Forest,** a 1.1-million-acre chunk of public land set aside by President Grover Cleveland in 1897. Forest headquarters is in Sheridan (2013 Eastside 2nd St.), just east of the I-90 Welcome Center (307/674-2600, www.fs.fed.us/r2/bighorn), with district offices in Lovell (307/548-6514) and Buffalo (307/684-7806) and an information office in Worland (307/347-5105). Any of these offices can provide detailed forest maps and listings of permitted local outfitters.

The **Big Horn Mountain Coalition** (www.bighorns.com) promotes recreation and development in the area and has links to local chambers of commerce. Another useful web source is www.bighornmountains.com.

This is multiple-use country, with recreation, grazing, and timber production the primary attractions. Commercial logging has gone on within the forest for almost a century, and old tie flumes are still visible near Dayton. At one time, vast numbers of sheep grazed the Big Horns, totaling perhaps half a million. Thousands of sheep and cattle still graze in these mountains, and sheepherder camps are common in the high meadows.

Most visitors simply drive through the Big

Horns on one of the three scenic highways, but the country is well worth stopping to savor, especially if you're a fan of waterfalls. There are many campgrounds, more than 850 miles of hiking trails, and good fishing for rainbow, cutthroat, brook, and brown trout. Come winter, the mountains become a popular destination for cross-country skiers, snowboarders, downhill skiers, and snowmobilers. More than 350 miles of groomed trails help make the Big Horns one of the top 10 snowmobiling destinations in America. Several mountain lodges rent the beasts.

There's quite a bit of wildlife to see here, too. Bighorn sheep have been reintroduced to the area and may be seen on the west slope of the mountains. No grizzlies roam here, but quite a few black bears live in the mountains, especially on the northeastern slopes. Also look for mule and white-tailed deer, elk, and moose. (The moose are not native; they were transplanted from Jackson Hole beginning in 1948.)

CRUISIN' THROUGH

Three paved highways cut across the Big Horn Mountains, providing popular connections between Yellowstone and the Black Hills. U.S. Hwys. 14 and 16 are both kept plowed through the winter, while U.S. 14A generally closes November–May. All three have Scenic Byway status, something that becomes more obvious with each mile you travel.

U.S. 16

U.S. 16 climbs across the southern end of the range from Ten Sleep to Buffalo and is the easiest way across the Big Horns. More than a dozen Forest Service campgrounds line the route. This was the original "Black and Yellow Trail," first proposed in 1912 as a link between Chicago, the Black Hills, and Yellowstone. The first caravan of automobiles made it over the old sheepwagon track the following year, reaching Yellowstone after 18 hard days on the road. By the 1920s, the highway was marked by poles with alternating black and yellow bands. For many years, this was the main route to Yellowstone.

East from Ten Sleep, U.S. 16 parallels cottonwood-lined Tensleep Creek, climbing past spectacular red and yellow cliffs. A cross and marker commemorate Gilbert Leigh, an Irish nobleman who fell to his death while hunting here in 1884 (he was caught in an October snowstorm and, unable to see his way, slipped over the cliff). Eventually the switchbacks take you up to **Meadowlark Lake,** a popular winter destination for both cross-country skiers and snowmobilers. The dirt road to **High Park Lookout Tower** is two miles east of here. Look for flower-bedecked **St. Christopher's Chapel of the Big Horns** as this side road climbs to the fire tower (not in use). Great views are to be had from the top. East of here, the road winds over Powder River Pass, providing breathtaking views into Cloud Peak Wilderness.

U.S. 14

Open all year, U.S. 14 offers an equally impressive passage over the Big Horns between Greybull and Dayton. Above the dot of a town called Shell the road passes a remarkably phallic rocky butte, and then catches Shell Creek and winds with it through the deep red rocks of dramatic **Shell Canyon,** past Shell Falls and the Antelope Butte Ski Area, before topping out at Granite Pass. (The name "Shell" appears repeatedly throughout the local topography thanks to the fossil invertebrate shells commonly found in the rocks.) At 120-foot-high **Shell Falls,** approximately eight miles east of Shell on U.S. 14, you'll find a visitor center with books and maps. It's open daily mid-May–mid-September. Nearby are several short walking trails with interpretive signs. Keep your eyes open for water ouzels, the water-loving gray birds that often nest beneath waterfalls. After joining U.S. 14A at **Burgess Junction,** the road continues to Twin Buttes, Sibley Lake, and the amusing jumble of rocks called Fallen City, before zigzagging sharply down to Tongue River Canyon and the town of Dayton. A Forest Service **visitor center,** 1.5 miles east of Burgess Junction near Twin Buttes, is open 8 A.M.–5:30 P.M. daily mid-May–late September and puts on occasional educational programs.

U.S. 14A

U.S. 14A (officially this is Alternate U.S. 14) is generally cleared of snow by Memorial Day, remaining open until mid-October. Engineers like this road, modeled after similar routes in the Alps. At the time it was built, it was said to be the most expensive stretch of road in America. Locals claim the "A" in "U.S. 14A" stands for adventure, and with three runaway truck ramps and 10 percent grades on some stretches, it's easy to see why. The climb to the top is *very* long and steep, but the views make the tough climb worthwhile. U.S. 14A rises over the Big Horns from Lovell to Burgess Junction, where it meets U.S. 14. Along the way you're treated to miles of open sage-and-grass country with timbered islands on Bald and Little Bald mountains, spectacular Bucking Mule Falls, and the famous Medicine Wheel. Watch for moose and deer in the meadows near Burgess Junction.

An enjoyable side loop is **Burgess Road** (Forest Road 15). The gravel road starts at Burgess Junction and continues approximately 20 miles to a junction with U.S. 14A near Bald Mountain. This side loop provides fine opportunities to view deer and elk, and it provides a grand vista from Burgess Road Overlook.

◖ MEDICINE WHEEL

High atop a windswept mountain plateau sits one of the best-known and least-understood archaeological sites in America, the Medicine Wheel. Measuring 80 feet across, this uneven "wagon wheel" of stones seems ready to roll over the nearby slopes. Twenty-eight rock spokes radiate from a central hub, with six smaller rock cairns scattered around the rim. A variety of lesser-known rock structures surround the Medicine Wheel on nearby slopes, including an arrow that supposedly points southwest to another "wheel" near Meeteetse 70 miles away, a large rectangle of stones, and more than 50 tepee rings. An ancient cairn-marked travois

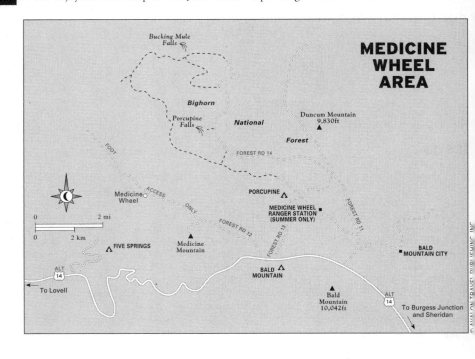

MEDICINE WHEEL AREA

trail continues northwest from Medicine Wheel over the Big Horn Mountains.

Origins

Medicine Wheel's origins are shrouded in time. White prospectors from the nearby gold-mining camp of Bald Mountain City (now entirely gone) discovered the Medicine Wheel around 1885. Carbon-14 dating of wood fragments found in one of the cairns yielded the date A.D. 1760, and scientists now believe the wheel was constructed some time between A.D. 1200 and 1700.

Prevailing theories about the purpose behind the Medicine Wheel fall into two schools: It was either an astronomical observatory or a site for sacred ceremonies. One of the most interesting theories was suggested by astronomer John Eddy in a 1977 *National Geographic* article. He noted that the 28 spokes are equal to the number of days in the lunar month and that two of the cairns served as horizon markers for sunrise and sunset, with the other four cairns marking the rising of three of the brightest stars. These could have signaled the summer solstice. Interestingly, similar alignments occur on a stone wheel in Saskatchewan, Canada.

Other scientists counter that the Indians would have little reason to care exactly when summer solstice occurred—since they were not farmers—and that the rocks probably served some religious function. These researchers point out the striking similarities between the wheel and medicine lodges used during Cheyenne and Sioux sun-dance ceremonies: Both have 28 spokes. The first published report (1885) described the Medicine Wheel as consisting of a central hub with spokes leading to stone huts: "It is said that these smaller huts were, during religious ceremonies, occupied by medicine men of different tribes, while the larger hut in the center was supposed to be the abode of Manitour." Various later reports attributed it to the Crow, Sheepeater, Arapaho, and Cheyenne tribes. University of Montana anthropologist Gregory Campbell considers the wheel a source of religious power to Native Americans and notes that it is a place where

Medicine Wheel

"powerful events come to the fore" for those who search for strength.

Regardless of its origins or earliest uses, the Medicine Wheel *was* used in historical times—and is still used today—as a place for prayer, meditation, renewal, and vision quests. Chief Joseph of the Nez Perce fasted here, and Shoshone Chief Washakie was said to have gained his "medicine" here. Because of the Medicine Wheel's location and the importance of ceremony in Native American life, it certainly remains a sacred site, whether or not it served any astronomical function.

Visiting Medicine Wheel

The signed gravel road into the Medicine Wheel parking area turns off U.S. 14A approximately 27 miles east of Lovell. You'll need to walk the last 1.5 miles to the site, although exceptions are made for people with disabilities and the elderly. Be sure to carry water with you, and take your time; at 9,800 feet in elevation you may get winded easily. The road passes an FAA radar dome on nearby Medicine Mountain; it's used to monitor air traffic in a three-state area and is a disturbing structure to find near such a significant Native American site. Medicine Wheel is open to the public all the time (except during Native American ceremonies), and interpreters provide information at the wheel 8 A.M.–6 P.M. daily July–September. The road to Medicine Wheel is usually covered with snow mid-October–mid-July. For more information, call the Forest Service office in Lovell (307/548-6541).

A wire fence surrounding the wheel is frequently festooned with strips of cloth, feathers, bells, herbs, flowers, sacred bundles, and other offerings left behind by Indians who come here on personal vision quests and other ceremonies. Such articles are particularly evident after solstices and equinoxes. Respect the importance of this religious site by not disturbing these items.

It is obvious why this mountain was chosen for the Medicine Wheel. The surrounding open country has scattered pine, juniper, and spruce, and the ridge drops off a 150-foot precipice just 50 feet away. From its 9,956-foot elevation, a vast panorama stretches to include the Bighorn Basin, the Wind River, the Absaroka Range, and the Pryor Mountains. Medicine Wheel is also a good place to look for hawks wheeling through the sky, especially red-tailed hawks and kestrels.

CLOUD PEAK WILDERNESS

Although maintained as a primitive area since 1932, the 189,000-acre Cloud Peak Wilderness did not receive official wilderness status until 1984. It's named for 13,175-foot **Cloud Peak,** a rocky mountain visible for 100 miles in all directions. At one time this entire range was glaciated, and reminders abound in the sharpened peaks, broad U-shaped valleys, and multitude of lakes in glacial tarns. There are even a few small patches of glacial ice. The Big Horns still get plenty of snow, leaving many hiking trails in the high country blocked until July. One oddly named mountain in the wilderness is **Bomber Mountain,** just south of Cloud Peak. An Air Force B-17 bomber crashed here in 1943, killing all 10 men on board. It was not found for two years. For the sad but fascinating story, see *The Bomber Mountain Crash: A Wyoming Mystery* by R. Scott Madsen (Buffalo, WY: Mountain Man Publishing).

With more than 140 miles of trails and thousands of acres more above timberline, hiking and horsepacking opportunities abound throughout Cloud Peak. Bears are not usually a problem in the Cloud Peak Wilderness. Backcountry users must fill out registration cards, available at the trailheads or local Forest Service offices. Be sure to camp at least 100 feet from water sources and trails and hang all food out of reach of black bears. Use existing campsites whenever possible to lessen your impact. No campfires are permitted above 9,200 feet. The Forest Service produces a free map/guide to the wilderness area, which lists additional precautions.

For complete trail and historical information on the wilderness, get *Hiking Wyoming's Cloud Peak Wilderness* by Erik Molvar (Helena, MT: Globe Pequot Press). Be sure to buy

CLOUD PEAK WILDERNESS AREA

FOREST SERVICE VISITOR CENTER

To Burgess Visitor Center and Sheridan

BEAR LODGE RESORT

14

Burgess Junction

To Lovell

BIGHORN MOUNTAIN LODGE

Big Horn

National

Forest

TIE FLUME

OWEN CREEK

To Shell

14

CABIN CREEK

RANGER CREEK

Coney Lake

Cloud Peak

Big Goose Falls

STULL LAKES TRAILHEAD

TWIN LAKES PICNIC AREA

RANGER CREEK

RED GRADE REGISTRATION BOX

Big Horn

LITTLE GOOSE

COFFEEN PARK

CROSS CREEK

Wilderness

Dutch Oven Pass

Shell Lake

Edelman Pass

Geneva Pass

Black Tooth Mountain

Cloud Peak Reservoir

EDELMAN TRAILHEAD

UPPER PAINT ROCK LAKE

MEDICINE LODGE LAKE

PAINTED LAKES TRAILHEAD

LOWER PAINT ROCK LAKE

Cloud Peak 13,175ft

Mount Woolsey

Bomber Peak

Lake Solitude

Elk Lake

HUNTER TRAILHEAD   To Buffalo

Florence Pass

COLD SPRINGS

BATTLE PARK TRAILHEAD

PAINT ROCK TRAILHEAD

WEST TENSLEEP LAKE

DEER PARK

Mather Peaks 12,348ft

Cloud Peak

Wilderness

16

MIDDLE FORK

PINES LODGE

THE HACK

CIRCLE PARK

SOUTH FORK INN

SOUTH FORK

SOUTH FORK MOUNTAIN LODGE

ISLAND PARK

SITTING BULL

DEER HAVEN LODGE

BOULDER PARK

Meadowlark Lake

MEADOWLARK LAKE RESORT

BIG HORN SKI RESORT

BULL CREEK

SHEEP MOUNTAIN LOOKOUT

CANYON

LOST CABIN

Big Horn

National

Forest

To Ten Sleep

16

TENSLEEP CREEK

LEIGH CREEK

To Burgess Junction and Sheridan

90

87

Sheridan

0   5 mi

0   5 km

topographic maps before heading out. Local bookstores and Forest Service offices sell a waterproof Trails Illustrated/National Geographic wilderness map; it's worth getting. Check with the Forest Service office in Sheridan, Buffalo, or Lovell for a list of permitted outfitters and wilderness regulations. Always practice "no trace" camping; if you don't know what this means, pick up a handout from any of the Forest Service offices.

Access into Cloud Peak Wilderness is via several entry roads along U.S. 16 on the southern border—most of the use comes from this side—and from the north (U.S. 14) at Cross Creek and Ranger Creek campgrounds and near Twin Lakes Picnic Ground. Other entrance points surround Cloud Peak, but many require long hikes up 4WD roads to get to the wilderness boundary.

Wayfaring Traveler Ranch (307/762-3536, www.tctwest.net/~wtr) offers guided llama treks to the Big Horn Mountains, along with llama rentals.

CRAZY WOMAN CANYON

One of the most fascinating drives in the Big Horns slices through Crazy Woman Canyon. Several stories exist for the origin of the canyon's name. One claims it's named for an Indian woman who went insane while living alone in her tepee here. Another version says it came from a white settler who was pushed to insanity when Indians murdered and scalped her husband. Soldiers from Fort Laramie reportedly found her wandering the area. Either way, it wasn't exactly a soothing name for migrants on the old Bozeman Trail! The canyon cut by cascading Crazy Woman Creek is a stunning one with steep—and sometimes bizarrely shaped—cliffs on both sides. A rough gravel road (high-clearance vehicles are recommended; this isn't for trailers or RVs) heads down from U.S. 16 and continues all the way to the mouth of the canyon and then out to Hwy. 196. The drive is actually more interesting (and easier on your brakes) if you do it from Buffalo westward, but be ready for a long and difficult trip in either direction.

RECREATION

You'll find plenty to see and do in the Big Horns, including Medicine Wheel and the Cloud Peak Wilderness. Stop by the Forest Service office in Sheridan, Buffalo, or Lovell for descriptions of other hiking trails.

Sheep Mountain Area Trails

Several trails take off from Sheep Mountain Road on U.S. 14A approximately 30 miles east of Lovell and three miles east of the turnoff to Medicine Wheel. **Littlehorn Trail** parallels the Little Bighorn River for 18 miles. Along the way you'll see 1,600-foot canyon faces and water fountaining off the limestone cliffs of Leaky Mountain. The trailhead is two miles up Sheep Mountain Road (Forest Road 14). Up the road 0.5 mile farther is the trailhead for **Porcupine Falls,** a 200-foot-tall cascade accessible via a very steep 0.5-mile path. Along the way the trail passes a 1930s-era gold mine. Much of the area here was burned in a 1988 forest fire.

One of the not-to-be-missed places in the Big Horns is spectacular **Bucking Mule Falls,** a 600-foot cascade dropping into Devil Canyon. The trailhead for Bucking Mule Falls lies 11 miles off U.S. 14A via Sheep Mountain Road and Devil Canyon Road, and the waterfall is a three-mile round-trip hike. You can also do an 11-mile hike by following the trail to the falls and then continuing south to Porcupine Campground.

Cloud Peak Wilderness Trails

The **Stull Lakes-Coney Lake Trail** is one of the shortest hikes into the lake country of Cloud Peak. It climbs three miles from the trailhead (0.25 mile west of the Twin Lakes picnic area), passes Stull Lake, and ends in the alpine country surrounding Coney Lake. Watch for elk and deer in late summer.

An excellent 21-mile loop hike begins at **Paintrock Lakes Trailhead** on the west side of the wilderness. This route traverses a wide variety of country, from dense timber to rocky mountain passes and small glaciers. The path climbs to a trail junction 1.5 miles west of Cliff Lake. From here, turn left and follow the trail to Geneva Pass (10,300 feet). The trail drops to

Lake Geneva and then follows East Fork Creek to the junction with the **Edelman Trail.** This path leads over Edelman Pass, around Emerald Lake, and then back down to the **Edelman Trailhead,** just 1.5 miles by road from your starting point. You'll find all sorts of other hikes and side trips in this area.

Another loop trip takes you to Lake Solitude. Begin at the **Battle Park Trailhead** approximately 15 miles north of Meadowlark Lake. Take the road to Tyrell Ranger Station and turn left after one mile, continuing up the rough gravel road to the trailhead. The trail climbs up Paint Rock Creek past Grace Lake and Lake Solitude to Mistymoon Lake. Beyond this you can either return on the same route or follow the trail down a steep valley to the waterlily-filled Lily Lake. Continue downhill to the **Paintrock Trailhead** on Forest Road 17, and turn right (northwest), following the road one mile back to your starting point. The loop is approximately 17 miles round-trip.

The easiest—and probably busiest—route to the top of Cloud Peak takes off from **West Tensleep Trailhead** on Forest Road 27. Plan on a strenuous 10 hours for the 11-mile climb up and back. This is not a developed trail and will require considerable rock hopping, but the spectacularly desolate scenery makes it worthwhile. Be prepared for sudden weather changes, and carry an ice axe into August. For detailed route instructions up Cloud Peak, get a topographic map and a copy of Erik Molvar's trail guide.

The **Elk Lake Loop** (19 miles round-trip) begins at **Hunter Trailhead** on the southeast side of the wilderness and involves lots of climbing. Follow the old jeep trail to Soldier Park, a scenic grassy meadow. Turn north at the trail junction and follow the path to Elk Lake. Along the way are some outstanding views across the alpine terrain to Cloud Peak. Turn left at Elk Lake, head up over a pass, and then south to **North Clear Creek Trail.** Follow it downhill to Soldier Park and back to the trailhead.

More Hikes and Caves

Black Mountain Lookout, west of Dayton on U.S. 14, offers surprisingly dramatic vistas from the top of a 9,300-foot peak. This old Forest Service fire lookout is open to the public and sits at the end of a one-mile trail. Get there by turning south on Forest Road 16 when it leaves U.S. 14 two miles west of the Fallen City area and follow it four miles to the trailhead.

The trailhead for **Tongue River Canyon** is 3.5 miles southwest of Dayton to the end of Tongue Canyon Road. This trail climbs up the canyon for a total of 11.5 miles, offering glimpses of the old McShane brothers' tie flume—built in 1894 and stretching for 26 miles—the fast-flowing blue-ribbon fishing stream (cutthroat, rainbow, brook, and German brown trout), and canyon walls reaching 1,000 feet into the air. Ambitious hikers may want to continue all the way to Burgess Junction. Locals float down parts of the river during the spring, when water levels are high.

Tongue River Cave is near the Tongue River Canyon trailhead and stays open all year. With more than one mile of passages, it's one of Wyoming's most popular caves but has been considerably vandalized with broken formations, trash, and graffiti. Because of its size, inexperienced spelunkers can become lost, so ask locally for someone willing to act as a guide. More than 100 other caves honeycomb this country; see the Forest Service for locations and precautions.

Another trail worth exploring if you want an out-of-the-way adventure is the **Little Bighorn River Canyon Trail** starting west of Ranchester along the Wyoming–Montana border. Contact the Forest Service in Sheridan for directions and details on this multiday trek.

An enjoyable waterfall is **Big Goose Falls.** Follow Forest Road 26 (it starts approximately five miles south of Burgess Junction on U.S. 14) to Big Goose Ranger Station, and then continue via Forest Road 296 to the end. The falls are about five miles below the ranger station along the East Fork of Big Goose Creek. They include plunge pools and water-sculpted rocks.

Cross-Country Skiing

The Big Horns provide some of the finest snow in Wyoming, with groomed cross-country ski trails at several locations. **Sibley Lake** has 15 miles of trails and a warming hut off U.S. 14; **Willow Park** has 23 miles of trails near Meadowlark Lake; and **Pole Creek** has 13 miles of trails and a warming hut off U.S. 16. Trail descriptions are available from local Forest Service offices. The rest of the forest makes for outstanding skiing most of the winter, but you'll need to break your own trail.

Downhill Skiing and Snowboarding

Big Horn Ski Resort (307/366-2424 or 888/244-4676, www.thebighorn.com) is next to Meadowlark Lake Resort along U.S. 16 (22 miles east of Ten Sleep and 42 miles west of Buffalo). This small area has an 800-foot vertical rise, with a double and a triple chairlift, a hand tow, lights on all runs, and extensive snowboard facilities that include three half-pipes and a terrain park. Snowmaking equipment lengthens the ski season, and ice skating is also available. The resort opens around Thanksgiving and closes in April. Lifts operate daily throughout winter, and full-day lift tickets cost $36 adults, $29 students, or $18 ages 8–12. Get food, drinks, and ski and snowboard rentals at the modern base lodge. Ski lessons are offered, and snowmobile rentals are available.

Antelope Butte Ski Area is a small family ski area along U.S. 16. It was closed through the 2005–2006 winter but may reopen. Call 307/674-2600 for the latest.

Snowmobiling

Snowmobilers will find 300 miles of groomed trails throughout the national forest; get a route map from chamber of commerce offices or the Forest Service. Rent snowmobiles at **Big Horn Ski Resort** (307/366-2424 or 888/244-4676, www.thebighorn.com), or **Bear Lodge Resort** (307/752-2444, www.bearlodgeresort.com).

ACCOMMODATIONS AND FOOD

Scattered throughout the Big Horns are seven mountain lodges and a guest ranch, most of which have bars and restaurants. Several of these are open year-round, providing a good base for snowmobiling and skiing adventures. Note that phone service can be spotty in the mountains, and you may not always be able to get through to the resorts.

Lodges Along U.S. 14

You'll find year-round accommodations at **Bear Lodge Resort,** at Burgess Junction at 8,300 feet in elevation (307/752-2444, www.bearlodgeresort.com). Modern motel rooms are $79 d; $119 for the hot tub suite. Rustic cabins cost $45, and modern condo cabins (two-night minimum stay) are $149–169 d. Guests will enjoy an indoor swimming pool and fitness center, plus the indoor and outdoor hot tubs. Pitch a tent for $8, or park RVs for $19. If you're staying elsewhere, take a shower for $3. The lounge is a great place to shoot a game of pool or tip a brew. Also here are a restaurant, gas pumps, laundry, and a gift shop with a few groceries and supplies. Winter snowmobile rentals are available.

Snowshoe Lodge (307/899-8995 or 800/354-8637, www.thesnowshoelodge.com) is six miles out a dirt road that turns off near Antelope Butte Ski Area (south of Burgess Junction on U.S. 14). Because of its mountain location at 8,300 feet, the lodge is popular with wintertime snowmobilers and skiers. It's also a favorite spot for summer weddings, family reunions, and mountain-biking. One room is available in the main lodge, along with three delightful modern log cabins with kitchenettes and private baths. Lodging is $165 for up to four people, with various packages available. Mountain bikes are provided, and snowmobile rentals are available. Other amenities include an outdoor hot tub, sauna, lounge, and double-deck porches facing the mountains. Winter is the busy season here, and you'll need to book well ahead for weekends in February and March. Snowshoe Lodge is part of the 250,000-acre Flintner Ranch, one of the largest in Wyoming.

Spend a delightful week in the Big Horn Mountains at historic **Ranger Creek Guest Ranch** (307/751-7787 or 888/817-7787, www.rangercreekranch.net), 16 miles east of Shell.

Guests (maximum 30) stay in rustic log cabins around a central bathhouse and enjoy horseback rides, trout fishing, day trips to Cody, evening barbecues, western dancing, and nature talks. The summer season is mid-June–mid-September, but the ranch is open year-round, with fall hunting trips and winter snowmobiling. All-inclusive six-night rates are $3,600 for two people, or $2,100 for two people for a three-night stay.

Near the crest of the mountains and one mile west of Burgess Junction, **Bighorn Mountain Lodge** (307/751-7599, www.thebighornlodge.com) is a large place with modern facilities that include a café, bar, lodging, gift shop, and gas. The cozy duplex cabins are $55 d (plus $5 for each additional guest); winter rates are $85 d. Two-bedroom kitchenette units sleep up to six for $100 (or $185 in winter), and all have private baths. RV parking is $25 with full hookups, and tent sites cost $15. If you aren't staying here, showers are $3.

Lodges Along U.S. 16

Deer Haven Resort (18 miles east of Ten Sleep on U.S. 16, 307/366-2424 or 888/244-4676, www.thebighorn.com) has a big variety of lodging choices. Least expensive are the plain-Jane rustic cabins ($49 d) with a separate bathhouse, or you can step up to a larger cabin ($115 d) or remodeled motel rooms ($85 d) with private baths. Also available is a chalet-style cabin ($210 for up to six) with two bedrooms, a full kitchen and dining room, and a beautiful four-bedroom ranch house ($475) that sleeps 10 and has its own hot tub. RV sites are $20. The resort is open year-round, and it also has a restaurant and lounge with a pool table and stone fireplace.

The same owners have **Meadowlark Lake Resort,** 22 miles east of Ten Sleep or 42 miles west of Buffalo along U.S. 16 (307/366-2424 or 888/244-4676, www.thebighorn.com), which has an equally diverse choice of lodging, including simple cabins ($79 for up to four) with a central bathhouse and motel rooms ($85–100 d). Families appreciate the cottages with kitchenettes and pull-out futons; one-bedroom units

are $129 for up to four, and two-bedroom units sleep six for $159. RV hookups are $25. The resort has Wi-Fi and rents rowboats, canoes, paddleboats, and fishing gear for the lake, as well as mountain bikes to explore surrounding country. The restaurant serves three meals a day, with a lounge and gift shop; open year-round.

The Pines Lodge, 14 miles west of Buffalo on U.S. 16 (307/684-9291 or 888/917-4637, www.pineslodgewyoming.com), has a wide variety of cabins, plus a restaurant and bar. Rates start at $38 d for a rustic cabin with separate bathhouse. Duplex cabins that share a bath are $52 d. Larger cabins have private baths and kitchens, and some contain fireplaces or wood stoves. These cost $65–125, with the biggest one sleeping eight. There's a minimum three-night rental on the larger cabins. RV hookups are $20, and tent spaces cost $15. Kids can throw in a line at the private fishing pond. The cabins and camping spaces are open May–October. The restaurant serves a Sunday brunch, and is open—along with the lounge—on winter weekends. Horseback rides are also available in the summer.

South Fork Mountain Lodge (307/267-2609, www.southfork-lodge.com), 16 miles west of Buffalo on U.S. 16, has simple cabins that sleep four guests for $99 (shared bathhouse), and an eight-person cabin with private bath, fridge, and TV for $200. Also here is a full-service restaurant and small bar, along with horseback rides and pack trips. The lodge is open May–November or by reservation only during the winter snowmobile season.

Constructed by the Civilian Conservation Corps in the 1930s, the Forest Service's historic **Muddy Guard Station** (307/684-7806) sleeps up to six for $40 per day. The log building has propane lights and a woodstove but no running water or electricity. This unique cabin, 25 miles west of Buffalo on U.S. 16, is open year-round.

Camping

With 34 Forest Service campgrounds ($8–11) in the area, you should have no trouble finding places to commune with nature. Most are above 5,000 feet in elevation, making for welcome escapes from summertime heat. During weekends in July and August, campgrounds along the main roads are frequently filled (get there before 2 P.M.), but harder-to-reach campgrounds usually have space. Reservations ($9 fee) are available for 10 popular campgrounds at 518/885-3639 or 877/444-6777, www.reserve-usa.com). Forest Service offices in Sheridan, Buffalo, and Lovell can all provide details on dates, cost, and access to these camping places,

or find the same information on the web at www.fs.fed.us/r2/bighorn. In addition to the official campgrounds, you can camp anywhere in Bighorn National Forest for free, as long as you are 0.5 mile off the main highways.

The BLM's delightful **Five Springs Campground** ($7, open year-round) is two miles off U.S. 14A, on the western border of the national forest. The road is steep and narrow, so no RVs more than 25 feet should travel this route. Scenic **Five Springs Falls** is nearby.

Sheridan

The attractive and vibrant small city of Sheridan (pop. 16,000) has plenty to see, several fine restaurants and art galleries, great country in the nearby Big Horn Mountains, and a genuine sense of history. At just 3,745 feet above sea level, it claims the lowest elevation of any Wyoming town, making for hot summer days. It's only 25 miles from Sheridan to the Montana border via I-90.

The country around Sheridan was settled by a broad mixture of Europeans—everyone from British lords to Polish coal miners. Their heritage carries on in such events as an annual polka festival and weekly polo matches at Big Horn Equestrian Center, the oldest polo club in the nation. Locals brag that Sheridan has a wealth of things to do and a surprising cultural richness without the crowds of Yellowstone and Jackson Hole. The town is, however, losing some of the hard-edged cowboy feel from the past and gaining more Western-wear boutiques, gift shops, galleries, antique stores, and eateries all the time.

Like other towns in the Powder River Basin, Sheridan was built on coal, cattle, farming, and the railroad. In 1882, John D. Loucks took a liking to the country here and decided to establish a town, drawing up a plat on a piece of brown wrapping paper. He named the new place for his commanding officer during the Civil War, General Philip Sheridan, and immediately set about getting others to come. For

several years Sheridan competed with nearby Big Horn City for the county seat, a title that ensured survival. Finally, in 1885, Sheridan promoters offered cowboys at the fall roundup free lots in the town. When most accepted, Sheridan finally had enough folks to incorporate. Almost overnight (literally, in some cases), businesses in Big Horn City moved to Sheridan, sometimes bringing their buildings along with them.

When the Burlington and Missouri Railroad reached Sheridan in 1892, the town suddenly changed. Now ranchers could get their cattle to market more easily and visitors could stay in the sumptuous Sheridan Inn. Farming became more profitable as investors built large grain mills and a sugar-processing plant. The first underground coal mines opened in 1883, but the Burlington Railroad didn't begin using the coal in its engines until 1903. For the next several decades these "black diamonds" were mainstays of the local economy. Sheridan soon had 1,500 people, wooden sidewalks, 30 saloons, six churches, and two opera houses. Small mining towns—Dietz, Acme, Kooi, Model, Riverside, and Carneyville—opened in the surrounding countryside, inhabited by thousands of European emigrants; newspapers often featured ads in both Polish and English. Electric streetcars were added in 1911, with frequent interurban service to the surrounding coal mines.

SHERIDAN

POWDER RIVER COUNTRY

To Decker, MT
To Ft Mackenzie
To Billings, MT
EXIT 20
BIGHORN MOUNTAIN KOA
337
87
90
KMART
SUPER 8 MOTEL
BRAMBLE MOTEL
FORT RD
KOOI ST
SEYMOUR ST
STEVENS AVE
WENZEL ST
TRAILS END MOTEL
STAGE STOP MOTEL
Goose Creek
BUDGET HOST MOTEL
14TH ST
ASPEN INN
SUPER SAVER MOTEL
SUNDOWN MOTEL
13TH ST
11TH ST
10TH ST
ALAMO MOTEL
9TH ST
8TH ST
PETER D'S RV PARK
7TH ST
6TH ST
SHERIDAN COUNTY HISTORICAL MUSEUM
VISITOR CENTER
To Wyarno
5TH ST
MOTEL 6
BIGHORN NATIONAL FOREST OFFICE
To Dayton
330
FAIRGROUNDS
HIGHLAND BLVD
CLAREDON AVE
4TH ST
BEST VALUE INN
336
EXIT 23
GAME & FISH OFFICE
WINGATE INN
SEE "DOWNTOWN SHERIDAN" MAP
LEWIS ST
3RD ST
2ND ST
1ST ST
VAL VISTA ST
MAIN ST N
GOULD ST
BROADWAY ST
SHERIDAN AVE
SPAULDING ST
GENERAL CROOK MONUMENT
TRAIL END STATE HISTORIC SITE
PIONEER RD
YMCA
MANDEL ST
ALGER ST
KROE LN
Kendrick Park
POOL
BEAVER ST
BRUNDAGE ST
ICE RINK
LOUCKS ST
GRINNELL AVE
331
Creek
WORKS ST
Goose
WATER ST
To Beckton
Big
WYOMING AVE
COFFEEN AVE
HOLIDAY LODGE
COLLEGE AVE
Washington Park
MAIN ST S
MONTANA ST
AVOCA AVE
SUGARLAND DR
90
BIG HORN AVE
Little Goose Creek
APPLE TREE INN
SUGAR LANE
WAL-MART
ALBERTSON'S
HOLIDAY INN
RIVERSIDE ST
EXIT 25
AIRPORT RD
SHERIDAN AVE S
LARIAT MOTEL
THE MILL INN
AIRPORT
BRUNDAGE LN
PARKWAY MOTEL
DAYS INN
COMFORT INN
14
To Gillette
87
6TH AVE E
SHERIDAN COLLEGE
To Buffalo

0   0.5 mi
0   0.5 km

World War II brought prosperity as local mines operated at full tilt and new technology allowed construction of the first open-pit mine. After the war, however, trains shifted to diesel and homes began burning less-polluting natural gas, so that by 1953 the last of the old coal towns had died. With increasing demand for western coal in the 1970s, Sheridan's population boomed again. Sheridan's economy now depends on a mixture of mining, the railroad, ranching, government jobs, and tourism. Many locals cross into Montana for jobs at the Decker and Spring Creek coal mines, while others work at the local veterans' hospital or the Burlington Northern switching yard. Coal-bed methane gas production has become an increasingly important part of the economy, and you'll see compressor stations and gleaming pipelines throughout the area.

SIGHTS
◀ Trail End State Historic Site

On spacious grounds overlooking Sheridan, Trail End State Historic Site (400 Clarendon Ave., 307/674-4589, www.trailend.org) is the city's best-known attraction. Trail End is open 9 A.M.–6 P.M. daily June–August and 1–4 P.M. daily March–May and September–mid-December, closed mid-December–February. Entrance costs $2 for nonresidents or $1 for Wyoming residents.

This was the home of John B. Kendrick, a wealthy rancher and a powerful Democratic politician. Born in Texas in 1857, Kendrick was raised as an orphan. He became a ranch hand by age 15 and, after trailing cattle north to Wyoming, fell in love with the country and took a job as a ranch foreman. At age 34, he married 17-year-old Eula Wulfgen, and they lived on a ranch in southeastern Montana for the next 18 years.

Through the years Kendrick acquired more than 200,000 acres of land in Wyoming and Montana, grazing tens of thousands of his cattle. He personally financed local homesteaders, friends, former employees, and relatives. Politics beckoned once Kendrick was firmly established as a rancher and businessman, and he

served first as governor and then as a U.S. senator until his death in 1933. One paper called him "the craftiest politician the state has ever produced." Kendrick helped expose the Teapot Dome Scandal and gained funding for the massive Kendrick Project, a series of dams and irrigation canals on the North Platte River.

Shortly before entering politics, Kendrick selected the site for his end-of-the-trail mansion high atop a hill overlooking Sheridan. Begun in 1908, Trail End took five years to complete and served primarily as a summer home because politics kept Kendrick away the rest of the year. The mansion is in the Flemish Revival style, with curvilinear gables on the third-floor windows, a red-tile roof, hardwood floors, mahogany walls, and exposed-beam ceilings.

Trail End State Historic Site in Sheridan

Many of the sumptuous original furnishings (including a 25-foot-long Kurdistan rug) are still inside. Look for photos of several of Kendrick's ranches upstairs.

The house cost $165,000 in an era when typical homes went for less than $1,000. Its 18 rooms include a third-floor ballroom with a loft where musicians could play without interfering with the dancers below. The built-in central vacuum system still works. Heating Trail End sometimes required up to one ton of coal each day.

Sheridan Inn

Built in 1893, Sheridan Inn (307/674-5440) was considered by many to be the premier hotel between Chicago and San Francisco. Visitors included Presidents Theodore Roosevelt, Taft, and Hoover, along with such celebrities as Will Rogers and Ernest Hemingway. Architect Thomas Kimball modeled the inn after a Scottish hunting lodge, with dormer windows on all 62 rooms; *Ripley's Believe It or Not!* labeled it "The House of 69 Gables," a name that has stuck through the years. Inside, carpenters added hand-hewn pine beams, three large cobblestone fireplaces, the Buffalo Bill Bar (imported from England), elegant oak furnishings, and the first electric lights in Sheridan. Colonel William F. (Buffalo Bill) Cody was later a co-owner of the hotel and used the veranda to audition performers for his Wild West Show. It was operated as a hotel until 1965 and later as a restaurant and bar.

On the corner of 5th and Broadway, Sheridan Inn is a registered National Historic Landmark, with a huge porch wrapping around the sides. Try to see if you can find all 69 gables. Step inside to explore this gracious place or enjoy a pleasant lunch or dinner at Wyoming's Rib and Chop House, housed in the old saloon. The impressive oak and mahogany back bar was built in England, shipped by rail to Montana, and finally delivered to Sheridan by ox-drawn wagon. The gift shop sells an interesting booklet about Kate Arnold, who lived here for 65 years and whose ashes are buried in an upstairs wall. Her ghost still shows up periodically to make sure the inn is well managed. Informative guided tours are available in summer for $5 adults, $2 seniors, free for kids under 12, but two days' notice is required. A self-guided tour brochure costs $2, and the basement houses a few historical items.

King's Saddlery

Well worth a stop is King's Saddlery (184 N. Main St., 307/672-2702 or 800/443-8919, www.kingssaddlery.com), a Sheridan-area fixture since the 1940s. When you step inside the doors, the smell of leather is almost overwhelming. The long, narrow shop has handmade saddles, leatherwork, ropes, spurs, chaps, belt buckles, cowboy hats, and various other tack for horses and their riders. Be sure to check out the miles of ropes filling racks in the back room (across the alley). Many top rodeo cowboys come in to buy their lariats, and King's sells 40,000 high-quality ropes a year.

The free **King's Western Museum** in the back is jammed to the rafters with 500 gorgeous saddles and thousands of other cowboy tools of the trade. It's one of the finest collections of cowboy memorabilia anywhere. Featured attractions include a Hope saddle (the earliest Western saddle), one owned by Gene Autrey, and the saddle used the only time the famous bronc Steamboat was ever ridden. Also here is an impressive display of Indian artifacts, including a beaded pottery vase and bridles made a century ago. Lots of trivia too: John Wayne's pants from *Red River,* Gary Cooper's cowboy hat, and even a unicorn cow. Leather craftsman Jim Jackson is in the back most days, carving intricate belts, checkbook covers, guest books, or other items. These are all by special order and very expensive—belts cost $150–300. King's Saddlery is fittingly named: Both Queen Elizabeth and the former king of Saudi Arabia have visited, and Presidents Clinton and Reagan were both given King's leather belts. King's Saddlery is open 8 A.M.–5 P.M. Monday–Saturday. The store also has a mail-order catalog.

Sheridan County Historical Museum

Sheridan County Historical Museum (850 Sibley Circle, 307/673-0644, www.sheridan-countyhistory.org, open 9 A.M.–6 P.M. daily late May–early Sept., reduced hours the rest of the year, $4 adults or $2 kids) is just off I-90 exit 23. Inside are displays on General Crook and the Sioux, historic photos, and dioramas of Sheridan in 1888 and the Tongue River tie flumes, along with changing exhibits.

Fort Mackenzie

Built in 1902, Fort Mackenzie never really served much of a military function. Pushed through Congress by Wyoming's powerful senator Francis E. Warren, the fort was ostensibly built as a base to put down Indian uprising on nearby reservations, but the last major Indian battles had occurred 20 years earlier. It was named for General Ranald S. Mackenzie, a veteran of the Civil War and various Indian battles. Through the decades, the fort shrank from 6,280 to 342 acres, and the last troops departed during World War I. In 1922, it became a 339-bed hospital for mentally ill veterans, but with facilities for other vets. You're welcome to walk around the grounds and admire the old brick buildings, but check in at the administration office first. Signs describe the various buildings.

Sheridan County Library

Sheridan's excellent library (320 N. Brooks, 307/674-8585) encloses a small collection of Indian artifacts and items from early settlers. The Wyoming Room has an extensive collection of old books, maps, and paintings, including a mural of the Wagon Box Fight; upstairs you'll find more historical exhibits and current artwork and a model of the Medicine Wheel. On the library walls are 11 paintings by Bill Gollings (1878–1932), a self-taught, but accomplished, cowboy artist.

Across the road is **Whitney Park,** a nice place to relax. On the grounds is a sod-roofed **log cabin** built in 1878. It served as Sheridan's first post office, and later it was used as a school, store, law office, and bank.

Other Sights

A historical marker on the corner of West Dow and Alger marks **General Crook's campsite.**

In 1876 the general camped here at the junction of Big and Little Goose creeks with 1,325 men and 1,900 pack animals after being forced to a stalemate by Sioux and Crow warriors on the Rosebud River. The fight took place just eight days before Custer would die at nearby Little Big Horn.

Directly across from the Sheridan Inn is the old red Sheridan **train depot,** built in 1892 and now housing a bar. Nearby is a huge Chicago, Burlington, and Quincy Railroad locomotive. Downtown on 3rd and Gould streets is a Sheridan **streetcar** from the early 1900s. History and architecture buffs should pick up a copy of the guide to Sheridan's **Main Street Historic District** at the visitor center.

One of the buildings mentioned—the **Mint Bar** (151 N. Main St., 307/674-9696)—offers a genuine taste of the West. The bar opened in 1907 and operated a backroom speakeasy throughout Prohibition. A mahogany bar stretches the length of the room, cedar shingles are burned with local brands, and an eight-foot rattlesnake skin holds center stage. Cartoonist Linda Barry's description of the Mint says it all: "Stuffed animal heads galore. Taxidermied fish galore. Burlwood carpentry galore." The bar even made it into a scene in the 1985 movie *Wild Horses.*

Across the road from the state rest area/information center on 5th Street, the **Wyoming Game and Fish Department Visitor Center** (307/672-7418, 8 A.M.–5 P.M. Mon.–Fri. year-round) contains several professionally produced and informative wildlife and fish displays. Although small, this collection is well worth a visit.

In summer you can hop on the **Sheridan Trolley** (307/672-2485 or 800/453-3650, $1) at the state information center for a ride through town. It runs all day Monday–Saturday.

ENTERTAINMENT AND EVENTS

A classic 1923 structure in the heart of town, **WYO Theater** (42 N. Main St., 307/672-9084, www.wyotheater.com) has live plays, dance performances, and musical events through-

out the year. **Carriage House Theater** at Trail End (307/672-9886, www.trailend.org) presents plays October–May and sometimes has children's theater in the summer. Drop by the Kendrick Park band shell for free Tuesday night **concerts in the park** in July and August. Music varies from polka to jazz.

For all-around fun and drinking with your friends, it's hard to beat the classic **Mint Bar** (151 N. Main St., 307/674-9696). Enjoy live rock-and-roll on weekends at **Scooter's Bar** at the Holiday Inn (1809 Sugarland Dr., 307/672-8931). Pool, snooker, and darts are featured attractions at the **Bruce's Caboose Bar,** in the old depot across from the Sheridan Inn.

Watch movies inside **Centennial Theatres** (36 E. Alger St., 307/672-5797), or visit one of Wyoming's few surviving drive-ins: **Skyline Drive In** (1739 E. Brundage La., 307/674-4532).

Cowboyography (www.cowboyography.com) is a fun mid-February festival of cowboy poetry and music.

Buffalo Bill Days (www.buffalobilldays.org) comes around the fourth weekend of June, celebrating the Old West with a grand Victorian ball, horse-drawn parade, Wild West Show, and living history demonstrations, all to benefit the Sheridan Heritage Center.

In existence for more than 75 years, the six-day **Sheridan WYO Rodeo** (307/672-2485 or 800/453-3650, www.sheridanwyorodeo.com) comes around the second week of July, bringing with it not just professional rodeo cowboys at the "world's largest one go-round rodeo," but also a parade down Main Street, bed races, a pancake breakfast, carnival, country-and-western bands, and street dances.

The third weekend of July is the **Prairie Rose Arts Festival,** held at the historic Sheridan Inn. This juried event attracts a wide range of artists, woodworkers, potters, and jewelers.

In early August, visit the **Sheridan County Fair** (www.sherfair.com) for 4-H displays, pig wrestling, a petting zoo, live music, and a free barbecue. It's followed by the **Sheridan County Rodeo** later in the month. The rodeo even includes stick-horse races for those under age four. **Big Horn Mountain Polka Days** is a fun Labor Day weekend event that attracts hundreds of polka enthusiasts. Oom-pa-pa!

See *Big Horn* (under *Around Sheridan*) for other popular local events: the Fourth of July fireworks show, Canyon Ranch Indian Paintbrush Festival in late August, and Don King Days over Labor Day weekend.

SHOPPING

You'll find a fine selection of Wyoming titles at **The Book Shop** (117 N. Main St., 307/672-6505) and **Sheridan Stationery** (206 N. Main St., 307/672-8080 or 888/266-5730). The Book Shop has occasional poetry readings and other literary events.

Western Gear

Custom Cowboy Shop (350 N. Main St., 307/672-7733) has quality boots, hats, saddles, and tack. Also be sure to visit **King's Saddlery** (184 N. Main St., 307/672-2702 or 800/443-8919; see *Sights*). **Little Willow Traders** (166 N. Main St., 307/672-0200) is a fun shop with distinctive gift items, furnishings, and knickknacks.

Bits and Spurs (655 Riverside, 307/672-8459 or 800/672-8459, www.tombalding.com) is a unique shop where you'll find beautiful bits and spurs welded by Tom Balding. In addition to his craftsmanship, the shop also sells cowboy music, leather goods, art, and jewelry.

Galleries

Several Sheridan art galleries provide enjoyable browsing, including **Bozeman Trail Gallery** (190 N. Main St., 307/672-3928) inside King's Saddlery, and **Bucking Buffalo Supply Co.** (317 N. Main St., 307/674-4999). The latter is a fun place packed with quality Western wear, home furnishings, and Indian-made items. **Wyoming Expressions** (250 N. Main St., 307/673-9698, www.bighornmtncreations.com) sells rustic Wyoming-made furniture.

Bella Gallery (38 S. Main St., 307/675-1007, www.belladisplay.com) has changing fine-arts exhibits in the front and a graphic arts business in the back.

Foothills Gallery (134 N. Main St., 307/672-2068, www.foothillsartgallery.com) showcases large oil, acrylic, and watercolor paintings, along with bronze sculptures, pottery, and blown-glass pieces.

RECREATION

Kendrick Park has a small game preserve where bison and elk are visible, plus a great playground for kids. Swim at the summer-only **outdoor swimming pool** (307/674-9434, www.sheridanrecreation.com) in the park, and feel like a kid again on the 90-foot-long water slide. The **YMCA** (417 N. Jefferson, 307/674-7488) has two swimming pools, plus racquetball and tennis courts and a fitness center.

Golfers will want to try out the 18-hole **Kendrick Golf Course** (307/674-8148, www.kendrickgolf.com) three miles west of town, or the acclaimed 27-hole **Powder Horn Golf Club** (307/672-5323, www.thepowderhorn.com) in Big Horn, six miles south of Sheridan.

Big Horn Mountain Sports (334 N. Main St., 307/672-6866, www.bighornmountainsports.com) has a big choice of outdoor gear and topographic maps. Much of this gear can also be rented, including cross-country skis, snowboards, snowshoes, tents, sleeping bags, backpacks, inline skates, and fly rods. **Back Country Bikes** (307/672-2453) inside Big Horn Mountain Sports rents mountain bikes and has helpful maps of nearby cycling trails.

Fly Shop of the Big Horns (227 N. Main St., 307/672-5866 or 800/253-5866, www.troutangler.com) has Orvis gear, classes in fly-casting and fly-tying, and guided fishing trips on the Big Horn and Platte rivers. Rent float tubes and fins here.

In the winter, the outdoor **Sheridan Ice Rink** (475 W. Brundage St., 307/674-9423, www.sheridanice.org) is open for public skating and hockey.

ACCOMMODATIONS

The Chamber of Commerce's website (www.sheridanwyoming.org) has an overview and web links to local lodging and campgrounds.

Most of Sheridan's motels lie along Coffeen Avenue and Main Street.

Under $50

Parkway Motel (2112 Coffeen Ave., 307/674-7259, $36 s or $38–50 d) is an OK low-priced choice, and most units have fridges and microwaves. Full kitchenettes available. **Stage Stop Motel** (2167 N. Main St., 307/672-3459, $42 s or $45 d) is a small place with minimalist rooms, all with microwaves and fridges.

The units aren't new, but they're clean and well-maintained at **Aspen Inn** (1744 N. Main St., 307/672-9064, $40–46 d).

$50-100

If none of the budget choices are to your liking, head to **Sundown Motel** (1704 N. Main St., 307/672-2439, $50–60 d) with a small heated outdoor pool on the premises, and Wi-Fi is available. (Same owners as the Aspen Inn.)

Find spacious and clean motel rooms, plus a continental breakfast, guest computer, and Wi-Fi at **Budget Host Motel** (2007 N. Main St., 307/674-7496 or 800/226-9405, www.budgethostsheridan.com, $45 s or $60 d). Also worth a look is **Holiday Lodge** (625 Coffeen Ave., 307/672-2407, $52 d) with remodeled rooms, all containing microwaves and fridges. Stay at **Apple Tree Inn** (1552 Coffeen Ave., 307/672-2428 or 800/670-2428, $50 s or $55 d) with decent rooms, most containing microwaves and small refrigerators

Motel 6 (911 Sibley Circle., 307/673-9500 or 800/466-8356, www.motel6-sheridan.com, $70 s or $80 d) is certainly one of the nicer (and more expensive) versions of the chain, with large rooms, an indoor pool, fitness center, and Wi-Fi.

Trails End Motel (2125 N. Main St., 307/672-2477 or 800/445-4921) has a mix of old and new rooms for $64–74 d. Family units are $78 for six people, and log cabins cost $54 d. An indoor pool is on the premises, and Wi-Fi is available in the lobby.

$100-150

Occupying a historic flour mill on the south side of town, the **Mill Inn** (2161 Coffeen Ave., 307/672-6401 or 888/357-6455, www.sheridan-millinn.com, $89 s or $99–105 d) lends a new meaning to the term "hitting the sack." The mill section of the building houses hotel rooms, while the old tower contains offices. Hotel amenities include an exercise facility and a filling breakfast (with waffles and fresh fruit).

Holiday Inn (1809 Sugarland Dr., 307/672-8931 or 877/672-4011, www.sheridan-wyo.com, $109–129 d) is the largest and most elaborate place to stay in Sheridan. A bit spendy, but the hotel features an atrium with a waterfall and two restaurants, plus a small indoor pool, sauna, hot tub, exercise room, Wi-Fi, and fitness center.

Sheridan's newest lodging place, **Wingate Inn** (1950 E. 5th St., 307/675-1101 or 800/228-1000, www.wingateinns.com), out of town near exit 23, features large rooms, an indoor pool, hot tub, fridges, microwaves, Wi-Fi, guest computer, in-room safes, and breakfast bar. Standard rooms are $99–139 for up to four, and suites cost $175 d.

Dude Ranches

The Sheridan area is home to a pair of classic dude ranches. The first in the region was run by the Hilman family, who took in their first paying dudes in 1889. It operated until the 1930s. Famous ◖ **Eaton's Ranch** (307/655-9285 or 800/210-1049, www.eatonsranch.com), 18 miles west of Sheridan, is one of the oldest, largest, and best-known dude ranches in America. The three Eaton brothers—Howard, Alden, and Willis—began ranching in North Dakota in 1879 but soon found themselves overwhelmed by visiting friends from the East. Eventually one offered to pay, and thus was born the first dude ranch. Initially these "dudes" (a term that both Buffalo Bill and Howard Eaton took credit for using first in this context) stayed wherever they could find space, eating the cowboy's grub and joining in on chores. In 1904, the brothers bought a ranch along Wyoming's Wolf Creek that would eventually grow to 7,000 acres. Fourth- and fifth-generation members of the Eaton family

Peter D's RV Park

still run the ranch. The ranch is a big one, accommodating up to 125 guests in modernized cabins. Many families return year after year to Eaton's. The emphasis—not surprisingly—is on horseback rides; this is one of the few dude ranches where experienced riders can head out on their own (with permission from the ranch). Other facilities include an outdoor pool, trout fishing, and a nearby nine-hole golf course. The ranch is open June–September with a three-night minimum stay. All-inclusive rates are $370–400 per night for two people.

High in the Big Horn Mountains 30 miles southwest of Sheridan, **Spear-O-Wigwam Dude Ranch** (307/674-4496 in summer, 307/655-3217 in winter, or 888/818-3833, www.spear-o-wigwam.com) has been in operation since 1923. This classic guest ranch—Ernest Hemingway wrote *A Farewell to Arms* while staying here—has comfy log cabins, a large lodge with a stone fireplace, a hot tub, pool tables, and horseback rides or overnight trips into the nearby Cloud Peak Wilderness (extra fee). A fishing guide is available to

teach fly-fishing. There's a three-night minimum stay, and all-inclusive rates are $380 for two people per night, or $2,400 for two people per week. The ranch plays host to a maximum of just 30 guests and is open mid-June–mid-September.

Camping

Many campgrounds ($8–11) are open within nearby Bighorn National Forest (see the *Big Horn Mountains* section).

Sheridan/Bighorn Mountains KOA (63 Decker Rd., 307/674-8766 or 800/562-7621, www.koa.com) has quiet tent sites for $21–26 and RV sites for $28–34. Basic cabins are $39–52 d. It's open year-round and has a pool, hot tub, minigolf, wireless Internet, and bike rentals. **Bramble Motel and RV Park** (2366 N. Main St., 307/674-4902, $25 RVs, no tents) has a handful of year-round RV sites. **Peter D's RV Park** (110 S. Joe St., 307/673-0597 or 888/673-0597, www.wyomingrvpark.com, $28 RV) is quiet and popular with retirees. Open April–October; no tents.

In addition to the official RV parks, many

folks hitch up their wagons in the old-time country setting of the Wal-Mart parking lot. No charge, and a delightful ambience to boot.

FOOD

Sheridan has a broad choice of eateries, including a remarkable number of notable restaurants. You'll find cowboy breakfasts, gourmet lunches, brewpub favorites, and an Italian bistro all within a few blocks of each other.

Breakfast and Lunch

Sheridan Palace Restaurant (138 N. Main St., 307/672-2391) is an old-time downtown establishment that opens at 6 A.M. and serves breakfast all day.

Java Moon (176 N. Main St., 307/673-5991) is a fun hangout place with a couple of streetside tables out front and a piano inside. Check out the daily lunch specials, including various panini sandwiches with soup or salad for $7. It also serves espresso, teas, smoothies, juices, freshly baked breads, salads, ice cream, and brick-oven pizzas. **Tumbleweed** (37 S. Main St., 307/672-5637) serves smoothies, fruit juices, wraps, and other healthy fare.

Burgers and Pizza

The best local burgers can be found—surprisingly enough—at **Dairy Queen** (544 N. Main St., 307/674-9379). **Golden Steer Restaurant** (2071 N. Main St., 307/674-9334) is a family dining place with good steaks.

Little Big Men Pizza (1424 Coffeen Ave., 307/672-9877) has reasonable pizza, burger, and salad meal deals, including all-you-can-eat lunch and dinner smorgasbords.

Fine Dining

Oliver's Bar and Grill (55 N. Main St., 307/672-2838, www.oliversbarandgrill.com) is a spacious and surprisingly chic downtown restaurant. Diners can watch the cooks at work in the open kitchen while sampling delectable appetizers, sipping a fine wine from the extensive list, or enjoying a dinner with such treats as chile-rubbed New York strip steak, grilled rack of lamb, or pepper-crusted

tuna. And oh, yes, those cooks make very tasty sweet-potato fries. Try to save room for desserts, including a decadent espresso crème brûlée cheesecake. Open dinners only ($12–39 entrées) most days, but it does have a great Sunday champagne brunch menu of grilled steak and eggs, Belgian waffles, and seasonal crepes. Dinner reservations advised. Owner and chef Matt Wallop is the son of former U.S. Senator Malcolm Wallop. **Brundage Street Wines** adjoins Oliver's and sells freshly baked breads, along with gourmet cheeses and wines. Check the calendar for upcoming wine tastings and other events.

On the corner of 5th and Broadway, the historic Sheridan Inn houses **Wyoming's Rib and Chop House** (307/674-5440), popular for lunch and dinner. Baby-back ribs, fresh grilled fish, and rib eye steaks are the main attractions, along with pasta jambalaya, Caesar salads, and Cajun-spiced fries. The front porch makes a delightful seasonal dining spot. Lunches and dinners are the same prices: $10–19, but call ahead for dinner reservations.

Empire Grill (5 E. Alger St., 307/674-4300, www.theempiregrill.com) is another star on the Sheridan scene, with an informal setting that attracts families, business folks, and travelers. The lunch menu encompasses sandwiches, salads, pastas, and small pizzas. Dinners add new pizza and pasta variations, along with fresh fish, Angus steaks, and such specialties as the cherry port–glazed pork loin chops. Most dinner entrées are $16–22, but you can also get small pizzas for $8 and up.

International

Get reasonably authentic Chinese cookery at **Golden China Restaurant** (in the T&C Shopping Center at Brundage and Coffeen, 307/674-7181). **Dragon Wall Restaurant** (425 N. Brooks, 307/673-6888) has a big Chinese buffet for lunch or dinner, including a not-so-Chinese salad and dessert bar. **Kim's Family Restaurant** (2004 N. Main St., 307/672-0357) is one of the only Korean restaurants in Wyoming.

Pablo's Restaurant and Cantina (1274 N. Main St., 307/672-0737) serves reasonably priced Mexican food and has a full bar. **Los Agaves** (922 Coffeen Ave., 307/674-0900) is also of note.

Pubs and Brewpubs

Sanford's Grub, Pub and Brewery (1 E. Alger St., 307/674-1722) is a popular pub with garage-sale flotsam and jetsam dangling from the ceiling, TVs in all directions, and rock tunes blasting over the speakers. The bar claims one of the largest beer selections in Wyoming with more than 125 brews, including 37 on draft. The diverse menu makes this a popular (and noisy) place to hang out with friends, but the food is nothing special.

Across from the post office, **Pony Bar and Grill** (3 S. Gould St., 307/674-7000) combines a sports bar with pub-grub burgers, quesadillas, buffalo wings, and other favorites, along with quart-size mugs of beer to quench your thirst. Pony Bar has 14 brews on tap, and its wraparound covered deck is a Friday after-work gathering place.

Groceries

Sheridan has several large grocers, including locally owned Warehouse Market and Sprout's Market, along with Albertsons, Safeway, and Wal-Mart SuperCenter.

INFORMATION AND SERVICES

The **Sheridan Visitor Center/State Information Center** (307/672-2485 or 800/453-3650, www.sheridanwyoming.org) is in the rest area at the 5th Street exit off I-90. Inside are various historical displays, a 3-D map, and a panoramic view of the Big Horns from the windows. The center is open 8 A.M.–7 P.M. daily late May–early September, 8 A.M.–5 P.M. daily till mid-October, and 8 A.M.–5 P.M. Monday–Friday the rest of the year.

The **Bighorn National Forest Supervisor's Office** (307/674-2600, www.fs.fed.us/r2/bighorn) is at 2013 Eastside 2nd Street.

Sheridan County Library (335 W. Alger St., 307/674-8585, www.sheridanwyolibrary.org) houses computers where you can check email. Check out the Wyoming Room, with a variety of Indian artifacts, including vests, moccasins, pipes, and weapons.

One of Wyoming's largest colleges, **Sheridan College** (307/674-6446 or 800/913-9139, www.sheridan.edu) was founded in 1948 and offers degrees in both academic and technical fields.

Wash clothes at **Econo-Wash Laundry** (19 E. 5th St., 307/672-7899), **Super Saver Laundromat** (1789 N. Main St., 307/672-0471), or **Sugarland Laundromat** (1842 Sugarland Dr., 307/672-5736).

Memorial Hospital of Sheridan County (1401 W. 5th St., 307/672-1000, www.sheridanhospital.org) has a 24-hour emergency room.

GETTING THERE AND AROUND
By Air

Sheridan airport is just southwest of town. **Big Sky Airlines** (800/237-7788, www.bigskyair.com) has daily nonstop flights connecting Sheridan with Denver and Billings.

By Car and Bus

Rent cars at the airport from **Avis** (307/672-2226 or 800/831-2847, www.avis.com) or **Enterprise Rent-a-Car** (307/672-6910 or 800/736-8222, www.enterprise.com). Get them in town at **Truck Corral Auto Rental** (1320 Coffeen Ave., 307/672-7955).

Powder River Transportation (307/674-6188 or 800/442-3682, http://gillette.coachusa.us) has daily bus service to Billings, Montana, and most towns in central and eastern Wyoming, continuing to Denver or Rapid City. Buses stop at Red Eagle Food Store (590 E. 5th St.).

The **Sheridan Trolley** (307/672-2485 or 800/453-3650, $1) leaves the information center Monday–Saturday in the summer, with tours of town.

Around Sheridan

RANCHESTER

Fifteen miles north of Sheridan, the little village of Ranchester (pop. 700) has a couple of interesting historical sites. **Connor Battlefield State Historic Site** is right in Ranchester's city park. It's a very pleasant place with picnic tables, year-round camping ($12 for nonresidents, $6 for Wyoming residents), and tall cottonwood trees along the Tongue River (so named because of a tonguelike rock along a tributary). Good fishing for brown trout can be found here. A cable footbridge leads across the river. Day use is $2 for nonresidents or $1 for Wyoming residents.

Despite its bucolic setting, the park has a gruesome history representing one of the worst atrocities in the Powder River Basin. The massacre took place in 1865 during a time of hit-and-run battles throughout the plains, set off by mass killing of the Cheyenne at Sand Creek in Colorado and continued in dozens of Indian attacks on settlers and emigrants. Red Cloud had just struck against Platte Bridge Station (see *Casper* in the *Central Wyoming* chapter) a few weeks before, killing 28 men, and the army was eager to avenge that raid as well as attacks along the Bozeman Trail.

General Patrick E. Connor—a proponent of the shoot-first, ask-questions-later school of military diplomacy—attacked Indian villages throughout the West, killing 200 Shoshone in an 1863 Utah attack and then rampaging through Nevada and Idaho. Connor's 1865 expedition to the Powder River included nearly 1,000 soldiers and 179 Pawnee and Winnebago scouts. Most of the effort was a failure as Indians kept ahead of the ponderous military wagons, but on August 29 Connor's men came upon Chief Bear's Arapaho village along the Tongue River. Connor ordered his men, "You will not receive overtures of peace or submission from the Indians, but will attack and kill every male Indian over 12 years of age." In a pell-mell rush, Connor's men slaughtered 63 men, women, and children, destroyed 250 lodges along with much of their winter supplies, and captured more than 1,100 ponies. Eight troopers died. No one ever determined whether the Arapaho they encountered were the same ones who had been attacking along the Bozeman Trail. The expedition ended when the government realized it was costing more than $1 million per month for transportation alone. A chastened Connor stashed his supplies at Fort Connor (later renamed Fort Reno) and returned to Fort Laramie.

Four miles west of here on U.S. 14, another monument marks the **Sawyer Fight.** Here, two days after Connor attacked the Arapaho along the Tongue River, Arapahoes retaliated against a 100-man road-building expedition led by Colonel James Sawyer. Three of his men were killed and the rest were pinned down for nearly two weeks before finally being rescued by Connor's troops.

Events and Recreation

Ranchester Days in June features a horseshoe tournament, horse-drawn parade, arts-and-crafts booths, and street dance. Children will enjoy the kid-designed **wooden playground** of forts and slides at the elementary school.

Practicalities

Stay at the clean and friendly **Ranchester Western Motel** (307/655-2212, www.ranchestermotel.com, $55–65 d), with microwaves, fridges, and continental breakfasts. **Lazy R RV Park and Campground** (307/655-9284 or 888/655-9284) has year-round RV sites ($21) and a couple of tent sites ($14).

Get groceries at **Buckhorn Groceries** (307/655-9766. The local minimall has a launderette.

DAYTON

The village of Dayton (pop. 670) contains the little log-cabin studio of watercolorist **Hans Kleiber** (1887–1966). The studio is now used as a combination museum and visitor center, with iffy hours in the summer only. Kleiber was known as "Artist of the Big Horns," and his works are internationally collected today. Inside are his press, art books, and several etchings. Dayton's old **bell tower,** built in 1910 to warn of fires, is now in the city park.

Dayton Days, held the last weekend in July, has the usual country favorites, including a parade, food and craft booths, a firefighters' water fight, Indian dancing, and a street dance.

Summerhouse Books (307/655-9714) sells both used (and some new) titles. Also worth a look is **Monastery Creations Gift Shop** (307/655-9013), with soaps, candles, salves, and other items crafted by the Benedicine Sisters of San Benito Monastery.

Anglers will find blue-ribbon trout fishing along the Tongue River. Dayton also has an outdoor seasonal **swimming pool** next to the Kleiber cabin.

Accommodations and Food

Foothills Campground and Motel (307/655-2547, www.foothillscampground.com) has cabins for $30 d, along with kitchenettes that cost $50 for up to five people; free Wi-Fi too. Camp along the river here for $15, or park RVs for $21. Noncampers can shower for $2. Both campground and cabins are open May–October only.

Whitehorse B&B (307/655-0245, www.whitehorsebedandbreakfast.com, $75–95 d) is a renovated 1903 inn in the heart of Dayton, with three Old West–style guest rooms, private baths, and a full breakfast. It has a flower-lined patio and a deck facing the mountains. Kids are welcome.

Branding Iron Restaurant (307/655-2334) is a good ma-and-pa café. Open daily, with Sunday buffet breakfasts for $12.

EAST OF SHERIDAN

Some of the prettiest plains country in Wyoming lies along U.S. 14, a quiet and scenic road that curls through miles of ranchland and winter wheat. The road heads southeast from Sheridan, gradually narrowing as it climbs through rugged hills and down a long green valley filled with fine ranches and modern homes. The

dinky settlement of Wyarno consists of a post office and the **Wyarno Bar and Grill** (307/737-2510), a locals' hangout and a favorite for bikers. It attracts folks from Sheridan with good food and cold beer.

Ucross

At the crossroads called Ucross, a huge red barn ("Big Red") dominates the view. The 22,000-acre Ucross Ranch is headquarters for the nonprofit Ucross Foundation (307/737-2291, www.ucrossfoundation.org), which operates an important retreat for writers, painters, poets, composers, sculptors, playwrights, photographers, and other artists. Each year about 100 selected artists enjoy a spring and fall residency program that includes individual work spaces, a printmaking studio, a gallery, and comfortable living accommodations. It's all to give artists the time to focus on ideas, theories, and works. Author E. Annie Proulx wrote both *Postcards* and *The Shipping News* while staying here; the latter won her a Pulitzer Prize in 1992. Drop in for a tour of the immaculate buildings or to check out gallery exhibitions.

The **Ucross Foundation Art Gallery** is open 8:30 A.M.–4 P.M. Monday–Friday all year, plus 10 A.M.–4 P.M. Saturday in summer. Big Red was headquarters for the enormous Pratt and Ferris Cattle Co., a spread that extended 35 miles along Clear Creek. At one time, more than 35,000 calves were branded each fall, and the huge barn could hold 30 teams of horses. The "U Cross" was its brand.

If you're in the area around the **Fourth of July,** stick around for food, games, live bluegrass music, and a spectacular fireworks display. It's a huge event attracting several thousand people.

Ucross is also home to **The Ranch at Ucross** (307/737-2281 or 800/447-0194, www.blairhotels.com), a luxurious guest ranch that fills with Tauck Tour buses during summer. The ranch typically has a few rooms available for other travelers, but don't expect to have the place to yourself. Guests stay in comfortable condo-type rooms or modern cabins for $249 d, including a full breakfast in the restaurant and access to the outdoor pool and tennis court. Horseback rides cost $20 per hour. The Ranch at Ucross is open May–September only.

Clearmont and Leiter Area

The 20 miles east from Ucross are some of the most distinctive in Wyoming. The road parallels cottonwood-bordered Clear Creek, winding its way down the grassy hillsides. The Big Horn Mountains form a dramatic Western backdrop, and large ranches dot the countryside with stone buildings and spreading old trees. It's easy to see why the Sioux fought so hard to keep this country out of white hands!

The largest settlement between Gillette and Sheridan, Clearmont is a pleasant place with a bit more than 100 folks, tall deciduous trees lining the handful of streets, a combination library/community center, and a pretty little town park with an old concrete jail. The town has a bar or two and meals, along with a convenience store/gas station. Be sure to stop at **Best Kept Secret** (307/758-4456 or 877/758-4456, www.thebest-keptsecret.com), an interesting quilt shop.

East from Clearmont is minuscule Leiter, with Joe's Motel, a bar, and the **Leiterville Country Club** (307/758-4343), locally famous for its steaks.

The highway crosses the Powder River at the little settlement called Arvada and then heads east to Spotted Horse. **Powder River Experience** (307/758-4381 or 888/736-2402, www.powderriverexperience.net) offers ranch vacations on a 24,000-acre spread three miles south of Arvada. Guests ride horseback and join in short cattle drives or other ranch activities. You can stay by the night or the week in the two comfortable guesthouses with shared or private baths; meals and lodging included. The ranch is open year-round and accepts a maximum of 15 guests at a time. Rates vary widely depending on the length of stay and activities included.

Spotted Horse

At Spotted Horse—named for a minor Cheyenne chief—the combination country store/gas station/saloon/café is worth a stop, if only to hang out with locals in the bar. Hard times

BEST WISHES FROM SPOTTED HORSE

May your horse never stumble
Your spurs never rust
Your guts never grumble
Your cinch never bust
May your boots never pinch
Your crops never fail
While you eat lots of beans
And stay out of jail
    –from a sign in Spotted Horse

show in the faces of local ranchers. The bar has a jukebox, a few fast-food items on the menu, and cold beer. Its walls are carpeted with an amusing collection of old junk, historic photos, and cheesecake biker shots.

The 1811 overland expedition of the Astorians passed through the Spotted Horse area. During the 1930s, tourists en route to Yellowstone posed on a stuffed bucking bronc in the back paddock, but once I-90 was completed, business plummeted and the local economy suffered a long decline.

Southeast from Spotted Horse, the highway curves toward the coal mines of Gillette and past an ever-increasing number of coalbed methane gas developments. The red scoria rock of the highway points through summer-green grass. (Also called clinker, this rock was created when coal burned underground, baking adjacent shale and sandstone to a bright red. Similar red roads exist all over Powder River Basin.) Old windmills pump water for cattle and sheep. From atop the hills a landscape of fences, phone lines, plowed fields, bales of hay, and horses spreads out in all directions. The sun darts between cotton-ball clouds as a lone cyclist pumps up the road, swerving around the smashed jackrabbits and passed by pickup trucks with gun racks and drivers with tipped-back cowboy hats. This is the true West, not the region cutesified for tourists. Red-sided buttes rise above the rolling plains. The new ranch

houses—trailer homes—stand next to aging farmsteads and collapsed log cabins; imported pickups sit in the driveways and satellite dishes guard the front yards. If you like grass and sky, brilliant starry nights, antelope, haystacks, and oil wells, you'll love this place. Stop for a while and listen to the silence broken only by the meadowlarks and the wind. God's country.

BIG HORN

Although I-90 cuts south of Sheridan toward Buffalo, U.S. 87 offers a much more interesting route, taking you through rolling ranch country and past cottonwood-lined draws. Along the way are the little settlements of Big Horn and Story and the historically rich country around old Fort Phil Kearny and the Bozeman Trail. The area's beauty has long attracted wealthy corporate executives and politicians, who come here to relax as gentlemen ranchers in ostentatious homes.

Tiny Big Horn was founded in 1879 by O. P. Hanna (local Indians called him "Big Spit" because of his tobacco chewing), a ceaseless promoter who sent glowing accounts of "Big Horn City" to various newspapers. A reporter decided to investigate and found that the town consisted primarily of a few outlaws, including "Big Nose" George Parrott and Jesse James's outlaw brother, Frank. A few homesteaders and settlers did take the bait, however: By 1884 Big Horn City had a hotel, three stores, two blacksmith shops, three saloons, a newspaper, a school, a church, and even a college of sorts.

Sights

Through the years, most of Big Horn's businesses moved to Sheridan, but still here is **Big Horn Mercantile** (307/674-1534), built in 1882 and considered the oldest business in northern Wyoming. In addition to the basics, the market also serves espresso, tasty sandwiches, burgers, and ice cream. Take a look inside for the photo of Queen Elizabeth, who visited this historically British area in 1984. From the same era is **Bozeman Trail Inn** (307/672-9288), where you'll find one of the oldest bars in Wyoming. Not fancy, but great burgers.

A historic 1881 blacksmith shop houses the **Bozeman Trail Museum** (open 11 A.M.–6 P.M. Sat.–Sun. June–August and on many weekday evenings; ask at Big Horn Mercantile for access when it's closed). The museum displays various local memorabilia, historical photos, and a small gift shop. The ceiling is "branded" with local cattle brands. No admission charge. The town park next door makes a pleasant picnic spot.

The **State Bird Farm** (307/674-7701), six miles south of town on Bird Farm Road, raises 16,000 pheasants each year. These birds are released around Wyoming shortly before the fall hunting season, just in time to get shot as "wild game." The farm also has show birds, including more than a dozen species of pheasants, along with peacocks, turkey, chukkar, and guinea hens. Come here in early May to see the cute pheasant chicks.

For a panoramic view of the surrounding country, follow Hwy. 335 west from Big Horn. The road turns to gravel after three miles and then continues into the Big Horn Mountains as **Red Grade Road** (Forest Road 26). The route's a bit rough and too steep for RVs, but it provides outstanding vistas after just a couple of miles. The road eventually connects with U.S. 14, but bring along a Forest Service map.

Polo

Certainly the last thing one might expect to find in Big Horn is a polo field, but the English tradition lives on at **Big Horn Equestrian Center,** south of town on Bird Farm Road (307/674-8687, www.bighornpoloclub.com). Tournament polo games are held on Sundays mid-May–early September, with practice games on Wednesdays and Fridays. The caliber of play varies, but you may see top-notch visiting players from South America.

Polo games began on the **Polo Ranch** (www.poloranch.com) a couple miles west of Big Horn before moving to the present equestrian center in the 1980s. The Polo Ranch is hard to miss, with an enormous white barn and immaculate white picket fences. It positively reeks of money. The owner is Joe Schuchert, an executive with American Standard, the toi-

let-fixture company, and a financial backer to right-wing Christian radio stations around Wyoming. The ranch was formerly owned by ex-U.S. Senator Malcolm Wallop, the grandson of Sir Oliver H. Wallop, seventh earl of Portsmouth (who served in the Wyoming Legislature before returning to England to sit in the House of Lords). Oliver Wallop and the two Moncrieffe brothers bought Western horses for the British Army during the Boer War, shipping 20,000 of them overseas. To test the ponies, the British purchasing officer would ride them the length of a polo field. Malcolm Moncrieffe trained a team on this field and later competed with them in England. Thus began what is believed to be the oldest polo club in America. Some of America's wealthiest individuals own spreads in the surrounding country, including Summerfield Johnston (Coca-Cola) and the members of the Mars (candy) family.

Events

The **Fourth of July** fireworks show at Big Horn Equestrian Center is the biggest in the Sheridan area and well worth seeing. The big annual event in Big Horn is **Don King Days** (800/453-3650) on Labor Day weekend, with steer roping and bronc riding, along with polo matches at the equestrian center. **Canyon Ranch Indian Paintbrush Festival** (307/673-9035) in late August is a very popular musical event held at the Wallop Ranch in Big Horn, with performances by the Wyoming Symphony and a variety of other artists.

Accommodations

In the cool pine forests seven miles west of Big Horn, ◖ **Spahn's Big Horn Mountain Bed and Breakfast** (307/674-8150, www.bighornwyoming.com, $110–140 d) is one of the most enjoyable B&Bs in Wyoming. Ron Spahn, a former geologist and lawyer who runs the place with his wife, Bobbie, a nurse, built this immaculate three-story log home. The house is off the grid, with solar panels providing most of the electricity. Enjoy a full breakfast on the porch, where the view extends all the way to Montana, 100 miles across Powder River Basin. It's a great place to watch distant lightning storms or to just soak up the quietude. Join one of Ron's evening wildlife safaris ($39 per person with dinner) for a 4WD trip into the mountains in search of moose, deer, elk, and other animals. Guests stay in three comfortable rooms inside the main house or in one of two cabins just a short walk away. The cabins are perfect for families or honeymooners who appreciate rusticity, but they're not to everyone's taste. Plan on spending several days here; there's plenty to do nearby, and the country is grand.

At **Bozeman Trail B&B** (307/672-2381, $75 s or $95 d), a graceful blue barn (built in 1919) has been transformed into a country bed-and-breakfast with four rooms and three baths, a tasty full breakfast, and a relaxing hot tub. Longhorn cattle and a horse graze in the adjacent pasture.

On a 3,000-acre ranch owned by the Wallop family, **Canyon Ranch Lodge** (307/674-6239, www.canyonranchbighorn.com) is a stylish building that rents for $165 per person. The price includes three meals a day, and a variety of guided fishing packages are available. You can also stay by the week at a cozy and remote cabin: $300 for up to six guests. (You'll need 4WD to get there.) There's a three-night minimum on lodging.

In addition to a championship 18-hole course, **Powder Horn Golf Course** (307/674-9545 or 800/329-0598, www.thepowderhorn.com) has furnished homes for rent next to the greens, including three-bedroom duplex homes for $350; these sleep six comfortably. Also available is a big old ranch house (not updated) that sleeps 10 for $280 per night. Guests at these receive discounted rates at the golf course.

◖ BRADFORD BRINTON MEMORIAL MUSEUM

In 1892, two Scottish brothers, William and Malcolm Moncrieffe, built a spacious two-story ranch house along Little Goose Creek. It became headquarters for their Quarter Circle A Ranch. A businessman and lover of the West, Bradford Brinton bought the ranch in 1923 and enlarged the home to 20 rooms, filled

it with elegant furniture, and lined the walls with his art collection. Bradford's sister Helen owned the house after his death in 1936, and upon her passing in 1960 the building became a museum honoring her brother. The museum (307/672-3173, www.bradfordbrintonmemorial.com, $4 adults, $3 seniors and students, free age 12 and under) is open 9:30 A.M.–5 P.M. daily late May–early September, with reduced hours till late December; closed the rest of the year. Excellent guided tours are offered of the home and a creekside cabin.

Step inside to taste the genteel life and to view works by some of the West's best-known artists, many of whom were friends of Bradford Brinton. Displays change throughout the year but always include items from the 600-piece collection by such artists as John James Audubon, Hans Kleiber, Charles M. Russell, Frederic Remington, and Will Gollings. Also here are impressive Indian handicrafts, a Jefferson peace medal originally given to an Indian chief, books, and historic documents. A small gallery in the museum sells quality gifts. The log lodge of Bradford Brinton sits along Little Goose Creek and is filled with big-game trophies. Horses are still raised on the 600-acre ranch, and the rural setting is most enjoyable: Mountains rise on two sides and big old cottonwoods border the drive. Get to the Quarter Circle A by heading five miles west on Hwy. 335 from the junction with U.S. 87. Signs point the way.

STORY

The town of Story (pop. 900) is surprisingly different from nearby Sheridan and Buffalo. The road into Story winds more than 1,000 feet above the valley floor to the pine-covered slopes of the Big Horns. Locals and visitors come up to escape the hot summer air, to enjoy the restaurants, and to look for deer, elk, moose, and wild turkeys. Story is the site of "Piney Island," a stand of timber used to build nearby Fort Phil Kearny in 1866. The town was named for Nelson Story, the first man to trail cattle north across the Powder River Basin. **Story Fish Hatchery,** established in 1907, raises trout for Wyoming lakes and streams. The visitor center has interpretive exhibits and is open 8 A.M.–5 P.M. daily mid-April–mid-September, 307/683-2234. **Piney Creek Pottery** (307/683-2181) sells ceramics and other artwork.

Accommodations

Several places provide relaxing lodging in the Story area. Set on five wooded acres, **Piney Creek Inn B&B** (307/683-2911, www.pineycreekinn.com) is a quiet place with a variety of accommodations, all with private baths. The rambling log house contains a guest room ($95 d) and two-bedroom suite ($145 for four people). Two cabins are also available. The larger one ($150 d) has two bedrooms, a kitchen, and spiral staircase, while the newer cabin ($150 d) is a favorite of honeymooners and contains a fireplace, kitchenette, and jetted bathtub. A hearty full breakfast is included, and guests will enjoy the hot tub off the main lodge, the large porch out front, and the pavilion for events. Children are welcome, as are horses (corral in the back). The friendly owners at Piney Creek also set up tours of the area, trail rides, and a variety of ranch activities.

Wagon Box Inn (307/683-2444 or 800/308-2444, www.wagonbox.com) has cozy cabins starting for $65 d, up to a secluded five-person cabin with kitchen for $99. Also available are shared-bath bunkhouse accommodations for $40 s or d. All guests can use the sauna and hot tub. Reserve at least a month ahead for midsummer visits here.

Story Pines Inn (307/683-2120 or 800/596-6297, www.storypinesinn.com, $69–74 d) is a small motel with modern accommodations, in-room fridges, Wi-Fi, and access to a hot tub and picnic area. The town launderette is also here.

Nestled along North Piney Creek, **Hitchin' Post Lodge** (307/683-3039, www.storybnb.com) offers three options for travelers: a loft room in the main house ($125 d), a suite ($145 d)—both including breakfast, and a three-bedroom home that sleeps up to 12 for $295. An outdoor pool and creekside hot tub are on the grounds.

Occupying a 1,000-acre spread south of Story, **Rafter Y Ranch** (307/683-2258, www .rafteryranch.com) has space for just 20 guests in comfortable log cabins with fireplaces, porches, and private baths. It's a good place to ride horses or just relax in the foothills of the Big Horns. No minimum stay, but most guests stay at least four days; $370 for two people per day all-inclusive. Open July–August.

Little Piney Ranch (307/683-2667, www.littlepineyranch.com) is south of Story and within walking distance from historic Fort Phil Kearny. Comfortable rental cabins are $125–150 with a two-night minimum; the larger one sleeps six. Horseback rides are also available. It's a pretty and peaceful setting.

Food

Wagon Box Inn (307/683-2444 or 800/308-2444, www.wagonbox.com) serves some of the best lunches and dinners in the area, with the house specialty—prime rib—plus steaks, pasta, chicken, seafood, and a substantial wine list. Entrées are $13–40. The Wagon Box has a large patio and occasional live music.

◖ **Piney Creek General Store** (307/683-2400, www.pineycreekgeneralstore.com) is an old-fashioned country store with crowded aisles and a surprising selection of groceries. A tiny café (Waldorf A' Story) here serves three wonderful meals a day, including homemade soups, creative sandwiches, and other treats. A few tables are inside, with more on the deck. There are nightly specials, including Saturday night ribs. Well worth a stop!

Tunnel Inn (307/683-2296) is an attractive log building with gourmet steaks, fish, and more served in an upscale setting.

THE BOZEMAN TRAIL

The discovery of gold in Montana during the 1860s triggered an avalanche of miners and businessmen. The fastest route to the Virginia City goldfields headed northwest from Bridger's Ferry (near present-day Douglas) through the Powder River Basin and then west across Montana. One of the pioneers who scouted and constantly promoted the "Montana Road" was John M. Bozeman (as in Bozeman, Montana). Before being killed by Indians on the Yellowstone River in 1867, he led several groups up the Bozeman Trail, as the route became known. Hundreds of others would die along Bozeman's route to the goldfields. Guide Jim Bridger knew that the Sioux would never stand for whites in their Powder River country—a place they had recently wrested from the Crows, the Shoshone, and the Arapahoes. Instead, he recommended a different route that would cut west of the Big Horn Mountains. Unfortunately, Bridger's advice went unheeded, and as attacks on emigrant wagon trains increased in 1864, so did pressure to protect them from the Sioux. Appeals to Washington brought military assistance in the form of forts filled with soldiers and cavalry. Parallels between the events that followed and America's experience in Vietnam—from the guerrilla warfare to the hurried exit of U.S. troops at the end of the conflict—are disconcerting.

Red Cloud's War

The first salvo by the army came in General Connor's savage wanderings through the Powder River in 1865 (see *Ranchester*). The following year, while treaty negotiations were being held at Fort Laramie, Colonel Henry B. Carrington and a battalion of infantry marched in, heading for the Bozeman Trail, where they planned to build new forts. Red Cloud, a fiery military leader of the Oglala Sioux, grew more and more angry, shouting:

> *Great Father sends us presents and wants new road, but White Chief goes with soldier, to steal road before Indian says yes or no....White man lies and steals. My lodges were many, but now they are few. The white man wants all. The white man must fight, and the Indian will die where his fathers died.*

The treaty was signed by older chiefs and the "Laramie Loafers," who hung around the fort, but not by Red Cloud. He and his warriors stormed out, arriving at Powder River ahead of Colonel Carrington.

Carrington was a strange man to direct this massive undertaking. A political appointee with no battlefield experience—let alone experience with guerrilla warfare—he approached the task of building forts and protecting travelers along the Bozeman Trail with a take-no-chances attitude that rankled his trigger-happy men. The troupe left Nebraska with a 30-piece brass band, carriages, and comfortable furnishings, earning the name "Carrington's Overland Circus."

Once finally in the Powder River country, Carrington split his men into three groups, stationing some at Fort Reno near present-day Buffalo (begun the previous year by General Connor) and sending others to build Fort C. F. Smith in Montana. These way stations were to provide military escorts for travelers and havens from Indian attacks. Instead, they came under attack, and Carrington's men nearly became prisoners inside them.

Fort Phil Kearny

In the heart of the Powder River country along Little Piney Creek, Carrington found good water, grass so thick that horses could barely walk through it, and timber close at hand. It seemed the perfect site for a fort. His guide, the famed Jim Bridger, pushed instead for a site farther north, away from the center of Sioux country. To Bridger, these "damn paper collar soldiers" seemed bound and determined to get killed.

Construction on the fort began on Friday, July 13th, 1866. The new garrison—named Fort Phil Kearny for a Civil War general—measured 600 by 800 feet and was entirely enclosed by a heavy log stockade. Big enough for 1,000 men, it never housed anything close to that many. Both Indian attackers and white defenders came to view this as the West's most-hated fort. From the first day, Carrington was harassed by the Sioux; by mid-December, more than 50 raids on the troops and civilians had left 17 military men and 58 civilians dead. Many of the horses and mules were stolen in the raids, and more than 700 cattle were lost when the Indians created a stampede by driving a herd of buffalo into them. With winter setting in, food and ammunition shortages

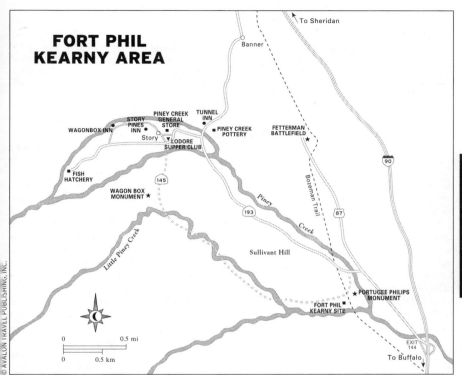

FORT PHIL
KEARNY AREA

© AVALON TRAVEL PUBLISHING, INC.

POWDER RIVER COUNTRY

made conditions worse, and even the nightly band concerts could not maintain morale. Jim Bridger revealed something of even greater concern after one of his scouting trips:

> Crow chiefs report that it took a half a day's ride to go through the villages of the war parties on Tongue River. The Sioux chiefs said they would not touch the new fort on Powder River [Fort Reno] but would destroy the two new forts, in their hunting grounds, meaning Phil Kearny and C. F. Smith.

Fetterman Fight

Again and again, the Sioux tempted soldiers into traps, drawing them away with attacks on the vital wood wagons (more than 4,000 logs

were used in the stockade) and workers cutting hay, or by stealing horses and then attacking the pursuers. Carrington's caution caused dissension in the ranks, and when a new company of cavalry arrived, led by Captain William J. Fetterman, the dissension edged on open revolt. Fetterman, like General George A. Custer, had achieved fame for his bravery during the Civil War and, like Custer, would meet an early death. Fetterman viewed the Sioux with reckless disdain, claiming, "I can take 80 men and go to Tongue River through all the Sioux forces." Jim Bridger responded to this boast by telling him, "Your men who fought down South are crazy! They don't know anything about fighting Indians."

On the morning of December 21, 1866, Indians attacked a wood train, and a force of cavalry and infantrymen under Captain Fetterman was sent out. Disobeying orders from Colonel Carrington, Fetterman responded to taunts by Sioux decoys (including young Crazy Horse) by following them into an ambush. Perhaps 2,000 warriors of Red Cloud, High Back Bone, Red Leaf, and Little Wolf suddenly appeared in the tall grass. Within a half hour, all 81 soldiers had been killed. Until Custer's last stand a decade later, this event was the worst annihilation of any American force. Carrington had lost his most experienced fighters. Perhaps 30 Sioux died in the raid. Troops sent out to investigate what had happened found the frozen bodies horribly mutilated. They buried the men in a mass grave.

After the Fetterman Fight, just 119 soldiers remained to guard against several thousand Sioux. Fearing further attacks, Carrington put the fort on full alert and sent messengers to Fort Laramie in a desperate bid for help. John "Portugee" Phillips made the 236-mile ride in four nights of hard riding, struggling through subzero temperatures and blinding blizzards and traveling at night to avoid Indian attacks. In a scene straight out of a Hollywood movie, Phillips staggered into a gala Christmas-night ball with the stunning news. His exhausted horse collapsed and died from pneumonia two weeks later. Because of bad weather, help did not reach Fort Phil Kearny for another two weeks, but the feared Indian attacks never came. Colonel Carrington was reassigned to Fort McPherson in Nebraska—accidentally shooting himself in the foot on the way out—and it took many years to clear his name of the Fetterman disaster.

Wagon Box Fight

Fearful of another attack, soldiers removed running gear from the woodcutter's wagons (used to haul logs for the fort), creating a makeshift fortress from the wagon boxes. They filled these boxes with ammunition and supplies in case of attack, and waited. The attack came on August 2, 1867, when Red Cloud's 3,000 warriors suddenly surrounded 32 woodchoppers and soldiers led by Captain James Powell. This time the tables were turned. Unbeknown

to Red Cloud, the soldiers were armed with new Springfield rifles that could fire up to 20 rounds per minute. Expecting the soldiers to take time to reload, Red Cloud sent waves of men, only to meet withering gunfire each time. Finally, after six hours of this devastation, soldiers from Fort Phil Kearny arrived with their howitzer and sent the Sioux fleeing. Four soldiers died in the Wagon Box Fight, while estimates of Indian casualties range from six to more than 1,000—Sioux warriors removed their dead after a battle, making it impossible to know how many had been killed.

The Fighting Ends

By late 1867, public sentiment had turned against the army's invasion of Sioux country, and the Bozeman Trail had become an anachronism, with miners heading to Montana via steamboat up the Missouri River. Besides, the Union Pacific Railroad was well on its way across Wyoming, and the diversion was no longer needed. (Some historians believe this was the primary reason for the building of the forts in the first place.) In 1868, the three Bozeman Trail forts were all abandoned. As the soldiers left Fort Phil Kearny, they turned back to see smoke on the horizon. The Sioux were burning it to the ground. Thus ended, at least temporarily, one of the most senseless conflicts in American history. Red Cloud finally returned to Fort Laramie to sign the treaty, having (he thought) forced the government to leave Powder River to the Sioux. Actually the treaty was ambiguous and contradictory, giving them rights to hunt buffalo on the Powder River but saying they would have to live on reservations in Dakota Territory. Six years later, the country would again boil over when another gold rush—this time in the Black Hills—brought General Custer north to fight the Sioux.

Exploring the Bozeman Trail

The site of **Fort Phil Kearny** (307/684-7629, www.philkearny.vcn.com) is now a National Historic Landmark and is managed by the Wyoming Department of Parks and Cultural Resources. The fort is 17 miles north of Buffalo and 21 miles south of Sheridan off I-90 (take exit 44). Day use at the fort costs $2 for nonresident adults, $1 for Wyoming residents; free for youths under 18. The fort is long gone—it was, after all, burned to the ground by the Indians—but a reconstruction project completed in 2000 includes two corner walls of the stockade and blockhouses on the original site. Also here is a CCC cabin from the 1930s that replicates a noncommissioned officer's room. Signs note former building locations, the cemetery, and the Bozeman Trail.

A fine small **museum** is open 8 A.M.–6 P.M. daily mid-May–September, and noon–4 P.M. Wednesday–Sunday October–mid-May. Inside, find an excellent model of the fort, videos about the Bozeman Trail and Fort Phil Kearny, and displays on Indian life.

The third weekend of June brings **Bozeman Trail Days** (www.bozemantrail.org) to Fort Phil Kearny, with archaeological tours of the fort and nearby battlegrounds, a living-history encampment, gold panning, and more. Another interesting website—www.bozemantrail.org—is maintained by the Frontier Heritage Alliance.

Other Bozeman Trail Sights

Ruts from the Bozeman Trail are still visible along much of its path, and the battle sites are all marked with monuments of various sorts. Portugee Phillips's ride is noted by a pyramid-shaped memorial not far from Fort Phil Kearny. Get to the site of the **Wagon Box Fight** by heading one mile south from Story (good road) or driving northwest from Fort Phil Kearny on a narrow, winding gravel road.

The **Fetterman Fight** is marked by a stone obelisk atop the hill where the final stand was made. Informative plaques provide a full description of events leading up to the battle and its consequences, and a one-mile interpretive trail crosses the battlefield. Access is only from the south; the north section of the road is blocked by a landslide.

Buffalo

At the base of the Big Horn Mountains, Buffalo (pop. 4,000) is one of those delightful small towns that seem to define rural America. Tourists and locals relax on summer mornings along Clear Creek, while dogs sit in the back of pickup trucks parked on Main Street. Despite the fact that Buffalo's Main Street curves along an old bison trail, the town got its name from Buffalo, New York—the name was picked out of a hat.

Buffalo—the Johnson County seat—is primarily a government, ranching, retirement, and tourism center for the area, with coalbed methane becoming an increasingly important source of jobs (and of royalty income for local ranchers). The county constitutes the heart of sheep ranching in Wyoming, and some of these flocks are still tended by Basque shepherds. Longtime residents of Basque heritage are now pillars of the local community.

HISTORY

During General George Crook's 1876 campaign against the Sioux, he had Captain Edwin Pollock build a supply center along the Powder River. Originally called Cantonment Reno, it was later renamed **Fort McKinney,** after Lieutenant John A. McKinney, who had been killed in the Dull Knife Battle. In 1878, Fort McKinney was moved 40 miles north to where the Bozeman Trail crossed Clear Creek. Gradually the new fort took shape, not as one of the stockade-walled structures generally thought of, but rather as a collection of barracks, mess halls, and two-story houses with board-and-batten exteriors. Soldiers marched from here to South Dakota's Pine Ridge Reservation to put down the Ghost Dance uprising in 1890. More than 150 Sioux and 25 soldiers died at Wounded Knee, the last major battle between Indians and whites in North America.

The establishment of Fort McKinney created

an immediate market for all sorts of businesses. Carpenters, blacksmiths, farmers, loggers, merchants, bartenders, and prostitutes arrived and quickly established the town of Buffalo two miles downstream. By 1883, a Cheyenne newspaper noted a dozen saloons and no churches. "Houses of dissipation" seemed more numerous than any other establishment. Much of the barley harvested locally went to supply two breweries. Buffalo had become the largest town in the northern part of Wyoming. This boom suddenly ended in 1894, when the army declared Fort McKinney excess property and abandoned it. The buildings became the Wyoming Soldiers' and Sailors' Home in 1903 and now house the Veterans' Home of Wyoming. It is still one of the county's largest employers.

After World War II, oil and gas exploration and development of the region's vast coal deposits turned Buffalo into an energy center. Today the coal resources of Johnson County remain essentially undeveloped, but substantial amounts of oil and gas are produced. Downtown Buffalo has undergone a facelift in recent years as new tourist-oriented businesses move in, selling gifts, artwork, antiques, espresso, fly-fishing gear, upscale kids' clothing, and health food.

SIGHTS

Jim Gatchell Memorial Museum

The Powder River Basin's rich history comes to life in the Jim Gatchell Memorial Museum (307/684-9331, www.jimgatchell.com, $4 adults, $2 ages 6–16, free for younger kids, and $10 for families), one of the finest small museums in the American West. The focus is on life in the 19th century, when a rugged mix of Indians, soldiers, miners, homesteaders, wealthy cattlemen, and outlaws brought turmoil to this land. Historic artifacts gathered by druggist Theodore James Gatchell form the core of a collection of 15,000 articles. The museum now fills two downtown buildings and an attached carriage house.

Displayed in the carriage house are several historic wagons, including the de rigueur sheepherder's wagon and chuck wagon. The front (annex) building contains historic photos, a model of Fort Phil Kearny, and traveling exhibits. Inside the main building are two floors; downstairs is the standard collection of old homestead and pioneer artifacts, along with walk-through re-creations of the past and a display on the Bozeman Trail. Upstairs is a treasure trove of unusual items, including one of the largest collections of Indian artifacts in Wyoming and a display on Bomber Mountain. Featured are detailed dioramas and displays of items found at the sites of various local battles, including the Wagon Box Fight, the Johnson County War, and the Fetterman Fight. Most touching is the flattened horn of bugler Adolph Metzger, one of the last to die at the Fetterman Fight. The note here says his body was the only one the Indians did not mutilate after the massacre; instead they covered it with a buffalo robe out of respect for his valor. Other stories say that after trying to fight off the warriors

with his hands and bugle, he was taken captive and tortured to death at the Sioux camp.

Scattered around the room are other surprises: an extensive photographic exhibit on the Powder River, a pair of Cheyenne medicine rattles used in the Dance of Victory after Custer's defeat at Little Big Horn, an arrowhead that belonged to Red Cloud, a cartridge belt made by mountain man Jim Bridger, along with hired gunman Tom Horn's spurs and a bridle he braided while awaiting execution. Ask the folks at the museum to point out a rifle probably used by the cavalry at Little Big Horn and a shell from Custer's handgun. Look around and you'll find even more surprises at this impressive small museum.

The Jim Gatchell Museum is downtown on the corner of Main and Fort streets. A gift shop sells historical books, old Wyoming license plates, and other items. The museum is open 9 A.M.–6 P.M. daily Memorial Day–Labor Day (closed Fourth of July), with reduced hours in the spring and fall. It's closed December–mid-April.

Occidental Hotel

Completed in 1910, the Occidental Hotel (10 N. Main St., 307/684-0451, www.occidentalwyoming.com) was the place where Owen Wister's Virginian "got his man." Through the years many famous people walked through these doors, including Teddy Roosevelt, Herbert Hoover (he stayed here two weeks in 1932), Calvin Coolidge, Buffalo Bill Cody, Butch Cassidy, and Calamity Jane. In later years it was a residential hotel before closing in 1985. Dawn and John Wexo bought the dilapidated building in 1997 and proceeded to lovingly return the hotel to its glory days. Many of the original fixtures and other items were returned, including the billiard table, stained glass, tin ceilings, light fixtures, piano, back bar, and even some of the original plants. Today the Occidental is operated as a combination museum, hotel, restaurant, and saloon. Free 15-minute tours of the Occidental are available upon request, and many are led by an octogenarian cowboy who really knows the

THE JOHNSON COUNTY WAR

Wyoming's history is a story of constant conflict – between emigrants and Indians, Chinese and white miners, big ranchers and homesteaders, sheepherders and cattlemen. The Powder River has seen more than its share of confrontations; one of the most notorious was the so-called Johnson County War of 1892, the setting for the 1980 box-office megaflop *Heaven's Gate*.

BARONS AND GRANGERS

The first white settlers in the Powder River Basin were the "cattle barons," men who owned enormous herds of cattle but who generally lived on the land only part of the year. During the 1880s, more and more homesteaders ("grangers") began to settle here, fencing their spreads and gradually forcing the large cow outfits onto less and less land. The barons tried to force homesteaders off the land, and several Johnson County grangers were found face-down in gullies, shot in the back. Homesteaders retaliated by appropriating cattle that wandered onto their land – and outlaws made off with other stock.

As rustling increased along the Powder River, the big ranchers found little sympathy in nearby Buffalo, the largest town north of the Platte River. Local juries, either sympathetic with or intimidated by cattle rustlers, failed to convict men who were caught, and even the Buffalo sheriff, "Red" Angus, was accused of being in cahoots with rustlers. The cattle barons feared for their lives. The small ranchers and homesteaders in Buffalo were soon openly at odds with the absentee cattle barons based in the largest town south of the Platte – Cheyenne.

THE INVASION

In 1892, the small Johnson County ranchers organized their own roundup, an action that proved too much for the powerful Wyoming Stock Growers Association. In a secret meeting, the association proposed a military coup d'état. On April 6, two days after the association's annual meeting in Cheyenne, a train headed for Douglas with 25 hired Texas gunmen (mostly ex-sheriffs and ex-U.S. marshals) and an equal number of Wyoming men. With them they carried a hit list of 70 suspected rustlers. Cutting the telegraph lines to keep advance word from reaching folks in Johnson County, and traveling in darkened railway cars, the "Invaders" headed north, stopping the train near Casper and continuing on horseback.

They first came to the KC Ranch – actually

Old West. At other times you can pick up a brochure for a self-guided tour and just wander the Victorian rooms, enjoying dozens of historical photos lining the walls.

Several other interesting structures line Main Street; pick up a walking-tour brochure of Buffalo's other historic buildings from the Chamber of Commerce.

Petrified Forest

One of the more unusual local sights is a petrified forest on BLM land seven miles east of Buffalo. Take the Red Hills exit from I-90 and follow the road another seven miles to Dry Creek Petrified Forest. The route can be muddy and slippery when wet, so don't head here if it has rained recently. An easy 0.75-mile trail loops through the hot sagebrush country, and markers along the way describe the geological history. About 60 million years ago, this was a swampy plain dominated by towering metasequoia trees. You can still count the growth rings on the petrified stumps, some of which are more than four feet in diameter and 60 million years old.

Other Sights

Two bronze sculptures occupy a small park across the street from First National Bank on South Main Street. Created by local sculptor D. Michael Thomas, they represent combatants in the Johnson County War of 1892. The war helped dissuade the Chicago, Burlington, and Quincy Railroad from coming through just a couple of cabins – and discovered two of the most notorious rustlers, Nate Champion and Nick Ray, holed up inside. In the daylong shoot-out that followed, Ray died quickly, but Champion managed to hold off the Invaders until dusk, when they finally torched the cabin and shot him as he ran for safety. A blood-stained diary found on Champion described his last hours. It ended: "Shooting again. I think they will fire the house this time. It's not night yet. The house is all fired. Goodbye, boys, if I never see you again. Nathan D. Champion."

After this initial success, the Invaders headed on to the friendly TA Ranch, 30 miles north, to rest up for their planned siege of Buffalo. But word got out, and the Invaders suddenly found themselves under attack by a mob of 200 well-armed grangers and rustlers led by Sheriff Red Angus (who was on the hit list). In the shoot-out that followed, two Tex-ans died. The tables had been turned, and the desperate Invaders faced almost certain an-nihilation. Meanwhile, word had gotten out to acting governor Amos W. Barber (a sup-porter of the Invaders), who cabled President Harrison for help. Troops from nearby Fort McKinney arrived before the townsfolk could attack with their tanklike wagon and dyna-mite bombs. Newspapers around the nation castigated the cattle barons for their effron-tery; the *Laramie Sentinel* noted, "of all the fool things the stock association ever did this takes the cake."

JUSTICE DENIED

The events that followed made a mockery of the legal system. After being rescued by army troops, the Invaders were taken to Cheyenne to stand trial. Not surprisingly, two trappers who had happened on the raid at the KC Ranch mysteriously disappeared until the trial was over, leaving no witnesses for the prosecu-tion. Everyone pleaded not guilty, but when the judge discovered that Johnson County was unable to pay for the prisoners' room and board, he ordered them all released on their own recognizance. After being paid by the cattle barons, the hired Texas gunmen imme-diately skipped town, never to be seen again. The Wyoming men involved in the raid were released when Johnson County had no more money to prosecute. Many of Wyoming's most prominent citizens, including Governor Barber and Senators Carey and Warren, would later be implicated as supporters of the raid. John-son County would take years to settle down after the battles of 1892, and for a while the big cattlemen lived in fear for their lives.

Buffalo, and for many years Buffalo remained America's largest inland city without a rail-way. Eventually a spur line was built, con-necting Buffalo to Clearmont. Locals called it BC&BM (Buffalo–Clearmont and Back, Maybe) but even it was abandoned in 1946 because of competition from trucking com-panies. Wyoming Railroad's **Engine 105** now rusts in the city park.

Children (and those who never really grew up) will love the antique **Carousel Park** (307/684-7033, www.bozemancrossing.com) on the east end of town behind Col. Boze-man's Restaurant. This is the only carousel in Wyoming and is open daily Memorial Day–Labor Day for just $1.50 per ride. It includes a dozen custom-carved Wyoming bucking horses. Also here are a 1936 Ferris wheel and a minigolf course.

Willow Grove Cemetery, on the south end of town, is an interesting place to ex-plore. Here you will find the graves of rus-tlers Nate Champion and Nick Ray, Sheriff "Red" Angus, homesteader John Tisdale, and others involved in the Johnson County War. The chamber of commerce has a little map of the gravesites.

Injured or aged veterans live on the grounds of the **Wyoming Veterans' Home** (old Fort McKinney), two miles west of Buffalo on U.S. 16. Of the original fort, only an old cavalry stable and the post hospital building are still standing. Check in at the office (307/684-5511) before sightseeing.

ENTERTAINMENT AND EVENTS

Buffalo has several places to go for live country-and-western tunes on weekends: **Cowboy Saloon** (177 U.S. 16 E., 307/684-5200), **Hoot N' Owl Pub** at the Best Western Crossroads Inn (75 North Bypass, 307/684-2256), **The White Buffalo** (U.S. 16 E., 307/684-0101), and the **Century Club** (14 S. Main St., 307/684-2821). Roll balls down the lanes at **Buffalo Bowl** (90 S. Cedar St., 307/684-2613).

Powder River Ranch Rodeo in June features a unique rodeo in which teams rather than individuals compete. In mid-June, the **Bighorn Mountain Music Festival** (www.bighornmountainfestival.com) features bluegrass, country, folk, and old-time music performances at the fairgrounds. Come to Buffalo in late June for a **horseshoe tournament.** The Jim Gatchell Museum's **Living History Day** in July includes mountain men, horse-drawn wagons, quilting, saddlemaking, Basque dancing, old-time cooking, and more.

All Girls Rodeos take place throughout the summer at the county fairgrounds. Every Wednesday night mid-June–August, the **Lions Club Rodeo,** has events at the fairgrounds; call 307/684-5649).

End the summer with a Labor Day weekend country-and-western music **Invitational Jam Session** at the fairgrounds. Buffalo's biggest annual event is the **Johnson County Fair and Rodeo** (307/684-7357, www.bighornmountains.com/jcf&r.htm), held in early August. A **Christmas Parade** comes to town the first Saturday of December.

SHOPPING

Get books on Wyoming from **The Office** (33 N. Main St., 307/684-2215 or 800/359-0209) or from the **Jim Gatchell Museum gift shop.**

Several local art galleries sell standard Western art prints, but much more distinctive is **Margo's Pottery and Fine Crafts** (1 N. Main St., 307/684-9406 or 877/825-4354, www.margospottery.com), where you'll find all sorts of playful earthenware from nationally known potters. Also sold here are blown-glass pieces, jewelry, and other works. The shop opens into Deerfield Espresso Bar Cafe.

Also worth a visit are **Amish Furnishings** (76 S. Main St., 307/684-2594), with beautiful furniture from Pennsylvania, and **Wolf's Den** (173 U.S. 16 E., 307/684-7337) for pelts, coats, and other furry items sure to make trapping opponents' blood boil.

RECREATION

The free **outdoor swimming pool** in Washington Park is one of the largest in the Rocky Mountains, stretching 120 meters by 80 meters. It has swimming lanes, two diving boards, a slide, and a wading pool for tots. Open 11 A.M.–6 P.M. daily during summer, this is a great place to play on a hot day.

Inside the modern **YMCA** (101 Klondike Dr., 307/684-9558), you'll find a six-lane pool, hot tub, weight room, and day care, along with racquetball and handball courts.

Buffalo's popular **Clear Creek Trail System** makes for a delightful afternoon stroll or bike ride. It follows the creek for 11 miles and is paved to the western edge of town, reaching all the way to the foot of the Big Horn Mountains. **Mountain Plains Heritage Park** (307/684-2693) on the east side of town has a mile-long nature trail.

Three miles out of town, **Triple Three Ranch** (307/684-2832, www.triplethreeranch.com) and **Little Piney Ranch** (307/683-2667, www.littlepineyranch.com) near Fort Phil Kearny offer horseback rides. Trail rides are also available from Pines Lodge and South Fork Mountain Lodge (see *Lodges Along U.S. 16* in the *Big Horn Mountains* section).

The 18-hole **Buffalo Golf Course** (307/684-5266), on the northwest edge of town, is one of the finest in Wyoming. One hole features a 90-foot vertical drop over 140 yards.

Buffalo has two good fishing shops: **Just Gone Fishing** (77 East St., 307/684-2755, www.justfish.com) and **The Sports Lure** (66 S. Main St., 307/684-7682 or 800/684-7682, www.sportslure.com). The latter also sells (and rents) hiking, skiing, mountain-biking, and backpacking gear. (See *Lake DeSmet* for other fishing options.)

ACCOMMODATIONS

You'll discover plenty of comfortable, exceptionally clean, and friendly motels to choose from in Buffalo, but it's a good idea to reserve well ahead for the midsummer, when tourists flood the area.

Under $50

Out on the west end of town, **Canyon Motel** (997 Fort St., 307/684-2957 or 800/231-0742) has some of the least expensive local rooms: $43 s or $50 d for standard rooms, or $58 d for two-bedroom units with full kitchens.

Arrowhead Motel (749 Fort St., 307/684-9453 or 877/277-6948, www.arrowheadmotel.com, $48–55 d) is a simple but clean place with microwaves and fridges in all rooms, along with four kitchenettes for those who prefer to dine in. Friendly owners, too.

$50-100

Z-Bar Motel (626 Fort St., 307/684-5535 or 888/313-1227, www.zbarmotel.com) features very nice log cabins for $52 s or $56 d, with fridges in all; cabins with kitchenettes are $6 extra.

Guests at **Mansion House Inn** (313 N. Main St., 307/684-2218 or 888/455-9202, www.mansionhouseinn.com, $66 s or $80 d) can stay in attractive Victorian-style rooms in a century-old home or comfortable motel units (some with fridges). Guests get a continental breakfast and access to the indoor hot tub.

Big Horn Motel (209 N. Main St., 307/684-7822 or 800/936-7822, www.bighorn-motel.com, $60–75 d) has nicely maintained rooms with microwaves and fridges. It's near the Clear Creek walking path.

It's hard to avoid using the word "cute" for the 17 clean and well-maintained log cabins at **Blue Gables Motel** (662 N. Main St., 307/684-2574 or 800/684-2574, www.bluegables.com, $45–80) on the north side of town. Some cabins contain fridges and microwaves. No phones are provided in the rooms, but the motel does have a heated outdoor pool.

You'll also find cozy modern cabins at the clean and friendly **Mountain View Cabins and Campground** (585 Fort St., 307/684-2881, www.mountainviewbuffalo.com). Cabins start at $50 d for one with a queen bed, up to $109 for a two-room unit that sleeps six. Free Wi-Fi.

Wyo Motel (U.S. 16 at I-25, 307/684-5505 or 800/666-5505, www.wyomotel.com) is a comfortable and modern place with a heated outdoor pool (with slides) and an indoor hot tub. Rates are $73–98 d; some rooms have fridges and microwaves. A six-person family unit with kitchen is $144.

$100-150

Buffalo's historic **C Occidental Hotel** (10 N. Main St., 307/684-0451, www.occidentalwyoming.com) is a four-star choice, with restored Victorian suites ($145–200) and cozy guest rooms ($110–125 d). Nicest is the four-room Wister suite, a much-improved version of the room where Owen Wister wrote *The Virginian;* it features a black marble fireplace, king bed, sitting room, and private balcony. Budget travelers will appreciate the "cowboy" rooms ($50 d) that share a bath, and one suite is wheelchair-accessible. A continental breakfast is included in the rates, and suites contain original furnishings. Rooms contain televisions and Wi-Fi, but no phones. Downstairs is a classy bar and restaurant.

Bed-and-Breakfast

For homey and historic lodging, stay at **Clear Creek B&B** (330 S. Main St., 307/684-2317 or 888/865-6789, www.clearcreekbb.com), an 1883 home with a wraparound porch and fossilized stone fireplace. Four guest rooms are available: Two share a bath and cost $65 d, and the other two have private baths and run $85 d. A filling breakfast is included, and kids are welcome.

Dude Ranches

Thirteen miles west of Buffalo on U.S. 16, **Paradise Guest Ranch** (307/684-7876, www.paradiseranch.com) is a longtime dude ranch with luxurious log cabins, an outdoor pool, an indoor hot tub, and space for 72 guests. In addition to the main attraction—horseback riding—the ranch has fly-fishing instruction and trips, chuck wagon cookouts, and special children's camp-outs, along with adults-only weeks in September. All-inclusive weekly summertime rates are $3,350 for two people. The guest ranch is open late May–September.

Another popular dude ranch is **Klondike Guest Ranch** (307/684-2390 or 800/362-2982, www.klondikeranch.com), 25 miles southwest of Buffalo along Crazy Woman Creek. Horseback riding and fishing keep folks busy, or you can join in the ranch work and help move cattle. Guests stay in log cabins with private baths and eat in the main lodge. There's also a hot tub for end-of-the-day relaxing. All-inclusive weekly rates are $2,350 for two people. The ranch has been owned by the Tass family and operated as a guest ranch since 1920.

One of the oldest dude ranches in America, **HF Bar Ranch** (307/684-2487, www.hfbar.com) has 32 comfortably restored cabins—mostly from the 1920s and '30s—on a historic 9,000-acre ranch 15 miles northwest of Buffalo. Guests get two horseback rides per day, access to the outdoor pool, plus all three meals. The ranch also offers a strong kids' program, guided fly-fishing, exercise and yoga classes, sporting clays, hayrides, and pack trips (extra fee). All-inclusive rates are $430 for two people per day; no minimum stay, but most guests stay at least a week. There's space for 135 guests at this big and well-known ranch. The dude ranch is open June–September.

Camping

There's camping ($6) at **Lake DeSmet,** eight miles north of Buffalo, but the sites can get steaming hot in midsummer. It is mostly for the RV crowd but has no water or hookups. Other nearby public campgrounds ($8–11) are in Bighorn National Forest approximately 15 miles west of Buffalo on U.S. 16.

Head two miles west of town on U.S. 16 to **Big Horn Mountains Campground** (307/684-2307, www.buffalocamping.com, $15 tents, $19 RVs, open all year), which has an outdoor heated pool. **Mountain View Cabins and Campground** (585 Fort St., 307/684-2881, www.mountainviewbuffalo.com, $15

tents, $27 RVs) is open May–October, with free wireless Internet.

The friendly folks at **Indian Campground** (660 E. Hart St., 307/684-9601 or 866/808-9601, www.indiancampground.com, $20 tents, $28–35 RVs) provide shady spots east of town off U.S. Hwy 16. Simple camping cabins are $40 d. Showers for noncampers run $5. It's open April–October.

Farther out on U.S. 16 is **Deer Park Campground** (307/684-5722 or 800/222-9960, www.deerparkrv.com, $18 tents, $29–32 RVs), with an outdoor heated pool and hot tub, wireless Internet, plus a pleasant creekside trail. Nightly ice-cream socials are a summertime ritual. Open May–September.

Also along U.S. 16 east of town, the **Buffalo KOA** (307/684-5423 or 800/562-5403, www.koa.com, $19–22 tents, $27–37 RVs) is open year-round, with a seasonal outdoor heated pool, hot tub, and pancake breakfasts. Tepees are $28, and basic cabins cost $45–59 d.

FOOD

Despite its small size, Buffalo has several pleasant eateries.

Breakfast and Lunch

DeerField Espresso Bar Cafe (7 N. Main St., 307/684-7776) is a delightful spot for filling breakfasts, soups, salads, sandwiches, espresso, and cinnamon rolls. The decor is bright and playful, with a patio for sunny days. Check your email on its computers or pop open your laptop to take advantage of Wi-Fi. It typically has live jazz on Thursday nights.

Just up the street is another recommended eatery, **Sagewood Cafe** (15 N. Main St., 307/684-7670), with homemade soups, sandwiches on bread fresh from the oven, and daily specials—including Friday seafood bisque. Open for lunch 11 A.M.–3 P.M. Monday–Saturday. The front of the building houses a gift shop.

Drop by **Tom's Main Street Diner** (41 N. Main St., 307/684-7444) for the best local breakfasts and a dose of Tom's politics. Popular for lunch too. Closed Tuesdays. **Seney's Drug Store** (38 S. Main St., 307/684-2253) has an old-fashioned soda fountain offering thick shakes and malts.

A good place for fast food, including excellent hickory-smoked fried chicken and ribs, is **Dash Inn** (620 E. Hart, 307/684-7930), a local legend. Try the potato wedges and chicken wings.

Dinner

Housed within the historic Occidental Hotel, **❮ The Virginian** (10 N. Main St., 307/684-0451, www.occidentalwyoming.com) serves a steak and seafood menu, with excellent dinners year-round for $13–24, including Friday and Saturday night prime rib. Closed Sundays. The hotel also offers informal dining in the enclosed gazebo on the deck along Clear Creek. This café is open three meals a day, with a wintertime pot-bellied stove to ward off the cold and a menu of breakfast quiches, with pizzas and pot pies the rest of the day. The same food is available in the no-smoking saloon till 11 P.M.

Winchester Steak House (117 Hwy. 16 E., 307/684-8636) has great steaks, prime rib, and seafood in a casual setting. Nightly specials too.

When folks are looking for an enjoyable evening away from town, they drive to Pines Lodge or South Fork Mountain Lodge (see *Lodges Along U.S. 16* in the *Big Horn Mountains* section).

Groceries

Get groceries from two markets on the west end of town: **Rocky Mountain Fresh Food IGA** (440 Fort St., 307/684-2239) and **DJ's Thriftway** (895 Fort St., 307/684-2518).

INFORMATION AND SERVICES

The **Buffalo Chamber of Commerce** office (55 N. Main St., 307/684-5544 or 800/227-5122, www.buffalowyo.com) is open 8 A.M.–6 P.M. Monday–Friday and 10 A.M.–4 P.M. Saturday–Sunday June–August, and 8 A.M.–5 P.M. Monday–Friday the rest of the year. It also operates a seasonal **Visitor Information Center** at I-90 exit 58, open 9 A.M.–6 P.M. daily May – September.

The **Johnson County Public Library** (171 N. Adams St., 307/684-5546 or 800/661-7071, www-wsl.state.wy.us/johnson) has Internet access.

Get information on Bighorn National Forest from the **Powder River Ranger District** (1425 Fort St., 307/684-7860, www.fs.fed.us/r2/bighorn). The BLM's **Buffalo Resource Field Office** (307/684-1100, www.wy.blm.gov) is in the same building.

Wash clothes at **Tanner's Coin Laundry** (334 N. Main St., 307/684-2205) and at **Squeeky Kleen** (631 E. Hart, 307/684-9666).

Johnson County Healthcare Center (497 W. Lott, 307/684-2228, www.buffalowyoming.com/hospital) has 24-hour emergency care.

GETTING THERE AND AROUND

Powder River Transportation (307/682-1888 or 800/442-3682, http://gillette.coachusa.us) connects Buffalo with the rest of northern and eastern Wyoming, with additional service to Billings, Denver, and Rapid City. Buses stop at Just Gone Fishing (77 East St.).

Rent cars from **Northside Car Sales/Avis** north of Buffalo (307/684-5136 or 800/831-2847, www.avis.com). The airport in Buffalo does not have scheduled service, so it came as quite a surprise one day in 1979 when a Western Airlines 737 carrying 94 passengers landed in Buffalo instead of Sheridan. Mistakes were made.

LAKE DESMET

Eight miles north of Buffalo is Lake DeSmet, a deep natural lake surrounded by open range country. The lake was formed when coal burned underground, leading to a collapsed area that filled with water. A stone **monument** to the Belgian Jesuit missionary Father Pierre Jean DeSmet (1801–1873) stands along the western shore. DeSmet was one of the few 19th-century men who maintained lifelong friendships with both Indians and whites. The Plains Indians called him "Blackrobe" and trusted him with various peacemaking roles at Fort Laramie. But the Indians viewed the lake named for DeSmet with suspicion, as did early settlers, who told of "Smetty the sea monster," which emerged at night from the seemingly bottomless body of water. When first found by DeSmet in 1851, it was a salt lake—the second-largest in the West (after Great Salt Lake)—but dams and dikes have increased its size and decreased its salinity.

Today Lake DeSmet is a popular place for local boaters and sailboarders. Try your luck at catching one of the mermaids, but you're more likely to pull in a big rainbow trout. Also here are brown trout, crappie, yellow perch, and rock bass. **Lake DeSmet Fishing Derby**(307/684-2755) is held each Memorial Day weekend and awards more than $55,000 in prizes and cash. Just north of the lake is a bed of coal that, in some places, is more than 200 feet thick—second in thickness only to one in Manchuria. No wonder Chevron-Texaco owns most of the land around Lake DeSmet!

Practicalities

You'll find **camping** ($6) at the Lake DeSmet recreation area along the water. The area has volleyball nets, picnic tables, and outhouses but no shade or drinking water.

Lake Stop Resort (307/684-8700 or 877/964-8700, www.thelakestop.com) has motel rooms ($59–79 d), four-person cabins ($39), and RV hookups ($19), plus a heated outdoor pool, café, convenience store, and bait shop. Fishing boats and personal watercraft are available for rent. **Angler's West** (307/684-5857 or 877/996-2626, www.anglers-west.com) guides boating and fishing trips to Lake DeSmet.

Kaycee

The town of Kaycee (pop. 250) is named for the nearby KC Ranch and serves as a bentonite, oil, and ranching center. Drive the side roads in spring or fall and you're likely to find yourself behind huge flocks of sheep being herded into or out of the Big Horn Mountains.

Frewen Castle

When the Powder River country was opened to white settlers in the late 1870s, it quickly attracted ranchers and farmers of all types, from homesteaders trying to prove up their 160 acres to wealthy international investors. Two of the most interesting were the English brothers Moreton and Richard Frewen, relatives of Sir Winston Churchill. Coming originally to hunt buffalo, the two saw the lush Powder River area and decided to invest in cattle. Near present-day Kaycee, they erected an elaborate two-story log house, filled it with furniture and fixtures from England, and even added an incredible luxury—a telephone. Frewen Castle, as it was soon called, became the center of an enormous spread with at least 60,000 cattle.

Their kingdom attracted English hunting parties and became something of an unofficial dude ranch. (To keep their ladies in the proper spirit, the Frewens set up relay stations to bring hothouse flowers from Denver on galloping horses.) The Frewens' Powder River Cattle Company, Ltd., attracted investments from the British royal family and various lords before reality struck. The cattle did not do as well as expected, competition from surrounding ranchers and rustlers cut into profits, and the disastrous winter of 1886–1887 forced the company to the brink of bankruptcy. The Frewens and many other "cattle barons" never really recovered. Today almost nothing remains of Frewen Castle.

SIGHTS

Kaycee's free **Hoofprints of the Past Museum** (307/738-2381) is open 9 A.M.–5 P.M. Monday–Saturday late May–October, closed the rest of the year. Inside is a nice collection of items from early settlers, outlaws, and the cattle wars. Look for the wooden potato planter. The museum offers historical tours of Hole-

© DON PITCHER

bull rider at Deke Latham Memorial PRCA Rodeo in Kaycee

in-the-Wall and the Dull Knife battlefield on the third weekend of June.

Just south of Kaycee, a marker describes the killing of rustlers Nate Champion and Nick Ray in the Johnson County War of 1892. The old **KC Ranch house,** where the two were killed by the Invaders, stood here. The Invaders holed up at the TA Ranch after raiding the KC Ranch (see *Accommodations*).

Ten miles east of Kaycee on Hwy. 192 is a marker noting the first buildings in northern Wyoming, constructed in 1834 by Portuguese trapper Antonio Montero. The log stockade and trading post (known as the **Portuguese Houses**) were abandoned around 1839, and nothing remains on the site. The site of old **Fort Reno** (1865–1868) is in the same general vicinity; ask in Kaycee for directions. A monument marks the place, and various remains are still present from this little-known fort.

Fans of country music will know that singer Chris LeDoux (www.chrisledoux.com) has a sheep ranch in the vicinity of Kaycee. LeDoux was a rodeo cowboy for many years, winning the 1976 PRCA world championship in bare-

back riding. He used his musical abilities to pay for his rodeo travels, and today he sings cowboy songs with a measure of authenticity lacking in other musicians. He still plays the rodeo circuit with his band, but he's also gained a national following.

EVENTS

Events in Kaycee include two sheepdog events: the **Sheepherders Rodeo and Dog Trials** on the first weekend after the Fourth of July and **Kaycee Challenge Sheepdog Trials** in early September. Don't miss the **Deke Latham Memorial PRCA Rodeo** (307/738-2431, www .dekelathamrodeo.com) in July. Kaycee is the smallest town in America with its own PRCA rodeo, and visitors will be impressed; the rodeo is one of Wyoming's best.

ACCOMMODATIONS

Cassidy Inn Motel (307/738-2250, $35 s or $42 d) has basic rooms in "downtown" Kaycee. The newest place to stay is just west of town at the **Kaycee Motel** (307/738-2213), next to the Sinclair station. The seven-unit motel is

THE WILD BUNCH

Glorified in the 1969 Oscar-winning film *Butch Cassidy and the Sundance Kid,* the Wild Bunch is one of the most famous of all Western outlaw gangs. The Wild Bunch consisted of a constantly changing membership held together by two friends, Robert Parker ("Butch Cassidy") and Harry Longabaugh (the "Sundance Kid"). In 1884, Parker, then a teenager, met up with a local ranch hand and part-time cattle rustler named Mike Cassidy. Rebelling against a strict Mormon upbringing, Parker picked up a few of the master's tricks before getting caught by the law and told to move on. But when he left Utah for Colorado and Wyoming, he took with him his mentor's name, Cassidy. (The "Butch" apparently came later, when he worked in several Rock Springs butcher shops.) Linking up with other outlaws, Cassidy held up the San Miguel Valley Bank of Telluride and then drifted back to horse stealing in Wyoming. Several years later, those horses landed him in the Wyoming State Prison in Laramie. Cassidy was pardoned by the governor after 18 months, reportedly after agreeing not to pursue that line of work in Wyoming anymore. Other places, however, were fair game.

THE GANG

If anything, prison made Cassidy more determined than ever to outwit the lawmen. Joining with Longabaugh (who picked up his Sundance Kid sobriquet while serving time in the Sundance, Wyoming, jail for horse thievery) and Harvey Logan, alias Kid Curry (a deadly and fearless Montana fugitive), Cassidy assembled a rogues' gallery of rustlers, drifters, killers, and wanted men soon known as the Wild Bunch. They operated from remote hidden canyons in the West, especially Brown's Park in western Colorado, Bighorn Canyon in Montana, Wyoming's Wind River Valley, and the famous Hole-in-the-Wall southwest of Buffalo, Wyoming – places where entire herds of stolen cattle could be hidden and where the finest horses could be trained for quick getaways.

The Wild Bunch achieved a measure of respect from local ranchers who bought horses and cattle at low prices and found ready workers when the outlaws needed to rest up awhile. For many, Cassidy seemed a modern-day Robin Hood, taking from the rich railroads, banks, mines, and cattle barons while leaving the small folks alone. To this day, locals in Kaycee, Wyoming, still talk fondly of the affable Butch Cassidy.

The gang's activities reached a peak in the late 1890s, with bank robberies in Utah, South Dakota, and Idaho (the latter to pay for a lawyer to clear a gang member on a murder charge). Cassidy – breaking his promise to Wyoming's governor – also led a train robbery in Wilcox, Wyoming, which netted $50,000, but only after he'd blown up the safe with 10 pounds of dynamite, sending money and banknotes in all directions. Within hours, a sheriff's posse was in hot pursuit, and in a gun battle near Casper the sheriff was killed. Somehow, the Wild Bunch managed to slip through the posse's lines for a clean getaway.

In 1900, they struck another Union Pacific train near Tipton, Wyoming (just east of Rock Springs). Amazingly, the same express messenger was present for both robberies; the first time he had refused to open the railcar door

$40 s or $50 d. The station also contains an ATM and showers.

Just across the road is **Powder River RV Park** (307/738-2233, $10 tents, $20 RVs, $30 cabins). It has a second location (Kaycee RV Park) on the south end of town, or you can camp for free at Kaycee town park.

Ranches

Famous **TA Ranch** (307/684-5833 or 800/368-7398, www.taranch.com) is approximately 30 miles north of Kaycee along Hwy. 87. Bullet holes are still visible in many of the wonderful old ranch buildings, which are being preserved for posterity. Still a working cattle ranch covering 8,200 acres, the TA takes in guests May–September and has a capacity of 24 people. The ranch specializes in horseback rides, cattle drives, and fly-fishing, but it also offers tours to the Hole-in-the-Wall area and other historic and was literally blown out with explosives. The second time the conductor persuaded him to open the door. Perhaps he knew that the safe held only $54; the train carrying $100,000 worth of gold had passed just a few hours before. Then the Wild Bunch was off to Winnemucca, Nevada, where a bank holdup netted them a cool $32,000. After a fling at Fanny Porter's Sporting House in San Antonio, the gang members bought some new hats at a Fort Worth haberdasher and, dressed as dudes, posed for the famous group portrait later used by Pinkerton detectives. Cassidy and two other gang members tried their hands once more at train robbery in 1901, taking at least $40,000 from a dynamited safe in Montana. The law was closing in, however. Of the gang members who stayed behind, all but one died a violent death. For Butch Cassidy and the Sundance Kid, the future lay in South America.

GRINGOS

In 1901, Butch and Sundance headed for Argentina. Accompanying them on the journey was Etta Place – a strikingly beautiful woman whom Sundance apparently met in Fanny Porter's Sporting House. (Butch later called her "a fine housekeeper, but a whore at heart.") There they settled with their ill-gotten wealth to a quiet life of ranching, traveling occasionally to Buenos Aires, where they stayed in the finest hotels and dressed in formal clothes befitting their new role as bourgeois American settlers. But even in South America, Pinkerton detectives managed to pick up their trail, and, sensing this, the three decided to try their skills in virgin territory. They robbed three banks in Argentina and a train in Bolivia before Etta Place came down with acute appendicitis. A hurried trip took the trio back to the States, but in Denver, where the operation was performed, the Sundance Kid got in trouble for shooting up his hotel room while drunk. Rather than face the law, he fled to New York, where he and Cassidy again boarded a steamer bound for Argentina. Etta remained behind.

The two outlaws now worked part-time at a Peruvian gold mine, using the work as a cover for their periodic forays into banks, trains, and stores in search of money. For many years, most believed that Butch Cassidy and the Sundance Kid died in a blaze of gunfire at a remote village on the Bolivian–Argentine border in 1909. Today, however, it appears that Cassidy escaped (and perhaps the Kid as well), using his reported death as a convenient opportunity to change his ways. According to Larry Pointer's *In Search of Butch Cassidy*, Cassidy later fought with Pancho Villa in the Mexican Revolution, met Wyatt Earp in Alaska, and settled down to running a Spokane machine shop, living under the name of William T. Phillips until his death from cancer in 1937. Several Wyoming residents, old friends of the famous outlaw, met him in Lander and Riverton on several occasions before his death. Cassidy reportedly spent considerable time in a fruitless effort to recover buried loot that he had stashed near Mary's Lake in the Wind River Mountains. Today, the Butch and Sundance legends refuse to die. Stop by the towns of Rock Springs, Lander, Laramie, Worland, Dubois, Baggs, or Kaycee, and you'll be regaled with more tales of their exploits.

sites. All-inclusive weekly rates are $2,400 for two people, or $370 per night for two guests.

Willow Creek Ranch at Hole-in-the-Wall (307/738-2294, www.willowcreekranch.com) is 35 miles southwest of Kaycee and offers one of the most authentic ranch experiences in Wyoming. The ranch covers 57,000 beautiful and remote acres in the Red Wall country made famous by the Hole-in-the-Wall gang. Guests take part in ranch activities, including branding and cattle drives. Photography, bird-watching, fishing, and hunting are other popular activities, along with the all-time favorite, kicking back and relaxing. Established in 1882, this working cattle and sheep ranch has space for a maximum of 12 guests, who stay in the renovated 1890 bunkhouse. In addition, two private cabins eight miles away offer the ultimate in solitude. The ranch is a great place to explore, with lots of outlaw history, plus Indian petroglyphs and tepee rings. All-inclusive stays are $470 per day for two people, and tt's suggested that you stay at least two nights because of the remote location; you'll certainly want to spend more time here. Open May–mid-October.

MORE PRACTICALITIES

You'll find all-American meals at **Invasion Bar Restaurant** (307/738-2211), and groceries, antiques, and espresso at **Kaycee General Store.**

Housed within a log building on the north end of town, **Kaycee Visitor Center** (307/738-2444, www.kayceewyoming.org) is open 9 A.M.–5 P.M. Monday–Saturday late May–early September, and 10 A.M.–5:30 P.M. Monday–Saturday in September and October. Closed the rest of the year.

HOLE-IN-THE-WALL COUNTRY
Outlaw Haven

The remote country used by the Wild Bunch and other outlaws lies about 30 miles west of Kaycee. Get here by following Hwy. 190 for 16 miles to where the pavement ends. At the road junction—maps call this Barnum, but there is no town here—a side road leads to Blue Creek Ranch (private), land once homesteaded by Butch Cassidy and the Sundance Kid. Surrounding you are gorgeous red-walled canyons rising above the Middle Fork of the Powder River. Its waters provide a fine place to fish for rainbow, brook, and brown trout.

Turning right (north) leads you to the **Dull Knife Battlefield,** named for an 1876 incident. General Crook's soldiers surprised Dull Knife's band of Northern Cheyenne in this remote valley. The attack killed at least 40 Cheyenne and ended what whites viewed as a campaign of terror and what the Indians viewed as retaliation for the invasion of their last stronghold.

To reach other area sites, turn left (south) on the graded gravel road that parallels the river. Follow the road five miles, past the Bar C Ranch, and bear right at the signed 4WD side road for Outlaw Cave. Beyond the intersection, the road is really only passable in high-clearance vehicles, so you may want to walk the last two miles to the cave. The road crosses a 0.75-mile-long stretch of prehistoric **rock cairns** and

then tops a knoll where you'll find **Outlaw Cave Campground** (free but no water). Stop here for impressive views of the Hole-in-the-Wall area.

From the campground, a steep 0.5-mile path drops 660 feet to **Outlaw Cave,** actually two small caves used as hideouts by the Wild Bunch and other outlaws. One of the caves is little more than a depression in the rocks, but the other is room-size. Take your fishing pole down to try for trout.

On the opposite side of the road from the campground and up another third of a mile is **Indian Rock Art Cave.** The cave (actually just a rock overhang) contains distinctive but faint Indian rock art, including a large warrior figure, bear claws, and shield designs. A major buffalo jump site (where Indians hunted buffalo by driving them over a cliff) is nearby, along with many tepee rings. The BLM office in Buffalo (307/684-1100, www.wy.blm.gov) can provide more detailed access information for the Outlaw Caves/Hole-in-the-Wall country.

Hole-in-the-Wall

The wealthy Frewen brothers who ranched here in the 19th century named this country after London's Hole-in-the-Wall Tavern. The "Hole" lies at the end of a steep V in the red cliffs bordering Buffalo Creek. It was accessible via a trail that cuts up the talus slope and into a narrow, funnel-shaped opening. The setting was perfect for rustling and as a hideout from the law, especially for gunmen such as Jesse James, the Logan brothers, and George "Flat Nose" Currie. About 30–40 bandits hung out here in six log cabins, including the most famous inhabitants, the Wild Bunch of Butch Cassidy and the Sundance Kid. The cabins have collapsed through the years, and today a few chunks of foundation are the only remaining evidence of the 19th-century rustlers who were based here. The cliff was easy to defend and offered a vantage point from where sentries could warn of approaching lawmen.

Hole-in-the-Wall is on public (BLM) land, but much of the surrounding land belongs to ranchers who guard their privacy closely. In addition, the unmaintained roads can turn into a quagmire when it rains and a rutted mess when the mud dries out. High-clearance vehicles are required. The BLM (307/684-1100, www.wy.blm.gov) has signed the route into Hole-in-the-Wall, and a 1.5-mile primitive trail crosses public land to the site.

Willow Creek Ranch (307/738-2294, www .willowcreekranch.com) offers informative all-day tours to Hole-in-the-Wall and the surrounding country for $85 per person, including

lunch. These summer-only 4WD tours start from the remote ranch, 35 miles from Kaycee. Reservations are advised since the route is not always passable. Kaycee Museum (307/738-2381) offers a **historical tour** to Hole-in-the-Wall the third weekend of June.

Historic Trails West (307/266-4868 or 800/327-4052, www.historictrailswest.com) has horseback trips across various parts of Wyoming, including a six-day Outlaw Trail ride through Hole-in-the-Wall for $1,500 per person.

Gillette

Campbell County proclaims itself the "Energy Capital of the United States," a title gained by producing more coal and oil than any other county in Wyoming. Although oil production is in decline, coal mining continues to increase every year, and 15 local mines shovel up an eighth of the total U.S. production of coal. In addition, the Powder River Basin has been the focus of extensive coalbed methane gas development in recent years. Energy companies predict that northeast Wyoming will have more than 20,000 natural gas wells by the year 2010. At the center of all this resource development is Gillette (pop. 25,000), Wyoming's fourth-largest city—and gaining on number three Laramie rapidly.

Gillette is a base for tours of nearby coal mines and coalbed methane gas projects, but it isn't otherwise known as a tourist destination. It does, however, provide a central location for exploring the wide-open spaces of northeastern Wyoming.

When you drive into Gillette, the sense of history permeating much of Wyoming quickly gives way to the raucous present. History is decidedly not Gillette's strong suit, even though the town is more than a century old. When the Burlington and Missouri route to Sheridan was being planned, it was originally set to go south of the present location, but astute surveyor Edward Gillette discovered a route farther north that saved construction of 30

bridges. Initially, the new company-platted town was to be called "Donkey Town" for its proximity to Donkey Creek, but instead it was named for Gillette. (Edward Gillette later served a term in Washington as a congressman from Wyoming; however, he preferred to live in the more scenic town of Sheridan than in his namesake.) The railroad reached Gillette in 1891, and the town was incorporated the following year. It became a shipping point for local ranchers and homesteaders and grew slowly through the ensuing decades.

Since the late 1960s, Gillette has ridden an enormous growth rocket, powered first by oil, then by coal, and most recently by coalbed methane. Gillette's oil boom began in the fall of 1967, when a drilling company hit an oil gusher that ignited an enormous fire. Firefighter Red Adair was called in to extinguish the flames, attracting worldwide attention. Hollywood soon followed—John Wayne's *Hellfighters* was based on these events. Other oil companies flooded the area with exploratory rigs, and almost overnight Gillette grew from a sleepy cow town into a major energy center. A frantic scramble for the almighty dollar ensued, with real-estate values quadrupling between 1966 and 1970.

Unlike the rest of Wyoming, where the oil boom of the '70s was quickly followed by the bust of the '80s and '90s, Gillette caught the coal wave just as the oil tide was heading back out to sea. With enormous reserves of

POWDER RIVER COUNTRY

DETAIL

2ND ST
1ST ST
ADVOCACY FOR VISUAL ARTS
3RD ST
ARROWHEAD MOTEL
VALUE INN
ROSS AVE
WARREN AVE
GILLETTE AVE
KENDRICK AVE
POST OFFICE
4TH ST
EMERSON AVE
OSBORNE AVE
BROOKS AVE
MILLER AVE
DOUGLAS HWY
5TH ST
CITY HALL
CAREY AVE

McManamen Park

BOOT HILL NIGHTCLUB

Burlington Lake

GURLEY AVE

To Airport and Sheridan

14
16
59

FOOTHILLS BLVD

FOOTHILLS TWIN THEATER

WARLOW DR

HANNUM RD

BROOKS AVE

AQUATICS CENTER

Burlington Northern Railroad

ECHETA RD

SEE DETAIL

To Buffalo and Sheridan

90

TOWER WEST LODGE
BUDGET INN EXPRESS
MOTEL 6
SUPER 8 LODGE

HAMPTON INN

EXIT 124

To Bell Nob Golf Course

ROCKPILE MUSEUM

COUNTY FAIRGROUNDS

2ND ST

GILLETTE AVE
KENDRICK AVE
MILLER AVE

MUSTANG MOTEL

DAN'S SUPERMARKET

BURMA AVE

CRAZY WOMAN

ICE ARENA

4TH ST

QUALITY INN

NATIONAL 9 INN

HOSPITAL

6TH ST

ECONO LODGE

WESTOVER RD

50

4 J RD

DOUGLAS HWY

RECREATION CENTER

EXIT 126

90

HUMPHREY'S

BOXELDER RD

GILLETTE VISITORS CENTER

HOLIDAY INN EXPRESS

WINGATE HOTEL

LIBRARY

COAL MINE TOURS

CLARION WESTERN PLAZA

DAYS INN

COUNTRY CLUB RD

LAKEWAY RD

KMART

WAL-MART

ALBERTSON'S/POWDER BASIN CENTER MALL

To Edgerton and Casper

JOST HOUSE B&B

LAKEWAY RD

EDWARDS RD

SAGE VALLEY JR HIGH/PLANETARIUM

LAKEWAY LEARNING CENTER/EINSTEIN'S ADVENTURARIUM

Gillette Fishing Lake

Dalbey Park

GILLETTE CAMPUS OF SHERIDAN COLLEGE

S 4-J RD

59

SOUTHERN DR

To Wright and Douglas

© AVALON TRAVEL PUBLISHING, INC.

GILLETTE

GARNER LAKE RD.

WARLOW DR.

To Moorcroft and Sundance →

16 14 90

EXIT 129

← CHALLENGER EARNING CENTER (OPENS 2007)

BUS DEPOT

EXIT 128

51

HIGH PLAINS ∧

To Wyodak Powerplant

■ CAMPLEX

BOXELDER RD.

GARNER LAKE RD.

0   0.5 mi

0   0.5 km

POWDER RIVER COUNTRY

low-sulfur coal throughout the surrounding countryside, Campbell County quickly became a major player on the energy scene and is now one of the most prosperous counties in Wyoming. The city's population continues to mushroom as coal mining, coalbed methane gas production, and the Wyodak power plant expand. Mining and drilling jobs—many paying $16–26 an hour—are plentiful.

Today Gillette is a prosperous version of the American dream: shopping malls, spreading suburbia, used-car lots, and fast-food joints, especially on the south end of town. Author Wallace Stegner's description of a California town could fit just as well here: "But mostly it is Main Street, Anywhere, a set used over and over in a hundred B movies, a stroboscopic image pulsing to reassure us by subliminal tricks that though we are nowhere, we are at home."

Environmental groups are very concerned by the impacts from coalbed methane development, but they are fighting an uphill battle because there is so much money involved. Visit the **Powder River Basin Resource Council**'s website (www.powderriverbasin.org) for details.

SIGHTS
History and Art
Gillette's fine **Rockpile Museum** (on U.S. 14/16, 307/682-5723, free) is open 9 A.M.– 7 P.M. Monday–Saturday and 1–5 P.M. Sunday June–August, and 9 A.M.–5 P.M. Monday– Saturday the rest of the year. This museum contains sheep wagons, a horse-drawn hearse— originally from Montana, its first eight customers died from gunshots—a blacksmith shop, an impressive arrowhead collection, and dozens of elaborate spurs and old rifles, and even floating rocks from Lake DeSmet. A big board shows a directory of several hundred brands. Out front is a minor local landmark for which the museum was named, along with a Burlington Northern caboose and a tiny one-room schoolhouse that could have served double duty as a doghouse. The metal building next door houses some strange sandstone rocks.

The **Campbell County Public Library** (2101 4-J Rd., 307/682-3223, www.ccpls.org)

POWDER RIVER COUNTRY

is one of the best in the state. Besides a large collection of books about Wyoming, it houses a remarkable collection of art, including paintings by Hans Kleiber, Gene Kloss, and Conrad Schwiering. Life-size bronze statues of cowboys and horses guard the exterior.

◖ Coal Mine Tours

During summer, free two-hour tours of **Eagle Butte Coal Mine** are offered through the Gillette Visitor center. These take place at 9 and 11 A.M. on weekdays June–August. Call 307/686-0040 or 800/544-6136 for reservations. The **Black Thunder Mine** also leads free tours; call 307/464-2201 for details.

Five miles east of Gillette on I-90 is the **Wyodak Mine** (307/682-3410), where tours are available. In existence since 1922, the mine feeds the adjacent Wyodak Power Plants (307/687-4280), which also offers tours. If tours aren't an option, you may want to peer into Eagle Butte Mine from an overlook five miles north of Gillette on U.S. 14/16. It's open during daylight hours, except when blasting is taking place.

Science Experiments

Kids of all ages will have a blast (pun intended) at **Einstein's Adventurarium** (525 W. Lakeway Rd., 307/686-3821, www.ccsd.k12.wy.us/adventuarium), housed in the Lakeway Learning Center. The finest science museum/kids' center in Wyoming, it is packed with ingenious science exhibits that make learning fun. You can play in the bubble room, learn about light and sound, or meet a parrot, chinchilla, South American lungfish, lizard, and ferret. The science center is open weekdays in the school year, or by reservation in summer.

Just up the road is another enjoyable family venue: the **Planetarium** (1000 W. Lakeway Rd., 307/682-2225) at Sage Valley Junior High. This sophisticated star chamber is one of the finest in any school district in America. A $14 million Challenger Learning Center and Science Complex near I-90 exit 128 was to replace both science venues in 2007.

Cam-Plex

Wyoming's premier multiuse facility, Cam-

240-ton truck at Black Thunder Mine

© DON PITCHER

Plex (307/682-0552, www.cam-plex.com) is east of town on Garner Lake Road. It's home to trade shows, concerts, and Broadway musicals in the beautiful 960-seat theater, conventions, plays, RV rallies, and rodeos. Out front is an odd collection of items from the past and present: Early-1900s log cabins and an old locomotive are just a few feet from a drilling rig and an enormous coal-hauling dump truck. The gargantuan tires make a great playground. Also here is **Cam-Plex Park,** with a shady picnic area, playgrounds, ornamental gardens, and hiking paths. Friday evening melodramas are a draw in June and July. A major expansion to Cam-Plex should be completed in 2007, including an ice rink and other facilities.

ENTERTAINMENT AND EVENTS

Head to Gillette City Park at 7 P.M. on Thursdays during June and July for the free **Concerts in the Park** series. Music varies from bluegrass to classical. The **Powder River Symphony Orchestra** (307/686-5767, www.prs.vcn.com) performs at Cam-Plex in the winter. You'll find community drama at its corniest during the **melodramas** (307/686-3025, www.cam-plex.com) held at Cam-Plex on Saturday evenings June–August.

For live country-and-western or rock tunes, check out the scene at **Jake's Tavern** (5201 S. Douglas Hwy., 307/686-3781), **Mingles** (2209 S. Douglas Hwy., 307/686-1222), or **Boot Hill Nightclub** (910 N. Gurley Ave., 307/686-6404). Mingles also has a half dozen pool tables.

POWDER RIVER COUNTRY

STRIP MINING

Wyoming's Powder River Basin has not always been the relatively arid place that it is today. About 55 million years ago the region was covered by freshwater lakes, creeks, and enormous peat swamps. These swamps were buried in sediments through the eons, and compression and heat combined to form thick coal beds.

Coal mining has been an important part of the Campbell County economy for many years. The first mines were underground, but once the technology developed to remove the overlying soil, strip mining became feasible. Today, 10 Campbell County surface mines (the industry's preferred term) are scattered along an enormous coal seam five miles wide, more than 70 miles long, and 70 -180 feet thick – enough to last hundreds of years. Together, the mines produce more than one-quarter of the nation's coal, and if Campbell County were a nation it would rank fourth in the world in coal reserves, behind the United States, Russia, and China! Most of the mines are owned by giant multinational corporations, including Peabody Energy, Kennecott Energy (Rio Tinto Group), RAG Coal West, and Arch Coal.

Coal production in these mines has risen rapidly in recent years and now tops a stag-gering 400 million tons annually. The North Antelope/Rochelle Complex (near Wright) is the largest mine in America, producing more than 80 million tons of coal per year, followed by the nearby Black Thunder Mine, which produces almost as much annually. Other giants are the Cordero Rojo, Jacobs Ranch, Caballo, and Antelope coal mines, all of which produce more than 25 million tons. The Wyodak Mine is the oldest in the Powder River Basin – it opened in 1922 – and feeds one of the world's largest air-cooled power plants (also on the site).

DIGGING THE COAL

Powder River Basin mines are heavily mechanized and highly efficient operations with relatively few employees; despite massive increases in production, the number of employees continues to drop. Mining coal here is a relatively simple process, made easier through the use of machinery and blasting equipment that are something beyond gargantuan; all the vehicles seem to be on steroids. Imagine a truck that carries 400 tons of coal – 2.5 railroad coal cars' worth – and is powered by a 2,200-horse-power engine. Try changing a flat on it – the tire stands 11 feet tall and weighs four tons! Even this
(continued on next page)

Movie houses are **Foothills Twin Theatre** (650 N. U.S. 14/16, 307/682-6766) and **Sky-Hi Cinema** (800 Shoshoni, 307/682-6766); find both places on the web at www.gillette-theatres.com.

All summer long you'll find racing on Saturday nights at **Thunder Basin Stock Car Track** on Garner Lake Road. Gillette's **Fourth of July** celebration is the biggest in northeastern Wyoming. In addition to an impressive fireworks show, you'll find a pancake breakfast, a parade, mud volleyball, firehose water fights, and even a Ping-Pong drop (a Ping-Pong drop?).

The **Wyoming Celtic Festival and Highland Games** (307/682-5785 or 877/688-6201, www.wyomingcelticfestival.org) takes place in early July. **Campbell County Fair** (307/687-0200, www.campbellcounty-fair.com) in early August includes livestock judging, arts-and-crafts exhibits, concerts, and other old-time favorites.

Cam-Plex (307/682-0552, www.cam-plex .com), a large and modern multievents center east of town on Garner Lake Road, frequently has concerts, livestock shows, rodeos, RV rallies, conventions, and other events. During summer, rodeos take place almost every weekend, the biggest being the **PRCA Rodeo** in late July and early August. In late November and early December, Gillette plays host to a series of **Christmas crafts fairs** (307/686-0040 or 800/544-6136).

SHOPPING

Gillette has many of the national discount stores on South Douglas Highway, including

---

STRIP MINING (cont'd)

behemoth is dwarfed by the dragline used at the Black Thunder Coal Mine. Its 300-foot boom pulls in a 170-cubic-yard bucket (a typical dump truck holds 12 cubic yards). Powered by electricity, the 3,600-ton machine waddles along like a duck, dragging its power line behind. Blasting loosens the overburden, which is then stripped away and dumped into waiting trucks. (Topsoil is stored for use in later reclamation.) Below this overburden lies the deep black coal seam that must be drilled and blasted. Electric shovels scoop up the loosened coal and dump it into the trucks for delivery to crushing and storage facilities.

The entire scale of the operation comes into focus by watching as 1.5-mile-long, 110-car trains move constantly through the loading facility, loading a car every minute. Workers can fill up to a dozen trains in a day – more than 150,000 tons.

ENVIRONMENTAL IMPACTS

The strip mining of coal has always been a controversial subject, with environmentalists concerned about the impacts from burning coal in an era of acid rain (97 percent of Wyoming coal is burned for electricity), global warming,

and escalating atmospheric carbon dioxide. They also question whether reclamation will really work on Wyoming's arid lands. The other impacts from mining are equally important: Access roads divide antelope and deer habitat, subdivisions for the workers spread out over the countryside (take a look at Gillette for a worst-case scenario), and wells draw down the water table. Mining companies, however, point with pride to herds of antelope grazing near the coal mines and believe that the land can be restored after the coal is gone. Besides, the low-sulfur coal found here is some of the cleanest-burning coal in America.

A visit to the coal mines is an eye-opening odyssey into the Super Bowl of strip mining. No matter what you think about strip mining, a tour of the mines is well worth taking, if only to see the enormous equipment and ponder what burning all this coal will do to the global environment. For tour information, contact the Gillette Visitor center (307/686-0040 or 800/544-6136, www .visitgillette.net). Learn more about coal mining at the Wyoming Mining Association's website, www.wma-minelife.com. For a look at the effects of coal on the global (and regional) environment, visit www.wyoming.sierraclub.org.

¡COWBOYS!
SCRAPE SHIT FROM
BOOTS BEFORE ENTERING

© DON PITCHER

a **Wal-Mart SuperCenter** (307/686-5166) and a **Kmart** (307/682-3212).

The nonprofit **Advocacy for Visual Arts** (509 W. 2nd St., 307/682-9133) provides a center for regional artists, with classes, concerts, poetry readings, and a gallery with changing exhibits.

RECREATION

Gillette has some of the finest recreation facilities in Wyoming, a reflection of the prosperous local economy. **Campbell County Recreation Center** (1000 S. Douglas Hwy., 307/682-5470, www.ccprd.com) houses an indoor pool with a diving well, the 383-foot Thunder Run Waterslide (summers only), weight rooms, racquetball and squash courts, a gym, and a sauna. Enjoy fabulous *free* summertime swimming at the **Gillette Water Park** (307/682-1962). Outdoors at Gillette and 10th, the park has a main pool with geysers and waterfalls, a wading pool with a slide for kids, a deep diving pool, and a sand play area. There's also an indoor **Aquatic Center** (307/686-3757) for competitive swimming events.

Bird-watchers should head to **McManamen Park,** north of town on W. Warlow Dr.,

where viewing blinds let you look for ducks and other birds.

Campbell County's modern **ice arena** (121 S. 4-J Rd., 307/687-1555) is open mid-October–mid-March. Roller-skaters will enjoy **Razor City Skateland** (885 Hannum Rd., 307/682-3529) and bowlers can roll their own at **Camelanes Bowling Center** (1005 W. 2nd St., 307/682-4811) or **Frontier Lanes** (5700 S. Douglas Hwy., 307/687-0261). Golfers hobnob at **Bell Nob Golf Links** (1316 Overdale Dr., 307/686-7069) or **Gillette Golf Club** (1800 Country Club Rd., 307/686-4774).

ACCOMMODATIONS

Gillette is dominated by chain motels; there aren't many independent places left in this boomtown. Rates tend to plummet in winter, but they escalate during the Sturgis Motorcycle Rally Week in early August, when everything fills up.

Under $50

Arrowhead Motel (202 Emerson Ave., 307/686-0909, $40 d) is one of the few surviving Gillette motels that isn't part of a national chain.

$50-100

Budget Inn Express (2011 Rodgers Dr., 307/686-1989 or 800/709-6123, www.budgetinngillette.com, $56 s or $66 d) has such amenities as an indoor pool, sauna, hot tub, Wi-Fi, and a light breakfast.

Get dependable economy accommodations from **Motel 6** (2105 Rodgers Dr., 307/686-8600 or 800/440-6000, www.motel6-gillette.com, $60 s or $66 d), including access to an indoor hot tub and sauna.

Best Value Inn (608 E. 2nd St., 307/682-9341 or 888/315-2378, www.bestvalueinn .com, $60–70 d) has an outdoor heated pool, in-room fridges, microwaves, Wi-Fi, and a light breakfast. This is an older motel, but the rooms have been recently updated.

National 9 Inn (1020 E. U.S. 14/16, 307/682-5111 or 800/524-9999, www.national-9gillette.com, $63 s or $69 d) has a seasonal outdoor pool and wireless Internet, along with fridges and microwave in some rooms. A café and lounge are also here.

Econo Lodge (409 Butler Spaeth Rd., 307/682-4757 or 800/553-2666, www.econolodge.com, $73 d) is a moderately priced motel with in-room microwaves and fridges, wireless Internet in the lobby, and a continental breakfast.

$100-150

A trio of modern corporate hotels close to I-90 offer the same upscale but cookie-cutter facilities that are popular with business travelers and families: large rooms with work tables and queen or king beds, an indoor pool, exercise room, hot tub, business center, wireless Internet, and breakfast bar. Summertime rates at all three are similar, around $130 d for standard rooms or $160 d for suites. The hotels are **Holiday Inn Express** (1908 Cliff Davis Dr., 307/686-9576 or 866/690-9800, www.holiday-inn.com), **Hampton Inn** (211 Decker Ct., 307/686-2000 or 800/426-7866, www.hamptoninn.com), and **Wingate Hotel** (1801 Cliff Davis Dr., 307/685-2700 or 800/228-1000, www.wingateinngillette.com).

Bed-and-Breakfast

Gillette's only B&B, **Jost House Inn** (2708 Ridgecrest Dr., 307/687-1240 or 877/685-2707, www.josthousebb.vcn.com, $69–79 d) is a modern home with two big guest rooms containing Victorian-style furnishings. Both contain king beds, and one has a sitting room and private bath. The expansive yard, gardens, and columned front porch add to the appeal. A big full breakfast is served each morning, and children are welcome.

Camping

Campers and RVers will enjoy **Crazy Woman Campground** (1001 W. 2nd St., 307/682-3665, $16 tents, $28–35 RVs, open year-round), a pleasant place with genuine shade trees—a rarity in eastern Wyoming's private campgrounds. Also here are a hot tub and an outdoor pool. The rather bleak **High Plains Campground** (Garner Lake Rd., 307/687-7339, $11 tents, $30–35 RVs, open year-round) has additional sites next to Cam-Plex on the east side of town.

FOOD

The Gillette restaurant scene tends toward middle-brow fare, but several places are a vast improvement over the rows of fast-food joints that border the main drags.

Breakfast

A cozy little locals' eatery next to the train tracks, **Lula Belle Cafe** (101 N. Gillette Ave., 307/682-9798) is famous for tasty pies and filling breakfasts. It's popular with smokers, so you'll get a dose of nicotine with your meal. Lula Belle's has been here since the early 1960s.

Get cappuccinos, lattes, and sweet treats at **Downtown Java Jae's** (300 S. Gillette Ave., 307/682-4199, www.javajaes.com). Pop open your laptop for free Wi-Fi access. Just up the block is **Coffee Friends** (320 S. Gillette Ave., 307/686-6119) with more espresso, plus light breakfasts and earthy lunches.

Lunch and Dinner

Humphrey's Bar and Grill (408 W. Juniper La., 307/682-0100) is a favorite lunch place for the business crowd, with a diverse pub-grub menu and Wednesday night ribs. Humphrey's has more than 50 beers on tap. The feeling is a bit formulaic: walls crowded with sporting photos and memorabilia and TVs tuned to all-sports channels.

The big salad bar/dessert bar at **Golden Corral** (2700 S. Douglas Hwy., 307/682-9130) makes for a bargain meal.

Bailey's Bar and Grill (301 S. Gillette Ave., 307/686-7667) is a fine place for such home-made lunch and dinner specialties as chicken-fried steak, burgers, and Mexican fare. Great finger food, too.

The award-winning **Prime Rib Restaurant** (1205 S. Douglas Hwy., 307/682-2944) is a very good place for prime rib—of course—but it also has a diverse menu of steak, pasta, chicken, and seafood, along with an extensive wine and champagne list.

Gillette's culinary standout, **☑ The Chophouse Restaurant** (113 S. Gillette Ave., 307/682-6805) is housed in a historic downtown brick building. It's a classy spot with white linen, a nice choice of wines, and gourmet dining. Dinner entrées cost $17–43, and featured items include slow-roasted prime rib of beef, steaks, barbecued ribs, Alaskan halibut, and more. It's also open for lunch, with salads, sandwiches, fish-and-chips, and other lighter fare. Closed Sunday.

International

Gillette is blessed with an excellent—and relatively authentic—Chinese eatery: **Hong Kong Restaurant** (1612 W. 2nd St., 307/682-5829). Lunch specials are $6, and the menu encompasses spicy orange beef, *moo-shu* vegetables, sizzling pork, and Chinese dumplings. Also of note is **China Buffet** (2701 S. Douglas Hwy., 307/682-7868), with popular lunch ($6) and dinner ($7) buffets, with more than 120 items, including that famous "Chinese" delicacy: chocolate brownies with icing.

In the Powder Basin Center Mall near Albertsons, **Ole's Pizza and Italian** (307/682-8484) has pasta, pizzas, and sandwiches, with a $5.50 lunch buffet on weekdays.

For Mexican food and great margaritas, try **Las Margaritas** (2107 S. Douglas Hwy.,

307/682-6545). Also of note is **Casa del Rey** (409 S. Douglas Hwy., 307/682-4738).

Groceries and Bakeries

Get groceries from Albertsons, Buttery, or the new Wal-Mart SuperCenter. **Breanna's Bakery** (208 S. Gillette Ave., 307/686-0570) downtown has doughnuts, sweets, pastries, sandwiches, and freshly baked breads. Stop by **Main Bagel** (2610 S. Douglas, 307/687-1616) for fresh bagels and bagel sandwiches; it's close to Albertsons.

INFORMATION AND SERVICES

The **Gillette Visitor Center** (1810 S. Douglas Hwy., 307/686-0040 or 800/544-6136, www.visitgillette.net) is next to the Flying J Truckstop at exit 126 and is open 8 A.M.–7 P.M. Monday–Friday, 10 A.M.–6 P.M. Saturday, and 10 A.M.–4 P.M. Sunday late May–early September, with reduced hours the rest of September–October; closed the remainder of the year.

At other times, go downtown to the **Gillette Chamber of Commerce** (314 S. Gillette Ave., 307/682-3673, www.gillettechamber.com), open 8 A.M.–5 P.M. Monday–Friday year-round).

Gillette is home to the state's fastest-growing junior college, the **Gillette Campus of Sheridan College** (300 W. Sinclair, 307/686-0254, www.sheridan.edu). The commuter campus offers a range of classes and degree programs from business to mining.

The **Campbell County Memorial Hospital** (501 S. Burma Ave., 307/682-8811, www.ccmh.net) has 24-hour emergency care.

GETTING THERE AND AROUND
By Air

Gillette Airport (307/686-1042, http://ccg.co.campbell.wy.us/airport) is five miles north of town. **Great Lakes Aviation** (307/433-2905 or 800/554-5111, www.greatlakes-av.com) operates daily flights between Gillette and Denver.

By Car and Taxi

Rent cars from **Thunder Basin Ford Rentals**

(307/682-4735, www.thunderbasinford .com), **Avis** (307/682-8588 or 800/831-2847, www.avis.com), **Enterprise Rent-a-Car** (307/686-5655 or 800/736-8222, www .enterprise.com), and **Hertz** (307/686-0550 or 800/654-3131, www.hertz.com). Avis and Hertz have cars at the airport.

For a taxi ride, call **American Couriers** (307/686-0905) or **City Cab** (307/685-1000).

By Bus

Gillette is headquarters for **Powder River Transportation** (1700 E. U.S. 14/16, 307/682-1888 or 800/442-3682, http://gillette.coach-usa.us), with daily bus service throughout northern and eastern Wyoming, continuing to Denver, Billings, and Rapid City.

WRIGHT

Wright sits right in the center of America's largest low-sulfur coal deposit. Established in 1976, the town quickly grew to 1,200 residents. Modern schools, a small shopping mall, and six churches popped up, along with trailer courts and suburban split-level homes on curving streets. Funded partly by Arco, Wright was built to house workers for nearby coal mines. It's a pretty weird place. Imagine an enclave of middle-class America plunked down in a setting straight out of *High Plains Drifter*.

Coal Sights

On the east end of town off Hwy. 387, the small **Wright Centennial Museum** (307/464-1222) houses homestead-era items. Out front is a 70-ton truck that was retired from hauling coal when it was replaced with much larger versions. The museum is open 10 A.M.–5 P.M. Monday–Friday and 10 A.M.–3 P.M. Saturday mid-May–mid-October. No charge.

Gargantuan strip mines surround Wright; all of them use Paul Bunyan–scale equipment and skeleton crews of employees to mine coal. Much of this is public land belonging to Thunder Basin National Grassland, meaning enormous revenues for the federal government and severance taxes for the state of Wyoming. The coal trains seem never to end.

Stop on the railroad overpass near the dot of a settlement called **Bill** and you'll see 100 cars of coal pass by every couple of minutes, with empty trains waiting on the sidings. Most of this coal is on its way to electric-generating plants in Texas and the Midwest. (Bill got its name from four early settlers, all of whom had the same first name.)

Thunder Basin Coal Company Mine is adjacent to Hwy. 450, approximately 10 miles east of Wright; stop to watch the trains and trucks at work. It could keep a four-year-old boy enthralled for hours.

Durham Buffalo Ranch

Four miles north of Wright is Durham Buffalo Ranch (307/939-1271), home to one of the largest private buffalo herds in existence. The Flocchini family owns a 55,000-acre spread here and is dedicated to returning the land to its original state, when bison and other native animals dominated the prairie landscape.

CROW COUNTRY

The Crow country is a good country; the Great Spirit has put it in exactly the right place. It is good for horses – and what is a country without horses? On the Columbia, the people are poor and dirty; they paddle about in canoes and eat fish. On the Missouri the water is muddy and bad. To the north of the Crow country it is too cold, and to the south it is too hot. The Crow country is just right. The water is clear and sweet. There are plenty of buffalo, elk, deer, antelope, and mountain sheep. It is the best wintering place in the world and has plenty of game. Is it any wonder that the Crows have fought long and hard to defend this country, which we love so much?

–Crow Chief Arapooish, describing Powder River Basin

Watch for some of the 2,500 head of buffalo along the highway. Herds more than 1,000 times this size once roamed across the land, and this is a rare opportunity to see bison today in a relatively natural setting. Tours are available for groups only ($150 per group).

Events and Recreation

The annual event here is **Wright Days,** held in late August, with games, a barbecue, and races. The town also has a fine **recreation center** (307/464-0198) with an indoor pool, racquetball courts, a weight room, and a gym. There's a nine-hole golf course nearby, **Haycreek Golf Club** (307/464-0747).

Accommodations and Food

Stay at **National 9 Inn** (307/464-1510 or 800/524-9999, www.national9inns.com, $60–70 d), with Wi-Fi; kitchenettes available.

Four miles north of Wright is **Durham Ranch Guesthouse** (307/939-1271), a historic stone house on this well-known buffalo ranch. The three-bedroom home sleeps up to seven for $35 per person (maximum $150). It's far enough off the road to enjoy the solitude of this picturesque spot and a good base for mountain-biking on the many dirt roads.

Sagebluff RV Park (307/464-1305, $7 tents, $19 RVs, open all year) is a mile west of town on Hwy. 387.

Get three meals a day—including buffalo burgers—at **Little Thunder Cafe** (307/464-1499) at the junction of Hwys. 387 and 59.

Information and Services

Wright Area Chamber of Commerce (307/464-1312, www.wrightareachamber.com, open 9 A.M.–3 P.M. daily year-round) is in the **Latigo Hills Mall.** The mall is Wright's focal point and includes a grocery store, café, a smoky bar, pizza-by-the-slice shop, library, credit union (with ATM), post office, bowling alley (Rolling Thunder Lanes), dentist, launderette, and hair salon. There's even a massage therapist.

POWDER RIVER COUNTRY

THE BLACK HILLS

In Wyoming's northeast corner, the Black Hills of South Dakota roll across an arbitrary state line, bringing a quiet beauty that differs greatly from other parts of the state. Here, the Belle Fourche River (bell-FOOSH, French for "Beautiful Fork") cuts northeast past rich pastures before taking a sudden right angle to the southeast as it heads to the Missouri River. Tiny towns nestle in the forested hills, and cattle graze on the riverbanks. Nearby, one of the most stunning of all sights—Devils Tower—seems almost alive in its abrupt rise from the pastoral landscape. South of the Black Hills in Weston County, the hill country quickly opens into the mixed-grass prairie of the plains. This out-of-the-way part of Wyoming is truly a special place. It's no wonder that the Sioux considered the Black Hills the home of the Great Spirit.

Only 13,000 people live in Crook and Weston counties, scattered on rural ranches or in the small settlements of Sundance and Hulett in the midst of Wyoming's Black Hills, along with Newcastle, Moorcroft, and Upton along the southern edge. Cattle grazing, bentonite mining, oil wells, logging, and tourism provide the jobs.

The Black Hills stretch in a long ellipse, 125 miles north to south and 65 miles across, rising 3,000–4,000 feet above the surrounding plains. South Dakota's Harney Peak, at 7,242 feet, is the tallest mountain in the Black Hills; in fact, it's the tallest peak between the South Dakota–Wyoming line and the Atlantic Ocean. The most famous attraction in this part of Wyoming is Devils Tower, but the Black Hills north of Sundance are captivating, especially in the spring and fall.

HIGHLIGHTS

MONTANA

Hiking in Devils Tower

Black Hills National Forest

Aladdin

Sundance

Gillette

Crook County Museum

Moorcroft

SD

Anna Miller Museum

Newcastle

Paleo Park

◖ Hiking in Devils Tower: This towering, flat-topped rock rises from the surrounding terrain like an apparition. There's a reason *Close Encounters of the Third Kind* was filmed here (page 648).

◖ Crook County Museum: Sure, it has exhibits on General Custer's 1874 march through the region, and a diorama of an Indian buffalo trap, but most folks come to view mementos—including a wanted poster—from the Sundance Kid's 18 months at the county jail for stealing horses (page 650).

◖ Black Hills National Forest: Most of the sights are on the South Dakota side, but travelers enjoy quiet campgrounds, an active fire tower, and hiking trails (page 653).

◖ Aladdin: Built in 1896, the bright red country store in this tiny town still has the old potbellied stove and post office boxes (page 654).

◖ Anna Miller Museum: A fun collection of the flotsam and jetsam of everyday ranch life a century ago (page 658).

◖ Paleo Park: A number of unusual dinosaurs—including an amazingly complete *Triceratops*—have been discovered at this remote ranch southwest of Newcastle. Tours and lodging are available; check out the commingled tracks of dinosaurs and birds from 60 million years ago (page 659).

LOOK FOR ◖ TO FIND RECOMMENDED SIGHTS, ACTIVITIES, DINING, AND LODGING.

From a distance, the dusky green carpet of ponderosa pine darkens the hills—hence the Sioux name *Paha Sapa,* meaning "Hills that are Black." The Black Hills are a blend of rocky hills crowded with pine and aspen forests, open meadows, and valleys lined with bur oak. This is one of the few places you're likely to see native oak trees in Wyoming.

White-tailed deer are abundant throughout the Black Hills, and herds of elk are found southeast of Sundance. Merriam's turkeys are a common sight all through this country. Introduced from New Mexico in 1948, they are now the most widespread game-bird species in northeast Wyoming.

PLANNING YOUR TIME

Devils Tower National Monument is the primary sight in this part of Wyoming. Some travelers (particularly rock climbers) come to the region specifically to explore the park, but most other visitors who come to northeast Wyoming are also seeing regional attractions in the Black Hills (Mt. Rushmore, Deadwood, Crazy Horse Memorial, and Jewel Cave) and Yellowstone National Park. Those looking to

relax can camp at Devils Tower or on nearby **Black Hills National Forest** land and enjoy hikes in the pine-covered hills.

Several small towns surround the Black Hills, including Sundance, where **Crook County Museum** features artifacts from the Sundance Kid's time in the local jail. Hulett is a little logging burg, and miniscule **Aladdin** consists almost entirely of a memorable country store. South of the Black Hills, the country abruptly opens into the mixed-grass prairie of the plains. Several more towns are here, including Moorcroft, Upton, and Newcastle, home to the interesting **Anna Miller Museum.**

Devils Tower National Monument

In the 1977 film *Close Encounters of the Third Kind,* Devils Tower was used as the contact point for aliens and humans. It was an appropriate choice. Rising 1,267 feet above the surrounding plain, this otherworldly apparition seems an appropriate metaphor for the mystery of life and our attempts to understand the universe. The flat-topped column of rock seems to push out of the earth like an enormous sawed-off stump from Paul Bunyan's forest. From a distance, Devils Tower looks as if some giant beast had scratched it, with parallel gouges running up the sides. Up closer, the gouges turn into enormous columns of rock molded into hexagonal columns (some have four, five, or seven sides). In the setting sun, Devils Tower glows a golden red long after the surrounding hills no longer reflect the sun's rays, and as night comes on, the stars and moon outline its bold shape against the horizon.

Ponderosa pine and bur oak forests surround Devils Tower, and the winding Belle Fourche River flows less than one mile away. A large colony of **black-tailed prairie dogs** prospers along the river just inside the park, with more than 1,200 of the little critters running around, much to the delight of tourists. You're also likely to see white-tailed deer feeding in the meadows. On top, Devils Tower is a fairly flat oval approximately 300 feet by 180 feet.

GEOLOGY

Geologists still dispute the precise way that Devils Tower formed, but they agree that the process began approximately 65 million years ago when a mass of molten magma was forced up through the overlying sedimentary rocks. As the igneous material cooled and contracted, vertical fractures formed in the magma, creating long columnar joints— the "scratches" up the side of Devils Tower today. (Some of these columns are 14 feet in diameter!) Eventually, precipitation and gravity eroded the softer sedimentary rock and the Belle Fourche River carried it away, leaving behind the harder core of Devils Tower. Surrounding the 1,000-foot-wide base of the

© DON PITCHER

Devils Tower National Monument

THE BLACK HILLS

black-tailed prairie dog

DEVILS TOWER NATIONAL MONUMENT

tower is a mass of talus from fallen pieces of columns, but erosion of this very hard igneous rock is very slow. The four prominent peaks of the **Missouri Buttes,** four miles northwest of Devils Tower, were formed in a similar manner. At 500 to 800 feet in height, they are not as dramatic and lie outside the national monument's boundaries.

HISTORY

Devils Tower is known to Native Americans by a variety of names, most commonly Bear Lodge, Tree Lodge, or Bear's Tepee. Fur trappers and early explorers certainly knew of the existence of Bear Lodge, but no note of it was made until 1857, when an exploration party led by Lieutenant G. K. Warren saw the rock from a distance. In 1875, Colonel Richard I. Dodge finally led a U.S. Geological Survey party to the formation. Dodge somehow came up with the name Devils Tower, claiming that the Native Americans called it "Bad God's Tower." Despite protests that "Bear Lodge" had long been the aboriginal name, the label Devils Tower stuck. Indians in the area regard the name Devils Tower an affront because they consider this rock a sacred place.

After the Indians had been driven from their traditional homeland in the 1870s, northeast Wyoming was opened to settlement by whites. Most lands were available to the homesteaders, but the General Land Office prevented developers from gaining this freak of geology. Wyoming already had America's first national park in Yellowstone, and support soon grew to make the Tower a second one. After years of effort, President Theodore Roosevelt proclaimed Devils Tower the country's first national monument in 1906. Unfortunately, the final monument was only 1,153 acres in size and excludes the Missouri Buttes.

In the early years of Devils Tower National Monument, the area served as a popular spot for picnics and camping, especially on the Fourth of July, when Independence Day celebrations attracted settlers from the entire region. The most famous of all these events came in 1893. Handbills announced that the "unclimbable" summit would be scaled and "On July 4th, 1893, Old Glory will be flung to the breeze from the top of the Tower, 800 feet from the ground by Wm. Rogers." The stunt was well planned. Several days before, two local ranchers, William Rogers and Willard Ripley, drove wooden pegs into a long crack that led to the top and tied the pegs together with strips of wood to make a ladder. They hauled a 12-foot flagpole to the top and returned on July 4 to scale the ladder in front of 800 people. Once on top (it took an hour to climb), Rogers unfurled a flag but a gust of wind blew it off. Wives of the promoters tore it up and sold the pieces as souvenirs (stripes cost $0.25, stars $0.50). The climb was a smashing success.

On July 4, 1895, Mrs. Rogers became the first woman to climb the ladder to the top of Devils Tower, and many other adventurous folks followed through the next several decades. The ladder was last climbed in 1927, but pieces of it are still visible today along the southeast side of the Tower. An iron stairway to the top, proposed by Wyoming's Congressman Frank Mondell as a tourist attraction, was never built.

For many years, Devils Tower remained undeveloped, and a bridge across the Belle Fourche River to the site was not built until 1928. During the Depression, the CCC constructed a log visitor center, new roads, trails, picnic areas, and a campground. Visitation increased as access became easier and more families acquired automobiles. One of the strangest events came in 1941, when George Hopkins—one of the top skydivers in the world—parachuted out of a plane to the top of Devils Tower as a publicity stunt. He had planned to descend on a 1,000-foot rope, but the rope landed on the side of the Devils Tower, leaving him stranded on top. Newspapers all over the country headlined his plight. Food and blankets were dropped to him, and for the next six days he spent a lonely vigil on top waiting to be rescued. Finally, Jack Durrance, a mountain climber who had scaled Devils Tower three years before, arrived to lead seven other climbers to the top and help Hopkins down. Many years later, in 1976, *Close Encounters of the Third Kind* was filmed here. Several hundred locals appeared in the crowd scenes. When the movie was released the following year, tourism here suddenly hit the stars. Today, more than 400,000 visitors come to Devils Tower each year.

KIOWA DEVILS TOWER LEGEND

The place we call Devils Tower was known to the Kiowa Indians as T'sou'a'e, meaning "Aloft on a Rock." Many tales are told about the origins of this mystical place, but the best known is that of the Kiowa.

Once upon a time, the people camped along a stream that had many bears. Seven sisters and their brother were playing nearby when the boy suddenly turned into a ferocious bear and began chasing the girls. In desperation, the girls climbed on a small rock and prayed, "Rock, take pity on us – rock, save us!" The rock started to grow, pushing them higher and higher as the bear clawed at the sides, trying to get them. Eventually the seven girls were pushed upward into the sky, forming the points of the Big Dipper. The gouges from the bear remain today on the sides of Devils Tower.

ACCESS AND INFORMATION

The monument is 33 miles northeast of Moorcroft. Access is from Hwy. 24, seven miles north of its junction with U.S. 14. Entrance costs $10 for vehicles, $5 for hikers or cyclists, and the passes are good for seven days. Annual passes to the monument cost $20, or you can buy a National Park Pass ($65), which lets you into all national parks and monuments. Seniors get in free with a Golden Age Pass (for a one-time fee of $10). The monument is open year-round 24 hours a day, although most of the more than 400,000 annual visitors arrive during summer.

Beyond the entrance station, it is approximately three miles along a paved road to the base of Devils Tower, where you'll find a pleasant old log **visitor center** (307/467-5283) and a parking lot that overflows on sunny summer days with rock climbers, day-hikers, and gawkers. The visitor center is open 8 A.M.–8 P.M. daily Memorial Day–Labor Day and 9 A.M.– 4 P.M. daily mid-March–Memorial Day and

Labor Day–mid-November (but these hours could change). Inside the visitor center, you can look at ecological displays and photos showing the dozens of climbing routes, and buy books on local lore. The center is closed mid-November–mid-March, but you can get information on winter weekdays from park headquarters. Contact the **Devils Tower National Monument office** at 307/467-5283, www.nps.gov/deto.

CLIMBING DEVILS TOWER

Although Devils Tower was first climbed in 1893 on a wooden ladder, the first ascent using modern rock-climbing techniques was not until 1937. Led by Fritz Wiessner, three New York City climbers made it to the top in a little less than five hours. Through the years, as climbing technology has improved and as more people have been attracted to the sport, Devils Tower has become one of the favorite climbing spots in the nation. During summer you're bound to meet several dozen climbers heading for the base of Devils Tower each morning. More than 60,000 people have reached the top, and the figure grows by more than 3,000 each year.

Climbing has not been without controversy. Some Indian leaders have called climbing the rock a sacrilege and demanded that it be closed, while climbers have trumpeted it as one of the premier crack-climbing areas in the nation. The Park Service came up with a compromise plan that includes a voluntary climbing closure for the month of June. Additional regulations were put into place emphasizing clean climbing techniques and restricting access to prairie falcon nesting areas mid-March–mid-May. Contact the monument for safety information and specifics on closures. If you're planning to summit Devils Tower, be sure to check in at the Climbing Registration Office or the self-registration kiosk. (In winter, check in at the Administration office.)

Displays in the visitor center and the kiosk describe climbing routes and techniques. For information on the various routes (at least 220 have been climbed), pick up one of the guidebooks in the visitor center, or talk with the climbing rangers who offer demonstrations daily in July and August. The monument website (www.nps.gov/deto) has details on climbing Devils Tower.

Those who want to climb Devils Tower but who lack the skills or equipment can choose from several permitted guide companies. Even rank beginners can summit the Tower if they are in good condition but they will need a day of climbing instruction, plus a second day to do the actual climb, for a total of $250 per person in groups of up to three climbers (higher for smaller groups).

You won't go wrong with Frank Sanders of **Above All Guiding/Devils Tower Lodge** (307/467-5267 or 888/314-5267, www.devils-towerclimbing.com), who has been climbing here since 1972. Other recommended guides include **Jackson Hole Mountain Guides** in Jackson (307/733-4979 or 800/239-7642, www.jhmg.com), **Exum Mountain Guides** (307/733-2297, www.exumguides.com), **National Outdoors Leadership School (NOLS)** in Lander (307/332-4784 or 800/710-6657, www.nols.edu), and **Sylvan Rocks Climbing School and Guide Service** in Hill City, South Dakota (605/574-2425, www.sylvanrocks.com).

❰ HIKING IN DEVILS TOWER

Four trails loop through this small national monument, providing fine views of Devils Tower and the surrounding country. Most popular is the 1.3-mile **Tower Trail,** which circles the Tower. It's an easy paved path with periodic openings offering impressive views of the summit, along with side paths to see the nearby Missouri Buttes and the Belle Fourche River. Be sure to look through the peep sight to find the old wooden ladder that once went all the way to the top of Devils Tower.

Red Beds/South Side Trail is a three-mile dirt path that also takes off near the visitor center but makes a longer, less-crowded loop around Devils Tower. Along the way you get nice views of the Belle Fourche River and the Red Beds—iron-stained bluffs near the river. A 30-minute side loop, the 1.5-mile **Valley View**

Trail, takes you to the prairie dog town and the Belle Fourche River.

You'll catch the finest views of Devils Tower from the **Joyner Ridge Trail,** a 1.5-mile path. Views from this hilltop trail are unforgettable, especially at sunrise and sunset. It's a delightful secret escape from crowds elsewhere.

EVENTS

Campfire programs are held several times a week during the summer at the campground amphitheater, with the standard Park Service fare of talks, tunes, and transparencies. Ranger walks and talks take place throughout summer; ask at the visitor center for upcoming events.

Each **Fourth of July** folks come from miles around to watch a big fireworks show put on by the KOA near Devils Tower.

PRACTICALITIES

Owned by climbing guide Frank Sanders, ⟨ **Devils Tower Lodge** (307/467-5267 or 888/314-5267, www.devilstowerlodge.com) is an attractive home hidden away on 21 acres near the base of Devils Tower. Four guest rooms are available, all with private baths and access to the hot tub and large indoor gym. Rates are $125–170 d, including breakfast (add dinner for $15 d). There's a spectacular view of Devils Tower from the hot tub. In addition to accommodations, Frank Sanders also offers several climbing packages for everyone from beginners to experienced climbers.

Families or groups of climbers enjoy **Canyon Ranch Guesthouse** (307/467-5555), a comfortable three-bedroom, two-bath home six miles from the Tower. This one has stunning views of Devils Tower, with space for 12. It rents for $145 d, plus $10 per person for additional guests, and has a full kitchen.

The Park Service maintains a fine **campground** ($12; open May–Oct.) 0.5 mile inside the entrance. In midsummer, get a space at the campground in the morning to be sure of having a spot. There's an eight-person limit at the campsites.

Just outside the monument are two private campgrounds. At **Devils Tower KOA** (307/467-5395 or 800/562-5785, www.devilstowerkoa.com), sites cost $24 for tents, $35 for RVs, and $55–60 d for simple cabins. The KOA has a heated outdoor pool plus wireless Internet, and it is open May–September. Horseback and hayrides are available, and if you haven't seen it before, you can watch *Close Encounters* on the TV. Most folks stock up on food in nearby towns, but the café here serves meals, ice cream, and espresso, and a general store sells limited supplies and gifts.

Devils Tower Trading Post (307/467-5295, www.devilstowertradingpost.com) is directly across the road from the KOA and stocks a few food items, gifts, and trinkets, and has a fast-food eatery. You can't miss its enormous American flag.

A **post office** (307/467-5937) stands just outside the park entrance gate.

Sundance and Black Hills National Forest

The quiet hamlet of Sundance (pop. 1,200) nestles at the foot of Sundance Mountain. The mountain—"Temple of the Sioux"—rises 1,000 feet above town and was an important sacred spot to the various tribes who claimed this land. Sun dances were performed at its base each year. Sundance got its start in 1879, when rancher Albert Hoge set up a trading post here. The town grew slowly until the 1950s, when Sundance Air Base arrived. Since its closing, the town of Sundance has settled into middle age, with the old standbys of ranching and logging its economic mainstays, although tourism is increasingly important.

SIGHTS

◀ Crook County Museum

The local museum (307/283-3666) is housed in the basement of the Crook County Courthouse on Cleveland Street. Hours are 8 A.M.–8 P.M. Monday–Friday June–August and 8 A.M.–5 P.M. Monday–Friday the rest of the year. Inside you'll find the usual collection of local paraphernalia, such as arrowheads, wooden wheelchairs, bison skulls, a Civil War battle flag from 1861, and cowboy gear, plus more interesting displays on the Vore buffalo jump site, a 1910 Studebaker buggy, along with dioramas of an Indian buffalo trap and of Custer's 1874 camp at Inyan Kara Creek. The real attractions are the mementos from Harry Longabaugh's visit to the town. Better known as the "Sundance Kid," Longabaugh spent 18 months in Sundance's Crook County Jail for horse stealing before being pardoned by the governor in 1889. The museum has his indictment and wanted poster, along with the criminal bar docket signed by Longabaugh during his trial and furnishings from the original courthouse. A replica (built in 1983) of the jail that once housed the Sundance Kid stands across the street.

Around Sundance

Access to 5,829-foot **Sundance Mountain** is via a dirt road that heads east from Hwy. 116 about 0.5 mile south of town. An enjoyable trail leads to the top, gaining 800 feet in elevation along the way. From the summit, you're treated with views of the nearby Black Hills and, on clear days, even the Big Horn Mountains 180 miles west. Call landowner Cecil Cundy at 307/283-2193 for permission to hike this trail.

Three miles west of the small settlement of **Beulah** (on the South Dakota border, 18 miles east of Sundance) is the **Vore Buffalo Jump,** where Indians drove thousands of bison into a pit between A.D. 1500–1800. The 200-foot-deep sinkhole is visible from I-90 and is marked by a small sign. Scientists believe 20,000 bison may have been killed here through the centuries.

The drive south from Beulah to Buckhorn provides a good taste of the Black Hills canyon country. Follow Sand Creek Road south from the freeway at Beulah, and you can drive for about 30 miles through canyons, the deserted mining town of Moskee, and on to Buckhorn along U.S. 85. In the spring and fall a 4WD may be needed for the muddy conditions, and the route is closed in winter. The Sand Hill Country Club and state fish hatchery at Ranch A are favorites of deer, especially in fall and early winter, when hundreds of deer are visible from the road. There's no hunting here, so you're likely to see several trophy-sized animals.

Eleven miles south of Sundance on Hwy. 116 is **Inyan Kara Mountain** (an Indian name meaning "Stone-Made Peak"), a 6,368-foot summit that dominates the surrounding country. In 1874, General George A. Custer led a large scientific expedition through this region en route to the Black Hills. Among others, Custer climbed the mountain, carving "G. Custer '74" on a rock near the summit. The inscribed rock is still here, but call landowner Marshall Nussbaum at 307/283-2851 for permission to cross his land on the way up the mountain.

EVENTS

The main event in Sundance is the **Sturgis Rally** during the first week of August (www.sturgis.com). Thousands of motorcyclists pass

SUN DANCES

The most spectacular religious ceremony of the Plains Indians was the sun dance. An annual event, it frequently attracted hundreds or even thousands of tribal onlookers, serving not simply as an important religious service but also as a social and political rally. Native American legends say that it originated centuries ago when a hunter was approached by a buffalo that suddenly spoke to him, offering a cure for sickness. Much later, an eagle came to another young man in a dream, prescribing the complete ceremony. The name is something of a misnomer because the dance was not a worship of the sun but a highly involved ceremony representing the creation of life and the triumph of good over evil. The specifics varied somewhat among the tribes. A common Native American term for it is "Thirsting Dance," referring to the long periods of dancing without water.

The sun dance was always held in late spring or early summer and led by a young man who spent considerable time learning the complex ceremonial steps from a priest. If he passed the test, the pledger gained immense status in the village as a fearless leader. The festivities lasted up to two weeks, with the main ceremony an intense four-day event. Central to the sun dance were an eagle representation (air), a buffalo head (earth), and a pole connecting the two to signify the sacred Tree of Life. The ceremony took place in a lodge, generally built around a central pole that forked at the top. After the sacred cottonwood tree had been selected by a scouting party, warriors attacked the tree in a furious charge. If it withstood this symbolic assault, the tree was cut down by a respected tribal woman and carried to the sun-dance site, where it was carefully erected. A bundle of brush (to represent an eagle or thunderbird nest) and a buffalo-skull altar were placed in the fork of the pole. Twelve other poles (the number varied with different tribes) were erected around the central one, with cross beams to the center. (Missionaries would later claim that the 12 poles around the central one were ritualistic representations of Jesus and the 12 apostles.) Brush was then laced around the outside to provide partial shade.

Supplicants spent four days without food or water, dancing, praying, blowing on eagle-bone whistles, and staring at the buffalo head, the sun, or a sacred doll as they waited for a vision of power. In most tribes, the sun dance also involved self-mutilation. Assistants commonly cut small pieces of skin from the candidates' arms and shoulders as a blood sacrifice to the Great Spirit. (According to several accounts, before the battle at Little Big Horn, Sitting Bull sacrificed 100 pieces of flesh in a sun-dance ceremony, after which a vision told him of the coming destruction of General Custer and his men.) Torture commonly went even further, as assistants cut slices into the back or chest of the dancers and slid bone skewers into the muscle. Thongs would be attached between the skewers and the central pole, while other skewers held heavy buffalo skulls to be dragged behind. Candidates would lean back until the ropes were taut, jerking as they danced. Eventually the skin and muscle ripped loose and the dancers collapsed on the ground. In some tribes, the dancers were actually lifted off the ground by these tethers.

Whites found the sun dance's torture difficult to understand and thought even less of such sexual aspects of the ceremony as the parading of a giant phallus. When the Indians were forced onto reservations, the sun dance was outlawed, although some tribes continued to practice it secretly. Finally, in the late 1920s, the government relented, and a more sedate version of the dance was resurrected. The traditional blood sacrifice still exists among some tribes but not in Wyoming. Today, the sun dance is performed in separate ceremonies by both the Shoshone and the Arapahoes on the Wind River Reservation. Visitors may watch but cannot take photos or videos.

The sun dance is now performed primarily as a thanksgiving ceremony, to cure disease, and to pray for the coming year. After several days of preparation, the main ceremony lasts for four days. Without food or water, the dancers move into a trance state that brings visions and power. On the fourth day, a bucket of water is passed around to signal the end of the sun dance, and that evening more dancing and feasting complete the ceremony.

through or stay in Sundance, and the town sometimes puts on special biker events.

If you're around in early August, don't miss the **Crook County Fair and Rodeo,** featuring sheepdog trials, various agricultural shows, pig wrestling, a parade, live music, and rodeo action.

RECREATION

Swim in the large **outdoor pool** (307/283-2133) at the grade school on the east side of town; open June–September. Golfers will enjoy the nine-hole **Sundance Country Club** (307/283-1191) on the east end of town.

ACCOMMODATIONS

Visitors will find five places to stay in the Sundance area. Be sure to book a room up to one year ahead if you plan to visit during the Sturgis Rally Week the first week of August. (Some local motels jack the rates up 50 percent for this event.)

You'll find very nice accommodations at **Bear Lodge Motel** (218 Cleveland, 307/283-1611, www.bearlodgemotel.com, $58–64 d). The hotel has wireless Internet, and some rooms contain microwaves and fridges. Right next door, **Arrowhead Motel/Budget Host** (307/283-3307 or 800/456-6016, www.budgethost.com, $59–69 d) has comfortable rooms. Closed January–February.

◖ **Sundance Mountain Inn/Rodeway Inn** (26 Hwy. 585, 307/283-3737 or 888/347-2794, www.sundancemountaininn.com, $69–79 d) offers attractive rooms with such amenities as an indoor pool and hot tub, continental breakfast, and wireless Internet in the lobby. Open April–November.

The town's fanciest lodging is the **Best Western Inn at Sundance** (121 S. 6th, 307/283-2800 or 800/238-0965, www.bestwestern.com/sundance, $91–121 d), on the east edge of town with a light breakfast and access to a pleasant indoor pool and hot tub.

Sundance Mt. Hideaway (42 Sundance Mountain Rd., 307/283-3766 or 877/838-0063, www.sundancemountainhideaway.com) rents out three modern log cabins with private baths, kitchenettes, and covered porches. These are a good deal: $80–125 d with a filling homemade breakfast.

Camping

You can reserve a spot at the Forest Service's fine **Reuter Campground** ($10, open year-round), just four miles northwest of Sundance, by calling 518/885-3639 or 877/444-6777 ($9 fee). Make reservations on the web at www.reserveusa.com. (Other public campgrounds in the Black Hills are described throughout this chapter.)

The private **Mountain View Campground** (307/283-2270 or 800/792-8439), 1.5 miles east of town, has tent sites for $20, RV spaces for $28–30. An outdoor pool is on-site. Open April–October.

FOOD

Open weekdays 6 A.M.–2 P.M., **Higbee's Cafe** (101 N. 3rd, 307/283-2165) cranks out dependably good American breakfasts and lunches; check the chalkboard for lunch specials. For three meals a day with daily specials, head to **Log Cabin Cafe** (1620 Cleveland, 307/283-3393) on the east side of town. **Aro Family Restaurant** (307 Cleveland, 307/283-2000) has homemade soups and Friday-night prime rib; it's probably the best place in town, but it can get smoky.

Country Cottage (downtown on Cleveland, 307/283-2450) serves frozen yogurt cones and Subway sandwiches. Get groceries from **Decker's Food Center** (106 N. 7th, 307/283-3155).

INFORMATION AND SERVICES

The small **Sundance Information Center,** in the rest area at exit 189 off I-90, 307/283-2440, is open 7 A.M.–7 P.M. daily mid-May–early September, and then 8 A.M.–5 P.M. daily until mid-October; it's closed the rest of the year. On the web, head to www.sundancewyoming.com.

The Forest Service's **Bearlodge Ranger District** is one mile east of town (307/283-1361, www.fs.fed.us/r2/blackhills). The **post office** is at 2nd and Main (307/283-3939) and the **Crook County Library** is at 414 Main Street (307/283-

1006). Get fast cash from ATMs inside the Texaco and Conoco gas stations.

GETTING THERE

Powder River Transportation (307/682-1888 or 800/442-3682, http://gillette.coachusa.us) has daily service connecting Sundance with other parts of eastern and northern Wyoming, continuing to Spearfish, Sturgis, and Rapid City, South Dakota. It also can take you all the way to Billings or Denver.

◀ BLACK HILLS NATIONAL FOREST

Black Hills National Forest lies primarily within South Dakota but reaches across the state line near Sundance. President Grover Cleveland established it in 1897 after a series of large forest fires focused attention on the need to protect the timber resource. The Forest Service's first commercial timber sale was held within the Black Hills, and the area is still a supplier for a Hulett lumber mill. Nearby, South Dakota's Black Hills contain a wide range of justifiably famous sites, including historic Deadwood—now a gambler's mecca—Jewel and Wind caves, Mt. Rushmore, Crazy Horse Memorial, and an enormous bison herd inside Custer State Park. Black Hills National Forest offices inside Wyoming can be found at Sundance (307/283-1361) and Newcastle (307/746-2782). Stop by for a forest map and information on camping and local sights, or find them on the web at www.fs.fed.us/r2/blackhills.

Scenic Drives

Many gravel roads wind up through the forested hills, and fall colors are brilliant along the aspen-lined stretches of the road just south of Cook Lake. A considerable amount of logging goes on within the ponderosa pine forests here, but it is selective logging, not clear-cutting, and hence not as visible. Be sure to stop at **Warren Peak Lookout** eight miles north of Sundance. The road is paved to this point, and you can climb the tower for a magnificent vista and a chance to visit folks at one of

---

JUST A-RIDIN'

When my earthly trail is ended
And my final bacon curled
And the last great roundup's finished
At the Home Ranch of the world
I don't want no harps nor halos,
Robes nor other dressed up things –
Let me ride the starry ranges
On a pinto hawse with wings!
Just a-ridin', a-ridin' –
Nothing I'd like half so well
As a-roundin' up the sinners
That have wandered out of hell,
And a-ridin'

—Charles Badger Clark Jr.

---

the few active fire lookouts remaining in Wyoming. Another interesting drive heads through the **Grand Canyon** area southeast of Sundance along Forest Road 863.

Hiking

Dozens of miles of hiking, biking, horseback-riding, and cross-country ski trails twist through the hills just north of Sundance. For details, pick up a *Sundance and Carson Draw Trails* map from the Forest Service office in Sundance or Newcastle. Good starting points for day hikes are the Cook Lake, Reuter, and Sundance campgrounds. Another interesting route is the **Dugout Trail** in the Sand Creek area.

Camping

Four campgrounds lie within the Wyoming section of the national forest, all open year-round (but not always accessible because of snow). **Sundance Campground** ($15) has campsites and horse corrals just three miles north of Sundance. **Reuter Campground** ($10) is five miles northwest of Sundance, and **Cook Lake Campground** ($11–15) is 16 miles north of Sundance on a tiny forest pond. You can make reservations for all three of these sites ($9 fee) by calling 518/885-3639 or 877/444-6777, or make reservations on the web at www.reserveusa.com. Camping is also available at small **Bearlodge Campground** ($5), seven miles west of Aladdin on Hwy. 24. In addition, free dispersed camping is allowed on Forest Service land throughout the Black Hills. Over on the South Dakota side of the line, you'll find more than two dozen additional Forest Service campgrounds.

Northern Black Hills Towns

◪ ALADDIN

Aladdin (pop. 10) was established in the 1870s to supply coal for gold smelters in Lead and Deadwood, South Dakota. During Prohibition, these mines housed moonshine stills. At 3,740 feet, it's the lowest settlement in Wyoming. Don't blink or you'll miss it, but if you do blink, turn around and stop for a visit. Aladdin is dominated by the fluorescent red **Aladdin Store** (307/896-2226), built in 1896 and operating continuously ever since. Out front is a "liar's bench" for local storytellers; inside is a potbellied stove, an ancient post office with the original boxes, and a few groceries. It's worth a visit for a taste of unspoiled Americana. An antique shop is upstairs with interesting collectibles from the area, and RVs can park in the old rodeo grounds across the street.

Next to the store is **2-2-2 Café** (307/896-2100), with all-American breakfasts and lunches in a smoky setting. Out back are modern motel rooms with microwaves and fridges for $64 d. You'll find a shady town park across the road.

Ten miles northeast of Aladdin is the **lowest point in Wyoming.** From here, the Belle Fourche River drops only another 3,125 feet on its several-thousand-mile descent to the sea via the Missouri and Mississippi rivers. Just east of Aladdin is the **Tipple Mine Historical Site,** with restored coal-loading chutes and other facilities. Approximately two miles east of Aladdin is a historical marker noting the still-visible tracks left by the party of 110 wagons, 2,000 animals, and 1,000 men led by General George A. Custer in the summer of 1874. Despite the Treaty of 1868 that reaffirmed this as Sioux Indian land, Custer's geologists, scouts, miners, and engineers had come to explore the Black Hills and investigate the rumors of gold.

Gold was indeed found by Custer's miners, and when word got out, the rush was on. Custer's own rush to judgment at Montana's Little Big Horn had also begun. He and all 268 of his men would die there just two years later.

On the other side of Aladdin, Hwy. 24 follows Beaver Creek past 150-foot-tall sandstone cliffs, ridge-top pines, and valley-bottom oaks. Old farmsteads appear, surrounded by fields filled with huge pyramid-like hay piles. The dot of a place called **Alva** (pop. 50) has a few old homes in the midst of the Bear Lodge Mountains but nothing in the way of services. West of Alva the road climbs into rolling grassy hills with trees in the draws and cattle grazing along the Belle Fourche River.

HULETT

The tiny logging and ranching town of Hulett (pop. 400) lies right along the Belle Fourche and is just 10 miles north of Devils Tower National Monument. Two lumber mills saw up timber from the adjacent Black Hills National Forest. The side of **Hulett National Bank** has burned-in brands from local cattle ranchers. A couple of miles west of Hulett you'll see bison grazing at a private ranch while magnificent Devils Tower looms on the horizon.

The summer-only **Rogues Gallery** (307/467-5849, www.devilstowermuseum.com) sells antiques, Indian artifacts, and the paintings of local artists Bob Coronato and Tom Waugh. There's a little museum in the back with Indian artifacts.

Entertainment and Events

For entertainment, head to **Capt'n Ron's Rodeo Bar** or **Ponderosa Bar** for a beer. **Hulett Rodeo** takes place on the second weekend of June each year and is a great local event. Actually, the biggest local event isn't in Hulett but in nearby Sturgis, South Dakota. Sturgis Rally Week (first week of August, www.sturgis.com) attracts thousands of motorcyclists to the Black Hills, filling every hotel and bar for 100 miles in all directions. Hulett's **Ham and Jam** (www.hulettrally.com)—a hog roast on Wednesday of Rally Week—is a huge local draw, with live music at the bars and throngs of bikers filling the streets, and a mechanical bull to test your manhood.

Recreation

Golfers will appreciate the elaborate 18-hole public course at **Devils Tower Country Club** (307/467-5773 or 877/467-5773, www.devilstowergolf.com).

Accommodations and Food

Hulett Motel (307/467-5220, www.hulettmotel.com) has comfortable rooms for $65 d, and suites for $85 d. Open mid-April–November with free Wi-Fi. Four new A-frame cabins are also available. **Pioneer Motel** (307/467-5656, $50 d) is simpler, but cozy, with fridges in most rooms.

Ten miles southeast of Hulett, **Diamond L Guest Ranch** (307/467-5236 or 800/851-5909, www.diamondlranch.com) houses a dozen or so guests at a time. The main activity is horseback riding, but you can also join in the chores and pretend to be a real ranch hand or just soak in the hot tub. There's a three-night minimum stay in the summer, but most guests book by the week. All-inclusive six-night rates are $2,500 for two people. Open mid-May–mid-September.

Whitetail Creek Outfitters (307/467-5625, www.whitetailcreek.com) has a lodge just four miles from Devils Tower. The seven guest rooms are $30 s or $60 d, including a full breakfast. **7 W Ranch** (307/878-4493, www.7wranch.com) contains a five-bedroom guesthouse on a 20,000-acre spread near Hulett. Lodging and three meals per day is $100 d. Both Whitetail Creek and 7W Ranch are popular with hunters in the fall and spring.

For food in Hulett, try **Ponderosa Cafe.**

Information and Services

Get Hulett information on the web at www.hulett.org. Hulett's **library** is in the high school. The town also has a country grocery store, a bank, a hardware store, and medical clinic.

ALZADA AND COLONY

North from Hulett, Hwy. 112 heads to the Montana border settlement of Alzada, cutting across land not unlike the foothills of California's Sierra Nevada. Cottonwoods and oaks fill the draws, and grassy meadows alternate with tree-topped hills. This land is very scenic, with an abundance of white-tailed deer all the way. The road doesn't really go anywhere that most tourists are heading; therefore, it is perfect for cyclists and anyone with an explorer's streak. From Alzada, U.S. 212 cuts southeast across Wyoming and to the South Dakota town of Belle Fourche. Along the way it passes a couple of bentonite mines in the grass-and-sage country around the nothing settlement called Colony. Antelope and cattle abound. Talk about confusion: Since there's no post office in Colony, Wyoming, locals have South Dakota addresses on a Montana delivery route!

OSHOTO

West and then south from Hulett is the tiny town of Oshoto (a Native American word meaning "Bad Weather"), accessible only via gravel roads. No services are available; all that's here is a post office. The **Brislawn Cayuse Ranch** (307/467-5394, www.cayuseranch.com) near Oshoto is one of the few places in America that has pureblooded mustangs—tough, small horses that were the pride of the Wild West. These are not the wild horses of the West, but true descendants of those brought by the Spanish. Bob Brislawn ("Mr. Mustang") started working to save the mustangs in 1925 and founded the Spanish Mustang Registry (www.spanishmustang.org) in 1957. He died in 1979, but his son Emmett carries on the tradition at the ranch.

MOORCROFT

Moorcroft (pop. 800) is a nondescript ranching and oil field town perched within a few miles of popular Keyhole Reservoir. It isn't particularly attractive, but it will do as a stop on the way to somewhere else. Because the famed Texas Trail passed through it, Moorcroft became an important cattle town. Up until the end of World War II, it served as the largest cattle shipping point along the entire Chicago, Burlington, and Quincy Railroad. The local historical stopping place is **Helen Robinson Zimmerschied Western-Texas Trail Museum** (200 S. Bighorn, 307/756-9300, open noon–4 P.M. Mon.–Fri. summers only; no charge). The name is almost bigger than the museum's collection of local items.

The main summertime event is **Moorcroft Jubilee Days** on the second Saturday in July, featuring a parade, games, barbecue, street dance, and bed races.

Practicalities

Find well-maintained older rooms—-some with fridges and microwaves—at **Cozy Motel** (219 W. Converse, 307/756-3486, $45–55 d). **Rangeland Court Motel and RV Park** (108 N. Yellowstone Ave., 307/756-3760, www.rt-connect.net/~rangeland, $50) is a spotless 10-unit place with rooms (some with microwaves and fridges). RV hookups cost $25.

The town's largest lodging place is **Moorcroft Motel** (214 Yellowstone Ave., 307/756-3411, $58 d), with fridges and microwaves in all rooms. Open April–mid-November.

Get meals at **Donna's Diner** (203 W. Converse, 307/756-3422) and groceries from **Diehl's Super Market** (N. Bighorn Ave., 307/756-3491).

There's no local visitor center; drop by **Town Hall** (104 N. Big Horn, 307/756-3526) for more about the moors and mores of Moorcroft. Moorcroft's **library** is at 105 E. Converse (307/756-3232).

KEYHOLE STATE PARK

Keyhole State Park (307/756-3596, http://wyoparks.state.wy.us) surrounds Keyhole Reservoir, a 14,720-acre warm-water lake that backs up water from the Belle Fourche River. (The name comes from the "keyhole" brand, used by a local ranch.) The dam was built in 1952 by the Bureau of Reclamation and supplies irrigation water for South Dakota farmers. Most of the visitors are locals, but it's an OK place to camp. Pine trees crowd hills to the east, while grass and sage grow around the reservoir's western shore. Anglers angle for the biggest walleye and northern pike in the state, bird-watchers watch for Merriam's turkeys and white pelicans, and snowmobilers 'bile around in winter.

Day use of the park is $4 for nonresident vehicles, $2 for Wyoming vehicles. **Camping** costs $12 for nonresidents, or $6 for Wyoming residents, at eight state campgrounds along the lake's east and south shores. Nicest are Pats Point and Pronghorn campgrounds. Make campsite reservations ($8.50 fee) at 877/996-7275, www.wyo-park.com.

Get to Keyhole State Park from I-90 by taking the Pine Ridge exit and continuing eight miles north. You'll find a swimming beach here, and the little settlement of **Pine Haven** (pop. 220; http://pinehaven.1wyo.net).

Every **Fourth of July,** the town of Pine Haven launches a grand display of fireworks over Keyhole Reservoir. **Keyhole Country Club and Golf Course** (307/756-3775) has a nine-hole golf course.

Keyhole Marina (307/756-9529) has supplies, RV electrical hookups ($15), and a convenience store with fishing gear. Open April–September. Get supplies, booze, and three meals a day from **Dugan's Bar and Grill** (307/756-9707).

Newcastle and Vicinity

Newcastle (pop. 3,000) sits at the junction of several major roads and serves as a gateway to the Black Hills. As in much of northeast Wyoming, the town's economy is a mixture of energy, ranching, and logging. Every half hour, day and night, traffic backs up on the railroad tracks across Main Street to wait as 100 soot-black coal cars rumble past bound for Midwestern power plants. A Newcastle refinery produces jet fuel for South Dakota's giant Ellsworth Air Force Base, and a natural-gas processing plant sits 25 miles south of town in the midst of the Finn-Shurley Fields. Large ranches encompass the town, dotted with oil pumpjacks, windmills, and Herefords.

HISTORY

The first white settlement of the Newcastle area came in 1875, when Professor Walter P. Jenney and Lieutenant Colonel R. I. Dodge led 432 soldiers and an army of mining engineers, scientists, and mapmakers to a base camp along Beaver Creek. They built the Jenney Stockade, which became a stage station and distribution point along the Cheyenne–Deadwood Trail. Many of the West's most famous characters stopped by en route to Deadwood, including Wild Bill Hickok, Calamity Jane, and Wyatt Earp.

Tubb Town

In 1888, the Chicago, Burlington, and Quincy Railroad announced plans to construct tracks across northeast Wyoming and into Montana. Speculators established Tubb Town, a ramshackle collection of saloons, hotels, and "sporting houses" along the proposed railroad route. All visitors were required to pay a toll (of sorts) on entrance: "set 'em up for the bunch." The party didn't last long—when the Burlington Railroad decided instead to build a town a few miles west at present-day Newcastle, Tubb Town faded into history. At Whoopup Canyon (so named because the spring floods came "a-whoopin' through"), a railroad worker attempted to pry the cap off a 25-pound can of black powder. After struggling without success, he decided to try a more forceful approach—using a pickax to punch a hole in the lid. His coworkers found little left to bury.

Wild Times

Coal was discovered in Cambria Canyon in the 1880s, and the coal-mining town of Cambria popped up almost overnight. It became a model community, with a water system, modern homes, three churches, electric lights, and some of the safest underground mines in the nation. Alcohol was banned, along with bawdy entertainment. At its peak, more than 1,500 people lived in Cambria, but when the coal ran out in 1928, the mines were forced to close.

The discovery of coal at Cambria led the Burlington Railroad to establish a townsite as near the mouth of Cambria Canyon as possible, with a spur to the four mines. The town was called Newcastle, after the English coal port of Newcastle-upon-Tyne. At first, the wide-open frontier sensibility of Newcastle contrasted sharply with that of quiet, sedate Cambria. When the new mayor, Frank Mondell (who had established the Cambria mines), decided to get rid of 20 of Newcastle's undesirables, a local hotel owner—fearing that he would lose most of his business—shot the mayor. Mondell (who later served for 26 years as Wyoming's lone congressional representative) carried the bullet in his spine the rest of his life.

In 1903 W. C. Clifton—known to most folks as Diamond L Slim—murdered a young couple to avoid paying a debt. He eventually confessed to the killings, but when the law seemed too slow, local vigilantes took matters into their own hands by hauling him out of jail in the middle of the night. Slim was dragged to a railroad bridge in Newcastle and hung. His last request, asking for "a long drop," was met—and then some; his head was torn from the body. Later, a mortician sewed his head on backward and propped the body in a window.

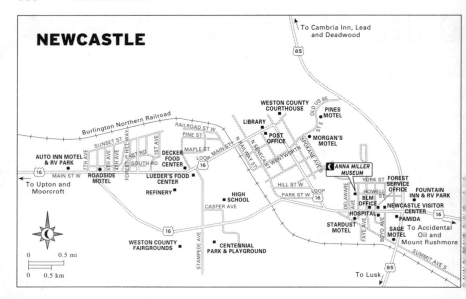

After the Cambria mines closed, the town of Newcastle faded, but with the discovery of huge oil deposits nearby in the 1950s it boomed again. By the mid-1950s more than 25,000 people crowded the surrounding countryside. A bust soon followed, only to lead to a similar cycle in the 1970s. Now Newcastle perks along on an economy of equal parts oil, coal, logging, and ranching. Folks from Nebraska or Kansas would feel right at home among the quiet streets, staid older homes, pickup trucks, and freight trains.

SIGHTS
C Anna Miller Museum
The Newcastle museum (Delaware St. and U.S. 16, 307/746-4188, open 9 A.M.–5 P.M. Mon.–Fri. all year; donation) is housed in the old National Guard Cavalry Barn, a stone structure built in the 1930s by the Work Projects Administration and now on the National Register of Historic Places. Inside the typical collection of local paraphernalia: items from the Cambria mines, a horse-drawn hearse, a noose (not, however, the one vigilantes used to hang murderer Diamond Slim Clifton from

the Newcastle railroad trestle), dinosaur bones, and a scale model of the giant KB&C ranch. Be sure to try a couple of cranks on the old noise-maker—it was used to disrupt newlyweds on their first night. And don't miss the old living quarters at the end of the barn, especially the children's room filled with historic toys. Anna Miller, for whom the museum was named, was a local school superintendent whose husband, Sheriff Billy Miller, was the last white man to die in a battle with the Indians in 1903.

Outside the museum you'll find a furnished one-room schoolhouse built in 1890, a homesteader cabin, and the **Jenney Stockade cabin** (built in 1875), the oldest building in the Black Hills. Ask at the museum for directions to the Cheyenne–Deadwood Trail ruts.

Downtown, the beautiful **Weston County Courthouse** is hard to miss; the Classical Revival sandstone structure was finished in 1911. President Taft spoke from these steps later that same year.

Accidental Oil Company
Certainly the most amusing sight around Newcastle is the kitschy Accidental Oil Company.

NEWCASTLE AREA CLIMATE

SNOWFALL — MAXIMUM TEMP.
RAINFALL — MINIMUM TEMP.

Average Maximum Temp.	59.2°F
Average Minimum Temp.	34.1°F
Annual Rainfall	15.12"
Annual Snowfall	36.1"

© AVALON TRAVEL PUBLISHING, INC.

In 1966 (around the time Jed Clampett of television's *Beverly Hillbillies* was "shootin' at some food, and up from the ground came a bubbling crude—oil, that is, black gold, Texas tea…"), Newcastle rancher Al Smith decided to dig a hole to see how far down it was to oil. Using a pick and shovel, and later dynamite, he reached it at 21 feet. The "world's only hand-dug oil well" is now a small tourist trap along U.S. 16 four miles east of Newcastle. Outside are steam-powered oil rigs and antique pumps. An old oil-storage tank encloses a rather nice gift shop, and you can walk down to view the oil-bearing rock under black light (which makes the seeping oil visible). It's more interesting than it sounds. Accidental Oil (307/746-2042,

www.trib.com/~debran) is open 9 A.M.–6 P.M. daily June–August; it's closed the rest of the year, although the gift shop stays open. Thirty-minute tours of the well, including a discussion of petroleum geology, cost $5 adults, $3 kids, or $15 families. Pure Americana.

(Paleo Park

On the 9,000-acre Zerbst Ranch, Paleo Park (307/334-2271, www.paleopark.com) is just about as remote as you can get—32 miles southwest of Newcastle and then 24 miles out a gravel road. The country consists of open grassland with to-the-horizon vistas and quietude almost lost elsewhere in America. The ranch lies near the center of the famous Lance Creek fossil area, where the late Leonard Zerbst discovered one of the most complete specimens of *Triceratops* in 1998. Named Kelsey Ann, this giant horned dinosaur roamed the land 65 million years ago, and the mounted skeleton now resides with the Children's Museum of Indianapolis. Other finds here have included a track site with the tracks of dinosaurs and birds together, the skull of a pachycephalosaur, a mummified duckbill dinosaur now at the American Museum of Natural History in New York, and even a *Tyrannosaurus rex* with skin impressions.

Owner Arlene Zerbst leads two-hour tours ($40 per person) that include the chance to see additional dinosaur bones in situ, check out a microsite filled with thousands of bone fragments and teeth (including a *T. rex*), plus a visit to the dinosaur track site. Overnight stays are $100 per person, including three meals and bunk accommodations. Call a day ahead for tour reservations and to make sure the road is passable. Open Memorial Day–Labor Day.

ENTERTAINMENT AND EVENTS

The **Dogie**—as in "Git along, little dogie"—(111 W. Main St., 307/746-2187) is the local movie house. The bar at **Old Mill Inn** (500 W. Main, 307/746-4608) has more than 100 beers, including many microbrews. Newcastle's live music scene is almost nonexistent; to party,

THE BLACK HILLS

© DON PITCHER

Black Hills north of Newcastle

locals head 50 miles away to happenin' Deadwood, South Dakota.

The biggest local event isn't in Newcastle. It's South Dakota's **Sturgis Bike Rally** (www.sturgis.com), which takes place the second week of August. It's not a good time to come through town on a Honda motorcycle! During the rally, locals pull out the stops with a **pig roast** at the Fountain Inn and **Bag Lady Days** at the Flying V.

Several events actually take place in Newcastle, including the **Spring Fling Rodeo** in late May. This unique professional event is the largest female rodeo in Wyoming. You're likely to find other rodeos going on at the fairgrounds most summer weekends. Also in May are **Living History Days,** when visitors will learn about the lives of pioneers.

The annual **Perino horse sale** in June brings people from all over the nation and is a great opportunity to see these beautiful animals. Newcastle's main local event is the **Weston County Fair,** held the first week of August, with 4-H exhibits, a livestock auction, junior rodeo, ranch rodeo, and barbecue.

RECREATION

Swim a few laps at **Kozisek Aquatic Center** (15 Stampede, 307/746-2713), or play a round of golf at the nine-hole **Newcastle Country Club** (2302 W. Main, 307/746-2639).

ACCOMMODATIONS
Motels

You'll find a good variety of lodging options in Newcastle. During Sturgis Rally Week (first week of August; www.sturgis.com), rates at many local motels rise sharply, and the rooms are often booked up almost a year in advance.

For rock-bottom rates, head to **Stardust Motel** (833 S. Summit, 307/746-4619 or 866/746-4719), where tiny rooms start at just $28 d. Larger, remodeled units with fridges and microwaves are $38–49 d. Families appreciate the apartment unit (full kitchen) that sleeps six for $60.

On the west end of town, **(** **Auto Inn Motel** (2503 W. Main, 307/746-2734 or 877/ 228-8646, www.autoinnmotel-campground .com, $49–59 d) is a good deal, with clean and comfy rooms, Wi-Fi, fridges, microwaves, and a continental breakfast. Kids appreciate the playground out back.

Two attractive and clean motels—**Morgan's Motel** (205 S. Spokane, 307/746-2715) and **Pines Motel** (248 E. Wentworth, 307/746-4334 or 800/946-4334)—have quiet, out-of-the-way locations just a few blocks off the main drag, with rooms for $50–100 d.

On the east end of town, **Fountain Inn** (307/746-4426 or 800/882-8858, www.barbarv.vcn.com, $65 s or $70–76 d) is the largest Newcastle motel (60 rooms), and the only one with an outdoor pool. Some rooms contain kitchenettes, and wireless Internet is available throughout the motel.

Other Options

Set amid majestic Black Hills country eight miles north of Newcastle, the **Flying V Cambria Inn** (307/746-2096, www.flyingv-cambriainn.com, $49 s or $69 d) offers country accommodations in a historic stone building. Built in the 1920s, the inn has a good restaurant and 10 guest rooms with a mix of antique and newer furnishings. Room rates include a full breakfast. Some rooms have shared baths. The Cambria is open June–December.

In the Black Hills 17 miles northeast of Newcastle, ◖ **EVA-Great Spirit Ranch B&B** (307/746-2537, www.wyomingbnb-ranch-rec.com/EVA.html, $80 d) is a roomy modern log home on more than 500 acres of ranch land. Owner Irene Ward cooks big country breakfasts and will fill you with details on the area's rich human and natural history. Three guest rooms have shared or private baths, and the back deck is perfect for relaxing in this remote and peaceful setting. Kids are welcome.

The ranch at remote ◖ **Paleo Park** (307/334-2271, www.paleopark.com) also has overnight lodging in a bunkhouse dorm. Lodging and three big meals is $100 per person per night (see *Sights* for tour information).

Camping

You can pitch a tent for free anywhere on nearby public lands within both Thunder Basin National Grassland and Black Hills National Forest. For access to the latter, head nine miles east on U.S. 16 and then turn north up Forest Road 117 (just a few hundred feet before the South Dakota border). **Beaver Creek Campground** ($8, open all year) is right on the Wyoming–South Dakota border 23 miles northeast of Newcastle near the place called Mallo. The Park Service's **Jewel Cave National Monument** (605/673-2288) has camping inside South Dakota, 25 miles east of Newcastle.

Directly in front of Fountain Inn, **Crystal Park Campground** (3 Seminoe Ave., 307/746-4426 or 800/882-8858, www.barbarv.vcn.com, $11 tents, $19 RVs, open Apr.–Oct.) has an outdoor pool and a fishing pond out front stocked with trout and bass. Showers for non-campers are $5.

Auto Inn Motel (2503 W. Main, 307/746-2734 or 877/228-8646, www.autoinnmotel-campground.com, $15 tents, $29 RVs) has year-round sites on the west side of town.

FOOD

For filling breakfasts, a good salad bar, steaks, prime rib, and homemade pies, head to **Old Mill Inn** (500 W. Main, 307/746-4608). The building itself is worth a look; places like this don't get built anymore. Completed in 1905, the mill produced Toomey's Flapjack Flour and Toomey's Biscuit Mix until going out of business in 1965. It was later transformed into a restaurant.

Historic ◖ **Flying V Cambria Inn** (307/746-2096, www.flyingvcambriainn.com), eight miles north of town on U.S. 85, serves delicious prime rib, steaks, seafood, and Italian meals. Big portions and good food in a nostalgic setting; open June–December only.

For fast food and sit-down meals in a friendly diner setting, head to **Hi-16 Drive In** (2951 W. Main, 307/746-4055).

◖ **Donna's Main St. Diner** (207 Main St., 307/746-2905) gets packed with locals who appreciate the smoke-free setting, hearty breakfasts (try the raisin Wyoming toast), and daily lunch specials that include homemade soups.

Isabella's (12 S. Sumner, 307/746-3500) mixes it up with Friday-night steaks and Chinese meals several nights a week, along with

THE BLACK HILLS

gourmet pizzas, sandwiches, salads, and ice cream all the time.

The best meal deals (and entertainment) in the area are across the South Dakota line. Deadwood's casinos (www.deadwood.com) serve a big variety of food, including inexpensive steak dinners. Lodging, however, is pricey.

Get groceries in Newcastle at **Decker's Food Center** (709 W. Main, 307/746-2779) or **Woody's Food Center** (622 W. Main, 307/746-3511). Decker's has a good bakery and deli.

INFORMATION AND SERVICES

Just west of the intersection of U.S. Hwys. 16 and 85, the **Newcastle Visitor Center** (307/746-2739 or 800/835-0157, www.newcastlewyo.com, open 9 A.M.–5 P.M. Mon.–Fri., 9 A.M.–5 P.M. Sat.–Sun. all year) has local information. While here, be sure to pick up *Beaver Creek: A Trip Through Time,* a booklet describing a loop tour of sites in the area; it's filled with fascinating descriptions of historic events.

Government offices include the **BLM's Newcastle Field Office** (1101 Washington, 307/746-6600, www.wy.blm.gov) and the Black Hills National Forest's **Hell Canyon Ranger District** (1225 Washington Blvd., 307/746-2783, www.fs.fed.us/r2/blackhills). Nearly all of the land the latter manages is across the border in South Dakota.

Check your email at the **Weston County Library** (23 W. Main, 307/746-2206, http://will.state.wy.us/weston).

Weston County Health Services (1124 Washington St., 307/746-4491) provides emergency care, with a doctor on call. Newcastle does not have bus or plane service.

FOUR CORNERS AREA

North of Newcastle, U.S. 85 climbs quickly into the pine-covered Black Hills, providing wide vistas over the town and across the open plains to the south. Eight miles north of Newcastle is **Flying V Cambria Inn,** constructed in 1928 as a resort for and memorial to the Cambria miners. It was completed just a few months before the mines closed down for good. Now listed on the National Register of Historic Places, the inn is open for meals and lodging. The ghost town of Cambria slowly crumbles on private land nearby.

Another nine miles north is **Red Butte,** a steep-sided sandstone peak rising right along the road like a miniature Devils Tower. A local landmark, it was said to have been used by both Indians and early whites as a lookout. Not far away is the site of the 1878 Canyon Springs robbery on the old Cheyenne–Deadwood stage route. A passenger and an outlaw died in the shoot-out, and at least $20,000 (some accounts claim up to $140,000) in gold was taken and buried nearby. Many years later, a local farmer digging potatoes near Red Butte apparently found some of the loot. Packing up his family, he split town without a word.

North of Red Butte, the land begins to open up into an undulating grassy terrain with rich red-black soil. Just a couple of miles up the road is a road junction country inn and post office. **Four Corners Country Inn** (307/746-4776 or 800/890-4776) has nicely furnished and economical rooms (shared or private baths, no in-room phones or TVs) for $25 s or $35 d. Add a breakfast for another $5 or dinner for $8 per person. RV sites with hookups are $25; no tents. Open year-round.

Mallo Road (gravel) heads east from Four Corners into South Dakota, offering a colorful fall drive as the aspens turn a brilliant yellow. The Forest Service's **Beaver Creek Campground** ($8, open all year) is six miles east of Four Corners and right across the state line inside South Dakota. Just one mile inside Wyoming is spacious **Mallo Camp and Resort** (307/746-4094), where modern motel rooms are $45 d, including access to two large communal kitchens. The resort is used for youth camps and other activities in the summer, and it attracts snowmobilers when the snow flies, with many trails on nearby Black Hills National Forest land.

HEADING SOUTH

South of Newcastle, U.S. 85 is an arrow aimed at the horizon, pointing across the almost-flat landscape of grass, wind, and antelope. A few bottomland trees line the creeks, and the Cheyenne River etches a narrow line through the land, which is nearly dry in the late-summer heat. This is the heart of the great mixed-grass prairie that borders eastern Wyoming and reaches into adjacent Nebraska and south into Colorado.

UPTON AREA

On the edge of Upton (pop. 870), a sign makes no bones about where you are: the "Best Town on Earth!" Who am I to argue? Like its neighbors—Osage and Newcastle—Upton lies right along the edge of the Black Hills, with ponderosa pines topping the picturesque ridge to the north (appropriately named Pine Ridge) and open-range country spreading to the south. The Chicago, Burlington, and Quincy Railroad established a depot here in 1892, and railroad tracks now form Upton's southern border. Beyond this point, Hwy. 116 climbs over gentle grassy hills through the heart of Thunder Basin National Grassland. It's a high-plains landscape filled with windmills and scattered ranches and grazed by sheep, cattle, antelope, and mule deer. The sky completely dominates the landscape. Upton's limited economy depends on local ranchers, oil pumping, and coal mining in nearby Campbell County. Much of "downtown" is now a ghost town of abandoned buildings.

Upton's tiny **Red Onion Museum** (307/468-2672, open 9 A.M.–noon and 1–5 P.M. Mon.–Fri.) houses pioneer items and local memorabilia, including the featured attraction: a two-headed Hereford calf born on a local ranch. Pick up the *Prairie to Pines* tour pamphlet for an interesting drive through gorgeous country northeast of Upton. On the east end of Upton is **Old Town,** an interesting cluster of a dozen reconstructed cabins (one built from sod) near the original townsite. They're open seasonally. Upton City Park is a good kid stop, with a fine playground. Find out more about Upton on the web at www.trib.com/~uptonwy.

Old Town Days in late June is the town's big event, with a pig roast, games, pie auction, dance, and homemade butter and ice cream. **Upton Fun Days,** held the third weekend of July, includes a pancake breakfast, parade, street dance, kids games and kids rodeo, tractor pull, and free barbecue.

Cedar Pines Country Club is a public nine-hole course three miles north of town on State 116.

Upton Practicalities

Stay at **Weston Inn Motel** (307/468-2401, $40 s or $53 d). **Remy's Diner** (307/468-2266) is popular with locals for all-American meals. **The Drug Store** (307/468-2770) claims the "best malts in Wyoming." Drop by to see for yourself.

Get groceries at **Joe's Food Center** (307/468-2372). You can hang out (or check your email) at the branch **library** (Pine and 4th Sts., 307/468-2324).

Osage

Halfway between Newcastle and Upton, tiny Osage (pop. 200) has a bar, its only surviving business, but not much else to show for having once been the center of the oil industry in northeast Wyoming. In 1920, a huge gusher turned the surrounding country into a madhouse of oil prospectors and transformed Osage into a tent city of 1,500 people. When the boom inevitably turned to bust, only a core of folks remained in what is now a railroad way station.

THE BLACK HILLS

THE MORAL OF THE STORY

If the reader thinks he is done, now, and that this book has no moral to it, he is in error. The moral of it is this: If you are of any account, stay at home and make your way by faithful diligence; but if you are "no account," go away from home, and then you will have to work, whether you want to or not. Thus you become a blessing to your friends by ceasing to be a nuisance to them – if the people you go among suffer by the operation.

–Mark Twain in *Roughing It*

BACKGROUND

The Land

Covering nearly 98,000 square miles, Wyoming is America's ninth-largest state. With just over 506,000 people in 2004—the smallest population of any state—Wyoming remains a remarkably undeveloped and unsettled place. Cattle outnumber people by nearly three to one. The population density averages just over five people per square mile, and in some counties there is nearly one square mile of land for each person.

GEOGRAPHY

On the map, Wyoming is simply a gigantic trapezoidal chunk of earth. Its straight-line border (375 miles from east to west and 276 miles north to south) is an arbitrary human creation that encompasses a surprising diversity of country. The Continental Divide wanders diagonally across the state's mountains from the northwest corner to south-central Wyoming, forming the barrier that separates waters flowing into the Atlantic and Pacific oceans. More than 71 percent of Wyoming's lakes, rivers, and streams drain into tributaries of the Missouri River, eventually reaching the Atlantic Ocean; most of the rest flow into tributaries of the Colorado and Columbia rivers and thence to the Pacific Ocean. Small sections drop into the Great Basin (Salt Lake) or the Great Divide Basin (between Rock Springs and Rawlins), where the water evaporates or percolates into the ground.

© DON PITCHER

Wyoming's mountains generally trend northwest to southeast, but smaller ranges break up this gross overall pattern. Northwest Wyoming is dominated by a complex mélange of mountains: the Absaroka, Teton, Gros Ventre, Wyoming, and Wind River ranges. North-central Wyoming is divided by the Big Horn Mountains, while the Laramie Range and the Medicine Bow Mountains dominate the south-central region. The far northeast corner holds the Black Hills. In among these ranges, the land spreads out in broad basins, including Bighorn Basin and Powder River Basin in the north, Wind River Basin in the west-central region, and the Green River, Red Desert, and Washakie basins in the southwest. The eastern section of Wyoming drops gently into the Great Plains. With an average elevation of 6,700 feet (and a range of 3,125–13,804 feet), Wyoming is the third-highest state in the nation. Only Alaska and Colorado are higher.

CLIMATE

Wyoming's climate mirrors its diverse geography, varying from arid deserts to cool mountain forests. The mountain ranges act as barriers to eastward-moving weather systems. Moist air is forced upward by the mountains, releasing rain or snow along the western slopes. By the time the clouds reach the east side, much of the water has been wrung out, creating a "rain shadow." Because of this, midwinter finds Togwotee Pass smothered under many feet of snow while Dubois, in the lee of the Absaroka Range, may have only a dusting on the ground.

Visitors to Wyoming discover weather typical of the West's high plains and mountains: hot, dry summers punctuated by fierce thunderstorms, and cold winters with a fair amount of snow. Conditions vary greatly throughout the state, however, with cooler summers and heavy winter snows in the mountains. July can sometimes be unbearably hot, with temperatures occasionally topping 100 degrees.

Extremes

Wyoming has a reputation for extreme conditions. Wintertime blizzards periodically lash the land, and strong winds pile the snow into huge drifts. Summertime thunderstorms—particularly in the mountains—can be an almost daily occurrence. Southeast Wyoming has an average of nine hailstorms per year—it's the hail capital of North America. Temperatures have been recorded from –66°F (Yellowstone National Park) to 114°F (the town of Basin). Precipitation shows a similar variation—high mountain ranges of northwest Wyoming see as much as 60 inches (mostly snow) per year, while parched desert areas in Bighorn Basin and Great Divide Basin receive only six.

Wyoming is well known for its wind. Throughout much of the state, the wind seems never to stop blowing, averaging more than 16 miles per hour along the eastern border. Buffalo Bill Cody, a man who symbolizes the West in the American conscience, once defended Wyoming when a friend complained of the wind:

You know where those winds come from? Well, this country up here is so close to paradise you can feel the breezes from heaven. That wind comes from the angels' wings. When they flap their wings the wind comes right down this valley.

Basin Weather

In the expansive basins that cover much of Wyoming, typical midsummer daytime temperatures are in the 80s and 90s, with nights dropping into the 50s and 60s. Low relative humidity makes the heat easier to take. The wettest months are April and May, with lots of sun in the summer. Afternoon thunderheads often build up, temporarily blocking the sun, but generally dropping more lightning than rain. Fall can be a most pleasant time of year, with shirtsleeve days and cool evenings.

When winter arrives in November and December, it can do so with a vengeance, pushing the mercury well below zero. Snowfall is not great, totaling 15–60 inches over the winter, but when combined with winds pushing 50 mph, it can look like a lot more. In places,

LIGHTNING SAFETY

Lightning is a significant hazard for travelers on foot or horseback in Wyoming, particularly in the high mountains such as the Tetons, Wind River Range, Snowy Range, or the Big Horns. Three people were killed by lightning strikes in 1998 and 1999 in the Snowy Range west of Laramie, and others are hit almost every year around the state. Perhaps the most famous incident came in the 1990s, when acclaimed writer Gretel Ehrlich was struck while riding a horse on her ranch at the foot of the Big Horns. Her long and excruciating recovery is detailed in *A Match to the Heart* (Random House, www .randomhouse.com).

CREATING A THUNDERHEAD

Thunderstorms are created by a combination of convective forces, moisture, and unstable air. On sunny days as the ground warms, heat begins to rise convectively. When the air above is unstable (much cooler at higher altitudes than closer to the ground), the warm air rises rapidly. As it rises, the air cools enough that tiny droplets of moisture precipitate out, forming clouds that may grow into thunderheads if there is enough moisture and atmospheric instability. This rapid development of thunderheads generates enormous amounts of energy that is released as lightning, wind, hail, and rain. During a lightning strike, an electrical charge reaches toward the ground and is met by an opposite charge rising from the earth. They connect in a brilliant flash of light, heat, and noise as 35,000 amperes of charge are released.

PROTECTING YOURSELF

Nearly 100 people die each year from lightning strikes in the United States, and hundreds of others are injured. Statistically speaking, golfers are the most likely to get zapped because they are often in open areas carrying metal golf clubs when a storm rolls in. Others at risk include softball and soccer players, mountain climbers, horseback riders, swimmers, and hikers.

Several factors are important in protecting yourself from lightning. One is to pay attention to building storms, even distant ones, and especially those that build quickly. Mountain thunderstorms – created when winds push air masses upslope against a mountain range – are five times more likely to occur than storms

---

snow fences extend for many miles beside the highways, attempting to blunt the blowing snow. Ground blizzards sometimes halt traffic along I-80 for days at a time. Locals joke that it snows only a couple of inches in December and then the snow blows back and forth across the state the rest of the winter until it is finally worn out. Actually, winters are not all so bleak, and temperatures occasionally rise into the 50s. You can expect sun 60 percent of the time. *Chinooks* (warm downslope winds) are common in the winters along the eastern slopes of the mountains, particularly around Sheridan, Dubois, and Cody.

Mountain Weather

Many of the favorite sites in Wyoming, including Yellowstone and Grand Teton national parks, lie primarily above 7,000 feet. Here, the weather is considerably cooler than in the basins. Summertime temperatures rarely top 80°F, while nights often dip into the 40s. Snow is possible at any time of the year. April and May are generally the wettest months. Spring comes late in the mountains, and drifts often block high passes until mid-July. Summer thunderstorms are common, especially in the northwest mountains, where they gather over the high peaks (and often nearby valleys) most afternoons. Mid-September brings fall conditions as mountain temperatures often drop 20–30 degrees below summer readings, quickly turning the aspen leaves a brilliant orange and sending most folks scurrying for warmer climes.

High-country winters are often severely cold and snowy, with temperatures below zero for days at a time. Snow depths often exceed over adjacent valleys. The color of thunderheads is another factor to watch; black bases mean significant amounts of moisture and may portend a more violent thunderstorm.

The most dangerous times are – surprisingly – before a thunderstorm comes directly overhead. Strikes can hit up to five miles in front of a fast-moving thunderstorm. In 1999, a Boy Scout was struck in the Tetons while watching a distant thunderstorm; overhead it was mostly blue sky! To determine your distance from an approaching storm, count the number of seconds between a lightning strike and the subsequent thunderclap, then divide by five to get the approximate distance in miles. If thunder arrives within five seconds, the storm is dangerously close, just one mile away.

If you see a storm approaching, get off ridgetops and other high places, move out of open fields, away from trees or other tall objects, and away from water. Lightning follows the path of least resistance, which usually means taller objects or those containing metal. Safer places are inside a car or house. If those options aren't possible, stay as low as possible and stand on an insulated pad or a four-foot square of polyethelene. Put your ankles and knees together and crouch down, or drop to your knees and bend forward, putting your hands on your knees. Do not lie flat on the ground. Move away from others in your group and avoid rocks and boulders if possible. Horseback riders should dismount and move away from the horse. Metallic and electronic objects attract lightning, so stay away from fence posts, golf clubs, cell phones, climbing gear, or metal objects in your backpack. Even a metal cap rivet can attract lightning. Don't stand in a group of people. If you're indoors when a storm hits, move away from windows, doors, appliances, pipes, and telephones.

Lightning strikes are sometimes preceded by a tingling sensation, and your hair may stand on end. If this happens, move immediately into the crouching position. If someone near you is struck by lightning, get immediate help by calling 911 and be ready to perform CPR. Injured people do not carry an electrical charge and can be handled safely. For additional lightning safety information, contact the nonprofit **Lightning Protection Institute** (800/488-6864, www.lightning.org).

six feet in the higher mountains. Grand Targhee Ski Resort receives 42 feet of snow over a typical winter! Fortunately, the relative humidity is quite low, making the temperatures easier to tolerate and creating fluffy powder snow conditions. One surprising winter feature is the presence of temperature inversions in intermountain valleys such as Big Piney and Jackson Hole. These often occur on cold, clear nights when the cold air sinks into the valley floors. Skiers who leave the lodge bundled in down parkas and polypro are often surprised to find temperatures 30 degrees warmer at the top of the mountain.

Flora and Fauna

VEGETATION

Wyoming's topography and climate are reflected in its vegetation, with dense forests in the mountains and dry grasses and shrubs at lower elevations. The vegetation can be classified into six broad categories (see map): mixed-grass prairie, sagebrush steppe, desert shrubland, evergreen forest, deciduous forest, and alpine tundra. Mixed-grass prairies dominate the eastern third of Wyoming and contain such species as grama grass, wheatgrass, junegrass, bluegrass, and sage. The western two-thirds of Wyoming contains vast areas of sagebrush steppe, a threadbare carpet of big sagebrush, wheatgrass, needle-and-thread grass, grama grass, tumbleweed, and other plants. This is the country most folks associate with Wyoming—sagebrush extending to the horizon. (An old cowboy saying goes, "I reckon the Lord done put tumbleweeds here to show which way the wind was a-blowin'.")

Wyoming also contains desert areas, notably the Red Desert and a large part of Bighorn Basin. Dominant plants in the desert shrublands include greasewood, saltbush, shadscale, and various kinds of sagebrush. At higher elevations, where more moisture falls, the land is covered with evergreen forests. Ponderosa pines dominate forested parts of eastern Wyoming, while lodgepole pine, Douglas fir, Engelmann spruce, and subalpine fir exist in mountains to the west. A few areas also have pinyon pine and juniper trees. Deciduous forests are scattered in small patches around Wyoming, consisting of cottonwoods along river bottoms, aspens in the middle elevations, and bur oak in the Black Hills. The tree line in much of Wyoming is around 9,500 feet. Above this line, one finds alpine tundra, where the dominant plants are low-growing herbs, grasses, and forbs.

WILDLIFE

When the first mountain men and explorers wandered into the vast land that became Wyoming, they found an incredible abundance of wildlife: herds of bison stretching to the horizon; antelope, elk, and deer grazing on the broad plains; and grizzly bears, wolves, coyotes, cottontails, and jackrabbits. Although wolves were poisoned to extinction, and only a few hundred bison and grizzlies remain, other animals fared better. Today, the two most common large mammals are mule deer and pronghorn antelope, both of which are found across much of the state. The sagebrush lands also provide cover for sage grouse, a large chickenlike bird (the males perform an elaborate X-rated mating display). In the mountains, one often hears the early-summer drumming of ruffed grouse. Rarest of Wyoming's animals is the endangered black-footed ferret.

Watchable Wildlife

Wyoming's undeveloped character makes it a mecca for those who enjoy watching wild animals. Yellowstone National Park is a favorite place to look for bison, elk, coyotes, moose, mule deer, bighorn sheep, river otters, and trumpeter swans. Both black and grizzly bears also live here, although they're less commonly seen. Another popular place is the National Elk Refuge in Jackson Hole, the winter home for a herd of more than 7,000 elk. Excellent places to see bighorn sheep are the Whiskey Basin Habitat Area, near Dubois, and the Bighorn National Recreation Area. Wyoming has around 3,500 wild horses; watch for them at Bighorn National Recreation Area near Lovell or in the Red Desert near Rock Springs. Mountain goats live in the Beartooth Mountains along Wyoming's border with Montana. The high mountains of the Tetons and the Wind River Range have such animals as pikas and yellow-bellied marmots, while the sagebrush country abounds with deer, antelope, coyotes, jackrabbits, cottontails, and prairie dogs. Certainly the most distinctive Wyoming critter is the jackalope. For a different sort of watchable wildlife, visit Wyoming in early May when pastures across the state are filled with wobbly baby calves.

SAGEBRUSH

Sagebrush is Wyoming's ubiquitous common denominator, a sweetly pungent bush found from the lowest deserts to 10,000-foot mountains. More sage grows here than anyplace else in North America. The volatile oils make it a last choice for cattle and act as a natural herbicide, preventing competition from other plants. Ranchers consider the plant less than worthless, but native animals such as sage grouse, antelope, and mule deer depend on sage for survival. You won't even find sage grouse where sage doesn't grow.

The terms sagebrush and sage are generally used interchangeably in the West. Note, however, that the spice on your kitchen shelf is not the same as the Wyoming plant (Artemesia), and any attempt to cook with sagebrush is likely to leave you gagging. Sage has been in the West for 25 million years and is well adapted to the poor soils and arid conditions of the desert. Sage survives by using its network of shallow roots to draw moisture from the ground as it percolates into the soil. Wyoming actually has at least seven different species of sage. Some of these exist only on very specific sites: Black sagebrush grows on windy ridges between 5,000 and 8,000 feet, where the soil is shallow and stony; alkali sagebrush grows in impermeable soils that are highly alkaline. The predominant species across much of Wyoming is big sagebrush, a bush that grows to three feet in height and often covers extensive areas.

Wyoming Game and Fish publishes **Wyoming Wildlife** (307/777-4600 or 800/710-8345, http://gf.state.wy.us, $13 per year), an attractive monthly publication, and also sell videos, T-shirts, caps, mugs, books, posters, cards, and other wildlife-related products.

Based in Casper, **Audubon Wyoming** (307/235-3485, www.audubonwyoming.com) is the Wyoming chapter of the National Audubon Society. It produces a bimonthly newsletter and sets up a number of birding day trips, bird banding, annual counts, and other activities. Chapter offices are in Cheyenne, Laramie, Cody, Casper, and Lander.

BEARS

Old-timers joke that bears are easy to differentiate: A black bear climbs up the tree after you, whereas a grizzly snaps the tree off at the base. Black bears live in forested areas throughout Wyoming, but grizzlies exist mainly in the northwest corner of the state, primarily within and around Yellowstone National Park. Both grizzlies and black bears pose potential threats to backcountry travelers, although you are considerably more likely to be involved in a car accident while driving to a wilderness area than to be attacked by a bear once you arrive. (See *Safety in Bear Country* in the *Essentials* chapter.)

Grizzlies once ranged across the entire Northern Hemisphere, from Europe across what is now Russia and through the western half of North America. When Europeans arrived, there were perhaps 50,000–100,000 grizzlies in what would become the Lower 48 states. Unfortunately, as white settlers moved in, they came to view these massive and powerful creatures (average adult males weigh 500 pounds) as a threat to themselves and their livestock. The scientific name, *Ursus arctos horribilis,* says much about human attitudes toward grizzlies.

Grizzlies still have healthy populations in Alaska and western Canada, but elsewhere they were shot, trapped, and poisoned nearly to the brink of extinction. In the Lower 48 states grizzlies survive in only a few of the most remote parts of Montana, Wyoming, Idaho, and Washington. By 1975, when the U.S. Fish and Wildlife Service listed them as threatened, fewer than 1,000 grizzlies survived south of Canada. Since that time the population appears to have recovered somewhat and includes 300–600 grizzlies in Wyoming's Greater Yellowstone Ecosystem.

BIGHORN SHEEP

These stocky mountain dwellers are named for the massive curling horns of the males (rams) and can be seen throughout the Rocky Mountains. They have a tan coat with a white rump patch. Bighorns were once abundant throughout the western United States, and early trappers in the mountains east of Yellowstone reported finding thousands of sheep in and around the present-day park. They were also an important source of food for the Sheepeater Indians who lived in Yellowstone before the arrival of whites. Bighorn sheep were virtually wiped out by hunters in the late 19th century, and domestic sheep overran their lands and brought deadly diseases. Within a few decades, the millions of sheep that had roamed the West were reduced to a few hundred survivors, though the population has since rebounded.

Both the rams and ewes (females) have horns that remain for life, but only the rams get the massive curl for which bighorn sheep are known. Rams are 125–275 pounds in size, with ewes 75–150 pounds. During the mating season in November and December you're likely to see the original head-bangers in action as rams clash to establish dominance. The clashes can be surprisingly violent, and to protect the brain, bighorns have a double cranium that absorbs much of the shock. Those with the larger horns are typically the dominant bighorns and the primary breeders. The young lambs are born in May and June. In summer the sexes separate, with the ewes and lambs remaining lower while the bachelor herds climb higher into the mountains. Bighorns use their ability to climb steep and rocky terrain as protection from predators such as coyotes, wolves, and mountain lions. Winter often finds bighorns in mixed herds at lower elevations. The best places to see bighorn sheep are in Yellowstone and the Whiskey Basin area near Dubois.

BISON

The bison is the definitive frontier animal and Wyoming's state mammal—its outline graces the state flag. Weighing up to 2,000 pounds, these are the largest land mammals in the New World. Bison commonly live 12–15 years. The calves weigh 30–40 pounds at birth and within minutes are standing and able to nurse. Two races of bison exist: the plains bison, primarily east of the Rockies, and the mountain bison (sometimes called wood bison) in the higher elevations. Technically, these huge, hairy beasts

are bison—the only true buffalo are the water buffalo of Southeast Asia—but the name buffalo is commonly used.

With their massive heads, huge shoulder humps, heavy coats of fur, and small posteriors, buffalo are some of the strangest animals in North America. They look so front-heavy as to seem unstable, ready to topple forward onto their snouts at any time. Despite this impression, buffalo are remarkably well adapted to life on the plains. A bison will use its strong sense of smell to find grass buried in a deep snowdrift and then sweep the snow away with a sideways motion of its head. The animals are also surprisingly fleet-footed, as careless Yellowstone photographers have discovered. In addition, the buffalo is one very tough critter. In 1907, a buffalo was pitted against four of the meanest Mexican bulls at a Juárez, Mexico, bullring. After knocking heads several times with the buffalo, the bulls fled and were saved only when bullfighters opened the chute gates to let them escape.

"Blackening the Plains"

When Europeans first reached the New World, they found massive herds of bison in the Appalachians and even more as they headed west. Daniel Boone hunted them in North Carolina in the 1750s; Pennsylvanians shot hundreds of buffalo that were invading their winter stores of hay. By 1820, settlers had nearly driven the buffalo to extinction in the east, but there were far more living to the west. As explorers, mountain men, and the first tentative settlers reached the "Great American Desert," they were awestruck by the numbers. Travelers told of slowly moving masses of buffalo blackening the plains and watched in astonishment as the herds stopped at rivers and nearly drank them dry. A fair estimate of the original population of buffalo in North America is 60 million. Even in the middle 1860s, travelers through Wyoming's Wind River Valley reported seeing 10,000 bison at one time. A pioneer Kansas settler named William D. Street recalled a trip in which a herd roared past his camp for an entire night. The next morning, he climbed

Bison are common in Yellowstone National Park.

a nearby butte and saw buffalo covering the plains below. According to Street:

> The herd was not less than 20 miles in width – we never saw the other side – at least 60 miles in length, maybe much longer; two counties of buffaloes! There might have been 100,000, or 1,000,000, or 100,000,000. I don't know. In the cowboy days in western Kansas we saw 7,000 head of cattle in one roundup. After gazing at them a few moments our thoughts turned to that buffalo herd. For a comparison, imagine a large pail of water; take from it or add to it a drop, and there you have it. Seven thousand head of cattle was not a drop in the bucket as compared with that herd of buffalo.

Indians and Buffalo

The Plains Indians depended heavily on the buffalo for food and—like the proverbial hot dog, which "contains everything but the moo"—they used every part of the animal. Hooves were carved into spoons, skins became buffalo robes and covers for boats and tepees, rawhide was used for drumheads, calf skins became storage sacks, hair was turned into earrings, and horns were formed into cups and arrow points. Everything that remained—including the muzzle, penis, eyes, and cartilage—was boiled down to use as glue for arrowheads. Their dried testicles and scrotum were used for rattles, and the ubiquitous buffalo chips became a cooking fuel on the treeless prairies.

Hunting techniques varied depending on the terrain. When possible, the Indians drove herds of bison into arroyos (dry gulches) with no exits, over cliffs, or into deep sand or snow, making them easier to kill. The arrival of Spanish horses in the 16th century made it far easier to hunt bison. In a surround, mounted hunters attacked from at least two sides, creating chaos in the herd and allowing buffalo to be shot with arrows or guns.

When whites first spread across the plains, they found the bison a plentiful food source but also viewed the massive herds as a hindrance to agriculture and cattle-raising. But these were not the only reasons whites wanted to destroy the buffalo. Killing off the bison would starve the Indians into submission and force them to take a more "civilized" way of life. General Philip Sheridan, commenting in support of white buffalo hunters, said:

> *Instead of stopping the [white] hunters they ought to give them a hearty, unanimous vote of thanks, and appropriate a sufficient sum of money to strike and present to each one a medal of bronze, with a dead buffalo on one side and a discouraged Indian on the other. They are destroying the Indian's commissary, and it is a well-known fact that an army losing its base of supplies is placed at a great disadvantage. Send them powder and lead, if you will; for the sake of a lasting peace, let them kill, skin and sell until the buffaloes are exterminated.*

This reckless slaughter did indeed endanger the Indians, but it also had an unwanted side effect: the Indians went on the warpath. The loss of their primary food source helped convince many Indians that their own extinction was next. The warriors who massacred Custer and his men at Little Big Horn had watched their people pushed to the brink of starvation by the destruction of the buffalo.

The Slaughter

Two factors propelled the slaughter to new heights in the 1870s: new railroads across the plains and a sudden international demand for buffalo robes and hides. Buffalo meat proved to be a readily available food source for railway construction workers, and hunters such as "Buffalo Bill" Cody provided a steady supply, generally taking just the hindquarters and hump and leaving the rest on the plains. Hundreds of thousands were killed. Once the railroads were completed in 1869, a new "sport" appeared—shooting buffalo from the moving railcars and leaving them to rot on the prairie. Wealthy gentry from the East Coast and Europe also discovered the joys of killing. One Irish nobleman had an entourage of 40 servants, with an entire wagon just for firearms; he killed 2,000 buffalo in a three-year carnage.

Conservationists tried to halt the buffalo slaughter through legislation in 1874, but President Grant's corrupt Secretary of the Interior, Columbus Delano, said, "I would not seriously regret the total disappearance of the buffalo from our western prairies, in its effect upon the Indians. I would regard it rather as a means of hastening their sense of dependence upon the products of the soil and their own labors." The legislation was pocket-vetoed by Grant.

In 1872, thousands of hide hunters spread through Kansas, Nebraska, and Colorado in search of buffalo. In the next three years, they brought in more than three million buffalo hides, with Indians killing another 400,000 bison for meat and robes. Good hide hunters could bring down 25–100 buffalo in a typical day, keeping five skinners busy from sunup to sundown. One hunter, Jim White, killed at least 16,000 buffalo in his career. Only the hides, cured hams, and buffalo tongues (which could be salted and shipped in barrels) were saved. When General Grenville M. Dodge toured Kansas in the fall of 1873, he noted that "the air was foul with a sickening stench, and the vast plain, which only a short twelvemonth before teemed with animal life, was a dead, solitary, putrid desert." Buffalo carcasses dotted the plains in such numbers that in later years bone pickers would collect massive piles of bones for knife handles, combs, and buttons or to be ground up for sugar refining, fertilizer, or glue.

When the buffalo of the central states approached extinction, hunters turned their attention elsewhere, reaching Wyoming, Montana, and the Dakotas in 1880. In 1882, more than 200,000 hides were taken, and another 40,000 the following year. By 1884, only 300 hides were shipped. The slaughter was nearly over; only a few private herds and scattered individual bison remained. The Indians who had once depended so heavily on buffalo for all the necessities of life were reduced to eating muskrats, gophers, and even grass. Some killed their horses, others stole settlers' cattle, and the rest had to beg the government for food. In only a couple of years, an entire culture had been devastated.

But the slaughter ruined the lives not just of

BLACK-FOOTED FERRETS

On September 25, 1981, near Meeteetse, Wyoming, a dog walked up to its master with a strange creature in his mouth. It was a black-footed ferret, a sleek, black-masked animal last seen in 1972 and feared extinct. Biologists soon discovered that a nearby prairie dog colony housed the only living population of ferrets, the world's rarest mammal. Ferrets eat prairie dogs and were once found in prairie dog colonies from Saskatchewan to Texas. The colonies were huge – one along the Cheyenne River in eastern Wyoming stretched for 100 miles – but the prairie dogs went the way of many other animals, hunted and poisoned by settlers and their land taken over by plowed fields. Although still present in Wyoming, prairie dog colonies are now far smaller and more isolated. The population of ferrets declined with their shrinking food source.

With the discovery of ferrets living near Meeteetse, national attention focused on saving the population from extinction. A 1985 outbreak of canine distemper threatened to kill all the remaining wild ferrets, so all 18 survivors were captured and taken to the Wyoming Game and Fish Wildlife Research Unit at Sybille. After inoculations, an ambitious captive-breeding program was begun. Only five of the animals actually reproduced, but the program proved so successful that the population was split up to reduce the chance that all might be killed in an accident such as a fire or in an outbreak of disease. The Sybille ferret center was closed in 2006, but populations are now at breeding facilities and zoos throughout the country.

REINTRODUCING FERRETS

The captive-breeding program has proven highly successful, but the ultimate goal is to reestablish at least 10 healthy ferret populations in the wild. Beginning in 1991, ferrets were released in Shirley Basin (north of the town of Medicine Bow). Unfortunately, sylvatic plague swept through the area, killing both ferrets and their prey, prairie dogs.

Most other efforts at reintroduction have also been hampered by plague, but ferrets are doing well in South Dakota, with limited success in Montana, Arizona, Utah, Colorado, and Mexico. A total of 300–350 ferrets now live in the wild at eight different locations. There are plans to eventually release them in Wyoming at Thunder Basin National Grassland if the population of prairie dogs recovers from plague outbreaks and hunting.

Because of their relatively short life span (three years in the wild) and their susceptibility to diseases and predators such as owls and coyotes, ferrets will almost certainly remain endangered for decades to come. The plague, continued destruction of prairie dog colonies by "varmint hunters," and poisoning by ranchers have all made it more and more difficult to find places to release wild ferrets. The habitat is becoming increasingly fragmented into "islands" separated by areas where the prairie dogs have been killed off; fewer than 10 large and healthy black-tailed prairie dog populations still exist in all of North America! It would indeed be sad if we managed to breed black-footed ferrets in zoos, but they were unable to survive in the wild because of habitat loss. Ferret out more information at www.blackfootedferret.org.

the buffalo or the Indians; hide hunters often spiked buffalo carcasses with strychnine, returning later to skin the wolves that had come to feed on the meat. Coyotes, kit foxes, badgers, vultures, eagles, ravens, and anything else that ate the meat were also killed. With both the buffalo and the "vermin" out of the way, Wyoming and the West were safe for domestic sheep and cattle.

Protection

The first federal legislation protecting buffalo (only in Yellowstone National Park, however) did not pass until 1894. The following year, only 800 buffalo remained in all of North America, a little over one-thousandth of 1 percent of their original numbers. Despite this dismal picture, the population has rebounded dramatically; today an estimated 65,000 bison roam across America. In Wyoming, small populations can be seen in Hot Springs State Park and Grand Teton National Park, while one of the few large wild populations remains in Yellowstone National Park.

A strong demand for buffalo meat has led some Wyoming ranchers to raise bison. It's a highly specialized ranching endeavor because the animals can flatten most fences, and standard roundup techniques don't work. Durham Buffalo Ranch near Wright has one of the largest private buffalo herds in the country: 3,500 head. Ranchers have discovered that bison are more efficient grazers than cattle, making it possible to produce more meat per acre, and they are less susceptible to disease. Perhaps someday the vast herds of bison may return to Wyoming's rangelands in the form of bison ranches.

DEER

Wyoming has almost as many deer as people. You can see two species along the state's roads: white-tailed deer—common in the Black Hills—and the larger mule deer, found across the state. Adult males (bucks) grow antlers each summer, and mating season arrives in November and December. Fawns are born in May or June.

Be especially careful when driving after dusk during the fall breeding season because the hormone-crazed bucks tend to leap out in front of cars. Nearly everyone who has lived in Wyoming has hit a deer under these circumstances, including the author. Slow down at night, especially in areas posted with Deer Crossing signs.

ELK

A majestic member of the deer family, elk (some biologists prefer the term "wapiti") are a favorite with both tourists and hunters. Elk inhabit much of Wyoming, with the largest herds along the western mountains. More than 30,000 elk graze in Yellowstone National Park alone. With bulls averaging 700 pounds and cows averaging 500 pounds, they are some of the largest antlered animals in the Americas.

Elk spend summers high in the mountains, feeding in alpine meadows and along forest edges. Mature bulls graze alone, but the cows and calves—generally born in late May and early June—group in large herds for protection. When the fall rutting season arrives, bulls attempt to herd the cows and calves around, mating with cows when they come into estrus and defending their harems from other bulls. During this time of year the bugling of bull elk is a common sound in the mountains, a challenge to any bull within earshot. When a competitor appears, a dominance display often follows—complete with bugling, stomping, and thrashing of the ground—to show who is the baddest bull around. In a fight, bulls lock their massive antlers and try to push and twist until one finally gives in and retreats. These battles help ensure that the healthiest bulls produce the most offspring, although other bulls often wait in the wings for battles over harems, and then rush in to mate with the cows while the larger bulls are sparring. The snows of late fall push elk to lower-elevation winter ranges, notably at the National Elk Refuge in Jackson Hole. When spring comes, the bulls drop their antlers and immediately begin to grow new ones. The elk head back into the high country, following the melting snowline.

Elk and bison both can be infected with brucellosis, a bacterium causing spontaneous abortions. Brucellosis is transmitted to other animals by contact with the dead fetus or birthing material and can cause undulant fever in humans. Ranchers worry that brucellosis can spread from elk and bison to cattle, particularly around elk feeding grounds in western Wyoming. To lessen the incidence of brucellosis, state employees now routinely vaccinate elk at the feeding grounds, shooting them in the hindquarters with vaccine-loaded pellets.

PRONGHORN ANTELOPE

One of the most commonly seen Wyoming animals is the antelope (biologists prefer the name "pronghorn"). More than 400,000 live in the state, constituting half the world's pronghorn population. Antelope survive on grasses, forbs, and sagebrush—perhaps Wyoming's most abundant plant. They are built for speed: Oversized

© DON PITCHER

elk at the National Elk Refuge

lungs and windpipes give them the ability to run for miles at 30 mph and to accelerate to twice that for short bursts. To watch for predators, they have the largest eyes by body weight of any mammal. One surprising trait in antelope is their inability to jump fences; instead they crawl under them. Fences that are too low will completely halt their migrations.

Despite their speed, pronghorn have an innate inquisitiveness that makes them relatively easy to hunt, an attribute that nearly drove them to extinction by market hunting early in the 20th century. Strict laws and careful management have brought antelope populations back.

Both males and females grow horns, and those on the males typically have a prong (hence the name). Dominant males (bucks) gather harems of females (does) and fawns and fight off other bucks in the late-summer rutting season. In May or June does give birth to 1–2 fawns.

WOLVES

The wolves are back! One of the most exciting developments for visitors to Yellowstone has been the reintroduction of wolves to the park, making this one of the few places in the Lower 48 where they can be viewed in the wild. Wolves once ranged across nearly all of North America, but white settlers regarded them—along with mountain lions, grizzly bears, and coyotes—as threats to livestock and unwanted predators on game animals. Even in Yellowstone, wolves were hunted and poisoned by both the army and the Park Service. By 1940, the wolf was probably gone from the park, although a few lone animals turned up briefly again in the early 1970s.

In the United States, until 1995 wolves could be found only in Alaska, in northern Minnesota, and in Isle Royale and Glacier national parks. With the more enlightened public attitude evident in recent years, ecologists and conservationists began pushing for the reintroduction of wolves to Yellowstone, considered one of the few remaining areas in the Lower 48 that could support a viable wolf population.

The U.S. Fish and Wildlife Service began reintroducing wolves to Yellowstone in 1995, initially releasing 14 gray wolves that had been captured in British Columbia. Additional wolves were set free the following spring. During subsequent years things have gone far better than anyone had predicted. By 2005, biologists estimated that 31 packs of wolves totaling 306 individuals inhabited the Greater Yellowstone Ecosystem from north and west of Yellowstone to the Pinedale area on the south, and eastward into Shoshone National Forest. Approximately half of these wolves are inside Yellowstone National Park. Because of the successful reintroduction, the status of wolves was changed in 2003 from endangered to threatened, and it's only a matter of time until wolves are removed entirely from the endangered species list.

Wolves are the largest members of the canids (dog family), with males averaging 70–120 pounds and stretching up to six feet long from head to tail. They are much more massive than coyotes, although the two are sometimes confused. Wolves live in packs of 2–8, led by an alpha male and female, and establish territories to exclude other wolf packs. Most pack members are from an extended family, but they may include outside members. The alphas are the only ones that generally mate, and a litter of six or so pups is born in early spring. Once they are weaned, the pack feeds pups regurgitated meat until they are large enough to join the hunt. Wolves hunt primarily in the evening and morning when their prey—elk, deer, moose, bison, and pronghorn—are feeding.

The Yellowstone website (www.nps.gov/yell) has additional details on wolves, and tips for watching them, or visit the U.S. Fish and Wildlife Service's gray wolf homepage (http://westerngraywolf.fws.gov) for regional information updated weekly. Also check out the annual "State of the Wolf" report from Defenders of Wildlife (www.defenders.org).

RATTLESNAKES

Everyone's least favorite reptile is the prairie rattlesnake, a heavy-bodied venomous creature with a telltale rattle. Prairie rattlesnakes often reach nearly one yard in length (the longest was 57 inches!) and are found in the plains and foothills of eastern and central Wyoming, generally below 7,000 feet. They're especially common around rock piles and in prairie dog towns. You *won't* find them in mountain country over 7,200 feet, in the Laramie area, in Yellowstone and Grand Teton national parks, or in the southwestern desert country (with the exception of the lower Green River Valley area). Prairie rattlers feed primarily on ground squirrels, rabbits, chipmunks, prairie dogs, and other small rodents, but they can also kill birds and lizards. They reproduce every other year, and large groups of rattlesnakes gather in dens to spend the winter in a dormant state.

Prairie rattlesnakes usually offer a warning of their presence—hence the name—but not all the time. At times aggressive, their size and appearance will certainly send your blood pressure up, but venom is actually less toxic than that of other rattlers and is usually only one-eighth the amount needed to kill a human. Because of this, snakebite fatalities are rare in Wyoming.

A smaller snake, the midget faded rattlesnake, is found in southern Wyoming within the lower Green River Valley around the cities of Green River and Rock Springs, and in Flaming Gorge National Recreation Area. They frequent rocky outcrops and, although smaller, are 10–30 times more poisonous than prairie rattlesnakes. Fortunately, midget faded rattlesnakes are quite timid and pose little threat to humans. They will coil and strike, but only if cornered.

The best defense against rattlers is to always use care when walking in their country and to keep your distance if you spot one. Be especially careful when clambering over rock piles or walking through dense grasses and sage. Shake out sleeping bags, boots, and bedding, and wear tall leather boots rather than sneakers.

If a rattlesnake bites someone, immobilize the area of the bite and immediately get him or her to a hospital or medical facility. If the bite is on an arm or leg, keep it below the level of the heart. Time is of the essence. Other treatments are possible for emergency situations when there is no chance of getting to a doctor in time, but the potential for harm is great if you don't know what you are doing. Take a good first-aid class to learn how to handle these situations, or talk with your doctor about where to get and how to use suction pumps. Your best bet is always preventing a bite in the first place. For more on rattlers and other crawly things, see *Amphibians and Reptiles of Wyoming,* by George T. Baxter and Michael D. Stone (Cheyenne: Wyoming Game and Fish Department, 1985).

History

Although Wyoming is a young state—reaching the century mark only in 1990—it seems to have more history per square inch than just about any other place in America. This history is a mixture of Indians and cowboys, settlers and outlaws, schemers and dreamers, railroad magnates and cattle barons, and plain folks clinging to plots of marginal farmland despite unbelievable odds. Wyoming's 19th-century frontier is a recurring theme in America's imagination, as revealed in countless books, songs, and movies. This rich treasure trove from the past is stored not just in the little-changed landscape, where the ruts from wagon trains are still visible and emigrant names remain carved in rocky buttes, but also in the cattle drives and rodeos and the weather-etched faces of sheepherders and cowboys working the range. It is hard to imagine a place with a richer past. An interesting web source for Wyoming history and historical photos is www.wyomingtalesandtrails.com.

NATIVE AMERICANS

Humans have been in Wyoming for perhaps 25,000 years. The Plains Indians—comprising 27 different tribes—were found from the Mississippi River to the Rockies, and from Texas to central Canada. The lives of these people revolved around the buffalo; they followed the vast herds, migrating where the buffalo led. Because of this nomadic lifestyle, everything they had was pared to the minimum. Pottery, so common in the southwestern deserts, was replaced by woven baskets on the plains. The tepee, an easily portable lodge, offered protection from the elements, and clothing was warm yet not burdensome.

Days of Glory

Although many people view the Plains Indians as existing in a state of balance with their environment, there is ample evidence that things were changing even before whites first pushed their way onto the plains. The arrival of horses and guns in the 17th and 18th centuries created a time of plenty that has rarely been known among nomadic hunting tribes. Horses made it easier to follow and hunt the huge bison herds, and tribes that had been at least partially farmers turned entirely to hunting. Native populations grew rapidly with the abundance of food. The warrior also gained importance with the changing culture as raiding parties stole horses and attacked other tribes. Villages grew larger as families gathered for mutual protection from their enemies.

The turmoil that resulted led to a constantly changing situation in Wyoming during the 19th century, as the tribes all strove for control. It was this turbulent society that greeted the first Euro-American explorers. Whites were accustomed to well-defined land ownership, with definite boundaries within which one lived; here the territories were in a state of flux, with tribes claiming overlapping areas.

During the 1700s, Indians from the Great Lakes and Canadian plains had moved into what would become Wyoming. By the 1850s, the Sioux were in Powder River Basin, the Crow in Bighorn Basin, and the Cheyenne and Arapaho south of the North Platte River. The Shoshone and the Bannock—originally from the Great Basin—had moved into the Green River and Wind River valleys, while their relatives, the Utes, held the Sierra Madre and desert land to the west. Communication between these diverse tribes was possible in a sophisticated sign language.

Treaties

During the first half of the 19th century,

FROM TAME EARTH TO WILD WEST

We did not think of the great open plains, the beautiful rolling hills, the winding streams with tangled growth as wild. Only to the white man was nature a wilderness, and only to him was the land infested with wild animals and savage people. To us it was tame. Earth was bountiful, and we were surrounded with the blessings of the Great Mystery. Not until the hairy man from the east came, and with his brutal frenzy, heaped injustices upon us and the families we loved, was it wild to us. When the very animals of the forest began fleeing from his approach; then it was that for us, the "wild west" began.

—Sioux Chief Standing Bear

American explorers, fur trappers, traders, and settlers began to push across Wyoming. As emigration westward increased in the 1840s, so did conflicts with Indians. Whites complained of random attacks and stolen horses. Indians complained of trampled grass, polluted water, and wasteful killing of bison. To deal with these problems, a great council was called at Fort Laramie in 1851, attracting 10,000 Indians from many different tribes. Indian agent Thomas Fitzpatrick was eager to gain permission for settlers to use the Oregon Trail across Indian lands in Wyoming. In exchange for gifts from the federal government in the form of annuities, the tribes agreed to stay within specified boundaries and to punish those who violated the accord or attacked white emigrants.

Father Pierre DeSmet drew up the boundaries, with allowances for hunting outside the "home" regions. The unstated long-term goal of the treaty was to transform the Indians from hunters into farmers. By developing a paternalistic system of dependency on the government, combined with educational programs and settlement, the Indians would—in theory—become like the whites. Violence erupted almost immediately among the tribes and between them and the Anglo emigrants. Soon, whites would be more concerned over how to dispossess the Indians of their land than how to get through it safely.

In 1861, the Fort Wise Treaty abrogated much of the Treaty of 1851, forcing the Arapaho and Cheyenne onto a desolate reservation at Sand Creek, Colorado, to get them away from the suddenly valuable land to the north. Some leaders signed the treaty, but only after the starving individuals saw that they would not receive their annuities without affixing their Xs.

The Battle Begins

Colorado's Sand Creek Massacre of 1865 proved a turning point in the history of Indian–white relations. A small band of Arapaho attacked a family farm, brutally murdering the family. When the mutilated bodies were put on display in Denver, public outrage pushed Colonel John M. Chivington—formerly a Methodist minister—to lead one of the most vicious and unwarranted attacks ever perpetrated by the army. Two hundred Cheyenne and Arapaho died in the daybreak attack on Chief Black Kettle's peaceful village.

The Indians—not just the Cheyenne and Arapaho, but also the Sioux—quickly retaliated by striking throughout Colorado and Wyoming, killing some 75 settlers around the Rock Creek Station (northwest of present-day Laramie) and destroying stage stations all along the Oregon Trail. During the next several years, hundreds died on both sides. The main focus of Indian attacks was the Bozeman Trail through the lush Powder River country of the Sioux. The army responded with an alternating series of military campaigns and peace overtures as the national mood flip-flopped between war and accommodation.

A major cause of these conflicts was the hysteria that gold created. Each new gold rush—California in 1849, Colorado in 1859, Montana in 1864, and finally the Black Hills in 1874—led to new incursions onto Indian lands. When whites found Indians standing in the way of development, they attempted to renegotiate the treaties or, failing that, to find some excuse to set them aside. Once gold had been found, the end of Indian culture was almost a given. Senator John Sherman noted: "If the whole army of the United States stood in the way, the wave of emigration would pass over it to seek the valley where gold was to be found."

Other factors also played critical roles in the destruction of the Indian way of life on the plains. Perhaps the most crucial was the loss of their primary food source, the buffalo. But many tribes were devastated as well by diseases brought by contact with Europeans, especially smallpox, cholera, whooping cough, and venereal diseases.

Cultural Mistrust

Many whites viewed the Indians with deep distrust. Writer James Chisholm reflected a typical frontier attitude, calling them "useless, strutting, ridiculous, pompous humbugs—lying, faithless, stealing, begging, cruel, hungry, howling vagabonds—cowardly, treacherous red devils." In 1869, General Philip Sheridan took matters even further by declaring, "The only good Indian is a dead Indian."

The Indians themselves were not entirely innocent. Attacks on wagon trains were frequent, and many of the trappers, stagecoach drivers, and ranchers who settled in Wyoming were murdered and their bodies mutilated by the Sioux, Cheyenne, or Arapaho. Scalping—a practice introduced by white traders—became commonplace. Whites complained that the federal government was arming and feeding the Indians at the same time it was leading military campaigns against them.

Evicting the Indians

More than 1,000 engagements were fought between Indians and whites in the late 19th century, killing at least 2,500 whites and twice as many Indians. On the plains, most of the battles involved the Sioux, Cheyenne, Arapaho, Kiowa, and Comanche tribes. The Shoshone under Chief Washakie always remained peaceful. The final drama came in the 1870s, beginning with the discovery of gold in the Black Hills of Dakota Territory. A flood of miners overwhelmed attempts by the government to keep them out of Sioux territory, and negotiations to buy the land bogged down when Red Cloud demanded a $600 million payment.

In 1876, General Sheridan led a three-pronged invasion to forcibly evict the Sioux from the Powder River region. He hadn't counted on two problems: the large numbers of Indians ready to do battle and the rashness of junior officer Colonel George A. Custer. At Little Big Horn on June 25, 1876, a combined force of Indians led by Crazy Horse, Sitting Bull, and others wiped out all 225 of Custer's men. This massive Indian victory quickly became the rallying cry for whites anxious to "solve" the Indian problem by forcing them onto reservations. Within five years, the last of the tribes had given up the fight. The uprising that led to the infamous Wounded Knee Massacre of 1890 was a last dying gasp in the attempt to regain land that had once all belonged to Native Americans.

Those who had lived in this land for centuries had been evicted by new peoples from another world. Chief Washakie of the Shoshones described the painfulness of this change (quoted in *Chief Washakie*, by Mae Urbanek):

The white man, who possesses this whole vast country from sea to sea, who roams over it at pleasure, and lives where he likes, cannot know the cramp we feel in this little spot, with the undying remembrance of the fact, which you know as well as we, that every foot of what you proudly call America, not very long ago belonged to the red man. The Great Spirit gave it to us. There was room enough for all his many tribes, and all were happy in their freedom. But the white man had, in ways we know not of, superior tools and terrible weapons, better for war than bows and arrows; and there seemed no end to the hordes of men that followed them from other lands beyond the sea. And so, at last, our fathers were steadily driven out, or killed, and we, their sons, but sorry remnants of tribes once mighty, are cornered in little spots of the earth all ours of right – cornered like guilty prisoners, and watched by men with guns, who are more than anxious to kill us off.

TRAPPERS AND EXPLORERS

The first Europeans to explore Wyoming were in a party of Frenchmen led by François and Louis-Joseph Vérendrye, who crossed northern Wyoming in 1743. Others occasionally passed this way in subsequent decades, and an inscription on a rock northwest of Pinedale had the initials M. A. and the date 1791; it's the oldest dated carving in the state. During the winter of 1807–1808, John Colter—a trapper and former guide for the Lewis and Clark Expedition—explored northwestern Wyoming in an attempt to develop the fur trade with Crow Indians. Other trappers in search of beavers soon followed Colter. It was a hazardous business, with the constant threat of Indian attacks and the many natural hazards such as angry grizzlies, disease, and injuries. Help was hundreds of miles away. The era of the mountain man lasted only until 1840, when demand for the furs plummeted, but the trappers' knowledge of the terrain proved invaluable. Many former trappers became guides for ci-

vilian and military expeditions, wealthy hunters, and government explorations of the West. The mountain passes they found (or, more likely, had been shown by Indians) provided a route for the exodus westward in the 1850s.

THE OREGON TRAIL

To 19th-century emigrants the Oregon Trail represented perhaps the best example of "Manifest Destiny"—the idea of an American nation reaching from the Atlantic to the Pacific. The Oregon Trail is actually a general term used to describe a whole series of wagon roads that headed west from Missouri. At different times, and along various paths, this route encompassed the Oregon Trail (to both Oregon and Washington), the California Trail (to the goldfields), the Mormon Trail (to Salt Lake City), and the short-lived Pony Express route. To emigrants it was not a trail but always "The Road."

Wyoming contains the least-changed and longest stretch (487 miles) of the Oregon Trail. From eastern Wyoming, the trail—actually a series of braided paths spreading across the river valleys—followed the North Platte and Sweetwater rivers upstream to the Continental Divide at South Pass. Travelers chose this route because of abundant forage for stock, good water, and a gentle grade over the divide.

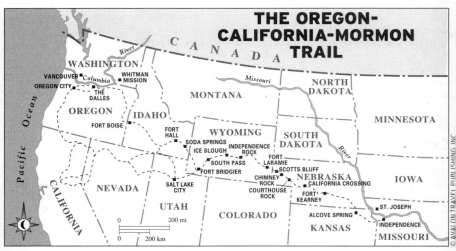

As the only route that met all three criteria, the Oregon Trail became a national thoroughfare to the Promised Land of the West.

"Oregon Country" was not simply the area that would become the state of Oregon, but the entire region west of South Pass. Thus the hills just beyond the Continental Divide in Wyoming became the "Oregon Buttes," and emigrants wrote of entering Oregon as they crossed the pass: "Today we entered Oregon. ... We nooned beyond at a small spring and drank the waters of the Pacific!" (The vast land collectively called Oregon actually belonged to the British, but this legal nicety was quickly pushed aside by the influx of Americans.) West of South Pass, the route divided at the "Parting of the Ways." California- and Utah-bound travelers turned south to Fort Bridger, while those en route to Oregon and Washington headed due west on the Sublette or Lander cutoffs.

Origins

Americans emigrated west for several reasons: to escape a severe economic depression in the East and falling crop prices, to get out of the crowded and polluted cities, to find religious freedom in Utah, to search for gold in the mountains of California, or simply to join in a great adventure in a new and undiscovered land. (More than a few also headed west to get away from debts or the law.) The first whites to cross the Continental Divide on what would become the Oregon Trail were a party of fur trappers known as the Astorians. They rode horses over South Pass in 1812, but it was not until a decade later that trappers really moved deeply into this country. The first freight wagons rolled over the pass in 1830, en route to a mountain-man rendezvous on the Green River. By the early 1840s, emigration westward was getting easier and more inviting. Fort Laramie, in eastern Wyoming, and Fort Bridger, in southwestern Wyoming, provided valuable way stations where travelers could rest up, repair their wagons, trade worn-out stock for fresh animals, and buy food, whiskey, and supplies.

The turning point in the history of the Oregon Trail came in 1843, when the Applegate Wagon Train left Independence, Missouri, with 875 people, 120 wagons, and 5,000 head of livestock. It was the largest wagon train

pulling replicas of Mormon handcarts along the Oregon Trail near Devil's Gate

© DON PITCHER

ever assembled. Under the leadership of Marcus Whitman (later killed in an Indian attack near present-day Walla Walla, Washington) and guided by mountain man Bill Sublette, the party made it all the way to the Columbia and Willamette rivers by September. It had taken six long months to travel the 2,000 miles, but they had shown that the route was feasible. The gates of history had been cracked open, and they could never be closed again. Soon, the trickle westward turned into a flood tide.

Rolling West

Most travelers tried to depart Independence or St. Joseph, Missouri, in the spring, leaving as soon as the grass would support their stock. Typically, each evening found the emigrant just 15 miles farther down the trail, and it generally took 5–6 months to travel from Missouri to California or Oregon. They had to be over the mountains before the first snows of winter struck, and those who erred—such as the infamous Donner Party of 1846—paid a high price.

Emigrants were forced to travel as lightly as possible to lessen the burden on oxen. Some traders grew rich on the castoffs from overburdened wagon trains, whereas others profited by operating toll bridges and ferries across the North Platte and Green rivers. (The toll at the Green River crossing was sometimes an amazing $16 per wagon!) Guidebooks—there were several; this was a big business even in the 19th century—described the crossings and camping places and suggested provisions for the 2,000-mile journey. A wagon, harness, and eight oxen cost travelers around $400.

Because of the scarcity of wood, Oregon Trail travelers used dry grass, sagebrush, or buffalo chips for fuel. Meals were simple but hearty, often consisting of a few staples plus whatever game might be found along the trail. Today, when you drive across the state it is easy to see how trying an experience this must have been for the emigrants—gale-force winds, dust, and lightning combined with the parched ground, the deceptively long distances, and the lack of shade. Wyoming can be a harsh and unforgiving land; it is not a place to wander into unprepared.

Perhaps one-tenth of the people who set out on the Oregon Trail never made it to their destination, and fellow travelers noted in their diaries the disturbing presence of graves—sometimes every 80 yards. Many died from diseases such as cholera or from accidents and drownings; others were killed by early winter storms and Indian attacks. Few of the graves are marked.

At the peak of migration in 1850—when California gold fever had struck America—55,000 men, women, and children pressed their way across the plains and mountains. One of the lesser-known facts was the two-way nature of the route; in 1851 vast numbers of disillusioned miners headed back east the same way they had come the previous years. The route was also heavily used in both directions by Mormon emigrants to Utah, many of whom returned east for supplies or to guide family members who had been left behind. In addition, stagecoach and freighting operations, along with a limited mail service, were established by 1852, operating in both directions.

It is easy to imagine the impact these wagons had with their thousands of cattle, horses, and mules. The grass quickly became overgrazed under this onslaught, and the already scarce water was badly polluted around popular campsites. Late-summer travelers were forced to range far and wide for better conditions, creating even more paths. The Indians who had lived here were shocked by the magnitude of the migration and began to realize not just what the whites were doing to their buffalo, but also how overwhelmed the native peoples would be by the newcomers. (The entire Plains Indian population probably numbered 40,000 individuals at its peak, and disease and war greatly reduced these numbers.) Indian attacks on Oregon Trail travelers were quite rare, and only 350 emigrants are known to have been killed by Indians. The biggest battles between Indians and Anglos came in 1865, more than a dozen years after the peak of westward travel on the Oregon Trail.

Finale

By 1870, perhaps 350,000 people had traveled across Wyoming by wagon train, stagecoach, horseback, and foot. It was the greatest peace-time migration in history. For most of them, this country seemed a worthless stretch of sage-brush and a barrier to the green lands farther west. It took the railroad to change this per-ception. Completion of the transcontinental railroad in 1869 turned the Oregon Trail into an anachronism. Suddenly one could cross the nation in relative comfort and in days instead of months. The trail continued to be used by freighters and some pioneers even as late as the turn of the 20th century, but most travelers turned to rail travel. An era had ended.

The Trail Today

It has been well more than 150 years since the first wagon train traveled along the Oregon Trail, but the mystique of the "great migration" continues to draw people from around the world. Much of the trail cuts across publicly owned land, and the tracks are readily visible in many places even after a century and a half. Explor-ers still discover artifacts strewn along the way. Visitors to Wyoming will enjoy delving into this rich past at such places as Fort Laramie, Oregon Trail Ruts, Register Cliff, Fort Caspar, Indepen-dence Rock, Devil's Gate, South Pass, Names Hill, and Fort Bridger. Hundreds of other lesser sights line the route, from the remains of old trading posts to countless emigrant graves. The recently opened National Historic Trails Center in Casper is a great place to get an in-depth look at the various trails that crossed the West. (See the *Southeast, Central, Wind River Mountains Country,* and *Southwest* chapters for detailed descriptions of sections of the Oregon Trail.) The nonprofit **Oregon-California Trails Association** (816/252-2276, www.octa-trails .org) works to preserve the trails.

THE PONY EXPRESS

On April 3, 1860, a lone rider galloped westward from the town of St. Joseph, Missouri. Nearly 2,000 miles away, another rider left the boom-ing city of San Francisco, heading east. One of the most celebrated passages in American history had begun. Although it lasted only 18 months and was a financial disaster, the Pony Express

caught the national imagination, proved that rapid mail service was possible even in the win-ter, and helped keep California in the Union.

The Pony Express was the brainchild of Wil-liam H. Russell, one of the great wheelers and dealers of the late 19th century and director of the Central Overland California and Pike's Peak Express Company. Russell, along with partners Alexander Majors and William Brad-ford Waddell, managed the largest freighting company in the West, a business that at one time owned 50,000 oxen for its 3,500 wagons and employed 4,000 workers.

In 1855, the firm of Russell, Majors, and Waddell secured a monopoly to supply all U.S. government military posts west of the Missouri River. Because of Mormon raids on the supply wagons and the failure of the War Department to pay the company for its services, it was soon in financial trouble. To escape, the company needed the contract for mail service between California and St. Louis, a route then held by the Butterfield Overland Mail Company. Butterfield's route took mail along a circuitous 25-day trek through Texas and Arizona into southern California. With the nation slipping rapidly toward the Civil War—and Texas on the side of the South—there were fears that mail service would be halted and that Califor-nia might join the Confederacy.

Express Mail

In 1859, the postmaster general signed a con-tract with Russell, Majors, and Waddell to op-erate coaches and horses along the central route to California. The Pony Express was born as a flamboyant symbol of the superiority of this route. Experienced young horsemen, some as young as 14 and none weighing more than 120 pounds, would ride the finest horses at a full gallop, carrying telegrams and mail through some of the most desolate land on earth. The trip was to take just 10 days.

Each horse had four mail pouches sewn into a leather *mochilla,* which could be easily trans-ferred between horses. (At $7.50 per half ounce, Pony Express mail was primarily urgent mes-sages and newspapers.) Riders changed horses

PONY EXPRESSIONS

We had had a consuming desire from the beginning, to see a pony-rider, but somehow or other all that passed us and all that met us managed to streak by in the night, and so we heard only a whiz and a hail, and the swift phantom of the desert was gone before we could get our heads out of the windows. But now we were expecting one along every moment, and would see him in broad daylight. Presently the driver exclaims: "HERE HE COMES!"

Every neck is stretched further, and every eye strained wider. Away across the endless dead level of the prairie a black speck appears against the sky, and it is plain that it moves. Well, I should think so! In a second or two it becomes a horse and rider, rising and falling, rising and falling –

sweeping toward us nearer and nearer – growing more and more distinct, more and more sharply defined – nearer and still nearer, and the flutter of the hoofs comes faintly to the ear – another instant a whoop and a hurrah from our upper deck, a wave of the rider's hand, but no reply, and man and horse burst past our excited faces, and go winging away like a belated fragment of a storm!

So sudden is it all, and so like a flash of unreal fancy, that for the flake of white foam left quivering and perishing on a mail-sack after the vision had flashed by and disappeared, we might have doubted whether we had seen any actual horse and man at all, maybe.

–Mark Twain in *Roughing It*

at relay stations—crude huts with station keepers and stock tenders—every 10–15 miles, continuing for 75–100 miles before passing the precious package to another rider. After a short break, the rider would speed back to his home station with mail headed in the opposite direction. The whole operation required military precision to keep the 119 relay and home stations stocked, make sure the horses were in good condition, and guard against attack. For their work, riders received $120 per month (including room and board).

The Demise

The threat of Indian hostilities became real when Nevada Paiutes, angry after decades of abuse and the theft of their land, began attacking white settlements, killing 16 of the men working at the relay stations, taking 150 horses, and burning seven stations. A full-scale war was avoided, but it took more than a month to get the Express back into operation, at a cost of $75,000. As it was already a money loser, this incident helped ensure the collapse of the Pony Express, but it was not just money that brought

down the Pony Express. Completion of the first continental telegraph line on October 24, 1861, also contributed; its mission replaced by a much more rapid means of communication, the Pony Express ended just two days later. Riders had delivered 34,753 pieces of mail, losing only one *mochilla* (both horse and rider were killed) in 616 cross-country runs.

The Final Chapter

The story of the Central Overland California and Pike's Peak Express Company does not end here. By late 1860, a year before the Pony Express ceased operations, Russell, Majors, and Waddell's firm already teetered on the verge of bankruptcy (its employees nicknamed it "Clean Out of Cash and Poor Pay"). To stave this off, William Russell met with a clerk in the U.S. Department of the Interior and received $150,000 in bonds belonging to the Indian Trust Fund. Russell collected more than $870,000 in illegal government funds before being caught.

The whole house of cards came tumbling down when partner Alexander Majors declared bankruptcy and Russell's partner in crime, Goddard Bailey, confessed. Russell spent Christmas 1860 in prison, but he somehow managed to escape prosecution, and he never repaid the money. With the start of the Civil War, Congress had greater concerns. In 1861, a joint agreement moved all western mail delivery to the central route, combining the forces of Butterfield's Overland Mail Company with the remnants of the Russell, Majors, and Waddell firm to avoid travel through the Confederate states. Later, Ben Holladay bought the bankrupt firm and transformed it into the Overland Stage Line. Both Russell and Waddell died poor men. Years later, one of the Pony Express riders, "Buffalo Bill" Cody, found Alexander Majors living in a tiny Denver shack. In a gesture typical of him, Cody put Majors on a cash retainer for the rest of his life.

THE OVERLAND TRAIL

Lesser known and shorter lived than the Oregon Trail, the Overland Trail was established by Ben Holladay, owner of the Overland Stage Company. Although the Oregon Trail had served for many years as the primary route west, by the 1860s a need was developing for a new path. Increasing Indian attacks made the Oregon Trail dangerous, and the rapidly growing mining town of Denver was too far away. After Holladay was given the contract to deliver mail to the West, he quickly rerouted travel along a trail originally scouted by Jim Bridger.

The new route proved 60 miles shorter than the Oregon Trail, but it passed directly through the difficult desert country of western Wyoming rather than along the relatively lush North Platte and Sweetwater rivers. Holladay established stage stations for changing teams every 10–15 miles and built home stations where travelers could stop for meals or lodging every 50 miles. Conditions at these relay stations were primitive at best; one traveler described southwestern Wyoming's Sand Springs station as "roofless and chairless, filthy and squalid, with a smoky fire in one corner, and a table in the center of an impure floor, the walls open to every wind and the interior full of dust." But the stations were better than sitting outside in the blazing hot sun or the bitter winter winds.

The stages covered 100–125 miles in a 24-hour period but were extraordinarily expensive for the time: $500 from Atchison, Kansas, to San Francisco. Still, emigrants began using the new route instead of the Oregon Trail; in a single year (1864), 17,584 men, women, and children used the Overland Trail, along with 50,000 head of livestock and 4,264 wagons.

Although the new route remained relatively free from attacks for several years, the 1865 Sand Creek Massacre sent Indians on the warpath throughout the plains. Stage stations were destroyed, stagecoaches were attacked, and many died on both sides. The attacks continued sporadically for the next two years. With completion of the transcontinental railroad in 1869, the Overland Stage rapidly faded in importance, and stagecoach service ended. The old Overland Trail continued to be used by wagons until the turn of the 20th century.

CONNECTING THE COASTS

More than any other event, the completion of the transcontinental railroad led to the settlement and development of Wyoming. Most of its major towns and cities originated along the railroad lines. Not only did the railroad bring Wyoming within a couple of days of either coast, but it also led to the opening of coal mines to fuel the engines, hastened development of the logging industry (for railroad ties and mine props), and made it easy to ship cattle to market. Settlers could order almost anything—Sears Roebuck even shipped prefabricated houses that filled two boxcars. It was no coincidence that Wyoming became a territory just as the railroad was being pushed across its southern border. An enduring impact from the railroad is a checkerboard pattern of public and private land ownership along the Union Pacific's route across Wyoming.

Surveying the Route

The Union Pacific's route was planned by General Grenville M. Dodge, a veteran of battles with the Sioux in the Powder River country.

The traditional Oregon Trail route ran too close to Sioux country, was too far from the gold-mining city of Denver, and didn't have the rich coal deposits of southwestern Wyoming. The course Dodge chose headed almost straight across southern Wyoming, climbing the Laramie Mountains west of Cheyenne and then cutting through the Laramie Plains and the Red Desert before winding across the mountains of eastern Utah.

Despite Dodge's efforts to avoid direct confrontation with the Indians and the government's diversionary tactic of building the Bozeman Trail through the Powder River country, the Arapaho did not take kindly to the presence of railroad surveying and construction parties in their traditional hunting grounds. They pulled up survey stakes, stole horses, and killed surveyors and loggers, forcing Dodge to request military escorts. Three forts (Russell, Sanders, and Steele) were built in Wyoming to house these troops.

Working on the Railroad

To span the continent, the Union Pacific headed west from Omaha, while the Central Pacific worked east from Sacramento. By July 1867 tracklayers had reached the main division point, which would become Cheyenne, and headed on west to found Laramie, Rawlins, Green River, and Evanston. Most of the Central Pacific's workers were Chinese contract laborers, whereas those on the Union Pacific were a mixture of Americans and emigrants, especially Irishmen. Great competition grew between the two groups, and a record was set as the tracklayers worked across the searing heat of Wyoming's Red Desert: The men laid 7.5 miles of track in a single day. Laborers were paid an extraordinary $2.50 per hour, but the work was equally dangerous; some estimate that the transcontinental railroad was built at the cost of 10 men's lives per one mile of track! Many were buried right in the roadbed. The tracklayers finally pushed their way into Utah and met workers of the Central Pacific at Promontory Point on May 10, 1869.

The railroad brought with it a gang of men who seemed to thrive on corruption, thievery, prostitution, gambling, drunkenness, and murder. As construction moved westward, temporary towns sprang up along the way; many were gone as soon as the tracks were out of sight. The entire procession of construction workers and hangers-on quickly became known as Hell-on-Wheels.

Worst of the temporary frontier towns was Benton, a few miles east of present-day Rawlins. Those who passed through called it "nearer a repetition of Sodom and Gomorrah than any other place in America" and a "congregation of scum and wickedness... by day disgusting, by night dangerous." There was no grass, little water, and the alkali dust stood eight inches deep. Murders were a nightly affair at the 25 saloons and five dance halls. The big attraction was gambling, with hundreds of men crowding the big tent each evening, paying for whiskey, dance-hall girls, or roulette wheels. Before the short-lived settlement could disappear in the alkali dust—just three months after its founding—more than 100 men lay buried in boot hill.

Newspaper reporter James Chisholm described these men in less than appealing terms:

I often speculate on what will finally become of all that rolling scum which the locomotive seems to blow onward as it presses westward. Will they get blown clean off the continent at last into the Pacific Ocean? One is gradually surrounded by the same faces in each successive town, the same gamblers, the same musicians playing the same old tunes to the same old dance, the same females getting always a little more dilapidated. As the excitement dies out of one town, and the railroad leaves it behind in a kind of exhausted repose, these old familiar faces die out to reappear in a new state of existence.

A rolling newspaper press tagged along with the flotsam and jetsam across Wyoming, printing the weekly *Frontier Index* in each new camp. Its editor, Legh Freeman, angered the primarily northern-born workers by constantly showing his support for the Confederacy; he once labeled General Ulysses Grant "the whiskey bloated, squaw ravishing adulterer, nigger worshipping mogul rejoicing over his election to the presidency." In Bear River City (long gone but near present-day Evanston), Freeman made the mistake of suggesting that several accused murderers then in jail should meet up with Judge Lynch. After a gang of vigilantes followed his suggestion by throwing a necktie party for the three, other ruffians destroyed the *Frontier Index* office and chased its editor out of town.

STATEHOOD

Because of its difficult climate, a paucity of good agricultural lands, and the lack of major deposits of gold, Wyoming was one of the last states to be settled. At various times, sections of Wyoming were parts of Indian country, Mexico, Louisiana, Missouri, Texas, Nebraska, Dakota, Idaho, Oregon, and Utah. In 1868, the Wyoming Territory was carved out of the Dakota Territory, a move primarily intended to keep the Democratic voters building the Union Pacific Railroad from overwhelming the Republican power base in distant Yankton. The folks out west were equally happy to gain independence from such a tenuous governmental link. It was not until May 19, 1869, that an organized government was established in the new territory. The first census of Wyoming, in 1870, found just 9,000 people, although the number would have been considerably higher had it counted Indians living in the state.

The word "Wyoming" comes from the Leni-Lenape Indians of Pennsylvania; their word "mecheweami-ing" meant "at the Great Plains." The term was first applied to the land that would become Wyoming in 1865, when Ohio's J. M. Ashley introduced a bill to form a "temporary government for the territory of Wyoming." Newspaper editor Legh Freeman has been credited with popularizing the name and having it inserted into the bill that created the Wyoming Territory in 1868.

A triumvirate of politicians—Francis E. Warren, John B. Kendrick, and Joseph M. Carey—governed Wyoming for much of its first half century. Carey, a Republican turned Democrat, was a founder of both the powerful Wyoming Stock Growers Association and the Cheyenne Club. He was a strong proponent of Wyoming statehood and introduced the enabling legislation in the U.S. House. During the debate, he claimed a Wyoming population of more than 110,000 people, an exaggeration that helped sway enough House votes to pass the measure. (The next year, the U.S. census found just 62,555 people in Wyoming.) The act was signed into law by President Benjamin Harrison on July 10, 1890, making Wyoming the 44th state. Interestingly, this was the same year that the director of the U.S. Census Bureau declared that the "frontier of settlement" was no more.

The Equality State

Wyoming's first territorial legislature passed an act granting women the right to vote. The measure was signed into law by Governor J. A. Campbell on December 10, 1869, making this the first government in the world to grant women the right to vote. (Technically, Wyoming was not the first state to allow women suffrage; New Jersey widows already had limited voting rights.) The name "Equality State" comes from this bold step. It would be another 50 years before the 19th Amendment was finally passed, giving all women in America the right to vote. Not everyone looked upon women's suffrage as such a good step. In 1871, Democrats in the second territorial legislature repealed the measure, and then came within one vote of overriding Governor Campbell's veto.

When the territory of Wyoming was seeking admission to the Union in 1890, the issue of giving women the right to vote—a measure included in Wyoming's new constitution—became a hotly contested topic. Alabama's Senator John T. Morgan led the fight against admitting the new state, with the argument that the other half of the population would be polluted by politicians (such as himself?): "It is the immoral influences of the ballot upon women that I deprecate and would avoid. I do not want to see her drawn in contact with the rude things of this world where the delicacy of her senses and sensitivities would be constantly wounded by the attrition with bad and desperate and foul politicians and men."

Wyoming's status as the home of equal rights took another big step in 1925 after the death of Governor William B. Ross. His wife, Nellie Tayloe Ross, was nominated to replace him and won the special election on a sympathy vote. She made no effort to get elected, noting, "I shall not make a campaign. My candidacy is in the hands of my friends. I shall not leave the house." She served ably as the nation's first woman governor and achieved considerable national attention. Despite a good record, Ross lost her bid for reelection, primarily because she was a Democrat in a heavily Republican state. In 1933, President Roosevelt appointed her as director of the U.S. Mint, a title she held for the next 20 years. She died in 1967 at the age of 101.

CATTLE COUNTRY
Opening the Range

Once the bison herds had been devastated and the Indians evicted, cattlemen found what seemed like a Garden of Eden in Wyoming: Land, grass, and water were essentially free for the taking. The cattle industry began innocently enough. In December 1863, Tom Alsop was returning to Omaha with a train of 50 wagons when a snowstorm pinned them down near present-day Cheyenne. Alsop abandoned the oxen and wagons on the plains and led his men safely home on horseback. The following spring, they rode back to recover the freight and were startled to discover that the cattle they had left to die of exposure had not only survived the winter but were thriving. The discovery soon attracted droves of ranchers.

The first cattle drive through Wyoming came in 1866, when a Montana merchant named Nelson Story decided that what the Virginia City miners needed was fresh beef. Heading south to Kansas with $10,000 sewn in the lining of his clothes, he filled a wagon with supplies, bought 3,000 Texas longhorns, hired 27 cowboys,

a bull near Pinedale

gave them the finest Remington breech-loading rifles, and headed north for the goldfields. At Fort Kearny (see *The Bozeman Trail* under *Around Sheridan* in the *Powder River Country* chapter for more on this notorious fort), Colonel Carrington forbade them from continuing north through Sioux country because they did not have the required 40 armed guards. (Some believe that Carrington actually hoped to requisition the cattle for his men; most of the army's had already been stolen.) In response, an angry Story thumbed his nose at the government, heading north under cover of darkness. Discovering his departure, Carrington was forced to cave in, sending 15 soldiers along to bring Story's force up to the legal minimum. Although one man died, the rest of the men and cattle made it to Virginia City on December 9. Nelson Story had gained himself a place in history.

Millions of cattle headed into or through Wyoming in the 1870s and 1880s. Ranching looked like a can't-lose business; dump a couple of thousand head of cows and calves on the range in spring and return a year later to round them up for market. What could be simpler? Investors from Omaha, New York, England, Scotland, and France quickly took note of the potential fortunes to be made.

By 1883, English and Scottish investors had poured some £6 million into Wyoming cattle and had turned Cheyenne into a country club for the European gentry. Some were more gullible than others; stories are still told of an Englishman who watched as the cattle he was buying were driven by to be counted, not noticing that the same cattle had come around the hill a couple of times before. The use of "book counts" also inflated the value of the herds; frequently, nobody bothered to make sure that numbers in the books equaled cattle on the range. The

BRANDS

Branding dates back to the Egyptian pharaohs, who branded not only their cattle, camels, and donkeys, but even their slaves. Slave branding was also practiced in America. The American tradition of cattle branding comes from the Spanish conquistadors and their *vaqueros* but was adapted to the spacious western plains. Because there were no fences, cattle belonging to various ranchers became intermixed, leading to inevitable questions of ownership, which brands helped answer.

Brands appear almost anywhere on an animal, and a given ranch may have a half dozen or more for its cattle, sheep, and horses. An individual animal often has several different brands or marks. To make them easier to identify on the hoof, cattle are frequently distinctively marked by cutting a notch in the ear, slicing the skin that hangs under the cow's throat (the dewlap), or hacking a flap of hide (a wattle) so that it hangs loose from the neck.

In Wyoming, having a brand is something of a status symbol, and the Wyoming Brand Book lists more than 28,000 in use. Not everyone who has a brand has stock; some are simply used for mailbox decorations on suburban ranchettes. The more complex ones aren't likely to appear on any cows because they become illegible as the scar heals. Brands that are hard to alter or of historic significance may sell for more than $5,000. Coming up with a design for a new brand can be a problem because the state looks askance on brands that resemble others in the same area or that might be easily altered by rustlers (they still exist). One 19th-century rancher, fed up with having his brand suggestions rejected, wrote the brand department, demanding, "Send me a brand P.D.Q." It complied by giving him the brand PDQ. Reading brands is an art gained by years of experience. They are read from left to right, top to bottom, and outside to inside.

Branding usually takes place in the spring, before cattle and calves are driven into the higher pastures or set loose on the plains. A branding iron is heated to a dull red in a fire and then pressed against the calf as it is held down. Freeze branding is also often used. Most male calves are castrated at the same time.

aristocrats were regarded with a mixture of humor and disdain by the hardened cowboys whose every other utterance was a swear word. One British lord rode up to a cowboy in his buggy, asking, "My good man, could you tell me where your master is?" The cowboy glowered back, spat out his tobacco, and proclaimed, "The son-of-a-bitch ain't been born yet!"

During the early years of ranching in Wyoming, cattle were allowed to roam at will and were not sorted out until the annual roundups. Sounds fine in theory, but in practice a few flaws showed up, notably the problem of mavericks. The term "maverick" refers to an unbranded calf or cow of questionable ownership or, as writer Struthers Burt put it: "A calf whose mamma has died and whose father has run off with another lady cow." Unbranded calves were generally divvied up among the ranchers on the basis of which herd they were with, but when herds became mixed together, conflicts were inevitable. In addition, multiple roundups meant that the first cowboys on the scene could pretty much decide for themselves which calves were theirs. Some even went so far as to slit the tongues of calves so they could no longer suckle and would not follow their mothers, thus becoming instant mavericks.

Cattle Barons and Rustlers

To curb the temptations for such "sooners," the powerful Wyoming Stock Growers Association—an organization dominated by the wealthiest of the cattlemen—gained the authority to dictate when roundups could be held. The organization dominated the political landscape of Wyoming for many years; by the 1880s, one-third of the state legislature belonged to the association. The 1882 Maverick Bill gave the association control over all cattle roundups in the territory, with proceeds from the sales of mavericks going into the association's coffers. It could blacklist cowboys as "rustlers" on the basis of hearsay, and cattle shipped without the association's permission risked being impounded by inspectors in Chicago or Omaha. Even worse, ranchers suspected of rustling (which seemed to include anyone except members) were some-

times ambushed and murdered by enforcers, the most notorious of whom was Tom Horn. Whole regions of Wyoming were terrorized by the practice of dry-gulching, in which suspected rustlers would be shot from behind and left in an out-of-the-way gulch.

Meanwhile, the big cattlemen—commonly called cattle barons—also ran into trouble, especially in the Powder River country. The fierce winter of 1886–1887 devastated their herds; some lost all of their cattle, whereas others had just 20–30 percent of the numbers from the previous year. Big ranching outfits also found themselves hemmed in by homesteading settlers who fenced the land. Fences created a hazard because cattle often moved with the winter winds until they hit the fences and then piled up there to die.

The big cattlemen accused these "nesters" not only of fencing the land but also of taking stray cattle for themselves. Using a "long rope" and a "running iron," they could easily alter the brands and soon have their own herd. The cattle barons decided to put an end to this thievery once and for all with the infamous Johnson County War of 1892, but the campaign proved a complete fiasco. Two men died on each side in pitched battles between the "barons" and the "rustlers." Although the Invaders managed to escape prosecution, the small nesters and rustlers had won the day. From that time on, the range would increasingly be fenced in.

SHEEP
History

Cattle arrived in most parts of Wyoming a decade or so before the first sheep munched their way across the grazing lands, but by 1902 the rangeland was crowded with close to six million sheep. Cattlemen considered the public land their own—by right of previous use—although legally it was all open range owned by the government. As competition increased, cattlemen declared "dead lines," across which no sheep would be allowed. Conflicts quickly erupted, and the single herder and his dogs proved no match for a gang of cattlemen on horseback. Herders were murdered throughout the state, and the violence escalated into the infamous Ten Sleep Raid of 1909, in which three sheepmen were brutally murdered. After this, things quieted down as the land became increasingly settled and government policies divided the areas. Some cattlemen even turned to raising sheep, but animosity still remains between sheepmen and cattlemen in some areas.

Sheepherding

Through the years, the number of sheep in Wyoming has steadily dropped; today there are about 450,000 sheep and lambs in the state. Sheep are generally moved up into the mountains each spring to graze in the high meadows and then brought back down in the fall. A long drive along country roads is a sight straight out of the history books. Sheep are sheared in spring, generally just before lambing season. By fall the lambs are big enough to send to market, and the ewes are bred.

Many of the first sheepherders in Wyoming were from Europe's Basque region. Many preferred to take sheep instead of a salary and so gradually gained flocks of their own. The frugal ones eventually became ranch owners in their own rights. The herding business has not changed much through the years, however, and herders still spend weeks at a time alone, seeing nobody but the camp mover when he arrives to help move the outfit to new feeding grounds. Today many herders are Mexican immigrants, although some Basque and American herders are still around. The herder's life is a simple and quiet one, with plenty of time for reflection. It takes someone with the right temperament to be a sheepherder.

The sheepherder's wagon—an early version of the RV—was invented by James Candlish, a Rawlins blacksmith, and later improved and marketed by Casper's Schulte Hardware Company. The design proved an efficient one, and a few herders still use the old wagons, although rubber tires have replaced wagon wheels and the roof is now tin instead of canvas. The layout is simple: A Dutch door opens into a small space filled with a bed at the back with drawers underneath and shelves above.

A small woodstove near the entrance is used for both heating and cooking. Almost every Wyoming museum seems to have one of these wagons tucked away in a corner.

ENERGY BOOM, BUST, AND BOOM

Wyoming's economy is heavily linked to the energy industry, with coal, oil, and gas all major employers. The state's first oil well was drilled in 1884, and by 1908—the year of the first oil boom—production approached 18,000 barrels per year. Production continued to climb through the decades, reaching a peak in 1970, when more than 155 million barrels were pumped. Since then, oil production has declined sharply as older fields have become exhausted, and by 2002, production had fallen below 60 million barrels.

The drop in oil production has been offset by dramatic increases in two other energy sources: natural gas and coal. Coal production, particularly in the Powder River Basin, has skyrocketed in the last two decades, topping 370 million tons in 2002. Wyoming is easily the nation's biggest coal-producing state, with nearly all of this being used in power plants. Natural gas is the latest boom, as thousands of wells are being drilled to extract coalbed methane in the Basin.

In the 1970s and '80s, Wyoming rode an economic bucking bronco as oil prices shot up and then suddenly dove, throwing this energy-rich state out of the saddle. The Arab oil embargo of 1973 and subsequent price increases turned Wyoming upside down. Oil-patch towns—particularly Casper, Rock Springs, Evanston, and Green River—became madhouses of pickup trucks, heavily muscled oil workers, honky-tonk bars, strip joints, fast-food outlets, and trailer courts. Drugs, crime, prostitution, and gambling rippled across the state. The population of Rock Springs doubled in two years. In the heady rush of new workers and high-paying oil jobs, many towns embarked on ambitious construction projects such as schools and housing developments, while trailer parks sprouted across the countryside. (Wyoming still holds top honors as the state with the highest percentage of mobile homes.)

This economic bubble collapsed with the sudden halving of oil prices in 1982, and Wyoming's population actually *dropped* by almost 3 percent during the 1980s. The bust left many towns struggling to survive as unemployment skyrocketed, the state government was forced into consolidation mode, and local residents were saddled with a bloated set of facilities.

Back Around Again

Wyoming has come full circle, and as of 2006, the state was in the midst of its latest boom, driven by high energy prices, discoveries of enormous gas deposits near Pinedale, and a continuing demand for coal and coalbed methane from the Powder River Basin. Towns such as Rock Springs, Gillette, Pinedale, and Rawlins have been growing rapidly, but the larger cities of Cheyenne and Casper are also prospering as regional centers. Northwest Wyoming, particularly Jackson Hole and Cody, continues to benefit from tourism, and Teton County now has the highest per-capita income of any county in the nation. The spillover effect of this development is even affecting formerly quiet Alpine and Star Valley, as Jackson Hole workers seek cheaper lodging. (The median home price in Jackson tops $680,000!)

The inevitable booms and busts associated with the energy and mining industries will affect Wyoming for the foreseeable future, but growing numbers of tourism and service-sector jobs may help cushion the blows next time around. The money may not approach that of the $24-per-hour coal-mining jobs, but at least a sales position at Wal-Mart pays the bills.

Government and Economy

POLITICS

Unlike in many states, where apathy reigns, Wyomingites take their right to vote seriously, with turnout during presidential election years sometimes topping 80 percent of registered voters. Wyoming has 64 elected state representatives (who serve two-year terms) and 30 state senators (elected for four-year terms). The elected statewide officials—governor, secretary of state, auditor, treasurer, and superintendent of public instruction—all stand for office every four years.

Republicans have controlled both houses of the legislature almost since statehood; Wyoming's congressional delegation has long been entirely Republican—including Vice President Dick Cheney—who served as the state's lone congressman 1977–1989. Despite a Republican juggernaut on other offices, Wyoming's popular governor—Dave Freudenthal—is a Democrat. The state last voted for a Democratic presidential candidate in 1964, so Sierra Club members and other liberals might want to keep a low profile in most parts of Wyoming. (Jackson Hole is the decided exception.)

WHO OWNS WYOMING?

Wyoming's economy is affected not only by private developments but also by the government. The federal government owns almost 47 percent of the land, while the state government holds another 10 percent, leaving 43 percent in private hands. The largest public land agency—the Bureau of Land Management (BLM)—owns nearly 18 million acres in Wyoming, but most of this exists in a checkerboard of small parcels with limited public access. The BLM manages only a few patches of wilderness scattered around Wyoming. The U.S. Forest Service has 8.7 million acres within nine national forests that cover the state's largest mountain ranges, and the National Park Service has another 2.3 million acres in five national parks, monuments, and recreation areas. Warren Air Force Base—the most important intercontinental ballistic missile (ICBM) base in North America—is in Cheyenne and represents the state's only major military installation. The military also owns land in other parts of Wyoming today, notably the Camp Guernsey training area

STATE SYMBOLS

The Great Seal of the State of Wyoming is filled with symbolism. The two dates commemorate establishment of the territorial government (1869) and statehood (1890). The Roman numerals (XLIV) represent Wyoming as the 44th state to be admitted to the Union; the male figures represent the livestock and mining industries, while the central female figure stands for political equality. In early versions the woman was unclothed, but legislators quickly sensed the problems inherent in nudity on Wyoming's official emblem and rejected the design. After a swath of cloth made everything acceptable, the symbol was finally adopted by the state legislature in 1893. The state flag includes both this symbol and the outline of a bison.

Wyoming's best-known symbol is its bucking horse, a figure that has appeared on state license plates since 1936. The silhouette was created by artist Allen True of Denver and was reputedly inspired by the rodeo cowboy Albert "Stub" Farlow. The bucking horse insignia was used earlier by Wyoming soldiers during World War I.

Despite jokes to the contrary, Wyoming's state tree is *not* the telephone pole! Wyoming has all kinds of other official designations: state flower (Indian paintbrush), bird (meadowlark), tree (plains cottonwood), stone (jade), mammal (bison), fossil (a fish called *knightia*), fish (cutthroat trout), and even a state dinosaur (triceratops). The state nickname seems to suffer from a split personality, being both "Equality State" and "Cowboy State." (To be honest, this really isn't a contest; I'll be the first to tell you that in the hearts and minds of all true Wyomingites, it's the COWBOY STATE.)

north of Wheatland and a Naval Petroleum Reserve at Teapot Dome.

Partly because of all this federal involvement, Wyoming residents are on the receiving end of generous federal monies; the state is second only to Alaska in per-capita federal aid. Interestingly, both states are also rich in oil and gas, have most of their land in federal ownership, are small in population, and suffered similar economic doldrums through the 1990s. You'll meet quite a few former Alaskans in Wyoming and an equal number of former Wyomingites in Alaska. Coincidence?

WORKING FOR A LIVING
Oil and Gas

Wyoming's economy steams along on a mixture of gas and oil extraction, coal and trona mining, cattle and sheep ranching, and tourism. Oil production—mainly in the Powder River and Bighorn basins—has long been the most important source of income, but it is increasingly being eclipsed by coal mining and natural gas production. Despite the recent decrease, about 1,000 Wyoming fields produce 52 million barrels of oil annually, sixth in the nation. Gas production has followed the opposite path in recent years, as production of coalbed methane from northeast Wyoming and natural gas from southeast Wyoming increased dramatically. Today, Wyoming produces an astounding 2 trillion cubic feet of natural gas annually, second in the nation.

Coal

A quarter of the nation's coal reserves lie beneath Wyoming, and it is easily the largest coal-producing state, far outstripping (pun intended) runners-up West Virginia and Kentucky. Nearly all of the more than 370 million tons extracted each year comes from enormous open-pit mines, primarily in the Powder River Basin. With perhaps one *trillion* tons of coal still below the surface, Wyoming is one of the largest energy storehouses anywhere on the planet. Eight of the nation's 10 largest coal mines are in Wyoming, and the low-sulfur coal produced is shipped by train to utility companies in 29 states.

THE RODEO

It may come as a revelation to many, but rodeo (in Wyoming, always pronounced ROE-dee-oh) is one of the most popular sports in America; more people watch professional rodeos than attend NFL football games! In Wyoming, where even the license plate is graced with a cowboy astride a bucking bronc, it's no surprise that rodeo is king. Every small town in the state has a rodeo of some sort during the summer, and the larger cities have world-class rodeos that attract hundreds of riders and ropers from the Professional Rodeo Cowboys Association (PRCA).

Although rodeo seems to have a few drops of the Spanish bullfight in its blood, and while many of the words – rodeo, bronco, lariat, arena, and honda – have Spanish origins, rodeo's true genesis was in the days of cowboys and cattle in the Wild West. Gradually, groups of cowboys got together to show off their riding and roping skills and to compete with neighboring outfits. Everyone argues over the official origin of rodeo, but credit is generally given to a bucking and roping competition between the Mill Iron and Hash Knife outfits, who met near Deer Trail, Colorado, in 1869.

As the West began to be fenced in, the cowboy events moved into the nearby towns as organized "buckin' shows." Buffalo Bill Cody probably had more to do with popularizing the sport than any other person. For many years his Wild West Show traveled the world, providing a spectacle that included several of the events in present-day rodeos. Lander lays claim to the oldest rodeo in Wyoming; begun in 1893, the Lander Pioneer Days rodeo still comes around each July. By far the most famous Wyoming rodeo, the "Daddy of 'em All," is the Cheyenne Frontier Days, one of the top four rodeos in the world. A good source for rodeo information on the web is www.prorodeohome.org.

Through the years, rodeo has become more professional and less connected to the true cowboy. Many participants today come from cities and have never spent time herding cattle or working on a ranch. Other cowboys still come from more traditional farming and ranching backgrounds, although they may work part-time at the local grocery store to fund their travels on the rodeo circuit.

Those who make it to the top do so the hard way. Grand Nationals winners are decided on the basis of rodeo earnings, which means that cowboys must compete almost continuously, flying from one rodeo to another and staying in cheap motels or living out of their RVs. Semipros and amateurs compete in the hundreds of smaller rodeos that dot Wyoming and the West, hoping to make it to the professional level. Most don't even come close, losing their stiff entry fees to more experienced competitors and taking home only bruises or broken bones.

Other Minerals

Vast deposits of trona (used primarily in glass and chemicals such as baking soda) occur in southwestern Wyoming, where mines produce 90 percent of the nation's supply. The state is also a major supplier of bentonite, helium, and sulfur. Uranium was once an important industry—one-third of America's reserves lie in Wyoming—but since the incident at Three Mile Island, production has dropped to almost nothing, with a single active mine north of Douglas.

Tourism

Nearly seven million people come to enjoy Wyoming's abundant recreational opportunities each year, and tourism contributes more than $2.6 billion annually to the economy. It is particularly important in northwestern Wyoming, where Yellowstone and Grand Teton national parks and other attractions are creating a booming Jackson Hole economy (and astronomical land valuations). Lesser levels of growth are taking place in other near-the-mountain towns such as Cody, Sheridan, Buffalo, Laramie, Pinedale, Dubois, Lander, Alpine, and Star Valley.

Agriculture

The state's most obvious industry—and the one that encompasses 90 percent of its land

The major rodeo events generally fall into two categories: riding and roping. Riding events include saddle bronc riding, bareback bronc riding, and bull riding; roping events include steer wrestling, calf roping, and steer roping. Women's barrel racing, clown bull-fighting, and chuck wagon races complete the roundup. In most of the events, luck has much to do with who wins. Much of the scoring is based on the difficulty of the ride; consequently, the toughest broncs or bulls are favorites because they mean higher scores. Times for ropers depend on the speed and behavior of the calf or steer they're trying to tackle.

One thing newcomers soon notice about rodeo cowboys is the clothes they wear — long-sleeve shirts, cowboy hats, Wrangler jeans (never Levi's — the seam is in the wrong place for riding), and cowboy boots. As writer Mary S. Robertson noted, "In no other sport but rodeo do the players and the spectators dress alike." Interestingly, the PRCA actually has a rule requiring long-sleeve shirts and cowboy hats; apparently at one time too many riders and ropers were wearing baseball caps and T-shirts, so the more traditional attire was made mandatory. One additional piece of attire is also worn by rodeo cowboys: the plate-sized silver and gold belt buckles. Top winners get these as awards for surviving a season of abuse; others buy them for flash and dash.

A title occasionally used for rodeo is "the suicide sport." It is, unfortunately, all too true, especially for bull riders. Accidents are common, and rodeos always have an emergency medical technician ready to tend to the inevitable smashed legs, kicked-in ribs, and broken collarbones. Many cowboys are crippled for life, and at least several die each year in the sport, including two at Cheyenne Frontier Days in the 1980s. I recall watching a man in a wheelchair behind the bull chutes at a Jackson rodeo as he encouraged the riders; he had been paralyzed two years earlier in a bull-riding accident at that same rodeo. Even the nation's top riders and ropers can be killed; Lane Frost, a champion bull rider, died at Cheyenne Frontier Days in 1989. Most dangerous of all are the bull rides, but just watching a "dogger" leaping off his horse onto the horns of a speeding steer can give the crowd pause. Rodeos are criticized by animal-rights activists as unnecessarily cruel to animals — steers occasionally die from broken necks and broncs sometimes injure themselves (and their riders) by trying to jump out of the chutes — but the cowboys really do all they can to prevent injury to the animals they ride or rope. Rodeo announcers always point out that the animals spend very little time in the arena; nearly all of their time is in the pasture.

base—is agriculture. Surprisingly, however, grazing and farming employ just 1.5 percent of the population. Wyoming is third in the nation in terms of sheep and lamb production and has 1.4 million cattle and calves. But it takes 30 acres to support a single cow (versus one acre per cow in parts of Nebraska!), which is why the average Wyoming farm is 3,743 acres—eight times the national average. Only 4 percent of the state is cultivated; primary crops are sugar beets, hay, barley, and corn. These are mainly grown within Bighorn Basin and Wind River Basin and along Wyoming's eastern plains.

Other Economic Mainstays

The state has no truly large manufacturing plants, although every town has its own specialty. The services sector of the economy—from flipping burgers to running copy machines—is the unheralded source of real growth in Wyoming, although the wages are nothing to brag about.

For detailed state economic information (including an annual almanac), visit the Wyoming Department of Administration and Information's website: http://eadiv.state.wy.us. The *Wyoming Business Report* (www.wyomingbusinessreport.com) is a monthly newspaper with articles on the state's economy.

ESSENTIALS

Getting There and Around

Public transportation is limited in Wyoming, although air service has improved in the last few years. Amtrak no longer offers train service through Wyoming, but the state has reasonably good bus service, even though this is minimal in some areas. Local buses operate in Jackson, Cody, and Cheyenne.

BY AIR

Commercial airline flights take you to the towns of Casper, Cheyenne, Cody, Gillette, Jackson, Laramie, Riverton, Rock Springs, Sheridan, and Worland. The resort town of Jackson has the best air service in the state—by far—with jet flights from Atlanta, Salt Lake City, Denver, Dallas, Chicago, Minneapolis, and Boise.

If you're flying to Jackson from Seattle, Los Angeles, or San Francisco, you will need to go through either Salt Lake City or Idaho Falls. The latter airport is served by Horizon Air (Alaska Airlines). Many folks opt to fly to either Salt Lake (275 miles away) or Idaho Falls (90 miles away) and pick up a rental car for the drive to Jackson.

Wyoming's primary air carrier is Cheyenne-based **Great Lakes Aviation** (307/433-2905 or 800/554-5111, www.greatlakesav.com), with

© DON PITCHER

DRIVING DISTANCES

flights connecting Denver with Cheyenne, Rock Springs, Riverton, Worland, Laramie, and Gillette. They code-share with United and Frontier, so you can book flights and get airline miles through either of these airlines.

BY CAR

Given the expanse and small population of Wyoming, it's no surprise that the automobile—and the pickup truck in many areas—is the primary means of transportation. The **Wyoming Department of Transportation** puts out a pamphlet detailing current road projects around the state. You can find it in many visitor centers or get this and much more, including webcams along main roads, on the web at www.wyoroad.info. For a recording with road conditions around the state, call 307/772-0824 or 888/996-7623.

Highway Safety

Wyoming drivers seldom slow down when meeting other vehicles, so flying gravel is a frequent problem on unpaved roads. It's even a problem on paved roads, so make sure your insurance pays for windshield repairs!

It's a long way between things in Wyoming. Be sure to gas up in the main towns before heading out, and have a spare tire and a cell phone. If you have little ones onboard, make the kids go to the bathroom before you depart because it's tough to hide behind a sagebrush plant. Rest areas (many solar-powered) are scattered across Wyoming along state highways, U.S. highways, and interstates.

Wyoming's official speed limits are 65 mph on most paved state highways (once you get away from the towns) and 75 mph on the interstate highways. Drive at those speeds and

RIDING INTO HISTORY

Several businesses attempt to re-create the days of the great westward migration with wagon trips along the historic Oregon Trail and in other historic areas. The trips are all-inclusive, with horses, meals, tents, and other gear provided; you'll need to bring a sleeping bag. They are typically limited to small groups, with a maximum of 12 or so on horseback trips. Wagon trains are larger – as were the original wagon trains – and may have up to 30 people.

WILD BUNCH RIDE

A unique way to discover the Old West is the **Outlaw Trail Ride** (307/864-2287 or 888/362-7433, www.rideoutlawtrail.com), a weeklong not-for-profit adventure in early August. This 100-mile trip follows the "Outlaw Trail" from the Hole-in-the-Wall country of Butch Cassidy and the Sundance Kid to Thermopolis. It isn't for dudes – you'll need to bring your own horse (although they can also be rented from HorseWorks), bedroll, and gear – but excellent meals are provided. A trail-ride fee of $875 covers catered meals, horse feed, nightly entertainment, and more.

WAGON AND HORSEBACK TREKS

Several companies offer Conestoga wagon or horseback trips across various parts of Wyoming, including the Oregon Trail. These typically last several days and include horses, meals, equipment, and tents. For details on the many options, contact: **Great Divide Tours** (307/332-3123 or 800/458-1915, www.dtoutfitting.com), **Historic Trails West** (307/266-4868 or 800/327-4052, www.historictrailswest.com), **SpiritRider Wagon Train Adventure** (307/472-5361 or 866/873-9397, www.spiritrider-wagontrain.com), or **Wagons A+Cross Wyoming** (307/859-8629 or 888/818-3581, www.wagonsacrosswyoming.com).

Multinight wagon-train treks are offered in Jackson Hole by **Wagons West** (307/543-2418 or 800/447-4711, www.wagonswestwyo.com) and **Teton Wagon Train/Double H Bar** (307/734-6101 or 888/734-6101, www.tetonwagontrain.com). Jackson isn't close to the Oregon Trail, but the scenery is grand.

you'll find yourself constantly passed by cars going well over the limit. But look out when driving through small towns throughout Wyoming; the cops vigorously enforce local speed limits. When darkness falls on the main interstate highways (I-80, I-15, and I-90), the trucks come out in force, like bats emerging from caves. It can be a bit intimidating if you're driving a compact car.

Travel Maps

Free Wyoming maps can be found at visitor centers across the state, but map aficionados should be certain to buy *Wyoming Atlas and Gazetteer* (www.delorme.com), which has detailed topographic maps of Wyoming. It is indispensable for travelers who are heading off main routes. National forest maps are also helpful for mountain driving in many parts of Wyoming; buy them at local Forest Service offices. The BLM produces a series of 1:100,000 maps for the entire state, and they are sold in sporting goods stores. They're especially helpful when you're planning to head out into areas with mixed private and public lands.

Car Rentals

You can rent cars in all of the larger towns, and those with airports generally have Hertz, Avis, and other national chains. If you plan to rent a car for an extended period, it's worth your while to check travel websites such as www.travelocity.com, www.expedia.com, or www.orbitz.com to see which company offers the best rates. Note, however, that these quotes may not include taxes, which can be substantial, especially if you rent at the Denver or Salt Lake City airports. If you're visiting in the summer, try to get a light-colored car; dark ones can get incredibly hot.

HORSES

For many people, the highlight of a Wyoming vacation is the chance to ride a horse into wild country. Although a few folks bring their own steeds, most visitors leave the driving to an expert local outfitter instead. (If you've ever worked around horses in the backcountry, you'll understand why.) Horsepacking is an entirely different experience from backpacking. The trade requires years of experience in learning how to properly load horses and mules with panniers (large baskets), which types of knots to use for different loads, how to keep the packstrings under control, which horses to picket and which to hobble, and how to awaken when the horses decide to head down the trail on hobbles at three in the morning. Add to this a knowledge of bear safety, an ability to keep guests entertained with campfire tales and ribald jokes, a complete vocabulary of horse-cussing terms, and a thorough knowledge of tobacco chewing, and you're still only about 10 percent of the way to becoming a packer.

Dozens of outfitters are scattered across Wyoming, but you'll find concentrations in the Jackson Hole, Pinedale, Cody, Dubois, Sheridan, and Saratoga areas. For a listing of permitted outfitters in a given region, contact local Forest Service and Park Service offices. The **Wyoming Outfitters and Guides Association** (307/527-7453, www.wyoga.org) maintains a statewide listing, and the **Wyoming State Board of Outfitters** (307/635-1589 or 800/264-0981, http://outfitte.state.wy.us) produces a directory of licensed outfitters.

Although horses are far more common, **llamas** are relatively common in some backcountry areas. You can't ride them, but they're easier to control than horses and do not cause as much damage to trails and backcountry meadows. Llamas are perfect for folks who want to hike while letting a pack llama carry most of the weight. Contact local Forest Service and Park Service offices for permitted llama- (and goat-) packers.

Winter Travel

Winter travelers need to take special precautions. Snow tires are a necessity, but you should also have emergency supplies, including tire chains, a shovel and bag of sand in case you get stuck, a first-aid kit, booster cables, signal flares, a flashlight with extra batteries, lighter and candle, transistor radio, nonperishable foods (granola bars, canned nuts, or dried fruit), a jug of water, ice scraper, winter clothes, blankets, a sleeping bag, ax, and tow strap. The most valuable tool may well be a cell phone to call for help—assuming you're in an area with reception.

If you become stranded in a blizzard, stay in your car. You're more likely to be found, and the vehicle provides shelter from the weather. Run the engine and heater sparingly, occasionally opening a downwind window for ventilation. Don't run the engine if the tailpipe is blocked by snow—you may risk carbon monoxide poisoning. For up-to-date road and travel conditions in Wyoming, call 307/772-0824 or 888/996-7623, or log onto www.wyoroad.info for updated information, webcams, and construction advisories. Get weather information at www.crh.noaa.gov/cys.

BY BIKE

Because of Wyoming's small population, cyclists will find uncrowded roads in many parts of the state. The long distances between towns, windy conditions, and frequent summer thunderstorms add to the adventure/danger. The Wyoming Department of Transportation publishes a useful *Bicycle Guidance Map*—on waterproof paper—showing the amount of traffic on each paved road, the width of paved shoulders, profiles of the steeper road grades, and general wind patterns. Anyone touring on a bike will find this map immensely valuable. Get a copy by calling the WYDOT Bicycle Coordinator at 307/777-4719.

Many thousands of miles of gravel and dirt roads provide excellent places to explore on mountain bikes; check with local bike shops for nearby routes. Get the BLM's 1:100,000-scale area maps (available at most BLM offices) before heading out. They show land ownership, contour lines, and all roads. On Forest Service lands, buy equally detailed maps from local district offices. Mountain bikes can be rented in most of the larger Wyoming towns.

BY BUS
Greyhound (800/231-2222, www.greyhound.com) serves only the southern Wyoming cities of Rock Springs, Rawlins, and Laramie. These daily buses continue south to Denver or west to Salt Lake City for onward connections to the rest of the country.

Based in Gillette, **Powder River Transportation** (307/682-1888 or 800/442-3682, http://gillette.coachusa.us) is Wyoming's primary bus company, with daily service to Basin, Buffalo, Casper, Cheyenne, Cody, Douglas, Gillette, Greybull, Lovell, Powell, Sheridan, Shoshoni, Sundance, Wheatland, and Worland. It also serves Colorado (Boulder, Denver, Fort Collins, and Greeley), Montana (Billings and Hardin), Nebraska (Kimball, Ogallala, and Sidney), and South Dakota (Rapid City, Spearfish, and Sturgis). Buses will stop at other towns en route—including Themopolis, Chugwater, and Moorcroft—but you'll need to call 24 hours in advance for a pickup. Powder River also offers summertime tours of Yellowstone and Grand Teton from Cody.

Alltrans/Jackson Hole Express (307/733-1719 or 800/652-9510, www.jacksonholealltrans.com) provides daily bus or van connections between Salt Lake City, Idaho Falls, Pocatello, and the resort town of Jackson.

Another option is **Wind River Transportation Authority/WRTA** (307/856-7118 or 800/439-7118, www.wrtabuslines.com), with scheduled trips connecting Lander with Salt Lake City, Jackson, and Rock Springs.

Tips for Travelers

FISHING AND HUNTING
For detailed fishing and hunting information, contact the **Wyoming Game and Fish Department** (307/777-4600 or 800/548-9453, http://gf.state.wy.us).

Fishing
Outstanding fishing opportunities abound throughout Wyoming, and several places—mostly in the Yellowstone area—have attained recognition as some of the finest in America. Cutthroat, brown, rainbow, brook, and lake trout are favorites of many anglers, but the state's waters also contain mountain whitefish, kokanee, grayling, channel catfish, smallmouth bass, largemouth bass, and others.

The Wyoming Game and Fish Department produces an excellent, free *Wyoming Fishing Guide,* with descriptions of the various river drainages, what fish you can catch in each, state record fish, and basic information on techniques, access, and maps. It's available in visitor centers across the state.

An exceptionally helpful online source for fishing information is the private **Wyoming Fishing Network** (www.wyomingfishing.net). Here you'll find details on where to fish, lures, local guides, and up-to-date fishing reports for various rivers and lakes.

Nonresident fishing permits cost $11 for one day or $76 for a season. Resident fishing licenses are $19 for the year. Nonresident youths (ages 14–19) pay $15 for the year ($3 for resident youths). With the exception of the one-day rate, you will also need to buy a $10 mandatory conservation stamp. Kids younger than 14 don't need a license if they're with an adult who has a valid fishing license. Buy permits at most sporting goods stores or from Game and Fish offices. Note that the Wind River Indian Reservation and Yellowstone National Park have their own regulations and permits (see appropriate sections

DUDE RANCHES

Wyoming has literally dozens of dude ranches and ranch resorts offering accommodations varying from spartan to so sumptuous that they bear absolutely no resemblance to ranch life. Not all dude ranches are created equal – some are slick and modern with tennis courts and hot tubs while others are funky and old-fashioned with delightful rough edges. The smaller ones offer more personalized service, but in larger ones you're more likely to find someone your own age (particularly important if there are teens in your entourage). Dudes normally sleep in log cabins. Conditions inside can vary widely, but don't expect TVs or phones in the rooms. The cabins are usually near a central lodge, where meals are served family-style. Many also have large libraries, along with outdoor games such as volleyball and horseshoes. Fishing and photography are other big attractions.

Dude ranch stays generally cost around $2,500-3,500 for two people per week, with lower rates for kids and surcharges for those staying by themselves. The price includes all meals, lodging, and horseback rides, but you'll usually pay more for features such as airport shuttles, rafting trips, guided fishing, beer and wine, or backcountry pack trips, not to mention local taxes and tips. The fanciest resort, Lost Creek Ranch in Jackson Hole, will set you back more than $12,000 for two people per week! Many guest ranches offer discounted rates in early June and late September and for repeat guests. A few also have special adults-only weeks. Most require that you stay a week, or at least three nights, although a few places offer overnight accommodations. To really get into the comfortably slow pace of ranch life, try to set aside at least a week.

Ask plenty of questions before you visit, such as what activities are available, what to bring in the way of clothing, what sort of meals to expect (vegetarians may have a hard time on some ranches), whether there are additional charges, whether it accepts credit cards (many don't), what the living accommodations are like, and how many other guests will likely be there at the same time – some house up to 125, others fewer than a dozen. Upon request, the better ranches will provide lists of references from previous clients. Note that it is considered proper to tip the ranch hands, kitchen help, and others who work hard to keep the ranch running. The standard total is 15 percent of your bill; some ranches add this automatically to the total. For many of them, this is a way to fund their college education (or buy a winter in Belize).

FINDING A RANCH

An outstanding source for detailed information about guest ranches in Wyoming (and elsewhere) is **Gene Kilgore's Ranch Vacations,** by Eugene Kilgore (www.ranchweb.com).

The **Wyoming Dude Rancher's Association** (307/455-2084, www.wyomingdra.com) has a useful website with links to more than 30 dude ranches in the state. Other useful sources are the national **Dude Ranchers' Association** (307/587-2339, www.duderanch.org), along with www.guestranches.com and www.dude-ranches.com. Nearly all dude ranches have their own websites, filled with beautiful photos of their ranch, glowing reports from past clients, and details on the packages available and their costs.

---

of this book for details). Report fishing violations and illegal fish stocking by calling 800/442-4331.

Hunting

Wyoming game laws are enforced with a vengeance, so out-of-state hunters must be sure they know and obey the regulations thoroughly. Access to private land is often available only for a fee, and trespassers are subject to stringent prosecution. For guided hunts, contact the **Wyoming Outfitters and Guides Association** (307/527-7453, www.wyoga.org).

FOOD AND DRINK

Wyoming is not known for its haute cuisine. This is cattle country, the land of the free and the home on the range, where juicy steaks and

WYOMING LINGO

Absaroka: Alternatively pronounced ab-SOR-ka or ab-SOR-aka, the word means "People of the Large-Beaked Bird" (hence the name of the Crow Indians, who lived here). The Absaroka Mountains lie east of Yellowstone National Park.

Arapaho: The word is often spelled Arapahoe. An Indian tribe of Algonquin stock originally living on the Canadian plains, the Northern Arapaho now live on the Wind River Reservation. The name comes from a Crow Indian term meaning "Tattooed People." They call themselves simply "Our People."

bentonite: A special kind of clay that originates from volcanic ash, bentonite absorbs large amounts of water, increasing in volume by 30 percent. Bentonite is used in oil drilling, to line ponds, and even in candy bars. Wyoming is the nation's largest producer of this mineral.

booshway: The boss at a mountain-man rendezvous.

buck-and-rail fence: Consisting of X-shaped supports and connecting poles, this is the classic fence of Jackson Hole, where the soils proved too rocky for ranchers to dig postholes. The abundant lodgepole pines made fine fences. Today, buck-and-rail fences are built more for beauty than function, and they are becoming less and less common in an era of metal fence posts.

calcutta: The auctioning off of various rodeo teams or contestants; it's a popular way to wager on rodeo events. Rules vary.

cattle baron: A cattle owner with extensive holdings; it was primarily used during the heyday of the giant cattle spreads in the 1880s.

cattle guard: Although immediately obvious to most Westerners, cattle guards are virtually unknown on the East Coast. These wide metal grates are used where fence lines and roads meet; cattle and horses won't cross them but vehicles can do so easily.

chaps: Pronounced SHAPS; protective leather leg coverings, useful when riding horses through brush.

chiselers: Ground squirrels, also called "ground cougars." The lemmings of Wyoming, they seem to delight in waiting until the last minute and then dashing toward car wheels. Lots of them get nailed on dirt roads all across the state.

coup: Pronounced COO; a Plains Indian word that signified an act of great skill and daring, such as striking an enemy in the midst of a battle or performing some other deed of valor. "Counting coups" was similar to gaining today's military medals of honor. Those with many coups wore warbonnets with many feathers.

coyotes: Fans of these ubiquitous critters call them ky-O-tees, whereas those who regard them as "varmints" tend to pronounce the word KY-oats.

creek: Everyone knows what it is, but old-timers in Wyoming pronounce the word CRIK.

dead line: A line established by turn-of-the-20th-century cattlemen who feared competition from sheep. Those herders who brought sheep across the imaginary line risked death and the destruction of their flocks.

dogger: A rodeo term used for steer wrestlers; it originated from Will Pickett, an early wrestler who threw steers to the ground by biting their lips in the manner of a bulldog. The name stuck, even though the lip-biting part didn't.

dogie: A motherless calf.

dog-trot: A type of log cabin common on old Wyoming ranches. Two cabins were connected by a breezeway, making a favorite place for dogs to hang out on hot summer days. This cabin style actually originated in the southern Appalachians.

dude: This term has changed meaning through the years. Writer Nathaniel Burt called the dude "any fancy-pants young man who wore a boutonniere and parted his hair in the middle." Later, the term came to mean a wealthy easterner vacationing on a western ranch, in contradistinction to "tourists," who were viewed as an inferior species. Today, Wyoming's many dude ranches are more proletarian. The wealthy elite generally prefer the term "guest ranches," which are really luxury resorts with a few horses thrown in.

emigrants: The dictionary defines emigrants as people who leave one place to settle elsewhere, in contrast to immigrants, who come into a new place. Guess it all depends on your perspective, but for some reason folks heading west on the Oregon Trail were almost always called emigrants, not immigrants.

hazer: A rodeo term used in steer wrestling. It refers to a cowboy who rides beside the steer to keep it in position for the dogger.

hog ranch: An establishment of ill repute where booze, gambling, and loose women were the primary attractions. The most famous were near military forts in Wyoming, notably Fort Fetterman and Fort Laramie. The name is generally attributed to the appearance of the women but may also refer to the tiny, squalid rooms where they plied their trade. Author David Lavender called them places offering "the poorest whiskey and women in the west."

hooey: A tie used in calf-roping events at rodeos. Three of the calf's feet are wrapped with a piggin' string and completed with a half hitch.

jackalope: An antlered jackrabbit found most commonly in the vicinity of Douglas, Wyoming, but proliferating throughout the West.

maverick: An unbranded cow or calf of questionable ownership. The term originated from Samuel Maverick, owner of a two-million-acre Texas ranch in the 1840s. Because many of his cattle were never branded, cowboys coming across unbranded cattle on the open range would joke that they were Maverick's. Eventually the term was applied to all unbranded cattle.

piggin' string: A short piece of rope used to tie a hooey around the feet of a roped calf or steer at a rodeo.

rendezvous: French for "appointed place of meeting." Between 1825 and 1840 the annual rendezvous was the big shindig for Rocky Mountain trappers, Indians, and traders. Modern-day versions try to re-create this trading and partying atmosphere.

runnin' iron: An improvised branding iron used by cattle rustlers.

rustler: A cattle thief or someone accused of taking cattle from the cattle barons; during the Johnson County War the term actually became a badge of honor in parts of Wyoming. "Packing a long rope" became the common term applied to folks who rustled.

sage hen: Another name for the sage grouse, a common bird across Wyoming. This was also cowboy slang for women.

scoria: A red rock commonly used on Powder River Basin roads. It was formed when coal beds caught fire and burned underground, baking adjacent shale and sandstone to create a bright red slag. The red comes from iron oxide. *Clinker* is another term commonly used for scoria.

Shoshone: An Indian tribe on Wyoming's Wind River Reservation. The word is also frequently spelled Shoshoni, and it's generally pronounced with a long e at the end.

Sioux: The word was derived from a derogatory term meaning "enemy" or "snake" and used by the Chippewa Indians to describe the Indians who lived just to their west. The Sioux actually called themselves Dakota, meaning "alliance of friends."

trona: A mineral (sodium sesquicarbonate) used in glass, detergents, baking soda, and other products. It's mined in huge underground mines west of Green River.

varmint: Any animal you don't like; especially used for prairie dogs, ground squirrels, and coyotes.

wapiti: Pronounced WOP-a-tee. The Indian word for elk, it is occasionally used by biologists who consider it a more precise term.

RANGE ETIQUETTE

Wyoming's land ownership pattern includes many areas where private and public lands are intermingled in a complex checkerboard. This arrangement creates all sorts of problems for management of and access to public lands and for private owners. The conflict is most apparent in grazing country, where many ranchers jealously guard their land from trespassers for any reason. There are places where access to public lands is blocked by private landowners who have had problems in the past. A gate left open by a careless visitor or sheep sent running by a barking dog can quickly sour even the most generous rancher. Many of them are living a marginal existence already, so every little problem becomes magnified, especially if created by a city slicker – or even worse, a city slicker with California license plates and a "Save the Planet" bumper sticker.

Private boundaries are not always marked by No Trespassing signs, so it's a good idea to use a detailed and up-to-date map (such as those sold at BLM offices throughout the state) to be sure you are walking on public land. This is a particularly big issue during the fall hunting season, when many ranchers require a hefty "trespass fee" for access. If you *do* hunt despite warning signs, don't expect any help from the state because Game and Fish officers are supportive of private-property rights. Also note that you need to get permission from the landowner – public or private – before collecting anything, including fossils. Because we're talking about ethical issues, here's some more advice: Never ask a rancher how many cattle he has; it's like asking someone how much money he or she earns.

then sit back for a big hunk of apple pie. For breakfast, it's pretty much standard all-American fare accompanied by a dark brew that folks in these parts call coffee. Real cowboy coffee, made only over an open smoky fire and not available within 20 miles of any town, is a potent medicine, not advised for children or the weak-kneed. Check local outfitters for a "café au grounds" prescription. Of course, all of the larger Wyoming towns now also have at least one restaurant or drive-through outlet selling lattes and mochas. Unfortunately, you'll also find the standard fast-food outlets that are turning regional differences into a bland mediocrity of frozen burgers and whipped-shortening "milk shakes." No wonder obesity is on the rise—here, and in the rest of the country.

Actually, Wyoming food is not quite as uniformly bland as might be imagined, and travelers will discover innovative restaurants in Laramie, Buffalo, Casper, Cheyenne, Jackson, Cody, Lander, Rawlins, and Sheridan, and relatively authentic Mexican restaurants scattered around the state. Jackson really stands out, with an amazing variety of dining choices—from all-American barbecue to gourmet cuisine.

Typical Wyoming breakfasts cost $5–7, with lunches running $6–9. Dinner prices show a greater range, from simple $5 burgers to complete steak, prime rib, chicken, or seafood dinners for $12–20 (higher for fine-dining establishments).

Smoke with Your Fries?

Until the last few years, Wyoming restaurants were bastions of smokers, but times are changing and even local greasy spoons are starting to go smoke-free. The city of Laramie has banned smoking in all public places—including bars. The Wyoming Department of Health (307/777-6494, http://sad.state.wy.us/Tobacco) produces a guide to smoke-free dining.

On the Town

In many Wyoming towns, drinking and carousing hold as much interest as eating, espe-

the finest prime rib can be found in every Podunk town in the state. (The two best steak houses may well be in the don't-blink-or-you'll-miss-it town of Hudson.) If you don't like that, try chicken-fried steak, the house specialty at every truck stop and greasy spoon in Wyoming. Wash it down with a beer and cially on Friday and Saturday nights. Every burg of any size has its resident country-and-western band, and saloon dance floors fill with duded-up cowboys and cowgirls out for a night on the town. Many of these bands also play Eagles-style rock tunes for variety. The larger cities and tourist towns have sev-

eral nightclubs, some with disc jockeys, others with basic rock-and-roll fare. Don't expect a steep cover charge to get in the door; most places are free.

Small breweries and brewpubs are in Cheyenne, Jackson, Laramie, Lander, Pinedale, and Rock Springs.

GETTING INTO THE WILDERNESS

To get a real feel for Wyoming, you need to abandon your car, get away from the towns, and head out into the vast and undeveloped public lands. Wyoming's most popular backcountry areas are in the Wind River, Medicine Bow, and Big Horn mountains, along with the entire northwest corner of the state, including Yellowstone and Grand Teton national parks. The Yellowstone region contains one of the largest nearly natural ecosystems and some of the most remote country in the Lower 48.

Many campers prefer to use horses for longer trips, but backpacking is very popular on the shorter trails, especially in the Wind River Mountains and in the national parks. Backcountry permits are required only within Yellowstone and Grand Teton. It is, however, a good idea to check in at a local Forest Service ranger station to get a copy of the regulations because each place is different in such specifics as how far your tent must be from lakes and trails and whether wood fires are allowed. Be sure to take insect repellent along on any summertime trip because mosquitoes, deerflies, and horseflies can be quite thick, especially in July and early August.

TRAIL INFORMATION

Many guidebooks offer detailed hiking information on Yellowstone, Grand Teton, the Big Horns, or the Wind River Mountains (see *Suggested Reading*). An overall source is *The Hiker's Guide to Wyoming,* by Bill Hunger (www .globepequot.com). The National Park Service and the U.S. Forest Service can also provide specific trail information and post much of this information on their websites.

The **Continental Divide National Scenic Trail** (303/838-3760 or 888/909-2382, www .cdtrail.org) stretches for 3,100 miles from

Mexico to Canada, including a long section that crosses the Sierra Madre Range and the desolate Great Divide Basin, before traversing the Wind River Mountains, Teton Wilderness, and Yellowstone National Park. Not all sections have been completed, and the route cuts across some desolate and hot places, including the Red Desert.

BACKCOUNTRY ETHICS

Wyoming's wilderness areas represent places to escape the crowds, enjoy the beauty and peace of the countryside, and develop an understanding of nature. Unfortunately, as more and more people head into backcountry areas, these benefits are becoming endangered. To keep wild places wild, always practice "leave no trace" hiking and camping. This means using existing campsites and fire rings, locating your campsite well away from trails and streams, staying on designated trails, not cutting switchbacks, burning only dead and down wood, extinguishing all fires, washing dishes 200 feet from lakes and creeks, digging "catholes" at least 200 feet from lakes or streams, and hanging all food well above the reach of bears. Your tent site should be 100 yards from the food storage and cooking areas to reduce the likelihood of bear problems. Wood fires are not allowed in many areas, so be sure to bring along a portable gas stove. And, of course, haul your garbage out with you. Burning cans and tinfoil in the fire lessens their weight (and the odors that attract bears), but be sure to pick them out of the fire pit before you depart – and make sure that the fire is completely out.

For detailed leave-no-trace brochures on minimizing your impact and treating the land with respect, contact the **Leave No Trace Center** (800/332-4100, www.lnt.org).

HIKING TRAIL ETIQUETTE

Because horses are so commonly used in Wyoming, hikers should follow a few rules of courtesy. Horses and mules are not the brightest critters on this planet, and they can spook at the most inane thing, even a bush blowing in the breeze or a brightly colored hat. Hikers meeting a packstring should move several feet off the trail and not speak loudly or make any sudden moves. If you've ever seen what happens when just one mule in a string decides to act up, you'll appreciate the chaos that can result from sudden noises or movements. Anyone hiking with a dog should keep it well away from the stock and not let it bark. Last of all, never walk close behind a horse, unless you don't mind spending time in a hospital. Their kick is *definitely* worse than their bite.

ACCESSIBILITY

The Park Service's free **Golden Access Passport** allows blind and people with permanent disabilities entrance to all national parks, historic sites, and recreation areas. The passport also provides a 50 percent discount for camping in the parks. Pick them up from any park visitor center or entrance station.

Many Wyoming motels, hotels, and B&Bs have wheel-chair accessible rooms for guests, and both Yellowstone and Grand Teton national parks provide accessible facilities, lodging, and campsites, plus some paved trails.

Contact **Wheelchair Getaways of Montana** (406/227-6524 or 800/630-8267, www.wheelchairgetaways.com) for accessible van rentals in the Yellowstone area. Boulder-based **Wheelchair Getaways of Wyoming** (303/674-1498 or 800/238-6920, www.wheelchairgetaways.com) serves the Cheyenne area.

Health and Safety

A common annoyance for Wyoming travelers is insects, especially mosquitoes and blackflies. These are most prevalent in early summer in the mountains; by late August mosquito populations thin considerably. Use insect repellents containing DEET to help keep them away.

Beaver Fever

Although Wyoming's lakes and streams may appear clean, you could be risking a debilitating sickness by drinking the water without treating it first. The protozoan *Giardia lamblia* is found throughout the state, spread by both humans and animals (including beaver). The disease is curable with drugs, but it's always best to carry safe drinking water on any trip or to boil any water taken from creeks or lakes. Bringing water to a full boil for one minute is sufficient to kill *Giardia* and other harmful organisms. Another option is to use water filters available from back-packing stores. Note, however, that these may not filter out other organisms such as *Campylobacter jejuni,* bacteria that are just 0.2 microns in size. Chlorine and iodine are not always reliable, taste foul, and can be unhealthy. The latest is the MSR Miox (www.msrcorp.com, $130), a purifier that uses an oxidant (not filtration) to clean water with little aftertaste.

Hypothermia

Anyone who has spent much time in the outdoors will discover the dangers of exposure to cold, wet, and windy conditions. Even at temperatures well above freezing, hypothermia—the reduction of the body's inner core temperature—can prove fatal.

In the early stages, hypothermia causes uncontrollable shivering, followed by a loss of coordination, slurred speech, and then a rapid descent into unconsciousness and death. Always travel prepared for sudden changes in the weather. Wear clothing that insulates well and that holds its heat when wet. Wool and polypro are far better than cotton, and clothes should be worn in layers to provide better trapping of heat and a chance to adjust to conditions more easily. Always carry a wool hat because your head loses more heat than any other part of the body. Bring a waterproof shell to cut the wind. Put on rain gear *before* it starts raining; head back or set up camp when the weather looks threatening, and eat candy bars, keep active, or snuggle with a friend in a down bag to generate warmth.

If someone in your party begins to show signs of hypothermia, don't take any chances, even if the person denies needing help. Get the victim out of the wind, strip off his clothes, and put him in a dry sleeping bag on an insulating pad. Skin-to-skin contact is the best way to warm a hypothermic person, and that means you'll also need to strip and climb in the sleeping bag. Do not give the victim alcohol or hot drinks, and do not try to warm the person too quickly because it could lead to heart failure. Once the victim has recovered, get medical help as soon as possible. Actually, you're far better off keeping close tabs on everyone in the group and seeking shelter *before* exhaustion and hypothermia set in.

Frostbite

Frostbite is a less serious but painful problem for the cold-weather hiker. It is caused by direct exposure to the cold or by heat loss from wet socks and boots. Frostbitten areas will look white or gray, and they'll feel hard on the surface and softer underneath. The best way to warm the area is with other skin; put your hand under your arm, your feet on your friend's belly. Don't rub the affected area with snow or warm it near a fire. In cases of severe frostbite, in which the skin is white, hard, and numb, immerse the frozen area in water warmed to 99°F to 104°F until it's thawed. Avoid refreezing the frostbitten area. If you're a long way from medical assistance and the frostbite is extensive, it is better to keep the area frozen and get out of the woods for help;

thawing is painful, and it would be impossible to walk on a thawed foot.

West Nile Virus

Most people who are infected with West Nile virus show mild (or no) symptoms, but the disease can be fatal. The virus is transmitted through mosquito bites, and it can infect not just humans, but also horses, many species of birds, and other animals—with potentially devastating impacts on wildlife populations. Reduce your chance of infection by applying insect repellents containing DEET. (A higher concentration lasts longer, but there's no benefit in using DEET in concentrations over 50 percent.) You can also spray your clothing with the repellent, wear long-sleeved shirts and long pants, and stay indoors at dusk and dawn, when the mosquitoes are their most active. The Wyoming Department of Health (877/996-2483, www.badskeeter.org) has details on the virus.

Hantavirus

This potentially fatal respiratory disease is spread by rodents, particularly deer mice. Contact with them or their droppings can lead to such symptoms as fever, muscle aches, coughing, and difficulty breathing resulting from fluid buildup in the lungs within 1–5 weeks. Once the symptoms appear, the disease progresses quickly, leading to hospitalization within 24 hours. More than one-third of those who come down with hantavirus die, and in the last decade, it has killed at least three Wyoming residents, including a young woman in 2002. Avoid contact with rodents and their feces or urine to minimize your chances of infection. Campers should never sleep on bare ground and avoid cabins if you find signs of rodents. Fortunately, the disease is not contagious from person to person. For additional information, visit www.cdc.gov.

Ticks

Ticks can be a real bother in parts of Wyoming, particularly lower-elevation brushy and grassy areas in the spring and early summer. They drop onto unsuspecting humans and other animals to suck blood and can spread several potentially devastating diseases, including Rocky Mountain spotted fever, Ehrlichia, and Lyme disease. All of these diseases have been reported in low numbers throughout Wyoming.

Avoid ticks by tucking pant legs into boots and shirts into pants, using insect repellents containing DEET, and carefully inspecting your clothes while outside. Light-colored clothing and broad hats may also help. Check your body while hiking and immediately after the trip. If possible, remove ticks before they become embedded in your skin. If one does become attached, use tweezers to remove the tick, making sure to get the head. Apply a triple-antibiotic ointment such as Neosporin to the area, and monitor the bite area for two weeks.

Lyme disease typically shows up as a large red spot with a lighter bull's-eye center and often causes muscle aches, fatigue, headache, and fever. Get medical help immediately if you show these symptoms after a tick bite. Fortunately, the disease can usually be treated with antibiotics. If untreated, it can cause a facial nerve palsy, memory loss, arthritis, heart damage, and other problems. A relatively effective vaccine has been developed for Lyme disease, but it requires a one-year regimen of doses and is expensive; check with your doctor for specifics. In Wyoming, where the disease is relatively uncommon, the vaccine is probably not warranted, and it may give a false sense of security because ticks can still spread other—and more dangerous—diseases. No vaccinations are available against either Rocky Mountain spotted fever or Erlichia, both of which sometimes kill people. The best action is to prevent tick bites in the first place. For more on tick-borne diseases, see the Harvard Medical School's website at www.intelihealth.com.

SAFETY IN BEAR COUNTRY

Bears seem to bring out conflicting emotions in people. The first is an almost gut reaction of fear and trepidation: What if the bear attacks me? But then comes that other urge: What will my friends say when they see these *incredible* bear photos? Both of these reactions can lead

to problems in bear country. "Bearanoia" is a justifiable fear but can easily be taken to such an extreme that one avoids going outdoors at all for fear of running into a bear. The "I want to get close-up shots of that bear and her cubs" attitude can lead to a bear attack. The middle ground incorporates a knowledge of and respect for bears with a sense of caution that keeps you alert for danger without letting fear rule your wilderness travels. Nothing is ever completely safe in this world, but with care you can avoid most of the common pitfalls that lead to bear encounters.

Avoiding Bear Hugs

Surprise bear encounters are rare but frightening experiences. There were just 23 bear-caused injuries in Yellowstone National Park between 1980 and 1997—one injury for every 2.1 million visitors. Avoid unexpected encounters with bears by letting them know you're there. Most bears hear or smell you long before you realize their presence, and they hightail it away. Surprising a bear, especially a sow with cubs, is the last thing you want to do in the backcountry. Before heading out, check at a local ranger station to see whether there have been recent bear encounters. If you discover an animal carcass, be extremely alert because a bear may be nearby and may attack anything that appears to threaten its food. Get away from such areas. Do not hike at night or dusk, when bears can be especially active. Safety is also in numbers: The more of you hiking together, the more likely a bear is to sense you and stay away.

Make noise in areas of dense cover or when coming around blind spots on trails. If you're unable to see everything around you for at least 50 yards, warn any hidden animals by talking, singing, clapping your hands, tapping a cup, or rattling a can of pebbles. Some people tie bells to their packs for this purpose, but others regard this as an annoyance to fellow hikers. In general, bells are probably of little value because the sound does not carry far, and they might actually attract bears. If bears can't hear you coming, don't be shy—make a lot of noise! It might seem a bit foolish, but loud voices may prevent

BLACK BEAR

No Hump

Straight Profile

3¾ in.   3½ in.   7 in.

GRIZZLY BEAR

Hump

Dish Face Profile

5½ in.   5¼ in.   9¾ in.

BOB RACE

Note: Color can't be used for identification.

an encounter of the furry kind. Unfortunately, it will probably scare off other animals, so you're not likely to see many critters, and other hikers may not appreciate the noise. Personally, I reserve yelling "Hey Bear!" for situations where I'm walking in brushy bear country with low visibility and have to contend with other noises such as a nearby creek. I wouldn't recommend doing so while walking the paved path around Old Faithful Geyser; you might get carried off in a straitjacket.

Hunters and photographers are the main recipients of bear hugs. Never under any circumstances approach a bear, even if it appears to be asleep. Move away if you see bear cubs, especially if one comes toward you, because mom is almost always close by. Dogs create dangerous situations by barking and exciting bears—leave yours at home (dogs are not allowed in the backcountry in national parks).

Never leave food around for bears. Not only is this illegal, but it also trains the bears to associate people with free food. Fed bears become garbage bears, and that almost inevitably means that the bear gets killed. Remember, bears are dangerous wild animals. This is *their* country, not a zoo. By going in you accept the risk—and thrill—of meeting a bear.

At the Campsite

Before camping, take a look around the area to see if there are recent bear tracks or scat and to make sure you're not on a game trail. Bears are attracted to odors of all sorts, including food, horse feed, soap, toothpaste, perfume, and deodorants. Your cooking, eating, and food storage area should be at least 50 yards away from your tent. Keep your campsite clean and avoid such smelly items as tuna, ham, sausage, and bacon; freeze-dried food is light and relatively odorless (although also relatively tasteless). Store food away from your sleeping area in air-tight containers or several layers of plastic bags, and be sure to hang all food and other items that bears may smell at least 12 feet off the ground and four feet from tree trunks. Bring 50 feet of rope for this purpose. Tie two cups or pots to it so you will hear if it's moved. Some Forest Service and Park Service wilderness areas provide food storage poles at campsites. In the Teton and Bridger wilderness areas, you can also rent bear-resistant backpacker food tubes or horse panniers from Forest Service offices. Camping stores in Jackson, Cody, and elsewhere sell similar containers.

Researchers have reported no evidence that either sexual activity or menstrual odors precipitate bear attacks. It is, however, wise for menstruating women to use tampons instead of pads and to store soiled tampons in double ziplock bags above the reach of bears.

Encounters of the Furry Kind

If you do happen to suddenly encounter a bear and it sees you, try to stay calm and not make any sudden moves. Do not run because you could not possibly outrun a bear; they can exceed 40 mph for short distances. Bear researchers now suggest that quickly climbing a tree is also not a wise way to escape bears and may actually incite an attack. Instead, make yourself visible by moving into the open so the bear will (you hope) identify you as a human and not something to eat. Never stare directly at a bear. Sometimes dropping an item such as a hat or jacket will distract the bear, and talking calmly (easier said than done) also seems to have some value in convincing bears that you're a human. If the bear sniffs the air or stands on its hind legs it is probably trying to identify you. When it does, it will usually run away. If a bear woofs and postures, don't imitate—this is a challenge. Keep retreating. Most bear charges are also bluffs; the bear will often stop short and amble off.

If a **grizzly bear** actually attacks, hold your ground and freeze. It may well be a bluff charge, with the bear halting at the last second. If the bear does not stop its attack, curl up face-

down on the ground in a fetal position with your hands wrapped behind your neck and your elbows tucked over your face. Your backpack may help protect you somewhat. Remain still even if you are attacked because sudden movements may incite further attacks. It takes an enormous amount of courage to do this, but often a bear will only sniff or nip you and leave. The injury you might sustain would be far less than if you tried to resist. After the attack, prevent further attacks by staying down on the ground until the grizzly has left the area.

Bear authorities now recommend against dropping to the ground if you are attacked by a **black bear** because they tend to be more aggressive in such situations and are more likely to prey on humans. If a black bear attacks, fight back with whatever weapons are at hand; large rocks and branches can be surprisingly effective deterrents, as can yelling and shouting. (This, of course, assumes you can tell black bears from brown bears. If you can't, have someone who knows—such as a park ranger—explain the differences before you head into the backcountry.)

In the rare event of a **nighttime bear attack** in your tent, defend yourself *very* aggressively. Never play dead under such circumstances because the bear probably views you as prey and may give up if you make it a fight. Before going to bed, try to plan escape routes should you be attacked in the night, and be sure to have a flashlight and pepper spray handy. Keeping your sleeping bag partly unzipped also allows the chance to escape should a bear attempt to drag you away. If someone is attacked in a tent near you, yelling and throwing rocks or sticks may drive the bear away.

Protecting Yourself

Cayenne pepper sprays (sold in camping goods stores) have sometimes proven useful in fending off bear attacks. Note, however, that these "bear mace" sprays are effective only at close range (10–30 feet). This is particularly true in open country where winds quickly disperse the mist or may blow it back in your own face. Another problem with bear mace is that you

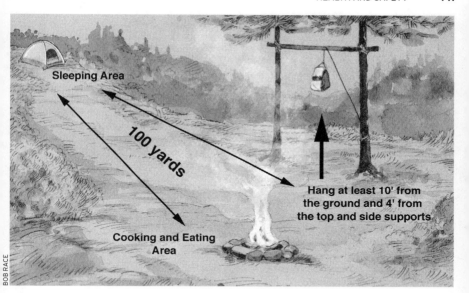

Sleeping Area

100 yards

Cooking and Eating
Area

Hang at least 10' from
the ground and 4' from
the top and side supports

BOB RACE

cannot carry it aboard commercial jets because of the obvious dangers if a canister explodes. If you do carry a pepper spray, make sure it is readily available by carrying it in a holster on your belt or across your chest. Also be sure to test-fire it to see how the spray carries. Although they *are* better than nothing, pepper sprays are not a cure-all or a replacement for caution in bear country. It's far better to avoid bear confrontations in the first place.

A good source for up-to-date bear safety information is the Yellowstone National Park website, www.nps.gov/yell. Two recommended safety books are *Bear Attacks: Their Causes and Avoidance,* by Stephen Herrero (www.ly-onspress.com), and *Bear Aware: Hiking and Camping in Bear Country,* by Bill Schneider (www.globepequot.com).

BACKCOUNTRY SAFETY TIPS

The most important part of enjoying—and surviving—the backcountry is to be prepared. Know where you're going; get maps, camping information, and weather and trail conditions

from a ranger before setting out. Don't hike alone. Two are better than one, and three are better than two; if one gets hurt, one person can stay with the injured party and one can go for help. Bring more than enough food so hunger won't cause you to continue when weather conditions say stop. Tell someone where you're going and when you'll be back.

Always carry the 10 essentials: map, compass, water bottle, first-aid kit, flashlight, matches (or lighter) and fire starter, knife, extra clothing (a full set, in case you fall in a stream) including rain gear, extra food, and sunglasses—especially if you're hiking on snow. To this list, you might want to add a cell phone. Most backcountry areas have no service, but in an emergency you might be able to find a high point where the phone can hit an antenna.

Check your ego at the trailhead; stop for the night when the weather gets bad, even if it's 2 P.M., or head back. And don't press on when you're exhausted; tired hikers are sloppy hikers, and even a small injury can be disastrous in the woods.

Information and Services

MONEY

Travelers checks (in U.S. dollars) are accepted without charge in most stores and businesses around Wyoming. It's not a good idea to travel with travelers checks in non-U.S. currency; they are accepted only at certain banks and are a time-consuming hassle. If you do arrive with pounds, yen, or Euros, several banks in Jackson, along with the park hotels inside Yellowstone, will exchange foreign currency for greenbacks.

Tipping is expected for many services, with 15 percent or more for wait staff at restaurants. In addition, tips are appreciated for other personal services, including river-rafting guides, taxi drivers, dude ranch employees, and hotel maids. The amount varies widely, but it is common for a wildlife tour guide to receive a $20 tip at the end of a day's assistance.

When traveling in Wyoming, I pay for expenses by credit card whenever possible, but I also keep an automated teller machine (ATM) card as a backup. You'll find ATMs in all the larger towns and increasingly in even the most remote Wyoming settlements. In this book, I've mentioned ATM locations in the smaller towns, but new ones are added all the time. Virtually all Wyoming ATMs tack on a charge—usually $1.50 per transaction—to your own bank's fees, making this an expensive way to get cash.

The major credit cards, especially Visa and MasterCard, are accepted almost everywhere. This is probably the easiest way to travel, especially if you can get airline mileage credit at the same time. The miles can quickly add up if you make all of your purchases this way, but so can your credit card bill!

TOURIST INFORMATION

Chamber of commerce information centers are described for each town in this book. You'll find large **state information centers** near Cheyenne, Evanston, Jackson, Laramie, Pine Bluffs, Sheridan, and Sundance.

For a helpful overall guide to Wyoming, along with a listing of events, chamber of commerce offices, and lodging and camping places, request a copy of the free **Wyoming Vacation Directory** from the Wyoming Travel and Tourism Division (307/777-7777 or 800/225-5996, www.wyomingtourism.org). Both summer and winter versions are available. It also has free state maps, or pick them up at any local visitor center.

FEDERAL AND STATE OFFICES

The U.S. government owns more than 30 million acres within Wyoming, primarily in national forests, national parks, and BLM lands. In addition, the State of Wyoming owns another 3.8 million acres, including more than 118,000 acres of state park lands.

National Park Service

The National Park Service manages 2.3 million acres in Wyoming, including:
Grand Teton National Park (307/739-3399, www.nps.gov/grte);
Yellowstone National Park (307/344-7381, www.nps.gov/yell);
Bighorn Canyon National Recreation Area (307/548-2251, www.nps.gov/bica);
Devils Tower National Monument (307/467-5283, www.nps.gov/deto);
Fossil Butte National Monument (307/877-4455, www.nps.gov/fobu);
Fort Laramie National Historic Site (307/837-2221, www.nps.gov/fola).

Forest Service

The U.S. Forest Service manages 8.7 million acres in Wyoming and has ranger district offices in Afton, Big Piney, Buffalo, Cody, Douglas, Dubois, Encampment, Evanston, Greybull, Jackson, Kemmerer, Lander, Laramie, Lovell, Moran, Mountain View, Newcastle, Pinedale, Saratoga, Sheridan, Sundance, and Worland. The following national forests cover parts of the state:

Bighorn National Forest (Sheridan, 307/672-0751, www.fs.fed.us/r2/bighorn);
Black Hills National Forest (Sundance, 307/283-1361, www.fs.fed.us/r2/blackhills);
Bridger-Teton National Forest (Jackson, 307/739-5500, www.fs.fed.us/r4/btnf);
Flaming Gorge National Recreation Area (Ashley National Forest, Manila, Utah, 435/784-3445, www.fs.fed.us/r4/ashley);
Medicine Bow-Routt National Forest (Laramie, 307/745-2300 or 800/877-9965, www.fs.fed.us/r2/mbr);
Shoshone National Forest (Cody, 307/527-6241, www.fs.fed.us/r2/shoshone);
Caribou-Targhee National Forest (Idaho Falls, Idaho, 208/524-7500, www.fs.fed.us/r4/caribou);
Wasatch-Cache National Forest (Evanston, 307/789-3194, www.fs.fed.us/r4/wcnf).

Bureau of Land Management

Although not well known by the general public, the BLM is one of the biggest landholders in America. In Wyoming, the agency manages nearly 18 million acres. The **Wyoming State BLM Office** (307/775-6256, www.wy.blm.gov) is in Cheyenne, with local offices in Buffalo, Casper, Cheyenne, Cody, Kemmerer, Lander, Newcastle, Pinedale, Rawlins, Rock Springs, and Worland.

Fish and Wildlife Service

The U.S. Fish and Wildlife Service has two staffed refuges in Wyoming: the **National Elk Refuge** (307/733-9212, http://nationalelkrefuge.fws.gov) in Jackson and **Seedskadee National Wildlife Refuge** (307/875-2187, http://seedskadee.fws.gov) northwest of Green River. Wyoming's other two refuges are **Hutton Lake National Wildlife Refuge** near Laramie and **Pathfinder National Wildlife Refuge** near Casper.

State Parks

Wyoming's **Department of State Parks and Historic Sites** (307/777-6303, http://wyoparks.state.wy.us) maintains 26 parks, historic sites, recreation areas, and archaeo-logical sites scattered across the state. Most of these charge day-use fees, or you can buy an annual day-use pass for $40 ($25 for Wyoming residents).

COMMUNICATIONS AND MEDIA
Newspapers

The **Wyoming Press Association** (www.wyopress.org) has a complete listing of newspapers in the state on its website. The *Casper Star-Tribune* (www.casperstartribune.net) is Wyoming's only statewide paper, and the letters to the editor provide a great way to check the pulse of Wyoming. They fill several pages every day and are sometimes quite amusing.

Other papers with daily editions include *Jackson Hole News and Guide* (www.jh-newsandguide.com), Cheyenne's *Wyoming Tribune-Eagle* (www.wyomingnews.com), the *Laramie Boomerang* (www.laramieboomerang.com), the *Gillette News-Record* (www.gillettenewsrecord.com), *Rawlins Daily Times, Riverton Ranger* (www.dailyranger.com), **Rock Springs Daily Rocket-Miner** (www.rocketminer.com), **Sheridan Press** (www.thesheridanpress.com), and Worland's *Northern Wyoming Daily News* (www.wyodaily.com). Most other Wyoming towns of any size have their own weekly papers; there's even one for Lingle (pop. 500).

Radio

If you like country-and-western music, you'll love traveling through Wyoming, where the radio dial is packed with country stations playing mournful songs about leaving small towns for greener pastures, hard times, loose women, and truck-driving men. My favorite has to be the one that begins:

> *You're the first thing that I thought of when I thought I'd drink you off my mind.*

Pretty much says it all.

Wyoming Public Radio (800/729-5897, www.wyomingpublicradio.net) is based in Laramie, with repeaters throughout the state

RODEO EVENTS

STEER WRESTLING

Steer wrestling, or bulldogging, involves leaping from a quarter horse onto the back of a 700-pound Mexican steer running at 25 miles per hour, grabbing his horns, and wrestling him to the ground. If you think that sounds easy, try it some time! Steer wrestling originated in 1903, when Bill Pickett, a black Texas cowboy (many early cowboys were black), jumped on the back of an ornery steer, grabbed its horns, bent over its head, and bit the steer's lower lip like an attacking bulldog. Soon he was repeating the stunt for the 101 Ranch Wild West Show. Others copied this feat, and although the lip-biting part has long since disappeared, the name bulldogging has stuck.

Steer wrestling is a complex endeavor involving two men: a dogger and a hazer. When the steer hurtles into the arena, the two spur their horses in quick pursuit, with the hazer trying to force the steer to run straight ahead while the dogger gets into position to leap onto the steer's horns and wrestle him to the ground with his feet and head facing the same direction. Because they are competing with other doggers on time, every second counts. Good doggers can get a steer down in less than seven seconds.

CALF ROPING

Calf roping originated in the Old West when ropers would pull down a calf and quickly tie it up for branding. Today, this is the most competitive of all rodeo events, and there is often big money for the winners. Calf ropers chase a 300-pound calf on their expertly trained horses, rope it, and then quickly throw it on its side. The piggin' string is wrapped around three ankles and secured with a half hitch ("hooey"), and then the calf is allowed to try to break free. If it can't within six seconds, the time stands and an untie man rides in to free the calf. Time is of the essence in calf roping, and a roper's horse is his most valuable asset. The best horses are in high demand and are often rented to other riders for a cut of any winnings.

STEER ROPING

The most controversial of all rodeo contests is steer roping, an event banned from most rodeos because it is so hard on the animals. Cheyenne Frontier Days is one place where you can still see it. The procedure is essentially the same as calf roping, but with a much larger animal. When the 700-pound steer is jerked back by the rope and thrown down with a thud, you can almost feel the impact. Fortunately, injuries to the tough old steers are uncommon.

SADDLE BRONC RIDING

When you say the word "rodeo," many people immediately think of saddle bronc riding. The oldest of all rodeo sports, it originated in cowboys' attempts to train wild horses. Rodeo saddle bronc riding is more complex than this, however; it requires a special "association" saddle and dulled spurs and is played by precise rules. It is a judged event, with points taken away for not being in the correct position or in control. The bronc is saddled up in the chute (a fenced-in enclosure along the edge of the arena) and the rider climbs on, grabbing a thick hemp rope in one hand and sinking his boots into the stirrups. When the gate opens the bronc goes wild, trying to throw the rider off. The smooth back-and-forth motion of a good saddle bronc rider makes it appear that he is sitting atop a rocking chair. Rides last only eight seconds (leading to lots of ribald cowboy jokes); when the horn sounds, a pickup man rides alongside the bronc and the rider slides onto the other horse.

BAREBACK BRONC RIDING

Bareback riding is a relatively recent sport, having arrived on the scene in the 1920s. The rules are similar to those for saddle bronc riding, but the cowboy rides with a minimum of equipment—no stirrups and no reins. A small leather rigging held on by a leather strap around the horse is topped with a suitcase-like handle. A second wool-lined strap goes around the flank of the horse to act as an irritant so that he bucks more. The cowboy holds on with one hand and bounces back and forth in a rocking motion, an effort akin to trying to juggle bowling pins while surfing a big wave. Eight seconds later it's over and a pickup man comes in to rescue the rider – if he hasn't been thrown to the ground.

BULL RIDING AND RODEO CLOWNS

Bull riding is in a class of danger all its own. Unlike a bronc, which just wants that man off its back, a bull wants to get even. When a bull rider is thrown off (and this is most of the time, even with the best riders), the bull immediately goes on the attack, trying to gore or trample him. Many bull riders are seriously injured and some die when hit by this 2,000 pounds of brute force. There are no saddles in bull riding, just a piece of thick rope wrapped around the bull's chest, the free end wrapped tightly around the rider's hand. A cowbell hangs at the bottom of this contraption to annoy the bull even more. When the chute opens, all hell breaks loose as the bull does everything it possibly can to throw his rider off – spinning, kicking, jumping, and running against the fence.

If the rider hangs on for the required eight seconds (style isn't very important), the next battle begins – getting out of the way of one very angry bull. Here the rodeo clowns come in. Dressed in bright red-and-white shirts and baggy pants, they look like human Raggedy Andy dolls. In reality they are moving targets. Clowns use every trick in the book – climbing into padded barrels that the bulls butt against, weaving across the arena, mocking the bulls with matador capes, and simply running for their lives to reach the fence ahead of the bull. Frequently, two clowns work in tandem to create confusion, one acting as the barrel man and the other as a roving target. The

rodeo clown also plays another role, that of entertainer between events. A clown's stock of supplies includes rubber chickens, trick mules, pantomime jokes with the announcer, and anything else that might keep folks from getting restless.

In a few of the larger rodeos there are clown "bullfights," in which a clown is pitted against a bull in a specially constructed small arena. He taunts the bull in every possible way, running past and around him, touching him, and maybe even leaping over him – all while trying to stay out of the way of those horns and hooves. These hijinks last only 45 seconds, but that seems like an eternity of danger. No wonder they call this the suicide sport!

OTHER EVENTS

One of the funniest of all rodeo events is the **wild horse race,** a zany event that since 1897 has ended each day at Cheyenne Frontier Days. Twelve teams of three cowboys try to rope, saddle, and then race a collection of the wildest horses imaginable. If they manage to get on the broncs, their next problem is convincing the horses to run around the 0.5-mile track in the right direction. It seems the definition of bedlam, with horses breaking loose and starting off in opposite directions, crashing into mounted riders and other horses. For sheer chaos, wild horse races would even put a Democratic Convention to shame.

Barrel racing – the only female-dominated event – is found at nearly every rodeo and consists of a triangular course around three barrels arranged 100 feet apart. The event requires riding a fast horse in a set pattern around these barrels, trying not to knock any over. The fastest time wins.

Many rodeos also have what is called a **calf scramble** – featuring dozens of children from the stands chasing a calf to get a ribbon off its tail – and a **colt race,** in which young colts are let loose in a race toward their mares. Both events are real crowd-pleasers.

providing in-depth morning and evening news from National Public Radio, along with Wyoming news reports and the *World Cafe* for eclectic music. It's a vast improvement over the Rush Limbaugh broadsides, Top 40 hit stations, and recycled rock pabulum found elsewhere on the radio dial.

WWWYOMING

Internet addresses are listed in the text for local chamber of commerce offices and a multitude of businesses. The official Wyoming state homepage is www.state.wy.us, and the state's tourism homepage is www.wyomingtourism.org.

Most libraries have computers with free Internet access; you'll find a listing of Wyoming libraries and links to their homepages at www.publiclibraries.com/wyoming.htm. In addition, the larger towns generally have Internet cafés or businesses with computer terminals for rent by the hour. More and more places also offer free wireless Internet (Wi-Fi) for laptop owners. These include many of the larger hotels and motels, plus cafés and coffeehouses in some Wyoming towns. Find updated listings on websites such as www.wififreespot.com.

Post Offices

Post offices generally open between 7 A.M. and 9 A.M. and close between 5 P.M. and 6 P.M.; only a few are open on Saturday. After hours, the outer doors usually remain open so you can go in to buy stamps from the machines. Some drug or card stores also operate postal substations where you can buy stamps or mail packages within the United States (you'll have to go to a real post office for mailing to foreign addresses or for other special services). Many grocery-store checkout counters also sell books of stamps with no markup.

RESOURCES

Suggested Reading

Note: Several of the following books are now out of print. You can find many of them in Wyoming libraries, or check the web for special orders or rare book auctions. Websites such as www.amazon.com, www.barnesandnoble.com, and others will also search used bookstores for out-of-print titles. **High Plains Press** (800/552-7819, www.highplainspress.com) specializes in niche books on Wyoming, primarily historical volumes.

DESCRIPTION AND TRAVEL

Anderson, Susan. *Living in Wyoming: Settling for More.* New York: Fodor's Travel Publications, www.fodors.com, 1990. A witty and insightful book about the people of Wyoming. Outstanding photos by Zbigniew Bzdak.

Burt, Nathaniel. *Wyoming.* New York: Fodor's Travel Publications, www.fodors.com, 2002. Provides a tour of Wyoming and its historical attractions. Photography by Don Pitcher.

Cook, Jeannie (ed.). *Buffalo Bill's Town in the Rockies: A Pictorial History of Cody, Wyoming.* Cody, WY: Park County Historical Society, 1996. A photographic visit to Cody's interesting past.

Ehrlich, Gretel. *A Match to the Heart.* New York: Pantheon Books, www.randomhouse.com, 1994. The harrowing story of the author's long recovery after being struck by lightning while working on the Wyoming range.

Ehrlich, Gretel. *The Solace of Open Spaces.* New York: Viking Penguin, www.penguinputnam.com, 1985. A stunningly beautiful collection of observations and stories about ranch life in Wyoming from one of America's finest writers.

Kilgore, Gene. *Gene Kilgore's Ranch Vacations.* Emeryville, CA: Avalon Travel Publishing, www.travelmatters.com, 2005. The definitive guide to dude and guest ranches in Wyoming and the rest of North America. Includes detailed, up-to-date descriptions of the best places to be a city-slicker cowboy.

Lewis, Dan. *8,000 Miles of Dirt: A Backroad Travel Guide to Wyoming.* Casper, WY: Hawks Book Co., 1992. Describes dozens of the state's most enjoyable back roads in a folksy but not always informative manner. (Example: The chapter on the Outlaw Cave drive doesn't bother to mention the cave's most famous inhabitant, Butch Cassidy!)

McClure, Michael. *Camping Wyoming.* Atlantic City, WY: WigRaf Publishing, www.campwyo.com, 1999. An amazingly detailed guide to virtually every possible Wyoming camping spot.

Munn, Debra D. *Ghosts on the Range: Eerie True Tales of Wyoming.* Boulder, CO: Pruett Publishing, www.pruettpublishing.com, 1991. A popular book filled with ghost stories from across the state.

Parent, Laurence. *Scenic Driving Wyoming.* Guilford, CT: Globe Pequot Press, www.globepequot.com, 1997. The best and most complete guide to scenic roads in Wyoming.

Pitcher, Don. *Moon Yellowstone and Grand Teton.* Emeryville, CA: Avalon Travel Publishing, www.moon.com, 2006. The companion guide to this one, with in-depth coverage for Wyoming's most-visited corner.

Roberts, Steven L., David L. Roberts, and Phil Roberts. *Wyoming Almanac.* Laramie, WY: Skyline West Press, 2001. Packed with almost 500 pages of Wyoming trivia, including such things as the average market price for Wyoming low-sulfur coal and the number of cabooses now used for other purposes. Hard to plow through it all (no index), but there are some real gems buried in this avalanche of facts.

Urbanek, Mae. *Wyoming Place Names.* Missoula, MT: Mountain Press Publishing, www.mountainpress.com, 1988. An excellent sourcebook for the names of everything from Abiathar Peak to the town of Zenith.

Williamson, Chilton, Jr. *Roughnecking It.* New York: Simon and Schuster, www.simonsays.com, 1982. A funny, insightful, and disturbing portrait of Wyoming during the oil-boom years of the early 1980s. Gonzo journalism at its best. Out of print.

Work Projects Administration. *Wyoming: A Guide to Its History, Highways, and People.* Lincoln, NE: University of Nebraska Press, www.unp.udl.edu, 1981. Reprint of a Depression-era guide to Wyoming originally printed in 1940, this classic guide still makes fascinating reading. Out of print.

GEOLOGY AND GEOGRAPHY

Blackstone, D. L., Jr. *Traveler's Guide to the Geology of Wyoming.* Laramie, WY: Geological Survey of Wyoming, www.wsgsweb.uwyo.edu, 1988. An excellent overview of Wyoming's geological history and how to see it in today's landscapes.

Largeson, David R., and Darwin R. Spearing. *Roadside Geology of Wyoming.* Missoula, MT: Mountain Press Publishing, www.mountainpress.com, 1988. Wyoming is perhaps the most geologically interesting of all the states. This is an invaluable road guide for anyone wanting to know more about geology without resorting to dense textbooks.

McPhee, John. *Basin and Range.* New York: Farrar, Straus and Giroux, www.fsgbooks.com, 1980. The book details how the landscape of Wyoming was created. Only this Pulitzer Prize–winning author could turn the complex story of plate tectonics into such an easy-to-read volume.

McPhee, John. *Rising from the Plains.* New York: The Noonday Press, 1986. A delightful intertwining of the story of Wyoming's complex geology and the life of its preeminent geologist, David Love.

Robinson, Charles. *Geology of Devils Tower.* Devils Tower, WY: Devils Tower Natural History Association, 1995. The definitive geologic story of this famous national monument.

FICTION

Ehrlich, Gretel. *Heart Mountain.* New York: Viking Penguin, www.penguinputnam.com, 1988. A touching novel about life in the Heart Mountain Relocation Camp near Cody, the forced home for hundreds of Japanese Americans during World War II.

Nye, Bill. *Bill Nye's Western Humor.* Lincoln, NE: University of Nebraska Press, www.unp.unl.edu, 1968. A collection of delightfully wry essays by one of America's best-known 19th-century humorists. Out of print.

Proulx, Annie. *Close Range: Wyoming Stories.* New York: Scribner, www.simonsays.com, 1999. Pulitzer Prize–winning novelist Annie Proulx now lives in Wyoming, and this book takes on the characters in her home state. Wyomingites may take umbrage at her unflattering portrayals, but take these stories for what they are—fiction. A good read.

Wister, Owen. *The Virginian.* Originally published in 1902 and now available from various publishers. The classic Western novel that established the cowboy hero and the lure of Wyoming.

BIOGRAPHY

Alter, Cecil J. *Jim Bridger.* Norman, OK: University of Oklahoma Press, www.oupress .com, 1979. The incredible story of the most famous of all mountain men.

Anonymous. *The Sweet Smell of Sagebrush: A Prisoner's Diary 1903–1912.* Rawlins, WY: Friends of the Old Penitentiary, 1990. This wonderful small volume contains the writings of an "anonymous" criminal (John Kirby), who served four terms in the Rawlins penitentiary for horse stealing and other crimes. It not only provides descriptions of his many escapades outside the law but also opens a window on the criminal mind.

Killoren, John J. *Come Blackrobe, DeSmet and the Indian Tragedy.* Norman, OK: University of Oklahoma Press, www.oupress.com, 1995. The story of Jesuit missionary Pierre Jean DeSmet, who spent his life in a futile attempt to protect the Plains Indians from the Manifest Destiny of American culture.

Olsen, Jack. *Doc: The Rape of the Town of Lovell.* New York: Dell, www.randomhouse .com, 1990. The true but hard-to-believe story of a respected physician who raped dozens of women in this small, religious town.

Pointer, Larry. *In Search of Butch Cassidy.* Norman, OK: University of Oklahoma Press, www.oupress.com, 1989. A thoroughly researched book that seems to show that Butch Cassidy's death in South America was a ruse and that he died much later in Seattle.

Rosa, Joseph G., and Robin May. *Buffalo Bill and His Wild West.* Lawrence, KS: University Press of Kansas, www.kansaspress.ku.edu, 1989. One of the newer books on Buffalo Bill, with a somewhat revisionist take on his life and times. Rich in detail on Cody's Wild West show.

Russell, Don. *The Lives and Legends of Buffalo Bill.* Norman, OK: University of Oklahoma Press, www.oupress.com, 1979. The most complete biography on the life of Buffalo Bill Cody.

Woods, L. Milton. *Moreton Frewen's Western Adventures.* Boulder, CO: Roberts Rinehart, www.roberts-rinehart.com, 1986. The strange tale of a wealthy British adventurer who made and lost his (and other folks') fortunes in Wyoming. Out of print.

OUTDOOR RECREATION

Additional recreation titles are listed under the headings for Jackson Hole and Grand Teton National Park and Yellowstone National Park.

Birkby, Jeff. *Touring Montana and Wyoming Hot Springs.* Guilford, CT: Globe Pequot Press, www.globepequot.com, 1999.

Fanselow, Julie. *Traveling the Oregon Trail.* Guilford, CT: Globe Pequot Press, www .globepequot.com, 2001.

Graham, Kenneth L. *Camping Wyoming and the Black Hills.* Guilford, CT: Globe Pequot Press, www.globepequot.com, 2001.

Graham, Kenneth Lee. *Fishing Wyoming.* Guilford, CT: Globe Pequot Press, www.globepequot.com, 1998. A 300-page tome that goes far beyond the standard coverage of Yellowstone and Jackson Hole.

Guillmette, Richard, Renée Carrier, and Steve Gardiner. *Devils Tower National Monument: A Climber's Guide.* Devils Tower, WY: Devils Tower Natural History Association, 1995. A detailed guide to one of the most varied and enjoyable rock faces in Wyoming.

Herrero, Stephen. *Bear Attacks: Their Causes and Avoidance.* Guilford, CT: The Lyons Press, www.lyonspress.com, 2002. An authoritative volume on the lives of bears and staying safe in their country.

Hunger, Bill. *Hiking Wyoming.* Guilford, CT: Globe Pequot Press, www.globepequot.com,

2003. A fine, detailed book that describes 75 different hikes in all parts of the state.

Kelsey, Joe. *Climbing and Hiking in the Wind River Mountains.* Guilford, CT: Globe Pequot Press, www.globepequot.com, 1996. Accurate information on most of the hiking trails and descriptions of hundreds of technical climbs.

Lewis, Dan. *The Floater's Guide to Wyoming Rivers.* Douglas, WY: Wyoming Naturalist, 1991. Filled with details on 27 Wyoming rivers and 1,700 miles of river trips.

Mitchell, Finis. *Wind River Trails.* Salt Lake City, UT: University of Utah Press, www.upress.utah.edu, 1999. A folksy, inexpensive guide by a man who hiked this country for 80 years.

Molvar, Erik. *Hiking Wyoming's Cloud Peak Wilderness.* Guilford, CT: Globe Pequot Press, www.globepequot.com, 1999. A complete guide to the Big Horn's dramatic wilderness country.

Phillips, Wayne. *Central Rocky Mountain Wildflowers: Including the Greater Yellowstone Ecosystem.* Guilford, CT: Globe Pequot Press, www.globepequot.com, 1999.

Retallic, Ken. *Flyfisher's Guide to Wyoming.* Gallatin Gateway, MT: Wilderness Adventures Press, 1998. An excellent guide; particularly helpful for anglers headed to Yellowstone.

Schneider, Bill. *Bear Aware: Hiking and Camping in Bear Country.* Guilford, CT: Globe Pequot, www.globepequot.com, 2001. A handy pocket-size book that is easy to read and up to date.

Travsky, Amber. *Mountain Biking Wyoming.* Guilford, CT: Globe Pequot Press, www.globepequot.com, 1999.

Woods, Rebecca. *Walking the Winds: A Hiking and Fishing Guide to Wyoming's Wind River Range.* Alpenbooks, www.alpenbooks.com, 1994. A useful guide to hiking trails in the Winds.

HISTORY

Baber, D. F. *The Longest Rope.* Caldwell, ID: The Caxton Printers, www.caxtonprinters.com, 1953. The fascinating story of the Johnson County War as told by William Walker, the only surviving "rustler" witness of the siege at KC Ranch. Out of print.

Bille, Ed. *Early Days at Salt Creek and Teapot Dome.* Casper, WY: Mountain States Lithographing, www.mtstlitho.com, 1978. The story of oil boom times in Wyoming's most famous oil fields. Many fine old photos. Out of print.

Brown, Larry K. *The Hog Ranches of Wyoming: Liquor, Lust, and Lies Under Sagebrush Skies.* Glendo, WY: High Plains Press, 1995. A playful book about the saloon/dance hall/brothels that sprang up around Wyoming's frontier forts.

Bryans, Bill. *Deer Creek: Frontiers Crossroad in Pre-Territorial Wyoming.* Casper, WY: Mountain States Lithographing, www.mtstlitho.com, 1990. A surprisingly engaging history of the Glenrock area, an important way station on the Oregon/Mormon/California Trail.

Burt, Struthers. *Powder River: Let 'er Buck.* New York: Rinehart, www.roberts-rinehart.com, 1938. A classic book on this famous part of Wyoming by one of the finest writers to come out of the state. Out of print.

Carlisle, Bill. *Lone Bandit. An Autobiography.* Pasadena, CA: Trails End Publishing, 1946. The story of the last of the old Wyoming outlaws, the "gentleman train robber" who later opened a popular Laramie motel. Out of print.

Coffman, Lloyd W. *Blazing a Wagon Trail to Oregon.* Springfield, OR: Echo Books, 1993. The experience and drama—much told in the participants' own words—of the "great migration," with details on Fort Bridger, Fort Laramie, Independence Rock, and other Wyoming stopping places.

Combs, Barry B. *Westward to Promontory: Building the Union Pacific Across the Plains and Mountains.* New York: Crown Publishers, 1986. How the West was really won. Includes a wonderful collection of historic photos by Andrew J. Russell. Out of print.

DeVoto, Bernard. *Across the Wide Missouri.* New York: Houghton Mifflin, www.hmco.com, 1990. Reissue of a 1947 book on the Rocky Mountain fur trade and how it shaped American culture. A classic.

Edgar, Bob, and Jack Turnell. *Brand of a Legend.* Greybull, WY: Wolverine Gallery, 1978. The story of the Pitchfork, one of Wyoming's most famous ranches. Includes many of Charles Belden's wonderful old photographs. Out of print.

Gowans, Fred R. *Rocky Mountain Rendezvous: A History of the Fur Trade Rendezvous 1825–1840.* Layton, UT: Gibbs Smith Publisher, 1989. Describes each of the rendezvous in detail.

Gowans, Fred R., and Eugene E. Campbell. *Fort Bridger, Island in the Wilderness.* Provo, UT: Brigham Young University Press, www.byu.edu, 1975. An excellent book about the first way station specifically built to serve emigrants on the Oregon Trail. Out of print.

Hafen, Leroy Reuben, and Ann W. Hafen. *Handcarts to Zion.* Lincoln, NE: University of Nebraska Press, www.unp.unl.edu, 1992. The true story of the Mormon handcart pioneers, told in a very readable manner.

Haines, Aubrey L. *Historic Sites Along the Oregon Trail.* St. Louis, MO: The Patrice Press, www.patricepress.com, 1994. Details many of the interesting places on this historic route.

Haines, Aubrey L. (ed.). *Journal of a Trapper: Osborne Russell.* Lincoln, NE: University of Nebraska Press, www.unp.unl.edu, 1965 (reprinted from the 19th-century original volume). The fascinating first-person account of a fur trapper from 1834–1843. A classic and surprisingly well-written book.

Hanna, Oliver Perry. *An Old-Timer's Story of the Old Wild West.* Casper, WY: Endeavor Books, 1984. Fascinating tales from the founder of Big Horn, Wyoming.

Hedgpeth, Don. *Spurs Were A-Jinglin'.* Cody, WY: Northland Press, 1975. Brief text follows the excellent photos by Charles J. Belden of cowboys and ranching in the early parts of the 20th century. Out of print.

Homsher, Lola M. (ed.). *South Pass, 1868: James Chisholm's Journal of the Wyoming Gold Rush.* Lincoln, NE: University of Nebraska Press, www.unp.unl.edu, 1960. Tales of life in the gold-mining town of South Pass shortly after the first wave of boomers had left. Very interesting.

Junge, Mark. *Wyoming: A Pictorial History.* Virginia Beach, VA: The Donning Co. Publishers, www.donning.com, 1989. A gorgeous coffee-table book filled with historic black-and-white photos from throughout Wyoming. Out of print.

Kahin, Sharon, and Laurie Rufe. *In the Shadows of the Rockies: A Photographic History of the Pioneer Experience in Wyoming's Bighorn Basin.* Powell, WY: Northwest Community College, www.nwc.cc.wy.us, 1983. Outstanding photos and interesting historical quotes on the Bighorn Basin. Out of print.

Larson, T. A. *History of Wyoming.* Lincoln, NE: University of Nebraska Press, www.unp.unl.edu, 1990. The definitive tome (663 pages worth) on Wyoming's history, with an emphasis on politics and development rather than on outlaws and Indian wars.

Lavender, David. *Fort Laramie and the Changing Frontier.* Washington, DC: Government Printing Office, http://bookstore.gpo.gov, 1984. An interesting little book filled with the history of the people who made Fort Laramie a primary center of trade and war in the West. Excellent illustrations, too.

Lindmier, Tom, and Steve Mount. *I See by Your Outfit: Historic Cowboy Gear of the*

Northern Plains. Glendo, WY: High Plains Press, 1996. An authoritative guide to what *real* cowboys wore. Filled with interesting historical photos.

Marcy, Randolph B. *The Prairie Traveler.* New York: Perigee Books, www.penguinputnam.com, 1859, reprinted in 1994. A telling portrait of life on the frontier as told by a U.S. Army captain. It was considered the essential handbook for travelers.

Mercer, Asa Shinn. *Banditti of the Plains* or *The Cattlemen's Invasion of Wyoming in 1892: The Crowning Infamy of the Ages.* Norman, OK: University of Oklahoma Press, www.oupress.com, 1976. A reprint of a classic book about the Johnson County War.

Morgan, Dale (ed.). *Overland in 1846: Diaries and Letters of the California–Oregon Trail.* Lincoln, NE: University of Nebraska Press, www.unp.unl.edu, 1994. A two-volume collection of diaries offering many fascinating insights into the lives of the emigrants.

Mothershead, Harmon Ross. *The Swan Land and Cattle Company, Ltd.* Norman, OK: University of Oklahoma Press, www.oupress.com, 1971. The story of the most famous of all Wyoming ranches, the million-acre spread begun by Alexander Swan in 1883. Out of print.

Munkres, Robert L. *Saleratus and Sagebrush: The Oregon Trail Through Wyoming.* Cheyenne, WY: Wyoming State Archives and Historical Department, 1974. This interesting small book offers eyewitness accounts from many travelers along the Oregon Trail. Out of print.

Murray, Robert A. *The Bozeman Trail: Highway of History.* Boulder, CO: Pruett Publishing, www.pruettpublishing.com, 1988. An attractively illustrated history of the West's most violent trail.

Osgood, Ernest Staples. *The Day of the Cattleman.* Chicago, IL: University of Chicago Press, www.press.uchicago.edu, 1929. An authoritative history of the 50 years when cowboys and cattle barons ruled Wyoming and Montana. Out of print.

Parkman, Francis. *The Oregon Trail.* New York: Viking Penguin, www.penguinputnam.com, 1886. A classic first-person account of the great westward migration. Reprinted in 1989.

Pinkerton, Joan Tregs. *Knights of the Broadax.* Caldwell, ID: The Caxton Printers, www.caxtonprinters.com, 1981. An account of the life of tie hacks in the upper Wind River country.

Rhode, Robert B. *Booms and Busts on Bitter Creek: A History of Rock Springs, Wyoming.* Boulder, CO: Pruett Publishing, www.pruettpublishing.com, 1999. A fine history of one of Wyoming's most turbulent cities.

Sandoval, Judith Hancock. *Historic Ranches of Wyoming.* Casper, WY: Mountain States Lithographing, www.mtstlitho.com, 1986. Details nearly 100 of the state's classic old ranches. Out of print.

Spring, Agnes Wright. *The Cheyenne and Black Hills Stage and Express Routes.* Lincoln, NE: University of Nebraska Press, www.unp.unl.edu, 1948. Tales from the early days of eastern Wyoming. Out of print.

Stamm, Henry E., IV. *People of the Wind River: The Eastern Shoshones 1825–1900.* Norman, OK: University of Oklahoma Press, www.oupress.com, 1999. The definitive source for the history of the Shoshones.

Thybony, Scott, Robert G. Rosenberg, and Elizabeth Mullett Rosenberg. *The Medicine Bows: Wyoming's Mountain Country.* Caldwell, ID: The Caxton Printers, www.caxtonprinters.com, 1985. An outstanding historical account of the Indians, explorers, miners, and tie hacks who called this scenic part of Wyoming home. Out of print.

Twain, Mark. *Roughing It.* New York: New American Library, www.penguinputnam.com, 1994. First published in 1872, this is one of the classics of American literature.

Samuel Clemens's witty descriptions of the Old West seem ageless.

NATIVE AMERICANS

Clark, Ella E., and Margot Edmonds. *Sacagawea of the Lewis and Clark Expedition.* Berkeley, CA: University of California Press, www.ucpress.edu, 1984. A fascinating investigation into the true stories behind one of the best-known women in American history. Bursts a few bubbles.

Flynn, Janet. *Tribal Government: Wind River Reservation.* Lander, WY: Mortimore Publishing, 1998. A good introduction to tribal government on the reservation, with a brief history of the tribes.

Frison, George C. *Prehistoric Hunters of the High Plains.* New York: Academic Press, www.academicpress.com, 1991. The authoritative source on the earliest inhabitants of Wyoming.

Hendry, Mary Helen. *Indian Rock Art in Wyoming.* Lincoln, NE: Augstams Printing, 1983. Detailed descriptions of rock-art sites in the state. The author's listed ages for the rock art are probably too recent, and she intentionally omits locations.

Lowie, Robert. *Indians of the Plains.* Lincoln, NE: University of Nebraska Press, www.unp .unl.edu, 1982. Famed anthropologist Robert Lowie presents a detailed picture of life on the plains before the arrival of whites.

Nadeau, Remi. *Fort Laramie and the Sioux Indians.* New York: Crest Publishers, 1997. A thorough historical account of the impact of Fort Laramie on the high-plains Indians.

Trenholm, Virginia Cole. *The Arapahoes, Our People.* Norman, OK: University of Oklahoma Press, www.oupress.com, 1986. The story of this important Wyoming tribe from prehistory to the tribe's forced relocation to the Wind River Reservation.

Trenholm, Virginia Cole, and Maurine Carley. *The Shoshonis: Sentinels of the Rockies.* Norman, OK: University of Oklahoma Press, www.oupress.com, 1964. The history of Chief Washakie and the Shoshone tribe.

Urbanek, Mae. *Chief Washakie.* Boulder, CO: Johnson Publishing, 1971. The fascinating story of the chief who led the Shoshone people for 60 years while always remaining a friend of whites. Out of print.

Utley, Robert M. *The Indian Frontier of the American West 1846–1890.* Albuquerque, NM: University of New Mexico Press, www .unmpress.com, 1984. An evenhanded portrayal of a half century of conflict between Indians and whites.

NATURAL HISTORY

Note: See also following sections on Jackson Hole, Grand Teton National Park, and Yellowstone National Park.

Baxter, George T., and Michael D. Stone. *Amphibians and Reptiles of Wyoming.* Cheyenne, WY: Wyoming Game and Fish Department, http://gf.state.wy.us, 1985. Everything you wanted to know about the state's snakes, frogs, toads, salamanders, and other cold-blooded critters.

Clark, Tim W., and Mark R. Stromberg. *Mammals in Wyoming.* Lawrence, KS: University Press of Kansas, www.kansaspress.ku.edu, 1987. The definitive guide to 117 native or naturalized Wyoming mammals: their identification, distribution, biology, and ecology.

Crowe, Douglas M. *Furbearers of Wyoming.* Cheyenne, WY: Wyoming Department of Game and Fish, http://gf.state.wy.us, 1986. A small book describing the state's fur-coated critters, with distribution maps.

Dorn, Robert D. *Manual of the Vascular Plants of Wyoming.* Cheyenne, WY: Mountain West Publishing, 1988. The authoritative key to Wyoming plants; a dense book with few illustrations. For botanists. Out of print.

Galvin, James. *The Meadow.* New York: Henry Holt, www.henryholt.com, 1993. A hauntingly beautiful book about a meadow on the Wyoming border near Tie Siding, and a century of the people who have lived there.

Knight, Dennis H. *Mountains and Plains: The Ecology of Wyoming Landscapes.* New Haven, CT: Yale University Press, www.yale.edu/yup, 1994. The definitive textbook on the ecology of Wyoming. Thorough and well written, but the $50 price may scare you away.

Petersen, David. *Among the Elk.* Flagstaff, AZ: Northland Publishing, www.northlandpub .com, 1988. The story of wapiti, with outstanding photos by Alan D. Carey. Out of print.

JACKSON HOLE AND GRAND TETON NATIONAL PARK

Note: Several natural history and geology books encompass both Yellowstone and Grand Teton national parks. See the following section on Yellowstone National Park for additional titles with overlapping coverage.

Geology

Good, John M., and Kenneth L. Pierce. *Interpreting the Landscape: Recent and Ongoing Geology of Grand Teton and Yellowstone National Parks.* Moose, WY: Grand Teton Natural History Association, www.grandtetonpark.org, 1996. This attractive book has the latest geologic research on the parks and presents it in an understandable format with excellent illustrations.

Love, J. D., and John C. Reed, Jr. *Creation of the Teton Landscape: The Geologic Story of Grand Teton National Park.* Moose, WY: Grand Teton Natural History Association, www.grandtetonpark.org, 1995. A small but authoritatively detailed guide to the geology of Jackson Hole and the Tetons.

History

Betts, Robert B. *Along the Ramparts of the Tetons: The Saga of Jackson Hole, Wyoming.* Boulder, CO: University Press of Colorado,

www.upcolorado.com, 1978. A substantial, detailed, and beautifully written book about the history of Jackson Hole.

Burt, Nathaniel. *Jackson Hole Journal.* Norman, OK: University of Oklahoma Press, www.oupress.com, 1983. Tales of growing up as a dude in Jackson Hole. Contains some very amusing stories.

Huidekoper, Virginia. *The Early Days in Jackson Hole.* Boulder, CO: University Press of Colorado, www.upcolorado.com, 1978. Filled with more than 100 photos from old-time Jackson Hole. Out of print.

Righter, Robert W. *Crucible for Conservation: The Creation of Grand Teton National Park.* Boulder, CO: University Press of Colorado, www.upcolorado.com, 1982. The story of how the Tetons were spared through a half-century battle.

Thompson, Edith M., and William Leigh Thompson. *Beaver Dick: The Honor and the Heartbreak.* Laramie, WY: Jelm Mountain Press, 1982. A touching historical biography of Beaver Dick Leigh, one of the first white men to settle in Jackson Hole. Out of print.

Natural History

Carrighar, Sally. *One Day at Teton Marsh.* Lincoln, NE: University of Nebraska Press, www.unp.unl.edu, 1979. A classic natural history of life in a Jackson Hole marsh. Made into a movie by Walt Disney. Out of print.

Clark, Tim W. *Ecology of Jackson Hole, Wyoming: A Primer.* Salt Lake City, UT: Paragon Press, www.paragon-press.com, 1981. An excellent scientific introduction to ecological interrelationships within Jackson Hole. Out of print.

Murie, Margaret, and Olaus Murie. *Wapiti Wilderness.* Boulder, CO: University Press of Colorado, www.upcolorado.com, 1986. The lives of two of America's most-loved conservationists in Jackson Hole and their work with elk.

Shaw, Richard J. *Plants of Grand Teton and Yellowstone National Parks.* Salt Lake City, UT: Wheelwright Press, 1981. Photos and descriptions of the most commonly found plants in the parks.

Travsky, Amber. *Mountain Biking Jackson Hole.* Guilford, CT: Globe Pequot Press, www.globepequot.com, 2001. Thirty-one rides in Jackson Hole, Grand Teton National Park, and surrounding areas.

Recreation

Carter, Tom. *Day Hiking Grand Teton National Park.* Garland, TX: Dayhiking Press, 1993. A pocket-size guide to 15 day-treks in the park.

Dufy, Katy, and Darwin Wile. *Teton Trails.* Moose, WY: Grand Teton Natural History Association, www.grandtetonpark.org, 1995. A useful guide to more than 200 miles of trails in the park.

Jackson, Reynold G. *A Climber's Guide to the Teton Range.* Seattle, WA: Mountaineers Books, www.mountaineerbooks.org, 1996. The definitive (415 pages!) climbing guide for the Tetons.

Prax, Brian, and Mark Schultheis. *The Book: Guide to Mountain Biking in the Jackson Hole Area.* Jackson, WY: Prax Photography and Productions, 2001. This spiral-bound book is the most complete guide to local cycling options and includes coverage on Teton Valley.

Rossiter, Richard. *Teton Classics: 50 Selected Climbs in Grand Teton National Park.* Guilford, CT: Globe Pequot Press, www.globepequot.com, 1994. A small and nicely illustrated guide to 50 climbing routes in the Tetons.

Stone, Robert. *Day Hikes in Grand Teton National Park and Jackson Hole.* Guilford, CT: Globe Pequot Press, www.globepequot.com, 2000.

Viola, Bob, and Thomas Turiano. *Jackson Hole Ski Guide.* Guilford, CT: Globe Pequot Press, www.globepequot.com, 1998.

Watters, Ron. *Winter Tales and Trails: Skiing, Snowshoeing and Snowboarding in Idaho, the Grand Tetons and Yellowstone National Park.* Pocatello, ID: Great Rift Press, 1997. A book that combines lucid writing on the area's rich history with guides to winter trails. More than 350 pages of details from an expert in the field.

Woods, Rebecca. *Jackson Hole Hikes.* Jackson, WY: White Willow Publishing, 1999. An excellent guide that includes trails in Grand Teton National Park and surrounding national forest areas. Easy to use and informative.

YELLOWSTONE NATIONAL PARK

Note: Several natural history and geology books encompass both Yellowstone and Grand Teton national parks. See previous sections on Jackson Hole and Grand Teton National Park for additional titles with overlapping coverage.

Geology

Bryan, Scott. T. *The Geysers of Yellowstone.* Boulder, CO: University Press of Colorado, www.upcolorado.com, 1995. The definitive guide to more than 400 geysers and other geothermal features in Yellowstone.

Fritz, William J. *Roadside Geology of the Yellowstone Country.* Missoula, MT: Mountain Press Publishing, www.mountain-press.com, 1986. All of the park roads are covered in this easy-to-follow Yellowstone geology primer.

Schreier, Carl. *Yellowstone's Geysers, Hot Springs and Fumaroles.* Moose, WY: Homestead Publishing, 1987. An attractive small book filled with color photos and brief descriptions.

History

Bartlett, Richard A. *Yellowstone: A Wilderness Besieged.* Tucson, AZ: University of Arizona Press, www.uapress.arizona.edu, 1989. The history of Yellowstone and the fight to prevent its destruction by railroad magnates, concessioners, and others.

Haines, Aubrey L. *The Yellowstone Story: A History of Our First National Park*. Boulder, CO: University Press of Colorado, www.upcolorado.com, 1996. A definitive two-volume history of the park. Volume one (history up to the park's establishment) is the most interesting.

Janetski, Joel C. *Indians of Yellowstone Park*. Salt Lake City, UT: University of Utah Press, www.upress.utah.edu, 1987. A general overview of the earliest settlers in Yellowstone and later conflicts with incoming whites.

Milstein, Michael. *Yellowstone Album: 125 Years of America's Best Idea*. Billings, MT: The Billings Gazette, www.billingsgazette.com, 1996. A delightful book filled with historical photographs, along with photos of postcards, souvenirs, and other tourist artifacts.

Schreier, Carl (ed.). *Yellowstone: Selected Photographs 1870–1960*. Moose, WY: Homestead Publishing, 1989. An outstanding collection of historical photographs from the park.

Natural History

Craighead, Frank J. *Track of the Grizzly*. San Francisco, CA: Sierra Club Books, www.sierraclub.org, 1982. The life of grizzlies in Yellowstone, by one of the most famous bear researchers.

Krakell, Dean, II. *Downriver: A Yellowstone Journey*. San Francisco, CA: Sierra Club Books, www.sierraclub.org, 1987. An extraordinarily moving journey down the magnificent Yellowstone River.

McEneaney, Terry. *Birds of Yellowstone*. Boulder, CO: Roberts Rinehart, www.roberts-rinehart.com, 1988. A guide to Yellowstone birds and where to find them.

Schullery, Paul (ed.). *Yellowstone Bear Tales*. Boulder, CO: Roberts Rinehart Publishers, www.roberts-rinehart.com, 1991. First-person stories of bear encounters from a range of travelers—including President Theodore Roosevelt—between 1880 and 1950.

Schullery, Paul. *Searching for Yellowstone*. New York: Houghton Mifflin, www.hmco.com, 1997. An eloquently written book by a long-time park ranger whose knowledge of the park goes far beyond the hype. Must-reading for anyone who cares about Yellowstone.

Scott, Douglas M., and Suvi A. Scott. *Wildlife of Yellowstone and Grand Teton National Parks*. Salt Lake City, UT: Wheelwright Press, 1990. A brief descriptive guide to Yellowstone and Grand Teton critters.

Shaw, Richard J. *Wildflowers of Yellowstone and Grand Teton National Parks*. Salt Lake City, UT: Wheelwright Press, 1992. Color photos and short descriptions of more than 100 wildflowers in the Greater Yellowstone Ecosystem.

Recreation

Anderson, Roger, and Carol Shively Anderson. *A Ranger's Guide to Yellowstone Day Hikes*. Helena, MT: Montana Magazine, www.montanamagazine.com, 2000. One of the best books for short park hikes.

Bach, Orville E., Jr. *Hiking the Yellowstone Backcountry*. San Francisco, CA: Sierra Club Books, www.sierraclub.org, 1998. A pocket-size guide to hiking, canoeing, biking, and skiing in the park.

Charlton, Robert E. *Yellowstone Fishing Guide*. Ketchum, ID: Lost River Press, 1995. A detailed guide to fishing in the park. Leaves no trickle unfished.

Henry, Jeff. *Yellowstone Winter Guide*. Boulder, CO: Roberts Rinehart Publishers, www.roberts-rinehart.com, 1998. A detailed guide to visiting Yellowstone in the winter; especially good for cross-country skiers.

Lilly, Bud, and Paul Schullery. *Bud Lilly's Guide to Fly Fishing the New West*. Portland, OR: Frank Amato Publications, 2000. The authoritative fishing source from the father of Western trout fishing.

Marschall, Mark C. *Yellowstone Trails: A Hiking Guide*. Yellowstone National Park, WY:

The Yellowstone Association, www.yellowstoneassociation.org, 1999. An excellent, up-to-date, and detailed guidebook to the park's 1,000 miles of hiking trails.

Parks, Richard. *Fishing Yellowstone.* Guilford, CT: Globe Pequot Press, www.globepequot.com, 1998. One of several authoritative guides, this one provides details on fly- and lure fishing, along with descriptions of more than 100 sites.

Schneider, Bill. *Hiking Yellowstone National Park.* Guilford, CT: Globe Pequot Press, www.globepequot.com, 2003. Clear maps and helpful trail profiles make this the most useful book for anyone heading out on Yellowstone hiking routes. Contains descriptions of more than 100 trails.

Stone, Robert. *Day Hikes in Yellowstone National Park and Jackson Hole.* Guilford, CT: Globe Pequot Press, www.globepequot.com, 2000.

Varley, John D., and Paul D. Schullery. *Yellowstone Fishes: Ecology, History, and Angling in the Park.* Mechanicsburg, PA: Stackpole Books, 1998, www.stackpolebooks.com. The comprehensive guide to the fish of Yellowstone, written by two authorities in the field.

Internet Resources

State of Wyoming
www.state.wy.us
This is the state's official home on the web and a good spot to learn more about history, events, state government, and a range of other subjects.

Wyoming Travel and Tourism Division
www.wyomingtourism.org
The state's tourism site has everything you'd expect in the way of an interactive visitor center and much more.

Wyoming Department of Transportation
www.wyoroad.info
This website has updated road conditions, webcams, and details on road construction projects.

Wyoming Public Radio
www.wyomingpublicradio.net
A good starting place for information on public radio stations around Wyoming.

Department of State Parks and Cultural Resources
http://wyoparks.state.wy.us
This site contains details on 26 state parks, historic sites, recreation areas, and archaeological sites scattered across Wyoming.

Wyoming Homestay and Outdoor Adventures
www.wyomingbnb-ranchrec.com
Better known as WHOA, this organization maintains links to several dozen bed-and-breakfasts, dude ranches, guest cabins, and other distinctive lodging options.

Wyoming Press Association
www.wyopress.org
Head here for a complete listing of newspapers in the state, including weblinks.

Wyoming State Library
www-wsl.state.wy.us
This site has information and links to the state's public libraries.

Wyoming Game and Fish Department
http://gf.state.wy.us
Head to this website for details on fishing licenses and seasons, along with current issues affecting fish. You can even download application forms.

Wyoming Fishing Network
www.wyomingfishing.net
An exceptionally useful online source for Wyoming anglers.

National Park Service
www.nps.gov

Wyoming contains two national parks (Grand Teton National Park, www.nps.gov/grte, and Yellowstone National Park, www.nps.gov/yell), two national monuments (Devils Tower National Monument, www.nps.gov/deto, and Fossil Butte National Monument, www.nps.gov/fobu), plus Bighorn Canyon National Recreation Area, www.nps.gov/bica, and Fort Laramie National Historic Site, www.nps.gov/fola. All of these are managed by the National Park Service.

U.S. Fish and Wildlife Service
www.fws.gov

The FWS has four refuges in Wyoming. The two largest have their own websites: the National Elk Refuge in Jackson, http://nationalelkrefuge.fws.gov, and Seedskadee National Wildlife Refuge northwest of Green River, http://seedskadee.fws.gov.

Bureau of Land Management
www.wy.blm.gov

Wyoming's largest landholder—it manages 18 million acres in the state—is the BLM. Its website has details on recreation opportunities and much more.

U.S. Forest Service
www.fs.fed.us

This federal agency manages land within eight national forests in Wyoming, mostly in the mountainous regions. They are Bighorn National Forest, www.fs.fed.us/r2/bighorn, Black Hills National Forest, www.fs.fed.us/r2/blackhills, Bridger–Teton National Forest, www.fs.fed.us/r4/btnf, Ashley National Forest (Flaming Gorge National Recreation Area) www.fs.fed.us/r4/ashley, Medicine Bow–Routt National Forest, www.fs.fed.us/r2/mbr, Shoshone National Forest, www.fs.fed.us/r2/shoshone, Caribou–Targhee National Forest, www.fs.fed.us/r4/caribou, and Wasatch–Cache National Forest, www.fs.fed.us/r4/wcnf.

ReserveUSA
www.reserveusa.com

Head here to book reservations at Forest Service campgrounds around Wyoming.

Wyoming Outfitters and Guides Association
www.wyoga.org

Interested in a backcountry pack trip? Visit this website to find outfitters for the area you plan to visit.

Wyoming Dude Rancher's Association
www.wyomingdra.com

This statewide organization's homepage has links to the websites of 30 Wyoming guest ranches.

Don Pitcher
www.donpitcher.com

Don Pitcher's website provides links to all the websites found in this book. You can quickly connect to websites for hundreds of chambers of commerce offices, regional sights, governmental agencies, lodging places, restaurants, campgrounds, and much more.

Index

HIKING

QR

RODEOS

SCENIC DRIVES

XYZ

Acknowledgments

God bless Wyoming and keep it wild.
– last entry in the diary of Helen Mettler, who died in the Tetons at the age of 15.

Now in its sixth incarnation, this version of *Moon Wyoming* includes a new organization and a chapter to orient travelers to the region. It would be impossible to thank all of the people who helped me update this book, but the following individuals deserve my heartfelt gratitude.

A special thank you goes to chamber of commerce and visitor center folks who opened doors to their hometowns and reviewed my manuscript for problems: Dee Woodall in Buffalo, Marlyn Black in Casper, Darren Rudlof, Janet Cowley, and David Troyanek in Cheyenne, Lee Anne Ackerman, Claudia Wade, and Lee Haines in Cody, Suzy Hahn in Cooke City, Gary Hirt in Douglas, Dorothea Stewart in Dubois, Peggy Rounds in Evanston, Chris Waters in Gardiner, Marcy Bowman in Gillette, Sue Anderson in Greybull, Kelly Barbello and Anna Olson in Jackson, Terry Picerno in Kemmerer, Rita Urbanek and Jackie Meeker in Lander, Erin Grimes, Liz Arthur, Jo Ann Davis, and Teresa Beyer in Laramie, Jackie Bredthauer in Lusk, Norma Shelton in Newcastle, Mindi Crabb, Marline Dingman, and Marline Dingman in Pinedale, Donna Boyd and Willy Maxwell in Riverton, Pat Robbins in Rock Springs, Stacy Crimmins in Saratoga, Melissa Butcher in Sheridan, Karen Hadderlie in Star Valley, Toddi Darlington in Thermopolis, Dick Fullmer in Torrington, Marysue Costello in West Yellowstone, Julie Minear in Wheatland, and Suzanne Rubio and Mike Willard in Worland. Without their help this revision would have been nearly impossible.

The following hard-working government employees provided a similar service for their areas of expertise: Roxanne Bierman from Grand Teton Natural History Association, Paul Blackman from Medicine Bow National Forest, Megan Bogle from Targhee National Forest, John Campbell from Flaming Gorge National Recreation Area, Linda Coates-Markle from Pryor Mountain Wild Horse Range, Christine Czazasty and Janet Hatfield from Devils Tower National Monument, Joe Ellis from South Pass State Historic Site, Marcia Fagnant from Fossil Butte National Monument, Steve Fullmer from Fort Laramie National Historical Site, Janet Hatfield from Devils Tower National Monument, Patrick McCune from National Historic Trails Interpretive Center, Linda Merigliano and Dorothy Neckels from Bridger-Teton National Forest, Jeanne Myoshi and Reid Rogers from Driggs, Marcia Rose-Ritchie from Medicine Bow-Routt National Forest, Jackie Skaggs from Grand Teton National Park, Jim Staebler from Bighorn Canyon National Recreation Area, Jeanette Timm from Black Hills National Forest, and Ryan Twomey from Shoshone National Forest.

I also wish to thank the owners of Apartment Suites in Saratoga, Best Value Inn in Cody, Plains Hotel in Cheyenne, Best Western Plaza Hotel in Thermopolis, Ramada Inn in Laramie, Spahn's Big Horn Mountain Bed & Breakfast, and Wyoming Inn and Wort Hotel in Jackson, along with Tom Mesereau of Mesereau Communications and Rick Hoeninghausen of Xanterra Parks & Resorts.

Thanks also to readers Ron Gordon, Merri Koolik, and Dave Moser for their comments and corrections from the previous edition.

This book was shepherded through the production process by my editor, Kay Elliott. Thanks to her and the rest of the gang at Avalon Travel Publishing for getting this book into your hands.

I offer a very special thanks to my wife, Karen Shemet, and our children, Aziza and Rio, for keeping me grounded while I researched and wrote this new edition. They make coming home more fun than traveling!

MAP SYMBOLS

▦	Expressway	【	Highlight	✗	Airfield	⚲	Golf C..
▦	Primary Road	○	City/Town	✈	Airport	P	Parkir., . ..
▦	Secondary Road	◉	State Capital	▲	Mountain	▲	Archaeological Site
▪▪▪▪	Unpaved Road	⊛	National Capital	✚	Unique Natural Feature	♟	Church
- - - -	Trail	★	Point of Interest			⛽	Gas Station
··········	Ferry	•	Accommodation	⚐	Waterfall	◯	Glacier
┼─┼─┼	Railroad	▾	Restaurant/Bar	▲	Park		Mangrove
▦	Pedestrian Walkway	▪	Other Location	🚩	Trailhead		Reef
▥	Stairs	Λ	Campground	⛷	Skiing Area		Swamp

CONVERSION TABLES

°C = (°F − 32) / 1.8
°F = (°C x 1.8) + 32
1 inch = 2.54 centimeters (cm)
1 foot = 0.304 meters (m)
1 yard = 0.914 meters
1 mile = 1.6093 kilometers (km)
1 km = 0.6214 miles
1 fathom = 1.8288 m
1 chain = 20.1168 m
1 furlong = 201.168 m
1 acre = 0.4047 hectares
1 sq km = 100 hectares
1 sq mile = 2.59 square km
1 ounce = 28.35 grams
1 pound = 0.4536 kilograms
1 short ton = 0.90718 metric ton
1 short ton = 2000 pounds
1 long ton = 1.016 metric tons
1 long ton = 2240 pounds
1 metric ton = 1000 kilograms
1 quart = 0.94635 liters
1 US gallon = 3.7854 liters
1 Imperial gallon = 4.5459 liters
1 nautical mile = 1.852 km

www.moon.com

For helpful advice on planning a trip, visit www.moon.com for the **TRAVEL PLANNER** and get access to useful travel strategies and valuable information about great places to visit. When you travel with Moon, expect an experience that is uncommon and truly unique.

HANDBOOKS • METRO • OUTDOORS • LIVING ABROAD

MOON WYOMING
Avalon Travel Publishing
An Imprint of
AVALON Avalon Publishing Group, Inc.
publishing group incorporated

1400 65th Street, Suite 250
Emeryville, CA 94608, USA
www.moon.com

Editors: Kay Elliott, Sabrina Young
Series Manager: Kathryn Ettinger
Acquisitions Manager: Rebecca K. Browning
Copy Editor: Karen Bleske
Graphics Coordinator: Tabitha Lahr
Production Coordinators: Jacob Goolkasian,
  Tabitha Lahr, Amber Pirker
Cover & Interior Designer: Gerilyn Attebery
Map Editor: Kevin Anglin
Cartographers: Kat Bennett, Mike Morgenfeld,
  Chris Markiewicz
Indexer: Rachel Kuhn

ISBN-10: 1-56691-953-3
ISBN-13: 978-1-56691-953-1
ISSN: 1542-8869

Printing History
1st Edition – 1991
6th Edition – May 2006
5 4 3 2 1

Text © 2006 by Don Pitcher.
Maps © 2006 by Avalon Travel Publishing, Inc.
All rights reserved.

Some photos and illustrations are used by permission
and are the property of the original copyright
owners.

Front cover photo: Mormon Row and the Tetons
© Don Pitcher

Title page photo: Mormon Row and the Tetons
© Don Pitcher

Printed in Canada by Transcontinental

KEEPING CURRENT

If you have a favorite gem you'd like to see included in the next edition, or see anything
that needs updating, clarification, or correction, please drop us a line. Send your comments via email to feedback@moon.com, or use the address above.